The
Complete Diary
of a Cotswold Parson

The
Complete Diary
of a Cotswold Parson

The Diaries of the Revd. Francis Edward Witts

1783-1854

in 10 volumes

Edited by Alan Sutton

Volume 8

The Man of Property

Diaries covering the Period

1845-1850

AMBERLEY

The Complete Diary of a Cotswold Parson

Volume 8

The Man of Property

First published 2010 by
Amberley Publishing
Cirencester Road
Chalford
Stroud
Gloucestershire
GL6 8PE

ISBN 978-1-84868-007-4

The illustration on page 2 is detail from Eyford Park, the home of Mrs Dolphin.

Typesetting and origination by Amberley Publishing
Printed in England by Hamptons Printing Bristol
Bound in Scotland by Hunter & Foulis

Contents

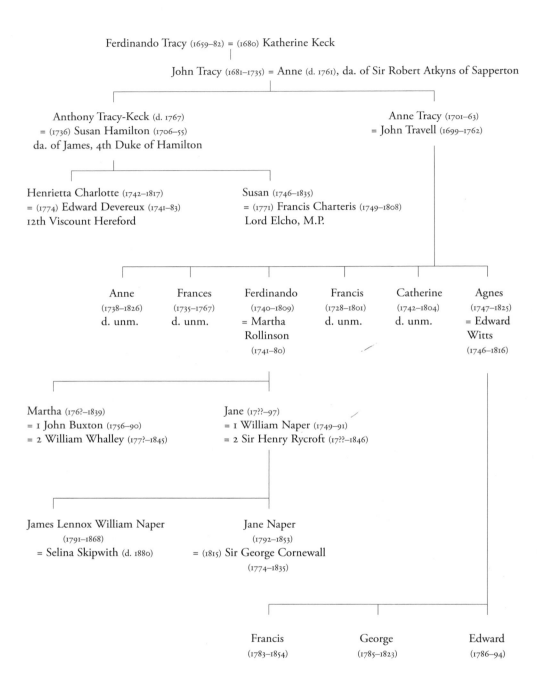

Ferdinando Tracy (1659–82) = (1680) Katherine Keck

John Tracy (1681–1735) = Anne (d. 1761), da. of Sir Robert Atkyns of Sapperton

Anthony Tracy-Keck (d. 1767)
= (1736) Susan Hamilton (1706–55)
da. of James, 4th Duke of Hamilton

Anne Tracy (1701–63)
= John Travell (1699–1762)

Henrietta Charlotte (1742–1817)
= (1774) Edward Devereux (1741–83)
12th Viscount Hereford

Susan (1746–1835)
= (1771) Francis Charteris (1749–1808)
Lord Elcho, M.P.

Anne
(1738–1826)
d. unm.

Frances
(1735–1767)
d. unm.

Ferdinando
(1740–1809)
= Martha
Rollinson
(1741–80)

Francis
(1728–1801)
d. unm.

Catherine
(1742–1804)
d. unm.

Agnes
(1747–1825)
= Edward
Witts
(1746–1816)

Martha (176?–1839)
= 1 John Buxton (1756–90)
= 2 William Whalley (177?–1845)

Jane (17??–97)
= 1 William Naper (1749–91)
= 2 Sir Henry Rycroft (17??–1846)

James Lennox William Naper
(1791–1868)
= Selina Skipwith (d. 1880)

Jane Naper
(1792–1853)
= (1815) Sir George Cornewall
(1774–1835)

Francis
(1783–1854)

George
(1785–1823)

Edward
(1786–94)

Edward Witts = Jane Hinton of Aldbourne (*m.* 1649)
(16??–1688)   (16??-1706)

Edward Witts = (2) Miriam Adams
(1650–1715)

Edward Witts = Sarah Broome
(1676–1736)

Edward	Richard = Jane Parish	George	Broome	John	Mary	Sarah = Thomas Hunt
(1701–54)	(1705–55)	(1710–16)	(1713–68)	(1707–30)	(1703–04)	(1715–66)

Broome   Richard Parish
(1738–69)   (1748–1828)
= Elizabeth
London
(1738–1837)

= Apphia
Anthony
(1713–60)

see pedigree on page 8

Broome Philips	Edward London	Maria Amelia = A. Rodick of
(1767–1845)	(1768–1841)	(1769–1830) Wellingborough
= Jane Lake	= Ann Parrott	

Jane	Emma	Broome	William	Maria	Edward	Henry	Unnamed	Unnamed
(1810–55)	(1812–99)	Lake	Frederick	(1822–1904)	London		boy	girls
= James	= R.	(1812–61)	(1818–84)	= John				
Currie	Allen	= Maria	= Ellen	Edward				
Duncan		Dickson	May	Woodroffe				
			Witts					

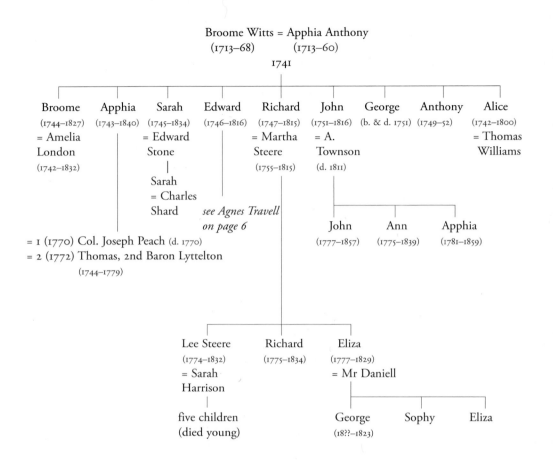

Broome Witts = Apphia Anthony
(1713–68)   (1713–60)
1741

Broome (1744–1827) = Amelia London (1742–1832)

Apphia (1743–1840)

Sarah (1745–1834) = Edward Stone
|
Sarah = Charles Shard

Edward (1746–1816)

see Agnes Travell on page 6

Richard (1747–1815) = Martha Steere (1755–1815)

John (1751–1816) = A. Townson (d. 1811)

George (b. & d. 1751)

Anthony (1749–52)

Alice (1742–1800) = Thomas Williams

= 1 (1770) Col. Joseph Peach (d. 1770)
= 2 (1772) Thomas, 2nd Baron Lyttelton
                 (1744–1779)

John (1777–1857)

Ann (1775–1839)

Apphia (1781–1859)

Lee Steere (1774–1832) = Sarah Harrison
|
five children (died young)

Richard (1775–1834)

Eliza (1777–1829) = Mr Daniell

George (18??–1823)

Sophy

Eliza

List of Illustrations

Anderson. Shropshire: Its Early History and Antiquities, John Corbett Anderson, 1864.

Bigland. Historical, Monumental and Genealogical Collections, relative to the County of Gloucester; printed from the original papers of the late Ralph Bigland. 1791.

BOTT. The Book of the Thames

CMAG. Cheltenham Museum and Art Gallery.

Corry. The History of Bristol, John Corry, 1816.

Crapelet. Souvenirs de Londres en 1814 et 1816, G. A. Crapelet, Paris, 1817.

DG. Delineations of Gloucestershire, J. & H. S. Storer and J. N. Brewer, 1826.

Evans. The History of Bristol, John Evans, 1816.

Glover. The History of the County of Derby, Stephen Glover, 1829.

Knight. Old England a Pictorial Museum of Regal, Ecclesiastical, Baronial, Municipal and Popular Antiquities, Charles Knight, 1845.

Lee. History of the Town and Parish of Tetbury, Alfred T. Lee, 1857.

Martineau. A Complete Guide to the English Lakes, Harriet Martineau, 1855.

PE. Picturesque Excursions, Arthur Freeling, c.1840.

Papworth. Papworth's Select Views of London,1816.

PTRT. Picturesque Tour of the River Thames.

Rudder. A New History of Gloucestershire, Samuel Rudder, 1779.

Rutter. Delineations of the North Western Division of the County of Somerset, John Rutter, 1829.

WFP. Witts Family Papers.

The codes in italics at the end of each illustration relate to the catalogue of the Alan Sutton Image Archive.

15. Old church, Bonchurch, Isle of Wight. *Nelson. A0930-19*

16. Bonchurch Pond, Isle of Wight. *Nelson. A0930-23*

17. St. Boniface, Isle of Wight, Arthur Freeling, *Picturesque Excursions, c*.1840. *A0903-98*

18. Bonchurch, Isle of Wight, Arthur Freeling, *Picturesque Excursions, c*.1840. *A0903-99*

19. Shanklin Chine, Isle of Wight, Arthur Freeling, *Picturesque Excursions, c*.1840. *A0903-100*

20. The Head of the Chine, Isle of Wight, Arthur Freeling, *Picturesque Excursions, c*.1840. *A0903-101*

21. Steephill, Isle of Wight, Arthur Freeling, *Picturesque Excursions, c*.1840. *A0903-96*

22. Ventnor Mill, Isle of Wight, Arthur Freeling, *Picturesque Excursions, c*.1840. *A0903-97*

23. Freshwater Cave, Isle of Wight. *Nelson. A0930-21*

24. Blackgang Chine, Isle of Wight. *Nelson. A0930-24*

25. Royal Sand Rock Hotel, Isle of Wight, Arthur Freeling, *Picturesque Excursions, c*.1840. *A0903-92*

26. Sand Rock Spring, Isle of Wight, Arthur Freeling, *Picturesque Excursions, c*.1840. *A0903-93*

27. Freshwater Gate Hotel, Isle of Wight, Arthur Freeling, *Picturesque Excursions, c*.1840. *A0903-102*

28. Freshwater Cliffs, Isle of Wight, Arthur Freeling, *Picturesque Excursions, c*.1840. *A0903-103*

29. Appuldercombe the home of the Earl of Yarborough, Arthur Freeling, *Picturesque Excursions, c*.1840. *A0903-91*

30. St Lawrence, Isle of Wight, Arthur Freeling, *Picturesque Excursions, c*.1840. *A0903-95*

31. Blackgang Chine, Isle of Wight, Arthur Freeling, *Picturesque Excursions, c*.1840. *A0903-94*

32. William Makepeace Thackeray. *C0119-01*

33. Osborne House, Isle of Wight. *Nelson. A0930-18*

34. West Cowes, Isle of Wight. *Nelson. A0930-26*

35. Bar Gate Southampton. *B1120-07*

36. Gaol and Bridewell. *B1120-08*

37. Southampton from the New Road. *B1120-09*

38. A broad gauge train. *C0203-12*

39. Waltham Abbey from the north-west, from *Old England a Pictorial Museum of Regal, Ecclesiastical, Baronial, Municipal and Popular Antiquities*, by Charles Knight, 1845. *A0916-67*

40. Northleach church. *C0125-03*

41. *Centaur*, A Daniel Gooch Fire Fly locomotive. *C0203-10*

42. Prinknash Park. *C0204-14*

43. Chevenage. *DG. A0924-35*

44. Harvesting scene from John Linnel's painting. *C0204-40*

45. Gloucester Docks and Cathedral 1842. *B1103-29*

46. Paddle steamers at Hotwells, Bristol. *C0203-24*

47. Boxwell Court. *DG. A0924-38*

48. Hawkesbury, Gloucestershire, from *Bigland. A0917-55*

49. Badminton. *DG. A0924-05*

50. A Fire Fly led train at Bristol Temple Meads. *C0203-11*

51. Holywell Street, looking west, showing the old house on the south side. From a drawing by T. H. Shepherd, 1851. *A0914-05*

52. The thatched house, said to have been Nell Gwynn's dairy, on the north side of the Strand. The tavern gave the name to Thatched House Court, which ran to the west end of Southampton Street. From a water-colour drawing by T. H. Shepherd, 1854. *A0914-08*

53. The shop of Richardson, the print seller, at the north-west corner of Villiers Street, Strand. From a drawing by

Introduction

Volume eight covers a period which might fairly be referred to as years of general 'slowing down'. Francis Witts was now a man of property with financial security and with high reputation in the County. The vexatious problems of his son and with his public duties were now behind him and he could look forward to the twilight years of his life in comfort and with satisfaction.

   Unfortunately it was not to be as idyllic as the ageing rector might have wished for. There were tedious matters to deal with — most notably the tiresome affairs of the Hunt family — but of equal annoyance was the difficulty in finding a suitable investment to replace the London property he had inherited from his uncle, Broome Witts. Alongside these troublesome issues there was the matter of his health. He suffered frequently from digestive problems and with chest pains which he realised were ominous. Last, but not least, was the failing health of his beloved wife, Margaret. She had always been in poor health, but in 1849 she went into serious decline and died the following year.

The volume begins in May 1846 following a gap in the diaries from July of 1845. During the winter and early spring of 1846 there were serious domestic upsets in the Howell family that eventually led Thomas Howell to sell the Prinknash estate. Thomas Howell was Francis Witts's closest friend and the affairs of that family affected him deeply. Howell's wife, Susan, had died at the same time of year back in 1842, from a haemorrhage following the birth of Macleod and further tragedy awaited; but first, the unknown domestic upset: *22 October 1846: . . . my Son and I left Gloucester in a fly for Prinknash Park, where we arrived about half an hour before its master, and we were very cordially and gladly received by Laura and Constance Howell. Emmeline is still in Devon, now on a visit to an old Gibraltar friend at Exeter. William had paid a hurried visit to his sisters yesterday: both he and Emmeline are, not without cause, aliens from the paternal home; yet it cannot be said that the Father is free from blame, though more sinned against than sinning. He had left London by a midday train, and came in good spirits, leading in his son Willougby, in his naval uniform, blue jacket, trousers, navy buttons, gold laced cap, and cutlass, as a naval cadet . . . . The evening was passed cheerfully, our host dwelling very fully and openly on many domestic matters, the sale of his property at Prinknash to Mr. Ackers, the coming sale of his Upton property, the purchase of a house in Town, &c. but observing a deep silence as to the painful events of last winter, the misconduct of Emmeline, William's eccentricities, and approaching marriage, the affair with the Widow Caldwell &c. My poor friend has an uncommon buoyancy of spirit, a great power of putting aside painful reflections, and, alas! Too entire a sympathy with this world and its engagements and pursuits . . . . One mourns that there is so much of levity, apparently so little of deep feeling on the eve of surrendering to others his parental property. The step is prudent, no doubt; for the events of last winter and spring have made the residence distasteful; his irritated temper has separated him from old friends and neighbours, without sufficient offence given by them; and a London life will be more congenial to his temperament, and, probably, suit better his views in placing out his sons yet unemployed: but more of seriousness, more of feeling, would have been more becoming. My son, who had been so greatly mixed up with the sad scenes of last spring, and so much interested in the position of Laura and Constance, was naturally impressed with deep emotion on this visit to Prinknash. We were both likely to feel acutely this, probably, the last visit we should pay to a place which for many years had been so familiar to us.*

From this entry it becomes clear that Edward was involved in some way in this upset. If so, it is further evidence to support the theory that Edward destroyed some diaries after his father's death, thereby explaining the gap of ten months. Whatever Emmeline did is unknown and it appears that William stood up for his sister, at the same time expressing affection for a lady of whom his father disapproved. Some comments seem to indicate instability on the part of Emmeline as she seems to be in need of supervision, and this is hinted at in an entry of a few weeks earlier: *6 September 1846: A letter from Howell: Prinknash Park is not yet sold; but he anticipates parting with it by private contract very shortly. A change has occurred in his plans. Owing to the illness of Mad. Frossard, the lady at Nismes to whose care Emmeline Howell was to have been consigned, that destination has been altered, and she is to reside with a Clergyman and his wife who are settled in Bucks or Bedfordshire; the lady of the Clergyman being sister to Mrs. Parsons, late of Upton St. Leonards.*

In November 1846 Thomas Howell purchased a house in Kensington garden terrace in readiness for when Prinknash Park was sold, but the sale became a protracted affair, not completed until the end of April 1847, and it was during this time that the next tragedy occurred. On 3 April 1847 the twins, Laura and Constance, accompanied by their young brother Macleod and an attendant, paid a visit to Upper Slaughter. They were due to be followed by their father in a few days; but then, the following day, a painful letter arrived at the rectory: *4 April 1847: Received a distressing letter from poor Howell, stating that on his arrival yesterday in Town, he had met with a letter from his friend, Major Sandham, communicating to him that a strong rumour prevailed that three Officers had been killed in an affray with the Kaffirs in South Africa of whom one was Frederick Howell, Surgeon in the Rifles, lately arrived in the Colony of the Cape of Good Hope. On receiving this intelligence Howell repaired to the Horse Guards, where he learnt that no official report of the affair had arrived, but that there was no reason to disbelieve the story. This sad news I had to communicate to the twin sisters, who were much distressed, but indulged in hope against hope. . . . 6 April 1847: . . . I received a letter from MW. informing me that Howell had written to his poor daughters, confirming the evil tidings he had communicated in his letter received on Sunday, and which, indeed, had been noticed in the London paper which I had seen at Gloucester this morning: the facts appear to be that on the Kei river in the Kaffir country, and beyond the limits of the Colony, a small military detachment had been stationed; Fred. Howell had charge of the sick and wounded there; with him was a Capt. Gibson, like himself of the Rifles; also an Hon. — Chetwynd, a son of Lord Chetwynd, an officer of another regiment: that these three had gone out to procure cattle, to increase their store of provisions; that they had advanced beyond the main body of their party, with four or five Hottentots; had met with a lot of cattle, perhaps, purposely placed as a decoy;*

had proceeded to drive this small herd, in the direction of their quarters: had so fallen into an ambush of savages; that poor Fred^{k.} Howell's horse was shot dead; himself killed & his two brother officers with two Hottentots, fighting in his rescue, were also massacred before the main body of their party which was a mile or two in the rear, and heard the firing, could come to their aid. . . . It was nearly seven o clock when I reached home: of course it was a melancholy evening of forced conversation, Laura and Constance being greatly overpowered.

Following the death of their brother, Laura, Constance and Macleod remained at Upper Slaughter (including a few days at Stanway) until the end of April, and then rejoined their father in London, to see their new home for the first time: *6 May 1847: A letter from Howell to announce his childrens safe arrival at his new house &c. — MW. received from Laura and Constance grateful notes, giving an account of their first impressions in Eaton Place West, and expressing their acknowledgements for our kindness to them while visiting us.*

Piecing together the thread of what happened during the period where there are missing diaries is interesting detective work. The diary entry for 18 May 1847 throws out a slight hint, but the exact circumstances remain veiled in fog. Presumably Emmeline had some form of relationship or possibly an elopement which ended in disgrace: *I received a letter from Howell, announcing the very unexpected intelligence that Emmeline had, at her place of seclusion, Mursley, in Buckinghamshire, where she is residing with a Clergyman named Horne, whose wife is sister to Mrs. Parsons, late of Upton St. Leonards, formed a connection with a medical Gentleman, named Wynter, practising at Winslow, a widower of 40 years of age, of respectable character, well spoken of by Mrs. Parsons and her Sister — Howell had gone down to see the parties, had given his consent to their marriage in July, and congratulates himself that this event will relieve him from much embarrasment, and solve difficulties. Under other circumstances the connection would not have been satisfactory; but it is not discreditable; and E. might have formed a bad connection: after what had passed in the winter of 1846 at Prinknash her return to her Father's house unmarried would have been prejudicial to her sisters, a cause of anxiety, and discord, and dread.*

William was in disgrace along with Emmeline and now had nothing to do with his father, but Edward Witts remained a friend and kept in touch: *26 September 1847: Cards sent by the post announce the marriage of Wm. Howell to Miss Willan. It has been a long engagement, and not very likely to end in prosperity: the lady is the daughter of a man who lived extravagantly, and was in latter years hardly sane. W.H. is eccentric, and alienated from his Father, who does little for him — He has recently undertaken the curacy of Tysoe in Warwickshire, where the new married will reside.*

The last information of note relating to the Howell family is when Thomas Howell becomes a grandfather, but presumably to a child he was never, ever, to see: *7 August 1848: . . . My son has engaged to go on Wednesday next to Tysoe in Warwickshire, returning home on Thursday, to be present at the christening of the first born child of William Howell, who is now residing there as Curate. His marriage to Miss Willan has been the result of a long attachment, but the lady brought him little fortune, and his father, very blameably, as I think, makes no pecuniary provision for him. It is true that William has displeased his father by his violence and eagerness of temper, particularly at the time of his sister Emmeline's strange misconduct, or derangement, whichever it might be; but the young man's general deportment is free from reproach, and it may be that mental infirmity would account both in him and in his eldest sister, for much that gives the parent just uneasiness & displeasure. Yet he never made a proper allowance to his son, and has, I grieve to say, failed generally in the paternal duties; turning his back, as it were, and leaving his eldest son and daughter without due countenance and provision; and not making himself beloved by his younger daughters.*

Away from the detailed diversion of the Howell family, volume eight commences with a four-and-a-half week holiday to the Isle of Wight. This enjoyable vacation was the last family holiday taken together, for Edward and Sophy had joined Francis and Margaret in the excursion and Margaret's health had held up reasonably well. On returning to Upper Slaughter Francis Witts set to work to find an investment for the £9,000 generated from the sale of the houses in Fenchurch Street. There had already been frustrations with other opportunities which had all come to nothing, but now Okey Farm in Haresfield seemed a likely possibility, together with a farm at Redmarley. At the same time negotiations were in hand with Joseph Jennings, Francis Witts's London agent, to find houses or ground rents to purchase. In the end, it was to be the latter. Jennings summoned Francis Witts to view a site in the east of London in February 1847, but being indisposed, Francis delegated the task to Edward, who reported back favourably. In July negotiations were entered into for ground rents in the parish of St George's in the East, an area immediately east of Whitechapel, between Stepney, Shadwell and Wapping. *1 September 1847: Rec^d. a letter from M^r. Jennings, announcing that he has, together with M^r. Warter, entered into an agreement on my part for the purchase of the Ground rents in S^t. George's in the East, subject to the approval of the Court of Chancery: price £9631: income £389 of which to the amount of £50 is leasehold. The ground rents are secured on about 190 houses of small size, a Chapel and a public house; the occupiers chiefly persons employed in the docks. The locality near the Blackwall railway. Many of the houses fall in at the expiration of 50 or 60 years, others 70 or more, extending to 90 years: the purchase is made on a calculation of something under twenty five years: therefore to pay 4 per C^t. and considering that the term of so many houses but little exceeds 50 years the profit may be considered equal to 5 p^r. C^t. — It is to be hoped we may not again be disappointed by finding the title of this property deficient.*

One other preoccupation of the Diarist was to secure an appropriate foundation for the fortune of his son. With Edward's family now growing he needed additional income and a larger home, and in July a likely opportunity appeared to be in view in the adjoining living of Stanton: *2 July 1846: A letter from E.F.W. who gives up all thoughts of the incumbency of Waltham Abbey, in which I think he acts wisely: for the labour and responsibility would be great, the remuneration inadequate, and the acceptance of the preferment would remove him from cherished connections and habits to a great distance, entailing on him duties and engagements alien to those to which he is now accustomed. My son admits that with an increasing family he finds his income inadequate, and though, no doubt, some indulgences might be abridged, it will be necessary and proper for us to increase his allowance, unless his means be increased from greater clerical emolument or any other source. While I was at Gloucester, I asked Mr. Jackson, Mr. Bloxsome's partner, whether it was in contemplation to part with the advowson or next presentation of the Rectory of Stanton, which belong to Mr.*

B's clergyman son, who is now in a very dangerous state of health, and, it is believed, cannot long survive. It appeared that the matter had been pressed upon Mr. W.H.B. but that he, not being convinced of the hopeless state of his health, was unwilling to part from the next presentation; that such a step was considered advisable by his friends; that, probably, the Advowson would not be sold. I requested Mr. J. to inform me if a resolution should be taken to sell the advowson or presentation. The acquisition of this preferment on reasonable terms would be advantageous to us, would be very agreeable to my son, to whom it would be a residence in his own neighbourhood and after his own heart, with an increase of income, and a benefice, moreover tenable at a future time with the living of Upper Slaughter, should such an arrangement be desirable. The value of the Rectory of Stanton, with the Curacy of Snowshill, is about £400 per ann.

In September the possibility of the Stanton living looked a little more hopeful, and Francis Witts arranged for his Cirencester solicitor, Sewell, to visit Mr Bloxsome senior, a solicitor in Dursley to discuss the matter: *Wrote to Mr. Sewell as to the purchase of the living of Stanton, mentioning what I had learnt yesterday from Mr. Malcolm, Rural Dean of Campden Deanery, that Mr. W. H. Bloxsome has acted illegally in some alterations made by him in the pewing of the Church there, giving great offence to some of his parishioners, and exposing himself to ecclesiastical censure, and to proceedings in the Ecclesiastical Court. Malcolm is to have a meeting with the parties to-morrow to endeavour to accommodate matters. It seems desirable that Sewell should be informed of this feud before his interview with the Solicitors in Dursley. This state of things will make Mr. WHB. more disposed to divest himself of the incumbency. . . . 7 September 1847: Mr. Sewell and my Son also met here to confer with me as to the purchase of the advowson of, or next presentation to the living of Stanton. After a long and close discussion of the subject in all its bearings, we came to the conclusion to offer £6000 for the advowson, or £4500 for the next presentation; these to be the utmost limits, but in the first instance to offer £4000 or £5500 . . . 15 September 1847: Received a letter from Sewell . . . W H Bloxsome positively refuses to part from the advowson, but will sell the next presentation for £4500 provided the fixtures be separately paid for at a valuation, and the next incumbent takes upon himself to do such matters in respect of repairs and alterations of Stanton Church as are in contemplation and discussion between WHB on the one hand, and the Churchwardens and parishioners on the other. After carefully considering the affair with E.F.W. and with his full concurrence, I replied to Sewell that I was willing to give £4500 for the next presentation inclusive of fixtures . . . 5 October 1847: E.F.W. sent his servant from Stow with a note, to inform me that he had had an interview with Mr. W H Bloxsome, who is eager to make arrangements for leaving Stanton, and for the sale of his furniture there. He wished to know my Son's views as to coming to reside at Stanton. My son had replied to him that such arrangements seemed to him premature, as the Bishop had not yet accepted the resignation tendered by WHB . . . 14 October 1847: I received letters form Mr. Bloxsome and his son Edward . . . Mr. E.B. flatters himself that before we meet at the Quarter Sessns. next week he shall have had interviews with Mr. Holt, and the Bishop: that the resignation will have been tendered and accepted, and the business all but settled . . .* But it was not to be. The Bishop took offence and refused to accept the resignation, so Edward's hope for the accession of Stanton to his cure came to an end: *9 November 1847: A letter came to-day from Mr. Sewell in which he reports that he met E. Bloxsome on*

Saturday last at Gloucester, and that their interview terminated in the cancelling of the contract for the purchase of the next presentation of Stanton. . . . Edward now needed augmentation to his income from elsewhere, and in the end it was a constant succession of cheques from his father.

European famine was not confined to Ireland; in 1845 it occurred more seriously in Belgium, Germany and Denmark, but whereas those countries were not so badly affected in 1846, Ireland experienced the blight to devastating effect. Slight recovery in 1847 and 1848 was of limited benefit due to the scarcity of seed potatoes. One of the consequences was a general increase in the price of grain and Francis Witts makes reference to this: *27 March 1847: Wrote to Davison, Newman and C⁰· to enquire the lowest price of Patna Rice in large quantities, some of the labourers being desirous of purchasing the article at a lower rate than it is sold in the village or country shops, as a substitute for flour, now at a high price. . . . 30 March 1847: Rec^d· a letter from Rowland Ingram Junr· acknowledging my contribution of £3. 3. 0. towards assisting the poor inhabitants of Giggleswick and Settle, not receiving parochial relief to obtain flour and oatmeal on moderate terms; he mentions the potatoe disease as having already shown itself this season in Craven . . . . 19 June 1847: called on M^r· Cook. Decided symptoms of disease in the potatoe plant.*

On Sunday 21 February there had been an appeal in church specified in a Queen's letter and a good response had been forthcoming from the parishioners of Upper Slaughter, but later in the year attitudes were hardening. Notwithstanding substantial press coverage and heart-rending engravings in the *Illustrated London News* the seriousness of the situation in south-west Ireland does not seem to have registered and Francis Witts is particularly hard-hearted. The grain harvest of 1847 in England had been good, but people were still starving in the streets in Ireland: *17 October 1847: This was the Sunday appointed for a thanksgiving to Almighty GOD for the great national blessing of an abundant harvest. . . . I preached on "Universal thanksgiving the duty of Christians," with a special application to existing circumstances, as required in the Queen's letter lately circulated, calling for a collection in aid of the distressed population in the Southern & Western parts of Ireland, and on the North Western coasts of Scotland. It is but too true that there is likely to be this winter also a great deficiency of food in those quarters, with great want. But this appeal for renewed charity to the Irish has been generally met with not only great coldness, but with strong disapprobation in some quarters, and a decided disinclination to liberal assistance. It is urged that an enormous fund has been already raised and remitted to Ireland for charitable succour in this year: that the nation has been heavily burdened by the advance of many millions to stay the evil in Ireland, with little prospect of repayment of much of the amount; that the people are incorrigibly idle and lazy, crying evermore, give, give: that there is a lack of energy in till^g· the soil, opening up fisheries &c.; that the agitators lay and clerical, clamouring for repeal and abusing the Saxon, relax not in their violent opposition to the government; that disorganization is rapidly spreading, agrarian disturbances, combination not to pay rents, and other disorders on the increase; that a secret conspiracy seems to exist, manifested by ruthless murders of persons of all classes, and many most worthy characters, even when going about doing good in their districts. Hence John Bull is resolved to shut up his purse, and keep his money at home, so that instead of the noble contributions of last spring, a very scanty supply may be expected as the result of the appeal made to-day by the Clergy in obedience to the Queen's letter. Our collection was £1. 15. 10 – in February last we received between £5 & £6.*

1848 was a year of revolution across Europe, but despite fears in Britain everything at home was relatively peaceful. In the 1820s Francis Witts had reported national and international events extensively in his diaries, but in later years this fell away. The events of 1848, however, led to numerous diary entries of interest: *5 March 1848: The newspapers announce the arrival at Newhaven on the Sussex coast of Louis Philippe, and his Queen, with two or three attendants. They were picked up at sea by a steamer, and taken on board from a French fishing boat. Great have been the perils and anxieties of these aged victims of a successful rebellion. Flying from Paris, without preparation, with hardly any money or clothes, in the most obscure vehicles, by highways & byways, in disguise, and under feigned names, making for the coast, forced to rely for succour and concealment on persons of humble means and humble station . . . The Duchess of Orleans and her boy princes have reached Dusseldorf in safety. . . . 12 March 1848: The results of the late French revolution develope themselves in other parts of the continent; it seems a contagion; or as if a shower of sparks issuing from a volcano spread wide conflagration in the surrounding circle. Fuel is every where ready, a torch only was wanting, and that is now supplied. A longing for liberty of the press, for a representative constitution, for the abolition of ancient class privileges, and for the correction of abuses, seem every where to prevail; yet for the most part there is no desire to fraternize with France. Italy is convulsed; Sardinia steps forward as the advocate of liberalism . . . There is little doubt that the convulsion will extend over the whole of Germany, and that the ancient realms of Prussia and Austria will be shaken: here, as in Italy, a rage for one empire to embrace all the German states is a dream which sanguine and stirring spirits will seek to realize — "Vaterland" is the cry — freedom of the press is loudly insisted on it, and a democratical spirit is spread far and wide.*

By far the most momentous coming change in Francis Witts's life in the period covered by the diaries in this volume is the decline of Margaret. On her birthday in 1848 he commented in optimistic terms: *24 August 1848: MW's birthday: entering on her 63ᵈ· year. May GOD protect and preserve her to be a comfort to her husband and children, and all connected with her! She has been my faithful and true partner for forty years and more, an affectionate wife and mother, a good daughter, bearing with the infirmities and faults of her nearest connections patiently, and doing her utmost to promote their peace and prosperity. Her health, though very indifferent, is not worse than it has long been; her removal hence would be a great blow to me, which GOD avert!*

Perhaps it was sub-conscious prescience that led him to make these comments, for from this time onwards her health continued to worsen. From December 1849 the diary entries are melancholy as they chronicle Margaret's slide towards the grave: *24 December 1849: M.W. has been of late so much indisposed, and appeared to suffer particularly to-day from the cold, and has such shortness of breath, with debility, and restless nights, that I wrote to desire Mʳ· Hayward to visit her; however, from some cause, he did not come . . . 25 December 1849: Christmas day —— Mʳ· Hayward visited MW. at breakfast time, and found her much out of order; much nervous excitability, a tongue very much furred, a bad pulse &c. but trusts there is no essential mischief at work, and that a course of alterative medicine with care may restore her to a comfortable state.*

On 8 January she was seen by Hayward and also the distinguished Dr. Baron who considered there was no serious mischief, but he was mistaken. Francis Witts clung to hope: *14 January 1850: . . . I fancied I observed some improvement in MW's health.*

Four days later the hopeful signs had disappeared: *18 January 1850: No improvement in my dear wife's health: the remedies applied yesterday do not seem to have succeeded in reducing the irregularity of the pulse, or relieving the impeded respiration — She continued in a very suffering, exhausted state; chiefly confined to her bed till towards dinner time, receiving her dear children, her grandchild and myself more or less in the sick chamber. Mr Hayward also paid his visit, prescribed a blister, and changed the medicine. In the evening we all passed some time in the sick chamber. — A very anxious and trying day.*

From this time onwards there is a growing realisation and on 15 February 1850 this turned into acceptance: *. . . Mr Hayward made an early visit, having been prevented attending yesterday. All seems much the same with our patient as of late; drowsiness, quick pulse, dry mouth, restless nights; the digestive organs, and the kidneys, appear in a better order, but the dropsical symptoms are not materially abated; and H. evidently considers them as serious, not denying, in answer to my questions, that there is anasarca, with a short cough common in that disease, and that MW's state may be feared to be a breaking up of the constitution . . .*

Margaret Witts had never been a confident and lively person and unlike Francis Witts's outgoing mother, Agnes, she did not force herself into the limelight but always remained quietly in the wings. Notwithstanding this lack of vibrancy she was a quiet and constant support for Francis. In his youth he had followed his mother being constantly in society; but due to Margaret's quieter propensities he settled to a rural domestic life and channelled energies into his business and magisterial life. Now, after a married life of forty years he was forced to contemplate losing his quiet domestic companion. The 'evil' was dropsy, or what today would be called congestive heart failure.

Margaret had always been delicate and in her younger years had suffered numerous miscarriages. We know from several diary entries that Francis Witts was of generous proportions and it may have been that Margaret was not of slender size; making heart disease more of a risk. From January onwards the decline was slow but unabating. As Francis Witts completed this notebook (later catalogued as diary F367) she was close to the end of her time in this world.

Each year Francis Witts mentioned his birthday, and this year he had cause to seek more strength from his Maker: *26 February 1850: My 67$^{th.}$ birthday; GOD be thanked for his loving kindness in granting me time to make my peace with him before I go hence & be no more seen! . . . Soften to me, O Lord, the heavy trial I now endure in the grievous sickness of my dear wife, and strengthen me and her to bear up patiently, and to meet the fatal issue to be expected at no distant day!*

Witts Family Papers F356

There is a gap in the diaries from 12 July 1845 and 18 May 1846. This gap also marks a change in presentation. Spaces amounting to almost one third of a line are introduced, as if to indicate paragraphs. A further and more radical change is also introduced in relation to the presentation of the dates. This diary F356 onwards shows dates in the form May 18. Monday as against the previous style of Monday May 18. This new style is continued until the end of his life.

During the winter and early spring of 1846 there were serious domestic upsets in the Howell family that eventually led Thomas Howell to sell the Prinknash estate. See 22 October 1846 and the footnote there. From this day's entry it becomes clear that Edward was involved in some way in this upset. If so, it is further evidence to support the theory that Edward destroyed some diaries after his father's death.

Diary — 1846

May 18. Monday.

After heavy rain during the night, a rainy day, yet not without frequent fine gleams, and the evening was fair.

After an early breakfast, left home with MW. in our close carriage, with man and maid servants, for Cheltenham, our first stage towards the Isle of Wight. Sent back our carriage, and at the Railway Station had the comfort of meeting Edward and Sophy, and their dear children, with a female attendant, who drove to Ashchurch, and there took the rail. Left the Cheltenham Station at 10.20. and arrived at the Gloucester Station by 10.40. Transferred ourselves, servants and luggage to the Cheltenham and Great Western line of rails,[1] starting by a train at 11 AM. Beautiful drive by Standish, Stroud and Brimscombe to the Sapperton tunnel; long obscurity, and emerged into a totally different Country: for the beautiful, narrow, and populous valley of Chalford entered on an upland, stone wall, Cotswold tract: called at the Tetbury road station, the Kemble or Cirencester Station, where a branch rail, and an engine convey people to and from |[2] Cirencester, the Minety station, the Purton Station

---

1. This was the notorious change from the Midland Station with the narrow gauge of rails, to the Great Western Station with the broad gauge of rails. The distance between the two stations was about 100 yards. The Midland Station was demolished in the late 1960s. Prior to that time, a covered way provided pedestrian access between the two stations. The current Gloucester Station is on the site of the Great Western Station.

Diary — 1846.

May 18. Monday — After heavy rain during the night, a rainy day, yet not without frequent fine gleams, and the evening was fair.   After an early breakfast, left home with MW. in our close carriage, with man and maid servants, for Cheltenham, our first stage towards the Isle of Wight. Sent back our carriage, and at the Railway Station had the comfort of meeting Edward and Sophy, and their dear children, with a female attendant, who drove to Ashchurch, and there took the rail. Left the Cheltenham Station at 10.20. and arrived at the Gloucester Station by 10.40. Transferred ourselves, servants and luggage to the Cheltenham and Great Western line of rails, starting by a train at 11 A.M. Beautiful drive by Standish, Stroud and Brimscomb to the Sapperton tunnel; long obscurity, and emerged into a totally different country: for the beautiful, narrow, and populous valley of Chalford entered on an upland, stone wall Cotswold tract: called at the Tetbury road station, the Kemble or Cirencester Station, where a branch rail, and an engine convey people to and from to the Swindon Station on the Great Western line, where a halt of twelve minutes gave us an opportunity of exchanging friendly greetings with our old acquaintance Newmarch, the father, whom we had not seen since his return from the Continent. — From Swindon Station to Reading Station, where we arrived at 2 P.M. and found waiting for us a conveyance provided by the landlord of the Reading Station hotel, to whom I had previously written, we freighted a clean omnibus, which he had procured, and which, drawn by a a pair of post horses, accommodated all our party and luggage – E.F.W. seated himself with the servant outside, the ladies, children, maidservants and myself within; it was rather close and warm within, and the motion of an Omnibus is always uncomfortable; but in a little more than an hour and half we reached our destination at the Basingstoke Station on the South Western railway. – We passed by a good road through a level, but richly wooded country, with much fine oak, and by several seats, especially by |3 Stratfield-Saye, the Duke of Wellington's, and near it the country residence of the Speaker of the House of Commons, Shaw Lefevre: much good farming, & some good land; but also much poor and uninclosed. As we approached Basingstoke the Chalk formation began, and we noticed some very deep and large chalk pits, where the material was excavated for sale. The distance from Reading to Basingstoke 16 miles: we did not enter the town, but drove past it to the Railway Station on the high ground near it; a very cold, breezy place, on down land, which surrounds the town in all directions. The station is near to a ruined church, with a churchyard now still used for interments, and the chancel is entire to receive the mourners with the corpse, where the service is performed: the view of the town from the station is pleasant, the houses are mingled with trees, and there is a roomy old Church with a low square tower. We arrived nearly half an hour before the train from London, by which we intended to proceed. It was about 4.45. P.M. when we took our departure for Gosport: the distance being 42 miles: the Stations |4 between Basingstoke and Gosport being the Andover road, Winchester, Bishopstoke, Botley, and Fareham stations. The Country is for the most part downland, in a state of good cultivation; Southdown sheep abound: the yellow broom grows as a native weed in great profusion, and full blossom: distant woods, and elevations; villages & seats here and there: the environs of Winchester, very near to which city the railway runs, with its cathedral, the Holy Cross Church, the Itchin river, the meadows on its banks &c. arrest attention, and induced a desire to visit these localities with more of leisure. At Bishopstoke Station the diverging line of rail to Southampton, six miles distant, conveyed the traveller to that port; at Botley, where one was reminded of Cobbett,[2] and still more decidedly at Fareham, we got into a level sea-shore tract: to our left the upper part of Portsmouth harbour. At the Gosport terminus we betook ourselves to a very clean, quiet, and comfortable Railway hotel, where we arrived soon after 6 P.M. and were all ready for a dinner in half an hour. The town of Gosport lay before us inclosed on the land side by a line of ramparts: the entrance into |5 the place being over a drawbridge, and through a gateway: near is a private gateway, and road, by which the Queen, on her journeys to and from the Isle of Wight, drives into the Royal Clarence Victualling yard, whence she embarks in her steamer for Osborne House:

2. William Cobbett, (1763-1835). Cobbett was a journalist and reformer. He published his radical *Weekly Political Register* until his death. His best known book is *Rural Rides*. He was born in Farnham, Surrey, not Fareham, Hampshire as seems to be hinted by Francis Witts.

*1. The break
in the gauges
Gloucester,
a Punch cartoon
of 1846.*

beyond the Victualling Yard is seen the Dockyard: to the right of Gosport is Haslar Hospital. After dinner strolled with E.F.W. into Gosport: as in other fortified towns, there is a broad unoccupied space of green fields, between the rampart and the Town; in the town are several populous streets, one wide and handsome, many narrow and more like alleys; not far from the entrance gate near the Victualling Yard is a recently built and consecrated Chapel of ease, a singular looking Church, devoid of all external ornament, yet interesting from its simplicity, in the earliest English style, with narrow lancet windows, nave, aisles, chancel, clerestory, with a small bell turret appended to the side of the North aisle — close by are spacious school rooms, somewhat in the Tudor style. Having partaken of tea, and arranged our plans for the morrow, we retired soon after |[6] ten to rest. —

	Distance travelled miles
Upper Slaughter to Cheltenham Station	16
Gloucester Station	7
Reading Station	18
Basingstoke Station	16
Gosport Station	<u>42</u>
	<u>159</u>

May 19. Tuesday.
Weather fine till evening.

Before breakfast, I strolled into Gosport, found my way to Cold Harbour, an open place by the harbour with good houses: obtained from an intelligent boatman information as to sights to be seen at Portsmouth, the Dockyard, the Victualling yard, Haslar Hospital, Nelson's ship, the Victory, lying in the harbour &c. — Repairs to the outworks going on: convicts

*2. Portsmouth
Harbour, c. 1830.*

employed. After breakfast at 10 AM. proceeded to the Packet Pier at the extremity of Gosport: exceedingly well arranged: embarked on board a very neat, clean, well appointed steam-boat for Ryde; weather beautiful, a fresh breeze, (we landsmen would call it) the wind a head, foam crowned waves — none of us sea-sick; but the children a little squeamish [7] made the passage in 50 minutes; distance five miles; had the wind been in our stern, would have crossed in half an hour. Mouth of harbour very fine: passed beneath two huge convict hulks: stood across to Portsmouth, took in a boatful of chiefly steerage passengers: fare for the stern passengers – eighteen pence each, servants a shilling, children sixpence each. Fort Monkton a bristling battery, on the shore, westward of Haslar hospital; other strong works for the sea defence in progress – Two men of war in the road, the Canopus, lately returned from the West Indies, and the Raleigh frigate: the evolution squadron sailed last week. Noted the buoy which marks the spot where the Royal George sank. Beyond Fort Monkton Westward, Anglesea, a Bathing place, with some villas and a row of lodging houses, said to be a bad speculation. Westward of Ryde, between it and Cowes, the Motherbank, where merchant vessels anchor, as contradistinguished from Spithead, the station of men of war. We saw before us the Northern shore [8] of the Isle of Wight from Cowes Westward, to nearly S[t.] Helens, Eastward; gently rising from the sea, with its slopes clothed with rich wood to the water's edge, especially about Ryde, which appeared what the French term <u>riant</u>, its numerous white villas crowded together in leafy groves: from the beach extends the Pier, half a mile into the sea, with a very well constructed and spacious head, on which we landed very conveniently; our luggage was consigned to a porter, and we pursued our course, much admiring, to the Pier Hotel. It was low water, and there was all the disadvantage of a great width of sand and mud, shingles forming the beach, and no good sands for exercise on horseback, in carriage, or in foot: but the Pier forms an excellent, breezy, but not cheap, promenade: to-day somewhat too windy for comfort. At the Hotel we were introduced to a House and lodging Agent, under whose guidance E F W. and I set out on a tour of inspection, and looked at several sets |⁹ of apartments; — near the sea, with a front view of the moving expanse, the price was higher than in more distant localities, not having a full seaview. We returned to report to the ladies, who accompanied us on a second survey, which ended in our engaging Nᵒˑ 3. Strand, otherwise Turret Villa, a house lately furnished and never yet occupied, on the Beach, commanding a glorious sea view: having a dining and drawing room, three best bedrooms, three secondary rooms, servant's bed room, and commodious offices. Our temporary abode is Eastward of the Pier, ᶜᵃˡˡᵉᵈ ᵀᵘʳʳᵉᵗ ⱽⁱˡˡᵃ near a mansion called the Castle, as built in a castellated form, from the turrets of wʰˑ I suppose, it̶ ᵒᵘʳ ᵃᵇᵒᵈᵉ takes its name. It is studiously furnished, with all manner of conveniences, and we are to pay five guineas a week, which includes some plate, all the linen and china, with the use of a cook, provided by the owner, living at our cost, but not sleeping in the house. This arrangement suits us well, as having three servants with us; and with the |¹⁰ children, it is better to be quite detached from other parties; here they have a little garden to run about in, opening on the beach. Our new abode is one of the last on the beach. Eastward: not far from us a beautiful hill crowned with timber, among which appear several Villas, with fine seaviews: this hill forms the boundary of a low valley, formerly, no doubt, covered at high tides by the sea, or a morass: the Western height flanking this valley is thickly studded with villas, and rows of houses, contiguous to which a handsome new church is in progress of erection. We dined at the Pier Hotel, and took possession of our new home by six P.M. — In the course of the day we strolled about the Town, making purchases for house-keeping, s̶t̶r̶o̶l̶l̶e̶d̶ ˢᵃᵘⁿᵗᵉʳᵉᵈ on the pier and beach &c.

Sophy was suffering from a bad cold and sore throat.

Received a letter from the County Chairman in answer to mine in which I had communicated to |¹¹ him the resolutions passed by the Guardians of our Union as to valuations of parishes for the purpose of the County rate: also from Mʳ Wells, Vice Chairman of the Northleach Union on the same subject, in answer to my letter to him inviting the co-operation of that Board of Guardians with ours.

May 20. Wednesday.
Fine till afternoon, when a shower or two fell: cold wind. —

Wrote to Mʳ Pearce a letter to be laid before the Valuation Committee of our Guardians to-morrow, or at their second meeting, if it should not reach Stow in time for the first: sent Mʳ Wells's letter received by me yesterday, and hints grounded on Purnell's letter also received yesterday.

Walked with MW. about the town: the Church which I noticed yesterday is consecrated, and used for divine service; the workmen are now employed in finishing the tower: there are two other churches, or rather, Chapels of ease to the Mother Church ᵃᵗ an inland village — Newchurch. – My old acquaintance, Spencer Phillips, is the |¹² Incumbent, but is now absent. Both these churches ᵃᵗ ᴿʸᵈᵉ are spacious, both modern, and both of the vile <u>Compo</u> order, so designated by Paget in Sᵗˑ Antholin's. At one of them, Sᵗˑ James's, Mʳ Sibthorp officiated before he went over to Popery, which he has ~~again~~ ^{in turn} recanted. There is a large Town Hall, connected with a spacious market house; also a theatre, and more than one meeting house. Union Street is the best and most frequented, with the best shops; in it also an Arcade, a very costly and elegant building with shops, but it is apparently not ~~much frequented;~~ ^{very popular} the shops contain fossils, stationery, playthings, prints, and the usual miscellaneous wares of a bazaar. — Villas and comfortable cottages, private residences and for hire, abound every where, nestling in shrubberies and gardens; at present the place seems thin, and dull. E.F.W. and Sophy explored the beach Eastward, and were much pleased with their walk. In the evening my Son and I walked in the same direction, below the grounds of Apley house, |¹³ along a sea wall, the tide being up: a charming view along the coast, oakwoods fringing the shore, gently rising with much luxuriance: we turned inland, and had an enchanting view of the interior of the Apley grounds, fine oak coppice, lofty and spreading single oaks, a luxuriant meadow nearby ready for the scythe, a beautiful vista of the sea seen through the stems or over the tops of the luxuriant oaks. The house spacious, backed by gardens, stables, and other villas not yet finished, looking towards Ryde, and commanding fine sea views, Westward. Returned by the grounds of St. John's, another large villa embosomed in trees.

A letter from Mr Dickins, in answer to my communication to him of the resolutions of our Guardians as to the valuation for the County rate: a deputation of guardians connected with the Gloucestershire parishes of the Shipston Union will meet our valuation Committee at Stow to-morrow, being desirous of acting in concert with us.

May 21. Thursday.
A fine day, but the wind Easterly. |¹⁴

Wrote a letter to Purnell in answer to the one I had received from him as to valuations for the County rate.

With M.W. and Sophy attended divine service in the forenoon at St. Thomas's Chapel: this being Ascension day. The pews high and narrow, galleries on three sides, a small organ, but neither Clerk, pew opener, or organist whom we could see. A small congregation of forty or fifty worshippers, chiefly ladies; no sermon preached; the prayers &c. well read by a young Clergyman with a weak voice.

E.F.W. made a long pedestrian excursion for twelve or fifteen miles to examine the geological structure of the Eastern point of the Island, visiting Brading, Sandown, Bembridge, Culver Cliffs, St. Helens, Sea View &c. with which he returned to dinner, pleased and fatigued.[3]

MW. Sophy, Broome and I enjoyed a long saunter or sitting on the Pier, watching steamers arrive and depart.

---

3. Edward's geological interests were probably the driving force behind the excursion to the Isle of Wight. Unfortunately the missing diaries covering the prior period result in this being conjecture.

*3. Iris paddle
steamer c. 1843.*

In the evening we all walked by the same delightful circuit which |[15] I took yesterday evening.

A letter from Bathurst about tithe and poor rate valuations &c.

May 22. Friday.
A very fine day.

Letter from M[r] Thornton with inclosures from M[rs.] Hunt, and Miss M. C. Hunt &c. on
Wadenhoe Trust matters. Wrote to Sophia Hunt on that affair. Letter from C. J. Geldard
covering the balance sheet of rents &c. received, money expended in repairs &c. on our property
in Craven. Also a letter from C Bathurst explanatory of one received from him yesterday —

Excursion to Carisbrooke Castle and back in an open carriage with one horse: distance nine
miles – The road from Ryde to Wootton Bridge, and a little further, very pretty: near Ryde an
abundance of elegant villas, with shrubberies and lawns, all commanding splendid sea views:
a fine gravel road, frequently ascending and descending. Country fertile, at a distance inland
lofty downs. Binstead, a village near Ryde, but the Church not seen; here other enjoyable
villas, and extensive stone quarries, rich in fossil remains. Further on to the |[16] right the
remains of Quarr Abbey, few and insignificant; this was the largest monastic establishment
on the island. Wootton Bridge lies on the Wootton river or Fishbourn Creek, when we
crossed it the tide was down; the water above the bridge, held up to supply extensive mills,
forms a beautiful small lake, fringed with oak coppice on the one side, and bounded by a
lawn attached to a handsome seat, Fern Hill, on the other; sloping heights crowned, clothed,
and pendant to the water's edge, with oak coppice to the right, present a sweet landscape
when the tide is high, and the mud covered: beyond a beautiful reach of the Solent Sea, and
the Hampshire coast ~~beyond.~~ Further on a tamer and less wooded tract, yet still not devoid of
oak wood and coppice, which abound in this part of the island: this tract recently enclosed.
Here to the North West we saw Osborne Tower, a late erection appurtenant to the Queen's
new residence of Osborne House, which lies below it, at the head of a wooded |[17] lawn

sloping down to the sea. Her Majesty has acquired considerable property here by purchase, the Barton farm, I believe, it is called, and by the roadside we passed an extensive brickfield, where brick, draining tiles &c. are fabricated for the improvement of the royal buildings and demesne. Beyond Osborne Tower is East Cowes on an eminence, overlooking the æstuary of the Medina river, which, taking its rise in the very south of the island, divides [it] into two nearly equal sections. Turning abruptly southwest, from the road leading to East Cowes, we approached Newport, the capital town of the island, with a population of 7000 inhabitants, situate on the Medina, which is navigable for small vessels: of the river we caught glimpses, from Newport to West Cowes, at its mouth. Before entering into Newport passed by a pretty suburb, Barton Village, with a new Church, a striking object, built after the Byzantine fashion: near to it is a lace manufactory. On the opposite side of the Medina lies Parkhurst forest, or what |[18] was anciently so called, high ground, with some extensive oak-woods. Here are seen, at a short distance from Newport, Albany Barracks, and Parkhurst prison. The former are capable of accommodating a force of 2000 men, and 1500 are often quartered there; the station being used as a dépôt for troops going out on foreign service, to Canada and other North American dependencies &c. – Here the detachments of various regiments combine in one dépôt, to be drilled until troop ships are ready to convey them to their several destinations. — Parkhurst prison is assigned to juvenile delinquents, to such as are sentenced to transportation, but are here imprisoned for a limited term before they are sent abroad, and are taught trades, to which they can apply themselves in the penal colony to which they are sent, being also duly instructed in a religious and practical course of education. — Newport, through which we drove, is a clean, neat town, with |[19] good streets, and many handsome houses; there is an old parish church, and in the outskirts a lately erected, apparently

4. Osborne House,
Isle of Wight

handsome, chapel, which we saw from
Carisbrook Castle. Carisbrook village
and its ruined castle are about a mile
beyond Newport: we passed through a
sort of suburb, known, I believe, as New
Village, containing numerous pretty and
comfortable residences and villas. The
village of Carisbrook lies at the foot of the
castle hill, separated from it by a rivulet, of
pellucid clearness. It is a considerable place,
with a handsome Church, its houses being
interspersed with trees: pretty villas of

5. *Carisbrooke Castle.*

recent erection are in its outskirts, among them one belonging to M[r.] Gunter, the London
confectioner, near which he has erected an infant school, which he endows for the benefit
of the children of the village: this is a pleasing symptom of the general state of feeling, and

very creditable to a generous individual.
At the foot of the Castle Hill my son and
I left the carriage, the Ladies proceeding
in it up the eminence to |[20] the Castle
gates: we ascended to the outer ramparts,
a beautiful stretch of short turf, forming
a delightful promenade, and commanding
a splendid view. Arrived at the Castle
gates we admired the beautiful ruined
entrance its arch, its flanking towers, its
machicolation Over the archway is inscribed
E. R. (Elizabetha Regina) 1598 — the gates
themselves are of wood, the ancient gates,
iron bound, with a low wicket, through

6. *Carisbrooke Castle.*

which we entered, admittance having been given by the guide from within, who resides in the
Governor's house, a modern pl pile, now never inhabited as an official residence: the present
Governor is Lord Heytesbury, now Viceroy in Ireland: some parts of the interior are

ancient, particularly, a lofty square tower-
like part of the house, but all modernized.
To the left, in complete ruin, are remains
of the apartments in which the unhappy
Charles the 1[st.] was imprisoned, and the
window is exhibited through which he
attempted to escape, but was prevented,
as |[21] he was unable to thrust his body
through. To the right on entering is a
modern chapel, probably, of the date of
the beginning of the 18[th.] Century, wherein
service used to be performed; but it is now

7. *Carisbrooke Castle.*

disused, except, I believe, when the municipal officers of Newport are annually sworn into office. Passing by the well house, and the old donkey, we ~~approch~~ approached the Norman Keep; here the view is exceedingly pleasing, the natural foliage of ivy, yew, and brushwood clothing the grey tower, and the rude flight of half decayed 72 steps, by which it is ascended. The summit commands a noble prospect, over Carisbrook, Newport, and along the valley of Medina; to the North West beyond Parkhurst forest, to Thorney bay; to the

8. Quarr Abbey, Isle of Wight.

South and South West, a fertile interior with valleys, and hamlets bounded by lofty downs. Refreshed by the contents of a basket which we had brought with us, and of which we partook at the top of the tower, we were greeted at the foot of the steps, by the offer of tumblers of milk made by |[22] the tenant of the pasturage within the circuit of the Castle walls, the extent of which is about twenty acres; the actual fortress covered about two acres. To the Well house, containing a very beautifully constructed ancient well, said to be 290 feet in depth: ~~290 fe~~ 210 feet to the water, 80 feet of water: the upper part surrounded with masonry, the lower hewn out of the rock: the water is drawn by a tread wheel, the donkey treading within it, as an old fashioned turn-spit would in a like wheel of small dimensions; the exercise seems not to disagree with the docile and patient animal; for he was stout and in good condition, through 20 years old, and his predecessor was shot on account of the infirmities of old age at 49 years. Experiments to shew the depth and beautiful construction of the well are made, by pouring a glassful of water down; it takes five seconds before the liquid dashes on the surface of the water below; and a lamp |[23] lowered by a coil of string to the surface of the water beneath reveals the accuracy with which the shaft has been sunk and constructed. Leaving the Castle we reached in a few minutes the village, where we rejoined our carriage, the horse having been baited. Visited the Church, an ancient early English Structure with a nave and South Aisle; badly pewed — of monuments one to the memory of

9. Carisbrooke Castle, Isle of Wight.

the lady of a former Governor of Carisbrook Castle, Sir N. Wadham, in the time of Hen. 7.: the charitable disposition of the deceased is testified by six figures of cripples, three on each side; the effigy of the lady being represented as kneeling in prayer. There is also a wooden tablet with quaint poetry, declaratory of the faith and hope of the departed, a Captain Keeling, who died in 1619, having been Groom of the Chamber to Ja[s.] 1. We returned home by five o clock, much pleased with our excursion.

May 23. Saturday.
A fine day.

Examined my Yorkshire accounts, and acknowledged to C. J. Geldard the receipt of his letter yesterday, |[24] with the half-yearly balance sheet. E.F.W. explored the Binstead Stone quarries, about a mile from Ryde on the Newport road, bringing back several fossils.

With MW. Sophy, and the children, being afterwards joined by E.F.W., sauntered on the beach and sands, and sea walls Eastward, below Apley, and by S[t.] Clare, the marine villa of Col. Harcourt, towards Puck Pool, a bay with two or three villas on the Beach, beyond which are Nettlestone point, and Sea View, a range of cottages for a quiet bathing station; a very pleasant stroll. — In the Evening, I explored the beautiful wooded bank to the Eastward of Ryde, inland, and stumbled on a very secluded, tree-encircled, modern built Church, in excellent style, by the side of the main road leading from S[t.] Helens and Brading, and the South eastern quarter of the Island to Ryde. An obliging person, whom I met and questioned, told me that the brook which descends by the valley near our house divides the parishes of S[t.] Helens and Newchurch; |[25] that the Church I had observed is a chapel of ease erected in 1843 in the parish of S[t.] Helens, endowed by some of the opulent residents having seats or villas in its neighbourhood, the Minister's income being increased by pew rents: that S[t.] James's Chapel, Ryde, formerly M[r.] Sibthorpe's, is a proprietary chapel, purchased by a M[r.] Hewitt, who now officiates there.

May 24. Sunday.
Fine weather. MW. and I went to S[t.] John's Church, which I had visited yesterday evening, where the service was well performed and a good sermon preached by a clergyman, names, I understand, Badger, the incumbent. The interior of the church is well arranged, to accommodate 300 worshippers, 150 being free seats: the style Early English, with lancet windows, ~~an~~ a nave, two transepts, a chancel, lofty, with a high-pitched roof, timbered beautifully, and stained to represent oak – the Chancel windows, a triple lancet, surmounted by a Catherine Wheel light, filled with well painted glass, with appropriate church designs; behind |[26] the Communion table, a réredos, an Arcade, with the Cross, gilt on light blue ground, in the centre compartment; the Lord's Prayer, Belief, and Commandments, in quaint, antique, and (a pity!) illegible, missal-like, characters in the other compartments – The sittings are very commodiously disposed, stall like, but fitted with doors, and wide enough for kneeling in the reserved pews — stalls in the nave for the free sittings, Sunday school children, who are taught in the nave before the service begins, and who join in the responses, being ~~taught~~ trained also to sing the Psalms, accompanying a small barrel organ.

The font near the only entrance, which is on the North side, as adjoining the road, is well designed with a carved wooden top — On projecting parts of the roofing timbers a few coats of arms, no doubt, of the contributors to the church or endowment. Nothing could be more pleasing than the service in this tasteful, churchlike, quiet structure, where the opulent and cultivated mingle with the humble, cleanly cottagers |27 and the neatly drest children of the school. – To evening service my son accompanied me to the same church: the ladies going to the new built Church of the Holy Trinity, at Ryde, not far from our house, at the upper end of Dover Street, where my son and daughter had worshipped in the morning.

In the evening E.F.W. and I explored the Villas in the Western quarter of the town, most of them beautiful retreats. A sermon by the Rev^d. A. Watson of Cheltenham was read by my son after we returned and before we retired to our rooms.

May 25. Monday.

Beautiful weather. We devoted this day to the visiting the interesting sights at Portsmouth and Gosport. Embarked in a steam boat from the Pier head at 10 AM. and in little more than half an hour reached the Pier at Portsmouth: a delightful, calm passage. The Canopus is now the only man of war lying in Spithead: the Raleigh sailed yesterday: the former ship is undergoing some repairs. Attended on our landing by an |28 intelligent boatman, whose boat and services we engaged at two shillings per hour, — a two-oared boat. At the end of the street by which we entered Portsmouth reached the interior harbour, which we crossed to the Royal Clarence Victualling Yard at Gosport. Objects of interest without number crowded upon us: our boatman proved a very good guide. Prominent was the Victory, now the Flag ship, the S^t. Vincent being absent with the evolution squadron. Further up the harbour magnificent ships in ordinary, ready to sail on short notice, calmly resting on the noble lake like harbour: Gosport to the left, with the Victualling Yard, which is, I believe, more accurately stated to be at Weevil; to the right Portsmouth, Portsea, the Dock Yard. Round the extremity of the Dock Yard, was stationed the excellent man of war, under the command of Sir Thomas Hastings, from which cannon were booming, and shots |29 ricochetting, or playing at duck and drake, across the interior of the harbour, this vessel being employed for instruction and practice in gunnery. At the head of the harbour, and distant from us, Porchester Castle. In the middle of the harbour a small island, once fortified, now used as a place of interment for the convicts, who die in the hulks. We noticed three or four huge old men of war used as hulks, also a stately and strange looking moving ship or structure, partly house-like, slowly crossing the harbour, the floating bridge between Gosport and Portsmouth, impelled by machinery, working on two powerful chains. Landed near the Victualling Yard: considerable works in progress; convicts, in russet garb, with one leg iron on one leg, working at laborious occupations, whaling materials, and the like. We were now not far from the terminus of the South Western railway and the hotel where we had slept on the night of the 18th. Passing under the |30 wall inclosing the Victualling Yard we came to a very elegant Archway by which admittance is gained into the Establishment. A party of Naval Police, attached to the Yard, was in waiting: on signifying our wish to be admitted, the question was asked whether we were natives of these Kingdoms, and the affirmative answer secured our entrance. At the office of the Inspector, an ill-tempered burly Jack in office, we entered our names, condition and residence, and joining a party already there, a Policeman was assigned to conduct us over the establishment. In theory the admittance is gratuitous, practically a douceur is given to the guide, to secure his attention, for otherwise the stranger would be hurried through the works, points of interest would be omitted, and only a very imperfect survey obtained. But this gratuity must be given, as the boatman cautioned me, "by the sly"; the guide cleverly rubs up against one, one hand in a conve-|[31] niently recipient position, and the necessary corruption is perpetrated. In the spacious square through which we passed were handsome houses, the residences of the superior officers of the yard; a second square, or rather space built on three sides, the fourth being open to the harbour, is devoted to warehouses and store houses. Through these squares her Majesty and Prince Albert, and their illustrious visitors, approaches the Steamer which carries them across to the Isle of Wight, when they have travelled to Gosport by the Railway. We were first ushered into a vast storehouse with barrels containing salted beef and pork for the use of the navy; others contain peas, oatmeal &c. We visited the mill, and all its departments, which are worked by steam: the great size of the apartments strike one, nor is one less impressed with the cleanliness, the airiness, the absence of bustle, the few hands employed, steam machinery performing most of the work: we traced the processes from a |[32] granary which contained eight hundred quarters of wheat through the mill, the boulting room &c.[4] vast was the din of wheels, millstones, and the necessary gearing: all was order, method, apt arrangement: but the most interesting sight was the Bakehouse, a vast apartment crowded with men and boys engaged in the process of baking sea biscuit: the temperature was very hot, the workmen scantily clad: on one side a long range of ovens, heated by coal, each attended by one man putting in to be baked, or taking out when baked, his oven full of flat biscuits: steam is here too the principal moving power; it moves machinery for forming the dough, machinery for kneading the dough, heavy rollers for rolling out the mass, machinery for stamping, cutting and marking the dough; the biscuits when baked are packed in bags each weighing a hundred weight, sowed up, and stored for use in a vast apartment which, when we visited [it] contained between 15 & 1600 bags. The |[34] flavour of the biscuit, as tasted warm from the oven, is excellent. — Leaving the Victualling yard we took boat again, and rowed higher up the harbour; observed a powerful, floating steam engine, ready for use in case any of the ships should catch fire: gazed with admiration on the mighty vessels ready to move to vindicate the honour, or punish the enemies of Britain; all is maintained in such order that on a very short notice these mountains of ships can be supplied with all the necessaries for their outfit, being brought close to the Dockyard, the masts, spars, cordage, rigging, guns and ammunition are speedily supplied: provisions are issued from the Victualling Yard, sailors from the receiving ships; and such is the advantage of order and arrangement that all is done without confusion, nothing omitted, all recorded, and in a space of time which strikes one with astonishment. It was our wish to have gone on board the Victoria and Albert Steam Yacht, the regal galley, which bears the Queen, |[34] her consort, and their court, on her voyages of pleasure, the exterior of which we had seen at Brighton, and the splendid fittings and apartments of which we would gladly have inspected: but she could not be shewn, as the painters and decorators were busy on board: however, we rowed

4.   Boulting room – bolting, sieving – a room where the flour is sieved.

round her, as also by the Royal George, the splendid sailing Yacht, built by Geo. IV in which he visited Scotland and Ireland, a sumptuously adorned ship, on board of which the Officers and Crew of the Victoria and Albert now live, until their own ship is complete in its refittings. To the Royal George we rowed, hoping to procure an order to be admitted on board of the Victoria and Albert. Thence we rowed leisurely by a long range of splendid men of war and frigates, lying in ordinary, at their moorings, to the Victory, anchored off the Common Hard, as it is called, the landing place to Portsea: this good old ship has never been at sea since the memorable battle of Trafalgar, when she |[35] bore the flag of Britain's hero, Nelson, and no wonder that men crowd around her, and visit her as a national shrine. A sort of staircase adapted to the exterior of the vast hull, gives easy access to the middle deck: here the stranger is required to inscribe his name, condition and residence in a book, and a warrant officer is directed to act as guide: him too it is expedient to propitiate with a douceur; and we found him a communicative and intelligent guide. There is a crew of 400 men on board the Victory: she is commanded by Capt. Pasco, a fine looking old Officer, who was Lieutenant in the Victory, when Nelson fell, and was to-day pacing the quarter deck with two midshipmen. A small brass plate inserted in to the deck marks the spot where Nelson fell, mortally wounded by a shot from above, from the rigging of the Redoubtable, enemy's ship: we afterwards visited the dark den off the hold, where the hero breathed his last, surrounded by the mourning friends, who watched the last ebbing breath, and received the last sigh. On the poop, |[36] above the case in which the signal flags are deposited, is inscribed Nelson's ever memorable last admonition "England expects every man to do his duty." The main deck, (I am not sure that I give it the right name) is now used as a school; we looked into the sick-bay or hospital; no bad cases are treated there: all such are taken to Haslar Hospital. Descended to the deck beneath; the kitchen and larder were pointed out to us, the mens mess tables, the barrels for biscuit, grog and vinegar attached to each. While we were on the upper deck: all hands were piped, by boatswain's whistle, to assist at lowering the hammocks, which had been airing aloft: every sailor took his own, was busily employed in rolling it up: the hubbub, the noise, the running to & fro, the indolence of some, the activity of others, were all interesting, and somewhat confounding; we descended into the hold, were shewn the water tanks, the magazines, where the Cabins of the Petty officers were, but not the interior of them, or of the principal cabins, or any |[37] officers private cabin. As it was our superficial view of the ship interested us exceedingly; it was a novel scene, calculated to expand one's notions; all about this great naval arsenal is on a grand scale, and impresses the beholder with high notions of his country's strength, wealth & power. Rowed on shore to Portsea: our Boatman preceded us to a tavern, the Keppel's head, where in a little back parlour we were soon busy with a luncheon of bread and cheese and beer, to recruit us before entering the Dock Yard. As we landed from our boat, the crowds congregated at the Dockyard gates struck us forcibly; it was not a groupe of hundreds, but of thousands; perhaps 3000 men are now daily working in the dockyard, and of these a large proportion were waiting for re-admission after their dinner hour. Soon after two o clock we applied for leave to go over the Yard, being received at the Police Station within the gates, where, having inscribed our names &c., we joined other sight seekers, and were escorted by a very intelligent |[38] Policeman, whose attention we secured by the same silver key which we had applied to other locks before. The first object of attraction was the mast houses, where the masts and yards for men of war from the smallest to the first rate are stored: every one is numbered or inscribed, as to its dimensions, or the ship to w^h. it belongs, and one is startled with the immense size of some among the largest. Next we visited the ropewalk a building 365 yards in length; steam machinery is here used; all is in the highest order and cleanliness, and method. We were shewn the very ingenious manner in which the yarn is drawn out and twisted into a cord, cords, into ropes, ropes into cables; in fabricating a cord a thread of coloured worsted is entwined into the substance so as to test the genuineness of the article, and to detect any fraud or improper conversion; for it is illegal to use this method of marking, as it were, the government cordage. — It would be endless to attempt to relate in detail much of |[39] what we say, saw or were told, or heard imperfectly: a few prominent points only can be noticed. For instance, the store of enormous anchors, of various shapes, and forms; — the many ships in building, or repairing in the dry docks, covered with timber or zinc roofing; the latter is preferred as being in less danger of conflagration; enormous steam frigates, first rate men of war, steamers on the principle of propulsion by the Archimedean screw; — an immense basin in the course of construction: — the blacksmith's shops and forges, huge dens of Cyclops, dark, lurid, of a suffocating heat; — the workshops where the copper sheathing is prepared; — timber stores, where mahogany is chiefly used, as being to the Government as cheap, if not cheaper than other woods: — vast quantities of waste timber, to be disposed of by auction: — offices and residences for the principal employés; — poor old and infirm Admiral Sir Hyde Parker, the Commander in chief, hardly released from a bed of sickness, creeping about to observe how |[40] matters were going on; other more vigorous and younger officers passing to visit, perhaps, some ship in progress of construction, destined to be placed under their command, and as to which they wishes to give some hint or make some suggestion. But of all the sights the most interesting is the making of Blocks, a most complicated and magical affair, by machinery of the nicest and most delicate, while, at the same time, powerful description, worked by immense steam power: a square piece of wood adapted for conversion into a block, passes rapidly through several distinct machines, each performing a separate part of the process, till at length it comes out with all the main qualities and characters of the block, needing only the last finish by hand. It is true one carries away only a general idea of this and other like wonders of mechanical skill here exhibited, but what one does see and learn thus superficially tends to enlarge the mind, to expand the range of thought, to make one zealous in love of a country capable of such great |[41] efforts of genius, and humble in the thought how little one individually knows, how much one has to learn. It was nearly four o clock when we left the Dockyard, and took boat to cross to the Gosport Pier to meet the Ryde Steamer, which, in fact, was under weigh when we neared her, and into which, not without a ducking to my wrapper, which, however I picked up as it floated, we scrambled, reaching the head of Ryde Pier in time to land by 5 o cl. at which hour we had, indeed, got to our lodgings, well pleased, and not disagreeably fatigued. As strangers we made at least one mistake, that is, the not taking return tickets by the Steamer, so expending four shillings more than was necessary.

May 26. Tuesday.

Lovely weather. E.F.W. went partly by coach, and partly on foot on an excursion to Sandown, Shanklin, Shanklin Brading Downs, &c. with which he was much delighted, and

10. Cadets' and Midshipmans' berths.

returned to dinner. M.W. and Sophy with the children strolled Eastward along the beach. I explored the road to Binstead, about a mile Westward of Ryde: a ~~beautiful~~ delightful walk; passing |[42] a number of beautiful villas, rich in roses, nestling in shrubberies, abounding in odd & quaint, or elegant outlines as to their architectural construction. The Church at Binstead, almost wholly rebuilt, is a sweet, rural, secluded place of worship, in excellent taste, of the Early English style; beyond it a spacious, thick oakwood or coppice, sloping to the beach, thro' a glade in which I found my way to the shore, expecting to be able to return on sand or shingle, but found myself entangled in a tenacious white mud, hardly practicable for walking, though intermingled with stones. Floundered along to a jetty, and a cottage on the shore, whence I obtained the guidance of the woman inhabiting it to prevent the intrusion of strangers on the private grounds of M^rs. Fleming, widow of a late MP. for Hants, who resides here. The usual silver key applied to the lock procured me a passage through the obscurer parts of the grounds of M^rs. F. to Binstead Church; ~~under the guidance of the~~ my guide having ascertained that the |[43] family or guests were not walking in that part of the grounds permitted me to cross a beautiful corner of the demesne laid out most tastefully in flower garden, and luxuriant in roses, fuchsias, and other delightful shrubs and plants. – Returned home by the Binstead Stone Pits, and the Newport road.

A letter from Miss Sophia Hunt on the appointment of a ~~trustee~~ Solicitor to the Wadenhoe Trust, and another from Mr Price, of Coln S^t. Dennis, in answer to mine addressed to him on the Valuation of parishes in the Northleach Union for the County Rate.

May 27. Wednesday.
Beautiful weather. At eleven o clock we left on an excursion to Shanklin, Broome accompanying his Parents and ourselves in an open carriage drawn by one horse. Our road led by the Church of S^t. Johns, and soon turned to the right leaving the road leading in the

direction of St. Helens, Sea View, and other places. It pursued a high tract, affording views of the interior of the Island, |[44] its high downs, its rich culture, its groves, and low vallies. For the most part the lanes are narrow, with high hedges, so as to prevent the traveller from seeing much of the surrounding country. Emerging from an oak coppice through which the road passed, we enjoyed to the left a fine view over Brading Haven, an inlet of the sea, which enters by a narrow channel between St. Helens and Bembridge downs. This space was now covered with a fine sheet of water, the tide being nearly at its height; at the ebb it presents an expanse of mud, so that we first saw it to the greatest advantage. The proprietors have made many attempts to exclude the sea, and to convert this inland water into productive meadow land, and that too in times long past, but the endeavours have been unsuccessful. The landscape, when the tide is in is very pleasing, soft, and gentle; meadow and coppice clothing the margin of the lake, contrasting well with the high-down land of Bembridge Peninsula. |[45] The village of Bembridge occupies a point of land at the extremity of the Peninsula, adjoining the entrance of Brading Haven, looking over it inland, and seaward to the open sea. There are lodging houses, and a Church in the course of erection. Yaverland is a hamlet towards Sandown Bay at the opposite extremity of Bembridge Down to that on which Bembridge is situate. The promontory formed by Bembridge downs terminates in the Culver chalk cliffs, a fine bold and lofty headland lashed by the waves of the broad sea. About a mile from Brading inland is Nunwell Court, the Estate and residence of the Oglanders an ancient family, the head of which is a baronet; it is a spacious Mansion at the foot of Brading down, nestling under fine oak and other timber. Beyond Brading down, Westward is Ashey down, with its seamark, and further still in the same direction Massley down. Brading itself is a poor decayed town, with a small old Market house near its ancient Church. We descended from our carriage to view the sacred edifice and its churchyard, ob-|[46] jects of lively interest of an adventitious kind. The Church has a porch surmounted by a spire at the West end, a Southern porch, a nave and side Aisles, each terminating in a chapel, and a chancel. The pillars are early English, greivously coated with white-wash, the pews of deal, of the most approved churchwardenish pattern, square, high and ugly. In the Chancel before the communion table is a beautiful incised slab, most elaborately wrought with inscriptions and ornamental bordering, niches for saints on each side of the effigy of a deceased Knight and Courtier of the time, I think, of James the 1st. the latine[5] which had been inserted into the stone is all gone, but the incision on the stone, a hard freestone, is nearly perfect, as also is the slab itself, and beautifully wrought. There are altar tombs, on each side of the Chancel, covered with slabs of Purbeck Marble; and one of the chapels, that at the East end of the South Aisle, being the burial place of the Oglander family, contains some monuments of |[47] recumbent knights of ancient renown, members of that family. The chapel at the Eastern end of the North Aisle is partitioned off as a Vestry. The incumbent is non-resident. But the main interest attached to Brading Church and Churchyard, w^{h.} causes many a pilgrimage hitherward, is based upon the love for worth and piety, which pervades so extensively the whole community, though not seldom bestowed on those whose characters exhibit those qualities a little too ostentatiously, denied to others who veil their goodness more humbly

---

5. Latine – latten. A yellow alloy resembling or identical to brass, hammered into thin sheets and used to make monumental brasses.

from the public view. Legh Richmond, a popular writer of the Evangelical class, author of the Dairyman's daughter, and other "short and simple annals of the poor," was for several years the curate here,[6] and resided at the Parsonage house in the Churchyard. "Little Jane" too lies buried here, a poor child trained in the ways of religion by Legh Richmond, a creature of early and warm piety, but doomed to a brief career; her tombstone remains with its touching inscription by her loving Pastor, and little village |[48] children crowd round the stranger at the churchyard gate, to remind him that "little Jani lies buried here". "Little Jane" alone appears as her designation on the tomb-stone, no surname being given: her parents were, it is said, vile and worthless; her cottage still stands, with the chamber in which she died, and is visited by the enthusiasts, the amiable tender hearted, whom one cannot but respect, through inclined to smile at their rapture. An inscription on another tombstone is pointed out as having been composed by "Little Jane", contain[g] a few pious lines. While we were inspecting the church, a gentleman and stranger, whose carriage had reached Brading before us, restrained as far as might be by a female, his companion, accosted us in an excited manner with some comments on "Little Jane"; inviting us to visit her tomb, to read the inscriptions &c. – while we were so doing he again intruded himself upon us — poor fellow! his manner indicated aberration; and we after-|[49] wards saw him on Shanklin Beach, but fortunately escaped a second encounter with him. We did not feel a call to deviate from our route to visit "Little Jane's" cottage, but pursued our way across the shoulder of the hill which is crowned with Brading down, descending afterwards a very steep and somewhat dangerous looking hill, owing to sharp turns in the road, into a more level tract bordering on the sea, apparently, in times long past, an inlet extending inland from the head of Brading Haven. In the interior, ranges of high down land with fertile valleys intervening between them; seaward the bold bluff chalk Culver Cliffs — not far distant. The Culver Cliff forms one extremity of a fine bay, Sandown Bay, stretching to Dunnose, the other extremity: the sea deep blue, calm, peaceful, studded with sails, from the stately three master to the minute pleasure boat: on the shore Sandown Fort, originally constructed in the reign of Hen. VIII. refortified and fitted out for the purposes of modern defence in the great wars of the early |[50] part of this century; now, I believe, again abandoned, and converted into a marine residence – Sandown village appears to be a rising place, and to the admirers of a fine expanse of sea would have great attractions: there are several villa residences to be sold or let, others, chiefly in the Tudor style, nearly finished, spacious and expensive erections, close on the beach: lodgings placarded on houses of less pretension; a disused range of Government Barracks, and last, though not least, a well designed, spacious, modern, and unfinished Church, nearly completed, to be furnished with a spire, in the Early English style, destined, it is to be hoped, to be a vital blessing to the place and neighbourhood. Shanklin village is a mile or two further on: with two picturesque hotels, at the head of a little dell, or, as it is locally called, <u>Chine</u>, down which an inconsiderable brook rushes to the sea; the houses are ornamental, in a sketchy style of building, detached, with flowers, ivy and creeping plants; a minute |[51]

---

6. Legh Richmond (1772-1827). Richmond was born in Liverpool and educated at Trinity College, Cambridge. In 1798 he was appointed to the joint curacies of Brading and Yaverland on the Isle of Wight. He was powerfully influenced by William Wilberforce's Practical View of Christianity, and took a prominent interest in the British and Foreign Bible Society, the Church Missionary Society and similar institutions.

museum, a shop or two, windows decorated with views of the Isle of Wight, a car or two waiting to be engaged. Here we partook of luncheon before setting out for the Beach and Chine, guided by E.F.W. who had visited the locality yesterday: Broome enjoyed his own special treat before we set out in a complete exhibition of Punch & Judy seen from the pretty garden of the hotel. Descended to the Beach by a well constructed path, passing several commodious lodging houses or villas, particularly one with a turret, embosomed in shrubbery and foliage on the very brink of the <u>chine</u>: before us a noble expanse of deep blue sea, Culver Cliff to the left, Dunnose to the right, Shanklin Down overlapping the latter point: a turn in the descending path brought us by a lovely combination, a cottage public house perched on the rocky margin of the dell, sheltered by an umbrageous bushy-topped old oak. On the beach at the mouth of the <u>Chine</u>, the Fisherman's hut, two or three Bathing machines, a boat just landed with a basket of mackarel |[52] from a Brighton fishing vessel lying off at a little distance, several villa looking lodging and bathing houses on the beach. We strolled some distance towards Sandown, and then, retracing our steps some distance towards Dunnose; hunting for shells, and fossils. The Cliff about us at its greatest height does not exceed 170 feet, the rock disposed in nearly horizontal Strata, Wealden, and sand rock, some parts, ~~which~~ on being broken with the hammer, yeilded casts of various old world shellfish fossils, dark and ferruginous, imparting an almost black hue to the sand beneath. Here we lingered long, and my son bathed, till we wended our way to the Village thro' the <u>Chine</u>. Be it known that <u>Chine</u>, in the dialect of Vectis, means a deep fissure or Chasm in the Cliff on the shore scooped out in the course of centuries by the constantly trickling or bounding of a streamlet seeking the sea. This is one of the most striking and picturesque: made accessible by walks, and |[53] steps, and seats, and points of view, kept in order by a person who has the privilege of conducting strangers through the little glen, each end of which is closed by a locked gate. In this dry season the rivulet was very scanty, forming, near the village, a diminutive kind of PisseVache fall of some twenty of thirty feet, into a dark hardly discerned basin, scooped out of the blackish sand-stone rock, if rock it can be called, which almost crumbles beneath the touch – the brooklet steals on amid brushwood; brushwood clothes the fissure on one side, on the other you have the naked rock, rising precipice-like overhead, or jutting forward at a height probably, never exceeding 200 feet, often much lower. It is a fairy dell, rich in ferns and other cryptogamous plants, and ever and anon, as the visitor looks backward, the mouth of the gorge presents the bright blue, sail-studded sea. Having regained our hotel, we left Shanklin, well pleased with our visit, and, in an hour and a half, having accomplished the nine |[54] miles of distance, were seated at the dinner table. —

May 28. Thursday.
Delightful weather. A letter from M[r] Thornton on Hunt concerns, with enclosures. —

A light yacht, of, perhaps, thirty tons burthen, which had been built, in a shed, near our house, on the Strand, was launched at half past one to-day. It belongs to a M[r] Fleming, a son of the lady residing near Binstead, into whose lovely grounds I obtained admission on Tuesday: he is Commodore of the Ryde Yacht club: the hull was safely launched to be g towed to Cowes there to be rigged and fitted out. Crowds on the beach greeted with loud hurrahs its descent into the water; we watched it as it came down the frame from a row boat, which we had engaged: MW. — my son and daughter, Broome & I then proceeded Eastward to Nettlestone Point, enjoying the calm bay as we rowed along by Apley, by St. Clare, the castellated Villa of Col. Harcourt Ver-|⁵⁵ non, Puckpool, the Swiss Cottage of the Architect, Wyatt, Springfield, a groupe of villa-like lodging houses close to the Beach, on a sea wall. At Nettlestone Point, where is the wide Sea stretching Eastward, and over against Hayling Island, is Sea View, a hamlet of lodging houses for those who seek privacy, and study economy; a pretty retired spot: beyond are St. Helens and Bembridge — This two hours trip suited the elder and the youngest of our party better than the intermediates, who suffered after their return from sea sickness; but, while on the water, it was agreeable to all. – Broome accompanied his Grandmamma and me for an hour on the Pier before dinner, and afterwards walked with me in the Evening by Apley and St. Johns.

May 29. Friday.
A continuance of the same lovely weather, though still an Easterly wind —

Wrote to Messrs. Hoare, desiring them to send me £60 in Bank post bills: — to Mr Thornton on the Hunt affairs: to H. D. Warter in answer to his letter of the 13th. Inst. on the |⁵⁶ failure of the treaty for the purchase of the Risington Property.

E.F.W. made a long excursion on a hired horse to-day to Freshwater gate, the Needles, Alum Bay, Scratchell's Bay, and the Westernmost quarters of the Island, to inspect ~~its~~ ^{the} geological features, and the magnificent sea and rock scenery there. He returned at teatime, very much fatigued, and suffering from a bad cold with cough: he had ridden 40 miles, and walked eight or ten.

MW. and I walked to Binstead village Church & back. I enjoyed an evening stroll by Apley and St. Johns.

In the forenoon MW. and Sophy, with Broome and myself attended divine service at the Church of the Holy Trinity, this being the Festival of the Restoration of the Royal family. A very small congregation: the prayers and service well performed by a young Clergyman. The church was opened for divine worship last year, being finished, except the tower, which is now in course of erection. |⁵⁷ It is of the early English, lancet windowed style, the Chancel being an apse with three windows of painted glass; a nave and two aisles, the Eastern windows of the latter being also of painted glass. The building is calculated to hold 800 persons, 500 in open sittings, free, which are in the nave; the close sittings are in the aisles, stalls with doors, as the other seats are stalls without doors. The reading pew, the pulpit, the communion rails, the roof, the stalls, all of dark oak, or painted to represent dark oak.

Saturday May 30.
Beautiful weather. My son had a day of rest, suffering much from fatigue and a bad cold.

Wrote to Miss Mansell, Postmistress, Stow, to desire her to forward our letters to Ventnor: and to Mr Pearce, acknowledging his letter to me, giving an account of the proceedings of the

Valuation Committee of our Union at their meeting on the 21ˢᵗ· and desiring that his future communications during my absence from home may be |⁵⁸ addressed to me at Ventnor.

With MW. and dear Broome enjoyed a pleasant row, for two hours, Westward, along the sweetly wooded coast, as far as the entrance to Wootton Creek and back.

This the 38th. anniversary of my wedding day: GOD has been and is very gracious and merciful to me and mine. MW. and I strolled out in the Evening.

May 31. Whitsunday.
Very fine weather. Received a letter from Messʳˢ· Hoare with an enclosure of £60 in Bank Post Bills. Attended divine service twice at the Church of the Holy Trinity: the services well performed: both the sermons by the same Clergyman, suited to the festival. Partook of the Holy Communion.

With MW. walked and sat on the Pier in the Evening. E.F.W. still suffering from a bad cold, cough, and fatigue.

Read a Sermon by Revᵈ· A Watson — ~~Ece~~ Brit. Mag. —

June 1. Monday.
Very beautiful weather. |⁵⁹ Wrote to the Newsagent London to forward the London newspaper to me at Ventnor: — wrote to Bathurst: — to Mʳˢ· Barr to condole with her and Mʳ Barr, on the death of Lt. Col. Barr, in consequence of his wounds received at the battle of Sobraon,⁷ a notification of which we had seen in the paper this morning. His loss will be severely felt in his family, and by the army in which he served, and had distinguished himself greatly.

M.W. walked with Broome on the beach Eastward, and I met them as I returned from a longer walk inland to Springfield by Sᵗ· John's Church, and by the beautiful grounds of Sᵗ· Clare; the hamlet of Springfield, of which we had only seen the row of lodging houses on the beach, as we rowed past to Sea View, contains some delightful villas at a little distance from the shore. My walk homeward was along the beach and on the sea wall, the tide being nearly full: very enjoyable.

E.F.W. and Sophy walked to Binstead with which they were |⁶⁰ much pleased, and back.

A stroll on the beach in the Evening. —

~~June~~
This being Whitmonday I attended divine service in the forenoon at Trinity Church.

---

7.   Major Marcus Barr (1802-1846). Barr was of the 29th Foot. He died of wounds, 26 March 1846. The battle of Sobrahan was fought on 10 February 1846 when Hugh Gough defeated the Sikhs there. It is interesting that the newspaper report should have reported his as being lieutenant-colonel.

June 2. Tuesday.
Brilliant summer weather.

Concluded our stay at Ryde, and proceeded
to Ventnor. Left our comfortable apartments
at 11 AM. giving our hostess, who had been
our cook, a written testimonial of our perfect
satisfaction with the accommodations &c.
Part of our luggage had been sent forward by
a carrier yesterday; we left our man-servant to
follow us in the afternoon by the coach,

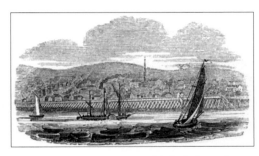

11. Ryde from the sea.

and we ourselves, with the children and maids, travelled in an open britska[8] with a pair of
horses from the Pier Hotel. The distance from Ryde to Ventnor is 13 miles. At Shanklin we
paused for a few minutes, while the horses had hay and water, and we looked once

more at the tiny waterfall at the head of the
Chine: the road to Ventnor |[61] is very hilly,
and very beautiful. Passing the parsonage, and
rustic diminutive church, both embowered in
fine timber trees, the ascent of Shanklin down
is slowly surmounted by a windy~ing~ road. My
son and I with Broome walked by a short cut,
for about a quarter of a mile, across the turf,
rejoining the carriage at the summit of the hill.
The views backward of Brading, the Culver
Cliffs, Sandown, and its bay, Shanklin village,
the rich valley lying between Brading

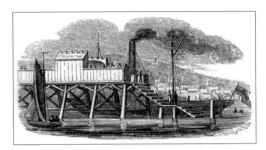

12. Ryde Pier.

and Shanklin downs, and the bright blue sea, were exquisite. The slopes of the downs,
very steep, browsed by sheep, and here and there diversified by a space of bare chalky soil,
reminded me of Salisbury Plain, or the Malvern Hills. From the hill above Shanklin we

descended into a sort of bason terminating on
the seashore in another chine, Luccomb Chine,
of the same general character, as forming
the drainage of the downs to the coast, but
without the romantic rock and wood features
of Shanklin Chine, |[62] yet very pleasing, with
its farm, its cottage orné, and its splendid
sea view. Another ascent, and we reached
what is called the East end, far below us the
sea, between it and the road high cliffs, a
continuance of the projecting headlands put
down on the maps as Dunnose

13. Assembly Rooms, Ryde.

---

8.   Britska – Britzka, an early nineteenth-century carriage, originating in Poland. An open carriage with calash top and
       space for reclining.

*14. Ventnor,
Isle of Wight.*

and Chine Point: here, at East End, one of the latest landslips recorded in the memorabilia of the Island occurred within the memory of man. We were now entered on that line of coast which is suitably named the Undercliff, being in fact formed by landslips, hundreds, perhaps, thousands of years ago, unrecorded at least in history, which have strewed the space between the Chalk Downs, and the Beach, on an average, a mile wide, with extensive debris, dislocated rocks, huge detached masses, clothed, more or less with rich foliage, timber and underwood, once a maze of rude beauty, now digested ~~more or le~~ by art and design, made the residence of the lovers of fine climate, picturesque grouping, and |⁶⁴ elegant retirement. Such Bonchurch affords, to which we now descended: once a little village of rude cottages, with a humble Church, built, centuries ago, among the debris, now a cluster of pretty villas enshrined amid roses and myrtles, and all the luxuries of the flower garden. Less than a mile further is Ventnor: fifteen or sixteen years ago it was a petty hamlet with its two or three cottages, its mill, and its rude cove: now it has sprung up into a town, and building goes on in every direction. Early attention was not paid to the laying out of the place, otherwise

*15. Old church,
Bonchurch, Isle of Wight.*

*16. Bonchurch Pond,
Isle of Wight.*

hilly and winding streets might have been avoided; but latterly a better arrangement has been observed, and the handsome Church forms a pleasing Centre, rows of houses, or villas, some climbing the down of S~t·~ ~Bonf~ Boniface, some close on the beach, or on the margin of the cliffs, risen or rising on every side. The opinion of medical men in favour of the mildness of the climate, recommending it for patients with tender |[64] lungs has ~tended~ ^operated^ to the rapid increase of the place, and made it a favourite resort of invalids in winter. At the entrance of the place is a singular looking Hotel, S~t·~ Boniface's, in the Italian Style, at the other extremity of the town, on the verge of the Cliff, commanding splendid sea views, are ~three~ ^two^ or three other hotels, at one of which, the Marine Hotel, we alighted, and were enchanted with the extensive sea prospect. Leaving the ladies and children E.F.W. accompanied me in search of lodgings, of which there seemed rather a dearth, at least sufficiently spacious for our party, not crowded by contiguous buildings, near enough to the cliffs, or beach, or commanding a sea view. At last we fixed on a detached cottage, opposite S~t·~ Boniface Hotel, at the foot of the Downs, commanding a considerable reach of sea, near the cliffs, having a beautiful view of Bonchurch, its villas, groves, and overhanging downs. For two sitting rooms, the drawing room spacious, and enjoyable, |[65] two best bedrooms, a good nursery, and two servants rooms, with use of plate, linen and china, the charge is three guineas a week; five shillings a week being paid to the landlady for her services in cooking, we to find coals. We returned to bring the ladies in a car to sanction our selection of a temporary abode, and we shortly afterwards sent the maids & children to take possession. Dined at the Hotel, and at teatime were comfortably settled in our new abode; our manservant arrived in the coach from Ryde, as we expected. The heat great. Aratrum Cottage is the name of our new domicile.

June 3. Wednesday.
Splendid weather.

Wrote to the Editor of the Gloucestershire Chronicle, desiring him to forward to me at this place the next two numbers of his publication.

Strolling, chiefly in the Bonchurch direction, at several times during the day, the heat very great till evening. On the cliffs overhanging the sea; not very high, |[66] now chalk, now indurated clay, or green sand. The herbage short; where undisturbed, rich in plants, as the bee orchis: haymaking in progress; on the beach, patches of sand, intermingling with dark masses of detached rock, and a shingle of exceedingly small pebbles — not any timber on the margin of the sea, but underwood in shady places: rich timber in the Bonchurch dells, interspersed with rocks, the deposit of ancient landslips; the cliffs still subject to

17. St. Boniface.

frequent land slips, and partial changes: hence access to the beach from the sea varying: the present cove, or landing place, for Bonchurch, altered within a few years; a few fishermen engaged in catching crabs and lobsters. The whole appearance of the district very much resembles the country near Lyme Regis; hilly, wooded, the same Geological character, the same tendency to landslip from the same causes; the springs insinuating themselves between higher and lower strata gradually produce a sort of launch |[67] of the higher down the lower. Here and there a copious spring steals almost unobserved to the edge of the cliff, percolates through the soil, and, bursting forth near the upper edge of the cliff, forms a waterfall on to the beach beneath: the springs are peculiarly pellucid. Explored Bonchurch, or, rather, S[t.] Boniface's Church, a low rustic Village Church, of ancient date, without any architectural pretensions, nestling amidst luxuriant trees, at the head of a meadow, sloping to the cliff, beautifully retired and obscure, but quite inadequate to the present population, or the requirements of a village of villas. For in every nook, on every eminence commanding a sea view, in every tree crowded dell, under the shadow of each rock, is a modern built, thatched or slated, villa; Italian, Gothic, Tudor styles abound; others there are in which square comfort, not external effect, is chiefly consulted. Not far from the Church a hugh detached mass of rock, as if pitched from above by a giant hand, and alighting on one end, stands in a |[68] field, ~~crowned with~~ surmounted by a flag-staff: higher up, nearer to the turfy slopes of S[t.]

Boniface's down, a like rock, similarly detached, stands prominent, a rude cross is on its summit, and marks the "pulpit rock." The ascent of S[t.] Boniface's downs immediately above Ventnor and Bonchurch is very precipitate, like the Malvern Hills, the views magnificent, the breeze refreshing, the air exquisitely balmy and soft. In a few years, doubtless, they will be made more accessible than at present by the tracing out of paths as at Malvern: the virgin soil is rich in rare plants, Thesium Linophyllum, Ophrys Apifera

18. Bonchurch.

&c. — Bonchurch, the sea cliffs, and Ventnor form a striking and diversified foreground: some would rather regret the hard outlined labyrinth ^of modern houses, of white stone and blue slate, however diversified in structure, which Ventnor now presents; ~~tints and~~ ^freshness not subdued by time, ~~nor~~ buildings not yet ~~clothed~~ ^relieved with foliage. —

19. Shanklin Chine.

June 4. Thursday.
The same brilliant weather. |[69]

Wrote to Maria Witts.

E.F.W. took a long geologizing ramble to Shanklin, Luccombe Chine, & the recent land-slip in that quarter (26 years ago) and returned much delighted with the scene.

Our walks were much restricted to the cliffs and beach; sitting on the former, or by the latter, to enjoy the breeze which mitigated the sun's rays, and ~~enjoy~~ the magnificent view across the channel. The cove is a shingly beach, (with a few pleasure boats,) on which materials for building may be landed from vessels lying at a little distance off the shore. Little is seen moving on the sea, as the coast here is not on the direct track of commerce, or route, up the channel, or to Portsmouth; but at this season, as to-day, an excursion steamer, with a pleasure seeking crew, coasting round the island, approaches Ventnor in its circumnavigation; starting from Southampton, Cowes or Ryde, & returning to those places at which it has called to take up passengers, or from which it has ~~st~~ set out. The circuit is usually accomplished in eight |[70] hours. Ventnor mill (for corn) is situate on the verge of the cliffs, wrought by a copious stream which, having done its duty, escapes to the sea in a really pretty miniature cataract, dashing & roaring with a gentle tone, down the rock, in a channel fringed with luxuriant weeds.

June 5. Friday.
Very hot and very hazy weather.

Wrote to Messrs. Hoare, directing them to sell the £530. 10. 1. 3 p^r Cent. Cons. standing in my name, and place the proceeds to my account, that I may apply the same in the investment of £1000 on Mortgage of Mr Lockhart's Bucks estates. Wrote to Messrs. Sewell, Sol^rs., Newport I.W., requesting a ticket of admission to be sent to enable us to inspect Lord Yarborough's mansion house at Appledurcomb, not far from Ventnor.

Rec^d. a letter from M^rs. C. Barr, in answer to mine of condolence on the death of Lt. Col Barr: she

20. The Head of the Chine.

transmitted a printed extract from a letter addressed to the Barr family on occasion of the decease of their brother by Sir Harry Smith, the distinguished |[71] hero of Aliwal, and the intimate friend of the excellent Marcus Barr; bearing testimony in most feeling language to the admirable qualities of the departed, as a Christian, a friend, a Gentleman, a soldier; ~~and~~ one whose ~~serv~~ advice was ever most highly valued, who died deeply regretted by the distinguished officers under whom he had served, a great loss to his friends, the army, and his country.[9]

My son left us by the Coach before breakfast, to explore the geological features of the Coast from Sandown to Luccumb Chine, and we went to meet him, (MW. Sophy, and myself,) in the afternoon, as he returned on foot. We went in a car, through Bonchurch, to the top of the hill above the Chine, to which we descended: at its head is a most secluded but beautiful Cottage residence, the property of a M[r] Cooper, embosomed in trees, with pleasure grounds, extending above and down one side of the Chine, even to its mouth and the sandstone cliff, over hanging the sea. Like Shanklin Chine in its formation by its being the outlet of a rivulet, which |[72] in successive ages has worn for itself a precipitous channel or cleft in the soft rock to the sea shore, it is unlike it by the lowness of the rocks overhanging the dell, by its chasm being narrower, and shorter, by the streamlet not tumbling down any considerable height, by the total absence of art or labour to make it accessible. In fact, to descend by a rugged, steep, difficult path is even more laborious than to ascend it, but the trouble is well compensated, and at the bottom on the sea shore, beneath the lofty cliffs, among the rocky debris of former convulsions, beside a little bay whose sand & shingle is partially covered with the decomposing, and, therefore, somewhat offensive sea wrack, there is a little nest of fishermens cottages, secluded and lonely, where live, no doubt, the descendants of a race of smugglers, whose lawless trade was favoured by the inaccessible character of the obscure dell at the foot of which their abodes were erected. Now, I apprehend, greater vigilance, less temptation, a better organized system of |[73] coast guard [have,] in a great measure, ~~have~~ annihilated a dangerous, unprincipled, and illegal course of life. Scrambling up the chasm or chine, accompanied by my Son, who was punctual in meeting us, we wended our homeward way thro' a lovely and most interesting tract, the site of the landslip which occurred within the memory of the living generation — entering on a labyrinth through which a winding, rocky footpath conducts, parallel to the cliffs overhanging the sea, amid the rich and dense underwood which clothes the fallen masses of rock, hazel, oak, ash, service & the like, with bright and glowing flowers variegating the velvet turf or moss growing in the interstices between the fragments of rock on every side — the foxglove, the honeysuckle, the cistus, the yellow clover, the vetch predominating. Above are overhanging cliffs, from which were severed the mingled masses of rock and soil through which our path led; to the left the lower range of cliff skirting the beach, and, further on, the wide sea, now, however, clouded by |[74] a curtain of haze.

At an earlier hour I had explored the base of the down in the opposite direction from Bonchurch, above the town of Ventnor and ascended by the road leading to Appledurcomb and the interior of the island. The haze prevented any extensive or clear view either by sea or land.

---

9.   Sir Harry George Wakelyn Smith Baronet (1787-1860). The main battle against the Sikhs was at Aliwal on 2 January 1846, that at Sobrahan consolidated the victorious position.

June 6. Saturday.

A continuation of the same broiling, hazy weather.

Rec^{d.} letters from Mr. Pearce with particulars of Poor Law matters relating to the Stow on the Wold union — from C Bathurst, lively and pleasant; — from Mr. Jennings with a balance sheet of the receipt of our Lady day London rents.

21. Steephill.

Strolled on St. Boniface down, attaining a further and a higher point than I had reached before; descended to Bonchurch by a blind footpath leading to a most curious and difficult, and nearly worn-out staircase, contrived in a fissure of the chalky cliff, not much unlike the spiral staircase of a ruined turret, which brought me to the level |⁷⁵ of the Bonchurch hotel, and of several other lodging houses or villas perched in gardens on a narrow terrace at the foot of the shrub clothed cliffs which overhang. A narrow path led to another steep stair below the Pulpit rock, of very many stone steps, conducting from the Bonchurch valley to the terrace I had left — crossed the road in the village of Bonchurch, and crept up a steep footpath leading to ~~another~~ ^{one} of the hundred dells or depressions in this romantic undercliff: here found an interior platform secluded by rocks, down, and foliage from every blast, spacious enough to hold four or five sweetly pretty secluded villas with their respective pleasure grounds, all having ready access to the cliffs overhanging the beach, screened from, but contiguous to, the village to which they belong, and at a very little distance from Ventnor.

In the evening explored the cliffs beyond the cove in the direction of Steephill and St. Lawrence, a delightful walk with a commanding sea-view. |⁷⁶

June 7. Sunday.

Trinity Sunday.

Very hot in the forenoon and afternoon, cooler in the Evening, the wind having changed from S.E. to West.

Attended divine service at the Church, which stands in a beautiful cemetery, overhung with foliage, tho' the situation is centrical in the town. The edifice is of a <u>false</u> Gothic, ecclesiastical in general effect, but full of anachronisms, and errors in detail – With a chancel scarcely projecting, gaudy painted glass exhibiting <u>green</u> angels over the Communion table – the interior one spacious room, with galleries, running the whole

22. Ventnor Mill.

length, besides a Western gallery for organ and school children, high pews, a pulpit surmounting a reading desk and clerk's pew, and all with their back to the chancel: a pew unlike the rest; luxurious & ostentatiously secluded, for the great man of the place, Mr Hambrough of Steephill Castle, adjoining the town; to whom, I believe, the ~~place~~ town is under great obligations, for it appears that he built the Church, and a school house; and with these good works has, no doubt, and, as was fairly |^77 due to himself, benefited his family in leasing out his property on building leases. Mr Coleman, who is the incumbent, preached a good sermon, memoriter, and very fluently, on the doctrine of the Holy Trinity, adducing scriptural proofs with judgment and a good arrangement; betraying, however, by his tone, and in certain passages, especially with reference to regeneration, which one could see he does not connect with baptism, the Evangelical School to which he belongs: this was further evinced in the mode of administering the ~~elements~~ consecrated bread at the Holy Communion, once reading or pronouncing to a whole company of communicants the formula which should be addressed to each individual separately, and the same practice being followed as to the cup. The service was read, except at the Communion table, by the Curate, Mr Sharp: who also performed the whole duty at the afternoon service, preaching a common place sermon in a common place manner. We did not attend the third service in the evening.

Rec^d. letters from Messrs. Sewell, Newport, with a ticket of admission |^78 to Appuldurcomb for Tuesday or Friday next: — from Messrs. Hoare, covering a power of Attorney, to be executed by me for the sale of my 3 p^r Cent. Cons. which cannot be effected till July 6. as the Books are closed: — from Mr Thornton with inclosures (a letter from Mr Hare, and the copy of one from Mr Thornton to Mr Hare,) on the subject of the appointment of a Solicitor to the Wadenhoe Trust. –

Strolled in the Evening by the seaside in the Cove, and on the Cliffs.

June 8. Monday.
Delightful weather.

Wrote to Messrs. Hoare, returning the power of Attorney for the sale of stock duly executed: also to G. F. Newmarch, explaining to him that I should not be able to pay £500, part of the money to be advanced on mortgage to Mr Lockhart, till after the 6th. July, when the sale of Stock could be effected: that I would desire Messrs. Hoare to remit to him £250 prior to the 23^d. Inst. in part of the sum to be lent to M^r L: that I should |^79 rely on his providing temporarily £750 to make up the £1000 — of which I should pay £500, when the Stock was sold, and the residue as soon as my accounts with my bankers would permit.

Set out in an open car at 11 AM. with MW., E.F.W., and Sophy on an excursion through the Undercliff to its extremity at Blackgang chine, the distance being seven miles. Passing the Ventnor hotel through an interior dell, secluded by a high cliff from the view of the sea, we soon reached the brow of a steephill from which a mansion derives its name, Steephill, the residence of Mr Hambrough already mentioned. It is perched on a platform rising out of the low valley, and backed by the cliff, or mural range, which from Ventnor to the termination of the Undercliff near Black Gang Chine rises above the labyrinth of beauty intervening between it and the lower cliff overhanging the beach. Steephill, occupying the site of an older residence, has been erected about thirteen years, and is a spacious mansion in the castellated form, |[80] standing in well timbered and spacious grounds, approached by a gateway and lodge, but so shut out from view that only glimpses of the interior can be obtained. Hay making and abundant crops of grass on each side of the narrow road; little oddly shaped fields, for the most part, of a most irregular surface, interspersed with masses of rock and brushwood, or overhung by luxuriant timber, with here and there some arable land with promising crops. Next came S[t.] Lawrance, where, almost wholly shut out by high hedges, lofty trees, or high walls, a large Elizabethan mansion, or villa, the property and frequent residence of the Earl of Yarborough, a nobleman with large estates in the Island, Lincolnshire & elsewhere, a great patron of Yachting, Commodore of the Yacht Club meeting at Cowes, and more commonly in favourable seasons to be heard of cruising in his favourite Kestrel than elsewhere;[10] — his Lordship's second son, Capt. Pelham, R.N. has a cottage residence contiguous |[81] to that of his noble father at S[t.] Lawrence. The scattered cottages of the village mostly nestle at the foot of a steep eminence, up which the road ascends, and at the summit, close by the highway, stands the picturesque and diminutive church of the little parish and rectory, an object of interest as the most tiny church of the Island, perhaps, of Great Britain. The church and churchyard are models of neatness, and the aged Clerk, "poor old John Green," as he calls himself, lingers there in fine weather, the live-long day, the poet, the guide, and the precentor of the place.[11] At 72 years of age, and after a service a Clerk of nineteen years, guardian of the grassy mounds, and nourishing the abundant flowers which deck the tombstones and the graves, he shews his little low browed edifice, tells how

23. *Freshwater Cave, Isle of Wight.*

---

10.   Charles Anderson Pelham, Baron Yarborough (1781-1846). Pelham was not to enjoy the *Kestrel* for much longer, for he died on board on the 5th of September off Vigo in Portugal.
11.   Little John Green with the ruddy face and crooked leg was the village schoolmaster. In the following year he wrote his memoirs and these were published in 1890.

24. Blackgang Chine, Isle of Wight.

it has latterly been lengthened from 25ft. 4¾ inches to 45 feet the breadth is 11 feet, and half an inch; height 11 feet 4¼ inches: the church yard is 60 feet long, in breadth 42 feet. Ivy profusely clothes the little bell turret: the interior is fitted up |[82] with dark coloured oak pews and benches; a large ancient font, small pulpit and reading desk, small communion table, and a transparency in the Eastern window, representing the resurrection, complete the description of this little house of GOD, where, as honest Green says or sings, — "You may join in prayer & worship GOD and, though the building is so low and small, you may be near to heaven, as at S[t.] Paul." The view from the Church yard is superb; below, the wide expanse of the British Channel, above, the towering range of cliff, the ~~Escap~~ escarpment of the Downs; forwards, the undulations of the Undercliff as yet unexplored by us, backwards, the dell of S[t.] Lawrence, with a striking view of Steephill Castle, Ventnor, and S[t.] Boniface Down. I should have mentioned, before the ascent to the Church, by the road side, a dark foliage-enshrined arch near Lord Yarborough's villa, veiling a copious well named after S[t.] Lawrence, a very pretty object to the passer, and interesting to the sketcher. On we went, |[83] up and down, twisting in every direction, now commanding fine sea views, now embosomed between high hedges, or over arching trees, now admiring the line of scar above, and its fringing of brushwood, now huge fragments of rock projected from on high in former wild convulsions, nor leaving unnoticed the exquisite natural carpeting of grass and wild flowers: while frequent on either side, and often where a level foundation could hardly be found, rose the larger or the lesser villa, mostly buried in rich wood, with cool grot and welcome shade, or sunny nook, and oaken rustic seats inviting to contemplation, or social conversation, purchance to sleep. Some of these scarce to be seen residences are ~~elegant,~~ refined, highly and tastefully decorated; among them one

25. Royal Sand Rock Hotel.

belonging to Sir Willoughby Gordon: all elegant retreats. Reached a valley descending in a cleft of the rocks from the interior of the island: here diverged to the left: the ~~rod~~ road to the right leads to the not distant village of Niton. |[84] To the left our road passed by the Sandrock Hotel, perched on a platform nearly a mile above the beach, commanding, no doubt, a noble sea view, and itself embowered in foliage with an enjoyable garden. Below, on the verge of the beach, accessible by a divergent road by which we did not descend, a modern light house with

26. *Sand Rock Spring.*

its accompanying offices, and adjacent several lodging houses for the accommodation of sea-bathers, and transient residents in the Island. This light house was completed in 1839, being greatly wanted for the safe guidance of shipping rounding or nearing the South of the Island in rough weather. The dreadful loss of the Clarendon, a West Indiaman on this coast in Oct. 1836 probably led to the erection of this beacon. At a little distance from it is the point called Rockenend, where a range of rocky fragments hurled in distant ages from the overhanging cliffs and heights of S[t.] Catharine extends sea-ward more than a mile. If a vessel having |[85] got too close to the land fail to round this point, and becomes embayed behind it in the lashing surge beating on the rock bound coast, its fate, like that of the Clarendon, would be inevitable destruction. There are many other projecting points further on between Rocken-end, and Freshwater bay, each bristling with its outlying reef of rocks. Signal beacons had been erected in times long past, and even a light house in later days, as warnings, to the mariner, from the summit of the S[t.] Catharine's down, but they were found inefficient, as this lofty hill, between 800 and 900 feet above the level of the sea, is in bad weather enveloped in mists. At the extreme West point of the Island, on the Freshwater Cliffs, overhanging the Needles rocks, is another light house: these rocky shores are thus rendered less dangerous to the seaman. Not far from the Sandrock Hotel is a chalybeate Spring. Pursuing our route, we entered on a most striking tract, the site of a landslip in 1799: here there has not been time for the growth of timber, or even of a luxuriant vegetation, and there is also |[86] little shelter of elevated ground to protect from the rough sea-blasts in winter; so that there is a comparative baldness, which, however, reveals the character of those natural convulsions by which the Undercliff has been ~~performed~~, the surface being strangely tossed about, a perfect maze of undulation, through which the road has been formed, tortuous, steep, and often carried along the edge of precipitous slopes: but here too the love of sea views, sea-air, bold and unusual scenery, and elegant seclusion has led to the erection of villas, not unfrequently in a style inconsistent with the spot selected; for instance, Italian villas contrast strangely with rugged treeless rock: and one thinks it somewhat strange to read in staring letters, that such and such a villa may be rented, and "furnished Apartments" oddly force themselves on notice. Unexpected too is it to meet the well loaded stage coach on the brow of some narrow, steep pitch, freighted with adventurous explorers, ~~making a circuit~~ travelling from |[87] Cowes ~~to~~ [by] Newport, and thence, purposely making a circuit ~~on the road~~ by the Blackgang Chine &

Sandrock Hotels to Ventnor, to open out at a cheap rate the beauties and the wonders of the Undercliff. Foremost among those beauties, as we approached the limit of the day's excursion, is the view of the Needles, Freshwater Cliffs, Freshwater Gate, and Bay, at a distance of 14 or 15 miles, all clearly ~~seem~~ seen across the deep blue sea on this brilliant day; almost without the assistance of our glass the minuter features were visible; and my Son, who had visited these localities from Ryde, was a good director. The character of the country here changes:

27. Freshwater Gate Hotel.

from the high ground on which the Blackgang Chine Hotel stands on the slope beneath the summit of S[t.] Catherine's Down, there is a descent to an apparently level tract extending Westward, and, to some considerable distance, inland, bounded on the North and West by Chalk downs and the Freshwater Cliffs, terminating in the Needles. The geological character of this level is ferruginous sand. At the hotel we [188] enjoyed superb sea views: beyond the Needles and Freshwater Cliff, we saw the indistinct outline of Purbeck Island, and Portland Island was, as our Landlord affirmed, who knew exactly where to look for it, visible at a distance of 54 miles. Having partaken of refreshment, we went forth to visit the Chine; entering on flower garden, we passed through a building occupied as a Bazaar, where all sorts of tempting articles were exposed for sale, mostly in some way or other connected with the Island, Guide Books, engravings, models of the Isle of Wight Churches, stationery, and all kinds of toys. In another building was exhibited the skeleton of a whale caught a few years since in a bay at the back of the Freshwater Cliffs: this monster of the deep was 80 feet in length; round the shed were exhibited abundant store of his whalebone in its natural state, as appended to the jaws to serve as a net to catch the molluscs on which the monarch feeds; his ~~mus~~ sinews hung there too, and they who had never seen [189] the living or recently dead fish would carry away a pretty accurate notion of it from what was here displayed. An Indian canoe, and planks thrown on shore by the waves, which had been perforated by the teredo,[12] attracted our notice. And now we commenced our descent of the chasm, not, like those of Shanklin or Luccomb, rich in foliage and luxuriant with plants, but dark, gloomy and steep, the descent being aided by steps formed in the black clayey mould, (neither mould, nor clay, or rock,) a sure footing being secured by pieces of wood so driven into the soil as to prevent the steps ~~for~~ crumbling away. The whole descent is about a quarter of a mile in length; the stream, which in winter, so doubt, is copious, was in this dry season, reduced to a trickling rill, apparently quite inadequate to produce the rift which it has wrought in successive centuries, while the black, clayey, ferruginous rocks towered above, diversified by occasional horizontal strata of light coloured sand stone. Scanty vegetation was not wholly [190] wanting, and the Statice Armeria, Arenaria Maritama,[na] Sedum Anglicum, Jasione montana, have their habitats in this triste locality. Having accomplished about half of the

---

12.   Teredo – a ship worm.

descent, we met the Fisherman Guide
on the road which crosses the chine at
some distance above the beach: and near
a house lately fitted up to accommodate
with lodgings such as may be inclined to
tarry for a season in so dark a dell, yet one
commanding a vast expanse of sea. The
remaining descent to the fisherman's cottage
close above the beach, is nearly of the same
character as ^{that} we had passed: seats are
provided to rest the weary climber – to
elicit a little loose cash from his pocket, the
Guide's wife has a table spread with knick-

28. *Freshwater Cliffs.*

knacks, boxes, watch-holders, taper & ring stands, turned, or said to be turned, out of
timbers of the shipwrecked Clarendon: there also stands a battered skeleton of a piano forte,
belonging to a family returning as passengers in the doomed vessel: they were close ~~on~~ ^{to} their
intended home; for friends had engaged for them a |[91] house at Newport, and they expected
to tenant it on the following day: the Guide had witnessed, and been present at the wreck.
^{The Clarendon} ~~It~~ neared the beach and the mouth of the Chine, as he stood on the road where
we met him; in two minutes he was on the beach, and the ship a total wreck. There are no
rocks on the beach; a smooth, steep shingle; but the resistless waves, lashing the black rocks
^{of the Chine,} drove the vessel impetuously onward, and the reflux pressed on her timbers with
such mighty force that, as ~~he~~ ^{our Guide} expressed himself, she was doubled up on herself, and
the miserable crew and passengers ^{were} rather crushed to death than drowned: of 27 souls on
board, three only were saved. A short distance from the Fisherman's Cottage is the base of
the rocky chasm, a dark cove of dank rock overhung by a projecting ledge, over which now
dribbled the tiny stream which in rainy seasons formed a fall of above 70 feet perpendicular,
not seldom caught and twisted into various forms, or broken into viewless spray, by the
cur-|[92] rents of wind: 500 feet above towers the black mass of rock through which the fissure
has been worn – in front is the shingly slope of beach, & the clear blue sea from the South
murmuring in froth-crowned wavelets, not now dashing in a mighty surge. The walk is
fatiguing, but, we thought, it well repaid the labour. About four o clock we left the hotel on
our return to our Ventnor home, and much had we enjoyed our morning's drive.

June 9. Tuesday.

A fine day, not so hot as it had been.

Wrote to Mr Jennings in answer to his letter received on the 6th. Inst. pressing him to look
out for an investment in good freehold houses, or ground rents in or near London, for the
£9000, the produce of the sale of our houses in Fenchurch Street, now that the treaty for
the purchase of the estate at Great Risington is broken off. – Wrote to Pearce in reply to his
letter rec^{d.} on the 6th. Inst. as to the Valuation of parishes in our Union for the purposes of
the County |[93] rate.

We started in an open car at one o clock to visit Lord Yarborough's seat at Appuldurcomb House. The distance from Ventnor is inconsiderable, not more, perhaps, than three miles; but the road is very hilly, passing over the extremity of Boniface Down by a deep cutting in the chalk: it is the direct road to Newport. Arrived at the summit of the hill, an extensive valley was stretched before us, chiefly arable land, surrounded principally by eminences bare of wood, except where the timber of Appuldurcomb Park creeps up the height, and on the opposite side where a grove is surmounted by a soi-disant ruin, erected by the builder of Appuldurcomb house, Sir Rob.t Worsley, and called Cooke's Castle, as an object to be viewed from the mansion house. Descending to the little hamlet of Wroxhall, the mansion and park open themselves out on the left: the former a large grey looking square ~~mansion,~~ house with four projections, one at each of the corners, [194] evidently not in the original design; lofty trees, some of them noble oaks, and beech, are fit accompaniments to the stately dwelling, which stands in an extensive flower garden, central in the park; above, on a bare down, is an obelisk raised in memory of the founder, Sir R Worsley, and deer are observed browsing. Turning from the main road by a very pretty Elizabethan Cottage, and passing by the gardens belonging to the mansion, we entered the park, still ascending towards the house, when we were admitted into the interior grounds, and by a back entrance received by the housekeeper, who ushered us into the suite of apartments on the ground floor, which contain the paintings and statuary, the principal objects of attraction here – They were collected, chiefly in Italy and the Levant, by Sir Richard Worsley, some sixty years since, at a great expence, and the statues and other marbles are elaborately [195] described in a splendid folio work, with engravings, entitled Museum Worsleyanum, to which we referred in the hall, where most of these antiquities are deposited: this fine volume was not published. This Sir R. Worsley's niece and heiress married Lord Yarborough, and so the property has passed into the Pelham family. Of this lady there is a beautiful bust in Lord Y's private room – The apartments shewn are a billiard room, the great hall, library, drawing room, private room, dining room, and an anteroom to the latter – In the billiard room there are exclusively marine pictures, chiefly of naval engagements, one fine representation of a shipwreck, and a drawing of his Lordship's late yacht. The hall is supported by eight beautiful Ionic columns of a composition resembling porphyry. Among the marbles is a most beautiful group of Bacchus, and his mythological favourite Acratus, winged as a genius; the wings exquisitely sculptured — an Egyptian priest in basalt; an Anubis in the same: an Hermæan [196] statue of Sophocles, found at Athens; Alcibiades from the same place; Anacreon; with many others well worthy of observation; particularly a large and very beautifully sculptured basso relievo of a bull, the "maxima victima" of Virgil, found in Magna Graecia, near the ruins of Crotona. The collection of paintings is not large, but some of them are very beautiful: among these Henry 8.th on pannel by Holbein; this was given by Henry himself to Sir James Worsley, then Governor of the Isle of Wight, after a visit to Sir James at Appuldurcomb: — Roxalana, in the Georgian dress, by Gentili Bellini: she was a Venetian, and married to Soliman the second, after having lived several years with him. Bellini painted the portrait at Constantinople, whither he had been sent for the purpose by the Doge of Venice, at the request of Soliman; she died in 1561. — Philip the fourth of Spain, and his wife Isabella of Bourbon, whole lengths, on horseback, by Velasquez; these pictures were brought [197] from Grenada: — Pope Alexander the 6.th a very fine head by Titian; this also was brought from

Grenada, where Alexander was born. There are other beautiful Titians; among them a very lovely portrait of a nun in a most stiff & unbecoming white dress. — head of one of the Medici family by Carlo Dolci: — Hobbes, the Philosopher of Malmsbury by Vandyck: there are other splendid portraits by this artist. There are some fine landscapes by Zucharelli — by Berghem — by Claude, and one by Gaspar Poussin, the figures by Nicolas Poussin: — Sᵗ· Catharine by Murillo; and by Tintoretto, a magnificent picture, the consecration of a bishop; Paul the third is represented as officiating. Many more might be enumerated. All these paintings and sculptures were seen in the pleasantest manner: the housekeeper did not intrude herself upon us, but had placed in our hands printed books, which were lying in each apartment, containing catalogues of the works of art, numbered correspondently with num-|[98] bers affixed to each picture &c. — In the drawing room there is a beautiful and costly French clock, representing by its machinery various astronomical details, such as the days of the month, week, & hours, minutes & seconds, with much more connected with astronomical science: it is now out of order; was the property of an eminent Frenchman of science before the French revolution, and sold when that political event reduced him to poverty; it had been previously valued at a thousand louis. In the library, a handsome and spacious gallery, there appeared to be a valuable, although not a very extensive collection of books; also many portfolios, containing a large collection of valuable drawings made by Sir Richard Worsley abroad. In the private room I noticed the portrait of a former lady Yarborough, I believe, by Sir Joshua Reynolds, in small size, a full length of a lady feeding chickens; tasteful and elegant: but unpleasing, as the dress of the day was closely copied; the hair dressed so as to |[99] be drawn upwards, and yeild no shade to the countenance; the costume a figured silk &c. — Lord Yarborough's ruling passion was displayed in the anteroom to the dining room, which is fitted up with compartments ~~fitted up with~~ containing beautiful models of the stems and sterns of some of the most celebrated ships of war, of all sizes; models of boats yachts, bomb vessels, canoes, anchors, and the like; among them two bottles one containing wine or other liquor fished up during the late operations for raising the remains of the wreck of the Royal George which encumbered the road-stead of Spithead – also another odd shaped bottle on which were adhering oyster shells; this was raised from the bottom of the sea, having sunk with some other ship long before the Royal George.

In this anteroom is also a strange-looking painted head without hair, with wide staring eyes of glass, and coarse copper complection said to be the <u>vera effigies</u>, a cast of the head of Oliver Cromwell. There is nothing very remarkable in the way of furniture; the marble floor of the hall is very beautiful, |[100] and it contains a beautiful inlaid marble table. We were allowed to walk round the flower garden; without the main entrance to the Hall, on each side of the door way, stand ancient marble Roman chairs of

29. *Appuldercombe, the home of the Earl of Yarborough.*

beautiful form, which we thought would with more propriety have been placed under cover within the house, for they were much worn by the influence of climate, stained with lichen &c. – The flower garden is extensive and formal; contains a fine stone basin with a large supply of water and a fountain not sporting a high jet. There is nothing remarkable in the plants or shrubs except the rich luxuriance & great size of the rhododendra. This place was originally designed and laid out by the old landscape gardener, Brown.[13] We returned home about four o clock.

30. St Lawrence.

A walk to Bonchurch with MW. before dinner.

Rec[d.] from the Accountant General of the Bank of England a printed letter announcing that a power of Attorney had been issued for the sale of stock standing in my name, and desiring an answer from me, |[101] stating to whom I had granted the power, and the amount of stock to be sold. This is a precaution recently adopted against frauds, especially such as have been practised of late by Barber and his confederates, personating holders of stock, and selling out by forged powers of attorney. I replied to this letter by return of post.

June 10. Wednesday.

A thick haze all the day, obscuring the sea, and coursing rapidly along the lofty down and higher cliff, not wetting in the lower region, but a Scotch mist on the upper grounds.

E.F.W. went on a geological excursion to Blackgang Chine, Atherfield Rocks &c., setting out before breakfast, and returning in the evening between our dinner and tea time, heavily laden with fossils, and having greatly enjoyed his day's work.

Received a letter from Mess[rs.] Hoare covering £20 in Bank post bills, which I had desired them to send.

I walked in the direction of S[t.] Lawrence, first on the cliffs beyond the cove, and afterwards by the road as far as S[t.] Law-|[102] rance's church, and back.

June 11. Thursday.

Very fine weather.

Received a letter from Sewell and Newmarch respecting the £1000 to be advanced on mortgage to M[r] Lockhart; also to mention a property at ~~Haref~~ Haresfield, between Stroud

---

13.   Lancelot Brown (1715-1783), better known as Capability Brown.

and Gloucester, now on sale, – 170 acres, let for £320 – price about £8500, which they thought might suit us as an investment for the £9000 arising out of the sale of the houses in Fenchurch Street. My son and I considered that such a property would meet our wishes; and I wrote an answer to S. and N. by return of the post, desiring that fuller particulars might be sent to me, and also to Mʳ H. D. Warter, as our Attorney in this business. Wrote also to Mʳ Warter on the subject.

31. Blackgang Chine.

With MW. took a long walk: achieved the steep ascent of Sᵗ Boniface Down to its summit near the road crossing the heights towards Appuldurcomb: pursued the level top of the hill to its extremity, overhanging the basin at the foot of which is Luccomb Chine; |¹⁰³ the crown of the hill is turf, scanty vegetation, furze — the Digitalis, the Vaccinium Myrtillus, the Calluna abound — minute fragments of flint cover the soil in patches. Most extensive and beautiful are the views, the range extends over the greater part of the Island, Sᵗ Catharine's Down, the downs in the direction of Freshwater, the chain of Chalk Hills running East and West, the Solent Sea, the coast of Hampshire, distant, and the internal valley of Appuldurcomb, stretching to Godshill, Newchurch &c. — At the brow of the Down above Luccomb the prospect is still finer, close below, the Undercliff, Luccombe Chine; on the same level with the Spectator, Shanklin Down; beyond, Shanklin, Sandown, the Culver Cliffs, Yaverland, Brading, its haven, Sᵗ Helens, Nettlestone point, Brading down, beyond which the line of Coast from Cowes by Wootton Creek to Ryde, Apley &c; then still more remote the Hants coast, Portsdown, Portsmouth, Gosport, Hayling Island, and the wide expanse of blue Sea, more particularly, the exquisite bay between the |¹⁰⁴ Culver Cliffs and Dunnose. We were amply repaid by these splendid scenes for the fatigue of the ascent and difficulty of the descent, nearly at the point where the footpath deviates from the main road to the recesses of Luccomb Chine. On the summit we encountered a party of Sappers, I believe, with their moveable huts, telescope & other surveying apparatus. The intelligent Corporal whom I addressed, and who appeared to be chief in the survey, explained to me that the object was to promote the accuracy of the Trigonometrical Survey as regarded the Undercliff, which was not very exactly pourtrayed in the Ordnance Maps. I entered one of the Huts which are used by these parties, being, in fact, little wooden square houses, with glazed window and door, folding table & stool, hammock and chests containing the necessary tools and appliances for the work of the surveyor. We returned home by Bonchurch –

June 12. ~~Thursday~~ *Friday*
Beautiful weather: very hot sun.

Received a letter from Mʳ Sewell, |¹⁰⁵ with further particulars as to the estate on sale at Haresfield; satisfactory on that point, also as to the £1000 to be advanced to Mʳ Lockhart. — A letter from R W Hippisley, soliciting a contribution towards the repewing of the

Church at Stow: this, probably, a circular to all the Clergy of the Deanery, as the appeal is made on the ground that the Visitations are held there. Such an application was expected.

Wrote to M[r] H. D. Warter, sending him an extract from Sewell's Letter as far as it related to the Haresfield Estate.

M[r] Coleman, the Incumbent of Ventnor, called, and sat for a considerable time. He stated it as his practice to wait on all visitors of the place that, if indisposition prevailed in any family, he might render his services as Minister. This he does under the conviction that ill health, i.e. consumptive tendencies, brings higher almost all the winter residents, and many of those who frequent the place at other seasons. In the winter he calls Ventnor a perfect hospital. I found him a polite, well informed, conversible man; with |[106] strong prepossessions against Peel and the Maynooth grant; strong leaning towards the Church Missionary Society, taking a great interest in the Jerusalem Bishopric, the Episcopate and Missions in New Zealand, and other topics which engage the energies of the Evangelical party. He told me that his is a district church with a district taken out of the parishes of Newchurch and Godshill; that eight years ago, when the Church was erected, there was a difficulty in shewing a population of 400; that now the population amounts to 2000; that in his three Sunday services he numbers, on an average, 1400 attendants.

Strolled at different times on the cliffs and in the beautiful slopes of the landslip near Luccomb Chine: also on the declivity of Boniface Down and towards the Pulpit rock.

My son busy in geological researches on the beech[14] below S[t] Lawrence, and Wolverton. –

June 13. Saturday.
Beautiful weather, but extremely hot with an Easterly wind. |[107]

Answered R W Hippisley's letter promising to subscribe £5 towards the repewing of his Church, but expressing doubts as to the congregation receiving an increase proportionate to the proposed an enlargement of accommodation, apprehension that he will find the appropriation of the sittings a source of contention, hope that there will be no novelties or peculiarities introduced which are likely to give offence to scrupulous people. Wrote to C Bathurst.

Received two letters from H. D. Warter, who wrote the former in answer to the one I addressed to him from Ryde as to the closing of the treaty for the Risington estate, and the payment of costs incurred, — as satisfactory as might be expected: — the other in reply to my letter to him of the 11[th.] Inst. respecting the estate on sale at Haresfield: he is of opinion that we cannot purchase at an auction, but only by private contract, supposing the property is not disposed of by public competition. That I suspected, and we must act accordingly.

---

14. *Sic.*

With |¹⁰⁸ MW. and Broome enjoyed a little excursion on the sea in a two oared boat, first rowing as far as Dunnose point, then out to sea, till opposite Sᵗ· Lawrence, then to the land at Ventnor Cove; very agreeable with a beautiful view of the coast.

A stroll on the Cliffs in the evening.

June 14. Sunday.
A continuance of the same fine weather.

To the morning service at Ventnor Church with MW. – E.F.W., Sophy and Broome went to Bonchurch Church, where the service was performed by two Clergymen, one of them being Archdeacon Hill, A. of Bucks, Rector of Shanklin and Bonchurch. Mʳ Coleman preached at Ventnor, Mʳ Sharpe read prayers. The former was clear, argumentative and impressive on a very questionable theme, the millenial reign of Christ, taking occasion from the concluding verses of the 72ᵈ· Psalm, arguing that Christ's kingdom on earth not being universal now, as predicted in the Psalm, the universal kingdom would |¹⁰⁹ follow his second advent, and he should rule with the Saints for 1000 years as foretold in the Book of Revelation: to show that this was the belief of the first three centuries he quoted <u>one</u> writer, Justin Martyr in his Dialogue with Trypho – the discourse was ingenious, delivered memoriter, and concluded with practical exhortations: the soundness of the doctrine might well be questioned, and the bias of the preacher was very apparent: the Roman Catholics hardly allowed to be Christians, regeneration predicated of anything but baptism &c. — To the afternoon service we all went together. Mʳ Sharpe officiated, and preached respectably.

Recᵈ· letters from a Solicitor in London, asking information which it is supposed we can furnish, as to the affairs of one Dodsworth, who, I believe, was tenant at Scale House more than forty years ago: — from a Clerk of Messʳˢ· Sewell and Newmarch, stating that his principals are from home, and that the matter on which I last wrote to them shall be attended |¹¹⁰ to when Mʳ Sewell returns on Monday: — from a Mʳ Mainwaring, a quondam protegé of Miss Witts, whom we long since saw for one day at Brecon, and who has been, I believe, in the East Indies, going out as a schoolmaster: he wishes to learn my cousin's address: — from H. D. Warter, saying that I have not given him the names of the London Solʳˢ· engaged in the sale of the property at Haresfield, and, therefore, cannot make enquiries.

Walked with MW. in the evening on the cliffs towards Sᵗ· Lawrence.

June 15. Monday.
Brilliant weather.

E.F.W. left us after luncheon to pursue his geological researches at Atherfield, and in its neighbourhood, going by a Newport and Cowes coach to ~~Atherf~~ Blackgang Chine Hotel, where he purposes to sleep, and to return to-morrow.

Wrote to Mʳ Warter in reply to his note received yesterday, sending him an extract from the Gloucestershire Chronicle, viz. an advertisement of the sale by |[111] auction at Gloucester on the 8th. July of the Okey estate at Haresfield, furnishing the names of the Solicitors concerned for the vendors &c. — to Mr Mainwaring, informing him of the death of my cousin, Anne Witts, and giving him the address of Captn. Witts, and his sister Apphia: — to Mr White of Barnard's Inn, that I am unable to give any information as to the affairs of Dodsworth, formerly tenant at Scale House: — to the Postmistress, Stow, desiring her to cease to forward letters and papers for us: also a letter to Mr Hare on Hunt affairs, (the appointment of a Solr to the trust) to be dispatched tomorrow.

32. *William Makepeace Thackeray.*

With M.W. enjoyed a row in the direction of Dunnose for an hour and quarter; and with the ladies and children a stroll on the beach by Horseshoe & Bonchurch coves in the evening.

Finished reading "notes of a journal from Cornhill to Grand Cairo, by way of Lisbon, Athens, Constantinople, and Jerusalem; performed in the steamers |[112] of the Peninsular and Oriental Company. By Mr M. A. Titmarsh (W M Thackeray) Lond. 1846" — an amusing book.[15] –

June 16. Tuesday.
No change in the weather: the midday heat scorching.

Wrote to Mr Thornton on Hunt affairs, sending him a copy of my letter of yesterday to Mr Hare, and returning the enclosures contained in Mr Hare's last letter.

My son returned to dinner from the excursion to Blackgang Atherfield point &c. — much pleased with what he had seen.

Strolled on the beach and on Boniface Down, near the Pulpit rock.

A letter from the Lunatic asylum, Gloucester, announcing a meeting of the Lunatic Asylum Committee for the 23d. Inst. –

---

15.   William Makepeace Thackeray (1811-1863), Thackeray used pseudonyms of Charles James Yellowplush, Michael Angelo Titmarsh, George Savage FitzBoodle. *Notes on a Journey from Cornhill to Grand Cairo* was published in 1846. Thackeray's most famous work, *Vanity Fair* was to be published in the following year.

June 17. Wednesday.
Continued hot and fine weather.

Received letters from Mr Warter and Mr Sewell as to the estate on sale at Haresfield.

Wrote to Messrs. Hoare, desiring them to pay £250 to the account of |^{*113*} Messrs. Sewell and Newmarch with the Gloucestershire Banking Company at Cirencester, towards the £1000 to be advanced on mortgage to Mr Lockhart: — to Mr Hardy, Newspaper agent, London, to forward the St. James's Chronicle to me at Upper Slaughter: — to the landlord of the Railway Hotel, Reading, to send a carriage to the Basingstoke Station on Saturday next at 8.20. AM. to meet our party there, and convey us to Reading.

Preparing to leave Ventnor on our way homewards to-morrow.

Strolled by the beach, and on the foot of St. Boniface Down &c. –

June 18. Thursday.
Brilliant weather.

Rose early, and breakfasted at 8 AM. to be ready to set out at 9 AM. by the coach to Cowes. Left Ventnor Hotel at half past nine, the coach having called for us at the other extremity of the place half an hour earlier. MW. and I with the nurse and Freddy in the coach, the others on the roof. The road leads by Wroxall and Appuldurcomb, a very long and steep hill to the summit of the downs — |^{*114*} afterwards a descent into the interior valley, but there are frequent hills, and the road is for the most part narrow, and far from good. Godshill is a very pretty village, the church standing in the centre on a knoll — from the Parsonage windows beamed the smiling countenances of a bevy of children, whom we had seen, our next door neighbours, at Ryde, the family of the Incumbent of the place: they recognized their late playmates on the beach. Godshill seemed a pleasant residence; several pretty cottages, in luxuriant gardens, a neat country inn &c. The country is diversified; here and there, rough commons, growing corn, meadow and pasture, the summits of the chain of downs crossing from Freshwater to Culver Cliffs, bare, ^{elsewhere} timber abundant: villas frequent. The valley of the Medina, the small river, which bisects the island from South to North, rising very near to the Southern shore, is narrow; near Newport the stream |^{*115*} passes through the chain of downs, ~~which it~~ the continuity of which it has interrupted: under the rising ground to the West, at the head of a wooded vally, is Gatcomb village and mansion, the latter the property of Lord As^hburton, and now the residence of Captain Berners. Approaching Newport, we noticed several villas, agreeably situate, and at the edge of the town a modern church, which I had observed from Carisbrook Castle. The town which we traversed in a different direction from that by which we had passed in our excursion to Carisbrook, appears a clean, thriving, and considerable place. About the centre is the ancient Church, grey and spacious, with no lack of Churchwardens architecture. We staid nearly a quarter of an hour in the place, before proceeding with fresh horses to Cowes. We soon reached the Albany Barracks, close to which we passed; they are very spacious, and neat, in

33. Osborne House,
Isle of Wight.

a fine airy situation, and commanding extensive views. The valley |[116] of the Medina, which is navigable to Newport at high water, is to the right, as we proceeded towards Cowes; must look to advantage when the tide is up; the banks are sloping, well cultivated, or fringed with coppice wood. Marching, drilling, & awkward squadding, were going on within the barrack inclosure: a little further on, on the same side, is the Juvenile Prison, where boys sentenced to transportation in the various courts of justice throughout the kingdom, and whose sentence it is proposed to carry out, are confined for a certain period, that they may be trained to habits of industry, and taught a trade, by which they may hereafter be enabled to earn an honest livelihood in the settlements to which they are removed. Many of the lads were busy in haymaking in the grounds attached to the prison as we passed. The system is well conducted: but, of course, reformation is not always the |[117] result. It has fallen to my lot to try prisoners under 20 years of age who, having been subjected to the discipline and tuition of this place, having been well instructed, removed to New South Wales, and served their time there, have found their way back to the haunts of their early vice, have attached themselves to their old bad companions, resumed their bad ways, and so, by the commission of some felony, subjected themselves to a ten years transportation. Northwood is a village to the right of the road, as we travelled from Newport to Cowes; on the opposite bank of the Medina we noticed, above East Cowes, its wooded promontory: ~~forming one of the~~ in the shady groves which crown the height is a castellated mansion, the residence of a M[r] Barwell; near it, on the top of the slope above E. Cowes, a few recently erected villas, somewhat staring, being the first and, perhaps, the last erections of a company which had schemed a grand group of detached residences of a |[118] superior class, to be called "the Park"; but even the near vicinity of the Royal residence has failed to attract purchasers or tenants, and the speculation is eminently unsuccessful. Further on is seen an Italian looking tower, or observatory, closely adjacent to Osborne House, the latter not being visible from this point; a subterranean communication connects the house and this tower; the building the latter is one of the main alterations which the Queen has made since her purchase of this property: with the Barton estate, and other lands acquired by her, a large tract in a ring fence is now her Majesty's demesne, but the house itself, though spacious, and containing some good rooms, has no architectural pretensions, and is at least half a mile from the shore, at the head of a well timbered lawn sloping to the sea, of which it commands a fine prospect, but not so varied, extensive, or lively, as if the house were situate nearer to Cowes harbour, where more |[119] shipping with yachts and boats usually lie. – Northwood park, the seat of M[r] Ward, overhangs with its groves the town of West Cowes, into which we descended, passing, as usual, in most parts of the Island, numerous villas, great or small. Nothing can be more unprepossessing than the crowded, narrow, twisting streets of Cowes, erected as a port in olden times, before luxury, superfluous wealth, and sea bathing abounded: through these lanes we soon reached our destination, an old fashioned, dirty looking, red brick Inn, calling itself the Fountain Hotel. Passing under an archway, we found ourselves in the Inn Yard, which is also <u>the</u> quay, ending in a small wooden pier, projecting into the harbour, built on piles, furnished with steps and inclined planes, to answer the various changes from high to low water. Here the steamers ply, and scarcely half an hour passes without the arrival or departure of one of more, ~~plying~~ keeping up the communication between this port, and Southampton, Gosport, Ryde, Poole, Yarmouth, Lymington &c. Having fixed ourselves |[120] in apartments here, a room looking out on the yard, quay, harbour, and opposite shore of East Cowes, ~~having~~ which had been bespoken for us, by the landlord of Ventnor Hotel on the preceding day, and having partaken of luncheon, we sallied forth to speculate on the place. The heat was so great that much walking was out of the question; an excursion on the water was, therefore, preferred by MW., Broome, & myself, which E.F.W. and Sophy declined, fearful of becoming seasick, to which they are liable by the motion of a small vessel. They contented themselves with a saunter and sitting on the seashore till dinner hour. We engaged a ~~two~~ boat with two intelligent watermen, and, hoisting sail, remained on the sea for three hours. Cowes harbour and road present a busy scene, and are very attractive: the mouth of the Medina affords a commodious harbour for small merchant vessels, steamers, |[121] yachts, and pleasure boats, and is, in fact, the great resort of the principal Yacht club: beautiful vessels were moored in all directions, and on the beach, at the edge of the town, is the Yacht Club house, with its signal post and flag staff. Just beyond, bathed by the tide, is the so-called Castle, being a modern mock castellated mansion built on what remains of a small fort erected by Hen. VIII., now only a semicircular platform with eleven guns mounted: the house is leased by government to the Marquis of Anglesey, as a marine residence. A little further Westward is a modern Chapel of the Church of England, built a little way distant above the beach, at the outskirts of the Town, and beautifully situate at the foot of a hill, stretching parallel to the shore, and densely covered with coppice wood. This sloping bank of wood forms a beautiful background to a range of elegant villas, and cottages, standing detached, and fronting |[122] the sea, from which they are separated by a vacant space of open ground, called "the Parade", extending for some distance along the beach, and forming a delightful promenade; the waves ripple close to the green turf, breaking softly in this fine summer weather on a shingly margin; in front, is the road stead, now studded with six or eight merchant men, three masters, or brigs of large size: two Americans, a Dane, a convict ship bound for Sydney, and waiting for a detachment of convict boys from Parkhurst gaol, were among the number. Opposite Cowes the Solent sea begins to narrow Westward, in the direction of Yarmouth & the Needles; large steamers, packets or Government vessels, were passing to Southampton or Portsmouth: among them one from the West Indies; another bearing, as it afterwards transpired, the Duke and Duchess of Saxe Cobourg & Gotha, with other members of that princely race, coming from Lisbon, where they had been visiting the Queen of Portugal & her consort, a Coburg Prince, |*123* and now bound on a visit to their Royal relatives of England, Queen Victoria and <u>her</u> Coburg consort, whose arrival at Osborne House is currently mentioned to-day, as likely to take place to-morrow. The Hampshire coast opposite to the Parade at Cowes opens to view the mouth of the Southampton river, Calshot Castle, and Eaglehurst, the seat of the Earl of Cavan. About a mile from Cowes Castle, along the beach, westward, close to the water's edge, is West cliff or Egypt, a castellated villa, the property of Sir T. Tancred, but usually occupied by some distinguished member of the Yacht club. So far we sailed, observing, beyond, the points of the Island forming the different bays, terminating in Freshwater & the Needles point; and in the evening we were among those who promenaded or sat on the parade: between the Castle and the parade are the bathing machines. But our excursion did not only lead us by the shore Westward, we made several tacks Eastward standing out into the mid channel, where we breasted the few foam crowned waves, |*124* and rocked on the swell, reaching a distance of five miles from the harbour. This carried us out beyond the roadstead crossing the course of the plying steamers and cruising Yachts, ~~brought us~~ within sound of the booming Artillery of Portsmouth, and within view of Anglesey and Alverstoke. Ryde, and its pier, and all the line of wooded Coast from Cowes to Nettlestone Point were clearly distinguishable, and we had a full and close view of Osborne House and grounds, ~~of~~ passing within the moorings of the Royal Steam yachts close by the landing place used by her Majesty in her naval trips, and by the marquée raised on the margin of the sea, ~~to~~ in which she & Prince Albert rest after their walks in the grounds, or take refreshments, and which being now pitched gave assurance of the speedy arrival of the Royal couple. Between Osborne and the Eastern point of Cowes Harbour is Norris Castle, the seat of Mr Bell; I was told he is the proprietor of the Journals, the Weekly Messenger, Life in |*125* London &c., and a very wealthy person. It is a fine marine castellated house, built by Lord Henry Seymour very substantially, clothed in great part with luxuriant ivy, with a frowning tower, and spacious accommodation for the largest family. It stands on high ground sloping to the sea with an abundance of luxuriant

34. West Cowes, Isle of Wight.

timber: the whole property along the beach is protected by a fine sea wall. It was once, in her youthful days, for a year or two, the residence of the Queen and her Mother; and its purchase would gladly have been made lately for the Crown, in preference to the adjoining estate of Osborne, but the proprietor demanded an exorbitant price. The sea view from this mansion must be extremely fine.

While we were at dinner a beautiful, long, slender, much gilded steamer glided rapidly up the harbour, before our window, and, having discharged its freight, or landed its passengers, soon after passed a second time in review before us; we judged rightly that she was the well known and much admired Fairy, the |[126] steam tender to the Royal Victoria and Albert yacht, arrived from Portsmouth, or rather Gosport, with attendants on the Queen, to prepare for her Majesty's reception to-morrow. This beautiful vessel draws little water, moves very fast, being built very sharp, and is perpetually plying for the use of the Court, when in residence at Osborne: the <u>fairy</u> bore her Majesty last summer up the Rhine and back.

My son and daughter crossed the harbour to East Cowes point after dinner, that the former might examine the geological character of the beach. MW. and I, with Broome, enjoyed a stroll on the Parade, passing thither by the shore and the Castle. I afterwards found my way through the lower parts of the town to the upper part of the harbour, where a ferry boat crosses from West to East Cowes: this gave me an opportunity of passing a large ship building yard, where three or four fine vessels, one a three master intended for the West Indian trade, were on the stocks; indeed, Cowes has long been |[127] celebrated for the excellence of the vessels launched from this yard. Even ships of war have been built here by contract; the yachts constructed here are unrivalled; and the ship wrights, particularly those in the employ of one eminent shipbuilder, are equal to the best workmen in the royal dock yards. –

June 19. Friday.
The weather very hot, and brilliant.

Wrote to M[r] Bloxsome, requesting him to send his half-yearly bill on the County, that I may examine it next week in preparation for the audit of the County accounts, on the 29[th.] Inst. — the day before the Trinity Sessions.

I took a walk before breakfast, by the Castle and Yacht Club house, the new Church in the vicinity of the Parade, by the entrances to the grounds of M[r] Ward's seat at Northwood Park, to the higher parts of the town, in search of the Church on the Hill, which, however, I missed, returning to the Hotel, by obscure, narrow and steep streets, leaving no favourable impression on the mind. The villas |[128] on and near the parade, and some lodging houses near the Yacht Club House, would be very enjoyable temporary residences; and the upper parts of the town include some houses in gardens, no doubt, commanding fine sea views, but, generally, the appearance of the town is unfavourable, although, probably, in the narrow streets lodgings may be found with good accommodations and views of the harbour and [the] lively, moving scene which it presents.

In the forenoon MW. and I sat for a long time in great enjoyment in a shady spot below the Castle, where an old man lets out chairs at a penny an hour. We had a delightful sea prospect. Every ship was dressed in colours, flaunting in all directions, from every mast, all the bunting each possessed being called into requisition, even on the ship destined to convey convicts to New South Wales, in honour of the expected arrival of the Queen and the Court, which was fixed for to-day, but the hour not exactly known. Flags waved from |[129] many of the houses on shore, from the Offices of the Consuls of Foreign powers, boats were plying, steamers passing and repassing, yachts cruising, and the scene altogether very attractive.

E.F.W. Sophy & the children lingered and loitered on the Parade and adjacent beach, collecting shells.

MW. myself and Broome indulged ourselves in a last short row up the harbour for a little view of the interior, the merchant vessels unlading, the yachts at their moorings, and the vessels in the building yards. We went to the Queen's private landing place at East Cowes, where she steps out of her Yacht on a private quay, her carriages being brought close to the pier beneath an archway which is opened when her Majesty has entered her conveyance: all is very plain, apartments to receive the luggage and attendants; a road ending at this quay leads directly to Osborne House, perhaps, not a mile distant. — Near the landing place is the Medina Hotel. We had fixed our departure by the Southamp-|[130]ton steamer, which leaves the Quay at a quarter before one, had embarked our luggage, & taken our places beneath the awning, when the rapacity of the servants of the hotel caused me some vexation and trouble, appeals being made to me on board by three fellows, a porter, an underwaiter, and a boots, whom I had already fully remunerated for their services, leaving the money with the head waiter. The pertinacity of one of these sharks, who would not be satisfied with my explanation, obliged me to land and state the facts to the landlady and her daughter, into whose presence I brought the insolent remonstrant, and expressed a strong opinion as to the extortionate conduct of their servants as disgraceful to themselves. I recovered my place on board the steamer, just before it unmoored, having successfully resisted the imposition, but not without temporary disturbance from the agitation.

We had a delightful transit |[131] to Southampton in an hour and five minutes, the distance being twelve miles. Sheltered beneath the awning, and cooled by the breeze, though the sea was exceedingly smooth, we experienced no inconvenience from the scorching sun, which both at Cowes and Southampton burnt with a fierce glare. At the mouth of the river on a level projecting point, the extremity of a narrow peninsula, on the West, stands Calshot Castle, one of Henry VIII's circular forts, still kept up, but, I should imagine, not a very formidable work either for the attack or defence. The fine arm of the sea up which we ~~are ea~~ were careering would have appeared to still greater advantage, if it had been the time of high tide; as it was, the muddy banks on each side detracted from the beauty of the firth. On the Westward bank, beyond Calshot Castle, is Eaglehurst, the seat of Earl Cavan; ascending the river, on the same side, is Cadlands, the seat of M[r] Drummond: Fawley, and Dibden are villages in the same direction; the ground rises gently from the |[132] water's edge, well wooded, with an undulating outline, and behind lies the New Forest. On the Eastern side, a creek runs

35. Bar Gate, Southampton.

up towards Botley: Hamble is a village full in view; villas and wood form the background: nearer Southampton, and pretty close on the water, shrouded among trees, are the picturesque remains of Netley Abbey, and its old castle, well worthy of a visit. Southampton occupies a projecting point, flanked on each side by creeks or minor bays; into that on the East flows the river Itchin, descending in a Southward direction from Winchester; into the Western and wider lake-like expanse runs the river Test, flowing in a Southerly stream from Stockbridge & Romsey: at the head of this branch of the Southampton Water is the village of Eling. As we ascended the river we passed many vessels either moored or sailing, some of considerable size, others of less dimensions. Among the larger was a Russian steamer, built, as I heard, in the United States of America, a very noble |[133] ship, freighted, it was said, in part, with presents for the Queen. Many of the crew of this vessel we afterwards saw sauntering in Southampton, a very neat, smart-looking, set of fellows, in white linen jacket and trowsers, with a blue border round the neck and wrist-bands, mostly wearing moustaches, and all black cloth caps, some of a very dark, almost Asiatic complexion, others fair: many were powerful, strong built men. Yachts and pleasure boats abounded round and near the pier and quay: as we drew close the town fronted us, and on our right, stretching Eastward on a level flat, we noticed the Terminus of the South Western railway, closely adjacent to the new and very extensive Docks. Both these establishments are of the greatest importance to the prosperity of the place, which has taken a great start in commercial speculation. Great steamship companies are established here, carrying on the communication with the Mediterranean, and by Alexandria with the East Indies, with the West Indies and South |[134] America: steam communications with ports to the West in the Channel, to the Channel Islands, and ports on the Coasts of France, Spain and Portugal are in great activity. To these may be added a considerable share in the Emigration business to North America (the British dependencies) the United States, and the remote Colonies at & beyond the Cape of Good Hope – for this speculation Southampton affords great facility; being now so easily accessible from the metropolis by railway, emigrants & their stores are promptly conveyed to the ship's side, so avoiding the delay and danger often incident to a tedious voyage from the Thames, down the straits of Dover and to the Isle of Wight, which being once passed, the risk is greatly diminished. But to increase, and, perhaps, to secure the prosperity of this rising port one thing is still lacking, — a direct railway communication with the manufacturing districts, and for this different projects are now under discussion before of |[135] Committees of the Houses of Parliament: one plan being a line from or near Cirencester, whereby a direct and continuous communication would be obtained by lines already formed, or others to be constructed, from Manchester to Southampton. From the Quay at its Western extremity, projects a pier, well constructed, but not very long, with a spacious head, and pavillion, provided with seats externally, commanding fine views of the harbour; carriages may be driven hither, to receive those who land, and require the accommodation; a broad footpath is separated by railing from the carriage road. At the extremity of this pier we landed from our Steamer, and as the Hotel to which we had been recommended, the Royal George, in the High Street, was not distant, we agreed to walk thither, our luggage being conveyed on trucks. At the pier gateway payment is made by those who use it. We here entered on a fine broad quay, extending on the Eastern side nearly to the terminus of the Railway and |[136] the entrance to the docks; to walk the distance may require more than five minutes: a few ships, colliers and the like, were moored by the quay, which projects opposite to the end of High Street, some way into the harbour. Handsome buildings, some of recent construction, faced the Western extremity of the quay: among them an unfinished hotel, and several large warehouses. Newly built warehouses were also in the High Street, at its lower extremity near the Quay, and our Hotel was a few doors from the Southern end of the High Street. We procured very comfortable apartments, as far as any can be agreeable on a day and night of great heat, and the provisions and attendance were good: one recommendation also this establishment possesses, that the landlord will, if desired, fix the amount to be given by his guests to the Servants; of this we availed ourselves, smarting under the extortion and pertinacity of the rapacious |[137] servants at the Cowes Hotel. We strolled out before dinner, and greatly admired the High Street; its direction is from North to South: being divided into an "Above Bar", and "Below Bar", by an ancient Gateway, modernized on its Southern front, which presents little but a heavy brick wall, but retaining on the North front the massive and very striking castellated architecture of the age in which it is ᵂᵃˢ built. The old fortifications of Southampton are for the most part obliterated by modern improvements; it would seem that the wall extended East and West of the bar — Westward to the water's side, along which they flanked the upper end of the Southampton Water, the mouth of the Auton or Test, in a Southerly direction, then proceeding along the Quay Eastward, where the principal remains are still to be seen in a massive Gateway, now, I believe, used as a Bridewell: thence they turned Northward till they met the wall stretching Westward from the Bar: some gates besides the |[138] Bar, and the Bridewell, are more or less visible, some have been removed, particularly a Water Gate, at the foot of the high street: some of the walls and towers are also traceable. The town has greatly outgrown on the land side its ancient dimensions. The High Street is wide, the shops handsome, generally, some with very elaborate fronts: the material of the houses mostly brick, but much modern intermingled with some old; a wide footpavement, here and there of asphalte – three churches are on the

36. Gaol and Bridewell.

Eastern side of the Street, one a very elaborate modern structure in the Grecian style, built more than half a century ago; another ancient, with a lofty spire, the architecture debased by churchwardens improvements, the mullions removed from, and not replaced in the windows &c; — the third church is of late erection, of brick, curtailed of its fair proportions, the spire which formed part of the design not having been raised, doubtless, for lack of funds; so |[139] that the top of the tower is boarded over, in the hope that at some future time the design may be completed. There are three or four very spacious hotels in the High Street. The heat prevented our walking much Northward of the Bar; what we saw there induced us to wish that it were prudent to continue our stroll in that direction — handsome houses, shady trees &c. In the quarter of the town between the High Street and the Western arm of the Southampton Water we noticed another ancient Church with a spire; here too was of old the site of the Castle; and in the older, less modernized, and narrower street of this part of the town, are to be seen as I have heard, some interesting specimens of ancient domestic architecture. MW. having retired to our hotel, I sauntered on the Quay, Eastward near the old walls and Bridewell Gate, on a promenade, called the Platform on which are ranged several cannon, peaceably reposing under rows of shady trees, where seats are provided, on one of which I rested, looking |[140] out on the harbour, among a few idlers of the humbler class, nurses and children. Not proceeding to the Railway Terminus or Dock Entrance, I returned to our hotel by some modern streets, Eastward of the High Street, and leading to it. It is on this side apparently, towards the Railway and Docks, that the town is extending itself by new Buildings & rows of houses. After dinner the cooler temperature tempted us abroad again; our walk was along the Beach, as it is called, on the platform, and under the trees lately mentioned, whence we commanded a fine view of the harbour: we afterwards visited the Pier, which appeared to be the favourite promenade, and where enjoyable seats with a delightful prospect across the water towards the New Forest ~~was~~ were found under the pavillion which is erected on the pier head. Here we watched the arrival of the last steampacket for the day from Cowes: before us lay moored several graceful yachts, others

37. Southampton from the New Road.

were sailing |*141* to and fro: one we watched with much interest for a long time. Two seamen plunged from her deck into the water, and swam towards the head of the pier, vigorously stemming the tide on the calm surface for a long distance and space, then turning and retracing their course to their vessel. From this yacht, which I heard belonged to a Mᵣ Pigot, an enthusiast in yachting, and which had lately returned from the Tagus, at 8 P.M. a shot was fired; the signal was instantly accompanied by a simultaneous lowering of flags from all the mast-heads of the elegant yachts in the harbour. While the sun was setting, and gleaming with mild effulgence across the Western arm of the bay, from Mᵣ Pigott's yacht streamed the melody of two well played bugles, executing various popular airs. Then came rushing on a twelve-oared boat from the Russian Steamer, bearing a single female to the pier: it transpired that this was the landlady of our hotel: she had accompanied the lady of one of the Russian |*142* officers, who had been on shore, to the vessel — and now was borne, like a Cleopatra, in the graceful boat with a crew of fine looking white jacketted & trowsered and mustachioed Russian seamen. I have since learnt that this magnificent Russian Steamer is, perhaps, the largest Steamship of war afloat, her dimensions being of 2300 tons: her name the Kamschatka; she had returned lately from the Mediterranean, where she had been in attendance on the Empress of Russia, who has lately been visiting Italy and Sicily to restore the impaired and exhausted state of her health — she came in to Southampton River, as on her voyage out, to coal & fit. — At length the shades of evening warned us to leave the pier, and return to our Quarters to enjoy a dish of tea, before retiring early to rest in preparation ~~of~~ ᶠᵒʳ our homeward journey to morrow. We experienced great heat in our sleeping apartments, and were disturbed by people moving about at midnight. |*143*

June 20. Saturday.
Very hot weather, bright sun — towards 3 PM. a haze and blight with, probably, a distant thunderstorm — a few drops of rain fell between 4 & 5 PM.

We rose early, and reached the Southampton Terminus of the South Western Railway, our luggage conveyed by porters on trucks, myself and two servᵗˢ· walking, and the rest of our party in a fly, by 7 AM just in time to start with the train, which conveyed us to the Basingstoke Station by twenty minutes past 8 AM. — There is near Southampton some rising ground, and a park with plantations; at Bishopstoke we came into the same line which we had travelled on May 18. from Basingstoke to Gosport. At Winchester a posse of merry, busy, bustling Winchester College boys, each with his portmanteau, going home for the holidays, were packed into the coaches. At Basingstoke Station we found awaiting us a coach dispatched, agreeably to my instructions sent from Ventnor, by the landlord of the Reading Station Hotel. It was a stage coach, and more |[144] easy and commodious than the Omnibus, which had been provided for us as we went to Gosport. The weather being so sultry, our vehicle had arrived last evening at Basingstoke, and three horses had been sent, that there might be the greater assurance of our punctually arriving at the Reading station at the hour we had fixed. From the Station, when our luggage had been packed, we drove into the town of Basingstoke, of which we know little, but that we found prepared for us, in the old fashioned Inn, an ample breakfast laid out in the old fashioned style of a coach passenger's breakfast, to which we severally did ample justice. At twenty minutes past nine we left Basingstoke, some on the roof, others, viz. MW and myself, Freddy and his nurse, in the coach, and, except for the inconvenience of a highly heated atmosphere, had a very enjoyable drive to Reading, which we reached at a quarter past eleven. — At 35 minutes past eleven we pursued our journey in the day mail train, which conveyed us to Glou-|[145] cester. We occupied a carriage in which were already seated two intelligent and conversible gentlemen — at Swindon we stopped for ten minutes, and took some refreshment: there our party was increased by the addition of Mr Lysons with a school-boy son, whom he had travelled from Hempstead to meet this morning at Reading, on his way home from school near Winchester for the holidays. – Much lively conversation with L. — After passing through the Sapperton tunnel we went cautiously along the incline at the head of the Chalford valley, one of the lines of rail being out of repair. It was 40 minutes past two o clock, when we reached Gloucester, and here we had to wait till a quarter past three o clock before we proceeded by the Birmingham and Bristol railway: this enabled us to take some slight refreshment, and to recognize one or two acquaintances on the platform. And now our family party was about to be broken up: M^rs. W. and myself with |[146] our Servants proceeding no further by the rail than to Cheltenham, but E.F.W., Sophy, their children and servant, going on to Ashchurch, where they had directed their open carriage to come to meet them, with a cart for their luggage. Our tender adieux were made as we steamed slowly to Cheltenham, for we went by a tardy train compared to that by which we had travelled from Reading to Gloucester, and so closed, where it had commenced, a family excursion, which in comfort, improved strength and health, acquisition of knowledge, and matter to look back upon, had fully answered our expectations. — Taking a fly at the Cheltenham Station, we reached the Plough Hotel about 4 P.M., remained there only a few minutes, and journeyed onward to Upper Slaughter in a chariot with post horses, provided by mine host Churchill, whose appointments, both in his hotel, and in his stable, are invariably of the best description — |[147] We reached our quiet, shady, rural home by half past six – Matters seemed to have gone on well in our family and village during our absence. Mr Colton had performed the Sunday duties, coming from and returning to Cheltenham each day, in a manner very satisfactory to my parishioners: — my crop of hay had been well got in several days ago. —

Letters awaited me: — from Mess[rs.] Hoare, who, conformably to my directions, had paid £250 from my account to the account of Mess[rs.] Sewell and Newmarch with the Gloucestershire Banking Company at Cirencester — this sum to form part of the £1000 to be advanced on loan to M[r] Lockhart. — from M[r] Ford, reminding me of the Decanal meeting to be held at Stow on Wednesday next, wishing my opinion as to the propriety of making a declaration of attachment to the Church of England, coupled with an expression of deep regret at the secession of many Clergymen of this and other |[148] dioceses to the Church of Rome; he gave me also an outline of the doctrine to be maintained by M[r] Sadler, in the paper he proposed to read to the meeting on the ordinary operations of the divine Spirit, on the soul of man: — from Sewell and Newmarch with further information as to the Okey farm in the parish of Haresfield, now on sale: — from M[r] Morgan, Stow, on the part of Harding, the Butcher, a request that I would recommend the latter to M[r] Morrison, to be employed by him, when he comes to reside on his Vicarage of Longborough; — from R W Hippisley, acknowledging the letter I wrote to him from Ventnor in reply to his application for a subscription towards new pewing the Church at Stow; — from Rob[t.] Waller, announcing the meeting of the Clerical Society at Stow on Wednesday next.

June 21. Sunday.
Fine weather; but the mercury falls in the Barometer. |[149]

Morning prayers — Evening prayers and sermon I preached on the conduct and character of Jael.

Rec[d.] a letter from M[r] Jennings as to the purchase of houses or ground rents in or near the Metropolis.

Wrote to M[r] Morrison to recommend to his notice for employment Butcher Harding. — To M[r] Ford approving the proposition of a declaration to emanate from the ruri-decanal meeting on Wednesday next, expressive of attachment to our church, a determination to

38. A broad gauge train.

abide in its bosom, and of regret for the late secessions to Popery. I prepared and forwarded such a document, partly grounded on a sketch sent to me by Mr Ford, but to which I thought exceptions might be taken. The Clergy of the Deanery of Hawkesbury in synod assembled have lately anticipated us in this course.

Preparing myself to take a part in the discussion of the doctrine to be propounded by Mr Sadler at the Decanal meeting on Wednesday next.

Read to the fami-|^{150} ly a section from Riddle's Commentary on the Gospel.

June 22. Monday.
Very hot weather in the forenoon and afternoon: early in the evening a very violent thundershower with impetuous wind; much thunder and lightning: lightning at night with much rain.

Wrote to Mr Warter as to the purchase of the Okey farm: — to Mr Jennings on the same subject, and as to the purchase of houses or ground rents: — to Sewell and Newmarch as to the purchase of Okey farm, and the advance to be made on mortgage to Mr Lockhart: — to Mr Colton, thanking him for his services, and requesting to be informed what is the amount incurred by him in travelling expences, that I may make him a remittance in remuneration for his services during our late excursion.

Attended a meeting of the Trustees of our Church and Charity Estate as to proceedings against the Cottage tenants who, |^{151} being greatly in arrear, have received notices to quit under the tenement act, and on other parish matters. Transacted parish business at home.

Rec^d a letter from Mr Pearce containing particulars as to what has lately passed as to Union business.

Transacted business with the Relieving Officer of the Union, and with the Superintendent of Police.

Visited sick and infirm parishioners.

Preparing myself on the question to be discussed on Wednesday next at the Decanal meeting.

Began reading Dr Wolff's narrative of his mission to Bokhara to ascertain the truth as to the presumed death or captivity of Lt Col. Stoddart and Capt. Conolly, two British officers employed as diplomatic agents in that barbarous country, and believed to have been executed by the Sovereign of the Country, or if not to be detained as Prisoners – A strange book, of strange adventures, by a strange man.

June 23. Tuesday.
Much rain had fallen during |^{152} the night; several showers fell during the day; the air cooler; more wind.

Justice business at home.

Preparing myself for the discussion on the doctrine of grace to be raised at the Decanal meeting to-morrow.

Dr Wolff's Bokhara.[16]

June 24. Wednesday.
Showery weather with some thunder and lightning.

Preparing for the subject to be discussed to-day at the decanal meeting.

Drove to Stow. Accompanied by MW. who called at the Cottage on the Vavasours, meeting there E.F.W. and Sophy, who had driven from Stanway. They were quite well, as were the dear children, and had found all going on properly at home on their return from their excursion. They returned to Stanway in the evening. M.W. returned to U. S. soon after her visit to the Cottage.

To the Library. Transacted business at the office of the Gloucestershire Banking Company.

Atten-|[153] ded divine service at the Church at Stow: Mr Hippisley read prayers: only a few of the Clergy present.

The Decanal meeting was held in the School room. The Rural Dean presided. Clergymen of the Deanery present were Messrs. Hippisley, Sadler, Clark, Estcourt, Pantin, Biscoe, Wiggin, Oakley Hill, Cooke, and myself. Of strangers, clergy, were present Messrs. Malcolm (Rector of Dunstew, Oxon) and Hutchinson (Rector of Batsford). Mr Sadler read an excellent, moderate, orthodox paper on the ordinary influences of the Holy Spirit, their manner and degree, and how they are known by their fruits – The Calvinistic errors were pointed out. — I followed, commenting in support of Mr Sadler's views, and adducing passages in confirmation of them from the writings of Bp. Bull, Whitby, Macknight, Paley &c. Most, indeed, all who were present made remarks on the subject, confirmatory for the most part

---

16. Joseph Wolff (1795-1862). Wolff was a Jewish Christian missionary, was born at Weilersbach, near Bamberg, Germany. Wolff was converted to Christianity as a child. In his travels in Bokhara he found the doctrine of the Lord's soon coming held by a remote and isolated people. The Arabs of Yemen, he says, "are in possession of a book called 'Seera,' which gives notice of the coming of Christ and His reign in glory, and they expect great events to take place in the year 1840." "In Yemen I spent six days with the Rechabites. They drink no wine, plant no vineyards, sow no seed, live in tents, and remember the words of Jonadab, the son of Rechab. With them were the children of Israel of the tribe of Dan, . . . who expect, in common with the children of Rechab, the speedy arrival of the Messiah in the clouds of heaven." In 1843 Wolff went to Bukhara to seek two British officers, Lieutenant Colonel Charles Stoddart and Captain Arthur Conolly who had been executed by the Emir of Bukhara, Nasrullah Khan in June 1842. As Wolff later described, he narrowly escaped death himself on account of the Emir laughing uncontrollably at Wolff's appearance in full canonical garb. His Narrative of this mission went through seven editions between 1845 and 1852. *Narrative of a mission to Bokhara, in the years 1843-1845, to ascertain the fate of Colonel Stoddart and Captain Conolly.* London, J.W. Parker, 1845.

of Mr Sadler's argument, and some important and interesting points thus came into |^{154} discussion. – The Rural Dean then proposed the declaration as to attachment to the Church of England, and of censure of those who had seceded to the Church of Rome, in the terms in which I had drawn it up, but without naming me as having prepared it. I enforced the propriety of putting forth such a document in observations which I addressed to the meeting, and no one dissented: though some exception was taken to one passage in which it was said that our pious forefathers had deliberately and in the fear of GOD gone forth from the Church of Rome. Mess$^{rs.}$ Wiggin, Biscoe, Hippisley &c. argued that the Reformers had not gone forth from the Church of Rome, that they were of the Church Catholic, and had succeeded in driving out the maintainers of corrupt papal doctrines, still continuing part of the Universal Church of Christ. As the point was more verbal than real matter of difference, and the sentence was complete, if it ended by saying |^{155} that the reformers had borne testimony against the errors of the Church of Rome, without adding that they had gone out of that corrupt Church, I recommended that the words objected to should be omitted — This was agreed to, and those present affixed their signatures, with the exception of Mr Estcourt, who probably acted under the feeling that in him to sign the declaration would be indelicate, as his brother is one of the Seceders. Mr Cooke also hesitated about attaching his signature, alledging that the document was an attack upon some fifty clergymen who had seceded from the Church of England, while we left unnoticed false doctrine held by a much larger section of the Clergy who still retained their station in the Church, while holding a doctrine at variance with the formularies, denying baptismal regeneration, and asserting regeneration to be something very different from what it is held to be by our Church. Mr Cooke, however, signed the declaration least |^{156} an inference should be drawn from his refusal that he has a leaning towards Rome — No doubt, he has imbibed to a certain extent Ultra High Church views, and symbolizes with the Hooks, Mannings, Coleridges &c. and no less doubt there is that similar opinions prevail among some of our younger clergy, Wiggen, Hippisley, Estcourt &c. — The question as to admitting parents to stand as sponsors, and allowing persons to act in that capacity, who ~~were~~ are not communicants, was started and discussed. It was concluded that such deviations from the strict and canonical order were justifiable on the plea of necessity, and that none might be excluded from the Church, on a ground not absolutely fundamental, deference being paid to the scruples of the weak brethren. — The next meeting of the Clergy of the Deanery was fixed for Sept. 21. and Mr Pantin announced as the subject of his Paper — "the Church of England Apostolical |^{157} in its origin, Episcopal in its Government, and Scriptural in its belief; wherein also its claims in opposition to Popery and Dissent are considered and asserted".

Afterwards followed the dinner of the Stow Clerical Society, at which Mr Hutchinson presided – Mr Waller was prevented by indisposition from being present as Secretary: other members present were Mess$^{rs.}$ Cooke, Ford, Hippisley, E. F. Witts, Winter, Clark, Griffin, Estcourt, Wiggin, and myself — The reunion was agreeable enough: Mr Hutchinson, late Student of Christ Church, nephew or great nephew of Cyril Jackson, the able Dean of Christ Church in my youth, and, I believe, the possessor of his library, is a man of considerable talent and research. He has just published the sermon which he preached at the last Archidiaconal Visitation at Campden, an elaborate and learned discourse, as it has been reported to me, aimed against the Tractarian, Newmanite, Ro-|*158* manizing doctrine of Development.

When the Clerical party broke up I accompanied E.F.W. to "the Cottage", where I partook of Coffee with the family circle there assembled — M^r and M^rs. Vavasour, M^r and M^rs. W. Vavasour, Emma Vavasour, and Sophy. —

Returned home to tea.

Received a letter from M^rs. Guydickens containing an offer to my son of the Perpetual Curacy of Waltham Abbey, Essex, vacant by the death of W. M. Whalley. The presentation rests with the representatives of the Trustees of th an Earl of Norwich — How the trust should have devolved to members of the Tracy family, and others connected with them I know not: but the Trust some years ago was limited by the decease of her Co-Trustees to M^rs. Guydickens, and renewed by her. At that time there was some talk of placing me on the trust, but it ended in nothing: the influence of the Whalley family prevailed: the present |*159* Trustees, I believe, are Miss Guydickens, Lord Wemyss, Mr Naper, Miss Harriet Whalley. – My Uncle Ferdinand Travell many years ago resigned the living in favour of his son-in-law W. M. Whalley. M^rs. Whalley had urged on Miss G. that her son or grandsons, if any in orders, should have a preference, when the living might become vacant: and the Whalleys having now declined to accept it, the offer is made to my son as a family connection. It is represented by M^rs. G. as of small value, not exceeding £100 per ann., and, probably, is not worth acceptance, but it appears by the Clergy list to be estimated at £237 per ann and, therefore, I recommended E.F.W. to make enquiry of his neighbour, William Whalley, who is likely to know the facts as to a piece of preferment so long held by his father. — The population exceeds 4000. — Rec^d. a letter from Mr Bloxsome, accompanying the half yearly bill of the Clerk of the Peace for business done for the county, to be examined |*160* by me before the Quarter Sessions.

39. Waltham Abbey from the north-west.

June 25. Thursday.
Some showers fell; otherwise fine weather.

Drove to Stow —

A letter from Mr Colton with particulars of the expence of his journeys to and from Upper Slaughter for the service of my church during my late absence from home: — from Messrs. Sewell and Newmarch, that they had rec^d. £250 remitted by Messrs. Hoare on my acc^t. which they had paid to Mr Lockhart, making up the balance of £1000 to be lent to him on mortgage, and would shortly, on their next visit to this neighbourhood, hand to me the security signed by Mr Lockhart — MW. rec^d. a letter from Miss Backhouse, who with her nieces Jane & Catherine proposes to visit us about the 16th. July.

To the Provident Bank, where and at the office of the Gloucestershire Bank^g. Company I transacted business.

To the Workhouse, where I had a conference with Mr Hunt, the District Audi-|[161] tor, who is now holding his audit there. Also conferred with Mr Pearce.

At the Justice room Messrs. Pole, Ford, and the Dean of Gloucester were my colleagues on the bench. Other Gentlemen whom I met to-day at Stow were Messrs. W B Pole, Oakley Hill and Polhill.

Wolff's Bokhara.

June 26. Friday.
Frequent showers.

Wrote to Mr Colton, sending him a cheque for £8. 13. 6 in payment of his services as a temporary curate; at the rate ^of a Guinea each Sunday, and £4. 9. 6 travelling expences. — to Mr Taplin, Mr Brookes's Clerk, as to a prosecution against a prisoner charged with felony, and to be tried at the Quarter Sessions next week: — to M^rs. Guydickens, acknowledging her kindness in offering the living of Waltham Abbey to my son, and requesting a little time for enquiry and consideration; — to M^rs. Marsh, Bell Hotel, Gloucester, that a bed may be reserved for me next week at the Sessions: — to Mr Pearce, in |[162] answer to a letter I rec^d. from him to day on Union matters.

Justice business at home.

Settled accounts with Harris, balancing the Lady-day rent of the Stanway Vicarage farm.

Wolff's Bokhara.

June 27. Saturday.
With the exception of one or two light showers, a fine day.

Wrote to Mr Polhill, forwarding to him the letter I rec^d from Mr Pearce yesterday, containing an explanation as to the circumstances under which leave to go to Broadwell for a day or two had been allowed to a pauper inmate of the Workhouse from that parish: — to Mr Rodwell, to order a book for the Stow Book Society.

Justice business at home.

Preparing a Sermon.

Examining Mr Bloxsome's half year's bill for business done for the County as Clerk of the Peace.

With MW. walked to Eyford, to call on M$^{rs.}$ Dolphin and Miss C. Knight: the former too much indisposed to receive us: |^{163} the latter we visited.

Visited sick and aged parishioners.

Rec^d a letter from E.F.W., who is disposed to decline accepting the living of Waltham Abbey — the income does not much exceed £200 per ann. — the population exceeds four thousand, mostly poor, with retired merchants, tradesmen &c. inhabiting villas adjacent to the town: the duties are necessarily very heavy: the parsonage a wretched house, which must be rebuilt or repaired at a great expence. It may be necessary to employ a curate: the character of the place and people is alien to the habits and tastes of my son and his wife; the increase of income above the amount of his Curacy not sufficient to tempt him to change; and the distance so great as to remove him quite away from his family connections.

Mr Aitkens called on us in the evening to request me to officiate at Lower Slaughter on July 5. to accommodate Mr Hippisley, who is going from home for three or |^{164} four Sundays, to be assisted by his neighbours; and Mr A., having undertaken the service at Stow on July 5., with the Sacrament to be administered, finds a difficulty in making arrangements for the duty at Lower Slaughter.

Sunday June 28.
Fine and cool weather.

Wrote to E.F.W. in answer to his letter received yesterday, that I by no means urged him to accept Waltham Abbey, concurring with him in the opinion that it was not an eligible preferment. My Son had thrown out a suggestion, grounded on a former conversation with me, that, as an increase of income with his increasing family is now becoming very requisite, it might be desirable, if convenient to me, to endeavour to purchase the advowson or next presentation of the living of Stanton, which is likely soon to be vacated by the expected decease of the incumbent, one of the Sons of Mr Bloxsome, the Clerk of the peace. Mr W.H.B. is in a very precarious state of health: indeed, his |^{165} father, in his letter rec^d by me on Wednesday, describes him as not likely long to survive. I promised my Son to make enquiries next week at

Gloucester as to the disposition of the family to dispose of the Advowson or next presentation. I apprehend that Stanton would be tenable with Upper Slaughter.

Visited the Sunday School.

Morning service, prayers and sermon: I preached on the joy there is in heaven on the repentance of a sinner. Afternoon service, prayers, after which the funeral of Jos. Wilcox, a native of this parish, brought from Quenington, where and at Bibury he has long resided — a labourer.

Received a letter from Mʳ Warter with particulars of the Okey farm; the Vendors solicitors offer to postpone the auction in order to treat with us; the title, as may be judged from the proposed conditions of sale, is not unexceptionable: Mʳ Warter could not approve of a postponement of the sale: it remains that, if a sale be not |¹⁶⁶ effected by auction, we may then, if so disposed, treat with the vendors for a purchase by private contract. I answered this letter that no further step should be taken in the matter until it be seen whether the property is sold by public auction. — A letter from Mʳ Hare on the debated point as to the appointment of a legal adviser to the Trustees of the Hunt Wadenhoe property.

Preparing for my journey to Gloucester to-morrow.

British Magazine — To the family a section from Riddle's Commentary on the Gospel.

June 29. Monday.
Fine weather.

After an early breakfast I left home for Gloucester in the open carriage, accompanied by M.W., who went no further than to Cheltenham, proposing to return home in the evening. I drove to the Railway Station, whence I proceeded to Gloucester, and took up my abode at the Bell Hotel.

To the Shire Hall, where engaged in the audit of |¹⁶⁷ accounts and county business generally with Messʳˢ· Purnell, Curtis Hayward, Baker and Goodrich — Messʳˢ· Bloxsome, Lefroy, Whitehead Keiley and Riddiford, as officials of the County, were in attendance. The indisposition of Mʳ Riddiford, who was suffering from Erysipelas was a drawback to the satisfactory audit of the public accounts.

The four Magistrates constituting the committee of accounts dined together at the Bell Hotel. Mʳ Sayers looked in upon us in the evening.

Busy with the accounts, and conferring with Purnell till a late hour. —

June 30. Tuesday.
A rainy morning, but the weather was fine afterwards.

Engaged with the County accounts before breakfast.

Breakfasted with Purnell. The Court was opened at the usual hour; Purnell in the Chair: the attendance of Magistrates was small, and the business light: no very debatable matter of general interest was |[168] brought forward, nothing calculated to induce a large attendance on the tapis. M[r] Mirehouse raised certain questions on which he was in a minority. The business closed between 3 & 4 P.M. Afterwards, according to the usage of old times, many Magistrates, of whom I was one, repaired to the County Gaol, & inspected many parts of it, especially the new buildings. M[r] Bloxsome received a note from Serjeant Ludlow, which made it doubtful whether he could attend to-morrow to preside in the Crown Court on the appeals & trials of Prisoners. A recent change in the Commissioners of Bankruptcy affecting the Court sitting at Liverpool seemed not unlikely to make it necessary for Ludlow to be at his post there to-morrow — Provision, therefore, was made that, in the event of his not coming, Curtis Hayward should take Ludlow's Chair, and I should sit in the second Court. And I wrote to MW. to acquaint her that my return might be postponed till Friday, in case I was called |[169] upon to act as Chairman. The contingency however did not occur, for Ludlow arrived late in the evening, having obtained the assistance of one of the London Comm[rs.] of Bankruptcy to sit for him for a few days at Liverpool.

Bathurst arrived from Lydney before the Court broke up, with whom, as usual, I passed much of the rest of the day.

The Magistrates dined together, a small but agreeable party at the Kings Head: those with him [whom] I was most in communication were Purnell, Curtis Hayward, Bathurst, Baker, Archd. Timbrill, Mirehouse &c.

July 1. Wednesday.
Fine weather: the air cool; a tendency to rain in the evening.

Wrote to MW. that, Ludlow being arrived, I should not be prevented from returning home to-morrow evening.

Breakfasted at the Bell with Purnell, Hale, Payne &c.

Attended throughout the day in Serjeant Ludlow's Court, excepting for an hour, when I went over to sit with Curtis |[170] Hayward, who needed a colleague. There were several appeals tried, one parish appeals, the others against orders of filiation. The Prisoners for trial exceeded 100, and several of these cases were disposed of in both courts.

Bathurst returned home to-day. I was one of a small, but agreeable, party of magistrates who met at dinner at the King's Head Hotel.

July 2. Thursday.
Fine weather.

Breakfasted at the Bell with M.ʳ Hale. Went into Court soon after nine o clock, and remained till twelve o clock, assisting Curtis Hayward in the trial of prisoners, and conferring with him on the plan which he suggests for the better management in future of the Lunatic Asylum, as respects the Subscribers and Counties, internal arrangements, classes of patients &c.

At twelve o'clock, accompanied Barwick Baker and M.ʳ Bernard to the quarterly meeting at the infirmary, where |¹⁷¹ the principal business was to read over and consider the regulations proposed by the Committee for the better management of the institution. These had been drawn up by Purnell, and involved great changes in the government, much closer supervision, greater economy, more checks against peculation. In particular, for the old House Committee, which had degenerated into a sort of family party, or clique, composed chiefly of subscribers residing at Gloucester, with a very careless and loose superintendence of the Establishment, is to be substituted a larger and wider committee to include gentlemen of the County, and to be responsible to another smaller and over-ruling Committee to meet yearly and on particular summons: alterations are proposed as to the officers of the Institution, the Treasurer, the Audit of accounts and the like. These innovations are objected to by some leading members of the old House Committee, who consider them as so much |¹⁷² of censure on their management, will not allow that the Infirmary was damaged under their government, and have struggled against the proceedings of some months past, by which the County party among the Governors has laboured to put the establishment on a better footing. But these gentlemen have little ground for a demand of confidence in themselves, under whose administration the late Secretary robbed the charity, and who never have been able to present a satisfactory balance of accounts. The regulations to be proposed to-day will have to be confirmed at the annual meeting in the Summer assize week. M.ʳ Gambier Parry, of Highnam Court, presided as a Vice-chairman — among those present were Purnell, Hale, B. Baker, Whitcombe, and Robinson (the latter a gentleman resident at Painswick,) who may be viewed as upholding the propositions of the Committee; Governors opposed to the rules now |¹⁷³ submitted by the Committee, were chiefly M.ʳ Avery, a Solicitor of Gloucester, a voluble speaker, one of the leaders of the old House Committee, Col. Cother, and M.ʳ Turner, the Treasurer — neutral, but rather leaning to the new system, Col. Hawkins, M.ʳ Coghlan (Rector of S.ᵗ Mary de lode,) M.ʳ Montague, Worthington, Clark, Martin — M.ʳ A Wood one of the surgeons of the Institution was decidedly in favour of the amended rules — M.ʳ C. Y. Crawley, acting as Chaplain, was also present – M.ʳ Avery and Col. Cother opposed the new system most warmly: I spoke in support of the plan recommended by the Committee, suggesting, at the same time, alterations, which were canvassed and adopted – G. Parry, Hale, and Baker supported the new arrangements, which were generally approved, and, having seen my friend Purnell safely across the bridge, I retired in time to leave Gloucester for Cheltenham by the train at half past four o clock. |¹⁷⁴

At Cheltenham I found my servant and carriage in waiting, with a note from MW. and I reached home by half past seven o clock.

A letter from E.F.W. who gives up all thoughts of the incumbency of Waltham Abbey, in which I think he acts wisely: for the labour and responsibility would be great, the remuneration inadequate, and the acceptance of the preferment would remove him from cherished connections and habits to a great distance, entailing on him duties and engagements alien to those to which he is now accustomed. My son admits that with an increasing family he finds his income inadequate, and though, no doubt, some indulgences might be abridged, it will be necessary and proper for us to increase his allowance, unless his means be increased from greater clerical emolument or any other source. While I was at Gloucester, I asked M[r] Jackson, M[r] Bloxsome's partner, whether it was in contemplation to part with the advowson or next presentation of the Rectory of Stanton, which |[175] belong to M[r] B's clergyman son, who is now in a very dangerous state of health, and, it is believed, cannot long survive. It appeared that the matter had been pressed upon M[r] W.H.B. but that he, not being convinced of the hopeless state of his health, was unwilling to part from the next presentation; that such a step was considered advisable by his friends; that, probably, the Advowson would not be sold. I requested M[r] J. to inform me if a resolution should be taken to sell the advowson or presentation. The acquisition of this preferment on reasonable terms would be advantageous to us, would be very agreeable to my son, to whom it would be a residence in his own neighbourhood and after his own heart, with an increase of income, and a benefice, moreover tenable at a future time with the living of Upper Slaughter, should such an arrangement be desirable. The value of the Rectory of Stanton, with the Curacy of Snowshill, is about £400 per ann. — Rec[d.] a letter from M[r] Colton in acknowledgment of my remittance to him — also from Mess[rs.] Hoare that they had received |[176] £20 paid in to my account by the Cirencester bank: I am at a loss to conjecture what this payment is.

July 3. Friday.
Fine weather.

Wrote to M[rs.] Guydickens, declining, on the part of my Son, the living of Waltham Abbey: — to E.F.W. with reference to his declining to accept the living of Waltham Abbey, mentioning what I had done as to the possible sale by the Bloxsome family of the Rectory of Stanton, what had transpired as to Okey farm, and what we were disposed to do in respect of the inadequacy of income of which he complained: viz. to give an addition of £100 during the ensuing twelve months: — to Mess[rs.] Sewell and Newmarch to enquire whether the £20 paid to my account at Mess[rs.] Hoare's bank had been remitted by them under any balancing of accounts between them and me, or, if not so, to enquire at the office of the Cirencester branch of the Gloucestershire Banking Company on what account it had been remitted: I also wrote to S. and N. about Okey farm. |[177]

Preparing sermons.

Visited sick and aged parishioners.

In the evening M[r] Aitkens called to remind me of the duty to be done by me at Lower Slaughter on Sunday next. M[rs.] Aitkens was confined last night; M[rs.] Waller on Sunday night last:

Received a letter from the Lunatic Asylum at Gloucester, a circular, announcing a meeting of the Visitors for the 14ᵗʰ· Inst. also from Merrett, tailor, Cheltenham, announcing his removal to another shop.

Justice business at home.

Wolff's Bokhara –

July 4. Saturday.
Bright and hot summer weather.

Preparing a sermon.

Wrote to C Bathurst on Lunatic Asylum matters: — to Mᵉ Thornton on the appointment of an Attorney to advise in matters relating to the Wadenhoe Trust:

Drove with MW. to Wick Risington, where called at the Rectory. Mᵉ Cook in Warwickshire; we were received by Mʳˢ· and Miss Caroline Cook: — then to call at Wyck Hill, where we were not admitted: Mʳˢ· Pole was out; Mᵉ P. in Town. |¹⁷⁸

A letter from Martin & Baskett, Silversmiths, Cheltenham with a bill.

Wolff's Bokhara.

July 5. Sunday.
Very hot weather till the afternoon, when, between 1 & 2 o clock, a thunderstorm, but not very heavy here: this cooled the air: the evening fine.

Visited the Sunday School.

Preparing a sermon.

Morning service at Upper Slaughter, prayers. — In the afternoon I officiated at Lower Slaughter for Mᵉ Aitkens. I preached on drawing near to GOD. — At six P.M. evening service at Upper Slaughter: I preached on Theft.

Recᵈ· a letter from Sophia Hunt: — from Merrett, tailor, Cheltenham, with patterns for trowsers: — from Alcocks, Birkbecks and Cº· with my half yearly balance sheet of banking concerns with them.

British Magazine.

July 6. Monday.
Showery weather.

Wrote to Martin, Baskett and C⁰· for particulars |*179* of the account which, they say, has been already delivered. We believe we do not owe them anything: — to Merrett, tailor, with a pattern for a pair of trowsers: — to Alcocks, Birkbecks & C⁰· desiring them to pay £250 to my account with Messrs· Hoare.

Examining my banking account with the Craven Bank.

Preparing a sermon.

Visiting sick parishioners.

Drove to Stow with MW. Transacted business with Mr Pain at the Provident Bank: — conferred with Capt. Polhill on Union matters; — called on the W. Vavasours at Maugersbury: saw M^rs· W. and Miss Vavasour: W.V. confined to his couch in consequence of injury received in the back by a fall from his horse two months ago, then neglected; now it seems he is seriously hurt in the vertebral cartilages.

A letter from Sewell and Newmarch, stating that the £20 remitted from the Cirencester branch of the Gloucestershire Banking Company was sent by advice from the Branch |*180* at Stow: on enquiry there, found that the remittance was by E.F.W's directions to his account with Messrs· Hoare, not to mine; and that the Clerks at Cirencester had ~~paid~~ ^sent^ the money to my account supposing that those at Stow had written E.F.W. for F.E.W. by mistake.

Wolff's Bokhara. |

1

Diary 1846

<u>July 7. Tuesday.</u> Fine, and cooler weather.

Wrote a note to E. F. W. whom I supposed
to be at Stow, playing cricket, respecting the mistake made in the remittance of £20 to my account
with Messrs Hoare, from the Gloucestershire Banking company's Cirencester Branch, instead of to
his account: received an answer that he and Sophy
had driven to Stow, intended to sleep at "the Cottage",
and to call on us to-morrow on their way home.

Preparing a sermon.   Justice business
at home.   Parish business with the Churchwarden.   I walked to Bourton on the
Water. Transacted parish business there with
Mr Wilkins: also with   Roff, and J. Gardner.
Called at Mr Aitkins', who was gone to play at
Cricket at Stow: a good report of his lady and
infant. Called at R. Waller's, who is recovering
from an indisposition which has hung upon him
for some time past. He gave a favourable account
of his lady and her infant. Harriet Hornsby is
on a visit there, cheerful as usual. R. Waller

Witts Family Papers F357

Diary 1846

July 7. Tuesday.
Fine, and cooler weather.

Wrote a note to E.F.W. whom I supposed to be at Stow, playing cricket, respecting the mistake made in the remittance of £20 to my account with Mess[rs.] Hoare, from the Gloucestershire Banking company's Cirencester Branch, instead of to his account: received an answer that he and Sophy had driven to Stow, intended to sleep at "the Cottage", and to call on us to-morrow on their way home.

Preparing a sermon.

Justice business at home.

Parish business with the Church warden.

I walked to Bourton on the Water. Transacted parish business there with M[r] Wilkins: also with Roff, and J. Lardner. Called at M[r] Aitkins', who was gone to play at Cricket at Stow: a good report of his lady and infant. Called at R. Waller's, who is recovering from an indisposition which has hung upon him for some time past. He gave a favourable account of his lady and her infant. Harriet Hornsby is on a visit there, cheerful as usual. R. Waller |[2] accompanied me part of my way homeward. We had previously visited the premises of his neighbour, D[r] Wing, who was busily engaged in arranging in the grounds surrounding his house, booths, orchestra, tents &c. for a rural fete to be given tomorrow on occasion of the annual meeting of the Bourton on the Water lodge of Odd Fellows, a society in which the little doctor takes singular interest. — Divine Service with a Sermon by the Rector open[g] the day; dinner, music, dancing, a concert, exhibition by an artist in that line of the attitudes of celebrated Grecian Statues, fire works, fire balloon &c. are the main attractions; large crouds are expected to attend.

Rec[d.] a letter from C. Bathurst on Lunatic Asylum arrangements: — also a circular from Gloucester Gaol, fixing a day for a meeting of the Board of Visiting Justices.

Miss C. Knight had called on us in the forenoon, to take leave of us before her departure from Eyford to-morrow.

Wolff's Bokhara.

July 8. Wednesday.
Showery weather: very unfa-|[3] vourable for the festivities at Bourton on the Water.

Justice business at home.

Preparing a sermon.

Wrote to C Bathurst on lunatic asylum matters: — to Mess[rs.] Hoare, desiring them to pay to my son's account £20. and to debit my account to that amount.

Received a letter from M[r] Thornton, who approves of my suggestion that the business of Whitby's mortgage be left in the hands of Mess[rs.] Cox and Williams, but that as to other concerns relating to the Wadenhoe Trust, some other Solicitor be employed to be named by M[r] Cox and M[r] Braikenridge: the former being the confidential adviser of M[r] Hare, and the latter of M[r] Geo. Hunt: — from M[r] Leonard, Cheltenham, Hardwareman, with a bill: — from Mess[rs.] Butt, Gloucester, with an invoice of wine sent: — from C Bathurst with a question as to the interpretation of an Act of Parliament.

Our dear children called on us as they returned from Stow to Stanway; they were quite well, and gave a good report of the two darling boys.

Visiting aged |[4] and dying parishioners — B. Carey and J. Betterton: both paid the debt of nature this day.

Called at M[r] Lea's on parish business.

Wolff's Bokhara.

July 9. Thursday.
Heavy rain in the forenoon; showers in the afternoon; a fine evening; rain at night.

Wrote to C Bathurst in answer to his letter received yesterday.

Preparing a sermon.

Drove to Stow. Transacted business at the Provident Bank; — at the office of the Gloucestershire Banking Company, and at the Workhouse with M[r] Pearce. — To the Justice room, where sat as Magistrate with M[r] Ford. He entered on the Case as to the Upper Slaughter Church and Charity Estate tenants, cottagers, in arrear of rent, and holding over after notice to quit: proceedings adjourned till next Thursday, when other Justices will be present. Mess[rs.] Winter and Polhill were our Assessors. —

Home to a late dinner.

Rec$^{d.}$ a letter from |^5 Sewell and Newmarch, covering a cheque for £83. 9. 10 — half a year's interest due by Mr Lockhart on the £4300 advanced to him by us on Mortgage, Income Tax being deducted: — from Mess$^{rs.}$ Hoare to announce the sale of the 3 p^r Cent Cons. standing in my name (£530. 10. 1) which brought £505. 16. 10 – after payment of commission and brokerage: — from Mess$^{rs.}$ Martin, Baskett & Co. — Silversmiths, Cheltenham, admitting that there is no charge against me on their books; but that the demand made upon me was a mistake.

Wolff's Bokhara.

July 10. Friday.
Showery weather.

Wrote to W. Newton, Guardian of the Hamlet of Wotton near Gloucester, with a remittance for the maintenance of Moses Roff, chargeable to that place, having received the amount from his Father: — to Mess$^{rs.}$ Hoare, desiring them to pay £500 to the account of Sewell and Newmarch with the Gloucestershire Banking Company at Cirencester; to go in further payment of the advance made to Mr Lockhart on Mortgage; |^6 Mess$^{rs.}$ H. to debit my account with them to that amount: — to Sewell and Newmarch, acknowledging the receipt of the interest from Mr Lockhart, forwarded by them, and advising them of the payment with I had directed Mess$^{rs.}$ Hoare to make to them, as above. — Justice business at home. Mr Ford came to assist me in it. He was on his way to visit Bowen, who still continues to suffer severely from his old complaint. M$^{rs.}$ Ford and her daughter Sophia have been very ill, but are now convalescent. Mr Pearce also came to give evidence as to the chargeability of the wife and children of the man who was brought before Mr F. and me for not allowing them to become so chargeable.

Visiting parishioners.

Rec$^{d.}$ a customary letter, announcing my appointment as one of the Visiting Magistrates of Gloucester Gaol: — a letter from an Attorney of Barnard's Inn, by name White, with an enquiry as to the Ex$^{ors.}$ of Dr Moorhouse's will; from this person I received a letter, when at |^7 Ventnor: he is endeavouring to investigate the affairs of the descendants of a Dodsworth, once a tenant of Scale House, and to whom Dr M. was indebted at one time, as it would seem, for a sum advanced on Mortgage, which was paid off, as the Scale House property has long been quite unincumbered. There seems an impression on the minds of these parties that, as representative of M$^{rs.}$ Backhouse and Dr Moorhouse, we possess information which would be likely to lead to the recovery of some property now lost, but supposed to have belonged to this Dodsworth: — a letter from Hoare that they have paid to my Son's account with them £20 taken from my account: — a letter from C Bathurst on Lunatic Asylum matters.

Wolff's Bokhara.

July 11. Saturday.
Fine weather.

Preparing a sermon.

Wrote to M⁻ White, Barnard's Inn, in answer to the letter received from him yesterday, stating that D⁻ Moorhouse had made no will, having by deed of gift conveyed all his property to M⁻ˢ· |⁸ Backhouse some time before his decease — that I had given answers to his queries more freely than most people would have done to a stranger; – and that if any further enquiry were made, I should refer him for an answer to my Solicitor.

Justice business at home.

Drove with MW. to call on the Winters at Daylesford, who were not at home. If afterwards appeared that M⁻ˢ· W. accompanied by Miss Penyston had drive to call on us, and we met them as we returned. Called on Lady Reade, with whom we found her old friend M⁻ˢ· Williamson: poor old Lady R. is somewhat feebler than she was, but otherwise tolerably well, and possessing her faculties at a very advanced age. Returning through Stow, we met and had a long parley with M⁻ Vavasour: he gave a poor account of the health of his wife and son. Transacted business at the office of the Gloucestershire Banking C⁰· and with M⁻ G. Pain.

A letter from C Bathurst on Lunatic Asylum |⁹ matters.

Officiated at the funeral of James Betterton.

Wolff's Bokhara.

M⁻ˢ· Dolphin had called during our absence. Also the Misses Hall from Bourton on the Water.

July 12. Sunday.
Very fine weather.

Visited the Sunday School.

Preparing a sermon.

Morning service and sermon. I preached on the effects of disobedience, as exemplified in the punishment of Saul. — Evening Service, prayers.

Received letters from Mess⁻ˢ· Hoare that Mess⁻ˢ· Alcocks & C⁰· had paid to my acc⁻ᵗ with them £250; and that they had paid on my account to Mess⁻ˢ· Sewell and Newmarch £500, as I had directed.

Funeral of B. Carey, Sen[r] – I wrote a note to M[r] Wells, Bourton on the Water, Registrar of Deaths and Marriages, recommending him to alter his register as to this death: he having spelt the name Kerry, which, ought to have been written Carey.

Report of the Soc. for Prop. of the Gospel for 1845.

To the family a section from Riddle's com-|[10] mentary on the Gospels.

July 13. Monday.
Beautiful summer weather.

Wrote to M[r] Hare, and to M[r] Thornton on the appointment of a Solicitor to the Wadenhoe Trust: to M[r] Pearce in answer to a letter received from him as to suggestions for better keeping of the Union accounts, and other improved arrangements for conducting the business of the Union, made by M[r] Hunt, the District Auditor, whose memoranda M[r] P. sent to me for my consideration: — to M[rs.] Barr, inviting M[r] C.B. herself and children to visit us from Friday next to the Monday following: we had learnt from Miss Daniell, that they would arrive on Saturday last from Leeds on a visit to M[rs.] Walker &c. at Henwick near Worcester: and we were at liberty to receive them on the days proposed, for MW. received to-day a letter from Miss. Backhouse of Wavertree, postponing the arrival of herself and her nieces till Tuesday |[11] the 21[st.] — Miss B. having had an attack of Influenza, which prevented them setting out ~~from~~ on their visit to us on the 16[th.] the day first proposed: — to E.F.W. informing him of the change of the arrangement as to the visit of the Backhouses, & that we ~~she~~ had invited the Barrs.

Justice and parish business at home.

My tenant Davis was seized to-day in a very alarming manner — paralysis with apoplectic symptoms. This is not the first attack of the same character. He had complained much of suffering by the late great heat, and was generally indisposed, his stomach being out of order. I found him speechless and paralyzed, soon after he returned from the field where he experienced the attack. Considerable delay occurred before M[r] Hayward was in attendance. He found the poor man in a very precarious state, and applied the most active means for his restoration, which, ~~partially~~ succeeded beyond his hope in abating the most dangerous symptoms, as the evening advanced — Hay-[1] |[12] called on us to report Davis's state.

Wolff's Bokhara.

July 14. Tuesday.
Beautiful weather.

M[r] Hayward breakfasted with us, whom I accompanied to visit poor Davis, who lies speechless, but sensible, and may survive the apoplectic seizure, but his state is very

---

1.   Francis Witts has forgotten to finish the name 'ward' on the change of folio on turning over the leaf.

precarious. Took his directions by signs, and interpreting his hardly articulate sounds, to make for him a short will, by which he leaves all his property to his wife – Hayward considered him quite competent to make such will, signed Davis's name by his direction, and witnessed the will with ~~M^rs·~~ ~~Jam~~ Mr James Merchant and myself.

Wrote to Sophia Hunt on the appointment of a Solicitor to the Wadenhoe Trust.

Visited B. Carey, the son of the poor old Schoolmaster, whom I buried on Sunday last; B.C. is at the point of death; paralyzed in body and mind, with a broken |^13 knee-cap, the effect of an accident some months ago. —

Transacted parish business.

A letter from Sewell and Newmarch, acknowledging the receipt of £500 forwarded on my account by Messrs· Hoare in part payment of the additional £1000 advanced to Mr Lockhart on mortgage of his Bucks estate; S.& N. propose to bring me the deed securing repayment shortly: — from F. Aston, announcing the sudden death of Mr Tordiffe, the Chaplain of Northleach Bridewell, on Saturday last, under the impression that I should like to communicate on the subject with Purnell: — from the R.O. Gloucester Union, acknowledging my remittance of £5.10.6 in payment of the bill for the maintenance of Mr Roff at the Lunatic Asylum: — a circular from the Gaol convening a meeting of V.J: — a letter from H. D. Warter informing me that Okey farm was not sold by auction as intended, and that the Vendors are willing to treat with us: the price asked is £8600: there is a doubt about the title. |^14

Report S.P.G. for 1845.
In the evening Miss S. Perkins called, and drank tea with us. She is at present visiting her brother at Lower Swell, whose wife and child are visiting their relations at Ryde.

July 15. Wednesday.
Fine weather: cooler air.

Justice business at home.

Visited J. Davis, who lies in a very precarious state.

B. Carey died.

Wrote to Capt. Somerset, Staff Officer of the District, who is expected tomorrow at Stow to pay the Pensioners, on behalf of the widow of B. Carey, that she may receive his quarter's pension: — to Mr Purnell to inform him of the decease of Mr Tordiffe, and a suggestion as to the appointment of a successor: — to F. Aston, in reply to his letter communicating the death of Mr Tordiffe: — to Curtis Hayward, asking him for information as to Okey farm: —

Received a letter from an Undertaker at Northleach requesting my attendance on Friday next at the funeral of poor Tordiffe. |[15]

M.W. received letters from Fanny and Jane Backhouse: the latter with her sister Catherine will join their Aunt on Tuesday next, and accompany her on a visit to us: but the young ladies do not think they can be our guests for more than a week; as they are to visit the Harford Battersbys near Clifton before the end of the month.

MW. heard also from Apphia Witts; a tolerable account of the health of our Shropshire cousins.

Drove with MW. to Bourton on the Water: called on the Misses Hall, who were from home: also on the Wallers: saw M^rs. RW. as well as R.W. and Miss Hornsby: the accouchée, and her infant well: fixed with RW. the day for holding the annual meeting of the Stow district Committee S.P.G. viz on Aug. 26

Report S.P.G. for 1845.

Wolff's Bokhara.

July 16. Thursday.
Showery weather.

Visited J. Davies, who is seriously ill.

Wrote to E.F.W. the letter conveyed by J Bateman, who went today to Cuts-|[16] dean to see his sister, Hannah West, who is dangerously ill.

Transacted parish business.

To Stow. MW. accompanied me in the carriage to L Slaughter turnpike gate, and walked home from thence.

A letter from F. Aston, inviting me to his house at N Leach to-morrow, that we may from thence go together to the funeral of Mr Tordiffe: — from M^rs. C. Barr, from Henwick, declining for herself and Mr B. our invitation to Upper Slaughter for a few days, because, having very lately arrived on a visit to his family, in sickness and sorrow, in consequence of the death of L^t. Col. M. Barr, they are unwilling to leave them, and so abridge even a few days of their proposed stay with them.

Transacted business at the Provident Bank, and at the office of the Gloucestershire Banking Company.

To the Workhouse, where I presided at the fortnightly meeting of the Guardians: there was much business: this being the first meeting at which I had been present for |[17] many weeks past; consequently there was much to be commented on, and regulations for better management to be made as suggestionsed by the auditor.

To the Justice room where sat with Mess[rs.] Ford, Pole, and R Waller as Justices, Mess[rs.] Winter, and Waller of Farmington being present. The business was heavy: our cottage tenants in arrear were adjudged to have held over contrary to the provisions of the small tenements act: warrants of ejectment were, therefore, directed to be issued in the customary manner.

Rec[d.] in the evening a reply to the letter which I had sent to E.F.W. by my son servant: all are well at the Vicarage: Lord Wemyss and his party arrived yesterday. My Son is going on Wednesday to Harvington on a visit to the Rev[d.] Winnington Ingram, a brother Geologist:[2] he returns on Friday, and wishes us to bring the Backhouses to pass some hours at Stanway on Saturday next, or on Monday in the week following.

When at Stow I had an interview |[18] with Capt. Somerset, the staff officer of the district as to the pension of the late B. Carey.

Wolff's Bokhara.

July 17. Friday.
Showery weather.

Called at M[r] Davis's: little, if any, improvement in his state.

Wrote to E.F.W. that, if the weather is fine, we shall probably call on the Wemyss family on Monday, and at the Vicarage, if they he and Sophy are at home: — to M[r] George Backhouse, inviting him to visit us during the stay of his Aunt and sisters at Upper Slaughter for as long a time as he can obtain leave of absence from the Foreign Office: — to B. L. Witts to make enquiry respecting a Rev[d.] M[r] Pyne, residing in the neighbourhood of Kingston on Thames, who professes to cure epilepsy by vital magnetism. A pauper from Lower Swell has been under his care, and wishes to return to make a further trial of the system.

M[r] Pearce called by appointment that we |[19] might together look over the minutes of yesterday's meeting, and make necessary arrangements for the supervision of the Union, during his absence for a fortnight or three weeks at Llandindrod Wells, for the restoration of his health, which is indifferent and which he hopes the waters of that Spa, considered to be efficacious in dyspeptic complaints, likely to restore.

A letter from E.F.W. of the same tenor as his note received yesterday; but written and despatched earlier in the day.

---

2.   Revd. E. W. Ingram, Prebendary of Worcester, Rural Dean, Rector of Harvingdon and Ribbesford, Worcestershire.

With MW. drove to Northleach, to visit the Astons, where we partook of luncheon, M[r] Ford joining our party. The whole family are at home, with the exception of George, out at sea with Evolution Squadron, from whom good accounts are received, he likes his profession. Frederick the younger has left the school at Rossal Hall, with a very good character; and is about to be placed at the Engineer College at Putney, to study civil engineering. The Astons |[20] pressed us to stay to dinner, to which we consented, and did not reach home till between 9 & 10 P.M.

M[r] Ford consulted me as to a letter which he had written but not dispatched, to M[r] Cooke, Cubbington, informing him that M[r] Pole, is grievously annoyed at the proposed placing of a stone communion table in the chancel of the Church at Wick Risington, and at the introduction of chanting into the service there; but chiefly at the former, which he considers objectionable, as being a badge of Ultra High Church or Tractarianism, and as declared illegal by the Judge in the Highest Ecclesiastical Court, Sir Herbert Jenner Fust, in his late Judgement as to the Stone Altar set up in S[t.] Sepulchre's Church at Cambridge. If persisted in, M[r] P. threatens to appeal to the Ecclesiastical authorities &c. — Ford very earnestly urges Cook[3] not to persist in his purpose, and thereby to come to a painful rupture with his squire, who with his |[21] family is so constant an attendant at Church, setting so good an example, being so liberal in the maintenance of schools, and other parochial charities. Our old friend Cooke is, no doubt, an Orthodox High Churchman, and very alien from Rome, but has a certain tenderness for some leaders in the Tractarian school, and in his advanced years yeilds too much to the influence of the younger branches of his family, who are smitten with prevailing fancies as to Church Antiquities, Architecture, Rubric, services &c. – and, resting too much on non-essentials, lack judgement, pushing their opinions even to the risk of peace, and edification. I concurred with the opinions expressed by Ford, and assented to his stating that I earnestly hoped ~~he~~ Cooke would with draw the objectionable stone table. Sir H. J. Fust's decision goes to the extent of affirming that a wooden table is the furniture required by the rubric; and the placing in a chancel a stone slab raised on legs and |[22] feet, and capable of being moved only by a great effort, probably, by machinery, even though colourably fitted with castors, cannot be a compliance with the law as laid down by authority, and rather savours of an unworthy evasion.

F. Aston and I walked to the funeral of M[r] Tordiffe at Ham[p]nett: M[r] Ford rode thither. It is an agreeable walk along the little valley behind the Bridewell, through meadows, at the extremity of which is the little straggling upland village, with its old fashioned secluded parsonage; its tower seen from afar crowning the hill; its one farm house, probably, once a mansion house for the Lord of the manor, close to the Church, which stands, as it were, in the centre of the extensive farm yards and buildings required for the management of a very large agricultural business – Poor M[r] Tordiffe, at all times, a nervous and excitable person, of irreproachable |[23] conduct, correct in the discharge of public and private duties, had, perhaps, never quite recovered from the painful shock his feelings had sustained, when an enquiry was instituted by the government some years since into the management of the Bridewell at Northleach, when his conduct as Chaplain was harshly assailed on grounds afterwards shewn to be erroneous. I had at that time the good fortune to detect and expose at the

3.   Francis Witts is inconsistent with his spelling of Cooke/Cook.

Quarter Sessions that gross oversight of the Commissioners on which was built their charge of neglect of duty against M[r] T. who was at the time too timid and too much agitated to discover the false imputation, and vindicate himself. He has ever since discharged the duties of the office most punctually & creditably, but the labour exceeded his strength, coupled, as it was, with the services of two Churches, Hampnett and Stowell, four services on every Sunday, and daily work at the Bridewell. His slender means appeared to justify this excessive |[24] labour, which, probably, undermined his constitution: he has been gradually getting thin and weak, but still appeared equal to the daily demands of duty, till on Saturday last, when M[rs.] T. thought him so unwell as to apply to M[r] Askew, the Master of the Grammar school at Northleach, to assist in the performance of part of her husband's duties on the following day: returning from Northleach, she found her husband laid down, but, apparently, only weak and languid, and able to converse: a change however, quickly ensued, he raised himself on his arm and fell back a corpse. Appearances after death lead to the conclusion that the immediate cause of dissolution was the rupture of a blood vessel on the brain. He leaves a widow and three or four children very slenderly provided for. The poor woman under the praiseworthy feeling of paying the last respect to her husband's memory, |[25] but, as it seems to me, unnecessarily, on account of the expence incurred, had invited all the neighbouring clergy, who had been well acquainted with, and shewn kindness to him. Those present were M[r] Daubeny, Rector of Hampnett, and Rural Dean of Cirencester, resident of Ampney, M[r] Ford, M[r] Aston, M[r] Guise, formerly curate of Hazelton, now of Staunton, Worcestershire, M[r] Wollaston, M[r] Price, M[r] Hill, Notgrove, M[r] Askew, M[r] Gibson, M[r] Newport, M[r] Thompson, Under Master of the school at Northleach, and myself. M[r] Tordiffe, residing at Ilfracomb, cousin of the deceased, and son of a late Clergyman resident at Northleach, and formerly curate of Hampnett, and Chaplain at the Bridewell, was present: he is an opulent person, and it is hoped will confer pecuniary favours on the widow and orphans. M[r] Bedwell, the Surgeon, of Northleach, M[r] Councer, Churchwarden of Stowell, M[r] Wells, Churchwarden of Hampnett, and M[r] Wood, a Schoolmaster at Northleach also attended. I was one of the |[26] Pall Bearers, M[r] Daubeny with M[r] Price and the medical attendant preceded the corpse, M[r] Price performed the Burial Service. Poor Tordiffe's age was 41. — The Village Church is a very interesting relic of the olden times, entering by a South Porch, to the West is a tower, with a belfry, separated from the Nave by a lofty pointed Arch; at the West end a stone immersion font, ancient: the Arch leading into the Chancel, Norman, highly carved, but the work miserably obliterated by coats of wash, yet still very

40. *Northleach Church.*

perfect, with capitals exhibiting sculpture of birds and a cup: there is the remains of an external entrance from the South to the roodloft: the chancel very singular, Norman of a late date, I suppose, if not Early English, reminding me of the engravings of the chancel of the Church at Elkstone, with much beautifully carved work in capitals, and pendants, pilasters & rib work to the arched roof, very uncommon, but all wretchedly disfigured with wash. The |[27] East window has been stopped up: the other windows of the Church are of a date posterior to the chancel, apparently, as late as Hen. VIII. – M[r] Wells's flower and kitchen gardens, adjoining his house, as that adjoins the Church, are patterns of neatness and good taste. Some conversation passed among the Clergy as to endeavours to procure an annuity for M[rs.] Tordiffe from the funds of the Diocesan Clergy Charity, also a house in Edwards' College, South Cerney, and an admission for a child into a Clergy Orphan School.

July 18. Saturday.
Showery weather.

M[r] Sewell called by appointment after breakfast, bringing with him the deed securing repayment of the additional £1000 lent by us to M[r] Lockhart on mortgage of his estates in Bucks. – Conferred with M[r] S. as to the purchase of Okey farm. He also proposed to us to buy a property at Redmarley, worth from £8000 to £8500 now on mortgage to D[r] Warneford and M[r] Capel, which must be |[28] sold under a foreclosure. – Consulted him also as to the possible purchase of the advowson or next presentation of the living of Stanton, from the Bloxsome family, desiring him to make calculations as to its value, in the event of its being offered to me, in consequence of a conversation I held with M[r] Jackson, when we met at the Trinity Sessions. M[r] Sewell, remained with us till after luncheon.

Rec[d.] a circular from the managers of the ~~Grea~~ North Western railway company, as to the shares originally allotted to me, but which I made over to Chr. Geldard. It appears that the Act is passed. Wrote to C. J. Geldard, forwarding him this circular, together with a cheque on Alcocks & C[o.] for £25, in favour of his father, as an acknowledgment for his agency in our affairs in Craven for the past two years.

M.W. called on Davis's family: there is small change for the better in his state.

Benj. Carey, the Pensioner, |[29] was buried this evening.

Wolff's Bokhara.

July 19. Sunday.
With the exception of a slight shower in the evening a fine day.

Visited the Sunday School.

Visited J. Davis, who continues in a bad state, paralyzed, speechless, depressed.

Morning Prayers: afternoon prayers and a Sermon. I preached on the temporal advantages of religion.

Preparing a sermon.

Received a letter from Curtis Hayward as to Okey Farm: he has taken much trouble in looking over and reporting upon it: if the title be good, and the price not excessive, the purchase would be eligible; but the property is not very improvable, nor the buildings in good repair.

MW. received a letter from Miss Backhouse of Wavertree who with her nieces, Jane and Catherine, purpose travelling on Tuesday next on a visit to us, from Wavertree, & Thelwall Hall near Warrington, where the Misses Backhouse and their mother are staying on a visit to the Nicholson family, relations of M^rs. B. |^30

Report S.P.G.

To the family a section from Riddle's commentary on the gospels.

July 20. Monday.
Showery weather, but not much rain fell.

Justice business at home.

Parish and Provident Bank business.

Visited the Davis's. It is thought there is a slight improvement in J.D's state.

Drove with MW. to Stanway. Called on Lord and Lady Wemyss, whom we found looking well; Lady Charlotte Fletcher and her daughter, Ladies Jane and Caroline Charteris, and Col. Wildman make up the domestic circle. We partook of luncheon there, and excused ourselves from any further visit, as friends are coming to stay with us to-morrow. We regretted to hear a very indifferent account of Lady Anne Charteris, now at Ryde with F. Charteris: since her confinement, five months ago, she has been in very delicate health, thin, with a bad cough: and the Infant boy then born, was born blind, with a congenital cataract, and apparently a weak |^31 constitution, for it is constantly crying, without apparent cause, so that an operation for the cataract dare not be ventured on till the infant has become stronger.

From the mansion house, we proceeded to the Vicarage, where we remained for some hours, partaking of an early dinner with our children, who were quite well, as also dear Broome; but poor Freddy looks very ill, much reduced in flesh, and delicate, having suffered from an attack of influenza, as it would appear, or bad cold, attended with much inward fever. He was, however, improving, and considered convalescent.

M^r and M$^{rs.}$ William Whalley called, while we were at the Vicarage. He took to himself a wife, a Miss Sawbridge, while we were in the Isle of Wight: the lady is lady-like, of a suitable age, a Clergyman's daughter; we had made her acquaintance before, when she was a visitor of Mr Francis, both at Upper Slaughter and Stanway.

Advised my son as to some business in which I found him engaged respecting the wills of two Parishioners, [32] Bassell and his niece.

Broome accompanied us on our road home as far as to Stump's Cross – we had tea late after our arrival at U. Slaughter.

July 21. Tuesday.
A showery day.

Visited sick parishioners: J. Davis considered to be rather better.

Wrote to Mr Warter about Okey farm, and the property at Redmarley offered for sale by Sewell and Newmarch – forwarded to him Curtis Hayward's letter, & the particulars of the Redmarley property.

Preparing a sermon.

Received a letter from Mr Geo. Backhouse, who is uncertain whether he can accept our invitation to meet his Aunt and Sisters: if he can obtain leave of absence from the Foreign Office, he may come late in the week: — from Mess$^{rs.}$ Butt, Gloucester, as to a hamper of Teneriffe wine which they have sent to me: — from Mr Hare, assenting to the proposition of Mr Thornton and myself, that the winding up of the business of Whitby's [33] mortgage shall be left in the hands of Mess$^{rs.}$ Cox & Williams; but that in all other business relating to the Wadenhoe Trust, in which the Agency or advice of an Attorney are wanted, one shall be employed who is wholly unconnected with the private affairs of any Trustee, or party interested in the Trust, such Attorney to be named either by Miss M.C. Hunt and Mr Geo. Hunt jointly, or by Mr Cox and Mr Braikenridge, as representing the interests of Miss M.C.H. & Mr G.H. — or by Mr Thornton and me.

Miss Backhouse with her nieces, Jane and Catherine, arrived from Wavertree & Thelwall Hall, to tea: having travelled by the Grand Junction and Birm. & Gloster railways to Cheltenham, and thence by post hither. Miss B. looks aged, as one expected, thin and with impaired vision, always wearing spectacles; lady like, reserved, but cordial: Catherine B., who has never visited us before, is taller than her sister, with a good figure, but plain; both are very pleasing, and lady like. [34]

July 22. Wednesday.
Fine weather.

Wrote to Curtis Hayward to thank him for his particular enquiries as to Okey farm; also about the Lunatic Asylum matters.

Justice & parish business at home.

Drove with MW. and the younger ladies to Stow, where I remained while they went to call on the Wiggins at Oddington, and the Vavasours at Maugersbury. Both the families were from home.

To the Workhouse: Mr Pearce had left home for Llandindrod Wells on Saturday last; I conferred with Miss Pearce, read the correspondence, and advised as to different matters.

To the library.

Transacted business with Superintendent Makepeace.

Rejoined the ladies as they returned through Stow: – home.

Rec^d. letters from Purnell in answer to mine as to the death of the Chaplain of Northleach Bridewell — from Sophia Hunt as to the appointment of a Solicitor [35] to the Wadenhoe Trust; S.B.H. and two of her sisters meditate an excursion up the Rhine.

Preparing a sermon.

July 23. Thursday.
Fine Weather.

Wrote to Mr Pearce on business relating to his office as Superintendent Registrar of Marriages. –

Drove to Stow: on my way met M^r and M^rs. Wiggin going to call on the Backhouses: stopped to parley with W. on parish matters at Oddington – misconduct of keepers of beer houses &c.

Called on the Baptist minister at Stow with reference to the registration business on w^h. I had written to Mr Pearce.

To the Workhouse; conferred with the matron.

To the Provident Bank.

At the Justice room the Dean of Gloucester, Messrs. Ford, Pole R Waller & myself sat as Magistrates – Messrs. Polhill, W. B. Pole, and Barrow were present: much business.

July 24. Friday.
Rainy in the forenoon and afternoon: the evening fair, but moist. [36]

Wrote to Harry E Waller, M. H. Estcourt, and W B Pole invitations to dinner on the 29th. Inst. – W. B. Pole declines accepting the invitation, as he is leaving home preparatory to his marriage on the 11th. Aug. to his cousin the daughter of Sir Peter Pole: the attachment is of 15 or 16 years standing; objections were formerly made by the Parents on both sides as to consanguinity, but these scruples are at last surmounted, and the lovers now no longer young, are to be united at last, with ample pecuniary means on both sides. Mr and Mrs. Pole, Wyck Hill, decline our invitation, having company at home — the Dean of Gloucester, the Wiggins, and the Maugersbury Vavasours accept.

Wrote to Perkins forwarding part of a letter which I received to-day from B. L. Witts in answer to my letter of enquiry as to the Revd. Mr Pyne, living near Kingston on Thames, who treats epileptic patients by vital magnetism — in other words, I sup-|37 pose by mesmerism. Mr Pyne is a friend of B.L.W. who is prejudiced in his favour, but admits that others and perhaps, a majority disapprove of his practice and system. BLW. writes from Everton, where he is on a visit to his sister Mrs. C. Duncan and her husband. Of news of his own family he writes that his Mother, two sisters and brother are going on a short tour to Geneva.

Received a letter from C Bathurst, who generously offers to give £30 to Mrs. Tordiffe, if the circumstances in which T. left his family justify call in my opinion for such an act of charity.

A letter from Messrs. Hoare announces that they have recd. from Lady Wilmot Horton, and placed to my account £194. 3. 4, as half a year's interest on Mortgage, Income Tax being deducted.

A letter from Mr Geldard, to acknowledge the receipt of my late remittance to him of £25, with particulars as to repairs at Giggleswick and Sherwood |38 House. It seems that the North Western Railway is to pass through a small portion of our Ravenflatt farm.

Wrote to H. D. Warter, enclosing to him the letter as to Okey Farm, which I thought I had sent to him on Tuesday last — the letter from Curtis Hayward — but which I found in my letter bag yesterday.

Preparing a sermon.

Visiting J. Davis, who still lies in a sad-paralytic state.

July 25. Saturday.
A promising morning, and ending in a showery day.

Wrote to C Bathurst as to the poverty of the Tordiffes, and the impression on my mind that his benevolence might very fitly be extended towards them.

Recd. a letter from Howell, he asks me to come to Prinknash – when I go to the Assizes at Gloucester: informs me that many enquiries are made as to his place now on sale, and to be put up to Auction in Town on Aug. 14: that his son Frederick is about to leave the Ionian Islands with his regiment for Jamaica: that |³² Edward has safely joined his regiment at Chambly in Canada.

A letter from Warter on the purchase of the farms at Redmarley or Okey.

With MW. and the Misses Backhouse, went to Stanway in our close carriage. On the road met and parleyed with the Astons, returning to Northleach after a visit of a day or two to Lord and Lady Wemyss. Also met and chatted with Mᵣ Wynniatt. The weather proved so bad, and the roads were so wet, that I was obliged to give up my intention of calling on Lord Wemyss, and walking from the Mansion to the Vicarage. E.F.W. and Sophy received us very hospitably: all were well, but our dear Freddy still looks very delicate, much pulled down. We partook of a luncheon dinner, and returned home to tea. Much rain on our way back. Miss Jane Backhouse and I, who sat in the hind seat were exposed to the pitiless pelting of the storm, but protected by an umbrella and cloaks.

We looked in |³³ vain for George Backhouse; but he did not make his appearance.

July 26. Sunday.
Fine Weather.

George Backhouse arrived to breakfast in a gig from Burford, where he slept last night, having left Town yesterday afternoon by an express train; which conveyed him to the Swindon station, whence he proceeded to Burford in a hired gig, arriving there too late to come on to this place. He is a lively, pleasant, quaint young man; well informed, peculiar in appearance, and undersized; but seemed pleased to make our acquaintance.

Visited the Sunday School, and J. Davis, who is slowly mending.

Morning prayers and sermon. I preached on the miracle of the loaves and fishes. Afternoon service.

A letter from Mᵣ Thornton who is very anxious for the settlement of the question as to the future solicitor to be consulted by the Wadenhoe Trustees. — A note from Mᵣ M. H. Estcourt; he declines our |³⁴ invitation for Wednesday next.

Wrote to Mᵣ H. Lindow inviting him to dinner on that day. — Also to Turner, fishmonger, London, for a dish of fish for Wednesday next.

July 27. Monday.
Fine weather.

Wrote to Mᵣ Thornton on the appointment of a legal adviser to the Hunt Trustees. – To R Waller, inviting him to dinner on Wednesday next. To Mᵣ Geldard on matters relating to our Yorkshire property.

Received a note from R Waller, leaving it uncertain whether he will dine here on Wednesday: – a note from H. Lindow, who accepts out invitation; a note from H. E. Waller, who declines it.

R Prosser having pressed upon me that it would be to my advantage to purchase for £900 eleven acres of excellent grass land in the parish of Lower Slaughter, late Smith's, which he (Prosser) had imprudently bidden for at the sale, and signed the contract to purchase, relying on one Johnson of Stow that he would be the [35] real purchaser – Johnson, however, failing to take the purchase, and now being incapacitated by a paralytic stroke from doing any act — I went to look at the fields, which would, I believe, be desirable for occupation either with the Rectory land here, or with the premises late Forty's; I was half tempted to engage in the purchase, although not having any ready money, my last savings having been invested in mortgage on Mr Lockhart's estate. Poor Prosser sadly hampered by his reliance on a treacherous and miserly person, who now fails him, has not the means to fulfil the engagement entered into by him at the Auction.

Mr Wiggin drove over to call on George Backhouse, & joined us at luncheon; he took G.B. back with him to Oddington; I accompanied them in Wiggin's carriage as far as the Lower Slaughter Turnpike Gate, from whence I walked home. George [36] Backhouse having accompanied his friend and relation to Oddington, was driven back by him to Stow, and thence returned on foot to join our family circle at dinner.

Preparing a sermon.

A cheerful domestic evening.

July 28. Tuesday.
Fine and very hot weather.

George Backhouse, in a Stow hired gig, left us at 5 AM. to arrive at Swindon in time to meet an express train to London which would bring him to the Paddington station by eleven o clock.

His sisters also took their departure in our open carriage for Cheltenham, after an early breakfast, at 8 AM. to proceed thence by rail to Bristol, whence they are going for two or three days on a visit to the Harford Battersby's. We parted with our young relatives with regret: they are much to be liked; serious, estimable, well informed, quiet, lady like: only a little too devoted to the ultra-high-church party. Miss Backhouse, the Aunt, continues our guest: sensible, well informed, rather reserved, but highly [37] principled, with some strong but subdued prejudices, and thoroughly right minded: her health is very indifferent.

I wrote to Howell.

Visited J. Davis.

Justice business at home.

Walked to Bourton on the Water: called at Messrs. Wilkins & Kendall's office. Conferred with Mr K. as to parish business, — the proceedings against the Cottage tenants under our Church estate trust, who hold over after notice giving to quit. Talked with Mr K. as to the land in Lower Slaughter, which Prosser has unwarily contracted to buy, and which he has asked me to purchase. M.^r K assured me that if I were disposed to become the owner, the money for the purchase should be advanced by himself and partner to me without mortgage, on my note, to be repaid as might suit my convenience.

Called at the Rectory; saw Mrs. R. Waller and Harriet Hornsby.

Rec.^{d.} a letter from Capt. Somerset, staff officer at Gloucester, complaining that |³⁸ he had not received the proper certificate and receipt as to the death and funeral of B. Carey, & the pension money paid to his widow. — A letter from Mr Thornton on Hunt matters — A letter from Mr Pearce as to the registration business, on which I wrote to him on Thursday last.

I wrote to invite Barrow to dine here to-morrow.

July 29. Wednesday.
Very fine hot weather.

Wrote to Capt. Somerset as to the pension paid to the late B. Carey.

Preparing a sermon.

Justice business at home.

Called on R. Prosser, and declined purchasing the land at Lower Slaughter, which he had offered to me. If I had the money unemployed, it would have been an eligible investment, but I do not like borrowing money to buy land.

Received a letter from Sewell as to the value of the advowson or next presentation of the Rectory of Stanton; — from H Warter, who returns Curtis Hayward's letter, and thinks that the Okey estate should be given up, at least for |³⁹ the present: — a note from Barrow, who cannot dine with us to-day, having a previous engagement at Wick Hill; a letter from C Bathurst as to prison regulations: a letter from Stokes on Mr Wells enclosing some of the land adjoining his farm on the Northleach road side.

A dinner party: the Dean of Gloucester, M.^r and Mrs. Wiggin, J. T. Rice, M.^r and Mrs. W. Vavasour, Miss Vavasour, and Henry Lindow made up our party.

W. Vavasour is still suffering severely from the accident by a fall from his horse which befel him in May last. He and his Father go to Dublin to-morrow. It is hoped that the spine is not injured, but the cartilages of the back are seriously strained. We heard from the V's, that Sophy accompanied Edward to Stow yesterday, and, while he was playing at Cricket, went to call on M[rs.] R. Waller at Bourton. |[40]

July 30. Thursday.
Fine Weather.

Wrote to C Bathurst in answer to his letter received yesterday.

MW. and Miss Backhouse accompanied me in the phaeton to Stow, returning as soon as they had set me down.

Transacted business at the Provident Bank with M[r] Pole &c.

To the Workhouse, where I presided for two hours at the meeting of the Guardians.

Afterwards sat at the Justice room with Ford as my colleague, the business being of a serious character, information being taken against a miscreant for an assault with intent &c. on a girl under ten years.

Received a letter from C Bathurst, enclosing a cheque for £30. in favour of poor M[rs.] Tordiffe: — a note from Acock, the Baptist minister at Stow, respecting a marriage intended to be solemnized under the Marriage Registration Act.

Home to a late dinner.

July 31. Friday.
Very fine and very hot |[41] weather.

Wrote to F. Aston, enclosing Bathurst's cheque for £30, and requesting him to present it to M[rs.] Tordiffe, but suggesting that the same be not handed to her till after Thursday next, on which day her claims for relief from the Clergy and Music meeting charity fund will be brought before the annual meeting of subscribers. As she will have to render an account of her resources, it is politic that they should not be swelled out by the insertion of this liberal benefaction from CB. It is intended to bring M[rs.] T. forward as a candidate for an annual allowance, and for a tenement in Edward's College.

M[r] Ford called by appointment, as did also M[r] Brookes and M[r] Hayward that the case against the Longborough wretch, who at the age of between 50 and 60 assaulted the child under ten years, might be fully gone into: the evidence was most |[42] conclusive, and the man was committed for trial at the coming assizes.

I walked with Ford as far as Wagbarrow Bush to meet Bowen returning to Upper Guiting from Little Risington, where he had been visiting the Fords. He came in F's carriage, driven by Henry F. who with his Father would accompany their friend to G. and return in the evening. Bowen is still suffering under his painful malady. I had sent my open carriage to bring Ford to U.S. to assist in the unpleasant case of assault.

A letter from Mr Thornton, inclosing one to Mr Cox, to be forwarded to him after I had perused it, respecting the nomination of a legal adviser to the Wadenhoe Trustees. We request Mr Cox to meet Mr Braikenridge, that they may fix on a professional gentleman to whom may be referred all matters connected with the trust, expect the completion of the business at as to Todd's mortgage, which |^{43} is to remain in the office of Mess$^{rs.}$ Cox and Williams.

Called on J. Davis who mends slowly, but is never likewis likely to be otherwise than a paralytic cripple.

Preparing a sermon.

Aug 1. Saturday.
Very hot and sultry: in the afternoon a very heavy thunderstorm for three hours or more: the lightning continued all the evening.

Preparing a sermon.

Justice business at home.

Wrote to Mr Hare on the appointment of a Solicitor to the Wadenhoe trust: — to Mr Thornton on the same subject: — to Bathurst as to his bounty to M$^{rs.}$ Tordiffe; and with a copy of the Gloucester prison rules of 1837, in compliance with a letter which I received from him to-day: — to E. Tombs, Clerk to Horne, Moreton, to order a supply of coals for distribution to the Poor, next winter, and some for myself and others. |^{44}

Sunday Aug. 2.
Showery weather, close and sultry, with thunder in the forenoon.

Visited the Sunday School.

Received a letter from E.F.W. the account good of all at the Vicarage, Stanway. Lady Wemyss indisposed: the family still remains in the country.

Morning service: prayers, and the holy Sacrament administered: 13 Communicants. Evening service; prayers & sermon. I preached on Elijah and the widow of Zarephath.

Preparing a sermon.

To the family a section from Riddle's commentary on the gospel.

Monday Aug. 3.
A showery day, close and sultry, with some thunder.

Wrote to M[r] Sewell, proposing to him to meet me at Gloucester on Wednesday the 12[th.] that we might together look over the property at Redmarley, which has been offered to us as an investment for the Trust money arising from the sale of the houses in Fenchurch Street.

Preparing a sermon.

Visited J. Davis. – |[45]

Parish business with W. Gregory.

Justice business at home.

The ladies drove out and called on the Fords at Little Risington, Aitkins's and Wallers, at Bourton.

Miss Perkins called during their absence.

M[r] Clark (Icomb) called late, and we detained him to dinner.

Received a letter from Howell, inviting me to Prinknash, while I am at Gloucester at the Assizes. His place is to be offered for sale by auction on the 15[th.] Inst. in London: many parties have applied, and looked over the property, with a view, no doubt, to its purchase. Frederick Howell's regiment is ordered from the Ionian Islands to the Cape of Good hope, which is the seat of harassing incursions by the Caffres.

Aug. 4. Tuesday.
Showery weather.

Preparing a sermon.

Justice business at home.

Wrote to Howell, excusing myself from accepting his invitation to |[46] Prinknash.

Drove to Stow with MW and Miss Backhouse, who went to Lower Swell to call at the Perkins's, taking me up on their return.

Visited the W. House, conferred with Miss Pearce on Union matters. I had received a letter from M[r] Pearce from Llandrindod Wells.

My son was at Stow, attending at the Cricket meeting: conferred with him, during a short interview, on several matters. He gave a good account of all at Stanway vicarage. Lady Wemyss is in better health.

Attended in the evening a meeting of the Upper Slaughter Church and Charity estate trustees, at the Vestry room to make arrangements with the Cottage tenants in arrear of rent as to the future occupation of their cottages.

Aug. 5. Wednesday.
Fine weather.

Conferring with W. Gregory on parish business, and preparing documents as to the Tenants of the Cottages held under the Church land Trustees, who are in arrear, with a view to their |[47] continuing in their occupations; and in the Evening they waited on me with W. Gregory to sign agreements to pay the arrears by instalments, and keep down the current rents.

Justice business at home.

Received a letter from M[r] Thornton concerning the appointment of a Solicitor to the Wadenhoe Trust.

With MW. and Miss Backhouse, visited M[rs.] Dolphin, who is an invalid. Bowen is ~~also~~ staying with her, very poorly.

Visited J. Davis, who slowly gains strength.

Aug. 6. Thursday.
A very fine summer day.

Wrote to M[r] Thornton on the appointment of a Solicitor to the Wadenhoe Trust, returning to him a letter on that subject addressed to him by Miss M.C. Hunt, which he had forwarded for my perusal.

Justice business at home.

Drove to Stow, accompanied by MW. who did not remain long there. Miss Backhouse did not accompany my wife, |[48] being somewhat indisposed.

To the Provident Bank, where I met M[r] O. Hill, and R.W. Hippisley.

To the Workhouse, where I visited the female wards, and conferred with the matron.

At the Provident Bank afterwards met Winter and R Waller.

In the Justice room R Waller, the Dean of Gloucester, and myself sat as magistrates; we were assessed by W. B. Pole, Winter, Clarke and two young Lindows.

Received a letter from Howell, urging me to visit Prinknash Park next week, and opening his mind to me as to his plans when the place shall have been sold: — from Mr Sewell who engages to meet me at Gloucester on Wednesday next, that we may from thence drive to Redmarley, and look over the property, which is thought of as an investment for the trust money arising from the sale of the houses in Fenchurch Street: — from F. Aston, who has presented to M^rs. Tordiffe the kind donation of C. Ba-|^49 thurst.

Jealousies, bickerings &c. love quarrels between John Bateman and Anne White begin to be very troublesome, and seem likely to end in their both leaving our Service.

Aug. 7. Friday.
A close, hot day; a rainy evening.

Wrote to Sewell and Newmarch making an appointment for Wednesday next, ~~in cas~~ as to going from Gloucester to Redmarley to see the land about to be sold: —— to E.F.W. acquainting him with this arrangement that he may accompany or meet us, if he is so disposed: — to Howell that my visiting Prinknash next week is quite out of the question: — to M^rs. Marsh, desiring that a bed may be reserved for me at the Bell Hotel during the early part of the Assize week.

Rec^d. a letter from Mr Thornton with an enclosure from Mr Cox Junr as to the appointment of a Solicitor to the Wadenhoe Trust.

As I expected, the misunder-|^50 standing between Bateman and Anne White has ended in our accepting from the latter a warning to quit our service, and giving a warning to the same effect to the former. AW. accuses JB. of neglecting her, after an engagement to marry her, of which we were cognizant, and of attaching himself to Farmer Dix's daughter; JB. says he is willing to marry AW. but cannot clear himself of the charge of slighting her, nor of the intimacy with the latter; though denying it; it seems generally the opinion that he has hampered himself with both: probably both Bateman and Anne are more or less to blame; but it was not for us to discriminate between the two, or give either a triumph by dismissing the one, and keeping the other: their matters began to be annoying; also they are both disposed to find fault without sufficient cause with their fellow servants; so to discharge both seemed the proper course, though inconvenient, as both are very good and trusty servants.

Preparing a sermon.

Preparing |^51 for the annual meeting Stow District Comm. S.P.G.

Aug. 8. Saturday.
Showery weather.

Preparing for the ann. meet^{g.} Stow Distr. Comm S.P.G.

Justice business at home.

Ford called on me to communicate what passed at the ann. meet^{g.} of the Subscribers to the Clerical Charity of the Diocese held on Thursday at Gloucester, at which he was present. A very liberal annuity was voted from the funds of the Charity to poor Mrs. Tordiffe, who is also to be accommodated with a house in Edward's College, South Cerney: the affairs of that College were much canvassed, but not with the bad spirit which F. had expected. He anticipated unpleasant strictures as related to himself, and the urging of courses with reference to that institution which would have been painful to him: but though much was said, and certain propositions partially discussed, which he did not approve, as a primary mover in |52 the institution, and executor of Mrs. Edwards, from whose noble bequest to the Clergy Charity the funds of the erection of the College were derived, he was treated with more courtesy than he expected from the party whom he believed to be disposed to act in an unfriendly way towards him, and who showed less disposition to unsettle former arrangements than he had anticipated. His self love, and position in the diocese, were also flattered & raised by an intimation conveyed to him at Gloucester in a note from the Bishop, that he purposes to appoint him, as an old, diligent and valued Rural Dean, to one of the honorary canonries in the cathedral of Gloucester, which the Bp. seems to reserve chiefly for Rural Deans, his chaplains &c. The regulation is that twelve honorary canons shall be appointed, one annually in each of the Cathedrals of Gloucester and Bristol, till the full number is made up, and then appointments are to be made as vacancies occur. At Gloucester, the Bp. began by nominating D^r |53 Warneford first, as the great Church Benefactor; next Murray Browne, his Lordship's Chaplain was appointed; then Malcolm, a recently appointed Rural Dean; but it so happens that Bp. Monk was admitted of Trin. Coll. Camb. under M. as Tutor; and now, greatly to his satisfaction, Ford is selected.

Rec^{d.} a letter from E.F.W. all well at Stanway: Sophy expects to be confined on an early day, and, therefore, Edwd. declines meeting me and Mr Sewell on Wednesday next, to look over the estate at Redmarley: on the purchase of which, as also on the possible purchase of the advowson or next presentation of the Rectory of Stanton my son comments.

Visited J. Davis.

Aug. 9. Sunday.
Fine weather.

Visited the Sunday School.

Preparing a Sermon.

Morning service — prayers and a Sermon. I preached on the unjust steward. Evening Service, prayers. |54

Rec^d. from Mr Thornton a letter on the appointment of a Solicitor to the Wadenhoe trust: he forwarded to me a copy of a letter on that subject which had been written by Mr Geo. Hunt to Caroline Hunt.

Wrote to   Haynes,[4] Ilmington, to order coals for the use of the poor of this parish &c.

Preparing for a journey to Gloucester to-morrow.

Aug. 11. Monday.[5]
Fine weather on the whole; the morning misty, in the evening a slight shower.

Justice business at home early.

After an early breakfast we left home in the close carriage, accompanied by Rebecca Backhouse, who left us to visit her friend M^rs. Evans, near Chepstow, before returning at the end of the month to Wavertree. She proposed going by Bristol and Clifton, and to spend the day with a friend at the latter place. But when we reached Cheltenham some of her luggage which had been sent forward by the carrier to meet her at the Plough was mislaid, and some time passing |^55 before it was found, both she and I were prevented from proceeding to Gloucester by the first train. I was, therefore, detained at Cheltenham till half past twelve, and Miss B an hour longer. MW. purposed to return home in the afternoon.

When I reached Gloucester I took up my abode at the Bell.

The business of the Assizes was begun — Maule presided in the Crown Court, the Lord Chief Baron of Common Pleas, Wilde, sat at Nisi Prius. Mr Bengough, High Sheriff. Marquis of Worcester, foreman of the Grand Jury. I took a seat in the Crown Court, and watched the proceedings there. Maule was suffering from Asthmatic affection, and seemed greatly indisposed. He exhibited lassitude, languor, and something closely akin to carelessness in the trials of prisoners: one might almost suppose that early and long indulgence in immoral habits had rendered him indifferent to virtuous principle, and tender to vice.

An adjourn-|^56 ment of the Quarter Sessions was held at two P.M. at which I attended with Purnell, (in the Chair) Sir W. Codrington, Browne, and other Magistrates; but there was little to be done; for the division of the County into Coroners districts is suspended until the documents are returned approved from the Privy Council; and no Candidates had offered themselves for the vacant Chaplaincy of Northleach Bridewell. As it seemed doubtful whether the Sunday services at that prison could be, or were, regularly performed, (though it transpired afterwards that the Under master of the Northleach Grammar School has temporarily undertaken the duty,) I wrote, with the concurrence of the County Chairman to offer Mr Colton the temporary service at Northleach Bridewell on Sundays, on the terms

---

4.   A space was left in the manuscript, seeming to indicate that another name would be added in at a later date.
5.   An uncorrected dating error.

on which he had performed my duties while we were absent in the Isle of Wight, and till the Michaelmas Quarter Sessions.

Resumed my place in the Crown Court, till a short time before the Judges rose, when |[57] I went to the usual Judges dinner, which was not very numerously attended by Magistrates and Grand Jurors. The Chief Baron alone received us; for Maule drove off to an hotel at Lansdown place, Cheltenham, alleging, and, probably, with truth, that his Asthmatic complaints would be greatly aggravated by sleeping in the close atmosphere of the Judges lodgings. Nothing was said publicly as to the inadequacy of the accommodation, but a new provision cannot be long deferred. The Chief Justice did not occupy them at night; but this probably arose from his being accompanied by Lady Wilde, ci devant Mademoiselle D'Este, who was lodged elsewhere. Whether it was an old acquaintance, or recently formed, while he was engaged as an Advocate in pressing the claims of the brother of the lady, Sir Augustus D'Este, to the Dukedom of Sussex, as Son to his R.H. by a marriage with Lady D'Ameland, a sister of Lord Dunmore, a marriage every |[58] way legal except as in contravention of the Royal marriage Act, and therefore disallowed, so as to prevent the succession to the title, is not well known: but the high born lady in mature life has wedded the low-born and talented lawyer. Wilde received his guests very courteously, and appeared an agreeable man in society: his elevation to the Chief Judgeship was unexpected by himself, arising out of the sudden-illness and death of the excellent Chief Justice Tindal, which occurred just as the Peel Ministry resigned to be succeeded by Lord John Russell's administration. Sir Tho[s.] Wilde was nominated Attorney General, and on that appointment went down to Worcester, to secure his re-election for that City; while there the death of Tindal resulted in his appointment to the vacant first chair in the Court of Common Pleas. He joined the Circuit at Stafford, the duties which would have been performed by Senior Judge devolving on a Sergeant put in the Commission for the |[59] purpose until the Chief Justice could join the Circuit. Wilde has long occupied a very high rank in his profession.

In the Evening the Bell party consisted of the Marquis of Worcester, Sir W. Codrington, Rob[t.] Hale, Purnell, two Brownes, (father & Son) two Sampsons, (father and son) Savage, Hicks &c. – a pleasant party. At the Judges lodgings I had sat by Lysons and Stoughton, had seen much of Curtis Hayward, Newman & others.

Aug 11. Tuesday.
Fine weather till towards the evening, when rain came on.

Breakfasted at the Bell.

A letter from M[r] Colton who declines taking temporary charge of the Bridewell duties at Northleach, as far as relates to the Sunday Services: — a letter from E.F.W. – with a good report of all at Stanway Vicarage: — a letter from Sewell, who purposes to meet me here at 9 AM. to-morrow to proceed with me in a fly to Redmarley.

To Court; took a seat on the Bench by the Chief Justice; |[60] and was much pleased by his manner of discharging his official duties: the case which I heard was not one of interest;

a controversy as to the ownership of a small house near Bristol, in which were engaged Sergeant Talfourd, Greaves, Keating & Skinner: the Judge exhibited much acuteness, close attention, collectedness, dignity and courtesy.

At one P.M. repaired to the Annual meeting of the Governors of the Infirmary, which was very largely attended. It had been expected that the Duke of Beaufort would attend: but his Grace was absent, cruizing on the coast of France. The Marquis of Worcester with Sir W. Codrington, Rob.ᵗ Hale, Brownes, & others attended, but only for a very short time, to express their good will, and intention to support the institution, and the new system about to be proposed; but they were obliged to return to their duties as Grand Jurors. The Lord Lieutenant was not present, though expected at Gloucester this evening to be in readi-|⁶¹ ness in case of his being called under a subpoena to give evidence on a trial expected to come on to-morrow, for a libel consisting in the superscription of an envelope sent by post at Cheltenham to Mʳˢ· Barker, with whom it is notorious that Earl Fitzhardinge lives in a criminal manner, such envelope having been traced to a Revᵈ· Disney Robinson, a Clergyman residing at Cheltenham, who, in intemperate zeal, addressed the envelope to Mʳˢ· B. "adulteress and Sabbath breaker." The proceedings, which can only terminate in the conviction of the libeller, are likely greatly to damage all parties, and it is no wonder that the hoary adulterer shrinks from meeting the gentry of the County on the eve of such an exposure. The Chair was taken and well filled by Mʳ Gambier Parry, as Vice President, and the Committee room was very much crowded – I may enumerate as County gentlemen, Sir M. H. Beach, Mʳ Crawley Boevy, Sir J. D. Paul, Messʳˢ· Hopkinson, Purnell, Curtis Hayward, |⁶² Baker, Machin, Bernard, Goodrich, Stanton, Vizards, Colchester, with many others, Revᵈ· Messʳˢ· Cornwall, Prowse Jones, Jones (Hempstead) Geo. Hall, Murray Browne &c. Of the inhabitants of Gloucester among the most conspicuous were Messʳˢ· ~~Wht~~ Whitcombe, Helps, Avery, Turner, Montague, Revᵈ· Hardwicke, Sayers & others. Mʳ Turner addressed the meeting in terms of congratulation, reporting, as Treasurer, considerable legacies and donations of recent date, with additional subscriptions, and that the receipts of the last year had exceeded the expenditure by £200 or thereabouts. The great business of the day being to confirm or annul the resolution passed at the last quarterly meeting, adopting the code of rules proposed by the Committee appointed to report upon the system of government existing in the Institution and to suggest alterations and improvements, Mʳ Purnell, as the organ of that Committee, proceeded to read the rules. A debate arose on the regulations prescribed to the medical officers of |⁶³ the institution, which were approved by the Senior Medical men, Dʳ Evans and Dʳ Wilton, but objected to by the Juniors, Dʳ Fletcher, Mʳ Wood, Mʳ Fletcher and Mʳ Buchanan. It appeared that the latter took umbrage at not having been especially consulted by the Committee, and at their seniors for acquiescing in the regulations proposed by the Comm. without giving the Juniors an opportunity of arguing the points. They also objected to the rules as being too stringent upon them, derogatory to their professional dignity, tacitly censuring them as to the past and distrusting them as to the future. The regulations required that the Med. Off. should keep a record of each case attended by them, of their prescriptions, of their being continued, suspended, or left off. It seems that this rule exists in the great Metropolitan hospitals, and was in no respect considered otherwise than reasonable or at all derogatory by Dʳ Evans and Mʳ Wilton. Dʳ Fletcher, & Mʳ A Wood warmly |⁶⁴ advocated their view of the matter, and several Governors, among whom I was one, spoke in support of the proposed rule. The general impression was in favour of the rule. An opposition was raised to the whole code on various grounds by different parties. M[r] Avery and M[r] Prowse Jones persisted in resisting it as a crude, indigested ill and not sufficiently considered system, needlessly superseding the old rules of the hospital, and requiring more mature deliberation, to which end it was proposed that the new rules should be printed and circulated among the governors, to be finally considered at a future meeting. To this several objected, among whom I spoke to the effect that the interests of the Institution were already compromised by long delay and by being left unsettled — that nine months had been already compromised in the investigation which, therefore, ought to be brought to a close — that the insufficiency of the old rules was sufficiently evinced by the bad state of the finances under the old administration, and the defal-[65] cations of the late Secretary — that a large meeting of Governors at a future time could not be expected — that while we were arguing & splitting on matters of detail, the poor sufferers were injured, for that disunion and procrastination would be sure to operate to the prejudice of the hospital, people would decline to support an ill regulated and disjointed establishment — I, therefore, pleaded with a Clergyman's feeling, conversant with the maladies of the Poor, that delay would be very prejudicial to the class whose benefit was intended — Some objected to a decision until a vote were taken on every rule seriatim, but it was clear that such a course would engage the Governors for many hours — Others, and chief among them Murray Browne, objected to the reconstruction of the rules as regarded the official dignitaries, Patron, President &c: heretofore the Bishop had been sole President, now he was nominated President jointly with the Lord Lieutenant, and so associated with a person [66] of lost character; so, at least, I supposed the worthy Bishop's chaplain felt in his secret soul, and wished to maintain the dignity of his patron; he was, however, overruled, as was the proposition that the Clerk, to which office M[r] Weaver was now permanently appointed, should be receive a salary of £80 instead of 50£. as settled by the rules. On all the divisions the supporters of the new regulations outnumbered the adverse party in the proportion of three to one. The main change in the constitution of the house is the appointment of a clerk with a low salary, in lieu of a Secretary well paid, the discontinuance of brewing and baking in the house, and the purchase of bread and beer by contract: the abolition of the old weekly board, which had become a clique, and the substitution of a Managing Committee, to be elected, and to consist of Governors living in the city and others resident within a moderate distance, such committee to be responsible to, and act under the directions of a Supervising Committee, chosen from the Governors, without limitation of distance, to consist [67] of a certain number of members of the Managing Committee and others, who are to hold an annual meeting, and make an annual report, and be convened at extraordinary meetings, when circumstances may call for their so doing. P A paid Auditor is also provided for, and the donations and legacies (the latter, at least, if not the former,) are to be founded. There is a reasonable expectation that the establishment may be carried on satisfactorily under these arrangements, if only the public will continue to support it by sufficient contributions; but the income is now barely adequate to the expenditure. The preponderance of favourers of the new code of rules precluded much wrangling: some favourers of the old system, M[r] Turner, M[r] Avery, M[r] Murray Browne, waxed somewhat warm; but though the discussion was not tame, there was no indecent warmth.

After the meeting had closed, I resumed my place in the Crown Court, and was present at |[68] the trial of the Longborough man whom I had committed on the charge of an assault with an intent &c. — he was found guilty, and sentenced to eight months imprisonment.

Dined at the annual Infirmary dinner at the Kings Head, at which about twenty five were present, and the Chair was filled by M[r] Hopkinson, the Sheriff of last year. Though under great anxiety in consequence of the dangerous and declining state of M[rs.] H.'s health, the Ex sheriff abounded as usual in all manner, of jokes and anecdotes. The party was agreeable: among those present were the High Sheriff, Purnell, Gambier Parry, D[r] Evans, Curtis Hayward, Newman, Pye, Turner, Whitcombe, Staughton, Savage, with many others. —

Aug. 12. Wednesday.
Heavy rain had fallen in the night, the day was very fine.

Breakfasted at 8AM. with Savage, Sampson Jun[r] and D[r] Greaves.

At 9 AM left Gloucester in a fly with M[r] |[69] Sewell, who had come from Cirencester, true to his appointment, for Redmarly, to look over a farm there which may suit us as an investment for the money arising out the sale of our houses in Fenchurch Street. The road and country beyond Over Bridge were quite new to me: we did not cross that bridge, but went over Maisemore Bridge, and then by the road from Gloucester to Ledbury, through the parishes of Maisemore and Hartpury, to Staunton in Worcestershire, a village just on the borders of that County and Gloucestershire, where are one or two Inns, and where the road from Tewkesbury to Ledbury, unites with that from Gloucester to the same place. We passed near the residences of M[r] Goodrich and M[r] T. Fulljames at Maisemore, of Cha[s.] Crawley, and M[r] Canning at Hartpury, but I do not think I saw either. The country is fertile, and picturesque, well timbered, with hedgerows; and the population seems to be |[70] scattered over the parishes in small groupes or single dwellings, not congregated into one considerable village: the houses and barns chiefly of brick, or lath and plaister — the country undulating. The Church of Staunton detached from the village, and overshadowed with trees, is an interesting object: beyond it, at more than a mile distant, on the right, is the seat of M[r] Dowdeswell, Down House, on rising ground. Here we deviated from the main road, and pursuing a village road, in less than a mile arrived at our destination, leaving our carriage at a little hamlet of road-side cottages, two miles, I believe, distant from the church at Redmarley. The farm we were to inspect is called Longbands, and is a quarter of a mile distant from the little hamlet, where we got out of our carriage. M[r] Aston, a decayed farmer, and Inn Keeper, is the nominal proprietor; love of pleasure, and sporting tendencies, seem to have brought him in mature years, for he ~~seems~~ appears about threescore years of age, almost to want — |[71] for when the farm is sold, and the mortgagees, D[r] Warneford and M[r] Capel, are repaid, nothing is likely to remain to him, but a cottage with a few acres of land. He joined us at the farm house, which is small, and not very substantially built, but is large enough for the farm, and the mortgagees, who, though they have not yet fore closed, have taken, with Aston's consent, the whole management into their hands, are about to repair some of the farm buildings, and erect others, the contracts being already made with a builder at Gloucester. The tenant, Clarke, is a clever young farmer, with a pretty young wife and child: he has occupied land at Longford near Gloucester, and entered on this farm in May, taking it from Lady day at a rent of £300 – for 14 years, determinable by either party at the end of seven years. The acreage is 160 – so that the rate is about 38/ per acre, which is less than is given for adjacent lands, let at 40/- |⁷² and 42/ per acre, and this farm has been let at £336 – but, probably, £300 per ann. is a full and fair rent now, for some of the arable land is foul and in bad condition, the late tenant having managed his land very ill, and left it, being ruined, after occupying it two years and a half. The property lies in a ring fence bisected, as it were, by the good parish road along which we came. It consisted till lately of two separate estates, Longbands and Applehurst, the latter having been bought by Aston a few years ago. The land is pasture, meadow, arable, and orcharding, with an abundance of fine thriving timber, principally oak. In the immediate vicinity are properties belonging to the Earl of Beauchamp, Dᴿ Beale Cooper, and Mᴿ Ricardo, whose seat at Bromeberrow is not far distant: the fine views of the Malvern Hills struck me much as seen from most of the fields. Redmarley is a very large parish, but the outgoings in the way of rates are comparatively small, |⁷³ and the tithe commutation has been settled at a ~~small~~ ᵐᵒᵈᵉʳᵃᵗᵉ rate per acre. Taking the rent of £300, and deducting £20 for land tax and average repairs, the value as estimated by Mᴿ Sewell, and which seems fairly calculated, would be about £8000 — the timber, to be taken at a valuation, might amount to from £500 to £700: the calculation is made on a 28 years purchase. We went over every part of the land, accompanied by Mᴿ Aston and the tenant Clarke, a fatiguing walk, followed by a luncheon at the farm house. As we drove back to Gloucester I agreed with Mᴿ Sewell to enter into treaty for the purchase, subject to the valuation to be made on our part by Mᴿ Hall of Cirencester, and to the title proving good, as to which I had no doubt, and agreed to afford us every facility to investigate it, by forwarding the Abstract to Mᴿ Warter. It was settled that Mᴿ S. |⁷⁴ should mention the matter to Dᴿ Warneford whom he was about to visit on Friday, and should breakfast with us on Saturday, when the arrangements might be further forwarded.

We arrived at Gloucester on our return at half past 3 o cl.: there I parted from Mᴿ Sewell, and at half past 4 I left the Railway station at Gloucester for Cheltenham. There I found MW. who had come in the carriage to meet me, and to see a person who had been named to her as likely to take the place about to be vacated in our family by the departure of Anne White. We left Cheltenham at about 6 PM. and reached home soon after 8 P.M.

A letter from F. Aston about Mʳˢ Tordiffe &c.

Aug 13. Thursday.
Frequent and heavy showers.

Wrote to C Bathurst, forwarding to him the letter which I recᵈ yesterday from F. Aston, and which contained an acknowledgement of the liberal benevolence of CB. to Mʳˢ Tordiffe, who had desired Aston |⁷⁵ to return thanks in her name.

Drove to Stow.

Attended at the Prov. Bank, where I met Mr O. Hill.

Transacted business at the Office of the Gloucestershire Banking Company.

At the Workhouse presided at the fortnightly meeting of the Guardians of the Union.

Met Mr Ford and the Dean of Gloucester as colleagues on the Bench at the Justice Room; Messrs. Winter and Polhill were present.

Dr Wolff's Bokhara

Aug. 14. Friday.
Fine weather.

Preparing for the Annual meeting of the Stow Distr. Comm. S.P.G.

Visited Davis.

Mr Lefroy arrived on one of his Constabulary circuits: he dined and slept here.

Aug. 15. Saturday.
Cloudy weather, with misty rain at intervals.

Mr Sewell came to breakfast from Lower Swell, where he had left M^rs. Sewell on a visit to her brother, now residing at the |^76 Bowle farm – Mr Hudson, M^rs. Sewell's father, has recently purchased the considerable estate, late belonging to the Atkyns Wright family, in Lower Swell, and is occupying that position of it, which was leased for many years by Jos. Clifford, placing one of his sons there to manage it. Mr H. is a very eminent agriculturist, a Norfolk farmer, and tenant formerly to Mr Coke, afterwards Earl Leicester — he now resides at or near Castle acre, having a large business there, but intends to keep in hand the farm at Lower Swell, having a strong opinion that a better style of farming will show that the Cotswold land is more productive than is generally believed. With Mr Sewell made further arrangements with reference to the purchase of the Longbands and Applehurst estate. S. returned to Lower Swell.

Lefroy left us after breakfast.

Wrote to H. D. Warter as to the purchase of the estate in Redmarley: to E.F.W. on the same subject, and on other matters. |^77

Preparing for the annual meeting of the Stow District Comm. S.P.G. –

Visited Hannah West, who is still very ill: she is staying with her relations, the Bryans at Lower Slaughter.

We dined at Daylesford with the Winters: a large and pleasant party — the Dean of Gloucester, M^r and Mrs. Wiggin, and John Talbot Rice, M^r and Mrs. C. Pole, Miss Adams, Mrs. W. Vavasour, and Emma V. and a Mr Pigot, a fellow of New College, a temporary Curate of Mr Twisleton at Adlestrop, with ourselves made up the circle.

Rec^{d.} from the War Office a letter about C. Lupton, a deserter.

Aug. 16. Sunday.
Fine weather.

Visited the Sunday School.

Preparing a sermon.

Morning service – Prayers. Evening Service: prayers and a Sermon. I preached on the vanity of human life.

Rec^{d.} a letter announcing a meeting of the Visitors of the Gloucester Lunatic Asylum |[78] on the 25th. August.

Preparing for the annual meeting Stow Distr. Comm. S.P.G.

To the family a section from Riddle's commentary on the gospel.

Aug. 17. Monday.
On the whole, a fine day: ~~symp~~ threatening of rain, but little fell.

Preparing for the approaching annual meeting of the Stow Distr. Comm. S.P.G. —

Wrote to Mr Hawkins, Secretary to the Soc. for Prop of the Gosp. requesting him to communicate to me any matters or documents of recent date, which it might be desirable that I should bring under the notice of the members of the Stow district Committee at the approaching annual meeting.

Drove with MW. to Stow and Longborough.

Shopping at Stow. At Longborough called at the Vicarage to pay our respects to our old acquaintances, M^r and Mrs. Morrison, now lately fixed there, on his preferment to the Vicarage by the favour of Lord Leigh. They were not at home.

Called on the Vavasours at "the Cottage", as we returned. Saw Mr V. who returned with |[78] his son from Ireland on Saturday last. Mrs. V. was gone to Maugersbury to see William V. who still continues to suffer much from the injury he sustained in his back, by a fall from his horse in May last.

Mr Henry Ford had called on us while we were absent, accompanying his sister Dulcy. Mr Barrow had also called.

Received from Craven two boxes with two brace of grouse in each: the one being sent by Christ. Geldard, the other by Henry Lindow.[6]

Aug 18. Tuesday.
The forenoon fine; afterwards heavy rain in frequent showers.

Wrote to Rodwell for a supply of books for the Stow Book Society. Wrote notes of invitation to dine on Friday next to the Fords, Hippisleys, Wallers, Barrow, Estcourt and Clarke — MW had written like notes to the Morrisons, Perkins's, and Aitkens's; the Morrisons accepted our invitation, the Wallers, Perkins's, Aitkens's declined it. Wrote to Chr. Geldard to thank him for his present of Moorgame. |[80]

Preparing a report for the Stow District Comm. S.P.G.

A letter from E.F.W. all well at Stanway Vicarage, and our dear Sophy expecting her confinement on any day. Joseph Higgins, their late servant, whose last weeks had been passed in lodgings at a relations at Stanway, while rapidly declining by consumption, and who received much attention not only from son and his wife, but from Lord Wemyss's family while at Stanway, and from the villagers, by whom on account of his gentle and unoffending manners he was much beloved, departed this life two or three days ago.

A letter from H. D. Warter in reply to my letter on the purchase of the property at Redmarley: this I forwarded to Sewell, as it mentioned Warter's engagements during the month of September.

Transacted Union business with R.O. of the Union.

Wolff's Bokhara.

Aug. 19. Wednesday.
A showery morning: the afternoon and evening fine.

Wrote to E.F.W. Rec^d notes from R W Ford & R W Hippisley. Mr F. accepts our invitation for himself, one of his |[81] daughters and his son Henry – Hippisley will also dine with us on Friday; but not Mrs H. who is a nurse.

A letter from Rev^d E Hawkins, Secretary S.P.G. with a small packet of Missionary Papers; he states that the Society greatly need suitable candidates for ordination, or, better still,

---

6. What was Henry Lindow doing in Craven? Perhaps Francis Witts offered him the opportunity of shooting on the Yorkshire estates from 12 August onwards when Lindow came to dinner on 29 July?

ordained Clergymen, prepared to undertake Missionary duty in Newfoundland or Southern India. A letter from Curtis Hayward on the business to be transacted at the meeting of the Visitors of the Lunatic Asylum at Gloucester on Tuesday next, which he presses me to attend, and invites me to his house at Quedgley, either on Monday or Tuesday, as may be most agreeable to me. A letter from Mess.ʳˢ Butt about a sample of Madeira, which they forwarded to me yesterday.

Preparing report for the Distr. Comm. meeting S.P.G. to be holden on Wednesday next. —

Journal of a Visitation Tour by the Bishop of Nova Scotia in 1844.

Justice |[82] business at home.

Transacting Parish business with the Churchwarden.

Visiting sick parishioners: very little amendment in the condition of J Davis.

M.ʳˢ and Miss. Ford called, when we were out.

Aug. 20. Thursday.
Heavy rain came on in the forenoon, which lasted for many hours.

Wrote to Curtis Hayward, that I would, if possible, attend the Lunatic Asylum meeting on Tuesday, but that I could not avail myself of his friendly invitation to Quedgley.

Drove to Stow. MW. accompanied me as far as to Lower Slaughter Turnpike Gate, whence she walked home.

Attended at the Provident Bank, where I met M.ʳ C Pole, M.ʳ O. Hill, & M.ʳ Hurd.

Afterwards attended at the Justice room with the Dean of Gloucester, and M.ʳ C Pole as my colleagues.

Reading D.ʳ Hook's strange latitudinarian sermon on National Education. It is addressed to the Bishop of S.ᵗ Davids.

Rec.ᵈ a note from Barrow who accepts our invitation to dinner for tomorrow. |[83]

A letter from Sewell, that his interview with M.ʳ Aston, the nominal owner of the Longbands and Applehurst farm, at which the sale of the property to our Trustees was to be discussed, is postponed till Saturday.

Aug. 21. Friday.
Moist weather, and showery, till the afternoon; then the weather fine.

Wrote to Anne Turner, our former cook, now in service at Cheltenham, desiring her to meet me at Cheltenham on Tuesday next to receive from me the amount of her deposits in the Stow Prov. Bank, which, under an authority she had given me, I had received yesterday.

Preparing report for the Stow Distr. Comm. S.P.G. annual meeting on Wednesday next.

Ford called on his way to Eyford to visit Bowen, now staying with M$^{rs.}$ Dolphin, intending to pass the interval there till time to dress here to dine with us. I accompanied him to Eyford; Bowen very poorly, returns to Guiting this afternoon. M$^{rs.}$ Dolphin much excited, the person to whom she had let |^{84} one of her farms having given notice of his determination not to abide by the agreement, he having heard from some quarter a bad account of the land. M$^{rs.}$ Dolphin walked back with me to U. Slaughter, descanting on her disappointment.

M$^{rs.}$ W. Vavasour and Emma V. rode to call upon us, giving but a very indifferent account of W. Vavasour, who is undergoing another course of blistering along the back bone, lying on a sofa.

Our dinner party went off well: our guests were Mr Ford, Henry & Dulcy F., M^r and M$^{rs.}$ Morrison, Mr Clarke, Mr Hippisley, Mr Estcourt, and Mr Barrow.

August 22. Saturday.
The weather, overclouded and close, but no rain.

Wrote to Mr Hawkins the Secretary S.P.G. with a remittance on account of subscriptions &c. rec$^{d.}$ by me as Treas. & Sec. of the Stow Distr. Comm. S.P.G. Preparing for the annual meeting of the Distr. Comm. fixed for Wednesday.

Drove with MW. to Wyck Hill to call on the Poles, and on M$^{rs.}$ and M$^{rs.}$ E. Rudge, now on a |^{85} visit there. Were not received; tidings having just arrived of the dangerous condition of Mr Rudge Senr of Abbey Manor near Evesham, and his son had just set out to visit his father, as anticipated on his death-bed. The elder Mr Rudge is 83 years of age, and has been in a precarious state for some time past. We met M$^{rs.}$ E. Rudge in the grounds, and conversed with her.

To Stow, where I answered a letter from Lewis Houldey, a Servant out of place, who had ~~by~~ offered to live with me, that I purposed being at Gloucester on Tuesday next, and would meet him there at the Bell Hotel.

Transacted business at the office of the Gloucestershire Banking Company.

Conferred with Mr Pearce at the Workhouse.

After we returned home, Mr C. Pole called, being very full on the uneasiness he experiences by the tendency of Mr Cooke and his family to introduce what he considers disturbing novelties into the Church and service, a stone altar-table, |^{86} chanting &c.

Dr Hook's letter on National education.

Aug. 23. Sunday.
Weather overcast, but hot and close, not rainy.

Visited the Sunday School.

Morning service, prayers and sermon. I preached on the reflections arising out of an abundant harvest. Afternoon, prayers.

Rec^d. a letter from Mr E. Cockey, written from his living at Hockley, Essex, in answer to my congratulations on his marriage: he appears happily settled, and writes in a cheerful, friendly tone. After the wedding the new married couple went abroad on a short excursion.

A letter from Geo. Baldwin, who is about to leave Mr Lindow's service, and would be glad to come into mine. He is now with M^r L's family at Cheltenham, where M^rs. L is in a poor state of health. I answered that I proposed being at C. on Tuesday, and would meet him at the Plough Hotel.

Preparing for the annual meeting of the Stow Distr. Comm. S.P.G. on Wednesday next.

To the family a Section from |^{87} Riddle's commentary on the Gospels.

Aug. 24. Monday.
Dull, close, and cloudy weather, but no rain.

Wrote to Messrs. Butt, Gloucester, ordering six dozen of Madeira, answering to the sample sent.

Preparing for the annual meeting Stow Distr. Comm. S.P.G. to be held on Wednesday.

Preparing for my journey to Gloucester to-morrow, looking over documents as to the Lunatic Asylum.

Rec^d. a letter from E.F.W. acknowledging my late remittance to him of £50. He gives a very good account of dear Sophy, and the children: the former seems to have made a sad miscalculation as to the time of her accouchement; it seems now not likely to take place for several days.

M^r and M^rs. Perkins, with his daughter, and sister Maria called upon us, and partook of refreshment here; they walked about our village &c. and I accompanied them on their way home.

Justice business at home. |^{88}

Visited J. Davis, who, in addition to his paralytic seizure, is suffering from a bowel complaint.

My dear wife's sixtieth birthday. May GOD protect and preserve her! She is an affectionate wife and mother, a kind hearted friend and neighbour, a sensible woman, diligently endeavouring to do her duty in the station in which GOD has placed her.

Dr Hook's pamphlet on National Education, with an able reply and exposure of the evil which it contains by Mr Burgess of Chelsea, a divine of a lower school, whose attention has been much directed to the subject of the education of the Poor, and who is secretary to the London, or Westminster, Distr. Comm. in aid of the National School Society.

Aug. 25. Tuesday.
Fine weather.

After an early breakfast set out for Cheltenham in phaeton, on my way to Gloucester, to attend a special meeting of the Visitors of the Lunatic Asylum.

As I passed through Cheltenham, met Anne Turner, to whom I [89] paid by a cheque on the Gloucestershire Banking Company £70. 5. 8, being the amount of her deposits, with accummulation of interest in the Stow Prov. Bank.

Proceeded to Gloucester by the Railway, and at the Bell Hotel, met Lewis Houldey, the servant who had offered himself as successor to John Bateman. His age, near 50, is against him, but I left it open whether I would engage him, subject to my interview with George Baldwin or others.

Walked to the Lunatic Asylum, where I found Curtis Hayward presiding at the meeting of Visitors; the other members present were H. C. Clifford, C. Crawley, A Sayers, T B Ll Baker, and D M Walker. – Purnell was absent, in town, but had written a letter, to explain his views, and urge a postponement of matters in dispute, with a view to a satisfactory settlement by further interviews between different parties, who are not yet fully agreed. The fact is, that P. made a proposition which the [90] visitors representing the subscribers will not agree to, but the latter are ready to consent to a proposal made by Curtis Hayward. The representatives of the subscribers, Mr Hyett, and Dr Baron, object to further argument or debate: they have taken their stand & made their concession, and will not be moved; and Hyett has a personal objection to a further conference with Purnell, apprehensive of its ending in angry disputation. Hyett had meant to have met the Visitors to-day, but met with an accident early this morning by a fall from his poney, by which he was strained. Messrs. C Hayward & Purnell on the part of the County, Dr Baron and Hyett, for the Subscribers, and D M Walker for the City had been a Subcommittee to deliberate on the best mode of regulating and arranging the Asylum, so as to secure its efficiency, its economy, and its capacity of holding an increased number of patients, without great outlay of public money. The subscribers claim a certain ownership in the best parts of the building, but are without |[91] funds except the profits derivable from the first class patients; the want of funds has prevented the admission of more charity patients for some time past: the pauper wards are inconveniently crowded, and insane patients of this class are constantly pouring in, owing to the recent enactment, which makes it imperative and so many persons in each district (Clergymen, Union Med. Officers, Relieving officers, parish officers) to move towards the conveying to the Asylums, wandering lunatics, lunatics neglected or ill used by friends, and pauper lunatics: greater accommodation is therefore absolutely necessary, and may best, as it seems, be provided, that is without incurring great expence in building, by appropriating and re-distributing those parts of the building over which the Subscribers have a controul. By the recent Act of Parliament, where a county or counties are associated with a body of voluntary Subscribers, the public body, or bodies, are made responsible |[92] for the repairs of the buildings, and this provision is continued in a bill now before Parliament; on this ground J C Hayward (and the same ground is taken by Purnell for his abortive scheme) proposes that the Counties shall, in consideration of their undertaking the future repairs, enter into occupation of certain parts of the building over which the Subscribers now have a controul: thus appropriating those parts more or less for public purposes, sufficient accommodation being reserved for Subscribers and charity patients. It is hoped that thus sufficient accommodation may be gained for increased numbers of pauper patients, together with a Chapel sufficiently large for the Institution so extended. But this plan involves the abandonment of the higher classes of Subscribers Patients, such as occupy spacious apartments, and for ~~her~~ whom a good table is kept: patients at five guineas and under to two guineas a week; these are uncertain; may be at times numerous, and yeild a good profit, but also may be few – the provision |[93] made for them is costly, ~~both~~ in respect of lodging, diet, and attendance; and as a good table must be kept for them, economy of housekeeping cannot be studied. But experience has shewn that a second class of paying & profitable patients are always to be had, tradespeople, professional persons, half pay officers and the like; and it is proposed that none of a higher grade than these be admitted, people whose friends would be contented with an inferior description of lodging, attendance, and diet, paying from 18/- to 30/- weekly, and maintained on an average of 12/- per week per head. This would release a large extent of room now occupied by the first class of opulents, so render the space gained available to other classes, and provide for increased numbers to be admitted as pauper patients. The arrangement would also allow of the admission of a limited number of charity patients, to be maintained from the profits of the ~~firs~~ higher class of patients, but on a scale |[94] little exceeding the dietary and accommodations of the pauper patients. And this would work favourably for the county, because, at present, the institution being closed against charity patients, cases often occur, when those who might be admitted as charity patients, are palmed upon the Establishment as pauper patients. On this general plan & outline the Subcommittee, Purnell alone dissenting, were agreed, and it seemed pretty clear that D[r] Baron and Hyett, for the Subscribers, would not consent to my other arrangement: as a probable settlement of a disjointed affair the arrangement seems very desirable: the County Visitors have been long battling hopelessly with the Visitors acting for the Subscribers; there now appears a fair prospect of their acting in harmony together, so that the financial concerns of the Institution may be conducted on a better footing; and to the Counties the proposition is recommended by its holding out the probability of the absolutely needed extension of accommodation being thus obtained at the least pos-|[95] sible outlay for buildings. But still there is a difficulty to be surmounted in the redistribution of the buildings, so as to obtain a Chapel of sufficient size; and this was pressed upon us to-day by M[r] T. Fulljames, who attended as County Surveyor, with plans &c. He, together with Purnell, proposes a Chapel in the space in front of the Crescent, accessible by Corridors from the main building; but the cost would, probably, not be less than £2000, and be likely to be warmly resisted at the Quarter Sessions, & in the Municipal council. All these matters and points were carefully considered to day, and the result was that, very much on my suggestion, the Visitors adopted the report of the Sub-committee, and recommended its being acted upon: subject, however, to such modifications, as to the same Sub-committee should appear fitting, in regard to the redistribution of the Space. It seemed to be desirable to come to this resolution, as a step in advance towards a final |[96] arrangement by which all parties might act in concert, to the best advantage of the different interests concerned. By the late Act of Parliament, whatever plans are proposed for material changes in any Lunatic Asylum, are to be submitted to the Commissioners in Lunacy, public officers, principally, if not wholly, of the Medical and legal professions, appointed by government to have a superintendence of all Lunatic Asylums, and by them to be reported on to the Home Secretary, whose sanction is necessary in the last resort: thus our present deliberations are brought before a higher tribunal, by which any erroneous views we may have taken will be corrected, if discovered. Another duty to be performed by the Visitors to-day was to settle as to the future government of the house, the place of resident Superintendent being now, & having been for some weeks, vacant by the removal of D[r] Huxley to a like post at the Lunatic Asylum at Maidstone for Kent. By the |[97] arrangements made more than a twelvemonth since, the resident Medical Officer had a salary of £100 per ann. with apartments, and a table kept: D[r] Hitch was allowed £300 per ann. to reside in Gloucester, but to be restricted from taking lunatic patients to reside under his care in his house: he was also bound to attend the Lunatic Asylum daily. The stipend to the Visiting Physician was as much too large, as that to the resident Superintendent was too low, and that was proved by the early departure of D[r] Huxley for a higher and better paid post. As we propose doing away with the high class patients, the expediency of restricting D[r] Hitch from taking patients into his own house falls to the ground; & by offering a higher salary to the resident Superintendent, a man of higher grade, likely to remain, may be secured. By putting an end to the system of a table for the resident Medical officer, it was |[98] calculated that about £50 per ann. might be saved; and by assigning to him such a position of the Crescent as would provide a moderately sized house, which might easily be isolated from the rest of the building, a communication being still maintained, that the Superintendent might at all times have ready access to the interior of the building, this officer would have accommodation for a family, if a married man, without the members of his household being in any way mixed up with the inmates of the rest of the building. Thus then we arranged the matter; to reduce the salary of D[r] Hitch to £150 per ann. not requiring daily attendance, but that he should visit three days in the week, being at liberty to take private patients into his own house: to advertise for a resident Superintendent with a salary of £300 – per ann. and detached apartments, but no board.

41. Centaur, a Daniel Gooch Fire Fly locomotive.

When the committee broke up, I walked into Gloucester with Clifford and Baker, and took a Sand-|[99] wich at the Bell, arriving at the Railway station in time for the train leaving Gloucester for Birmingham at 3.20. P.M.

By this train I travelled to Cheltenham in the same coach with M[r] Holland, who was returning to Dumbleton from Cirencester, where he had been visiting the Agricultural College, of which he is one of the most active managers, and which he represents as advancing very satisfactorily.[7]

At Cheltenham I was met by two servants out of place, desirous of living in my service: one of them is very likely to suit me, George Baldwin, now in the service of M[r] Lindow as butler, but leaving him, as he finds the habits of the family irregular, and the work fatiguing, owing to the different members of the family taking their meals at uncertain times; the offices also are on the basement floor at Lower Slaughter, causing a perpetual running up and down stairs. G.B. is about forty years |[100] of age, with a wife and family settled at Cheltenham, the woman being a dress maker, and letting lodgings.

After a short parley with Lefroy, whom I met in the High Street, I left C. so as to reach home by 7 P.M. suffering a good deal from defluxion, owing to my having, when I arrived at the L. Asylum, much heated with my walk from Gloucester, sat in a strong draught in the Committee room, of which I was not aware till the evil was done, and the result will, doubtless, be a severe cough and cold to which I am so liable.

Rec[d.] a letter from Mess[rs.] Hoare, announcing that M[r] Jennings had paid to my account with them £69. 14. 0 – also a receipt from the Treas. S.P.G. for £15. 10. 3 remitted by me on Sunday morning last.

---

7.   The Royal Agricultural College was established in 1844. One of the leaders in the early days was Earl Bathurst.

Wolff's Bokhara.

<u>Aug. 26. Wednesday.</u>
Fine day, but cloudy.

Preparing for the annual meeting Stow distr. Comm. S.P.G. to be held today.

Wrote to Mr Lindow for the character |[101] of George Baldwin, and to George Baldwin, that I will take him into my service, if the character be satisfactory. Mr Lindow and the ladies of his family are now at Cheltenham; for medical advice, Mrs. Lindow being much indisposed.

MW. accompanied me to Stow in the open carriage, and returned after the Missionary meeting was over, accompanied by Jemima and Dulcy Ford, whom she had by previous arrangement met there, and brought back to dinner.

A letter from Sewell; a dispute between Mr Aston, the proprietor of the Longbands and Applehurst farm, with his tenant, interposes a probably temporary obstacle to the progress of our treaty for the purchase of ~~that~~ the estate.

A letter from S. F. Sadler, explaining that an engagement which he could not put off prevents him from attending the meetings at Stow to-day.

A note generally circulated, but without signature, intimates that the Marquis of Worcester having sent venison as a |[102] compliment to the yeomanry of the neighbourhood of Stow, has intimated his intention of meeting them at dinner on Friday next, on which occasion my attendance is requested. Lord Redesdale is expected to preside.

The annual meeting of the Stow District Committee of the S.P.G. was well attended. The Dean of Gloucester presided. Messrs. Ford, Waller, Hurd, Wiggin, Barrow, Pantin, Morrison, Smith, Potter, Houghton, Clarke, Estcourt, Winter, Hutchinson & myself were the Clergy present – Several ladies, Mrs. Witts, Mrs. Morrison, Mrs. W. Vavasour, Miss Vavasour, the Misses Ford, together with the wives and daughters of tradesmen, professional gentlemen and farmers in and near Stow, were present, together with a few laymen; in all probably, 50 or 60 persons were present. I read the annual report which I had drawn up; and was the principal speaker as to the state of the missions prosecuted by the Society. This district now contributes to a considerable annual amount. I had remitted during the |[103] year which had elapsed since the last annual meeting more than £70. — Messrs. Wiggin and Smith (Curate of Naunton) spoke at some length, Messrs. Ford, R Waller, Morrison and Barrow more briefly.

The third-Clerical dinner for the season followed, being the last in the year: Mr Hutchinson presided, and Mr Wiggin was elected Chairman for next year. The clergy present were the Dean of Gloucester, Messrs. Hutchinson, Winter, Barrow, Billingsley, Waller, Potter, Estcourt, Wiggin, Ford, Clarke and myself.

I returned home with Ford in his carriage, who rejoined his daughters at our cheerful tea table, leaving us for Little Risington, before ten o clock.

I had been suffering all day from the violence of the cold I had caught yesterday; coughing, defluction and hoarseness being very aggravated, and rendered worse by the exertions I was obliged to make. While at Stow I had conferred with Mr Hayward's assistant, not |^104 being able to meet his principal, and brought home medicine to alleviate the attack.

Aug. 27. Thursday.
Fine weather.

So overcome with the severe catarrh under which I was labouring that I forbore going to Stow, to attend to my usual Thursday's business.

Wrote notes — to Mr Pain on Provident Bank and library matters — to Mr Pearce, that indisposition prevented me from presiding at the Board of Guardians to-day: — to Mr Morgan that the bad-cough which confines me to the house to-day will prevent my meeting the Marquis of Worcester at the Yeomanry dinner to-morrow.

Wrote to H. D. Warter inclosing to him the letter I had received from Mr Sewell yesterday as to the Redmarley property.

Arranging my accounts and papers as to the S.P.G: this consequent upon the meeting of the Distr. Comm. held yesterday.

Preparing a sermon.

Quarterly Review for June.

Aug. 28. Friday.
Fine weather.

The |^105 cough and its accompaniments very troublesome.

Justice business at home.

Mr Pearce called on Union business.

M^rs. Dolphin called.

Wrote to E. Hawkins, Sec. S.P.G. with a remittance for subscriptions &c. rec^d. from members of the Stow Distr. Comm. £19. 12. 6.

Visiting my parishioners.

A letter from Lindow with a fair character of George Baldwin; also a letter from the latter as to his coming into my Service.

Quarterly Review.

Aug. 29. Saturday.
Fine weather.

Still suffer much from the catarrh: Hayward called, and prescribed expectorants.

Wrote to George Baldwin to come into our service on Sept. 10: and to Lewis Holdey, to inform him that I have engaged another Servant, and so cannot take him into my place.

Wrote to E.F.W.

Justice business at home.

Parish Business.

Visited sick neighbours; J. Davis and Hannah West; both great |*106* sufferers.

Anne White left our service.

MW. received a letter from M^rs. A. Currer, from Canada, announcing the death of her sister, M^rs. Langton, at 80 years of age. The illness was short, and very trying to A.C. who feels her last tie to earth unloosed. One would suppose that she will pass her few remaining months or years, for she is between 70 & 80, in the distant land whither she accompanied her sister: the niece, Miss Langton, was suffering from an illness when her Mother died: the brother John Langton, was from home, in attendance on his wife, who had lately been confined at her father's house at Peterborough, a colonial town, forty miles distance from Blythe, the location of the Langtons – the infant had died. It is to be hoped that the aged Aunt will be kindly treated by her nephew and nieces, and sink peacefully into a far-off grave.

Aug. 30. Sunday.
Fine weather.

Suffering much from catarrh; still I got thro' my clerical duties pretty well, although much |*107* fatigued.

Visited the Sunday School.

Wrote a note to Mr Wells, Med. Off. of the Union, directing his attention to the case of a poor girl of the village, who had dislocated her wrist. —

Morning, prayers: — Evening – prayers, and Sermon. I preached on prayer.

Preparing a sermon. A letter from Treas. S.P.G., acknowledging the receipt of my remittance of £19. 12. 6 made on Friday last.

Eccl. Gazette.

Aug. 31. Monday.
Fine weather till evening, when the sky overclouded, and slight shower fell.

Much oppressed with a cough.

My son arrived from Stanway to breakfast, having heard at Upper Guiting on Saturday that I was indisposed. He remained with us for two hours, and then went on to Stow, this being the last day for the season of the meeting of the Cricketers. He gave a good account of his dear wife's condition: she has strangely miscalculated, but well, hoping, however, to be soon otherwise, and |[108] to recover happily from the crisis of a trying hour. The children well: but Broome taking medicine rather for prevention than because actually out of order.

Justice business at home.

Wrote to Dr Hitch for a report of the state of Moses Roff, a patient in the Gloucester Lunatic Asylum.

Drove with MW. to Maugersbury, to call on the W. Vavasours: saw them and Emma Vavasour; W.V. suffers much from the injury sustained in his back; in great pain; and there seems little difference, whether he takes moderate exercise, or confines himself to the coach: he has been again blistered and leeched.

In the evening transacted parish business as to the Church estate cottage tenants in arrear.

Quarterly Review for June.

Sept. 1. Tuesday.
Fine weather.

My cough, though better, still very troublesome.

Wrote to C Bathurst about the Lunatic Asylum arrangements.

Preparing |[109] a sermon.

Transacting Parish business with W. Gregory &c.

Rec^d. a letter from Messrs. Butts, Gloucester, who have forwarded to me six dozen of Madeira.

M^r M H Estcourt called.

Quarterly Review for June.

Sept. 2. Wednesday.
Very fine weather.

Wrote to T. J. Howell.

Justice business at home.

Drove with MW. to Oddington; called at Lady Reade's: she had not left her room. We were received by M^rs. Matthews, late Miss Emily Reade of Bath, now the wife of a gentleman resident on his property in Somersetshire, without any profession, not far from Wincanton; also by Miss Reade, daughter of Sir. J.C.R. It is announced that her sister Clara is ere long to be married to John Talbot Rice, the Dean of Gloucester's youngest Son, not in any profession; not having passed an examination for a degree at Oxford, where he was of Exeter College: |^110 One feels vexed that so pleasing a young person as Clara Reade should have engaged herself to a young man, with so little mental power; in moral character he is very respectable. Her health is delicate: it is said they are to reside at the Rectory, Great Risington, and he, whose present occupation is farming, will, probably, manage the Rectory farm.

At Stow, called at the Library, and shopped.

Received a letter from Geo. Wellford: – also from Dr Hitch as to the state of Moses Roff, a lunatic patient at the Gloucester asylum.

Quarterly review for June.

Sept 3. Thursday.
Very fine weather.

Wrote a note to R W Hippisley, with a copy of the Thesis on which Mr Pantin proposes to write an essay to be read at the next decanal meeting.

Preparing a sermon.

Drove to Stow, accompanied by MW. who returned shortly afterwards.

Transacted business at the Provident Bank, |^111 where I met Perkins; and at the office of the Gloucestershire Banking Company.

To the Workhouse, where I conferred — with Mr Pearce on Union business.

To the Justice room, where I sat with the Dean of Gloucester and Mr Ford, as Colleagues. Mess$^{rs.}$ Winter, Polhill, and Clarke were present.

My cough does not leave me: I have, probably, caught a fresh cold: it was very troublesome to-day.

British Magazine. Quarterly review for June.

Sept. 4. Friday.
Fine weather.

Still much oppressed with cough.

Preparing myself for the discussion on the Anglican Church to be brought forward at the next decanal meeting.

Visited J. Davis: he has got down stairs, but continues very paralytic.

Quarterly Review for June. British Magazine.

Sept. 5. Saturday.
Weather fine.

Little amendment as to my troublesome cough. |^{112}

Preparing myself for the discussion as to the Anglican Church expected at the coming decanal meeting.

Justice business at home: interview with Mr Kendall as to paupers settled at Eyford, respecting whom M$^{rs.}$ Dolphin is anxious.

Drove to Broadwell: left our cards at the Rectory for M^r and M$^{rs.}$ Potter: he has lately fixed there, as Curate, in the room of Mr Underwood; apparently from the North Country, and a sensible man, of whom the Bp. of Hereford, in whose diocese he has been curate, speaks in favourable terms.

Rec$^d.$ a letter from J. Round: also from C Bathurst, who is on the eve of a tour in the Netherlands &c: also from Mr Rawlinson, Chipping Norton, proposing Lt. Col. Dawkins, of Over-Norton as a candidate for admission into the Stow Book Society.

Called at the Library, Stow, that Col. Dawkins's name be circulated among the members of the Book Society, as a candidate for admission. |^{113}

Quarterly Review – Brit. Magazine.

Sept. 6. Sunday.
Rain had fallen during the night: the day fine, but hot; distant thunder heard.

Visited the Sunday School:

Preparing a Sermon.

Wrote to Mr Rawlinson in answer to his note received yesterday.

Morning Service: prayers and Sermon. I preached on the good Samaritan. Evening Service; prayers.

A letter from Howell: Prinknash Park is not yet sold; but he anticipates parting with it by private contract very shortly. A change has occurred in his plans. Owing to the illness of Mad. Frossard, the lady at Nismes to whose care Emmeline Howell was to have been consigned, that destination has been altered, and she is to reside with a Clergyman and his wife who are settled in Bucks or Bedfordshire; the lady of the Clergyman being sister to M^rs. Parsons, late of Upton S^t. Leonards. |^114

Preparing a sermon.

Eccl. Gazette – British magazine.

Sept. 7. Monday.
Fine weather, after a foggy morning, till evening, when distant thunder, and a shower.

Preparing a sermon.

Mr Pearce called, with whom conferred on Union matters.

Preparing for the expected discussion on the Anglican Church at the next Decanal meeting.

Quarterly review for June.

Sept 8. Tuesday.
Cloudy, but fine weather.

Preparing for the discussion at the next decanal meeting, fixed for the 21st. Inst.

Accompanied MW. on a drive to call on the Biscoes at Turkdean: when we arrived within a mile of the village, we met Mr B. Miss Middleton, and a brother of hers on a visit to the Biscoes going to call on the Astons at Northleach: just as we were entering into M^r B's premises, we met M^rs. B. going to walk with her children; we declined going into the house: M^rs. B. |^115 joined us, and sending the carriage forward; we walked for some distance with her on our way home.

A letter from a Dr Williams, Hayes, Middlesex, accompanying some very satisfactory testimonials as to his professional skill, talents, and general character. Dr W. is a candidate for the vacant situation of resident superintendent of the Gloucester Lunatic Asylum. A letter from Mr Wilton, Treasurer of the County of Gloucester, accompanying the yearly balance sheet of the receipts and expenditure of the County, to be examined by me, as it has already been by Purnell and Dr Timbrill.

Quarterly review for June.

Sept 9. Wednesday.
A showery morning; the weather afterwards fine.

Engaged in examining the Abstract of the County Treasurer's accounts, forwarded to me yesterday.

Justice business at home.

Visited J. Davis: he is able now to go out in a wheel chair, or low |^116 poney chaise; but is very paralytic.

Received a letter Mr Pearce as to the estimate of number of rations to be charged in Union accounts to the establishment account for the maintenance of the officers table. A circular from a clergyman in the Isle of Man, begging for a contribution of eighteen pence towards the building of a parsonage. Circular letter from the Gloucester lunatic asylum, announcing a meeting of Visitors on the 15th. Inst. to select three names from the list of applicants for the office of Superintendent, from whom one to be chosen at a subsequent meeting.

Quarterly Rev. for June.

Sept. 10. Thursday.
Very fine weather.

Parted from my servant, John Bateman: his successor, George Baldwin, arrived.

Drove to Stow. MW. accompanied me, and returned soon after we reached the place.

Transacted business at the Provident Bank, at the office of the Gloucestershire Banking Company, |^117 and at the office of Mr R. Brookes.

To the Workhouse: presided at the fortnightly meeting of the Guardians of the Union.

Joined the Dean of Gloucester and Ford, sitting as magistrates at the Unicorn; Winter and Lewes were also present. An affray occurred on Sunday evening last, in the public house at Barrington Wharf, it being the night of Barrington feast, which ended in the death of a man present, and the serious wounding of another, both injuries being caused by rash or unlucky blows inflicted by a Police Constable, Probert, stationed at Northleach, and detached on duty at Barrington, with three others of the Constabulary. Barnett, as Coroner, has held an inquest, which he has adjourned: the evidence given is said to be very contradictory; it is presumed that the P.C. was too rash: the Coroner is wont to protract enquiries, where the probability |[118] is that persons holding office are censurable; and where excitement prevails.

Quarterly Review for June.

Sept. 11. Friday.
Fine weather.

Wrote to M[r] Wilton, the County Treasurer, returning the abstract of the accounts of Income & Expenditure by the County for the year ending at Easter Sessions 1846 which I had examined and signed. Drew his attention to one error.

Preparing for the discussion at the next decanal meeting.

With MW called on M[rs.] Dolphin at Eyford: she is in good spirits, having succeeded in letting a farm to distant people.

Anderson's history of the Church of England in the Colonies.

Sept. 12. Saturday.
Fine weather.

Preparing for the discussion on the Church of England, expected at the next decanal meeting.

Justice business at home.

Walked to Joiners downs, to see the repairs now in progress to the Wear at the |[119] Water meadow there.

M[rs.] W. Vavasour and her sister called: they had driven to Stanway yesterday, and seen all at the Vicarage quite well: dear Sophy in good spirits, wondering at the delay of her accouchement, and expecting it at any hour. The ladies gave but an indifferent report of the health of Will. Vavasour.

M[rs.] Aitkins & the Misses Hall with other ladies from Bourton had called on MW. when I was out.

Anderson's History of the Church of England in the Colonies.

Sept. 13. Sunday.
Very fine weather.

Visited the Sunday School.

Preparing a sermon.

Morning service – prayers. Afternoon service, prayers and a Sermon. I preached on reading the Scriptures.

British Magazine.

To the family a section from Trowers short lectures on the Gospels.

Sept. 14. Monday.
Fine weather.

Preparing a sermon.

Preparing for |[120] the discussion at the approaching decanal meeting.

Wrote to E.F.W. – also to Mr Waterfall about a bill due by us to late Walls and Fisk; — also sent eighteen pence to the Clergyman in the Isle of Man who had begged for that sum towards the erection of a parsonage house.

My parishioner; Joshua Dix, dreadfully injured by a threshing machine: the spindle when the machine was at work, caught him by the right arm, broke the bone & greatly lacerated the flesh: the fracture is between the shoulder and the elbow. Visited him; found him calm, composed, and quite sensible. The medical men from Bourton are in attendance upon him; amputation has been talked of, but not performed. At 77 years of age, it may be difficult to determine on the proper course to be adopted.

Drove with MW. to Stow, shopping; as we returned met the elder Vavasours, who had been calling upon us.

Anderson's history of the Church of England in the Colonies.

Sept. 15. Tuesday.
Fine weather.

Visited |[121] Joshua Dix, and administered to him the Holy Communion: he lies in a calm state of body and mind; resigned to die, which he anticipates as near at hand, and by mortification. The arm has been bound up by Mess$^{rs.}$ Wells & Wing, but no mention now made of amputation.

Preparing for a discussion at the coming Decanal meeting.

Rec$^{d.}$ a letter from Mr Wilton, the County Treasurer: he admits & corrects the error which I detected in the County Accounts: — a circular from R. W. Hippisley, giving notice of the Decanal meeting fixed for Monday next.

Anderson's Church of England in the Colonies.

Sept. 16. Wednesday.
Fine weather.

Visited Joshua Dix who remains in the same state as yesterday.

Justice business at home

Preparing for the coming Decanal meeting.

Called on M$^{rs.}$ Dolphin, expecting to have found Bowen on a visit at Eyford: but he is only to arrive there to-day.

Anderson's History of the Church of |^{122} England in the Colonies.

Sept. 17. Thursday.
Fine weather.

Visited and prayed with Joshua Dix: his life is not expected to be long protracted.

Preparing for the discussion at the approaching Decanal meeting.

Drove to Stow: MW. accompanied me, and returned home soon after our arrival there.

To the Provident Bank, where I met Mr Oakley Hill, Perkins, and Winter.

To the Workhouse: conferred with Mr Pearce on Union business.

To the Justice room: sat with the Dean of Gloucester, and Ford, as my colleagues on the bench. Other gentlemen present were Mess$^{rs.}$ Winter, Polhill, C Lindow, Clarke &c.

Rec$^{d.}$ a note from Vavasour. M$^{rs.}$ V. had received a letter from dear Sophy, who describes herself as quite well, but hourly expecting her confinement.

Anderson's History of the Church of England in the Colonies.

Sept. 18. Friday.
Fine weather, but dull and overclouded.

Preparing for the |[123] discussion at the Decanal meeting on ~~Tues~~ Monday.

Visited sick parishioners.

A letter from the Gloucester Lunatic Asylum, announcing a meeting of the Visitors in order to elect a Superintendent on the 22[d.] — A letter from E.F.W. with a very good report of all at Stanway; save that the suspence as to Sophy's confinement still subsists.

As I walked to and from the turnpike gate at Lower Slaughter, had a long parley with M[r] Lindow.

We dined at the Fords, meeting a large party. A bride and bridegroom, M[r] and M[rs.] Fenton, were staying in the house: M[r] F. a young officer, lately present at the battles (one or more of them) on the Sikh frontier, and returned without wound, an agreeable, unaffected young man, a nephew of M[rs.] Ford: his lady was a Miss Salmon, from near Chepstow. We met also, M[r] and M[rs.] Morrison, and their eldest daughter, M[rs.] Aston, her eldest daughter, and young |[124] Frederick, who goes for the first time next week to study at the College for civil Engineers at Putney; M[r] and M[rs.] Biscoe, with her brother, M[r] Middleton; M[r] Lewes, and ourselves with the Ford family at home, M[r] & M[rs.] F. Henry, and three sisters, filled both dining and drawing rooms: — a pleasant party enough. –

Sept. 19. Saturday.
Fine weather.

Preparing for the Decanal meeting on Monday next.

My tenant Forty, who has evaded the Bailiffs for two years past, was arrested this morning, and conveyed to Gloucester Gaol at the suit of M[rs.] Scott, of Banks fee, for the costs in the action which she brought against him, and in which a Verdict passed against him. I wrote to M[r] Morgan, Sol[r] to M[rs.] Scott, on the occasion, as to my position as his landlord in respect of rent due at Mich[s.] and received an answer from him explaining the proceedings taken, the course likely to be pursued by Forty, and the remedies in my power as to recovery of rent. |[125]

Visited Joshua Dix, who still lingers; but there now appears to be a possibility that his limb may be set, and his life spared.

Justice business at home.

Anderson's Church of England in the Colonies.

Sept. 20. Sunday.
Fine weather.

Visited the Sunday School, which was taught for the first time in the new Schoolroom — a very great improvement on our old plan of teaching in a cottage kitchen or Forty's parlour.

Visited Joshua Dix, who is going on well.

Morning Service Prayers and Sermon. I preached on the love of our enemies, and the forgiveness of injuries. Evening Service — Prayers.

Preparing for the discussion at the Decanal meeting to-morrow.

To the family a section from Trower's Exposition of the Gospels.

Sept 21. Monday.
Weather fine, but an approaching change indicated by the fall of the Mercury in the Barometer. |[126]

Preparing for the discussion at the Decanal meeting to-day.

MW. accompanied me to Stow, and soon returned home.

Attended divine Service at Church, — the feast of S[t.] Matthew; — the desk service performed by R. W. Hippisley; M[r] Ford and RWH. officiated at the Communion: only ten communicants out of the whole clergy of the Deanery; alas! for the lukewarmness; the lack of professional feeling, which this betrays — I believe there are 34 Clergymen resident in the deanery — those who attended were Mess[rs.] Ford, Hippisley, Wiggin, Haughton, Pantin, Helliar, Potter, Morrison, Witts, Talmage — and the last was a stranger to the deanery — of the diocese of Oxford.

After divine service half an hour elapsed during which I visited the Workhouse, accompanied by M[r] Morrison, before we joined the rest of the Clergy assembled at the National School room.

To the names mentioned above I have only to add those of M[r] Smith and M[r] Clarke. The Rural Dean |[127] took the Chair. The declaration passed at the last decanal meeting, expressive of regret at the Secession of so many Clergymen of our Church to Rome, and of affectionate adherence to the Church of which we are ordained ministers, which had been generally signed by the Clergy of this deanery, had met with the approval of the Bishop, and ~~had~~ it was arranged that it should be forwarded for publication in the Ecclesiastical Gazette.

M[r] Pantin read a very able paper, shewing great research, in a very rapid manner. His thesis was handled with very judicious method: he shewed that Christianity was planted in Britain in the first century, by apostolical men, at least, if not by an Apostle, and that there was a great probability that St. Paul himself had preached the gospel on our shores; he shewed that the British church so planted was Episcopal, and independent of any foreign Church |¹²⁸ so continuing for many centuries; that it was a struggling, and oppressed church during the centuries of trouble and intestine commotion which marked the early history of England: that it was driven by the Saxon invaders into the mountainous recesses of the West of the Island, there, however, keeping up an intercourse with Gaulish, Irish and Scottish Christians: that the Roman mission into Britain under Augustine in the 6th. Cent. was followed only by a partial conversion of the Saxons chiefly in the South of the Island, and was not in its early proceedings widely extended, at least not very successfully carried on; that the British Church refused to attach itself to the Roman mission, or to acknowledge any dependence on Rome; that the larger portions of the Anglo Saxon country were evangelized by British, Scotch and Irish Missionaries; that Roman rituals and especially the Roman computation of Easter were long repudiated; that the Papal |¹²⁹ influence did not begin to spread itself, or to take firm root till towards the close of the seventh Century; and that there was always a more or less sturdy protestation against Papal supremacy down to the time of the Reformation, when it was entirely cast off; — the reader showed further that our church was scriptural, was allowed to be a pure branch of the Universal and Apostolical Church, except by the Papists, was held in high respect and greatly commended by the early continental Protestant divines, the leaders among whom recognized its Episcopacy as derived from primitive times, and lamented that local circumstances prevented the establishment of Episcopacy generally among Protestants — lastly he shewed ~~its~~ ^{the} claims of the Anglican Church as opposed to dissent on the one hand, and Romanism on the contrary. — As the Senior present, I followed with a comment on the various matters of history and antiquity brought forward in M^r |¹³⁰ Pantin's ~~history,~~ ^{Essay} dilating more fully on the different matters which he had touched. I urged the evidences as to the probability of St. Paul having evangelized Britain, explained the legend of Lucius, shewing how far the monkish story relating to him was probable; I pointed out the independence of the British, Irish & Scotch Churches; adverted to the British Bishops who had been present at Continental councils, shewed the efforts which had been made in Britain, with the aid of Gaulish Bishops, to suppress Pelagianism by preaching, and at a Synod, to which the Church of Rome was no party; I descanted on the state of independence of great portion of the Anglo-Saxon church, showing that they derived their Christianity more from British, and Scottish than from Roman sources, the Southern Kingdoms of the Heptarchy only having been brought into the pale by the Romish Missionaries. I pointed out how they and the Clergy succeeding them gradually acquired ascendancy, and in the 7th. Century, by the |¹³¹ influence mainly of Wilfrid, the able advocate for Romish opinions and ritual, ^{who} in the time of the Metropolitan Theodore, Archb. of Canterbury, a Greek, sent from Rome, under peculiar circumstances, of which the Pope artfully availed himself, contrived, after a long and difficult struggle, to obtain a footing for Papal pretensions, which was slowly and gradually improved during the subsequent ages of the Heptarchy – Others of the Clergy followed, but none entered fully into the historical question. Mr Clarke was inclined rather to trace Christianity in Britain to the Oriental Churches. Messrs. Smith and Haughton, Hibernicé, harping on the one string, talked much of the Council of Trent, as contradicted by those of Nice & Ephesus, one or both, but with no very distinct notion which: the latter was particularly national in his oratory, grotesque gesticulations, elevation and depression of voice, assumed pathos of solemnity, so as to move his brethren to the limits of hearty laughter. |[132]

M[r] Hippisley read a long and laboured letter rec[d.] by him from M[r] Cooke, the incumbent of Wick Risington, reminding him and the members of our decanal meeting of what he considered a promise made at the June meeting, that, as a set off, as it were, to the declaration then made of regret at the sessions to Rome, and [of] firm adherence on our parts to the Church of England, we should put forth a declaration censuring those of the Clergy who, remaining within our Church, hold the tenet of Regeneration non-baptismal. The observations which it occurred to me to make as to this letter of our worthy, but injudicious, and, perhaps, irritable friend, appeared to concur with the opinions of the Clergy present: that because we had expressed regret at certain parties leaving the church, and our own determination to abide in it, it did not follow as a reasonable consequence, that we were to protest against those who, holding opinions different from us on a question which had been matter of dispute among Protestants, almost, if not quite, from the |[133] beginning, who still remained in our Church, conscientiously, no doubt, thinking that their position was not irreconcileable with their tenets, and were not excluded on account of those tenets from the ministry, by the ruling authorities of the Church. It was added that mooting this question was likely to engender strife, and interrupt harmony among ourselves. M[r] Hippisley, therefore, was requested to give a brief answer to the effect that the Clergy of this deanery, assembled at their periodical meeting, did not hold themselves to have given any pledge to make such a declaration as that required by M[r] Cooke, but would be ready to entertain the question, if brought forward hereafter by him. The fact is, my good old friend is sore; has an affection for many who hold opinions verging to the extreme of Tractarianism; though he repudiates Romanism, and fights against it manfully in his own way, he is entangled in the mazes of ecclesiastical archaeology, stone altars or |[134] tables &c., aware that non essentials have been raised into undue importance, and yet leans in that direction, postponing his own sounder judgment, and, amiably, tho' weakly, deferring too much to the younger members of his family, who overrate the fringe, and think not enough of the material to which it is appended.

Other clerical matters were touched upon before the meeting separated.

Before returning home I had an interview with M[r] Stokes on Turnpike road matters.

Anderson's Church of England in the Colonies.

Sept. 22. Tuesday.
The weather overclouded: a blight with a tendency to rain; heavy rain at night. Preparing a Sermon.

Justice business at home.

Visited Davis and Dix: the former less well than he has been; the latter is improving in his condition.

M^r and M$^{rs.}$ Rudge, accompanied by M^r and M$^{rs.}$ Henry Pole, called on us from Wyck Hill.

Anderson's Church of England in the Colonies. |^{135}

Sept. 23. Wednesday.
Heavy rain had fallen during the night, and heavy showers fell during the day.

Preparing a sermon.

Wrote to Shirer and C$^{o.}$ Cheltenham with a remittance for goods supplied.

Justice business at home.

Anderson's Church of England in the Colonies.

Sept. 24. Thursday.
Showery weather.

Justice business at home.

Drove to Stow, accompanied by MW. who, suffering much from a cough, consulted Mr Hayward at his house before she returned.

To the Provident Bank.

To Mr Brookes's office; transacted business at both places.

To Mr Morgan's office, whom I consulted as to the position in which I am placed relatively to Forty, as an insolvent.

To the Workhouse, where I presided at the fortnightly meeting of the Guardians.

R. Dunford, R.O. there put into my hands a letter as to his |^{136} pecuniary embarrasments, in which he asks me to draw up a statement of his losses, and difficulties, in order that he may solicit donations towards extricating himself from them.

At the Justice room, sat with the Dean of Gloucester, Mr Ford, and Mr Pole, as Magistrates: other gentlemen present were Mess$^{rs.}$ Winter, W. Vavasour, Polhill, Aitkens &c.

When I got home I found M^r and M$^{rs.}$ Aitkens and M$^{rs.}$ R. Waller, visiting my wife, and waiting for my return: the former came to take leave, on their departure for Staffordshire, where Mr A. is about to settle himself on his incumbency of Castle Church. M$^{rs.}$ RW. gave an indifferent account of her husband's health and spirits. He suffers from diarrhoea, is very deaf, and moped, requiring what he thinks he cannot have change of air, and scene: no arrangements have yet been made by him to secure a successor to Mr Aitkens, as Curate of Lower |^{137} Slaughter and Clapton.

Anderson's Church of England in the Colonies.

Sept. 25. Friday.

A fine day. An early messenger from Stanway brought a letter from E.F.W. with the glad tidings that our dear Sophy had been safely delivered of a Son last evening; she had a good and a short time, and both the Mother and the infant are going on quite well. GOD be praised for this great mercy! Replied to my son's note.[8]

Preparing a sermon.

Mr Pearce called by appointment, with whom I conferred on various Union matters, and principally as to the expediency of altering our system of granting out-relief to non settled paupers to be repaid by the Unions to which they belong: and repaying relief given by other Unions to non-resident paupers of our Union settled living within their Unions. Such a course seems now to be inexpedient, since the new act came into force, about a month since, |^{138} granting the privilege of irremoveability to persons who have resided five years in any place, so making them chargeable to such place, as long as they continue to reside there; the length of residence to make out five years being computed so as to exclude any portion of time during which they shall have been receiving parochial or other ^{quasi} eleemosynary relief,[9] or otherwise not been living on their own resources, or by the wages of their labour. I prepared a letter to the P.L.C., to be sent by M^r P, developing our views on this subject, and shewing why it appears to us advisable to refuse henceforth the advantages we have given to the paupers of other Unions resident in ours, and to decline sanctioning the relief of paupers having settlements in our Union by the Guardians of other Unions in which they reside, relieving on our account. Requested the P.L.C. to report communicate at an early date their view as to this matter.

Called with MW. at Eyford, expecting to have found Mr Bowen on a visit to M$^{rs.}$ Dolphin, |^{139} but he has declined coming this week. We found with M$^{rs.}$ D. A M$^{rs.}$ Mills, daughter of the Agent, Mr Paxton, who was also at Eyford.

Visited J. Davis; not so well as he has been. Joshua Dix is improved in his state of health.

Arranged with Mr Gregory as to the retirement of his daughter A.M.G. from the office of mistress of the parish daily school, with a view to the appointment of Mary Forty in her room.

Anderson's Church of England in the Colonies.

---

8.   George Backhouse Witts (1846–1912).
9.   Eleemosynary – compassionate, mercy; a person who is dependent on alms.

<u>*Sept. 26. Saturday.*</u>
Showery weather.

Preparing a sermon.

A letter from Mess.ʳˢ· Shirer and Cᵒ· with an acknowledgement of the remittance I had made to them.

Visited and enquired after sick parishioners.

In the evening Mʳ Pain called from Stow to ask permission to be absent on Tuesday next from the annual meetings of the Soc. for Prom. Christ. Knowledge, Stow district, and the Stow Book Society. Mʳ |¹⁴⁰ Pain's wife's mother lies dead at Oxford, and the funeral is fixed for Tuesday. He shewed me the balance sheet of his accounts as Librarian of the Book Society, and having charge of the depository of Books of the S.P.C.K. and went forward to Little Risington on a like errand to Mʳ Ford. Of course his presence will not be insisted on.

<u>*Sept. 27. Sunday.*</u>
Showery weather.

Visited the Sunday School.

Preparing a Sermon.

Morning service; prayers; Afternoon service, prayers, and a sermon. I preached on the Tree of life — a sacramental sermon; the Communion to be administered on Sunday next.

MW. received a very satisfactory account of dearest Sophy & her infant from Mʳˢ· Vavasour, who wrote that she had driven to Stanway on Friday, on the morning after the accouchement, and found both mother and infant going on as well as possible.

Eccl. Gazette.

To the family a section from Trower's Exposition of the Gospels. |¹⁴¹

<u>*Sept. 28. Monday.*</u>
Showery weather.

Justice business at home.

Interview with Mary Forty, who engages to undertake the office of School mistress for the daily Parish School; but considers the stipend too low, and is likely to resign, should any better situation present itself.

R. Dunford, R.O. called, with whom I conferred, declining to draw up any petition or statement of his embarrasments, with a view to his soliciting donations, expressed my own readiness to help him by contributing two Sovereigns, if others yeilded such assistance, cautioned him not to apply generally for such aid, as the avowal of difficulties would lead some to doubt the safety of entrusting him with public funds, advised him to make concessions as to a quarrel between him and Foreshaw of Great Risington, where both parties were to blame, and F. had threatened an action. Conferred with D. on Union matters.

Preparing for the annual meeting of the Stow Book Society |[142] to-morrow.

Mr Morrison walked over from Longborough, accompanied by his son, a fine lad of fourteen, and a pupil of the same age. Returned part of the way with them, accompanying them till we came in view of Lower Swell.

Mr Clarke called on us afterwards.

Received a letter from E.F.W. with a very excellent account of his dear wife and her baby.

Andersons History of the Church of England in the Colonies.

Sept. 29. Tuesday.
A fine autumnal day.

Preparing for the annual meeting of the Stow Book Society to be held to-day.

Drove to Stow with MW. who returned home soon after we arrived there.

At the Workhouse conferred with Mr Pearce on Union Matters.

At the library engaged with Mr Ford in auditing the annual accounts of the district committee S.P.C.K. and the Book Society.

At the Annual meeting of the district comm. S.P.C.K, there was lamentable proof of the coldness and indifference not only of |[143] the laity, but of the Clergy of this district in attendance upon meetings for the furtherance of Christian and Church purposes. They need to be stimulated, invited, tempted by the expectation of something to gratify curiosity. It is a sad sign of the general lukewarmness that six Clergymen were all who attended. The Dean of Gloucester presided: the report was read by Mr Ford, the Treasurer and Secretary – Mess$^{rs.}$ Pantin, Hippisley, Barrow and myself made up the number above stated.

The annual meeting of the Stow Book Society, and the dinner followed. This also was poorly attended, but a pleasant party. M^r C Pole presided; the other members present were Mess$^{rs.}$ Ford, Hippisley, Barrow, Winter, Pantin, Capt. Leigh, Hutchinson, my Son, and myself.

Lt Col. Dawkins, J. T. Rice, & Mr Morrison were elected members of the Society; Col. Dawkins to preside next year.

E.F.W. brought very gratifying accounts of dear Sophy, the infant, and his other treasures at Stanway. He gave a very indifferent report of Will. |^{144} Vavasour's health, whose spine is, I fear, injured: perfect rest in a reclining posture is prescribed, to which he will not entirely submit. My son rode home after the dinner party broke up.

I brought Mr Barrow home with me to tea, who left us about ten o clock.

Sept 30. Wednesday.
Fine weather.

Engaged with my Co-Trustees of the parochial Church and Charity estate in laying out for the use of the cottagers the ground contiguous to the new School room, examining the state of the Cottages, giving orders to Mason and Carpenters &c.

Mr Hayward visited and prescribed for MW: whose cough continues obstinate, the biliary system being deranged.

Visited Parishioners.

Preparing a sermon.

Making up the Minutes and Accounts of the Book Society – Wrote to Rodwell with an order for books.

Examining with R Blizard the bills for the erection of the New School room.

Anderson's church of England in the Colonies. |^{145}

Oct. 1. Thursday.
Fine, but cloudy weather: a slight tendency to rain in the Evening.

Preparing a Sermon.

Justice business at home.

MW. Very hoarse, has nearly lost her voice.

Wrote to the Clerk of Gloucester infirmary, to ascertain whether there will be room for a patient on the 8th Inst.

I drove to Stow.

To the Provident Bank, transacted business there.

To the Workhouse: audited the bills of the last quarter.

The Dean of Gloucester and Mʳ C Pole sat with me at the Unicorn as Magistrates. Mʳ Winter was present – Much business – Committed to the H. of C. Northleach a rogue and vagabond, who had been levying contributions in July last in this vicinity, from the opulent, by a false statement, furnished with false signatures of leading people, as having given liberally, such as Lord Dynevor, C Pole, C Greenaway – R. W. Ford, R Waller, and myself – An |¹⁴⁶ attempt had been made at the time to detain the fellow, but he escaped, to practice the same fraud in the vale of Gloucester, for which he was sentenced to two months imprisonment in the H. of. C. at Lawford's Gate, on the expiration of which term he was apprehended by the police on a warrant issued by me. Several parties engaged in the same fraudulent occupation seem to have infested this County of late.

An information against J. Smith, the keeper of a disorderly beer house at Lower Slaughter, for offences against the law and the tenor of his licence, fell to the ground, in consequence of the witness, a Police constable, not being able to prove the sale and delivery of the liquor; but matters transpired connected with the granting of the licence, shewing great negligence or irregularity in the part of the Excise officer, together with the granting of a false certificate as to rating by the late Overseer of the parish, a Brother in law of the Beer house keeper, which will require further in-|¹⁴⁷ vestigation, either by the local Magistrates, or, on their representation, by the Commʳˢ· of Excise, which will, probably, lead to the putting down of the Beer house, which is, and has for some time past been, a great nuisance, & injury to the lower classes. Mʳ Carter, soi-disant Attorney of Winchcomb, appeared for the Beerhouse Keeper, and, as usual, was vulgar, bullying, and offensive in his manner.

Anderson's Church of England in the Colonies.

Oct. 2. Friday.
A rainy day, with but little intermission.

Preparing a Sermon.

Justice business at home.

Visited J. Davis and Josh. Dix.

MW. not so hoarse as yesterday, but still much of an invalid.

Recᵈ· a letter from Mʳ Jennings with the Midsummer Balance sheet of London rents received by him.

Anderson's Church of England in the Colonies.

Oct. 3. Saturday.
Fine weather. |[148]

Justice ~~meeting~~ business at home.

MW. less unwell, but not sufficiently recovered to venture to accompany me to Stanway.

I drove thither; near to Stumps Cross, met and held a parley with M[r] Billingsley.

Found all at the Vicarage as I could wish: my dear daughter so wonderfully recovered as to be dressed, sitting in the drawing room, in excellent spirits, looking as if nothing had happened to her. The dear infant not so large a child as its elder brothers had been, at the same age, but a very lovely baby, perfectly healthy. It is to be name George Backhouse, the former name being given in memory of my deceased brother, the latter out of respect to the ~~family~~ family and maiden name of my dear wife. Broome and Frederick were bright, blooming boys, seemingly delighted to welcome grand-papa, the only drawback being the absence of Grandmamma, and its cause. Freddy's complexion and whole condition much improved ~~wh~~ since I last saw him, when he looked deli-|[149] cate, hardly recovered from slight feverish attack. I remained two hours with the dear party, taking luncheon with them. The two elder boys came with me in the carriage to the top of Stanway Hill, returning with the nurse who walked to meet them.

Called on M[r] Bowen at ~~Temp~~ Temple Guiting, whom I found in better health than he has of late been; but still a greater sufferer from his chronic complaint. With whom was M[r] Walsh, the Curate of Cutsdean, making a visit: this gentleman has resigned his curacy on account of delicate health, and is going abroad, to Malta, as he suffers from a pulmonary affection.

Received a letter from the Clerk of the Gloucester Infirmary, that there will be room for the patient whom I propose to send on the 8[th.] Instant: — from M[r] Pantin a voluminous epistle, with quotations and references to authorities on the many points involved in the paper read by him, and in the comments theron made by me at the late Decanal meeting. |[150]

MW. Received a letter from M[rs.] C Barr, with a very favourable report of herself and family.

While I was at Stanway, my son rec[d.] a letter of congratulation from John Witts, who gave a very indifferent account of his wife's health.

During my absence from home, M[r] Moore, the Med. Off. of Distr. 3. of this Union called.

Brit. Magazine – Anderson's Hist. of the Church of England in the Colonies.

Oct. 4. Sunday.
Fine Weather.

Visited the Sunday School.

Wrote to Mr Pantin, inclosing a recommendation of Thos. Cook of Westcote to the Gloucester infirmary.

Morning ^{service} – prayers, sermon, & Sacrament. I preached on Christ coming to Judgment – 23 Comm. Evening service – prayers.

Mrs. Dolphin, with her visitors, Mrs. Curtis Smith, and Miss Humphris called on us after evening service.

Received a letter from Sewell and Newmarch on the subject of Longbands farm. It seems that the nomi-|¹⁵¹ nal owner, Aston, having quarrelled with the tenant, Clarke, the latter has relinquished his holding, and surrendered the farm to the mortgagees, who, finding matters thus come to a crisis, have resolved on immediately putting in force their power of sale; the property is, therefore, advertized to be sold by auction by Hoggart and Norton, at Gloucester, on the 27th. Inst. on which day they sell Howell's Upton land. The purchase by auction on the part of our Trustees, I suppose, is out of the question: if, therefore, a bidding beyond the low reserved bidding is made at the sale, our chance is gone; if the farm be not sold by auction, we may, if so disposed, endeavour to buy by private contract.

Preparing a Sermon.

Ecclesiastical Gazette.

To the family a section from Trower's exposition of the gospels.

Oct. 5. Monday.
Showery weather.

Wrote to H. D. Warter, forwarding to him the letter which I received yesterday from Sewell and Newmarch as to the Redmarley |¹⁵² property, desiring to know his opinion, as the matter now stands: — to Sewell and Newmarch, acknowledging their letter, informing them that I had put myself into communication with Warter on the subject, but still apprehended that we could not purchase by auction: — to Mr Jennings acknowledging his late letter, and explaining to him how we are circumstanced as to Longbands farm, and my doubts whether we shall be able to invest the money proceeding from the sale of our Fenchurch Street property in that property; requested him to look out for ground rents or house property of an eligible description in London or its vicinity, in the event of our not buying a farm.

My son having driven early to-day to Stow, to breakfast with the W. Vavasours at Maugersbury, and to be ready to play at Cricket with such members of the Club as might be so disposed, if the weather would allow, before the annual Cricket Club dinner, which is to be held today, sent his servant over to enquire after his |¹⁵³ Mother's health, who continues indisposed, suffering from spasm, as well as by a bad cough. The news from Stanway as to the health of dear Sophy, and her children excellent. I wrote to E.F.W. with particulars as to the actual state of things as regards the Redmarley estate.

Preparing a Sermon.

Visited the daily parish school, held to-day for the first time in the new School room, Mary Forty having entered upon her new office.

M^{rs.} and Miss Wynniatt called: the former so lame and helpless as to be unable to get out of her carriage, into which MW. entered, & there received her visit.

Anderson's History of the Church in the colonies.

Oct 6. Tuesday.
The morning rainy: the afternoon ~~fine~~, and the evening fine.

Wrote to Mr Thornton on Hunt Trusteeship matters.

Transacted parish business with M^r E Lea, Overseer, consulting with him as to the propriety of now procuring a valuation of the parish, for parochial pur-|[154] poses, and at the same time to satisfy the demands of the County rate Committee, who require from us, and most other parishes in this neighbourhood, a new valuation for the County rate.

Mr Ford called, and shewed me notes which he had received within these few days from Mr Barrow, which indicated great nervous irritability, proneness to take offence, a morbid feeling that his acquaintance slight or insult him, in short, a condition of mind which leads to fears for his sanity. It is a sad thing; and difficult to say whether any steps should be taken to apprize his connections of his frame of mind: certainly his fancies are perfectly groundless, he having been treated by everybody with great civility and attention.

A letter from the Lunatic Asylum, Gloucester, announcing a meeting of Visitors on the 15th. Inst.

In the evening Mr Stokes called to apprize me of a meeting of Comm^{rs.} of the Foss and Cross Turnpike road intended to be holden at Adlestrop Turnpike Gate on the 16th. Inst. To |[155] consult as to the course to be taken in respect of the passing of the Worcester and Oxford and Wolverhampton railway at the point, whether on a level, or by a deviation and bridges: some difficulties have been raised by Lord Leigh or his agent, Mr Jones.

Justice business at home.

British Magazine.

Oct. 7. Wednesday.
Very showery weather: in the evening and at night heavy rain and boisterous, with thunder and lightning.

Preparing a Sermon.

Received a letter from Mr Warter's managing Clerk, by which it appears that he is in Scotland, and not likely to return till the 19th. Inst. my late letter to him on the purchase of the Redmarley estate together with its enclosure, the letter on that subject from Sewell and Newmarch, has been forwarded to M^r W.

MW. rec^d. a letter from Sophia Hunt, who with her brother Thomas, and sisters Maria and Fanny are lately returned |^156 from a tour on the Rhine, and in Switzerland. She gives hurried but ample details of their adventures.

Visited the parish School.

MW. did not feel sufficiently well to accompany me to dine at Longborough with M^r and M^rs. Morrison: I had a very stormy drive thither and back: they had been disappointed of some expected guests: those who came, besides myself were Mr Ford, Henry and Dulcy F. and Mr Clarke. The Misses Morrison are very pleasing girls, and musical. An agreeable party.

Oct. 8. Thursday.
Fine weather: only a slight tendency to rain.

Wrote to Sewell and Newmarch, forwarding to them the note I had received yesterday from Mr Warter's managing Clerk: — to Mr Wells, Hampnett, in reply to a question he had put to me so long ago as when I attended the funeral of Mr Tordiffe, respecting his being allowed to enclose part of a wide space of turf adjoining the turnpike |^157 road and his farm between Leygores hill and Northleach: explained to him the reluctance of the Comm^rs. of the Foss and Cross road to make any such accommodation.

Drove to Stow.

Transacted business at the Provident Bank, and at Mr Brookes's office.

To the Workhouse: where I presided at the fortnightly meeting of the Guardians of the Union.

To the Justice room, where the Dean of Gloucester, Mr Ford and R Waller were my colleagues on the bench, Messrs. Winter, Polhill and Aitkens being present. As to the case against the Beer house keeper at Lower Slaughter, we desired Mr Brookes to forward to the Comm^rs. of Excise a letter which he had prepared, containing a statement of the case, with particular reference to the irregularities chargeable on the Officers of the Excise in this district; desiring to know whether, in the opinion of the Board, any and |*158* what proceedings can be taken against the parties. It seems, however, that the Excise Officers have, since the hearing on Thursday last, abated the nuisance by recalling the defective licence, and insisting on the party not selling any more liquor either in or to be consumed out of the house. —

While I was at Stow, Sir John C. Reade called with his daughter Clara, who is taking leave of her friends under her maiden name and condition, being on an early day to be married to John Talbot Rice; pity that so delicate, pleasing and intelligent a young person should have attached herself to a young man of so little mind, and without profession: but her home is distasteful to her, owing to the violence, weakness, and intemperate habits of her father, and, if report does not mistake, of her brother. The young people are to live in the Rectory house at Great Risington.

"The Expedition to Borneo of H.M.S. Dido, for the suppression of Piracy; with extracts from the Journal |*159* of James Brooke Esqr of Sarāwak – (now agent for the British Government in Borneo) by Captain the Hon. Henry Keppel RN. 2 Vols 8vo." A very interesting publication on a very new, important and interesting topic – the exploring of Borneo, the suppression of the pirates harboured there, the opening of commercial intercourse with the Borneon Governments and inhabitants, mainly by the intervention of one of the most remarkable men of the age, Mr Brooke, who has not only, at his own charge, and without the aid of government, opened a communication with this hitherto almost unknown region, but has acquired there a sort of province, which he rules in a kind of feudal sovereignty, as Rajah or chief of Sarāwak.

Oct. 9. Friday.
A stormy and rainy day prevented our going to Stanway to visit our dear children and grand children.

My wife's cough is going off, and she considers her general health better.

Wrote to Rodwell |*160* to order books for the Stow book Society: also some for myself.

Wrote to Howell.

Drove to Naunton, by appointment, to see a poor girl who is insane, and as to whom I had signed an order for her conveyance to the Lunatic Asylum at Gloucester: the law requires the Magistrate personally to examine the party sent: found her raving: learnt that the attack is supposed to originate in agitation in consequence of her younger sister being committed for trial at the approaching sessions for a trifling theft committed on her master, a tailor at Naunton; the poor insane girl is bound over to give evidence against her sister, as to an article stolen. Conferred with the Prosecutor, who would gladly now be excused proceeding with the charge: his wife, who is also bound by recognizance to give evidence, ~~as~~ ^is on the very eve of her confinement; so unable to attend on the 21st. and, as the wife and the insane girl are the material witnesses, the trial must be postponed till the Epiphany Sessions, unless the |[161] prisoner be discharged in Court, no evidence being adduced by the Prosecutor. To ~~pre~~ postpone the trial for three months seems a great hardship on the prisoner, who has already suffered several weeks imprisonment for a slight offence; at the ~~next~~ Epiphany Session the sister may not have recovered her senses, or the appearance in Court as witness may again disturb her mind. But it is a difficult and delicate matter: I, therefore, considered it desirable to acquaint R Waller, as Committing Mag., and M[r] Wilkins, as engaged to conduct the prosecution, with the circumstances, and, before I returned home, drove to ~~Naunton,~~ Bourton, where I had an interview with the latter, deliberating with him how the object might be accomplished, and leaving him to confer with RW. on the subject.

Received a letter of Hunt Trust matters from M[r] Thornton, who has lately returned from a Continental tour.

Keppel's Borneo.

Oct 10. Saturday.
A very rainy forenoon: |[161] fine in the latter part of the day.

Wrote to J Round.

Justice business at home.

Called on J. Davis.

The weather had prevented our driving over to Stanway. MW's health continues to improve.

Keppel's Borneo.

Oct. 11. Sunday.
Very showery weather: heavy rain.

Visited the Sunday School.

Morning service – prayers. Afternoon Service – prayers and a sermon. I preached a charity sermon, under the authority of a Queen's letter in aid of the funds for the relief of the sufferers by the dreadful fire, which destroyed three fourths of the City of S[t.] John's, Newfoundland on June 9[th.] Collected £1. 19. 0

Rec[d.] A letter from M[r] Sewell as to the Redmarley Estate with particulars, plan, and Conditions of sale. He purposes breakfasting here on Friday morning, to explain the propositions he has to make with a view to the farm being purchased by us, with our Fenchurch Street funds, if it be |[162] not disposed of by auction.

A circular came from the County Gaol announcing a meeting of the Board of Visiting Justice's on Friday next.

Preparing a Sermon.

Eccl. Gazette.

To the family a Section from Trower's exposition of the Gospels.

Oct. 12. Monday.
A foggy morning, a fine forenoon and afternoon, a windy and rainy evening.

Justice business at home.

Wrote to Mr Sewell that we should be glad to see him on Friday.

With MW. Drove to Stanway, and had great pleasure in visiting our dear children and grandchildren. Sophy seems to be quite recovered, and the baby thrives greatly. Broome & Frederick lovely boys. A most cordial reception. M^r and M$^{rs.}$ Vavasour had, like ourselves, come on a morning visit. A cheerful party at Luncheon. M$^{rs.}$ Holland, accompanied by one of her children, and a lady, called before we left the Vicarage.

We reached home to a late dinner — |^{163} MW. did not seem the worse for her little excursion.

A letter from Mr Thornton with an enclosure from Mr Cox, and a copy of M^r T's answer to Mr C. on Hunt Trusteeship affairs.

Keppel's Borneo.

Oct. 13. Tuesday.
Weather cold, but fine.

Wrote to Mr Geo Hunt, Mr Thornton, and Mr Cox, on Hunt Trust business.

Preparing a sermon.

Justice business at home.

A letter from Howell.

A circular from the Clerk of the Peace announcing a meeting of the County rate Committee for the 19$^{th.}$ Inst.

Visited the daily school.

Keppel's Borneo.

Oct. 14. Wednesday.
A very rainy day, with little intermission.

Preparing a sermon.

Justice business at home; M.ᵣ Pearce came to complain of drunkenness and misbehaviour on the part of a pauper inmate of the Workhouse, whom I convicted and committed to Nleach Bridewell. Conferred with M.ᵣ P. on Union affairs. |*164*

Wrote to Sophia Hunt on Wadenhoe Trust matters a note sent with a letter from MW.

Visited the daily school.

Keppel's Borneo.

Oct. 15. Thursday.
Showery weather.

Attended a parish vestry, at which it was agreed that the parish should be mapped, measured, and valued for Parochial purposes, under the Parochial Assessments Act, both to give greater satisfaction to some rate payers, and with a view to furnish such a valuation as should be satisfactory to the County rate Committee.

Drove to Stow.

Rec.ᵈ a letter on Hunt affairs, enclosing one from M.ᵣ Cox, who refuses to be a party to the appointment of a Sol.ᵣ to the Trust in lieu of his successors, Mess.ʳˢ Cox & Williams.

To the Provident Bank, where I transacted business.

To the Gloucestershire B.ᵏᵍ Co.'s office, where I had business.

To the Workhouse, where I had a long and somewhat disagreeable investigation as to the |*165* manner in which M.ᵣ Hayward's assistant, M.ᵣ M.ᶜGreal, had conducted himself generally in his intercourse with the officers, nurses & paupers, and particularly as to two cases, which appeared on his Medical report book. Wrote to M.ᵣ Hayward and M.ᵣ M.ᶜG. to attend: the former was not at home: the latter came. I pointed out to him that he had made entries which could not be justified by the Poor law regulations, which were on matters alien from his province, in which an authority was assumed greater than belonged to the Office of Med. Off. — that he had not been sufficiently explicit in his entries, had acted with a harshness calculated, in possibility to injure a patient — cautioned him to be very circumspect in his conversation and manner in visiting the sick, and in his intercourse with the officers and Servants. I found him very respectful and civil to myself, but ^he is, I suspect, a swaggering, swearing, over bearing, ignorant person, |[166] hasty and ill-educated in his intercourse with the paupers and servants; nothing appeared to impeach his medical skill. I afterwards saw Mr Hayward, and explained myself ~~more~~ unreservedly to him as to the faults which on careful inquiry I found in the conduct of his Assistant.

At the Justice room sat as Magistrate with the Dean of Gloucester. Messrs. Winter, Lewes, and Stevens, Fellow of New Coll. and Curate of Burford, were present.

John Talbot Rice and Clara Reade were married on Tuesday last.

Keppel's Borneo.

Oct. 16. Friday.
A foggy morning, and fine day afterwards, but not without a tendency to rain.

Mr Sewell came from Cirencester, on his way to Lower Swell, and Bourton on the Hill, and breakfasted with us. Conferred with him as to the sale of the Redmarley farm, as to our purchase of it by private contract, if not sold by auction, as to its value, |[167] which, it is now admitted, has been overrated, and does not exceed £7000. The tenant whom I saw there, and who has quarreled with the owner, ~~and~~ has thrown up the farm, which he had agreed to hold for £300 per ann (the preceding tenant having given £336 per annum), and a respectable and substantial farmer has offered to take it at £260 per ann. for 14 years. Mr Sewell confidently asserts that the title is good, but admits that objections might be raised by crotchety counsel or attornies.

As Mr Sewell remained till between 11 & 12 o cl. I did not attempt to fulfil an engagement to meet the Comm^rs. of the Foss and Cross Turnpike road at Adlestrop Bridge at one o clock to deliberate as to a deviation at the road at that point, rendered expedient by the construction of the Oxford, Worcester and Wolverhampton railway, which crosses the Tpike road at that point. The works on this |[168] line are in progress, but not in our vicinity.

My Son rode over from Stanway, took luncheon with us, and remained two hours or more, bringing a very good account of our dear Sophy and her children.

Rec^d. from Mr Cox a letter as to the matter in dispute respecting the Hunt Trust.

Visited the daily School.

Keppel's Borneo.

Preparing a Sermon – Wrote to M^rs. Marsh, Bell Hotel, Gloucester, to reserve a bed for me at the Sessions next week.

Oct. 17. Saturday.

A rainy morning, a fine afternoon and evening.

Preparing a Sermon.

Wrote to Mʳ Thornton on Hunt affairs, forwarding to him the letter which I recᵈ· from Mʳ Cox yesterday: also to Mʳ Hunt at Boreatton, forwarding to him the letter from Mʳ Cox to Mʳ Thornton, which the latter had enclosed to me for my perusal.

Wrote to Mʳ H. D. Warter, sending him the letter I had recᵈ· from Sewell as to |¹⁶⁹ the Redmarley property, in which he proposed coming to confer with me on the purchase, also the printed particulars and conditions of sale, and gave him an account of my interview with Sewell yesterday.

Transacted Justice business at home with Mʳ R Brookes &c. previous to the Sessions.

Recᵈ· a letter from Mʳ Thornton with further comments on Hunt affairs: — from Mʳ H. D. Warter from a remote part of Scotland, where he has been visiting his brother Edward, that he returns to Town on the 20ᵗʰ· and will then attend to the Redmarley matter: – from Howell that he shall not reach home (Prinknash) till Wednesday next, being delayed in town in consequence of having obtained a naval cadetship for his son Willoughby, on board the Rattlesnake, a vessel to be employed on surveying service in the Torres Straits. I had previously written & posted a few lines |¹⁷⁰ to Howell, that I proposed, if possible, visiting him at Prinknash on Thursday next. —

Keppel's Borneo.

Oct. 18. Sunday.

A rainy day.

Preparing a sermon.

Morning Service. Prayers and sermon. Morning service. I preached on – "the Church the harvest: ~~the labourers~~ her ministers the labourers". Evening service – prayers.

Received a letter from Sewell with a query as to the Valuation of Bourton on the Hill parish: what valuer would be approved by the county rate committee? – Also from Morrison, to whom it is inconvenient to go to the Quarter Sessions on Tuesday to take the oaths on his preferment to the Vicarage of Longborough: he enquires of me whether it is absolutely necessary.

Answered both these letters.

Preparing for the Quarter Sessions.

To the family a section from Trower's Exposition of the Gospels. |

1

Diary
1846

Oct. 19. Monday — A foggy morning, a fine day, a wet night. —— Early breakfast: — to Cheltenham in the open carriage on my way to Gloucester: — to the Railway Station; thence by rail-road to Gloucester. — To the Bell Hotel: — conferred with the County Chairman: — to the Shire Hall: — meeting of the Committee of accounts: — Messrs. Purnell, C Hayward, Baker, Goodrich: auditing accounts. — Meeting of County rate Committee: — Messrs. Purnell, C Hayward, Witts, Kenney, Fulljames: — officials present, Messrs. Blossome, Riddiford, Wilton, Whitehead, Lefroy, Keiley, Fulljames. — Dinner at the Bell: Messrs. Purnell, C Hayward, Goodrich, Baker, Witts. — In the evening, till past midnight, auditing accounts, deliberating on public business — Somewhat indisposed; flatulency and spasm in the back and sides.

Oct 20. Tuesday — A fine day, rain at night. — Auditing accounts before breakfast — Wrote to MEO. — Breakfasted with Purnell. — To the Shire Hall, where engaged all day in Court on the County business. — Took the usual part as Chairman of the Committee of accounts, and spoke on other points — the valuations for the County rate, the maintenance of the Rural police on its present footing &c. —

Witts Family Papers F358

Diary 1846

Oct. 19. Monday.

A foggy morning, a fine day, a wet night.[1] — Early breakfast: — to Cheltenham in the open carriage on my way to Gloucester: – to the Railway Station, thence by rail-road to Gloucester. — To the Bell Hotel: — conferred with the County Chairman — to the Shire Hall: — meeting of the Committee of accounts: — Mess[rs.] Purnell, C Hayward, Baker, Goodrich: auditing accounts. — Meeting of County rate Committee: — Mess[rs.] Purnell, C Hayward, Witts, Kenney, Fulljames: — officials present, Mess[rs.] Bloxsome, Riddiford, Wilton, Whitehead, Lefroy, Keiley, Fulljames. — Dinner at the Bell: Mess[rs.] Purnell, C Hayward, Goodrich, Baker, Witts. — In the evening, till past midnight, auditing accounts, deliberating on public business. — Somewhat indisposed, flatulency and spasm in the back and sides.

Oct. 20. Tuesday.

A fine day, rain at night. — Auditing accounts before breakfast — Wrote to MW. — Breakfasted with Purnell. — To the Shire Hall, where engaged all day in Court on the County business. — Took the usual part as Chairman of the Committee of accounts, and spoke on other points – the valuations for the County rate, the maintenance of the Rural police on its present footing &c. — |[2] Among the leading Magistrates present were the Lord Lieutenant Lord Ducie, Sir W. C. Codrington, Sir M. H. Beech, the Hales, father and son, Archdeacon Timbrill, Mess[rs.] Curtis Hayward, Baker, Lysons, Mirehouse, &c. My son came from Stanway with a very good report of his dear wife and children. — He took up his abode at the Bell – where the Magistrates dined and spent the evening; a pleasant and rather large party.

Oct. 21. Wednesday.

After a rainy night a cold, showery day. — Breakfasted at the Bell – Wrote to MW: —— also to M[r.] W. Court, Inspector of Weights and Measures, Coleford, on county business, as Chairman of the Committee of accounts. — Rec[d.] a letter from Howell, who returns from Town to Prinknash to-morrow, and expects E.F.W. and me to dine and sleep there: — also from MW. with a good report of herself. — To the Shire Hall, where sat all day in the ~~County~~ Crown Count; one parish appeal – several trials for felony, some of interest. Sergeant

---

1. After a change in presentation in F357 whereby Francis Witts started using spaces as assumed paragraph marks, he presumably concluded that he did not like how it looked. Although persevering in the style right up to the end of the diary, he used the opportunity presented by a new blank book to revert to his older methods – that of dashes short and long.

Ludlow presided, by whom I sat, taking a leading part in the business — The Magistrates dined at the Bell, a good party; and agreeable. Serg.ᵗ Ludlow, Mess.ʳˢ Purnell and son, C. Hayward, Hale Sen.ʳ D.ʳ Timbrill &c. &c. — Curtis Hayward presided in the second court.

Oct. 22. Thursday.

A very rainy forenoon, the afternoon and evening fine. — Wrote to M.ʳ Churchill, Plough Hotel, Cheltenham, to desire that a fly might be sent to morrow morning to Prinknash Park to convey E.F.W. and me to Cheltenham on our |³ way homewards. — Breakfasted at the Bell — Shopping — Visited W. Forty in the debtors prison: he has been very unwell, and is still very much indisposed. — To Court, till past twelve o clock, sitting by Serg.ᵗ Ludlow, trying prisoners. — With M.ʳ Hale to the Infirmary — Quarterly meeting: numerously attended M.ʳ Gambier Parry in the Chair: present, among many more, Mess.ʳˢ Purnell, Hyett, Baker, Whitcomb, Hall, Avery, Cols. Cother and Hawkins, Mess.ʳˢ Helps, Clarke, Worthington, Walters &c. — Some favourable to the new system of rules, others opposed to them. – Mess.ʳˢ Murray Browne and Shute so hostile as to withdraw by letter their subscriptions – M.ʳ C. Crawley, the Chaplain, resigns his office, being offended with the stringency of the rule as to his office, requiring daily attendance, and that the Visitors, or Weekly board, shall sanction the substitute whom the Chaplain may name desiring his occasional absence. M.ʳ Hyett proposed a resolution, which was carried, for the raising of fund by donations or subscriptions, to be called the Chaplain's fund in aid to secure to the office, if possible, £60 per ann. in addition to the £60 now paid from the funds of the institution. |⁴ M.ʳ H. is sanguine of success. – The Bishop to have the appointment, as by the rules; M.ʳ C. Crawley to continue his services till the new Chaplain appointed. — Memorials from the Medical officers, who object to the rules as laid down for them as too stringent, and implying distrust, and derogatory. On this point had appeared a letter in the public journals, reflecting on the Committee for preparing the rules, and especially on their Chairman, Purnell, written & signed by D.ʳ Fletcher, in which he improperly made use of certain expressions in a private letter from Purnell, to M.ʳ A. Wood, one of the surgeons; not only quoting them, but quoting them unfairly, and not fully; as to which expressions, as to his own leaning and feelings, and as to the disposition of the Committee to deal in a proper spirit with any remonstrance or suggestion of any of the officers, Purnell spoke temperately, calmly, and in a conciliatory tone. By the rules the memorials of the medical gentlemen were referable to the Supervising Committee, |⁵ and the question was in what form such reference should be made. M.ʳ Avery endeavoured to discuss at length the objections raised by the Chaplain and medical staff; found fault with the course which had been adopted by the Committee for preparing the rules, and the meetings of a general character by which they had been adopted, and ended by proposing as a resolution that the memorials of the Medical officers should be referred to the Supervising Committee, with a recommendation from this meeting that they should relax and alter the rules, so as wholly or in part to meet the views of these officers: others, especially, M.ʳ Sturge, the Quaker Corn Merchant, advocated the cause and complaint of the Medical men. On the other hand it was urged by M.ʳ Whitcombe, M.ʳ Purnell, myself, and others, that the resolution should be a mere reference of the matters in dispute to the Supervising Committee; for that it was inexpedient, and appeared mistrustful, to couple such reference with a re-|⁶commendation, instruction, or dictation, (whichever it might be called,) as if the Committee would treat the affair under prejudiced views; and as ^{if} it were not a governing body, by the constitution of the Society. An amendment, therefore, was made to Mr Avery's resolution, and, on a shew of hands, the amendment was lost, the numbers being eleven to nine, the resolution was then carried — After taking refreshment, about four o'cl. my Son and left Gloucester in a fly for Prinknash Park,[2] where we arrived about half an hour before its master, and we were very cordially and gladly received by Laura and Constance Howell. Emmeline is still in Devon, now on a visit to an old Gibraltar friend at Exeter. William had paid a hurried visit to his sisters yesterday: both he and Emmeline are, not without cause, aliens from the paternal home; yet it cannot be said that the Father is free from blame, though more sinned against than sinning. He had left London |⁷ by a midday train, and came in good spirits, leading in his son Willougby, in his naval uniform, blue jacket, trousers, navy buttons, gold laced cap, and cutlass, as a naval cadet, having passed at Portsmouth, and being appointed by Lord Auckland to the Rattlesnake, surveying ship, which is going out under the command of an eminent and scientific officer, Capt. Stanley, son of the Bishop of Norwich, to survey Torres Straits, the coast of Carpentaria &c.[3] Howell has also the promise of a naval Cadetship from Sir. C. Adam, one of the Lords of the Admiralty, for his next son, Johnny. The evening was passed cheerfully, our host dwelling very fully and openly on many domestic matters, the sale of his property at Prinknash to Mr Ackers, the coming sale of his Upton property, the purchase of a house in Town, &c. but observing a deep silence as to the painful events of last winters, the misconduct of Emmeline, William's eccentricities, and approaching marriage, the affair with the Widow Caldwell &c. My poor friend has an uncommon buoyancy of spirit, a great power |⁸ of putting aside painful reflections, and, alas! Too entire a sympathy with this world and its engagements and pursuits, to the exclusion of the unseen world, and the fitting preparation of futurity. But much of this is the result of circumstances, the force of habit, and the constitutional tendency of the mind. One mourns that there is so much of levity, apparently so little of deep feeling on the eve of surrendering to others his parental property. The step is prudent, no doubt; for the events of last winter and spring have made the residence distasteful; his irritated temper has separated him from old friends and neighbours, without sufficient offence given by them; and a London life will be more congenial to his temperament, and, probably, suit better his views in ~~furthering~~ placing out his sons yet unemployed: but more of seriousness, more of feeling, would have been more becoming. My son, who had been so greatly mixed up with the sad scenes of last spring,[4] and so |⁹ much interested in the position of Laura and Constance, was naturally impressed with deep emotion on this visit to Prinknash. We were both likely to feel acutely this, probably, the last visit we should pay to a place which for many years had been so familiar to us.

2.   Presumably he intended to write 'my Son and I left Gloucester'.

3.   The Torres Strait separates Papua New Guinea from Queensland in Australia, almost 100 miles at its narrowest point, with islands in between. Carpentaria was an old name for this region of Australia, still used in the name for the large 'U' shaped gulf in the north of Queensland, named the Gulf of Carpentaria. The officer in command was Captain Owen Stanley (1811-1850).

4.   The diary recording these events is missing. As this entry states that Edward was 'mixed up with the sad scenes of last spring' it is possible that Edward destroyed the diary that contained unfavourable references to himself following his father's death.

42. Prinknash Park.

Oct 23. Friday.

A fine day. – After breakfast E.F.W. and I left Prinknash in a fly which came from Cheltenham, as ordered. Architects were busy in the Hall, employed by the new purchasers, M.r Ackers, to plan alterations in the Mansion house, and those designed seemed for the most part very judicious, and likely to make the house very handsome and commodious. Cold and sunless in autumn, winter, and spring, it must ever be, from its aspect and situation: but a delightful summer residence, and at all seasons it exhibits all the advantages which ª noble prospect, fine timber, the slope of the hill, verdure, foliage, and undulating ground afford. — We reached Cheltenham by twelve o clock, where we found our respective carriages and Servants |¹⁰ arrived, with letters from home, conveying good news both from Slaughter and Stanway. — As my son and myself were busy shopping, we parted soon, to meet again, and partook of luncheon together before we directed our steps homeward, he to Stanway, and I to Slaughter, about two o clock – In a little more than two hours I reached home, finding MW. pretty well, and being myself, barring a little fatigue, and dyspeptic spasms, in tolerable health. — Several letters awaited my return; – from M.r Sewell, as to the Redmarley estate, that M.r Hall would write to me his opinion as to its value as an investment; and, accordingly, M.r Hall reports the land to be much out of order, but he considers it worth £7000 as an investment. – A letter from Warter on the same subject; and his views are given as to the course to be pursued relatively to the estate, if not sold by public auction. — From M.r Thornton and M.r Geo. Hunt there were letters on Hunt matters: — and a circular from the Secretary of the Gloucester and |¹¹ Berkeley canal Company, with a dividend warrant, entitling MW. to receive 2/6 on each of three shares, late M.rs. Backhouse's, being this year's dividend. — Keppel's Borneo.

Oct. 24. Saturday.

Showery day. — Settling accounts with tradespeople, this being the day of Stow fair. — I drove to Stow, and remained for three or four hours at the Provident Bank, transacting business there: the heavy rain prevented me from going to other places, or transacting other business — Met there Winter, and his wife's nephew, Hastings Woodman, an officer in the King of Bavaria's service. — Home by dinner time — Keppel's Borneo.

Oct. 25 Sunday.

A damp morning; fine afternoon. — Visited the Sunday School — Preparing a Sermon. — Morning service: – prayers — Afternoon Service – prayers and sermon; I preached on circumspection of conduct. – Eccl. Gazette – To the family a section from Trower's Exposition of the Gospels.

Oct 26. Monday.

A foggy morning, a fine after-|[12] noon. — Preparing a Sermon. – Settling Stow fair accounts with tradesmen. – Parish business with the Churchwarden. — Called on J. Davis — Wrote to Rodwell for a supply of books for the Stow book Society. — Keppel's Borneo.

Oct. 27. Tuesday.

A foggy day, but dry and fair. — Justice business at home. — Parish business with the Overseer, on whom I called (E Lea) and for whom I wrote the draft of a letter to be copied by him to Mr Croome, Surveyor, Tewkesbury, requesting him to state the terms on which he would value this parish under the Parochial Assessment Act, and when. — Wrote to Mr Marshall, Snowshill in respect of a poor man, late his servant. — Walked to Bourton on the Water, to hand to Roff the account due for his son's maintenance &c. in the Gloucester Lunatic Asylum; saw his wife and daughter. — Rec^d a letter from Miss Talbot, Guiting, written under an error, requesting my interference in preventing the licencing of a beer house in that parish. Wrote in reply, explaining that Guiting is in Winchcomb division, in which I do not act, and that Beer house |[13] licences are granted by Excise officers, irrespectively of Magistrates — Preparing a sermon — Keppel's Borneo. — Remitted to the Cashiers Bank of England £3. 6. 0 being the amount of Collections made at U Slaughter (£1. 19. 0) & Stanway (£1. 7. 0) in aid of the sufferers by the fire at St Johns, Newfoundland.

Oct. 28 Wednesday.

A very fine autumn day — Justice business at home. — Parish business as to Income Tax &c. also as to work on the Church land estate. — With MW. drove to call on the newly married couple at Upper Swell; M^r & M$^{rs.}$ W. B. Pole: before arriving there met Mr Lambert,[5] and learnt from him that there was great distress at Wyck Hill, poor Mr Rudge being dangerously ill, and great fears entertained. It is a melancholy dispensation; just after the death of his father in extreme old age, and so just come to the enjoyment of a large fortune; himself in middle life, as people are want to say, of those not much beyond fifty years of age, with a numerous young family: a man of blameless character, quiet, sensible,

5.   Lambert Pole.

well informed, gentlemanly. He has been poorly for |[14] sometime past, but serious alarm has not been entertained. We were not received at the Rectory U Swell; W. B. Pole, as we understood was at Wyck Hill. — Shopping at Stow. — Keppel's Borneo. —

Oct. 29. Thursday.

A fine day, but foggy. — Wrote to M[r] Newton, Wotton with an enclosure, a remittance for the amount of the bill for maintenance of M. Roff at the Gloucester Lunatic Asylum — Preparing a Sermon. — Drove to Stow. — Letter from Sewell: the Longbands and Applehurst farm was sold on Tuesday last for £8200 to Fergus O'Connor the Chartist: M[r] Miles of Bristol being his competitor; this was £1000 above the reserved bidding, and £1200 above M[r] Hale's valuation to me. Sewell offers for our consideration as an investment M[r] Hudson's Swell Wold farm: but I am disposed to decline dealing for this, as it must be worth £16000 and above, and in that case we must recall our money, now on a good mortgage of Lady Wilmot Horton's Cheshire property, paying a higher interest than land; and the purchase would |[15] have to be divided between different trusts, viz. our marriage Settlement, and the trust affecting our London property. — A letter from Butts Gloucester, to accompany a sample of Marsala wine. — A circular from M[r] Bloxsome's Office, my nomination of Visiting Mag. of Gloucester Gaol. — To the Provident Bank, where transacted business, and met M[r] Oakely Hill. — To M[r] Morgan's office, where transacted business with him as to Income Tax &c. — To the Workhouse; visited the wards, examined the minutes of the last Board day; conferred with M[r] Pearce and M[r] Wilkins on Poor law matters; met M[r] Perkins there, with whom inspected the house. — To the Justice room, where not much business to be done: M[r] R. Waller was my colleague M[r] Ford from home — the Dean absent — M[r] Pole did not come, owing, no doubt, to the indisposition of poor M[r] Rudge: who is considered a little better to-day. — Miss Vavasour accompanied me home in my carriage, coming to us on a visit for a day or two and to accompany us to-morrow to Stanway, |[16] to be present at the Christening of my infant Grandson. – Will. Vavasour and his wife, the latter to be godmother, went to Stanway to day; the former is reported as better in his health: M[r] and M[rs.] Vavasour are at Clifton on a visit to Lady Arbuthnot.

Oct. 30. Friday.

A beautiful day on the Hills: but foggy in the morning and evening; and fog in the vale, but not damp. — Preparing a Sermon – Letter from M[r] Marshall, Snowshill, in answer to my note to him as to Elias Jones; he declines interfering in his favour. — From the Cashiers of the Bank of England, an acknowledgment of my remittance of the collections made on behalf to the sufferers by the fire at S[t] John's, Newfoundland. — After breakfast, with MW. and Miss Vavasour, went in our close carriage to Stanway, to attend the Christening of my third grandson, who received the name of George Backhouse: the former out of respect to the memory of my departed brother, the latter out of regard to the family of my dear wife, and as her maiden name. The party present were M[rs.] W. Vavasour, Emma |[17] Vavasour, & M[r] Lefroy: my son performed the rite, his excellent wife and the promising children, Broome & Frederick, with my wife and myself, and the attendant nurses, were the rest of the congregation. I stood as proxy for M[r] Charles Barr, as one of the Godfathers, the other, the Rev[d.] M[r] Ashworth, an uncle of my dear Sophy's, being the husband of her mother's sister, was represented by Mr Lefroy. Mr Ashworth had promised to attend in person, but was prevented by business. GOD bless the dear young Christian! William Vavasour remained at the Vicarage, reclining; his unfortunate malady, injury of the spine by a fall from his horse in May last, though somewhat relieved, is still very serious; and he had suffered by the drive from Maugersbury yesterday: however he joined us at the luncheon table, where the loving and cheerful party were increased by the accession of M^r and M$^{rs.}$ W. Whalley from Toddington. Other friends, Billingsley, and Mr Coucher Dent, were expected to dinner. After the departure of the Whalleys, about |^{18} a quarter past four o clock, M$^{rs.}$ W. Emma Vavasour and I drove home to a late dinner, having much enjoyed our visit to Stanway, and talking over all the little events of the day. GOD be thanked for his mercies to me and my wife in blessing us with affectionate children, and lovely grandchildren.

Oct. 31. Saturday.

A fine, but foggy day. — Preparing a Sermon. — Miss Vavasour left us for Maugersbury; we were much pleased with our guest: sensible, lady-like, well principled, and accomplished $^{\&}$ of agreeable manners, she conciliates esteem and regard. — I conveyed her in the phaeton to Stow, whence she went forward in the carriage to Maugersbury, to await the arrival of her sister and William Vavasour from Stanway. — I was engaged with R. Waller, whom I had appointed to meet me in transacting Justice business, in respect of parties whom I had committed for re-examination on a charge of felony: the husband was finally committed to Gloucester Gaol for trial at the |^{19} Epiphany Sessions, on a charge of stealing a pair of boots: the wife committed under a suspicion of swindling some tradesmen at Oxford, was discharged, the prosecutors not appearing against her, on the plea that they feared the property obtained under the false pretences could not be identified. — MW. received a letter from Canada, written by Miss Langton, communicating the intelligence of the death of poor Alice Currer, about six weeks after the decease of her sister, M$^{rs.}$ Langton. She was carried off by an epidemic fever which has been prevalent in the district of Upper Canada, where the Langtons are located. Miss L. had suffered from the same fever, but had recovered, and wrote from Peterborough, a town some forty miles from their settlement at Blyth, which was free from fever, and to which, with her brother and his wife, as we suppose, she had gone. A.C. was far advanced in years; a woman of considerable talent and information, of warm attachment to relations and early friends, my wife's first cousin once removed; she had visited us here, |^{20} and we had been much in her society in Yorkshire, but many years had passed since we have met: and her removal with M^r and M$^{rs.}$ Langton, and their son and daughter, into Canada, some years since, precluded any probable chance of our meeting again in this world. My wife felt the loss of an old friend and connection; but at her advanced age, and with a delicate constitution it did not take us by surprise. — Keppel's Borneo.

Nov. 1. Sunday.

All Saints' day. — Fine weather. — Visited the S. School. — Wrote to Mr Lefroy, respecting J. Lait, who solicited me yesterday to procure for him a situation in the Constabulary force. — Morning service, and sermon. I preached on the use of Saints days. — Evening prayers. — A circular from Gloucester, signed by Mr Hedley, announcing a meeting of the diocesan board of education to be held at the Palace, Gloucester at which the Bishop will attend on the 4[th.] Inst. — Preparing a Sermon. — Eccl. Gazette — To the family a section from Trowers exposition of the Gospels. |[21]

Monday Nov. 2.

Fine Weather — Wrote to E.F.W. with a cheque for £5. 17. 6 for the price of a poney bought at Stow fair, which I promised to give to my eldest grandson: — to Sewell and Newmarch, declining to purchase the Swell Wold farm; —— to H D Warter, enclosing the last letter from S. & N. with particulars as to the sale of the Redmarley farm to Fergus O'Connor, that I had declined treating for the Swell Wold farm, and that he and M[r] Jennings might now look out for an investment in ground rents or houses in or near London. — M[r] Pearce called; with whom a long conference as to Union matters. — M[r] Barrow called: notified his intention of quitting his curacy, and visiting Germany to try the so-called Water-cure. — With MW. walked to Eyford to call on M[rs.] Dolphin, who was not at home: M[r] and M[rs.] Frobisher are visiting there — Visited the weekly school. — Suffering from cold in my head, with cough and diarrhoea. — Keppel's Borneo.

Nov. 3. Tuesday.

A damp and somewhat rainy day — Did not leave the house, being oppressed by |[22] a cold and cough. — Wrote to M[r] Jennings as to the Redmarley estate being sold, and requesting him to look out for an eligible investment in ground rents or houses in or near London. —— Much engrossed with parish and Justice business — M[r] Lea called with a letter from M[r] Croome, Land Surveyor, of Tewkesbury, as to the terms on which he would undertake the valuation of this parish. Assisted M[r] L. in writing a reply to this letter. — A letter from M[r] Waller, Farmington, brought by his keeper, with an information against a trespasser in pursuit of game. H.W. desires information as to the valuations insisted upon by the County Rate Committee. This imposed on me the trouble of answering his letter at considerable length. —– Other justice business. — A letter from C. J. Geldard enclosing a receipt prepared by him for the signature of MW. and myself, which purports that we have sold for £18. To M[r] Foster of Clapham, certain sheepgates to which we |[23] are entitled in a common in the parish of Avoncliff in right of our Sherwood House and Helwith Bridge estate. The owners of sheepgates &c. on this common have agreed to inclose the common into allotments proportioned to their rights; but our right is so small that to enclose the very small portion of land which would come to our lot would cost more than value of the allotment. We had, therefore, agreed to sell to M[r] F. for such price as should be settled by M[r] Geldard our title to an allotment, so that the portion coming to us might be included by him in one piece with his allotment, and be enclosed by one mound.[6] This receipt is so worded as to preclude the necessity of a more formal conveyance. — Preparing a Sermon. — Keppel's Borneo.

Nov. 4. Wednesday.

A moist and showery day. — Wrote to the Editors of the Gloucestershire Chronicle that my paper had not reached me on Sunday last, nor by any later post, desiring another to be sent, and the paper in future to be properly forwarded. — Wrote |[24] to C. J. Geldard returning

---

6.   Mound – in this particular sense, a fence or a hedge.

the receipt for the sheepgates sold to Mr Foster signed by MW and myself. — Much engaged in preparing drafts of letters to the P. L. Comm$^{rs.}$ to be sanctioned by the Guardians of our Union tomorrow, and to be written by the Clerk — on the County rate valuations, and on the right construction of the late act concerning removal of the poor. — Rec$^d.$ a letter from Mr Lefroy, intimating that he does not consider James Lait eligible to be a Constable – from Sewell that as the purchase must be made under two distinct trusts, he considers Swell Wold would not be a suitable investment. — A letter from Rebecca Backhouse inclosing £7. 10. 0 in two post office orders, as our share of the last remittance from Virginia on account of the claims of the Backhouse family, but the letter does not state whether the orders are drawn in favour of me or my wife, consequently we do not know which of us is to sign and |^{25} present them; therefore we must trouble Miss B. with further enquiry on the subject — Still harassed with cough, cold in the head, and wheezing. — Parish business. — Keppel's Borneo. —

Nov. 5. Thursday.

A moist day, some slight rain, but generally fine. — Wrote to Miss Backhouse for information to which of us, MW. or me, the Post office orders, which came yesterday, were made payable. — – Preparing a Sermon. — To Stow, in the phaeton, accompanied by MW. — who went afterwards to call on M$^{rs.}$ W. Vavasour, and her sister at Maugersbury, before she returned home. — Letters from Mr Warter, acknowledging my last communication to him — from Mr Horne, Moreton in Marsh, as to a person ~~residing~~ in his service having a claim on the Gloucester Prison Charity — from the Clerk of the Gloucester Union, covering an acknowledgment for the money forwarded by me in payment of the maintenance and sustentation &c. of Moses |^{26} Roff in the Gloucester Lunatic Asylum — also a notification that W. Forty has filed his petition as an Insolvent Debtor, addressed to me as one of his Creditors. — Transacted business at the Provident Bank: — at the Office of the Gloucestershire Banking Company, and at Mr Morgan's office. — To the Workhouse: presided at the fortnightly meeting of the Board of Guardians: fully attended — Mess$^{rs.}$ Hippisley, Hurd, Perkins &c. – Much business to be transacted, especially as regards the new law as to removal of paupers, and the County rate Committee's demand of new valuations: the letters which I had prepared to be forwarded by the Clerk to the P.L.C. were adopted by the board. — To the Justice room, where Mr Pole and Mr R. Waller sat with me as Magistrates: present Mess$^{rs.}$ Winter, Capt. Leigh, C Lindow, H. Ford, Polhill — detained late; two game cases &c. — A more favourable report of the health of Mr Rudge and M$^{rs.}$ Lindow: — I am still oppressed |^{27} by a cough and cold but not to severely as I was. — Keppel's Borneo. –

Nov. 6. Friday.

Foggy in the morning and afternoon, the midday fine. — Wrote to Mr Horne, Moreton in Marsh, as to the man claiming a reward from the Prison Charity fund at Gloucester — to Mr Rodwell ordering books for the Stow Book Society. — Superintending work in the Village on the Church Trust land – Studying Lumley's Commentary on the new law as to pauper removals. — Preparing a Sermon — Visited John Davis — Visited the weekly school. — Keppel's Borneo.

Nov. 7. Saturday.

Foggy weather, and raw; but not damp — Wrote to Mr Thornton on Hunt Trust affairs. — Preparing a Sermon — Unpacking parcel of reports and quarterly papers for the members

Stow distr. Comm S.P.G. — Received a letter from Miss Backhouse, that the Post Office orders which she sent were made payable to me. —A letter from E.F.W. – very pleasant accounts of all dear to us at Stanway. — Keppel's |²⁸ Borneo.

Nov. 8. Sunday.

Foggy weather; damp in the forenoon, dry in the afternoon —Visited the Sunday School. — Wrote to the Postmaster, Moreton in Marsh, forwarding the Post office orders made payable to me by Miss Backhouse, with my signature desiring the amount to be sent to me. — Morning prayers; evening prayers and sermon. I preached on the resurrection. — Preparing a sermon — Eccl. Gazette — British Magazine — To the family a section from Trower's exposition of the gospels.

Nov. 9. Monday.

A cold, dry, less foggy day. — Settled for rent and Sunday School stipend with M. Forty — Justice business at home. — Wrote to E.F.W. with a remittance for £30. — Also to Miss Moorhouse, with a remittance for £5. — A letter from Mᵣ Vavasour requesting me to do duty at the Workhouse on Friday next: he and Mʳˢ· V. continue at Clifton on a visit to Lady Arbuthnot: — With MW. drove to call at Guiting Grange: saw Mʳˢ· and Miss Wynniatt. — |²⁴ The Postmaster at Moreton sent me the amount of the Post office order obtained by Miss Backhouse. — Keppel's Borneo. Mᵣ R. Waller called, when we were out. —

Nov. 10. Tuesday.

Very fine weather. — Wrote to Mᵣ Vavasour that I would perform the duty at the Stow Workhouse on Friday next. — Justice business at home. — Preparing a Sermon — Preparing the reports and quarterly papers S.P.G. for circulation to the members of this District Committee. — Recᵈ· a circular from the Lunatic Asylum, Gloucester, announcing a meeting of visitors for the 18ᵗʰ· Inst. — Mᵣ and Mʳˢ· W. B. Pole called, while we were taking a walk. — Visited Mᵣ E Lea, who is suffering from rheumatism on Parish business. — Keppel's Borneo — Mʳˢ· Abell's (late Miss L.E. Balcombe's) recollections of Napoleon at Sᵗ· Helena. — Amusing and interesting.

Nov. 11. Wednesday.

Very fine day. — Wrote to Mᵣ Pantin, thanking him for the loan of a volume of Stillingfleet's works, which I am about to return, and adverting to the subject |²⁵ discussed at our last decanal meeting — the introduction of Christianity into Britain, and the independence of the British and Saxon Churches, for centuries, and until supremacy was gradually extorted by Rome. — Preparing the Reports &c. S.P.G. for circulation among the members of the Stow Distr. Comm. — Justice business at home. — Visited Mᵣ E. Lea, an invalid, and conferred with him on Parish business — Letters from Purnell and Curtis Hayward, both strongly pressing for my attendance on the 18ᵗʰ· Inst. at a meeting of the Visitors of the Lunatic Asylum, Gloucester, on matters of material importance; the latter inviting me to his house at Quedgley. — Mʳˢ· Abell's recollections of Sᵗ· Helena.

Thursday Nov. 12.

Fine weather: the air towards evening somewhat moist. — Wrote to Purnell, that I propose to attend the Lunatic Asylum meeting at Gloucester on the 18[th.] — To Curtis Hayward to the same effect: and that I will dine & sleep at Quedgley on that day. — To Mitchell of Cutsdean, measurer and mapper, to desire him |[26] to call here on one of the three days named, to measure and map this parish previous to valuation — Drove to Stow: MW. accompanied me, and returned shortly. — Received a letter from M[r] Thornton on Hunt matters, with an inclosure, a letter from him to M[r] Hare, to be perused and forwarded by me, if approved. — Transacted business at the Provident Bank: — at M[r] Morgan's office — at the Workhouse. At the latter conferred with M[r] Pearce on union matters, met Perkins, and with him inspected the house. A pauper of bad character, whom I had committed lately to Northleach Bridewell for misbehaviour in the Workhouse, now returned, and either really ill, or feigning to be so, brought forward several charges against M[r] Pearce and the Matron on improper dealing with the Stores of the House, and other irregularities in the management. Though emanating from a bad and vindictive spirit, such allegations must be sifted, and I proposed to take down in writing the man's statement to-morrow. — Joined the Magistrates afterwards at the Unicorn — Mess[rs.] |[27] Ford, Pole, Dean of Gloucester, sat with me — Mess[rs.] W. Vavasour, Winter, W B Pole, Lewes, Barrow, H. Ford, Wilkins were also present — M[rs.] Abell's recollections of Napoleon. —

Nov. 13. Friday.

Fine weather — Drove to Stow, after breakfast, accompanied by MW. who soon returned home. — Preformed divine service at the Workhouse to the paupers of the establishment, a congregation of about seventy, attentive, clean, orderly. The children, led by the Schoolmaster, sang the morning hymn: Governor and Porter and Nurse present. — Conferred with M[r] M[c]Greal, the Ass[t.] Med. Off. — Took down in writing the complaint of John Wilkins, the pauper who is endeavouring to ruin M[r] and Miss. Pearce by charging them with malversation and irregularities in the management of the establishment. If is clear that he is a bad, malignant fellow, full of deceit, and, as the M.O. believes and asserts, pretending illness. The charges are of no great weight. I left them with M[r] Pearce to prepare his answers to them: the matter to be brought |[28] before the Guardians on the next Board day. A letter has been received from the P.L.C. in answer to one dictated by me, and sent by the Clerk, shewing the sense in which, on the authority of the Attorney and Solicitor General, the recent act as to the removals of the Poor is to be interpreted, the construction being the same as suggested by me. — Paying tradesmens bills — Conferred with M[r] Pain as to arrangements respecting the Library, printing new catalogues &c. — Met and parlayed with M[r] Pole, and M[r] Twisleston. — Walked home by Lower Swell, where saw M[r] Perkins, who accompanied me part of my way home. — Recollections of Napoleon. — Preached to my poor hearers on the general resurrection.

Nov. 14. Saturday.

Fine Weather. — Engaged with M[r] Lea, Overseer, in giving directions to W. Mitchell as to measuring and mapping this parish, preparatory to a Valuation for the County rate, and under the Parochial Assessm[t.] Act: agreeing upon terms &c. — Superintending work at the Church and Chancel. — |[29] Wrote to M[r] Hare, on Hunt Trust business, forwarding M[r] Thornton's letter to him, sent for my approval and to be posted to M[r] H. — Justice business at home — Rec[d.] a pleasant letter from E.F.W. with a very good account of himself and his belongings:

they purpose being with us on Monday next. — Sir R. H. Bonnycastle (L^t· Col. Engineers) Newfoundland in 1842 — Walked to Joiners downs to inspect some work done there, a new floodgate on a new construction, for irrigating our watermeadows. — Rec^d· a packet from Mr Pearce: with his answers to the charges made yesterday by John Wilkins, a note from himself on that subject: and a copy of the P.L.C.'s letter on the Poor Removal Act.

Nov. 15. Sunday.

A dry, cold, foggy day. — Visited the Sunday School. — Morning prayers, and sermon: I preached on family religion; family prayer &c. – Evening prayers. — A letter from Messrs· Hoare, announcing that Mr Jennings had paid to my account with them £69. 14. — One of my horses being ill, sent for J. Pegler, the Veterinary Surgeon, |^30 who pronounced the disease, inflammation of the lungs, and treated it accordingly. J.P. sat with me sometime in the evening. — Eccl. Gazette — Preparing a Sermon — To the family a section from Trower's Exposition of the gospels. ——

Nov. 16. Monday.

Cold, dry, dull weather — Transacting business with the Parish Church warden. — J Pegler came to visit the sick horse, and with him I went in his gig to Stow: the poor horse very ill, but improved in his state as the day advanced. — Justice business at home. — At Stow met R Waller, and sat with him as Commissioner hearing appeals against assessments to the Property tax. — Visited the Workhouse, Mr Pearce was gone to Cheltenham; conferred with the Matron. — Walked home. — Visited the daily School. — Mr Ford had called during my absence. — Our dear children and grand children arrived from Stanway: a happy reunion de famille.

Nov. 17. Tuesday.

A rainy day. — The sick horse believed to be worse, and fears entertained |^31 that it would not recover — Justice business at home, and preparing for public business to-morrow and Thursday. — An unpleasant conversation with our man servant, Baldwin, who seems inclined to be master; or to quit his service. — Enjoying the society of our dear children & grand children. —

Wednesday Nov. 18.

A foggy morning, showery day afterwards — Rose and breakfasted early: a better opinion given as the to the sick horse. — Left home in the phaeton for Gloucester, borrowing one of my Son's horses to run with my second horse. Reached Andoversford Inn by nine o clock, where a fly met me which I had desired might be sent from the Plough at Cheltenham, and which conveyed me to the Cheltenham rail road station by ten o clock, in time to leave by a train coming in from Birmingham — Met and conversed with Mr Viner, who, like myself, was on the way to attend the meeting of Visitors at the Lunatic Asylum. Dr Timbrill also |^32 came for the same purpose by the train from Ashchurch, with whom I proceeded in the same carriage; and accompanied him in a fly to the Lunatic Asylum. There were assembled a numerous body of visitors; of those representing the County of Gloucester there were present Messrs· Curtis Hayward, in the chair, Purnell, Baker, Clifford, Timbrill, Viner, Baker, Sayers, Walters, ^J· ^Niblett & myself; Mr Hyett represented the Subscribers; neither of the Visitors appointed by the City of Gloucester attended. A long discussion took place as to arrangements for the future occupation of the Asylum, as between the Counties on the one hand, and the Subscribers on the other; it had been understood that the settlement come to in August last was nearly final; but, points being left open to the Sub committee, a new and amended proposal was suggested by them, which was this day generally approved, and agreed to be acted upon so far as that Counsel's opinion should be take upon it, and the plan matured under the ~~opinion and~~ advice of Counsel be |33 submitted for approbation to the Secretary of State, as required by the Lunatic Asylum Act. The meeting broke up before three o clock; but Messrs. Hayward, Purnell, Dr Timbrill and myself remained in consultation with Mr R. Wilton, the solicitor to the Asylum, when it appeared that the whole matter was surrounded with legal difficulties, and would probably break down as many other suggestions for a satisfactory arrangement between the Counties and subscribers had already done. The Archdeacon of Gloucester left earlier than Messrs. Hayward, Purnell and myself: the former walked with me to Gloucester, and we rejoined the latter, who had preceded us in a fly, ~~to~~ at the Bell Hotel, where Curtis Hayward's carriage was ready to take us to dine and sleep at Quedgley. We were kindly received by the pleasing Mrs. Hayward, and in due time the party was increased by the arrival of Mr Lysons, with two ladies, from his house at Hempstead, connections of his, a mother and daughter, whose names I did |34 not catch, and a Mr Le Marchant, Curate of Hardwick. A Miss Nisbet, a niece of CH's was also one of the party staying in the house. We passed a pleasant evening, with music, and looking at portfolios, especially those brought by Lysons containing a valuable collection of engravings of antiquities, especially of tesselated pavements, both from Italy, Spain, & France, & from England. These had been acquired by his Uncle and Father, the celebrated Antiquarians, and were now produced in consequence of Purnell's having lately discovered the remains of a Roman Villa on his property at Stancombe. Interesting books of engravings as to the revival of the arts in Italy were also shewn by Curtis Hayward. He & I, on our walk into Gloucester from the Lunatic asylum, had looked into a Chapel attached to some Almshouses on the London road, between Northgate Street and Wootton, which has lately been refitted internally, principally at the expence of Mr J. A. Whitcomb, after an approved plan conformable to the views of the |35 Ultra High Church party – with painted windows in the Chancel, glazed tiles below the Communion table, the table decorated with emblematical cloth and fringe of divers colours appropriate to divers seasons, the chalice candlesticks, and brass clasped books upon it, no reading pew, but a lectern, the minister to perform the prayers, in front of the Altar, in a state nearly approaching to prostration at one time, and, at another, kneeling before & at the table, in both cases with his back to the congregation, seated on benches, or keeling, or standing, in the nave. Daily morning and evening service is performed here by the incumbent, a Mr Norman, once Curate of St Mary de Crypt church: a weekly Sacrament in also administered, and a miscellaneous congregation from different parts of Gloucester and its suburbs are collected. We found a gentleman, I believe, a retired officer of the Navy, busy in directing the suspending of certain hangings in this chapel: he is, I apprehend, a lay enthusiast, and would be, with the other members of this congregation, popularly termed a Puseyite. |36

Nov. 19. Thursday.

A very fine day. — Early breakfast at Quedgley; after which Purnell and I took leave of our friendly host and hostess, proceeding in his open carriage to the Gloucester Railway

Station — My train, to Cheltenham, left the platform at a quarter past ten AM. — being a train to Birmingham, and that by which P. was to travel to the Dursley Station set out a quarter of an hour later:[7] leaving him at the Station, a quarter of an hour brought me to that at Cheltenham, where, as I had appointed, a fly from the Plough was waiting for me, in which I set out for Andoversford, at wʰ· place I found my servant and carriage awaiting my arrival, with a satisfactory note from my wife, and a better report of my sick horse. Much business being in store for me at Stow, I did not deviate to Upper Slaughter, but pursued the straight course to the former place, where I arrived before 2 P.M. — and at the library had an interview with Mᵣ Ford on two or three points of business. — Thence proceeded to the Workhouse, where a large Board of Guardians was assembled, and business already |³⁷ begun, certain important points being postponed till my expected arrival. On these I directly entered, and obtained the concurrence of the Guardians in a resolution to act upon the new Poor Law Removal Act in conformity with the construction put upon it by the Attorney & Solicitor General, and promulgated by the Poor Law Commᵣˢ· — Explained to the Guardians the proposed arrangement, whereby half the cost of medical attendance on the Poor, half the cost of the Education of poor children in Workhouses, and the whole cost of the audit of accounts of Unions, is henceforth to be borne by the Government, and paid out of the Consolidated fund. — Entered on & went through with the charges preferred against the Governor and Matron by the pauper John Wilkins, with the defence and answers of Mᵣ Pearce, a statement prepared by me as to what had occurred in this matter under my own knowledge, together with a report by the Assᵗ· Med. Officer, and other documents. The accuser and Mᵣ Pearce were confronted: the only witness called was the nurse, Sister |³⁸ of J.W., and whose testimony wholly discredited him: the Guardians came to an unanimous resolution that the charges were frivolous and vexatious, and that there was no occasion to carry the investigation further. — The malignant temper of the accuser was abundantly manifest, his falsehood, ingratitude, deception, and character most apparent. A second resolution was passed, expressive of confidence in and approval of the conduct and management of the Govᵣ. and Matron. — Among others were present, Messᵣˢ· Hippisley, Perkins, Wiggin, & E.F.W. — Thence attended the Justice meeting, where Messᵣˢ· Ford & R Waller sat with me on the bench, Messᵣˢ· Winter, Perkins, E.F.W. &c. being our assessors. The principal matter was a very intricate case of felony charged against a man who had gone off with the wife, money and goods of a labourer at Lower Swell; he had been traced into the neighbourhood of Birmingham, and there apprehended: but the woman remains at large; and the course of the enquiry with a view to the |³⁹ conviction of the prisoner as a felon, and wʰ· is nearly, if not quite, complete, is to prove the man and woman guilty ad of adultory, after a delivery of the goods from the woman to the prisoner. The pris. was remanded till Thursday the 26ᵗʰ· — Home to a late dinner. — A letter from C. J. Geldard covering copies of mergers of the tithes of our property in Horton in Ribblesdale and Kirkby Malghamdale.

---

7.   This station on the Gloucester – Bristol main line was closed to passengers in 1963. From 1856 until 1963 its name had been changed to Berkeley Road. The station now named Dursley and Cam, was built in 1856 and from then until 1968 named Coaley Junction, for in 1856 a branch line was built to the town of Dursley, and a new Dursley Station was to become the terminus.

Nov. 20. Friday.

A rainy, or showery, and very stormy day. — Justice business at home — Mᵣ Pearce called, with whom engaged in preparing minutes and resolutions of the proceedings of the meeting of Guardians held yesterday, especially as regarded the line to be taken touching the Poor Removal Act, and the charge brought by J. Wilkins against Mᵣ P., with the exculpation of the latter. — Took a walk with Sophy and Broome — ^{A letter from Revd. C. B. Trye on} Union business. ——

Nov. 21. Saturday.

Finer weather than yesterday. — Wrote to C. J. Geldard in answer to the letter received from him with the mergers |⁴⁰ of tithe — to Mᵣ Alder, Stationer &c. Cheltenham, to order paper to be mounted for the map to be made by Mitchell of this parish. — To Mᵣ Morgan, Stow, returning to him with my comments thereon, a letter addressed ~~by him~~ to him on Tax business by Mᵣ Longhurst, the Surveyor of Taxes, who, as it appeared to me & other Commissioners, had taken a liberty in seeming to dictate to us. — Mʳˢ· W. Vavasour and her sister Emma came to take luncheon with us. — Mʳˢ· R Waller, and two of her boys also called — I walked with dear Broome to the Turnpike Gate for our post, and received a letter from Mᵣ Thornton one being enclosed from Mᵣ Hare to Mᵣ T. & the latter sending me a copy of his answer to Mᵣ H. for my perusal. Mᵣ Hare refuses to concur with Mᵣ T & myself in the appointment of another Solicitor to the Hunt Trust in the room of Mᵣ Cox, so putting himself in opposition to us. As Mᵣ T. points out, no other course appears to be left to us than to nominate a Solicitor, without consulting |⁴¹ whom we shall declin~~ing~~ᵉ acting in any special matter requiring legal advice. ^{Answered the letter recd. from C. B. Trye.}

Nov. 22. Sunday.

A very rainy forenoon, and showery day. — E.F.W. rode to Stanway after an early breakfast, and performed the duties of his parish, returning to a late dinner — Visited the Sunday School. — Morning, prayers: afternoon, prayers and Sermon. I preached on anger. — Preparing a Sermon. —

Nov 23. Monday.

Justice business. — Preparing a Sermon. — Walked with my dear Sophy and Broome. — Damp weather. ——

Nov. 24. Tuesday.

Showery morning; fine afternoon. — Justice business at home. — Mᵣ Clarke called, and partook of luncheon with us. — Walked with MW. and Broome. — E.F.W. and Sophy rode out, as they had done on Saturday. — My sick horse convalescent. – Recᵈ· a letter from Mᵣ Sewell, as to the valuation of the parish of Bourton on the hill to the County rate. — Wrote to Mᵣ Thornton, returning to him the enclosure forwarded by him in his letter recᵈ· by me on Saturday, and concurring with him in his view as to our |⁴² present position in respect of the Hunt Trust. Omitted to mention a letter which I wrote to Walker of Northleach, Corn merchant, for a supply of oats.

Wednesday Nov. 25.

A wet day. — Preparing a sermon — Justice business at home. — Wrote to Mᵣ Sewell in answer to his letter rec^d. yesterday. — A dinner party: M^r and M^rs. R. Waller, M^r J Wynniatt with his sisters, Susan and Anne, Mr J. T. Rice, Mr H. Ford were our guests. — We had expected Mr Wiggin, who is indisposed.

Nov. 26. Thursday.

Fine weather — Drove to Stow in my open carriage drawn by one horse, the sick horse, though convalescent, not considered fit for work. Sophy drove me to the Lower Slaughter Turnpike gate, Edward behind: from thence they walked home. — A note from Alder, Cheltenham, as to mounting paper for parish map. — Attended at the Provident Bank — to the Workhouse, conferred with Pearce on Union matters. To the Justice room: much business; principally, the completion of the matter postponed last |^43 Thursday, the prisoner, John Williams, committed for trial at the Epiphany Q.S. evidence in great measure circumstantial, but strong. — Present, Magistrates, Messrs. Pole, Ford, R. Waller, and myself: by standers, Winter, Hippisley, Perkins, W B Pole &c. — M^r and M^rs. F. Biscoe and Miss Middleton had called during my absence — E.F.W. and Sophy had ridden to call on the Fords at Little Risington — The elder Vavasours are returned to the Cottage from Clifton.

Nov. 27. Friday.

A fine morning and forenoon — the afternoon rainy or foggy. — E.F.W. went to attend a Justice meeting at Winchcomb, and returned to dinner. — Mr Ford called, and partook of luncheon with us: with him went to the Church, to point out how M^rs. Dolphin may be accommodated with a stove in her pew, and her pew enlarged, if she wishes to provide and maintain a ^stove pew at her own expence. He proceeded to Eyford to lay the matter before her. She represented to F., on the authority of her medical visitor, Mr Bainbrigge, the dangerous dampness of |^44 the church, and that she was prevented attending divine service from fear of injury to her health. Alas! in fine summer weather she seldom comes, and perpetually makes excuses. The Church is less damp than most village churches, with far better pews than most can boast; more airy, more air-tight, and with more light. She wished a stove to be put into the church, and tended and provided with fuel by some subscription, offering £10. towards the first cost, and a moderate contribution towards the fuel & attendance. But it is hopeless to expect anything from the farmers, or from a church rate, and the Church and Charity Trust cannot be made to meet the cost: besides, with an habitual shortness of breath and tendency to cough, any stove would be most irksome to me: I cannot promote one, but will not oppose one. If, therefore, the lady insists upon one, let her provide it at her own expence in her own pew, to be lighted when she chooses. It is the only place in the Church, where it can be placed with safety. |^45 Received a letter from Howell: he has purchased a house in Kensington garden terrace; to which he talks of removing from Prinknash Park ~~from~~ about Christmas: proposing to us to receive Laura and Constance in transitu from Gloucestershire to London, to go thither when the new house is ready to receive them.

A letter from Mr Francis, late Curate of Great Risington, and who for a few weeks took the duty here and at Stanway, during our absences at Dover and Scarborough, to inform us of his preferment to the living of Shottisham near Woodbridge, Suffolk.

Nov. 28. Saturday.

Fine weather. — Our dear children left us for Maugersbury House on a visit to the W. Vavasours, to remain till Wednesday next, and on the Tuesday to join the assembled neighbourhood at Stow Ball, revived under the stewardship of the Hon. Henry Leigh, eldest son of the Lord Leigh, now and for some time past resident at their seat at Adlestrop, which has been an engrossing topice with the young and gay. — A circular letter from the Clerk of Gloucester and |[46] Berkeley canal, as to raising money by shares for extending dock accommodation on the side of the canal. — Quarterly review for October.

Nov. 29. Sunday.

Beginning of Advent — A very hard frost, and cold day. — Visited the Sunday School — Morning Prayers and sermon: I preached on the love of GOD in the incarnation of Christ. Evening Prayers. — A letter from Walker, Northleach, with an invoice of five quarters of oats with which he has supplied me: — also from Mr Clerke, Rector of Eydon, Northamptonshire, about a pauper resident in that village, whose settlement is at Great Barrington, addressed to me as Chairman of Stow Union — Preparing a Sermon — To the family a section from Trower's exposition of the gospels — Eccl. Gazette. —

Nov. 30. Monday.

Hard frost, cold and dry weather. — Wrote to Mr Francis, congratulating him on the preferment he has obtained — To Mr Clerke, Eydon, in answer to his letter received yesterday. — Preparing a Sermon, — Justice business at home. — Walked |[47] with my dear Broome. On our return we found his parents with M^r and M$^{rs.}$ W. Vavasour had driven from Maugersbury; they only made a short stay with us. A good report of the infant. — Called on J. Davis — Quarterly review for October.

Dec. 1. Tuesday.

A hoar frost and rime, in the afternoon a tendency to thaw. — Justice business at home. — A walk with dear Broome ——— A circular announcing annual Provident Bank meeting for the 9$^{th.}$ Inst. — A letter from Mr Sewell acknowledging my last to him as to valuation to the County rate. — Stow Ball — Quarterly Review. —

Dec. 2. Wednesday.

Frost suspended; fine day. — Preparing a Sermon — Wrote to Mr Cockey. — Walked with Broome to Lower Slaughter Turnpike & back; met Mr Clarke, who had called on me; with whom conferred as to the case of a pauper resident at Icomb. — As I returned met Mr Haughton, the Curate of Oddington, who had called and who returned with me. A strange, vain, diffuse, talking, florid Irishman, violently |[48] Anti papist, eccentric in manner. His object being to urge me to adopt his views, which he represents as supported by the Dean of Gloucester, Mr Ford, Mr Hippisley and others, as to obtaining from the Guardians of our Union a vote of extraordinary remuneration for one year to Mr Moore, the Med. Off. of Great Risington district, in consideration of his good services & extraordinary expence in attending on the poor of Great Risington, during a late period of epidemic typhoid fever there: also a subscription in favour of Dunford, the Rel. Off. was advocated by him. — Our dear children & the infant returned from Maugersbury to the delight of the elder boys, and our great comfort — M^r & M^rs. W. Vavasour & Emma V. conveyed them back. Much amusing detail of last night's Stow Ball.

Dec. 3. Thursday.

A good deal of snow had fallen during the night, the day fine, frost hard, and roads very slippery. — After an early breakfast, I drove in the phaeton, with some difficulty, the horses shoes not being rough, |^49 to the foot of Stow hill, whence I walked to Stow, fearing an accident, if I attempted to ascend the hill, and sending back the carriage with directions that the horses shoes should be turned up. To the Workhouse to a meeting of the Guardians, at which I presided, called at an unusually early hour, to allow time for revising the pauper lists, and accommodating them to the new state of things under the late Poor Removal Act; in this we proceeded, referring certain points to the Poor Law Commissioners on which doubt arose. — A full meeting attended by the Dean of Gloucester, Mr Hurd, Mr Hippisley, Mr Ford, Mr Perkins; of whom the Dean and Mr Ford urged on the Guardians the propriety of presenting Mr Moore with a gratuity in acknowledgment of his extraordinary and valuable Services, as Med. Off. Of the 3^d. District, in respect of a fever lately prevailing and not yet subdued at Great Risington. The feeling was kind |^50 and, probably, the merits of the officer great; but the proposers were, by their systematic neglect of the business of the Union, and ignorance of the details of Poor Law Administration, and the existing law, unacquainted with the principles and practice which govern the remuneration to Medical Officers, and ill informed as to facts, supposing Mr Moore's emoluments to be much lower than they actually are. Hence I had the disagreeable office of explaining to them, and the board generally that the proposition was at variance with the regulations, unjust and uncalled for. The exposition w^h. I gave of the law and practice, of the manner in which funds were procured for payment of the Medical Off. Salaries, of the real amount of their annual receipts &c. at once put a close to the project: which the Dean very handsomely gave up: and the end will be a private compliment made to the Officer by the parties interested, the proprietors and occupiers of Great Risington. |^51 At three o clock, I went to the Justice room, where Ford was my colleague, Whitmore Jones, Winter, and E.F.W. who had walked to Stow, were assessors. There awaited me a good deal of business, and some which called for caution and tact. — E.F.W. returned home with me to a late dinner. Fatigued, but enjoying the society of my dear children and grandchildren.

Dec. 4. Friday.

Hard frost, cold and fine weather. — Wrote to Mr Brookes on a matter of justice business, and received an answer from his Clerk, with documents for my signature. Afterwards Mr Brookes called, with whom conferred on Justice business — Wrote to the Dean of Gloucester, ~~that~~ explaining to him — what, I understood from Mr Haughton, had been misrepresented to him, my views as to assistance to be given to the Rel. Off. Dunford, who is in pecuniary embarassment: but as to whom I deprecated an appeal to the charity of the neighbourhood, by way of petition or memorial. — E.F.W. |^52 and Sophy with Broome went in the forenoon to Bourton to be present at the christening of R. Waller's youngest son, they being Godfather and Godmother: the name Raymond Edward. — Mr Wollaston the other Sponsor. They returned after partaking of luncheon at Bourton Rectory. I met and enjoyed a walk with them and dear Broome. Afterwards we all (the Seniors) went to dine with the Wallers at Bourton; meeting Harry Waller, two Misses Larkin, Captain Pettatt, Mr Wollaston, M^r and M^rs. Winter. A pleasant party – Home late. — In the forenoon I was engaged with Mr Pearce in Poor Law matters, preparing a letter on the operation of the Poor Removal Act to be ~~submitted~~ addressed to the Poor Law Comm^rs. — requesting further instruction &c. — Mr Hastings Woodman was also a guest at the Wallers, brought by his relations, the Winters. —

Dec. 5. Saturday.

Frost, milder weather, and fine. — Justice business at home. — Our dear children and grandchildren returned to Stanway, |^53 leaving us very lonely, but grateful for so much enjoyment of their society. — Wrote to Messrs. Hoare, to pay £35 from my account to that of E.F.W. and to send me the continuation of my account: — to Davison, Newman & Co. with a remittance for groceries supplied, and an order for more. — A letter from Bathurst; the first received from him since his return from a three months tour on the Continent: — a circular from the Secr. of the Prop. of the Gospel, as usual at this Season. — Quarterly review for October. —

Dec. 6. Sunday.

In the early part of the night there had been a thaw, so that the snow had greatly melted away, but a hard morning frost caused the roads to be very icy and slippery: the frost continued through the day, with rising Mercury. — Visited the Sunday School. — Morning service — Prayers – Afternoon Service. – Prayers and sermon — I preached on the presence of the Messiah the glory of the second temple. — A letter from an official assignee at Bristol as to a small sum owing by me to _____ Leonard, of Cheltenham, |^54 an Ironmonger, a Bankrupt. — Preparing a Sermon. — To the family a section from Trower's Exposition of the Gospels.

Dec. 7. Monday.

A frosty day, roads very slippery; in the afternoon it thawed. — Wrote to the official assignee at Bristol as to the trifle due by me to the estate of H. Leonard, which had been misstated: — to Bathurst in answer to his letter rec^d. on Saturday. — Mr Wynniatt called. — Conferred with R G K Brookes as to Justice business; an unpleasant interview — there is a probability that the commitment of Charles Lupton on Thursday last for want of sureties will be called in question, Mr Griffiths, Sol^r, Campden, having applied to Brookes for a copy of the examinations. Also a great mistake has been made in the commitment of one Daubeny to Northleach H. of C. on Thursday last — in which the Clerk was much to blame, and the Magistrates negligent. — Quarterly Rev. for Oct. — After a short conversation with the Servant, Baldwin, who seemed dissatisfied with his place three weeks since, he expressed |^55 a desire to remain in the Service, to which we assented. Quarterly review for October. —

Dec. 8. Tuesday.

The thaw continues: weather raw and damp: some rain in the evening, and at night. — After breakfast, drove to Stow, to Mr Brookes's office, to meet the parties who had laid informations against Charles Lupton, to reduce their evidence into formal examinations, that copies may be forwarded to Mr Griffiths, Campden: also as to the commitment of William Daubeny gave further instructions to Mr Brookes. — Called at the Workhouse, and conferred with Mr Pearce; also at the library, to parley with Mr Pain; and had an interview with Mr Makepeace at the Police Station. — Home to a late luncheon — Mr Clarke & Mr Barrow called: the former to obtain my testimonial, previously to his receiving Priest's orders. — Received a letter from Davison, Newman & Co. acknowledging my late remittance — a letter from Messrs. Hoare, covering the continuation of my account to this time: — and |^{56} a letter from Mr Geldard, accompanying the quarterly balance sheet as to our Yorkshire rents &c. — Dined at Mr Wynniatt's, Guiting Grange, meeting M^r and M^{rs}. Lee Warner, with two daughters, on a visit there and M^r and M^{rs}. J. T. Rice, together with the Wynniatt home circle. A pleasant party.

Dec. 9. Wednesday.

A moist foggy day. — Engaged in arranging my Yorkshire accounts. — Drove to Stow to attend the annual meeting of the Stow Provident Bank: present the Dean of Gloucester in the Chair, Messrs. Pole & Perkins, Capt. Leigh and myself. Everything goes on steadily, uniformly, and accurately. The total sum for which we are responsible has been considerably lessened within the last two years, but this was expected: speculation is rife, and the diminution of interest allowed to depositors in Savings Banks tempts many to look out for other and often less safe security. — To Mr Brookes's office, where conferred with Mr Taplin on Justice business. — Called at "the Cottage," Mr Vavasour was not in, but I found M^{rs}. V. and with her Miss^{rs}. W.V. & Emma V. |^{57} whom, indeed, I had met before in the library. — A letter from E.F.W. all well at the Vicarage, Stanway, having arrived safe there on Saturday, though the roads almost impassable from the ice covering them. — A letter from Mr Morrison, about some paupers receiving relief from the Union, chargeable to his parish — Home sometime before the dinner hour — Quarterly review for October.

Dec. 10. Thursday.

A fine morning and forenoon; in the afternoon a hail-storm, followed by frost and snow, and a rough night. — Wrote to Mr Morrison, in answer to his letter rec^d. yesterday. — Received a letter from Mr Thornton on Hunt affairs. — Drove to Stow. — Attended at the Provident Bank: then with R Waller, an appeal against assessments to the Income tax: — then a long conference with Mr Pearce, and the Auditor of the Union, Mr Hunt: at last, at the Justice room, business with Messrs. R Waller, Ford, and Pole as my colleagues, Winter, Perkins, W. Vavasour, Clarke, as Assessors. — Came to an |^{58} arrangement that henceforth Justice meetings shall be held on alternate Thursday, viz. on those days on which the Board meetings are not held. This system I have long desired; but did not propose, as it looked like a personal accommodation to myself; it was suggested by Mr Ford; and further it was agreed that Justice business should begin punctually at one P.M. — Dressed at the Unicorn for dinner at the Rectory, Stow, MW. calling for me in the carriage. A pleasant party: M^r and M^{rs}. R. Waller, M^r and M^{rs}. Winter, Mr Hastings Woodman, M^r & Miss Hutchinson with a lady friend, and a School girl sister of M^{rs}. R Hippisley.

Dec. 11. Friday.

A hard frost, a scattering of snow on the ground: very slippery roads. — Wrote to E.F.W: — also to Mr Thornton on Hunt matters — Settling my banking account for the past year with Messrs. Hoare. — notes passed between Mr Pearce and me on Union business — I walked to Eyford: called on M^rs. Dolphin, who is an invalid, and much harassed with troubles, very much self sought, and the |^59 result of her own indiscretion, proneness to act on impulse, and real inaptitude to business. Had a few moments interview at Eyford with Miss Walmsley and W. Vavasour. The latter had walked over to call on Miss W. who is visiting M^rs. D. and the lady was returning part of the way homeward with the Gentleman. — Rec^d. a letter from Mr Jennings with the Mich^s. Balance Sheet of our London rents: — also from Mr Clerke, of Eydon, Northamptonshire, in answer to my letter to him as to an irremoveable pauper residing in his parish, but settled in Great Barrington: the Gentleman, though an ex. officio Guardian, is not very conversant with the law and the practice. — Quarterly review for October.

Dec. 12. Saturday.

A snow shower had fallen during the night: a hard frost, bad travelling — Wrote to Mr Jennings in answer to his letter received yesterday: to Mr Geldard in reply to his late letter, accompanying the Martinmas Balance Sheet as to our Yorkshire concerns: — |^60 to Messrs. Alcocks & Co. desiring them to direct Messrs. Barnard Dimsdale & Co. to pay £250 to my acc^t. with Messrs. Hoare. — Rec^d. a letter from Sophia Hunt. — MW. heard from Constance Howell: it would seem likely that the visit of herself and sister, which we expected about Christmas, will be postponed, as the completion of the purchase at Prinknash Park by Mr Akers is delayed, so that the Howells will not break up their establishment there as early as was expected. — The keeper of the House of Correction at Northleach came over to confer with me as to the defects in a warrant of commitment signed by me at Stow on the 3^d. Inst. and the best way of correcting the error. — Wrote to Mr Pearce on a Workhouse dietary matter. — Visited J Davis, who seems less well, and fears are entertained of a slight paralytic seizure on the right side. Visited at John Illes, whose aged mother seems to approach to her end. — Quarterly review for October.

Dec. 13. Sunday.

Hard frost, bright cold weather. — Visited the Sunday School. — Morning prayers and Sermon — I preached on the obstacles and dangers attending the profession of Christianity |^61 — Evening Prayers — Conferring with Churchwarden &c. as to the state of the Widow James & her son, living together — the former very old and deranged: the latter infirm in body and mind; a very difficult case to be dealt with — Old Widow Illes died last night. — Preparing a sermon — Ecclesiastical gazette — To the family a section from Trower's exposition of the Gospels. —

Dec. 14. Monday.

Hard frost, cold, clear weather. — Busy in correcting for the press the Book Society catalogue; writing to Lane, the Printer, therewith. — Funeral of Anne Hope, from the Workhouse. — Visited J Davis, who was worse yesterday, but rather recovered today. — Justice business at home. — Quarterly review for October.

Dec. 15. Tuesday.

Hard frost, cold and fine wintry weather, with a tendency to snow, one short shower falling. — Transacting Income Tax business with some of my parishioners &c. — Wrote for Thos.

Collett to R G Smith at Ramsgate. — Preparing a Sermon. — Quarterly Rev. for October. |⁶² Wrote to Cotterill and Rich, Kensington, for a supply of candles. —

Dec. 16. Wednesday.

A hard frost; fine winter weather. — Preparing a sermon — Received a note from Mʳ Pearce with correspondence on Union business from the P.L.C. to be considered by me before the fortnightly meeting to-morrow, and answered the note. ——— The funeral of Mʳˢ· Illes, aged 90 years. — Visited Mʳ Davis, who is confined to his bed-room in a condition calculated to give uneasiness to his friends — Justice business at home. Quarterly Review for October.

Dec. 17. Thursday.

A slight thaw in the night had dissipated some of the snow covering the ground, but there was a hard frost in the morning, which continued with a Northerly wind all day. — Drove to Stow. — Attended at the Provident Bank — Corrected a sheet of the catalogue of Books in the library. — To the Workhouse: presided at the fortnightly meeting of the Guardians, which was numerously attended. The business heavy, owing to the Severity of the weather, making many poor chargeable for want of employment. — |⁶³ Much discussion and correspondence arises out of the altered state of the law as to removal of the Poor: and much needless labour was caused to-day by revision of the pauper list of the parish of Longborough, owing to an ill judged, but well meant interference on the part of Lady Leigh, (a lady bountiful) who, in charitable visits to the Cottagers of that parish, in which Lord L. has property, has been imposed upon by artful and untrue tales of destitution. It appeared that the complaints of insufficient relief alledged by her ladyship were almost; if not altogether, groundless: but such a course causes dissatisfaction, and consumes to no good purpose valuable time. — Looked in at the Justice room, where not much business had been done by Messʳˢ· Ford & Waller, met there and at the Provident Bank Messʳˢ· Hippisley, Pole and Twisleton; also Mʳ Barrow. – Messʳˢ· Ford, Waller, Hippisley, Twisleton and Barrow were going to dine together at the Unicorn on |⁶⁴ occasion of the annual meeting of the Trustees of the Cope Charity: I declined joining the party, as I have also declined for several years past, — being unwilling to risk injury to my health by returning home at a late hour in an inclement season, and that after incurring fatigue in the transaction of public business for some hours before. — Letters from C Bathurst on Constabulary matters &c. and from Mʳ Thornton on the appointment of a new Solicitor to the Hunt Trust. — Quarterly review for October. — Recᵈ· information of the decease of our old friend and neighbour, Lady Reade, at Oddington, which happened yesterday. Her ladyship had passed her 90ᵗʰ year: had long been a frail being, subject to frequent inflammatory attacks, but retained her faculties wonderfully till nearly the last. She was a charitable, amiable, pious woman and her loss will be great to her family and to the poor of Oddington. —

Dec. 18. Friday.

A continuance of the same frosty, cold weather; but towards night there |⁶⁵ were symptoms of a thaw. — Engaged for several hours with Mʳ Pearce on poor law business, making up minutes and resolutions of the meeting of the Guardians yesterday, and writing to Mʳ Morrison a long letter and statement as to the alleged insufficiency of relief granted to the out-door poor of Longborough, to be communicated by him to Lady Leigh. — Visited Davis, who continues confined to his bedroom, in, I fear, a precarious condition — M. Forty, the Schoolmistress, is also seriously unwell — Quarterly review for October. —

Dec. 19. Saturday.

A rapid thaw, weather fine overhead. — Wrote for W. Dix a letter to the Secretary of the Post Office as to the mistake in the post office orders of which he had been apprized yesterday. He had procured two at Gloucester in payment of rent in favour of John Blandford, and the Christian name had been written Thomas in error. — Wrote to C Bathurst — Preparing a Sermon. — A meeting of the Trustees of the Upper Slaughter Church and Charity Estate held in my study. |[66] Messrs. Lea and Collett, and Churchwarden Gregory were present. — Rec^d. a letter from Messrs. Hoare, announcing that Messrs. Alcock & Co. had paid to my account with them 250£ — Dear Freddy's birthday — 3 years old. — Quarterly review for October — Justice business at home.

Dec. 20. Sunday.

Moist weather and mild air, a shower or two fell. — Preparing a Sermon — Morning prayers — Afternoon prayers and Sermon. I preached on the Sacrament of the Lords supper. — Rec^d. a letter from Ramsgate written on behalf of R. G. Smith, late of Bourton on the Water, in answer to mine to him on the business of Income Tax charged on Thos. Collett, in respect of a mortgage held by him on Smith's property at Bourton. — Eccl. Gazette — To the family a section from Trower's Exposition of the gospels.

Dec. 21. Monday.

Mild, showery weather — Preparing a sermon — Wrote to Messrs. Hoare to pay £250 on my account to Messrs. Mastermen to be placed to the account of Messrs. Sewell |[67] and Newmarch, with the Gloucestershire Banking Co. at Cirencester in repayment to them of the advances made by them when £1000 was lent on Mortgage to Mr Lockhart in addition to the money before lent by us on mortgage of his property in Bucks: — to Messrs. Swell Sewell and Newmarch, that I had so done: — to Mr Warter as to advertising for ground rents in London, wherein to invest the proceeds of the sale of the Fenchurch Street houses: — to Mr Thornton, in answer to his last letter, desiring him to communicate to Mr Hare and Mr Cox that we had fixed on Mr Tilleard as our Solicitor to be consulted on Hunt affairs, when necessary: — to Mr Bloxsome, desiring him to forward to me in next week his half yearly bill against the County, that I may look over it before the approaching Sessions. — Rec^d. a letter from Mr Pearce, covering one from Mr Moore, as to reporting on the nuisance at Great Bar-|[68] rington, and asking for further instructions, to which I replied with necessary information, desiring P. to forward my letter to Mr M. — Visited at Mr Davis's, who still continues a great invalid; on Mary Forty, also ill, on Churchwarden Gregory, on parish business. — Quarterly Review for October.

Dec. 22. Tuesday.

A sharp frost, and fine day. — Transacting business with the Church warden. — Making minutes of the meeting of the Parish Trustees lately held — Preparing a Sermon. — With MW. called on M^rs. Dolphin and Miss Walmsley at Eyford: but the former was engaged on business, and the latter had walked out. — A letter from C. Bathurst in answer to my last to him. — Quarterly Review for October. ——

Dec. 23. Wednesday.

Some snow had fallen during the night, which partially covered the ground, but there was no frost: sleet or snow fell for the greater part of the day. — |[69] John Jones and Elizabeth Benfield were married. — Preparing a Sermon — Engaged with the Churchwarden &c. in parish business. — Justice business at home — A letter from Mess.rs Hoare announcing that they had paid on my account to Mess.rs Masterman £250 to be placed in the acc.t of Mess.rs Sewell and Newmarch with the Gloucestershire Banking Company at Cirencester — from Mess.rs Cotterell & Rich, Kensington, that they had forwarded a box of candles agreeable to my order: — from M.r Warter, that he had advertized for ground rents for purchase, but that as yet none had been offered worthy our consideration — Quarterly review for October. ——

Dec. 24. Thursday.

A very sharp frost, rendering the travelling bad; snow heavy on the hills, light in the valleys; snow storms fell, but not of long continuance. — Transacting business with Churchwarden Gregory — Preparing a Sermon. — Drove to Stow — A cir-|[70] cular from the County Gaol, announcing a meeting of visitors for Wednesday next. — To the Provident Bank: transacted business there, and with M.r Morgan, as Clerk to the Comm.rs of Taxes. — Met M.r Potter at the Savings Bank. — Transacted business at the Office of the Gloucestershire Banking Company. — Called on M.r RW Hippisley at the Rectory: saw him, his lady, and her sister; business with RWH. as Comm.r of land tax. — Looked ~~her~~ with him into his now dilapidated chancel which, at this inclement season, he has, I think, unwisely unroofed, thus beginning a large repair and repewing, and somewhat increasing the accommodation ~~on~~ ᵒᶠ of his church. — With M.r Ford sat as Magistrate for three hours at the Unicorn: a case of felony, orders of removal, abating a nuisance &c. M.r W B Pole and Barrow our assessors. I brought the latter homewards in my carriage from Stow to Lower Slaughter Turnpike Gate. — Quarterly Review for October. |[71]

Dec. 25. Friday.

Christmas day. — A hard frost — Preparing a Sermon — Morning Service, prayers, sermon, and sacrament: 18 communicants: I preached a sermon on the Nativity of Christ. — Afternoon — prayers. — Letters – from Stanway, to MW. from E.F.W. and Sophy: a very pleasant account of all there; – from Eliza Daniell to MW. and myself, with little presents of warm woollen netting or knitting for the neck: — from M.r Thornton with a copy of the letter he has written to M.r Hare, to acquaint him that we have fixed on M.r Tilleard as the Sol.r to be consulted by us on Hunt matters, when there is occasion. —— British Magazine. —

Dec. 26. Saturday.

A fine, frosty day. — Preparing a Sermon — Wrote to the Keeper of the House of Correction at Northleach with reference to the discharge of Daubeny, a prisoner whom I had committed — to M.r Rodwell with an order for books for the Stow Book Society. — Visited sick parishio-|[73] ners, M.r Davis (who was fatigued, and could not admit me) Eliz. Wilcox, — Townsend, with whom I prayed. — Quarterly Review for October. ——

Dec. 27. Sunday.

Festival of John Ap. and Evan. — A thick fog or rime continuing all day: a suspension of frost, yet not a thaw. — Visited the Sunday School. — Morning prayers and Sermon. I preached on the Christian's fellowship with GOD and Christ. — Afternoon Prayers. — Preparing a Sermon. — British Magazine — To the family a section from Trower's Exposition of the Gospels. —

Dec. 28 Monday.

A sharp frost in the morning: afterwards foggy and rime with a gentle thaw. — Preparing a Sermon. — Justice business at home. — Wrote to Mr Moore, Med. Off. as to giving evidence on the information laid by him of a nuisance at Great Barrington. — Wrote to my Son with a remittance on account of the Stanway Charities — to Miss E Moorhouse with a cheque |^73 on the Craven Bank for £2. a present from MW. at this inclement season. — A letter from Howell; the conveyance to Mr Ackers of Prinknash Park will not ^be completed for some weeks: ~~he~~ ^Howell will Keep up his establishment there till shortly before he yields possession: at the last will have a sale of furniture; before that wishes us to receive Constance, Laura and Macleod, till he has prepared for them a lodging in Town, near Wilton Place West, where he has bought a house, which will not be ready for him before the end of March. — Visiting sick and aged parishioners. — British Magazine — Quarterly review for October. — Sir Bonnycastle's Newfoundland.[8] ——

Dec. 29. Tuesday.

Very slippery in the roads — a gently thaw. — Preparing a will for W^m. Collett, to be executed by him in favour of his daughter, who has long been his faithful attendant: he has only his few household goods to leave, and three poor and hungry sons with |^74 large families, living in adjacent villages. Attended the execution of the will; and, later in the day, administered the sacrament privately to him; three brothers, a Sister, and his daughter partaking with him. It was a striking scene, the humble garret in which the old man of 81 was stretched, in great infirmity of body, crowded with his homely, humble kindred; the youngest of the family party, save the daughter, being 69 years of age; all inhabitants throughout their lives of this village: all having saved a humble competence, all on good terms with one another. — The sister is wife of a labourer possessing a little independence: the daughter of the dying man single, perhaps, fifty years of age. — Wrote to Howell in reply to his letter received yesterday, explaining that we should be ready to receive Laura, Constance and Macleod at the time most suitable to them, provided an attendant to wait on M^cL. accompanied them. — Wrote to E.F.W. to explain what I had done as to Howell, |^74 offering to keep McLeod here, when his sisters should be visiting at Stanway, since the addition of the child into their nursery would be very inconvenient. — Visited J. Davis, who is rather better, and has come down stairs — Rec^d. letters from Morrison, who acknowledges my letters to him concerning the administration of Out. Relief at Longborough, he forwarded my letter to Lady Leigh;

---

8. Sir Richard Henry Bonnycastle (1791-1848). Bonnycastle wrote two works at this time; *Considerations upon the Political Position of Newfoundland* (London: The House of Commons, 1841; and *Newfoundland in 1842,* 2 vols. (London 1842).

is ready to take an active part as Manager of the Savings bank: announces the engagement and approaching marriage of his eldest daughter to Mr Scott, of Banksfee, with which he and M^rs. M. are greatly pleased: she is a fine, well looking, well educated young woman; her intended must be a good deal her Senior, and is a strange looking, unprepossessing man, almost unknown in the neighbourhood, but, I daresay, sensible, and well informed, hitherto chiefly residing in town: M. speaks very favourably of him from personal observation, |^75 and the report of others: at all events, it will be what is called a good match, the Lady's fortune being I suppose, <u>nil</u>, and the Gentleman son & heir of an old lady of good property and Estate. — from F. Aston, with a pretty good account of himself, wife and children; his letter came with his wonted Christmas present to me of an Oxford Almanach for 1847: — from E.F.W. a long and very satisfactory letter, with good tidings, of all the dear household, and with much comment on Justice business, particularly to two cases of neglect of duty on the part of Cooke, the Coroner, which he has been called upon to bring under the notice of the Sessions next week; as to which he craves my advice, and sends me the letters and documents. — British Magazine — Bonnycastle's Newfoundland.

Dec. 30. Wednesday.

The same kind of weather a very gradual thaw with fog. — Wrote to E.F.W. in answer to his letter received yesterday: — |^76 to Morrison with congratulations on the approaching marriage of his daughter; — to F. Aston, a reply to his letter received yesterday: — to Mr Clarke, Icomb, acknowledging a remittance made by him in a note today, as his subscription to S.P.G. — Examining into the law as to Coroners — A candidate for the place of schoolmistress at the Union Workhouse called upon me – widow of John Privett, our late butcher. — Rec^d. a few lines from Mr Bloxsome, accompanying his half year's bill for business done for the County, and a notice of a Prison Committee meeting fixed for Monday next at Gloucester. — Bonnycastle's Newfoundland. —

Dec. 31. Thursday.

Rime and fog, the roads very slippery, and travelling bad: the moisture freezing as it settled on the ground. — Drove to Stow. — Attended at the Provident Bank, where met Winter and the Dean of Gloucester. — Presided at the fortnightly meeting of the Guardians of the Union:—— |^77 which commenced to-day at eleven o clock: remained there till nearly two o clock. — Transacted business at the office of the Gloucestershire Banking Company. — To the Justice room, where much business, the Dean of Gloucester and Mr Ford being my colleagues. — Proceedings to abate a nuisance at Barrington — enquiry as to a felony at Broadwell; the evidence not sufficiently strong to justify a commitment — two orders of removal &c. — Messrs. Winter, W B Pole, and Polhill &c. present. — I remained to dress at the Unicorn, where MW. called for me in the Chariot to accompany her to a dinner party at "the Cottage." — present M^r & M^rs. W B Pole, Miss Walmesley, on a visit to the Vavasours, Dr Twisleton, M^r and M^rs. W. Vavasour, Emma Vavasour and Mr Clarke: a cheerful, pleasant party — Home at midnight.

1847

Jan. 1. Friday.

A sharp frost, with a clearer atmosphere, but a tendency to sleet and snow: |[78] towards night it thawed. — Wrote to M[rs.] Marsh to reserve a comfortable bed for me next week at the Bell at Gloucester. — Engaged in auditing M[r] Bloxsome's bill for business done for the County. — Visiting old & sick parishioners: — conferring with Churchw[dn.] Gregory — Entertained the Singers at Supper. — Bonnycastle's Newfoundland. — Entered on a new year, which I may not survive: GOD give me grace to amend, and to live, while I am on earth, as far as human frailty will permit, a truly Christian life, on sound Gospel principles, not according to the false maxims of this world, but referring to the law and to the testimony, doing as much good as I can, and ceasing, by the aid of the Holy Spirit, to do evil! —

Jan. 2. Saturday.

An Easterly wind, sharp frost: the roads and paths very icy and slippery. — Engaged in auditing the Clerk of Peace's bill, and in making other preparations for the Quarter Sessions next week. Justice business at home. — Rec[d.] a note from |[79] M[r] Clarke, Icomb, as to the amount of his subscription to the S.P.G. — Bonnycastle's Newfoundland. —

Jan. 3. Sunday.

An Easterly wind; hard frost; very cold and icy: some snow fell towards night. — Morning service, prayers: afternoon service, prayers and sermon. — I preached on the name of Jesus: a sermon for the new year. — Wrote to M[r] Clarke, Icomb, with a receipt for his subscription to S.P.G: — also to Mess[rs.] Sewell and Newmarch, expressing surprize that they had not acknowledged the receipt of £250, which I had desired Mess[rs.] Hoare to pay to Mess[rs.] Masterman to be placed to the account of S. and N. with the Gloucestershire Banking Company at Cirencester; and which had been so paid, according to advice I had received from Mess[rs.] H. — Preparing a Sermon. — Preparing for a journey to Gloucester to-morrow. — To the family a section from Trower's exposition of the gospels.

Jan. 4. Monday.

A good deal of snow lying on |[80] the ground, a thaw, thick fog, and cold damp weather. — Left home at 8 A.M. after an early breakfast for Cheltenham in the phaeton; drove to the Station, proceeded by train, with Lefroy, to the Bell, Gloucester — met and conferred with Purnell, and to the Shire Hall, where business of the County till dinner time — Comm. of Accounts – Curtis Hayward and Baker, the former an invalid, Goodrich, unwell, could not attend: Prison improvements and alteration committee, — present D[r] Timbrill & M[r] Surman, besides those before mentioned — County rate Committee business — Purnell, Hayward & myself. — D[r] Timbrill joined Purnell, Baker and me at dinner at the Bell — Till midnight engaged with auditing accounts, preparing business for to-morrow &c. — Wrote to MW. ——

Jan. 5. Tuesday.

Cold, raw, damp weather. Before breakfast engaged in auditing bills &c. Wrote to MW. that if Curtis Hayward were prevented by illness from attending to-morrow, |[81] my services would be required as Chairman in the second court, which would delay my return till Friday or Saturday. — Breakfasted with Purnell, and with him opened the Court — A short attendance of magistrates in the early part of the day, but the Court fully attended from two till four: the Marquis of Worcester, and Lord Fitzhardinge present. — I went thro' the usual routine bills, as Chairman of the Committee of accounts. — My son came to make a charge of neglect of duty, and misconduct against Cooke, the Coroner, E.F.W. conducted his case with great propriety, and was supported by Purnell and myself, meeting the general acquiescence of the Court in the censure passed upon the delinquent, who was warned that his age and infirmities amounted to a disqualification, and that he ought to resign. But the old man is past feeling, and in abject poverty, and little impression was made upon him. He was advised without delay to appoint a deputy, and given to understand that neglect or misconduct hereafter must be followed by application |[82] to the Lord Chief Justice of the Queen's bench for his removal. — Many magistrates flocked in from Cheltenham to oppose any vote for building Judges lodgings, Craven Berkeley, as MP. for Cheltenham, at their head. But the Chairman had no intention to propose such a measure; the question had been adjourned to this Sessions, and he proposed a further postponement till the Epiphany Sessions this time twelvemonth. Thus there was no fight on this point: but the Magistrates who had come to earn popularity by opposing any building expence, were unwilling to go home without a contention, and when the Chairman moved the Court to build a new Chapel at the County Gaol, making at the same time, and under the same expenditure, other necessary alterations for better accommodation in various ways, he was vehemently resisted by Craven, Berkeley, Capt Sinclair, Col. Jenner, Sir John Guise &c. – It was in vain to urge on these gentlemen that the alterations proposed were |[83] merely the completion of designs already planned and sanctioned by the Court, an appendage without which the separate prison could not be properly occupied, and the non completion of which would render the management of the Gaol according to the system now established not only difficult, but almost impossible, the Magistrates in question took a one sided view of the matter, the Chairman gave offence by some observations which he made, as if the work ought to be done, because approved by himself and the Prison Committee, and the question was eventually put and decided by a shew of hands. True, it was decided in favour of the Chairman's proposition by a division of 13 to 7 — but a kind of personal attack had been made, and the Lord Lieutenant, pleading insufficient information, and that he had not had an opportunity of acquainting himself with the facts of the case, observed a neutrality, which greatly offended the Chairman, who considered the compact broken on which he had accepted the Chair — namely that the Earl |[84] should support him in his office; he, on the other hand, consulting the Lord Lieutenant before entering on any great work, which he considered himself virtually as having done with regard to this expenditure of £3000 or £4000, which he viewed as being, as it really is, only part of the great alterations & improvements in prison & bridewells which the County had distinctly sanctioned already. What may [be] the result of this day's proceedings is doubtful: Purnell will write his sentiments to Lord Fitzhardinge, and on the reply which he receives will depend whether he will continue to hold his office or resign his Chair. That the latter alternative should be the issue would be a matter of regret: P. makes himself unpopular, is proud & vain, perhaps, and he might transact the business with better judgement and discretion, keeping a straight forward course, and not caring for, or consulting great people, otherwise than as their rank and wealth make it |[85] fitting to shew deference; but change is an evil, and there is no person on whose shoulders the mantle could fitly fall, who is in many, not to say all, respects eligible. — The business was concluded by 4 P.M. and the Magistrates met at dinner at the King's head, a small party, at five o clock. In the evening after we had risen from table, Bathurst came in, having arrived two or three hours before, not intending to join the dinner party, or to be present at the business in Court. He was in good health and spirits, and contributed greatly to make the Evening pass off pleasantly. ——

Jan. 6. Wednesday.

Damp, close weather — After breakfast to the Court, which had been opened by Sergeant Ludlow, who had arrived yesterday evening. — A note from MW. — Curtis Hayward came from home: his indisposition greatly removed by rest and good nursing yesterday, so that my services as a Chairman will not be required — An interesting appeal against an order of removal made by D[r] Tim[9] |[86] and E.F.W. which by common consent is to be taken to the Court of Queen's Bench, and will raise the question as to the true legal construction of the much debated clauses of the late Poor Removal Act. — An appeal against a conviction of a publican for permitting drunkenness in his house, (Beckford Inn) was otherwise interesting, and to me especially because the conviction had been made by D[r] Timbrill & my son; it was confirmed. — Trials for felony &c. kept the Court engaged till between six and seven P.M. when rather a larger party met at dinner than yesterday, and a pleasant party it was — At nine, Purnell, Bathurst, E.F.W. and myself with some others adjourned to the Shire Hall to attend a Choral Concert, arriving between the first and second part. There was a large audience, chiefly of the middle classes, professional persons, tradespeople &c. — and the performance was very creditable: perhaps 150 male & female Singers, with no other music than the occasional assistance of a piano, all under the manage-|[87]ment of one Higgs, a baker, who is a person of much musical talent, and rare powers of training and organizing, and keeping in order so large a body of musical amateurs of all ages from twelve or thirteen to five and thirty. The performers were more numerous than when I attended one of these choral concerts some months ago — we lost the first part — sacred music — what we heard was a very pleasing selection of glees, choruses, and the like. It is gratifying to see so many hundred persons of the middle, or somewhat below the middle class spending an evening so harmoniously, in so refining an amusement, not devoting the hours to scandal, or gossip, tea, tippling, or tobacco: and this branch, at least, of the Gloucester Mechanics Institute merits the encouragement it receives. — Three or four, Purnell, his son, Bathurst, Halliwell and Edward & myself had tea together at the Bell after the Concert was over.

Jan. 7. Thursday.

A raw, foggy, damp day. |[88] — Preparing to return home, settling bills &c. at Gloucester. — After breakfast attended in Sergeant Ludlow's court for two hours. Transacting business with Riddiford as to County finance, and other matters — Bade adieu to Bathurst, who with Purnell and others were was going to a Quarterly meeting of the Governors of the

---

9.   This is presumably Dr. Timbrell. Francis Witts has forgotten to complete the name on turning over the leaf and commencing the new folio.

Infirmary. Left Gloucester station for Cheltenham, at a little before one o clock, and arrived at the Plough Hotel, where I found my carriage and servants &c. with a note from MW. — Shopping — and reached home by 5 P.M. finding my wife pretty well. — A letter from Howell, whose Prinknash Property will not be conveyed to Mr Ackers till towards the end of February: he writes to me for information as to the Assessment of Prinknash to the County rate: does not mention when the twins and Mc Leod are to visit us — In the evening a cheerful, pleasant note to MW from dear Sophy, with an excellent account of herself and children in reply |^89 to a note and parcel which MW. had forwarded by a chance messenger to Stanway to-day. E.F.W. intended to return from Gloucester to Stanway this evening, setting out two or three hours later than I did — Bonnycastle's Newfoundland. ——

Jan. 8. Friday.
Cold, raw, and foggy weather — Wrote to Howell in answer to his letter which awaited me yesterday, sending him a copy of the last printed county rate — also to the Waiter at the Bell Gloucester desiring him to send back a sovereign to which amount I had overpaid him in settling my bill with him yesterday. — A letter from Newmarch with an acknowledged of £250 which I remitted to him just before Christmas, with a statement of my cash account with them, ^S. and N. now closed, and with the intimation that he had paid to my account with the Gloucestershire Banking Company at Stow the half year's interest on mortgage due by Mr Lockhart. — Bonnycastle's Newfoundland. |^90

Jan. 9. Saturday.
A cold, dry fog: with Easterly wind. — Wrote to Sewell and Newmarch in answer to their letters received yesterday: — to W B. Pole that I had searched in the Clerk of the Peace's Office at Gloucester for the award of the Inclosure Act of Upper Swell without success: — to Mr Pearce to desire him to come hither early in next week to confer with me on Union matters: — to Chr. Geldard to request him or his father to attend on Tuesday next at Ravenflatt to meet parties connected with ^cerned in the North Western railway as to roads to connect the portions of our property there through which the line of rails will be carried, severing one part of the farm from another: this letter I wrote in consequence of one received to-day from the Secretary of the North Western railway, giving notice that a deputation would visit our land on Tuesday next to set out such roads — Justice business at home — Preparing a Sermon — Bonnycastle's Newfoundland. |^91

Jan. 10. Sunday.
A sharp frost, and cold weather — Visited the Sunday School. — Morning prayers and sermon — I preached on the golden rule of equity. — Evening prayers — Preparing a Sermon. — Brit. Magazine — To the family a section from Trower's exposition of the gospels.

Jan. 11. Monday.
Hard frost: fine weather. — Wrote to Mr Holt, Secretary to the Bishop of Gloucester, requesting him to forward to me a form of return, such as is made by incumbents of livings annually at this season, as I had mislaid or lost that which my Son had given me at Gloucester, and which had been addressed to him as Minister of Stanway. — Arranging my papers on

public business, making minutes and memoranda arising out of the transactions at the Quarter Sessions — Rec^d· a note from Mr Moore, Med. Off. of a district of the Stow Union, craving my advice as to certain points in the discharge of his official functions. Replied briefly that an engagement |^92 at Eyford prevented my ~~repl~~ answering his letter fully, that the subject of it required consideration, and that I would communicate with him upon it in a day or two — M^rs· Dolphin sent to desire me to call on her: I went, accompanied by MW. We found her alone, in a very languid and depressed state, alarmed by recent seizures, and fainting, which had caused her to call in the aid of Mr Hayward: yet she rallied enough to go into a long detail of distresses and grievances. She then seemed likely to sink, but a cordial revived her, and I promised to administer the sacrament to her tomorrow. I doubt whether her malady is so serious as she apprehends; loneliness, having just now no visitor, recurrence to the loss of her mother at this season last year, vexations and embarrassments, unwise resort to sedatives, confinement to the house, and self indulgence, not keeping early hours, and a proneness to nervous disorders, will account for her present pitiable state. — A letter from Howell, chiefly |^93 as to his own concerns: Laura and Constance and Macleod will probably not visit us till late in February, when the establishment at Prinknash will be broken up: — A letter from Bathurst, with particulars at to the Infirmary meeting on Thursday last, and what passed at the QS. on Tuesday, when the Lord Lieutenant failed to support the Chairman under an attack at him by the Castle adherents: CB. from the printed report collects that Purnell came off with credit. — Bonnycastle's Newfoundland — While we were at Eyford Mr Vavasour Senr with M^rs· William V. & Emma V. called having walked hither & meaning to walk back.

Jan. 12. Tuesday.

Hard frost: cold weather and foggy, but not damp. — Wrote to Mr Moore in answer to his letter received yesterday. — Mr Pearce came with minutes, correspondence, and other documents relating to our Union, conferred with him on many points, drew up letters to be addressed to the P.L.C. and minutes. The |^94 Rel. Off. Dunford also called on Union business. — M^rs· Dolphin sent to say she was too ill to see me to-day — The only letter a circular announcing my appointment as Visitor of Gloucester Gaol. — Bonnycastle's Newfoundland.

Jan. 13. Wednesday.

A frost, and dry fog: the weather rather softer in the afternoon, slightly thawing. — Wrote to my Son. — Busy in preparing for public business to-morrow. — A message from M^rs· Dolphin that she continues very ill, and wishes to postpone seeing me till ~~to-morrow or~~ Friday. — Letters from Alcocks, Birkbecks & Co· with my half yearly balance of banking account — from a person named Rudge, canvassing for the vacant situation of housekeeper to the Gloucester Infirmary — from Messrs· Butt, Gloucester with a bill for wine delivered by the carrier yesterday. — Visited J. Davis, who is as well as one expect to see a paralytic cripple – Visited W. Collett, who has rallied & is down |^95 stairs. — Read a pamphlet, "A few words on the Corn. Laws," which was published some months ago by C Bathurst, but not with his name, and acknowledged by him only to a few particular friends. He sent it me by to-day's post. It is ably written, a clear & well argued exposition of the fallacies by which restriction is usually justified; very acute, impartial as to political factions, the work of a mature scholar & soundly deep thinker. It has not obtained a wide circulation, but deserves it.

Jan. 14. Thursday.

A hard frost; very foggy forenoon, the afternoon clear, and the sun melted the frost; freezing in the evening. — To Stow — Letters from Rev^d. Jas. Commeline, Redmarley, who recommends to my support Anne Crowse, a parishioner of his, who is a candidate for the vacant place of Housekeeper to the Gloucester Infirmary: — from C Bathurst, who asks my advice and opinion as to the propriety of subscribing at the request of his Vicar to purchase for the Church at Lidney new Sacramental Plate, |^196 particularly a flagon and basin to receive alms. — Attended for a short time at the Provident Bank, where transacted business, and at the Gloucestershire Banking Company — To the Workhouse, where presided at the fortnightly meeting of the guardians of our Union; a heavy day's work, and a full board: much distress in the lower classes, owing to the severity of the season, and the rapidly increasing price of the necessaries of life, coupled with the scarcity, high cost, and frequently total want of potatoes.[10] — Detained at the Board from 11 AM. till after 4 P.M. — My Son looked in upon me there late in the day: he had ridden with Sophy to Stow, to "the Cottage;" all at Stanway were quite well: ~~the~~ E.F.W. & S. would return home this evening. — Bonnycastle's Newfoundland. —

Jan 15. Friday.

A frosty morning with fog; the sun in the afternoon melted the frozen earth where it shone; frosty evening — Replied to the letters I had received yesterday |^197 from Bathurst and Mr Commeline: — wrote to M^r J D Charles, Stow, with a remittance for insurance in the Sun Fire Office — Rec^d. a letter from the Official assignee of the Bankruptcy of H Leonard of Cheltenham, admitting that I am only indebted to the estate in 2/9. — and desiring that sum to be remitted by post office order, or in post office stamps. — Parties called on Justice & other business — Visited M^rs. Dolphin, who continues a great invalid, and harrassed in mind. Administered to her the holy Sacrament. — Bonnycastle's Newfoundland.

Jan. 16. Saturday.

Some rain had fallen, frost had followed, and the roads were very slippery: a cold, raw, damp air, yet freezing generally — Justice business at home. — Wrote to Messrs. Alcocks, Birkbecks & Co. acknowledging the receipt of their half yearly balance sheet, and pointing out an inaccuracy — Wrote to W. Newton, Wotton, Gloucester, with a remittance on account of the maintenance of Moses Roff in the Lunatic Asylum near Gloucester, I had |^198 brought the account with me from Gloucester and received the amount from his father: the poor fellow is returned home cured, still a relapse may be feared. – Rec^d. a circular from the office of the Clerk of the Peace. — Also a notice that a Turnpike meeting for the Crickley Hill district of roads will be held at Northleach on the ^10 9th. February. — Engaged at Mr Davis's in a settlement of accounts with him, which his illness has very inconveniently postponed; proceeded in examining into the debtor & creditor relations, and deferred a final balance until early in next week, when I can more fully look into the items, & strike a balance. — M^r & M^rs. Winter called upon us. — Bonnycastle's Newfoundland.

---

10. This is the first diary reference to the potato famine. The previous November the potato crop had failed for a second year in Ireland.

Jan. 18. Monday. [17. Sunday]

A hard frost: cold weather; a thick fog, but dry. — Visited the Sunday School. — Morning service, prayers: afternoon service, prayers and a Sermon. I preached on fornication. — A letter from the Infirmary, announcing that one Cook |[99] of Westcote, admitted on my recommendation is declared to be incurable, and should, therefore, be removed. — A letter from the Gloucester Lunatic Asylum, announcing a meeting of visitors on routine business. — Preparing a Sermon. — Eccl. Gazette. — To the family a section from Trowers' exposition of the Gospels.

Jan. 18. Monday.

A hard frost, dry, cold weather without fog. — Wrote to Mr Pantin requesting him to take measures to remove from the Gloucester infirmary Thos Cook, whom I had caused to be admitted there on his recommendation. — Remitted to E M Miller, Official Assignee, Bristol, 2/9 in postage stamps, in payment of a debt due by me to the estate of H Leonard, late Ironmonger, Cheltenham, now a Bankrupt. — Made the annual returns required as to the ~~Benf~~ benefices of Upper Slaughter and Stanway. — Mr Pearce came, with whom engaged for three hours in preparing letters on Poor law business to the P.L.C, and advising with him on many points of poor law and Union Management. — Received |[100] a letter from C Bathurst in answer to mine on Sacramental Utensils &c. — Bonnycastle's Newfoundland. — Transacting parish business. —

Jan. 19. Tuesday.

Weather less severely cold: hard frost: clear. — Wrote to W. J. Walker, Northleach, with a remittance for oats supplied to me by him: to Messrs Garaway and C^o Nurserymen and Seedsmen, Durdham Down, for a supply of garden seeds — Justice business at home — Making out accounts with J. Davis and others. — Called on JD. to settle accounts with him. — The Misses Hall paid a morning visit. — Preparing a Sermon — Received a letter from Mrs Barr, with a good account of herself and family. — Bonnycastle's Newfoundland – A letter from Mr Mayer, Clerk to the Gloucester Union acknowledging my late remittance to Mr Newton on account of the maintenance of Moses Roff in the Gloucester Lunatic Asylum. |[101]

Jan 20. Wednesday.

A frost, in the afternoon a snow shower, and snow or sleet fell more or less till night. — Settling accounts with J W Harris, as to the rent of Stanway Vicarage farm, and other matters. — Drove with MW. to Stow and back; the snow beginning to fall soon after we had set out. – Transacted business at the office of the Gloucestershire Banking Company; paying bills to various tradesmen at Stow, ordering sheets, counterpanes, calico and flannel to be distributed among the poor of Upper Slaughter; called at the library &c. — A letter from C Bathurst, inclosing one from Mr Mirehouse as to the right interpretation of the recent Nuisance Act. — A circular from Mr Maitland, librarian to the Archb. of Canterbury, with enquiries as to any ancient printed books, hidden in old parochial or school libraries, with a view to some publication on the antiquities of printing and printed books. — A circular from the National Society with some tables to be filled up as to the numbers of children educated in their parish in Church of |[102] England Schools. — A letter from Mrs Mountain, a candidate for the office of Housekeeper at the Gloucester Infirmary. — Bonnycastle's Newfoundland.

Jan. 21. Thursday.

From daylight, snow & sleet began to fall unremittingly, with a tendency to thaw, and in the afternoon rain fell: much snow lying, and the roads a good deal impeded. — Drove to Stow. — Attended at the Prov. Bank, where met Mr Hippisley, and transacted business with Mr Morgan. Mr Ford came and joined me as Magistrate at the Justice room, where we transacted a good deal of business — Home late to dinner. — Mr Clarke was our assessor. — Rec^{d.} a letter from Mr Chesshyre Attorney, Cheltenham, with an enclosure as to Prov. Bank business, respecting the deposits of Jane Busson of Stanway, deceased. — A letter from Messrs. Garaway & Co. as to a packet of seeds forwarded according to my order. Bonnycastle's Newfoundland. |[103]

Jan. 22. Friday.

A thaw, without much rain, the snow slowly melting. — Wrote to Mr Chesshyre in answer to his letter received yesterday. — To Rodwell, for a supply of books for the Book Society. — Preparing a Sermon — Justices business at home — Visited the Daily School – transacting business with E Lea &c. as to Land Tax & parish trust concerns — Called at J. Collett's on business. — Rec^{d.} letters from Mr J. W. Pantin, on behalf of his father, who is ill, acknowledging my letter to him as to a patient in the Gloucester infirmary. — from Miss A. K. Settree, a candidate for the vacant office of House Keeper at Gloucester Infirmary: — from Mr Geldard, (Chr) as to the severance of our land at Ravenflatt by the line of the North Western Railway. The Directors mean to suggest to us and to Mr Garforth such an exchange of lands as will preclude the necessity of any bridge or other mode of communication across the line, by Mr G. taking as much of our land on his side the railway in exchange for so much ^{of hin} |[104] on our side of the line, that the Railway shall be boundary to each: — from J^{as.} Walker, Northleach, acknowledging my late remittance of his of £7. 0. 0 for oats. — The debates on the Queen's Speech and address, Parliament having met on the 19th.

Jan. 23. Saturday.

A thaw; the snow rapidly going. — Justice business at home. — Preparing a Sermon. — A note from Mr Barrow respecting books which he wishes me to order into the Book Society: — an acknowledgement from the Official Assignee at Bristol, as regards 2/9 which I remitted in postage stamps in payment of a bill to Leonard, late Ironmonger &c. a Bankrupt. – A letter from the Office of Messrs. Vizard & Leman Sol^{rs.} — London, addressed to me by error: should have been addressed to E.F.W; as one of the Ex^{ors.} of the late Lady Burdett; forwarded it with a few lines to my Son by return of post. — Mr Barrow called |[105] upon us: I walked back with him part of the way towards Wick. — The debates on the address in answer to the Queen's speech.

Jan. 24. Sunday.

Very rainy day, with little interruption till the Evening. — Wrote to Mr Barrow some remarks on the value of different commentaries on the Bible, Grotius, Pole's Synopsis, Calvert^{vin} &c. – chiefly taken from Hartwell Horne's Introduction to the Scriptures: thus conveying to Mr B. more accurately the opinions I had given offhand in conversation with him yesterday, when he consulted me on the purchase of the Commentary of Grotius. — Morning Service: prayers and sermon. I preached on "Life a Journey." — Evening service, prayers. — Preparing a Sermon. — Rec^d. a letter from Mr C. Aitkens, making enquiries as to the Pincott Charity, a fund from which, as I had told him, assistance may be obtained towards the erection of a Parsonage: – from Messrs. Hoare, ~~ackn~~ acquainting me that Lady Wilmot Horton |[106] has paid to my account with them the half yearly interest on Mortgage, £194. 3. 4 Income Tax being deducted from £200. — Eccl. Gazette. — To the family a Section from Trower's exposition of the Gospels. –

Jan. 25. Monday.

The forenoon fine, the afternoon showery. — Wrote to Perkins, requesting information as to the Pincombe Charity, by which he benefited in the erection of his parsonage, that I may be able to communicate with Aitkens on that subject. — to Jackson Clark that, if the weather were fine on Wednesday, I would call on him to accompany me to the Turnpike meeting at Bourton on the Hill: — to Hayward, requesting him to send his bill for attendance and medicine. — Justice business at home — Preparing a Sermon. — Received a letter from E.F.W. all well at Stanway: – also a note from Jackson Clark asking me to take him to Bourton on the Hill to-morrow, a request which I had anticipated by my note to him — Visiting sick and aged parishioners — distribu-|[107] ting charitable alms kindly furnished by Mr Lumbert. — Bonnycastle's Newfoundland. — Wrote to Mr Maitland, librarian to the ~~Apr~~ Arbp. of Canterbury, in answer to his circular to the Clergy requesting information as to ancient printed books contained in old church or school libraries, that I knew of none in this neighbourhood; I named two such collections which had come under my observation, one at Ashby de la Zouch, one at Skipton.

Jan. 26. Tuesday.

A fine forenoon and afternoon; as evening closed in, rain, and a windy storm during the night. — Wrote to Mr C. H. Aitkens, forwarding the note I had received yesterday respecting the Pincomb Charity: — preparing a return to the Secretary of the National Society as to Church Schools in this parish, and writing a letter to go with it: — wrote to M^r R G K Brookes, requesting him to let me have the population returns of 1841, which I suppose are in his office. — John Talbot Rice and his lady called upon us; they are now residing at Great Risington. — Visited Mr Davis, to settle accounts with him, also M^rs. Ryan & her daughter |[108] at Eyford, to enquire about M^rs. Dolphin, who, I heard, returned yesterday from Cheltenham. — A letter from Messrs. Alcocks, Birkbecks & Co. who have received from Mr Geldard on my account £1. which he had omitted to pay them before, so correcting an error in M^r G's accounts with me. — A note from Mr Hayward, accompanying his bill for medical attendance. — Finished Bonnycastle's Newfoundland. Began Stanley's memoir and correspondence of Dr Arnold, the eminent late Head master of Rugby school.[11]

Jan. 27. Wednesday.

A fine day; rain and wind in the evening: a stormy and rainy night. —— Drove to Bourton on the Hill, to attend a meeting of the Trustees of the Evesham 2^d. Distr. Roads, and of

11. Arthur Penrhyn Stanley (1815-1881) *The life and correspondence of Thomas Arnold, D.D.: late head master of Rugby school, and regius professor of modern history in the University of Oxford*. London: 1844. 2 volumes.

the road from Chapel House to Bourton on the Hill. — Conveyed Mr Clark, of the Bank, who is Treasurer of the Evesham 2^{d.} Distr., from Stow to Bourton on the Hill, and back. — Called on Dr Warneford, whom we found in firm health, considering his age and chronic infirmity: his faculties of mind unimpaired, sight and hearing good. |¹⁰⁹ He still takes the same lively interest in what regards the Church and the State; is still acute, and diligent in the management of his private affairs, and in conducting his great and systematic charities. — The Turnpike meeting was attended by Lord Redesdale, Mr Malcolm, Mr Jarret, W B Pole, & myself — Messrs. Brookes, Stokes, Taplin & Clerk,[12] officials in attendance. The Evesham 2nd. District is now out of debt, £250 being ordered to be repaid to me, which is the last incumbrance. The Chapel House and Bourton on the Hill road is still heavily burdened. Transacted ordinary business — offered two vacant gates to be let, but as the bidders were few, and did not offer what we considered their value, we intend to hold them in hand — Called at Stow at the library &c. — Rec^{d.} a letter from the Dean of Gloucester, now in residence there, drawing my attention to ill-conduced beer-houses in the parish of Oddington, & other matters of justice business in which the Dean is interested. — Returned home by dinner time, and found a letter from Mr Pearce with inclosures from the P.L.C. on |¹¹⁰ the appointments of Schoolmaster and Schoolmistress, and on relief to able bodied families in times of scarcity. — Read the Premier's exposé of the calamitous state of Ireland in respect of famine, and of the temporary and permanent remedies proposed.[13] — Mr Barrow called during my absence. —

Jan. 28. Thursday.

After a very rainy night, a cold, damp, but not rainy day. — Mr Davis having sent me a cheque for the arrears of rent due to me up to Mich^{s.} last, wrote to him acknowledging the receipt of the same. — Drove to Stow. Attended at the Prov. Bank, and transacted business at the Office of the Gloucestershire Banking Company. — To the fortnightly meeting of Guardians, which was fully attended several weighty matters for consideration — Fixed the proposed salaries of Schoolmaster and Schoolmistress at £10 each with diet in the house. Acceded to the recommendation of the P.L.C. that during the pressure arising from high prices of |¹¹¹ articles of necessary consumption, relief, if any be given to the able-bodied heads of large families by offering to admit into the Workhouse one or more of the children. — Raised the salary of the Rel. Off. from £90 to £100 per ann. — Postponed till next Board day the further consideration of an application by the Matron for an increase of salary of £5 from £20 to £25. — Applications for relief many and urgent. — Messrs. Hippisley and Perkins present. — Joined Mr Ford at the Provident Bank, whom I found there with Mr Morrison. — a meeting of the Foss. and Cross, and Stump's Cross districts of roads had

---

12.   *Sic.*
13.   Sir Robert Peel had been forced out of office in June 1846 by Lord John Russell and a Whig administration dedicated to a laissez-faire policy. Neither Irish landlords nor the Poor Law unions could deal with the burden of a huge starving population. In January 1847, with Peel sniping from the opposition benches Russell's administration modified its non-interventionist policy. Money was made available on loan for relief, and soup kitchens were established. The potato crop did not fail in 1847, but the yield was low. Then, as hundreds of thousands of starving people poured into the towns and cities for relief, epidemics of typhoid fever, cholera, and dysentery broke out, and claimed more lives than starvation itself.

been held, at which it was resolved to repay me £50 of the amount of mortgage I still hold on the Foss. & Cross road, — £200. — Transacted some Justice business with M[r] F. — then he accompanied me as far as the Lower Slaughter Turnpike on my way home, he having sent his carriage forward from Stow. A fatiguing day, followed by a slight attack of indigestion — The debates on the relief |[112] of Ireland.

Jan. 29. Friday.

A frosty morning – a very fine day. — Wrote to E.F.W: — also to my dear Broome to be received by him on his birthday – the 31[st.] Inst. — also to Rev[d.] C. James, Evenlode, acknowledging a letter I had received from him yesterday respecting an application for relief made by one of his Parishioners, explaining the principle on which relief, in a certain way had been accorded to one, & denied to another: — dispatched to the Secr. of the National Soc. my report as to the Church Schools in this Parish, with an explanatory letter — Walked with MW. to Eyford; called on M[rs.] Dolphin, whose health is better, but her perplexities increase upon her, and cause great excitement. Bowen visiting at Eyford; is in better health. Met Ford there, come to call on Bowen. — Learnt the death of poor M[rs.] Lindow in Town, of a disease in the womb: she had been considered for some time in a hopeless state. — Stanley's life of D[r] |[113] Arnold.

Jan. 30. Saturday.

A frost in the morning; a little rain about mid-day: weather otherwise fine — Busy all the forenoon in appropriating and distributing to the poor, according to their necessities, and the size of their families, sheets, coverlets, calico and flannel, to the amount of £10 from the funds of the Church and Charity Estate; being assisted by Churchwarden Gregory, and M[rs.] Lea, as the wife of one of the Trustees. — Preparing a Sermon. — Received a letter from M[r] James, Evenlode, as to relief given on Thursday to one of his parishioners; my letter to him yesterday will answer the question put by him. — A letter from Serg[t.] Jones, P.C. stationed at Combe Hill, near Tewkesbury, soliciting from me a recommendation to aid him as a Candidate for the office of Inspector of Borough Police Tewkesbury. — Justice business at home with Superintendent Makepeace. — Heard of the miserable end of M[r] Ireland, Chaplain to the House of Correction, Northleach, who committed suicide on Wednesday night. He was elected at the Mich[s.] Sess[ns.] came into duty early |[114] in December, was understood to be a person of doubtful character: but this not known till after his election; he had brought good testimonials. He was an elderly man, with a wife & children, not resident at Northleach, but at or near Malmsbury, where he had held a Curacy, or chaplaincy of a Workhouse, is said to have a son at University: probably, poverty unsettled his mind, and led to the sad catastrophe. — A pamphlet, being a reprint of an article in the English Review adverse to D[r] Hook's late pamphlet on the Education of the Poor: the writer is, I believe, D[r] Wordsworth, now Canon of Westminster, late Headmaster of Harrow School: able & strong for the Church against latitudinarian views; has been much circulated; lent to me by D[r] Warneford. – Wrote a note to E.F.W. to be conveyed by John Bateman, who is going to-morrow to Cutsdean, where my Son is expected to officiate for the Curate, who is absent. –

<u>*Jan. 31. Sunday.*</u>
A frost, fine, cold weather. — Wrote to Sergeant Jones, Glorshire Constabulary, such a letter of commendation as he may shew |[115] to those who have the appointment of Inspector of the Tewkesbury Borough Police, promising to procure for him, if possible, testimonials from Mᵣ Ford and Mᵣ R. Waller: — to whom I wrote notes, requesting them to sign a document in Jones's favour, which I propose to send with his letter to me, and the notes I have written to them by a Policeman to-morrow. — Attended the Sunday School. — Morning service, prayers: Afternoon Service, prayers and sermon. I preached on the love of Christ to mankind a standard of the Christian's love to the brethren. — Preparing a Sermon. — British Magazine — To the family a section from Trower's exposition of the gospels.

<u>*Feb. 1. Monday.*</u>
A snow shower had fallen during the night; a frost; in the course of the day the snow chiefly melted, but partially remained on the ground. — Justice business at home — Prepared and sent for the signature of my brother Magistrates a testimonial in favour of Serjeant Jones. — Engaged in parish accounts &c. — Wordsworth's Review of Dᵣ Hook's pamphlet on education. – |[116]

<u>*Feb. 2. Tuesday.*</u>
A snow shower had fallen during the night: frost in the morning, but melting in the forenoon and afternoon: snow or sleet continued to fall but not heavily during the most of the day. — Busy in writing and making a remittance to the Secretary of the S.P.G. – settling the accounts of the Stow District Comm. &c. — Recᵈ a letter from Mᵣ James, Evenlode, who is very much dissatisfied with the order made by the Guardians on Thursday last as to the case of Baylis, a pauper of that parish, and purposes to bring the matter under the notice of the P.L.C. — A packet containing the Queen's letter in aid of the Collection now being made for the starving Irish and Western Highlanders. — Wordsworth's Review of Dᵣ Hook's pamphlet on the education of the poor.

<u>*Feb. 3. Wednesday.*</u>
More snow had fallen during the night, and some little fell in the forenoon, but melted, there not being a frost after sunrise. — Wrote a note to Dᵣ Warneford to accompany the pamphlet by Wordsworth on the education of the Poor, which I returned. — Sorting and preparing for |[117] distribution among the members of the Stow district Comm. S.P.G. a packet of Quarterly Papers of the Society. —— Mᵣ Pearce called by appointment, with whom a long conference on Poor Law Union matters, drawing up a letter as a Settlement, removal, and relief, to be written to the Poor Law Commᵣˢ· — A letter from Mᵣ Jennings, as to certain ground rents offered to us for purchase; suggesting that I should come to Town to see and judge of the fitness of any of those which have been offered. — Called on J. Davis — Stanley's life of Arnold. —

<u>*Feb. 4. Thursday.*</u>
A sharp frost; the remains of snow on the ground and on the roads: fine day. — Driven to Stow by Baldwin, the House Servant, John Cox, the coachman, being invalided by an attack of Lumbago. — Walked home after business was over. — Received letters from

H. D. Warter, with particulars of a property in ground rents in the Wandsworth road offered to us for purchase for my consideration; one of the same of which Jennings referred in his letter received yesterday: — from C Bathurst, who purposes to send me a |¹¹⁸ copy of the memoirs and correspondence of his uncle, Visc^{t.} Sidmouth, lately published by his son in law, the Dean of Norwich, Hon. & Revd. Dr Pellew.[14] — from Mr Coyle, Blockley, inclosing a cheque in payment of his annual subscription S.P.G. — From my son, with a good and pleasant account of all at Stanway: – from Revd. Hedley, Gloucester, a printed solicitation for a subscription to a church now in course of erection in the suburbs of Gloucester. — At Stow, transacted business at the Gloucestershire Banking Company's office, settling my Turnpike mortgages accounts with Mr Clark — had an interview with Mr Morgan on Tax matters — attended at the Provident Bank, meeting there Winter, Morrison &c. — To the Justice room, where Ford and R. Waller sat as my colleagues: Messrs. Winter, W B Pole, Perkins, Mangin, Oakley Hill, Barrow, being our Assessors. — Stanley's life of Arnold. —

Feb. 5. Friday.

A milder day, no frost, a little tendency to rain. — Wrote to H D Warter and |¹¹⁹ Jennings as to the investment in ground rents, intimating that my son and I shall probably think it desirable to go for two or three days to Town, to consult with Mr Warter & Mr Jennings, and to view the localities of proposed purchases, when the time is come for action: — to Mr Coyle in acknowledgement of his subscription S.P.G: — to the Dean of Gloucester as to the beer houses at Oddington: — to Rodwell, London, for a supply of books for the Book Society: — to Messrs. Alcocks, Birkbecks & Co., directing them to pay £150 to my account with Messrs. Hoare. ———— Our dear children rode over from Stanway to visit us, and remained more than two hours, returning home to a late dinner: conferred with them as to investment in suburban ground rents, a journey to Town &c. – much pleasant conversation; a good report of our dear grandchildren; — Rec^{d.} from G. B. Hayward an acknowledgment of the remittance I had made to him yesterday: — from Messrs. Hoare intimation that they had received from Jennings £64. 3. 7 |¹²⁰ to my account: — from the Treasurers S.P.G. an acknowledgement of the remittance I had made to them on the 3^{d.} Inst. — Received also a packet containing the promised life of Lord Sidmouth, sent by Bathurst's orders from a London Bookseller — 3 handsome 8vo. volumes. — Stanley's Life of Arnold. —

Feb. 6. Saturday.

Showery weather. — Wrote a long letter to C Bathurst, thanking him for his kind present of the life of Lord Sidmouth and alluding to many topics on which he had touched in former letters, and to which I had not adverted. — Preparing a Sermon. — Visited sick and aged parishioners: — also my cotrustee, Mr Lea, as to Parish Trust matters. — Stanley's Life of Arnold. —

---

14. Charles Bathurst's father, Charles Bragge Bathurst (1754-1831) had married Charlotte Addington, the youngest sister of his close friend Henry Addington in 1788. Bragge Bathurst was an influential member of Parliament. Henry Addington (1757-1844) was prime minister 1801-1804, and elevated to the peerage as Viscount Sidmouth in 1805. George Pellew (1793-1866), Dean of Norwich 1828-66. *Life of Sidmouth* (London, 1847).

Feb. 7. Sunday.

A snowy day, till towards the evening, but, there not being much frost, little snow lay. — Visited the Sunday School. — Morning service: prayers and sermon. I preached on the ministry of Sᵗ Paul. — Evening service, prayers. — A letter from Mᵣ Jennings in answer to mine of Friday last, with some |¹²¹ particulars as to other ground rents at Chelsea, and houses, near the Blackwall terminus on sale. — Preparing sermons. — British magazine — To the family a section from Trower's exposition of the gospels.

Feb. 8. Monday.

A hard frost: snow fell almost without interruption from 10 AM. till evening; a heavy fall. — Wrote to E.F.W. forwarding to him the letter received from Jennings yesterday, with my views respecting a journey to Town next week to look at the properties offered for sale, and confer with Jennings & Warter: — wrote to Jennings to the same effect. — Mᵣ Pearce called with a packet received from the P.L.C. as to the case of J. Baylis of Evenlode, which Mᵣ James has submitted to the P.L.C. complaining that the relief ordered by the Guardians was inadequate. The P.L.C. call for our observations on the case: prepared an answer to the P.L.C. to be submitted to the Guardians on Thursday next. — Justice business as home — Preparing a Sermon. — Stanley's Life of Arnold. |¹²²

Feb. 9. Tuesday.

A frost; fine till after mid-day, when heavy snow showers were frequent: the snow deep. — Preparing a Sermon. — Engaged with one of the persons employed in measuring the parish, and with Churchwarden Gregory in giving information as to the breadth of the roads, and other matters requisite to the making a correct map. — Recᵈ a letter from Mᵣ Warter, who will be disengaged next week, and ready to confer with my son and me as to an investment in ground rents or otherwise. — Stanley's Life of Dᵣ Arnold.

Feb. 10. Wednesday.

A frost: deep snow on the ground; a clear sky over head. — Wrote to E.F.W. — forwarding to him the letter I recᵈ yesterday from Warter, and fixing our departure for London from Stanway for Tuesday next: — to Mᵣ Warter, & to Mᵣ Jennings, announcing our intended journey to Town, and making an appointment with the latter to accompany us on Wednesday to view the properties offered for investments: — |¹²³ to Miss Sophia Hunt on Hunt affairs — Received a letter from Messʳˢ Hoare, announcing that the Cirencester Branch of the Gloucestershire Bkᵍ Cᵒ has paid to my account £350: – from Jennings saying that he shall hold himself disengaged to transact business with us on Wednesday and the following days: — from the Assist. Chaplain, Gloster Gaol, soliciting my subscription to a book he is about to publish — "the Clergyman in the Gaol." — Preparing a Sermon. — Stanley's Life of Arnold. — Visited a poor person at Lower Slaughter. ——

Feb. 11. Thursday.

A fine frosty day; snow still deep on the ground; but travelling in this quarter not much impeded. — Wrote to Messʳˢ Hoare, informing them that I expected they would soon receive a remittance on my accᵗ of £150 from the Craven Bankers, and desiring them to invest £650 in 3 p^r C^t· Cons. in my name, when that money from Yorkshire sh$^{d.}$ have been paid in. Also desired them to pay £8. to the Relief Association for the destitute |^{124} Irish and Scotch, £5 as my subscription, £3. as that of my wife. — Wrote to the Rev$^{d.}$ G Heaton requesting him to add my name to the list of subscribers to the forthcoming work — "The Clergyman in the Gaol." Drove to Stow — Letters from C Bathurst, and from Serg^t· Jones, Glouc. Const. thanking me and other Magistrates for our recommendation, but the vacancy expected in the Inspectorship of Police at Tewkesbury, which he hoped to obtain, did not occur. — Transacted business at the Provident Bank. — Presided at the fortnightly meeting of the Guardians of the Union: a full attendance, and a heavy day's work. Matters of chief interest — the Correspondence with the PLC. as to the alleged insufficient relief given at the last meeting to a pauper of Evenlode, of which Mr James had complained to the Comm$^{rs.}$ the letter I had prepared indicating the course taken, with further facts shewing that the man's condition was not so bad as represented, was adopted and dispatched. — The application of the |^{125} Matron for an increase of £5 to her salary was negatived. — The Guardians agreed to petition both houses of Parliament, that the law of settlement may be done away with, and that a National fund be created for the relief of the poor, wherever their destitution might arise, to be levied on all landed, personal, and other property, professions or employments producing profit, to be distributed by Boards of Guardians as at present constituted, with fit machinery to prevent extravagance or abuse in the distribution. I was requested to prepare such a petition — My Son looked in upon me at the Union W.H. he had ridden with Sophy from Stanway, to transact Provident Bank business at Stow: gave a good account of the children; was returning to Stanway, accompanied by Emma Vavasour; arranged with me for our Journey to Town next Tuesday: it is proposed that MW. and I shall go to Stanway on Monday, and my wife will remain there with Sophy and the children till our return from London on Friday. — Late home, much tired, with a bad cold, and something of a cough. — |^{126} Stanley's Life of Arnold.

Feb. 12. Friday.

Hard frost, snow lying thick on the ground, fine overhead till the afternoon, when more snow fell, but not much. — Wrote to Perkins, requesting him to do my duty here on Ash Wednesday, which he consented to perform in the afternoon. — Wrote to Rodwell, Bookseller, London, with an order for books for the Stow Book Society. — Mr Pearce called by appointment, with whom long engaged in preparing minutes and resolutions of the Union, according to the proceedings at the Board meeting yesterday; also I draw up a petition for the abolition of the law of settlement &c. to be laid before the Guardians for their signature at their next meeting. — Parish and Justice business. – A letter from Hoare announcing the receipt of £150 to my account from Alcocks, Birkbecks & Co· – A letter from my Son, who returns the letter and sketch from Jennings, which I had forwarded to him, and writes on the arrangements for our journey to London next week: all which we settled when we met |^{127} yesterday: he had not thought of coming to Stow when he wrote. — Cold and cough very troublesome — Stanley's Life of Arnold.

Feb. 13. Saturday.

A frost in the morning; but less hard than of late, and symptoms of a thaw. — Wrote to M$^{rs.}$ C Barr: also to Mr Wellford — Visited sick parishioners — Rec^d· a letter from Mess$^{rs.}$ Hoare, who have brought for me 3 p^r Cent. Cons. £717. 14. 10 with £650 money – 90½ per C^t. Very unwell with Cough, feverish cold, asthmatic difficulty in breathing & expectorating. Much indisposed in the Evening and during the night.

Feb. 14. Sunday.

A rapid thaw. — Performed the morning service of my church – prayers: but too much indisposed to attempt the Evening duty — Sent for Mr Hayward, who prescribed for me, and considered that I was under the influence of a violent cold. A very uncomfortable evening, irritation in the air passages, a hard cough, defluxion, languor — the remedies taken before bed time relieved me, so that I passed a more comfortable night than the preceding. — A parcel arrived from C Bathurst, a very |^{128} handsomely bound copy of the poetry of the Antijacobin 4$^{to.}$ — A letter from the Revd Ernest Hawkins, Sec. S.P.G. in answer to one of my official letters, the last written, to the Society, in which I had remarked that the visit of some^{one} of the official Advocates of the Society, to our next annual meeting, might be productive of good: he holds out a prospect of himself coming, or sending some other help — A letter from Mrs Mounsain, a candidate for the vacant situation of Housekeeper to the Gloucester Infirmary. — Eccl. Gazette — Brit. Mag.

Feb. 15. Monday.

Heavy rain in the morn^g snow nearly melted away; a shower or two, but for the most part fine weather. — Found myself so much indisposed as to make it unwise to leave home for Stanway, or to carry out the plan of a journey to London — Dispatched the groom with a letter to my Son, desiring him to go to Town without me, and to make needful arrangements with Messrs Warter and Jennings — To this he and Sophy immediately responded by |^{129} riding over in the kindest manner to see me, and they remained with us two hours — I gave E.F.W. further necessary instructions as to business, and promised, if well enough, to go to Stanway for a few days on Friday, to meet my Son on his return home. — Very much indisposed in the evening, a violent cough, & discharge from the nostrils, great want of appetite &c. Wrote to Hayward to visit me to-morrow. — Good reports of our dear Grand children — Stanley's Life of Arnold. — A very restless and uncomfortable night.

Feb. 16. Tuesday.

A fine morning: rainy afternoon: evening fine. — Mr Hayward called on me, and prescribed: considers me as suffering from congestion on the lungs, and in the bronchial tubes: my state requiring medicine, care, and watching: the remedies administered: squills and tartarized antimony, very Sickening and lowering: appetite bad; general languor; great labouring in cough and expectoration: much indisposed — but more comfortable after I had retired to bed. — Brit. Mag. — Stanley's Life of Arnold. – |^{130} Letters on Hunt affairs from Sophia Hunt and Mr Hare.

Feb. 17. Wednesday.

Moist, damp afternoon after a fine looking morning – stormy and windy in the Evening. — Hayward visited me and considered me a shade better than yesterday; but great care with medicine requisite, so as to make it clear that I must not think of going to Stanway on Friday, or officiating on Sunday either here or there. Pursuing the same course of medicine with a little change: the cough and defluxion bad, languor and nausea uncomfortable: appetite not good. — Wrote to E.F.W. at the Burlington Hotel, that our visit to Stanway must be given up: begging him, as he had promised, to procure assistance on Sunday at Stanway, and to come on that morning, and undertake my duties here: remaining with us till Monday morn^{g.} — Wrote also to the same effect to dear Sophy. — Rec^{d.} a letter from Mr Pole, who sends me his proxy as to the Election of a Housekeeper at the Gloucester Infirmary, under a conviction that I have the best means of |[131] ascertaining who of the candidates is most likely to fulfil the duties well. — Perkins came in the afternoon to perform the Ash Wednesday duty, and remained with me after service for an hour or more. — Stanley's Life of Arnold. — British Mag. — Wrote to Pearce to send for my perusal any correspondence he may have with the P.L.C. —

Feb. 18. Thursday.

A damp, dull, and sometimes rainy day. — Little change in the state of my health. Visited by Mr Hayward, who changes the medicine. — Wrote to Mr Pole, in answer to his letter rec^{d.} yesterday. — Brit. Mag. and Stanley's Life of Arnold.

Feb. 19. Friday.

A cold day, free from rain, but windy. — Very little difference in my condition; Mr Hayward called: much oppressed in the head and chest, with hard cough. — Mr Ford called. — Rec^{d.} a letter, very short, from E.F.W. from London: he promises to be here on Sunday, to do the duty, and report what he has seen and done in business matters: — a few lines from Sewell, offering a mortgage for £3000, if we have such a sum |[132] to invest. — Brit. Mag. and Stanley's Life of Arnold. —

Feb. 20. Saturday.

A fine dry day. — Little change for the better in my health: the cough and expectoration continue, with much defluction from the head: not permitted to go out; confined to the fire side, but not taking so much medicine. Hayward called, and encouraged me by saying that I was slowing mending —— Justice and Union business, a refractory pauper being brought before me by Mr Pearce, and convicted; sentenced to 42 days imprisonment at Northleach H. of C. — Pearce submitted to me correspondence rec^{d.} from the P.L.C. — Letters from Gloucester, circular, announcing meetings of the Gloucester and Berkeley Canal proprietors, and Visitors of the Lunatic Asylum — M^r & Mrs. W. Vavasour called on horseback to enquire after me, but did not dismount. — Brit. Mag. and Stanley's Life of Arnold – Wrote to Messrs. Sewell and Newmarch that I had no £3000 at liberty for investment in a mortgage. —

Feb. 21. Sunday.

A fine open day. —— My son |[133] arrived from Stanway to breakfast, having returned from his London journey on Friday – he rode over; left his wife and children well. The Curate of Cutsdean undertook the Stanway duties E.F.W. performed the two services at my church, administering the Sacrament in the morning; prayers and no sermon; reading prayers & preaching under the authority of a Queen's letter in aid of the collections made for the relief of the sufferers by famine in Ireland, and some parts of Scotland. Collected.

Hayward called to visit me. I suffered less today than I have from the cough, but still the complaint maintains its hold, or relinquishes it slowly; and both in the head and chest is heavy. Confinement to the house, perseverance in expectorants, watchfulness as to the general state of the health necessary. Occasional violent paroxysms of coughing. — Much conversation with my Son as to the business which took him to Town. I am quite satisfied with what he has done in concert with Mr Jennings & Mr H. |*134* Warter, and trust that matters are now put into such a train that we shall be able to accomplish at no distant time an investment in ground rents, houses, or both on good terms, and profitably. — Brit. Mag. ——

Feb. 22. Monday.

A very mild, fine day. — My son returned to Stanway about twelve o cl. his visit having been a great comfort to us. — Parish business with Churchwdn. Gregory and Mrs. Lea. — Wrote to Mr Jennings expressing my approval of, and concurrence in all that had been arranged as to the purchase of ground rents &c. – between him, my son, and Mr Warter during E.F.W.'s visit to London last week. — Mr Waller came from Bourton, agreeably to a request I had made to him by note yesterday, to officiate for me in the interment of a poor woman, a settled parishioner in Sesincote, but residing here for some months past with a sister. He sat for an hour with me. — Mr Hayward came, and paid a long visit in the evening, he considered me to be slowly improving but noticed the tenacity of my chronic cough. — |*135* Stanley's Life of Arnold. — Mr Moore called.

Feb. 23. Tuesday.

A cold, raw day. — Wrote to Mr H. D. Warter on the subject of investment in ground rents in the neighbourhood of the metropolis, sanctioning the line taken in the late consultations on the subject between him, my son and Mr Jennings. — Preparing a Sermon. — Justice business at home — Mr Vavasour and Mrs. W. Vavasour called: the former offered to perform my duties on Sunday next. — My health seems better; the cough and visitation of the air passages diminished: no visit from Mr Hayward to-day. — Stanley's Life of Dr Arnold.

Feb. 24. Wednesday.

Cold, Easterly wind, and frost: fine overhead. — Mr Hayward called, considered my improvement in health satisfactory, but enjoined great caution as to exposure to the air: advising me to avail myself of Mr Vavasour's proffered services for Sunday next; to whom I wrote accordingly: — much less cough, and oppression in the head, yet expectoration and defluxion going on. — Transacted Justice and Union business at home with Mr Makepeace, |*136* Mr Pearce and others. — Mr Ford called upon me: so also our dear children, who had ridden from Stanway to Stow, and called on us, as they returned home. — A letter from C Bathurst, kindly anxious as to my health. — Stanley's Life of Dr Arnold.

Feb. 26. Friday.

A frosty morning, dry day, and Easterly wind. — My 64th. birthday. GOD be thanked who has prolonged my life thus far and granted me time for repentance! May his grace be with me, that during the remainder of my earthly course I may run a stricter race of virtue & piety! that I may renounce the false maxims of this world, and act on sound Christian principles!

that I may redeem the time, not waste the precious privileges which are granted to me! that I may receive the divine dispensations, whether they be good or evil, gratefully and patiently! that I |*137* may have a lively faith in the merits of Christ Jesus, and give evidence of that faith by the general purity and correctness of my life and conversation! — I passed a comfortable day, free from much coughing, the lungs being less loaded and the respiration freer: but the cold biting air forbade my attempting to leave the house. M^r. Hayw^d. called and directed a continuance of the squill and Ipecacuanha pills. — Transacted Justice business at home. — Wrote on Trust business to Sophia Hunt — Rec^d. a kind letter of enquiry after my health from F. Aston. — Brit. Mag. — Stanley's Life of Arnold. —

Feb. 27. Saturday.

A continuance of the same cold, frosty weather with Easterly wind. — Free from much cough, with less defluxion, and altogether improved in health: but I dared not venture out. — Wrote to E.F.W. and to F. Aston. — M^r. Makepeace called. – A letter from H D Warter as to the amount deposited with the Accountant General of the Court of Chancery, the produce of the sale of houses in Fenchurch Street. — British Mag. — Stanley's Life of Arnold. |*138*

Feb. 28. Sunday.

Cold, raw, frosty weather, with Easterly wind. — Wrote to J. W. Harris for a supply of coals. — M^r. Vavasour came to do the duties of my church, accompanied by M^rs. W. Vavasour, and remained with us from 11 AM. to 4 P.M. — Received a letter from C Bathurst. — M^r. Hayward called, and considered me convalescent: the cough nearly gone, the pulse and appetite good, the chief evil being pain over the left eye, the consequence of an irritated state of the mucous membrane, shewing a remnant of catarrhal affection. — Brit. Magazine.

Mar. 1. Monday.

A flickering of snow in the morning: wind Easterly, air cold. — Wrote to M^r. Pearce in answer to a note received from him on Union business. — After luncheon left home with MW. on a visit to our dear children in the Phaeton; did not experience any inconvenience in the way of coughing or oppression on the chest, from exposure to the air, though still suffering from what is called Brow Ague.[15] Our children not having received my letter written on Saturday, were uncertain whether to expect us or not, and |*139* had gone out to ride when we reached the Vicarage. – The dear children received us, all quite well, and pleased to see us. — A happy domestic evening.

Mar. 2. Tuesday.

Weather fine, wind easterly. — Took a walk with our dear children to Didbrook, where met and parlayed with M^r. & M^rs. W^m. Whalley: — I was somewhat tired and heated with my first walk for a fortnight: the cough and catarrh rather diminished. — A day of enjoyment in the Society of our children and grand children.

---

15. Brow ague – strictly supra-orbital neuralgia of malarious origin. The first Oxford English Dictionary reference to the word is in 1855 and this may have been a fashionable word to use in the prevailing medical jargon.

Mar. 3. Wednesday.

A slight tendency to rain, but fine weather, on the whole — Wind Easterly — Wrote to C Bathurst — A note on Union business from M͏ͬ Pearce. — Not so much fatigued with my walk to-day as yesterday — Called on M͏ͬ Cook. — A day of domestic comfort with those dearest to us.

Mar. 4. Thursday.

Cold, raw weather: — Easterly wind. — Settling accounts with my son &c. — Wrote to Mess͏ͬˢ· Hoare, desiring them to place £50 to the credit of my son with them, debiting my a/c to that amount. — Enjoyed a walk to Church Stanway, in the pleasure grounds on the mansion |¹⁴⁰ house &c. — I feel, thank GOD, more than convalescent. — Much pleasant talk with, and enjoyment of our dear children and grand children. — Rec͏ͩ· a letter from Howell: his establishment at Prinknash is not likely to be broken up till towards the end of the month, at which time, I suppose, Laura & Constance, with Macleod will be our guests. –

Mar. 5. Friday.

A moist morning; cold N.E. wind: a dry forenoon & afternoon. — Left our dear children and grand children, and returned home, after a most comfortable visit, in better health. — M͏ͬ Morrison paid us a morning visit. — M͏ͬ Ford called upon us. – M͏ͬ Brookes called to solicit me to give testimony to his character and fitness for the office of Clerk to the district Court about to be established at Stow, under the Small Debts Act of last Sessions: the appointment rests with the newly appointed Judge of the Gloucestershire District of these Courts, M͏ͬ Francillon, of Gloucester, a Provincial Barrister, to whom M͏ͬ B. requests me to write in his favour. — Received letters from M͏ͬ Warter & M͏ͬ Jennings, as to the amount deposited with the Accoun-|¹⁴¹ tant General of the Court of Chancery, — the produce with accumulations of the price for which our Fenchurch Street property was sold, and as to the purchase of the ground rents in Larkhall Lane &c. with the freehold house in the Wandsworth road, the latter being approved as an investment by M͏ͬ Jennings, if it can be bought worth the money — A letter from M͏ͬ Thornton on Hunt matters: he returns to me the balance of Trust monies, forwarded to me by M͏ͬ Hare; also M͏ͬ Hare's letter to me by which it was accompanied, both of which I had sent for his perusal. — A letter from the Clerk at the Lunatic Asylum; fixing a meeting of visitors for the 16͏ͭʰ· Inst. on which important business is to be transacted. — Memoir of J. W. Smith, a recently deceased eminent and rising Barrister, by M͏ͬ Warren, Barrister, published in a late number of the Blackwood's Magazine.

Mar. 6. Saturday.

A cold, raw day. Easterly wind. — Wrote to M͏ͬ Francillon in recommendation of M͏ͬ R. Brookes: — To M͏ͬ J. Clark, Glouc. Bank͏ᵍ· C͏ᵒ· Stow, with a cheque, and received his reply with £20 for my cheque. — |¹⁴² To M͏ͬ Jennings and M͏ͬ Warter in answer to their letters received yesterday, instructing them as to proceeding in the negociation for the ground rents and other property in Clapham and Chelsea. — To Howell, in answer to his letter received at Stanway, and that we shall be ready to received Laura & Constance with Macleod, when the establishment at Prinknash is broken up; — (MW. rec͏ͩ· to-day a letter from Laura Howell, by which it appears that the Sale of furniture at Prinknash is fixed for the Tuesday in

Easter week; so that we may expect the sisters and their little brother in Passion week) — to Randall, hatter, St̶ Oxford, ordering a new hat: — to C Bathurst in reply to a note received from him to-day, asking information as to payment of some of the officers of Unions out of the consolidated fund. — Rec^d. a circular from the Secretary of the Gloucester & Berkeley Canal Company as to certain resolutions passed at a late meeting of the Shareholders. — Transacting parish business with M^r Ed. Lea, Mr Davis, Mr Gregory & |^143 Mr J. B. Collett, calling on the three latter at their respective houses. — Mr Warren's memoir of J. W. Smith. — Rec^d. a note from J. Bryan, Stow, Undertaker, announcing the death of Mr Smith, farmer of Bledington, and that it is proposed that he be interred at Upper Slaughter on Tuesday next: he was for very many years a tenant resident at Eyford, and some of his children are buried here.

Mar. 7. Sunday.

Showery, raw and cold weather, with a North Easterly wind. — Preparing a Sermon. — Morning service; prayers — Afternoon – prayers and sermon. I preached on the power of conscience. — Rec^d. a letter from Bathurst, on the law of settlement, and several other points — Brit. Mag. — Fatigued with the duties of the day, and a touch of lumbago came over me; otherwise pretty well in health.

Mar. 8. Monday.

A fine day: the wind no longer Easterly. — Wrote to E.F.W. — A parish meeting was held at my house: to nominate persons fit to serve as parish constables: also to settle as to re-letting the Church |^144 and Charity Estate for another term of seven years to the present tenant, M^rs. Griffin, at the same rent, £65 per ann. — Present Messrs. E Lea, John Brain Collett, W Gregory and myself. — Wrote to M^rs. Griffin to inform her of the resolution passed in her favour — Preparing a Sermon. — Justice business at home — Drove with MW. to Stow. Rec^d. a letter from Messrs. Hoare, that they had paid £50 from my account with them to that of my Son; – from C Bathurst, more on the law of settlement &c. — Shopping — Business at the Library: — also with Mr Pearce at the Workhouse. — Called at "the Cottage": M^rs. Vavasour gone to see the family at Maugersbury – Emma Vavasour ill with measles. — Saw Mr V. but did not go into the house. — Warren's memoir of J W Smith — Stanley's Life of Dr Arnold. — Except as a slight attack of rheumatism in the back, little to complain of in respect of health.

Mar. 9. Tuesday.

A cold, raw, day: a slight tendency to snow. — Wrote to Rodwell for a |^145 supply of books for the Stow C̶l̶e̶r̶i̶c̶a̶l̶ ^Book Society. — Engaged in the forenoon at the School room with Mitchell and his son, who produced the map of the parish which they had made, that the owners and occupiers of land might give information as to the ownership and occupancy, and name of each parcel of land, house, cottage &c. — J B Collett, W Gregory, Jos Reynolds, S. Collett, Geo. Lea, Price &c. attended. — Rec^d. a letter from Mr Francillon in answer to mine on behalf of the R G K Brookes, to whom I forwarded the letter. It is probable that Mr B. may be appointed a deputy to Mr Anderson, of Cirencester, who is nominated Clerk of a district of which Stow forms a part. — A letter from Mr Thornton, covering a letter w^h. had been forwarded to him by Mr Hare, from Messrs. Cox and Williams, who forward the report of a Surveyor as to the premises by the River side in London, held by the Hunt Trustees as security for money lent on Mortgage. A sale of the property is recommended. — A circular from the Weekly board of the Gloucester Infir-|[146] mary, as to the names, ages, and testimonials of the Candidates for the office of Matron of the Infirmary at Gloucester. — Justice business at home. — M[r] Hayward called. He considered me as recovered from my late attack; but I am now, though not severely, suffering from lumbago. — M[r] Smith from Bledington was buried here to-day. — Stanley's Life of D[r] Arnold.

Mar. 10. <u>Wednesday.</u>

A cold day; wind Easterly: snow showers till the evening, but much did not lay on the ground. Towards night frost. — Wrote to M[r] Hare and to M[r] Thornton on Hunt affairs, respecting the sale of the Red Lion Wharf, Thames Street. — Wrote to C Bathurst. — Preparing a Sermon. — Justice business at home. — Received a letter from M[rs] Mountain, Cirencester, one of the Candidates for the office of Matron at the Gloucester Infirmary: she requests again my support, and that I would allow the Misses Hall of Bourton, who had given me their proxies to vote for whom-|[147] soever I should consider the most competent person, to vote for her. Wrote in answer that I should beg those ladies to vote as seemed them best: but that I should not vote for her, as her age, 54, as compared with that of two other candidates with equally good testimonials, was against her: more particularly, as the weekly Board recommends Governors not to support candidates younger than 30, or older than 45. — Wrote to Miss Hall with a copy of my letter to M[rs] M. begging her and her Sister to use their own judgement without respect to me. — Stanley's Life of D[r] Arnold.

Mar. 11. Thursday.

A hard frost — in the early part of the morning, wind Easterly: afterwards to the West, but cold. — Drove to Stow. — Rec[d] from some member of the H. of Commons a copy of the bill now before Parliament for the more speedy trial and punishment of the Juvenile offenders. — To the Provident Bank, where I transacted business – To the Workhouse, where presided over the Board of the Guardians from ½ past 11 AM. to 3 P.M. – the usual routine business. Returned to the Provident |[148] Bank, where I met Mess[rs] Winter, Lewes, W. Vavasour, and H. Lindow. — The latter gave a very bad account of his father's state, who was seized on Tuesday night with an attack of Paralysis, not unaccompanied by Apoplexy. His speech is inarticulate, he has lost the use of one side, and the best hope is a partial recovery, and that very doubtful. – As I returned home, I was accompanied to the Turnpike gate at Lower Slaughter in my carriage from Stow, by M[r] Barrow. – Stanley's life of Arnold. — My health good, and not fatigued by the business of the day — A little Justice business at ~~home.~~ Stow. — Stanley's life of Arnold.

Mar. 12. Friday.

A frost in the morning, with a sprinkling of snow — the day afterwards fine — Justice business at home. — Preparing a Sermon. — Walked with MW. to Eyford, to call on M[rs] Dolphin, who was indisposed, and had not left her room. — As we returned, met and parleyed with ~~G.~~ M[r] Wynniatt, on horseback, who was accompanied by James Goodrich, now staying at Guiting Grange. — A circular from Gloucester Gaol, announcing |[149] a meeting of Visiting Magistrates there for Thursday next. — Stanley's life of Arnold. —

Mar. 13. Saturday.

A fine day. — Preparing a Sermon. — Drove with MW to Great Risington, to call on M[r] and M[rs.] J. T. Rice, who were from home. — As we returned called at Little Risington on the Fords, being received by M[rs.] Ford, Dulcy, and Sophia. — A letter from E.F.W. — who returns me letters from H Warter, Jennings and Bathurst, which I had sent for his perusal. All well at Stanway Vicarage. — Stanley's life of Arnold.

Mar. 14. Sunday.

A frosty morning, and fine, but cold day. — Visited the Sunday School. — Morning service. Prayers and Sermon: I preached a funeral discourse, this being the first Sunday since the internment of the late M[r] Smith. — Evening prayers. — Preparing a Sermon. — Ecclesiastical Gazette. — To the family a section from Trower's exposition of the gospels. — Wrote to R. Waller to meet me at Stow on Thursday next, to assist me in Magisterial business, as M[r] Ford will be from home, and so not able to attend. |[150]

Mar. 15. Monday.

A fine day. — Preparing a Sermon. — Called on J. Davis. — Rec[d.] a circular from Bloxsome, announcing a meeting of the County rate Comm. at Gloucester fixed for the day preceding the Sessions. — Stanley's life of Arnold.

Mar. 16. Tuesday.

A frosty morning, fine day, cool air. — I left home after an early breakfast in the phaeton, to attend a special meeting of Visitors of the Lunatic Asylum at Gloucester; — at the railroad Station met and parleyed with J W Martin &c. — Reached the asylum by 11 AM. where were assembled Curtis Hayward, Purnell, D[r] Timbrill, M[r] Brooke Hunt, Clifford and Hyett: the last representing the interests of the Subscribers, the former those of the County. M[r] Meyler represented the interests of the City of Gloucester. The business was to read and agree upon drafts prepared by the Sol[r] M[r] R. Wilton, with the advice of counsel, M[r] Prance, for the dissolution of the partnership now existing between the Subscribers on the one hand, and the County & City on the other: |[151] and for the reunion of the same parties on a different basis: the object being to assign certain parts of the building to the Counties, other parts to the Subscribers exclusively, other parts to be held jointly, that so the property being divided, the Counties might pay a certain balance to the Subscribers for such parts of the buildings as could not be nicely divided, and rent part of the superfluous space allotted to the Subscribers, which they could not apply to the purposes of their charity on account of insufficient funds; the Subscribers gain would be more ample funds from renting of their superfluous space to be expended in their charity, while the Counties would gain by acquiring at a moderate rate more space for pauper patients which is now ~~much~~ much wanted, and which, if this arrangement cannot be carried out, must be procured by the Counties in obedience to the Lunatic Acts now in force at a much heavier expence. The arrangement made by the Committee to-day is the fulfilment of the plan sketched out at a meeting of |[152] the visitors in November last, and to be final must be approved by a majority of the Visiting Board, and by the Home Secretary. We were unanimous. I left the meeting so as to reach the Railway Station in time for the train leaving for Birmingham at 3.25 PM. which conveyed me to

Chelten^m. — where I found my servant ready with the carriage, and arrived at home by a little before 7 P.M. — A letter from Howell, to say that his daughters, Laura and Constance, will be with us for a visit on the 3^d. April, bringing McLeod & his attendant. — The Astons had called here while I was absent. — Stanley's life of Dr Arnold.

Mar. 17. Wednesday.

A fine day. — Wrote to Howell, that the arrangements proposed by him as to the arrival of his daughters with their little brother here on Apr. 3. would be very agreeable to us. — Preparing a Sermon. — Justice business at home. — Mr R. Waller, and Mr Clarke called upon us. — Stanley's life of Arnold. — Heard of the recent decease of our old acquaintance Lady |^153 Imhoff, at an advanced age, in Town. —

Mar. 18. Thursday.

A fine day. Preparing a sermon — Drove to Stow. MW. accompanied me, and soon returned home. — Rec^d. a letter on Hunt affairs from Mr Hare; also from Mr Hyett on the approaching election of a matron at the Infirmary: this letter I ans^d. while at Stow. — Attended at the Provident Bank, where I met Mr Morrison & R Waller. – Transacted business at the office of the Gloucestershire Banking Company. — At the Justice room R. Waller was my colleague: Messrs. W. B. Pole and Westmacott assessors. — Stanley's life of Arnold. —

Mar. 19. Friday.

Fine weather. — Wrote to Mr Rodwell with an order for a book for the Stow Book Society, — to Mr Ford, urging him to vote for the House candidate at the approaching election of a matron to the Infirmary; — to Mr Westmacott, with explanations as to the case of Baylis, a parishioner of Chastleton, but chargeable to Evenlode: sending to him for his perusal the notes written to me by Mr James on the man's case; and disclaiming, as I did yesterday, any imputa-|^154 tion as entertained by me on the parish of Chastleton, as having tampered with the man, to induce him to establish himself at Evenlode to the prejudice of the rate payers there. Baylis's wife has died after child birth, and in distress, charity being withheld from the family both by the Chastleton and the Evenlode people who might have bestowed ^it, but for the pique and ill feeling which has sprung up in consequence of the supposed scheme on the part of the rate payers at Chastelton to throw a burden on Evenlode. — Walked with MW — to Eyford, to call on M^rs. Dolphin, who is ill, and had not left her room. A bad account also of poor Bowen — Mitchell has brought the map of the Parish, with its measurement and reference book of owners and occupiers. – I examined it with him. — Stanley's life of Dr Arnold. Justice business at home with Mr Makepeace &c. —

Mar. 20. Saturday.

A little rain fell in the morning and evening, otherwise the day was fine, but cold where the Sun did not reach. — |^155 Called on E Lea, and conferred with him on various parish matters, — survey and valuation, appointment to parish offices &c. — Wrote to Mr Croome, Tewkesbury, desiring him to make his valuation of this parish as soon as he could. — Justice business at home. — Preparing for business at the Sessions next week. — Received a letter from Mr Lefevre as to the valuation of the parish of Toddenham, for the country rate: — from Mr Pole, desiring me to use his proxy in voting for a matron to the Infirmary as I should judge best: he gives an indifferent report as to poor Sir Charles Imhoff: — to this letter I replied: — from Mr Thornton with inclosures from Mr Hare on Hunt Trust property, — the sale of property by the Thames in London held by the Trustees in foreclosure of a mortgage: — a letter from C Bathurst. — Stanley's life of Dr Arnold. — Preparing a Sermon. — I have been suffering from cough for a day or two. —

Mar. 21. Sunday.

Showery, but not much rain. — Wrote to Mr Hare and Mr Thornton on Hunt Trust matters. — Preparing a Sermon. — |[156] Morning prayers. — Afternoon prayers and Sermon. I preached on the duty of repentance illustrated — Received a circular letter from Mr Graves, Assistant Poor Law Commissioners, addressed to Chairman of Unions in his district, inviting information respecting the deficiency in the Potatoe Crops, and the disease in that plant. — From Mr Pain a note requesting my signature, as one of the Trustees of the Stow Prov. Bank, to a Draft on the Commrs. for the Reduction of the National debt for £650 to supply cash for the payment of recalls beyond the amount of floating cash in the hands of the Gloucestershire Banking Company. I signed the same, to be forwarded to G. P. by the post to-morrow. — Preparing for the Sessions at Gloucester. — Eccl. Gazette — Much inconvenienced by a cough. —

Mar. 22. Monday.

Fine weather. — An early breakfast: Left home for the Sessions at Gloucester: MW. accompanied me in the phaeton to Cheltenham, where she remained at the Plough, passing the day, and sleeping there; shopping, going to the dentist, visiting Mrs. |[157] Keyshall &c. Sent back the Servant, carriage & horses: — I went on to the Railway Station, with Lefroy, whom I accompanied to Gloucester — Took up my quarters at the Bell Hotel. — Conferred with Purnell as to County business — To the Shire Hall: where attended from 12 to 6 PM. to the business of the Committee of Accounts, and two other Committees, on the County rate, and Prisons. There were present Purnell, Curtis Hayward, Baker, (now hors de combat, as being High Sheriff,) Raymond Barker, Danl. John, T. Niblett, with the usual officials, Bloxsome, Riddiford, Wilton, Whitehead, Lefroy, Keiley &c. Ordered compulsory surveyors for the County rate as to several parishes near Stow, letters insisting on professional surveys to be sent to many parishes backward in furnishing them. Considered and reported upon the proposal made at the last Sessns. by Mr Hanford for an interchange of constabulary between the Worcestershire and Gloucestershire force, in respect of those parishes between Tewkesbury and Broadway, which alternate-|[158]ly project into one or the other county. — The Chairman reported that the Home Secretary had sent his consent to the alterations proposed and carried at the last Sessions as to Chapel, Governors apartments, and offices in the Gaol, some modifications and improvements being made. — Purnell, Curtis Hayward & I dined together at the Bell: much consultation as to the business of to-morrow, auditing of accounts, & business with Riddiford — A good deal troubled with cough and expectoration. —

Mar. 23. Tuesday.

A bright morning: heavy rain in the forenoon; a fine afternoon and evening — Rose early: busy auditing County bills till breakfast time. — Breakfasted with Purnell — Court opened

– Few Magistrates — the only one of rank present, the Lord Lieutenant — I went through my usual budget of bills, relative to the County expenditure in the last quarter. — The Rev^{d.} — Thorpe was elected Chaplain of Northleach House of Correction in the room of Mr Ireland, deceased. — A very long and |¹⁵⁹ tedious document, but well and carefully prepared, was read, referring to an investigation made by the Vis. Jus. of Little Dean H. of C. into the conduct of all the officers of that prison, Keeper, Matron, Wardsman & Schoolmaster, developing all sorts of irregularity, drunkenness, profligacy, swearing, violence of temper, on the part of some or all of the parties, brought to light by quarrels between the Keepers and Wardsman, resulting in their suspension by the Vis. Justices, with a recommendation from them to dismiss all: to this the Court almost unanimously assented: much interest taken in the case as the Keeper had been a confidential and favourite non-commissioned officer of 36 years standing in the Gloucestershire Militia of which Lord Fitzhardinge is Colonel, Jenner, Lt. Col. — It was feared that a party would be made to support the man, but the case was too gross, the Peer threw the Keeper overboard, and Jenner contented himself with not voting for his dismissal. Being obliged to return home for the duties of the fast day to-morrow, I left the Court between |¹⁶⁰ three and four P.M. and before another case came on of much interest — a charge against the Clerk and deputy Governor of the County Prison, who had charged the Governor with a total disobedience of the rules laid down for the management of the prison, speaking of them as dead letter & not to be regarded &c. But this serious charge Moore, when required to substantiate it, failed to make good: so that it seems likely that he must be dismissed, though, in fact, the charge made by him is to all intents and purposes correct, though, probably, not capable of being proved by direct evidence, though the Governor is notoriously inefficient, and his deputy an active and effective officer. The result of Moore's probable dismissal is utter confusion in the Prison Management, and the full exposure of Mason's incompetency. — All this I could not help leaving in the hands of others. — In the course of the day, I had been much in intercourse with Purnell, Curtis Hayward, Timbrill, Price &c. |¹⁶¹ At the Gloucester Station had a parley with Col. Browne, Mr Clutterbuck, and Mr Teast, and with the latter walked from the Cheltenham Railway Station to the Plough. There joined MW. at about half past five P.M. and soon after set out homewards in a Plough Chariot, arriving at U Slaughter towards eight o'clock — My cough very troublesome. — Letters from Ford, who sends me his and Bennett's proxies for the ~~office~~ election of a Matron at the Infirmary; from Mr Westmacott, in reply to my letter to him as to the case of Baylis of Evenlode, and the relief afforded to his family by the Guardians of the Stow Union. — EFW. also wrote with a pleasant account of himself and family, except that poor little Freddy set himself on fire by a rushlight which caught his night dress on Saturday: providentially the nurse was near at hand, and extinguished the flames before he had been much burned; the injury to the arm was, however, such that the assistance of the Apothecary was required. — Justice business awaited me |¹⁶² when I returned home. —

Mar. 24. Wednesday.

Rain had fallen during the night – the day was dry, and air cold. – Wrote to E.F.W. — This being the day appointed for a general national fast, to acknowledge the many and great sins of the people, generally and individually, whereby we have deserved GOD's wrathful judgements, and to beseech him to relieve this nation from the grievous famine and disease now prevailing in Ireland and Scotland, and devastating certain localities with frightful calamity, divine service was performed by me to good congregations both in the forenoon and in the afternoon. I preached on the bad and good uses to be made of GOD's judgements on others. — A note from Hippisley (circular) announcing a meeting of the Stow Deanery Clerical conclave for the 7th. April: — a note from Bloxsome inclosing 1/6 for the Inspector of Weights and Measures in this district. W.B. had paid me yesterday £1. 8. 6 for this officer, whereas he is entitled to £1. 10. 0. — Brit. Mag. — Eccl. Gazette — Much oppressed with a cough. |[163]

Mar. 25. Thursday.

A sharp hoar-frost in the morning: fine, but cold during the day. — Drove to Stow. — To the Provident Bank. — To Mr Brookes's office, where I heard evidence against a prisoner charged with felony, sufficient to justify his commitment for re-examination. — To the Workhouse, where I presided at the fortnightly meeting of Guardians, fully attended. Lord Redesdale has written a long letter, promises to present our petition for an abolition of the law of settlement, and payment of relief to the poor from a national fund; but dissents from our views, more particularly from payment by a national fund. — Again to the Provident Bank, where I met Watson Pole, Morrison &c. as I had met Perkins at the Board. — Called on Hayward, who gave me a box of pills to relieve my cough, which was very troublesome — MW also is suffering from pain in the face, which is much swollen. — Received a letter from Mr Thornton covering others on Hunt Trust business from Mr Hunt, and his solicitor, Mr Braikenridge, — also from Mr Croome, the land surveyor, who pro-|[164] poses to be at Upper Slaughter for the purpose of valuing the parish about Apr. 12th. or 13th. — Brit. Mag. —

Mar. 26. Friday.

Fine weather. — Wrote to Mr Croome, requesting him not to delay beginning his valuation of this parish beyond the 12th. or 13th. April. — Wrote to Messrs. Hare & Thornton on Hunt Trust business, but kept back my letters, because the post brought me a letter from Mr Thornton, covering one from Mr Hare to him, which requires to be commented on by me, and to be returned to Mr T: — my letters of to-day, therefore, will be opened, and added to, and dispatched to-morrow. — Wrote to Rodwell for a supply of books for the Stow Book Society, but this also I kept back, Mr Pain having sent to inform me by post of other books which Mr Lockwood desires to have ordered into the library. — Wrote to Mr Pearce on Union business — Recd. a letter from C Bathurst, also a present of a very fine piece of sturgeon, caught, I suppose, in the mouth of the Severn. — Preparing for the |[165] Ruri-decanal meeting on Apr. 7. — Still suffering from a heavy cold with cough: MW. also from a bad swelled face. — Stanley's life of Dr Arnold.

Mar. 27. Saturday.

A foggy, moist morning, small rain in the forenoon, a fine afternoon and evening. — Added to and posted the letters written yesterday to Mr Hare, Mr Thornton, and Mr Rodwell. — Wrote to C Bathurst. — Justice business at home. — Preparing for the approaching ruri-decanal meeting. — Called at Davis's &c. — Wrote to Davison, Newman and Co. to enquire the lowest price of Patna Rice in large quantities, some of the labourers being desirous of purchasing the article at a lower rate than it is sold in the village or country shops, as a substitute for flour, now at a high price. — Still much affected with a cold, and coughing. MW. also much plagued with a cold and swelled face. — Stanley's life of Dr Arnold.

Mar. 28. Sunday.

Palm Sunday. — A very steady fall of rain from morning till evening — My cough continues very troublesome: MW. |[166] less annoyed with cold and swelled face, but afraid to venture to Church. — Morning service, prayers and sermon. I preached on the merits of Christ's passion. — Afternoon service, prayers. — Preparing Sermons. — Received a packet on Emigration from the Colonial Office. — A letter from Mr Wiggin, dated Deanery, Gloucester, who is in trouble, in consequence of a servant of his late strange curate of Oddington, Mr Houghton, persisting in holding a cottage of which Mr H. had the occupation as Curate, to the great inconvenience of Mr Williams, the present Curate, and annoyance of the Dean and Wiggin — Mr Williams is directed to call on me, and this letter is to prepare me for his visit, and to request me to take some steps as a Magistrate to eject the woman: — MW. rec^d. a note from M^rs. Aston in which I am requested to apply to Mr Cockey, Mr Birkbeck &c. to obtain votes for the admission of |[167] one of the children of the late Mr Tordiffe of Hampnett, into the Wanstead orphan asylum. — Brit. Magazine.

Mar. 29. Monday.

A frosty morning: frequent showers of cold rain, and sleet: — Wrote to Mr Birkbeck to obtain the votes and interest of two ladies of his family, and of Mr Redmayne, ~~Sett~~ Stainforth, in favour of M A Tordiffe's admission into the Wanstead Infant Orphan Asylum, either at the approaching or the November election: in the same strain wrote to Mr Cockey: also to F. Aston that I had so done; and to Mr Wiggin, in reply to his letter received yesterday, pointing out the course to be adopted under the circumstances stated in his letter ~~received yesterday.~~ — Much engaged with Magisterial business at home. — W B Pole called. — Received a pleasant and satisfactory letter from E.F.W. all well at the Vicarage, Stanway, with the exception of the burn on Freddy's arm; that wound is |[168] healing. — A circular with a detailed account of the subscriptions received, sums collected after sermons in churches within this diocese, and the expenditure of the whole, as regards the amount (over £9000) raised in 1844, towards the building of ten churches in populous parts of the diocese, where districts were formed, and Incumbents appointed, under Peel's act: to this fund I was a subscriber. — Stanley's Life of Dr Arnold.

Mar. 30. Tuesday.

A fine day. — Wrote to Messrs. Hoare, desiring them to transfer £45. 5 - from my account to that of my son. — Rec^d. a packet of papers with a letter from Mr Pearce, to which I replied – all on Union business — Preparing a Sermon. — Received a letter from Mr Hare with inclosures relating to the sale of the mortgaged property on the Thames side — Hunt Trust. — from the County Gaol, a circular announcing a meeting of the Visiting Committee: — from |[169] C Bathurst: — from Davison, Newman and C^o. with the price of Patna Rice by the bag, as I had desired by a letter I had written to them on Saturday last: — a circular from R Waller, announcing the Stow Clerical meeting to be held on the 7th. Apr. — Walked to Bourton – to pay my insurance from fire at Palmer's shop: — called on the Wallers, who were out: met R.W. afterwards, who walked with me nearly to U.S. on my way home. — Our dear children rode from Stanway, arriving just after my return from Bourton, and passed an hour or more with us very agreeably — all well at the Vicarage, and Freddy's wound healing — A very bad account of the state of our neighbour M[r] Lindow, who is said to have experienced another apoplectic or paralytic attack. — My cough less troublesome. – MW. suffering less from swelled face. — Stanley's life of Arnold.–

Mar. 31. Wednesday.

A cold day; occasional |[170] flickering showers of sleet and rain. — Wrote to M[r] Hare and to M[r] Thornton on Hunt Trust business: — to Purnell, requesting him to be the bearer of our Proxies for the election of a matron to the Infirmary at Gloucester on Thursday next: — to the Clerk of the Infirmary with the Proxies of MW. – Rev[d.] R. W. Ford, M[r] Pole, and M[r] Bennet and myself in favour of Miss Setree, the rule being that proxies should be deposited with the Clerk three days at least before the Election: — to Davison, Newman & C[o.] to order Patna Rice for my poor neighbours. — Rec[d.] a note from the Governor of Glouc. Gaol, announcing that the day of meeting of the Vis. Just. is changed, and that the Board will meet on Monday next at one P.M. — Preparing a sermon — Stanley's life of Arnold. – |

Diary
1847.

Apr. 1. Thursday. — A heavy snow had fallen during the night or early in the morning; frequent snow showers during the day: snow rapidly melted under the influence of a still air, and gleams of sun. —— A parish meeting in my study: present Shea, W. Gregory, J. B. Collett, W. Dix — overseers accounts audited: new Overseers nominated: Highway accounts passed: new Surveyors elected. — Drove to Stow. — Attended at the Prov. Bank, where met Mr. Morrison — transacted business at the Office of the Gloucestershire Banking Company. — parleyed with Mr. Hippisley. — To the Workhouse, where sat for an hour, auditing accounts with Mr. Perkins, and three other guardians. — To the Justice room, where Messrs. Ford and R. Waller sat as my Colleagues, and much business was done: — passing the Highway accounts; appointing fresh Overseers; appointing Assessors and Collectors of taxes; with ordinary cases of magisterial duty. — Messrs. W. B. Pole, Clarke, and Turner

Witts Family Papers F359

Diary — 1847

Apr. 1. Thursday.

A heavy snow had fallen during the night or early in the morning; frequent snow showers during the day: snow rapidly melted under the influence of a still air, and gleams of sun. — A parish meeting in my study: present E Lea, W Gregory, J B Collett, W Dix — overseers accounts audited: new Overseers nominated: Highway accounts passed: new Surveyors elected. — Drove to Stow. — Attended at the Prov. Bank, where met Mr Morrison — Transacted business at the Office of the Gloucestershire Banking Company: — parleyed with Mr Hippisley. — To the Workhouse, where sat for an hour, auditing accounts with Mr Perkins, and three other guardians — To the Justice room, where Mess$^{rs.}$ Ford and R Waller sat as my Colleagues, and much business was done: — passing the Highway accounts; appointing fresh Overseers; appointing Assessors and Collectors of taxes; with ordinary cares of magisterial duty. — Mess$^{rs.}$ W B Pole, Clarke, and Turner |^2 were present: the latter is the gentleman about to undertake the Curacy of Lower Slaughter and Clapton, residing at Bourton on the Water: he appears a sensible, intelligent man, and is a Son of a recently deceased incumbent of Hagley. — Home to a late dinner — Letter from E.F.W. brought by a messenger from Stanway, who came for a calf which I had sold to J. Court: a good report of all at the Vicarage: — a circular from the Glouc. Infirmary as to the approaching election of matron; — a letter from Mess$^{rs.}$ Hoare, that they had passed £45. 5. 0 from my account with them to that of my Son. — Stanley's life of Arnold.

Apr. 2. Friday.

Good Friday. — A cold day, frequent transient showers of snow and sleet — Wrote to Mr Brookes on Magistrates' business; to M$^{rs.}$ Marsh, Bell, Gloucester, desiring her to keep a bed for me on Monday next, when I purpose attending at the Assizes: — to Mr Graves, Ass^t Poor Law Comm^r with such information as I was able to give respecting the |^3 Potato disease, and the cultivation of that root in this district — Divine service — morning prayers and a Sermon; "the sufferings and death of Christ practically explained and applied." — Letter from Mr T. Birkbeck, who promises that M$^{rs.}$ B. shall vote for the admission of M. A. Tordiffe into the Wanstead Orphan Asylum. — Preparing for the Ruri-decanal meeting on Wednesday next.

Apr. 3. Saturday.

Cold and raw weather, with flickering snow at intervals, and a heavy snow shower for an hour in the afternoon. — Wrote to F. Aston inclosing Mr Birkbeck's letter received yesterday. — A person called to serve me on the part of the North Western Railway Company with a notice and schedule calling on me to make within 21 days my claim for compensation for the land on our Ravenflatt farm, about 3 acres, which the directors propose to take for their line. Wrote to M[r] Sharpe, Lancaster, the Secretary to the Company, requesting him to send duplicates of [4] these papers to M[r] Chr. Geldard; wrote also to Chr. Geldard on the business, desiring to hear from him when he and his Father have fully considered this business, and are prepared to advise as to the course to be taken, price of land to be asked &c. — Preparing for the ruri-decanal meeting on Wednesday next. — Settling accounts with a tradesman. — Laura, Constance, and Macleod Howell arrived on a visit to us; having finally left Prinknash Park this morning, as also their Father, who is gone to Town, to furnish his new house to receive them at the end of the month. The sale of furniture at P. takes place next week, and M[r] Ackers's servants and furniture are already there; but the purchase by M[r] A is not finally completed. — A letter from Howell brought by his daughters. — A letter from F. Aston.

Apr. 4. Sunday.

Easter day. — Cold and sour weather. — Visited the Sunday School — Wrote to M[r] Walker, Corn-dealer, Northleach, desiring him to furnish me with five quarters of [5] oats. — Divine Service; morning, prayers. Administered the holy sacrament to 18 Communicants. — Afternoon prayers and sermon. I preached on the resurrection of Christ. — Preparing for the ruri-decanal meeting on Wednesday next. — Received a distressing letter from poor Howell, stating that on his arrival yesterday in Town, he had met with a letter from his friend, Major Sandham, communicating to him that a strong rumour prevailed that three Officers had been killed in an affray with the Kaffirs in South ~~America,~~ Africa of whom one was Frederick Howell, Surgeon in the Rifles, lately arrived in the Colony of the Cape of Good Hope. On receiving this intelligence Howell repaired to the Horse Guards, where he learnt that no official report of the affair had arrived, but that there was no reason to disbelieve the story. This sad news I had to communicate to the twin sisters, who were much distressed, but indulged in hope against hope. — A letter from M[r] Chr. Geldard, who had been over [6] the line of the North Western Railway, as far as it crosses our Ravenflatt property, with the Engineer of the company: C.G. points out the course most proper to be taken in the business, and seems quite competent with his father to advise in, and conduct the business. — A letter from M[r] Thornton on Hunt Trust business; he returns to me a letter which I had forwarded for his perusal, addressed to me by M[r] Hare.

Apr. 5 Monday.

A cold, raw day, with some rain. — Left home after breakfast for Gloucester; to Cheltenham in the phaeton: thence to Gloucester by the railway; travelling with M[r] Keating, the Barrister, and M[r] Wiggin. The latter was returning from Oddington to the Deanery at Gloucester; he had managed to obtain possession of the cottage, respecting which he had communicated with me; M[r] Houghton's female servant had given up the Key, and left the house, and the property of M[r] H. had been removed. It is not, [7] however, unlikely that M[r] H. will cause some trouble to M[r] W. before the connection between them is entirely closed. — Took up my quarters at the ~~Kings~~ Bell Hotel. — Attended a meeting of the Visiting Justices of Gloucester Gaol, which lasted three hours, and at which some important business was transacted — There were present — Mess[rs.] Purnell, Curtis Hayward, Ellis Viner, Surman, R. Davis, C.

Crawley, Sayers, and myself — The High Sheriff, Baker, came, attended by his Under Sheriffs, Wilton and Burrup, to take possession of his Gaol, according to custom: he had come in from Hardwick Court with a large cortege of horsemen, yeomen &c. whom he had feasted at his mansion, and again regaled at Gloucester. — The city was very crowded and bustling — the Commission day of the Assizes, Sheriff's dinner, Easter Monday, and a large fair, caused a great concourse of people. The High Sheriff's equipage and appointments, his liveries and Javelin men, & other parapher[1] — |[8] were all in very good style. His brother in law, Murray Browne, officiated as Chaplain — My son joined me at the Committee room in the Gaol, having come in from Stanway, and, like myself, taken up his abode at the Bell; he brought a good account of all dear to us at Stanway — and grieved with us for the accumulated distress of the Howell family — The Sheriff escorted the Judge into the town about six P.M. — M[r] Serg[t.] Gaselee preceded M[r] Justice Maule, who arrived at a later hour from Monmouth; M[r] Baron Platt being seriously ill was incapacitated from going the circuit, and Serg[t.] Gaselee officiated in his room. — There was a large attendance of country gentlemen at the Sheriff's dinner; fifty three attended, most of them Magistrates or connected with the magistracy of the County. This was, of course, a gratifying testimony to the High Sheriff of respect and regard. Only one of the Members for the County was present — Grantley Berkeley, who disgraced himself |[9] by giving utterance to language expressive of his personal animosity to his brother the Lord Lieutenant, on whose health being given in the usual routine, he disclaimed participating in the compliment paid to one whom he designated as an adulterer at once with two mens wives, and the coercer of his brother. This outbreak was met by very intelligible marks of disapprobation by the company present — None of the peers connected with the County were present – After dinner I joined a party to take coffee with the High Sheriff in his private apartment. The magistrates with whom I was most in communication during the evening were Purnell, Curtis Hayward, Niblett, Wallington, D Pyrke, Ludlow Walker, Sir M B. Crawley, John Browne, W H Hyett, Hopkinson, Crawley, R. Onslow &c. —

Apr. 6. Tuesday

Weather uncertain; a tendency to rain at times, but no very heavy shower — Breakfasted with other magistrates at the Bell — Called with Col. Browne and the |[10] Rev M[r] Pye, on the High Sheriff at the Kings Head, whence to the Cathedral, where divine service was performed, and a very good, and suitable Sermon preached by the High Sheriff's Chaplain, Murray Browne — The cathedral very cold; the Dean and Archdeacon Wetherell the members of the chapter in attendance: M[r] Serg[t.] Gaselee only was present: his brother Maule not appearing, probably excusing himself on the score of bad health — A large concourse of the lower orders at the Service. The Courts opened about half past twelve, M[r] Serg[t.] Gaselee taking his seat in the Crown Court: the Marquis of Worcester acted as foreman of the Grand Jury. While I remained I was for the most part seated by the presiding Judge, and in communication with him and his officials, on the business before the Court. Three or four trials took place before I left the Shire Hall in which I could not help thinking the |[11] learned Sergeant deficient in dignity and self-possession, wanting in that à plomb, which should be the attribute of a criminal judge, and without

---

1.   The end of the word was omitted by accident on turning the leaf. Presumably the intended word was paraphernalia.

any fixed principle as to the amount of punishment to be awarded in minor cases: at least, he did not hesitate to change his views as to the sentences to be passed on hearing what I had to say on the matter, when he referred to me; and his intercourse with me, a stranger, was very unreserved, easy and conversational, and off-handed, as if I had been an old acquaintance with whom he was in habits of familiar conversation — His minute features, slender form, peering short-sighted eyes, and overpowering wig were oddly contrasted, and the tout ensemble not very judge like. I left the Court about 3 P.M. took leave of my Son, who proposed remaining till to-morrow, and repaired to the Railway Station, which I left at half past three for Cheltenham — From the Cheltenham Station into the Town |[12] I walked with M[r] Townsend, the Vicar of Cold Aston, who was returning from Gloucester — at the Plough I engaged a fly to convey me to Andoversford, where my Servant was to meet me with the Phaeton — Here I received a letter from MW. informing me that Howell had written to his poor daughters, confirming the evil tidings he had communicated in his letter received on Sunday, and which, indeed, had been noticed in the London paper which I had seen at Gloucester this morning: the facts appear to be that on the Kei river in the Kaffir country, and beyond the limits of the Colony, a small military detachment had been stationed; Fred. Howell had charge of the sick and wounded there; with him was a Capt. Gibson, like himself of the Rifles; also an Hon. — Chetwynd, a son of Lord Chetywnd, an officer of another regiment: that these three had gone out to procure cattle, to increase their store of provisions; that they |[13] had advanced beyond the main body of their party, with four or five Hottentots; had met with a lot of cattle, perhaps, purposely placed as a decoy; had proceeded to drive this small herd, in the direction of their quarters: had so fallen into an ambush of savages; that poor Fred[k.] Howell's horse was shot dead; himself killed & his two brother officers with two Hottentots, fighting in his rescue, were also massacred before the main body of their party which was a mile or two in the rear, and heard the firing, could come to their aid. (I should have mentioned on Monday that I wrote to Howell to condole with him; to invite him to visit us, if his business would allow of his quitting London; and to assure him that we should do all in our power to mitigate the blow by attention to his daughters & little Macleod.) By my carriage the Howell's maid Servant came from Upper Slaughter, and proceeded in the fly which brought me to Andoversford to Cheltenham, there to call on a lady of the |[14] acquaintance to make needful arrangements as to procuring of mourning for the young ladies and their little brother – The maid is to return by a Cheltenham carrier to-morrow evening — It was nearly seven o clock when I reached home: of course it was a melancholy evening of forced conversation, Laura and Constance being greatly overpowered. — The following were the letters which awaited my return home: from Chr. Geldard an envelope containing a tracing shewing the exact proposed line of the North Western Railway across our Ravenflatt property — from a M[r] Rawlins a canvassing letter soliciting my vote and interest in his favour for the vacant situation of Clerk and ~~Depute~~ Deputy Governor of Gloucester Gaol, in the room of Moore, dismissed at the last Quarter Sessions; — from M[r] Wiggin, on the subject of the cottage at Oddington, now relinquished by M[r] Houghton's maid Servant: this letter |[15] had been written by M[r] W. on Sunday at Oddington, and its purport had been communicated to me orally by ~~M[r]~~ him when we met on Monday. — Some anxiety exists in the village in consequence of a young woman, daughter of one of my parishioners, a labourer, having returned home on Saturday evening, clandestinely, as it would seem, from a distance; (it is supposed Birmingham) with an eruptive disease, which Mr Wills, the Med. Officer of the Union pronounces to be smallpox — What could be done to isolate the family has been done.

Apr. 7. Wednesday

A cold, windy day. — Called on the Churchwarden, W Gregory, ^& Mr E. Lea, and conversed with other parishioners, as to the alarm of Smallpox in the village: also directed the School-mistress to close the free school for a short time, being fearful least the congregating of the children together might increase the risk of the dissemination of the supposed variolous infection. — Drove to Stow. — Received a letter |[16] from Mr Betterton, Inspector of this Tax District, inclosing a form for my signature, by which I am to acknowledge the receipt of the land tax for the Rectory of Bourton on the Water in that parish, Lower Slaughter, Upper Slaughter, and Clapton, payable to me by Robt Waller — attended the Ruri-decanal meeting, or Synod, as some of my brethren love to call it, held at the National School room at Stow: The Rural Dean in the Chair. Owing to the present condition of the Church and Chancel at Stow, now in progress of being repewed, with extensive alterations and repairs, divine Service could not be performed; and, therefore, the Secretary, M^r R W. Hippisley, read short prayers from the liturgy to the Clergy assembled in the School room. These consisted of Messrs. Biscoe, Morrison, Townsend, Oakley Hill, Clarke, Dolphin, Hillier, Hill (Notgrove) Pantin, R Waller, Hunt (Curate of Great Risington) Williams (Curate of Oddington) Potter, F. E. Witts, Hutchinson (Batsford) – The subject proposed for a paper to be read by the Rector of Adle-|[17] strop, but which was not forthcoming, was "the Divinity and eternal generation of our blessed Saviour" — the disappointment arose from the unexpected decease, a few days since, of Lord Saye and Sele, whose barony and considerable estate descends to my old friend and neighbour, Fred^k Twisleton. Last week he was hurried up to town, but not to find his cousin alive; and in a letter to the Rural Dean received this morning he expresses himself as not recovered from his bewilderment in finding himself a Peer with property to the amount of £6000 per ann. superadded to his former position of Canon Residentiary of Hereford and Rector of Adlestrop — As to the promised paper, he says, "pendent opera interrupta" — his presence under the circumstances was not to be expected, and it remained to see how far without a leader a discussion could be raised. In this, however, there was no great difficulty, for several were prepared to enter on the subject, and seniority marking me out as the front rank man, I opened the subject, |[18] speaking of the Catholic doctrine of the divinity of our blessed Lord, touching upon the various heresies of early and of late ages, and more particularly of on the false views entertained by the Unitarians in our own country — In discussing these matters I dwelt especially on some leading texts, chiefly from the gospel according to St John, and the Epistles of St Paul and St John, treating them in an exegetical manner, with critical remarks on the Greek text, and references to Fathers of the first three Centuries — Messrs. Pantin, Oakley Hill, Clarke, Potter, Hunt, and others followed me, not to question, but rather to confirm my positions, and add other comments with other references in aid of the line of argument which I had taken up. The discussion on the whole was interesting and well maintained, in a very good spirit. — The Rural Dean then made to us a communication: from the Bishop of the Diocese, being the purport of the convention |[19] of the Rural deans with the Bishop at the Palace at Stapleton in the week before last. The most material point was to ascertain the feeling of the Clergy of the Diocese as to the acceptance of the measure in respect of national Education recently propounded by Government in Parliament, as developed in the minutes of the Committee of Council on Education in August and December 1846 — This matter is now exciting great attention: ~~it~~ the Government plan is generally approved in the Church of England, generally disapproved by the Protestant dissenters: the latter maintain that the effect of the ministerial scheme will be to throw the education of the people almost wholly into the hands of the Clergy of the Establishment — that the scheme suggested is unconstitutional and subversive of civil and religious liberty: that government has nothing to do with education, and should leave the thing wholly to voluntary effort, &c. &c. — The real fact is that the dissenters find from experience that the proportion between Church and Dissent is such that, where |[20] 18/9 out of every pound under the Parliamentary grants goes to the Church, 1/3 only falls to the lot of dissent — and why? because the National Church is, after all, the Church of the people, and ~~that~~ the energy and zeal all on that side; the dissenting body being a minority, divided into sections, not animated by liberality or activity. How far the government may have confidence, courage and firmness to resist the torrent of Dissenting opposition and parliamentary petitions, may be doubtful: but it is clearly the policy of the Church to uphold the Government, to acquiesce in the scheme as propounded, and so to give a sanction to the outline and mechanism sketched out: therefore, altering two or three too generally expressed phrases in an address to the Lord Bishop proposed by the Rural Dean, we set our hands to a document hailing with cordial assent the measures involved in the minutes of Council; and |[21] acting upon a semi-official authority which, it is to be hoped, is good, that aid from Government will not be extended to schools not using the authorized version of the Bible, (whereby Romish schools & Unitarian seminaries would be without the pale,) we attached our signatures to petitions to both Houses of Parliament expressive of our adhesion to the scheme promulgated by government. But, while we declared our readiness to come into the scheme traced out in the Minutes of council, as far as the circumstances of our respective parishes and schools would allow, the tone of the different clergymen who took part in the discussion concurred with my feeling openly expressed, that the progress of education in the small rural parishes of this district, with any and all the aid to be obtained from the Privy Council Committee on Education, would be very slow, and that we of the Ministry had great difficulties to encounter in promoting the education of the poor children of our flocks, |[22] which would not easily be surmounted, even with Government assistance. — Other minor matters were discussed, and the meeting was dissolved, M[r] Morrison having engaged to propose as the subject for discussion, at the next synod the sixth chapter of S[t] John's gospel, and its reference to the Sacrament of the Lord's supper — The Clergy who were members of the Clerical Society, or about to be elected, (such, at least, as were disposed to remain) adjourned to the Unicorn Inn, and dined together. The members present were but few: — R. W. Hippisley took the chair in the absence of Wiggin; the Rural Dean, Mess[rs.] Winter, Hutchinson, Waller, Williams, Hunt, Clarke & myself — I returned home before nine o clock. —

Apr. 8. Thursday.

Fine, with a boisterous wind. — After breakfast I drove to Stow — To the Provident Bank, where I transacted business. — To the Workhouse: the first meeting of the newly elected Board of Guardians — |²³ Most of the old and experienced guardians continue in office; and of those newly elected one half have served before. Mᴿ Hippisley has not been re-elected; there is an unfavourable prejudice against him among the rate payers of Stow in certain quarters — Mᴿ Perkins is re-elected. The retirement of Mᴿ Shelton, the guardian for Longborough, is to be regretted. — I was re-elected Chairman, with Mᴿ Beman as Vice Chairman. There was nothing out of the ordinary course in the day's proceedings, which terminated about 3 P.M. Some inconvenience arose from the absence of the Rel. Officer from serious injury by a scald to his leg. — Returned to the Provident Bank, where met Mᴿ Winter, with whom I sat for an hour before driving home. — Two letters from Howell, with further details as to the death of poor Frederick. H. declines coming to Slaughter; his business in Town will not allow of his coming — a circular from the Secretary of the Gloucester |²⁴ Diocesan Board of Education, announcing a meeting of the members on the 15ᵗʰ· Inst. for the Election of Exhibitioners as Training Mistresses. — A letter from Mᴿ Sharp of Lancaster, Secretary to the North Western Railway, in answer to mine of the 3ᵈ· Inst. and making some suggestions as to the arrangements between the directors and the proprietors of land on the line.

Apr. 9. Friday.

Fine weather, but cold. — Parish business — calling on some parishioners, chiefly with reference to the alleged case of small pox. Mᴿ Wells called on me last evening, and stated that he had no doubt that the young woman had experienced an attack of that disease, but that the eruption was of nearly a fortnight old when she returned home, and, therefore, the risk of infection less than if it had been recent, still he considered that there was some fear that the disease might spread. — Visited Mʳˢ· Ryan, who is ill, at Eyford; also Mʳˢ· Dolphin; |²⁵ — A letter from Chr. Geldard acknowledging mine of the 3ᵈ· Inst. he and his father consider that they shall be able to drive a harder bargain with the directors of the North Western Railway Company in my absence, than if I were to be present; but suggest the propriety of my visiting Craven, when an exchange of lands is negociated between Mᴿ Garforth and us, after our treaty with the company has been closed. — A letter from one Bees, an officer in the Bristol Gaol, soliciting my vote and Interest that he may be elected Keeper of Little Dean Bridewell. — A letter from the Clerk of the Gloucester Lunatic Asylum, announcing a meeting of Visitors to be held on Apr. 20. — Read a Fast Sermon, preached by Geo. Wellford at Bray on the 24ᵗʰ· Ult. printed by him, and now forwarded by him to me by the Post yesterday.

Apr. 10. Saturday.

A mild day, with some showers. — Justice business at home. — Wrote to Dᴿ Williams, Superintendent, Gloucester Lunatic Asylum, and Mᴿ Illes of the Fairford Luna-|²⁶ tic Asylum, to ascertain whether Moses Roff of Bourton could be admitted into either of these asylums, he having relapsed into a state of insanity. — Wrote to Mᴿ Sharpe, Lancaster, in reply to his letter received on Thursday, that I had transmitted it to Mᴿ Geldard, of Settle, who would communicate with him on its contents. Wrote to Chr. Geldard, to whom I forwarded Mr Sharpe's letter, desiring him to answer it as he and his father judged best, and in acknowledgement of his late letters respecting the land on the Ravenflatt property to be taken by the Directors of the Northwestern railway Company, desiring him and his father to act for us and treat for us according to the best of their Judgment. From Chr. Geldard I received a letter by the post, mentioning an application made to him by the Attorney of the North Western Railway to the same effect as the contents of Mr Sharpe's letter to me. C.G. recommended that the proposal so made should be declined, |²⁷ and wished me to write a letter to him to that effect: this I did, and will dispatch it by to-morrow's post with my letters already written to Mr Sharpe and Mr C. Geldard. — Wrote to Mr Wells, Med. Off. of the Union, desiring him to visit an aged parishioner, who has been taken ill, and whom I visited. — Sent to Mr Betterton, Receiving Inspector of Taxes for this district, a document, which he had forwarded to me for signature, purporting that I had received the amount of the land tax chargeable on the living of Bourton on the Water, in the parishes of Bourton, Clapton, Upper and Lower Slaughter: such land tax redeemed by a late Incumbent, but not exonerated, having been purchased by me some years since. — Mr Wilkins of Bourton on the Water and his son called on me, partly on Magisterial business, partly to request me to ~~afford~~ ᴸᵉⁿᵈ some documents to the young man to assist him in bearing his part in a discussion likely to be entered upon in a debating Society in Town, of which the young-|²⁸ ster is a member, – being a law student. The subject is the present state of the Poor Laws — I furnished him with some pamphlets &c. — Received a short letter from Howell, accompanying ~~anoth~~ a newspaper, containing further details as to the lamentable loss of his son Frederick. — E.F.W. rode over from Stanway to dine with us, remaining more than two hours: we had expected him and Sophy yesterday or to-day to pass the morning with us: he came to explain that they had been prevented by the serious illness of the Baby, who had been suffering from a violent cold and congestion of the lungs – He seemed to consider the dear child better, and the danger over; but one cannot but feel much anxiety on its account. It was arranged, unless unforeseen circumstances should prevent it, that Laura and Constance Howell shall go on a visit to Edward and Sophy for a week or ten days, on Wednesday next. E.F.W. & his wife quite well; the elder children have colds. — Wrote to |²⁹ J. W Harris for a supply of coal.

Apr. 11. Sunday.

Very rainy in the forenoon, fine in the latter part of the afternoon, and evening. — No Sunday School opened in consequence of the alarm as to the Smallpox, though I am not very apprehensive of its spreading. — Morning prayers and Sermon. I preached on "eternal life the gift of GOD in his Son." — Afternoon prayers — Preparing a Sermon. — Received a letter from Mr H. D. Warter: he has agreed for the purchase of Courland House at £1822 and of ground rents in Courland ~~road~~ ᴳʳᵒᵛᵉ and Lark hall lane, yeilding £123. 5. at 22 years purchase — another party having stept in and bought the remainder of Mr Selby's ground rents, yeilding £52. 10. — at 25 Years purchase: this, ᵃᵍʳᵉᵉᵐᵉⁿᵗ ᵇʸ ᴹʳ ᵂ. ᶠᵒʳ ᵒᵘʳ ᵖᵘʳᶜʰᵃˢᵉ, ⁱˢ of course, subject to the approval of the Court of Chancery. This will serve as an investment of £4533.10 of the Trust money to be laid out, and leave about £4000 or £4500 to be expended in |³⁰ another investment. — A letter from Mr Croome, the land surveyor, who is about to value this parish for a Poor Rate Assessment, that he may be expected here on Tuesday. — H. D. Warter gives a very indifferent account of the health of my cousin, John Witts. — To the family a section from Trower's Exposition of the Gospels. —

Apr. 12. Monday.

A warm, genial, spring day. — Wrote to E.F.W. a note which I dispatched by the groom, to enquire after the health of the dear infant; he brought back a letter with a greatly improved report. I sent to E.F.W. the letters I had received yesterday and on Saturday from H. D. Warter, and C. J. Geldard, which my son returned. — Domestic annoyance from disagreements among the Servants; the House servant, Baldwin, gave warning — Visiting sick parishioners, M^rs. Ryan, at Eyford, Shepherd Townsend — Called on J. Davis, |^31 and W. Gregory on parish matters. — Preparing for the expected arrival to morrow of Mr Croome, the Surveyor who is to value the Parish under the Poor Rate Assessment Act. – Received a letter from Sophia Hunt: — from Mr Graves, Ass^t. P.L.C., acknowledging my communication to him on the Potato disease; — from J. W. Harris, that he will send in coal within a few days.

Apr. 13. Tuesday.

A cold raw day; wind Easterly, with rain in the afternoon. — Wrote to Mr Warter and Mr Jennings on the purchase of ground rents near London — Mr Croome, the Land surveyor, called; with whom engaged for two hours or more in directing and explaining what is to be done as to the valuation for the Poor Rate Assessment in this and other Parishes — Mr Pearce also came, who assisted in the matters, as far as his duties are involved as Clerk of the Union — When Mr Croome went, I transacted business with Mr Pearce as to Union concerns, chiefly as to a |^32 letter to be addressed to the Poor Law Comm^rs. — Received a letter from Howell, desiring to know his daughters address, and if they were gone to Stanway, when they would return — from Mr Cockey, in answer to my letter addressed to him: he has ceased to subscribe to the Wanstead Orphan asylum; while he wrote his wife was confined of her first child — a little boy: — from E.F.W. a note written on Sunday, giving an improved account of the Baby, but the account received by our servant yesterday was later and still more favourable; — from Mr Illes, Fairford Lunatic Asylum, that they would receive M. Roff at 12/- per week; — from Dr Williams, Superintendent Gloucester Lunatic Asylum, that my letter to him respecting M.R. would be laid before the Committee of Visitors yesterday; and that I should hear further on the subject. — M^rs. Dolphin called upon us.

April 14. Wednesday.

Easterly wind, cold, |^33 and showery. — Wrote to F. Aston to inform him that Cockey ~~was~~ ^is no longer a subscriber to the Wanstead Orphan Asylum; and to Cockey, to congratulate him on the birth of his firstborn — Justice business at home. — Preparing a Sermon. — Laura and Constance Howell left us for Stanway, being conveyed in our carriage to visit Edward & Sophy, and remain till the 23^d. Inst. Macleod and his attendant are left with us. — A letter from Curtis Hayward as to the admission of Moses Roff into the Gloucester Lunatic Asylum — from C. J. Geldard as to the treaty with the Directors of the Northwestern Railway Company, and the conveyance to Settle of the title deeds of the Ravenflatt property: — a circular from the office of the Gloucester and Berkeley Canal Company, as to the resolutions passed at a late meeting of the Shareholders. — Walked to Bourton on Water; conferred with Mᵣ Wilkins, Mᵣ Wells, and Thomas Roff, as to the conveyance of Moses Roff to the private house |³⁴ at Fairford for the reception of insane persons, to which it seems most convenient that he should be taken. — Reading a pamphlet by C Bathurst lately published on the law of settlement and removal, and poor law generally. — Our servant brought back from Stanway a letter from E.F.W. to his mother, with a very satisfactory account of the convalescence of the dear infant, and of the health of the remainder, each in their different ways so dear to us.

Apr. 15. Thursday.

A fine day, but very cold wind. — Wrote to Howell. — Preparing a Sermon. — Drove to Stow accompanied by M.W. — who called at Maugersbury House on Mʳˢ W. Vavasour, and Emma Vavasour before she returned home. — Transacted business at the Provident Bank, at Mᵣ Brookes's office, at Mᵣ Morgan's office and with Mᵣ Pearce and others at the Workhouse. — Met Mᵣ Morrison at the Provident Bank. To the Justice room, where much Magisterial busi-|³⁵ness with Messʳˢ Ford and R. Waller, as my Colleagues, Messʳˢ Winter, W. Vavasour, and W. B. Pole being present. — Received a letter from H. D. Warter; progress is being made in treating for the Ground rents in Radnor Street, Chelsea. — When I returned from Stow, found my son's servant with a note, intimating that he had been sent to desire Anne Bateman to go to Stanway to supply the place of Sophy's cook, who is leaving them in a hurried, unhandsome manner; so that annoyance in respect of servants visits them as well as us. A good account is given of all; the children ail but little now. — Finished the perusal of Bathurst's pamphlet on the Settlement and Removal of the Poor. —

Apr. 16. Friday.

Weather fine, but a hard frost in the morning, and the wind cold. — Wrote to Messʳˢ Davison, Newman & Cᵒ with a remittance and an order for groceries: — to C Bathurst to acknowledge the receipt of his pamphlet on the Poor laws; — to Assᵗ P.L.C. Graves with a |³⁶ paper on the cultivation and disease of the Potatoe, which I received yesterday from Mᵣ Scovell, Bailiff to Lady Cockerell. — Preparing a Sermon. — Visiting Townsend, an aged and sick parishioner. — Letters from Mᵣ Thornton and Mᵣ Hare, with inclosures from Messʳˢ Cox & Williams, Mᵣ George Hunt, and Mᵣ Braikenridge, as to the sale of the Red Lion Wharf, Thames Street. — Life of Dᵣ Arnold. —

April 17. Saturday.

A frost in the morning; a fine day, wind cold. — Wrote to Mᵣ Hare, Mᵣ Hunt, and Mᵣ Thornton on the business to which the letters received by me yesterday from Mᵣ Hare and Mᵣ Thornton related. — Received a note from Mᵣ Hare, covering a letter on the same business from Mᵣ Braikenridge, which Mᵣ B. had addressed to Mᵣ Thornton and which the latter had forwarded to Mᵣ Hare. — Justice business at home. Drove with MW. to Bourton on the Water; called on the Wallers, seeing both RW. and his lady: |³⁷ — called on the Misses Hall, where met Mᵣ Morrison and his Son. Miss Sarah Hall has lately returned from London, where the operation for cataract has been successfully performed on one eye by Mr Alexander, the celebrated oculist: — made a first call on M^r and M$^{rs.}$ Hunt, and M$^{rs.}$ Angus, now occupying the house lately inhabited by M^r and M$^{rs.}$ Aitkens: M$^{rs.}$ Angus, a lady from Liverpool, mother of M$^{rs.}$ H., has taken the house for six months, until after her daughter's confinement, and until M^r and M$^{rs.}$ H. remove into a very small house at G$^t.$ Risington lately built by the Dean of Gloucester, and assigned by him for the residence of his curate. — Life of Dr Arnold — Wrote to E.F.W. sending my letter by A. Bateman with Bathurst's Pamphlet on the Poor Laws, and Wellford's Fast Sermon. –

Apr. 18 Sunday.

Cold, but dry weather. — Morning service prayers – afternoon, prayers and sermon — I preached on "Swearing." — Rec$^d.$ a letter from M^r |^{38} Chr. Geldard with further details as to the negociation with the ~~Trustees of~~ Directors of the North Western Railway, which seems to make a satisfactory progress. It appears that four acres of the Ravenflatt farm will be wanted, and that the Company offers £650, about 65 years purchase for the land: we ask £800, & expect to get £700. — A letter from Mess$^{rs.}$ Davison, Newman & C$^{o.}$ acknowledging the receipt of my remittance on Friday last; — a letter from F. Aston in reply to my letter of Wednesday last: — a letter from Howell in answer to mine of Thursday last. — Preparing a Sermon — M$^{rs.}$ Dolphin called after evening service. — To the family a section from Trower's commentary on the gospels — Eccl. Gazette. —

Apr. 19. Monday.

A fine and dry, but cold day. — Transacting business with M$^{rs.}$ Griffin, the tenant of the Church and Charity Estate; — with W. Mitchell, the Measurer and Mapper, in whose favour I wrote a commendatory |^{39} letter to Mr Dent, Sudeley Castle; — Justice business at home. — Wrote to Chr. Geldard, in answer to his letter received yesterday: — to Mr Hare, acknowledging the receipt of his note and its enclosure yesterday: — to Mr Thornton, to whom I returned the letter from Mr Braikenridge which Mr Hare had forwarded to me yesterday: — to Curtis Hayward in reply to his letter received on Wednesday last. — Mr Lefroy came about mid-day, and, having ridden on to Stow and Moreton, to visit the Police Stations there, returned to dine and sleep here. — Received a pleasant letter from C Bathurst. — W. Vavasour called to leave a letter he had received from Charles Clift, a former servant of his and his father's, now in service in London, which he is about to leave, as not suiting his health. W.V. had written to inform him that we want an indoor servant; and he expresses great desire to accept the place.

Apr. 20. Tuesday.

A frosty morning, and cool |^{40} air, but fine day. — Mr Lefroy left us after breakfast. — Wrote to Sophia Hunt — Justice business at home. — Preparing a Sermon. — Drove with MW. to call, first, on the W. Vavasours at Maugersbury, to learn the address of Charles Clift. Saw M$^{rs.}$ W.V. and Emma — the former an invalid, had been seized with a fainting fit on Sunday; but is better. Thence to Daylesford, to the Winters, to call on them, and on Sir Charles Imhoff, now visiting them. Saw M$^{rs.}$ W. & Sir C. who is much aged, and infirm, but in comfortable health and spirits, having revived greatly since the death of Lady I. and his removal into the country — Winter confined to his bed with an attack of Influenza.

— Received a letter from Mr Hare, and an enclosure, both relating to the matter of the Red Lion Wharf — MW. received a letter from Apphia Witts; her brother has been very weak and ill, but is now better: M$^{rs.}$ JW. very infirm; so also M^r and M$^{rs.}$ Warter. — A letter from |^{41} Reeves, an officer of the County Gaol, a candidate for the vacant office of Keeper of Littledean Bridewell. — In the evening, hearing that my neighbour Lea was about to send a horse to Stanway to-morrow, to be shewn to my son, with a view to his buying it, I wrote a letter to him. — Finished the memoirs of Dr Arnold, a very interesting book.

Apr. 21. Wednesday.

A fine, and a mild day — Wrote to Mr Hare returning to him the copy of the letter from Todd & Son which he had forwarded to me yesterday. — Wrote to Charles Clift, as to his coming into my service, wages work &c. — Wrote to M$^{rs.}$ Sadler, with whom C.C. has been living in Town, to enquire his character. — Parish & Assessed taxes business at home. — Mr Morgan called on the latter — Mr Hunt from Bourton on the Water called. — Received a packet of documents from the Committee of Privy Council on Education with a letter from Mr Jelinger Symons, the Barrister, who is employed by government |^{42} in collecting Statistical information on Educational matters, as he has been on other subjects of internal policy; who requests me to give my sentiments as to the establishment and constitution of penal schools for juvenile criminals. Mr S. is a talented man, practises on the Oxford circuit, and at our Sessions, where I have become acquainted with him, when I have acted as Judicial Chairman; he was at one time Radical Candidate for Stroud, and opposed Lord John Russell, who soon neutralized him by giving him temporary employment as a Commissioner of enquiry, as to hand loom weavers. — A letter from Mr Thornton with an enclosure from M^r H ^{Hare} to Mr T. on Hunt Trust matters. — A letter from F. Aston as to a servant out of place, who might perhaps suit us. — A letter from Chr. Geldard, announcing the arrival at Settle of the box containing the deeds of the Ravenflatt Estate. — |^{43} A letter from C Bathurst, on sundry county matters. — In the evening rec$^{d.}$ a letter from my son, brought by one of the young Leas, who had gone to Stanway this morning to shew a horse which, it was supposed, would suit Edward — He gives a good account of the health of all at the Vicarage. — Began the perusal of the Life of Lord Sidmouth by the Hon. E. Pellew, Dean of Norwich — an interesting work —

Apr. 22. Thursday.

A fine day, but cold — Wrote to F. Aston, to thank him for his letter received yesterday, mentioning that I was in treaty with C. Clift, and expected to engage his services, but, if that failed, then I would request him (Aston) to make enquiries as to the servant mentioned in his letter received yesterday. — Drove to Stow, accompanied by MW. who, after shopping, returned home — To the Provident Bank — To the Workhouse, where met and became acquainted with Mr Graves, Ass$^t.$ P.L.C. now in charge |^{44} of the district comprizing our Union. Accompanied him in visiting the house: his principal enquiries were as to the Schools, with a view to ascertain the competency of the present Schoolmaster; this ended in the provisional appointment of Hornsby, to be made permanent, if, at the expiration of a few months, he acquires greater proficiency in arithmetic. It was arranged that the advertising for a Schoolmistress be for the present postponed, and be made dependent on the arrangement to be made as to Hornsby — The accommodation for vagrants was another point investigated by Mr Graves — He attended the meeting of the Board – Points discussed before him were the proper construction of the late removal Act under certain contingencies; — the policy of relaxing the rule which prohibits granting out-relief to widows with children having given birth to bastards subsequent to the decease of their husbands; and ^to single women Mothers of |^45 bastards; it was settled that the Guardians should submit certain special cases to the P.L.C. for a relaxation of the rule. Other matters were discussed, on which Mr G. discovered great familiarity with the law and practice, and liberal views: the usual business of the Board proceeded; and at its close, past four o clock, Mr G. accompanied me in my carriage to dine & sleep at Upper Slaughter – We found him a very well informed man, a barrister, connected with the Graves family of Mickleton; he has fixed his residence for the present at Cheltenham, as tolerably central in his district, which includes more than fifty Unions, the extreme points being from Amersham, Bucks, to Cleobury Mortimer, in Salop, and in another direction Chepstow & Banbury. — Received a letter from Mr Hunt accompanying a copy of a letter from Mr Braikenridge to Messrs. Cox and Williams on the sale of the Red Lion Wharf — Also a letter from Chr. Geldard, who with his Father has |^46 completed an apparently very satisfactory agreement as to the Sale of that portion of the Ravenflatt farm which is required for the North Western Railway; the price given by the directors is very liberal, and the mutual arrangements dependent on certain contingencies are fair.

April 23. Friday.

A warm and genial forenoon, but somewhat overclouded as with a blight, led to light rain increasing to heavy showers in the afternoon, with distant thunder and lightning; at Stanway the thunderstorm was heavy. — Mr Graves left us for Cheltenham after breakfast. — Mr Ford called as Rural Dean to visit our Church, in which he found no cause to complain of neglect on the part of Rector or Churchwardens – I walked with him some distance on his road to Lower Swell — Wrote to E.F.W. in answer to his last letter, sending him those from Bathurst, Chr. Geldard, Apphia Witts &c. in which I thought he |^47 would take an interest: this ^packet I sent by the Servant with the open carriage, which conveyed little Macleod Howell and his attendant to pass the morning with the children at Stanway, & to return accompanied by his sisters. They arrived here safe after 5 P.M. pleased with their visit to Stanway, and bringing a very good account of the dear circle at the Vicarage; also a letter from E.F.W. who sent back the various letters and papers which I had forwarded to him. — Letters were received by me from M^rs. Sadler with a satisfactory character of Charles Clift, who appears not to have behaved quite well to her, on leaving his situation, yet as well as Servants generally do: — a letter from one Carrington, with printed testimonials, who is highly recommended, as a Candidate for the vacant office of Clerk and Deputy Governor of Gloucester Gaol: — a letter from Lord Saye and Sele, forwarding a cheque for £3. subscriptions from Adlestrop to the District Committee at Stow of the S.P.G. — I wrote to |^48 Messrs. Hoare, directing them to transfer ~~£48.~~ £51. 19. 0. from my account with them to my Son's account: — a letter to Mr Thornton on Hunt Trust matters, with enclosures forwarded by him to me which I returned with comments. He is about to go abroad for a few weeks, so that he will not be able personally to take part in any proceedings under the Trust now pending. — Reading the debates in the House of Commons on the Minutes of the Committee of Council as to the Education of the People — Lord John Russell's speech –

April 24. Saturday.

A fine and mild day, but hazy. — Wrote to M^rs. Sadler & Charles Clift about the latter entering into my service: — to Chr. Geldard expressing approbation of the arrangements made by the'm on our behalf with the Directors of the North Western Railway; — to Mr Hunt, as to the sale or reletting of the Red Lion Wharf, returning the copy of the letter from Mr Braikenridge which he had |^49 forwarded to me: — to Lord Saye & Sele in answer to the letter I received from him yesterday, and congratulating him on his accession to his title. — The speeches of Lord J. Russell, and Mr Macaulay on the Government scheme in aid of the Education of the People. — There was a good deal of rain in the evening. —

Apr. 25. Sunday.

A very fine, mild, spring day — Preparing a Sermon. — Morning service — prayers and Sermon: I preached the first of a series of three sermons on Baptism; afternoon service, prayers. — From C. Clift a letter as to his coming into my service: — from Ass^t. Comm^r Graves an official acknowledgement of my second letter to him as to Potatoes: — from Messrs. Hoare that they had transferred from my account with them to my Son's £51. 19. 0 — To the family a section from Trower's Exposition of the gospels.

Apr. 26. Monday.

After much rain during the night a fine, but somewhat cloudy, cold, and windy day. — Preparing a letter to Mr J. C. Sy-|^50 mons on the subject of penal Schools — Preparing a Sermon. — Walked with Laura and Constance Howell to Bourton on the Water and back. — They received a letter from Stanway, with a good account of our dear children and grandchildren — A letter from one Webb of Cirencester, formerly a School master at Stow, asking testimonials and advice from me with a view to his offering himself as a candidate for the vacant post of Clerk & deputy Governor, Gloucester Gaol. Finished Macaulay's speech on the Minutes of the Committee of Council on Education —

Apr. 27. ~~Monday.~~ ^Tuesday

Rain had fallen during the night: there was a tendency to rain during the day, but the high wind kept off the rain — Finished and dispatched a letter on penal Schools to Mr Symons. — Wrote to M^r R Webb, Cirencester, declining to give a testimonial to him on the ground that I had never much opportunity to judge of his competency to discharge difficult official duties, |^51 and that he had for some years been removed from my observation; discouraged him from applying for the Situation of Deputy Governor, and Clerk of Gloucester Gaol — Wrote to Mr Stokes respecting the repair of the side gate at Lower Slaughter Turnpike. — With MW., Laura, & Constance Howell, to Stow. On the way met and had a long parley with Mr Pole, who is come from Town to pass a few days at Wick Hill — To the Library, where met and had a conference with M^rs. Vavasour, and M^rs. W.V. the latter was at Stanway Vicarage yesterday, where all were well. Her husband and sister are ~~staying at the~~ visiting a lady at Chester: she is staying at "the Cottage". — To the Workhouse, where visited the different wards, school &c. with Laura and Constance Howell, who were much interested with all they saw and heard. Conferred with Mr Pearce & his sister. — Received letters from Howell, who suggests that his children should remain |^{52} with us till Monday next, and then rejoin him in Town: — From M$^{rs.}$ H Sadler, and Charles Clift, making it sure, as far as anything is sure, that the latter will come into my service on May 17$^{th.}$ — Further speech of Lord John Russell on the Education scheme proposed by Government, and adopted by a large majority in the House of Commons, though vehemently opposed by the dissenters. —

Apr. 28. Wednesday.
After rain in the night, a windy, rather cold day, with now and then a slight shower. — Wrote to Howell, that we should be happy to keep his children till Monday next, when the coach would convey them to Oxford, whence they would proceed by the Railway. — A long conference with Mr Pearce, who came from Stow, and brought the draft minute book that I might draw up some special minutes: he and other officers of the Union are rendered uneasy by the exacting, harsh, and over-bearing manner of the Auditor. — Preparing a Sermon. — |^{53} Our dear children and two elder grandchildren drove over from Stanway to pass two or three hours with us, taking luncheon, and returning to a late dinner. They visit M^r and M$^{rs.}$ Vavasour at "the Cottage" next week, and, perhaps, come to us for a fortnight in the week following: — they, too, have experienced annoyance from the misconduct of a servant. —

Apr. 29. Thursday.
A showery day. $^{thunder\ at\ a\ distance}$ — Preparing a Sermon — Posting accounts. — Drove to Stow, accompanied by MW. and Laura Howell, who returned after shopping. — Attended at the Provident Bank, where met Mr Pole, Mr Perkins, Mr Morrison & Mr Ford — Transacted business at the office of the Gloucestershire Banking Company. — To the Workhouse, where conferred with Mr Pearce on Union matters. — To the Justice room, where Mr Ford was my colleague, Mr Williams (Oddington) and Mr Barrow assessing us. — Constance Howell with Macleod came up in the carriage to accom-|^{54}pany me home to dinner —

Apr. 30. ~~Thursday~~ Friday.
Frequent showers, with distant thunder, the forenoon mild, the afternoon chilly. — Wrote to Mr Morrison, forwarding to him a receipt for the annual subscription S.P.G. which he had paid to me yesterday for M$^{rs.}$ Scott. — Wrote a few lines to E.F.W. by a person, who came from Stanway with a load of coal. — Wrote to Mr Pearce, cautioning him against allowing to pauper inmates of the Workhouse liberty to leave the establishment to walk in or about Stow, which seems to have become a practice, and which justly gives offence to rate-payers, especially when the characters of the parties so indulged is bad. — Walked with Laura and Constance Howell to Eyford &c. — Called on M$^{rs.}$ Ryan, who still continues a great invalid. — Called to enquire after M$^{rs.}$ Dolphin, who is at home, after a short absence in London and at Cheltenham; she is much indisposed; |^{55} and, it is stated, has been informed by a Physician that she is labouring under an affection of the heart.

May 1. Saturday.

A fine, showy morning, followed by an afternoon and evening of steady rain. — Posting accounts — Rec^d. a letter from Mr Hurst, enclosing a letter from Todd and Son, forwarded to him by Mr Hare, which I had before seen. —

May 2. Sunday.

Forenoon fair, afternoon rainy — Visited the Sunday School, closed during the last month from fear of infection by small-pox. — Morning service; prayers: afternoon service, prayers and sermon. I preached the second of a course of three sermons on baptism — To the family, a lecture from Trower's exposition of the gospels. — Preparing a sermon. —

May 3. Monday.

Cold, cloudy, and showery, though the promise of the morning had been bright. — Our young friends, Laura and Constance Howell, with their little brother, left us, after an early breakfast, to join their Father |^56 at his new house in Town; travelling ~~to Oxford~~ in a fly to the foot of Stow hill, thence by the coach to Oxford Station, and thence by railway. The girls had made themselves very acceptable to us, having acted with great propriety, and right feeling. — Received a welcome letter from my Son; he & his promise us a visit of a fortnight to commence on this day week; the children caught cold by the searching wind on the day on which they visited us: the whole party purpose going to "the Cottage" tomorrow on a visit of a week to the elder Vavasours. — Wrote to Mr Hare, returning to him the letter from Todd & Son, which I had received under a cover from Mr Hunt on Saturday. — Received a letter from Mr Stokes in answer to one I had written to him about the repair of a gate post at Lower Slaughter Turnpike — Preparing a Sermon — Posting accounts — Justice & Tax business at home. — Memoirs of Lord Sid-|^57 mouth — "The School in its relations to the State, the Church, and the Congregation, being an explanation of the minutes of the Committee of Council on Education" — an able pamphlet put forth to illustrate the movement now being made by the Government to aid voluntary efforts towards the general education of the lower classes, which, after loud and vain opposition by the dissenters, being adhered to by the Church, is likely to be carried out beneficially. — Wrote an answer to the note I had received from E.F.W. to meet him at Stow to-morrow.

May 4. Tuesday.

A fine day. — Preparing a sermon — Posting accounts. — Walked to Bourton on the Water, MW. accompanying me as far as to the turnpike at Lower Slaughter and returning thence alone. — A circular announcing a meeting of Visitors of the Gaol at Gloucester for the 11th. Inst. — At Bourton left my card at the lodgings of Mr Turner, the new curate, who was from home — Met and |^58 parleyed with Mr Wilkins — Called at the Rectory; saw M^rs. R. Waller; the children suffering severely from hooping cough. — Life of Lord Sidmouth. —

May 5. Wednesday.

A tendency to rain; not much fell till the evening, and then only a passing shower: the air cold, with cloudy sky — An early breakfast. — Drove with MW. to Cheltenham, where arrived before 11 AM. — and left it at 6 P.M. — My wife visited Mr Tibbs, the Dentist,

to have her mouth renovated; the operation went off successfully, to all appearance —
Shopping. — Saw and parleyed with Lefroy, Capt. Sinclair, Messrs. Moore (Brimpsfield)
Fendall (late of Cowley) &c. — Home by 8 P.M. — A note from Mrs. Vavasour gave us a
good account of our dear children and grandchildren, now on a visit at "the Cottage" — A
letter from Mr Hunt, inclosing a report by a Surveyor, as to the State of repair, and other
circumstances |[59] connected with the Red Lion Wharf – A letter from Mr Charles Trye, as
to Union business — A letter from Howell to announce his childrens safe arrival at his new
house &c. — MW. received from Laura and Constance grateful notes, giving an account of
their first impressions in Eaton Place West, and expressing their acknowledgements for our
kindness to them while visiting us. ——

May 6. Thursday.

A showery forenoon, the afternoon fine. — Drove to Stow — Attended at the Provident
Bank office — Transacted business at the office of the Gloucestershire Banking Company.
— To the Workhouse; presided at the fortnightly meeting of the Guardians of our Union:
a full attendance; the usual amount of business detained me from 11 AM. to 4 P.M. — My
son joined me there for the last hour. — Accompanied him to the Cottage, where only
found Mr Vavasour and my infant grandchild: Mrs. V. and Sophy with Broome and Freddy
were gone on a |[60] walk. E.F.W. drove homeward with me to the foot of the hill leading to
Burford. — Received a circular from the Gaol at Gloucester, summoning me to a meeting
of the Visiting Justices on the 11th. Inst. to consider the testimonials of the candidates for
the office of Deputy Governor of the Prison. — British Magazine — Life of Lord Sidmouth.
— Mr Barrow called, when I was at Stow. —

May 7. Friday.

Showery weather, though not much rain fell. — Wrote to Mr Hunt on Wadenhoe Trust
matters — also to Mr Hare on the same: forwarding to the latter the report on the Red Lion
Wharf which Mr Hunt sent me, and which reached me on Wednesday. — Wrote to Miss
Moorhouse, forwarding a cheque on the Craven Bank for £7. in her favour; viz. £5., the
half yearly aid afforded to the Misses M. by MW., with £2. extra in consideration of their
plea of bad health. — Wrote to |[61] Mr C. Trye, in answer to his letter on Union business
received on Wednesday. — Justice business at home, in order to attend to which my Son
came from Stow, it having arisen in his district. He remained with us during the forenoon,
and till it was time for him to return to dine with the W. Vavasours at Maugersbury:
fishing occupied part of the time: I accompanied him by the brook Side. He brought a good
account of his children, but his dear wife is suffering from a cold — Life of Lord Sidmouth.

May 8. Saturday.

A moist or rainy day; one very heavy shower; otherwise wetting fog or small rain. — Wrote
to Howell and Bathurst — also notes to Messrs. Hunt, Turner, Barrow, and Clarke to invite
them to dinner on Friday the 14th. — Brit. Magazine — Rec^{d.} from the office of the Clerk
of the Peace a circular, giving notice of a meeting of the Prison Committee at Gloucester on
the morning of the 18th. Inst. before the Adjourned Sessions at one P.M. — |[62] Life of Lord
Sidmouth — Mr Hunt declined, Mr Turner accepted our invitation. —

May 9. Sunday.

Showery in the forenoon; a fine afternoon and evening — Visited the Sunday School. — Morning Service: prayers and Sermon. I preached the third and last of a set of three Sermons on baptism. — Afternoon Service — prayers. — Preparing a Sermon — British Magazine — Trower's Exposition of the gospels to the family. —

May 10. Monday.

Very fine spring weather. — Preparing a Sermon — Posting accounts — Justice business at home — Wrote a note to R Waller requesting him to meet me at Stow on Thursday for the transaction of Magisterial business, as Mr Ford will be from home. — Walked with MW. to Eyford; called on Mrs. Ryan at the garden, who is recovering from a severe illness — Called on Mrs. Dolphin; found her in better health, but excited. With her were Capt. and Mrs. Frobisher. — On our return |⁶⁴ home, found our dear children and grandchildren arrived from Stow, accompanied by M^r and Mrs. Vavasour, who left us after a short visit. — Mr Turner had called during our absence. — E.F.W. was suffering from a cold and bad headache: Sophy also has the remains of a cold and cough. The dear children very well and happy. —

May 11. Tuesday.

Showery weather — Wrote a note to invite Mr Potter to dine with us on Friday: he accepted the invitation. — Brit. Mag. — Posting accounts. — Justice business at home. — Transacting business with Tradesmen bringing Stow Fair bills. — My son and daughter rode to Broadwell to lunch with Capt. Leigh, and meeting his niece Anna, who is visiting there: M^r & Mrs. Vavasour, and M^r and Mrs. W. Vavasour met them there. — Received a letter from Mr Hare, on Hunt affairs, he returns to me the Sketch and report by Mr Edwards as to the Red Lion Wharf, which I had forwarded to him. — A delightful evening |⁶⁴ with the Children. —

May 12. Wednesday.

Very showery weather. — Stow fair day. — Wrote to Turner, fishmonger, London, to order a dish of fish for a party to morrow. — E.F.W. rode to the fair, and returned earlier than I did. — I drove to Stow and back, going thither before 11 and returning before 5 P.M. — Transacted business at the Provident Bank, where met Mr Winter, Mr W. Vavasour, E.F.W. &c. — To the Workhouse, where conferred on Union matters with Mr Pearce. — To the Office of the Gloucestershire Banking Company, where transacted Union business with Raymond Cripps, the Treasurer of our Union, meeting the Hon. & Rev.[2] Gustavus Talbot, H. Lindow &c. — Met and parleyed with W. Vavasour. — A pleasant domestic evening.

May 13. Thursday.

Showery weather — Stow second fair-day. — Drove to Stow, accompanied by MW. who returned soon afterwards to Upper Slaughter — Transacted |⁶⁵ business at the Provident Bank, where I met Mr Morrison — To the Justice room with Mr R. Waller, as my colleague,

---

2. An interesting change of usage where 'Rev.' appears in place of 'Revd.' The later diaries contain much less use of 'Revd.' anyway, and Francis Witts uses the term perhaps only to one third or so of the extent used in the 1820s.

E.F.W. with Broome, and W. Vavasour, being assessors. A good deal of business. E.F.W. had driven Sophy, with his two elder children, to Maugersbury to luncheon at the W. Vavasour's; thence they brought the children to the fair. I joined them for a few minutes, when I met Mᴿ Vavasour, Mʳˢ· W.V., Mᴿ Westmacott &c. — Broome returned home with me, and delighted in the fair & fairings: the rest followed not very long afterwards.

May 14. Friday.
Showery weather. — Parish business with W. Gregory. — Wrote to Mᴿ Brookes, Stow, with a draught of a case to be sent up to the Editors of the "Justice of the Peace" respecting a doubtful point, which occurred in the decision of a matter at the Magistrate's meeting yesterday, asking for an opinion on the subject. — Received a letter from Mᴿ Francis, Incumbent of Snottisham, [166] now absent from his living, because his parsonage is under repair, and offering to take my duty temporarily, if we wish to make a summer excursion — Also a letter from Howell, with an indifferent account of Macleod: H. sends me a cheque for the money I advanced to his daughters for their journey to London, and forwards for my perusal a letter he received some time ago from his friend, Major Wright, dated Algiers, and giving an amusing and interesting account of Valencia, Algiers &c. — Mᴿ Lefroy came from Cheltenham to dine and sleep here. — We had a dinner party — of gentlemen; Mᴿ Vavasour, Mᴿ R Waller, Mᴿ Turner, Mᴿ Potter, and Mᴿ Barrow were our guests. — All passed off pleasantly.

May 15. ~~Friday~~ Saturday.
A fine day till the Evenᵍ· when rain fell. — Mᴿ Lefroy left us for Cheltenham, making a tour of Stations by Stow, Moreton, Campden &c. — Wrote to Howell in answer [167] to his letter received yesterday: — also to Mᴿ Francis that we had no present intention of leaving home, & so that I did not require clerical assistance. — Received a letter from Howell, who has dispatched a box of Raisins as a present to be divided between MW. and Sophy — Brit. Magazine. —

May 16. Sunday.
A showery day — Visited the Sunday School twice — Morning Service E.F.W. officiated, reading prayers: he not returning to his duty at Stanway, which Mᴿ Walsh had undertaken. — Evening prayers were read by me, and my son preached on preferring the praise of GOD to the praise of men. — A letter from Purnell as to the business to be transacted on Tuesday next at Gloucester, at the Adjᵈ· County Sessⁿˢ· A letter from H. D. Warter, stating that the title to Mᴿ Selby's property, ground rents &c. on the Wandsworth road, proves bad, and that the purchase proposed must be given up. This is very annoying — [168] To the family a section from Trower on the Gospels. —

May 17. Monday.
Fine weather — Wrote to Mᴿ Warter in answer to his letter received yesterday, desiring him, with the assistance of Mᴿ Jennings, to endeavour to procure another suitable investment in ground rents or houses, in or near the Metropolis, for the money to be laid out in a purchase to replace the property sold by us in Fenchurch Street. — Wrote to Mᴿ Jennings to the same purpose with a copy of my letter to Mᴿ Warter. — Preparing a Sermon. — Mᴿ & Mʳˢ· Ford.

Dulcy Ford, M^rs. W. Ford, and her two elder children called. — M^rs. W. Vavasour called. — Walked with MW., Sophy and her two elder boys. — E.F.W. fishing — G Baldwin left our service: Charles Clift entered into it.

Tuesday May 18.

A damp morning, cloudy day, and rainy evening. — I breakfasted early, and left home in the phaeton for the Cheltenham Railway Station, where I met |^69 Mr Ellis Viner, Lefroy &c. — and proceeded by rail to Gloucester. — Transacted business at the office of the County Treasurer. — To the Shire Hall, where met several members of the Prison Visiting Board, and of the Prisons Committee, — Purnell, Curtis Hayward, Dr Timbrill, Ellis Viner, Price, Brickdale &c. — The business of the Prisons Committee was to receive and consider tenders made for the building of the new Chapel and other alterations in the County Gaol, estimated at £3000 — but no tenders were sent in: no doubt, in consequence of the state of the money market, rendering it very difficult to obtain accommodation from Bankers, coupled with the great works on railways now in progress, causing a great demand for labourers and artificers, and the doubt as to the price of labour for some time to come, owing to the very advanced, and still advancing prices of the necessaries of life, dearth of provisions, and dread of famine. The Committee resolved to recommend to the Court to com-|^70 mence the works, under the management of a good Clerk of the Works, acting under the direction of the County Surveyor, who has had experience in such a case, the great work of a Lunatic Asylum for the North Welsh Counties, in course of erection at Denbigh, being now in progress under him, as Architect, without the intervention of contractors. — The Visiting Justices present at their meeting on the 11th. Inst. had carefully gone through the testimonials of thirty three candidates for the vacant office of Clerk and Deputy Governor of the Gaol, and had selected out of the list four persons as possessing the greatest claim for support, being very highly recommended, and having had experience in Prison management. Of these one Maconochie, had been in the Scotch Fusilier Guards, Inspector of Police on the Eastern Counties railway, and for four years a Wardsman at the Pentonville Prison: he was strongly com-|^71 mended by Major Jebb, Surveyor of Prisons — S. Hudson, Supervisor at the Millbank Penitentiary, was provided with excellent testimonials: Benwell, Clerk and Deputy Governor of the Bristol Gaol, had high pretensions; all the above appeared before us: not so one Price who was highly spoken of, having served in the army, and being now a Superior Officer in a military prison in Scotland, but prevented by his duties there from personal attendance at Gloucester. Of the above we selected as the most promising, and, therefore, to be nominated by the Visiting Justices, Maconochie: but the others, especially Benwell, were unexceptionable — At one PM. the Court was opened, and was soon very much crowded: the L^d. Lieut. attending, backed by a long train of obsequious followers, ready to support their Whig leader. The first business was the appointment of a Governor, Matron, and Turnkey for Littledean House of Correction, in the room of the Officers dismissed at the |^72 last Sessions. There were several candidates; but the Vis. Justices of the Bridewell strongly recommended Shepherd and Bennett, a Sergeant of the Rural Police, and a Constable of the same force, who had been acting pro tempore as Governor and Turnkey. These men were unanimously appointed. But as to the appointment of Clerk and Deputy Governor of Gloucester Gaol there was no such unanimity: the Lord Lieut. and his tail were bent on bringing in a broken Clothier of Uley, one Jeens, who was supported by a long list of sponsors, testifying to his talent, integrity, familiarity with accounts &c. Argument availed nothing against a foregone conclusion: it was in vain that the Chairman urged ably and calmly the great importance of choosing a candidate highly recommended by competent judges, capable of conducting the gaol in the absence of the governor, with judgment, firmness, and that readiness w$^{h.}$ |73 familiarity with prison duties gives; that the person elected should be thoroughly conversant with the modern system of prison management required by the government — in short, with the Pentonville system; that such an appointment would go far to recover the character which of late years the Prison had lost, since it could not be denied that it had not latterly maintained its ancient rank: it was in vain that Curtis Hayward urged all these points more warmly and energetically, declaring that the Visiting Justices ought not to be held responsible for the good management of the gaol unless they were allowed officers of experience and intelligence on whom they could rely: it was in vain that I upheld the views entertained by the Chairman and Assistant Chairman, urging, as a fresh argument for the selection of a Candidate having practical experience in Prison management, that the new plans as to secondary punishment, abolishing transportation to penal colo-|74nies, and involving imprisonment on the separate system in the provincial gaols, made it necessary that thoroughly trained officers should be appointed; and that with scarcity confessed it could not be doubted that crime was likely to be increased, and, so, the Gaols would probably, be more occupied than for two or three years of past prosperity, such circumstances evidently requiring the selection of men of experience: — all this availed nothing, but on the votes being taken the result was that thirty four voted for Jeens, and 26 for Maconochie. The only Magistrate who spoke on the side of the victor besides the Lord Lieut. was Capt. Sinclair: the only argument used was that, if there was a situation vacant, to which a salary was attached, and a Gloucestershire man presented himself with testimonials as to talent and integrity, he ought to take precedence of a stranger; that if Mr Jeens were as yet unversed in prison |75 management, his duties might be taught him by his principal, and he might learn, while his qualifications as an accountant were peculiarly good. From the speeches made by the Chairman, Curtis Hayward, and myself Capt. Sinclair inferred that we considered the Governor, Mason, incompetent; and this seemed in certain quarters to give great offence. No such assertion had been made directly, nor had the Governor been named, but true it is that the inference was not unfairly drawn. The whole transaction of this election was truly discreditable; a packed majority flocked together to carry the pet of a party, careless whether they appointed a man quite ignorant of his business, or excluded one thoroughly instructed in it; careless also whether the Establishment were well or ill officered, so that the pet of the party were pitchforked into the place. – As soon as the object was gained, there was a rush to get away; |76 the sixty magistrates dwindled down to a dozen or a Score, some few finally remaining to transact important business still to be done, chiefly as to the building of the chapel and other works at the Prison. Of the number who so remained I was not one, being obliged to leave that I might return to Cheltenham by the train leaving Gloucester at half past four. I partook of some refreshment at the Bell, before repairing to the Railway Station, where several Magistrates were waiting to go in the direction of Cheltenham &c. or towards Bristol. Among them were Mess$^{rs.}$ Hanford, Colchester, Talbot & others, with the latter of whom I travelled to Cheltenham, rain having now steadily set in for the evening. At the Plough Hotel I found my Servant ready, and was soon on my homeward route, reaching

Upper Slaughter shortly before 8 PM. — My son and daughter with their children had been at Stow and Maugersbury; |[77] at the former place the members of the Cricket Club had met; at the W. Vavasours there had been luncheon given; but our party had returned home to dinner, the rain having prevented the cricketers from returning to their game after their mid-day repast. Edward had been a little hurt and shaken by coming in collision with a player in running to catch a ball — he was, however, not seriously injured. —— I received a letter from Howell, announcing the very unexpected intelligence that Emmeline had, at her place of seclusion, Mursley,[3] in Buckinghamshire, where she is residing with a Clergyman named Horne,[4] whose wife is sister to M[rs.] Parsons, late of Upton S[t.] Leonards, formed a connection with a medical Gentleman, named Wynter, practising at Winslow,[5] a widower of 40 years of age, of respectable character, well spoken of by M[rs.] Parsons and her Sister – Howell had gone down to see the parties, had given his consent to their marriage in July, and congratulates him-|[78] self that this event will relieve him from much embarrasment, and solve difficulties. Under other circumstances the connection would not have been satisfactory; but it is not discreditable; and E. might have formed a bad connection: after what had passed in the winter of 1846 at Prinknash her return to her Father's house unmarried would have been prejudicial to her sisters, a cause of anxiety, and discord, and dread. — I received a letter from one Halling of Cheltenham, a man in a humble station, whose son was ~~trans~~ sentenced to transportation for stealing Bread from a Baker's barrow in Cheltenham. He was tried with two other boys, his companions & accomplices, at the Gloucestershire Adjourned Sessions in 1845, and a prior conviction having been proved, sentence of transportation was passed on him, as an old offender, and the other boys were sentenced to three |[79] months imprisonment each. The Father soon afterwards wrote to me to beg me to recommend ~~him~~ to the pro~~perty~~ authorities the case of his son, with a view to a remission of the sentence of transportation, alleging that he was of weak intellect &c. I declined interfering, leaving it to the friends to memorialize the government, & holding myself in readiness to forward to the Home Office a copy of my notes when they should be called for. It is now alleged that a boy, who was the principal and most material witness against the lads convicted, has made a statement to the effect that he perjured himself: this witness has, it seems, been taken before the Cheltenham bench of Magistrates to be sworn to the truth of his present statement, but they decline to administer an oath to him, as it would lead to the prosecution of the party for perjury on his own confession. I am referred to the Magistrates for the correctness of this story, or I may be |[80] furnished with a copy of the statement as made in writing before a lawyer, and I am requested to represent the facts at the Home Office, and to solicit a pardon. — Received a circular soliciting my vote at the General Election for the Rt. Hon. W. Gladstone, as MP. for the University of Oxford, in the room of M[r] Estcourt, who has intimated his intention to resign on the ground of his advanced age, and infirmities. Three candidates are put forward; ~~in this~~ Gladstone, Cardwell, Charles Round; the first of Christ Church, the two others of Balliol College, all men of talent, and high character. Gladstone, besides being distinguished as a prominent member of Sir Robert Peel's administration, is the author of a work on the

---

3.   Mursley is a village in between Buckingham and Leighton Buzzard.
4.   Thomas Horne, rector of Mursley.
5.   Winslow is a market town, a little over one mile south-west from Mursley.

Church in which very high Church opinions are held: Cardwell is a pupil of Sir R. Peel, a pleasing speaker in Parliament, a good man of business, held office under |⁸¹ the late government, is of an independent fortune, and is believed to hold high-church, but not ultra-high-Church principles: Charles Round, relation of my old friend the MP. for Maldon, is of the legal profession, an excellent man of business, of independent property, a Chairman in Essex, the Northern division of which County he represents, and is proposed by those who fear that Gladstone is verging towards Romanism, and that Cardwell, as a Peelite, will be the advocate of expediency, not unlikely to consent to the endowment of the Romish Priests in Ireland, or other liberal measures in that direction; while Round is considered as pledged to strictly Protestant views, having opposed the endowment of Maynooth College, and being understood to be adverse to concessions to the Roman Catholic party.

May 19. Wednesday.

Some showers in the morning; but afterwards the weather fine. — The Churchwarden, Gregory, transacted business with me before |⁸² breakfast — Mᵣ Pearce called to submit to me some letters received on Union business from the Poor Law Commissioners, as to out relief in certain cases to single women or widows, the mothers of illegitimate children, and inmates of the Workhouse: and as to the provisional appointment of Hornsby as School-master in the Workhouse, and the appointment of a Schoolmistress. — Mᵣ Palso laid before me a private letter recᵈ by him from Mᵣ Hunt, the Auditor of the Union, together with a letter addressed to the Chairman & Guardians of the Union, which, coupled with a former private letter addressed to Pearce, and the tone of conversation in his intercourse with the officers held by Mᵣ H., require careful consideration. It is true that Mᵣ Hunt has passed the half year's accounts; but he has expressed in such broad terms his disapproval of the manner in which the Union is conducted, and so reproved the officers, in a way to shew that he ~~emput~~ imputes to them, espe-|⁸³cially to the Clerk and Governor, Pearce, either incompetency, or negligence, or misconduct, that it seems necessary to require explanations from him, and to invite examination and enquiry, appealing to the Poor Law Commissioners — for, as matters stand, the Auditor not only subjects the accounts to a strict audit; but dictates, directs, censures, and interferes in a manner wʰ· the Act of Parliament defining his powers does not seem to justify. — Mᵣ and Mʳˢ· Vavasour came from Stow about one P.M. to take luncheon here, and remained with us till after five o clock. While with us, we all walked to Eyford to call on Mʳˢ· Dolphin, who was so much of an invalid as to be unable to receive us; but we visited her friend, Miss C Knight, who arrived on a visit, a few days since; and we met there Miss Browne from Salperton. Walked with the Vavasours, Sophy, the dear children & EFW. about the Eyford grounds and gardens. — Received a letter from Mᵣ Warter, who mentioned that no further correspondence had taken |⁸⁴ place between him and the Solicitor for the Vendors of the Chelsea ground rents, the price demanded by the latter being higher than Mᵣ Jennings considered the true value; also that he was not aware whether any thing more had been done as to the houses near the terminus of the Blackwall railway; he talks of again advertizing for ground rents; suggests whether some of our settled Yorkshire property might not be sold to serve as an investment for the produce of the sale of the Fenchurch Street houses &c. — Recᵈ a circular in favour of Mᵣ Cardwell's pretentions to the representation of the University of Oxford. — In the evening consulting my Son as to the Course to be recommended to the Guardians of our Union to-morrow in respect of the correspondence ~~we~~ submitted to me to-day by Mᵣ Pearce, both as regards the letters from the P.L.C. and those from the Auditor. —

May 20. Thursday.

Weather fine. — Wrote |⁸⁵ to Howell, congratulating him on the prospect of Emmeline's marriage, not as an event likely to give unmixed satisfaction, but as likely to relieve the family from much difficulty and anxiety. — Wrote to Halling, the father of the lad sentenced by me to transportation in the spring of 1845, intimating that it does not belong to me to initiate any proceedings in the matter; that it is not my duty to investigate the facts stated as to the readiness of the witness to confess thast he swore falsely on the trial: but that the proper course is to forward a memorial for remission of the sentence to the Home Office, stating all the facts, and accompanied with proper documents; that the probable result of such course will be the Authorities referring to me for a copy of my notes taken at the trial, which I shall readily send, and feel glad if the lad be restored to his parents. — Drove to Stow — Attended at the Prov. Bank, where I regretted to find Mᵣ Pain very unwell — |⁸⁶ We have also lost our other Clerk, who had been long and from the very beginning connected with the institution — Mᵣ J. D. Charles of Stow, who has been sinking for some time, suffering from a liver complaint, and died two or three days since. — Transacted business at the office of the Gloucestershire Banking Company. — Had an interview on Tax business for a parishioner with Mᵣ Longhurst, surveyor of taxes. — At the workhouse, presided for more than four hours at the meeting of the Guardians of our Union; there were a crowd of applicants for relief, owing to the increased price of the commodities of life especially of bread, which has reached one shilling per quartern loaf. The value of wheat is nearly doubled since this time twelvemonth; scarcity is confessed; the stocks both of home grown and of foreign corn are small; food riots have broken out in some localities, especially in the West of England: government |⁸⁷ gives warning of dearth, and a strong feeling is abroad of the absolute necessity of economizing the grain used for human food, by abstaining from the use of the finest flour, lessening consumption, substituting coarser articles of food. The farmers have generally raised the wages of the labourers, the highest rate given being 12/ per week, the general rate 10/- per week, and to-day the Guardians raised the rate of relief proportionally. — The arrangements as to Schoolmaster, Schoolmistress, and Nurse, proposed by me were unanimously adopted. — I brought forward the correspondence of Mᵣ Hunt, the Auditor, with a view to challenge him to an explicit statement in a formal manner of his imputations against the Clerk and Governor, and Relieving & Medical Officers, and of his censure on the guardians as to the general management of their business — The universal feeling was that Mᵣ H. exaggerated minor errors, (although |⁸⁸ his blame of the Medical Officers was not without sufficient cause) that he outstepped his province in finding fault with the established regulations of the Union, and in urging points in such a manner as to amount to dictation. It was unanimously resolved that I should address the Auditor by letter to the effect that the Guardians, having under their consideration his public letter of the 15th. Inst. to the Chairman and Guardians, together with his private letters to the Clerk of the 1st. and 15th. Inst., having also heard the statements of the Clerk and Rel. Off. as to the tone of censure in which he addressed himself to them respecting their individual conduct, and the general management of the Union by the Guardians, and considering the conduct of the Clerk and Governor, & Rel. Off. as substan-|[89]tially correct and unimpeachable, those officers having acted under the directions of the guardians, have it in contemplation to submit M[r] Hunt's letters coupled with necessary comments on them to the P.L.C. requiring from them directions as to the proper course to be taken thereon. Whether this measure should be adopted would materially depend on the answer M[r] H. should make to the communication I was instructed to make. If he apologizes, and states that the construction put on his letters and conversation is erroneous, and withdraws his censure of the officers and the Guardians, then the appeal to the P.L.C. not to be made. If how he persists then the whole affair to be referred to them. — M[r] Hurd attended the Board: so also M[r] Perkins, who though an old acquaintance of M[r] Hunt, fully concurs in the view taken by the Guardians as to his interfering improperly & censuring without |[90] sufficient cause. — MW. received a letter today from Eliza Daniell, from which it appears that M[r] Barr has been for some time her guest at Leamington, in bad health, consulting D[r] Jephson. M[rs.] C. Barr and the children are there also. — A circular from Oxford, recommending the support of M[r] Charles Round as Representative for the University. — E.F.W. and Sophy had ridden to call at Great Risington on M[r] & M[rs.] J. T. Rice. — I was much fatigued & overpowered with sleep in the Evening. —

May 21. Friday.

A very fine day. — Wrote to M[r] Hunt, as stated in the Diary of yesterday — Justice business at home. — The Rev[d.] M[r] Walsh came from Winchcombe to dine and sleep here. This pleasing young man was ordained Deacon and Priest as Curate of Cutsdean, but resigned his Curacy last autumn, from ill health, with fears of a pulmonary complaint. A voyage to Malta, and temporary residence there, together |[91] with a journey home through Italy and France, including a tour in Sicily and a visit to Naples and Rome, seem to have restored his health, and he has returned to his residence at Winchcomb, with which place, however, he has no connection, except his partiality to the country and neighbourhood, and where he now resides without any clerical charge. He has often assisted my Son in his duties, and hence an intimacy has sprung up, which induced us to invite him — Received a letter from my old friend, John Round, MP. for Maldon, bespeaking my support of his relation and friend C G Round who is to be proposed as a representative for the University in the room of Estcourt. —

May 22. Saturday.

Fine weather. — Lost our dear children and grandchildren, who returned to-day to Stanway: their departure left a great blank — M[r] Walsh also left us. — Received from the Gaol at Gloucester a circular, announcing a meeting of the Visiting Magistrates on special business for |[92] Saturday the 29[th.] Inst: it is added that the County Chairman & Curtis Hayward, whose signatures were attached to the requisition upon which the meeting is called, particularly wish for my attendance. I expect that some important matter will be discussed arising out of the proceedings of the Adjourned Sessions on Tuesday last. — M[r] Pearce called, with further documents to exculpate himself from the blame cast on him by M[r] Hunt, the Auditor, and with a letter, a circular, received from the P.L.C. referring to the scarcity of wheat and other grain, and suggesting for the consideration of the Guardians some arrangement whereby relief may be given with bread of a wholesome, but inferior sort. — Memoirs of Lord Sidmouth. — Preparing a Sermon.

May 23. Sunday.

Wet weather in showers. — Visited the Sunday School. — Whitsunday. Prayers, Sermon, and administration of the Holy Communion. I preached |[93] on the descent of the Holy Ghost on the Apostles: — 21 Communicants. — Preparing a Sermon. — Evening Service, prayers. — Ecclesiastical Gazette. — To the family a section from Trower's Exposition of the Gospel. — Omitted to mention on Saturday that I received a letter from H. D. Warter, writing from Cruck Meole, whither he had gone to visit his mother, who has been seriously indisposed, as to the final closing of the negociation for the purchase of the Wandsworth ground rents. — I had written to him on the same business on Saturday, stating my unwillingness to interfere with our settled property in Yorkshire in such a manner as that it should descend otherwise than as an inheritance from my wife's family.

May 24. Monday.

Fine weather — Preparing a sermon — Justice business at home. — Received a letter from Christopher Geldard as to the fence to be made by the Railway directors t̶o̶ across our lands at Ravenflatt — he had stipulated that it should be a stone |[94] wall, both for the sake of shelter, and that the cattle might not be injured by becoming entangled in the iron wire fence proposed by the company, or, forcing through it, stray on the line of the railway. It is settled that we are to be allowed 14/ per rood to build such wall, but it will cost a shilling or two more, which the Geldards think will be well laid out in the erection of a secure fence. — Drove with MW. to call on M⁛ and M⁛⁛ W. B. Pole at Upper Swell. We were not admitted, as the lady was prepared to go out on horseback, and her horse was at the door. — Transacted business at M⁛ Brookes's office, Stow — Called at the library: M⁛ Pain is a great invalid, but slowly recovering. — Looked into the Church: the new pewing and alterations are in a very forward state, and the improvement is very great, the work being well executed, and on good principles. The chancel is fitted with stalls, the floor |[95] partly laid with encaustic tiles. — Drove to Lower Swell: called on the Perkins's: much conversation with him as to M⁛ Hunt, the Auditor, with whom he has been long acquainted, and whose appointment he warmly advocated, but whose present proceedings as to this Union he wholly disapproves, and mentioned some passages of M⁛ H's early life which were discreditable, and lessen one's surprize at his present overbearing and offensive tone and conduct. — Transacted some Justice business at Lower Swell. — Memoirs of Lord Sidmouth. —

May 25. Tuesday.

Fine weather — Wrote to Round, declining at present to pledge myself to support either of the Candidates for the representation of the University, being desirous of further time for consideration and observation — expressed that it would give us great pleasure to receive a visit from Round, which he leads us to hope he may make during the summer. — Wrote to Chr. Geldard, |[96] approving the arrangements he has made as to the fence with the directors of the North Western Railway. — Preparing a Sermon — Posting Accounts. — Received a letter from M⁛ George Hunt, with copies of a correspondence inclosed between M⁛ Braikenridge, and Mess⁛⁛ Cox and Williams on Hunt Trust matters — a letter from W. Cripps MP. — asking my vote for M⁛ Cardwell, in whose favour I rather incline, and commenting on the shameful conduct of Lord Fitzhardinge and his party at the Adjourned Sessions held at Gloucester on the 18th Inst. — A letter from Mess[rs] Hoare, announcing that they have received to my account from M[r] Jennings £59. 3. 6 – From Settle printed circulars soliciting my subscription towards the relief of the Poor of the townships of Giggleswick and Settle in consideration of the present high price of provisions — the application is signed by Rowland Ingram, the |[97] Vicar, as Chairman of a meeting held on the 18th Inst. — Memoirs of Lord Sidmouth — Wrote to R. Waller, requesting him to attend at the Justice meeting at Stow next Thursday.

May 26. Wednesday.

Fine weather — Wrote to W. Cripps, in reply to his letter rec[d] yesterday, declining to pledge myself to support Cardwell, as candidate for the representation of the University, but not refusing him my vote, if on further consideration he sh[d] appear to me the most eligible of the three competitors. Adverted also to the late proceedings at the Adjourned Sessions at Gloucester — Wrote to Rowland Ingram, Vicar of Giggleswick, with a check on Mess[rs] Alcock, Birkbecks & C[o] for £3. 3. 0 as my subscription towards the fund for assisting the poor inhabitants not receiving parochial relief resident in the townships of Giggleswick & Settle to purchase the necessaries of life in this season of scarcity. — With MW. drove to call on M[r] and M[rs] Boudier at Farmington, whom |[98] we found at home. — Rec[d] from M[r] Hare a letter accompanying a voluminous packet of correspondence on the disputed affair of the Red Lion Wharf, (Hunt Trust concern) between Mess[rs] Cox and Williams on the one part, and M[r] Braikenridge on the other. — Memoirs of Lord Sidmouth. — Justice business at home.

May 27. Thursday.

Very fine weather — With MW. drove to Stow, who returned after calling at the library and one or two shops. Transacted business at the Provident Bank, where I met Mess[rs] Ford, Winter, Morrison, Perkins &c. — Called on business at the Office of the Gloucestershire Banking Company. — To the Workhouse, where conferred with M[r] Pearce on Union matters — At the Justice room Mess[rs] Ford and Waller sat as my Colleagues: Mess[rs] Winter, W. B. Pole, Turner and Barrow were our Assessors — Rec[d] from Butt & Sons, Gloucester an invoice of wine sent by the |[99] carrier on Tuesday. — Memoirs of Lord Sidmouth.

May 28. Friday.

Beautiful summer weather. — Wrote letters to M[r] Geo. Hunt, and M[r] Hare on Hunt Trust business. — Also a note to M[r] Pearce on Union matters — Transacted parish business with M[r] Lea, M[r] Gregory &c. — Received a letter from J Round as to the pretensions of his relative to the representation of the University of Oxford; also from W. Cripps on the claims to the same honourable post of his friend Cardwell. — from M[r] Geldard the half-yearly balance sheet of rents received and repairs and improvements from & on our estates in Craven. — On the controversy as to the "heavenly witnesses" — the summary contained in the 4th Vol. of Hartwell Horne's Introduction — Memoirs of Lord Sidmouth. ——

May 29. Saturday.

A heavy thunder storm, till about one AM. — some slight rain in the afternoon, otherwise very fine weather. — I breakfasted early, and left home for Gloucester to attend a meeting of the Board |[100] of Visiting Justices of the County Gaol. At the Cheltenham stationed met

Mr Viner, with whom travelled to Gloucester. — A full meeting of Vis. Justices in the Committee Room at the Gaol — present Purnell, Curtis Hayward, Timbrill, R. Davies, Price, Sayers, Goodrich, Viner, Clifford, C. Trye, Surman & myself. Much deliberation as to the course to be adopted in consequence of the vote of the Majority at the Adjourned Sessions on the 18$^{th.}$ whereby Mr Jeens, now in office, was elected Clerk of the Gaol. By the regulations it is laid down that the ~~V~~ Governor shall propose to the Vis. Justices such officer of the Prison whom he shall select as his Deputy Governor, and the understanding was that the Clerk and Deputy Governor should be combined offices. Such appointment, however, was subject to a veto on the part of the Vis. Justices. Insisting on our principle declared on the 18$^{th.}$ that it is indispensably necessary to have a |^{101} deputy Governor experienced in prison management on the Separate System, we determined to exercise that Veto, and, on the Governor nominating Mr Jeens, we refused to sanction his appointment, and directed that pro tempore the duties of Deputy Governor should be performed, when necessary, by Reeves and Cooper; two officers of ~~tried~~ good standing in the Gaol. With this resolution we combined another proposed by Mr Purnell, that the office of Storekeeper of the Prison be abolished and that its duties be performed by Jeens together with those of Clerk, so that he shall have sufficient work for his salary; for, as he is elected to an office in the prison by the Court, he cannot be displaced. It was agreed also as part of the same plan that it be proposed to the Court at the next Sessions that an officer be appointed as Deputy Governor and Chief Warden of the Separate Prison, such officer being a person thoroughly conversant with Prison Manage-|^{102}ment and the separate system, and that Government be requested to nominate three competent persons from whom the Court to select one, his salary to be £150 per ann. This will involve an alteration of our Prison Rules, which would, no doubt, be sanctioned by the Home Secretary. — This arrangement, or one to the same effect, has been contemplated as requisite at a distant period, when the new building for separate prisoners should be completed, and ready with its Chapel and other appendages. Then an increase of the staff would be wanted, and, indeed, sufficient work can be found for such an officer as is proposed now, since extraordinary watchfulness is required while the buildings are in progress. It is proposed also that all the officers with the exception of the Governor shall wear a uniform. Some doubt existed among us, whether to advise the early |^{103} appointment of Chief warden and Deputy Governor, or to procure a vote of the Court sanctioning such appointment and deferring the actual appointment; but on consideration it was judged expedient to fulfil the scheme at once, for such a feeling now subsists as to the unbecoming manner in which Jeens was brought in by a party for party purposes, in opposition to the Chairman, Visiting Justices, and leading Magistrates engaged in conducting the business of the County, by a packed majority, mainly consisting of inexperienced and inefficient men, that it will be easier now than hereafter to carry points by a sort of reaction. It was distinctly stated by the County Chairman to-day that, if this measure were not carried, he should resign, and the Vis. Justices responded to him by an assurance that they would cease to hold that office unless they had such a staff of gaol officers as they considered adequate to the satis-|^{104}factory management of the Prison. Mr Mason hesitated as to nominating a Deputy Governor to-day, saying that he did not consider Jeens as yet sufficiently acquainted with the duties of the place, but fully expected he would in time be fit for it: but, being pressed, he did nominate Jeens. He was evidently out of humour; (Mason) and shewed, as usual, his own incompetency: and made but a lame defence, when charged by Purnell with mis statements or at least unauthorized statements to one of the candidates on the 18th Inst. as to the salary and perquisites of the Office of Deputy Governor and Clerk. Before the Visiting Justices separated, it was agreed that private solicitations should be made to induce Magistrates not statedly attending the Sessions, but inclined to uphold the Chairman & Visiting Justices, to support |[105] them at the Trinity Sessions. Such measures are constantly used by the adversary, and we are driven to resort to the like. The meeting broke up at about half past one, but as no train left Gloucester for Cheltenham till half past three, I was detained till that hour. — Part of the time I occupied by visiting the Petty Sessions of County Mag. in the City Grand Jury room at the Shire Hall, where W. Guise, Price & Sayers were administering Justice. — Met Lysons, R Davies, C Hayward &c. in the Street, and with them continued to discuss the business which had engaged us at the Gaol. — In the coffee room at the Bell, where I took some refreshment, met M[r] R. Beman, who attends Gloucester market, and from whom I learnt that diseased potatoes of this year's growth had been exhibited there this forenoon. D[r] Timbrill confirmed this by telling me that the blight was plainly to be seen on the leaves of young |[106] potatoe plants in gardens at Beckford — At half past three went to Cheltenham by railway, travelling thither in the same carriage with Timbrill & Viner. — At Cheltenham, met and parleyed with Lefroy and M[r] Bold Williams; and setting out with little delay in my carriage, I reached home by half past six P.M. — Letters awaited me from E.F.W. with a very comfortable report of all at Stanway Vicarage — from Howell to say that the box of raisins had been dispatched from town; — from G. Pain, respecting a book to be ordered for the Stow Book Society. — M[rs.] Dolphin and Miss C Knight had called to-day, and mentioned certain matters as to alleged misconduct of servants at Eyford, which were likely to be brought under my cognizance; and accordingly I had to hear the complaint of a party considering himself aggrieved, whose case, however, I could not deal with magisterially, but it became necessary for |[107] me to communicate upon it by note to M[rs.] Dolphin. — M[r] and M[rs.] W. B. Pole also called to-day, and left their cards. —

May 30. Sunday.

Trinity Sunday. — Very beautiful weather. — The 39th anniversary of my Marriage — great reason have I to thank GOD for the many blessings and comforts bestowed on me through that union with a virtuous, amiable, sensible, and affectionate partner! May GOD preserve us both, as long as it seems good to him, to live in harmony and mutual endeavours jointly & separately to fulfil our duties towards each other, towards our children, servants, neighbours, & all with whom we are brought into contact, constantly striving to be useful and beneficial to others, to set a good example to others, to prepare for eternity, and to correct the errors of past years! — Wrote to Howell, that we had safely received the box of raisins: — to Rodwell, Bookseller, London to order two books for the Stow library. — Visited the Sunday School |[108] twice. — Morning service, prayers. Afternoon service. I preached on the Trinity — Miss C. Knight called between the services. — Rec[d.] a letter from Rowland Ingram Jun[r] acknowledging my contribution of £3. 3. 0. towards assisting the poor inhabitants of Giggleswick and Settle, not receiving parochial relief to obtain flour and oatmeal on moderate terms; he mentions the potatoe disease as having already shown itself this season in Craven — Preparing a sermon — Eccl. Gazette — To the family a Section from Trower's Exposition of the Gospels. —

May 31. Monday.

Beautiful weather — Busy with Yorkshire accounts, and Geldard's half-yearly balance sheet of rents received and expenditure. — Wrote to M^rs. R Waller, in answer to a note received this morning, that I should have much pleasure in going to tea at the Rectory, Bourton, on Friday next, the annual meeting of the Benefit |^109 Society being fixed for that day, at which it is my custom to attend as one of the Trustees. MW. declined visiting Bourton on that day of probable heat and bustle. — Wrote to E.F.W. a long letter on various topics public and private to be conveyed to him when he is at Stow, at the Cricket meeting to-morrow. — Wrote to Bowen, expressing an anxious hope that his intended removal from home to place himself at Brentford under the care of a Dr Costello, a medical man who is reputed extremely skilful in calculous complaints, and who has visited Bowen at Guiting, but did not find him in such a state as to justify his performing an operation, may be beneficial to him. The poor old man is suffering pitiably from Stone and disease of the Prostrate gland, and is bent on the forlorn hope of relief by this journey, which, one would fear, may be more than he can bear. Of his intention we had learnt from Miss C Knight yesterday, and from Mr Ford, who called to-day on his |^110 way to see his old friend before his departure which is fixed for Wednesday next. Mr Ford partook of luncheon with us. At a later hour Mr Turner called; and after him Mr Lumbert, whom I saw rep respecting digging stone on his land to erect a wall to mound out the road in my rectory fields, Pease Hill & Short Riff Hill, on the way to the Cheltenham turnpike road. — Rec^d. a satisfactory letter from Mr Hare on Hunt trust matters. — Life of Lord Sidmouth. —

June 1. Tuesday.

Very fine summer weather. After an early breakfast MW. and I started in our open carriage for Cheltenham, where we arrived before eleven o clock AM. and were engaged for two hours shopping &c. — Afterwards repaired to the house of our good old friend M^rs. Keysall, with whom we passed some hours pleasantly, taking an early dinner & tea with her — We left her at half past six P.M. and returned home between eight and nine P.M. — Rec^d. a letter |^111 from Mr Hunt the Auditor of our Union in reply to mine of May 21. he disclaims dictating to the Guardians as to their manner of conducting the business of the Union; but persists in his allegations and imputations against the competency, integrity, or diligence of the Clerk and Governor. — A letter note from E.F.W. to his mother mentions that all at the Vicarage, Stanway, are quite well. — Mr Davis sent me a cheque on the Gloucestershire Banking C^o. for £100 in payment of his half year's rent due at Lady day last. —

June 2. Wednesday.

Beautiful weather — Transacting business with W. Gregory as to the Church and Charity Estate Cottage rents and their expenditure, change of a tenant &c. — Wrote to Mr Davis, acknowledging the receipt of the cheque which he sent me yesterday. — Wrote to Mr Geldard on the balance sheet forwarded by him as to our Craven Rents and expenditure, which I received some days ago. — Wrote to Mr Pearce, in-|^112 forming him that I had received a letter from Mr Hunt, the Auditor, and what was its tenor. — Considering the proper course to be adopted as to the letter written by the Auditor, and preparing for the meeting of the guardians of the Union to be held to-morrow. — Memoirs of Lord Sidmouth.

June 3. Thursday.

Fine summer weather — Drove to Stow. — Attended at the Prov. Bank, and transacted business there, where I met M.ᵣ Winter. — At the office of the Gloucestershire Banking Company, where I had business — Paying a bill. — To the Workhouse. Presided for four hours at the fortnightly meeting of the Guardians: very heavy work, mainly owing to the blame imputed by the Auditor, with little cause, to the officers, Clerk and Governor, and Medical Officers. Investigated his charges against the latter, Messʳˢ· Hayward and Wells being present, and both had |¹¹³ been guilty of omissions of duty as the the keeping of their books; Mᵣ Wells, through weakness of understanding, and being entrapped in a private conversation with Mᵣ Hunt, had made unnecessary admissions to him, contrary to the fact, and had deviated from the line of duty by obeying the suggestions which Mᵣ H. had made without authority: he also had neglected keeping his proper books. Mᵣ Moore, having accompanied poor Bowen yesterday on his journey to Brentford, was not present, but had written a letter in which he denies the assertion of Mᵣ Hunt that the Med. Off. of this Union order extras to persons not under medical treatment; which Mᵣ Hayward also emphatically denied having done. I proposed to the Guardians a Series of resolutions grounded on Mᵣ Hunt's letters, and charges against Mᵣ Pearce, to the effect that the whole correspondence with comments thereon, to be drawn up by me with the assistance of a |¹¹⁴ committee, be submitted to the P.L.C. that they may give such directions thereon, as may seem to them expedient: it being impossible that the business of the Union can be carried on with the present officer lying under the stigma of the Auditor, until those allegations which he has made are investigated under the central authority, or declared by ~~them~~ that authority undeserved and frivolous. — After the business of the Union, I was engaged for nearly an hour, as a Magistrate, in hearing the complaints of Mᵣ Polhill and Mᵣ Potter as to an unwholesome nuisance at Broadwell; and in making an order for the removal of a poor insane woman from Adlestrop to the Lunatic Asylum at Gloucester. — MW. recᵈ· a letter from Mʳˢ· C. Barr. Mᵣ B. has reached Henwick near Worcester from Leamington, convalescent as ~~his~~ regards his late severe attack of chronic gastritis, but very weak. They de-|¹¹⁵ cline our invitation to visit us here before their return to Leeds, whither his business as Banker calls him as soon as the state of his health permits. — Memoirs of Lord Sidmouth.

June 4. Friday.

Fine summer weather. — After breakfast, Justice business at home. — Drove with MW. to Bourton on the Water, callᵍ· on the way at Prosser's, Lower Slaughter, on Prov. Bank business. Recᵈ· a letter from Newmarch Senᵣ, or, rather, copies of a correspondence between him and Lord Sherborne relative to the disagreement between them as principal and agent, which have been existing for some years past – N. considers himself aggrieved, and, probably is so: his desire seems to be that his and his Son's clients should be in possession of his case against Lord S. and his L'ship's evading to do him justice. — A note from George Baldwin, requesting from me a certificate as to character to enable him to procure from the Town Commᵣˢ· a licence to keep a wheel chair. ᵃᵗ ᶜʰᵉˡᵗᵉⁿʰᵃᵐ — MW., having escorted |¹¹⁶ me to the outskirts of Bourton, returned to U. S. I joined the honorary members of the Bourton Friendly Society, of which I am one of the Trustees, and preceded the train of ordinary members, about 50 in number, to the Church. Mᵣ Ford, R Waller, Mᵣ Turner, Mᵣ Hunt (Gt. Risington) Messʳˢ· Bryan, Bennet, &c. were of the number of honorary members. Mr Turner preached a very good, plain, & suitable sermon, after prayers read by R. Waller. The funds of the Society, which has been steadily and slowly increasing for ten years, exceed £360 — new members were added to-day. At two o clock the dinner took place at the New Inn, R Waller presiding, and all went off pleasantly, as far as heat, punch and cigars with pipes w^d. permit — cordiality prevailed, compliments and good advice, formed the staple of the speeches, song and recitation went round; and without the Inn door, booths, toy shops, and the omnium gatherum of |^117 a rural festival prevailed – Between four & five the high table broke up to repair to the Rectory where M^rs. Waller regaled with tea & coffee the Rev^d. Messrs. Ford, Hunt, Turner & myself – also Mr Stenson – the Waller children delighted in the band, and flags. — Good tidings had reached Bourton, through Mr Moore, the Med. attendant, as to the success which had attended the operation for the Stone, by crushing, which had been performed on Bowen by Dr Costello at Brentford yesterday.[6] Ford had accompanied his friend to Oxford, whence Mr Moore proceeded with him. — Good accounts from Stanway Vicarage by John Bateman. — Home to tea. — Memoirs of Lord Sidmouth.

June 5. Saturday.

Fine weather — Wrote to George Baldwin giving him a character for steadiness, sobriety, attention, and honesty, to be used in procuring a licence to keep a wheel-chair at Cheltenham. — Wrote to G. F. Newmarch with reference to the documents forwarded to me which arrived yesterday, as to |^118 late correspondence between Lord Sherborne and his Father, regretting that it was not more satisfactory, and expressing my good will to N. and persuasion of his integrity. — Justice business at home. — Mr Pearce called — Engaged with him for two or three hours in perusing and preparing documents relating to the controversy between him; the other officers, & Guardians of our Union, and Mr Hunt, the Auditor. — Called on John Davis. — A letter from Mr Hare on Hunt matters. — Memoirs of Lord Sidmouth.

June 6. Sunday.

After a shower early in the morning a fine summer day. — Visited the Sunday School twice — Morning prayers and Sermon. I preached on the love of relations and friends. — Afternoon service — prayers. — Miss C Knight called after afternoon service: M^rs. Dolphin has received a very indifferent account of Bowen's state: he has suffered greatly since the operation was performed. — Rec^d. a letter and enclosure |^119 from Mr Thornton on Hunt Trust matters — Also a letter from Mr Geldard explaining a mistake made in the last balance sheet: he does not urge my coming down to Craven to negociate an exchange of lands with Mr Garforth, unless I desire it. — A circular with reference to the approaching contest for the representation of the University of Oxford. — Preparing a Sermon — Brit. Mag. — To the family a section from Trower on the Gospels. —

June 7. Monday.

Fine weather, but a blight, which has prevailed much of late, will prove injurious to fruit. — Justice business at home —— Wrote to Mr Thornton on Hunt Trust matters, sending him for his perusal a letter from Mr Hare. — Wrote to Mr Geldard in answer to his letter received

---

6.   Dr. Costello was the medical superintendent at Wyke House Asylum near Isleworth.

yesterday, that I shall avoid the fatigue and expence of a journey to Craven this summer, unless some particular occasion should arise rendering my presence necessary. — With MW. drove to Longborough, to call on the Morrisons, whom we found at home. A sister |¹²⁰ of Mʳˢ· M. is their guest. Mʳˢ· M. looks very delicate, and has been a great invalid. The marriage between the eldest daughter and Mʳ Scott is still contemplated; has been postponed in consequence of the gentleman's ill health. We saw all the young people except the affianced one, who was with her future mother in law. Called at Longborough on Mʳˢ· Coates, Mʳˢ· Backhouse's old Servant. — At Stow called at the Library: the town was enlivened by holiday folks, bands of music &c. this being the day of annual meeting of the Friendly Societies of the place. — Life of Lord Sidmouth. — Wrote to Mʳ Croome, desiring him to forward the valuation of this parish for the Poor and County rate with as little delay as possible.

June 8. Tuesday.

A showery day. — My son rode from Stanway, and breakfasted with us, bringing a very good account of his dear wife and children. — Wrote to Messʳˢ· Hoare, directing them to transfer £40 from my |¹²¹ account with them to that of my Son. — Preparing for a meeting of a committee of Guardians to be held on Thursday, some comments on the correspondence of Mʳ Hunt, the Auditor, to be forwarded to the Poor Law Commissioners — E.F.W. left us for Stow to join in a game at cricket. — Received from the Home Office a packet from the Under Secretary, requesting a report of the evidence taken on the trial of James Halling and others at the Adjᵈ· Sessions for Gloucestershire in 1845, at which I presided, together with memorials, correspondence &c. as to a remission of the sentence of transportation then passed on Halling, after a previous conviction for felony, on the ground that the principle witness on the trial now declares that his testimony was false. — Preparing such report, with observations on the case. — A circular as to subscriptions to be raised for four new Colonial Bishoprics lately formed at the Cape of Good Hope, Adelaide, Port Philip, and Newcastle, the three latter |¹²² dioceses being in Australia, forwarded from the Office of the Society for the Propagation of the Gospel: the object being to provide supplies towards sending out additional Clergymen &c. to those colonies. — Life of Lord Sidmouth. —

June 9. Wednesday.

A few showers fell; otherwise the day fine — Wrote to the Secretary of State in relation to the case of James Halling. — Preparing Upper Slaughter Church and Charity Estate accounts, to be submitted to the Trustees at a meeting this evening. — Mʳ T. Wynniatt called — Accompanied MW in a drive to Northleach to call on the Astons, whom we found at home, viz. Mʳ and Mʳˢ· A. and Mary, and heard good accounts of their about children: fork luncheon there.⁷ — In the evening a parish meeting. The Churchwarden's accounts were passed, and H Gregory and E Lea nominated as churchwardens: the latter by me vice |¹²³ Davis, whose infirmities prevent his longer holding the office — The accounts of the Church and Charity Trust were also passed. — Brit. Mag. — Life of Lord Sidmouth.

---

7.   A fork luncheon was a meal that could be eaten with a fork alone, as if necessitated by standing – as at a function for instance. This is a difficult transcription point. It is possible that as on most previous occasions he wrote 'took', but the word looks distinctly like 'fork'.

June 10. Thursday.

A fine, but chilly day after rain in the night. — To Stow, accompanied by MW. who soon returned home after a little shopping. — To the Provident Bank, where transacted business, and met Mr Pole, Mr Morrison &c. — Mr Pole and his lady are returned to Wyck Hill from Town — Business at the Office of the Gloucestershire Banking Company. — To the Workhouse, where met Messrs. Beman, Wilkins, Morgan and Comely, and with them, as a Committee appointed on the last Board day, arranged the terms of the representation to be made by the Guardians as to the correspondence and controversy with the Auditor, which has been so much discussed — Mr Potter accompanied Mr Beman, to confer with me, and take |^124 my advice respecting a dispute which has arisen on parish matters in the pugnacious parish of Broadwell. — To the Justice Room, where the Dean of Gloucester, now at Oddington, Messrs. Ford, and R Waller acted with me as Magistrates, Mr Winter, Mr Potter &c. being assessors —— Home by 5 PM. — Rec^d. a packet of letters between Mr Braikenridge and Messrs. Cox and Williams on Hunt Trust matters, sent with a letter by Mr Hare; — also from Geo. Hunt a letter on the same business; — also from Messrs. Hoare a letter noting that they had passed £40 from my account with them to that of my Son; — also circulars from Mr Gladstone's and Mr Round's Committees for furthering the return of those gentlemen as representatives for the University of Oxford. — Life of Lord Sidmouth.

June 11. Friday.

Fine weather. — My haymaking begun. — Wrote to Mr Thornton on |^125 Hunt trust matters, forwarding to him the packet of letters, which I had received yesterday from Mr Hare, with my comments thereon: — also to Mr Hare, with observations on the present state of the discussion as to the Red Lion Wharf. — Walked with MW. to Eyford: called at M^rs. Dolphin's, who was out in her open carriage: called on the Ryans in the garden: still doubtful when M^rs. D. goes abroad. — Letters from Mr Hare with further documents, (a letter from Mr Cox sent to Mr Thornton, copied and sent to Mr Hare,) on the debated matter of the Red Lion Wharf; — from Howell, who writes that Mr Ackers has now paid the whole price of Prinknash — MW. received letters from our old friend Miss Rollinson, who leads us to expect a visit from her during this summer; — and from Constance Howell, with an account of their seeings and doings; also that Macleod is very poorly. — British Magazine — Life of Lord Sidmouth. —

June 12. Saturday.

Fine weather — Wrote to |^126 Hare, returning to him the copy of the letter from Mr Cox to Mr Thornton, which he had forwarded to me with comments on it. — M^r and M^rs. Polson called on us, and passed an hour with us on their way homewards (Woolston, Berks) from the Billingsleys at Wormington, whence they had brought their younger boy, as also a little girl, a daughter of the Billingsleys; it was pleasant to see the kindly warmth with which the Polsons revisited old neighbours. — Drove to Wyck Hill, to call on the Poles; met Mr P. by the way, and were not admitted to see M^rs. P; who might be in her garden. — Thence to Little Risington; called on the Fords: Mr F. not at home: saw M^rs. F. and her daughters: the mother looks very ill, just recovered from a serious inflammatory attack. — While we were out M^rs. Dolphin and the Misses Hall had called. |^127 Letter from Mr Geo. Hunt, urgently pressing me to insist on a speedy settlement of the Hunt Trust matters now under discussion. — MW. rec^d. a letter from Sophia Hunt, who with her sisters and brother are visiting Caroline & Maria at Clifton. She announces a decision on the part of Caroline, suggested by Mr Whitcomb, which will give offence to George Hunt, and render still more unpleasant the existing controversy about Trust matters. — Brit Mag. — Life of Lord Sidmouth. — Justice business at home.

June 13th. Sunday.

Rainy weather, with scarcely any interval of fine gleams. — Visited the Sunday School. — Preparing a Sermon — Morning Service: prayers — Afternoon service, prayers and sermon; I preached on the duty of forgiveness — Gave Prayer Books and Reward books to the children after saying the catechism in Church. — A letter from Mr Hare accompanying one to him from Sophia Hunt, announcing that Caroline Hunt refuses to |^128 concur in any reference of the matters now in dispute respecting the Hunt Trust: — a letter from Mr Croome, the land Surveyor, who promises the valuation of this parish within a few days. — Eccl. Gazette — To the family a section from Trower on the gospels. –

June 14. Monday.

A rainy forenoon; showers in the afternoon. — The weather prevented us from fulfilling an intention of driving over to Stanway to pass the day with our children — neither would the rain allow of my walking to Bourton on the Water to meet Messrs. Ford & R Waller to transact magistrate's business fixed for this day. — Wrote to Mr Thornton on Hunt business, forwarding different letters I had rec^d. and copies of what I had written — Preparing a sermon. — Mr Clarke paid a visit, in calling between four & five o clock. — Life of Lord Sidmouth. –

June 15. Tuesday.

The forenoon and afternoon |^129 very fine showery, the evening fine. — Wrote to Sophia Hunt on the controversy as to the Red Lion Wharf, shewing the error Caroline Hunt had committed in refusing to be a party to an arbitration — Wrote to Mr Croome, the Surveyor, as to the valuation of this parish, in reply to a note which Mr E. Lea had received from him desiring to know whether any lands in this parish were subject to Tithe or rent charge. — Rec^d. two letters from Mr Hare on the interminable dispute as to Whitby's wharf: he incloses a letter he had received from Mr Thornton. — Rec^d. a note from Jemima Ford, desiring me to order a new book for the Book Society, to which I replied in a jocose style to correspond with that in which her note was written. — Preparing a Sermon — Posting accounts. — Life of Lord Sidmouth.

June 16 Wednesday.

A rainy day almost without intermission, which prevented us from going to visit our children at Stanway. We heard, however, a good account of them, |^130 MW. having received a note from E.F.W. written at Stow yesterday, by which it appears that they have an engagement on Friday, so that our visit must be delayed till Saturday. — Wrote to Mr Hare on Hunt Trust affairs, returning to him the letter from Mr Thornton which he had sent for my perusal. — Preparing a Sermon — Posting accounts — British Magazine. — A letter, (circular) announcing a meeting of the Visiting Justices of Gloucester Gaol. Life of Lord Sidmouth.

June 17 Thursday.

Fine weather. — Wrote to Howell. — To Stow, MW. accompanying me, and very soon returning home. — Transacted business at the Provident Bank, there meeting M[r] Pole, and conferring with him — Received a strange, incoherent, eccentric note from Miss Ford, as to books ordered into the Stow library. — Met and conferred with M[r] Moore, the Surgeon of Bourton on the Water, who read to me a letter he had just received from D[r] Costello, |[131] under whose care poor Bowen is now staying near Brentford, from which it appears that he has been attacked with Bronchitis so severely, as to cause D[r] C. great alarm, who writes for information as to the friends whom he ought to apprize of M[r] B's danger, and expresses a wish that M[r] M. were with him. The latter seems evidently to consider the alarm not ill founded. I recommended him to communicate the letter to M[r] Ford, and to take his advice and directions upon it. In the evening I wrote to M[rs] Dolphin an account of the contents of D[r] C's letter; she had been informed by letter from her servant Gillman, now in ~~communication with~~ attendance on Bowen, that there was a change for the worse, but the nature of the attack had been mistaken by Gillman. M[rs] Dolphin, with M[r] and M[rs] Frobisher called on MW. to-day. M[rs] D. has made her arrangements for setting out for the German baths on Saturday, meaning to call on Bowen on her road to Town. — Transacted |[132] business with M[r] Croome, Land Surveyor, at Stow, on the subject of the valuation of the parish of U Slaughter, under the Parochial Assessments Act, and made an appointment with him at my house on Saturday morning — Attended the fortnightly meeting of the Guardians of our Union, at which I presided. Investigated the manner in which M[r] Moore discharged the duties of his office as Med. Off. of Distr. 3. in order to ascertain how far he was liable to, or exempt from the Censure passed by M[r] Auditor Hunt on the medical department of our Union; he seems to have punctually discharged all his duties. Much business; contracts made for bread, and other articles for the ensuing quarter. A sample of cheap bread, hominy mixed with flour in a small proportion of the former,[8] was laid on the table, as made by the Matron according to a receipt furnished by the Poor Law Comm[rs] and it was considered very |[133] good; the saving would be about two pence on a quarter loaf at the present price of bread. It was agreed to decline contracting for the bread used in the Workhouse, and to prepare hominy bread for the use of the workhouse. The contract made with the Bakers, conditional, in case we elect to supply home made bread to the outdoor paupers, was for each district at 10[d]½ per quartern loaf: meat, beef without bone, & mutton at 7[d]½ per lb. — I was detained late at the Workhouse, and afterwards by conferring with Pole on Prov. Bank matters &c. and by others applying to me on magisterial business, so that I reached home late to dinner, and tired. — Received from M[r] Thornton two letters on Hunt Trust disputes, with a proposition that the matters under discussion be referred to M[rs] Whitcomb, on the part of Miss Hunt, and M[r] Braikenridge on the part of M[r] Hunt — All the papers and documents relating to the controversy with the Auditor |[134] have been transmitted to the P.L.C., M[r] Graves, Ass[t] P.L.C., and M[r] Hunt. — but no answers yet received. —

---

8.   Hominy is a maize hulled and ground and prepared for food by being boiled in water or milk. Its name comes from the Algonquian word *uskahomen*. During the potato famine the British Government ordered large stocks from the USA but the starving Irish did not know how to prepare it and tried to use the grain as a direct substitute for wheat, leading to severe digestion problems from stomachs hardly able to cope with food through severe malnutrition and stomach enzymes accustomed to potatoes.

June 18. Friday.

A very showery forenoon and afternoon, – evening fine. — Wrote to Mͬ Thornton in reply to his letters received yesterday on Hunt Trust disputes; agreeing to the plan that Mͬ Whitcomb, for Miss H., & Mͬ Braikenridge, for Mͬ Hunt, should meet and endeavour to settle, or otherwise refer to arbitration the matters under discussion. — Wrote to Mͬ Bloxsome, requesting him to forward to me early in next week his bill on the County for the half year ending Trinity Sessions, that I may examine it previously to the meeting of the Committee of accounts on the 28ᵗʰ· — Brit. Mag. — Posting accounts. — Justice business at home. — Visiting and reading prayers with an aged and sick parishioner, W. Collett. — Life of Lord Sidmouth. –

June 19. Saturday.

Fine weather. — Mͬ |¹³⁵ Croome, the Surveyor, and Mͬ E. Lea, as Churchwarden, designate, and principle rate payer in the parish, waited on me by appointment, when we went through the new assessment for poor rates which Mͬ Croome has made, correcting some trifling errors. — After breakfast MW. and I drove to Stanway to pass the day with our children and grandchildren, calling, by the way, at Temple Guiting, to make enquiries at the Vicarage house as to the last accounts of poor Bowen, which were bad. Mͬˢ· Dolphin, who left Eyford this morning, has taken his housekeeper to visit and attend upon him; Mͬˢ· D. means to see him on her road to London. — Found all the dear children quite well, and pleased to see us, took luncheon, and an early dinner with them, rambled about near the house, and on the farm; called on Mͬ Cook. Decided symptoms of disease in the potatoe plant. — Lady Phillips from Middle Hill called, accompanied by her unmarried daughter in law, and a Mͬ Fenwick, an Oxonian to whom the young lady is |¹²⁶ engaged. — We returned home to tea between 8 and 9 PM. — Received a letter from Howell; Emmeline is to be married to Mͬ Wynter, Medical practitioner at Winslow, on the 29ᵗʰ· Inst. — Johnny Howell has brought back from school at Gosport the measles, which his sisters and Macleod are likely to catch. — A letter from Mͬ Thornton in reply to one of mine on Hunt Trust matters. — A letter from C Bathurst, who has been a great invalid for several weeks, and is still much indisposed. — Lord Redesdale has brought in a bill to relieve parishes from a burden entailed on them by the operation of the Act for securing the irremovability of the Poor who have resided five years in any parish, as relates to contiguous parishes, in one of which the expenditure on the paupers has been increased in a certain proportion by relief granted to irremoveable paupers settled in the other parish; the object is also to check |¹²⁷ the disposition to reduce the number of cottages in any parish below that which is sufficient for the accommodation of an adequate number of hands for the cultivation of the parish.* —— Resumed haymaking, suspended during the week by the very rainy weather: some of my grass is a good deal damaged: but the crop abundant.

* Lord R has sent me a copy of the Bill. ——

June 20. Sunday.

Anniversary of the Queen's accession. — A dull, close, overcast day; a shower of rain in the evening. — Visited the Sunday School. — Morning prayers and Sermon. I preached on the tribute-money. — Afternoon prayers. — Preparing a Sermon. — Eccl. Gazette — Recᵈ·

a letter from C. J. Geldard; Mr Garforth declines making an exchange of lands with us, as regards the portions of Ravenflatt severed by the Railway, so that we have to carry out an agreement with the railway directors by which they purchase on liberal terms our severed parts, and we buy certain other parts belonging to them as severed from |^{128} other properties which lie contiguous to our land, to the Eastward of the railroad line — To the family a section from Trower's exposition of the gospels.

June 21. Monday.

Showery weather. — Wrote to C. J. Geldard in answer to his letter received yesterday: — to Howell, in reply to his letter received on Saturday; — and to C Bathurst, in answer to his letter received on the same day. — Harry Waller called and partook of luncheon here: he explained the low condition to which Vernon Dolphin has sunk, a state almost approaching to want. It appears that Mrs Dolphin has for some time ceased to supply him with funds, and H.W. had been at Eyford, expecting to find her, and prevail on her to assist him; the departure of the lady for Town on her way to the Continent seems likely to militate against any such arrangement. It would seem that V.D. has never left England, but lived in obscurity in some retired place on the |^{129} allowance furnished by his wife, but of late with-held, as is supposed, from a sense that his bad habits are still persevered in, and that he lives with a mistress; not Miss Ling, who is married. It is lamentable to think how low a man of fine fortune is brought by extravagance, and vicious habits. — H.W. mentioned that Mrs Ford has had a relapse, and is understood to be in a state causing much anxiety to her family — Rec^d a letter from Sophia Hunt on the litigated Hunt Trust matters. — Life of Lord Sidmouth.

June 22. Tuesday.

Showery weather. — Wrote to E.F.W. a note to be given to him at Stow, where he is expected to play at cricket. — Wrote to Sophia Hunt, in answer to her letter received yesterday, and to Mr Hare; both letters being on the subject of the disputed matter of the Wharf. — Visited sick parishioners, J. Davis, (who met with an accident by falling ~~from~~ in his house on Sunday) and W. Collett. — Walked to Bourton on the Water, calling for my letters at the Turnpike gate: there was one from |^{130} Mrs Dolphin to M.W. from Town, giving a better account of ~~her~~ poor Bowen, whom she found at Wyke House, (Dr Costello's establishment) greatly relieved from the attack of bronchitis, but suffering from his other complaints and very weak. — Called at Bourton on Mr Moore, whom I informed as to the state in which Mrs Dolphin had found his patient, Bowen — Called at the Rectory, where I saw Mrs R. Waller, and Harriet Hornsby, who were prepared to walk to U Slaughter to call on us, and who accompanied me home, and sat some time to rest themselves. MW. had come back from L. Slaughter, whither she had accompanied me on my way to Bourton. — Hay making does not advance very prosperously owing to the rains of last week and the showers of this. — Life of Lord Sidmouth. — In the evening a strange incoherent note from Jemima Ford, alluding to the odd note written by her to me last week, and to which she seems to expect an answer. She names her mother's late serious relapse of |^{131} illness, and that she is going to accompany her to Cheltenham for change of air, and to try the waters; the note written in a jocose style; I answered it in a graver mood, hoping that Mrs F. would benefit by change of place &c., and assuring her that, as Secretary of the Book Club, I would soon send for the book which she wished me to order.

June 23. Wednesday.

Showery weather. — Justice business at home. — Preparing myself for the discussion about to take place at the approaching decanal meeting. Rec^d. from Round, a letter offering us a visit next week; I replied by return of post, regretting that the Sessions would prevent my receiving him, but inviting him to come on the 6th. July, or, indeed, on any other day in the month. — A letter from Bloxsome with the usual halfyear's bill against the County for his services as Clerk of the Peace, to be audited by me before the Sess^ns. From the Bishop a circular, announcing the places and times of the approaching Visitations and confirmations — at Stow on Aug 25 and |^132 26th. — Round informs me what is stated in the paper, that Cardwell has declined the contest for Oxford. — M^r and M^rs. Pole called upon us. — Life of Lord Sidmouth — Preparing a Sermon. —

June 24. Thursday.

Showery weather, very hindering to the hay, much of which must be damaged. — Preparing a Sermon. — Drove to Stow — to the Provident Bank, where met Messrs. Pole, Winter, Morrison &c. — Conferred with Mr Morgan, in the library, and with Mr Clark in the Bank. — Visited the W.H. with Perkins; conferred with Mr Pearce; gave directions as to repairs of the Well, alterations at the Vagrant ward, baking hominy bread &c. — To the Justice room, where sat with Ford and Waller, as my colleagues, Lewes & Price being ~~my~~ assessors. — Business lasted till past four o clock. — Mr Ford left M^rs. F very ill yesterday at Cheltenham, a bilious affection — passing gall-stones. — Mr Sewell gave |^133 a very unfavourable report of Dr Warneford — suffering from gout, influenza &c. — his age 83. Received a letter from E.F.W. who, with his wife and children, came from Stanway to-day. Edwd. & Sophy with George to the W. Vavasours at Maugersbury, Broome & Frederick to "the Cottage" — the inducement being a proposed al fresco gathering of Col. & M^rs. Colville's friends to-morrow on Adlestrop Hill. ——E.F.W. has been asked to become one of the Clerical Stewards of the approaching Gloucester music meeting: — writes about hominy bread; and the approaching election at Oxford. — MW. received a letter from Laura Howell; hitherto none of the family have caught the measles: Johnny has had the complaint lightly. — Life of Lord Sidmouth. —

June 25. Friday.

Still showery weather: but with a prospect of improvement. — Wrote to Dr Williams, Superintendent, Gloucester Lunatic |^134 Asylum, for information as to the condition of a poor woman from Adlestrop, whom I lately sent thither. — Wrote to Mr Brookes in regard of two trials to come on at the approaching Q Sess^ns. — Wrote to the Bishop of Gloucester, inviting him to make our house his resting place, at the time of the Visitation &c. if it should so be that illness or other cause should prevent his visiting Mr Ford. — M^r E Lea consulted me as to encroachments made on the waste and street of the parish by mowing the grass and turning out cattle, in which W. Dix is the principle aggressor, contrary to the understanding come to two years since, when Counsel's opinion was taken, as to the proper means of correcting the great nuisance of the open parts of the Village being used as a common pasture. Advised him to act as recommended in the opinion then given by impounding any cattle found straying, as Surveyor of the Highways, so leaving the party whose |^135 cattle shall be impounded to his remedy of proceeding by action against the impounder; the effect of which would be to lay on the plaintiff the burden of proof that he had a right of common, which would be, if possible, attended with great expence. Afterwards walked to Bourton on the Water, and called on Mr Kendall, as Attorney for the parish, whom I instructed to act, if necessary, on our part, in this business, and who concurred in the advice I had given to E Lea — Rec^d. a note from E.F.W. from Maugersbury. He promises to breakfast with us to-morrow: answered his note. — A letter from C. Bathurst in answer to my last: he seems to be mending in health, though he employed his wife as amanuensis. — Life of Lord Sidmouth. — A circular from Mr Round's committee at Oxford, again soliciting my vote at the approaching election. — Met Mr Moore at Bourton, who had received more favourable accounts of poor Bowen: he is to undergo another operation to-morrow. — |^{136}

June 26. Saturday.

Very fine weather, much to the advantage of the hay. — E.F.W. did not come to breakfast, as we expected, but arrived with dear Sophy ^{on horseback, en route for Stanway from Maugersbury,} to take luncheon with us, and passed two hours here, which was a great pleasure to us. The children with their nurse, returned to Stanway, in Mr Vavasour's carriage, from "the Cottage" and Maugersbury. — Finished auditing Mr Bloxsome's bill against the County: — preparing for the approaching quarter sessions. — Preparing a Sermon. — Visiting a sick parishioner, W. Collett. — A letter from Round, who is unable to visit us, as I proposed, in the week after next; but hopes to find an opportunity during next month. — M^r R W Hippisley sent a statement of the receipts, disbursements, and deficit, relating to the new pewing, and restoring of Stow Church, which is to be opened for divine service on Tuesday the 6th. July, when he invites the Clergy to attend in gowns; full |^{137} service, morning and evening, is to be performed, two ~~services~~ sermons preached, and a collection made. It is not stated by whom the Sermons are to be delivered; Dr Hook and Archdeacon Wilberforce have both declined. The friends and acquaintances of the Hippisleys are invited to luncheon at the Rectory. RWH also announces the Ruri-decanal meeting as fixed for July 7. — A circular from the Lunatic Asylum, Gloucester, giving notice of a meeting for the 7th. July, to complete the dissolution of the partnership between the Subscribers to the Asylum on the one hand, and the County and City on the other, and to renew the partnership on other terms, as agreed upon in a contract for such dissolution and renewal of partnership submitted some months since to the Secretary of State for the Home department, and now approved by him. — A letter from C Bathurst on the appointment of a Deputy Governor to the Gaol at Gloucester, as intended to be proposed by the Chairman and Visiting |^{138} Justices of the Prison on the 29th. at the Sessions. — Mr Pearce called, with whom conferred on Union matters. — Life of Lord Sidmouth. — Wrote to Rodwell with an order for books for the Stow Library. —

June 27. Sunday.

Fine weather, but cloudy and close. — Visited the Sunday School — Morning service — prayers — Evening Service prayers & sermon. I preached on Confirmation, giving notice of the rite to be performed on Aug. 26 — Rec^d. a letter from the Bishop of Gloucester, who cordially accepts our invitation to visit us at the time of the visitation, if he should be prevented going to Little Risington, by Mrs. Ford's illness, or otherwise – MW. received a note from Jemima Ford, dated Cheltenham, which speaks of her Mother as still much indisposed:

J.F. writes to beg that a book which she has desired me to order into the Stow library may be sent to her at Cheltenham when it arrives. Her eagerness on this matter, at such a time, indicates |[139] a disturbed and unquiet mind. — M[rs.] Aston writes to MW. that she and her husband and two daughters will visit us from Monday till Thursday in next week. — A letter from M[r] Croome, land-surveyor, as to valuations for the Poor rate of parishes in this neighbourhood, including that of Upper Slaughter, to be sent in as to-morrow to the Clerk of the Peace. — My son's servant came with my horse, which I lent to E.F.W. yesterday: all the dear party reached home yesterday well. — Preparing papers for the Quarter Sessions —

June 28. Monday.

With the exception of a brief shower in the evening the weather fine. — After an early breakfast, set out in my phaeton with MW. to Cheltenham, on my way to Gloucester. Reached the station by ten o clock. MW. proposed to pass a few hours at C. and to return in the evening to U Slaughter. — At the Railway Station joined M[r] Lefroy, and accompanied him to Gloucester. — To the Bell Hotel; where conferred with Purnell on |[140] county business. Then to the Shire Hall, where attended to county finance business. M[r] Gambier Parry, of Highnam Court, recently appointed a magistrate, and member of the Committee of accounts, was initiated into that business: Curtis Hayward and Goodrich were the other colleagues with whom and the Chairman I worked: Baker, who, as High Sheriff, is precluded from acting as a magistrate, came in and assisted his friend Parry. — A very important meeting of the Visiting Justices of the Gaol, at which attended the County Chairman, Mess[rs.] Surman, Brooke Hunt, D[r] Timbrill, R Stevens, Clifford, C Hayward, Price and myself, who determined on a report to be made to the Quarter Sessions to-morrow, embodying the views and resolutions entertained by the Board of Visiting Justices on May 29. with but little change, which we to-day communicated to the Governor, Mason, and his Clerk, Jeens: this occupied much |[141] time and thought, as also in the evening, & past midnight, when the County Chairman and I closed our deliberations. — Continuing our labours of finance, we broke up at past six P.M. to dine together at the Bell — Purnell, Curtis Hayward, Timbrill, Goodrich, Gambier Parry and myself. Towards nine o clock, the County Chairman and I were left alone, and worked at public business till twelve o'clock — assisted by M[r] Riddiford. Other officials with whom [we] were engaged during the day were, Mess[rs.] Bloxsome, Lefroy, Keiley, Whitehead, Fulljames &c. — A letter from D[r] Williams, the Superintendent of the Lunatic Asylum, in answer to mine requesting a report of the state of Sarah Willoughby.

June 29. Tuesday.

Very fine weather. Rose early and engaged in preparing for the business of the day. — Breakfasted with Purnell. — To the Shire Hall, to attend the Court on the County business, where sat till between three |[142] and four o clock. — A very large attendance after one o'clock; in all 74 Magistrates present. Among these the Marquis of Worcester, Sir Chr. Codrington, Sir M H Beach, Sir M B Crawley Boevey &c. I went through the financial business satisfactorily to myself, with only a little sparring with Coroner Barnett. — The business of the day, which called together so large a concourse was the expected discussion as to the Gaol appointments. The Lord Lieutenant, together with his particular adherents and Justices chiefly under his influence, absented himself, but had privately written a cross letter to the County Chairman. The latter had taken pains to gather a large muster of those adverse to the Peer, and likely to support himself and friends, so that the latter probably amounted to 50, against 24. Mr Purnell read a firm, able, explanatory, argumentative, temperate, conciliatory report from himself, in which he introduced |^{143} the report agreed to yesterday by the board of Vis. Justices of the Gaol as to the offices of Clerk, Head Officer of the separate prison, and Deputy Governor. P. intimated decidedly that he should retire, unless he were supported, and continued to enjoy the confidence of the County. The Marquis of Worcester moved the adoption of the report of the V.J. of the Gaol, that it should be acted upon &c. which being seconded — Mr Prowse Jones, (Uncle of Mason, the Governor) commenced a fierce attack upon the County Chairman, second Chairman, and myself, on the ground that we, backed by the board of Visitors, were prejudiced against the Governor, depreciated his merits, sought to supersede him, or to fetter and dictate to him, grounding the charge on inferences drawn from our speeches on May 18. and adding offensive remarks, as applied to P. & Curtis Hayward, abstaining from such as related to myself. He was well, but rather confusedly answered by C.H. I followed in |^{144} a reply as to the mistaken inferences drawn from what I had said, speaking also to the fitness of the course adopted by the Vis. Board, repelling the charge of prejudice or dictation. I spoke to my own satisfaction, and I believe with general approval; and was followed by Purnell, who very briefly and temperately defended himself from the imputations thrown out against him by the Rev^d advocate of the governor. The motion of the M. of W. was carried almost unanimously, as was also a Vote of confidence in the County Chairman proposed by the same nobleman – Thus a signal triumph was gained: even Capt. Sinclair making a civil and conciliatory speech; a few Magistr. spoke shortly and pointedly in favour of the line taken by the Chairman and visiting board; and it would seem that the administration of County business as superintended by the leaders now in the ascendant is strengthened by the result of |^{145} the day's discussion. My son arrived early; bringing a very good report of his wife and children. Other Magistrates with whom I was in frequent communication were Archd. Timbrill and Onslow, Mr Mirehouse, Curtis Hayward, Lysons, Ford, R Waller &c. When the Court broke up, sauntered for an hour or more, in the Streets, and at the Spa &c. with E.F.W. and R. Waller — Afterwards sat quietly in my room, till it was time to dress, to go to dine at Hempstead, with the Lyons's; an unusual variation from my general rule of dining at the Magistrates dinner. Drove thither in a fly by Lanthony Abbey, the Docks, and fields near Newark, Mr Higford Barr's mansion. A very agreeable party at Hempstead. M^r & M$^{rs.}$ Lysons (his second and lately married wife, sister of Curtis Hayward,) his five children by his first wife, Sir Michael H. Beach, and his friend Mr Smith of Southerop, a very agreeable travelled man, and a distant relation of the Vavasours |^{146} of Rochdale, i.e. of Marmaduke V., M$^{rs.}$ V. of "the Cottage" &c. — Mr Winston Hayward, a Clergyman, Brother of Curtis Hayward, lately married to a Miss Phelps of Chavenage, a nice couple, Mr Gambier Parry and myself made up a party of eight: not reckoning the children — Good cheer, good wine, pleasant conversation; in the library, music, and a most interesting portfolio of early sketches and drawings and engravings by Sir T. Lawrence, of whom also Lysons possesses four very good family portraits — Reached the Bell at a little before eleven; one hour spent pleasantly in conversation with Purnell, his son, E.F.W. and R. Waller. —

43. Chevenage.

<u>June 30. Wednesday.</u>
Very fine weather — Breakfasted at the Bell with the Magistrates, Playne, Hale, Stokes, Purnell, R. Waller, E.F.W. &c. — To the Court, where joined Sergeant Ludlow, who presided at the trial of appeals, which lasted nearly all day: only two or three prisoners being |[147] tried in the evening. — Received a letter from MW. all well at home — she forwarded to me a letter received from Howell. — Dinner at the King's Head; a small party of Magistrates — Serg^t. Ludlow in the Chair — Purnell, Hayward, Mirehouse, Timbrill, Hale &c. — Wrote a few lines to J. Perkins; begging him to communicate to his parishioner, Betterton, the mother of S. Willoughby, the account I had received from Dr Williams as to the state of that lunatic. —

<u>July 1. Thursday.</u>
Very fine weather. — E.F.W. left Gloucester at 7 AM. for Worcester by the Railway, to join in a Cricket match to be played between the Stow and Ombersley Clubs this day — Breakfasted with Mr Hale. — Shopping &c. — Attended in Serg^t. Ludlow's Court from 9 AM. to ½ past 2 P.M. when I left to proceed to Cheltenham by the Railway train leaving Gloucester at half past three for Cheltenham. — Travelled from Gloucester to Cheltenham with RGK Brookes. Shopping &c. at Cheltenham, where I met my Servt. |[148] and carriage with a note from MW. – Arrived at home by a little after 7 P.M. — The haymaking no ^{now} advancing satisfactorily. — Letters none, excepting circulars, and from Apphia Witts to MW. – with a pretty good report of John Witts and his wife, and a bad account of M$^{rs.}$ Warter —

July 2. Friday.

An overclouded day, cool, but without rain, gleams of sunshine. — Wrote a note to G. Pain, desiring him to forward to Miss Ford at Cheltenham, when it arrives, the book which she has lately desired me to send for, to be placed in the Stow library. Business with the parish Churchwarden — Arranging my accounts and papers after the Sessions. — Mr Wynniatt called; also Mr Barrow. — Preparing a Sermon; also a lecture on the Apostles Creed to be read to the candidates for confirmation, thirteen of whom I met in the School room in the evening, being the first beginning of preparation for the rite |[149] to be administered at the close of next month. — A letter from Howell — Emmeline was married on Tuesday last: — Constance and Macleod have caught the measles, likely to be communicated to Laura and Henry. — Life of Lord Sidmouth.

July 3. Saturday.

Very beautiful weather — Made great progress in the hayfield. — Preparing a sermon. — Preparing for the Decanal meeting on Wednesday next. — Rec$^d.$ a letter from Mr Holland Corbett, requesting the character of George Baldwin: to which I replied. — MW. had notes from M^r and M$^{rs.}$ Vavasour, who had spent two days at Stanway Vicarage this week, and returned on Thursday Evening, leaving Sophy and the children quite well. E.F.W. not then returned from Worcester. — M$^{rs.}$ Wynniatt, with Susan W., — accompanied by Mr Lee Warner, Junr and his lately married lady, called upon us. — An indifferent account of poor Bowen's state — Life of Lord Sidmouth.

July 4. Sunday.

Fine weather — Attended |[150] the Sunday School. — Morning prayers and sermon. Preached on the Rich man and Lazarus. — Evening service – prayers. — Preparing a sermon. — Preparing for the Decanal meeting on Wednesday next. – Received a letter from C. J. Geldard informing me that the directors of the North Western Railway Company will pay the price of the land taken for their line across Ravenflatt, (£725) either immediately, or on Feb. 14. next, with Interest at 5 p^r Cent. — He rather recommends the latter course. — To the family a section from Trower's Exposition of the gospels. —

July 5. Monday.

Beautiful weather. — Wrote to J Round, expressing a hope that he will visit us shortly: — to Chr. Geldard, in answer to his letter received yesterday. — Preparing for the approaching decanal meeting — M^r and M$^{rs.}$ Aston with Mary and Sophy Aston came on a visit for a few days. — Cheerful and agreeable evening. — |[151] Justice business at home. —

July 6. Tuesday.

Very fine weather. — After breakfast, drove to Stow in two carriages — the chariot with post-horses, and our phaeton, conveying the Astons, to be present at the re-opening of the church after being renovated and repewed. The service was well performed; the prayers being read by the Rector, and the Sermon preached by the Rural Dean. This was as it should be; better than had been contemplated; an endeavour had been made to procure the oratorical aid of stranger and wandering stars, Dr Hook, Archdeacon Wilberforce, Mr Villers &c.

— but it had failed. The choir of the parish accompanied by the organ chanted the service, performing anthem and the hundredth psalm very creditably. Mr Ford preached a good and suitable sermon, and a collection was made amounting to rather more than £23 — which was increased to about £36 in the evening, when divine service was again |^152 performed, M^r R W Hippisley reading prayers and Mr Wiggin preaching. But at this latter service we did not attend. – The alterations in the Church are very well done, under the directions of a skilful architect:[9] more than 300 new sittings are obtained; aid has been liberally afforded by the Incorporated Church building Society, and by the Diocesan Association for the same purpose: besides the expenditure on the Chancel, which falls on the Rector, £630 have been laid out in the Church, towards which the receipts by donations and grants amount to nearly £512 – so that the deficiency was £118, now reduced by the contributions of this day to above £80. The floor of the Church and Chancel has been entirely new laid, with a current of air made to pass under it. The coved ceiling of the chancel has been removed, and the timber roof stained in dark oak colour; unsightly pews have given place to a range |^153 of twenty or thirty substantial antique oak-stalls, to day wholly appropriated to the clergy who attended in their gowns, to the number of eighteen; not reckoning the reader & preacher. The chancel has been cleared of some heavy table and mural monuments, the portion adjoining the communion table has been laid with encaustic tiles; other encaustic tiles, not in patterns, but black and red squares are laid as a border in the other part of the chancel, the central floor being composed of dark blue ancient stone monumental slabs: the picture of the Crucifixion, a large piece of considerable merit, of the Flemish School, presented to the former Rector, Vavasour, for the chancel, as an altar piece, has been removed from its late position over the Communion table, and is now suspended on the South Wall of the Chancel; a memorial painted window, by Wales of Newcastle, has been set up to record the death of M^rs. Frances Anne Hippisley, my old and worthy |^154 friend, Aunt of the present Rector; other Chancel windows have been coloured of a greenish hue to suit the picture, and take off a glaring light; thus an almost excessive gloom was given to the Chancel. In the nave and aisles the space has been apportioned in a range of low, single, open pews, to be assigned to the parishioners, very well arranged, of deal, to be f varnished with a slightly brown tint, only partially done at present. An unsightly western organ gallery, and plaister ceiling, still remain; but a very chaste and well designed Southern Porch, with an immersion font are in good keeping. All this has not been accomplished without some sore feeling and heart-burning: but RWH. is not of a very sensitive temperament ~~and~~ and is very persevering; fine as the day was, the attendance both of clergy and laity was not so large as might have been wished, though as to the higher classes, M^r and M^rs. Hippisley |^155 had been very liberal and general in their invitations to refreshment after the service performed. Of the poorest there were hardly any present, and there was ample space for a large addition to the congregation. The same defective attendance marked, as I understood, the Evening Service — Among those present were the Rural Dean and two daughters, Aston and family with ourselves, Mr Askew, Headmaster of Northleach

---

9. The architect was John Loughborough Pearson (1817-1897). This was his first commission outside of the East Riding of York. He later built Quarwood, a Gothic country house for R. W. Hippisley, 1856-9, and described as 'outstanding'. It was originally a strange combination of Victorian Gothic and French chateau style, but subsequently remodelled to a more modest Cotswold style in the 1950s. Pearson undertook numerous other commissions in the Cotswolds after his work at Stow.

School, and family, the Dean of Gloucester, M^r and M$^{rs.}$ Wiggen, Mr Lockwood and family, Miss Penyston, Misses Wynniatt and two brothers Rev$^d.$ Mess$^{rs.}$ Hutchinson, Morrison, Jarrett, Sadler, Clarke, Turner, Williams, Mangin &c. — all of whom partook of M^r and M$^{rs.}$ Hippisley's hospitality in an abundant collation, prepared for a much larger company, and set out in the pleasure ground of the Rectory, but unfortunately so arranged that the principal table with its substantial dishes, delicacies, and guests was exposed to the fervid rays of a burning Sun. — |^{156} We left Stow on our return home about two o'clock, our party being increased by the addition of Mr Sadler, the worthy and agreeable Rector of Sutton under Brailes, who was pleased to be our guest for the day at bed and board — M^r and M$^{rs.}$ Aston, Sadler & myself explored the beauties of Eyford before dinner, at which our circle was increased by the addition of Mr Turner, and we passed a cheerful and pleasant evening. — A note from Jemima Ford as to the book which she has desired me to order for the Stow library, but which cannot yet be procured: probably is not yet published. She and her mother are returned from Cheltenham; the latter is still very much indisposed.

July 7. Wednesday.

A heavy thunderstorm during the night, followed by a fine day. — Leaving the ladies, Mr Sadler, F. Aston and I went to Stow at 11 AM. to attend the Ruri-decanal meeting. On the way received a letter from my Son with a good report of those most dear to him and us at Stanway, and an acc$^t.$ |^{157} of his proceedings at Ombersley and elsewhere, since we parted at Gloucester. The cricket match at O. ended in the signal defeat of the Stow Club after two days contest — A letter from Mess$^{rs.}$ Alcock, Birkbecks & C$^o.$ with a statement of my account with them for the half year now expired. — A letter from Mr Thornton on Hunt Trust business. — A circular giving notice of a meeting of V.J. at Gloucester gaol. — Attended divine service, afternoon prayers, at the Church: Mr R. W. Hippisley officiated — about a dozen Clergy present. — Afterwards to Mr Morgan's office, where signed a requisition to the Marquis of Worcester and Sir C W Codrington to stand for the ~~West~~ Eastern division of the County, for the representation of which a movement is made by the Radical party at Stroud, Cheltenham and Gloucester, and elsewhere, who put forward Mr Holland; he has issued an address, responding to the requisition presented to him, promising to come forward in advocacy of his principles, |^{158} but declining to spend any money, or to ask any vote. Such an opposition can only be annoying; without a chance of success the low party seems to aim at teazing and wearying, and seek an opportunity of publicly divulging extreme opinions. — Then to the decanal meeting, at which the Rural Dean presided, and the following Clergymen were present — Mess$^{rs.}$ Hutchinson, Jarratt, ^{Mangin} and Aston, not of the Deanery of Stow, — of the Deanery, R W Hippisley, Hunt, Sadler, Pantin, Hillier, Williams, Clarke, Wiggin, O. Hill, Morrison, Barrow, Turner, Biscoe, & myself. — Mr Morrison read a very good paper on the 6$^{th.}$ Chapt. of St John's Gospel, and how far it had relation to the Sacrament of the Lord's Supper. He held that if any reference to the Holy Communion was intended by our Saviour, it was not the direct meaning of the passage ^{as} relied on by the Romish Church, |^{159} but merely an obscure anticipation of the Sacrament hereafter to be instituted by him, — that the interpretation ~~was~~ $^{is\ of\ a}$ spiritual $^{eating\ and\ drinking}$ and purported^s that faith in Christ ~~was~~ ^{is} signified by the terms of eating and drinking, flesh and blood: — that in this sense the early church had understood and expounded the passage, though they had used it by way of application to the Sacrament: that the Romish doctors had perverted it to support their doctrine of transubstantiation: that the Protestants generally, and the Anglican Reformers in particular, had been opposed to the sense of an oral and sacramental manducation as set forth in the chapter, though some writers of note, Hooker, Andrews &c., had interpreted the passage of the Lord's supper. — I followed with further illustration and enforcement of the views upheld in the Essay, quoting passages from the ancient Fathers, and adverting to Waterland and Beveridge in our own Church: shewing also that some eminent Romish writers disallowed |[160] the reference to the Sacrament of the Lord's Supper. M[r] Pantin followed me with further evidence from Anglican divines of note, shewing the sense of antiquity, and the opinions of many learned Roman Catholic writers, to be opposed to the Sacramental interpretation. M[r] P., as usual, displayed much research and book learning. M[r] Barrow and others followed in short addresses, all taking the same view, with the exception of M[r] Clarke who had taken up the Sacramental interpretation. — It was announced that on the next occasion M[r] W B Pole would read a paper on the Connection between the Church and State, and with an enquiry how far the objections of the Dissenters to such connection are just. — After the meeting M[r] Sadler returned to Sutton — I visited the Workhouse, and conferred with M[r] Pearce. — At four o clock most of the Clergy who had attended the decanal meeting |[161] dined together at the Unicorn Inn; as Members of the Stow Clerical Society, Mess[rs.] Aston an Jarrard, and Mangin being present as guests of myself, M[r] Hutchinson, & M[r] Ford. Other clergymen present were Mess[rs.] Wiggin, in the Chair, R W Hippisley, Hunt, Williams, Clarke, Barrow, Turner &c. The party broke up before 7 P.M. when M[r] Ford and his friend M[r] Mangin, followed F. Aston and myself to Upper Slaughter, and passed the remainder of the evening with us round the tea table &c. in a right cheerful mood.

July 8. Thursday.

A shower about 2 P.M. — otherwise a fine day. — The Astons left us for Northleach. — MW. accompanied me to Stow, returning after having called at one or two shops. — A letter from J Round, who proposes to visit us on the 19[th.] Inst. coming from Belmont near Hereford, whither he goes for a few days next week; his ward, grandson or grandnephew of the late Rev[d.] D[r] Prosser, is about to |[162] come forward as representative for Herefordshire. — To the Provident Bank, where met Mess[rs.] Ford, Morrison, W B Pole, Winter &c. — To the Workhouse, where met M[r] Davis, Guardian of Oddington, and was busy for an hour or more auditing accounts. — To M[r] Morgan's office with M[r] Ford, as a Committee for the return of Lord Worcester and Sir C W Codrington. They have issued spirited addresses to the Electors of East Gloucestershire, in consequence of M[r] Holland coming forward on the Whig Radical Interest. M[r] Morgan had obtained the signatures of many freeholders to the requisition calling on Lord Worcester & Sir C W Codrington to continue in the representation of the division. — To the Justice Room with M[r] Ford as my Colleague, Mess[rs.] W. Vavasour & Whitmore Jones being our assessors: a good deal of business. —— Home |[163] to dinner by 5 P.M. — E.F.W. and other members of the Stow Cricket Club gone to Cirencester to play a match in Lord Bathurst's park with the Purton Cricketers. — Life of Lord Sidmouth. —

July 9. Friday.

Fine weather, except a slight shower in the afternoon — Justice business at home — Wrote to Round expressing our readiness to receive him for a few days in the week after next — and that we shall be most happy to see him ~~in the week after next~~ on the 19th. Inst. — Wrote to E.F.W. in answer to his letter received on Wednesday, and inviting him with his wife and children to come and meet my old friend Round, and spend with us the week after next. — Settled my Yorkshire Banking Accounts, and wrote to Birkbecks the Bankers, desiring them to cause their correspondents in Town, Barnard, Dimsdale & Co. to pay for them to my account with Messrs. Hoare £250. — Visited sick parishioners, J Davis, |164 W. Collett, and W. Gardner. — A circular from the Lunatic Asylum, Gloucester, announcing an adjourned meeting of Visitors for the 14th. Inst. — In the Evening met 18 candidates for Confirmation at the School room, and read to them a lecture on part of the Apostle's Creed, examining them as to their knowledge of the first elements of Xtian truth. — Life of Lord Sidmouth.

July 10. ~~Friday.~~ Saturday

A close, sultry, still and cloudy day. In the afternoon and evening some small rain fell in showers. — Justice business at home — Preparing a Sermon. — Wrote to Mr Hare, forwarding a note which I received from Mr Thornton on Wednesday: — also to Rodwell with an order for books ~~from~~ for the Stow Book Society. — Recd. a strange letter from C. Ackerley, requesting me to see to the preparation of a statement of the services of Anderson, |165 now Porter at the Stow Union Workhouse, as an Artillery soldier in the last American war, with a view to his obtaining some remuneration from government — A. was subsequently Mr Chamberlayne's servant, and C. Ackerley lodged with him, and employed him in the same capacity. — "From Oxford to Rome," — a recent publication, partly narrative, and fiction, partly grounded on events of notoriety as to what has been called the Oxford movement, shewing the steps by which an able, pious, enthusiastic student, trained by Newman, entered into the Church of England, ministered as Curate, and passed over to the Church of Rome: intended also, it would seem, to shew that such a step is not necessary in point of conscience, for that the Anglican Church principles and practices, fully carried out, suffice to meet the utmost longings of the pious, and satisfy the demands of those who aspire to carry out the principles |166 of the Catholic Church: — a fascinating book, and therefore to be distrusted, liable to all the objections which may be brought against works of fiction and tales applied to religious and controverted questions: a state of mind is presented in attractive lights, which exceeds the sober frame of the commonalty of the Christian world; it is a portraiture of what may be called the superesaltate: but it is a little work exhibiting much talent and deep feeling, and intimacy with the modes of thinking and acting adopted by the Romanizing party in the Church. It was lent to me by Mr Turner. — Life of Lord Sidmouth.

July 11. Sunday.

A fine summer's day — Visited the Sunday School — Preparing a sermon. — Morning prayers: afternoon service; prayers and a sermon. I preached on rash judgment. — After evening service John Perkins Senior called; and sat for |167 an hour with us after dinner: he and his aged wife are now visiting their son at Upper Swell; the old man is much broken, slightly paralytic; his mind somewhat weakened, bursting into tears on accosting an old friend. — "From Oxford to Rome" — a section from Trower's exposition of the Gospels to the family. –

July 12. Monday.

Very fine summer weather. — Finishing the hayrick, and beginning to clear the brook, catching fish. — Preparing a Sermon. — Wrote to Howell. — Received a letter from E.F.W: he & Sophy propose visiting us on Tuesday in next week to stay till Saturday: we are to send for Broome and Frederick on Monday Morning: that day is fixed for an archery meeting &c. under the auspices of Mᵣ Colville at Stow, E.F.W. Sophy and George are to sleep at the W. Vavasours that night: the following day will be devoted to Cricket, till it be time to come to U Slaughter. On Wednesday E.F.W. |[168] goes to Town to bring Helen Dryden to visit her relations at Stow, Maugersbury, and Stanway: returns on Friday. To-morrow my Son and daughter will be at Stow: cricket the weekly attraction. — Life of Lord Sidmouth.

July 13. Tuesday.

Brilliant weather. — Wrote a letter to my son to be delivered to him by me at Stow, where he would be so much engaged at Cricket that I should not find an opportunity of conversation with him. — Preparing a Sermon. — Drove to Stow with MW. Received ᵃ letters from Mᵣ Thornton on Hunt matters, covering one from Mᵣ Whitcombe to Mᵣ Braikenridge, from which it appears that the disputed matter of the Wharf must, after all, be submitted to Counsel for an opinion. — Met E.F.W. at the Unicorn, where conferred with him, and on the Cricket Ground; he was suffering from a slight attack of diarrhoea, owing, no doubt, to over exertion and the heat of the weather. — |[169] To Maugersbury House, where found the W. Vavasours at home, with Emma, who is lately returned from visits to Lady Styles at Chester, and Mʳˢ· Donnington Jefferson in Yorkshire — Sophy and her mother afterwards came to Maugersbury, from "the Cottage:" and all afterwards met together at the latter abode, whence E.F.W. and Sophy set out to return to Stanway, when MW. and I went home to a late dinner. — I had also visited the Workhouse, and had an interview with Mᵣ Pearce, and the Porter, Anderson, taking down from the mouth of the latter, an old Artillery man, a statement of his military services in Canada, where he escaped wounds, imprisonment and death, though in the thickest of many well fought actions with the Americans. Mᵣ C. Ackerly conceives him entitled to some remuneration from the Crown, agreeably to a late Order in Council, and I shall cause the above statement to be forwarded to him to be presented |[170] by him on Anderson's behalf in the proper quarter. — Transacted business at the Office of the Gloucestershire Banking Company — Parleyed with the Dean of Gloucester. — Life of Lord Sidmouth. — |

1

Diary

1847

July 14. Wednesday. — Fine summer weather; a hot close day. — Wrote to Mr Lambert, enquiring whether the report is true that
he meditates selling his property at Upper
Slaughter: explained to him how I am circumstanced as to the investment in lands or
other freeholds of the proceeds of the sale of our
houses in Fenchurch Street; and that I
should be prepared to buy his farm here
on reasonable terms, if the price and title be
such as would be approved in the Court of
Chancery. — Wrote to Mr Thornton and
Mr Hare on Hunt trust matters, forwarding
to the latter the last note received by me from
Mr Thornton, together with its enclosure, a
letter from Mr Whitcombe to Mr Braikenridge. — Wrote a note to Mr C. Ackerley
to accompany a statement of Jos. Anderson's

Witts Family Papers F360

July 14. Wednesday.

Fine summer weather; a hot close day. — Wrote to Mr Lumbert, enquiring whither the report is true that he meditates selling his property at Upper Slaughter: explained to him how I am circumstanced as to the investment in lands or other freeholds of the proceeds of the sale of our houses in Fenchurch Street; and that I should be prepared to buy his farm here on reasonable terms, if the price and title be such as would be approved in the Court of Chancery. — Wrote to Mr Thornton and Mr Hare on Hunt trust matters, forwarding to the latter the last note received by me from Mr Thornton, together with its enclosure, a letter from Mr Whitcombe to Mr Braikenridge. — Wrote a note to Mr C. Ackerley to accompany a statement of Jos. Anderson's |² military services in Canada, to be sent to-morrow, and to be presented by Mr A. at the office of the Secretary at War, in the hope that A. may receive some gratuity. — Received a letter from Mr Hare, who returns to me a note from Mr Thornton to me, which I had forwarded for his perusal: he writes from Western super mare; and gives me his address for many weeks to come at Earnshill near Langport. — A letter from Mr Jennings, accompanying the Lady day balance sheet of London rents received &c. — together with a mention of enquiries made by him as to ground rents on sale in or near Town, but nothing definitive on that subject. — In the evening attended a Vestry meeting, where met Messrs. Lea, Gregory and Dix, parish officers, as to the making out a new Poor Rate on the Valuation lately finished by Mr Croome. All passed off amicably. — "From Oxford to Rome." — Life of Lord Sidmouth. |³

July 15. Thursday.

Very fine summer weather. — Drove to Stow. MW. accompanied me, and after calling at some shops, returned home. To the Provident Bank, where I met Messrs. Winter, Morrison, and W B Pole: transacted business there. — To the Workhouse, where I presided at the fortnightly meeting of the Guardians. A schoolmistress was elected — Ann Pearce, niece of the Clerk and Governor, by a majority of three or four voices above her competitor Sarah Walker, a young person from Banbury. — Also Charlotte Wilkins was chosen as nurse by a bare majority over her competitor, Clara Hookham. — The Poor Law Commissioners have at length replied to the communications made to them from the Guardians respecting the imputations thrown out by the District Auditor against the Clerk and Governor, Medical Officers &c. – The Comm^rs. express an opinion |⁴ that Mr Hunt has not exceeded the line of his duties, remind the Guardians that it is to be expected that in the discharge of his functions the Auditor is likely to make comments unpalatable to Guardians and their officers, trust that the Guardians will reconsider the matter, and thus the Commissioners seem disposed to uphold the Auditor, and let the question drop. The consideration of this business was deferred till the next Board day. — Home to a late dinner. — A letter from J. Round, now attending the Assizes at Chelmsford: he proposes being with us by dinner time on Monday next, and remaining till Thursday, unless parliament should be prorogued on that day, in which case he will leave us on Wednesday. — Life of Lord Sidmouth. —

July 16. Friday.

A hot, close day; a strong blight. — Justice business at home. — Preparing a Sermon. — Wrote to M[r] Ford, forwarding to |[5] him Rodwell's bill for books supplied to the Stow library. — Wrote to Rev[d.] E. Burridge, whom I presume to be Curate of Blockley, who had applied to M[r] Pain, expressing a wish to become a member of the Book Society at Stow. Told him, if recommended by a Subscriber, he might be elected at the annual meeting in September, and have books from the library as soon as he chose. — Visited aged and sick parishioners. — Rec[d.] a letter from E.F.W. dated yesterday in London; he had seen M[r] Jennings, and accompanied him to look out [at] some ground rents on sale in Whitechapel, within the compass of our Fenchurch Street Trust money, which they consider a desirable investment. This business delays my Son in town till Saturday morning, or rather afternoon, when he proposes leaving by train for Stanway with Helen Dryden, and I wrote to him a letter by return of post, with my considerations on the purchase, to guide him in an interview which he will have with M[r] Jennings to-morrow morning. — Received a letter from Mess[rs.] |[6] Sewell and Newmarch acquainting me that they had paid to my credit with the Gloucestershire Banking Company at Stow £102. 18. 2. the amount of half year's interest, less income tax, received for money lent on Mortgage to M[r] Lockhart: acknowledged the receipt by letter to Mess[rs.] S. & N. — A letter from M[r] Bayly, Vicar of Brookthorpe near Gloucester, Steward of the Gloucester Music meeting in 1844. Great difficulty is found in obtaining the consent of Clergymen to act at the coming meeting this year. Among others application had been made to my son, who declined as being unbeneficed. Lord Saye and Sele had been Solicited under an impression that he had not served the office. He replied that he had acted in that capacity on my nomination, having been my successor in 1826; but offered to serve again in 1850, if I would take the office this year, and again appoint him my successor. Wrote to M[r] Bayly that I must be excused setting a new precedent of serving twice. — "From Oxford |[7] to Rome" — Life of Lord Sidmouth. —

July 17. Saturday.

A close, cloudy day, with blight, not so hot as of late; one shower in the forenoon, and a moist atmosphere generally. — Justice business at home. — With MW. drove to Cheltenham, setting out at 9 AM. and returning at 6 P.M. our errand being to meet a cook, of whom we had heard that she was likely to suit us, and willing to take our place; but it proved that the mistress with whom she lived had re-engaged her at higher wages. — Shopping. — Met John Bateman, who had come with E.F.W's horse from Stanway to meet him and Helen Dryden. B. gave a good account of his mistress and the dear boys. — There is an opposition made to the return of M[r] Craven Berkeley for Cheltenham: offence has been taken at some incautious remarks made by him as to the salubrity of the place, and his re-election is opposed by some of his supporters of old, and by those who have always been adverse to him. A Sir Willoughby Jones, a |[8] resident at Cheltenham, is brought forward to compete with him. — Mr Holland retires from the contest for East Gloucestershire; — it is expected that parliament will be prorogued on Wednesday next, and dissolved on Thursday. — A letter from F. Aston with two little books, (an exposition of the Church Catechism,) one of which I am to give to Mr Wiggin. — Mr Hale, M.P. for West Gloucestershire, sent me a parliamentary return as to the Constabulary serving in various counties, the expence &c. – Life of Lord Sidmouth.

July 18. Sunday.

Very fine and clear weather. — Visited the Sunday School — Preparing a Sermon. — Morning service, prayers and sermon — I preached on Jesus, the prophet whom Moses and other Jewish Phrophets foretold — Part 1. — Afternoon Service. — A letter from Sophia Hunt on Hunt affairs: she wishes us to fix at what time we will visit her and her brother and sisters at Stoke |^9 Doyle: it would seem that about Aug. 9. w$^d.$ be the most convenient time. — A circular from Rev$^d.$ — Hedley, Gloucester, as to the Diocesan Education Board: and from the Gloucester Lunatic Asylum, fixing a meeting of visitors. — Wrote a few lines to Sophy, in addition to what MW. had written, to be taken to Stanway to-morrow, when we send the phaeton to bring the children hither: — also a note to Lady Wemyss, now at Stanway, with my Lord and the family, having, as we suppose, arrived there on Friday last, apologizing for not calling there this week, as we shall have friends staying with us. – A note to Mr Clarke, inviting him to dine here on Tuesday. — "From Oxford to Rome." — To the family a section from Trower's exposition of the gospels. —

July 19. Monday.

Very fine summer weather. — Sent our phaeton to Stanway to bring our grandchildren to visit us. Broome and Frederick arrived after having gone to Stow |^{10} to deposit their cousin, Helen Dryden, with her grandpapa and grandmamma Vavasour. The children all shewed themselves on the Archery ground where a large party was assembled for a fete. My son and daughter came from Stanway to this gathering, and proposed sleeping at Maugersbury House, whence, after a game of cricket, they will come to us to-morrow, with dear George. I received a few lines from E.F.W. who reached Stanway with his niece late on Saturday Even. He sends me the printed particulars of the Ground rents in the parish of S$^t.$ George's in the East, the purchase of which we are contemplating — A letter from Howell, which my son brought with him from Town — A few obliging lines from Lady Wemyss in answer to my note of enquiry addressed to her Ladyship —— Preparing a Sermon — Mr Pearce called by appointment with whom conferred on Poor Law matters. — Received a few lines from Round, dated from |^{11} Belmont near Hereford, apprizing us that he will arrive here to-day, but must leave us on Wednesday morning, as the prorogation of Parliament is to take place on Thursday. — A note from Ford, who is going to Town, and to visit poor Bowen. F. wishes me to name to him any order for books into the Stow library emanating from his daughter; observing on the enthusiasm of young heads: the singular eagerness of Miss F., with a certain religious bias, urging her to desire the introduction of books of a certain class into the collection, will thus be checked, and I shall be relieved from a slight embarrasment. — Our old friend Round arrived by 5 PM from Hereford, and seemed please to revisit us. He appears to enjoy good health, and is a hale man for his years, but very deaf. His eldest son and daughter are travelling in Germany, but soon rejoin him at Brighton, where he will henceforth generally reside. His second son, the Usher of the Green Rod, is likewise abroad, at the German Baths. His youngest |[12] Son, who is married is the junior partner in a provincial Bank at Chelmsford. My old friend retires finally from parliament at the approaching dissolution, relinquishing his seat for Maldon. His spirits are good, and he abounds in anecdote.

July 20. Tuesday.

A very fine forenoon, early in the afternoon a very violent shower with thunder and lightning, which cleared off towards the evening. — Justice business at home. — With Round took a drive in the phaeton: to Maugersbury, where we met E.F.W. and Sophy, with Emma Vavasour on their way to Stow; my son to the Cricket field, my daughter to "the Cottage" — EV. returning to her sister who is indisposed. — We proceeded to Daylesford: called on the Winters: W. kindly accompanied Round and myself in a drive thro' the grounds attached to Adlestrop House, and by the Daylesford approach to D. House, over which, full of its reminiscences of Hastings, Winter conducted us; we afterwards partook |[13] of luncheon at Daylesford Rectory, and drove home in the thunderstorm. — A note from M[r] Sadler, requesting me to forward to him the last quarterly paper S.P.G. — Our children, with their youngest little boy arrived from Maugersbury an hour after our return; and at six o'clock friends came to a dinner party — M[r] and M[rs.] Winter, M[r] amd M[rs.] R. Waller, and M[r] Clarke. A cheerful evening.

July 21. Wednesday.

A dull foggy morning, followed by a hot day. — Breakfasted at an early hour with Round, my son rising to take leave of our friend, whom I conveyed in my open carriage to Northleach, to proceed thence with post horses to Cirencester, where he would take the railway train to Town; he was desirous of reaching London in time to attend the last sitting of the House of Commons w[h.] it is understood, is to be prorogued to-morrow, and dissolved on the day following. R. is about to relinquish parliamentary life after a long |[14] service for Ipswich and Maldon. He seemed to enjoy his short visit to us, which was also very acceptable to me. — After he set out for Cirencester, I baited my horses, and called at the Vicarage, on the Astons, all of whom I found at home except the naval cadet. — Letters from M[r] ~~Hare,~~ [Thornton] inclosing others from M[r] ~~Thornton~~ [Hare] on Hunt Trust matters; — and from M[r] Burridge, Curate of Blockley, as to his becoming a subscriber to the Stow Book Society. — Wrote to M[r] Sadler in answer to his letter received yesterday. — Justice business at home. — My son left us about three o clock for Leamington, Sophy and myself walking with him to the Turnpike gate at Lower Slaughter, where he was joined by R. Waller, and W. Stenson in a fly: the party being formed to journey together into Warwickshire for a Cricket match at Stoneleigh to-morrow, the Stow club being to try their strength with the Stoneleigh Club, and, probably, to sustain a defeat. This cricketing by the Stow party, of which my |[15] son is the Secretary, consumes too much time, and is too expensive. — M[r] Barrow called upon us, and walked with us to Lower Slaughter Turnpike, whence Sophy and I returned together, meeting the dear children by the way. — A comfortable domestic evening.

July 22. Thursday.

Some rain had fallen during the night: the day very fine. — Drove to Stow, accompanied by MW. and Sophy, and her two elder boys. Called with them at "the Cottage," where saw M^r and M$^{rs.}$ Vavasour, and whence MW. returned home with Frederick, leaving Sophy and Broome at "the Cottage." Transacted business at the Provident Bank, where I met Mr Morrison: — also at the Office of the Gloucestershire Banking Company; ~~where~~ from "the Cottage" to the Workhouse, where I met J. Perkins, and with him visited the Establishment, making a report as to the state of the house, and conferring with the Clerk & Governor: — At the Justice room I sat alone; my colleagues being all absent; transacted |^{16} such business as came within the jurisdiction of a single magistrate; postponing several cases for a fortnight. Mess$^{rs.}$ W. B. Pole and Winter sat with me during part of the sitting. — Returned home to a late dinner, accompanied by Sophy and Broome. A pleasant domestic party. — A letter from Mr Lumbert, who acknowledges the receipt of mine of the 14$^{th.}$ Inst: he does mean to sell his farm at Upper Slaughter, but not unless for a higher price than I should be at liberty to give for property purchased under sanction of the Court of Chancery: — a letter from Mr Ackerley, with a copy of one written by him to the Secretary at War, to whom he has transmitted the statement of Jos. Anderson's services in Canada: Mr A. supplies me with a number of crazy papers about his healing lamp: as incoherent as all his usual compositions — A circular, announcing a meeting of the Visitors of the Gloucester Lunatic Asylum for the 27$^{th.}$ Inst. — There were two or three transient |^{17} showers about breakfast time. —

July 23. Friday.

Very fine weather. — Justice business at home. — Wrote to Mr Thornton, Mr Hare, and Mess$^{rs.}$ Cox and Williams, as to Hunt Trust matters: — to Mr R. G. Smith, Ramsgate, on business of Thomas Collett; — to Miss S. Hall, requesting her to give an order into the infirmary in favour of a man in the Workhouse nearly blind; — to Mr Jennings, acknowledging the receipt of his last letter containing the quarterly balance sheet of rents received & money paid; also urging him to proceed, if possible, to a treaty for the purchase of ground rents offered for sale in the parish of S$^t.$ George's in the East. — to Mess$^{rs.}$ Hoare, enquiring whether they have received and placed to my account the sum of £250, which I have directed Mess$^{rs.}$ Alcocks & C$^o.$ to cause to be paid in, but of which I have not been advised. — Accompanied MW., Sophy, and Broome to the Turnpike gate at Lower Slaughter, whence |^{18} MW. returned home, Sophy and I proceeding with Broome to Bourton, where we called on M$^{rs.}$ R. Waller. I also called on the Misses Hall, and obtained a promise that the patient of whom I wrote above should be admitted to the infirmary at Gloucester on Miss S. H's order — The ladies from Salperton, Miss Browne and M$^{rs.}$ C. Pettatt, called while we were at the Rectory, at Bourton — M$^{rs.}$ R. Waller with three of her boys accompanied us on our way home as far as to Lower Slaughter. — E.F.W. rejoined us before dinner, from Leamington, the match at cricket having terminated in the defeat of the Stoneleigh Cricketers. — He had seen Eliza Daniell at Leamington, from whom he heard an indifferent account of Mr Cha$^{s.}$ Barr. — In the evening met at the School room the Candidates for confirmation. —

<u>*July 24. Saturday.*</u>
Very fine weather. — Our dear children and grandchildren left us after breakfast to return to Stanway; we sent |[19] our carriage to convey the nurse and two younger boys. When the servant returned in the evening, he brought a note from E.F.W. announcing their safe arrival, and accompanying a letter from Mr Croome, the surveyor, of Tewkesbury, to whom Mr Billingsley, at my son's desire, had mentioned that we are looking out for a freehold investment. He names an estate at Eldersfield in Worcestershire, the property of Mr Terrett, of Tewkesbury, on sale by private contract, which may, perhaps, answer our purpose: but we have so often been disappointed, that I am far from sanguine as to any offer made. — Justice business at home. — Wrote to Sophia Hunt on Wadenhoe Trust matters, and proposing that MW. and I should visit her & the rest of the brother and sisterhood at Stoke for a few days early in August — from the 9th. to the 14th. — Preparing a Sermon. — Walked with MW. to Eyford. Visited the Ryan family at the Mansion House; the daughter |[20] an invalid. No tidings have arrived from Mrs. Dolphin, who has now been absent five weeks. — A letter from Mr Jennings. It appears that the proprietor of the Ground rents near the Commercial road will not accept our offer, being desirous of selling to a purchaser, whose money is promptly forthcoming, which would not be the case with us, as our affair must drag its slow length through the Court of Chancery; so were again disappointed. — A letter from Messrs. Hoare, announcing that Lady Wilmot Horton has paid to my account with them £194. 3. 4 being the half year's interest on mortgage — less income tax. — Visited an apparently dying parishioner, W. Collett. — "From Oxford to Rome" — Life and Correspondence of Lord Sidmouth. — Wrote to Mr Wills, Med. Off. of the Union in respect of the infant child of a parishioner, now ill.

<u>*July 25. Sunday.*</u>
A very fine day, after a |[21] thunderstorm and copious rain during the night. — Attended the Sunday School. — Preparing a Sermon. — Morning service; prayers — Afternoon service, prayers and sermon. I preached on Christ, the prophet whom Moses and the other Jewish prophets foretold. — A letter from Messrs. Hoare, in answer to mine of the 23^{d.} saying that Messrs. Alcock and C^{o.} had some days since remitted to Messrs. H. on my account £250. which they had inadvertently failed to advise. — A letter from C Bathurst, now in Town, and in tolerable health: he and Mrs. B. had travelled with E.F.W. lately to London in the same railway coach. — A circular from Mr C. G. Round's Committee at Oxford announcing that the election for the University is fixed for Thursday next. Parliament was prorogued on Friday last, and dissolved in a Gazette published the same evening. It is my intention to be neutral. I cannot consistently vote for Gladstone, though a |[22] man of great talent, and experienced statesman, and excellent scholar. His opinions are on matters relating to the Church not very intelligible: one knows not how far they may lead him; he has sympathized warmly ^{with} and supported by his votes in Convocation the Tractarian party; and his tendencies seem Romeward; every opportunity should be taken to check Puseyism in the Church and in the University: but I do not vote against him, because I fear that C. G. Round has low church tendencies; he is not a man of commanding talent, though a scholar, and a man of business; he comes also recommended to one by his relationship to my old friend; yet still I withhold my vote from him, though he numbers among his supporters most of the Heads of Houses,

but he is too openly upheld by the low Church party and the Protectionists. Besides, my Son's preference is for Gladstone; and I do not wish to run counter to his [23] views, which I am unwilling to blame, because with those of his standing Ultra High Churchism is predominant, and by my declining to vote he may also be induced to be neuter. — "From Oxford to Rome:" — to the family a section from Trower's exposition of the Gospels.

July 26. Monday.

Fine weather, but at times overclouded with a threatening of rain, though little or none fell. — Wrote to E.F.W. at Stow, whither he goes to-day accompanied by Sophy and George, to play in a cricket match between the Stow and Ombersley Clubs; the return match; at Ombersley Stow was beaten: E.F.W. and Sophy go to "the Cottage," to sleep &c. and remain at Stow to-morrow, which is the weekly cricket day of the Stow Club; perhaps, too the match may not be played out to-day. I sent my Son for his perusal the letter I received on Saturday from M[r] Jennings, announcing that the Vendors of the ground rents in the parish of S[t] George's in the East decline to treat with us. — Wrote to M[r] Croome, explaining to him how [24] we are circumstanced as to the purchase of an estate, and desiring him to procure for us further particulars as to the Eldersfield property now offered for sale. — Wrote to Mess[rs.] Hoare, desiring them to invest £250 of the balance in their hands to my credit in the purchase of 3 P[r] C[t.] Cons. — Drove with MW. to Stanway, to call on the Wemyss family: politely received by Lord and Lady W. — Lady Jane, & Lady ~~Catherine~~ Caroline Charteris, Lady ~~Eliza~~ Charlotte and Miss Fletcher, and M[r] Wildman. Lord & Lady W. in their usual state of health: we partook of luncheon with them. F. Charteris is now a candidate for the County of East Lothian, but is opposed by Sir David Baird, yet there is reason to expect that the former will succeed: F.C. abides by his moderately Conservative line of politics: adhering to Sir Robert Peel. — Passed an hour at the Vicarage, Stanway, with dear Broome and Frederick. — Home by 7 P.M. having made [25] enquiries by the way at Upper Guiting of poor Bowen's housekeeper, as to the late accounts of her Master, which are very indifferent; he suffers great pain, and is much reduced; further surgical operations for the stone are in reserve. — Justice business at home — "From ~~Rom~~ Oxford to Rome." — Life of Lord Sidmouth. — M[r] and M[rs.] Boudier called while we were from home.

July 27. Tuesday.

Very fine summer weather. Wrote to M[r] Clark of the Gloucestershire Bank[g.] C[o.] at Stow with a cheque for £20, and received his answer and the money — To Sophy at "the Cottage," to inform her that we had left our dear grandchildren well yesterday afternoon. — Understood by our messenger on his return that the match game between the Stow and Ombersley Clubs had terminated in favour of the Stow Cricketers. — Wrote to M[r] Hare on the matter of the Turnpike Bonds Interest belonging to the Hunt family. — Reading the Annual Report S.P.G. for 1846 with a [26] reference to the annual meeting of the Stow district Committee to be held in September. — Life of Lord Sidmouth. — Posting accounts.

July 28. Wednesday.

Fine weather — Justice business at home — Preparing for the meeting of the Board of Guardians to-morrow. — Posting accounts — Report S.P.G. for 1846. — Letter from

Messrs. Hoare announcing that they have bought for me £281. 13. 10 — 3 P^r. C^t. Cons. with £250 cash — from one E. Gardner, asking advice as to the recovery of arrears under an order of filiation; the case has come before me frequently — from M^rs. Grecy, Ramsgate, on behalf of R G Smith, in answer to my letter to him of the 23^d. Inst. which has answered its purpose — a note from Mr Turner with regard to a pauper receiving relief, to which I replied. — Life of Lord Sidmouth — Visited Thos. Collett as to the letter received from M^rs. Grecy.

July 29th. Thursday.

Very brilliant summer |^27 weather — Colonial Church Chronicle — With MW. drove to Stow: she shortly afterwards returned home. To the Provident Bank, where met Messrs. Pole, Morrison, Lewes, Barrow. — To Mr Brookes's office, where transacted business as to magisterial matters. — To the Workhouse, where presided at the fortnightly meeting of the Guardians. — After some debate, and a division, the reply to the P.L.C. respecting the matters in controversy with the District Auditor which I recommended was adopted: the purport is to challenge investigation into the management of the Union and the conduct of the officers, or that the P.L.C. should state that they see nothing in the allegations made by the District Auditor which requires investigation. — An act of Parl^t. recently passed modifies the law as to the expence incurred by the relief of paupers irremovable on account of a five years residence; where it can be proved that such paupers received relief from the |^28 place of their settlement or presumed settlement in the year preceeding Aug 26. 1846, — the expence incurred on their account by the place of their residence is to be charged to the general account of the Union, and to be defrayed by all the parishes and places in the Union in proportion to the average expenditure: this is a step in the direction of a Union Settlement. — Returned home before 5 PM. Mr Barrow accompanying me in the carriage as far as to L Slaughter Turnpike Gate. — A note from J W Harris as to the supply of coal. — Life of Lord Sidmouth.

July ^30 29th. Friday.

Very fine weather — Wrote to Mr Pearce, desiring him to ascertain whether Mr Hayward recommends one Latham to be sent to Gloucester Infirmary on account of defective sight, that I may in that case procure an order for his admission from Miss S. Hall: — to E Gardner, explaining to her, in answer to her letter |^29 to me, the proceedings which may be taken to recover money due to her under an order of filiation: — to Mr Turner, informing him what are the real facts of the relief given to Widow Cross and her family. — Justice business at home. — Wrote to Turner, fishmonger, London, with a cheque for £4. 18. 6 for fish supplied. — Colonial Church Chronicle, with a view to the coming annual meeting of the Stow Distr. Comm. S.P.G. — Preparing Quarterly papers and Diocesan lists of the S.P.G. for circulation in the district. — Posting accounts. — Met in the School-room in the evening the Candidates for Confirmation. — The Misses Hall and a nephew from Shropshire called in the evening. — Life and correspondence of Lord Sidmouth. — Wrote to J. Perkins, now at Oxford, requesting him to pay for me a bill I owe to Randal, Hatter — A circular from Oxford intended to prejudice Gladstone in the opinion of voters. |^30

July 31st. Saturday.

Very fine summer day — Quarterly papers S.P.G. — Visited a sick parishioner, W. Collett; also the Free School, and the Churchwarden. — Posting accounts. — Drove with MW. to call on Mr & Mrs. J. T. Rice at Great Risington, whom we found at home, and with them the Dean of Gloucester. — Called at Bourton on the Water at the Rectory, and at Mr Hunt's, but found both families at dinner, and were not admitted. — Letters from Mr Hunt on the sale of the Red Lion Wharf, with inclosures from Mr Braikenridge & Maria Hunt: — from Sophia Hunt, accepting our proposed visit to Stoke Doyle on the 9th. August, but urging us to prolong our stay there, so as to remain till the 16th. or 17th. — Life and Correspondence of Lord Sidmouth.

Aug. 1. Sunday.

Very fine weather — Visited the Sunday School. — Morning service — prayers and sermon. I preached on |[31] frequent attendance at the Holy Communion, having given warning of the administration of the sacrament on Sunday next. — Afternoon prayers. A letter from H. Turner, Fishmonger, London, acknowledging the remittance I made to him on the 30th. — Preparing a Sermon. — Quarterly papers S.P.G. —— To the family a section from Trower's exposition of the gospels.

Aug. 2. Monday.

For the most part a fine day: it was overclouded in the afternoon, and blighting; a shower fell, which cleared the air — Wrote to Mr Hunt, and Mr Thornton on Hunt Trust business; forwarding to the latter the enclosures which I had received on Saturday from Mr Hunt together with his note to me. — Mr Frobisher called from Eyford: this gentleman being with his lady intimate friends of Mrs. Dolphin, has come, bringing his Children, from their house at Cheltenham to take up their temporary residence at Eyford; he was at Church yesterday: a retired officer of the |[32] Bengal army: I certified to his being living with a view to his obtaining pension, or half-pay. No tidings of Mrs. Dolphin. — Wrote to Mr Ford, to enquire as to the state of Mrs. F's health, and whether he thought it likely that he should be able to receive the Bishop at his house at the time of the Visitation; it being understood that if Mrs. F's ill health should prevent the Bishop going to L Risington, he should be our guest. — Wrote to R Waller, requesting him to come to Stow on Thursday to assist me in the Justice room, as Mr F. would probably be attending the Clerical Charity meeting at Gloucester on that day; enquired whether Sept. 8 would suit RW. for the annual meeting of the Stow Distr. Comm, S.P.G. and the Clerical Society's dinner: — lastly asked him, if convenient, to assist me with one duty at U Slaughter on the 15th. Inst. to enable me to extend my visit at Stoke Doyle by two or three days. — |[33] He replied that he would meet me at Stow on Thursday; doubtfully as to assistance on the 15th. and gave no answer as to Sept. 8th. — Received a letter from E.F.W. with a good account of all at the Vicarage, Stanway. Emma Vavasour is now their guest, W.V. and his wife having gone to the Isle of Wight, in the hope of benefitting the health of the latter. — A letter from Mr Hare, who assents to my making in Northamptonshire such arrangements as may seem expedient as to the Interest on the Hunt Turnpike Securities. — Transacting business with the parish churchwarden, collector of taxes &c. — Report of the Mission at Barripur, Bengal. — Life of Lord Sidmouth.

Aug. 3. Tuesday.

Very fine weather — Transacting business with the Parish Churchwarden, making out a new rate on Mr Croome's valuation. — Received a letter from Mr Ford; M$^{rs.}$ F. is in a very weak state of health, so as to render it doubtful whether the |^{34} Bishop can be received at the time of the Visitation at Little Risington; Ford proposes a communication to be made to his Lordship nearer the day of visitation in a manner which would be at variance with the correspondence which has passed between the Bishop and me as to his being our guest. I replied to F. that some other course should be taken, sending for his perusal and guidance the letter I had received from his Lordship in reply to my invitation to visit us, if M$^{rs.}$ F's health prevented his going to the Rural Dean's. F. sent me a letter of a late date from poor Bowen, who seems in a very suffering and precarious state. At a late hour I met F. in Stow, and conferred with him as to the arrangement touching the Bp. but no decision was come to. F. does not like to acknowledge that M$^{rs.}$ F. is in a precarious state, nor to lose the little credit of receiving the Bishop – so the matter |^{35} is left open for a few days. — Preparing for the approaching annual meeting of the District Committee S.P.G. —— Preparing for a special meeting of the Guardians of our Union, held today at Stow. — Drove thither, presided at that meeting from 2 to 5 PM. — a pretty large muster of guardians: discussed the recent Act as to paupers irremoveable under the Act of last Session; and made out a list of those paupers whose relief shall be placed to the account of the Union funds. — Revised the pauper lists. — Had a transient interview with my son, who was attending at the weekly game of cricket at Stow. — A poor woman from Eyford was buried in the evening. — Life of Lord Sidmouth.

Aug. 4. Wednesday.

A fine forenoon and afternoon; rain in the evening — Assisted W. Gregory in making out a poor rate assessment — Justice business at home — Preparing a Sermon — Parish business — With MW. walked to Eyford; |^{36} called on Capt. and M$^{rs.}$ Frobisher. A letter has been received from M$^{rs.}$ Dolphin, dated Wildbad. — Harry Waller and his cousin, John Dolphin, called: the latter is now on a visit at Farmington, the father of seven children, and an amiable, respectable Norfolk Clergyman. — Life of Lord Sidmouth.

Aug. 5. Thursday.

Fine weather till the evening when some rain fell. — Engaged with the Churchwarden in making out a poor rate assessment. — Drove to Stow. — Attended at the Provident Bank, where met Mr Morrison, Mr O. Hill &c. — Transacted business at the office of the Gloucestershire Banking Company, at the Office of Mr Brookes, and at that of Mr Morgan. — To the Workhouse, where conferred with Mr Pearce and the Matron, and went over some of the Wards. — To the Justice room, where R. Waller attended as my Colleage, and we heard and settled several cases. Mr Perkins, Mr W. B. Pole, Mr Lewes, and Mr Price Lewes were our assessors. — Perkins kindly promised |^{37} to undertake the Service of my church on the afternoon of Sunday the 15$^{th.}$ to enable us to prolong our stay in Northamptonshire by three or four days. — Mr Gladstone has been returned as MP. for the University of Oxford by a majority of 173 over Mr Round. — Colonial Church Chronicle. — "From Oxford to Rome" — Life of Lord Sidmouth. ——

Aug. 6. Friday.

Fine weather. — Busy with the Churchwarden in making an assessment for poor rate. — Preparing a Sermon. — Justice business at home. — Wrote to Mr Croome, Surveyor, directing his attention to some small errors and omissions in his valuation of this parish, and requesting an answer to the letter I had written to him on July 26th· — to Mr Lefevre, Toddenham, with information which he had requested yesterday as to the County rate Act, and Parochial Assessments act, and proceedings as to valuation of parishes. — To Mr Lane, printer, desiring him to print some notices of the Annual l^38 meeting of the Stow district Committee. S.P.G. — to Perkins, requesting him to procure for me a new Master's gown from Oxford — to Mr Morgan, as to whether a labourer of this parish is eligible as a competitor for one of the prizes to be given by the Stow and Chip^g· Norton agricultural Association. — Visiting sick parishioners — Met the Candidates for confirmation at the School room, and instructed them. — Life of Lord Sidmouth — The Marquis of Worcester and Sir C W Codrington were quietly elected representatives for the Western division of this County on Wednesday last.

Aug 7. Saturday.

Weather fine in the forenoon and evening, overclouded with a wetting mist and showers in the afternoon. — Preparing a Sermon — Justice business at home — Preparing papers referring to the Hunt Trust concerns to be taken into Northants next week. — Colonial Church Chronicle &c. with a view to approaching annual meeting of the Stow District Committee S.P.G. — l^39 Captain & M^rs· Frobisher called. — MW. received a note from Dulcy Ford, written by her father's desire, saying that considering M^rs· F's weak state it has been determined to decline receiving the Bishop of Gloucester at the time of the Visitation at Little Risington, on the understanding that he shall be our guest. — A note from J W Harris about a supply of coal. — Life of Lord Sidmouth. — I wrote to E.F.W. —

Aug. 8. Sunday.

A fine day; cooler weather — Visited the Sunday School. — Morning service: prayers, and the communion of the Lord's Supper: 18 Communicants. — Afternoon service; prayers and sermon. I preached on Christian responsibility in the Education of children, as applicable to a collection made under the authority of a Queen's letter in aid of the funds of the National Society for the Education of the Poor in the principles of the Established Church. Collected £1. 17. 0. — Wrote a note to Mr Pearce, desiring him to write to me, during my absence, if any letter l^40 came from the Poor Law Commissioners as to the controversy with Mr Hunt, the district auditor — also to Mr Pain, desiring him to come or send Henry Stone to rectify a time piece which is out of order. — Wrote to the Bishop of Glouc. & Bristol, as to his being our guest at the time of the Visitation at Stow. — Received a letter from Mr Croome, as to the Eldersfield estate on sale by private contract: the value exceeds our amount to be invested under Trust, and for entail: but possibly I may be able to supply funds of my own to purchase a part on my own account. — Two applications from Free trade partizans at Leeds and Manchester, in which my vote is sought for the Election of Cobden, already returned for Stockport, as Free Trade colleague for the West Riding of Yorkshire, to displace the conservative and protectionist former member, Denison. — According to the latest accounts furnished in the

Gloucestershire Chronicle, Grantley Berkeley, as Candidate |⁴¹ for West Gloucestershire, is considerably ahead of Grenville Berkeley, his cousin and opponent. R B Hale's majority is far above both. — To the family a section from Trower's exposition of the Gospels.

Aug. 9. Monday.

A dull day, with but little sun, and a stirring wind. — After breakfast MW. and I set out on our Northamptonshire journey, accompanied by the lady's maid. Travelled to Cheltenham in our open carriage. There met with Mᴿ Lefroy, who went with us to different shops &c. — Learnt that Grantley Berkeley on Saturday last was elected by a very large majority over his cousin, Grenville Berkeley, to the great annoyance of Lord Fitzhardinge, thus beaten twice in his own county, & shorn of his seats for West Gloucestershire and Cheltenham. As Grantley is a Whig radical, like his cousin, and withal a man of damaged fortune, and bad character, he owes his success mainly to the feeling prevalent that he has been ill used by his brother and patron the Lord Lieutenant |⁴² in the family quarrel which has been so long and so disgracefully before the public, and to the strong desire of very many to evince their marked disgust at the immoralities and deep disapproval of the general and political conduct of Lord Fitzhardinge. — Left the Plough for the Railway Station in a fly, and the Station for Birmingham by a train starting at one P.M. — While stopping at Ashchurch had a conversation with Mᴿ Edwards, the Clergyman of Prestbury. — Harvest generally begun; the wheat and barley yeild fine crops; the beans are miserably blighted. — Reached the Birmingham terminus by half past three, where procured a slight refreshment, and proceeded by the North Western Railway at four o clock, as far as to Blisworth Station. Had not travelled on this line before. — It is carried through a flat, fertile, and dull country: branching & connecting railways, some completed, and more in progress, in many directions; also we were in frequent |⁴³ sight of canals, on which a considerable traffic was going on. — At the Coventry Station a railway branches off to Leamington and Warwick. Saw little of Coventry, but its tapering spires at a distance. Of Rugby saw nothing, but the Station there is very extensive; and other railways meet and diverge from hence. — The Kilsby tunnel near Weedon is very long; but probably not so long as the Box tunnel on the Great Western railway. — At Blisworth the railway to Northampton & Peterborough joins the North Western, which we left at this point. It was nearly a quarter of an hour before the down train from London arrived on its way to Birmingham, part of which was destined for the Northampton and Peterborough line, as we also were together with other passengers who had travelled by the same train as ourselves from Birmingham. In a few minutes after starting from Blisworth we reached the Northampton Station at half past six o clock: thence the line |⁴⁴ proceeds along the level of the meandering little river Nen, by a long valley, the meadows rich, and the arable land productive, but the country dull & flat, and not abounding in trees. Every where village Churches, mostly marked by tapering spires. Stopped at several stations, the leading ones being contiguous to Wellingborough, Higham Ferrers, and Thrapstone. A fellow traveller explained to me the great advantage to the farmer by the opening of this line: the grain produced in the district about Oundle &c. formerly was conveyed to Birmingham at a cost of nearly seven shillings per quarter, taking a fortnight in its transit, now it costs half a crown per Quarter, and reaches its destination the next day. The country too is better supplied with coal, chiefly from Derbyshire. The station near Oundle, where we arrived at about 8 P.M., is nearly a mile from the town; here, by the

44. *Harvesting scene from John Linnell's painting.*

kind arrangement of the Misses Hunt, we found a commodious carriage |[45] waiting for us, by which we were conveyed, thro' the town of Oundle, to the village of Stoke Doyle, distant about two miles from O. where, as the evening closed in, we were most kindly received by the Hunt family — Sarah, Sophia, Fanny and Thomas. — I suffered much from a very bad cold and cough, with difficulty of respiration, hoarseness, and impeded expectoration. —

Aug. 10. Tuesday.

Showery weather — Received a letter from M[r] Thornton on Hunt Trust affairs — Wrote to M[r] Croome, Tewkesbury in answer to his letter received on Sunday, requesting some further information respecting the Eldersfield estate, whether it was capable of being divided so that the greater portion might be bought with the Trust monies, the lesser being paid for by me out of my own private resources. — Wrote to M[r] Warter on the same subject, espressing a readiness to treat for the Eldersfield property, if a suitable arrangement could be made as to the funds with which it must be bought, and if no other |[46] treaty for the purchase of ground rents &c. has been entered upon on our behalf by M[r] Jennings or himself. — After luncheon we drove, M.W., Sophia & Fanny Hunt, and myself, in a comfortable carriage, the same which had brought us last evening from the Oundle Station, to Benefield, a distance of about five miles. We skirted the town of O. and took a line of turnpike road leading towards Market Harborough. Biggin Hall, the seat of M[r] Watts Russel, a wealthy proprietor in this County and in Derbyshire, is on high ground, surrounded by old timber and modern plantations to the right about two miles from O: to the left some extensive woods, and a piece of water. A mile further is the village of Benefield, situate in a sort of bason, with undulating ground encircling it, and consisting of detached groupes of farmhouses and cottages, some of both sorts being recently erected by M[r] Watts Russel very substantially in the Elizabethan Style: the |[47] Church, Churchyard [and parsonage] crown a Knoll central in the village, backed by wood on higher ground. The living of Benefield was formerly held together with that of Stoke Doyle by M\ Ed^d. Hunt, the father of our friends, and the parsonage of B. was their residence. We called at a M^rs. Berkley's, a widow with a Son and daughter living in the village, and thence walked to the parsonage, a rambling, but apparently commodious residence, chiefly old with some late additions. Here we were introduced to the Incumbent & his lady M^r & M^rs. Day, pleasing persons. Mr Day was tutor to some part of Mr Watts Russel's family, and is a Cambridge man. Mr W.R. presented him to the living, when it was vacated, about a year and half ago, by the secession to Rome, of his son, Mr Mich^l. W.R., who with his wife went over to the popish Church, about the same time that Mr Faber, Incumbent of Elton, Huntingdonshire, professed himself a Roman Catholic. These perversions attracted great |^48 attention at the time, and particularly in this neighbourhood. Mr Day was so kind as to show us his church, which has lately been almost entirely rebuilt, and the work of restoration of the Chancel, and erection of the Church Spire has cost about £12000, defrayed by Mr Watts Russel. The Church yard has been levelled, not without offence to the families of those interred there, whose remains were disturbed. We entered by the Vestry, near the Chancel, and were struck at once by manifest indications of a Popish tendency. A painted window, with the legend "Ave Maria, gratiæ plena," first struck my eye: the ceiling of the Vestry was painted in party-colours,[1] very rich and gilded, texts of scripture occupying every compartment, in Old English characters illuminated, and inscriptions being even inserted into the sides of the archway leading from the Vestry into the Chancel. Another narrow arch leads into a small opening on one |^49 side to the Chancel, and provided with finely carved stalls: this was originally meant as a seat for the family of the patron and great proprietor, Mr W.R: but, as he prefers sitting with the congregation, the rich with the poor, the chapel is now appropriated to school children. In it are some beautifully executed modern painted glass windows, one of them being a memorial window to one of the W.R. family, who died in childbirth: the inscription at the foot is from Ecclesiasticus, a symptom of Romanizing. Our obliging guide conducted us into the body of the Church, which is quite new, Derrick of Oxford being the Architect:[2] it is a beautiful building of three aisles, the pillars exquisitely wrought and chaste with capitals all dissimilar, in the Early English Style, the windows painted, but in a chaste, subdued tone of browns, in pattern work: the seats are substantial, of oak, the font of a beautiful Early English pattern: there is a Clerestory, & oak timbered roof. The tower of the former |^50 church, surmounted with a low spire, has been allowed to remain as the foundation of the present graceful and lofty spire; at the angles from which the spire rises are four emblems of the four Evangelists, the lion, ox, eagle &c., of carved stone projecting like gargoyles. The interior of the lower part of the tower is open to the church, with a painted Western Window, representing the law & the Gospel, Moses & the Saviour. Looking Eastward, the gorgeous decorations of the Chancel appear somewhat subdued from the lower part of the Church, but, viewed near, they are elaborately rich & even gaudy. The Eastern painted glass window, by Evans of Shrewsbury,[3] represents in five compartments the

---

1. Party-colours – parti-colours – partly one colour and partly of another – variegated.
2. John Macduff Derick (1810-1859). J. M. Derick had links with the Oxford Movement, and was Pusey's architect at St. Saviour, Leeds.
3. David Evans of Shrewsbury. Evans was possibly responsible for a window *c.*1850 at Salperton, and at Ashley near Tetbury.

Saviour & the four Evangelists; below is a richly carved Altar piece, of stone, painted and gilt in blues & greens, with stars &c. — The Lord's prayer, Creed & Commandments, with select sentences, referring to the Holy Communion from John 6 – |[51] of course interpreted as a prediction of the rite of the Lord's supper, occupy niches, being traced in old English characters with quaint flourishings &c. To the North of the Communion table, or rather Stone Altar, is a wooden credence table, with an appropriate inscription. On the Southern side of the Chancel are three Sedilia, with an elaborately carved reading desk in front, the recesses of the Sedilia being painted in gaudy colours, or lined with crimson. There are no rails in front of the Altar; the windows on the North and South sides of the Chancel are of painted glass; the floor both of the Church and Chancel are of encaustic tiles of a complicated pattern. The walls and roof of the Chancel are still undecorated; but it is intended that they should be painted & gilt in keeping with the Altar and its screen. All this part of the building was completed under the incumbency of the late Mich[l.] W. Russel, prior to his Secession from the Church, and betrays the strong leaning which |[52] resulted in his renouncing the faith of his fathers. As a work of art, allowing for some incongruities, one cannot but admire the whole of this very unique & striking Church; how far one sympathizes with the spirit and taste in which it has been raised is another consideration. — We reached Stoke Doyle by five P.M. — I still suffer much from cough and cold.

Aug. 11. Wednesday.

A very fine day. — Drove with MW., Sophia, and Fanny Hunt, to Wadenhoe, distant between two and three miles. — Met there M[r] Tebbutt, the Steward of the estate, and with him and Sophia looked at many improvements, repairs, and alterations which had been made as to the farm houses, farm buildings, cottages &c. in the Village; the whole parish, excepting the Rectorial allotment, belongs to the Estate of the late T. W. Hunt. Since the decease of M[rs.] M. Hunt great improvements have been made; especially a new and very good |[54] Schoolroom has been built, capable of accommodating sixty children. Great and judicious repairs have been done as to the Church, which we visited, and much remains to be done as to the shapeless tower, which is in a very poor state. The interior is exceedingly well arranged with open stalls, of ancient oak. In the floor of the Chancel is inserted a black marble slab, recording the death of M[rs.] M. Hunt: a marble tablet records the melancholy deaths of Tho[s.] Welch Hunt and his lady by the murderous attack of banditti near Pæstum. The Church is evidently built on the site of an old fortress, or military outpost, castle or other work of defence, crowning a knoll, rising from the banks of the Nen, and surmounted by a tuft of trees. The view is very pleasing; rich meadows, a winding stream, the seat of Lord Lilford, backed by timber, the elegant spire of Achurch Church, the more distant tower of Tichmarsh, the wooded grounds of Wadenhoe House rising above the river, are |[54] the principle features – We partook of luncheon, by appointment, with M[rs.] Praed, the lady of the tenant of Wadenhoe House, her husband being absent in town, on his business as a banker, being a partner in the firm of Praeds & C[o.] We found M[rs.] P. an elegant and polite hostess, surrounded with a fine young family, partly her own children, partly M[r] P's by a former wife. — Leaving Wadenhoe, accompanied by M[r] Tebbutt, we drove to the Woods, a distance of more than a mile from W. being a large tract of Oak timber and underwood, intersected by ~~walk~~ grass rides, meeting in a centre — The road formed through fields is rather rough, as our carriage testified, for, when we reached the centre of the wood, we discovered a startling fracture of part of the undercarriage, which let down one set of the springs, yet without danger to the party. A couple of cords, with which the driver was prepared, judiciously applied, preven-|⁵⁵ ted further mischief. Mᵣ T. drove MW. in his gig accross the rough field road to the main road; the Misses Hunt and I walked to the same point, satisfying ourselves that there was no risk in our all resuming our seats in the broken vehicle, which at a funereal pace brought us safely back to Stoke by dinner time — My cough still very troublesome. —

Aug. 12. Thursday.

A warm, close day, without sun. — Received a letter from Mᵣ Croome, Tewkesbury, in answer to mine of the 6ᵗʰ· Inst. requesting explanation as to his survey of the parish of U. Slaughter for a Poor rate, as to one or two points; such information he affords. MW. received a letter from Eliza Daniell, giving the very melancholy intelligence that poor Mᵣ C. Barr, though his serious complaint, gastric fever, has been cured, is sinking from great debility, has been to Leamington to consult Dᵣ Jephson, and is returned with Mʳˢ· Barr to Henwick, little hope being |⁵⁶ given of his recovery. — Accompanied Sophia Hunt in a walk to Pilton Furze to visit one of the farms on the Hunt Estate, a small farm: the land and buildings in good order. Distance walked to and fro about three miles — Company arrived to dinner: — Mᵣ Isham, a fine old Clergyman, but very deaf, father of the late Mʳˢ· T. W. Hunt, Rector of Polebrook, and formerly Vicar of Oundle: he was accompanied by his daughter, Mʳˢ· Currie, the wife of a Clergyman, an agreeable woman. Mᵣ George Capron, the Incumbent of Stoke Doyle, a pleasing young man; ᵗʰᵉˢᵉ were the guests.

Aug. 13. Friday.

Very fine weather — Letters from Mᵣ Thornton on Hunt Trust matters, and particularly, as to Whitby's Wharf: — from E.F.W. with a very pleasant report of himself and those nearest and dearest to him: — from the Bishop of Gloucester, fixing on the evening of the 25ᵗʰ· after the Visitation at Stow as the time of his coming |⁵⁷ to be our guest at Upper Slaughter: — from Maria Witts, announcing her approaching marriage to a Mᵣ Woodroffe, a Barrister of Lincoln's Inn, of Irish extraction, and asking me to give her away, standing in the place of her deceased Father: the ceremony to be performed at Kingston upon Thames by her eldest brother, in about a fortnight — We had heard rumours of this event as being on the tapis: — from Mᵣ Wynniatt, inviting me to dinner on the 16ᵗʰ· to meet Barwick Baker, coming with his lady, I suppose, to attend the Archery meeting at Stow on the 17ᵗʰ· — this note I answered by the post, explaining that it would not be in my power to accept his invitation, as we should not return to US. from Northamptonshire till the 18ᵗʰ· — At eleven o clock left Stoke in the hired Clarence,⁴ with MW. Sophia and Fanny Hunt, on an excursion for some hours to Peterborough. Passed thro' Oundle to the Railway Station. Transacted Hunt Trust business at Messʳˢ· Yorkes, Ban-|⁵⁸ kers, Oundle. O. a still, dull, but decent country market town, with a handsome Church and lofty spire, and some good houses occupied by respectable families. The Nen flows thro' rich meadows adjacent. Proceeded to the railway Station, where we

---

4. A Clarence was a four-wheeled closed carriage with seats for four inside and two on the box.

took return tickets for Peterborough, and made the transit thither in about half an hour, the distance being about thirteen miles thro' the valley of the Nen, a fine fertile tract. Passed through a pretty long tunnel – Stations at or near Elton, Wansford, Castor and Overton. Elton is the parish of which the seceding M[r] Faber was the incumbent, where perversion to Roman doctrine and discipline occupied much of the public observation nearly two years ago. The village is in Huntingdonshire, and Lord Carysfort is owner of a large estate here. At the Wansford Station, passengers leave the Rail to go by coach to Stamford. Wansford is a town at some distance to the left of the line, |[59] in the direction of Stamford. Castor is a Village with a Church tower of very elaborate Architecture, and, I believe, worthy of observation. It was in sight to the left, as we proceeded towards Peterborough. In the same direction is also Fotheringhay, there are no remains of the Castle, the prison of the hapless Mary of Scotland; but the Church tower is lofty and commanding, and the whole edifice worthy inspection. To the left hand of the travelling[er] journeying by the railway to Peterborough, is a fine old seat of Earl Fitzwilliam. Other noblemen, Lord Westmoreland, Lord Cardigan, Lord Aboyne &c. have seats and estates in this part of the Country. Several other villages with rural Churches, with tapering spires or low towers, met the eye as we were whirled along. — The Station near Peterborough is very extensive and seems very well arranged. There is a junction here with the Eastern Counties line, by which a communication is opened to Ely, Stamford, Norwich &c. The Peterborough Station adjoins the river Nen being nearly opposite to the Bishop's Palace |[60] and Cathedral which rears its noble Western facade boldly above the encircling low buildings of the little city. Proceeding to the bridge by which Peterborough is entered, we passed thro' several streets and a spacious Market place with an old Town Hall, seeing nothing striking except the fine ancient gateway leading to the Minster Yard. Our friends took us to visit a Miss Cox, a lady of fortune resident here, whence, leaving the Misses Hunt to make another call, we retraced our steps to the Cathedral. In its purlieus is the usual mixture of incongruous architecture, ecclesiastical stillness and repose, with neatness, shade, foliage and lofty walls sheltering the passerby from noontide sun. To the right of the enclosure at the Western end of the Cathedral is the Bishop's Palace, to the left inclosed by lofty walls, the Deanery and its gardens. We looked in at the gateway; the present [late] Dean, D[r] Turton, now Bishop of Ely, has greatly improved this residence, since it was occupied |[61] by the Bishop of Gloucester, the new parts being of a more ecclesiastical style than the old, which ill suited the beautiful adjacent cathedral. The palace is approached by a gateway of ancient architecture, but we did not look within to observe the character of the Episcopal residence. There appeared to be a road leading quite round the Cathedral, and, doubtless, affording advantageous views of the structure; but we had not time to explore the exterior, which seems to present much of interest in many remains of the olden time, and former Abbey, in ruined Cloisters, ancient walls, columns, arches &c. — The restoration of this Cathedral, which was completed about seventeen years ago, was carried on under the directions of Bp. Monk, then the Dean, large sums being collected from the city and neighbourhood, and distant lovers of Ecclesiastical Architecture and Antiquity. Blore was the skilful Architect employed, and the operative workmen were almost entirely found among the inha-|[62] bitants of the place. The grand features are the exquisite Western façade; of early English Architecture; the outer choir, so also the choir, with the Transepts; and the Eastern part, or apse, is more recent, of the age of Henry Seventh, with beautiful groined ceiling. The whole edifice is small, compared with many cathedrals, but kept in the neatest manner; the outer choir is not disfigured by mural monuments; the tablets to departed members of the Chapter are chiefly in the Lady's Chapel, where several bishops are interred; among the memorials to other good men, I noticed tributes to the worth of Dr Tournay, Warden of Wadham, and Mr Parsons, formerly Schoolmaster at Elmore; the one was elected to the headship not long after I ceased to reside at his College, where in later years I had partaken of his hospitality: he was an excellent man of business, a good scholar, consulted on matters of grave concern, peculiarly agreeable in society, and might have risen, had he been |[63] so disposed, to the highest rank in the profession; the latter was my first instructor. The inner Choir is most commodiously and chastly fitted up with oak stalls, pews, throne, closets &c. — There are several remains of very ancient monumental sculpture, in tombs & slabs of old Abbots, and we were shewn the covering Stones of the graves of the Queens Mary of Scotland, and Catherine of Arragon. While MW. and I examined the interior of the Cathedral, the Misses Hunt were preparing for our hospitable reception at the house of Dr James, one of the Canons, formerly a Curate and Schoolmaster at Oundle, and author of some very useful practical essays on the Collects, and other parts of the service of our Church. Mr Roberts, the Rector of Wadenhoe, who with his lady was on a visit to Miss Cox at Peterborough, was sent to conduct us to the Prebendal residence of Dr James, which is but at a short distance from the Cathedral, an ancient low-browed, rambling, priest- |[64] like looking house, with a shady court or garden in front. The worthy Doctor received us cordially, and refreshed us with luncheon. M^r and M$^{rs.}$ Roberts with Sophia & Fanny Hunt making up the party. Dr Bliss, the Registrar of Oxford, and his lady, were on a visit to the good Canon, but did not appear, as the former suffered from an attack of gout. One topic of condolence and regret was the sudden death at Edgware, of which parish he was the Incumbent, of Mr Hughes, a Canon of Peterborough, who had lately left the place in apparently good health, but had died with but short notice of his approaching end, from disease of the heart. He was brother of M$^{rs.}$ Monk the wife of the Bishop of Gloucester. As the afternoon service at the Cathedral was at hand, and time permitted us to attend at least the earlier part of the prayers, we adjourned from Dr James's house to the Cathedral, where, in one of the privileged ~~Cloisters,~~ closets we enjoyed the commencement of |[65] the service, and retired unnoticed before the Anthem began. M^r and M$^{rs.}$ Roberts accompanied us to the Railway Station: by the way I stopped to purchase an engraving of the beautiful Western façade of the Cathedral — At 4 P.M. we started homeward from the Peterborough Station, travelling in the same carriage with a communicative Alderman of London, Sir Chapman Marshall. Half an hour brought us to the Oundle Station, and another half hour brought us safe, but rather tired with the day's excursion, to the quiet cottage at Stoke.

Aug. 14. Saturday.

Fine weather. — Received a letter from Mr H. D. Warter in answer to one I had addressed to him on the 10$^{th.}$ Inst. respecting the purchase of Mr Terrot's property at Eldersfield — Wrote to Maria Witts, congratulating her on her approaching marriage, and promising, if it were possible, to be present at the Wedding, and to give her away. — Wrote to E.F.W. — With Sophia Hunt and her brother |[66] Thomas drove out in the hired Clarence with a pair of horses, our first point being Thrapston distant six or seven miles. Passed by Pilton, a village embosomed in trees. Crossed the river Nen by two very badly constructed bridges, and one of them much out of repair, not creditable to the neighbourhood, and close by Lilford Hall, the seat of Lord Lilford, a fine old mansion of the close of the 17th. Century, standing on rising ground with a descent to the river. The grounds are well timbered, and the place has much the air of a nobleman's seat. Passing Achurch with its elegant spire to the right, the road led us to Thorpe, where we crossed the railway on a level, and the so-doing does not appear practically so great an inconvenience as one would imagine it.[5] The Village of Tichmarsh, with its handsome Church was left by us on an eminence to the right; Thrapston comes next with an ancient and elegant spire, and modern- built nave, aisles and chancel. — Transacted business at the Thrapstone Bank relating to the Hunt |[67] property. — While Sophia Hunt and Thomas called at the parsonage, I walked round the Churchyard and to the railroad Station in the outskirts of the small town, which has a large Market — Rejoined the Hunts at the parsonage, being introduced to the incumbent, Mr Bagshaw, and his family. — Then called on M$^{rs.}$ Yorke the lady of the Banker and principal inhabitant of the place in the outskirts of the Town; her husband was at his farm. I had met him formerly, when I was at Wadenhoe, as Executor, at the time of M$^{rs.}$ M.H.'s decease. — Getting again into the carriage we drove two miles further, crossing the railway at the Station on the level, to Twywell, a small village, where there is a farm belonging to the Wadenhoe trust. — To our right, near Thrapstone is Islip, a village with a Church decorated by a beautiful spire. — We followed the Wellingborough road. The Church at Twywell, which is a small village, is not any way remarkable. Miss S.H. and her brother went to call on some acquaintances at the Parsonage: I |[68] remained at Miss Hunt's farm, which is not large, being received by the tenant, a Widow, and was there met by Mr Tebbutt, the Steward of the Hunt property, who walked with me over some of the land, which is of a superior quality to most on the Hunt Estate, being, as Mr T. expressed himself, Miss H's plum. — After partaking of some refreshment here, we returned homeward through Thrapstone, deviating from the direct road to view the Church at Tichmarsh. This fine building has been of late years well restored under the judicious oversight of a competent architect. The exterior is regular; the interior well arranged with open sittings, and in every respect what one admires. There is some remainder of early English Architecture, chiefly about the Chancel; and I particularly noticed the restoration of a Hagioscope in the screen dividing the Chancel from a Chantry to the North. In this are some handsome ancient monuments to former families having property in the parish, and among them a |[69] gossiping old tablet recording the history of the Drydens, especially of the poet, as connected with this parish: the inscription was set up by an octogenarian lady related to the family, and priding herself on the connection — The poet was born at Aldwinkle, a village near Wadenhoe; and the present seat of the Drydens is at Canons Ashby in the Southern part of Northamptonshire. — Returned home to a late dinner.

Aug. 15. Sunday.

Very fine weather — Preparing a sermon. — Morning Service — prayers; the duty performed by Mr Geo. Capron, the Rector: afternoon service, prayers and sermon; M^r

---

5.   This is the first reference to a level crossing, and this subject must have been on the mind of Francis Witts in relation to the Ravenflatt property in Yorkshire.

G.C. officiated in the reading desk, and I in the pulpit. I preached on the Obstacles and dangers attending the profession of Christianity. — The Church is a handsome building of its class, but very unecclesiastical; more like a town church, or chapel in a Nobleman's grounds than a village church. It was, I believe, erected more than 100 years ago. A tower is at the West: there is no chancel projecting from the single |[70] aisle. The windows large, round headed, Grecian or Roman; a singing gallery to the West — square pews for the principle properties, smaller pews, all in excellent repair and handsome of their kind, as are the pulpit and reading desk. The Church is ceiled; over the Communion table a Venetian Window; two bronze-looking Angel in Statuary, adoring, surmount the Altar piece, they were the gift of a late Rector, Mr Shillibeer; on the North side of the Communion table, preserved, no doubt, from the old church, is a mural monument, with inscription, to some former proprietor — a gentleman and lady, ruffed, and furbelowed,[6] kneeling at a prayer desk, with the effigies of their progeny beneath. Near to this a mural monument, said to be Chantrey's,[7] and, at all events, issuing from his workshops, but not of first rate execution, in memory of the wife of Dr Roberts, formerly Curate of Stoke, when Mr Edward Hunt was the incumbent: the dying lady lies on a couch, the kneeling & afflicted husband bends towards her, as if to |[71] take the last farewell. Dr R. was father to Mr R. the Rector of Wadenhoe and Aldwinkle All Saints. Near the Communion table is, on the South side a monument in memory ^of the wife of Dr Hunt, a former Rector, of the same family as our friends. On the South side, not far from the Communion table is a costly mural monument, erected by Mr Capron, Father of the present Rector, in memory of his parents, formerly inhabitants of this parish; they had sunk in the world, but were pretty well connected, and the present Mr Capron, with good abilities has aquired wealth as a London Solicitor, having risen greatly in the world – he has purchased the principal property at Stoke, and other estates in the neighbourhood, among them Southwick, beyond Oundle, where he resides. But it remains to notice a very elaborate and costly monument by Rysbrack to the memory of Sir Ed^d. Ward, once Chief Justice of Common Pleas, who died in 1714. It is a gorgeous affair; the Judge reclining in full length of white marble in the panoply of Judicial robes and wig — all admi-|[72] rably executed; behind these is a pyramidal background, beneath, on a sort of altar tomb, a very complimentary and prolix inscription, recording a kind of biography of the distinguished Judge, and his immediate descendants. These had no heirs in the male line, so that Sir Edwd. Ward's Estates eventually came by a marriage of one of his daughters into the Hunt family — this is true of the Northamptonshire Estates, if not of some of the Shropshire Hunt property. The Stoke Doyle property has, indeed, been alienated; but the Wadenhoe, and Oundle and other property once possessed by Sir E.W. form the bulk of the estate now held for life by Caroline Hunt. The really very fine monument to the Judge stands in a chapel, if so it may be called, opening into the Church by an arch near the Altar on the North, having been erected at the same time as the Church for a family Vault, and containing only this stately memorial. — In the evening read a sermon to the family.

---

6. Furbelow – a gathering or pleated border on a skirt or petticoat; a flounce, a ruffle.
7. Sir Francis Chantrey (1781-1841).

Aug. 16. Monday.

A rainy forenoon; the after-[73] noon dull, but fine overhead. — Wrote to Mess.[rs.] Yorke, Oundle, and to M.[r] Eland, Thrapstone, on Hunt trust matters — re. Turnpike bonds. — Conferred with Sophia Hunt on this and other subjects relating to the Wadenhoe Trust. — Walked with M.[r] Thomas H. to Pilton, a village about a mile distant – on the opposite bank of the Nen is Lilford Hall — looking on the finely wooded Pilton Meadows, central in which, detached from the Village, in a tuft of trees, is the beautiful, but somewhat dilapidated Church, with an elegant spire, and, close adjoining, an ancient manor house, which Lord Lilford is now converting into a parsonage, taking the parsonage, which is at some distance from the Church as a residence for a Steward. — M.[r] Geo. Capron joined our party at dinner.

Aug. 17. Tuesday.

After a very heavy thunderstorm during the night, a dull, close day, with.[t] rain till late in the evening — Received a letter from M.[r] Pearce, forwarding a copy of a letter from the P.L.C. in reply to my last official [74] communication to them respecting the charges made by M.[r] Hunt as to the management of the Union at Stow, and misconduct of the Clerk and other officers. The P.L.C. answer, as I suggested and wished, that in reviewing the correspondence they do not see anything alleged of sufficient weight to require an investigation into the conduct of the parties concerned in the management of the Union. — A letter from P. B. Purnell, inviting me to his house on the 24.[th.] Inst. to meet M.[r] and M.[rs.] Curtis Hayward, and M.[r] and M.[rs.] Lysons, at dinner and to sleep, and on the following day to view the site of the Roman Villa which he has been disinterring on his grounds at Stancombe Park, and which he proposes to open to public inspection on three days, the 23.[d.], 24.[th.] and 25.[th.] receiving on the last day at a dejeuner all those of his friends and acquaintance, and others introduced by them who may favour him with their company. The remains are not remarkable for their tesselated pavements [75] but chiefly for their extent, covering six acres, and exhibiting in the foundations the whole arrangement of a Roman mansion, and its appendages. Even the road to the front door can be traced, and the ancient well remains with its original stone walling. It would seem that the remains of this ancient villa, after it was deserted, had served for a quarry whence were obtained building materials for houses, when our forefathers began to erect them of stone. P. is not famous for hospitality, and his place enjoys many recommendations as the residence of a man of good fortune and virtu, situate in a beautiful part of the Country. I regretted, therefore, my inability to accept this invitation, as the 25.[th.] is the day fixed for the Visitation at Stow, and on which the Bishop and his Chaplain are to be our guests at U Slaughter – Wrote to P. to this effect. — With MW, Sophia and Fanny Hunt drove out to visit Polebrook, where there is a farm belonging to the Wadenhoe Estate. Our road led us through Oundle, where we called [76] at the Bankers, with whom I had some trust business to transact — Walked round the exterior of Oundle Church, which is a fine spacious building with a beautiful and lofty spire: the interior needs reparation and renovation, and much of the outer walls requires to be restored, where dilapidated by time, or deformed by injudicious patching. A considerable subscription has been raised with this view, and M.[r] Watts Russell has promised a very liberal contribution in condition of being allowed to name the Architect to be employed: but some misunderstanding has led to delay, and the project appears to be suspended.

There is a good endowed grammar School in the Churchyard, and other parts of the still, quiet town shew Alms houses. In the town are several good old fashioned houses, formerly and I believe still inhabited by families of the class of gentry, or professional men; one of these belongs to the Hunt Trust. — Crossing the Nen and |[77] the Railway, close to the Oundle Station, we proceeded by Ashton, a hamlet in the parish of Oundle, to the Village of Polebrook, situate in a basin, about three miles from Oundle. It was the week of the Polebrook feast, and there remained one or two booths, with a sprinkling of idle vagabond foreigners, Musicians, Organ grinders, Broom Girls[8] & the like. These feasts are still kept up in the Northamptonshire Villages, and on a Sunday, so being very prejudicial to the morals of the people. MW. & F.H. left the carriage here, going to the parsonage, (M[r] Isham's) to await the return of Sophia and myself from Polebrook Lodge, distant, perhaps, a mile, whither we went to look at that farm. Ascended by a long acclivity, the soil, as we approached the top of the hill, becoming more sour, and less fertile. Received by the old tenant and his wife; the farm house and buildings in good repair; but the land unproductive and not capable of much improvement. Having looked round us, and walked over some of the fields, and |[78] taken a luncheon of bread and cheese, we returned to Polebrook, and rejoined our party at the Parsonage, being politely received by the aged Rector and his lady. Here in a comfortable small house, in a pretty small garden, M[r] Isham shewed us portraits of his lamented daughter and son in law, M[r] and M[rs.] T. Welch Hunt, which had been taken about the time of their marriage, and departure for the continental tour from which they never returned.[9] Contiguous to the Rectory is the very interesting village Church, with, as usual in this county, a very elegant spire; but it is modern & very recent, being, however, a facsimile of its predecessor, and looking venerable from antiquity, as built stone for stone, of the materials of the ancient tower and spire. The interior of the Church needs greatly renovation and repewing, being full of unshapely boxes with[t.] lids; but there is much to admire; an Early English pointed Arch separates the Chancel from the Nave, and the Eastern Window is |[79] of three lancet lights, with detached shafts after the manner of the Purbeck shafts in Salisbury Cathedral &c. – there is also a perfect piscina of Early English pattern. The nave is divided from the North and South Aisles, by columns and pointed Arches; and there is a transept projecting to the North, with a series of very elegant pointed Arcades; this was, no doubt, a distinct Chapel or Chantry. The tower surmounted by the spire is at the West end of the Church, and on the North side, is a very curious porch, with Zig Zag mouldings to the Arches, of beautiful, but much dilapidated work. Thus here, as in other instances, the main entrance to the Church was on the North side, not on the South, as is the general rule, the other being the exception, for the very good reason that the main road through the Village ran to the North of the Church, East & West. — Leaving Polebrook and returning by Oundle we arrived at Stoke by the usual dinner hour. — In the forenoon I had walked to the parsonage at Stoke, to call on M[r] George Capron, who was from home. It is a quaint |[80] old dwelling, with antique Oriel windows, at the bottom of a carriage drive, a little further than the Church. —

---

8. Broom Girls were usually Flemish broom sellers, who frequented fairs as well as selling door to door.
9. Thomas and his young wife, Caroline, were murdered by bandits in Italy. The assailants attacked them as they were returning in their carriage from the ruins of Paestum in December 1825. *See* the entry for 24 March 1835.

Aug. 18. Wednesday.

A dull, moist morning: rain had fallen during the night; but little fell during the day. — Left our obliging friends at Stoke, driving in <u>the</u> Clarence to the Oundle station, whence we set out by the railway on our homeward journey at half past eleven A.M. – At Blisworth we were detained about half an hour, waiting for the down train from London, by which we were to proceed to Birmingham. — Arrived at the Birmingham Station at half past three P.M. — There we remained for three quarters of an hour, and had refreshment. At a quarter past four we pursued our journey by the Birmingham and Gloucester railway, which brought us to the Cheltenham station at five minutes past six P.M. — Thence to Mrs. Forget's shop, about engaging a cook, which ended in nothing; took a chariot and post horses at the Plough, |[81] and arrived safe at home by nine o clock. — A letter from Maria Witts; her wedding had been fixed for the 26th.; was postponed till the 28th. to suit my engagements; but has been further put off, and no day fixed, owing to the Settlements being not yet ready. — A letter from poor Bowen, from the establishment of Dr Costello, near Brentford, expressing what agony he has endured, but written in the confident hope of a final operation for the Stone being near at hand, and that he shall be able to return to Guiting early in next week: he wrote in answer to a friendly letter I addressed to him on the eve of his departure from home. — A letter from Howell, from Dawlish, whither he has gone with Laura, Constance, and Macleod. He forwards to me a letter he had received from R. J. Cooper, the Chaplain of Gloucester gaol, who seeks to obtain the post of Prison Inspector vacant by the recent death of the Revd. Whitworth Russel, and solicits Howell's interest with the members of the adminis-|[82] tration – The failure of his application may be certainly anticipated; but a very indifferent Chaplain would make a still worse Prison Inspector. —

Aug. 19. Thursday.

A fine day. — Wrote to P. B. Purnell, forwarding to him for his perusal R. J. Cooper's letter to Howell, that he might know, if he had not otherwise been informed, that his brother, the Chaplain, was seeking office as Prison Inspector. — Settling acc^{ts.} and arranging my papers after my Journey — Drove to Stow. — Rec^{d.} from Mr R. Wilton, Gloucester, a packet containing the deed of dissolution of the alliance or partnership in the Gloucester Lunatic Asylum between the Subscribers on the one part, and the County of Gloucester, and County of the City of Gloucester on the other part: it had received the signatures of most of the Visitors, at a meeting at the Asylum, which I had not attended. This document will be approved and signed by the Home Secretary, and is preliminary to another |[83] deed by which the divorced parties will be reunited on different terms already agreed upon, and so arranged as to meet the altered circumstances of the several parties, and cause this valuable institution to be conducted with greater efficiency. Signed the deed, which was witnessed by Mr Lefevre, and returned it by post to Mr R. Wilton. — Informed of the marriage of Mr Scott of Banksfee to Miss Morrison, eldest daughter of the Vicar of Longborough: this match long delayed on account of the Gentleman's ill health for some months past, took place on Tuesday. — At the Provident Bank had a long conversation with Mr Pole, who is much annoyed by his Rector G L Cooke making alterations in the Church Service at Wick Risington, chanting &c. which are distasteful to the Poles, and to the congregation, but on which Mr Cooke insists. — Met Mr Croome, land surveyor, and conferred with him on the survey made by him of the parish of

U Slaughter &c. making an appointment to meet him to-morrow for further |[84] examination of the Valuation, and for more particulars as to M[r] Terrett's[10] Eldersfield Estate. — To the Workhouse, where communicated with M[r] Pearce, M[r] Perkins, and M[r] Wilkins on Union and other matters. — Looked with the Dean of Gloucester and M[r] R W Hippisley into the Church of Stow, where a new painted window, to the North of the Communion table, has just been placed, opposite to the memorial window inscribed to the late M[rs] Frances Hippisley. Both are by Wale, a skilful artist at Newcastle; the new window is a present by the Rector's lady, with which she has agreeably surprized him. It represents in two compartments our Saviour's tender regard for little children. — With the Dean of Gloucester and M[r] Ford sat in the justice room, hearing cases. Capt. Leigh was present, making an application as to a Broadwell grievance, as to which we had no jurisdiction. — I dressed for dinner at the Unicorn Inn, where MW. called |[86] for me in the Chariot. We proceeded to dine at M[r] Winter's at Daylesford; where we met Marmaduke Vavasour and his daughter Penelope on a visit there, M[rs] Vavasour and her husband with Emma V., M[r] and M[rs] Pole, M[r] and M[rs] Colville — A pleasant party. — M Vavasour looks well, and his daughter appears to be a very pleasing girl.

Aug. 20. Friday.

Fine weather. — Engaged with Churchwarden Gregory and M[r] Croome, who waited on me by appointment, in finally settling the valuation of this parish in order to the making of a rate. Conferred with M[r] Croome as to the purchase of M[r] Terrott's estate at Eldersfield, which may turn out an eligible investment. Suspended further proceedings in this matter till after Sept. 8 before which time I shall not have leisure to look at the property. — Wrote to M[r] Illes, Lunatic Retreat, Fairford on behalf of Roff, of Bourton, who called on me for advice as |[86] to his son, a patient in confinement there, and the future arrangements necessary in the event of the fund being exhausted which is now applied to the poor man's maintenance — Wrote to E.F.W. sending my letter to Stanway by our groom, who goes to bring back our single harness, which we had lent, but which is wanted at home, as one of my horses is suffering from inflammation of one eye. — Wrote to M[r] Turner, — an invitation to meet the Bishop of Gloucester, and others here on Wednesday evening next. — Our dear children rode over from Stanway, and staid two hours with us very agreeably; partaking of luncheon; they brought a good account of their precious boys, and promised to come to us on Wednesday to meet the Bishop and sleep here. — MW. received a letter from E. Daniell, who gives a slightly improved account of M[r] C. Barr. — Conferred with W. Dix, whose brother in law, R. Yearp, is more or less deranged, and had disturbed us |[87] during the night, by knocking at our doors on a vain pretence. — Attended at the School room in the evening to meet the Candidates for confirmation; but all being engaged in harvest, none appeared. — Life of Lord Sidmouth.

Aug. 21. Saturday.

Very fine weather — Wrote to M[r] Clarke and M[r] Perkins, to invite them to join our Episcopal party on next Wednesday Evening. — Wrote to M[r] Illes, Fairford, having, in mistake, forwarded to him yesterday, a document lying on my table folded as a note, and looking like the letter I wrote, which I afterwards found I had not sent, so dispatched it to-day. — Justice

---

10. *Sic.* Francis Witts seems uncertain whether it is Terrett or Terrott.

business at home. — Capt. Frobisher, accompanied by Ryan, Mrs. Dolphin's gardener, and his daughter, called respecting a troublesome affair, which had been brought by Mr Wilkins under the notice of the Magistrates on Thursday, and as to which we considered we had no jurisdiction. It concerns Mrs. D. one of her tenants, her steward, and the Ryans, acting |[88] as M^{rs.} D's agents. Legal proceedings are threatened against the tenant by adverse parties, acting at the suggestion of a discreditable Cheltenham lawyer, and the tenant looks to Mrs. D. for indemnification. Walked with Mr F. to call on Mr W. at Bourton, and advise with him on the matter; discussed it with Mr W. so that Mr F. might understand & communicate to Mrs. D. all the bearings of the case. — Wrote to M^r E Hawkins, Secr. S.P.G. with a remitance of subscriptions recieved by me from members of the Stow district Comm. S.P.G., fixing Sept. 8. as the day for the annual meeting of the Distr. Comm., and suggesting that a deputation from the Parent Society should attend the meeting. — Received a letter from P. B. Purnell, who returns to me his brother's letter to Howell, which I had forwarded to him — A letter from E.F.W. written on the day before yesterday, the information in which he had anticipated by his visit yesterday. — Visiting poor old William |[89] Collett, who still survives, but is almost senseless — Life of Lord Sidmouth. —

Aug. 22. Sunday.

A fine day, rain having fallen during the night. — Visited the Sunday School — Morning service; prayers. — Afternoon service, prayers and sermon. I preached on contentment enforced by the consideration of GOD's general and particular providence — M^r and Mrs. Frobisher called after morning service. — Met the candidates for confirmation in the School room in the evening. — Preparing a Sermon — Wrote to the Superintendent of Police at Stow — Business with Churchwarden Gregory — S.P.G. Tracts in preparation for the approaching annual meeting. — To the family a section from Trower on the Gospels.

Aug. 23. Monday.

Fine weather, with a cooler air. — Wrote to Howell, returning R. J. Cooper's letter to him: — to the Treasurer of the National Society, with a remittance of £1. 17. 0 being the amount of the Collection made in our church on the 8th. Inst. |[90] under the authority of the Queen's letter; — to Mr Rodwell with an order for books for the Stow Book Society: — to Chr. Geldard thanking him for a box of grouse sent by him, and which greeted us on our return from Northamptonshire. — Mr Turner called on us at breakfast time, desiring to be present at the hearing of a case of larceny charged against a boy, Son of one of his parishioners of Lower Slaughter. Remanded the case for final hearing at the next Petty Sessions — Preparing a Sermon. — Drove with MW. to Stow: called at the Workhouse and library: — shopping: — met and parleyed with Emma Vavasour. — Rec^{d.} a letter from Mr Illes, Fairford, who returns to me the paper which I had forwarded to him by mistake. — In the evening my son's Servant came on his own business to the Village, and brought a letter from his master with a good account of all at Stanway Vicarage. — Life of Lord Sidmouth. |[91]

Aug. 24. Tuesday.

Fine weather. — Wrote to Mrs. C. Barr, at Henwick Hall, with enquiries as to her husband, and expressing a hope that the amendment in his health lately mentioned by E. Daniell had been progressive: — Wrote to C Bathurst. — Justice business at home. — Preparing a report for the annual meeting of our district Committee S.P.G. — Received a letter from the Rev^{d.} — Fagan, Ass^{t.} Sec^{y.} S.P.G. in answer to mine to Mr Hawkins of the 21st. Inst. Mr F. holds out a hope that he shall be able to prevail on the Revd. W. Bullock, a Nova Scotian Missionary, now in England, to attend our Meeting on the 8th. Sept. as a deputation from the parent Society: — from Maria Witts who announces her wedding as fixed for the 9th. Sept. and expects me to be present at it; — from Dr Williams, Superintendent of the Lunatic Asylum, Gloucester, to inform me that poor Mrs. Willoughby, of Adlestrop, a patient in that institution, sent thither |⁹² by me, and who, when taken out for exercise with others, beyond the boundaries of the asylum, had escaped, had been recovered and was again returned. The poor woman had gone to Cheltenham to an acquaintance, who apprized the police of her having eluded the keepers, so that she was only absent one day and night. A keeper had been sent by Dr W. to Adlestrop on Friday or Saturday last to seek her, and apprize her friends of her escape: he had also waited on me to acquaint me with the circumstance — Life of Lord Sidmouth. —

Aug. 25. Wednesday.

Fine weather till the evening; rain fell as the evening closed in, and during the night. — Wrote to Maria Witts, explaining that my engagements on Sept 8. would preclude my being able to be present at her wedding on the day following. — Preparing a lecture to be addressed on Sunday next to the young persons of my parish who shall be confirmed tomorrow. — Drove to Stow, to |⁹³ attend the Bishop's Visitation — Received a letter from M^r W H Bloxsome, Rector of Stanton, announcing that his health continues to be so bad as to render him unable to perform clerical duties, and therefore to have resolved to sell the next presentation to his living; of which determination he gives me the first notice, as he had learnt that I had been making enquiry respecting it of his brother's partner, Mr Jackson, a twelvemonth ago; — from the Treasurers of the National Society, acknowledging the receipt of my remittance of £1. 17. 0. forwarded on the 23^{d.} Inst. — I joined the Bishop, his Chaplain, Murray Browne, and others of the Clergy, at the Rectory, Stow. His Lordship and Chaplain came from Northleach, where he had held a confirmation yesterday, and had been Aston's guest. — After twelve o clock Evening service commenced, performed by R W Hippisley: it was prolonged by the chanting and singing of the choir, ambitious to exhibit their skill, and do honour to the occasion. |⁹⁴ The sermon was preached by F. Biscoe, V. of Turkdean, and was an excellent, unpretending, well compacted discourse, setting forth the privileges and responsibilities of the Clergy. One clearly saw that the Preacher, had he desired, was competent to have selected and discussed higher and more difficult points — his subject was handled with delicacy and right feeling, and the language very correct: his delivery somewhat feeble, his voice being weak, but simple, impressive, and unaffected. — The Bishop's charge was long and somewhat heavy, chiefly occupied with the engrossing topic of national education, as connected with the recent regulations of the Committee of Privy Council on Education, which he advocated warmly, counselling his clergy to avail themselves of the aid offered by the State as far as possible: his Lordship traced rather diffusely the whole history of national Education, as it has developed itself in this country of late years. Towards the close of his |⁹⁶ charge he adverted with just reprobation, and with feeling energy, to the four perversions to Popery which had occurred of late within his own diocese – lamenting the apparent disingenuousness of those who must have entered into the Church with minds already entangled in the mazes of Romanism, making at last the desparate plunge, by which they adopted all Roman error, purgatory, transubstantiation, and "the worshipping of the ~~relics~~ bones of dead men and women, whom the superstitious of a barbarous age had raised into the rank of saints." — A large party of the Clergy attended the Visitation dinner, which passed of much as usual,[11] with abundance of compliment, and courtesy. The Bishop announced that a proposition had made to him[12] from the Bp. of Oxford for the union of the two dioceses in carrying out the schemes for National Education by combination as to Training Schools, in such a manner that there should be one training school for matters common to both dioceses at Headington |[96] near Oxford, and one for Mistresses, in like manner to answer for both dioceses, at Gloucester — The dinner over, I hastened in my carriage homeward to receive the Bishop and Murray Browne, and they followed very closely on my steps. The party whom we had invited to meet his Lordship were M[r] Ford with his daughters Dulcy and Sophia, my son and his wife, who had arrived from Stanway this afternoon with the baby, and who slept here, M[r] and M[rs.] Hippisley, who were accompanied by their Visitors, Miss Digby, and M[r] Raikes, a young brother of M[rs.] Hippisley; M[r] and M[rs.] W. B. Pole, who brought with them M[rs.] Vavasour; Mess[rs.] Perkins and Potter, whom I brought in my carriage from Stow, Mess[rs.] Hunt, Turner and Clarke — Tea and Coffee, with a cold supper at 9 P.M., with conversation, were the arrangments of our Episcopal soirée. —

Aug. 26. Thursday.

A fine day — After breakfast the Bishop and his Chaplain |[97] took leave of us, and went to Stow to the Confirmation — My son and daughter and their baby left for Stanway about mid-day. — I followed the Bishop to Stow very shortly after he set out, and rejoined his Lordship &c. at the Rectory. — On my way received from M[r] Hedley, Secretary to the Diocesan Board of Education for the Archdeaconry of Gloucester notice of a meeting fixed for Tuesday next, at which the Bishop will preside to consider the propriety or feasability of making a Union with the diocese of Oxford as to the Establishment of training schools for the common use of the two dioceses. — Morning service at the Church, M[r] R. W. Hippisley officiating; again a superabundance of chanting and singing made the service very long. Many clergymen in attendance from whose parishes came the candidates for confirmation, of whom more than 400 of both sexes received the rite — More than two hours were occupied in the service — Afterwards the Bishop and |[98] Murray Browne proceeded to Moreton, where also his Lordship confirmed. He was afterwards the guest of Lord Redesdale at Batsford Park, whence he proceeds to-morrow to hold a Visitation at Campden. — I called at "the Cottage," and partook of luncheon with the Vavasours, meeting Marmaduke V. and his daughter Penelope, also W. Vavasour, who with his wife returned yesterday from the Isle of Wight, where they have been sojourning at Ryde for a month, and both are in better health. — At the Provident Bank met M[r] Pole, M[r] Winter, and others. — Late in the day to the Workhouse, to attend the fortnightly meeting of Guardians: but few were present;

---

11. Presumably he had meant 'passed off much as usual.'
12. *Sic.*

business had been begun, but I took the chair to conclude it — Returned home fatigued. — Sir F.B. Head's very interesting book — The Emigrant[13] —

Aug. 27. Friday.

Fine weather. — Wrote to the Rev^d. W. H. Bloxsome and to Mr Sewell as to the purchase of the Advowson, |^99 or next presentation of the Rectory of Stanton; — to the former that I would desire Messrs. Sewell and Newmarch to communicate on the subject with Messrs. Bloxsome, and ~~Wells~~ Jackson — to the latter, recalling his attention to the conversations and correspondence on the matter which had passed between us last year: desiring him to conduct a treaty on our behalf with B & Jackson on the part of W.H.B. — Preparing a report for the coming annual meeting of the Stow district Committee S.P.G. — Reading papers touching on the Missionary operations of that Society — Received a letter from Howell, from Dawlish: he is coming to town, on his way to a visit to the factories in the Cheshire part of his country: he invites me for Monday and Tuesday next to Eaton Place West, under the impression that I may then be in London or its vicinity to attend the wedding of Maria Witts. — A letter from C. Bathurst, written from Town, in pretty good health and spirits; he wishes me to |^100 procure for him some Neckar wine.[14] — A letter from Mr Illes, Fairford Lunatic Retreat, as to the condition of his patient, Moses Roff. —— M^rs. W. Vavasour called with her sister Emma; the former improved in health by her visit to Ryde. — "The Emigrant." —

Aug. 28. Saturday.

Fine, but close weather, till towards evening, when a mist came on which ended in rain. — Wrote to Mr Winter about procuring Neckar wine for C Bathurst — To Howell, explaining to him that I am prevented from going to Town or its neighbourhood to be present at the marriage of Maria Witts. — T. Roff from Bourton came, with whom conferred as to the state of his lunatic son, the demand of support made on the father by the son's wife, the necessity that the parties should have recourse to parochial relief, and the manner in which their claim to relief ought to be substantiated: wrote on all these points to Mr Wilkins, as |^101 Guardian of the parish of Bourton on the Water, desiring T.R. to hand to him my letter with that which I received yesterday from Mr Illes. — Preparing a report for the annual meeting Stow Distr. Comm. S.P.G. — Received a letter from Mr Jennings, which announces that the negociation for the purchase of the Ground rents in the parish of S^t. Georges in the East, for which we had been treating, had been revived with some prospect of a successful issue — A friendly letter from J Round. — Mr Lefroy called and partook of luncheon with us. — With MW. drove to Stow: shopping. — "The Emigrant."

Aug. 29. Sunday.

Weather fair, except that a thunderstorm of short duration fell about noon. — Visited the Sunday School. — Wrote to Mr Jennings desiring that the Treaty for the purchase of the

---

13. Sir Francis Bond Head (1793-1875). *The Emigrant. The United States Democratic Review*, volume 20, issue 103 (January 1847).
14. Neckar wine. The Neckar is a tributary river to the Rhine. It runs north-west to Mannheim where it falls into the Rhine. The wine referred to is what would now be called Württemberg. The area has long been known for the quality of its wine, among the finest in Germany. The reason for Mr. Winter being involved is unclear, but his wife, being an Imhoff clearly had useful connections.

Ground rents in St. Georges in the East may be proceeded with. Though conversations and correspondence with Mr Croome have been conducted with |*102* a view to the purchase of the Eldersfield property from Mr Terrett, yet that affair has not reached a point from which one could not well recede, and it is probable that the investment in gound rents will be more eligible, and pay better interest than the Estate. The treaty as to the latter may be renewed if that for the former fails. — Preparing a Sermon. — Morning Service and sermon; I preached on 2. Pet. 1. 3. Afternoon service, prayers — after which I addressed from the reading-desk the young people who were confirmed on Thursday last. — Received a letter from Eliza Daniell, announcing the decease of Mr C. Barr, at Henwick Hall, on Friday last. This foreseen event is a great affliction to his poor wife, and will be heavily felt by his brothers and sisters; he was a good, benevolent, well principled man. Probably, he has left his wife and children well provided for. Of course they will remove from Leeds; but nothing, I apprehend, has been |*103* settled yet as to the future. — Eccl. Gazette — To the family a section from Trower's Essays on the gospels.

Aug. 30. Monday.

Fine weather, but dull. — At the desire of Eliza Daniell, wrote to Captain Witts to inform him and his sister Apphia of the death of poor C Barr. — Wrote to Mr Morgan, Stow, as Secretary of the Stow & C Norton agricultural Association with a certificate to procure for my parishioner Samuel Jones, a premium at the approaching annual meeting of the Association, on the score of thirty years service on one farm in this parish under three successive tenants, all of the same family. — Preparing notes & summonses to be delivered to the members of the Stow Distr. Comm. S.P.G. announcing the annual meeting to be held on the 8th. September. — MW. received a letter from our friend Miss Rollinson, now ~~at~~ ^{on} a visit to M^r and Mrs. Davy at Cowley, fixing the 18th. September as the day on which she will come on a visit to us — In the mean time she proposes |*104* visiting the Bowlys at Siddington, the Wallers at Farmington, and the Poles at Wyck Hill. — My aged parishioner W. Collett died today. — "The Emmigrant." —

Aug. 31. Tuesday.

Weather dull and threatening in the morning, but fine afterwards. — Wrote to E.F.W. to meet him at Stow today, to inform him that the treaty for the purchase of the ground rents in the parish of St. George's in the East had been renewed with a prospect of a favourable issue: — also to acquaint him with the death of M^r C Barr — Sent out notes, hand bills &c. annual the annual meeting of the district committee S.P.G. At Stow on Sept. 8.[15] — After breakfast MW. and I proceeded in our phaeton to Cheltenham, where I remained an hour or two shopping; and leaving my wife there, went on by the railway to Gloucester. — This day had been fixed for the consecration of the district church of St. Mark's, built near the Kingsholm Turnpike, by the side |*105* of the road leading to Tewkesbury, and for the accommodation of a large and ~~popu~~ poor contiguous population: I walked as far as the Church, but could not enter it, the doors being closed as the communion was in course of administration, after the consecration to the Bishop and Clergy, and others who remained for that sacred rite.

---

15. The handwriting is quite clear here, but Francis Witts presumably intended to write 'announcing the annual meeting . . .'

Mr Edward Niblett, son of Mr N., the Magistrate, my old acquaintance, is the Architect, and the design does him great credit. The edifice is small: the tower surmounted by a spire, fronts the road, the nave and aisles receding from it: the style is Early English, very chaste and pleasing, with a striking look of newness; being built of free stone it wore the appearance of a huge model of biscuit China. A Clergyman of the name of Barlow, I believe, is the appointed Minister; the sermon was preached by Mr Clements, the Perpetual Curate of Upton St Leonards. There was a large gathering of Clergy from adjacent and some from dis-|^{106} tant parts of the diocese; among the latter my neighbour Ford with Dulcy and Sophia; Mr Biscoe, with Miss Middleton; and Mr Malcolm. The long consecration service caused a delay in holding the meeting at the Palace, which I came to attend, and which took place about 3 P.M. Of members of the Diocesan Board of Education for the Archdeaconry of Gloucester there were present, the Bishop presiding, Curtis Hayward and Gambier Parry, — laymen — $^{Revd.}$ Mess$^{rs.}$ Ford, Malcolm, Murray Browne, Attwood, Hedley, Sir Geo. Prevost, Close, Perkins (Wotton under Edge) Raymond, Sir Geo. Seymour, Coghlan, and ~~Barrow~~ two or three others whose names were unknown to me. Mr Attwood and Mr Hedley are the Treasurer and Secretary of the Diocesan Board for the Archdeaconry of Gloucester, and Mr Barrow, an Incumbent at Bristol, and Chaplain to the Bp., is Secretary of the Diocesan Board for the Archdeaconry of Bristol. This gentleman |^{107} was also present. The actual state of the diocese as to Training Schools at present is that there are small but efficient Establishments both at Bristol and Gloucester: at the ~~former~~ ^{latter} for school mistresses, at the former for School ~~mistresses~~ ^{masters} — that the Boards, their institutions, and their funds are distinct; that the income arising from subscriptions is in both cases scanty; that a liberal contribution for Educational purposes is not to be expected; and that any arrangement which would tend to break up the separate establishment at Bristol would be probably distasteful to the supporters of it. — The advantages proposed by the Committee of Privy Council for Education can only be obtained by so considerable a fund subscribed or otherwise raised, that there is very little reason to suppose that the necessary sum can be furnished by any one diocese; therefore unions of dioceses are under consideration, that from two or so combined a sufficient fund may be obtained, on the under-|^{108} standing that the Privy Council will consider such unions as separate institutions to which they will extend the pecuniary grant and other advantages now held forth to a single diocese. With this view a Union of the dioceses of Oxford and Gloucester and Bristol has been contemplated, on the basis that the Training School for Masters shall be at Headington near Oxford, where a Church is about to be built, to which the Training School shall be appended, and the Training School for Mistresses be at Gloucester. This arrangement would involve the discontinuance of the Training School for Masters at Bristol, which might be seriously objected to by its supporters. Doubts are also entertained whether Oxford, or its immediate vicinity, are eligible situations for a Training School for Masters. All these considerations made the subject for deliberation to-day difficult and delicate. If the actual limited good enjoyed in its two Training schools be withdrawn from the diocese of Gloucester |^{109} and Bristol, a serious evil would be incurred, unless success attended the establishment of schools on a larger and more comprehensive plan: we should be giving up a present certain advantage for a doubtful though greater and more complete arrangement, which might never be carried out. All present were fully aware of the great difficulty of raising large subscriptions or donations in the diocese of Gloucester and Bristol; none were sanguine of success in a large scheme; so the meeting came to resolutions not very likely to terminate in any amalgamation if the dioceses of Oxford and Gloucester and Bristol for educational purposes: — viz. that the meeting considered the union of the dioceses for such purposes desirable — that, as a step towards it, delegates from the Educational Boards of the Archdeanconries of Gloucester and Bristol (if the Bristol Board adopted the view) should put themselves in Communication with the Oxford Educational Board, and report progress to their respective Boards: that Messrs. |¹¹⁰ Mess^{rs.16} Attwood, Hedley and Murray Browne should be delegated from the Diocesan Education Board for the Archdeaconry of Gloucester. With these resolutions passed the meeting separated after an hour and half spent in deliberation. — At half past five P.M. I left the railroad station on my return to Cheltenham. I walked from the Palace thither with Ford; there and at the Palace I was principally in communication with Curtis Hayward, Malcolm, and Davies, now a Clergyman in the Forest of Dean, formerly Vicar of Sherborne and Windrush, and others. I travelled to Cheltenham in the same coach with M^r and Mrs. Close, whom I found very conversible and agreeable. Mr Ford was my companion in the Omnibus from the Station to Cheltenham: there I joined MW. at the Plough; we set out for U Slaughter at half past six, and reached home by half past 8 P.M. — A letter from Mr Sewell, who has appointed to meet Messrs. Bloxsome and Jackson to treat on our behalf for the purchase of the |¹¹¹ advowson or next presentation of the living of Stanton: — from Mr Warter as to the purchase of the Ground rents in St. George's in the East; — from the Apparitor at Gloucester;¹⁷ a summons to attend there to vote for Proctors for the Diocese in Convocation: — from Mr Fagan, Ass^{t.} Sec. S.P.G., that the gentleman whom he had named as likely to be able to attend at Stow on the 8th. Sept., as a deputation from the Parent Society, is otherwise engaged, and cannot come: — from Messrs. Hoare that Mr Jennings has paid to my account with them £69. 11. 6.

Sept. 1. Wednesday.

Fine weather. — Wrote to Mr Sewell as to the purchase of the living of Stanton, mentioning what I had learnt yesterday from Mr Malcolm, Rural Dean of Campden Deanery, that Mr W. H. Bloxsome has acted illegally in some alterations made by him in the pewing of the Church there, giving great offence to some of his parishioners, and exposing himself to |¹¹² ecclesiastical censure, and to proceedings in the Ecclesiastical Court. Malcolm is to have a meeting with the parties to-morrow to endeavour to accommodate matters. It seems desirable that Sewell should be informed of this feud before his interview with the Solicitors at Dursley. This state of things will make M^r WHB. more disposed to divest himself of the incumbency. — Preparing a report for the approaching annual meeting of the Stow Distr. Comm. S.P.G. — Rec^{d.} a letter from Mr Jennings, announcing that he has, together with Mr Warter, entered into an agreement on my part for the purchase of the Ground rents in St. George's in the East, subject to the approval of the Court of Chancery: price £9631: income £389. of which to the amount of £50 is leasehold. The ground rents are secured on about 190 houses of small size, a Chapel and a public house; the occupiers chiefly persons

---

16. *Sic.*
17. Apparitor – a servant or attendant of an ecclesiastical or civil court.

employed in the docks. The locality near the Blackwall railway. Many of the houses fall in at the expira-|[113] tion of 50 or 60 years, others 70 or more, extending to 90 years: the purchase is made on a calculation of something under twenty five years: therefore to pay 4 per C.[t] and considering that the term of so many houses but little exceeds 50 years the profit may be considered equal to 5 p.[r] C.[t] — It is to be hoped we may not again be disappointed by finding the title of this property deficient. — A letter from Winter, who promises to procure the Neckar wine for C Bathurst. — "The Emigrant."

Sept. 2. Thursday.

The weather fine, but not without a tendency to rain. — Wrote to E.F.W. with particulars as to the purchase of the Ground rents in S.[t] Georges in the East, and of the advowson or next presentation to the Rectory of Stanton: — to M.[r] Croome, Tewkesbury, that, having agreed for the purchase of ground rents in the Metropolis, I give up all further thoughts of purchasing M.[r] Terrot's property at Eldersfield — Drove to Stow with MW., who very shortly returned to U Slaughter. — Letters from Warter & |[114] Jennings conveyed further details as to the purchase of ground rents in S.[t] George's in the East. — Transacted business at the Provident Bank, at the office of the Gloucestershire Banking Company, and at M.[r] Brookes's office, and at the Workhouse, where I met M.[r] Vavasour, and M.[r] J Perkins — Joined M.[r] Ford at the Provident Bank, with whom and the Dean of Gloucester I sat in the Justice Room, M.[r] Turner being our Assessor. Much business was transacted. — Conferred with M.[r] Morgan as to S. Jones's application for a premium from the Stow & C. Norton agricultural Society on account of long service on one farm — Home to dinner — Afterwards officiated at the funeral of the aged W Collett. — "The Emigrant".

Sept. 3. Friday.

A showery day — Wrote to M.[r] Jennings and M.[r] Warter as to the purchase of the Ground rents in S.[t] George's in the East: — To M.[r] Ford and M.[r] Potter respecting the part which I wish them to |[115] take in moving and seconding a resolution at the ann. meeting of the Stow Distr. Comm. S.P.G. on the 8.th Inst. Wrote to M.[r] Bloxsome, Clerk of the Peace, on behalf of W. Dix, Overseer, who has made a blunder as to the duties of his office in respect of the registration of County Voters. — Preparing Report for the Propagation of the Gospel meeting on Wednesday next. — The Colonial Chronicle. — "The Emigrant."

Sept. 4. Saturday.

Fine weather. — Preparing report for the Ann. meeting Stow Distr. Comm. S.P.G. — Justice business at home. — Frederick Aston Jun.[r] called, and partook of luncheon with us. — Walked with MW. to Eyford: called on the Frobishers; he was at dinner with his children; so we were not admitted: he has left M.[rs] F. in London for a few days for medical advice — Letters from M.[r] Sadler, who regrets that he is unable to attend at the meeting of the district Comm. S.P.G. on Wednesday next; — from M.[r] Turner, who expresses his |[116] readiness to become a member of the Stow Distr. Comm. S.P.G. — MW. received a letter from Maria Witts to whom she had written, on sending her a china ornament, as a little souvenir on her approaching marriage. She proposes bringing her husband to visit us towards the close of October, as they return from Devonshire, whither they ~~propose~~ are going to pass the honey-moon. — This evening old Joshua Dix died with but very little warning. — Colonial Chronicle — "The Emigrant." —

Sept. 5. Sunday.

Showery weather. — Attended the Sunday School. — Called on the Dix family, to make enquiries as to the almost sudden death of Joshua last evening. — Morning Service: prayers. Afternoon Service; prayers and Sermon. I preached on Acts. 20. 32. — Mr Frobisher and his children called after morning service. — A letter from E.F.W. — Preparing a Sermon. — Colonial Chronicle — To the family a section from James on the Collects. — |¹¹⁷

Sept. 6. Monday.

Fine, except as to two or three showers in the afternoon. — Preparing report and other work for the meeting of our district committee S.P.G. fixed for Wednesday next. — Wrote to Hoares with directions to transfer £20 from my account with them to my Son's account with them. — A letter from Mr Sewell with particulars of his interview with Mr E. Bloxsome as to the purchase of the Advowson of, or next presentation to, the living of Stanton. Immediate resignation is contemplated by M^r W H Bloxsome: the next presentation is what it is meant to sell, but offers will be received for the Advowson. A higher value is set by the Vendor on the next presentation than we are likely to give; but Sewell seems to think that less will be taken than is asked. He purposes to come hither to-morrow to advise with us, as to further proceedings in this matter, and has written to E.F.W. to meet him here. — A letter from the Rev^{d.} E Berridge Curate of Blockely, who is desirous to become |¹¹⁸ a member of the Stow district Comm. S.P.G. — A letter form Mr Croome in answer to mine addressed to him on the 2^{d.} Inst. — A letter from Geo. Wellford, full of polemics; written in a kindly feeling towards me and mine, but with bitter antipathy to the Tractarian school. — A letter from John Witts acknowledging mine to him announcing the decease of M^r C Barr: the health of himself and M^{rs.} J W. is pretty good, but the account of Mr Warter's state is very sad. — When we were walking Mr Potter called. — The Emigrant. —

Sept. 7. Tuesday.

A cloudy, but fine day till towards the evening, when heavy rain fell. — Preparing for the meeting of the Distr. Comm. S.P.G. to be held to-morrow. — Justice business at home. — M^r and Mrs. Perkins with their daughter called upon us. — Mr Sewell and my Son also met here to confer with me as to the purchase of the advowson of, or |¹¹⁹ next presentation to the living of Stanton. After a long and close discussion of the subject in all its bearings, we came to the conclusion to offer £6000 for the advowson, or £4500 for the next presentation; these to be the utmost limits, but in the first instance to offer £4000 or £5500 — The Bloxsomes Estimate the gross receipts of the living at £414 per ann. Sewell estimates the net annual value at £330: there is an excellent parsonage house in good repair built some years ago by Mr Wynniatt, and fitted up and enlarged by Mr W. H. Bloxsome — two churches — single duty at each, and the Bishop cannot, by act of Parliament, insist on double duty at either, the population being under the rule laid down in the Act. There are two farms, with buildings in good repair, one at Stanton, the other at Snowshill; also a rent charge on an estate at Snowshill. Mr W.H.B. engages to resign immediately. We parted on the understanding that we should meet again |[120] at Stow to-morrow to consider the matter once again; Mr Sewell engaging in the meantime to obtain all the information which Mr Wynniatt can afford as to the living, which he sold to Mr Bloxsome a few years since. Sewell has an early engagement with Mr Wynniatt to-morrow. — Mr S. came from Mr Hudson's farm at Lower Swell — My son from Stow, whither he had come today from Stanway, accompanied by Mrs Walsh and Sophy, to play at cricket. They purpose going home to Stanway this evening. The dear grandchildren are quite well — Received a letter from Mr Thornton as to the controversy respecting the Red Lion Wharf; he forwarded to me letters from Mr Hunt and his Solicitor, Mr Braikenridge — I felt very much oppressed today by a cough and cold which have hung upon me for several days past.

Sept. 8. Wednesday.

After heavy rain during the night a fine day. — Preparing for the |[121] annual district meeting of S.P.G. fixed for this day. — MW. accompanied me in the open carriage to Stow. — Recd a letter from Mr Wiggin, with the list of subscribers to the Parochial Association S.P.G. at Oddington — from Mr Fagan, Asst Secy S.P.G. with a ~~doc~~ fragment of the forthcoming printed report of the Parent Society for 1847, which he supposed might be useful to me today: — from Messrs Hoare, announcing that they had transferred £20 from my acct with them to my Son's account with them. — Met Mr Sewell by appointment at Stow, and renewed with him the conference as to the purchase of the advowson or next presentation to the Living of Stanton. He had seen Mr Wynniatt, and learnt from him that the price given by Mr Bloxsome to him for the Advowson some years ago, was £4600 — but W. was then in want of money, the value of Church property was depreciated, and the title was not without a defect. Since that |[122] time Mr B. has completed the house, and expended on the premises from £1200 to £1500 — agreed with S. to abide by the calculations we had made yesterday; and under no circumstances to exceed the sums fixed on by us as the extreme limits. My son was not able to meet us, but came shortly after Mr Sewell left me, and gave his full concurrence to what had been settled. — The Ann. Distr. Comm. meeting commenced about 2 P.M. I had been engaged for some time before in receiving subscriptions, and making with some of the Clergy arrangements for the order of the business. The Dean of Gloucester presided. The following Clergymen were present — Revds R W Ford, F.E.W., C. B. Turner, E. F. Witts, Walsh, Clarke, Crompton, Potter, Pantin, Hippisley, Winter, Morrison, Waller, Wiggin, Hunt and Williams. — Several ladies attended — Mrs Witts, Mrs Hippisley, Mrs W. Vavasour, and her sister, Mrs Potter, the Misses Ford |[123] &c. also many friends of the Society of the middle classes from Stow, Maugersbury, Lower Swell &c. farmers, tradesmen, and their wives, daughters &c. — so that the Ball room at the Unicorn was tolerably full. I read the report which I had prepared, presenting a view of the Missionary Operations of the Society in some of its most promising and interesting fields — Mr Ford proposed a resolution having reference to the late increase of the Colonial Episcopate and the efficiency of Theological Schools & Colleges connected with the S.P.G. in the Colonies, and he was seconded by Mr Potter, who furnished some very pertinent and valuable details and statistics, illustrating his remarks by a reference to a map of the world pourtraying the religious privileges, or the religious destitution, as still subsisting after all that has been done in evangelizing mankind: shewing that however successful the friends of the Missionary work may have been here and there, |[124] a dreary void and desert wilderness of vast extent remains to be invaded and cultivated. In return to the customary vote of thanks to the Treasurer and Sec[y.] – which was proposed by M[r] Wiggin in a very judicious tone, and with very suitable remarks on the general subject of Missions, I made a speech of some length, in which I touched on a variety of matters, which had not come within the compass of my report, dwelling especially on the brighter prospects of solid success in missionary labours beaming on the Christian world by the spreading of the Gospel in a systematic manner through an apostolically constituted and Episcopal Church planted in the several Colonies & dependencies of the British Empire — The meeting closed between 4 and 5 P.M. — Most of the Clergy remained to attend the third dinner for the Season of the Clerical Society, for which I was altogether unequal; suffering severely from cough and cold in |[125] the head. — After I reached home I felt greatly oppressed, fatigued and languid, during the evening. —

Sept. 9. Thursday.

Very fine weather — Settling the accounts of the transactions at the Annual Distr. Comm. meeting S.P.G. yesterday; monies received &c. — Drove to Stow. — A letter from parties engaged in the conveyance of Emigrants to the Cape of Good hope, addressed to me as the Chairman of Stow on the Wold Union. — Attended at the Provident Bank. — A letter from M[r] Westmacott, as member of the Stow Book Society, consulting me as to the propriety of his withdrawing the work of Chevalier Bunsen on "the Church of the future" which has been procured on his order: he doubts its being a book suited for general circulation. — Transacted business at the Office of the Gloucestershire Banking Company — Presided at the fortnightly meeting of the Guardians of the Union; — a thin attendance — Returned home by 4 P.M. to attend the funeral of Joshua Dix. — "The Emigrant." — |[126] Less indisposed than for some days past with cough and cold.

Sept. 10. Friday.

Fine weather. — Wrote to Tagart, Chemist, Cheltenham for a box of Squill pills: — to M[r] Pain, that L[t.] Col. Dawkins is nominated Chairman of the Book Society annual meeting to be held on the 28[th.] Inst: — to M[r] Westmacott in reply to his letter received yesterday: — to M[r] Thornton, returning to him the letters from M[r] Hunt and M[r] Braikenridge, which he had forwarded for my perusal, and discussing general the Hunt Trust matters. — Settling accounts of Distr. Comm. S.P.G. — Justice business at home — Visiting a sick parishioner. — Received from M[r] Wilton, County Treasurer, the Annual Abstract of monies received and expended on the account of the County of Gloucester, to be audited by me, as it has already been examined by Purnell and D[r] Timbrill. — "The Emigrant." — Suffering much today from my very troublesome cough, |[127] being generally oppressed and unwell.

Sept. 11. Saturday.

Very fine weather. — Wrote to M[rs.] C. Barr. — Examining the County Treasurers abstract of accounts. — Drove with MW. to call on M[rs.] Wiggin at Oddington, by whom we were received, but neither the Dean of Gloucester nor M[r] Wiggin were at home: on our return we met the latter coming back from Great Barrington. — We also drove to Daylesford House, and left our cards for Sir Charles Imhoff, and Baroness Klock, who had driven out.

The aged General has accomplished, since we met him at Mr Winter's in the Spring, soon after the decease of Lady Imhoff, a voyage and Journey into the Interior of Germany, to visit his connections there, and, in spite of old age and infirmities, has borne the fatigue and ~~exeat~~ excitement well; bringing back with him on a visit his half sister, a widowed Baroness Klock, the daughter of his father Baron Imhoff, by his second wife, whom he married after his divorce from his first wife, afterwards M$^{rs.}$ Hastings — |^{128} Baroness Klock was, I believe, the youngest child by the second marriage: the elder daughters & a Son of Baron Imhoff, as also his widow, were resident at Weimar, when my Father & Mother, with my Brother and myself passed two Winters there in 1798 & 1799: we were much acquainted with them; the elder, Amalia von Imhoff, was already an accomplished writer, a poetess; Demoiselle d'honneur to the Reigning Duchess of Weimar: this lady afterwards married a Swedish officer, Von Helwig, who died a General of Artillery in the Prussian service; Mad. de Helwig is also deceased; she maintained her literary reputation by many works of poetry and fiction. — The second daughter died a widow, many years since; the Son was an Officer in the service of the Duke of Weimar; Mad. de Klock has a daughter now Demoiselle d'honneur to the present Reigning Duchess of Weimar. — Called at the library, Stow. — Rec$^{d.}$ a letter from Mr H. D. Warter, who complains that I have not |^{129} answered his question whether the ground rents in S$^{t.}$ George's in the East are to be conveyed wholly to the Trustees, or partly to them, and partly to myself: that is, such a portion to the Trustees as amounts to the exact fund disposable, and the small portion remaining to me as bought out of my private funds: but I wrote to him on the 3$^{d.}$ Inst. that I wished the whole of the property to be conveyed to the Trustees. — A letter from Mr Morgan, that the Committee of the Stow and Chipping Norton Agricultural Association had awarded to my parishioner, Sam$^{l.}$ Jones, £1. on account of thirty years service on one farm under different masters of the same family. — "The Emigrant." —

Sept. 12. Sunday.

A sour looking day, with close air: in the evening a tendency to rain. — Visited the Sunday School. — Wrote to Mr H. D. Warter, repeating to him the purport of my missing letter to him of the 3$^{d.}$ Inst. — Morning Service: prayers and Sermon. I preached on the parable of the Wheat and the |^{130} Tares. — Afternoon Service, Prayers. — Capt. Frobisher and his children called after the morning service — Wrote to Mr Wells, Med. Off. of the Union, desiring him to attend Matt. Davis, who is suffering from a wound in the leg, and whom I visited. — Preparing a sermon. — Rotheram on Establishments, with a view to the coming discussion at the Decanal meeting on the 21$^{st.}$ Inst. — To the family a section from Dr James on the Collects.

Sept. 13. Monday.

Mild, but steady rain from morning till evening. — Engaged with Churchwarden Gregory in making a rate from Mr Croome's valuation of this parish. — Audited the County Treasurers Abstract of accounts, which I forwarded to Gloucester with a note to him. — Settling accounts and arranging papers of the Stow Distr. Comm. S.P.G. — Rotheram's Essay on Establishments. — Bishop Wilberforce's History of the Protestant Episcopal Church in America. — I am not yet quite recovered from the cough, which |^{131} hangs on me, making me languid and heavy. —

Sept. 14. Tuesday.

Weather fine, though there was a slight tendency to rain. — Visited Matt. Davis, who is ill, and the family of W^m. Dix, with reference to Rich^d. Yearp, who is not in his right mind. — Justice business at home. — Drove to Stow, to attend the annual meeting of the Stow and C Norton Agricultural Society, held this year at Stow. — MW. accompanied me, but very soon returned home. — Much engaged during the day in the Show Yard, where was a very respectable display of cattle, horses, sheep, pigs, and implements, and a large attendence of gentry, yeomanry and farmers. Of the latter several were desirous of shewing me the best specimens: Messrs. Beman, Shelton, D. Smith, ~~By~~ Bryan &c. went round with me to the objects most worthy of observation — A fat short horned cow of Mr Beman's gained the prize as the best animal in the yard: a fat long horned cow of Mr Penson's, gained a prize, and rivalled Mr Beman's — |[132] Mr Beman's. Mr David Smith's, Mr Hemming's sheep were of excellent quality. — Mr Bryan's and other bulls merited great commendation. — On the shew-ground I had also much intercourse, with Lord Redesdale, Sir W. Codrington, the Dean of Gloucester, Messrs. Jarratt, Westmacott, Clarke, Polhill, Winter, W. Vavasour, Langston, Barter &c. — Transacted some Justice business at Mr Brookes's office, where I met Mr Morrison, and my son came to assist me, if necessary — he brought a good account from Stanway of his dear wife and children. — About four o clock the principal gentry present, with some of the Clergy, assembled at the Unicorn Inn for dinner, the farmers congregating in the Ballroom, where the repast was to be served, or loitering in groupes round the Inn, attending a sale by auction of the Prize Hunter, bred by Mr T. Cook of Fox Farm, and bought by Sir C W Codrington. — The Marquis of Worcester arrived to preside at the entertainment, coming |[133] from Gopsall Hall, the seat of his Father in law, Lord Howe, in Leicestershire. — Very unpleasant rumours in circulation as to the finances of the Duke of Beaufort. He is going abroad, if not gone, on a very limited income, as it is said, the bulk of his revenues being assigned to the payment of creditors to a great amount. Such a denouement has been long anticipated. Of those who took the high table seats at the Dinner, the Marquis of W. Lord Redesdale, Mr Phillips, of Weston Park, Mr Evans, of Dean, Col. H. Dawkins, Mr Colvile, Col. Colvile, Mr Langstone, Mr Dickins, may be mentioned together myself and my son; other gentlemen & clergymen present were Messrs. Barter, W. Vavasour, Huxtable, Jarratt, Winter, Clarke, Berridge. — The leading farmers of the district, with several professional men and tradesmen, and others made up a party of about 130. — Grace before and after dinner was said by me, and I also responded to the toast of the Bishops and Clergy. — There were present three |[134] professional singers, Messrs. Ransford and two others associated with him, now on a professional tour in the neighbourhood: they performed in a very spirited and pleasing manner, Non nobis Domine, following up the toasts with suitable or unsuitable songs, some serious, some comic, adding much to the pleasure of the evening. I was very pleasantly placed between Col. Dawkins & Col. Colvile, two Waterloo men. The Chairman, Sir C. Codrington, Col. Colvile, Lord Redesdale, Mr Langston, Mr Phillips, Mr Evans, made speeches more or less to the purpose, and Mr Beman, after some sensible agricultural comments, proposed the health of the Rev^d. Mr Huxtable, whose acknowledgment of the compliment was the speech of the Evening. This Gentleman, who married Miss Langston, a good deal his Senior, with her large fortune, is beneficed, I believe, but, at all events, settled near Blandford in Dorsetshire, and has of late years devoted himself to Agriculture & Agricultural Che-|[134] mistry. He has become an oracle by his system of stall feeding, artificial manures, and ingenious arrangements for forcing an extraordinary produce from the soil, economising; and adapting means which may be applied more or less in all farms. Being a man of ready speech and ready wit, clever in expedients, skilful in chemistry, and full of self confidence, he has acquired much celebrity, lectures at the annual meeting of the British agricultural Association, is visited by the Patrons & lovers of Agricultural pursuits, and certainly has obtained great results, though whether it may not have been at a great outlay of money is to himself best known. He has, it is well known, a long purse, and is an agreable talker, and no doubt, a good and successful experimentalist. — After this Gentleman had delivered himself of two speeches, of considerable interest, I retired, accompanied by my son, and, I believe, the rest of the Gentry were not long in following me. — E.F.W. accompanied me home, & passed |[135] the night here. — I did not feel the worse for exposure to the evening air, the cough being today much less troublesome. — The marriage of Maria Witts to Mᵣ Woodroffe was announced to us today by the customary compliment of cards sent by the new couple reaching us by the post. —

Sept. 15. Wednesday.
Fine weather till night fall when it was stormy and rainy. — My Son left us for Stanway after post time. — Received a letter from Sewell, accompanying copies of letters from him to E. Bloxsome Junᵣ and of the reply of the latter. On our part S. had offered for the advowson of Stanton £5500, and for the next presentation £4000, to include fixtures &c. W H Bloxsome positively refuses to part from the advowson, but will sell the next presentation for £4500 provided the fixtures be separately paid for at a valuation, and the next incumbent takes upon himself to do such matters in respect of repairs and alterations of Stanton |[136] Church as are in contemplation and discussion between WHB on the one hand, and the Churchwardens and parishioners on the other. After carefully considering the affair with E.F.W. and with his full concurrence, I replied to Sewell that I was willing to give £4500 for the next presentation inclusive of fixtures &c., but on the understanding that the next incumbent should have nothing to do with any matters in dispute between the present Rector and his Parishioners — should incur no responsibility on that account, nor be liable to any pecuniary obligation. We expressed our willingness that the fixtures should return to the owner of the Advowson at the expiration of my Son's incumbency, as they had been received, as far as is consistent with ordinary wear and tear. If the Bishop should accept the resignation of W.H.B., we would buy on these terms, not making any claim for dilapidations: if our terms were not agreed to, then the treaty at |[137] once to close. — Wrote to Mᵣ Westmacott with information as to J W Harris's milking cows for sale at his auction at Broadwell, on Monday next, Mᵣ W. having desired me yesterday to obtain some information on that point. — Walked with MW. to Eyford; called on Mᵣ & Mʳˢ· Frobisher, but they were from home. — Visited J. Davis, and the daily school. — Rotheram on Establishments.[18] — Bp. Wilberforce's American Church.[19]

---

18. John Rotheram (1725-1789). *An essay on establishments in religion. With remarks on the confessional.* Newcastle upon Tyne: 1767. 8vo.
19. Samuel Wilberforce (1805-1873). Wilberforce was the third son of William Wilberforce. He graduated in 1826, and in 1828 was ordained and appointed curate-in-charge at Checkenden near Henley-on-Thames. In 1841 he was chosen Bampton lecturer, and shortly afterwards made chaplain to Prince Albert, an appointment he owed to the impression produced by a speech at an anti-slavery meeting some months previously. In October 1843 he was appointed by the archbishop of York to be sub-almoner to the Queen. In 1844 appeared his *History of the American Church.* In March of the following year he accepted the deanery of Westminster, and in October the bishopric of Oxford.

Sept. 16. Thursday.

The weather disposed to rain, but not much fell: the wind very high and stormy. — Burke's judgment of Church establishments from his work on the French revolution. — Tax business at home — Drove to Stow. — Attended at the Provident Bank — at the office of the Stow Branch Gloucestershire Banking Company, and at the Workhouse, where I conferred with Pearce on Union matters — At the Prov. Bank met Messrs. Pole, Morrison, Ford and R. Waller — With the two latter adjourned to the |[138] Unicorn, where transacted Tax and Justice business. — Returned home to dress for dinner at Mr Pole's at Wyck Hill, where we ^{were} received at a sumptuous repast. W B Pole was confined to his room owing to a hurt in the leg: M.^{rs.} WBP. was of the party. Miss Rollinson was on a visit to the Poles, having arrived on Tuesday last from Farmington Lodge; she promises to come to us on a visit on Monday next. She appears in good health and spirits; somewhat deaf and not equal to much walking, but not much aged, since we met last. — M.^r & M.^{rs.} R W Hippisley, accompanied by his sister Jane, — M.^r & Mrs. W. Vavasour with Emma — Mr Wynniatt with his son Tom, and his daughters, Susan and Harriet, — Mr Lewes and Mr Clarke, made up the party. — As I drove home from Stow, Mr Vavasour accompanied me in the Carriage as far as to Lower Slaughter Turnpike, discussing with me the pending treaty with Bloxsome. — |[139]

Sept. 17. Friday.

Rainy weather till the afternoon. — Wrote to Revd. E. Hawkins, Secr. S.P.G. with a remittance of the balance in my hand of subscriptions &c. rec.^{d.} from members of the Stow Distr. Comm. — A circular from the Gloucester and Berkeley Canal Company, announcing a meeting of proprietors. — Bp. Ellys on Establishment and Dissent. — Bp. Wilberforce. Hist. of the American Church.

Sept. 18. Saturday.

A showery day. Wrote to C Bathurst. — Wrote to Bowen, directing to him at Wyke House, Brentford, where I suppose him still to be under the medical care of Dr Costello. — With MW. drove to Bourton on the water. Called on the Hunts. Mrs. H. was out; received by Mr H. and Mrs. Angus, Mrs. Hunt's mother: — Left cards at the Misses Hall, who are absent from home. — Mr Turner, on whom I called also absent. — Received a letter from Sewell, who has little doubt that on Tuesday next a |[140] formal agreement will be signed by him on my part, and by M.^r E Bloxsome on the part of his brother for the purchase of the next presentation to the living of Stanton on the terms stipulated in my letter of the 15.th. Inst. — Emma Vavasour rode over to call on us. — Wilberforce's History of the American Church.

Sept. 19. Sunday.

Cold, raw weather, with a shower or two before dark, wind and rain afterwards. — Wrote to E.F.W. as to the purchase of the living of Stanton, and the letter received from Sewell yesterday: invited him, Sophy, and Broome to dine and sleep here on Friday next, to meet Miss Rollinson. — Wrote to Turner, Fishmonger, London, to order a dish of fish for a dinner party on Tuesday. — Visited the Sunday School. — Morning service, prayers: afternoon service, prayers and sermon. I preached on confession of sins, and prayer for others, especially in sickness. M.^r and Mrs. Frobisher called after morning service. —

Received a |[141] letter from a woman at Long Compton, complaining that George Cooper, formerly Police Officer at Bourton and afterwards at Long Compton, having had a child by her, did not contribute to its support; requesting me to speak to him on the subject. He is now an Officer in the County Gaol at Gloucester: I was instrumental in procuring him that situation. — A letter from the Receiver S.P.G. acknowledging the remittance which I made on the 17th. Inst. — Preparing a Sermon — Reading with a view to the question on Establishments to be discussed at the Decanal meeting on Tuesday next. — To the family a section from James on the Collects. ——

Sept. 20. Monday.
Cold weather, with a shower or two. — Wrote to the woman at Long Compton from whom I received a letter yesterday. — Also to Mrs. Keysall, offering the Curacy of Stanway, should my Son vacate it, to Mr Bradford, a respectable Clergyman, who married Mary Keysall, |[142] daughter of my old friend and Curate Charles Keysall. Mr B. lately removed from the Curacy of Castle Eaton, Wilts, in consequence of the death of the Incumbent, and may not have fixed himself permanently in another curacy. — Justice and Poor Law business at home. — Reading with a view to the discussion to come on at the Decanal meeting to-morrow — Received a letter from Mr Thornton on Hunt trust matters, with enclosures from Mr Geo. Hunt, and Messrs. Cox and Williams. — Our good friend Miss Rollinson came from Wyck Hill to pass a few days here.

Sept. 21. Tuesday.
Rain or wetting fog till the evening. — Preparing for the decanal meeting held to-day. — Drove to Stow — Received a letter from H. D. Warter, accompanying the agreement for the purchase of the Ground rents in St George's in the East, to be signed by me: — a letter from Sewell, mentioning that E. Bloxsome had postponed till Thursday the meeting between him & Sewell, |[143] for signing the agreement for the purchase by me of the next presentation to the living of Stanton: — from Mr Braikenridge, by Mr Thornton's desire, a letter written by him to Mr B. on Hunt affairs, to be perused by me, and then returned. To Stow — St. Matthew's day. Attended divine service, performed by R W Hippisley — no sermon — a pretty full congregation, with more of the laity, male and female, than I had expected to see: the choir chanted, and a hymn was sung: I enjoy this sacred music now and then exceedingly. The Holy Communion followed, administered by the Rural dean and R W Hippisley to 26 Communicants, including 14 Clergymen. Revd. Messrs. Ford, Hippisley, Sadler, Wiggin, Biscoe, Williams, W. B. Pole, Hunt, Potter, Clarke, Morrison, Crompton, Hillier, and myself. — The Decanal meeting was held afterwards at the National School room, being attended by the |[144] above named Clergymen, with the exception of Wiggin, who went to Gloucester to join the party assembled at the Deanery, to attend the Music meeting, which begins to-day. — Mr W. B. Pole read a very good paper vindicating church Establishments and the Union between Church and State, and particularly as among us; shewg. the weakness of the objections maintained by the Dissenters. — No one expressed any discrepancy in opinion. — I addressed the meeting on the subject at considerable length; Messrs. Clarke, Hunt, Potter, Hillier and Crompton also spoke. — The Rural Dean and myself afterwards explained to the Clergy present what had passed at the meeting held at the Palace, Gloucester, as to the

establishment of training schools in conjunction with the Bishop of Oxford and his diocesan board of Education. — I returned home before 4 P.M. — Entertained a party at dinner. — M^r and Mrs. R. W. Hippisley, Miss Jane Hippisley, M^r and M^{rs.} R Waller, M^r M^{rs.} and Miss |¹⁴⁵ Morrison and a young lady accompanying them, were our guests: with Miss Rollinson there was a party of twelve; which passed off pleasantly.

Sept. 22. Wednesday.

Fine, mild weather – Returned to Mr H. Warter the agreement for the purchase of ground rents in St. George's, which I signed, and my son witnessed the signature. He rode over to luncheon, and passed two hours with us. All well at the Vicarage, Stanway, except that Sophy has a cold. It will not be in my Son & Daughter's power to come to dinner on Friday, as we wished. — Mr Ford called upon us, as he went to Upper Guiting to visit poor Bowen, who is returned from Wyke House in a better state of health, but is languid, weak, and likely to relapse into a suffering state from accumulation of stone in the bladder — Received a letter from Mr Wilkins on the case of Moses Roff, the poor lunatic, and as to his settlement — Justice business at |¹⁴⁶ home. — MW. and Miss Rollinson took a drive. — A letter soliciting a shilling subscription towards the erection of a Church in Essex.

Sept. 23. Thursday.

A fine day, mild weather — Forwarded a shilling subscription towards the rebuilding of the church at Clacton in Essex. — Drove to Stow. — A letter from Mr Thornton respecting Hunt Trust matters — Whitby's Wharf. — Attended at the Provident Bank, where I met Messrs. Pole, Senr and Junr and W. Vavasour — Rec^{d.} a note on Union business from Mr Morrison. — Attended the fortnightly meeting of the Guardians of our Union, at which I presided from 11 AM. to 3.30 P.M — Mr Vavasour accompanied me part of the way home in my carriage, conversing with me as to the contemplated purchase of the next presentation of the living of Stanton. — Passed a pleasant evening in conversation with MW. & Miss Rollinson.

Sept. 24. Friday.

Fine weather — Justice |¹⁴⁷ business at home; received a note from H Lindow respecting it, to which I replied – Wrote to Mr Braikenridge on Hunt affairs — MW. and Miss Rollinson drove to Salperton, to call on the Brownes, but were not admitted: some of the family were at the Music Meeting; Miss Browne indisposed — Received a letter from Mrs. Keysall, who has forwarded my letter to Mr Bradford; but she supposes him to be so far engaged as to a curacy in Wilts that he will not be able to accept that of Stanway, should my Son vacate it. — Visited parishioners, Davis, Dix, M Davis, P.S. &c. — Transacted business with the Overseer in the Evening.

Sept. 25. Saturday.

Fine weather for the most part; one or two slight showers. — Wrote to Mr Thornton, Mr Hare, and Messrs. Cox and Williams on Hunt Trust business. — Visited the ~~Sund~~ Parish School with Miss Rollinson and MW. — After luncheon our good friend, Miss Rollinson |¹⁴⁸ left us to visit R W Hippisley at the Rectory Stow: I believe we had mutually enjoyed each others Society; Miss R. is a little prejudiced; but well principled, sensible, & well informed

— Received a letter from Sewell; he reports that he has entered into contract on my behalf with M^r E Bloxsome for the purchase of the next presentation of Stanton Rectory: that the terms are satisfactory, being conformable to those to which I had agreed; it is considered advisable that the details should for the present not be divulged to the principals, as secrecy and caution on such occasions are very necessary; M^r S impresses the prudence of not making the transaction generally Known; recommends close reserve; will announce when that reserve is no longer requisite. All, I presume, to be settled as far as relates to vendor and purchaser, but the former must obtain the Bishop's assent to his resignation before the bargain becomes operative; and the Bishop may interpose |^{149} difficulties. — A letter from Mr Bradford expresses regret that he has engaged to take the curacy of Rushall, Wilts, and so cannot accept that of Stanway, should it be vacated. — Bp. Wilberforce's History of the American Church.

Sept. 26. Sunday.

Fine weather — Visited the Sunday school. — Morning service; prayers and sermon. I preached on the Sacrament of the Lord's Supper. — Afternoon service – prayers. – M^r and M$^{rs.}$ Frobisher called after morning service, to take leave; they quit Eyford for Cheltenham on Tuesday next. — Rec$^d.$ a letter from C Bathurst — Cards sent by the post announce the marriage of W$^{m.}$ Howell to Miss Willan. It has been a long engagement, and not very likely to end in prosperity: the lady is the daughter of a man who lived extravagantly, and was in latter years hardly sane. W.H. is eccentric, and alienated from his Father, who does little for him — |^{150} He has recently undertaken the curacy of Tysoe in Warwickshire, where the new married will reside. — MW. received a letter from Emma Witts: there is reason that we should expect a visit from M^r and M$^{rs.}$ J. E. Woodroffe about Oct. 22: the bride and bridegroom are now on a tour in North Devon. — Ecclesiastical Gazette — To the family a section from Dr James on the Collects.

Sept 27. Monday.

Beautiful weather — Preparing a Sermon. — Justice business at home — Preparing for the annual meeting of the Stow Book Society to be held to-morrow. — In my walk met and parleyed with the Hippisleys and Miss Rollinson, who were taking a drive — Received a visit from Sir Charles Imhoff, and his half sister, the Baroness von Klock – Poor Sir C. is heart-whole,[21] but very feeble; yet he has accomplished during the summer a tour up the Rhine into Germany, to visit his family connections, and has |^{151} brought back with him a sexagenarian widowed Baroness, daughter of his father by his second wife, whom in my youth I knew well at Weimar. I believe this lady had not then emerged from the Nursery — her brother and two sisters, whom I knew intimately, were her seniors, and of them Mad. de Helwig, then demoiselle d'honneur, to the Duchess of Weimar, was even in her youth distinguished as a poetess, and possessed of much literary taste and talent. Madame de Klock is a ladylike

---

20. *Sic.*
21. Heart-whole. There are three meanings, 1. unimpaired at the heart; having the spirits or courage unimpaired; undismayed. 2. Having the affections free; with the heart unengaged. 3. Whole-hearted; free from hypocrisy or affectation; sincere, genuine. It is difficult to know which meaning was intended, but probably the last.

person, and has a daughter demoiselle d'honneur to the Reigning Duchess of Weimar: the Baroness has to learn English, but has already profited by the instruction of her relations, Sir C. Imhoff, and Mrs. Winter. — Received from Mr Westmacott a note as to his subscription &c. to the Stow Book Society. — Bp. Wilberforce's History of the American Episcopal Church.

Sept. 28. Tuesday.

Very fine weather. — Preparing for the Stow Book Society meeting — |^{152} Giving directions to Workmen, as to repairs, painting, slating &c. — Justice business at home. — With MW. drove to Stow; she went to call at the Rectory on Mrs. Hippisley and Miss Rollinson, and then returned home — Received a letter from Mr Sewell, who desires me to send him the Mortgage deeds as to the security on which we have advanced £5300 to Mr Lockhart, that when the arrangement as to the living of Stanton is complete, that security may be transferred to M^r W H Bloxsome in payment of the £4500 stipulated, we receiving the balance, £800: – the transaction with M^r WHB not sufficiently matured to allow of its being made public. — A letter from Mr Hare, who demurs as to laying the case respecting the Wharf prepared by Messrs. Cox and Williams before Mr Braikenridge, as Mr Geo. Hunt's Sol^r: he considers that the Trustees ought first to see it: — however I also received a letter from Messrs. Cox and Williams, by which it appears that they have |^{153} already forwarded the case to Mr Braikenridge — Engaged with Mr Ford and Mr Pain in auditing the accounts of the Stow Book Society, and Stow District Committee of the the the Society for Promoting Christian Knowledge — Afterwards the annual meeting of the Distr. Comm. S.P.C.K was held at the Unicorn Inn, when Mr Ford, as Treasurer and Secretary, made the customary report. The Dean of Gloucester presided: others present were Messrs. Wiggin, Pantin, Hippisley, Morrison, and myself. It is a bad sign of the clerical feeling and spiritual zeal of the Clergy of the district, that this anniversary is so lightly esteemed; it shews sad indifference and laxity; there may be a lack of energy in the Treasurer and Secretary; a love of old, cold ways; but the carelessness and apathy are very censurable in all who stay away. — Accompanied my son, who had come from Stanway to attend the annual Book Society dinner, to "the Cottage," where |^{154} I found Sophy, whom he had driven up to dine with her parents, and would drive home in the evening. They gave a good report of their dear children. A brief parley as to Stanton living. — The annual dinner of the members of the Book Society followed; here was no coldness, no indifference, no backwardness to attend; it was a secular engagement, and, therefore, shunned by none. L^t. Col. Dawkins of Over Norton presided, and with spirit, obliging and complimentary. — Mr Pole, Mr Rawlinson, E.F.W., Mr Lockwood, Mr Wiggin, Mr E. Rudge, (Mr Pole's Grandson,) Mr Ford, Mr Hippisley, Mr Hutchinson, Mr Winter, Mr Morrison, Mr Malcolm and myself made up the party. Mr Ford was reappointed Treasurer, as I was Secretary. Lord Saye and Sele nominated as Chairman for the next meeting. — I got home by 8 P.M. — Rec^d. a note from Mr Pearce with the Valuations of the parishes |^{155} of Upper Slaughter and Icomb.

Sept. 29. Wednesday.

Beautiful weather — Giving directions to workmen. — Visiting Mich^l. Cook, who is ill, and has received a wound from a pitch fork in his labour: also called on Mrs. Collett. — Examining papers as to the closing of the treaty for the purchase of Stanley Hill's property at Great

Risington. It has transpired that the Solicitor for the sale has expressed to Messrs. Wilkins & Kendal, that he considers the negociation with us as still pending. Whatever Mr Clarke may think, I believed the business closed, relying on the assurance of Mr H. D. Warter to that effect. — Wrote to Mr Sewell, and sent to him at Lower Swell the Mortgage deeds which we hold as our Security for £5300 lent to Mr Lockhart. These are to be transfered to Mr W. H. Bloxsome in payment of the sum agreed upon for the grant of the next presentation of the living of Stanton, £4500, we receiving back £800 from W.H.B. |^156 — Wrote to Messrs. Hoare, directing them to transfer £47. 15. 0 from my account with them to the account of E.F.W. — Rec^d. a letter from M^rs. Barr, written under a deep feeling of bereavement, with a tone of earnest piety. She proposes to fix her residence near Worcester, when she can meet with a suitable house, for the present she means to make Malvern Wells her temporary abode, after having visited Leeds, and settled her affairs there: she writes from Henwick Hall, where she is staying with the Barrs, and M^rs. Walker. — M^rs. R. Waller and M^rs. Aitkens called: M^r and M^rs. A. are on a visit to the Wallers at Bourton, M^rs. A in indifferent health. — Wilberforce's Hist. of the American Episcopal Church.

Sept. 30. Thursday.

Fine autumnal weather — Preparing papers for business at Stow — Visited Michael Cook. — Drove to Stow. — Rec^d. a letter from Mr Thornton on the business of the Red Lion Wharf. — Transacted |^157 business at the Provident Bank. — To the Workhouse, where engaged in auditing bills — M^r and M^rs. Aitkens and M^rs. Waller met me there by appointment. I had long ago promised to shew M^rs. R.W. over the establishment, which she had a curiosity to inspect. Went over all the wards, schoolrooms, store rooms &c. — At the Justice room sat with Messrs. Ford and R. Waller as Magistrates, Mr Pole being present for a short time — Mr Aitkens and Mr Winter also attended; there was a good deal of business — Had an interview with Mr Kendall, who informed ^me that Mr Clark, of Shipston on Stour, had stated to him and Mr Wilkins by letter that he considered the negociation for the purchase of Stanley Hill's property at Great Risington, as still pending between the Vendors & our Trustees under the private Act of Parliament. I shewed Mr Kendall my correspondence with Mr H. Warter to disprove that assertion. It seemed that we |^158 ought to have insisted on a formal release. — Drove home to dress for dinner at the W. Vavasours at Maugersbury House. MW. accompanied me in the Chariot: a pleasant party: met besides W.V. his wife & Emma, Mr Franks, who is on a visit to the Vavasours, M^r and M^rs. Wiggin, the Dean of Gloucester, Miss Penyston and a friend of hers, — Miss Sterling, T. Wynniatt, with his sisters Susan and Anne, and Mr Clarke.

Oct. 1. Friday.

A drizzling morning; fine & dry weather afterwards. — Justice business at home — Wrote to Mr Warter to acquaint him that Mr Clarke considers the negociation for the purchase on our part of the Great Risington property as still subsisting; asked for an explanation on that point; as I had, on HDW's assurance, viewed the matter as long since closed. — Called on the Ryans and on Mich^l. Cook. — Superintending workmen employed on my premises, painters, glaziers, plaisterers &c. — Rec^d. from |^159 Messrs. Hoare a letter to announce that they had transferred £47. 15. 0. from my account with them to that of my son. — Wilberforce's History of the American Church.

Oct. 2. Saturday.

Dull, but dry weather. — Superintending workmen. — Walked to Bourton on the Water to consult with Mr Kendal as to proceedings to be taken against Henry Collett, son of J. B. Collett, of this parish, a very turbulent, ill-conditioned young man, who had attempted pound breach yesterday morning, when George Lea, by order of his Father, as Road Surveyor, had impounded a cow belonging to Farmer Price, and a horse the property of R. Humphris, which were found straying on the village green. This had been done in pursuance of counsel's opinion given when we submitted a case to the right of turning out cattle, pigs &c. in the Village Street. The practice, discontinued when notice was given that proceedings would be taken against parties offending, had been |^{160} of late partially revived, and among the lower orders, and some who should know better, an angry feeling had been excited, with a mistaken opinion that rights were infringed. H.C. not only obstructed G.L. in the execution of his Father's directions, but used very vulgar and insulting language, and challenged his cousin (G.L.) to fight. I arranged, in the absence of R Waller, but with M^r RW's acquiescence, that a Petty Sessions should be held at Mr Kendal's office on Tuesday next, when the case should be heard by Mr Ford, and Mr Waller. To the former I wrote, informing him of the proposed meeting. R. Waller, with Mr Aitkens and Mr Stenson, were gone to Westwell to shoot. — I took luncheon with Mrs Waller and Mrs Aitkens — Transacted Prov. Bank business with Mr Hartwell at Bourton. — Called on Edwd Lea to inform him what I had arranged for Tuesday next at Bourton. — Rec^d a letter from Mr Sewell who expresses his regret that the treaty between |^{161} us and the Bloxsomes has become so public, as he considers secrecy in such transactions very essential to their successful issue, but he trusts all the will be satisfactorily concluded in a few days. — In another letter Sewell writes that a gentleman not far from Cirencester wants £1000 for six months, on his note with the deposit of title deeds of property worth £2000; interest to be at 5 P^r C^t. — S. proposes to use to this purpose the £800 coming from W H Bloxsome, and that I should make up the sum by £200 from my own resources — A circular from the Bishop of Tasmania soliciting subscriptions for Church & Missionary purposes in his diocese. MW. received a letter from Jane Lonsdale: her nephew, Thomas Cooper, died lately of consumption. — Bp. Wilberforce's American Episcopal Church. —

Oct. 3. Sunday.

Fine weather, but a dull day — Wrote to Mr Sewell that I had no objection to the employment of £1000 for a time in |^{162} the way proposed by him in his letter received yesterday: — to Messrs Hoare, directing them to pay on my account £200 to be placed to the account of Messrs Sewell and Newmarch with the Gloucestershire Banking Company at Cirencester: — to Messrs Alcocks, Birbecks and C^o desiring them to instruct Messrs Barnard, Dimsdale and C^o to pay on my acc^t £200 to my account with Messrs Hoare. — Visited the Sunday School. — Morning Service — Prayers and the Communion: 20 Communicants. — Evening service, Prayers and a Sermon. I preached on Behaviour at Church. — Received a letter from Sophia Hunt, dated Clifton, giving a very alarming account of the health of her sister Caroline: the Medical attendants speak very doubtfully of the issue, in fact, give little hope of recovery: dropsical symptoms increase rapidly, strength is wasting: there is an idea of her being removed to the sea, to Teignmouth, but this seems hardly practicable: probably, |^{163}

her life may not be long protracted: — a letter from a Clerk in Mr Warter's office: Mr W. is in Shropshire: the Clerk does not suppose there is ground for uneasiness as to the contract for the purchase of the Risington Estate being insisted upon by the vendors. — Preparing a Sermon — Ecclesiastical Gazette. —

Oct. 4. Monday.

Fine weather, but a dull day. — Wrote to Rodwell for a supply of books for the Stow Book Society. — To Mr Thornton, in reply to his letter rec^d. on the 30th. Ult.: returned to him the enclosure from Mr Hare which he had forwarded to me; sent him a letter lately received by me from Mr Hare; apprized M^r ~~Hare~~ Th. of the bad state of Caroline Hunt's health. — Justice business at home. — Preparing a Sermon. — Mr Ford called at the door on his way to visit Bowen, who continues in the same weak state as for some time past. — Received a letter |^164 from Mr H. D. Warter from Cruck Meole; he will, on returning to Town within these few days, write to Mr Clark as to the contract made for the purchase of the Great Risington Estate, which he supposes to be still operative. Mr W. considers that we have long ago notified to the different parties our abandonment of it. Mr W. sends a good account of the health of my cousin John Witts and his wife; but M^r and M^rs. Warter are great invalids. — Visited E Lea (as to the Justice business to be transacted at Bourton to-morrow,) Davis, M. Cook &c. — History of the American Episcopal Church.

Oct. 5. Tuesday.

Fine weather. — Wrote to my Son, forwarding several letters for his perusal, and proposing that we should visit him and Sophy from Monday till Thursday in next week. Sent this letter to meet E.F.W. at Stow, where he is expected to-day at the annual Cricket dinner — |^165 Wrote to Mr H. D. Warter, cautioning him, when he writes to Mr Clark about the Great Risington Estate, not to mention Lord Dynevor or the Dean of Gloucester as contemplating the purchase of it — Walked to Bourton to meet Messrs. Ford and Waller at Mr Kendall's office to hear the complaint of George Lea against Henry Collett, for attempting to rescue the cattle impounded at U Slaughter, challenging him to fight, and other blackguard and turbulent conduct. I sat as Amicus Curiæ, not as Magistrate. H.C. was fined £2. to cover costs, and bound in his own recognizance in £10. for six months to keep the peace towards G.L. — Saw M^rs. Waller and M^rs. Aitkens at the Rectory, but declined remaining there to luncheon. R Waller, who was driving Messrs. Turner and Stenson to Stow to join the Cricket party, conveyed me as far as to Lower Slaughter Turn- |^166 pike gate on my way home. — Rec^d. a letter from Messrs. Hoare, announcing that they have paid £200 on my account to the account of Messrs. Sewell and Newmarch with the Gloucestershire Banking Company at Cirencester. — E.F.W. sent his servant from Stow with a note, to inform me that he had had an interview with M^r W H Bloxsome, who is eager to make arrangements for leaving Stanton, and for the sale of his furniture there. He wished to know my Son's views as to coming to reside at Stanton. My son had replied to him that such arrangements seemed to him premature, as the Bishop had not yet accepted the resignation tendered by WHB. — but that, if it could be accomplished, he should prefer getting into the Rectory at Stanton as early as might be convenient to all parties — I wrote in reply to my Son's note, cautioning him not to say or do anything as a party concerned until the resignation had been |[167] accepted; perhaps not until he had been instituted to the living. — Wilberforce's History of the American Episcopal Church.

Oct. 6. Wednesday.

A rainy day; stormy and windy in the Evening. — Preparing a Sermon — Justice business at home — Received a letter from M[r] Sewell: M[r] E. Bloxsome has not yet announced to him that the Bishop has accepted the resignation of the living of Stanton. M[r] N. Marling is the party to whom the temporary advance of £1000 is to be made: he is a clothier near Stroud — A letter from M[r] G. F. Newmarch, who writes to enquire whether M[r] Polson is still looking out for a living to purchase: some years since M[r] P. applied to N. on that subject, having met him with me: S. & N. now know of preferment on sale. — Bp. Wilberforce's History of the Episcopal Church in the United States of N. America.

Oct. 7. Thursday.

A rainy forenoon: the |[168] afternoon and evening fine. — Wrote to M[r] Polson, enclosing to him the letter I received from G. F. Newmarch yesterday. — Preparing for the business at Stow to-day. — Looking over the Acts of the last Session of Parliament. — Drove to Stow. — Received a notification of a meeting of the Visitors of Gloucester Lunatic Asylum to be held on the 16th Inst. — Presided at the fortnightly meeting of the Guardians of the Union. M[r] Ass[t] Comm[r] Graves attended. Detained there for nearly four hours. — Transacted business at the Provident Bank, and at M[r] Brooke's office — On my return home, met and held a parley with M[r] William Pole. — Bp. Wilberforce's History of the American Protestant Episcopal Church.

Oct. 8. Friday.

Fine weather, but for two or three transient showers. — Wrote to M[r] Bloxsome requesting him to send me his bill on the County for examination and audit — Preparing a Sermon. — Justice business at home. |[169] Received a letter from M[r] Hare on Hunt Trust matters: he incloses a letter he has received from Mess[rs] Cox and Williams as to the Red Lion Wharf, and a letter which he proposes to send to Mess[rs] Williams, Deacon & C[o] as to the payments to be made henceforth to Miss M. Hunt. — MW. received a letter from Eliza Daniell: M[rs] C. Barr is now at Leeds, winding up her matters there: she purposes to pass the winter with M[rs] Walker and the Barrs at Henwick Hall — Bp. Wilberforce's History of the Protestant Episcopal Church in America.

Oct. 9. Saturday.

A moist morning; rain in the forenoon, a damp air throughout the day. — Wrote to M[r] Thornton, M[r] Hare and Sophia Hunt on Hunt trust matters. Received a packet from M[r] Thornton, containing a letter from him to me, letters from M[r] George Hunt to M[r] T. for my perusal, and the copy of a letter from M[r] Thornton to M[r] Hunt. As to the proceedings of the Trustees, |[170] particularly M[r] Hare, as to Mess[rs] Cox & Williams, as to the affair of the Red Lion Wharf especially, M[r] George Hunt manifests a lamentable wrong-headedness, is impetuous, overbearing, dictating, and deluded: he seems unmanageable, and cannot view things calmly; one fears over excitement. — A letter from M[r] Sewell: it seems that M[r]

W. H. Bloxsome has executed in my favour a grant of the next presentation to the living of Stanton; but the Bishop has not yet accepted his resignation. — A letter from Mʳ H. D. Warter with a copy of a letter he has written to Mʳ Clarke, the Attorney for the vendors of the Great Risington Estate, purporting that we have long since abandoned the purchase. — A letter from Messʳˢ· Hoare, announcing that Messʳˢ· Alcock, Birkbecks & Cº· have paid to my account with them £200. — Finished Bp. Wilberforce's very interesting history of the Protestant Episcopal Church in the United States of America. |¹⁷¹

Oct. 10. Sunday.

A very rainy day — Morning service and sermon. I preached on the man healed of the palsy. Afternoon service, prayers. MW. received a letter from Sophia Hunt, from Clifton with a very indifferent account of the health of her sister Caroline. — Ecclesiastical Gazette — To the family a section from Dʳ James on the Collects.

Oct. 11. Monday.

A very fine, mild day — Wrote a note to Mʳ Pearce, and received a reply to the effect that Mʳ Assᵗ· Commʳ Graves had expressed himself satisfied with all he saw at the Workhouse on Thursday last; that he had found no fault with the management. Mʳ P sent for my consideration different papers from the Poor Law Commissioners, correspondence &c. — Superintending workmen. — Transacting business with the Churchwarden. — Recᵈ· a letter from my Son, which should have arrived a day or two ago, expressing that he & Sophy anticipate a visit |¹⁷² from MW. and myself to-day with much pleasure. — A letter from Mʳˢ· Woodroffe, who with her husband, after a tour during the honeymoon in North Devon &c. is now on a visit to her relations, Mʳ and Mʳˢ· Ruddle, at Walton House near Tewkesbury; Mʳ and Mʳˢ· W. propose visiting us about the 21ˢᵗ· or 22ᵈ· Inst. I replied that we should have much pleasure in receiving them after my return from Gloucester Sessions on the 22ᵈ· Inst. — Left home for Stanway before 1 P.M. in our phaeton with post horses, our own horses being unwell. — Called at Temple Guiting on poor Mʳ Bowen, who returned some time back from Wyke House, near Brentford, where he has been under the care of Dʳ Costello, a celebrated operator in calculous diseases: B is now comparatively easy, though still suffering, and purposes another visit to Wyke House, that he may be subjected to further discipline. He is much reduced in strength, and aged in appearance; but still clings to the hope of complete recovery, and |¹⁷³ though verging on fourscore, does not resign himself to the prospect of approaching death as one could wish. It is natural to long for life, and to hope against hope, but one wᵈ· like to see in an aged Minister a greater readiness to depart. — We reached Stanway at half past three P.M. and were affectionately received by our children and grandchildren. — I took a walk with E.F.W. and Sophy — Our conversation then and in the evening naturally turned much on the prospect of a removal to Stanton.

Oct. 12. Tuesday.

Beautiful weather: very mild and spring like; Treacherous, though delightful. I sat in a draught, and caught a bad cold, of which I became sensible almost at the moment when the mischief was done — Wrote a letter to Mʳ Thornton on Hunt Trust matters, and returned to him the letters, which he had sent for my perusal. — E.F.W. having written to Mʳˢ·

W. H. Bloxsome to request permission to bring his |[174] mother and me to see the Rectory at Stanton, if her husband's health would permit, an answer was given in the affirmative, and we drove thither in the afternoon. Mr W.H.B. received us politely and cordially; looked very ill, wearing a black skull cap, with scars on one cheek, excited, insisting on accompanying us all over the house, and grounds, and church; M^rs. Bloxsome near her confinement, a pleasant, active person. M^r W H B. very desirous to remove from Stanton to Nibley, where they have a house, and propose to reside, has made arrangements for a sale of his effects at Stanton in the very beginning of November. He mentioned having received a letter from the Bishop couched in kind terms. His Lordship cautions him not to be hasty in resigning his preferment: trusts that he is not so dangerously ill as he apprehends; hopes he may recover; suggests that he had better not personally confer with him on the subject, but delegate some friend to apply to him, or |[175] through his secretary, Mr Holt. Mr W.H.B. considers this letter favourable to his retirement from the living, only for propriety sake his Lordship suggests delay and consideration. It certainly no where appears in it that the Bishop will accept the resignation. Mr W.H.B.'s precipitancy in announcing and arranging the sale of his furniture seems to me very ill judged; he should have waited for the Bishop's consent to his resignation. It will be advisable that my son should take some part of the furniture at a valuation; principally what is made up to fit the rooms, carpets, curtains, book-cases &c. but these articles should be taken subject to his being eventually Rector of Stanton — The Rectory ^House is spacious & very commodious; very well built, somewhat in the Tudor style, under the incumbency of Mr Wynniatt, and shortly before he sold the advowson to Mr W.H.B: the latter has also added some rooms, a lodge, and out offices, and |[176] much increased and improved the accommodation. There are a good entrance hall, hall and staircase, study and library, dining and drawing rooms: several very good bedrooms and dressing rooms, and excellent offices. The Rectory stands in a moderately sized garden with a small field adjoining, and sufficient kitchen garden, quite detached from the village, but adjacent to the Church and Church Yard; without distant view, or indeed, any view except into the small pleasure ground; some fine timber is seen encircling the premises, but only one large tree, an elm, on the Rectory land. The Church is ancient, with a beautifully tapering spire: at present in a transition state, for Mr W.H.B. has, at his own expence, done much and well towards rearranging the interior, with open sittings; but he has given great offence to his parishioners by taking down, without the consent of the Parish, a singing gallery, and using up the materials, as they say, to mean purposes of |[177] his own. Hence an appeal to the Bishop: and the matter referred to the Rural Dean. His unauthorized interference as to the gallery has given great offence, and it is insisted that he restore it, or make such additions to the accommodation as shall satisfy the parish, or abide the consequences of proceedings in the Ecclesiastical Courts. At present it is in contemplation to build a North Aisle, where anciently there was one, and so compensate for the loss of the Gallery sittings; but "pendent opera interrupta" — there is much good work in open sittings, and much incongruous, and in bad taste and worse repair, in pews, pulpit, reading desk, decayed open sittings &c. — With a considerable outlay, and under judicious superintendence, the Church might be restored to vie in correctness and elegance with the most well appointed Village Churches; but at present the prospect is not very encouraging, and the good and new contrasts unpleasantly with the bad |[178] worn out parts. — Mʳ W.H.B. has made himself unpopular — a hasty temperament, seclusion of himself from his parishioners, a proud manner, and a disinclination to visit the lower sort at their homes, want of affability, and kindness, and an obliging demeanour, have militated against his usefulness, respectability and comfort. — We returned to Stanway by Berry Wormington, meeting dear Sophy and Broome on his poney. S. got into the carriage, and her dear boy cantered by or before us, as we returned to Wood Stanway. —

Oct. 13. Wednesday.

Fine, mild weather, but not as warm as yesterday. — Held a sort of family council, and came to a definite arrangement as to my Son's future income and position, in the event of his becoming Rector of Stanton. — Walked with Edwᵈ· and Sophy to Church Stanway, and over the hill home: very enjoyable, except as I was suffering from the severe cough and cold caught yesterday. — Enjoying the Society |¹⁷⁹ of my dear and promising grandchildren. Broome makes good progress in learning.

Oct. 14. Thursday.

A cold, raw day. — After breakfast left our dear children, and proceeded in our phaeton with post horses to Stow, where the usual public business of the day awaited me. — At Stow, as we arrived met Emma Vavasour on horseback, on the way to call at the Vicarage, Stanway. — MW. proceeded homewards. — I went to the Provident Bank, and to the office of the Gloucestershire Banking Company. — At the former place met Mʳ Hurd, who accompanied me to the Workhouse, where met Mʳ Perkins, and transacted Union business with the latter and Mʳ Pearce — Returned to the Provident Bank, where met Messʳˢ· Pole, Winter, Morrison, Lewis & Waller — Conferred with Mʳ Pole as to the assuring £2000 on my Son's life in the event of his becoming Rector of Stanton. |¹⁸⁰ This is a necessary part of the negotiation for the purchase of the next presentation, to provide, in the event of my Son's early decease, that something approaching to one half of the purchase money may be recovered to our family. — Conferred with Mʳ Wilkins as to the sale of my Son's two cottages at Bourton on the Water, in the event of his being instituted to the living of Stanton: he will then need them no longer as a qualification for a vote for the Eastern division of Gloucestershire; and their value will be very useful to him in the purchase of furniture. — Conferred also with Mʳ Wilkins as to the position in which I am placed with respect to the Estate of Great Risington late Stanley Hill's. — There was much business in the Justice Room: I sat as Magistrate with Messʳˢ· Ford and Waller. Messʳˢ· Polhill, W. Vavasour, and Turner, and two gentlemen, friends of Mʳ Turner, |¹⁸¹ were present. — My open carriage was ready to take me home to dinner after the business was over. — I received letters form Mʳ Bloxsome and his son Edward: the former reminding me that his bill on the County is sent half yearly, not at the Michˢ· but at the Epiphany Sessions; the latter forwarded a copy of the Bishop's letter to W.H.B. in answer to the one he had written to announce his intention to resign his living; it answered to the account given to me by Mʳ W.H.B. as to its contents, on Tuesday last. Mʳ E.B. flatters himself that before we meet at the Quarter Sessⁿˢ· next week he shall have had interviews with Mʳ Holt, and the Bishop: that the resignation will have been tendered and accepted, and the business all but settled — Received letters from the office of the Clerk of the Peace to apprize me that the County rate Committee and Prison

Committee will meet at the Shire Hall, Gloucester, on |[182] the 18th. Inst: — A letter from Mr Thornton, who returns to me a letter from Mr Hare, which I had forwarded for his perusal. — Very heavily oppressed with a cold and a cough.

Oct. 15. Friday.

A dull, cold day with showers. — Justice business at home. — Arranging my papers on my return from Stanway. — With MW. drove to Wyck Hill House: called on Mr and Mrs. Pole, whom we found at home; also Lt. Col. Pole and his lady. He is one of Mr Pole's younger Sons, and has lately returned with his regiment from foreign service: having been stationed for many years in New South Wales and India. His marriage to the daughter of an Officer in the army took place in India: his regiment is now quartered at Chatham, whither he soon returns. Lt. Col. P. has enjoyed good health, & in an unfavourable climate has risen rapidly in his profession. — Suffering much from cough. — The Crescent and the Cross.

Oct. 16. Saturday.

A dull morning, but the |[183] day fine. — Wrote to Cotterell and Rich Chandlers, Kensington, with a remittance, and an order for candles. — Preparing for the Quarter Sessions next week, arranging my papers &c. — Justice business at home. — M.W. received a letter from the Clerk of the Gloucester and Berkeley canal, announcing a dividend payable on our shares in that concern. — Recd. a letter from Mr Winter respecting Neckar wine procured for Mr Bathurst. — Much indisposed with a cough. — "The Crescent and the Cross."

Oct. 17. Sunday.

Beautiful mild weather — Wrote to C Bathurst, sending to him the letter I received from Winter yesterday, announcing the arrival and delivery of the Neckar wine; — to Winter that I had communicated with C.B. and expected shortly to remit to him the money for the wine supplied to him. — Attended the Sunday School. — This was the Sunday appointed for a thanksgiving to Almighty |[184] GOD for the great national blessing of an abundant harvest. A very suitable form of prayer had been prepared. Morning Service prayers; evening service prayers with a Sermon. I preached on "Universal thanksgiving the duty of Christians," with a special application to existing circumstances, as required in the Queen's letter lately circulated, calling for a collection in aid of the distressed population in the Southern & Western parts of Ireland, and on the North Western coasts of Scotland. It is but too true that there is likely to be this winter also a great deficiency of food in those quarters, with great want. But this appeal for renewed charity to the Irish has been generally met with not only great coldness, but with strong disapprobation in some quarters, and a decided disinclination to liberal assistance. It is urged that an enormous fund has been already raised and remitted to Ireland for charitable succour in this year: that the nation has been |[185] heavily burdened by the advance of many millions to stay the evil in Ireland, with little prospect of repayment of much of the amount; that the people are incorrigibly idle and lazy, crying evermore, give, give: that there is a lack of energy in tillg. the soil, opening up fisheries &c.; that the agitators lay and clerical, clamouring for repeal and abusing the Saxon, relax not in their violent opposition to the government; that disorganization is rapidly spreading, agrarian disturbances, combination not to pay rents, and other disorders on the increase; that a secret conspiracy seems to exist, manifested by ruthless murders of persons of all classes, and many most worthy characters, even when going about doing good in their districts. Hence John Bull is resolved to shut up his purse, and keep his money at home, so that instead of the noble contributions of last spring, a very |[186] scanty supply may be expected as the result of the appeal made to-day by the Clergy in obedience to the Queen's letter. Our collection was £1. 15. 10 – in February last we received between £5 & £6. — Received a letter from Mrs. Woodroffe, who with her husband is now staying at Cheltenham: they promise to come to us on a visit on the 22d. Inst. — Busy in preparing for a Journey to Gloucester to-morrow. — To the family a Section from Dr James on the Collects — I continue to be oppressed by a heavy cough and cold.

Oct. 18. Monday.

A foggy morning, a damp, dull day. — After an early breakfast, left home in our open carriage with MW. for Cheltenham, where she proposed passing some hours, and returning in the afternoon. — I proceeded by the Railway to Gloucester, travelling in the same coach with Mr Barnett, the Coroner. — To the Bell Hotel, where took up my |[187] quarters in my usual apartment. — There had a conference with the County Chairman, Mr Surman, and Mr Riddiford — Thence to the Shire Hall, where I engaged as usual with other members of the Committee of Accounts, in auditing bills &c. There were also two other Committee Meetings — a meeting of the Prison Committee, and a meeting of the County rate Committee — Much business was transacted. The Magistrates present were [Purnell,] C Hayward, Lysons, Goodrich, Sir M. B. Crawley, Gambier Parry, Dr Timbrill, and some others, including C Bathurst, who being kept out of his house at Lidney Park by repairs going on there, is, with Mrs. Bathurst, staying in Gloucester, in a small lodging in the Westgate Street. The officials with whom I was in contact to-day were Bloxsome, Lefroy, Keiley, Riddiford, Wilton, Whiteheart, |[188] Fulljames &c. — Conferred with George Cooper, one of the Prison Officers as to an allowance to be made by him to an illegitimate child of his at Long Compton, the Mother having solicited my interference to procure some assistance from him towards the support of the child — The usual dinner party at the Bell was attended by Purnell, C. Hayward, Timbrill, Lysons, Gambier Parry, and myself. — At nine o oclock resumed our work of auditing accounts, being assisted by Riddiford: the others withdrew, by ten o cl. but Mr Purnell and I were busy till midnight. — I received by the Hereford Mail a bulky packet from Mr Thornton. It contained the case for the Wadenhoe Trustees prepared by Cox & Williams to be laid before Counsel, with pencil notes on the margin by Mr Braikenridge and George Hunt; also a letter from Mr Thornton to myself; a letter from George Hunt to Mr Thornton — The copy |[189] of a letter from Mr Braikenridge to Messrs. Cox and Williams, with a letter from the latter to Mr Thornton. — My cough still very troublesome, but not so trying as it has been. —

Oct. 19. Tuesday.

Rainy weather till the Evening. — Engaged in the audit of the accounts, and in preparations for the business of the Quarter Sessions before breakfast — Breakfasted with Purnell, and accompanied him to Court. — The usual average attendance of Magistrates; among them the Lord Lieutenant and his recreant brother, Grantley Berkeley: they glowred at each other, but there was no hostile outbreak: neither of them addressed the Court on any subject, though it was understood that Grantley came intending to make some comments on the assignment of the districts to the Coroners, as injudicious, leading to expence, and delay; so meaning to please the Foresters, who complain without much |[190] cause — There does not appear to be any relaxation of the feud raging in the house of Berkeley. The Peer cannot comprehend that his influence in the County is lessened by his immoralities, and bitter animosity against some of his own family: he cannot stomach the rejection of his brother, Craven Berkeley, by the Electors of Cheltenham, and of his Cousin and Nominee, Grenville Berkeley, by the Electors of the Western division; he cannot brook the election of his brother Grantley Berkeley, by a combination of Conservatives, acting out of opposition to Lord Fitzhardinge, with the radicals who have rebelled against his Lordship's dictation; and he meditates the ejection both of the new member for Cheltenham, Sir Willoughby Jones, and of Grantley by petition to the House of Commons against those returns; in the meantime the family feud continues unabated; the language of Grantley's letters, as far as the Newspapers will print them, and the tone of his speeches, |[191] continues to be fierce, insulting, exaggerated. Thus two profligate brothers expose and fight against themselves and each other; and the unnatural war serves to exhibit the truth of that text — "be sure your sin will find you out." — Sir W Codrington and Rob[t.] Hale attended — As Chairman of the Committee of accounts I brought forward and conducted the ordinary financial business of the County. — As a Clerical member of the Board of Visitors of the Gaol it fell to my lot to make some comments on a rather delicate topic, the intercourse of Chaplains of Gaols with Prisoners, with respect to the discovery of offences committed by them or others. It appeared from the Chaplain's Journal that he had been in correspondence with a lady at Cheltenham in whose house a burglary had been committed, and plate stolen. Two lads had been apprehended, tried, and sentenced for the offence; one of them was |[192] remaining in the Gaol as a convict, awaiting his removal under sentence of transportation to Millbank Prison. The lady had not an unreasonable curiosity to know more about this burglary, perhaps, hoping to trace and recover her plate, perhaps to find out whether her servants were implicated: she writes to the Ass[t.] Chaplain, begging him to discover from the Prisoner more particulars as to the robbery: he replies that the Prisoners under his charge are the untried: that the Prisoner in question has passed under the superintendence of the Chaplain, to whom he refers the lady: the Chaplain listens to her request; urges the prisoner to confess; repeatedly presses for information: the prisoner has no more to tell, or will not tell more; the Chaplain makes entries in his journal to this effect; and that he had written to the lady to name that his endeavours to procure the information sought are unsuccessful. The impropriety of this course was strongly felt |[193] by the members of the Visiting Board under whose notice it was brought yesterday, and I was deputed to bring the subject forward, as the Chairman, being brother to the Chaplain, would perhaps, incur the charge of personal ill-will towards him, it being known that they are not on good terms. – I began by reading the entries in the Journal, and admitting that the task I had to perform was a delicate one; because I entirely felt that no one ought to intrude between the Minister and the Prisoner, as to the spiritual intercourse which passed between them; that the duty of the Chaplain clearly was to inculcate the duties of restitution and confession; that it would often and perhaps generally be incumbent on him to addess the Prisoner personally, to press his own guilt upon him, not to content himself with vague and general admonition, but to say |[194] with Nathan, thou art the man: but then the intercourse of the Chaplain with the prisoner should have spiritual ends solely in view, not secular ends. I admitted that the wish of the Lady was natural, though she had erred in making application to the Chaplains; but that the Chaplain ought to have declined to be the medium for obtaining the information sought. I touched lightly on the duty of the Chaplain in the case of a confession being made to him; there would be a question as to revealing what he heard, and the fitness of so doing would mainly depend on the peculiar circumstances of each case; but generally, I thought, the Chaplain would feel it right not to reveal the matter confided to him. By acting as Mᵣ R J Cooper had done, he lowered his position, having entered on the province of the Police-man, and he ran great risk of losing the attachment, respect and confidence of the Prisoners, withᵗ· which his services would be of little benefit. |¹⁹⁵ I expressed my persuasion that the Chaplain had erred through inconsideration, and concluded by moving a resolution that it be an instruction to the Chaplain from the Court that in his intercourse with the Prisoners under his charge, he should confine himself to their spiritual interests, and not seek any secular ends in his communications with them. — C Bathurst, who had not been prepared, nor heard of the matter till I rose, followed me by a warm approbation of all I had spoken; urging like views as grounded on his own former experience as Chairman, and wondering that Mᵣ R. J. Cooper should have made an entry in his Journal so condemnatory of himself. — Archd. Timbrill formally seconded my motion. — The County Chairman fully concurred, explaining the duties of the Chaplain as defined by law & in the Prison Rules. My motion passed by |¹⁹⁶ unanimous assent, and several magistrates afterwards expressed to me their full satisfaction with the matter & manner of my speech. — Nothing more occurred requiring particular notice. — E.F.W. arrived to attend the Sessions, bringing a good account of his dear wife and children — From Edwᵈ· Bloxsome I learnt that he had seen the Bishop's secretary, Holt, and had confided to him that the next presentation to the living of Stanton had been bought by me for my son; Holt, as E.B. considered, had no doubt that all will be satisfactorily concluded in a few days. The Bishop is engaged to-day in the consecration of a new church at Kemerton; and a like consecration is to be performed at Fretherne on Thursday next. On the latter occasion the resignation of Mᵣ W. H. Bloxsome will, probably, be formally presented to his Lordship. — Eighteen Magistrates dined together |¹⁹⁷ at the Bell — a pleasant party — Sir W. Codrington, the two Hales, Archd. Onslow and his son, Archd. Timbrill, E.F.W. &c. were of the party. — At nine o clock I went to pass an hour with Mᵣ and Mʳˢ· Bathurst at their lodgings, taking tea with them, and before retiring to bed a walk with CB. in the College Green &c. — My cough very troublesome. — Wrote to MW. —

Oct. 20. Wednesday.

Very fine weather — Breakfasted with my brother magistrates staying at the Bell. — Recᵈ· a letter from MW. who forwards a letter from Sewell which had arrived at U Slaughter: its contents much to the same purpose as the communication made to me yesterday by E Bloxsome. Sewell proposes being with us at breakfast on Saturday morning, to report progress as to the Stanton living, and to obtain my signature to the transfer of the mortgage on Mᵣ Lockhart's property |¹⁹⁸ to W H Bloxsome. — I wrote to Sewell that we should be glad to see him on that day. — Wrote to Mʳˢ· Hughes, Long Compton, the result of my conversation ~~yesterday~~ on Monday with G. Cooper, that he agreed to pay through Mᵣ Baughan, Churchwarden of Long Compton, 25/ each Christmas towards the Schooling of

45. Gloucester Docks and Cathedral.

his illegitimate child, and that he would do more as the child grew older; advised her not to irritate him by writing angry letters. — I attended in Sergeant Ludlow's Court, at the hearing of appeals against convictions of Magistrates under the Alehouse acts, and trials for larceny. I observe with regret the increasing irritability of the Chairman; his eagerness of temper leads him more and more, and more unpleasantly to interrupt counsel, to find fault, and use ~~unpleasantly~~ ^{courteously} the authority which his position and standing in his profession should lead him to exert in moderation. A frequent squabbling with |*199* the counsel engaged is very indecorous, and protracts business, which L. is desirous of hurrying on rather too fast. — Our young friends, the Bride and Bridegroom from Cheltenham, M^r and M$^{rs.}$ Woodroffe, found Edward and myself in Court, having come over for the morning. We accompanied them on a walk, after they had sat for some time observing the business in Court. We went over the Gaol very fully, to the Docks, the Spa &c. Mr W. is a gentlemanly, lively, clever young Irishman, full of spirits & humour, but with an unmistakeable brogue, and his studies for the bar in England have not wholly obliterated his Milesianism.[22] — Maria Woodroffe, as usual, pleasing and agreeable in look and manner. They returned to Cheltenham, after evening service at the Cathedral. — Met an old acquaintance Barwick Lechmere, the Rector of Hanley Castle, Worcestershire, son of Sir A. Lechmere, and Brother of Mr Lechmere, the Banker, of |*200* Worcester and Malvern. He informed ^{me} of a sad grief in his family, the conversion of a young girl, his brother's daughter, to the Church of Rome. She is first cousin

22.   *See* the footnotes for F324. Francis Witts uses the term in his comments on O'Connell.

of Compton Reade, and his sisters, having lost her Aunt, the wife of Sir John Reade, who, with her sister, M^rs. Lechmere, was a Miss Murray, of the Elibank family. It would seem that Miss L. had been secretly alienated from the Protestant faith of her family, by some Roman Catholics resident near Malvern, into whose society, as being of the neighbouring gentry, she had been thrown. Under the patronage of the Hornyhold family an establishment of Popish devotees, Sisters of Mercy, I believe, with a Flemish Priest, has been fixed for sometime in the parish of Hanley. It is not long ago that Miss Lechmere was staying on a visit at her Uncle's Rectory house, on a Sunday, and rec^d. the communion at his hands. In the Evening of the same day, she forsook his house, and placed herself under the charge of the Roman |^201 Catholic Priest and the Sisters – lamentable duplicity — a victim, probably, of secret tampering with a weak, susceptible, and imaginative mind. — But few magistrates dined together, at the Bell, under the presidency of Serg^t. Ludlow, but it was an agreeable party — E.F.W. and I had some conversation with the elder Bloxsome as to the resignation by his son of the living of Stanton; in talking of it, he spoke of my son's succession as almost <u>un fait accompli.</u> — A small party at tea, which C Bathurst joined, consisting of Purnell, ~~Ro~~ Hale, W H Hartley, E.F.W. myself and one or two more. Much varied and agreeable conversation.

Oct. 21. Thursday.

Rain had fallen during the night: there was a heavy shower in the course of the day. — After an early breakfast at the Bell, went into Court, and sat with Serg^t. Ludlow &c. hearing trials for felonies &c. till 12 o clock. — |^202 Left Gloucester Station for Cheltenham by rail at half past twelve. — My son proposed returning home at a later hour. — I remained at Cheltenham till past 3 o cl. — Shopping, and making enquiries for a cook, as ours is likely to leave us, being engaged to be married. — Returned home in my phaeton, which had been sent to meet me. A note from MW. — I reached U Slaughter at half past five — Found a letter from Mr Polson in answer to that which I had lately addressed to him: he has given up all thought of purchasing a living — A letter from Cotterell and Rich, Kensington, chandlers, acknowledging the remittance of a cheque I had sent them in payment of a bill for candles. — A circular issued by a committee asking for a subscription towards a memorial proposed to be offered as a testimony of the great services to the Church of Earl Powis, as being mainly instrumental in preserving the two ancient |^203 Sees of Bangor and S^t. Asaph, which it was proposed to unite, with a view to obtain funds for the new See of Manchester, now recently created, without such extinction of one of the Welch Bishoprics, from other resources. It is proposed to endow by subscription one or more scholarships in one or both of the Universities, to be held by young Welsh students about to enter into holy orders; the study of the Welsh language for the purposes of the Ministry is a prominent object in the scheme. — The Crescent and the Cross.

Oct. 22. Friday.

A cold, cloudy day; a tendency to rain, which came on in the evening. — Preparing a sermon. — Justice business at home. — Wrote to Mr Bloxsome on County business: I had omitted to bring back from Gloucester the Valuation Books of the parishes in this neighbourhood, which I had taken with me, and which had been allowed and passed by the County rate committee: requested that they might |^204 be forwarded — Engaged in arranging my papers on my return from the Quarter Sess^ns. — Read over the case which has been prepared to be submitted to

Counsel as to the disputed questions respecting the Red Lion Wharf — Hunt Trust business. — Walked to Wick Risington to make my first call on M⁻ Terry, a new curate lately arrived there, to replace M⁻ Barrow. He is, I believe, a fellow of Lincoln College, and has been Curate of Norton near Gloucester. I did not find him at home, but left a card for him with an invitation to dinner on Tuesday next. — MW. received a letter from Apphia Witts, who, with John W. and his wife, is pretty well. — Shortly before dinner time Maria Woodroffe and her husband arrived from Cheltenham, on a visit to us. We found them very pleasing and agreeable. He is about 25 Years of age: a very talented and well educated man; having passed through Dublin College with |[105] credit. His Father, D⁻ Woodroffe, now resident at Dublin, and infirm ⁱⁿ health, retired from his profession, was for many years an eminent Surgeon at Cork, and has many children – three sons in the legal profession: one an Irish Barrister, another at the English bar, our guest, a third a Solicitor. The English Barrister has a fine flow of spirits, and much Irish humour, with great fluency, and little reserve. He is young, and, therefore, eager, and a warm encomiast of every person and thing connected with Ireland, at least as relates to the lawyers, and the University, esteeming the land of his birth to have a high preeminence in talent, science &c. This will wear off by greater commerce with Society on a wider scale. His health has been indifferent, and he does not appear to be strong.

Oct. 23. Saturday.

A very rainy day. — M⁻ Sewell came from M⁻ Hudson's at Lower Swell to breakfast with us: conferred |[106] with him as to the living of Stanton, and other matters connected with the proposed purchase of the next presentation. — Wrote to M⁻ Thornton on Hunt trust disputes. — A letter from Bathurst about his Neckar wine and county matters. — M⁻ Terry, the Curate of Wick Risington, returned my call; he appears an intelligent, not very polished person, not reserved, and somewhat deaf. — M⁻ Lefroy arrived from Cheltenham to pass a day or two with us. —

Oct. 24. Sunday.

A fine day. — Attended the Sunday School. — Morning Service and Sermon. I preached on "the one thing needful." — Afternoon service – prayers. — A letter from Bathurst respecting occurrences at the Sessions; — from M⁻ Thornton on Hunt Trust matters — After dinner M⁻ Sewell called from Lower Swell to shew me a letter he had rec^d· from M⁻ Edward Bloxsome, by which it appears that the Bishop interposes difficulty, |[107] at least delay, as to the acceptance of W. H. Bloxsome's resignation of the living of Stanton. A communication has been made from M⁻ Holt to E.B. that his Lordship considers it kind and right to take further time for consideration of the matter. E.B. looks on this notification as ill-omened, and proposes indirect ways of reaching the end ~~prop~~ designed. To Sewell and me the prospect seems lowring, and the suggestion of E.B. not to be entertained. But as the matter requires careful consideration, I engaged M⁻ Sewell to dine here to-morrow, when he will have an opportunity of meeting my Son, with whom we may further deliberate.

Oct. 25. Monday.

After heavy rain in the night, a very fine day. — Stow fair — Much engaged with tradesmen calling for payment of their bills — with Churchwarden Gregory, and with justice business at home. — M⁻ Lefroy left us after break-|[108] fast, returning to Cheltenham by a circuitous route, visiting Police Stations on his way. — Drove to Stow, accompanied by Mr Woodroffe, and attended at the Provident Bank, where met Winter and W B Pole. — J W Harris called there and made a payment to me on acc^t of rent for the Vicarage farm, Stanway. — Transacted Justice business at Mr Brookes's office. — Called with Mr Woodroffe at "the Cottage," where we saw M^r and Mrs Vavasour, with whom we partook of luncheon. Mr Vavasour afterwards ~~called~~ went with us into the fair. — Transacted business at the Office of the Gloucestershire Banking Company. — Called at the Workhouse, and conferred with Mr Pearce. — Shopping. — Mr Woodroffe and I walked home by Lower Swell. — A letter from the Gaol, Gloucester giving notice of a meeting of Visiting Justices — MW. received a letter from Sophia Hunt, with a very alarming account of the declining state of her sister Caroline. — |^{109} Our dear children and grandchildren arrived from Stanway on a visit to us. — Mr Sewell dined and spent the evening with us. In conference between him, E.F.W., and myself as to the state of the negociation respecting the living of Stanton, it was agreed that Sewell should endeavour to have a meeting with M^r E Bloxsome tomorrow; that we should not take any indirect course to obtain the end desired; that it is our wisdom to sit still, leaving the Bloxsomes to fulfil their engagement by obtaining the Bishop's acceptance of his resignation, till when we have no locus standi. — The more this affair is considered the more unpleasant it appears: and the more doubtful that we should succeed in our object. It is most probable that the publicity given to the treaty by W H Bloxsome has displeased the Bishop.

Oct. 26. Tuesday.

Fine weather, but cold, and towards evening damp. — |^{110} Wrote to Mr Rodwell for a supply of books for the Stow book society: — to Mr Winter, forwarding to him a cheque which I had received from C Bathurst by E.F.W. yesterday, to pay for the Neckar wine which he has been supplied with: — to Bathurst to know how much more of the same he wishes to have. — Settling accounts, and paying tradesmens' bills — Justice business at home. — Drove to Stow fair. MW. accompanied us to the Turnpike gate at Lower Slaughter, walking home. — Mrs Woodroffe and my dear Broome were my companions onward in the Phaeton — E.F.W. drove Sophy and Mr Woodroffe. — Drove to "the Cottage," where our party partook of luncheon; afterwards visited the fair, Mrs W. Vavasour and Emma V. being added. — With my Grandson treated myself to a sight — in a shew — a learned poney &c. — Transacted Justice business at |^{111} Mr Brookes's office — At the Provident Bank we met Mr Winter — Visited the Workhouse — Home to dinner — Mr Terry, the new curate of Wick Risington joined our circle: — a plain looking and not very polished man, but well informed. — A letter from Mr Bloxsome as to the Valuations of parishes in this Union, and the amount at which they are assessed to the County Rate.

Oct. 27. Wednesday.

After rain in the night a fine day. — Justice business at home — Wrote to Mr Hare a letter to accompany the case as to the disputed points in respect of the Red Lion Wharf, which I am about to forward to him with letters and copies from Messrs Thornton, Braikenridge, Cox and Williams &c. — Accompanied E.F.W. and Sophy, and M^r & Mrs Woodroffe in a walk to Eyford. Mrs Dolphin is not yet returned home, but is expected soon. — Mr Terry called while |^{112} we were absent. — A letter from Mrs Hughes, Long Compton as to the affair I had arranged for her at Gloucester with Geo. Cooper.

Oct. 28. Thursday.

After rain during the night a foggy morning and evening; the midday and afternoon were fine, though rather damp. — Forwarded to the Cashiers of the Bank of England a remittance for the collections made on the day of Thanksgiving (Oct.17) for the blessing of an abundant harvest — such collections to be in aid of the fund for the relief of sufferers from anticipated scarcity of food in parts of Ireland and Scotland: together with the amount of what had been received in this parish, I remitted what had been collected by my Son at Stanway, and by Mr Terry at Wick Risington, in all only £5. 1. 8. — Visited a sick parishioner, R. Yearp, of whom it is hard to say, whether he is more diseased mentally or bodily. — Drove to Stow with MW. who shortly after returned, taking |[113] back with her in the carriage Mr Vavasour, who joined the party at the Rectory at luncheon, and was brought back by E.F.W. & Sophy in their carriage in which also they conveyed Mr Woodroffe to Stow and Maugersbury. — I transacted business at the Provident Bank, at the office of the Gloucestershire Banking Company, and at the Union Workhouse. — At the Magistrate's room R Waller and I ~~were~~ sat as Justices, assisted by the Dean of Gloucester. Lord Redesdale, Mess$^{rs.}$ Polhill, Winter, E.F.W, Pole, and Woodroffe were also present. — Mr Woodroffe returned with me in my carriage — E.F.W. drove Sophy home. — Mr Hayward visited our dear grandchild Freddy professionally: poor little fellow, his bowels and liver are a little out of order, and he looks pale, suffers also from toothache. Mr H. prescribed for him, and there is no reason for uneasiness. — Received a letter |[114] from Sewell, who was not able to meet either of the Mess$^{rs.}$ Bloxsome at Dursley yesterday, but had an interview with Mr A. Jackson, their partner, who agreed in the opinion that the publicity given to the transaction as to the purchase of the next presentation of the living of Stanton had been most unfortunate, and unwise, and that W H Bloxsome had in so divulging it acted with great imprudence, and in a manner calculated to offend the Bishop, as if he set at defiance his power to refuse to accept the resignation. More particularly, they censured WHB's rash and premature sale of his goods which is fixed to take place on Tuesday next; his friends have urgently advised him to stop the sale, but do not expect to prevail with him, such is his impracticability. Sewell explained to Mr Jackson that we should remain quiescent, and that it behoved the Bloxsomes to extricate themselves, if they could, from their embarra-|[115] sing position with the Bishop. — Rec$^d.$ a letter from Chr. Geldard; information is required as to the date of the decease of M$^{rs.}$ Moorhouse, of Newcastle, and her children, as to the payment of the legacies left in Dr Henry Moorhouse's will, and as to the date and place of my wife's baptism: all this with reference to the sale of a portion of the Ravenflatt estate to the directors of the Railway Company. — I omitted to mention yesterday that MW. had rec$^d.$ a letter from Eliza Daniell, whom we had invited to pass some time with us. She declines coming, alleging that she is too poor — the fact being that, through some mismanagement on the part of trustees or lawyers, she has not received some dividends to which she is entitled with the usual punctuality: and perhaps she dislikes a country visit in cheerless November.

Oct. 29. Friday.

Foggy and damp weather, but without decided rain. — An early |[116] breakfast to allow of M^r and M$^{rs.}$ Woodroffe being in time to proceed by Oxford to reach Town in the Evening. A fly took them to meet the Wonder coach at the foot of Stow Hill. — We were pleased with the young couple, and loth to part: still more sorry to lose our dear children and grandchildren, who took their departure for Stanway at half past nine o clock. My son having an engagement at Winchcomb to-day to meet his brother magistrates, we lost him and his family a day earlier than usual. — Felt flat and uncomfortable when all were gone — Preparing a Sermon. — Wrote to Chr. Geldard in answer to his letter received yesterday. — Received a letter from Mʳ Thornton on Hunt Trust affairs — Visited Dix's family to advise with them as to the afflicted state, both mental and bodily of their kinsman, and my parishioner, Richᵈ˙ Yearp — The Crescent and the Cross. |[117]

Oct. 30. Saturday.

Fine, but moist weather — Wrote to Miss Sophia Hunt, and to Mʳ Thornton on matters relating to the Hunt family. — Preparing a Sermon. — Visiting sick parishioners. — Walked with MW. to Eyford. — The Crescent and the Cross. —

Oct. 31. Sunday.

A very fine day. — Preparing a sermon. — Visited the Sunday School. — Morning service, prayers — Afternoon service, prayers and a sermon: I preached on steadfastness in religion, and adherence to the Established Church recommended. — Received from Mʳ Robert Wilton, Gloucester, a letter, accompanying a deed of contract signed by many Visitors of the Gloucester Lunatic Asylum, and waiting for my signature, whereby the Keeper of a licenced private mad-house at Hook-Norton engages for nine shillings weekly for each patient to maintain and treat twenty pauper lunatics, chargeable to pa-|[118] rishes in this County, or to the County, being chronic cases, and the overflowings of the Lunatic Asylum, for whom there is no room. Others are sent under a like contract to the private licenced Mad house at Fairford; such is the increase of mental disease among the lower classes, and, indeed, all classes. When the Lunatic Asylum was built, it was designed for the accommodation of a certain number of opulent patients, sixty charity, and sixty pauper patients: now more than 200 pauper patients are crowding the building, and yet nearly forty are sent out to Fairford and Hook Norton. The number of ᶦⁿˢᶦᵈᵉ paupers detained in Union Workhouses, or in the cottages of the poor is, indeed, much diminished: the provisions of the late Lunatic Asylum Act are very stringent, Magistrates, Clergymen, Med Officers, Rel. Officers, Governors in Unions & Workhouses, and Parish Officers, are bound to give notice of cases of insanity, and to provide for the conveyance |[119] of the insane to proper houses of detention; and convenience, humanity, and a more enlightened state of the public mind as to this dreadful malady, concur in promoting the due attention to this afflicted class. — A letter from Mʳ Bloxsome announced, as usual, my appointment as one of the Visiting Magistrates of Gloucester Gaol — A letter from the Bank of England acknowledging the receipt of my remittance of the sums collected at Upper Slaughter, Stanway and Wick Risington on the 17ᵗʰ˙ Inst. for the famine-stricken in Ireland and the West of Scotland. — A letter from Sophia Hunt communicates a much worse account of the state of her sister Caroline, who may have already departed this life, and cannot, it would seem, last many days — Ecclesiastical Gazette. — To the family a section from James on the Collects. —

Nov. 1. Monday.

Very fine weather — Justice business at home. — Signed and |[120] dispatched to D[r] Timbrill for his signature the contract for the maintenance of pauper lunatics belonging to Gloucestershire at Hook Norton licenced mad-house. — Wrote to E.F.W. at length in the forenoon in answer to a note I received from him this morning, brought by a coal waggoner from Stanway, chiefly as to the Stanton affair. It seems that M[r] W H. Bloxsome persists in selling the furniture of the Rectory by auction on Tuesday next, although urged by his friends at Dursley not to persevere in a course so likely to offend the Bishop, and to prevent the accomplishment of the arrangement made for the sale to us of the next presentation. In the afternoon I received another note from my Son with further information as to his arrangements with W H Bloxsome, in the event of E.F.W. making any purchases at the sale, that those purchases should be conditional, dependent on the living being resigned, and my Son being instituted — |[121] Strongly advised my Son not to be present at the sale — A third letter came by the Post from E.F.W. inclosing one to him from M[r] Walsh to whom the Curacy of Stanway had been offered in the event of my Son's removal to Stanton, but which he declines, as not likely to hold any curacy long. My Son sent me a note he had received from M[r] Murray Browne as to the appointment of a chaplain to the Workhouse of the Winchcomb Union, who should be also a Curate of the Incumbent of Winchcomb. This arrangement had been planned at the time of the Bishop's visitation, and my Son had been mixed up in it, and received the Bishop's approval of the part he had taken in it; as an Ex-officio Guardian of the Winchcomb Union, [he] used his influence in procuring the appointment of a Chaplain to the institution in such a manner as to promote the Spiritual interests of the parish of Winchcomb and its hamlets. — Preparing a sermon — |[122] Received from Sophia Hunt a letter announcing the death of her sister Caroline which took place on Saturday night; she summons me to Clifton, as one of the Executors of her sister's will, and I propose setting out early to-morrow morning. — From M[r] Hare I received a packet with letters which I had forwarded to him from Mess[rs.] Thornton, Cox and Williams, and Braikenridge, as to the disputed matter of the Wharf: M[r] Hare consents to the proposition made by M[r] Thornton and myself that the case respecting the Wharf, as to the legality of the management of that affair by the Trustees under the advice of Mess[rs.] Cox and Williams, shall be referred to M[r] George Turner, an eminent chancery Barrister. — Rec[d.] a letter from C Bathurst as to another order of Neckar wine. — Wrote to M[r] Sewell as to the living of Stanton — to M[r] Thornton, acquainting him with the death of poor Caroline Hunt; — to Mess[rs.] |[123] Hoare, desiring them to place £35 to the account of my Son — to M[r] Robert Waller, as to Justice business to be transacted, and to which I shall not be able to attend, owing to my proposed journey to Clifton, and as to the Service of my Church on Sunday next, in case I am unable to return home before that day. — M[r] Wiggin called on us to-day.

Nov. 2. Tuesday.

A very foggy morning, followed by a very fine sunny day: foggy towards evening. — Rose early; early breakfast — Left home at 7 AM: reached Cheltenham at half past nine: left the Station near Cheltenham for Bristol at eight minutes after ten; arrived by the railway at the Bristol Station at half past twelve; and Clifton was reached by me in an omnibus at one P.M. — Found Sophia, Fanny, and Maria Hunt as well as could be expected after the great anxiety and fatigue, and grief |[124] which they had gone through. — Mr Tebbutt, the Steward of the Wadenhoe property, had arrived on the preceding day, not aware of Miss Caroline Hunt's death, but anticipating the event, and wishing to obtain instructions as to the future — After luncheon, the will of our deceased friend was opened and read by me in the presence of her sisters. It is dated in 1836, and Sophia Hunt and myself are appointed Executors and Trustees. The small freehold cottage belonging to her at Wadenhoe is to be sold, the refusal of it to be given to the Owner of the Estate — now George Hunt, who, by Caroline's decease, succeeds to the whole life interest which she held, and is to enjoy in perpetuity under T. W. Hunt's will the Northamptonshire estates, together with the personalty which is considerable; as to the whole Mr Hare, Mr Thornton and I are in trust. — All the property of which Caroline died possessed after payment of debts, funeral and testamentary expences, and |[125] a few legacies, is to be equally divided between her brothers and Sisters, — Thomas, Edward, Sarah, Sophia, Fanny, and Maria in equal proportions: but the portion coming to Edwd is to be in trust, to be invested in the public funds or on real securities, the interest to be paid to E.H. during his life, and the principal, after his decease, to all and any of his children; failing such, to all and every his brother and sisters then living, and to the issue of those who shall have died. (This Edward is a weak man, who was, for some misconduct into which he fell, or was led by bad example or advice, reduced from the East India Company's military service, with a small pension, on which he subsists at or near Bombay, living, it is believed, with a native woman. His family have had little or no intercourse with him by letter for several years past: all attempts to extricate him from his degraded position have been ineffectual.) — There is a legacy to me of |[126] £105 — and three others of £19.19.0 each, of which two are to Ward Hunt, Mr George Hunt's eldest Son, and to Mr Hare. The assets of Miss MCH. may be roughly estimated at exceeding £10000 in the gross, consisting of rents due, considerable balances in her Bankers hands, and £5000 for which she holds a policy of insurance dated many years back. — It would have been in her power, during the twelve years enjoyment of a considerable life income, to have realized largely, for she lead a retired life, mixing little in society, and maintaining a respectable, but not expensive establishment: such, however, was not her plan; satisfied to leave a comfortable addition to the means of every one of her family, she delighted in expending the surplus of her income in works of charity, with great liberality, and without ostentation. Her private charities to persons of genteel connections with confined resources were numerous; to the poor destitute she was ever |[127] bountiful: to public charitable institutions, for the sick and helpless, for the extension of education, for missionary purposes, for extending church accommodation, she was very liberal in donations and subscriptions: her loss to many will be severe; she was a gentle, amiable, humble Christian; slow and procratinating[23] in her habits, constitutionally feeble, and of late years greatly afflicted by a uterine complaint, which ended in dropsy, a lingering illness, and death, neither preceded nor attended by severe suffering or pain — Before dinner walked with Tebbutt by Clifton down, St Vincent's rocks, the Hotwells &c. conversing on Hunt affairs — In the interview with the undertaker in the evening the arrangements for the funeral and removal of the corpse for interment at Wadenhoe were settled. — Much discussion of Executorship matters.

---

23. *Sic.*

46. *Paddle Steamers at Hotwells, Bristol.*

Nov. 3. Wednesday.

A foggy day, no rain — Before breakfast engaged with Mᵣ Tebbutt in |¹²⁸ settling various matters connected with the funeral. At 11 P.M.²⁴ he set out on his return to Northamptonshire. — Wrote to MW: — to Mᵣ Winter, requesting him to order six dozen of Neckar wine for C Bathurst. — Conferring with Sophia Hunt on Exorship concerns: and wrote letters relating to them to Messʳˢ· Coutts, Bankers, the Secretary of the Crown Life Insurance Company, Mᵣ Roberts, the Rector of Wadenhoe, and Mᵣ Whitcombe, Solicitor, Gloucester. — Took a short walk before dinner. The hurry and anxiety of my present engagements had brought on a bad attack of diarrhoea, which ended in the evening in a violent bilious attack, with profuse vomiting, making me very wretched, and driving me, after vain efforts to exert myself, to my bedroom at half past nine. I had consulted a Chemist and been supplied with medicine before dinner time. When my stomach was relieved I enjoyed a comfortable night's rest. — |¹²⁴

Nov. 4. Thursday.

Very fine, mild weather — Much relieved by medicine and a good night; indeed, comfortably well — Wrote to MW. and recᵈ· a letter from her. — Wrote to Bathurst about the order for a fresh supply of Neckar wine. — A letter from Mᵣ Thornton on Hunt Trust matters, to which I replied — Took two short walks — Constant conference with Sophia Hunt and her sisters as to our Executorship.

---

24.   This was probably an error, and presumably A.M. was intended.

Nov. 5. Friday.

Beautiful weather for the season. — My transient indisposition quite gone. — Wrote to Edward Hunt, at Bombay, explaining to him the disposition made in his favour by his sister Caroline, how he will now be affected by a division of the £2000 in which she had a life interest under Mrs. Mary Hunt's will, which is to be distributed between her Brothers and Sisters, and desiring instructions from him as to payments to be made |¹²⁵ to him. — A letter from E.F.W: all well at Stanway Vicarage: dear Freddy recovered after taking the medicine prescribed by Mr Hayward. — The sale of W H Bloxsome's furniture &c. at Stanton took place on Tuesday; what my Son bought is only to be his, if he becomes Rector of Stanton. — A letter from Sewell who has received that which I wrote to him on Monday last: to the legal questions respecting the treaty for the purchase of the next presentation of Stanton living he does not reply, not having had time to consider them. He forwards a copy of a letter which he has received from Edward Bloxsome: it is proposed that W.H.B. shall shortly wait on the Bishop with certificates of his bad health, and press his acceptance of the resignation of the living of Stanton. — A letter from the Crown Life Assurance office as to the claim of £5000 to which the Estate of M C Hunt is entitled: — from Messrs. Coutts with a statement of the balance standing on |¹²⁶ their books to her credit. — Walked to Bristol to consult Mr Wood, an Attorney there, as to the termination of M C Hunt's tenure of the house in the Mall, Clifton, which she holds under an agreement, as Under-tenant to a Miss Leech. Mr Wood had been consulted when Miss Hunt took the house some years ago. In the afternoon, by appointment which I made, Mr Wood called, and Sophia Hunt and I, as Executors, signed the necessary notices to give up the house. — I returned from Bristol in a fly. – Mr Hare arrived from Bath before luncheon time, and remained with us till after tea time, returning home by the last train. Held much conference with him on the Trust concerns in which we are mutually en interested, and on the present Exorship affair. — Mr George Hunt having intimated by letter to Sophia Hunt that the indisposition of one of his children, (apprehended measles) will prevent his attending |¹²⁷ the funeral at Wadenhoe on Tuesday next, Mr Hare was invited to be present. Mr Ward Hunt, now of Christ Church, Oxford, Son of George Hunt, has been requested to attend. There has been some thought of my being one of those present. I have, on account of the fatigue, distance, and recent attack of indisposition, been allowed to excuse myself. — Walked with Mr Hare on Clifton Hill, and on the Downs. — After his departure, engaged in looking over papers and accounts, and arranging various matters. — Wrote to Messrs. Coutts. |

Diary
1847

Nov. 6. Saturday – Very fine weather. –
After an interview with the Undertaker before
breakfast, and having breakfasted, I left
the Misses Hunt, and drove to the Bristol
Railway Station in a fly. — Left at 11 A.M.
by the Mail train for Cheltenham, travelling
in the same coach with Mr Josephs, an intelligent resident at Cheltenham, an acquain
tance of some years standing. — Reached
the Cheltenham Station by ½ past 1 P. M.
and the Plough Hotel by 2 P. M. — There
I met MW – who had come to meet me in
the Chariot, suffering from pain in the face.
— She had been endeavouring to engage a
cook. — Took some refreshment at the
Plough, and reached home by 6 P. M. —
Received a letter from Mr Thornton covering
a copy of the last letter Mr Hare had written
to him on Hunt Trust business: of this letter

Witts Family Papers F361

Diary 1847

Nov. 6. Saturday.

Very fine weather. — After an interview with the Undertaker before breakfast, and having breakfasted, I left the Misses Hunt, and drove to the Bristol Railway Station in a fly. — Left at 11 A.M. by the Mail train for Cheltenham, travelling in the same coach with Mʳ Josephs, an intelligent resident at Cheltenham, an acquaintance of some years standing. Reached the Cheltenham Station by ½ past 1 P.M. and the Plough Hotel by 2 P.M. — There I met MW. – who had come to meet me in the Chariot, suffering from pain in the face. — She had been endeavouring to engage a cook. — Took some refreshment at the Plough, and reached home by 6 P.M. — Received a letter from Mʳ Thornton covering a copy of the last letter Mʳ Hare had written to him on Hunt Trust business: of this letter |² Mʳ Hare had already sent me a copy. — In answer to my letter of Monday last Mʳ Sewell writes that he is persuaded that our contract with W. H. Bloxsome is in no respect simoniacal, and is, agreably to the latest legal decisions on the subject, unimpeachable: I was disposed to think that, as related to the Vendor, he might by possibility be thought to have approached the borders of simony, as far as he was a party; but in this view Mʳ E. Bloxsome, his Solicitor and adviser, did not concur. On the whole, considering Mʳ W.H.B. to be an unmanageable, wayward and wilful person, so that his rash proceedings may lead us into further difficulties: and looking to the Bishop's evident reluctance to accept the resignation; Sewell judges it most prudent to rescind the contract, and has made an appointment with E.B. for this |³ day, with that view: hoping that the negociation may be renewed under better caution. Altogether we are placed in a very disagreeable position: I have acted with good faith, in the full confidence that I was taking no step not warranted by law, to my own prejudice, & with risk of serious pecuniary loss, but with an eye solely to promote the comfort and preferment of my Son and his family. — A letter from Messʳˢ. Hoare announces that they have transferred £35. from my account to that of my Son. — "The Crescent and the Cross." —

Nov. 7. Sunday.

Mild and fine weather in the forenoon, followed by rain in the afternoon, wind and rain in the evening. — Visited the Sunday School. — Mʳand Mrˢ. W. Vavasour and Emma Vavasour came to accompany us to Church. This unusual proceeding springs from an unpleasant feeling respecting the Church at Stow, which has led W.V. |⁴ with others to memorialize the Rural Dean on the great discomfort experienced by some of the Parishioners whose seats adjoin the Chancel, owing to draughts of air penetrating through the interstices of the boards under the slates — which shrink in dry weather, not being dovetailed or ploughed and tongued:

expanding in moist weather. It is alleged that the rush of cold air so introduced gives colds, rheumatism and the like — This has led to a remonstrance to M[r] Hippisley, who has replied offensively, and a painful controversy is the result. — After morning service W.V. left us to call on Henry Lindow, and accompany him to Lower Slaughter Church; the ladies took luncheon with us, and went to our afternoon Service; after which they left us, calling for W.V. by the way. — At Morning service prayers and Sermon. I preached on the attributes of GOD. — Afternoon Service, prayers. — Received a letter from M[rs.] C Barr, who has finally left Leeds, whither she went to settle her affairs, and is now staying for the winter months with M[rs.] Walker and the Barrs at Hen-|[5] wick Hall near Worcester. — MW. received a letter from Apphia Witts, who seeks by the desire of the Misses Harness, ladies resident at Malvern, any information which I may be able to give, as Ex[or] to the will of my Aunt Lady Lyttleton, respecting the tenure on which the houses were held in which during my Aunt's life time her school of industry and school for infant children were kept on Malvern Common, whether freehold, leasehold, or otherwise. — Preparing a Sermon. — Reading Bishop Monk's charge delivered at his late Visitation, a copy of which has been sent to me in common with other beneficed Clergy in his diocese. — To the family a section from D[r] James on the Collects.

Nov. 8. Monday.

A bright morning was soon exchanged for a rainy forenoon and afternoon: the weather altered for the better before the darkness came on. — Engaged with M[r] Lea, the Tax Collector, with M[r] Pearce and M[r] Dunford: with the two latter on Union and Poor Law business. — M[rs.] Griffin, the tenant of the Church and Charity |[6] estate called to pay her Michaelmas rent. — Employed in settling my accounts — Examined the Executorship papers as to the Estate of Lady Lyttelton, to see whether I could ascertain anything certainly as to the tenure of the cottages on Malvern Common in which her Infant School and School of industry had been kept; but c[d.] meet with nothing to the purpose — Received a letter from M[r] Whitcomb, who does not anticipate any difficulty or objection in or to my acting as Executor to Caroline Hunt's estate, although I am Trustee of the Wadenhoe property, and as such there may be a claim against the Estate which it might be my duty to make. M[r] W. answers other points adverted to in the letter I addressed to him from Clifton last week. — Visisted M[r] E Lea's family; his second daughter, a very lovely, interesting, amiable girl of eighteen, is rapidly declining to the grave: nor is this the only calamity apprehended: the second son is suffering from defective vision, and fears are entertained that |[7] his lungs, like his sister's are affected with disease. — Received a note from W B Pole, as to a parishioner of his at Condicote, Union business, to which I replied. — Wrote to E Moorhouse, Longpreston, with a cheque on Alcock & Birkbecks, for the sum which we usually give to this fallen branch of MW's family at this season: £5. 0. 0. — "The Crescent and the Cross."

Nov. 9. Tuesday.

A fine day. — Wrote to Apphia Witts that I have not been able to find anything as to the tenure of the Cottages on Malvern Common, in which my Aunt's schools were formerly held — though I have looked thro' all the Executorship papers. — M[r] Collins, Surgeon, Bourton on the Water, called as to visiting R. Yearp, to ascertain the State of his mind, whether a lunatic, and fit to be removed to the Lunatic Asylum. — Wrote a letter on Hunt affairs to

Mr Thornton — E.F.W. and Sophy rode over from Stanway to call upon us, remaining two hours, and then returning. Much anxious conversation as |^8 to the living of Stanton, and my Executorship and Trust business with relation to the Hunt family. — A letter came to-day from Mr Sewell in which he reports that he met E. Bloxsome on Saturday last at Gloucester, and that their interview terminated in the cancelling of the contract for the purchase of the next presentation of Stanton Rectory. Further particulars he will give vivâ voce, he says, this evening, when he proposes dining with us, on his way from Bourton on the Hill, whither he goes to see Dr Warneford. I gather from Sewell's letter that thus ends our concern with the living of Stanton, and intimated as much to Edward and Sophy, but their sanguine tempers suggested that the negociation was only broken off to be revived in a better and less objectionable manner; that is in a way to which the Bishop could make no objection. — Soon after they had left us Mr Sewell came, |^9 remaining here till 9 P.M. and going back to sleep at Mr Hudson's, Lower Swell. — His explanation of the breaking off the treaty with the Bloxsomes is this: — he insisted on cancelling the agreement, because no reliance could be placed on WHB's discretion, who was taking the very course to defeat the object by rashly acting as if the Resignation must be accepted by the Bishop. The agreement being cancelled, Sewell urged E.B. to call at once on Mr Holt, the Bishop's Secretary, and learn what was the impediment to the acceptance of the resignation, and whether it could be surmounted. Mr Holt readily explained that his Lordship peremptorily refused to accept the tendered resignation, because he considered the transaction, as respects the Incumbent and Vendor, to have been conducted in too open and undisguised a manner, to have been publicly divulged by him, so that the Bishop was informed of the intention as long ago as on his visitation at Campden, when it was intima-|^{10} ted to him by a third party that he intended to keep the advowson, but to sell the next presentation with the assurance of an early avoidance, which of course would greatly increase the value, and this the Bp. regards, I apprehend, as a culpable trafficking. His Lordship seems to have been offended with his persisting in his intentions after a caution on his part, conveyed in the letter in which he desires him not to be too hasty, but to reconsider the matter, — with the publicity given to the affair by the announcing a sale of the effects at the Rectory, the Bishop's acceptance of the resignation not having been obtained. This he seems to have regarded as an act of defiance of his authority, and setting at nought the exercise of his discretion, whether the resignation should be accepted or not. He therefore declares his resolution not to accept the resignation, but at the same time, his readiness to grant to WHB. a licence for non- |^{11} residence, as he well knows his inability from ill health to perform clerical functions. It is thus, as it would appear, that his Lordship expresses his Episcopal dislike of sales of presentations with the understanding that there will be an early avoidance, although the Courts of law have of late years expressly ruled that such sales are legal. It is possible, but not probable that the Bishop may not even know that we were the parties in treaty for the purchase of the next presentation. It is also possible, but very unlikely, that the Bishop may change his mind. What may most readily be anticipated is that when WHB. applies to his Lordship formally to accept his resignation, it will be intimated to him that the acceptance is refused, but that he may have a licence for non-residence. I directed Sewell to fix an early appointment to meet Mr Holt, and to explain to him fully our part in the transaction. If the living be again for sale the first offer will be made to us by the Bloxsomes: |^{12} but I consider it almost a matter of certainty that no contingency will arise by which the acquisition of this preferment for my son can be effected. The disappointment to E.F.W. and Sophy will be very great, and I much regret it; and as far as one could foresee, the asquisition of this preferment was in a worldly point of view very desirable; but I mean not to say that the failure of the scheme is to be lastingly deplored, for I am thoroughly convinced that all is overruled for the best by that wise and merciful Providence which governs all things, and directs all for our real benefit. — Rec^d. from Messrs. Coutts a letter re. the affairs of M C. Hunt, in answer to one written to them by me from Clifton on Friday last. —

Nov. 9. Wednesday.[1]

A foggy morning followed by a very fine day. — Justice business at home. — Wrote to E.F.W. a very full account of all I had learnt from Mr Sewell |[13] as to the living of Stanton, the cancelling of the contract for the purchase of the next presentation, and the Bishop's determination to accept W. H. Bloxsome's resignation. At a later hour my son sent over his servant with a note from himself, and a letter he had received to-day from W. H. Bloxsome, who states that he had waited on the Bishop, who had refused to accept his resignation, but had granted him licence of non-residence. — So ends the dream of Stanton, never, I expect, to be revived. E.F.W. and Sophy still cling to the hope that the negociation may be renewed, or that by becoming Curate of Stanton, my Son may yet be able to remove to so spacious and commodious a house; but from this idea of taking the Curacy, I strongly dissuaded E.F.W. in a second letter which I wrote, sending both letters by the Servant. We received a good report of all at the Vicarage. — Wrote to Sophia Hunt, now at Stoke Doyle, forwarding to her the letter I had received yesterday from M^r |[14] Whitcombe, informing her that I should not decline the Executorship and Trusts under Caroline Hunt's will, but that I trusted and expected ^she (Sophia) would attend to the details, and relieve me from much of the labour: advised her to forward the will to Mr Whitcombe for probate, when she returns to Clifton — Answered Mr Whitcombe's letter received yesterday to the same effect as I had just written to Sophia Hunt. — Received from Mr Roberts, Incumbent of Wadenhoe, a reply to the letter relative to the interment of Caroline Hunt which I had addressed to him last week from Clifton. M^r R's answer had been directed to me at Clifton, and forwarded to me from thence. — A letter from Mr Grazebrook, the Undertaker, from Clifton, notifying that he had sent me the usual compliment of silk on occasion of Caroline Hunt's funeral, which also arrived. "The Crescent and the Cross." —

Nov. 11. Thursday.

A fine day, but gloomy. |[15] Transacting business at home with the Churchwarden and Overseer – Called on T. Collett on tax business, and on Rich^d. Yearp, where I met Mr Collins, the surgeon, who would not pronounce R.Y. to be insane; therefore his removal to the Lunatic Asylum is out of the question. — Drove to Stow, accompanied by MW., who soon returned to US. — To the Provident Bank, where I was much engaged in business, meeting Messrs. Pole, Ford, Morrison, R. Waller, and Winter. — To the Justice room, where I sat with Ford and Waller as my colleagues: a long sitting. — Messrs. Winter, W Vavasour, and Polhill were present. — "The Crescent and the Cross."

---

1.   An uncorrected dating error. It was 10 November 1847.

Nov. 12. Friday.

A bright morning followed by a rainy afternoon, and windy evening. — Transacting parish business with the Churchwarden, Gregory — Mʳ Pearce called by appointment, with whom I was engaged in Union business. — Received a letter from Sophia Hunt, from Stoke Doyle, giving particulars of the |¹⁶ funeral of her sister on Tuesday last. — Mʳ Hare attended; also Mʳ Ward Hunt: — Thomas Hunt of Stoke was present, but hardly equal to encounter the exertion. S.H. incloses for my perusal a note from Mʳˢ· Hunt, stating that her husband, George Hunt, had fallen into a depressed and dejected state of mood, since Caroline's decease. This note MW. forwarded to Fanny Hunt at Clifton by Sophia's desire. The letter of the latter contained much Executorship business, to which I replied, and also wrote a letter to Messʳˢ· Yorke, Bankers, Oundle, which S.H. will send to them, directing them to honour her drafts &c. on the Exorship accᵗ· as if they had my signature. — Wrote to George Pain on Provident Bank business. "The Crescent and the Cross." —

Nov. 13. Saturday.

A fine day for the season — a slight shower of rain — Justice business at home. — Visited Thoˢ· Collett on Tax business — also W. Dix as |¹⁷ to the bad condition of ~~the~~ his kinsman, R. Yearp. — Advised with Forty as to one of my horses, ailing under a chronic inflammation of one eye. — Prosser called on me about Prov. Bank business. — Preparing a copy of a letter to be written by Mʳ Pearce to the Poor Law Commʳˢ· as to the valuation of lands in this parish. — Received from Mʳ Moore, Med. Off. of one of the districts of our Union, a note suggesting that measures should be taken by the Guardians to improve the sanitary state of the villages, especially under the probability that Asiatic Cholera, which has long been steadily advancing from the East towards the West, and has shewn itself on the Eastern borders of Europe, may again ere long visit this country. — I replied that I would ~~brink~~ bring the matter before the Board at the next meeting. — "The Crescent and the Cross."

Nov. 14. Sunday.

A fine day till the afternoon, when rain fell. — Wrote to Mʳ Hay-|¹⁸ward and Mʳ Wills, the Med. Off. of the two other districts of our Union, informing them of the purport of the note I had received yesterday from Mʳ Moore, the Med. Off. of the third district, stating that I should bring the matter before the Guardians on Thursday next, and inviting suggestions from them either vivâ voce, or by letter. —— Attended the Sunday School. — Mornᵍ· service – prayers — Afternoon Service, — prayers and sermon. I preached on drawing near to GOD. — Preparing a Sermon — Ecclesiastical gazette — To the family a section from James on the Collects.

Nov. 15. Monday.

Fine weather, very mild for the season. — Justice business at home. — Mʳˢ· Lea called and gave us a very unfavourable report of the health of her children — the second daughter fast sinking under a decline; the second son with symptons of a tendency to consumption, and moreover with very im-|¹⁹paired vision. —— Drove with MW. to Stow. — Shopping — Visited the Workhouse; conferred with Mʳ Pearce on Union business — Called at "the Cottage" — saw Mʳˢ· Vavasour — "The Crescent and the Cross." — A letter from Mʳ Thornton on Hunt affairs.

Nov. 16. Tuesday.

A wetting fog amount[g.] to rain in the forenoon, fine afternoon, and evening. — Wrote to M[r] Thornton on Hunt affairs. — Justice business at home. — Brit. Magazine — Visited the day-school; also Mary Davis, and R. Yearp. — Rec[d.] a letter from M[r] Sewell, who has had an interview with the Bishop's Secretary, M[r] Holt. The latter assures Sewell that neither my Son or myself are at all compromised with the Bishop in respect of the late transaction for the purchase of the next presentation of the living of Stanton; for our names were not officially communicated to him as being parties in the affair. – However this maybe, I have little doubt that his Lordship |[20] is not ignorant that we were in the negociation; — and may have entertained on that account an unfavourable prejudice against us. M[r] Holt observed that it would be both unwise and improper, either that E.F.W. or myself should communicate on the matter with himself or the Bishop. Sewell considers that perfect quietness, while we wait the chapter of accidents, is the course to be persued: he is of opinion that if W. H. Bloxsome should die within a few months, his representatives will hand over to us the grant made in our favour, but I do not understand how that can be properly done, we having cancelled the agreement: Sewell seems to suppose the grant of the next presentation may still be made available, and so professes not to entirely abandon the expectation that the living may yet be secured for my Son, but advises the utmost caution and secrecy in any future transaction, and that such be kept from my Son's knowledge till completed. — |[21] He to be warned against holding any intercourse on the subject with the Bloxsomes. For my own part I ~~like~~ [look] upon the whole as an affaire manquée. — A circular from Gloucester Gaol announcing a meeting of Visitors. — "The Crescent and the Cross."

Nov. 17. Wednesday.

After heavy rain during the night a fine and much colder day than of late. — Wrote to E.F.W. forwarding to him the letter which I had received from Sewell yesterday. I dispatched my packet by our groom, who brought me back my Son's reply. He and Sophy are greatly disappointed, but exonerate me from all blame, kindly saying that in all transaction respecting Stanton I have acted with great liberality and earnest endeavour to promote their interest and wishes. They greatly blame the Bloxsomes who, as they think, have acted with great indiscretion: they incline to the opinion that the affair may not have been well managed by Sewell, and they blame the Bishop as being ready to wink at |[22] a proceeding which he does not approve, if it be managed so as to avoid publicity & notoriety, but takes offence if it be conducted openly, sufficient deference not being shown to him, and resents the apparent defiance of his power to refuse to accept a resignation. They suspect that he would do indirectly what he objects to doing openly. But I am disposed to think that the Bishop has acted conscientiously and on principle, though, perhaps, erroneously. He is very likely to be censured by many who hear of the matter; for the many are always prone to think ill of those in authority, and his Lordship is not generally popular. Besides one cannot understand why, when it was in his power to secure an efficient Rector for Stanton and Snowshill, he retains a man utterly inefficient as regards bodily health, habits, and temper. And, again, why does the Bishop oppose an arrangement now which he approved a few years ago under the same circumstances |[23] as the present? When M[r] Wynniatt sold his advowson to M[r] Bloxsome it was with the understanding that he should have immediate possession. W. resigned: the same Bishop accepted the resignation, and instituted Mr B., an untried man, and a younger man than my Son: no scruples were raised then; why now? — E.F.W. sent for my perusal a letter he has received from Bowen, who is still at Wyke House under the care of Dr Costello, considers himself better, and looks forward to returning in a fortnight. — Justice business at home. — Wrote to M$^{rs.}$ C. Barr. — Preparing to circulate Reports and Quarterly Papers S.P.G. to the members of our District Committee. — British Magazine — Received a letter from a M$^{rs.}$ McNeile, a widow residing at Sydney in the Colony of Cape Breton, seeking information as to a person of Scotch extraction, to whom she supposes herself related, and whose property, as she has heard, was left to be |^{24} equally divided among all her relations. I am applied to, as being resident in the neighbourhood of Stow, where the applicant understands the rich deceased to have lived. I imagine some Missionary of Cape Breton may have found my name and abode in some list of the Members of the Society for the Prop: of the Gospel. — Poor woman! I shall have to disappoint her by my reply; no such person having lived at or near Stow. — Preparing for the meeting of the Guardians at Stow to-morrow. — "The Crescent and the Cross."

Nov. 18. Thursday.

A hard frost: very fine and seasonable weather. — Drove to Stow: MW. accompanied me, but soon returned. — Transacted business at the Provident Bank, and with Mr Croome, land surveyor, at the Unicorn Inn. — To the Workhouse, where I presided at the fortnightly meeting of the Guardians of our Union. |^{25} There was a full board and a great deal of business. — Mr Auditor Hunt has been at Stow for some days, auditing the Union Accounts for two past quarters: he has not finished his labours; but we had no intercourse with him, as he did not attend at the Workhouse; but Mr Pearce and the Rel. Officer complained that he exhibited towards them and the parish officers a very sour temper, as being much incensed by the late correspondence which has passed between him, the Guardians, the Poor Law Comm$^{rs.}$ and the paid officers; his manner is unbending, he shews a great disposition to find fault, and harrasses the officers by his minute and captious examination into the accounts, giving great trouble and annoyance to all parties — After consulting with the Med. Off. (Mess$^{rs.}$ Hayward) and having before us the letter addressed to me together with another entering more into detail from Mr Moore, and a note from Mr Wells, a resolution was passed at my |^{16} suggestion, that the attention of the Med. Officers of the Union should be directed to the provisions of the late Act for the prevention of nuisances, to the end that they might take the initiatory proceedings in any care in which they might apprehend danger from contagion arising from accumulations of noxious matter. Thus precautions may with propriety, and with a reasonable prospect of a successful issue, be taken against cholera or any other contagious disease: the Medical Off. applying to the Guardians, & the latter to the Magistrates, that so the necessary remedies pointed out by the Statute may be employed. And it was ordered that hand bills should be largely circulated in the Union that so the attention of all classes, the Magistracy, the Clergy, the Parish authorities, and Rate-payers generally, may be drawn to a matter of so great interest to all. — After the business of the Workhouse was over, I returned to |^{17} the Provident Bank, where I met Mess$^{rs.}$ Pole, W. B. Pole, Winter &c. — "The Crescent and the Cross." —

Nov. 19. Friday.

A frost, very fine weather — Justice and Tax business at home — Wrote to Rodwell with an order for books for the Stow Book Society. — To Mᵣ Moore, in acknowledgment of his letter addressed to myself and the Guardians of the Union received yesterday at the Board meeting, in which he had very ably treated on the necessity of taking precautions to arrest the progress of cholera or other contagious diseases. I explained to him the resolutions passed by the Board with a view to carry out his very proper suggestions. — To Mʳˢ· Mᶜ·Neile, the person resident at Sydney, Cape Breton, from whom I had received a letter, informing her that no such person as Jane Ellis, respecting whom she inquired, was known as having resided at Stow, or in its neighbourhood; neither were the parties mentioned by her as |¹⁸ the Executors of her will at all known in this neighbourhood. — Recᵈ· a circular from the Lunatic Asylum, Gloucester, announcing a meeting of Visitors as fixed for the 25ᵗʰ· Inst. — Mᵣ Ford, in his capacity of Rural Dean transmitted to me this day a packet containing a letter addressed to me in common with several others of the Clergy of the Deanery, suggesting to us the propriety of concurring in a memorial to Lord John Russell, as Prime Minister, remonstrating with him on the presumed intention on his part to raise to the Episcopal bench the Regius Professor of Divinity at Oxford, Dᵣ Hampden. The Rural Dean had drawn up such a memorial which he requested us to sign. Two names only were affixed to it, those of Mᵣ Morrison, and Mᵣ Wiggin, though the document had been sent to others. The death of Dᵣ Vernon, Archb. of York, at a very advanced age, has made a vacancy on the Episcopal Bench; and |¹⁹ it is generally understood that Dᵣ Musgrave, Bishop of Hereford, is to be translated to York, and that the See of Hereford is destined for Dᵣ Hampden. — I wrote to the Rural Dean giving him some reasons why I declined signing the proposed memorial. — We only know by common rumour, and on newspaper authority, that Dᵣ Hampden is selected; — a remonstrance to the Premier from a small knot of rural Clergy seems an unusual course, likely to be of no service; and if such a measure were desirable, it should have been communicated by the Rural Dean at a meeting of the Clergy of his deanery regularly summoned; it seems every way objectionable to make such a measure the act of a few clergymen selected from the whole body of the Deanery; and in this instance unanimity could not be anticipated; for Lord Saye and Sele, one of our number, is not only well known to advocate the Interests of Dᵣ Hampden, and to have upheld him |²⁰ during the controversy which agitated the University when he was appointed Regius Professor several years ago, and to have persisted in the same friendly view of his case, but, as a Canon of Hereford, will have to vote on the case when the congé d'elire is sent out to that body. Besides, it is a dangerous course to rush into a contention; the best interests of the Church would seem to be jeoparded by unwise agitation. The lower Clergy would do well to wait for a demonstation from the rulers of the Church. — To me the appointment of Dᵣ Hampden appears most rash and unwise; he is a marked man, and a suspected man; and though his opinions may be sound, and his piety and learning eminent, yet his published works have an appearance of heterodoxy – he has used a language, and adopted terms, and taken a line of argument, which have led men of learning to doubt his orthodoxy, |²¹ and have puzzled and confused the unlearned. I voted, as a member of convocation of the University of Oxford, with the great majority who curtailed him of some of the powers and privileges attached ordinarily to the holder of his chair; the charges against him then were brought forward by low churchmen, high churchmen, and Ultra High Churchmen; his opinions, as developed in his Bampton Lectures, and in a pamphlet in which he advocated the admission of dissenters into the University, had excited general alarm and uneasiness — there appeared a tendency to latitudinarism, a resistance to the system of articles and creed, and a favourable leaning towards dissent, which justified the strong measures adopted against him. Since that period he has not retracted any of the objectionable language used by him, but, in his subsequent publications, sermons, and lectures, he has betrayed no token of heterodoxy. It is true also that since the vote of censure was passed against him, the |[22] University has passed a vote of confidence in him by giving him a voice in a committee to which is intrusted the selection of professors of divinity for chairs recently founded; and when a motion was made in the University Convocation to restore to D[r] Hampden those prerogatives of his Regius Professorship which had been refused to him, the majority of votes against him was very much diminished. He is also generally esteemed to be an amiable, high-principled, pious and learned divine: but still he is unfortunately compromised by rash and incautious language heretofore adopted in published writings, and he ought to pay the penalty of indiscretion, not seeking episcopal dignity, nor sought by the Minister. It is better that D[r] H. should remain in a secondary position than that the peace of the church should be disturbed by his elevation to the Bench. But Lord John Russell is a bold, some would say a rash minister: he probably |[23] considers D[r] Hampden an ill used man; and wishes to select for a bishop one who has been from the beginning opposed to the Tractarian and Romanizing section in the Church. — The British Magazine — "The Crescent and the Cross."

Nov. 20. Saturday.

No frost: dry, but hazy weather. — Wrote to Sewell in answer to his letter received on Tuesday last. — Preparing packets of S.P.G. books, tracts and reports for circulation to the members of the Stow district Comm. — Drove with MW. to Bourton on the Water: called at the Rectory; M[rs.] R. Waller at home. — M[r] Turner, the Curate, is about to leave Bourton for a better curacy in Worcestershire. — Received a letter from Sophia Hunt from Stoke Doyle, on Exorship matters: she proposed to return to Clifton next week: — also a letter from Mess[rs.] Yorke, Bankers, Oundle, with a Balance Sheet, shewing the amount standing in their hands to the credit of Caroline Hunt — |[24] Brit. Magazine — "The Crescent and the Cross."

Nov. 21. Sunday.

Dull, hazy weather; heavy rain towards night. — Visited the S. School — Morning prayers and sermon. I preached on Christian Charity. Evening prayers. — Eccl. Gazette. — Preparing a Sermon. — To the family a section from D[r] James on the Collects.

Nov. 22. Monday.

After a rainy night a fine day; more rain towards nightfall — Wrote to Sophia Hunt on Executorship business. — Justice business at home — M[r] J W Harris called to make a payment on account of rent, and settle accounts with me. — Drove [with] MW. to Stow, where transacted business at the office of the Gloucestershire Banking Company. — Thence to Upper Swell, where we left our cards for M[r] and M[rs.] W. B. Pole, who were from home, but whom we met afterwards at Maugersbury House, where we made a call; finding M[rs.] W.V. and Emma at home. — "The Crescent and the Cross." |[25]

Nov. 23. Tuesday.

A rainy forenoon; the afternoon fine. — Preparing packets of S.P.G. for distribution — Preparing a Sermon. — M[r] and M[rs.] Vavasour called — Rec[d.] a letter from C Bathurst, who is now in London: — also from Mess[rs.] Hoare, who notify that M[r] Jennings has paid to my account with them £69. 11. 6. — "The Crescent and the Cross." —

Nov. 24. Wednesday.

A hoar frost: fine day. — Preparing a sermon. — Justice business at home — Wrote to C Bathurst. — Walked to Eyford, where, having heard that M[rs.] Dolphin had returned home, I called to enquire after her: was not admitted; but soon after I had reached home she called upon us, in high health and spirits; being very diffuse as to her late tour in Germany and Switzerland, her visits to the German Baths, her complete recovery under the care of D[r] Granville &c. — Received a packet from Cirencester; by the seal I judge that it was dispatched by M[r] Powell: its contents |[26] two printed documents stimulating the Clergy to vigorous resistance to the appointment of D[r] Hampden to the vacant see of Hereford. Strong measures are counselled – petitions, memorials, addresses to the Queen, to the Minister, to the Archbishop of the Province, to the Bishop of the Diocese, deprecating the elevation of a person under the censure of the University for presumed heterodoxy: that an address be presented to the Dean and Chapter of Hereford, praying them not to elect him on the congé d'elire,[2] and so to incur the penalty of præmunire:[3] to the Archbishop of Canterbury urging him to refuse confirmation and consecration; lastly, if all prior efforts fail, it is proposed to stand forward and oppose the confirmation at Bow Church after the somewhat doubtful and rare precedents which ecclesiastical history presents: the opposition to be on the score of false doctrine. All this violence, & zeal with little judgment is |[27] greatly to be regretted, but not to be wondered at, as emanating from the Ultra High Church or Romanizing party. — "The Crescent and the Cross." —

Nov. 25. Thursday.

A very foggy, damp day. — Preparing for business at Stow. — Drove to Stow. — Received a latter from Sophia Hunt, dated from Stoke Doyle, and covering a copy of a letter which she has rec[d.] from M[r] Whitcombe on our Exorship business. S.H. returns in a day or two to Clifton. — A letter from the elder Newmarch, who informs me that his younger Son, having been obliged in consequence of ill health to relinquish his profession as a sailor, — an officer on board an East Indian Trader, — has employed himself, not unprofitably, in telling his tale of what he had seen in his voyages to and from India and China, in a publication which has lately appeared, entitled, "Five years in the East by J. N. Hutton" — why he assumes a name is |[28] not explained. It is intended to present me with a copy, and I am requested to promote the sale of the book. — A letter from E.F.W: all well at

---

2. Congé de élire – royal permission to a cathedral chapter to fill a vacant See.
3. Præmunire – originally a writ charging a sheriff to summon a person accused of asserting or maintaining papal jurisdiction in England, so denying the ecclesiastical supremacy of the monarch. Also, the statute of Richard II on which this writ was based, later applied to various actions seen as questioning or diminishing the royal jurisdiction. Presumably Francis Witts used this in reference to Hamden's support of dissenters.

the Vicarage. He and Sophy come to the Vavasours at Maugersbury on Tuesday next to attend Stow ball, returning on Wednesday or Thursday. It had been contemplated that they should be accompanied to M. by the youngest boy, and that the two elder should come for the short time to us, which would have been a great pleasure to us: but the season is unfavourable, and it has been judged better not to remove the children from home, and the prudence of this arrangement cannot be denied. — Attended at the Provident Bank, where I transacted business: also conferred with Mr Pearce, for whom I sent from the Workhouse. — The Auditor has left Stow, having made himself very disagreeable, and shewn his ill-temper by disallowing several |^29 items of the Unicorn accounts for very trifling errors, none of them involving any real loss to the institution, or damaging any person, parish or party. — Met Mr Pole at the Provident Bank. — There was much business at the Justice room — the Dean of Gloucester, Ford, Waller, and myself were the Magistrates present — Capt. Leigh, Messrs. Potter, Polhill, Winter, W. Vavasour, and J. T. Rice ~~were~~ also attended. — "The Crescent and the Cross."

Nov. 26. Friday.

A fine day for the season. — Justice business at home. — Wrote to Mr Newmarch in answer to his letter received yesterday. — Visited W. Dix to advise as to the condition of R. Yearp, who continues in a melancholy state of mind and body. — A letter from a Clergyman at Devonport, — a circular craving a contribution towards a Church &c. — British Magazine — "The Crescent and the Cross." – |^30

Nov. 27. Saturday.

Very foggy and rainy weather. — Wrote to Sophia Hunt and Mr Hare on Exorship matters. — Justice business at home. — A letter from Mr Geldard with the balance sheet of our ~~Michaelm~~ Martinmas rent-day in Craven — receipts and expenditure. British Magazine. — Finished "The Crescent & the Cross" — a spirited, clever, interesting book.

Nov. 28. Sunday.

A very wet and foggy day. — Visited the Sunday School. — Morning service – prayers. Afternoon service, prayers and sermon. — I preached on the Lord coming to his Temple. — Preparing a Sermon. — A letter from Sophia Hunt on Exorship business; forward^g. for my perusal a letter from Mr George Hunt. A letter from C Bathurst. — A letter from Rev^d. F. Fulford, Editor of the Colonial Church Chronicle, requesting me to promote the circulation of that periodical. — British Magazine — |^31 To the family a section from James on the Collects.

Nov. 29. Monday.

Fine weather — Settling my Yorkshire accounts. Wrote to Mr Geldard, acknowledging his letter received on the 27th. – with the balance sheet of rents &c. — Wrote to E.F.W. — Justice business at home. – Called on J Davis on a matter of justice business. — Mr Morrison and his son called on us. They walked from Longborough, and we conveyed them back as far as to Stow, in our open carriage, MW. accompanying me thither — Called at the library. — Shopping — To the Workhouse: there conferred with Mr Pearce on

Union business, and arranged that he should visit me to-morrow for a further conference. — Began the Life of Sir Sam[l.] Romilly.[4] —

Nov. 30. Tuesday.

A soft, fine day, but moist atmosphere. — Justice business at home. — Wrote to Mess[rs.] Alcock, Birkbecks & C[o.], desiring |[32] them to pay £200 to my account with Mess[rs.] Hoare. — To Sophia Hunt on Executorship matters; returned to her the letter from M[r] George Hunt, which she had forwarded for my perusal. — To M[r] Pearce, on Union business, in answer to a note which I received from him, he being prevented from waiting on me, as had been arranged. — Received from M[r] Thornton a short note, stating that he is leaving home for a fortnight, and his movements will be so uncertain that he is unable to give me his address. — Called on John Davis, and settled with him the Mich[s.] half year's rent of his farm, he giving me a cheque on the Gloucestershire Banking Company for the amount. — Life of Sir. S. Romilly.

Dec. 1. Wednesday.

A fine, open, mild day. — Preparing a Sermon. — M[r] Pearce called. Engaged with him for some hours on Union business, chiefly with reference to the complaints made, and faults found, |[33] by M[r] Hunt, the Auditor, who has made several disallowances and surcharges on Presiding guardians, paid Officers, (Clerk and Relieving Officer) Parish Officers &c. arising out of the transactions of the two quarters which he has been lately auditing. According to him the affairs of our Union are very badly conducted, but he has failed to shew any injury or injustice done to any party, has proved no substantial wrong; only pointing out and exaggerating inconsiderable errors and deviations from rule, and trifling inaccuracies. It is manifest that his censure is dictated by a bad feeling, and that he acts under the impulse of pique, because his views have not been fully adopted, and a disposition has been manifested not to yeild to his dictation. Conferred with Pearce on the whole matter, and assisted him in preparing minutes, resolutions and correspondence rendered necessary by this very unpleasant controversy. — Received letters from the elder M[r] Newmarch |[34] and his son Charles with reference to the book published by the latter, and the copy which he had promised to send to me by the carrier, but which, by some mistake, has not been forwarded. — A letter from M[r] Hare in answer to mine addressed to him on the 27[th.] – Ult. He has received from M[r] Thornton a letter which he forwards to me to the same effect as the note I rec[d.] from him on Tuesday: M[r] T. will agree to any measure taken by M[r] Hare and me during the time when, by reason of his absence from home, he is unable to maintain a correspondence with us. M[r] H. forwards also a balance sheet shewing the amount due from the trust to Caroline Hunt at her decease. — M[r] Moore, Med. Off. of the Union called, but when I had gone out for exercise. — Rec[d.] a note from M[r] Ford, asking me to furnish him with the form of a testimonial for orders, that he may send a copy of it to M[r] Fullarton, the Curate of Cuts-|[36] dean, who is about to take Priest's Orders at the approaching ordination of the Bp. of Worcester. M[r] F. is a man of whom very unpleasant rumours are current, impeaching

---

4. Sir Samuel Romilly (1757-1818). *The Life of Sir Samuel Romilly* in Two Volumes, London: 1842. Romilly was a law reformer who worked tirelessly to reduce the offences and laws, many dating back hundreds of years, for which captial punishment — hanging — was the only sentence.

his moral character. He has been a Cavalry officer, and a Gentleman Commoner of Magd. College, Oxford; his father, recently deceased, has left him a large fortune, and his habits are more suitable to a layman than a clergyman: yet Ford and Bowen are not unwilling to concur with M[r] Strickland, Rector of Bredon, in giving him testimonials. He has, indeed, made himself useful to Bowen by assisting him in the Clerical duties of Temple Guiting, which B. could not discharge, owing to his absence and bad state of health, and M[r] F. is said to officiate well; but, by all accounts, he ought not to go further in the profession, and cautious men would hesitate to give him testimonials. Bowen Ford reports as on his return from D[r] Costello's establishment near Brentford to Guiting, having gone through many operations [36] for the stone, and being now, it is said, quite relieved from that complaint. I sent to Ford the form of a testimonial. — Life of Sir Sam[l.] Romilly. —

Dec. 2. Thursday.

A fine day — Drove to Stow. — MW. accompanied me; returning after calling at one or two shops. — Transacted business at the Provident Bank, and at the Office of the Gloucestershire Banking Company. — Presided at the fortnightly meeting of the Guardians of the Union; — a full board, and very heavy business. — Much discussion and explanation, with correspondence rendered necessary by the objections, disallowances, and surcharges lately made by the Auditor. It is necessary to appeal to the Poor Law Commissioners, and before such appeal a preliminary correspondence is unavoidable. I went through all the points, discussing them, and recommending as to the course to be pursued, as relates to the unfavourable [37] comments made by the Auditor on the general management of the Union by the guardians, and the particular disallowances and surcharges. The line which I advised was adopted. There were also very many applicants for relief, so that I was obliged to leave the business unfinished, and under the charge of others, at four P.M. Before leaving the Workhouse E.F.W. and W. Vavasour came to seek me. My son and his wife had been staying since Tuesday at Maugersbury, and had been present at Stow Ball on that night. I met Sophy and Edward afterwards at the door of the library with M[rs.] W. Vavasour and Emma Vavasour. The former were on the point of setting out for Stanway — Conferred with several parties to-day as to parochial valuations as required by the County rate Committee. — Returned home, much tired with my day's work. — Life of Sir Sam[l.] Romilly. — [38]

Dec. 3. Friday.

A damp, foggy day, with some rain. — Wrote to P. B. Purnell, to consult him as to allowing the parishes of Longborough, Donnington, & Stow, to employ Mess[rs.] Bravender and Trinder, of Cirencester, to make valuations of those parishes under the Parochial Assessment Act; and that the County rate Comm. should withdraw the directions they had given to those Surveyors to value those parishes for the purposes of a County rate only. The occupiers of these parishes had resisted the applications made to them from the County rate Comm. requiring them to furnish a satisfactory professional valuation. Therefore the Comm., under the County rate Act, sent their own valuers to make a compulsory survey and valuation. This, the occupiers found, would entail on their parishes an expence, without benefit; for the valuation would not be useful for parochial [39] purposes. They, therefore, now find it prudent at the eleventh hour, to submit to the requirements of the Comm. and solicit my interposition that they may be allowed to have a valuation under the parochial Assessment Act. I consented to interfere only on condition that they should employ as Surveyors the Valuers whom the Comm. had directed to make the valuation on their account. — Wrote to Messrs. Hoare, desiring them to place £35 from my account to the acc^{t.} of my Son. — Wrote to Messrs. Garaway & Co. Nurserymen, with an order for seeds &c. — Wrote to Sophia Hunt on Exorship matters — Justice business at home. — Rec^{d.} a letter from the Poor Law Comm^{rs.} on the charges made by the Auditor, Hunt, as to mismanagement and improper modes of proceeding on the part of the Guardians and paid Officers of our Union. A copy of Mr Hunt's report to the P.L.C. is forwarded. — ~~Rec^{d.} a letter from Sophia Hunt on Exorship~~ Rec^{d.} a letter from Sophia Hunt on Exorship |⁴⁰ business In the letter ~~from Sophia Hunt~~ she ~~business. She~~ forwards as statement of accounts from Mr Tebbutt, the Steward of the Northamptonshire Hunt Estates. — Life of Sir S. Romilly. —

Dec. 4. Saturday.

A fine day: very windy at night. — Justice business at home — Wrote to Mr Hare on Hunt Exorship concerns. — To the Poor Law Comm^{rs.} in answer to their letter received yesterday. — A letter from the Clerk of the Gloucester Lunatic Asylum, announcing a meeting of Visitors for the 15th. Inst. — to consider the testimonials of candidates for the office of Matron now vacant by the death of the late matron, and to deliberate on plans for enlarging the building so as to receive a greater number of Paupers. — Life of Sir S. Romilly. —

Dec. 5. Sunday.

Rain had fallen during the night, a cold, but a fine day. — Morning prayers and sermon. I preached on the "Prince of Peace." Afternoon |⁴¹ prayers. — Received a letter from Messrs. Hoare, announcing that they had transfered £35 from my account to that of my Son. — A letter from Miss E Moorhouse, announcing the death of her sister Alice, my wife's first cousin once removed, and intreating some pecuniary help to enable her to meet the charges of the funeral. — Preparing a Sermon. — British Magazine — To the family a section from Dr James's work on the collects. —

Dec. 6. Monday.

A very stormy and rainy day. — Transacted Union and Justice business at home with the Relieving officer. — Wrote to E. Moorhouse, forwarding a cheque on Messrs. Alcock and C^{o.} for £3. to assist her in meeting the expence of the funeral of her sister Alice. — Wrote to Sophia Hunt on Exorship business — Visited   Watts, a poor woman at Eyford, who is in a dangerous state from cancer in the bladder. — Life of Sir S. Romilly. — |⁴²

Dec. 7. Tuesday.

A windy day; a little, and but very little rain. — Went to Eyford; administered the holy Sacrament to   Watts: her four married daughters and two aged inhabitants, the Pinchins, were also communicants. — Preparing a Sermon. — Copying the report of the annual meeting of the Stow District Comm. S.P.G. for 1846. — A letter from Mr H. D. Warter, who announces to me that the purchase of the Ground rents in the parish of St. Georges in the East is nearly completed; and that he shall soon call on me for a remittance of £200; of which £150 will be required for the purchase of stamps, and £50 to pay for a small piece of Leasehold included in the purchase, but which must be bought out of my private funds, as the Trust money cannot be employed in buying any thing but freehold — A letter from Purnell on County business. In reply to mine of the 3ᵈ· Inst. he assents to |⁴³ my proposition as to the valuation of Longborough, Donnington, and Stow, as far as may be done without the express authority of the County rate committee, which may be obtained at the Epiphany Sessions. — A letter from Mᵣ Hare as to the amount of payments due from the Personal Estate of T. W. Hunt at the time of Caroline Hunt's death to her estate, on which point he will consult Messʳˢ· Cox. and Williams, and report the answer he receives from me — A letter from Messʳˢ· Hoare announces that Messʳˢ· Alcock & Cᵒ· have paid £200 to my account with them. — The promised book, "Five years in the East" by Hutton alˢ· Charles Newmarch came to-day. — It appears to be written in a pleasant light, gossiping style, & gives much, but not deep, information on the many countries visited, mixed with personal narrative. — Life of Sir S. Romilly. —

Dec. 8. Wednesday.
There had been a sprinkling of snow: a sharp frost; fine day. — Wrote to H. D. Warter that I should be ready |⁴⁴ when called on to remit to him £200, as desired by him in his letter received yesterday. — Copying report Stow Distr. Comm. S.P.G. for 1846. — Drove to Stow — Received the usual annual circular from the Secretary S.P.G. desiring a remittance of subscriptions &c. received by the local Treasurers in their respective districts to the close of the year: — from the Clerk of the Peace's office a notice of a meeting of the Prisons Committee for this County on Dec.15: — from Mᵣ Potter a letter in which he charges Mᵣ Hayward, as M.O. of the 1ˢᵗ· Distr. of our Union, with neglect of his duties, inattention to the sick poor, the lying in, and the sufferers by accidents requiring surgical attendance, in the parish of Broadwell – Called on Hayward; conferred with him on the above letter, which I left with him, that he might refer to the cases alleged by Mᵣ Potter, and prepare to defend |⁴⁵ himself against the charge. — Attended the annual meeting of the Stow Provident Bank, at which the Dean of Gloucester presided. Mᵣ Pole, who usually attends to lay before the meeting the Balance sheet, and comment on the business of the past year, was absent on business in London. I did my best to supply his place. – Messʳˢ· Ford, Morrison, Hippisley and W. B. Pole were the other Trustees or Managers present. On the whole, considering the depression in monetary matters which exists, as it has for some months prevailed, the high prices and scarcity of the necessaries of life during the past twelvemonth, the low rate of interest given, and the consequent temptation to withdraw capital to invest elsewhere at a higher rate of interest, the transactions of our Savings Bank have been satisfactory. The amount of deposits with interest due exceeds £49000: and the number of depositors this year on the books is only twenty three below the number at the last annual meeting. |⁴⁶ The routine business of the day was transacted, and Mᵣ Lefevre, who, since the decease of Mᵣ J D Charles, had been attending as Assistant Clerk, was permanently appointed to that office. — An extraordinary meeting of members of the Book Society was held, at which Mᵣ Barter, of Sarsden, was elected a subscriber. — Transacted business (tax & County rate matters) with Mᵣ Morgan and Churchwarden Lane. — Went with Mᵣ Hippisley to the Workhouse, to investigate a matter alleged on common report in the town, that an aged female pauper had lost her life by apoplexy superinduced by being long detained in the open

air in the cold of last Thursday evening, waiting with others until the Rel. Off. was ready to distribute relief to the applicants. She had been found dead on the following morning in the Almshouse which she occupied. Directed M[r] Pearce to inquire and report as to this allegation. — |[47] Much indisposed all day, particularly in the evening, by an attack of diarrhoea with flatulence &c. — Newmarch's Five years in the East. — Life of Sir S. Romilly.

Dec. 9. Thursday.

Mild, moist weather, with occasional drizzling rain. — Drove to Stow. — Received a latter from E.F.W. — a good account of all at Stanway Vicarage. — Attended at the Provident Bank, where I met Mess[rs.] Morrison, R Waller, and Ford. — To the Workhouse: conferred with M[r] Pearce on Union business, especially as to the surcharges and disallowances made by the Auditor, and the matters alleged by Capt. Leigh as to relief improperly administered, as he conceives, in the parish of Broadwell. This charge, though supported by M[r] Polhill, will, I fully believe, prove to be without reasonable ground, and originates very much in personal antipathy against M[r] Beman, which Capt. L. indulges, and in a jealous feeling towards the same party |[48] entertained by others. — Ascertained that there is no foundation whatever for the report mentioned yesterday by M[r] Hippisley that the old widow Wilkins had met her death by exposure to cold when attending on Thursday evening last to receive parochial relief. On the contrary she had received every attention, and even indulgence. I communicated the facts in a note to M[r] Hippisley — At the Justice room I sat with Mess[rs.] Ford and R Waller as my colleagues — M[r] Polhill & W. Vavasour attended. — M[r] Hayward explained to me the particulars of his defence against the charge preferred by M[r] Potter that he neglected his Union patients at Broadwell. —Consulted Hayward as to the attack of diarrhoea under which I still suffered, though it had abated. He prescribed for me. — Life of Sir S. Romilly. —

Dec. 10. Friday.

A moist, dark day. — |[49] Wrote to M[r] Potter in answer to his letter received on Wednesday, requesting him, if so disposed, to prefer his charges against M[r] Hayward at the meeting of the Guardians of Thursday next, when I had desired M[r] Hayward to attend. I told M[r] P. that M[r] H. expressed a desire for an investigation, & that he considered himself to have a full justification for his conduct in the case to which M[r] P. alluded in his letter to me. — Wrote to M[r] Hayward, informing him of the terms of my letter to M[r] Potter, pointing out to him wherein his defence appears to me deficient. — Wrote to M[r] Rodwell, with an order for the supply of books to the Stow library. — M[r] Pearce called, with whom I was engaged for several hours, considering Union business, preparing an answer to the Auditor's imputations of mismanagement &c. — Received a letter from M[r] H D Warter, who desires me to cause £200 to be paid to his |[50] account at Childs', Bankers, London: — to meet the cost of stamps for the conveyance of the Ground rents in S[t] Georges in the East, as also the price of a small leasehold connected with them. — Rec[d.] a letter from Sophia Hunt, with enclosures from M[r] Whitcombe; it is proposed that I should meet her at Gloucester next week, to be sworn with her by commission to the due discharge of our duties as Executors of the will of her lately deceased Sister. — M[rs.] W. Vavasour and her sister called on us. — Life of Sir S. Romilly — Newmarch's Five years in the East. — My indisposition abated; but the disorder in my stomach and bowels not entirely removed.

Dec. 11. Saturday.

A fine, mild day. — Wrote to Messrs. Hoare, directing them to pay £200 from my account with them to the account of Mr H. D. Warter with Messrs. Childs. — Wrote to HDW. that I had so done. — Wrote to Sophia Hunt, returning |^51 to her the letters from Mr Whitcombe which she had forwarded, and engaging to meet her at Mr Whitcombe's office on Friday the 17th. – Inst. to be sworn with her to the due discharge of our duty as Executors to her late sister. — Wrote to Mr Whitcombe that I should attend at his office to meet S.B.H. on the 17th. – Inst. unless I heard to the contrary. — Wrote to my Son in answer to his letter received on the 9th. In the evening came a note from E.F.W. to his Mother. All well at the Vicarage, Stanway. — Visited S. Watts. Eyford, a sick person. — Brit. Mag. — Life of Sir S. Romilly

Dec.12. Sunday.

A fine, mild day. — Visited the Sunday School — Morning service – prayers — Afternoon – prayers and sermon. — I preached on the Evidences of Christianity. — Preparing a Sermon. — Brit. Mag. — To the family a Section from Dr James on the Collects.

Dec. 13. Monday.

Fine weather. — A long |^52 conference with Mr Pearce and Mr Dunford on Union matters, preparing answers to Mr Hunt's charges of incorrectness and mismanagement — Justice business at home — Visiting a sick parishioners, Mary Davis, a great sufferer. — Received a letter from Mr Griffiths, Subwarden of Wadham, soliciting my vote in Convocation for Mr Michell, of Lincoln Coll., formerly of Wadham, who is a candidate for the office of Public Orator, likely to be vacated by Mr Jacobson, of Magd. Hall, formerly of Exeter Coll., of whom it is stated that he will be raised by Government to the Regius of Professorship of Divinity, about to be resigned by Dr Hampden, when elevated to the see of Hereford. The proposed appointment of Jacobson is considered a good one; he entered the University an unknown aspirant for promotion, without family interest or patronage: rose in estimation by the force of talent and application – has published a valuable work |^53 on the Apostolic Fathers, if I mistake not: distinguished himself by his judicious management of Magd. Hall, and the character of his tuition – (was my Son's Tutor there) and has filled the office of Public Orator with credit. Mr Michell is Prælector of Logic. I gave him my suffrage when he obtained that appointment; he is a good and sound scholar, and much respected, and well calculated, say his friends, for the office of Public Orator. His Uncle, Michell of Wadham, was my tutor at College. — Life of Sir S. Romilly. —

Dec. 14. Tuesday.

Fine weather — Wrote to Messrs. Davidson, Newman and C^o. with a remittance for groceries supplied, and an order for more: — to Mr Griffiths, promising my vote in favour of Mr Michell as Candidate for the office of Public Orator — Our cook, Elizabeth Painter, married this morning by me to William Pugh, of this village. — Drove to Stow. Attended a meeting of Comm^rs. of Taxes: appeal under the Income |^54 Tax, Schedule D – trade & professions — Messrs. Ford and R Waller sat with me as Comm^rs. Messrs. Betterton and Morgan were the Officials: the former a very pleasant and intelligent man, is an officer of the higher grade with charge of a wide district, and makes a half yearly circuit to receive the taxes. — Mr Polhill joined us as an appellant. — A letter from Sophia Hunt engaging to meet me at Mr Whitcombe's office at Gloucester on Friday next. — from Messrs. Hoare, who have paid £200 from my account with them to Mr H. D. Warter's account at Childs' — Life of Sir S. Romilly. —

Dec. 15. Wednesday.

A fine forenoon, a rainy afternoon and evening — Parish business in the morning at home. — Justice business at home. — Wrote to Messrs. Hoare, desiring that the continuation of my account may be sent. — Received a letter from Mr Potter, who persists in his charges against Mr Hayward. — |^55 Received from Oxford a packet of papers in favour of Dr Hampden, rebutting the charges against him, and advocating his fitness to be raised to the Episcopal bench. The controversy respecting him is in a state of great activity. Thirteen Bishops, among them the Bp. of Gloucester, have addressed a memorial to Lord John Russell, praying him to abandon an intention to appoint as a Bishop a under the censure of his University, and of doubtful orthodoxy; shewing that great injury is likely to accrue to the Church by such appointment, a large section within the Church being conscientiously hostile to such appointment, and praying that in some manner his orthodoxy and the tendency of his writings may be tested. To this remonstrance the Archbishop of Canterbury is not a party, but it is understood that he disapproves of the appointment, and has intimated to the Minister his dissatisfaction with it. I consider that this movement on the |^56 part of these Bishops is right, and the far properer course than petitions, complaints, and demonstrations emanating from the inferior clergy. Lord John Russell answers the thirteen bishops in a respectful, but firm tone, contests their views, argues that Dr H. was condemned on insufficient grounds, by a tumultuous vote of a popular and not very deliberative body, that compensation for the wrong done him is his due, and manifests no disposition to abandon his purpose of placing him on the Episcopal bench. Of the thirteen Bishops, Dr Philpot of Exeter addresses Lord J.R. in a long, laboured, able, argumentative, caustic, pungent, and polemical reply to the letter which the Minister sent as an answer to their Lordships. The Bp. of Exeter's production is quite characteristic of his style and temper, and power in controversy, but also such a letter as a moderate man, seeking peace, and the |^57 furtherance of unity, and the cultivation of charity, would have abstained from ~~righting~~ writing. Nearly five hundred laymen of the nobility and gentry have also memorialized Lord John Russell against the appointment of Dr Hampden. To them his reply seems not to indicate any intention of reconsidering the matter: on the contrary rather shews a design to persist in it, thereby shewing hostility to the Ultra High Church and Romanizing party. The latter certainly take the lead in opposing the appointment; but moderate men both of High Church and Low Church tendencies, deprecate the selection. — Received a note from Winter informing me that Bathurst's Neckar wine is arrived in London. —— E.F.W. and Sophy, bringing with them their two elder boys, drove over from Stanway to visit us; partaking of luncheon here, and passing two or three hours. All were in good health. We were most pleased to see them, and loth to part from them; |^58 the more so, as they left us in heavy rain. — In the evening a parish meeting was held in my Study; the Church land Trustees, Messrs. Lea and Collett, with Church Warden Gregory, consulting with me, and concurring in a list of those poor parishioners to whom out of the funds of the Church and Charity Estate coal is to be distributed during several weeks at the low rate of sixpence the hundred weight. Other parish business was transacted. — Life of Sir Samuel Romilly.

Dec. 16. Thursday.

Moist, not to say rainy weather throughout the day. — Wrote to C Bathurst to announce to him the arrival of the Neckar wine. — Drove to Stow — Attended at the Provident Bank. — To the Workhouse, where I was engaged from 12 o cl. to 4 P.M. presiding at the fortnightly meeting of the Guardians of the Union. There was much to be done; and the administration of relief had hardly begun |⁵⁹ when I quitted the Board. — The leading business of the day was the passing of various resolutions, observations, and explanations prepared by myself and Mᵣ Pearce, to rebut the allegations made by the district Auditor against the management of the Union, and with a view to obtain a reversal of his disallowances and Surcharges. — Next followed an investigation as to a charge preferred to the Poor Law Commᵣˢ· by Capt. Leigh, who complained of relief granted by the Board to a pauper of Broadwell, named Hardiman, a labourer in the employment of Mᵣ Beman, a man of infirm health, and with a large family, at low wages. Captain Leigh, Mᵣ Polhill, and Mᵣ Potter were present. The gravamen as to Hardiman was that Mᵣ Beman enjoyed his services, in a responsible situation, as attending to a thrashing machine worked by steam, an employment requiring judgment, on wages of only five |⁶⁰ shillings weekly, so that the parish funds were needed to supply what the necessities of the man's large and young family required. It was urged that he should have been paid good wages for important services — but the answer was that the law under which Guardians are appointed and act has nothing to do with regulating wages — that Beman employed a very sickly man in light and easy work, whom none of the other farmers would employ at higher wages. From documentary evidence produced by Mᵣ B. it appeared that the man was in a deplorable state of health from fistula, often incapacitating him for many weeks together; this was confirmed by Mᵣ Hayward. Mᵣ Dunford testified that he had pointed out to the rate payers the cost incurred by the parish on account of Hardiman's low wages and large family, but no one had offered him higher wages than Mᵣ Beman; Mᵣ B. stated that the work at which he was employed |⁶¹ could be done by a lad at low wages; and from the man's appearance and evidence it appeared that he had for many years been very infirm, and that the allegations made by Capt. Leigh in his communications to the Poor Law Commᵣˢ· that he could ride, shoot, &c. were exaggerations based on very slight foundation. The Guardians considered the charge made to have been disproved, and agreed that the Evidence should be forwarded to the P.L.C. who will, doubtless, exculpate the Board from an improper administration of relief in this instance as charged against them by Capt. Leigh. — Mᵣ Potter afterwards brought forward his charge against Mᵣ Hayward, confining himself to one case of alleged neglect of a woman whom he had been required to attend in her confinement. Mᵣ P. conducted his case steadily and cleverly; with a strong prepossession against the Medical Officer; ready to take advantage of any point which might arise unfa-|⁶² vourable to the accused: and it was obvious that he had been seeking out for matter of charge against him among his poor parishioners. The case also selected by him was stale; the woman had been confined in last spring; had herself brought forward no complaint either then or subsequently; and there was every reason to expect that the circumstances of the case had escaped Hayward's recollection in the multiplicity of his professional engagements, and so might be unfairly pressed against him. Hayward also has an irritable, nervous, hesitating manner, is totally unused to such proceedings, and was likely, as he did, to meet the charge with warmth and indiscretion. The woman in question, who had gone through her labour well, and had recovered from it without any extraordinary debility or ailment, her husband, who had gone to Mr Hayward's surgery on the evening of the confinement, and obtained medicine, a girl who had been sent |^63 as a messenger for Mr H., but who had been wrongly instructed by those who sent her, and neither knew that the woman was in labour, nor brought any message but that M^r H's attendance was required, so that he believed he had been summoned only to a person labouring under another attack, and not to a midwifery case, and the boy Ferris, Hayward's nephew, who assists in his uncle's surgery, were examined; — from all whose testimony it seemed to the Guardians that the blame or error in the case, and the apparent neglect of the Med. Off. in not attending at the delivery was not chargeable on him, but on the parties themselves, who had failed to send a proper and explicit message when the confinement took place. It appeared also to the Board that Mr H. was justified in his subsequent treatment of the case, and in charging the parish with the fee to which he was entitled for attendance as in a midwifery case. — At the same time it must be confessed that Hayward |^64 is deficient in method and arrangement in the conduct of his business; often has no assistant, which was the case at the time alleged, whereas his medical engagements imperatively require that he should never be without an experienced Substitute; and would carry on his business with more satisfaction to himself and others, if he kept his books more accurately, and filed more carefully the notices and orders sent to him from the Union Officers. Of his experience & skill, and attention in Serious cases, whether in the higher or lower classes of his patients, too much cannot be said in commendation. — I returned from Stow much tired. — Mr Terry called when I was absent. — Rec^d. a letter from H. D. Warter in acknowledgment of the receipt of the £200 which I had directed Messrs. Hoare to pay to his account with Childs. He expects very soon to complete the purchase of the ground rents in S^t. George's in the East. — Rec^d. a letter from |^65 Messrs. Davison, Newman and C^o. in acknowledgment of the remittance of £5. 6. 0. which I had made to them. — Life of Sir S. Romilly.

Dec. 17. Friday.

A rainy day – rough wind in the afternoon and evening. — Early breakfast. — With MW. in the open carriage to Cheltenham, where we arrived by 11 A.M. — To the Plough Hotel. — At Mr Forget's engaged as Cook an elderly woman, subject to the reply to be made to the enquiry to be made of her last mistress as to her character. — Leaving MW. at Cheltenham, I proceeded from the Great Western Station by a short train to Gloucester at twelve o clock. It was my first journey by this road now lately opened on the broad gage System from Cheltenham to Gloucester, & traversing, on a complicated system of rails, the same line as is pursued on the narrow gage system by the British and Birmingham railway. On arriving at the Gloucester Station I waited for the train from |^66 Bristol by which Sophia Hunt had promised to travel to meet me. It soon arrived, and with it our friend from Clifton, who was also met by Miss Louisa Davies. S.H. gave a very unfavourable report of her brothers and sisters at N°. 8 West Mall, Clifton, they being attacked with the prevailing epidemic, the influenza, which also affected their Servants: nor was Sophia free from the complaint. She accompanied me in an Omnibus to Mr Whitcomb's office, where we took the Oaths as Co executors of the will of Caroline Hunt, which were administered by Mr Hardwick, the Rector of S^t. Michaels Gloucester, in which parish Mr Whitcomb's office is situate, and in which, therefore, S.H. and I were locally and temporarily resident, ^{being the Commissioner.} After some conference with S.H. and Mͬ Whitcomb on Executorship business, I left them, S.H. proposing to pass a day or two with her friend Miss Oakley at Gloucester. I did not reach the Railway Station in time to return to Cheltenham |⁶⁷ by the 1.30. short train of the Cheltenham and Great Western line, which had just departed as I came. I was, therefore, obliged to wait till 2 PM. when an engine with two or three Carriages was dispatched to meet a train in the line leading direct from London, Swindon & Stroud to Cheltenham, without calling at the Gloucester Station: this meeting takes place about a mile from the Gloucester Station, where a small station will be built (now there is only an open platform:) here I was transferred from the carriage in which I had come from Gloucester to the train it had joined, and a few minutes brought us to the Cheltenham Station, occupying part of Jessop's garden, and not remote from the centre of the High Street — Having rejoined MW. at the Plough, and taken a slight refreshment, we left Cheltenham for Upper Slaughter soon after 3 PM., arriving at home in heavy rain and wind between 5 & 6 P.M. — A letter from Messʳˢ· Hoare, with the continuation of my banking account. — Mͬ Ford had |⁶⁸ called during our absence. — Life of Sir S. Romilly.

Dec. 18. Saturday.

Very rainy weather — Settling my banking account with Messʳˢ· Hoare, who having omitted to receive for me some dividends on 3 Pͬ Cͭ· Cons. standing in my name, I wrote to remind them of the neglect, and to request that it may be remedied. — Wrote to Messʳˢ· Hitchman & Cᵒ· Chipping Norton with an order for four Gallons of Brandy. — Justice business at home. — Received a letter from Mͬ Warter, who informs me that the conveyance of the Ground rents in Sͭ· George's in the East is nearly concluded, and that he will send for my signature a power of Attorney to enable him to draw the money out of the Court of Chancery, to which I am entitled as accumulation of interest on the sum so long impounded there: this document I ~~must~~ ᵐᵃʸ expect by Tuesday's post, and must, if possible, return it by the post |⁶⁹ to London of the same day; otherwise delay may be caused by the office of the Court of Chancery being closed for Christmas. — British Magazine — Life of Sir S. Romilly.—

Dec. 19. Sunday.

A cold, raw day, no rain — Visited the Sunday School. — Morning Prayers and a Sermon. I preached on the usual objections made to the habitual receiving of the Lord's Supper. — Afternoon Service, prayers. — Received a letter from C Bathurst, now in London, as to the forwarding to Lidney of his Neckar wine — Also from the Clerk of the Gloucester infirmary a letter with reference to a patient there under my recommendation — Preparing a Sermon. — Ecclesiastical Gazette — to the family a section from Dͬ James on the Collects — Dͬ Hampden's appointment to the Bishopric of Hereford appears in the Gazette — The Minister, therefore, will not concede to the calls made upon him, but persists in his ill judged appointment. |⁷⁰

Dec. 20. Monday.

A cold, raw day; moist without being rainy. — Wrote to Mͬ Winter about forwarding the Neckar wine to Lidney for C Bathurst. — Also to the Clerk of the Gloucester Infirmary with a fresh recommendation of Hannah Clapton as an in-patient — Mͬ Pearce called: with whom a long sitting, in which we prepared minutes, resolutions, and notes of evidence as to the two cases which were subjects of enquiry before the Guardians on Thursday last, — the charges brought forward by Captain Leigh, and M[r] Potter.

Dec. 21. Tuesday.

Cold, but dry weather: a frost towards sunset. — Drove to Bourton on the Water, calling by the way at the Turnpike Gate for letters. There I received, as I expected, a packet from M[r] H. D. Warter, containing a power of Attorney to be executed by me in presence of an Extra Master in Chancery, to enable M[r] Warter to receive on my behalf from the Accountant General |[72] of the Court of Chancery, the sum, exceeding £700, to which I am entitled, as the accumulation on the capital impounded there, under the private Act of Parliament, which empowered the sale of the houses in Fenchurch Street entailed by my Uncle Broome Witts's will. This amount will all be swallowed up in the law and other expences incident on the purchase of ground rents to be settled under the Trusts of the same will; in the same gulph will be swallowed the sum of £200 recently remitted by me to M[r] H D Warter: nor will these sums suffice; a heavy balance will, I fear, still remain to be paid. But it is to be observed that these heavy costs embrace the tedious, expensive and abortive effort to purchase the late M[r] Stanley Hill's Great Risington Estate, as also lesser sums expended in enquiries after other freehold investments which were from time to time suggested, but which proved ineligible. Called at M[r] Wilkins's office and there |[73] executed the power of Attorney, writing to M[r] H. D. Warter, and returning to him the power of Attorney. — Walked to Eyford, and called on M[rs.] Dolphin, who has recently returned from Cheltenham, and who is again about to leave home. — With her I found Miss Knight, and Bowen, who had come from Temple Guiting, whither he returned some time ago from Wyke House, and from under the medical charge of D[r] Costello. His grievous malady, the stone, has been very much relieved by a series of painful operations, in lithotrity,[5] and by severe discipline; but there is room for apprehension in respect of the future health of one so aged, and with so strong a tendency to the formation of calculus. — Life of Sir Samuel Romilly.

Dec. 22. Wednesday.

A hard frost, and fine winter's day. — Engaged with Churchwarden Gregory and [in] settling the list of poor |[74] parishioners entitled to receive each a portion of bread at this season under an old parish bequest. — Wrote to M[rs.] Dolphin, sending her a copy of that part of the Valuation of this parish by M[r] Croome which relates to the land occupied by her, and to the rates payable by her. — Visited poor Emily Lea, far gone in consumption, and whose days are numbered: prayed with her, — an interesting and lovely girl of eighteen: her parents and her Aunt Tysoe were present. — D[r] Hampden has addressed a letter to Lord John Russell, in which he vindicates himself from the imputation of heterodoxy, and sets forth a personal confession of second faith. He enters into the history and character of the proceedings formerly taken at the University against him, and complains of the attack now made against him. The controversy is maintained with great eagerness: his enemies

---

5. Lithotrity – the operation of crushing a stone in the bladder into minute particles which can be expelled through the urethra.

are "lively and strong" — the church and the public mind are greatly agitated on |[75] the subject. — British Magazine — Life of Sir Sam[l.] Romilly. —

Dec. 23. Thursday.

Cold weather, and a sharp frost. — Drove to Stow. — Rec[d.] a letter from M[r] H. D. Warter accompanying a deed to which my signature is required, by which I covenant to produce, when necessary, such title deeds in my possession as may [be] required from time to time to support the titles of the purchasers of certain portions of the Estate in S[t.] George's in the Fields, which we have recently bought of M[r] Furze, and of which the conveyance has now been made to us, so that the ground rents are now ours, & will be paid to us from and after Christmas. — Executed the said deed in presence of M[r] Pain and M[r] Lefevre. — Rec[d.] a letter from the Clerk to the Gloucester Infirmary. It appears that the letter which I received from him on the 19[th.] was written by error; and that the patient therein men-|[76]tioned has been discharged, greatly recovered. The fresh recommendation which I sent has, therefore, been cancelled. — At the Provident Bank met M[r] and M[rs.] Winter, M[r] Lewes, Baroness de Klock, M[r] Ford, M[r] R Waller — Engaged for more than an hour at the Workhouse with M[r] Pearce, auditing accounts, and giving directions. — Returned to the Provident Bank, where I met the Dean of Gloucester. — To the Justice room, where transacted Magisterial business, assisted by Mess[rs.] Ford and R Waller — Lord Saye and Sele, Mess[rs.] Polhill, Winter, W B Pole, W. Vavasour, and R W Hippisley were in attendance. — Several of these dined together at the Unicorn Inn, this being the Anniversary meeting of the Trustees of the Cope Charity. At so severe a season I am afraid of exposure in an open carriage to the night air, and have for several years declined dining with my brother Trustees — |[77] J N Hutton's (Ch[s.] Newmarch's) Five Years in the East — Life of Sir S. Romilly.

Dec. 24. Friday.

Frost gone: milder weather. — Wrote to C Bathurst about sending to him the Neckar wine. — To M[r] Warter, returning to him the deed which I had received yesterday, and had executed. — To M[r] Bloxsome, requesting him to send me his half yearly bill on the County, that I might examine it before the Quarter Sessions — to M[r] Croome, Land Surveyor, with reference to some correction required in his valuation of this parish — to M[r] Gilby, Incumbent of S[t.] James's, Cheltenham, respecting a pauper settled at Lower Slaughter, as to whom he had addressed a letter to me — Received a letter from E.F.W: all well at the Vicarage, Stanway. — a letter from Mess[rs.] Hoare who have now received the Dividend on 3 p[r] C[t.] Cons. standing in |[78] my name which they had neglected to receive in July last. — a letter from the Clerk to the Lunatic Asylum at Gloucester, announcing a meeting of the Visitors to be held at the Shire hall, Gloucester, on the 3[d.] Jan. – the day before the Sessions — a letter from Sophia Hunt of Hunt Trust and Executorship matters. Sarah Hunt is in a very weak, perhaps a declining state, and her brother Thomas an invalid — MW. received a letter from Apphia Witts, with an indifferent account of her own health and that of her brother and his wife: — she also heard form Dublin from M[r] Woodroffe, now arrived there on a visit to his family with his wife, having suffered much by a very stormy passage from Liverpool. M[r] W. writes about the buying two Irish Poplin dresses; one intended for MW.

and one which she means to present to Sophy.[6] — I called on J Davis; and at Eyford on Sarah Watts who still lingers in a very distressed state. — British |[79] Magazine — Newmarch's five years in the East. — Life of Sir S. Romilly.

Dec. 25. Saturday – Christmas day.

Raw, damp, dark weather, but no rain — Morning prayers with a Sermon, and the Sacrament of the Lord's supper administered. I preached on the preeminence of the Christian dispensation. — 18 Communicants — Evening Service — prayers. — Received a letter from Broome Lake Witts, who announces to me his approaching marriage to a lady of the name of Dickson, daughter of a late Major Dickson: the young people are to be united in next month; it would seem that the lady is well connected, but, I fear, has very little fortune; and his income is not large. They will reside at Hersham near Kingston on Thames, where he is the incumbent of a district Church. — Received a notification of a meeting of Visiting Justices at Gloucester Gaol, which is fixed for the 30th. |[80] Inst. — British Magazine.

Dec. 26. Sunday. Martyrdom of St. Stephen.

Open weather, fine, but cold. — Visited the Sunday School. — Morning service, prayers — Afternoon Service, prayers and sermon. I preached on the Martyrdom of St. Stephen. — A letter from Howell. — A letter from C Bathurst. — A letter from Mr Hare on Hunt Trust business, covering a letter on the same affairs from Messrs. Cox and Williams. — Preparing a Sermon — British Magazine — To the family a section from James on the Collects.

Dec. 27. Monday.

A frost; fine weather. — Wrote letters to Mr Thornton, Mr Hare, and Miss Sophia Hunt, on Hunt Trust and Executorship matters, sending to Sophia H. a copy of the letter from Messrs. Cox and Williams which Mr Hare had forwarded to me: the original I sent on to Mr Thornton by Mr Hare's desire. — Administered the sacrament |[81] privately to Mr and Mrs. Davis — Called at E. Lea's, and prayed with Emily Lea. — Received a letter from Mr Croome, land Surveyor, in answer to one which I wrote to him lately; he furnishes a correction of his valuation of this parish, as relates to lands held by Mrs. Dolphin and James Merchant. — Mr Brookes called to consult me as to appointments of days for holding the annual meetings of the Foss and Cross and Evesham 2d. Distr. of Turnpike roads — Life of Sir S. Romilly.

Dec. 28. Tuesday.

A sharp frost, and a fine day. — Wrote to E.F.W. making a remittance to him on account of the Stanway Charities distributable at this season. — Wrote to B. L. Witts, congratulating him on his approaching marriage — Received a letter from Mr Thornton, who is returned to Lanwarne, but has heard nothing of the progress of our Hunt Trust concerns: — A letter from |[82] Mr Potter, who finds fault with the minutes and resolutions of the Board of Guardians at Stow in regard to the late investigation as to alleged neglect of duty at Broadwell, by Mr Hayward, as Med. Off. of the Union. Mr P. wishes to re-open that question, and to prefer

6. The writing here is very clear and definitely refers to Mr. rather than Mrs. Woodroffe. The meaning, perhaps, is that Mr. Woodroffe will procure two dresses for MW of which MW will present one to Sophy.

other charges against Mr H. — A circular from the Clerk of the Peace's office announces a meeting of the County rate committee to be held at the Shire Hall, Gloucester, on Monday next — the day before the Quarter Sessions. — M$^{rs.}$ Hughes, of Long Compton, who has heretofore solicited my interference on her behalf in respect of alleged neglect by Geo. Cooper, one of the Officers of the County Gaol, and the father of an illegitimate child, to which she had given birth, writes to me to complain that Cooper has not sent her money as promised. — Justice business at home — Brit. Magazine. — Life of Sir S. Romilly. |[83]

Dec. 29. Wednesday.

A sharp frost, and a cold day. — Justice business at home — Drove with MW. to Stow — Called on Mr Hayward, and conferred with him both at his own house and at the Stow Workhouse as to the charges preferred against him by Mr Potter. Mr H., by his inaccuracy and deficiency of precision, has misled us; having mis-stated certain facts, but those not of importance to the points at issue: still such mistakes give an advantage to his accuser. Advised with Mr Pearce, after carefully perusing the minutes of evidence, and the resolutions passed by the Guardians on the last Board day, as to the course to be taken at the meeting to-morrow in respect of the charges against Mr H. — Mr Turner, who had called at Upper Slaughter after we left home, followed me to Stow, where I signed his testimonial to satisfy the Bishop of Worcester of his orthodoxy |[84] and good moral character. He is going from Bourton on the Water on Saturday next, leaving that curacy to take the charge of the parish of Shelsley Beauchamp, in Worcestershire. — Transacted business at the office of the Gloucestershire Banking Company. — As we returned home we met Mr Clarke who had been calling upon us — Received a letter from Mr H. D. Warter, and with it a packet, containing a frighful book or books of law-charges, Surveyor's bills &c. amounting in all to more than £1200, incident on the abortive treaty for the purchase of the Great Risington Estate, and the now accomplished acquisition of the Ground rents in St George's in the East; of this all is paid off out of the accumulations of the fund in the Court of Chancery, and money lately remitted to me to Mr H. D. Warter, except about £280, which I must provide as soon as I can. — Received a letter from Mr Bloxsome accompanying his half yearly |[85] bill on the County to be audited by me in readiness for the meeting of the Comm. of accounts on Monday next. — Received a printed circular from the Committee appointed to defend Sir Willoughby Jones's seat for Cheltenham, against whose return for that borough a petition has been presented to Parliament, by the Whig-Radical supporters of the defeated candidate, Craven Berkeley. The application is for a subscription towards the expences already incurred, and hereafter to be provided for: it being argued that the affair regards not only the local interests, but the general cause of Conservatism, so that a claim on the Conservative gentry of the County is set up. — Life of Sir S. Romilly.

Dec. ~~29.~~ 30. Thursday.

A good deal of snow had fallen in the night, a thaw came on, which partially melted it, but frost returned in the evening. — Preparing for business at Stow — Conferred with Mitchell, the land |[86] measurer, as to the map he has made of this parish, with a view to settling the boundaries between Upper and Lower Slaughter at one point. — Drove to Stow — Received a letter from Mr Hare, covering a letter which he proposes to address to Mess$^{rs.}$ Cox and

Williams on the Hunt Trust business – particularly as to submitting a case to counsel. He wishes the sanction of Mr Thornton and myself to be given to this letter, which, therefore, I must forward to Mr T. — Received a letter from Sophia Hunt on Executorship and Hunt Trust matters: she gives a bad account of the state of health of those at 8 West Mall. — Received a letter from Winter as to the cost of the Neckar wine procured for C Bathurst. — Received a letter from M^rs. Dolphin in answer to mine in which I sent her a copy of the Upper Slaughter parish valuation as far as relates to the land in her occupation. — To the Provident |187 Bank — To the office of the Gloucestershire Banking Company: at both of which places I transacted business. — Presided at the Union Workhouse at the fortnightly meeting of the Guardians till 3 P.M. — Mr Hayward was in attendance to meet any charge which might be preferred against him by Mr Potter: but that gentleman did not come, sending a letter to me, and pleading illness as preventing him: so this matter remains in abeyance. — The Rel. Off. unable to attend, suffering from serious illness. The Influenza very prevalent at this time, and very severe. — After leaving the Board returned to the Prov. Bank, where I met Winter and W.B. Pole, and transacted some justice and parish business with Mr Taplin and James Merchant. — Life of Sir Saml. Romilly.

Dec. 31. Friday.

Snow or sleet falling occa-|188 sionally throughout the day: no frost, but the snow does not dissolve quickly — Wrote to Mr Potter in answer to his letter received yesterday, detailing the proceedings of the Guardians as to his charges against Mr Hayward, so furnishing him with particulars of what took place yesterday. I declined further private correspondence or conversation on this affair, which is now become public and formal, being likely to go on to ulterior proceedings and reference to controlling authorities — and to measures the progress and end of which it is not easy to anticipate or foresee. — Wrote to Mr H. D. Warter, acknowledging the receipt of his packet containing letter, bills &c. which came to hand on the 29th. Said that I was unable at present to examine the acc^ts, or as yet to discharge the balance due to him, but that I would do both these things as soon as I conveniently could. — Wrote to Jackson Clark that the illness |189 of R. Dunford had prevented me yesterday from drawing up an appeal which he proposes to make to the Gentry and Clergy resident within the Stow on the Wold Union, for pecuniary assistance to enable him to extricate himself from embarrasments into which he has fallen by the loss of more than one horse used by him in his office of Relieving Off. of the Union. He has been very unlucky in this respect, and has had illness in his family, with a severe injury from a fall, which have entailed heavy medical expences. The man is a punctual, attentive, honest, and active public servant with a large family; and deserves to be helped: and as Chairman of the Union, it seems but fair that I should bear my testimony to his worth and usefulness. — Wrote to Mr Pearce with a sketch of minutes and resolutions to be inserted in the Minute Book of the Union, as concerns the charges brought by M^r |190 Potter against Mr Hayward. — Engaged in examining and auditing Mr Bloxsome's bill for business done for the County for the past half year. — Justice business at home. — A letter from Mr Thornton approving the contents of the letters I had written to him and Mr Hare on Hunt Trust matters on the 27th. Inst. — Life of Sir Sam. Romilly.

1848

Jan. 1. Saturday.

With the commencement of a new year are combined thoughts as to the past and future: serious self reproach for opportunities and talents, and favours misapplied, unimproved, neglected, and earnest prayer for grace to repent and amend; and a deep sense of the frailty of life, now daily more and more brought home to me as my years increase, and I am literally well stricken ⁱⁿ years. In Thee, O GOD, do I put my trust: for the Saviour's sake, pardon and help me! for of myself |⁹¹ I cannot do any thing ~~could,~~ ^{good} and through thee only can avoid the greatest evil — A cold, raw, day: not much moisture falling: the weather in a sort of equilibrium between frost and thaw. — Justice business at home — Wrote to Mʳ Thornton and Mʳ Hare on Hunt Trust affairs. — Wrote to F. Aston to thank him for his customary Christmas present of an Oxford Almanac for 1848. — I afterwards received a kind letter from him — Wrote to Mʳ Brookes on Justice business: — also ~~th~~ to the Revᵈ· Ernest Hawkins with a remittance of all the money I had received as Treasurer of the Stow Distr. Comm. S.P.G. to the close of 1847. — Audited Mʳ Bloxsome's bill on the County. — Visited the Lea family: prayed with Emily Lea in presence of her parents and Sister. The fatal disease is making rapid strides, and her life cannot be protracted much longer. It was my |⁹² trying duty, at the suggestion of her friends, to communicate to her the great and imminent peril of death. The poor, amiable girl bore the interview with great patience and meekness, and joined devoutly in prayer, with as much energy as her feeble state would permit. — Visited Mary Davis, another sick parishioner. — Life of Sir S. Romilly. —

Jan. 2. Sunday.

A thaw, the snow rapidly dissolving: the morning foggy; in the forenoon the sun broke out: the afternoon was dull. — Morning service, prayers and sermon: I preached on the New Year. — afternoon Service, prayers. — A letter from Sophia Hunt on Executorship and Trust matters: she forwards for my perusal a letter from Mʳ Whitcomb — A letter from H. D. Warter, who desires me not to pay the balance due to him till it is quite convenient to myself. — A letter from Mʳ Coyle, Blockley, covering his annual subscription to the Soc. for the Prop. of the Gospel. — |⁹³ Recᵈ· the usual copy of queries sent through the Bishop of the diocese, which are to be answered at this season, respecting the benefice of Upper Slaughter. — Preparing a sermon — Getting ready my papers for the Quarter Sessions in anticipation of my proposed journey to Gloucester to-morrow — To the family, a section from James on the Collects. —

Jan. 3. Monday.

Damp and rainy weather. After an early breakfast I left home at 9 AM. in my open carriage for Cheltenham where I arrived at the Great Western Station so as to start by the Railway to Gloucester at half past eleven o cl. — Took up my usual quarters at the Bell Hotel — To the Shire Hall, where closely engaged in public business till 6 P.M. — There was a meeting of Visitors of the Lunatic Asylum to consider of the enlargement of the building, so as to accommodate a greater number of pauper pati-|⁹⁴ents, a measure which is positively necessary — In a meeting of the Prisons Committee it was agreed by a majority that the parties petitioning for leave to erect an Organ in the Great Hall of the County should be allowed under certain restrictions so to do: this will be a popular and acceptable measure, and promote good feeling and rational amusement, enabling the choral Society in the City to give concerts with better effect. — The members of the County rate Committee present passed many valuations of parishes, and settled the amounts at which they should be severally assessed to the County rate — The usual business in the audit of accounts was gone through under my presidency. — The Magistrates present were Mess.rs. Purnell, Curtis Hayward, Hyett, P. Price. Archd. Timbrill, Sayers, Lysons, Goodrich, & Brooke Hunt, and Sayers: — the officials in attendance were Mess.rs. Bloxsome, Riddiford, Wilton, Whitehead, Fulljames, |.95 Lefroy and Keiley. — The Magistrates dining together at the Bell were Archd. Timbrill, Purnell, Lysons and myself — Purnell and I were occupied with the County accounts, and arrangements for the business of the morrow till midnight. —

Jan. 4. Tuesday.

Fine weather, and a mild day — Preparing business for the meeting on the first day of the Sessions, auditing bills, examining accounts &c. before breakfast. — Breakfasted with the Chairman. Before we went into Court, Curtis Hayward came to solicit my assistance in his place as Chairman of the second Court for the trial of prisoners. This owing to the dangerous illness of his sister, Miss Hayward, who is now under medical attendance at Gloucester, the symptoms yesterday being such as to cause great fear that she may not survive many days. Should she rally, he promises to release her me as soon as he can with propriety. I consented to preside for him. — I attended in the Grand Jury room at the |.96 opening of the Court, and transacted the usual business as to financial matters, in my capacity of Chairman of the Committee of accounts. — The attendance of Magistrates was very small — The Lord Lieutenant was present. — The Court agreed to the erection of an Organ in the Hall, as had been arranged yesterday in Committee. — The extension of the Lunatic Asylum for the reception of Pauper Patients at an expence of, I think, £5000 was voted. This, in fact, is a matter of necessity. — I took a leading part in an investigation, originating in a statement made through the Rural police, from which it indirectly appeared that M.r Barnett, Coroner, had possessed himself of a sum of money found on the person of a tradesman at Newnham, who was seized with Apoplexy and found by a constable, and conveyed home a corpse. At the inquest held on him the money, of which the Police Officer had taken charge, was taken from him by the Coroner, who kept it, and had not restored it to the Executor of the |.97 deceased. M.r B. justified his conduct, and threw out imputations against the Constable, as having been officious, rude & unfeeling in his behaviour. He complained of being watched, and disadvantageously reported of by the Police &c. It came out also that M.r B's Clerk had written to the friends of the deceased, offering to withdraw his name from the list of inquests held, so that it should not appear, as was expressed, "among paupers," on the payment of £5. The friends had declined the offer, and the inquest was inserted in the bill as usual: but the expence charged was under £4. — This conduct also M.r Barnett justified, stated that it was the common practice of Coroners, and quoting.ed instances of it, rather taking credit for his practice, as being a saving to the County purse, questioning the right of the Court to require any explanations from him as to his demeanour in his office, the Magistrates power being limited to allowance or disallowance of the bills. There was a strong impression on the minds |.98 of those who had considered the subject that Barnett had acted improperly in taking possession of the money found on the deceased, and that probably he had unjustly imputed blame to the constable. It was also felt that his practice of taking payment from the friends of deceased parties for the Inquest held was very improper, and indefensible, and might, perhaps, call for a representation to the Lord Chancellor, or Lord Chief Justice, as to malversation in office, such complaint to emanate from the Court. But as the proceeding was openly confessed, as the practice might be common, and as the other Coroners of the County, one only of whom was present, and observed a guarded silence, might also so act, it was deemed the more prudent course not to dwell further on the points elucidated in part, but not fully developed, by the enquiry, so far as it had gone, and, no doubt, an ulterior investigation will be hereafter resorted to, when the matter has been more maturely considered, and more |[99] facts have been ascertained. — Wrote to MW. — In the course of the morning conferred with M[r] Whitcombe on Hunt Trust and Executorship business. — There was but a small party of Magistrates present at the dinner at the King's Head. — Most of them, and myself among the number, adjourned to the Shire Hall to attend a concert given by the members of the Gloucester Choral Society: a vocal performance with no other music than an accompaniment on the Piano-forte. The first part consisted of sacred music, the second of glees, madrigals, quartetts, choruses &c. — It was a very creditable exhibition of skill by a large number of amateurs of the middling class under the direction of a clever amateur director, a Baker and Maltster. The performers do not seem to have much improved since I heard them before: probably their promised organ will be of service towards perfecting them. |[100]

Jan. 5. Wednesday.

A rainy morning, the middle of the day fine, rain at night. — Attended till noon in the Court in which Serg[t.] Ludlow presided. There was one appeal – When the Grand Jury had returned some bills, I took my seat as Chairman in the second court, where I was engaged in trying prisoners till half past six P.M. — I tried nine or ten cases, and fourteen Prisoners — Met at dinner a party of twelve Magistrates, Ludlow and Purnell being of the number.

Jan. 6. ~~Wednesday~~ *Thursday*

A rainy morning; fine weather afterwards — Took my seat in the second Court at nine A.M. and continued trying prisoners with only a few minutes cessation till half past six P.M. — A note from Curtis Hayward intimated that the alarm as to his sister's condition having subsided, he proposed to release me from the labours of the second chair to-morrow — Mess[rs.] Brickdale, and R Davies, Lord |[101] Ellenborough, Mess[rs.] Goodrich, John Purnell, O. Jones &c. were the Magistrates who more or less sat with me during the day. I tried 21 prisoners in 19 cases. — Wrote to MW. that I expected to be released to-morrow — The dinner party at the Kings Head was small. Ludlow was afraid of joining the party, being somewhat indisposed: these were only present, Purnell, Curtis Hayward, Brickdale, Mirehouse, Bloxsome and myself. —

Jan 7. Friday.

A rainy morning: snow covered the Cotswold range, but melted in the Course of the day: the sun broke out, and the afternoon was fine. — Sat for an hour in the second Court, transacting County business, as to County rate returns &c. with M[r] Riddiford and others — Received a letter from MW. who had forwarded a letter from Mr Potter, chiefly on the subject of the Broadwell valuation for the County rate. — I left Gloucester railway |^102 Station by a train at a quarter past eleven — Shopping at Cheltenham, which place I left in a fly before one o clock, and reached home before 3 P.M. — Found all well. — Letter from Mr Thornton as to Hunt Trust matters — An acknowledgment from the S.P.G.. of the remittance made by me on Jan. 1. — Life of Sir S. Romilly. —

Jan. 8. Saturday.

A snowy morning; snow or sleet fell during the greater part of the day: there was no frost, but the evening was windy, with a colder atmosphere. — Arranging papers and accounts after my return from Gloucester. — Justice business at home. — Wrote to Mr Wilkins, Bourton, on the case of Moses Roff, a lunatic, who has relapsed, and as to whom some measures must be taken by the parish of Bourton, to convey him to the Lunatic Asylum, and to fix the expence of the maintenance of him and his wife and child on the parish to |^103 which they are legally chargeable. — In consequence of a letter received from Sophia Hunt, I wrote to Messrs. Miles, Bankers, Bristol, in whose hands are some of the funds of the late MCH; desiring them to honour S.B.H's drafts and direction as to such money, as if my signature as Executor was attached to them, as well as her own. — Wrote to Mr Potter respecting the Broadwell County rate, and parochial valuation. — Life of Sir Saml. Romilly. — Preparing a sermon.

Jan 9. Sunday.

A hard frost, and an Easterly wind. — Visited the Sunday School — Morning service — Prayers — Afternoon Service — prayers and Sermon. — I preached on the Epiphany. Rec^d. a letter from Messrs. Alcocks, Birkbecks and C^o. who forwarded the half yearly balance sheet of my banking account with them. — Preparing a sermon. — British Magazine. |^104 To the family a section from James on the Collects.

Jan. 10. Monday.

A hard frost: the East wind not so keen as yesterday. — Wrote to Messrs. Alcock, Birkbecks and C^o. in acknowledgment of having received yesterday the half yearly balance' sheet of my banking account with them; — to Miss Sophia Hunt on Hunt Executorship and Trust matters: — to C Bathurst with particulars as to the cost of the Neckar wine supplied to him: gave him some account of proceedings at the late Quarter Sessions — to George Cooper, Officer at the County Gaol, whom I had not seen when last attending the Sessions: I forwarded to him the letter I had received some time ago from the woman at Long Compton, by whom he has an illegitimate child, and who accuses him of not fulfilling his promise to help her in the support of that child: urged him to make good the payments he had promised: — to Mr Turner, Banker, Gloucester, and Treasurer of Gloucester Infirmary, with a |^105 remittance for infirmary subscriptions due at this season from MW. and myself, from the Stow on the Wold Union, from the charity funds of this parish, and of Stanway. — Wrote to Mr Lea, Bookseller, Cheltenham, requesting him to send me a parcel of Bibles and Prayer Books, suitable for use in the Congregation, nicely bound and portable: that poor Emily Lea may select two of each, which she wishes to present as a memorial of affection to her two elder Brothers, a significant warning and pledge of attachment from her dying bed. Visited this amiable and patient sufferer, now nearly worn out: prayed with her and her afflicted parents and other near relations. — Rec^d. a letter from E.F.W. He and his wife and children have been visited with bad colds, which prevented my son from attending the Quarter Sessions last week. — A letter from Garaway & Co. Nurserymen, near Bristol, with an invoice of garden seeds sent. — Life of Sir S. |^106 Romilly.

Jan. 11. Tuesday.

A frosty morning and foggy weather; thawing in the afternoon, freezing in the evening. — Wrote to F. Aston: — to M^rs. Dolphin with particulars of the Valuation and Assessment of the Eyford property to the County rate, and of some items in the Parochial Assessment of this parish: not knowing whether she was at Eyford, or from home, I walked thither; but though she had not left Eyford, found she was about to set out to-morrow, and was so engaged as to be unable to see me: left my letter. — Visited Sarah Watts of Eyford, still lingering in a very suffering state. — Received a letter from Messrs. Coutts, who forward to me for my ~~paper~~ signature a paper empowering them to honour the drafts and instructions which Sophia Hunt may draw or give as to the Executorship account standing in our names. — Constable W. Jones, Glorshire Constabu-|^107 lary, stationed at Marshfield, writes to consult me as to offering himself as a candidate for the vacant office of Keeper of the House of Correction at Horsley. — A letter from Mr Potter in answer to mine of Saturday last respecting the valuation of Broadwell for the County rate. — A circular from the County Gaol, announcing a meeting of Visiting Magistrates to settle the rota of visiting for the quarter. — Life of Sir Saml. Romilly. —

Jan. 12. Wednesday.

A slight frost in the morning, followed by a ground thaw — Wrote to Messrs. Coutts, returning to them with my signature the order which I had received from them yesterday. — Wrote to Mr Croome respecting an error which I have detected in the Upper Slaughter parochial Valuation. — Wrote to Const. W. Jones in answer to his letter received yesterday. — Received a letter from |^108 M^rs. Dolphin in reply to mine left for her at Eyford yesterday: she is gone to visit a friend in Wiltshire. — A letter from Messrs. Butt, wine merchants, Gloucester, with an invoice for wine, which they had forwarded by the Carrier, and which arrived yesterday. — A letter from the Rev^d. — Gilby, Incumbent of a Church at Cheltenham, as to relief withheld from a pauper settled at Lower Slaughter, but resident at Cheltenham. — A note from Mr Lee, bookseller, Cheltenham, who has sent a packet of Bibles and Prayer books, from which Emily Lea may select such as she may wish to present to her brothers. — Called at Mr Lea's; visited the afflicted daughter, whom I found sinking rapidly. — Life of Sir Saml. Romilly.

Jan. 13. Thursday.

Fine weather overhead; mild and foggy. — Mr R. C. Lumbert called, and left in my hands the very liberal donation of Three Pounds to be distributed at my discretion among poor people of this place. |^109 Drove to Stow. — At the Provident Bank met my son, who with Sophy came to Stow yesterday, on a visit to the elder Vavasours, and intend to return to Stanway to-day, calling on MW. at Upper Slaughter by the way. — From E.F.W. I heard a full account of what passed on Tuesday last at a large meeting of the Clergy of the Archdeaconry of Gloucester, which had been summoned at the requisition of a numerous band to consider the propriety of addressing the Bishop of the diocese, thanking him for joining with the other twelve prelates in remonstrance against the elevation of Dr Hampden to the see of Hereford, and pressing for further endeavours to avert that measure. The requisitionists were mainly clergymen entertaining high-church opinions; but with them were mingled some of low church principles, evangelicals, or so esteemed, who on religious grounds ~~were~~ ^{are} opposed |¹¹⁰ to the alleged latitudinarian tendencies of Dr Hampden. Many, among them, myself, deprecated this meeting is ill-judged, and dangerous. I considered Hampden disqualified for the episcopate because his theological writings were so couched as to lead both learned and unlearned to apprehend his opinions unsound: he may be orthodox, but his language is obscure, and inferences may be and have been drawn from his words which do not seem unfairly drawn, but which would shew him to hold unsound doctrine. He disavows such inferences, but that they can ^{be} and are drawn is a proof that he is an unsafe person to be entrusted with a ruling authority in the Church. Therefore I with others deprecated the proposed meeting, which was likely to lead to acrimonious contention, as it would array in open opposition two contrary sections of the Clergy: it being understood that the low church party would |¹¹¹ attend in considerable force, and make a strenuous resistance to the proposed measure. And the very long, laboured, special pleading letter of the Bishop of Exeter addressed to Lord John Russell in censure of the appointment of Dr Hampden, not conceived in a good tone, together with a late correspondence of Dr Wilberforce the Bishop of Oxford, one of the thirteen remonstrant bishops, but now exhibiting something of tergiversation, contributed to render the public agitation of the question inopportune. Better would it have been if an expression of thanks to the Bishop of Gloucester for the late remonstrance of himself and his brethren had been prepared and privately circulated in the Archdeaconry. But this, I believe, was disapproved by Dr Timbrill, the Archdeacon, who also greatly disliked and dreaded the meeting, and availed himself of the plea of indisposition to avoid attending it. |¹¹² Nearly, if not quite, 100 clergymen were present, and Canon Selwyn, in residence, was called to the chair, a person of feeble health, and habits, I believe, and nearly unknown in the diocese. The motion for the address of thanks was proposed by Mr Edmund Estcourt, Vicar of Newnton, a worthy man, who has through life maintained low Church opinions, though probably his tendencies towards high Church principles have been latterly fostered by the Tractarian bias of two Sons in the church, one of whom has gone over to Rome, and the other, lately Curate of Great Risington holds strong Puseyite opinions. Mr Estcourt was seconded by Kennaway, Vicar of Campden, also bred in the Low Church School, well known in Cheltenham and Brighton, as a preacher, and the writer of theological and devotional publications, but having likewise imbibed some of the inclinations of the Tractarian party. M^r |¹¹³ Kennaway supported the motion in a long and able speech, and in a moderate tone impugned the doctrines of Dr Hampden, or shewed from his writings his unfitness to be raised to the Episcopal bench, shadowing forth the evil results likely to follow. — Dr Jeune, Master of Pembroke College, Oxford, and Canon of Gloucester, a personal friend, and strong partizan of Dr Hampden, also a scion and pillar of Evangelicalism, moved the amendment or counter resolution in a speech of great ability, vigour, and tact. He was seconded by Mr Close the Incumbent of Cheltenham, whose fluency and energy were not without personal attacks and allusions which would have been better spared; and such was the pointed language used that the Chairman was constrained to implore his brethren not to forget that they were Clergymen and Christians, — Mr Murray Browne, the |^114^ Bishop of Gloucester's chaplain replied to Dr Jeune and Mr Close, vindicating with spirit the course taken by the requisitionists and the line adopted by Messrs Estcourt & Kennedy.[7] Mr Riddle followed in an abrupt tone, and with an offensive manner, which the meeting would not endure, and upon a division the numbers were for an address of thanks to the Bishop of Gloucester 71. — against it 28. No resolution was proposed to the effect that further proceedings should be taken by the Bishops to resist the elevation of Dr Hampden to the See of Hereford. — My son had attended this meeting, having a strong feeling adverse to the appointment of Dr Hampden, and having attended a meeting of the Clergy of his deanery at Campden, where that measure was the subject of disapproval: he was also invited so to do by Canon Murray Browne, with whom he happened to be in correspondence as to the appointment of a Chaplain to the Workhouse |^115^ at Winchcomb. — E.F.W. accompanied me to the Office of the Gloucestershire Banking Company, and to the Workhouse, where we parted. — Presided for four hours at the fortnightly meeting of the Guardians of our Union: the business was heavy. From Mr Hunt, the Auditor, disagreeable letters had been addressed to the Officers, but there was no communication from the P.L.C. either as to our controversy with that functionary, or as to the charge preferred by Capt. Leigh. This, indeed, I expect will die a natural death, as not being substantiated. — Mr Potter addressed me in a public letter, in which he maintained his charge against Mr Hayward, and desired to be heard on other charges against him. The Guardians, acting under my suggestion, resolved to decline receiving any further charge against Mr Hayward which Mr Potter may have to prefer: |^116^ for his letter shewed that he considered the late decision of the Board in M^r H's favour to have been partial, not borne out by the evidence, and based on false inferences. Under these circumstances intimation will be given to Mr P. that the Guardians will await such directions from the P.L.C. as those authorities may give in consequence of any appeal which may be made to them by Mr Potter. — Returned home by 5. P.M. — E.F.W. and Sophy had called on their Mother, proceeding hence to Stanway. — The Misses Hall had called. — Rec^d from Mr Hare a letter and a packet, containing a further correspondence between Messrs Cox and Williams and Mr Braikenridge, which the former gentlemen consider ought to form part of the case to be submitted to Mr Geo. Turner: after perusing this correspondence I am requested to forward it to Mr Thornton. — A letter from Mr Pole as |^117^ to the character of a young woman said to be resident in my parish, and who has offered her services as an under laundry maid at Wyck Hill. — A letter from George Cooper, Officer in the County Gaol, who assures me that he has more than fulfilled the promise he made to me at the Mich^s Sess^ns respecting assistance to be given towards the education of his natural child by a woman at Long Compton. — Life of Sir S. Romilly.

Jan. 14. Friday.

A fine, open, mild day. — Busy on parish matters with Churchwarden Gregory both before breakfast and in the evening. — Justice business at home: wrote to Superintendent Makepeace, who afterwards called in the afternoon to confer with me on the matters which

7.   This should have read Kennaway.

had been the subject of my note to him — Wrote to M^rs. Hughes, Long Compton, declining any further interference between her and George Cooper: — to Mr Rodwell, |^118 with an order for books for the Stow Library; — to the Rev^d. J. D. Gilby as to the relief heretofore granted to a pauper settled at Lower Slaughter, but living at Cheltenham; and informing him that our Board has resolved to discontinue out relief to non resident paupers — to those who live beyond the limits of our Union: — to Mr Pole in answer to his enquiries about Elizabeth Alcocks: — to the Misses Hall with receipts for the S.P.G. subscriptions left ~~th~~ by them, when they called on M^rs. W. yesterday. — With my wife visited Emily Lea; put up prayers with her and others of her family: found this poor young suffering^er in a very declining state: not long for this world. — Visited other parishioners — A letter from C Bathurst, who sends a cheque in payment for the Neckar wine which I have procured for him. — A letter from Mr Turner, Treasurer of the Gloucester Infirmary, with receipts for the |^119 annual subscriptions to that institution which I had remitted to him. — Cards forwarded by the post in the usual nuptial fashion announced the marriage of B. L. Witts and Miss Dickson on the 12th. Inst. — Life of Sir S. Romilly. —

Jan. 15. Saturday.

Very fine weather, open and bright. — Justice business at home — Wrote to Mr Winter, sending him the cheque I received yesterday from C Bathurst, in payment for the Neckar wine supplied to him. — Wrote to Mr Lee, Bookseller, Cheltenham, returning to him the parcel of Bibles and Prayer books which he had sent, that Emily Lea might select two of each for a dying present to her elder brothers. She had made her choice, which I intimated to-day, desiring Mr L. to procure for me and forward two exactly like ~~the one~~ those chosen, in binding &c. — But death has arrested her career; she has not lived to present her pious and affection-|^120 ate momento to those she loved. She died at 7 P.M. this evening: and the Brothers will receive from another hand the parting token of her love and concern for their welfare. — Wrote to Mr Thornton, forwarding the packet which I received yesterday from Mr Hare, and which I perused this morning: – an angry correspondence between Mr Braikenridge and Messrs. Cox and Williams; shewing, on the part of the former and his Client, no abatement in the asperity with which the whole transaction and controversy as to the Wharf has been carried on. – Mr Hunt views the whole of the Trust management in the most prejudiced light – very unjustly, very intemperately, very irritatingly. — M^r and M^rs. Ford and their daughter Dulcibella paid us a morning visit — Received a letter from a Clergyman at Audenshaw near Manchester soliciting eighteen pence to help him to pay off a debt on account of his new church |^121 for which he is responsible — Received from the Lunatic Asylum, Gloucester, a notice of a meeting of Visitors on the 25th. Inst. — Received from the Office of the Clerk of the Peace a notification that I am appointed one of the Visiting Magistrates of the County Gaol. — Life of Sir S. Romilly. —

Jan. 16. Sunday.

A sharp hoar frost, and a fine day. — Did not attend the Sunday School, the Schoolmistress being confined with an attack of Influenza, now very prevalent. — Morning service, prayers and sermon. I preached on the miracle performed at the marriage feast at Cana in Galilee. — Evening service — prayers. — A letter from the Rev^d. E. Francis, now settled as Incumbent of a living in Suffolk, who recommends to me, and requests me to subscribe to a new work about to be published by his nephew, Dr F., a Med. officer, in the East India Company's ser-|^{122} vice, but now at home on account of ill health. The publication will be a series of engravings illustrating Indian scenery and manners, and particularly as throwing light on customs recorded in Scripture. — A letter from Mr Pole in answer to mine of Friday last respecting Eliz. Alcock. — A letter from the legacy duty office as to the Executorship and will of Miss M C Hunt. — A letter from one Baughan, Churchwarden of Long Compton, who writes to inform me that M$^{rs.}$ Hughes of that place had made a false statement to me as to the alleged neglect of George Cooper, Officer at Glouc. Gaol, in fulfilling his promise to make some provision for his natural child by her: B. shews what C. has done, he (B.) having been Cooper's agent in the affair — Forwarded to the Incumbent of Audenshaw eighteen pence as desired by him in the letter which I received yesterday. — Preparing a sermon. — Ecclesiastical Gazette. |^{123} To the family a section from Dr James on the Collects. —

Jan. 17. Monday.

A rainy day, with little intermission. — After an early breakfast drove with MW. to Cheltenham, both of us having cause to require the prompt assistance of a dentist. — Reached the Plough Hotel soon after 11 AM. — Engaged with Mr Tibbs, the dentist. — I called on Mr Lefroy, at the Police Office, and conferred with him on constabulary matters. — Shopping. — Left Cheltenham by 3 P.M. and home soon after 5 P.M. — A letter from Mr Croome, Land Surveyor in in reply to the last which I addressed to him. — Life of Sir S. Romilly.

Jan. 18. Tuesday.

A sharp frost: Towards night-fall a scattering of snow. — Justice business at home. — Wrote to George Cooper as to the transaction between him and M$^{rs.}$ Hughes, Long Compton: — to Mr Francis, promising to subscribe |^{124} to his nephew's publication, so far at least, as that the Stow Book Society shall take a copy: — to C Bathurst, acknowledging the receipt of his draft for the Neckar wine supplied to him. — Received a letter from M$^{rs.}$ C. Barr: — a letter from Sophia Hunt with an inclosure of accounts relating to our Exorship concerns: — a letter from F. Newmarch, apprizing me that the half year's interest due on Mr Lockhart's mortgage has been paid to my account with the Stow Branch of the Gloucestershire Banking Company: — A note from Mr Purnell, accompanying a copy of the Gloucester Journal, which he sends that I may have an opportunity of reading Dr Jeune's speech at the late meeting of the Clergy of the Archdeaconry of Gloucester, to present a vote of thanks to the Bishop of the Diocese for having with other Bishops remonstrated against the appointment of Dr Hampden to the See of Hereford. Purnell |^{125} is anxious to have my opinion as to that speech, and on the subject generally. — Visited the Lea family: the anxiety and grief attendant on the death of his daughter has deranged the health of her father — Life of Sir Sam. Romilly. —

Jan. 19. Wednesday.

A cold day: a slight frost in the morning, thaw at midday, frost again at night. — Wrote to Mess$^{rs.}$ Sewell and Newmarch, acknowledging their letter received yesterday: — to Miss S. Hunt, on Executorship and Trust matters, and in reply to her letter received yesterday. — To Mess$^{rs.}$ Butt, Gloucester, to inform them that in one of the hampers of Marsala wine received from them yesterday, and which was binned to day, only 2 dozen and 10 bottles were found: there should have been three dozen. — Preparing a Sermon — Received a letter from Mr Thornton: he has returned to Messrs. Cox and Williams the correspondence between them and M^r |^126 Braikenridge which I forwarded lately, and has desired them to submit the case thus enlarged to Counsel without delay. — We dined at Mr Ford's: met M^r & M^rs. John Scott from Banksfee; M^r and M^rs. R. Waller; M^rs. and Miss Mary Hornsby, now on a visit to the R. Wallers; Mr Albert Boudier, Mr Hunt, and Mr Terry.

Jan. 20. Thursday.

A little snow had fallen early in the morning: frosty, cold, and wintry weather. — Drove to Stow — Transacted business at the Provident Bank, and at the office of the Gloucestershire Bk^g. Company: at the former met with Ford, R Waller, and Morrison. — Shopping — To the Workhouse where conferred with Mr Pearce on Union and Workhouse matters, and met Mr Perkins. — Sat in the Justice room with Ford and R Waller: — transacted a good deal of business. — Mr Lefroy had come from Cheltenham, whither he returned, that he |^125 might be present at an investigation as to Policemen not paying the toll for a carriage in which witnesses were conveyed on their way to give evidence at the Q.S. and in which they also had seats. We held that the privilege accorded to the Constabulary of travelling toll free when on duty did not extend to cases when they went in carriages hired to convey witnesses: for in such a case they availed themselves of the conveyance for their own convenience; the rules of the force being that Constables going to attend Q.S. as witnesses should walk: or if they travelled otherwise it should be at their own expence. — There was also another enquiry; an allegation had been made that a Constable had received money at Gloucester, to be paid to a witness in a case for expences, and had withheld such money so received. It appeared that this imputation was unfounded, and we dismissed |^126 the case. — Rec^d. a letter from E.F.W. — he and his are well, and he proposes soon to bring Sophy and Broome to dine and sleep here — Life of Sir S. Romilly. —

Jan. 21. Friday.

A dull, cold day: frosty, with a scattering of snow on the ground — Wrote to G. Pain, Stow, as to books ordered into the library: — to Mr Wells, Med. Off. of the Union, requesting him to visit a sick woman, Townsend, whom I also visited: — to E.F.W. in answer to the letter rec^d. from him yesterday, begging him to bring Sophy and Broome to dine and sleep here on Feb. 1. or the first fine day afterwards: — to Messrs. Hoare, desiring them to transfer £35 from my account to that of my Son. Poor Emily Anne Lea was buried to-day: I preceeded the corpse from the house to the Church: her Father suffering from rheumatism, but able to attend. — Life of Sir Sam. Romilly. —

Jan. 22. Saturday.

Hard frost, calm, cold |^127 weather. — Wrote to Purnell by his desire fully on the Hampden controversy, and matters connected with it: especially as to the speech lately made by Dr Jeune at the recent Archidiaconal meeting at Gloucester — Justice business at home. — Rec^d. a letter from Messrs. Butt as to the deficiency in the hamper of wine lately sent by them: — from C. Bathurst a poetical jeu d'esprit purporting to be answer from the Bp. of Gloucester to the late address received by him from the Clergy of the Archdeaconry of Gloucester, assembled at the recent meeting convened to thank his Lordship for joining with other Bishops in remonstrance against the appointment of Dr Hampden to the See of Hereford. — Visited sick parishioners — M. Forty and Townsend. — Life of Sir S. Romilly. –

Jan. 23. Sunday.

Same weather as yesterday. — The Schoolmistress being ill, there |^128 was no attendance at the Sunday School — Morning service, prayers. — Afternoon Service, prayers and Sermon. I preached a funeral sermon. — All the mourners, & connections of the Lea family, who had attended on Friday at the interment of Emily Lea, were present. — Preparing a Sermon. — Rec^d. a letter from one Gibbs, formerly of this parish, but now residing in Warwickshire, who asks me for some information as to the family of his Grandfather, for many years long since, living in U Slaughter, named Wood: this in the forlorn hope that he may be able to prove himself heir at law of the well known James Wood, Banker of Gloucester. The old miser, and millionaire, has left an abundant harvest for lawyers, excited the cupidity of all credulous and ignorant people of the name of Wood, or reckoning a Wood in their family, for a wide circuit around Gloucester, and |^129 still scope is left for further litigation, and wider spreading of fallacious hopes, and petty profits to attornies: — A letter from the official assignee of Turner, our London Fishmonger, who is a bankrupt, and to whom we owe a small bill for fish supplied — A letter from Messrs. Hoare, who have transfered £35 from my account to that of my Son. — Eccl. Gazette — British Magazine — To the family a section from James on the Collects. —

Jan. 24. Monday.

A frost in the morning; in the afternoon it thawed; the evening was windy: a flickering of snow in the forenoon. — Wrote to John Gibbs, in answer to his letter received yesterday: — to Mr Jennings, requesting him to pay the little bill due to Turner, the Fishmonger, and to send me the Balance Sheet of the Mich^s. Bucklersbury rents: adverted to the lately acquired ground rents in S^t. George's in the East. — Mr Pearce |^130 called with some letters from the P.L.C. on a settlement question, on relief to the poor, and on the increase of vagrancy: conferred with him on Union matters — Visited, and prayed with Townsend's wife. — Life of Sir S. Romilly. —

Jan. 25. Tuesday.

A very cold day, hard frost, and East wind — Wrote to Mr Lyne, Auctioneer, forwarding a cheque in payment of poles and faggots bought at Wyck Hill wood-sale — Justice business at home — Visited John Davis — Rec^d. a circular from Gloucester gaol, announcing a meeting of Visiting Justices — A letter from Mr Hare, who names that the the case prepared as to Whitby's Wharf has been submitted to counsel, and that an opinion may soon be expected. — A letter from Messrs. Hoare announces that Lady Wilmot Horton has paid to my account with them the half year's interest due on mortgage — £194. 3. 4 — less Income Tax. — By a |^131 person coming from Stanway we heard a good account of the health of our dear children and grandchildren. — Brit. Mag. — Life of Sir S. Romilly.

Jan 26. Wednesday.

A very cold day, & hard frost with an Easterly wind. — Engaged in going through the voluminous accounts sent in by Mᵣ H. D. Warter, as to the business done by him and others, in the purchase of Ground rents in Sᵗ· George's in the East, and the abortive treaty for the purchase of the Risington Estate &c. — Called on the Lea family — Life of Sir S. Romilly. —

Jan. 27. Thursday.

Very hard frost: fine weather: easterly wind — Drove to Stow. — Attended at the Prov. Bank where I met Mᵣ Winter — To the Workhouse. — Presided at the fortnightly meeting of the Guardians of our Union from 11 AM. to 3 P.M. — Transacted business at the office of the Gloucestershire |¹³² Banking Company. — A letter from E.F.W: all well at the Vicarage, Stanway: they propose visiting us for a day next week — A letter from a law-publisher in London announces that a work on summary punishments by Magistrates, to which I have subscribed, is on the eve of publication. — Life of Sir S. Romilly.

Jan. 28. Friday.

A hard frost: a cold day: a flickering of snow in the forenoon: a fine afternoon snow fell at night. — Engaged in wading through the bills for business done in the attempt to purchase the Risington Estate, and in the purchase of Ground rents in Sᵗ· George's in the East. — Wrote to Mᵣ Rodwell for a supply of books for the Stow book Society. — Visiting sick parishioners at Eyford and Upper Slaughter — Mʳˢ· Ryan, Watts, & Townsend. — Recᵈ· a note from Mᵣ Lyne in acknowledgement of the cheque I had sent him to pay for poles and faggots bought at Wyck Hill. — |¹³³ Life of Sir S. Romilly. —

Jan. 29. Saturday.

Much snow on the ground in the morning, which melted afterwards under the influence of a gentle thaw — Still engaged in going through the mass of accounts transmitted to me by Mᵣ H. D. Warter. — A circular from the Lunatic Asylum, Gloucester, announces a meeting of the Visitors for Feb. 9. — Brit. Magazine — Life of Sir S. Romilly.

Jan. 30. Sunday.

Anniversary of King Charles's Martyrdom — A rapid thaw; the weather much milder: some heavy rain fell. — Visited the Sunday School. — Morning Service; prayers and sermon. — I preached a sermon suitable to the anniversary. — Evening service – prayers. — Preparing a Sermon — Brit. Magazine — To the family a section from James on the Collects. —

Jan. 31. Monday.

A slight frost in the morning, fine overhead: dirty walking. |¹³⁴ The birth day of my beloved Grandson, Broome; he is this day eight years old: a very fine, healthy promising boy: may he be well brought up, and prove a blessing to all connected with him! — Justice business at home. — Preparing a sermon. — Wrote to Howell. — Recᵈ· a letter from my cousin Mʳˢ· Shard; a kind enquiry after me and mine; written in an excellent hand and full of matter; a remarkable letter for a person of seventy eight: dwelling on the events of a long life, and with lively interest on passing events: tracing and noticing the changes in our family, writing on its various members with a lively interest; mentioning old books reperused; adverting to marriages and deaths: going back to jeux d'esprit of nearly a century ago: and, among other anecdotes, she mentions what I had never heard, or had forgotten, that Abp. Secker was a cousin of my Grandfather Witts.[8] — Visiting sick parishioners — Life of Romilly. — |[135]

Feb. 1. Tuesday.
A hard frost, and very fine day. — Preparing quarterly papers S.P.G. for circulation — Copying report of the Stow Distr. Comm. S.P.G. — Brit. Mag. — Justice business at home — Our dear children, accompanied by Broome, came from Stanway to luncheon; dined & slept here; Passed with them a very agreeable afternoon and Evening. —

Feb. 2. Wednesday.
Beautiful weather; a slight frost in the morning: bright sunshine; but the walking very dirty — Walked with E.F.W., Sophy, and Broome to Bourton and back. Called at the Rectory; saw Robert Waller, Mrs. W., and Miss M. Hornsby. — Rec^{d.} a letter from Howell, full of levity and gossip. — About 3 P.M. our dear children and grandchildren left us to return to Stanway. We had greatly enjoyed the short visit. — Copying the Stow Distr. Comm. Ann. report S.P.G. — British Magazine — Life of Sir S. Romilly — |[136] The Hampden controversy has been vigorously prosecuted. The Ultra impugners of the elevation of this divine to the Episcopal Bench have made good their pledge to oppose the measure to the last. Accordingly three Clergymen have put themselves forward as opponents in the Court in which Bishops elect are confirmed. These vehement men are Mr Powell, the Incumbent of Cirencester, Mr Huntley, of Boxwell, both in this diocese, and both very estimable, but over strenuous Clergymen, with whom I have been long acquainted, and Mr Jebb, an incumbent of the Diocese of Hereford. — In the ceremony of confirmation which takes place in Bow Church, London, before Judges of the Civil Courts, delegated by the Archb. of Canterbury, according to ancient precedents, the confirmation is ordinarily a mere matter of form. In its course proclamation is made – by which opponents are invited to come forward, and allege any |[137] objections they may have against the confirmation of the proposed bishop: and two instances of ancient date, since the Reformation, are quoted, when such opposition was made on the ground of false doctrine or immorality. But these cases occurred in times when the law was not well settled, or rather unsettled by reason of political and religious feuds: and the authorities seem to have been overawed or borne away against their better judgment by prejudice or clamour. — When the proceedings at the Confirmation of Dr Hampden had arrived at a certain point; the opposers preferred their claim by advocates to be heard: but the Ecclesiastical Judges sitting to preside overruled the claim, and maintained, that, though proclamation had been formally made that all opposers should appear, or else for ever after hold their peace, that they could not be heard, for that the statute |[138] of Præmunire, with

---

8.   Thomas Secker (1693-1768); bishop of Oxford 1737, archbishop of Canterbury 1758-1768. The nature of the
      relationship is unknown. It does not appear that they could have been first cousins. Secker's mother's maiden name
      was Brough, Francis Witts's great-grandfather, Edward Witts married Sarah Broome. In *The Correspondence of Bishop
      Secker* (A. P. Jenkins, Oxfordshire Record Society 57, 1991) there are three letters between the Witts family and Secker,
      but none imply any particular closeness.

its heavy penalties, precluded them from any other course than obedience to the mandate imposed upon them by the Crown, to confirm the person Elected Bishop, by the majority of voices in the Chapter of Hereford. There too a struggle had been made: the Dean with some of the Canons having refused to vote for the Election of Dᵣ Hampden, so exposing themselves to the penalties of præmunire, while a majority carried the election under a protest from the minority. Thus baffled in the lower Court, the opposers forthwith applied to the Court of Queen's Bench for a mandamus to the inferior jurisdiction to entertain the plea of the opposers. Lord Denman, with Coleridge, Patteson, and Erle Judges, sat to hear the arguments, and the ablest counsel were arrayed on both sides. The case was argued with very great ability and learning, and research. On the one hand it was maintained by the Crown Law-|[139] yers that the opposers were called upon not to impugn the moral character or the doctrine of the Bishop Elect, — that was beyond their competency — that was matter already considered & determined upon by the Crown, as head of the Church, holding the supremacy once wrested from the Pope; but that the matters to be enquired into and opposed, if need be, were whether the Election was valid; — whether the person elected was qualified by law, whether he had the plurality of votes, whether the Electors were persons legally entitled to elect &c. – And, I own, it appears to me, on the whole, that a right view of the matter was here taken, and that the precedents referred to were not such as were tenable. Of course the opposite opinion was very ably and learnedly maintained: and the arguments were long, and very interesting. The judges were divided in opinion: Lord Denman & Erle decided |[140] that the opposers could not proceed on the ground of unsound doctrine; Coleridge and Patteson held the contrary opinion; and the Court being equally divided ~~the court~~ gave no decision; cadit quæstio: the opposers oppose in vain; and Dᵣ Hampden is confirmed. — Great is the disappointment, and very heavy the expence incurred by the opposers, and the Ultra party who supports them — Coleridge may have

47. Boxwell
Court.

been biassed by his attachment to Tractarian views, and Patterson may have been influenced by his friend and Brother in law; but it is time that the antiquated processes of congé d'elire, and confirmation should be swept away: and, as is now the case with Irish and Colonial Bishops, that the English prelates should take their sees by a simple nomination by the Crown, the responsibility being thus thrown on the Minister.

Feb. 3. Thursday.

A slight frost in the morning: the weather afterwards open, |[141] but cold. — Brit. Mag. — Drove to Stow with MW. who soon returned home — I attended at the Provident Bank, where I met Mess[rs.] Morrison, Winter, and W B Pole. — The last had accompanied me thither from the Workhouse, where I had met him, making enquiry as to the course to be pursued as to a Lunatic pauper. — I had been conferring with M[r] Pearce on Union matters — To the Justice room, where I sat alone, transacting such business as was within the competency of a Single Magistrate. Ford was detained at home by indisposition, and had written to me to that effect. R Waller was at home, somewhat rheumatic, and indolent, who might & would have attended, had he not expected that Ford would have met me. — Mess[rs.] Winter, W B Pole, W. Vavasour, H. Lindow, and Turner were present. The last on a visit to |[142] R Waller, but has resigned the curacy of Bourton, and is on the eve of departure — A note from Sup[t.] Makepeace explained that he was detained on Police business elsewhere. — Rec[d.] from M[r] Jennings a letter accompanying the balance sheet of the Mich[s.] Quarter rents from houses in Bucklersbury. — A note from Lord Saye and Sele, inviting MW. and me to dinner on Tuesday next to meet the Bishop of Madras. To this I replied in the affirmative from Stow. — Life of Romilly. —

Feb. 4. Friday.

Rain in the forenoon. In the afternoon moist and foggy weather — Wrote to M[r] Ford (a Latin letter with notes &c. – a jeu d'esprit) returning a bill forwarded to him as Treasurer of the Stow Book Society by Rodwell, which I had looked over, and found correct: — to M[r] Jennings, acknowledging his letter rec[d.] yesterday, and the correctness of the Mich[s.] balance sheet. — J W Harris called and paid |[143] up the Mich[s.] rent for the Stanway Vicarage farm. — Settling other accounts with tradesmen. — Life of Sir S. Romilly.

Feb. 5. Saturday.

A wet day; almost constant rain. — Wrote to M[rs.] C. Barr in reply to her last letter, and condoled with her on the death of her late husband's brother, M[r] Martin Barr, which took place last week: he was domiciliated at Henwick Hall with M[rs.] Walker & Miss Maria Barr, M[r] George Barr, and M[rs.] C. B. and her children, a united and attached family party: disease of the heart carried him off. He was a useful man of business, whose loss my cousin will have reason to regret — three brothers dying in succession, with but a few months interval between the decease of each, has been a heavy trial in that family: the third, Marcus Barr, was a military officer who had served with great distinction on the Staff in India, particularly |[144] in the last great war in the Punjaub. — Justice business at home — Transacted business with W. Forty, as to the premises which he rents of me. — Conferred with W. Gregory, Churchwarden, on parish matters. —— Concluded the very interesting life of Sir S. Romilly — and began the life of Lord Loughborough, one of the series of lives of the Chancellors, lately published by Lord Campbell in seven volumes.[9] —

Feb. 6. Sunday.

A mild, spring-feeling day, but somewhat damp. — Visited the Sunday School — Morning Prayers — Afternoon prayers and Sermon. I preached on the duties of the aged. — Received a letter from my old friend J Round, now residing at his house at Brighton — he begs me to make some enquiry as to the conduct and character of Commander Story R. N. whom his only daughter has met at Baden, and who has proposed for her hand. The lady has attached herself to her admirer, |[145] but the good Father hesitates, as it is not many months since the gentleman lost a second wife, and to be so early a suitor appears strange. Capt. Story is well connected, but my old friend wishes for information as to the circumstances attending the decease of his last wife, who left one infant child. It appears she died at Shipston, and R. thinks I can procure intelligence. — Preparing a Sermon — Colonial Church Chronicle. —

Feb. 7. Monday.

A soft, mild day: some rain in the afternoon, which afterwards cleared off. — Preparing a Sermon. — Wrote to Mr Sadler, Sutton under Brailes, as residing in the neighbourhood of Shipston; to make enquiry as to Capt. Story, agreeably to the request made to me by Mr Round. — Mr Ford called here, on his way to see poor Bowen, who is again a great sufferer, an abscess having formed in his bladder: he is considered to be in a |[146] precarious state. F. called to shew me a letter he had received from Mr Murray Browne, the Bishop of Gloucester's chaplain. It seems that an arrangement has been made, that the principal towns in the Diocese should be visited between the 13$^{th.}$ and the 23$^{d.}$ Inst. by a deputation from the Society for the Propagation of the gospel in Foreign parts. This deputation is to consist of the Bishops of Madras and Antigua, Mr Thomson, a former Missionary of the Society in the diocese of Madras, and Mr Vernon, one of the Secretaries of the Parent Society. They are to be accompanied and introduced by Murray Browne, and the Bp. of Gloucester is to be present at the meetings fixed for Bristol, Chippenham, and Gloucester. The Bp. of Madras, who arrives to-day, on a visit to Lord Saye and Sele, will advocate the cause of the Society during the earlier part of the time above named, but not towards its close, when the deputation visits this part of the |[147] Diocese, Murray Browne having fixed the 22$^{d.}$ Inst. for a meeting at Stow; and desired Ford to communicate on the subject with Hippisley as Rector of the parish, and with me as Secretary of the district Committee. — Drove to Stow with MW: called at the Rectory: saw M^r and M$^{rs.}$ Hippisley, & Miss Jane Hippisley: M$^{rs.}$ H., lately confined, looked delicate. Conferred with Hippisley as to the proposed extraordinary meeting in aid of the funds of S.P.G. — Called at the Workhouse, but did not meet with Mr Pearce: — at the printer's to give directions for hand bills &c. to announce the proposed meeting on the 22$^{d.}$ Inst. — Rec$^{d.}$ a letter from E.F.W. with a good account of all at the Vicarage, Stanway: he & Sophy with Broome meditate a visit to the Vavasours at the Cottage to-morrow, to sleep there one night, as they did with us last week. — In the evening I was called to visit Sarah Illes, who was seized with an |[148] alarming

9.   John Campbell, 1st Baron Campbell (1779-1861). *The Lives of the Lord Chancellors and Keepers of the Great Seal of England from the Earliest Times till the Reign of King George IV.*

attack of illness this forenoon. Her family anticipate the worst. I prayed with her and those in attendance upon her. — Lord Campbell's life of Lord Loughborough.

Feb. 8. Tuesday.

A fine, open, mild forenoon and afternoon: the evening and night rainy and stormy. — Visited S. Illes, who is very ill, but apparently not in immediate danger. — Wrote to Murray Browne as to the proposed meeting in aid of S.P.G. to be held at Stow, on the 22ᵈ· Inst. pointing out the arrangements which I propose, but expressing a doubt whether, particularly at this season of the year, a numerous assemblage or considerable contribution can be expected. I begged to invite himself with the Bishop of Antigua, and one of the other gentlemen forming the deputation, to accept the hospitality at our hands, and to consider themselves engaged to dine and sleep here after the meeting at Stow — Wrote to E.F.W. inclosing a cheque for £40, to meet him at "the Cottage" this |¹⁴⁹ evening. — Preparing a Sermon — Preparing for the expected meeting S.P.G: drawing for the printer MS. of handbills, notes &c. — Recᵈ· a letter from C Bathurst as to the proceedings at the Epiphany Sessions, Gloucester, in regard to Mʳ Barnett, the Coroner. — A letter from Sophia Hunt on Trust and Executorship concerns. — Officiated at the funeral of Sarah Watts of Eyford. — In the evening went with MW. to Adlestrop, to dine with Lord Saye & Sele — A very bad, dark, stormy, and rainy night, both as we went and returned. Our first visit to the Peer since he has succeeded to the title. His appointments suitable to his present rank and fortune, both in respect of table, wine, and attendance. — A large & agreeable party: the Bp. of Madras, the Rural dean, Ford, with his daughters Jemima and Dulcibella, Mʳ and Mʳˢ· Winter, Mʳ and Mʳˢ· Potter, Mʳ Sadler, Mʳ Westmacott, Mʳ Cameron, Mʳ Williams |¹⁵⁰ (Curate of Oddington) Sadler and Cameron were staying in the house: the latter I had not seen for a long time, he having been abroad, but now is returned and is residing with his wife and children at his benefice of Honington. When the gentlemen went into the drawing room to rejoin the ladies, I enjoyed a long téte à tete with the Bishop of Madras. Our conversation was animated, open and interesting on Missionary matters, particularly in India, on the Church at home, her divisions and prospects. I found Bp. Spencer an ardent, zealous, right-minded, clear headed, well informed and sound theologian, excepting as to delicate health very well adapted for his arduous work. He is an Oxford man, of University College, Brother to the Bishop of Jamaica, once Bishop of Newfoundland. They are not distantly allied to the family of the Duke of Marlborough; the wife of the Bp. of Madras is a Sister of Sir J C Hobhouse. He has been returned from |¹⁵¹ the East about eight months, and if his health will permit purposes to return to his immense diocese towards the close of the year; but he wants rest, and complains that he cannot get it. In fact, he may blame himself; for his zeal in the Missionary cause is such that he is always seeking rather than avoiding opportunities of labouring at public meetings to promote it. — Questioned Sadler as to any knowledge he has of the Captain Story respecting whom J Round has written to me. I collected that he is one of a large family of brothers and sisters, children of a Clergyman of good family and fortune, but a man of very extravagant and unsteady habits and conduct: that the general impression as to the character of the present generation is unfavourable, though one of the sons, in the army, is respectable. One of the daughters is married to Lord Dillon, a man of loose character, and wild; of Captⁿ· S. my informant knew nothing decidedly to his preju-|¹⁵² dice: but still a doubt hangs over the character of the family generally. Having lost his first wife, — of the Baring family, he married a grand daughter of Sir John Dashwood, whose widowed mother lived at Leamington: he took his lady thither to be with her mother during her confinement: she bore him a daughter: hardly had she recovered from her confinement, when they proposed a visit to Lord and Lady Dillon at Ditchley: set out and travelled one stage to Shipston, where very alarming symptoms shewed themselves; a puerperal fever and delirium came on; in ignorance, but with good meaning, he administered cordials which aggravated the complaint; they could not proceed on their journey, and having sunk, in a constant state of delirium, there she died, leaving him a widower with one child. There seems to have been no unkindness on his part, though something of levity. — And one cannot but fear that the connection is such as J R. would do |[153] well to break off, if he can.

Feb. 9. Wednesday.

A stormy and showery day. — Wrote to Round, giving him the information as to Mr Story which I had obtained yesterday from Sadler. — Wrote to Ford, giving him an outline of my proposed arrangements for the coming Special meeting in aid of S.P.G. and the reception of the deputation at Stow and at Upper Slaughter. — Preparing a Sermon — Visiting sick and infirm parishioners — S. Illes delirious, if not exhibiting symptoms of insanity. — Much illness at E. Lea's. — Life of Lord Loughborough by Lord Campbell. —

Feb. 10. Thursday.

After heavy rain during the night a fine day. — Visited S. Illes, who is calmer to-day. — Drove to Stow with MW. who soon returned to U. S. — Transacted business at the Provident Bank, and at the office of the Gloucestershire Banking Company: — also at |[154] the Printer's — To the Workhouse, where I presided till 3 P.M. at the fortnightly meeting of the Guardians. — Returning to the Savings Bank, met there Mess$^{rs.}$ Winter, W B Pole, and Morrison. — Rec$^{d.}$ a letter from G. F. Newmarch naming Mar. 15. as a convenient day for holding the annual meeting of the Turnpike trust at Northleach. — Life of Lord Loughborough. —

Feb. 11. Friday.

A fine day. — Wrote to M$^{rs.}$ Winter to acknowledge a note which I had received from her yesterday, containing a cheque for £4. 4. 0 in ~~app~~ payment of arrears of subscriptions to the S.P.G. due by the late Lady Imhoff. — To G. F. Newmarch that the 15$^{th.}$ Mar. would suit me very well for the Turnpike meeting at Northleach; but that I doubted whether I should attend. There are sufficient active Trustees resident along the line of road, so that an old man may be excused, and |[155] take a less active part: the same feeling will operate upon me as to the meetings of other Turnpike Trusts at Bourton on the Hill. — Justice business at home — Folded and directed nearly 100 notes to be circulated or sent by post announcing the Special meeting in aid of the Society for the Propagation of the Gospel fixed for the 22$^{d.}$ Inst. at Stow. — Rec$^{d.}$ a letter from E.F.W., acknowledging the cheque which ~~he h~~ I had sent him. All are well at the Vicarage, Stanway. — A letter from R W Ford in answer to mine detailing the arrangement as to the coming S.P.G. meeting; all which he approves. — Visited S. Illes; there seems to be a breaking up of the constitution both in body and mind. — Life of Lord Loughborough.

Feb. 12. Saturday.

Fine weather — Dispatched by a messenger and bill-sticker a large packet of notes and hand bills |*156* announcing the approaching meeting S.P.G: the circulation to be within the limits of the District Committee — Preparing a Sermon — Rec^d. a letter from Murray Browne, who accepts our invitation for the Bishop of Antigua, himself, and one other of the deputation from S.P.G: the fourth of the party is to be lodged at Mr Hippisley's at Stow. M. B. approves of the proposed arrangements, but talks of a second evening meeting at Stow or elsewhere, which I think would be a failure, nor have I sanguine expectations as to the morning gathering — A letter from Mr Barrow, late Curate of Wick Risington, now settled on a curacy in Sussex, Yapton, near Arundel: he forwards for my signature a testimonial, which Ford has already signed, and which he requests me to lay before Hippisley or R Waller, that one of them may vouch with Ford and myself as to his orthodoxy, and fitness to hold a cure in the diocese of |*157* Chichester. — Barrow in his letter gives aggreeable details of his present situation, and of his late tour in Germany &c. — Visited old & sick parishioners. — S. Illes, P. Carey, Eliz. Wilcox. — Life of Lord Loughborough. —

Feb. 13. Sunday.

A fine day, till the evening, when rain and wind came on. — Visited the S.S. — Morning service: prayers & a Sermon. I preached on the evil of corrupt communication. — Afternoon Service; Prayers. — Rec^d. a letter from Sophia Hunt on Hunt Trust and Executorship affairs. — The papers announce the death of the venerable, aged and excellent Arbp. of Canterbury, Dr Howley. The event has been for some time expected. His Grace was eminent for piety, prudence, meekness, calmness, discretion; firm without being peremptory or dictatorial: gentle without weakness; moderate in opinions; learned, but not brilliant nor |*158* presuming; and so an admirable head of the Church for a long course of years. — He filled the See of London before he was advanced to the primacy. — Preparing a Sermon — Eccl. Gazette & other papers in preparation for the coming S.P.G. meeting on the 22^d. Inst. —

Feb. 14. Monday.

Fine weather in the early part of the day: the afternoon and evening rainy. — Justice business at home. — Union business with the Relieving Officer — Rec^d. a note from Mr Wilkins, making an appointment at Bourton on the Water for Wednesday next, for the removal of the wife and child of Moses Roff to the presumed place of her husband's settlement.[10] — Wrote to Lord Saye and Sele, R W Ford, & R W Hippisley, as to the meeting S.P.G. fixed for the 22^d. Inst., inviting them to dine here to meet the deputation from the Parent Society. — Colonial Church Chronicle, — and preparing for the same |*159* meeting, drawing up resolutions &c. — Life of Lord Loughborough.

Feb. 15. Tuesday.

After rain in the night, a foggy morning, and a fine day. — Justice business at home. — At the desire of Sophia Hunt, to whom the measure has been suggested by a Col. Ottey, of the E.I. Company's service, I wrote, as Exor of M C Hunt, to Major Rowley, Superintendent of

10. If someone threatened to become reliant on parish relief and could not satisfy the strict guidelines for legal settlement they were liable to be removed to the place of their last legal settlement. A removal order was applied for from the local Justices of the Peace. This would usually involve an Examination as to Settlement carried out before the local justice, overseers and another ratepayer in order to ascertain the place of last legal settlement.

Pensioners, Bombay, as to Edward Hunt, who is on the Bombay pension list, who has not answered the letter I wrote to him on Nov. 5. respecting his Sister's will, the interest he has under it, and the portion otherwise coming to him under the will of Mrs. M. Hunt. I requested the interposition of Major Rowley, that E.H. may be prevailed upon to answer my letter, and give directions as to the money due to him, and the interest on money vested in the funds on trust to be hereafter paid to him. — Wrote to |¹⁶⁰ Sophia Hunt, sending a copy of what I had written to Major Rowley. — Rec^{d.} a letter from E.F.W. chiefly on Union business, as to the Chaplain and Med. Off. of the Winchcomb Union. My Son forwards for my perusal letters from the Medical Officers, and on the part of himself and Mr Holland, the Chairman of the Union, requests my views and thoughts as to the salaries & allowances of Medical Officers, with particulars as to the salaries and other perquisites of the medical officers of our Union. — E.F.W, Sophy, and the children are well; they purpose coming to Maugersbury next week to attend the special meeting of our district committee S.P.G. — A letter from Sadler, in answer to mine about Capt. Story: he repeats what he told me at Lord Saye & Sele's. — Visited sick people — S. Illes, and E. Lea's family — Life of Lord Loughborough. —

Feb. 16. Wednesday.

A hard frost, and a fine day. — Wrote to Mrs. Shard — Preparing |¹⁶¹ for the meeting of S.P.G. fixed for the 22^{d.} Inst. — Drove with MW. to Bourton on the Water. She went on to call on the Fords at Little Risington. I remained at Mr Wilkins's office, where I met Rob. Waller, and was engaged with him in reading over documents, and hearing evidence, and making an order of removal to Long Compton, of the wife and child of Moses Roff, now confined in the Lunatic Asylum at Gloucester: and as to whom an adjudication was made yesterday by Curtis Hayward and Lysons, fixing the payment of the costs of maintenance of Moses Roff on the same parish. A difficult case, attended with considerable expence. Mr Wilkins with several witnesses had attended at Gloucester yesterday. The examinations, order of removal, and adjudication, in both cases, had been drawn by Greaves, the Counsel. — MW. brought Dulcy Ford back with her in |¹⁶² the carriage to Bourton. Met and parleyed with M^{rs.} R Waller. — On our return home found Mrs. W. Vavasour and her sister Emma, who had walked from Maugersbury to call on us. I accompanied them on their way back ~~till~~ ^{to} near Swell. They gave a good account of our children and grandchildren whom they had seen at Stanway on Monday. — A letter from R W Hippisley who accepts our invitation to dinner on the 22^{d.} Inst. and comments on the arrangements proposed for that day. — A letter from J Round in reply to my letter stating what I had learnt as to Capt. Story: the good father has given his consent to his daughter's marriage to that officer. — A letter from one Breakspear of Oddington as to rates being charged on one Hunt, a labourer of that parish — Life of Lord Loughborough.

Feb. 17. Thursday.

A frost: fine weather — Wrote to E.F.W. my thoughts on the payment of Medical officers of Unions; afterwards |¹⁶³ I procured from Mr Pearce returns which he had prepared on the same subject, as to the emoluments of those officers in our Union, the regulations observed by us as to medical relief &c. these I forwarded with my letter to my Son, returning the documents which he had furnished me with — MW. accompanied me to Stow, but soon returned home. — Attended at the Prov. Bank. — Transacted business at the office of the Gloucestershire Banking company —

Conferred with Mr Pearce at the Workhouse on Union matters. — At the Unicorn, presided at the annual meeting of the Comm^rs. of the Turnpike road leading from Stow to Burford: present Messrs. Ford, W. B. Pole, R Waller, and Winter — R W Hippisley was also present at the Justice meeting, which followed: I was assisted in transacting magistrate's business by Ford and R Waller. — Rec^d. a circular, announcing a meeting of the diocesan |^164 Board of Education for the Archdeaconry of Gloucester to be held there to-morrow. — Lord Campbell's Life of Lord Loughborough.

Feb. 18. Friday.

A sharp frost, and fine day — Wrote to Mr Barrow, forwarding to him his testimonial, signed by R W Hippisley and myself — Justice business at home. — Rec^d. a letter from Lord Saye and Sele, who accepts our invitation to dinner on Tuesday next. — So also Mr Terry, to whom I sent a note of invitation this morning. — A letter from C Bathurst respecting a series of bills for regulating proceedings of Magistrates on summary convictions, commitments for trial, and holding of Petty Sessions lately brought into the House of Commons by the Attorney General. — Life of Lord Loughborough.

Feb. 19. Saturday.

A sprinkling of snow on the ground in the morning, which soon melted; the weather afterwards fine. — Justice business at home. W. Vavasour |^165 called, having detected a poacher in the exercise of his calling yesterday evening — Wrote to Sophia Hunt on Hunt Trust and Executorship matters. — Preparing for the S.P.G. meeting to be held on Tuesday next — Life of Lord Loughborough.

Feb. 20. Sunday.

A rainy forenoon: weather afterwards cold, but fair. — Visited the Sunday School. — Morning Service — Prayers. — Evening Service – Prayers and a Sermon. — I preached on the due observance of the Lord's day. — Preparing a Sermon — Rec^d. a letter from Messrs. Hoare, announcing that Mr Jennings had paid to my account with them £61. 5. 3 — A circular giving notice of the annual meeting of the Comm^rs. of the Crickley Hill Turnpike Trust, to be held at Northleach on Mar. 18. — Preparing for the S.P.G. meeting fixed for the 22^d. Inst. — To the family a section from James on the Collects. — |^166

Feb. 21. Monday.

A fine morning, but a rainy afternoon. — Preparing a Sermon. — Justice business at home — Union business with the Rel. Officer at home. — Preparing for the meeting S.P.G. to-morrow. — Life of Lord Loughborough. —

Feb. 22. Tuesday.

A very stormy day, with frequent showers and boisterous wind — Preparing a Sermon. — Drove to Stow accompanied by MW. to attend the extraordinary meeting in aid of the objects of S.P.G. We were soon joined at the Unicorn by M^r & M^rs. Ford and two daughters. — With F. I went to the Rectory to meet the deputation, who had come from Cheltenham, and driven thither. Mr Hippisley was refreshing them with luncheon. Murray Browne introduced the Rural Dean and me to the Bishop of Antigua — The Rev^d. H. J. Vernon, and the Rev^d. — Thompson — delegated

to advocate the Interests of the Parent Society — |[167] They had held two meetings (morning and evening) yesterday at Micheldean — slept last night at Gloucester, and come from thence to day. Arranged the order of proceeding according to their notions: they came provided with resolutions to be moved. Adjourned to the Unicorn Inn, where a platform had been prepared in the Ballroom — The attendance did not exceed sixty or seventy persons: the very bad weather was greatly in our disfavour; and there is indifference & lukewarmness as to this and other religious objects, with a distaste for such displays. The season of the year was also unpropitious. Among those present were Lord Saye and Sele, R Waller, Pantin, Williams, (Oddington) Potter, E.F.W, — Mrs. Potter, Mrs. W. Vavasour, Mrs. E. F. Witts, Miss Jane Hippisley. — Ford, as Rural Dean, presided. — The first Resolution was moved by Lord Saye & Sele in a few words, and seconded by the Bp. of Antigua in a long and earnest speech. Dr Davis is a Sexage-|[168]narian, of West Indian parentage, educated in England, and of Pembroke College, Oxford. He has passed through all the graduations of his profession in the West Indies, as Curate, Rector, Archdeacon and Bishop — He appears a very right minded, clear-headed, earnest person; not of commanding talent, nor preeminent eloquence, nor very attractive by elegance or polish of manners; but his speech was effective, interesting, somewhat egoistical, full of unction, and gave much insight into the working of the Church & of Episcopacy in the West Indies, how it had little influence, and was little cared for, and set at nought heretofore; but now is respected and firmly fixed in the affections both of the descendants of English forefathers, and of the negro race, as far as that race has been since the emancipation brought within its pale – Of course much was to be told as to the emancipation, as to devastation by earthquakes and hurricanes, and while there is great cause for encouraging hope, there lack not ~~motives~~ grounds of uneasiness. — |[169] The second resolution was moved by Mr Thomson, formerly a Missionary in the diocese of Madras, but now a Curate of a parish in Wilts, having been compelled some years ago to relinquish his Oriental Sphere of duty by suffering from liver complaint: he and his wife having left India with very impaired health. Mr T's speech, of course, turned chiefly on the Evangelization of Southern India, and his details were exceedingly interesting; but here again one's taste is offended with the almost unavoidable egotism of such narratives. Mr T. is an energetic, laborious, sincere, & earnest man, and seems to have done very good service, in organizing and superintending schools, in translating Scripture and religious writings into Oriental dialects, and in preaching the Gospel. His speech was rather provincial, he being a North Country man, bred at the Durham University; and so his elocution was unprepossessing; but he abounded in anecdote, read extracts from correspondence from native converts or |[170] pupils, gave us samples of the Tamil tongue, shewed us little religious manuals of the Brahmins, from which he made translations &c. — Of Finnwelly &c. he spoke with confidence & hope; of the Bp. of Madras with admiration and affection; of the exertions of the Church Missionary Society's agents he spoke with great respect; not so of the Missionaries of Protestant dissenters, and as to the labours of the Roman Catholic Missionaries he treated them as being almost worthless, translating their converts from one form of idolatry to another, from Hindoo devil worship to Mariolatry – From his brother delegates I gathered that Mr Thompson shone to greater advantage in addressing an evening meeting of the lower and less educated classes than in speaking before a more refined audience. With the latter he is under constraint, with the former he indulges in more pungent anecdotes & details, and gives vent to his humour and taste for putting things in a broad light. —
(Continued in another book) |

Diary
1848

1

Feb. 22. Tuesday — (Continued from another book)
— M.ʳ Vernon seconded the resolution moved
by M.ʳ Thomson. M.ʳ V. is an elegant young
man, lately appointed Under Secretary of
the S. P. G. — a very ~~elegant and~~ agreable
person, who has been Curate of M.ʳ Spencer
Phillips at North Church in the Isle of Wight.
He spoke with great fluency and correctness;
touching on many miscellaneous points connected with the parent society — with the
state of the finances, the need of copious sup-
plies, the importance of parochial contributions &c. He also dwelt on the case of the
emigrants to the North American provinces,
and of the successful efforts made in prea-
ching the gospel to the North American
natives, the Red Indians. — Resolutions
of course, with short speeches, wound up
the proceedings of the day. A vote of thanks
to the Bishop of Antigua was moved by
R. Waller, and seconded by me. — M.ʳ —

Witts Family Papers F362

Diary

1848

Feb. 22. Tuesday. — (Continued from another book)

Mʳ Vernon seconded the resolution moved by Mʳ Thomson. Mʳ V. is an elegant young man, lately appointed Under Secretary of the S.P.G. — a very ~~elegant and~~ agreable person, who has been Curate of Mʳ Spencer Phillips at North^ew Church in the Isle of Wight. He spoke with great fluency and correctness; touching on many miscellaneous points connected with the parent society — with the state of the finances, the need of copious supplies, the importance of parochial contributions &c. He also dwelt on the case of the emigrants to the North American provinces, and ~~of~~ ^on the successful efforts made in preaching the gospel to the North American natives, the Red Indians. — Resolutions of course, with short speeches, wound up the proceedings of the day. A vote of thanks to the Bishop of Antigua was moved by R. Waller, and seconded by me. – Mʳ |² Hippisley moved thanks to the Chairman, and was seconded by Murray Browne. — The collection made amounted to £15. 17. 2½ — There was little opportunity of intercourse with our dear children who had been staying since yesterday with the W. Vavasours at Maugersbury, and returned to Stanway after the meeting ended. — MW. and myself hastened back to U Slaughter to receive our guests. Murray Browne soon brought with him in a fly from Stow the Bp. Antigua and Mʳ Vernon: these three dined and slept with us. Hippisley brought Mʳ Thomson to dinner, and took him back to sleep at the Rectory, Stow; Lord Saye and Sele, Mʳ Ford, with his daughters, Jemima and Dulcibella, and Mʳ Terry made up our party. — In the course of the evening Lord S. and S. opened to me the very anxious position in which he has been placed by the necessity of proving his right to his title before a Comm. of the H. of Lords. The matter is still pending; nor can he take his |³ seat, till it is determined in his favour. His father, Dʳ Twisleton, Archd. of Ceylon, and a younger Brother of the Lord S. and S. of that day, was a very gay and dissipated young man. Even when a pupil at Westminster School he devoted himself to private theatricals, and at a very early age became entangled with a Miss Wattell a Stage heroine, as young and giddy as himself. Her he married, and poverty, dissention, and separation were the result of the ill conditioned union. She bare him no live child, and on their being parted, she went on the stage as a means of support, he prosecuting his studies at Oxford. At Edinburgh, as an actress, she became the mistress of one Stein, a merchant, who kept her until she had borne him a Son, and eventually separated from her. This connection enabled Mʳ Twisleton to obtain a divorce; after which he married a Miss Ashe, the mother of the present Lord and his two brothers. – Till Lord S & S. succeeded to the title and estates, which were left to him by his deceased cousin — who had never married, but had lived a dissipated & eccentric life, always of late years |⁴ recognizing his cousin, the Rector of Adlestrop, as his heir and successor, these not very creditable family histories had been lulled to sleep, and were hardly remembered, except as recorded in one to two memoirs of persons long since deceased, particularly in those of one Reynolds, an Actor & wit, and companion of the early life of the Archdeacon. — Now it became necessary to revive them; and chiefly to prove that the Son of Mʳˢ· Twisleton, born after her separation from her husband, and before their divorce, could not be his Son by reason of non-access. Extraordinary success has attended the researches made by Lord S. & S's Solicitors. They have discovered, still living, an octogenarian, the Mʳ Stein who cohabited with Mʳˢ· Twisleton, the Actress, at Edinburgh, who, having survived to this period, seems to have felt it a point of honour and justice to declare the truth; admitting that he lived with Mʳˢ· T. as man and wife, that a Son was the produce of that connection, whom he considered as his own, and whom he educated for many years, inten-|⁵ding to place him in a respectable situation. But losses in trade & crippled means prevented the fulfillment of that design, and the Son eventually became a private sailor in the commercial marine. He, therefore, was sought after by Lord S & S's agents, and was, after long and difficult enquiry, discovered at some seaport at ᵒⁿ the eve of embarking on a distant voyage; a common sailor of fifty two years of age, the person who might put in a claim to the peerage — but the estates were all securely conveyed so as to be without his reach. He readily confirmed the statement made by Stein, whom he considered his father, who had treated him as his son ᵇʸ whom he had been educated &c. — It remained to prove that circumstances precluded access between Twisleton the husband and his unchaste wife, so as to negative his being the Father of the Sailor. And this could be done; for a correspondence which had been preserved shewed that during part of the time of gestation and before it, Mʳ T. had been hiding himself from his Creditors in the West of England, — |⁶ and that during the remainder of the time he had been keeping term at Oxford, which could be proved by the production of the battle books of his college – Sᵗ· Mary Hall. The decision of the case will not be long deferred; and it is fully expected a decision favourable to the Rector of Adlestrop: for the law of non-access is not construed so strictly now as formerly, when it was required that the parties should not both be inter quatuor Maria. — I believe I was wrong in saying that there was no child born alive to Archd. Twisleton by his first wife: there was a daughter recognised as his own: he has a daughter also by the second marriage, married to a Mʳ Gisborne. — When at Stow I recᵈ· from Mʳ Pearce a large packet of correspondence relative to Union matters from the Poor Law Board, but had not leisure to peruse them ˡᵉᵗᵗᵉʳˢ — My parishioner, Sarah Illes, died to-day rather suddenly; a happy release, as she was broken both in body and mind. |⁷

Feb. 23. Wednesday.

After heavy rain during the night, a bright but cold morning: towards sunset showers began to fall. — Our guests, the Bp. of Antigua, Murray Browne, and Mʳ Vernon, left us after breakfast, between 11 & 12 o cl. – as I trust, mutually pleased with each other: we had much free and pleasant conversation on general subjects, on the state and prospects of the church, and more particularly on the very awkward state of things at the present conjuncture arising out of the elevation of Dʳ Hampden to the Episcopal bench: and specially with regard to the late meeting of Clergy of the Archdeaconry of Gloucester, as to which Murray Browne admitted that all were in a false position, and that dissention had been fostered by what passed there. — The deputation proceeded to Moreton in Marsh, where a meeting is to be held: by the way, they proposed calling at Bourton on the Hill to enquire after the excellent D[r] Warneford, |[8] the bountiful patron of the church both at home and abroad, but it was not expected that he would admit them owing to his infirm health, and the indisposition under which at this season of the year he labours — From Moreton the Bishop and his fellows proceed to Campden, where a Sermon is to be preached in aid of the S.P.G. and its advocates are to be the guests of the Vicar, M[r] Kennaway. — Tomorrow their circuit closes with a public meeting at Tewkesbury — Busy in settling the accounts of the meeting at Stow yesterday — and in considering the correspondence on Poor Law matters which had been placed in my hands by M[r] Pearce yesterday. — Visited the Lea family: still does sickness prevail among them: the second Son has visited D[r] Baron, at Cheltenham, for his advice, and that eminent physician holds out very faint hopes of his long surviving. With an appearance of health in the coun-|[9] tenance, and a seemingly athletic frame, consumption has already made considerable inroads on his constitution — Called at J. Illes's. — I caught cold yesterday and felt fatigued with my exertions. — Life of Lord Loughborough.

Feb. 24. Thursday.

A very showery day — Transacted business with my Churchwarden. — Also Justice business at home — Wrote to M[r] Brookes, Stow. —— Drove to Stow. — Rec[d.] a letter from Sophia Hunt on Executorship affairs. — To the Provident Bank, where I transacted business; also at the Office of the Gloucestershire Banking Company. — At the Workhouse presided at the fortnightly meeting of the Guardians of our Union. The chief matter to be discussed was the letter rec[d.] from the P.L.C. as to the matters in dispute between the Board & its officers, and M[r] Hunt, the Auditor. The documents forwarded by the P.L.C. were read, and further consideration of them was postponed for a fortnight: they are then |[10] to be considered in the first instance by a committee sitting earlier than usual, to report to the Board when the Guardians meet at the ~~usual~~ wonted hour — Returned to the Provident Bank, where I met M[r] Winter, and transacted Justice business with M[r] R. G. K. Brookes &c. – Life of Lord Loughborough — Somewhat inconvenienced by a cold.

Feb. 25. Friday.

With the exception of a shower, the weather fine overhead till evening, when heavy rain came on, and continued during the night. — Justice business at home. — Wrote to Rodwell for a supply of books for the Stow Book Society. — Wrote to Rev[d.] Ern. Hawkins, Sec. S.P.G. with a remittance and statement of subscriptions &c. rec[d.] from members of the Stow district Comm., including the collection made at the special meeting on the 22[d.] Inst. — Rec[d.] a letter from the Rev[d.] M[r] Jones, |[11] Rector of Hempstead, near Gloucester, who, acting as Secretary to a body of Clergymen of this Archdeaconry associated for the purpose, forwards for my approbation and signature, if I be so disposed, a copy of an address which it is proposed to ~~be~~ present to D[r] Hampden, when he shall have been consecrated Bishop of Hereford: — the address being congratulatory and expressive of full confidence in him, and conviction of his orthodoxy. The address is so drawn up as to avoid any censure of, or anything disrespectful to our own diocesan, but it is manifestly intended as a declaration of opinion contrary to the resolution of thanks voted to the Bp. of Gloucester by the majority of the clergy of the Archdeaconry assembled at the late unwise meeting at Gloucester. Seventy Clergymen of the Archdeaconry, beneficed and Curates, have signed this address: they are mostly men of low Church opinions, & low in politics. — Rec^d. a packet of parlia-|[12] mentary proceedings sent by Robert B. Hale, MP. for West Gloucestershire, being the series of bills lately brought in by the Attorney General for regulating the proceedings of Magistrates in Petty Sess^ns, protection of Magistrates, rules of practice &c. — The Bp. of Chester, D^r J B Sumner, is gazetted Archb. of Canterbury. This appointment will be distasteful to the Ultra High Church party, satisfactory to moderate men, and gratifying to the Evangelical section in the Church. — It is probably intended by the Minister as an indication that extreme high Ch. opinions are ~~up~~ unpalatable to those holding high office in the State. Dr Sumner is the author of some useful works in theology, not exhibiting profound learning, but very valuable as guides to and incentives of piety. In his administration of the very populous and important diocese of Chester, he has been very earnest and indefatigable; |[13] and particularly has greatly promoted the erection of new Churches, with the establishment of new pastoral districts; being also a zealous patron of Church Societies, and among them a powerful friend to those most fostered by the Evangelical Section in the Church; — the Bible Society, Church Missionary Society &c. — His brother, the Bp. of Winchester partakes, perhaps even in a greater measure, of his low church opinions; but is a very estimable and zealous prelate. — Very serious disturbances broke out at Paris on the 22^d. & 23^d. inst. and order does not seem to be reestablished. For some months past there has been an uneasy feeling, and a great outcry on the subject of what we should call Parliamentary Reform; very numerous public meetings and public entertainments have been held, at which very strong language has been used, and a very determined spirit exhibited. Louis Philippe and his ministry headed by that eminent Statesman, Guizot, |[14] have given no indication of concession to the ~~popul~~ popular cry: and in the chamber of deputies the question has of late been eagerly and angrily debated: ministers pronouncing such meetings to be illegal, and their opponents maintaining the reverse. The latter determined on bringing the point to an issue: convened a large reform banquet for the 22^d. at Paris; dared the government to suppress it. The result of this measure appears to have come on both parties by surprize: the favourers of reform, alarmed at the indications of disturbance, declared at the eleventh hour that the meeting would not be held — ministers on their part had collected a great military force to put it down. But the mob of Paris took the matter into their hands; rioting soon amounting to insurrection was the order of the day; collisions occurred between the populace, the police, & the military; barricades were erected, and vigorous^ly defended in the Streets of Paris, |[15] after the manner of 1830: the National Guard seems to have sympathized more or less with the disturbers of the public peace: in the Chamber of deputies the opposition impeached the government; and the last accounts shew that Guizot has resigned and that the King has called upon Count Molé, to form a new Ministry. Whether this concession will calm the troubled sea, remains to be proved, and may be doubted.[1] — Officiated at the funeral of Sarah Illes — Life of Lord Loughborough.

---

1. The revolt in Paris was due to the failure Louis Philippe's reign, the economic depression and the prohibition of reform banquets. On 24 February Louis Philippe abdicated in favour of his grandson, the Comte de Paris, but a Republican Provisional government was proclaimed under Alphonse Lamartine.

Feb. 26. Saturday.

A stormy day of almost continual rain — My birthday. I am this day sixty five years of age — a monument of GOD's gracious goodness and long suffering: yet an unprofitable servant, to whom much has been granted, who has enjoyed many great privileges and advantages, but not borne proportional fruit. Much will be required from me: am I able to render a good account? Alas! I am very deficient in the graces and virtue of a matured Christian. Lord! Give |[16] me strength of body and mind, give me grace to repent and amend my ways; with a repentance not to be repented of may I be enabled to combine greater constancy and steadiness in the paths of true religion! — Justice business at home — Preparing a Sermon. — Replied in the following terms to the letter I received yesterday from the Rev[d.] — Jones, Hempstead. — "In returning to you the copy of the proposed address to the Bishop of Hereford, and in declining to attach my name to it, I think it right to say that though I did not take a part in the late movement at Gloucester, because I doubted whether the agitation of the question was well timed or expedient, I nevertheless approved of the remonstrance made by the thirteen Bishops, and after mature reflection both now, and when the matter was brought before the Convocation of my University, I entertain a strong opinion that whatever may be the personal piety, or |[17] personal orthodoxy of D[r] Hampden, which I am far from presuming to impugn, the tone of his publications was such as to create a reasonable doubt of the soundness of his faith; and consequently to disqualify him from occupying any of the more eminent Stations in the Church." — As much conversation had passed on this subject when the Bp. of Antigua visited us, I deemed it right to inform Murray Browne by letter of the tone of my reply to M[r] Jones. As chaplain, he possesses the ear of the Bishop of Gloucester, and I am desirous that the view I have taken of this affair should be properly represented to his Lordship. — Rec[d.] a letter from F. Aston — Engaged in perusing and considering the Parliamentary bills forwarded to me by R B Hale. — Life of Lord Loughborough — Hutton's (Newmarch's) Five years in the East.

Feb. 27. Sunday.

A day of almost constant rain; at night stormy, wind and thunder — Summoned early to the bedside of Eliz[a.] |[18] Collett, wife of T. S. Collett, who has very lately been confined, and is in a state of great debility: so that her life is considered in danger. Administered to her the Sacrament. — Morning service, prayers and sermon. I preached on the parable of the Sower — Evening service, prayers. — A letter from Sophia Hunt, who forwards a letter she has received from M[r] Archbould — Exorship business. — Preparing a Sermon — Eccles. Gazette — To the family a ~~Sete~~ Section from Dr James on the Collects. — The news from Paris very calamitous: the disturbances have ended in a revolution. The concession made by the King in the dismissal of the Guizot Ministry, and the attempt to form an administration under the Count Molé, failed to appease the violence of the mob, who continued to acquire strength and power hourly: the government, the military commanders, the higher and the middle orders, seemed para-|[19]lyzed: nowhere firmness, decision, or resistance. Paris soon became the stronghold of a reckless mob, the multitude of ~~reckless,~~ godless, republican & Socialist workmen, without employment, becoming masters of the metropolis under unscrupulous leaders, plundering and devastating on all sides. A feeble attempt to recover authority was made by the King offering to Thiers and his friends, the opposition leaders in the Chamber of deputies, the posts of ministers; but Thiers and Odillon Barrot, and their adherents, acting as Servants of a monarch however limited in power, would no longer satisfy the violent populace. On the storm raged, and the Sovereign and Royal family were invaded in their palace: by an apparent fatality the army was not called into action; but a feeble resistance was made: there was no confidence in the defenders, or a panic seized on the King and Princes of his house. Pressed and threatened and urged, Louis Philippe abdicated & |[20] sought refuge in a hasty flight, without dignity, without preparation, without guards, without money, in disguise; and so it fared with the Princes and Princesses, all scattered, separated, none knows where, a perfect sauve qui peut. The abdication was said to be in favour of the Grandson of the King — the young Duke of Orleans, — his widowed Mother, accompanied by the Duke de Nemours, with her boy princes in her hand, was conducted into the Chamber of Deputies; there an effort was made to procure for the elder of the Princes a recognition of a Regency by his mother till he attained his majority; and there were deputies and statesmen anxious to rally round, and uphold this last hope of monarchy. But the mob pressed on, forced an entrance, filled the tribunes; the galleries, the centre of the hall; fierce and intoxicated, with maddened energy, armed and unarmed, with vehement gesture & |[21] in the rudest garb of the lowest people, whom nothing would satisfy, but the subversion of the monarchy, and a reign of terror and licence. Gradually, and with difficulty, retiring before the wave, the Princes were borne out of the Hall, and placed in a carriage, which bore them to some place of obscure and temporary security. The Chamber of deputies was tumultuously dissolved: the populace were in an uncontrollable ascendancy: a republic was declared by acclamation, and a Provisional Government of a motley kind instantly installed. Of these rulers thus forced into a perilous preeminence, being men of talent, and popular on account of the extreme opinions which they hold, and the powerful tone in which they advocate them, the leaders are the aged Dupont de l'Eure, the poet Lamartine, the scientific Arago, the democratic Ledru Rollin — others are well known in Paris as ultra politicians, more or less implicated in the secret machinations which must have been long approaching to |[22] maturity, and among the leading persons destined to ride on the whirlwind, and control the Storm, are the clever editors of various journals holding extreme opinions on political matters, who have mainly contributed to produce that state of public opinion and feeling which has eventuated in this thunderclap of a revolution.

Feb. 28. Monday.

A windy, bright day, after a turbulent night; some slight showers — Justice business at home. — Wrote to Sophia Hunt on Exorship affairs — M[r] Pearce called: with whom I was long engaged in perusing and considering letters and papers from the office of the P.L.C. bearing upon our controversy with the district Auditor: making memoranda on the subject for future use. — Visited sick parishioners — T. S. Collett's wife, now considered to be out of immediate danger; baptized her infant privately: — also M. Cook's wife, Mary Davis, M[rs.] |[23] Davis &c. — Life of Lord Loughborough.

Feb. 29. Tuesday.

A fine forenoon: the afternoon very rainy; stormy and windy at night. — Transacted business with Churchwarden Gregory. — Justice business at home. — Wrote to R Waller, requesting him to attend the Petty Sessions on Thursday next. — To Lord Saye and Sele,

Mr Wiggin, and Mr Bowen, sending to each of them acknowledgments for their subscriptions &c. to S.P.G. — Rec^d from S.P.G. an acknowledgment of my remittance to the Treas. of the Society on the 25th. — A letter from Mrs C. Barr from Henwick: she describes Mrs Walker as being very unwell: but, if she recovers in some degree, M^{rs} CB. proposes paying a visit with her children to Mrs E. Daniell at Bullingham, near Hereford, and from thence coming on a visit to us. — A letter from C Bathurst: he imagines I must be ill, as I have not written to him lately. — |^{24} Engaged in considering the bills as to jurisdiction of magistrates lately brought into the House of Commons by the Att^y Genl Finished Lord Campbell's Life of Lord Chancellor Loughborough, and began his Memoir of Lord Chancellor Erskine – these are very interesting and amusing pieces of biography.

Mar. 1. Wednesday.

Rainy morning, the afternoon fine — Justice business at home — Wrote to C Bathurst with comments on the bills regulating Magisterial office and duties lately brought into the House of Commons by the Att^y General — Wrote to E.F.W. inviting him and his to visit us from the 13th to the 18th Inst. — Mr Terry called: walked with him part of the way to Wick Risington — Rec^d a letter from Mr Thornton as to the controversy respecting the repair of Whitby's Wharf. It seems that Mr George ~~Thornton~~ Turner delays giving his opinion on the |^{25} case submitted to him, probably, because a Junior Counsel has not been associated with him. — There seems to be a lull in the storm lately raging in the French metropolis: several members of the Royal family have succeeded in escaping, and have reached this country, in disguise; with great difficulty, Princes separated from their Wives, escort^g those of their brothers, and the like. Some members of the late French ministry have also arrived in England. One fruit of this foreign disturbance, and of the impatience loudly expressed at home, against a proposed measure of our Government — the raising of the Income Tax from 3 to 5 Pr Cent, has been that Ministers have abandoned that project. It is also very wisely declared by the Premier that it is not intended in any way to interfere in the internal affairs of France. British hospitality will be afforded to the refugees, but we shall not assume a hostile attitude as regards the de facto go-|^{26} vernment of France. — Lord Campbell's Life of Lord Erskine. ——

Mar. 2. Thursday.

A bright morning, and cloudy noon. — Preparing for business at Stow. — Drove thither, accompanied by MW., who shortly after returned home. On the way, at the Lower Slaughter Turnpike gate, met Mr Terry by appointment, who took a seat at the back of our carriage, he being desirous of visiting the Workhouse under my guidance. — At the Provident Bank transacted business, as also at Mr Morgan's office, and with Mr Croome at the White Hart Inn. — At the Workhouse, conferred with Mr Pearce, Mr Dunford, and Mr Wilkins on Union matters. Visited the different wards, school rooms, dining hall &c. — Returned to the Provident B^k where met Messrs Winter, W B Pole, Ford, R Waller, Morrison, and Terry. — Thence |^{27} to the Justice room, where sat with Ford and R Waller — Winter, W B Pole, Terry, and W. Vavasour, being present. — Rec^d a letter from Mr Hare, who forwards for my perusal a letter from Messrs Cox and Williams as to Whitby's Wharf, and the case as to the duty of repairing it, whether incumbent on the Trustees, and what course is to be taken by them in order, now that the life tenant is no more, to be released from their trust. — Lord Campbells's Life of Lord Erskine. ——

Mar. 3. Friday.
Fine weather — Wrote to M[r] Hare, M[r] Thornton, and Mess[rs] Cox and Williams on the case to be laid before counsel as to the Red Lion Wharf — to F. Aston that I apprehended it would not be in our power to accept his invitation to luncheon on the day fixed for the Turnpike meeting at Northleach, it being very doubtful whether I should attend it, and the more unlikely, as my son |[28] and daughter and their children would be our guests at that time — to Otway, our former Stow Policeman, now Porter at Blenheim palace, to thank him for a present he lately sent, a fine eel from the Blenheim lake, a mark of his gratitude and attachment, very acceptable, and not the first proof of his right feeling — to M[rs] C Barr, that it will give us great pleasure to see her and her children on a visit after she has been with the Edw[d] Daniells at Bullingham — Visited the day-school and different sick parishioners — Rec[d] a letter from C Bathurst in reply to the one I addressed to him on the 1st Inst. — A long and pleasant letter from E.F.W. on various subjects — the French revolution — Union matters — late meeting at Stow in aid of S.P.G. &c. — a good report of all at Stanway Vicarage — |[29] MW. rec[d] from Apphia Witts a tolerable report of her self, her Brother John, and M[rs] John Witts. — From France the tidings are ~~not~~ more favourable than could be expected: matters proceed under the Provisional government with more tranquillity than might have been supposed. No certain tidings of the King and Queen of the French, nor of the Duchess of Orleans and her children — Examining the Bills relating to Magisterial duties & proceedings introduced into the H. of C. by the Attorney General — Lord Campbell's Life of Lord Erskine. ——

Mar. 5. Saturday.[2]
Fine weather — Justice business at home — Wrote to M[r] Croome, Surveyor, respecting an error which has crept into our parish Valuation: — to Mess[rs] Hoare, desiring them to transfer £50 from my account to that of my Son with them: this sum is a present, not on his income account. — Making a transcript of the |[30] Parish Registers, to be transmitted to the Registrar's office at Gloucester. Drove with MW. to Stow: called at "the Cottage," where we found M[r] and M[rs] Vavasour at home, and met M[rs] W. Vavasour and her sister. — Life of Lord Erskine — Newmarch's five years in the East.

Mar. 5. Sunday.
A rainy day. — Preparing a sermon. — Morning service, prayers. Afternoon service, prayers and Sermon. I preached on Christian charity. — The newspapers announce the arrival at Newhaven on the Sussex coast of Louis Philippe, and his Queen, with two or three attendants. They were picked up at sea by a steamer, and taken on board from a French fishing boat. Great have been the perils and anxieties of these aged victims of a successful rebellion. Flying from Paris, without preparation, with hardly any money or clothes, in the most obscure vehicles, by highways |[31] & byways, in disguise, and under feigned names, making for the coast, forced to rely for succour and concealment ~~to~~ on persons of humble means and humble station, concealed near Harfleur, and in communication with the British Consul at Havre, M[r] Featherstonehaugh, the persecuted ex Sovereigns, lately esteemed so

2. An uncorrected dating error.

puissant & so secure, under the assumed name of Smith, in a blouse and a peasant's cap, as regards Louis, and in a humble mourning gown & bonnet, as regards the Queen, landed, almost literally without a change of clothes, with one carpet bag, or portmanteau: forced to remain at the humble inn of the obscure port till clothing could be procured from London. — The Ex minister, Guizot, has reached Town from Ostend in a state of utter destitution: his aged mother with the Statesman's daughters had preceeded him by a few days and by another route. The Duchess of Orleans and her boy princes have reached |³² Dusseldorf in safety. — Ecclesiastical Gazette — to the family a section from James on the Collects. —

Mar. 6. Monday.

A fine day. — Busy with workmen employed in repairing our laundry. — Engaged with Mr Pearce and Mr Dunford, conferring on Union matters, chiefly as to the course to be taken respecting our controversy with the Auditor; and as to a new system of keeping Union accounts, requiring an alteration in our practice — MW. rec^d. a letter from our dear Sophy which gives us a prospect of seeing her with her husband and children on a visit to us on the 13th. Inst. — Life of Lord Erskine.

Mar. 7. Tuesday.

A fine day. — Justice business at home — Preparing a sermon. Wrote to Mr Francis, suggesting that his nephew's forthcoming publication on India; to which I have promised the subscription of the Stow Book Society, be forwarded to Rodwell, our bookseller in Town, who should |³³ pay for the same, charge the price in his acc^t. with us, and forward it to us. — Wrote to R. Waller that an aged parishioner of his at Lower Slaughter had caused an application to be made to me that I would call and pray with her: that I had referred her to him, and promised to write to him on the subject. I fear that the visitation of the sick and aged has been neglected latterly at L. Slaughter: there being as yet no settled curate since Mr Turner left the situation. — Drove with MW. to Stow and Maugersbury: called on the Willm. Vavasours, who were not at home. — Called at the library & some shops at Stow — Returned home by Lower Swell. – Called on M^r & M^rs. Perkins — Rec^d. a letter from Messrs. Hoare, announcing that they had transfered £50 from my account to that of my son. — Life of Lord Erskine. —

Mar. 8. Wednesday.

A dull morning: rain for an hour or two in the afternoon; fine weather afterwards. — Wrote a few lines on |³⁴ Poor Law matters to E.F.W. to accompany a note from MW. to Sophy: — Wrote to Randall, hatter, Oxford, for a new hat. — Preparing a Sermon — Brit. Magazine — Divine service in the forenoon, this day being Ashwednesday. — Rec^d. a letter from Sophia Hunt on Executorship and Trust Matters — A circular from the Glouc. ~~Lunatic Asylum~~ ^gaol announcing a meeting of Visitors for the 15th Inst. — Life of Lord Erskine. — The spirit of misrule has, as was to be expected, crossed the Channel. In such perilous times great commotion among the refuse of Society must be expected. Outbreaks have occurred at Glasgow and in London: in the former place the Chartists and the mob appear to have gained a considerable ascendancy, and were not put down by the authorities, when the latest accounts came away. In Town the disturbance arose from the circumstance of a would be demagogue, a self conceited Mr Cochrane, who has offered his services as a |³⁵

mob candidate for Westminster, convening by placards a meeting in Trafalgar Square to petition for the abolition of the income tax. At his bidding an assemblage was collected of a huge rabble of Chartists and sympathizers with the French Revolutionists, the numbers being swelled, by the thoughtless, the idle, the curious, the mischief lovers, and the pickpockets: much rioting, blackguardism, and alarm ensued for some hours, but the disturbance was promptly & efficiently suppressed by the Police.

Mar. 9. Thursday.

A damp day; rain falling in the afternoon and evening with wind; but the forenoon fine and mild — Drove early to Stow. — To the Workhouse where met several guardians in Committee; deliberated on the course to be taken in respect of the charges made against the Clerk and Rel. Off. by the Auditor: agreed to follow out the suggestions of the P.L.C. by writing to M[r] Hunt for information when and where he would receive the books |[36] and other documents necessary to be seen by him, that he may give his reasons for the disallowances and surcharges made by him: the Clerk to convey such books &c. and to bring them back when ʰhe ~~has~~ Auditor had entered his reasons in them — Agreed also on certain modifications of our practice as to ~~subsis~~ extras given in out relief: these changes being made necessary by an alteration in the system of keeping the books and accounts enjoined by the P.L.C. and now about to be adopted by us: necessary also to avoid intricacy and needless labour of the Clerk and Rel. Off. — When the Committee had settled the report to be made on the matters submitted to them, the measures recommended were adopted by the Guardians assembled in their ordinary meeting, and the usual business of the Board was transacted. — I afterwards attended at the Provident Bank, where I met M[r] Barter, M[r] Morri-|[37] son and M[r] Lewes. From Barter I heard such an account of the Story family, of their levity of character, and habits, that I much fear that Constantia Round has small hopes of happiness in wedded life, and that my poor old friend will have much anxiety in his latter years arising out of the injudicious attachment formed by his darling daughter. — Transacted business at the Provident Bank, at the office of the Gloucestershire Banking company &c. — Received a letter from M[r] Hare on Hunt Trust business, particularly as to the Red Lion Wharf — Lord Campbell's Life of Lord Erskine.

Mar. 10. Friday.

A cold wind, and boisterous day with gusty showers. — Justice business at home. — Wrote on Hunt Trust and Executorship matters to Sophia Hunt, M[r] Hare, and M[r] Thornton. — The riots at Glasgow have been suppressed; but not without a hard struggle, and loss of life. At Manchester disturbances |[38] are apprehended. In London the Trafalgar Square rioting degenerated into street rows, window breaking, pilfering a few shops, and annoyance to the residents in different streets in Westminster, and were well kept under by the Police. The inhabitants of the Metropolis are coming forward, from the highest rank down to the artizan and labourer, as special constables. — Newmarch's five years in the East. — Life of Lord Erskine.

Mar. 11. Saturday.

After very heavy rain and wind during the night, a cold, stormy day, with frequent hail showers and rain. — Wrote to Chr. Geldard to make enquiry as to the settlement of the business between us and the directors of the North Western Railway Company, in respect of the purchase of part of our Ravenflatt property, for which payment had been promised on Feb. 15. — Preparing a Sermon. — Justice business at home. — Superintending workmen – repairs of laundry &c. — Received a letter from Sophia [39] Hunt, accompanying one from the Secretary of the Crown Life Assurance Company, as to payment of £5000 to the Estate of M. C. Hunt. The question is whether I should go to Town to receive the money, or whether it can be done by the intervention of bankers &c. — It seems irregular that neither of the Exors should attend. I replied that I should be ready to go to Town for the purpose, but not before the 27th. Inst. — that if Sophia Hunt made her election to go to London to transact this business, I should be perfectly satisfied that she should undertake it; so leaving the matter open. — Visited J. Davis and T. S. Collett's wife — Lord Campbell's life of Lord Erskine. —

Mar. 12. Sunday.

A cold, stormy day: but little rain fell. — Visited the Sunday School — Morning service. — Prayers and Sermon: I preached on "the righteous delivered;" with reference to Lot's rescue from Sodom. — Administered the holy Sacrament to [40] fourteen communicants. — Evening service, prayers. — Received a circular addressed by Mr Estcourt, late MP. for the University of Oxford, addressed by him as Secretary to the Committee of subscribers to the erection of a memorial to record the merits of the late Lord Edward Somerset, as a distinguished officer, and an excellent and tried representative of his County for a long series of years. The projected tower is now completed: it stands on very high ground at Hawkesbury Upton in the vicinity of the ducal residence of his family at Badminton. The expence has exceeded £1600; and more than £300 are required to make up the deficiency in the subscriptions: to deliberate on the means of raising this sum a meeting of the subscribers is summoned for Mar. 30, being the second day of the Lent Assizes at Gloucester — Preparing a Sermon — Brit. Magazine — To the family a Section from Dr James's work [41] on the Collects. — The results of the late French revolution develope themselves in other parts of the continent; it seems a contagion; or as if a shower of sparks issuing from a volcano spread wide conflagration in the surrounding circle. Fuel is every where ready, a torch only was wanting, and that is now supplied. A longing for liberty of the press, for a representative constitution, for the abolition of ancient class privileges, and for the correction of abuses, seem every where to prevail; yet for the most part there is no desire to fraternize with France. Italy is convulsed; Sardinia steps forward as the advocate of liberalism: the Pope favours the new views, and encourages the ruling passion for a Kingdom or state to embrace all Italy. Naples is on the eve of a revolution and Sicily almost sure to be severed from her. Austrian supremacy in the North of Italy totters on its seat. In Germany, the Southern states are greatly agitated; [42] the people every where call on their rulers for liberal concessions, and generally obtain them: Bavaria, Würtemberg, Baden, Nassau, and Neufchatel are thus disturbed — There is little doubt that the convulsion will extend over the whole of Germany, and that the ancient realms of Prussia and Austria will be shaken: here, as in Italy, a rage for one empire to embrace all the German states is a dream which sanguine and stirring spirits will seek to realize — "Vaterland" is the cry — freedom of the press is loudly insisted on it, and a democratical spirit is spread

48. Hawkesbury.

far and wide.[3] In Belgium there is unexpected tranquillity: in fact gradual ameliorations & concessions have left little real cause for complaint: and the same is the case with us: the concessions to public opinion of the last eighteen years have removed the grounds of grumbling. Yet in many large towns, – Edinburgh, Manchester, Hull &c. the populace are |[43] restless and riotous, but the movement is confined to the lowest ranks, to those who bawl for the six points of the Charter, and have plunder in their view. The Government is sending troops to the quarters where disturbance is threatened, and the partial outbreaks are every where suppressed.

Mar. 13. Monday.

Fine weather, but cold — Wrote to Howell — Justice business at home — Preparing a sermon. — A letter from Murray Browne in answer to the one I had addressed to him on the Hampden controversy: he forwards to me a copy of a proposed address to the Archb. of Canterbury, praying him not to consecrate Dr Hampden, until he shall have been purged of the imputation of heresy or unsoundness of doctrine by an inquiry into his writings by some competent authority. This address emanates from the High Church party, rather from the Ultra section of that party. — A letter from Mr Croome, the land-surveyor as to the Map and |[44] valuation of this parish: he proposes calling on me on Saturday next. — Our dear children and grandchildren arrived from Stanway on a visit of a few days, to our great pleasure.

---

3. The European Revolutions of 1848, appeared to be a revolutionary wave which erupted in Sicily and then, further triggered by the French Revolution of 1848, soon spread to the rest of Europe. Although the revolutions were put down quickly, there was horrific violence on all sides, with many thousands tortured and killed. Most obvious, immediate political effects of the revolutions were quickly reversed; nonetheless the long-term reverberations were far-reaching. The United Kingdom, the Netherlands, the Russian, and Ottoman Empires were the only major European states to go without a national revolution over this period.

49. Badminton.

Mar. 14. Tuesday.

Very fine weather — Walking with E.F.W., Sophy &c. — M^rs. R. Waller and her two boys, John and Sidney, came to pass some hours here, partaking of luncheon — others who called, so that we held a kind of levée, were M^r and M^rs. Vavasour, and M^r and M^rs. Hippisley — A letter from C Bathurst on County business, as to Coroners, and the investigation into alleged misconduct on the part of Barnett, the Coroner, at the Epiph. Sess^ns. — A letter from Mr Hare on Hunt Trust matters. ——

Mar. 15. Wednesday.

A foggy morning, followed by a fine day. — Wrote to Mr Murray Browne; returned to him the copy of the proposed address to the Archb. of Canterbury, which I had received from him |[45] ~~yesterday~~ on the 13th. — Stated why I declined affixing my name to it: — that public opinion has been already sufficiently declared for and against Dr Hampden — that his elevation to the Bench cannot now be prevented — that the prolonging the controversy perpetuates and increases the irritation — that rest rather than agitation is desirable for the Church. — I also explained my views as to the meeting of the Clergy of the Archdeaconry of Gloucester held at the Cathedral library in January last. It may be as well to copy what I wrote — "Whatever may have been reported by any one who mistook what I said, my objection to the meeting in the Cathedral library referred to the prudence of the measure, to the inexpediency of agitation, and the risks of collision: more especially after the letter of the Bp. of Oxford had been published. You will remember too that the clergy were invited in the advertisement to stimulate the Bps. to further efforts — a course which was afterwards very properly abandoned. |[46] But at the same time I expressed a strong opinion that the appointment of Dr H. was a very bad one. I doubt the discretion of addressing the Abp. of Canterbury in the terms proposed. There can be no question but that his Grace has made up his mind, and intimated his intention to consecrate Dr Hampden, which may be looked upon almost as a "fait accompli." To what end, then, to heap protest on protest? Those who object to the consecration have already significantly protested directly and indirectly; what has been said and done will not be strengthened by a final and ineffectual protest; but ill feeling may be embittered. The words "has for many years laboured &c." seem to be loosely expressed, as if it were meant that D^r H's late teaching, as Professor, was of unsound doctrine &c. Might it not be answered that many Bps. required a certificate of his lectures having been attended by Oxford candidates for ordination, and so |^{47} an imputation pass on those Bishops, and a sort of admission be made that a large section of the younger Clergy had been trained in unsound doctrine? &c." — MW. and Sophy drove to Moreton and back, shopping — E.F.W. was diligently fishing — Broome accompanied me in a walk to Eyford, the roaring well &c. — A letter from Howell, very full on the French revolution, politics, disturbances in London &c. — It seems to be generally felt that the disturbances in the Metropolis need not cause uneasiness, for that the middle classes are loyal and well disposed. A recent meeting of Chartists and sympathizers with the foreign republicans held on Kennington common, which had been the cause of much apprehension, passed off without disturbance: the exhibition of revolutionary tendencies was less formidable than was expected. — In Dublin and other great towns in Ireland very outrageous language is used by Repealers of both sections; |^{48} the moral force and the physical force party are alike violent in their abuse of government, and unequivocal language is hazarded by those ultra men who uphold republican principles, and sympathize with the French revolutionists. The Government is strengthening itself with military force, and taking great precautions against a threatened out-break on the 17$^{th.}$ St Patricks day. — No great fear is entertained as to riots in the manufacturing districts of England; yet there alarm is not altogether ungrounded. — In France the failure of banks, and much financial embarrasment, augur ill for tranquillity; the mob now in the ascendent insist on claims which cannot be satisfied, and so hinders judicious administration by the provisional government. — A letter from Miss S. B. Hunt, covering one from Mr Conyers, the Secretary of the Crown Life Assurance ~~Soc~~ Company. She wishes me to go to Town |^{49} on the 27. Inst. to receive from that office the £5000 due to the Estate of Caroline Hunt. — A circular from the office of the Deputy Clerk of the Peace, announcing meetings of Committees at Gloucester on the 20$^{th.}$ Inst. the day before the Quarter Sessions. — A letter from Mr Thornton on Hunt Trust matters: he returns a letter from Mr Hare which I had forwarded for his perusal. —

Mar. 16. Thursday.

A very rainy day — Wrote to Mr Conyers, Crown Life Assurance office, London, informing him that I purpose to receive the £5000 due from that establishment to the Estate of M C Hunt — and shall probably call on him on the 28$^{th.}$ Inst. — Wrote to Mr Lyne, Auctioneer, with a cheque for timber bought at Sesincote wood sale. — Wrote to Mr Croome, land surveyor, that I shall be glad to see him on Saturday next. — Drove with Sophy to Stow; left her at "the Cottage" to pass some hours with her Mother, &c. E.F.W. rode |^{50} to Maugersbury and Stow, and returned to dinner. Transacted business at the office of the Gloucestershire Banking Company — At the Provident Bank conferred with Mr Wilkins on a matter to be heard by the Magistrates today, — the refusal of Mr F. Taylor, a dissenter, and a farmer at Notgrove, to pay Church rates — Mess.rs. Morrison, Waller &c. were in attendance at the Savings Bank – At the Justice meeting Mess.rs. Ford and Waller sat with me on the bench: others present were E.F.W., W. Vavasour, W B Pole, and Winter. There was much business, and the Notgrove Church rate case attracted attention. The recusant is a rabid dissenter, a would be fine gentleman and orator, professes a conscientious objection to the payment of Church dues, but cannot prove any irregularity in the proceedings of the vestry, or in the summons. He does not mean to carry the matter into |51 another court: so an order of payment was made — Called at "the Cottage" for Sophy, where I saw M.r and M.rs. Vavasour: we got home to a late dinner. — A letter from Chr. Geldard: the Directors of the North Western Railway company have not fulfilled their engagement to pay for the land bought of us by them for the purpose of their line through our Ravenflatt property, pleading the scarcity of money, & considering it enough if they pay interest at 5 P.r C.t. — As I had written to C. G. that I had occasion for some part of the money expected from the Railway directors, he offers to advance what I may want to meet my engagements. — C. Bathurst sends me part of a letter written by M.r Estcourt, formerly MP. for the Univ. of Oxford, and Chairman of the Wilts Q.S., respecting Coroners accepting presents from the friends of deceased persons over whom they hold inquests. — M.r Pearce being |52 gone to meet M.r Hunt, the District Auditor, at Chipping Norton, by appointment, accompanied by M.r Dunford, the R.O., respecting the surcharges and disallowances made by the Auditor in regard to certain items of their accounts, sent for my perusal, as I was sitting in the Justice room, sundry letters and documents relating to Union matters which had been received, which I looked over, and gave directions as to some of them. ——

Mar. 17. Friday.

Cold, raw, damp, and rainy. — Wrote to C Bathurst on the subject of Coroners misconducting themselves in their office, receiving compliments in gratuities from the families of persons over whose bodies they have held inquests — CB. means to bring the matter before the Court at the approaching Quarter Sess.ns. A letter from Howell — M.rs. W. Vavasour and her sister called upon us: drove hither, and walked back: E.F.W., Sophy, |53 and myself accompanied them part of the way to Lower Swell. — A very enjoyable domestic evening

Mar. 18. Saturday.

A cold, raw, and rainy morning: the forenoon and afternoon fine — M.r Croome, Surveyor, called in the morning, and met M.r Lea, Churchwarden: examined the Valuation of the parish with the map: made some corrections of errors which had crept in, so as to secure accuracy both as to measurement and value. — My son left us in the forenoon, riding to Winchcomb, there to attend a meeting of the Board of Guardians, whence he would proceed to Stanway to rejoin his wife & children, who left us, to our very great regret, in the afternoon — Wrote to Chr. Geldard in answer to his letter received on the 16th: accepted his offer of an advance of money to the amount of £200, to be repaid when the directors of the North Western Railway Company pay for the land which they |54 have taken at Ravenflatt — the £200 to be paid to my account with Mess.rs. Hoare — Rec.d. from the S.P.G. an abstract of the receipts and expenditure for 1847 — From the Glouc. Lunatic Asylum a circular announcing a meeting of Visitors on Mar. 29. — A circular from Mess.rs. Aplin and Wilkins giving notice of a turnpike meeting at Chipping

Norton fixed for Mar. 21. — A letter from Mr Lyne, Auctioneer, with an acknowledgment of a remittance from me (£10. 4. 0) for timber bought at Sesincote wood sale. — From Mr Hayward a certificate that the wife of T. Edginton, Shoemaker, Stow, is so dangerously ill, that her life cannot be calculated on from day to day, so that her husband's attendance on the Jury at the Quarter Sessions at Gloucester should be dispensed with. — M. A. Ryan called in the Evening, to inform us that M^rs. Dolphin had been returned to Eyford a fort-|^55 night since; that she was ill, and in much distress of mind; that she had expressed herself as hurt at apparent negligence on our part in not having called on her or enquired after her. Desired MAR. to assure her that we only heard of her return home yesterday. — Life of Lord Erskine.

Mar. 19. Sunday.

A raw, cold day, after a foggy morning; a heavy hail storm about 4 P.M. and a rainy evening. — Wrote to M^rs. Dolphin to explain our apparent inattention as arising from our not knowing that she was come home. — Visited the Sunday School — Morning service — prayers — Afternoon service – prayers and sermon — I preached on the moral infirmity of human nature — A letter from C Bathurst as to misconduct of Coroners in taking gratuities from the friends of deceased persons as to whom they have held inquests: — from Mr Lumbert that the valuation of the parish of Bourton on the Water which he has been making will not be |^56 ready to be submitted to-morrow to the County rate Committee at Gloucester: — from the Clerk to the Gloucester and Berkeley canal Company, announcing a meeting of Shareholders — from G. F. Newmarch the annual statement of the Crickley Hill turnpike road trust — From the Home office a well timed document, printed for circulation among magistrates &c. being an abstract of the duties of all classes of people in the time of riot and popular disturbances: extracts are contained in this paper from Chief Justice Tindal's admirable exposition of the law on this head in his address to the Grand Jury on the special commission appointed for the trial of the Bristol Rioters in 1830. — The dreaded meeting of repealers and sympathizers with foreign revolutionists held at Dublin on the 17th. went off quietly; the authorities were well prepared, and the disturbers of the public peace overawed — In Germany the revolutionary spirit is making rapid progress, and very widely dissemi |^57 nated: it is manifest that great and organic changes are at hand in that great section of Europe: but there is no apparent disposition to fraternize with France. — As to the latter country it is alleged that serious variances and feuds exist among the members of the Provisional Government: the great masses of the people, the populace of Paris, and the unemployed workmen, who have, in fact, carried the revolution, and overthrown the Monarchy, press upon the government now established, with much vehemence, and with extravagant claims, which cannot be yeilded to without a breaking up of social order: great financial difficulties cause additional embarrasment, the Bank of France is driven to cease from cash payments; the Government is interfering with the Savings Banks, prohibiting depositors to withdraw from them more than a certain limited sum on each account: trade is every where brought almost to a stand-still: English artizans and servants, the multitudes employed on railways, in cotton |^58 factories &c. are hunted out of France — The Queen of England has given birth to another princess — Wrote to C Bathurst, in answer to his letter rec^d. to-day, a note to meet him on his reaching Gloucester to-morrow. — Preparing papers for the Quarter Sessions — To the family a section from James on the Collects.

Mar. 20. Monday.

During the night a total eclipse of the moon. — In the morning a hard frost: a fine day. — After an early breakfast left home for Gloucester, to attend the Quarter Sessions: reached Cheltenham in my open carriage by half past nine o'clock, and Gloucester by railway at ten. Took up my Quarters at the Bell. — Conferred with the County Chairman on business likely to come forward at these Sessions. — To the Shire Hall, where I was joined by other members of the Comm. of accounts, and was engaged in auditing bills and other financial work. Two other Committees also met, that for regulating the |[59] prisons, and that for assessing the County rate. — The Magistrates present were Mess[rs.] Purnell, Curtis Hayward, Lysons, Baker, Brooke Hunt, Surman, Henney, Sayers — The officials present were Mess[rs.] Bloxsome, Riddiford, Lefroy, Keiley, Wilton, Whitehead, and Fulljames. — Mess[rs.] Purnell, Baker, Curtis Hayward, and myself, dined together at the Bell — Engaged from 9 to past mid-night in the audit of County accounts. — C Bathurst arrived from Town, accompanied by M[rs.] B. and they betook themselves to the Spa Hotel. I did not see him; but two or three notes passed between us, respecting the business which he means to bring forward to-morrow — the illegality of the practice of Coroners accepting payment or gratuities from the families of deceased persons on whose bodies they have held inquests.

Mar. 21. Tuesday.

A snowy morning, and very wet in the forenoon: the afternoon dry and fine weather. — Arranging and looking |[60] over the public accounts before breakfast — Breakfasted with the County Chairman — Attended the Court, at which few Magistrates were present, and not many auditors. — I went through the usual routine, of presenting, commenting upon, and passing the County bills for the Quarter. — The most interesting matter of the day was in reference to M[r] Coroner Barnett, who was not present, though he had received notice to attend. The Chief Constable produced evidence and letters with other documents in vindication of the conduct of a Constable who had been represented by M[r] Barnett at the last Q.S. to have exceeded his duty, and acted offensively in respect of a poor man on whom M[r] B. held an inquest at Newnham. The explanation was most satisfactory, and the correspondence and statements coming from the friends of the deceased were very condemnatory of the Coroner, who had |[61] very grievously misstated the facts, and misbehaved himself. In the same case M[r] B. had attempted to induce the family of the deceased to pay him a compliment in money, exceeding the amount charged to the county for the expences of the inquest, which they declined doing: and this practice he had vindicated, when the question was before the court at the last Sessions. It was now blamed by C Bathurst in a very able speech, which he concluded by proposing two resolutions declaratory of the law, and of the disapproval of the practice by the Court. The County Chairman, M[r] Curtis Hayward, and myself followed M[r] B. in speeches condemning the practice. Of the Coroners present M[r] Ball declared that he never had, and never would accept any gratuity or payment from the family of deceased parties on whose bodies he had held an inquest. M[r] Joyner Ellis by his silence left one to suppose that the practice had been followed by him, but |[62] what has passed publicly to-day will, no doubt, check it in this county hereafter, if it do not wholly suppress it. — When the business of the Court was over, walked with M[r] Davies some distance on the Bristol road. Met M[r] Jelinger Symons, Barrister, and one of the Commissioners employed by the Comm. of Privy

Council on Education, as also by the Poor Law Board in prosecuting enquiries, and making arrangements in furtherance of the education of the Poorer Classes. His commission extends into Gloucestershire, South Wales, and adjacent counties, and he has lately made a report on the state of education in Monmouthshire which has been circulated by the Comm. of the Privy Council on Education. Yesterday, as it appears, he had visited the Stow Workhouse, and to-day had been on a like errand at Whitminster. His object and that of his principals seems to be to raise the standard of edu-|⁶⁴ cation of the poor, as regards useful information, arithmetic, geography, industrial training &c. To this end a better class of school masters and school mistresses than are now generally employed in Workhouses & Village schools are needed; and, where the numbers in each school are limited, one does not see how means are to be found to pay for an improved system: hence concentration in district schools is desired: but this involves great outlay, and, if to be provided at the cost of rate payers, how are those to supply their quota who, though rate payers, hardly rise above the class of paupers? Mᵣ S. is a clever man, and a Liberal. — My son came to Gloucester about mid-day — The Magistrates who dined at the Bell were P. B. Purnell, Hale Senᵣ, Brickdale, Holland Corbet, B. Baker, George, W P Price, J. Purnell, Davies, E.F.W. and myself. To these add Mᵣ Bloxsome — C. Bathurst joined us in the Evening. — |⁶⁵

Mar. 22. Wednesday.

Cold, showery weather — Wrote to MW. — After breakfast with the Magistrates quartered at the Bell, repaired to the Court, and sat all day with Sergeant Ludlow, who presided in the Crown Court. There were no appeals. — Lamented the irritability of our Chairman, who is perpetually contending with counsel; and thus angry sallies with impetuous remarks are elicited both from the bench and the bar. With Mᵣ W. H. Cooke there was a very unpleasant altercation. Ludlow's increasing deafness, his interference with the manner in which Counsel conduct their cases, his careless and succinct way of taking notes, and his testy temper, are hardly compensated by his great practical experience, and his ~~reli~~ rare knowledge of criminal law and of the law of evidence. — The dinner at the Bell was attended by Ludlow, Purnell, |⁶⁶ Curtis Hayward, Mirehouse, Lysons, Hale, Brickdale, George, J. Purnell, E.F.W., myself &c. – C. Bathurst joined us in the Evening.

Mar. 23. Thursday.

Showery weather, but there did not fall much rain, and the air was milder. — After breakfast attended the Court, which opened at 9 AM. — Sergeant Ludlow was less irritable than yesterday, but still contrived to enter into angry and hasty discussions with counsel. — Left the Court at 12 o clock, accompanied by my son. — Travelled by railway to Cheltenham, where we were met by my Son's servant with his carriage and horses; our dear Broome also gladdened us by his appearance, having been driven over to meet us. — Shopping — I called on the Dentist, who found little to do in respect of teeth stopped when I last visited him. — Accompanied my dear Grandson to an exhibition of wax work figures, which, though not of first rate merit, interested him exceedingly. — Left Cheltenham at 3 P.M. |⁶⁷ for Stanway, where we met MW. who had arrived from Upper Slaughter this forenoon in our open carriage. It was a pleasant renunion de famille — We were happy in the lively circle of our beloved children and grandchildren — Received a letter from Mᵣ George Hunt, a disagreeable one, as usual, on Hunt Trust matters. — Also a letter from Bowen, who after a very serious attack of illness, connected with his calculous malady, has again rallied, but is still a great invalid — Our conversation in the evening turned very much on the best way of increasing the accommodation at the Vicarage, so as to render it more commodious as a permanent residence for my son and his family. This pressed upon us by the failure of the negociation for the purchase of the living of Stanton, the principal recommendation of which was the commodious parsonage. With no other than a life tenure of the Vicarage of Stanway, |⁶⁸ and at my advanced time of life, it would have been desirable not to lay out money in the enlargement of the Glebe House, but the situation, as a residence for my Son, is so ~~desirable~~ eligible in every point of view, and he and his wife are so attached to it, and his sphere of usefulness here is so wide, that I must not hesitate to ~~lay out~~ expend (say) £400, in improvements which may be available to my Son's comfort and that of his family for a few years, should my life be protracted.

Mar. 24. Friday.

Milder weather, and no rain. — Wrote to Mr Jennings and to Mr Warter, apprizing them that I ~~proposed~~ being in London next week, and requesting them to fix a time when I could meet them — Justice business at Stanway. — Much engaged with E. Chidley, Stanway, the builder, in planning, considering estimates for building, &c. — Came with him to a final arrangement as to the enlarge-|⁶⁹ment of the Vicarage by the erection of a drawing room and bedroom over it, with a passage for entrance, and a laundry — also for a new stable, detached from the house, removing the old stable. This alteration will make the Vicarage very comfortable, providing for my son a commodious study and business room on the ground floor, in the present dining room, the present drawing room being converted into a dining room; one good bedroom will be added, and a dressing room upstairs will be at liberty and henceforth used as a sleeping apartment. In the nursery also a little alteration will greatly increase the comfort. — Left our dear children and grandchildren for Upper Slaughter at 3 PM. — Called on Mr Bowen, who, though much recovered from the late attack, continues in a feeble and unsatisfactory state. Much conversation with him about Mr and Mrs. Dolphin – It appears |⁷⁰ that the latter has conceived, as, indeed, we had been informed before by M. A. Ryan, the scheme, of prosecuting not only a separation but a divorce from her husband, being moved thereto by information of his continued habits of profligacy: hence she withholds from him those pecuniary supplies on which he wholly depends, and he complains bitterly in letters to Bowen, whom he endeavours to persuade that the misconduct imputed to him is greatly exaggerated — We reached home to a late dinner — MW. received a letter from Mrs. Barr, who purposes coming with her children to visit us on the 10th. April. — From Mr Crompton I received a packet of printed papers having reference to the controversy as to the elevation of Dr Hampden to the See of Hereford: — copies of a petition to the Archb. of Canterbury not to consecrate Dr H. &c. Mr Crompton is an Ultra High Churchman — what is called a Puseyite. — Justice business |⁷¹ awaited me at home. — The news from the Continent are very startling – Every where there are revolutionary movements, every where concessions to popular demands — At many points riots have occurred, collision with the authorities, civil and military, bloodshed and insurrection. Berlin and Vienna have been frightfully agitated. The King of Prussia, yeilding to force, has placed himself at the head of the popular movement in Germany, and in so doing has taken a stride in advance of the Emperor of Austria; but how far these revolutionary schemes can be carried out in the different states of Germany without serious conflicts, and how far the several states can be brought into one federal union, under one head, and one system of political administration, and how far war with Republican France can be avoided, or Russia kept in the background, restraining herself, |[72] or being restrained by circumstances, from interfering in the general melée of the central and Southern parts of Europe, are problems of which time only can dispose. — In Ireland the uncompromising, undisguised, open & prominent talkers and publishers of sedition, Smith O'Brien, Meagher, and Mitchell, have been bound by recognizance to answer the offences imputed to them at the Bar of the Court of Queen's Bench. — A monster meeting of the Physical Force Repealers, held at Dublin on Monday last, turned out to be a very small monster, as far as numbers were concerned; but very monstrous in the abundance of seditious talk: there was, however, no riotous disturbance, the government having made great military preparations, and so prevented an outbreak.

Mar. 25. Saturday.

Very fine weather — Transacted parish business with Churchwardens Lea and Gregory. — Justice business |[73] at home. — M[r] Brookes called. — Wrote to M[rs.] Perkins a note of enquiry as to the health of her husband, of whom I had been informed that he had experienced a paralytic stroke on Monday last — Received two letters from M[r] Pearce on Union matters, chiefly relating to the disputes with M[r] Hunt, the Auditor. — Answered them — also wrote to M[r] Pain to send me my watch, which he had undertaken to repair; — and to M[r] Brookes on Justice business. — Giving directions to workmen as to repairs necessary on our premises. — Arranged papers and settled accounts after the Sessions, and in anticipation of a journey to London on Monday next. — Wrote to M[r] George Hunt, in answer to his letter received yesterday; and promised to have an interview next week, when in town, with his solicitor, M[r] Braikenridge, according to his request. — Received from Miss Sophia Hunt, |[74] by post a registered document, – the policy of insurance for £5000, which I am to receive at the Crown Life Assurance office, as Ex[or.] of Miss Caroline Hunt, whose life was assured for that sum: — with this came a letter from Sophia Hunt, on Executorship and Trust business, in which she presses me to seek a conference with M[r] Braikenridge, and relates what had passed between herself and M[r] Geo. Hunt during her late visit to his family at Buckhurst. — A letter from M[r] Chr. Geldard who will place or cause to be placed to my account with Mess[rs.] Hoare, £200 — on Monday next. —

Mar. 26. Sunday.

The morning and forenoon very rainy: the afternoon and evening fine — Morning service, prayers and sermon. I preached on the great danger of denying the Saviour — Afternoon Service — prayers. — Received a letter from Mess[rs.] Hoare, announcing that M[r] Chr. Geldard had paid £200 to my acc[t.] with them. — Wrote to him to acknowledge |[75] the same — Wrote to M[r] Brooke Hunt, as one of the Visitors of the Gaol of Gloucester, respecting a lad from Cheltenham of the name of Halling, ~~respecting~~ as to whom I had a correspondence some time back with the authorities of the Home Office. This youth, the son of a labourer, had been tried at the Assizes in 1844 — and sentenced to a short imprisonment — released from that, he had been detected in stealing loaves with other boys from a baker's barrow: for this offence he was tried before me at the Quarter Sessions in 1845 – and sentenced to seven years transportation. The parents urged me to apply to the Secretary of State for a remission of the sentence. I declined, but left them to memorialize — then followed a statement of the case by me to the Home office, and the petition of the parents was refused: but it was again urged, perhaps, with electioneering influence to support it: another correspondence passed between the Home office and myself: eventu-[176] ally a pardon was granted, and the lad came back to his friends in 1847: returned to his old evil habits, was tried at the late Q.S., and again sentenced to seven years transportation: it is intended to make a full statement of this case, as to which much pertinacity in applications for remission of punishment, and much manoeuvring & false statements have been exhibited, to the Home Office. It furnishes an instance of the hopelessness of recovering a boy of vicious habits by the processes of trial and imprisonment, and of the desirableness of trying some system of moral and industrial training by the state, removing the party from old associations, subjecting him to moral discipline, & sending him, when taught an useful trade, to exercise it in the colonies, or in some other remote sphere of life, severed from home, and bad connections. — Wrote to M[r] Rodwell for a supply of books for the Stow Book Society — Received a note from M[rs.] J. Perkins: her husband is gradually and [177] slowly recovering from his late attack of paralysis. — Busy in collecting and preparing my papers for my visit to London.

Mar. 27. Monday.

In the morning and forenoon a cold and wetting fog; the afternoon and evening fine. — After breakfast I left home in my open carriage for Cheltenham, to take a train for the metropolis. — At the foot of Dowdeswell hill passed a coach full of convicts from Gloucester Gaol going to Northleach House of Correction, with four horses — surely it would be better that a Prison Van be procured available for such removals, and also to convey prisoners from the Gaol to the Court for trial, convicts to be sent to Millbank penitentiary to the Railway Station &c., that so the carriage might shew externally to all passers by the purpose for which it is used. At present the prisoners are marched with guards from the gaol to the Shire Hall, a considerable distance, exposed to the gaze of the people in the Streets, who crowd to the exhibition, and communicate with the [178] prisoners more or less on the way. — A little further Lord Fitzharding's foxhounds were collected by the road side, ready for the chase: and as I proceeded, a crowd was gathered in a wide part of the Turnpike road, horsemen, foot people, and many in carriages. As I drove up, the Peer rode from Cheltenham, and we met in the Crowd, he recognised me with a smile, amused with the address of the rencontre: the bystanders closed round, & prevented my carriage from proceeding; and a circle was quickly formed of which the Lord Lieutenant was the centre. Immediately a Gentleman on horseback, M[r] Only, took out of his pocket a sheet of paper, from which he read a long address to his Lordship, purporting to emanate from inhabitants of Cheltenham, recounting in complimentary terms the great benefits which it was alleged had been conferred upon the town by his Lordship having for so many years made it his residence during part of the winter, and for several months in each season the head quarters of his hunting establishment. The address [179] went on to express a hope that the connection thus subsisting, and so valuable to the town and its inhabitants, might long be continued. His Lordship replied in a well considered, carefully worded, measured tone, looking back to a connection for forty years, not disguising his persuasion that he had been of service to the place, and trusting that, though now advanced in years, health and strength might still permit him to follow his sporting pursuits among them, and that other circumstances might not occur, which might have the effect of severing the connection — The crowd then separated and the Peer again gave me a nod in passing, as much as to say, this is a droll position for you, the Conservative, not able to help yourself, but accidently made a prominent figure in a troop of my Whig Satellites — All this has no doubt a reference to the representation of Cheltenham, wrested at the last election by the Conservative party from his Lordship's |[80] grasp: Craven Berkeley was thrown out, and Sir Willoughby Jones brought in: but a petition against the return of the latter has been presented on the score of bribery and corruption. It is very possible that the Blue member may be unseated, then the yellows will make a vigorous effort to recover the lost seat, and the Peer's long purse will be again placed in requisition to reestablish his brother in what, since the Reform Act passed, has been treated very much as a family borough appendant to Berkeley Castle. — The delay occasioned by my rencontre with the Peer and his Myrmidons did not hinder my arriving at the Great Western Station at Cheltenham in time to take a place in the train starting for London at half past twelve o clock; by which I proceeded, having a prosperous journey, and reached the Paddington Station at fifty minutes past four o clock: so that shortly after five o clock, I reached the Queen's Hotel, Cork Street, which had been recommended to me by my friend, Purnell, and where I obtained comfortable |[81] accommodation. — Here I found waiting for me a note from Mr Jennings, fixing Wednesday at a quarter past eleven as the hour at which he would call to accompany me to see the locality of the ground rents lately purchased in St George's in the East. — also a note from Mr H. Warter who desired me to fix my own time for calling on him on the same day. — Replied to these notes that I would be ready for Mr Jennings at the hour proposed, and would call on Mr Warter at 2 P.M. — Wrote part of a letter to MW. — Well satisfied with my hotel: the coffee room in which I dined & spent the evening, has very much the air of a private family apartment, and the rule seems to be that the inmates fall into general conversation with each other. One gentleman, who like myself dined, was conversible and agreeable. —

50. A Fire Fly led train at Bristol Temple Meads.

Mar. 28. Tuesday.

Fine weather after a rainy night; rain fell again at night. — Breakfasted in the Coffee Room, meeting an agreeable com-|[82] panion — Received a letter from C. Bathurst, from Gloucester: he proposed to arrive in Town to-day; and hopes to see me in the evening. — Went into the City, partly walking, partly taking a Cab, and at the Office of the Crown Life Assurance Company in Bridge Street, Blackfriars, received, in a cheque on the Bank of England, the sum of £5000, for which amount Caroline Hunt's life had been insured in that establishment. — With this valuable document betook myself to the Banking office of the Mess[rs.] Coutts, in the Strand, where I paid it to the account of myself and Sophia Hunt as the Executors of her sister Caroline, introducing myself in the capacity of Executor, and giving directions as to the division of the £5000 under the will among the Brothers & Sisters of the deceased. — Thence I went into Lincoln's Inn Fields, and called on Mess[rs.] Cox and Williams, as Solicitors to Mess[rs.] Hare, Thornton and myself, in our character of Trustees to the Estate of the late T. W. Hunt: found that the business of the Trust was conducted by the |[83] Junior partner, M[r] Williams, with whom I had a long conference on the affairs of the Trust. — Went to Brunswick Square, where I called on the Witts's and Woodroffe's, who live together; did not see M[rs.] Witts, but found Emma Witts and Maria Woodroffe at home, with a friend, a Miss Thomas. M[r] Woodroffe was at his chambers. — Engaged myself to dine with them in the evening. — Returned to my hotel: finished the letter to MW. which I had begun yesterday evening. — Wrote to Sophia Hunt: also to M[r] Braikenridge, requesting him to fix a time at which I might call on him on Thursday. — My next object was to call on Laura and Constance Howell in Eaton place West: I knew that their father was absent from Town on a factory circuit. Walked part of the way, and took a cab for the rest. The young ladies were gone out for the day. — Proceeded to Hans Place, where I called on the Backhouses, and found M[rs.] B, with her |[84] daughters, Fanny and Catherine, and Jane, and Miss Backhouse from Wavertree still on a visit to her sister in law and nieces. The latter was about to avail herself of orders for admission into the House of Lords, which she had obtained from Lord Harrowby, to see the new Chamber, & begged me to escort her, which I was much pleased to have time to do, not having seen the splendid apartment. Therefore accompanied Miss B. in a carriage which waited for her, and arrived there, so as to be able to pass half an hour in the House before I was under the necessity of leaving it to prepare for my dinner engagement. Met Lord Redesdale, and, under his auspices, were admitted into the interior part of the chamber, where the peers sit, so as to have a full view of the whole. It is, indeed, a most splendid and gorgeous apartment, in the most exquisite style of florid gothic, and as brilliant as gilding & painting can make it. Too brilliant, perhaps; but a London atmosphere will soon dim its lustre. The compartments for the Fresco histo-|[85] rical pictures are nearly all filled, some of these may be liable to unfavourable criticism. The windows are for the most part fitted with painted glass. The arrangements for the members of the house are very much on the same plan is in the former houses of peers. When the business of the House commenced, I removed without the bar, and Miss B into the Seat of Sir Augustus Clifford, the Usher of the Black rod. Several distinguished peers entered the house, and took part in the proceedings. The Chancellor, Lord Shaftesbury, and Lord Campbell, were commissioners to pass certain bills. Others were brought up by the House of Commons. Certain petitions were presented by Lords Campbell, Redesdale &c. After leaving the House Miss Backhouse set me

down at my hotel: she goes very shortly to
Wavertree. — I dined in Brunswick Square,
— a family party — M$^{rs.}$ Witts, Emma, M^{r}
and M$^{rs.}$ Woodroffe, Miss Thomas, and
myself. An agreeable evening. |^{86} It was so
late when I got home to my hotel that I was
prevented from going to Arlington Street, to
see Bathurst, from whom I had received a
note requesting me so to do, he and M$^{rs.}$ B.
having arrived to-day from Gloucester.

Mar. 29. Wednesday.

A very fine day. — Received a note from
Laura Howell before I was dressed, which
I answered, and promised to call in Eaton
Place West to-morrow. — Wrote to C
Bathurst to explain to him that it was
so late when I returned from Brunswick
Square last night, that I could not call on
him – Breakfasted at my hotel — Soon after
11 o cl. Mr Jennings called to accompany
me to the "far East," to shew me the
property lately purchased in S$^{t.}$ Georges in

51. Holywell Street.

the East. We journeyed thither on foot and in an Omnibus, and returned in a Cab. Much
conversation on business, and of a general sort with Mr J., whom I found, as I ever had before,
a judicious well-informed, and right minded person. Beyond Fenchurch Street I came into a
land |^{87} hitherto unknown to me. Passed through Whitechapel, and along the Commercial road
into the vicinity of the London docks, and adjacent to the line of the Blackwall Railway. There
we left our Omnibus, and deviated from the Commercial road into a network of small streets
occupying the space between that great thoroughfare, & another parallel to it, but not of such
note or traffic. In these streets is situate our property, a little quarter of small houses, dingy
red brick tenements, with dirty unpaved ways, looking as if the very place for Cholera, the
tenements averaging about £20 per ann. each to rent, in more or less good repair. The houses
are chiefly occupied by persons labouring in the docks, some householders, some lodgers,
with petty shopkeepers, houses of public entertainment, perhaps worse. — We called, and
made ourselves known to some of the tenants, an Engineer, a Hallier, a Coaster of Chichory,
a timber dealer &c. — |^{88} Explained that we called in the capacity of Ground landlord and
his agent, spoke as to rents due and to be received from the leaseholders, or renting tenants,
and were generally received with civility. I was glad to find that one tenement called a Chapel
was not in the hands of dissenters, but used as a day school under the direction of one of the
Parochial Clergy. Left the quarter with no very high notion or admiration of the locality: it is
likely to pay well as an investment, and hereafter to acquire more and more value as the houses
fall in to the Ground Landlord: being near the Commercial road and the London docks, the
property is not likely to be depreciated by any changes in business. The Blackwell railway runs

52. The thatched house, said to have been Nell Gwynn's dairy, on the north side of the Strand.

also in this direction; crossing one of the streets — Having made our survey, Mr Jennings & I got into a ~~Cab~~ cab, and betook ourselves to Mr H. Warter's office in Carey Street, where we conferred with him as to the St George's Ground rents, and M^r |[89] Jennings took with him from thence a number of deeds relating to ~~it~~ the property which he will want as a guide in receiving the Ground rents. Here I parted from Mr Jennings, and remained for some little time with Mr Warter, conversing with him on business, as to the payment of the balance due to him on his account for business done &c., and as to our mutual friends and connections in Shropshire. — I next resorted to the office of Messrs Cox and Williams, where I had reason to expect that I should find Mr G. Turners opinion on the case submitted to him with a Junior Counsel, as to the Wadenhoe Trust affairs; but was disappointed. Conferred with Mr Williams. — Returned to my hotel — C Bathurst had called upon me; went to Arlington Street, to endeavour to meet with him; but he and Mrs B. were out — Wrote to MW. — Dined at my hotel — Retired early to rest; fatigued & sleepy. — |[90]

Mar. 30. Thursday.

A fine day. — Wrote to Mr Jennings, requesting him to colour a plan of the Estate of Mr Furze in Ground rents in St George's in the East, as lithographed with the particulars of the property offered for sale by auction, that I might be able to distinguish the portion bought for us, and keep it as a memorandum for reference. — Received a letter from MW. — who forwards a letter addressed to me by Reeves, the Keeper of the House of Correction at Northleach, who doubts as to the accuracy of a recent game commitment of mine. — I replied that on my return home I would look into the matter — A letter from Miss Sophia Hunt, who answers that which I wrote to her on the 28th and gives me directions as to Executorship business to be transacted with Messrs Coutts. — After breakfast betook myself to the bank of Messrs. C. where I was engaged for some time in giving directions as to the distribution of the £5000 paid in by me on the 28th. Between |^91 the brothers and sisters of Caroline Hunt, and also as to the distribution of the Stock standing in the names of Mr Hare and myself, £2179. 16. 8 — 3 P^r C^t. Cons. – divisible, under M^rs. M. Hunt's will, between Caroline's brothers and sisters on her decease. — Thence I proceeded to Bartlett's Buildings, Holborn, to the office of Mr Braikenridge, Mr George Hunt's Solicitor, with whom I had a long and confidential interview, respecting the controversies as to the Hunt affairs, the management of the trusts, the advice given by Messrs. Cox & Williams to the Trustees, the relative positions of the Life tenant and Remainder man, the errors into which it was is alleged the Trustees have been betrayed by their Solicitors, the prejudices of Mr Geo. Hunt, and the best way of winding up the Trust. — Mr B. appeared to me a very candid, fair, cautious, right-minded man, but somewhat irritated by the correspondence into

53. The shop of Richardson, the print seller, at the north-west corner of Villiers Street, Strand.

which |^93 he had been drawn, by Messrs. Cox & Williams' mode of conducting the Trust affairs, which, I suspect, has not been in all respects judicious; and that errors have been committed. I have little doubt. It seems the object of Mr B. to terminate this intricate and tedious business as quietly and amicably, as he can, consistently with his duty to a very suspicious, prejudiced and overbearing client, whom he cannot drive, but hopes to lead. — Called on Messrs. Cox and Williams, but finding the latter engaged, and hearing that Mr G. Turner's opinion is not yet received, I left the office without an interview with Mr W. — To Messrs. Hoare, the Bankers, where I looked at my banking account, and gave directions for the payment at Messrs. Childs, Mr H. Warter's bankers, of the balance due by me to Mr W. on account of business done, £281. 19. 8. — My next movement was to the "far west," — to Eaton Place West, to call on Laura and Constance Howell, partly |^93 on foot, partly in a cab: — received with kind warmth by the young ladies — Macleod improved in appearance — found them very comfortably housed, but in rather a dull street — was taken all over the house, which is very nicely furnished — conversing on many interesting subjects — Prinknash — Upper Slaughter — Stanway — and their inmates. — The kind hearted girls ordered their carriage, a nice Clarence with one horse, and drove me to Arlington Street, where I called on the Bathursts; in less than half an hour Laura and Constance took me up again, and I prolonged my visit to them very agreeably, by driving with them in Hyde Park till 6 P.M. when they set me down at my hotel, where I dined, and in the evening wrote a long letter to Sophia Hunt. —

54. *Grosvenor Gate and the New Lodge.*

Mar. 31. Friday.

A slight tendency to rain; otherwise a very fine day. — Packing up for my departure home. — Breakfasted I[94] at my comfortable hotel at 9 o cl. Left in a cab at ½ past nine: — reached the Paddington Station at a quarter before ten o clock, in time to take my place for Cheltenham in the express train, which starts at 9.50 AM. — I had not previously travelled by an express train, but found it very pleasant; one is hardly sensible of the very rapid movement, as compared with the ordinary rate of going. We accomplished the distance to Didcot, – 53 miles — in one hour: This was the first station at which we stopped: and then proceeded without calling at any intermediate station to Swindon station, where was the usual halt of ten minutes.[4] Called at the Tetbury road, Stroud, and Gloucester stations, and reached the Cheltenham terminus at 12.37. P.M. so accomplishing a distance of 120 miles in two hours and forty seven minutes: the rapidity of the motion caused the engine wheels to catch fire, as we proceeded between Stroud and Gloucester: the grease was melted, and smoked up, but with the frequent application of buckets of water from the I[95] tender no mischief ensued. — MW. had sent my servant with the phaeton to meet me; being prevented from coming

---

4.   It was at Swindon station that the railway refreshment room first acquired its unsavoury reputation. The G.W.R. directors had unwisely let the management of the railway hotel on a long-term contract to S. Y. Griffiths the proprietor of the Queens Hotel Cheltenham, with a clause to the effect that all regular trains should stop at Swindon 'for a reasonable period of about ten minutes' so that passengers might refresh themselves. This enforced stop at Swindon became a bane to the Company, especially when the monopoly was abused. The poor quality of the coffee provided by Griffiths there was the subject of a stinging retort from to Brunel to Griffiths:

Dear Sir,

I assure you Mr Player was wrong in supposing that I thought you purchased inferior coffee. I thought I said to him I was surprised you should buy such bad roasted corn. I did not believe you had such a thing as coffee in the place; I am certain I never tasted any. I have long since ceased to make complaints at Swindon. I avoid taking anything there when I can help it.

Yours faithfully,
I. K. Brunel.

55. Coffee room at Paddington Station.

herself by a cold which affected her eyes. — Remained for two hours at Cheltenham, while the horses baited; walked about with Lefroy and J. W. Martin. From the former I heard a good report of my children and grandchildren, he having been very lately at Stanway. — I reached home by 5 P.M. — A letter from Mr Betterton, Receiver of Taxes, who forwards for my signature an official acknowledgment of the Land tax on the living of Bourton on the W. redeemed, but not exonerated, which I purchased of the heirs of the late Mr Croome, and which Mr R. Waller pays to me. — From Messrs. Butts, Gloucester, I heard as to samples of Madeira sent by them. — From the County Gaol, Gloucester a circular as to a meeting of Visitors — Messrs. Sewell and Newmarch notify that Mr Marling ~~has~~ will repa~~y~~id with interest the tem-|^100 porary loan made by me of £200: ^on Apr. 16. S & N offer me an investment on Mortgage for £1000 — Rec^d. a letter from Mr Brooke Hunt as to Halling, the convict, being a reply to my letter to him of the 27th. inst. — From E.F.W. a letter came with plans and estimates for the stable and other work proposed at the Vicarage, Stanway — he gives me a good account of all his circle. —

Apr. 1. Saturday.

Beautiful weather — Wrote to Mr Betterton in answer to his letter received yesterday: sent him a receipt for the amount of land-tax due to me, although I have not yet been paid by Robt. Waller, who is generally tardy in this matter. — Wrote to E.F.W., consenting to the building of the stable at Stanway Vicarage, agreeably to the estimate received by me yesterday, which I returned — Wrote to Sewell and Newmarch, requesting them to place to my account with the Gloucestershire Banking Company at Stow, the £200 with |^101 interest thereon about to be received from Mr Marling; informed them that it was not in my power at present to advance £1000 on mortgage; requested them to send their bill for the business done in the abortive treaty for the purchase of the next presentation of the Living of Stanton. Arranging and settling my papers and accounts on my return

56. Ealing Haven Station.

from London. — Called on the Churchwardens Lea and Gregory on parish business, and otherwise. — Met Harry Waller in the village, on his way to Eyford: long conversation with him as to the concerns of M^r and M$^{rs.}$ Dolphin; — the desire of the latter to procure a divorce, her determination to with hold any pecuniary supplies from him; his evil habits, and low connections. — A letter from C Bathurst as to whether Coroners should have a power granted to them to bail in cases of manslaughter. A bill to that effect has been brought into the House of |^{102} Lords by Lord Campbell. — Preparing a Sermon — Lord Campbell's Life of Lord Erskine. —

Apr. 2. Sunday.
Very fine weather. Distant thunder heard. — Visited the Sunday School — Morning Service – Prayers — Afternoon service, prayers and sermon. I preached on Joseph a pattern of forgiveness. — After the afternoon service M. A. Ryan called with a painful account of M$^{rs.}$ Dolphin's state of health, and depression of spirits — Eccl. Gazette — To the family a section from Dr James on the Collects. —

Apr. 3. Monday.
Fine, warm weather: thunder at a distance. — Wrote to Mr Thornton on Hunt Trust business — Also to C Bathurst on Coroners having the power to bail persons on whom a Coroner's Jury shall pass a verdict of manslaughter — Received a letter from Reeves, the Keeper of Northleach Bridewell, who incloses |^{103} for my signature a form of warrant of commitment properly filled up as to the case of a person committed by me for a trespass in the pursuit of game. — The authorities at the Home Office require to see the warrants of commitment in game cases, and are very exact in respect of them, ordering to the discharge of prisoners in whose commitment there is any informality. — Justice business at home — Walked with MW. to Eyford; but not admitted by M$^{rs.}$ Dolphin, who is confined to her room by indisposition resulting from agitation of mind — Life of Lord Erskine.

Apr. 4. Tuesday.

A very fine day. — Wrote to Mr Hare on Hunt Trust affairs — Also to Mess$^{rs.}$ Edwards and Pell, Glass-dealers, London, to order four glass milk bowls for use in our dairy. — Walked to Lower Swell, and called on Perkins, whom I saw, as also his wife and daughter. |^{104} Perkins is more recovered from his late attack than I had expected; his speech is articulate, and the paralysis much relieved, though he is somewhat lame and very weak, requiring much care and attention: his constitution seems very delicate, and prematurely worn out. — Rec$^d.$ a letter from Sophia Hunt on Hunt Trust and Executorship matters; she forwards to me a power of Attorney already signed by herself, to be signed also by me as her Co-Executor and trustee, under the will of Caroline Hunt, in respect of the money bought into 3 P^r C$^t.$ Cons. in her name and ~~mind~~ ^{mine} as Trustees for Edward Hunt, being his share of £5000, received from the Crown Assurance Office. — A letter from a Stranger, a Mr Prentice, dated from Cheltenham, a botanist, who asks for a direction to the true habitat of Thlaspi perfoliatum, a rare plant, known as indigenous by Bobart,^{5} afterwards lost, as was supposed, but re-discovered some years ago by my son and Mr Billingsley, |^{105} growing on a rough banks, which had never been turned by the plough, or otherwise cultivated, at the back of my Rectory farm, in Bowman's hay, Joiners downs, and adjacent steep banks on E. Lea's farm. The plant has since been found in other like places on the oolite formation. — Life of Lord Erskine.

April 5. Wednesday.

Cooler weather than for two or three days lately, but fine and seasonable. — Justice business at home — Wrote to Mr Prentice with directions as to the habitat of Thlaspi perfoliatum — to Sophia Hunt on Trust and Executorship matters — Received a letter from Mess$^{rs.}$ Cox and Williams with a copy of the opinion given by Mr Geo. Turner on the case submitted to him as to the Hunt Trust affairs. — A letter from C Bathurst who sends a copy of Lord Campbell's bill for giving Coroners power to bail in cases of manslaughter with comments thereon. |^{106} C.B. also enquires as to a late Clerk of Mr Bloxsome's tried at the Assizes last week for a fraud, having obtained money from the County Treasurer, by a fraudulent document purporting to emanate from the Clerk of the Peace in the shape of an order of payment on the Treasurer for costs to Prosecutors and witnesses in a case tried before the Quarter Sessions — A circular from Mr Bloxsome's office announces that I am appointed a Visitor of the County Gaol. — Called on the Leas, Davis, and other parishioners. — Life of Lord Erskine.

Apr. 6. Thursday.

After heavy rain in the night, or early in the morning, a fine day, but cold and cloudy. — To Stow in the carriage, accompanied by MW., who soon returned home — To the Provident Bank, and Library. — To the office of the Gloucestershire Banking Company. — To the Workhouse: the first meeting of the newly elected board of Guardians, by whom I was again chosen the |^{107} Chairman of the Union, and Mr Beman the Vice Chairman. The business of the fortnightly meeting detained me from 12 to 4 PM. — This day we began the new system

---

5.   Jacob Bobart (1599-1680). Born in Brunswick, Bobart moved to England in 1632 as superintendent of the Oxford Physic Garden. In 1648 he published an anonymous catalogue, in alphabetical order of sixteen hundred plants then under his care *Catalogus Plantarum horti medici Oxoniensis*.

of keeping the books and accounts required by the Poor Law Commissioners. — Returned to the Provident Bank, where met Mr Winter, W B Pole, and Morrison. — Justice business at home, and at Mr Brookes's office. — Lord Campbell's life of Lord Erskine.

Apr. 7. Friday.

An Easterly wind — the day for the most part fine, but the air cold: in the evening a hailstorm. — Engaged in the forenoon at a parish meeting in the vestry, auditing the accounts of the Overseers, and nominating their successors for the year ensuing: — also auditing the accounts of the Road Surveyors, and electing Surveyors for the next year. — Received letters from Mr Thornton and Mr Hare who approve what I had done in London, in respect of |[108] the Hunt Trust. — M^r and Mrs Biscoe, accompanied by Mary Aston, called on us. Frederick Aston the younger has been removed from the Engineers College at Putney: his father had deplored to me the immorality prevalent there; but in what educational establishment, where many young men are congregated, does not vice shew itself? It is now alleged that the prospects of persons entering on the profession of Engineer are less good than formerly, the state of the country being such that Railway projects are in a great measure abandoned, and reduced within a narrower compass: but the tide may turn again, and there will never be a lack of employment for scientific men. I fear our young friend lacks energy, or application, or useful talent, and loves an idle, or sporting life, and, with moderate prospects, will remain without productive employment or a profession. — Justice business at home. — I walked to Eyford to call on Mrs Dolphin, but either she had |[109] not left her room, or was gone out: I did not see her. — Finished Lord Campbell's Life of Lord Erskine, and began his memoir of Lord Eldon. —

Apr. 8. Saturday.

An easterly wind, a cold day; rain with little intermission. — Wrote to Messrs Cox and Williams, and to Mr Thornton on Hunt Trust business — Also to C Bathurst as to the fraud committed by Bloxsome's clerk on the County Treasurer. — Justice business at home — Rec^d letters from Miss S. B. Hunt and Mr Hare on Hunt Trust business. — Life of Lord Eldon.

Apr. 9. Sunday.

In the morning showers of rain, and a flickering of snow: the day afterwards cold, with a N. E. wind — Visited the Sunday School — Preparing a Sermon. — Morning Service – prayers and a sermon. I preached on the endurance and improvement of affliction. Afternoon service, prayers. — A letter from Messrs |[110] Edwards and Pell, Southampton Street, Strand, who announce that they have sent, by the Carrier, four glass milk pans, according to my order — While MW. and I were attending the Sunday School between morning and afternoon service, Mrs Dolphin called accompanied by Miss Walmsley, now on a visit to her. — British Magazine — To the family a section from James on the Collects. —

Apr. 10. Monday.

A bright morning, soon exchanged for rain, sleet, and snow, falling heavily at noon, but clearing off later in the day; cold and raw. — Wrote to Mr Thornton on Hunt Trust matters: — to Mr Hare on the same: — To Messrs Coutts, Bankers, as to the 3 Pr C^t Cons. now standing in the name of Mr Hare and myself, a third of which is now divisible between her surviving brothers and sisters on the decease of Caroline Hunt, as directed in the will of M$^{rs.}$ M. Hunt. — A letter from E.F.W: except that the children have colds, all are well at the Vicarage, |^{111} Stanway — M$^{rs.}$ C. Barr with her little boy and girl, arrived from Mr E. Daniell's at Bullingham, near Hereford, on a visit to us. M$^{rs.}$ B. in better spirits than I had expected; her children look healthy, and are lively and intelligent.

Apr. 11. Tuesday.

A cold day, rain at night — Wrote to E.F.W. in answer to his letter received yesterday: invited him, Sophy and Broome, to visit us next week; to come on Monday, dine and sleep; to meet M$^{rs.}$ Barr. — Wrote to Mess$^{rs.}$ Hoare, desiring them to transfer to my son's account with them from my account, £47. 15. — Transacted parish business with Churchwarden Gregory — Justice business at home — Drove to Eyford in the phaeton with MW. and M$^{rs.}$ C. Barr: called on M$^{rs.}$ Dolphin and Miss Walmsley — Received a letter from Mr Hare on Hunt Trust business: he encloses a balance sheet from Mess$^{rs.}$ Cox & Williams. — Received a note from |^{112} C Bathurst about the Coroner's bill in progress through the House of Lords. — Lord Campbell's Life of Lord Eldon. —

Apr. 12. Wednesday.

A cold, raw, showery day — Wrote to Sophia Hunt on Hunt Trust and Executorship business, sending her a copy of Mr G. Turner's opinion; also of my last letter to Mess$^{rs.}$ Coutts as to the distribution of that portion of the 3 P^r C$^t.$ Cons. now stand$^g.$ in the names of Mr Hare and myself which is divisible on the death of M C Hunt. — Visited the day-school. — Justice business at home. — Rec$^d.$ a letter from Mr Thornton on Hunt Trust affairs — Also from Mr Estcourt, a circular, respecting the subscriptions required to make up the deficiency of the cost of the tower built at Hawkesbury Upton as a memorial of the late Lord Edward Somerset. — Rec$^d.$ from the Secretary a notice of the next meeting of the Decanal Clergy to be holden at Stow on |^{113} the 26$^{th.}$ Inst. — It appears from the newspapers that the greatly dreaded and threatened monster meeting of the Chartists at Kennington common on Monday last was a great failure. After much boasting of what should be done the people assembled did not exceed 15000 at the utmost: of these many were attracted by curiosity, and were not of the disaffected: a meeting was held, speeches were made, and resolutions were passed; but the petition to the House of Commons which was agreed upon was not taken in procession, as had been arranged, to the House, but this design was abandoned, and two or three cabs or flys conveyed the ponderous document and some of the Chartist committee. The government had made great and wise preparations to counteract, and, if necessary, to suppress the movement; a large military force was judiciously distributed, but kept out of sight, and its services were never required; |^{114} an overwhelming body of special constables was in readiness to act, assembled at convenient points of rendezvous, but their services were not needed; all the dispersion of the mob that was necessary was effected by the police; and thus a threatened emeute^6 and revolution à la mode de Paris were frustrated.

---

6.   Émeute – crowd, uprising – a popular rising or disturbance.

57. *Chartist rally,*
Kennington Common.

Apr. 13. Thursday.

A milder day, for the most part fine, but some rain fell about 5 o clock. — I went to Stow, accompanied by M^rs. Barr and her children, who returned in the phaeton. — Transacted business at the office of the Gloucestershire Banking Company, and at the Provident Bank, where I met Messrs. Lewes, Morrison, and R. Waller. — At the Workhouse presided for an hour and half at a special meeting of the Guardians of our Union, held for the revision of the pauper lists. — Sat in the Justice room with R. Waller as my colleague, where much business detained us late. — Rec^d. a letter from C Bathurst |^115 as to the bills now passing through the H. of C. for the regulation of magisterial business &c. — with comments on different clauses.

Apr. 14. Friday.

A fine, but cold day. — Justice business at home — Wrote to Messrs. Edwards and Pell, Glasswarehousemen, London, that of the four glass milk pans sent to us by them, which arrived yesterday by the carrier, two were broken, in consequence of bad packing. — Wrote to Sophia Hunt on Hunt and Exorship matters, particularly as to Mr Hare having paid M^rs. Miles, an annuitant under T. W. Hunt's will £48 per ann. instead of £40 as specified in the will: forwarded to S.B.H. two letters I had received from Mr Hare on that subject. — Wrote to Mr Hare, returned to him a balanced cash account of Messrs. Cox and Williams, which he had forwarded to me — Rec^d. letters from Mr Thornton and M^r |^116 Hare on Hunt Trust business, — particularly, as to Mr G. Hunt claiming a watch, once the property of Mr T. W. Hunt, and which Mr Hare considers as having been given to him by M^rs. Rowland Hunt after her son's decease: but it is very questionable whether she had any right to dispose of it. — Walked to Lower Swell: called on Perkins, who is slowly recovering. — Received a letter from Messrs. Hoare, who announce that they have transferred £35 ^47. 15 from my account with them to that of my Son, as I had desired — Rec^d. a circular from the Rev^d. Mr Michell, of Lincoln College, Oxford, thanking me for my promised vote, to assist in his election as Public Orator of the University. It seems that the party set up in opposition to him has withdrawn from the contest, and that the election will take place without competition to-morrow. Mr M. already holds the prælectorship of Logic, and it is understood will be appointed by Dr Macbride, the Principal |^117 of Magdalen Hall, to succeed Dr Jacobson as Vice Principal of that body. It is the elevation of Dr Jacobson to the Regius Professorship of Divinity which has caused the vacancy in the Public Oratorship and in the Tutorship of Magdalen Hall — That appointment to the Regius Professorship is, I believe, very generally approved: Dr J. has obtained it by his ability and learning, not by family or other interest, having come to the University, to Exeter College, as I have been told, a poor and unfriended, but talented youth; he was early noted and obtained a good degree: was highly esteemed as a Tutor at Magdalen Hall, and published a valuable edition of the apostolical Fathers. Mr Michell also is held in high consideration in the University; he was in the first instance a Member of Wadham College: he is no supporter of Ultra High Church doctrines; indeed, opposed to the Pusey and Newman party: and recently has declared himself an advo-|^118 cate for Dr Hampden: so may be considered of the moderate school. — Isaac Barrow – concio ad clerum, de potestate clavium. —

Apr. 15. Saturday.

A cold, raw, and dull forenoon, ending in a very rainy afternoon and evening. — Justice business at home. — Wrote to Mr Hare on the claim made by Mr Geo. Hunt to a watch formerly T. W. Hunt's; doubting whether M^rs. R. Hunt had a right to give it to Mr Hare, I suggested, though I did not directly advise Mr Hare, that he should give up the watch so claimed. In this I acted in conformity with the views of Mr Thornton, as expressed in the letter I received from him yesterday. — Drove to Stow, accompanied by MW. and M^rs. Barr, who left me at the Unicorn Inn, where I met by appointment Mr R. Waller, and was engaged in a long and intricate investigation as to a felony committed long since by two trampers, recently apprehended, who stole two asses from two different parties, in different neighbourhoods, |^119 but both from Gloucestershire; there were many witnesses from a distance to be examined, and a voluminous chain of evidence, but very complete. Committed the two men for trial at the Trinity Sessions; discharged one who had been apprehended on suspicion, but whom the evidence did not touch. — While I was thus employed, my ladies paid visits to M^rs. John Scott at Banksfee, and to M^rs. W. Vavasour, and her sister, at Maugersbury — As I returned home, I was much exposed to the pelting of the pitiless storm, and may lay my account to a bad cold, or fit of rheumatism. — From Mr Hare a letter, with extracts from letters of Mr Braikenridge, and of Messrs. Cox & Williams, as to transfering to Mr Geo. Hunt the personal estate of the late T. W. Hunt, reserving for the Trustees a certain portion as an indemnity, in the event of Mr Hunt taking any proceedings against them, which they might be entitled to combat at the cost |^120 of the Trust Estate. — From Messrs. Coutts a letter with a power of attorney to be signed by me to enable them to transfer stock standing in the name of Mr Hare and myself to the amount of £2179. 16. 8 - 3 P^r C^t. Cons. — being distributable under M^rs. Mary Hunt's will between the surviving brothers and sisters of Caroline Hunt at her decease. — From Mr H. D. Warter a letter with receipts for the various bills I have paid him for business done in his profession, as also for other Attornies bills, surveyors &c. who have been engaged at my cost in the purchase of ground rents in St. George's in the East, or in the abortive treaty for the purchase of the Great Risington Estate: — From Revd. W. Hicks, Cubberley, a letter requesting me to find for him a house servant, one whom I recommended to him some years ago being on the point of leaving him. — From the Clerk to the Gloucester Poor Law Union, a circular on the subject of the formation of district pauper schools, to which objections are made |¹²¹ by the Guardians of that Union, on the ground of expence, and that it is unreasonable that pauper children should have a better education than falls to the lot of those of the poorer contributors to the poor rate, who would thus be unreasonably taxed. There is reason in this; the recent visits to the Gloucestershire Unions of Mr Jelinger Symons were likely to elicit this feeling. — From Barto Valle, Wine merchant, London, with a bill for Claret which he has lately supplied to me. — From the Clerk to the Gloucester Lunatic Asylum a notice of a meeting of Visitors fixed for Apr. 25. — From the Bank of England an application to ascertain whether I had given a power of attorney for the sale of Stock standing in my name and in that of Mr Hare, and to whom. This measure has been now for sometime adopted by the Bank to guard against frauds, such as were practised by Barber and his confederates, presenting fictitious |¹²² and forged powers of Attorney for sale of stock — From Sophia Hunt, on Hunt Trust and Executorship affairs, chiefly as to Mr George Hunt's claim of the watch given many years ago by Mrs. Rowland Hunt to Mr Hare — From Messrs. Sewell and Newmarch with their bill for business done for me in the matter of the abortive negotiation for the purchase of the next presentation of the Rectory of Stanton, which as it ended in a failure, they have calculated on a very low scale, and charge £19. 16. 6., a sum much below what I expected. S. & N. have also paid to my account with the Gloucestershire Banking Company at Stow £204. 17. 1 being the £200 which we lent to Mr Marling, with interest thereon. — While I was out, Mr Moore, Med. Off., called.

Apr. 16. Sunday.

Palm Sunday. — A cold, raw day, ending in rain at night. — Visited the Sunday School — Preparing Sermons. — Morning service, prayers. |¹²³ Evening service – Prayers and sermon – I preached on the sacrifice and satisfaction of Christ. — Rec.^{d.} a letter from the Gloucester and Berkeley Canal office, with a report of the half yearly meeting of the proprietors — To the family a section from Dr James on the Collects. —

Apr. 17. Monday.

A fine day. — Wrote to Mr Hare and Mr Thornton on Hunt Trust matters. — To Messrs. Coutts on the transfer of stock from the names of Mr Hare and myself to the names of the five ^{Hunts} (brother and sisters) now in England: the two shares for the brothers in India to remain in the names of Mr Hare and myself till we receive their directions respecting them. I had forwarded to Mr Hare a power of Attorney as to this affair, which Messrs. Coutts had forwarded to me, and which I executed on Saturday: Mr Hare, when he has signed it, will return it to Messrs. Coutts — |¹²⁴ Wrote to the Accountant General of the Bank of England that I authorized such sale and transfer — Rec.^{d.} from Mr Hare a letter which had been addressed to him by the Accountant General, Bank of England, on the same sale and transfer, which he had rec.^{d.} and signed, and which I filled in with the amount of Stock, and the names of the Attornies in the transaction. — Wrote to Barto Vallé, London, sending a cheque on Messrs. Hoare for £8. 7. 6 – the amount of the bill for Claret, with which he has lately supplied me. — Rec^d. a letter from E.F.W. who with Sophy and Broome promises to visit us to-morrow, and stay till Wednesday. — Justice business at home — Transacted business with the Relieving Officer of the Union. — Walked with M^rs. C. Barr to the Turnpike Gate at L. Slaughter: as we returned met Mr W. B. Pole, who had called upon me to consult me on a matter of Justice business, he returned home with |^125 us, and paid a visit. — One of our servants being ill, Mr Collins, from Bourton on the Water, was called in, with whom I had an interview respecting her state of health — Lord Campbell's Life of Lord Eldon. —

Apr. 18. Tuesday.

A dull morning: rain came on at mid-day, and continued with little or no interruption till night. — I had been taken ill during the night, with a violent attack of acute rheumatism in the left arm and shoulder, aggravated by a fit of indigestion, caused by incautious indulgence at dinner yesterday. Sent for Mr Hayward who prescribed purgative medicine, and a draught to correct the peccant stomach, also a powerful embrocation to be rubbed on the parts affected. I suffered great pain, with languor from interrupted sleep, and was much indisposed all day. No doubt the exposure to pouring rain on Saturday contributed to my malady, as it caused M^rs. Barr, a very bad attack |^126 of brow ague. — Wrote to Mr Hicks in answer to his letter received yesterday — To Sophia Hunt, on Hunt Trust and Executorship business. — Received from her a letter chiefly respecting the payments made by Mr Hare to M^rs. Blake, a legatee under the will of Mr T. W. Hunt — From Mr Hare a letter as to the watch which Mr G. Hunt claims, and which, I suppose, Mr Hare will give up; also as to the property to be made over by the Trustees to Mr Geo. Hunt as advised by Mr G. Turner. — From Mr R. Waller notice of a meeting of the Clerical Society for Wednesday next. — Justice business at home. — Our dear son and daughter, accompanied by darling Broome, came before luncheon to pass the remainder of the day and part of to-morrow with us. Great pleasure in their society, although I am so unwell. — They left dear Freddy and Georgy quite well at Stanway. —

Apr. 19. Wednesday.

Slight showers once |^127 or twice, but the day generally fine. — I had a sleepless night, suffering great pain from rheumatism in the arm: languor and much suffering during the day; in the evening greatly overpowered with pain and drowsiness; unable to leave the house, or accompany my children and M^rs. Barr in their rambles. Mr Hayward attended me — I am to continue the medicines now prescribed, and to hope for early convalescence. E.F.W. busy fishing in the forenoon. — He and his left us after luncheon, to return to Stanway. — Wrote to Mr Hicks, sending my letter by one Rogers, a servant out of place, who, perhaps, may suit him. R. married a sister of our old servant, T. Andrew's wife, and has been with his wife for some time past lodging with T.A. — Wrote to Sophia Hunt on Hunt Trust and Exorship business. — Wrote to Messrs. Sewell and Newmarch, with a remittance of £20 — as a renume-|^128 ration for their professional services in the matter of the proposed purchase of the next presentation of the Rectory of Stanton — M^rs. Dolphin called on us, accompanied by her brother, Mr Hutchinson and her friend Miss Walmesley. — Received a letter from Sophia Hunt on Hunt Trust and Executorship business: — also from Barto. Vallé an acknowledgment of my remittance to him in payment of wine supplied by him.

Apr. 20. Thursday.

A mild and cloudy morning and forenoon; a dull and rather damp afternoon; a rainy evening. — Though I had slept well, and suffered less pain, I judged it prudent not to venture to Stow today; therefore sent notes by my Groom to Mr Hayward, Mr Pearce, Mr Pain, and Mr Clarke; from Mr Clarke I received a note to the effect that Sewell and Newmarch had paid to my account with the Gloucestershire Banking Company at Stow £204. 17. 1: from the others I received verbal |[129] answers. — Rec^d a note from my son, sent by Harris's carter, who brought a load of coal, and took back sawed timber for the new stable at the Vicarage, Stanway. — Wrote to E.F.W. in reply. — Also to Sophia Hunt on Hunt Trust and Executorship matters, and to Mr Thornton, to inform him that I had reason to believe that Mr Hare did ˢⁿ does not mean to maintain his right to the watch which Mr George Hunt claims. — Wrote a note to Mr Brookes on some magistrates business — Walked in the Village, to the school &c., and called on some parishioners, who are unwell. Mrs Barr and her children accompanied me. — A letter came, addressed to Revd F. E. Thornton, U.S. with the Bath post mark. I suspect it to have been written by M^r or Mrs Hare, and through some blunder directed F.E.T. instead of F.E.W. – did not venture to open it: shall forward it to Mr Thornton |[130] — The Post brought a packet containing a form of prayers to be read by the authority of the Privy Council to-morrow, being Good Friday, and on four Sundays following, for the maintenance of peace and tranquillity. This order very properly issued, considering the disturbed and agitated state of the public mind, both in this country, where the Chartists are seeking to unsettle the government, and in Ireland, where the repealers are pursuing a very turbulent and threatening course, and apparently paving the way for a revolution by insurrection. — Mr Hayward called and, in addition to other medicines, prescribed Dover's powders to be taken at night as a sedative. — Two of our female servants are ill: the Cook confined to her bed with influenza — and the Housemaid with swelled face, but somewhat better. — Lord Campbell's Life of Lord Eldon.

Apr. 21. Friday.

Good Friday. — A dull, foggy, damp day. — Wrote to M^r– |[131] Thornton; forwarded to him the letter rec^d yesterday, directed Revd F.E.T. Upper Slaughter Rectory &c. — Morning Service, prayers and sermon. I preached a discourse suitable to the day. — Preparing myself for the discussion at the Decanal meeting on Wednesday next — on the power of the Keys, absolution &c. — Looked into Barrow de potestate clavium, and Whitby's notes on the leading texts. — Justice business at home. — I had slept well, probably, under the influence of Dover's powders; suffered considerable pain in my left arm, but less intense than it has been: rather fatigued by my Clerical duties of the day. —

Apr. 22. Saturday.

For the most part a dull, cloudy, and foggy day. — Mr Hayward called. I had slept well, but suffered much pain and weakness in my left arm: same medicines continued. — Preparing for the approaching discussion at the Decanal meeting, fixed for |[132] Wednesday next, by looking into Bingham, Hooker, Mant's prayer-book, Burnet on the Articles, Whitby, Barrow &c. — making extracts. — Justice business at home — Called a̶ ᵒⁿ my parishioners, the Leas: illness still lingers in that family: privately baptized an infant lately born. — Visited Mʳˢ· Jos. Collett, and Mʳˢ· Gregory, both being unwell. — Recᵈ· a letter from the Revᵈ· Griffith, Wadh. Coll. announcing that Mʳ Michell had been elected Public Orator of the University of Oxford: Mʳ G. had canvassed me in his favour. — A letter from Mʳ Hicks, that he has hired Rogers, the servant whom I had named to him. — A letter from Sewell and Newmarch, acknowledging the letter and remittance sent by me on Wednesday last — Campbell's life of Lord Eldon.

Apr. 23. Easter Sunday.

A fine day — Still suffering severely from rheumatic pains in the left arm; but my general |¹³³ health improved — Preparing a Sermon — Preparing for the discussion on Absolution at the Ruri-decanal meeting on Wednesday next. — Morning Service, Prayers and Sermon. I preached on the resurrection of Christ. — Administered the Sacrament of the Lord's supper to 22 Communicants. — Received a letter from Sophia Hunt, who forwards for my perusal two notes received by her from Mʳˢ· Hare, announcing that Mʳ Hare is very ill, and prohibited from all correspondence or attention to business — A letter from C Bathurst on public matters — Evening Service, Prayers. —

Apr. 24. Monday.

Rain in the morning and forenoon; the afternoon dry, cold and cloudy, with Easterly wind. — Full of rheumatic pains: Mʳ Hayward called, & prescribed for me. — Wrote to Mʳˢ· Hare in consequence of the serious indisposition of her husband, and to Mʳ Thornton, |¹³⁴ forwarding to him the two notes from Mʳˢ· Hare respecting her husband's illness which she had written to Sophia Hunt, and which S.H. had sent for my perusal. — Wrote to Sophia Hunt on Hunt Trust and Executorship matters: — also to C Bathurst in answer to his letter received yesterday. — Preparing for the discussion on Absolution which will be the subject of debate at the decanal meeting on Wednesday next. — Lord Campbell's Life of Lord Eldon. —

Apr. 25. Tuesday.

A cold air; an ungenial Northerly or Easterly wind. — Still suffering from rheumatism, especially at night. — Wrote to Howell; — to Messʳˢ· Butt, Gloucester, with an order for Madeira Wine — Preparing for the discussion on Absolution at the ruri-decanal meeting to-morrow. — My son rode from Stanway to see us: poor Sophy was unable to accompany him, as she is suffering from tooth-ache, and a swelled face. — E.F.W. partook of luncheon |¹³⁵ with us, amused himself with his fishing rod, and remained with us till between 5 & 6 PM. — I accompanied him to Lower Slaughter, and by the brook-side. — The ladies drove to Bourton on the Water, and called on Mʳˢ· R. Waller, and the Misses Hall — Justice business at home. — Received a letter from Mʳ Thornton on Hunt Trust business. He sends back the letter which I had forwarded to him, as being directed Revᵈ· F. E. Thornton, U. Slaughter, and which proves, as I suspected, to have been intended for me, and written by Mʳˢ· Hare, who blundered Witts into Thornton, to a̶c̶q̶u̶a̶i̶n̶t̶ inform me of the serious illness of her husband — Recᵈ· a letter from George Pain, Stow, in his capacity of actuary of the Prov. Bank, respecting my signing a draft for £700, on the Commʳˢ· for the reduction of the National debt, as a Trustee of our |[136] Savings Bank, that ~~some~~ sum being required from our funds in the hands of those Commissioners, to meet recalls of deposits. — Lord Campbell's Life of Lord Eldon. —

Apr. 26. Wednesday.

A rainy morning; a ~~dull,~~ cold cheerless day; sun and showers alternating. — Justice business at home. — Wrote a note to M[r] Lefroy, to be taken by a young man who is desirous of entering into the Constabulary force. — Although still suffering from rheumatism, and weak in my left arm, I drove to Stow — Consulted M[r] Hayward — Called at Geo. Pain's, where, as Trustee of the Provident Bank, I signed a draft on the Comm[rs.] for the Reduction of the National debt for £700. — To the Rectory: called on M[r] Hippisley: conferred with him as to the business likely to be brought to-day, before the Clergy of the Deanery at their decanal meeting. The Rural Dean joined us at the Rectory, and was accompanied by his daughters, |[137] Dulcibella and Sophia — Attended the afternoon prayers at the Church, commencing after twelve o clock, and read by R W Hippisley to a very small congregation, about half a dozen clergymen, and the two Misses Ford being the only persons present. Some new painted glass windows have been added to those previously in the Chancel. — After service, to the Decanal meeting held in the National Schoolroom. The Rural Dean presided: the Clergy present were Mess[rs.] Hill, Witts, Sadler, Morrison, Hutchinson, Williams, Terry, Boggis (the new curate of Bourton on the Water) Hurd, Hunt, Biscoe, and Potter. — Biscoe read a very judicious and well studied paper on the nature and extent of the sacerdotal power of Absolution: the general purport of his doctrine was that Absolution is ministerial, not judicial. — In the comments made by the |[138] clergy on the subject of the paper I led the way, taking a view of the power of the Keys, of the errors of the Roman Church, of the fault of Protestant dissenters in regard to Absolution. I shewed the judgment of antiquity, quoting the Fathers, and developed the views of several of the best Anglican divines, — Hooker, Jer. Taylor, Bp. Burnett, Archb. Secker, Nicholls, Sparrow &c. — Others who spoke on the subject were R W Hippisley, Potter, and Hunt, all more or less confirming the views entertained by Biscoe and myself, yet with shades of difference, as in each the bias inclined either to High or Low Church principles. — The Rural Dean made a communication from the Bishop of the diocese to the Clergy present, as to certain arrangements which he proposes to make for the benefit of the Church in this diocese. His Lordship has lately called his Rural deans together at Stapleton, to consult with them on the design |[139] which he had formed. His plan is to devote a large sum, over which he has entire controul, and which he might without blame appropriate to his private purposes, above £9000, to the erection of parsonages in small benefices in the diocese the income of which is under £200 per annum. This sum he intends to invest as a Trust funds in his own name, and in that of the two Deans and two Archdeacons of the Diocese; so that the Bishop and these dignitaries shall be at all times trustees of this fund. The Bishop reserves to himself the right of nominating the first eighteen Churches to which parsonages shall be attached from this fund; to each, I believe, he proposes to assign £200, to be met by further contributions of a local or personal character, and grants from Queen Anne's bounty, the fund derived from D[r] Warneford's charity for the purpose of aiding in the building of parsonages, or from other |[140] resources. The Bishop contemplates the reduction of the original fund of £9000 to a capital of £5000;

but means to provide that the interest and accumulations on the latter sum be a perpetual fund for building and repairing parsonage houses on benefices in this Diocese under £200 a year. – The £9000 thus devoted by the generous Bishop will arise partly from private savings made by his Lordship out of his income, as Bishop, and devoted by him to church purposes, and also from the sale of his interest, as Bishop of Gloucester, ~~in the sale~~ to the Ecclesiastical Commissioners, of the Manor of Horfield near Bristol. This is a very valuable property, leased on lives, and now held on the single life of a person aged 87 years, at whose demise, the Bishop, should he survive him, which is fully to be expected, considering his general health and age, would be entitled to secure, if he so chose, the valuable property to his own family, by |[141] putting in the lives, say, of three of his own children, aged 18, 20, and 22 years. Should he adopt this course, he might, calculating on the average duration of human life, secure to himself and descendants a property exceeding £200,000; for it is estimated that, at the demise of the remaining life by which the property is now held, it will be worth from £5000 to £6000 per ann. Now the Bishop foregoes the right he has, as Bishop antecedently to the late laws for regulation of Cathedral and Church property, to retain this prize in his family, by leasing it in his family for lives, should he outlive the now remaining life: with the Ecclesiastical Commissioners he contracts that they shall enter into the immediate enjoyment of the revenues of the Horfield Estate, as soon as the present life drops, so as to apply the proceeds to the advantage of the Church generally, stipulating only that the sum be paid to him which he has devoted |[142] to this fund for the erection of parsonages on small benefices in the diocese, and that the income of the incumbent of Horfield be increased by £100 per annum. This is highly liberal and praiseworthy: it might, indeed, have been censurable, had his Lordship insisted on his right to apply to his own uses all the advantages within his grasp, if the manor of Horfield should fall in during his episcopate, and he would, probably, have been charged with nepotism; but he might without blame have benefited his family to a considerable extent, say, £20000 or £30000: but now he renounces all personal or family advantage, and only insists on such a benefit as will enable him to secure to the poor livings in the diocese the great improvement of a residence – It was unanimously agreed that the Rural Dean, in the name of the Clergy present; shall offer to the Bishop their best acknowledgments and thanks for this new and |[143] extraordinary proof of his great liberality — Mr Hippisley proposed to the Clergy to join in a petition against the enactment of a Proviso intended to be moved for insertion in a clause of a bill now before Parliament, for the correction of heresy, schism, and false doctrine in clerical persons, to the effect that, when the charge made is touching any matter of doctrine set forth in the 39 Articles, no opinion shall in any court be considered false doctrine, unless it contradicts the doctrine contained in the Articles. This Proviso has been submitted to the consideration of the Bishops, but has not received their sanction, and they have probably come to a right conclusion regarding it, but their reasons have not been set forth. The Bp. of Exeter, however, has expressed a strong opinion on the subject, considering that the proposed proviso amounts to the setting up of a new test of heresy; the articles being made, as he supposes, the sole test, to the |[144] exclusion of doctrines set forth and developed in the Liturgy, and especially in the Church Catechism. The view taken by Bishop Philpotts has been warmly taken up by Clergy in that diocese and elsewhere, and petitions against the Proviso have been drawn up and signed; and are strongly advocated in the English

Churchman, a journal which speaks the sentiments of the Tractarian or Ultra High Church party. In this diocese Archdeacon Thorp advocates the same views, and our old neighbour Crompton strongly urges remonstrance and appeals to Parliament; thus ultra high church men are moving in the direction. But I judged it premature to take any step in advance, and prevailed with the Clergy present to sit still. I argued that we were called upon to adopt the inference from the words of the proviso, which the Bp. of Exeter and others have drawn, but which does not appear certainly to follow from the expressions used. The parties drawing such inference might be in error — the proviso might |[145] never be proposed, — might be withdrawn, or over-ruled — might, when properly explained, turn out to be unobjectionable; – so that the safer course would be to defer the matter, at least to wait till we had some further insight into it, and some intimation of the leaning and opinions of our own diocesan upon it. It seemed to me also wrong to take a course which might seem to under-rate the authority of the articles. — When the decanal meeting closed about 4 PM. I returned home, not thinking it prudent in my present state of health to join the Clergy at the meeting of our Clercial Society, assembled at the Unicorn to dine together. — Rec$^{d.}$ a letter from C Bathurst — Lord Campbell's Life of Lord Eldon — Tired, and suffering from rheumatic pains.

Apr. 27. Thursday.

Rain in the morning and evening; in the forenoon and afternoon the air chilly, and the wind cold, when the sun, which shone out at times, had no influence. — |[146] Preparing a sermon — Drove to Stow, accompanied by M$^{rs.}$ Barr, her two children, and their nurse. With M$^{rs.}$ B., accompanied by R W Hippisley, visited the church at Stow. — M$^{rs.}$ B. &c. returned to U. Slaughter. — I transacted business at the Provident Bank. — At the Workhouse I examined the minutes of the last meeting of Guardians, and conferred on Union matters with Mr Pearce — Joined R W Ford at the Savings Bank, with whom sat at the Unicorn, as Magistrates, where we had much business. — Mess$^{rs.}$ Winter and W B Pole were present with us. — Home by 5 PM. — A letter from J. Round announces that his daughter ~~was~~ is $^{to be}$ married to Capt. Story on the 9$^{th.}$ ~~Inst.~~ May. — From Howell a letter with many details and comments of and on passing events: — ~~and~~ a letter from parties writing on behalf of the Glassware-housemen from whom we recently bought some glass milkpans, two of which were broken |[147] in the carriage: it seems that these tradesmen are insolvent, and the people winding up the concern insist on full payment being made for the broken pans. — A letter from M$^{rs.}$ Hare: her husband's health is improved, but is still very indifferent — In the Evening I felt heavy, drowsy, and fatigued: the rheumatic pains are abated, but still continue.

Apr. 28. Friday.

A finer day, and a clearer sky than for a long time past. — Wrote to Mr Jennings, inclosing to him the invoice as to the glass milk pans, and the correspondence about them, requesting him to pay the bill, making the best bargain he can. — Copied a document relating to the Wadenhoe Trust, and prepared a letter to Mr Thornton on Trust matters — Justice business at home, in which I was assisted by Mr Ford, who came for the purpose; Mr Taplin also came to act as our clerk — Rec$^{d.}$ a letter from M^{r-} |[148] Thornton on Hunt Trust matters, he returns to me the two notes from M$^{rs.}$ Hare to Sophia Hunt, which I had forwarded for his perusal — Rec$^{d.}$ from the Gloucester lunatic Asylum the annual report of that institution. — Walked with MW., M$^{rs.}$

Barr, and her children to Eyford &c. — M^r. Terry overtook us, as we returned, accompanied by a stranger friend, whose name I did not catch: the two gentlemen called upon us — I am tolerably free from rheumatism during the day, but the pain is very wearing at night.

Apr. 29. Saturday.

Fine weather — Preparing a sermon — J. Perkins called, accompanied by his father and daughter. He has recovered greatly from his late attack of paralysis; but is still very weak and likely to continue so. The old man is very much broken, and feeble both in body and mind — M^rs. W. with M^rs. Barr and the children drove to Bourton &c. I walked to Eyford, meaning to call on the party at M^rs. Dolphin's — Found that Bowen |^149 had returned to-day to Temple Guiting; and that M^rs. Dolphin had taken Miss Walmesley to Stow to visit M^r and M^rs. Vavasour till Monday. M^r and M^rs. Frobisher were at home, and I visited them. — Visited several poor and sick parishioners. — Read portions of Izaak Walton's life of Hooker. — Suffered a good deal from flying rheumatic pains; also from flatulence.

Apr. 30. Sunday.

Very fine weather — Preparing a Sermon. — Attended the Sunday School. — Morning service – prayers – Evening Service, prayers and sermon. I preached on peaceful submission to the laws, ~~enforced~~ and respect for those who administer them, enforced on the sure authority of holy Scripture. My subject was selected with reference to the late convulsions in foreign lands, and the late attempts at distubance at home by the Chartists and mob leaders, which have given occasion for the prayers |^150 for the maintenance of peace and tranquillity now put up in all congregations of the Church of England by authority of the Queen in Council — Much indisposed with rheumatic pains and flatulence.

May 1. Monday.

Fine weather. — M^rs. Barr and her children left us for M^rs. Walker's at Henwick, near Worcester, now her temporary residence until she fixes on a house for herself, which she desires to find in the neighbourhood of Worcester, that she may remain near her late husband's surviving relations, and in a neighbourhood, where he meant to have fixed himself had he lived to execute his project of retiring after a few years from his engagements as a banker. M^rs. Walker's health is very precarious: with her reside her unmarried siiter, and an unmarried brother, to both of whom M^rs. C.B. is attached, as they are to her & her children. — It is much to be lamented that the children are ill regulated; they are fine, stout and promising in appearance; clever, |^151 and intelligent withal; but sadly spoilt, wayward, wilful, disobedient, and somewhat artful. Allowances should be made, as during Mr Barr's fatal illness, and since, as inmates of M^rs. Walker's, they have been necessarily more or less allowed to run riot, and indulged: and, in fact, have, I suspect, never been properly ruled, nor does the Mother's system, or want of system, seem likely to train them steadily to habits of obedience and subordination. She is an excellent, well informed, and very agreeable person, but appears to lack firmness and judgment as to the education of little ones — Justice business at home. — Wrote a note to Mr Clark of the Gloucestershire Banking Company's Branch at Stow, with a cheque for £20 — my messenger brought back the money. — Wrote to Mr Thornton on Hunt Trust affairs. — Preparing a Sermon. — Lord Campbell's Life of Lord Eldon. —

May 2. Tuesday.

Fine weather. — Justice |[152] business at home, and at Bourton on the Water, whither I drove, accompanied by MW. and met M[r] Ford at the office of Mess[rs.] Wilkins & Kendal. — When at Bourton, left our cards for M[r] Boggis, the new Curate of the parish, who, with a mother and brother, have taken lodgings in the Village. The gentlemen and the lady were from home. — Wrote to Round, congratulating him, as far as might be, on his daughter's approaching marriage: but there is reason to fear that she is not about to make a very eligible connection. — Wrote to E.F.W. that we propose calling on him and his at Stanway next week. — It appeared from Hayward, who visited me, that my son is to-day at Stow, this being the first meeting for the season of the Stow Cricket Club. — M[r] Hayward prescribed for me: I am still suffering from flatulence, with aches and pains, and restless nights. — Engaged in parish matters with W. Gregory, and J B Collett. — A begging letter from a poor |[153] Clergyman in Cambridgeshire. — Lord Campbell's Life of Lord Eldon. —

May 3. Wednesday.

Very fine weather — Wrote to M[r] Thornton on Hunt Trust matters — Preparing a Sermon. — Walked to Lower Swell Vicarage: called on the Vicar. Visited him & his wife, his father and mother, and sister: J.P. Jun[r] continues in the same state of health as when we met lately: the old man is very declining. — Rec[d.] a letter from Sophia Hunt in Trust and Executorship business: she forwards for my perusal letters from M[r] Hare & Geo. Hunt — A letter from Mess[rs.] Butt, Gloucester, as to six dozen of Madeira which they forwarded to me by the Carrier yesterday — M[rs.] R. Waller called, but in the absence both of MW. and of myself. — My health improved to-day: though rheumatic and dyspeptic pains still haunt me. — Lord Campbell's Life of Lord Eldon. |[154]

May 4. Thursday.

Fine weather. — Justice business at home. — Drove to Stow; MW. accompanied me, but soon returned to U. Slaughter. — Rec[d.] a letter from M[r] Hare, who forwards letters to him on Hunt Trust matters from Mess[rs.] Cox and Williams, and M[r] Thornton. M[r] Hare is much recovered from his late illness, but is still a great invalid. — A letter from E.F.W., who hopes to see us at Stanway on Monday next: on Tuesday he & his go to Stow and Maugersbury to visit the Vavasours, of the elder and younger house, for the rest of the week — A letter from Rodwell as to a book which he had supplied to me some time ago, but which I had lately discovered to be very defective; several pages being left out. — Transacted business at the depository of the Books of the Society for Promoting Christian Knowledge — at the Provident Bank Office; — at the office of the Gloucestershire Banking Company; — and at M[r] R G K Brookes's office — |[155] To the Workhouse, where presided for more than three hours at the fortnightly meeting of the Guardians of the Union — Consulted Hayward, who continues to give me medicine to correct the derangement of the stomach; still suffering from rheumatic pains in the shoulder — Lord Campbell's Life of Lord Eldon. —

May 5. Friday.

Very fine weather — Busy in superintending workmen stripping slate off part of our roof, where repairs are necessary. — Wrote to M[r] Hare and M[r] Thornton on Hunt Trust affairs.

— Preparing a Sermon — Walked with MW. to Eyford: called on M$^{rs.}$ Dolphin and Miss Walmesley. — While we were absent the Rev$^{d.}$ J. Boggis & his brother called. — Received a letter from Mr Thornton on Hunt Trust business — MW. heard from M$^{rs.}$ Barr who reached Henwick in safety with her children on the day on which they left us. — Called on J Davis and W Gregory — |^{156} Lord Campbell's Life of Lord Eldon.

May 6 Saturday.

Fine weather, with the exception of a slight shower in the afternoon — Engaged with Churchwarden Gregory on parish business — Justice business at home. — Wrote a note to R G K Brookes — Wrote letters on Hunt Trust business to Mr Hare and Mr Thornton. — Drove with MW. to call on M^r and M$^{rs.}$ Boudier at Farmington, but on our way thither, before we turned from the Turnpike road, we met them in their carriage going towards Bourton. We, therefore, proceeded to call on the Biscoes at Turkdean, whom, however, we did not find at home. Mr B. has greatly improved his parsonage, and the pleasure ground, with the approach, adding a new drawing room with other apartments and accommodations, which seem very judiciously arranged. — Lord Campbell's Life of Lord Eldon.

May 7. Sunday.

Fine weather. — Visited |^{157} the Sunday School. — Visited Joiner Collett's wife, very recently confined, and in a very exhausted and precarious state — Morning service; prayers and Sermon; I preached on the Error of Balaam — Afternoon Service, prayers. — Distributed prayer books and tracts to the children, who during Lent had repeated the Catechism in Church. — Preparing a Sermon — To the family a section from James on the Collects — My health is very tolerable now; during the day time I experience but little pain, but rheumatic aches disturb me at night.

May 8. Monday.

Fine weather — Drove with MW. to Stanway. — On the road overtook and chatted with our old neighbour, Bowen, who, at present, is tolerably free from his harrassing complaints, and able to walk out for a short time. — Spent three hours very enjoyably at the Vicarage, Stanway, |^{158} with our dear children and grandchildren. Inspected the alterations, particularly the new stable and laundry, which are nearly completed, and very commodious. — We all walked to Church Stanway, where an ornamental garden has been laid out on the site of an old cottage near the Churchyard lately taken down. — We returned home to dinner — Lord Campbell's Life of Lord Eldon.

May. 9. Tuesday.

Fine weather — Justice business at home. — Wrote to Sophia Hunt on Trust and Executorship business, sending her copies of parts of my late letters to Mr Thornton — Received a letter from Mr Hare who forwards to me the Trust accounts in T. W. Hunt's Trust, as prepared by Mess$^{rs.}$ Cox and Williams; when I have looked at them I am to forward them to Mr Thornton — Received a letter from C. J. Geldard. It appears that the land sold by us from the |^{159} Ravenflatt farm to the North Western Railway Company will reach the amount of £1700 — about £725 of which represents land actually traversed by the line, the rest land severed from the farm and bought by the Directors. The transaction appears a very favourable one to us; for, while the Tenants of the farm will be satisfied with a reduction of £20 per ann., our income will be improved by nearly £50 per ann. But this depends on the solvency of the company, of which, however, there is no reason to doubt: though, probably, the directors may not be prepared to pay the whole amount down, but will require, for part at least, that it remain for a certain period, bond being given, at 5 Pr Ct. Interest. — Lord Campbell's Life of Lord Eldon.

May 10. Wednesday.

Fine weather — Justice business at home — Wrote to Mr Hare and Mr Thornton on Hunt Trust busi-|[160] ness, forwarding to the latter the Trust accounts which had been sent to me by Mr Hare, and which I received yesterday. — Wrote to Mr C. J. Geldard in answer to his letter recd. yesterday. — Received from Mr Hare a packet of bills for business done by Messrs. Cox and Williams in the matter of the Hunt Trust; these bills to be looked over and to be forwarded to Mr Thornton — Also a letter from Mr Thornton on Hunt Trust concerns. — The Messrs. Boggis again called when we were out. — Lord Campbell's Life of Lord Eldon.

May 11. Thursday.

Very fine weather — Wrote to Mr Thornton, forwarding to him the packet of bills for business done in the matter of the Hunt Trust by Messrs. Cox & Williams, which Mr Hare had forwarded to me; commented on them, and partly answered Mr Thornton's letter received yesterday. — Wrote to Mr Hare, commenting on the above mentioned bills which I had received from him yesterday. — |[161] Drove with MW. to Stow; who proceeded to Maugersbury, where, at the W. Vavasours she called, meeting our dear Sophy and her children, who had arrived there on a visit on Tuesday. Miss Graydon, an elderly relation of the Vavasours, is also on a visit at Maugersbury. The day was fixed for a pic-nic fishing party of the W. Vavasours, with my son and daughter and others, on my land at Joiners downs; and MW. made her carriage useful by conveying to Upper Slaughter Sophy and Broome, with Emma Vavasour, who walked to Joiners downs from our house. — I went to the Provident Bank, where my Son met me, and accompanied me to the Workhouse, where I conferred with Mr Pearce on Union business. Thence I returned with E.F.W. to the Unicorn Inn, where I assisted him in hearing a case of assault on an officer of the Gloucestershire County Court, committed at Evenlode, and therefore under my Son's jurisdiction, as a Worcestershire Magis-|[162] trate. — When my Son had transacted this business, he went to Maugersbury to join the pic-nic party. — R. Waller joined me in holding a Petty Session till 4 PM. — Messrs. Winter and W B Pole were present. — Mr Ford is now at Gloucester, taking Cathedral duty, as an Honorary Canon, to supply the place of Archdeacon and Canon Wetherell, the Canon in residence, who is in infirm health. This new arrangements brings the Honorary Canons, if they be so disposed, into active service; and they receive a portion of the stipend allotted to the Residentiary whose duties they undertake. — When the Petty Sessions was over, I met and parleyed with the Dean of Gloucester, Mr Wiggin, and Mr Potter. — Saw Mr Hayward, who wishes me to continue for sometime longer the draughts which I am now taking — composed of Alkali, Taraxacum and Salicene — My health is now pretty good; but I still suffer pain and uneasiness in my left arm and shoulder, |[163] particularly at night. — Wrote to Mr Wells, Med. Off. of the Union, desiring him to attend a poor sick parishioner. — Lord Campbell's life of Lord Eldon.

May 12. Friday.

Very fine weather — Stow fair day — Drove to Stow — MW. accompanied me to within a short distance of the Town, and then returned — I was joined in the Fair by my son and W. Vavasour, who accompanied me to the Provident Bank, where we met Mr Winter — To Mr Brookes's office, where several cases of magistrates business awaited E.F.W. and myself. — Thence to "the Cottage," where joined M^r and M^rs. Vavasour, dearest Sophy, and my beloved grandchildren, and partook of luncheon with them — Afterwards returned with my son and eldest grandson to Mr Brookes's office, where further cases of Justice business were ready for us. — Perambulated the fair with Mr Vavasour and Broome — |^164 To the Provident Bank, and to the office of the Gloucestershire Banking Company, where heard of the lamentable death by brain fever after a short illness of William Cripps, MP. for Cirencester; he leaves a widow and four orphans, and will be a great loss to his family. I always found him a pleasant acquaintance, and occasional correspondent, ready to comply with any little suggestion or request I had to make — As a Barrister, he had attained a fair position, had attached himself to Sir Robert Peel, under whom he had held the office of a Lord of the Treasury, and been employed in Commissions. In the House of Commons, and particularly on Committees, he was a very useful person, and not long ago had signalized himself by a strong, but well merited censure and castigation of Feargus O Connor, the Representative of Nottingham, and dangerous Chartist leader. — Informed today that Henry Lindow is likely to be appointed a Magistrate for the County of Gloucester — |^165 His father continues miserably infirm and incapacitated by paralysis, a wreck in body and mind, so that the charge of the parent & his concerns has devolved on the Son, who is nowise deficient in ability, but is less steady, sober, and settled in habits than might be wished. As to politics he, like his father, professes Whiggism, and so has been noticed by Lord Fitzhardinge, whose hunt he has joined, & the Peer enlists him for his own & his party, by proposing to call him to the bench on an early cold seal being issued. If so he will become my colleague, and, probably, to me less distasteful than to others with whom I act. Whether he will be a useful Magistrate remains to be seen — Received a letter from Sophia Hunt on Executorship and Trust business. She has now taken up with energy a minor point in these concerns respecting which she blames Mr Hare, as to extra payments to an annuitant under T. W. Hunt's will, Sarah Blake — |^167 Other contorversies as to this entangled Trust are far more important, but so it is that people forget the old adage of Defoe — "In trouble to be troubled, is to have your trouble doubled." — Returned home to dinner — Lord Campbell's Life of Lord Eldon.

May 13. Saturday.

Very fine weather. — Attended a vestry meeting — The two Churchwardens and myself alone present. The Churchwardens accounts were passed, and the former Churchwardens re elected. The accounts of the parochial Church and Charity Estate were examined and allowed. — Settled at home parish accounts, paying tradesmens bills &c. — Wrote to Sophia Hunt on Hunt Trust matters. — Visiting a sick parishioner — Lord Campbell's life of Lord Eldon.

May 14. Sunday.

Very fine weather: very hot and sultry with bright sun: the evening cloudy; distant thunder, but no rain fell here. — Visited the Sunday School. — Preparing a Sermon — Morning service, prayers: — |*168* Afternoon service, prayers and sermon. I preached on the difficulties of a Christian life — W. Vavasour came to attend the evening service here, being still very uneasy about the state of the chancel of the church at Stow, and reluctant to go thither, alledging that the ill constructed roof still admits such draughts of air as to be very unpleasant, causing him to catch cold and inflicting rheumatic pains. His applications for redress to the Rector and Rural Dean have been of little avail, and he thinks of preferring a complaint before the Archdeacon at the approaching Visitation. He has some grounds for the complaint, as, no doubt, the roof has been ill constructed, and Mr Hippisley and the Rural Dean have evaded the matter, and shewn a disinclination to remedy the mischief: but there is also a sore feeling and unfriendliness between the Rector and his Parishioner, much to be regretted. — Received a letter from Mr Thornton with enclosures on the |*169* Hunt Trust concerns: he has transmitted to Mr Braikenridge the bills, which I forwarded to him, that he may examine them on the part of his Client, Mr Hunt. — Received an impudent letter from Heneage Lupton, praying me to shorten the period of imprisonment of a poacher of the name of Harding whom I ~~have~~ committed to Northleach House of Correction, and whom H.L. met in that resort of bad and blackguard characters. It is amusing that the Prisoner committed for an assault on a Police Constable should intercede with the Committing Magistrate on behalf of a brother prisoner suffering the punishment adjudged to him by the same Magistrate! — Ecclesiastical Gazette — To the family a Section from James on the Collects.

May 15. Monday.
Very fine weather. — Mrs. Griffin called to pay the Ladyday rent, for the land which she holds under the Trustees of the Church and Charity Estate in this parish. — J W Harris called to pay £50 |*170* on account of the Ladyday rent due for the Vicarage farm at Stanway. — Justice business at home. — Wrote to Mr Hare on Hunt Trust matters, returning to him letters from Messrs. Cox and Williams, wh. he had forwarded for my perusal, and which I had received back from Mr Thornton, to whom I had transmitted them. It is proposed that the Stock standing in our names as Trustees be transfered into the name of Mr Geo. Hunt, a small portion being reserved to meet any expences to which the Trustees may be put by any adverse proceedings which Mr G.H. may be advised to take, and which may be chargeable to the corpus of the estate: and the title-deeds of the landed property are also to be handed over to Mr G.H. — Recd. a begging letter from a Clergyman near Boston, praying for aid towards payg. off a debt on the erection of a new church. — Lord Campbell's life of Lord Eldon. |*171*

May 16. Thursday.
Fine weather — Drove to Stow, accompanied by MW. who returned almost as soon as we had arrived there — The day of the Archdeacon's Visitation. — Poor Dr Timbrill in great distress. His eldest son lies almost at the point of death, from an abscess of long standing near the spine externally; a very promising youth of 20 years of age, an Undergraduate of Worcester College — now at Beckford; Mrs. Timbrill also is in a deplorable state of health with a chronic spine complaint, at Clifton — The old man expressed to me privately the deep grief he felt, but publicly bore up manfully, going through firmly the duties of the day. — R W Hippisley read the Prayers, and Morrison preached a good, sound, sermon, but in a dull monotonous tone. His subject and text were the same as I had selected some years since

for my Visitation Sermon at Campden, but very differently treated: the treasure in earthen |[172] vessels. — The Archdeacon's charge was good and strong; chiefly directed against the Papists and Romanizing party in the church, he was very earnest for the Protestant cause: It seemed to me a defect that when he pointed out the risk to which the church was exposed by extreme opinions on the one side, he omitted to notice the danger arising from laxity and indifferentism and latitudanarianism on the other: About 28 or 30 Clergy of the Deanery attended to answer to their names. — At the Library and at the office of the Gloucestershire Banking Company. — Met and conversed with M[r] and M[rs.] W B Pole, M[r] and M[rs.] and Miss Morrison, and M[rs.] R A Scott — At the Unicorn, while waiting the return of the Archdeacon from the Church, where he was meeting and conferring with the Church wardens, the Dean of Gloucester, the Rural Dean and myself were together. Ford had |[173] arrived from Gloucester to attend the Visitation. He is very full of his engagements there as substitute for a Residentiary canon, calls his residence very dignified but very dull; yet likes the pomp and ceremony of a Cathedral dignitary, and, perhaps, still more, the pecuniary remuneration which he expects. He returns to Gloucester to-morrow. — It seems that Hippisley has tacitly admitted the justice of the complaints made by W. Vavasour as to the imperfect state of the roof of the chancel of Stow church; for workmen have been employed yesterday in nailing strips of wood over the interstices between the planks under the slates to shut out the air pouring through. The matter has been brought before the Archdeacon, and if further complaint be made it is arranged that a report shall be made to the Archdeacon by a Builder as to the alleged defects. — I had an interview with Hayward; he wishes me still to continue taking the medicine which he has lately ad-|[174]ministered, and recommends me to take a journey to the seaside, when I can conveniently leave home; chiefly that I may enjoy repose and cessation from business and professional duties for a short time, in a bracing and enlivening air & place. It is true that I am still annoyed by rheumatic and dyspeptic pains, particularly at night — At the Visitation dinner the party was not large, and some complaints were made as to the absence of several of the Clergy — Those present were the Archedeacon, the Dean of Gloucester, the Rural Dean, Morrison, Hippisley, R Waller, Boggis, Clarke, W B Pole, Sadler, Lewes, Hurd and myself — Also M[r] Burrup as Archdeacon's registrar — Ford returned with me to Lower Slaughter Turnpike gate, where, leaving him to proceed to Little Risington in his own carriage, I got into mine, which had followed us. The Archdeacon went to hold |[175] his Visitation at Campden to-morrow. — Received a letter from M[r] Thornton on Hunt Trust matters: he forwarded for my perusal letters from M[r] Tilleard and M[r] Braikenridge — A letter, as to the sale of land from the Ravenflatt farm to the Directors of the North Western Railway company, from Chr. Geldard. — A note from M[r] Pearce with enclosures as to Union business. — Lord Campbell's Life of Lord Eldon.

May 17. Wednesday.

A fine day on the whole: about noon a few heat drops fell, and distant thunder was heard. At night there was wind, and a shower of rain. — Wrote to Mess[rs.] Cox and Williams on Hunt Trust business, urging them to complete the transfer of the greater proportion of the Stock held by the Trustees to M[r] Geo. Hunt, and to deliver up the title deeds to M[r] Braikenridge as his agent. This I did on the suggestion of M[r.] |[176] Thornton in his letter received yesterday — A meeting of the Upper Slaughter Church and Charity estate Trustees was held in my study respecting repairs wanted in one of the cottages which is about to be tenanted by my house servant. — Transacted Provident Bank business at home. — Walked with the Carpenter to Joiner's downs barn, with a view to its being repaired this year, and to its being rebuilt next year. — Lord Campbell's Life of Lord Eldon. —

May 18. Thursday.

A showery day. — Drove to Stow: MW. accompanied me, and soon returned home after setting me down at the Provident Bank, where, later in the day, I met Winter and Morrison. — To the office of the Gloucestershire Banking Company, and to Mr Brookes's office, where I transacted business — At the Union Workhouse presided at the fortnightly meeting of Guardians |[177] from 11 AM. to 3 P.M. — Laid before the Board a letter addressed to me as Chairman from the P. L. Commrs. — (like letters having been addressed by them to Mr R. Cripps, as Treasurer of the Union, and to Pearce, as the Clerk) purporting that they had confirmed the surcharge made by Auditor Hunt on Mr Pearce. At the same time it should be observed that the offence imputed to him, at the utmost, only amounted to an irregularity, or technical error in the management, he having committed no moral offence, nor done any injury to the Union at large, or to any parish, or any individual. — The Auditor had surcharged one of the Guardians, (West of Icomb) for a supposed misconduct in the chair, which he had upon some occasion occupied during the absence of myself or the Vice Chairman; but this surcharge the P. L. Commrs. do not confirm, and so imply a tacit censure on the Auditor — |[178] The vast increase of trampers, as they are called, poor wanderers, wayfarers, and mendicants, claiming shelter and food, and lodging, at the Workhouse, came under consideration. This is a very serious evil: and the hardship is great on the parish in which the Workhouse is situate; for, as the law now stands, such paupers are chargeable on that parish exclusively. The crowd of nightly applicants, of whom by far the largest proportion are Irish, and most filthy or diseased, — many also insolent and turbulent — has latterly greatly increased, as the knowledge that they are admissible has been spread through this class of people. The apprehension least any such travellers should be cast away from want has led to the indiscriminate admission of all applicants, under the dread of incurring censure from the Central Authorities, who have, perhaps, too urgently pressed the |[179] duty of relieving casual paupers on the officials. The subject has been pressed by memorials & correspondence from different unions, and by our Guardians among others, on the P. L. Commrs. and by petitions on the Houses of Parliament; and it is expected that some legislative remedy will be devised, whereby the expence of maintenance may be more fairly met; also that restrictive orders may be issued, to ~~cheq~~ check indiscriminate admission — Received a letter from Chr. Geldard with the balance sheets of May-day rents received from our tenants in Craven, money disbursed &c. — A letter from Sophia Hunt on Hunt Trust and Executorship matters. — A letter from Mr Whitcombe on the same. A letter from Mr Thornton on the same — Lord Campbell's life of Lord Eldon.

May 19. Friday.

A rainy day; little interval between the showers, an enriching rain — Examined and posted Yorkshire accounts, |[180] and replied to the letter which I received yesterday from Chr. Geldard, sending him a cheque on Alcock & Co. for £200 in repayment of that sum which he advanced to me on loan towards the end of March last. — Copied a letter from Mʳ Tilleard to Mʳ Thornton on Hunt Trust concerns, which the latter had forwarded for my perusal. — Received a letter from Messʳˢ Cox and Williams as to the names and proper designations of the Hunt Trustees, the amount of Stock standing in their names, and the payment of the balance of bills due to Messʳˢ C. & W. for professional services to the Trustees. — Preparing a sermon – Wrote to G. Pain, Stow, on Provident Bank business — Transacted Prov. Bank business at home. — Lord Campbell's Life of Lord Eldon. — France has just passed through, or is passing through, the horrors of the second |¹⁸¹ revolution within the short space of three months. On the assembly of the National Convention, the Provisional Government resigned their authority into the hands of that body. Thus Lamartine and his Associates, motley men of various grades and shades of democracy, abdicated their power; but only to resume it in another modification of parties; for, a Commission of government being appointed by the National Assembly to exercise the functions of government until the new Constitution should have been settled and decreed, the same parties as before, with a few exceptions, and especially Lamartine and Ledra Rollin, have been nominated to carry on the public service. Moderate views are in the Ascendancy among the representatives of the people in the National Assembly, and of these Lamartine appears to be the advocate, and the leader of those Republicans, who do not hold extreme opinions. The minority, however, in the National Assembly, a firm, strong, active, |¹⁸² and unprincipled body, of whom Ledra Rollin is the leader, hold extreme republican views, and consists more or less of communists or socialists, or, as we should call such men, Chartists. These sympathize with the canaille of Paris, and congregate in Clubs, indulging in violent speeches and threatening assemblages. Their plans seem well organised, and they would appear to be ripe for any mischief. In contrast with them are the Bourgeoisie, who, for the most part, hold moderate opinions, and these form the great bulk of the National Guards — On the 15ᵗʰ the Communist and Clubbist mob invaded the Hall of Assembly, took it by storm, drove out the Moderates, expelled the members of the Executive Government, and declared the National Assembly dissolved; establishing a Provisional Government by their own chiefs, and so, for a brief season, usurped the supreme authority. But, as the Evening advanced, the National |¹⁸³ Guards recovered possession of the Hall of the National Assembly and of the Hotel de Ville, suppressed the mob, and made several arrests of the leaders — At home too our Government have a difficult game to play. In Ireland Smith O'Brien, and Meagher, have been indicted for sedition, but it has proved impossible to obtain a conviction against them. They were discharged, because the Juries could not agree on a Verdict. This is alarming, and such a state of things is calculated to encourage the Repealers, whether the moral force men whom O'Connel leads, rather by the Prestige of his Father's name than by his own waning influence, and who will probably soon dwindle into insignificance, or the Physical force Confederates, excited by such violent spirits as Smith O'Brien, Meagher, Dillon, O'Gorman, Doheny & others, who, in fact, are little better than openly revolutionary. Among them stands preeminent one Mitchell, a publisher of undisguised sedition in his most outrageous |¹⁸⁴ Journal. Still these men have not yet resorted to a declared and open out-break, and so the Government lacks the opportunity of suppressing them by the strong hand. |

(Diary

1848

1

May 20. Saturday — A showery forenoon; the afternoon fine. — Wrote letters to Cox and Williams, and to M.ʳ Thornton on Hunt Trust matters. — E. F. W. came from Stanway to luncheon, bringing a good account of his dear wife and children. We invited them all to pass a fortnight here from June 5. I accompanied my son in a ramble by the brook side, while he was fishing. About 5 P. M. he left us to return home. — Received a letter from M.ʳ Hare on Hunt Trust business. — Lord Campbell's Life of Lord Eldon.

May 21. Sunday. — Dull weather; a blight falling at times; a damp atmosphere — Visited the Sunday School. — Morning Service — Prayers and Sermon. — I preached on keeping the commandments — Evening service — prayers. — M.ʳˢ Dolphin called after morning service. — A letter from

Witts Family Papers F363

Diary — 1848

May 20. Saturday.

A showery forenoon; the afternoon fine — Wrote letters to Cox and Williams, and to Mr Thornton on Hunt Trust matters — E.F.W. came from Stanway to luncheon, bringing a good account of his dear wife and children We invited them all to pass a fortnight here from June 5. I accompanied my son in a ramble by the brookside, while he was fishing. About 5 P.M. he left us to return home — Received a letter from Mr Hare on Hunt Trust business. — Lord Campbell's Life of Lord Eldon.

May 21. Sunday.

Dull weather; a blight falling at times; a damp atmosphere — Visited the Sunday School. — Morning Service — Prayers and Sermon. — I preached on keeping the commandments — Evening service — prayers. — M$^{rs.}$ Dolphin called after morning service. — A letter from |^2 Mr Thornton on Hunt Trust affairs; he forwards for my perusal a letter he has received from Mr Braikenridge — Preparing a Sermon. —

May 22. Monday.

A dull morning; the afternoon and evening fine — Wrote to Mess$^{rs.}$ Cox and Williams on Hunt Trust business, as suggested by Mr Thornton in his letter received by me yesterday. — Copied the letter from Mr Braikenridge to Mr Thornton, which the latter had forwarded to me — Justice business at home — Drove to Stow with MW. — At the Library conferred with G. Pain as to supplying books to Mr Kennaway, the incumbent of Campden, who wishes to become a member of our Book Society, and whom my son proposes to nominate. I had previously written to Mr K. on the subject. — At the library met and conversed with W. B. Pole. — Called on the Vavasours at "the Cottage", but |^3 as they were from home, we left our cards — To the Workhouse, where I conferred with Mr Pearce on Union business, looked over the minutes, visited the wards &c. — Gave directions to Superintendent Makepeace as to apprehending and searching trampers and Mendicants — Lord Campbell's Life of Lord Eldon.

May 23. Tuesday.

Fine weather. — Wrote to Mr Whitcombe on Hunt Trust and Executorship matters, answering the letter which I received from him last week. — Preparing a sermon. — Walked with MW. to Eyford. We called on M$^{rs.}$ Dolphin and Miss C. Knight. M$^{rs.}$ D. took me aside, with whom I had a long and painful téte à téte, she being much agitated. The subject was a design eagerly taken up by her, to obtain a divorce from her husband on the ground of his irregularities of conduct, and living in a state of disgraceful concubinage. It seems that he has never left |⁴ England, as has been generally supposed, but has been residing, at least of late, at or near Fareham in Hants, where he keeps a mistress, having lived on the supplies furnished to him by Mʳˢ· Dolphin, not exceeding £200 per ann, for several years past, but now discontinued, on account of the disgust excited by his hopeless profligacy, of which she has procured, as she alleges, ample testimony. In common with other friends to whom she has intimated her design of suing for a divorce, (Bowen, Harry Waller &c.) I strongly dissuaded her, pointing out that although her conduct had been beyond censure, yet there were circumstances in her case nearly, if not quite, amounting to a condonation of her husband's crime — that the Legislature wisely interposes difficulties in the accomplishment of such a design as she meditates, requiring the case to be most fully established, and the wife to be free from all possible suspicion or ap-|⁵ pearance of having directly or indirectly countenanced her husband's immoralities. I reminded her that, while the issue was uncertain, a most painful exposure, and expensive process were inevitable; and urged her strongly not to take any step without the clearest sanction on the part of lawyers of known eminence in the management of such delicate and difficult business. — On our return home we found that Mʳ and Mʳˢ· Vavasour and Miss Grayson, their guest and relation, had called upon us. — Lord Campbell's Life of Lord Eldon.

May 24. Wednesday.

Very fine weather — Wrote to Sophia Hunt, sending her a copy of the letter which I wrote yesterday to Mʳ Whitcombe, and answering her last letter on Hunt Trust and Executorship business. — Justice business at home. — Received a letter from Chr. Geldard, who now for the first time informs me that the £200 which he remitted to me at the end of March, and which I |⁶ understood to have been a loan made by him, was, in fact, received from the North Western railway company in part payment of the land at Ravenflatt which we have sold to them. He, therefore, asks, whether he shall pay to the company the cheque for £200, which I lately sent to him in repayment of his supposed accommodation, and so leave the whole amount of the purchase made by the Company in their hands at 5 per Cent Interest, or whether he shall return me the cheque. — We drove to Farmington, and called on Mʳ and Mʳˢ· Boudier: the former was engaged in superintending the repair and restoration of the Chancel of his Church, the funds for which have been kindly supplied to him by some of his former pupils. The Chancel and Aisle of the Church present some interesting specimens of Old Norman and Early English Architecture, but the building has at various times, and even of late, been sadly |⁷ modernized and mutilated. — Harry Waller has lately built a school room for the children of the parish. — On our way to Farmington we met and parleyed with Mʳ and Mʳˢ· Biscoe driving out with their children — Lord Campbell's Life of Lord Eldon.

May 25. Thursday.

Beautiful weather — Wrote to Chr. Geldard, desiring him to return to me my cheque for £200. — Justice business at home. — Drove to Stow with MW. who soon returned to Upper Slaughter — Received a letter from C Bathurst, who enquires my opinion of the character of Mʳ Heaton, the Assistant Chaplain of the County Gaol. — A letter from Mʳ Thornton on Hunt Trust business: he returns to me different letters which I had sent for his perusal. — To the Provident Bank — To the Workhouse, where I conferred with Mʳ Pearce on

Union matters. — At the Justice room sat with R Waller as Magistrate, W B Pole being our Assessor. — |[8] Tax business awaited us as well as Justice business. — The Misses Hall called on MW. during my absence at Stow — Lord Campbell's Life of Lord Eldon. —

May 26. Friday.

Fine summer weather — Wrote to C Bathurst in answer to his letter received yesterday. — to Mess[rs.] Coutts, desiring them to transfer to the account of Captain John Hunt one seventh share, with the dividend due thereon, of the Stock divisible under the will of M[rs.] M. Hunt, on the decease of Caroline Hunt: — to the Secretary of the Comm. of the Privy Council on Education, that I had received a volume of reports on Education in Wales, which had been sent to me by reason of my holding the situation of Chairman of a Union — Preparing Quarterly papers S.P.G. for circulation among the members of the Stow Distr. Comm. — Received letters from the Bank of England as to the powers of Att[y.] granted by the Hunt Trustees for the sale |[9] and transfer of Bank Stock and 3 P[t.] C[t.] Cons. standing in their names, about to be made over to M[r] George Hunt. This is a recent provision intended to obviate a fraudulent dealing with stock by forged powers of Attorney, such as were imposed on the Bank by a Solicitor named Barber, who was tried and convicted of the offence some time ago — Lord Campbell's Life of Lord Eldon.

May 27. Saturday.

Very fine weather — Returned to the Chief Accountant of the Bank of England the papers which I had received yesterday, having properly filled them up, with the amount of 3 P[t.] C[t.] Cons. and Bank Stock to be transferred to M[r] Hunt by the Wadenhoe Trustees, Mess[rs.] Cox & Williams being the parties to whom we have granted the powers of Attorney — Copying reports of the Stow Distr. Comm. S.P.G. — Posting accounts. — Justice business at home. — Received a letter from M[r] Hare, who forwards to me |[10] the powers of Attorney for the transfer of Hunt Trust Stock to M[r] G. Hunt, that I may execute them: he also sends a letter from Mess[rs.] Cox & Williams. — A letter from M[r] Thornton, who returns to me a copy of a letter of mine to Mess[rs.] Cox & Williams which I had sent for his perusal. M[r] T. Comments on Hunt trust affairs. — MW. received a letter from Sophy: all well at the Vicarage, Stanway: they promise to visit us from June 5[th.] to 17[th.]

May 28. Sunday.

Delightful weather — Visited the Sunday School — Preparing a Sermon. — Morning service, prayers; Afternoon service, prayers and a Sermon. I preached on the destruction of the Canaanites — M[rs.] Dolphin called here after the morning, and Miss C. Knight after the Evening service — Received a letter from Chr. Geldard, who returns to me the cheque for £200, which I had sent him. — Preparing for the approaching discussion |[11] at the Ruri-decanal meeting — Ecclesiastical gazette. — To the family a section from James on the Collects. —

May 29. Monday.

Very fine weather; in the evening a copious and beneficent shower of rain. — Wrote to M[r] Thornton and to M[r] Hare on Hunt Trust matters; sending to the former, now visiting his connections near Town, the powers of Attorney for the transfer to M[r] George Hunt of the Hunt Trust Stock, and to the latter a copy of a late letter of mine to Messrs. Cox and Williams; gave Mr Hare a sketch of what I take to be the present state of our matters as regards all the parties concerned. — Copying Report Stow Distr. Comm. S.P.G. — Drove to Stow with MW. who went on to call on M^rs. Potter at Broadwell, and took me up, when she returned. — Called on Mr G. Pain and Mr J. Clark, whom I got to witness my execution of the powers of Attorney which I sent from Stow to M^r. |^12 Thornton by the post. — Called at the Workhouse: Mr Pearce absent: visited the Girls' school there. — Met and chatted with Perkins, Wiggin &c. — M^r and M^rs. W. B. Pole had called on us during our absence from home. — Mr Terry called after we returned. — Concluded Lord Campbell's very amusing life of Lord Eldon.

May 30. Tuesday.

Very fine weather — Visited the daily school — Justice business at Stow. — Wrote to Alcock, Birkbecks and C^o., desiring them to direct their London Correspondents to pay £200 to my account with Messrs. Hoare, and A.B. & Co. to debit my account with them to that amount. — Wrote to Howell — M^r and M^rs. Aston, with their daughter Mary, visited us, partook of luncheon, and spent two or three hours here. — Rec^d. a letter from Mr Boye, Paymaster of the Bombay Pensioners, with a full account of the present circumstances of |^13 Mr Edward Hunt. This letter is a reply to one written by me on Feb. 15. last to Major Rowley Superintendent of Pensioners, Bombay establishment. — In the evening E.F.W. called on us, drinking tea with us on his return to Stanway from Stow, where he had been playing Cricket — All were well at the Vicarage. — Ranke's History of the Reformation in Germany.[1] —

May 31. Wednesday.

Fine weather in the forenoon and evening: a beneficent shower in the afternoon. — Wrote to Sophia Hunt, forwarding to her the letter received by me yesterday relative to her brother Edward. — Copying reports Stow Distr. Comm. S.P.G. — Posting accounts. — A letter from Messrs. Coutts, announcing that they had transferred from the account of Mr Hare and myself, as Trustees, to that of Capt. John Hunt, one seventh part of the 3 P^r C^t. Cons. divisible under the will of M^rs. M. Hunt upon the decease of Miss M. C. Hunt, between |^14 her surviving brothers and sisters. — John Mitchell, the Editor of "United Irishman", a Dublin inflammatory newspaper, having been indicted for a treasonable felony under a recent act for the security of the Queen's person, throne, and dignity, has been found guilty, and sentenced to fourteen years transportation. This has created a great sensation in Ireland, but has not led to any positive outbreak on the part of the confederated body and their adherents, who are probably preparing for insurrection. Mitchell after his conviction avowed and gloried in his offence, and was wisely removed without delay on board a steamer, which conveyed him to Cork, whence he is to be shipped by a vessel of war dispatched for the purpose to the hulks at Bermuda. Not only did the convict boast of his offence, but his Counsel sympathized with him, joining in the denunciation against Judges, Sheriff, and Jurors as corrupt and packed — |^15 — Ranke's history of the Reformation in Germany.

---

1. Leopold von Ranke (1795-1886). *History of the Reformation in Germany* (1845-47).

June 1. Thursday.

A cold air; occasional showers; rain at night. — Drove to Stow — MW. accompanied me, but returned after having set me down. — A letter from Sophia Hunt, who forwards to me copies of a letter on Trust business which she had received from one of M⁺ G. Hunt's daughters, written by his desire, and of the answer she (S.H.) had sent in reply, which is not calculated to smoothe matters. — A letter from M⁺ Hare on Hunt Trust affairs — A letter from M⁺ Thornton on the same interminable and annoying subject. — From R Waller a note announcing the next meeting of the Stow Clerical Society as fixed for June 7ᵗʰ. — A letter from the Dean of Gloucester on a nuisance of which he complains — that R. Beman works a steam thrashing portable machine so near the highway at Broadwell as to be |¹⁶ dangerous to persons riding or driving by it. — At Stow met and conversed with M⁺ Sewell. — Attended at the Savings Bank, meeting there Winter, W B Pole, Morrison, and the Dean of Gloucester. — Transacted magistrate's business with M⁺ Brookes and his Clerk at their office — Presided at the fortnightly meeting of the Guardians of our Union — Ranke's Hist. of the Reformation in Germany.

June 2. Friday.

With the exception of two or three passing showers, a fine day — After breakfast drove to Bourton on the Water to attend the annual meeting of the Friendly Society. MW. accompanied me to Bourton, and then returned home. I joined the honorary and ordinary members of the Club at the Club room, where I met Messʳˢ· Ford, R. Waller, Boggis &c. — Walked in procession to the church. The prayers were read by R Waller, the sermon preached by M⁺ Boggis, who |¹⁷ delivered a good, plain, and suitable sermon, though rather dull and monotonous. — Afterwards followed the Club dinner, with its disagreeables, Punch and Tobacco: yet not unsatisfactory, as a discharge of duty in countenancing a praiseworthy institution, and keeping up a kindly feeling between the employers and the employed. Ford having an engagement did not dine with us; but, with R. Waller in the Chair, there were present, of honorary members, Messʳˢ· W. and Jos. Bryan, Wilkins, Stenson, J. Bennett, Palmer, Ransfords, Senʳ and Junʳ — &c. — The younger Ransford, the London Singer, on a visit to his family, and on a professional tour with his musical son and daughter, giving concerts in country towns, like a Scottish Wilson, indulged us with many songs well sung with a fine voice. — It appears that the Club numbers 54 ordinary members, with a fund of £421. This is the |¹⁸ eleventh anniversary, and it is somewhat remarkable that the amount of payments made to sick members ⁱⁿ ᵗʰᵉ ˡᵃˢᵗ ʸᵉᵃʳ hardly exceeded £4. — Left the Club room at 5 P.M. — partook of coffee at the Rectory — Mʳˢ· R Waller absent from home, visiting her relations at Eton. — I walked home — From two servants from Stanway, who were at the Club, we had good accounts of our dear children and grandchildren — Ranke's Hist. of the Reformation in Germany. —

June 3. Saturday.

A few occasional showers: otherwise fine. — Wrote to M⁺ Thornton, to whom I sent for his perusal copies of letters which had passed on Hunt Trust business between Miss Sophia Hunt, and her cousin, a daughter of M⁺ Geo. Hunt; Sophia had sent me these letters for my perusal — Received a letter from M⁺ Pearce with enclosures relative to an application to be made by the Relieving Officer, Dunford, |¹⁹ for the remission of the surcharge imposed upon him by

M[r] Hunt, the Auditor of the Union. D. memorializes the Poor Law Comm[rs.] — Wrote a note to Pearce in reply. — Justice business at home. — Walked with MW. to Eyford: called on M[rs.] Dolphin, and M[rs.] Hutchinson, wife to M[rs.] D's brother, who, with her sister, Miss C Knight, is now on a visit at Eyford. — M[rs.] Dolphin, as usual, in great agitation, and much excited, having received fresh details of the profligate habits of her husband, from whom she is now more and more bent upon obtaining a divorce. — MW. received a pleasant note from dear Sophy: all well at Stanway Vicarage. — Preparing for the business to come on at the Ruridecanal meeting on Wednesday next. — Ranke's History of the Reformation in Germany.

June 4. Sunday.

A showery day. — Visited the Sunday School. — Morning service, prayers, and sermon. I preached on |[20] the Ascension of our Saviour. — Afternoon service, prayers. — A letter from Fred Aston, with an invitation to us, and our party, — E.F.W. — Sophy and Broome — to pass next Friday at the Vicarage, Northleach. — A letter from M[rs.] Barr, with an indifferent account of herself and children, and the other inmates of Henwick Hall. — Preparing for the discussion appointed for the ruri-decanal meeting on Wednesday next. — To the family a section from James on the Collects.

June 5. Monday.

Showery weather — justice business at home — Replied to the letter I had received yesterday from Aston, accepting his invitation to Northleach for Friday next. — Preparing for the approaching discussion at the Decanal meeting at Stow. — Our dear children and grandchildren arrived from Stanway on a visit to us.

June 6. Tuesday.

A very fine forenoon; a |[21] heavy shower in the afternoon; a fine evening — Justice business at home. — This day being appointed for the playing a match at Cricket between the members of the Stow Club, and those of the Ombersley Club, Worcestershire, my son and daughter, with their eldest boy drove to Stow – E.F.W. to play, and Sophy and Broome to be spectators, and visit the Vavasours at "the Cottage"; they left with us the two other dear boys as pledges of their return, and came home after 9 P.M. – the match not being decided. — Received a letter from Mess[rs.] Hoare, announcing that they have received on my account from Mess[rs.] Alcock, Birkbecks and C[o.] £200. — Wrote to Mess[rs.] Hoare, desiring them to invest that sum for me in £ 3 P[r.] C[t.] Consols. — Preparing for the discussion expected tomorrow at our ruridecanal meeting — Rec[d.] a letter from the wife of a poor Lincolnshire Clergyman, begging for charity. — M[r] Moore, Med. Off. |[22] of the Union called in the evening to request from me an order into the Gloucester Infirmary for a poor boy at Great Barrington which I gave.

June 7. Wednesday.

A showery day — E.F.W. accompanied me to Stow in the phaeton after breakfast. He went up to join the Cricketers, and play out the match commenced yesterday: the Stow party was victorious: their Worcestershire opponents left them in good humour after an early dinner at the Unicorn. — E.F.W. returned home without waiting to accompany me in the evening, after my Clerical engagements — On reaching Stow I went to the Workhouse, and transacted Union business with Mr Pearce — I was also occupied with Justice business at Stow. — At twelve o clock went to afternoon prayers at the Church, Mr Wiggin officiating for Mr Hippisley, who was suffering from a bad cold. After service the Clergy met at |²³ the National School room for a ruri-decanal gathering under the presidency of Mr Ford. There were present Messrs· Hippisley, Biscoe, Terry, Potter, Wiggin, Morrison, Hill (of Notgrove) and myself. R W Hippisley read a paper on the following thesis — "the Church of Christ: — the ministers are divinely appointed, and Episcopal ordination is necessary." The essay was orthodox and moderate, and in a right spirit — I followed at some length with observations corroborating the opinions which had been laid down, touching on all the points, as to the antiquity and Apostolical origin of Episcopacy, the errors of the Roman Church as to ordination, shewing that the Primitive ages recognized only the three orders, Bishop, Priest and Deacon, that the inferior orders were modern, resting on no warrant of Scripture or antiquity. I pointed out the errors of dissenters in rejecting Episcopacy and in ordination by Presbyters. My views I |²⁴ corroborated by references to and quotations from the Fathers, and from Hooker, and other standard divines of our Church — Mr Biscoe followed with a few remarks confirmatory of what had been said by Hippisley and myself. — There were present at the Clerical dinner at the Unicorn Inn, Morrison, occupying the Chair, Messrs· Ford, Winter, Wiggin, Potter, Boggis, Terry, Hippisley, and myself — I brought home Mr Boggis in my carriage, who passed the evening with us; the family circle clustering round the tea table, & offording to my wife & me great pleasure.

June 8. Thursday.

A rainy forenoon; the afternoon and evening fine — Began mowing for my haycrop. — Drove to Stow; attended at the Provident Bank, where I met Messrs· Winter and R Waller — Transacted business at the office of the Gloucestershire Banking Company. — |²⁵ To the Workhouse, where I conferred with Pearce and Dunford on Union business. — At the Justice room, sat as magistrate with the Dean of Gloucester, Ford, and Robt· Waller. Messrs· W B Pole, and Winter were our assessors — A good deal of business. — As I returned home to dinner two of my dear grandsons met me at Lower Slaughter, and enjoyed a drive home in the phaeton — E.F.W. and Sophy had ridden to Maugersbury to the W. Vavasours, with whom and Mr Henry Rice they went on horseback to Blockley, Northwick &c. Received letters — from Mr Thornton, who returns to me the copies of the correspondence between Miss M. Hunt, Sophia H. and Mr Geo. Hunt, on Wadenhoe Trust business, which I had sent for his perusal — from Messrs· Cox and Williams with a copy of a letter from Mr Braikenridge addressed to them on the subject of the Turnpike securities, which I hold — |²⁶ from Messrs· Hoare, announcing that they have invested for me £200 in the purchase of £236. 13. 8. 3 P^r C^t· Cons. — Sent a donation of one shilling to the Rev^d· F. Sturmer, a Lincolnshire Clergyman, from whose wife I had received a begging letter. — An enjoyable domestic evening.

June 9. Friday.

A fine forenoon; in the afternoon heavy rain came on, and continued to fall without ceasing till bedtime. — Visited and prayed with a sick parishioner — Wrote to Messrs· Cox and Williams on Hunt business, and dispatched to them from Northleach a packet of documents, being the securities for the Northamptonshire Turnpike-roads money, formerly lent ~~but~~ ^{by} the Hunt family, and now due to the Wadenhoe Estate, to the legatees of Mrs. M. Hunt, to the Messrs. Briggs, and to Mr Hare in different proportions. For some time past I had held |²⁷ these securities for the different parties; and they are now to be handed to Mr Braikenridge, as Solicitor for Mr Geo. Hunt, to whom, as proprietor of the Wadenhoe ~~pro~~ estate the greater share in this mortgage loan belongs, and who is therefore the proper party to hold the Securities. — Received a letter from Sophia Hunt, who forwards for my perusal a letter received by her from her Brother Edward in India — I also received a letter addressed to me by E.H. writing from Daprolee Camp, near Bombay, where he resides — a pensioner on the Bombay pension list. — A letter from Mr Thornton on Hunt Trust matters, who forwards to me for my perusal one which he has rec^{d.} from Mr Braikenridge — With MW. Sophy and Broome drove to Northleach to visit the Aston family, E.F.W. riding thither, and calling ~~at~~ ^{on} the Biscoes at Turkdean by the way. All F. Aston's family at home. The midshipman, my |²⁸ godson, George, is a very fine and promising lad, now on leave for a few days to visit his family: since he entered into the service he has been on board the St Vincent man of war, one of the largest and finest ships in the Service, stationed at Portsmouth, Lisbon or Cork &c, or cruizing with an experimental Squadron in the Channel and Atlantic, bearing the Admiral Sir Charles Napier's flag. Thus he has had the best advantages for a naval education, and is well reported of. It is to be lamented that his elder brother, Frederick, has no occupation, no profession. He has been a student at the Engineer's college at Putney, but his parents have removed him from thence under a feeling that the establishment is likely to injure his moral character, from the dissipated habits of the students, while he is not likely to benefit by the studies of the place: in fact, the professional services of |²⁹ men versed in engineering are not now in such demand as when the railway mania was at its height, and when the country had not experienced a reverse of prosperity and a scarcity of capital, checking the progress of all great enterprizes, and extinguishing many; so that only the most skilful and scientific are called into employment. This, however, may be a temporary suspension only. But the truth also is that the young man and his parents are somewhat fastidious — the lad not being fond of steady and persevering application; though possessed of very fair abilities, he seems to like an idle lounging life — would devote himself to fox-hunting, cricket and the like with great energy, being of an excitable temperament. It is much to be lamented that he has not yet fallen into a settled and steady course of occupation — Sophy, the younger daughter has left, or is immediately about to leave, the school at Cheltenham at which she has |³⁰ been educated, and is a very pretty and pleasing girl of seventeen. — The two boys and Broome accompanied me to visit the Bridewell, where every thing appeared to be very clean, and in good order. Inspected the prison minutely, particularly the new or altered parts, and those in which the separate system of imprisonment is in operation; also the School for boy prisoners. The prison is very crowded. — Returning, found the others from the Vicarage viewing the fine old church; my son had now joined the party. — An early dinner followed, at which Mr Gibson, Rector of Chedworth, was a guest, a sensible, quaint old bachelor. — Music was the accompaniment of our coffee, after partaking of which we left our hospitable friends, reaching home by 9 P.M. — The close carriage protected us, but Edward was drenched with the rain, as he rode home.

June 10. Saturday.

Fine weather till the |³¹ evening, when rain fell — Soon after breakfast my son left us for Winchcomb, to attend the meeting of the Guardians of that Union, and thence going to Stanway to be ready for his duties to-morrow: he purposes to return to us to-morrow to dinner. — Preparing a sermon. — Justice business at home — Walked with dearest Sophy and her children to Joiners downs, and back: enjoying a little domestic pic-nic of our own, by the "Seven wells." — On our return I found a most unexpected note from Vernon Dolphin, dated Broadwell, in which he begs me to meet him at noon to-day at Messʳˢ· Wilkins and Kendall's office; if I could not come, he would call on me. Fortunately for myself I did not receive his note till five hours after the time appointed, and so have thus far been spared a very unpleasant interview. There seems to be at hand a crisis in the affairs of the misguided pair who have so sadly engaged the |² conversation of the neighbourhood; both by their folly, he by his vices. I believe I should have gone at his request to meet him, on the principle that having been cognisant of Mʳˢ· Dolphin's complaints of his misconduct, and heard her story, it would be unfair not to listen to him; but I should have gone resolved not to mix myself up in their disputes. She, I believe, has been this week in Town, consulting lawyers as to her project of obtaining a divorce, and seeking evidence of his adulteries, which it is expected a cast off mistress will afford. His object, after so many years absence from Gloucestershire, in coming so near to Eyford, and "fluttering his Volscians in their dove cote" remains to be seen.² Perhaps he hopes to intimidate his wife into a restoration of those pecuniary supplies which she has latterly withheld, or may have hopes to set aside the arrangement by which she has |³ long been mistress at Eyford. — MW. had received a letter from Fanny Hunt who is now with Maria on a visit at Gloucester: Sophia remains with Thomas and Sarah at Clifton, the latter in so declining a state that no attempt can be made at present to remove her to Stoke Doyle. —

June 11. Sunday – Whitsunday.

A fine day, though cloudy and close: only a few drops of rain fell. — Visited the Sunday School. — Wrote to Vernon Dolphin explaining to him that I did not receive his letter till 5 P.M. yesterday, and therefore could not meet him at Bourton at the hour he had named. — Enclosed my note under cover to Mʳ Polhill, to whom I wrote a few lines, requesting him to forward my note to V.D. if he had left Broadwell — Wrote to Turner, fishmonger, London, for a dish of fish for a party to dinner on Wednesday. — Morning service. Prayers and the administration of the |²⁴ Holy Communion: 22 Communicants — Afternoon Service — prayers and sermon. I preached on "the nature and office of the Holy Ghost." — Walked with Sophy and dear Broome to Eyford to meet E.F.W. returning from Stanway. Encountered Mʳˢ· Hutchinson and Miss C Knight, with whom conversed as to the agitating affair of Vernon Dolphin's visit to Mʳ Polhill at Broadwell. The latter had not invited, nor expected him, and, on finding him at his house, came to Eyford to announce to Mʳˢ· Dolphin the arrival of her husband. As far as the ladies explained what had taken place, V.D. has not presented himself at Eyford, nor sought an interview with his wife; but has caused to be

2.   The Volscians were an ancient warlike people formerly inhabiting the east of Latium in central Italy, subdued by the Romans in the fourth century BC.

made to her some proposition ^{to} which she cannot and will not accede — neither can I, as it is believed, consent to the proposition Mr D. meant to make to me. — Mrs. D. had |²⁵ gone to consult Mr Bowen at Guiting, and had been in communication with Mr Kendall — E.F.W., returning from his duties at Stanway, met us at Eyford. —

June 12. Monday.

A fine, but dull forenoon; a rainy ^{after}forenoon and evening. — Wrote to Mr Clarke, Icomb, to invite him to dinner on Wednesday next; — to Messrs. Hoare, desiring them to transfer £35 from my account to the account of my Son — Preparing a sermon — Justice business at home. — MW. with Sophy, and the two elder boys drove to Stow and back, shopping: it had been their intention to have gone on to Moreton; but meeting Mrs. Vavasour, Mrs. W.V. and Emma Vavasour on their way to call here, they returned to receive them, and after they had left, went out again in the Carriage — E.F.W. accompanied me in a walk to Lower Swell, to call on J. Perkins. We found him languid and feeble — |²⁶ Received a letter from Messrs. Cox and Williams who acknowledged having received from me the Hunt Turnpike bonds, to be handed to Mr Braikenridge.

June 13. Thurssday.

A showery day — Wrote to Mr Thornton on Hunt Trust matters, returned to him a letter from Mr Braikenridge which he had forwarded for my perusal. — Preparing a Sermon. — E.F.W. went to Stow, to join the Cricketers, but came back to dinner. — Sophy and Broome rode to Bourton to call on Mrs. R. Waller. I met them near Lower Slaughter as they returned, and walked home by their side. — Met Mr Clarke, who declines our invitation for dinner to-morrow. — So also Mr Boggis whom I had asked to join our party. — It appears as if Vernon Dolphin had abandoned his intention of seeking an interview or otherwise communicating with me. |²⁷

June 14. Wednesday.

Very little rain to-day — Justice business at home. — Preparing a Sermon. — Rec^{d.} a letter from Messrs. Hoare, informing me that they had transferred £35. from my account with them to that of my Son. — A circular from Gloucester Gaol announcing a meeting of the Board of Vis. Justices. — A letter from a Capt. Tucker, R.E. from Wakefield. This officer is engaged in the Ordnance Trigonometrical Survey, and seeks information from me as to the boundaries of the Townships of Coniston and Otterburn on our Ravenflatt Estate. It seems that Mr Garforth, the principal land owner in Coniston, asserts a different boundary from that which is recognized by the inhabitants of the respective townships. Mr G. relies on the tithe map of Coniston, and a map of the manor of Coniston: a reference to the Estate Map of Ravenflatt is requested. To this I |²⁸ referred, and it confirms Mr Garforth's assertion: but this does not settle the question, because it is probable that our estate map may have been based upon the Coniston maps produced by Mr Garforth, as far as the laying down of the boundary. I traced the line as laid down on our Estate map, and sent the tracing to Capt. Tucker, with my comments thereon, referring him for further information, if any were required, to Mr Geldard — Walked with dearest Sophy to Eyford slate quarries, whither E.F.W. had preceded us to collect any fossils which the Quarrymen might have put aside for him, and whom we found in the Slate Quarries. We all returned together by the Thorn Valley — a delightful walk. — A dinner party. Our company consisted of M^r and M^rs. Wiggin, M^r and M^rs. W. B. Pole, M^r and M^rs. J. T. Rice, M^r and M^rs. |²⁹ W. Vavasour, and Emma Vavasour.

June 15. ~~Friday~~ Thursday.

Fine weather — After breakfast drove to Stow, accompanied by my daughter and the two elder boys, who were going to "the Cottage" by appointment, that from thence they might visit the Cricket field, where a match was to be played between the members of the Stow and Purton Cricket Clubs; this was the return game, the Stow Cricketers having been beaten, I believe, last year by their Wiltshire antagonists at Purton. E.F.W. rode to Stow, and met us there. As we drove up we overtook R Waller, & Mr Stenson, accompanied by Mr Barnes, a Berkshire or Oxfordshire Clergyman, and a noted Cricketer, a member of the Stow Club, on whose skill and good play much depends. Chatted with Stenson as we slowly ascended the hill. — Learnt from Mr Wilkins that Vernon Dolphin had quitted the neighbourhood, some arrange-|³⁰ ment having been made as between the husband and wife, in which Harry Waller and Mr Polhill were the negociating parties. It appears that he wished to see me to make oath before me, as a magistrate, that he was not guilty of certain matters imputed to him. It is clear that I should have overstepped my duty as a magistrate, if I had listened to such a proposition, or administered an oath to him, there being no matter pending in which I possessed any jurisdiction — To the Provident Bank, where I met Mr Pole, who with M^rs. P. has lately arrived from Town at their seat, Wyck Hill — To the Workhouse, where I was engaged from 11.½ to 3 PM. presiding at the fortnightly meeting of the Guardians of our Union. — Sophy and her dear children joined me at the Provident Bank office, and we drove home to dress for dinner at Mr Ford's, MW. accompanying |³¹ us. E.F.W. was prevented from going, as the match at Stow was not played out. — The party at Little Risington consisted of ~~himself~~ M^r F and wife and three daughters, M^r and M^rs. Pole, Mr Lewes, Mr Wiggin, Mr Hutchinson, with his two sisters, and ourselves. In the latter part of the evening we were joined by a Clergyman from Berks, a member of the Purton Cricket Club, and, as such, one who had been engaged in the match at Stow; he is married to one of Mr Ford's numerous nieces; his name Harene — On our return home, between 11 & 12 o clock, we found E.F.W. awaiting us, having enjoyed a good day's sport, with every prospect of concluding the game by beating the Purton Club to-morrow. — Received letters from Mr Thornton and Mr Braikenridge on Hunt Trust matters — Mr B. sends a correspondence between Mr Thornton and Messrs. Cox and |³² Williams for my perusal.

June 16. Friday.

A beautiful summer's day. — E.F.W. went, after breakfast, to conclude the cricket match at Stow, returning to a late dinner, victorious over the Purton players. — Wrote to Mr Braikenridge on Hunt Trust matters — Received from Sophia Hunt a letter with enclosures; she forwards a balance sheet of accounts of bills paid at Clifton &c. relating to our joint executorship to the will of her sister Caroline — she returns to me the letter from Mr Boye respecting her brother Edward, which I had forwarded for her perusal. The account which she gives of her eldest Sister, Sarah, is very unfavourable: it will not be possible, apparently, to remove her alive to Stoke Doyle – Her death seems near at hand. — MW. and Sophy, with Broome and Frederick, drove to Oddington, and had luncheon there with the |[33] Dean of Gloucester, and the Wiggins — Justice business at home — Greatly enjoying the society of my dear children and grand children.

June 17. Saturday.

Very heavy rain had fallen in the night, and continued in the morning: the weather later in the day fine — Parted with great regret from our dear children and grand children, who returned to Stanway. We had greatly enjoyed their society. Our open carriage conveyed some of the party, and when it returned in the evening we received a note from E.F.W. announcing that all had arrived at home safely. — Justice business at home — Wrote to M[r] Hare on Hunt Trust matters. — M[rs.] Dolphin and Miss C Knight called on us; no mention made of V.D. — I am suffering from a bad cold. — Ranke's Hist. of the Reformation in Germany. —

June 18. Sunday.

After heavy rain during |[34] the night, a rainy morning; the forenoon and afternoon were fine; the evening wet — Visited the Sunday School — Trinity Sunday. — Morning service, prayers and sermon. I preached the first of two sermons on the Trinity. — Evening service – prayers. — Received a letter from M[r] Thornton on Hunt Trust business; he forwards for my perusal two letters which he had received from M[r] Braikenridge — I received also a letter from M[r] Hare, and another from M[r] Braikenridge, all on the very annoying, and, apparently, interminable affair of the Wadenhoe trust, which is protracted by the ill temper, suspicions, grasping, jealousies, and irritability of some or all the parties concerned. The Trustees would gladly be released: but the adverse claims and demands of the Representatives of the late life tenant on the one hand, and the remainder man on the other, with |[35] the bickerings of attorneys, preclude an amicable arrangement. — Rec[d.] circulars from the Clerk of the Peace's office, giving notice of committee meetings at Gloucester in the Sessions week, on June 26, as to the County rate assessment, and erection of new buildings in the Prisons, with other points of Prison administration. — Preparing a sermon. — Ecclesiastical Gazette — To the family a section from James on the Collects. — Oppressed with a cold and hoarseness. —

June 19. Monday.

Very fine weather — Justice business at home. — Wrote to D[r] Williams, Superintendent of the Lunatic Asylum at Gloucester, respecting a pauper lunatic of the parish of Condicote, who is confined at M[r] Mallam's private Madhouse at Hooknorton, and of whom it is reported that she is sufficiently recovered to return home. This is one of a number of pauper lunatics placed out at the |[36] Hooknorton establishment, in consequence of the accommodations at the Gloucester Lunatic Asylum being insufficient for the reception of all the County Lunatic paupers. — Wrote to M[r] Braikenridge and M[r] Thornton on Hunt Trust affairs; returned to the latter the letters from M[r] Braikenridge which he had sent for my perusal. — M[r] Price of Coln S[t] Dennis, and his youngest daughter by the first wife, called on us, and partook of luncheon. He came to confer with me on the County rate valuations, and the proceedings of the County rate committee — Drove with MW. to call on M[rs.] Pole at Wyck Hill, who was not at home. M[r] Pole was gone to London — Left my card for M[r] Terry at Wick Risington, where M[r] Cooke is building, and has nearly finished a Schoolroom, with cottage for Schoolmistress attached — Met and chatted |[37] with M[rs.] W. Vavasour and Emma V. who were driving to call on Miss Lindow. — I felt much indisposed with rheumatic or dyspeptic aches and pains. — Ranke's History of the Reformation in Germany.

June 20. Tuesday.

Beautiful weather — Wrote to Sophia Hunt and M[r] Hare on Hunt Trust business, returning to the former the letter from her brother Edward which she had sent for my perusal. — Justice business at home. — Copying report of the Stow Distr. Comm. S.P.G. for 1847. — Preparing a sermon. — Less indisposed to-day than yesterday. — Ranke's History of the Reformation in Germany.

June 21. Wednesday.

Very fine summer weather. — Wrote to M[rs.] C. Barr. — Rec[d.] a letter from M[r] Bloxsome respecting his half yearly bill on the County for business done as Deputy Clerk of the Peace — The bill itself also arrived with a |[38] letter from M[r] Riddiford. — A letter from M[r] Thornton on Hunt Trust matters; he forwards to me a letter which he had received from M[r] Braikenridge to the same effect as the last which I received from that gentleman. — A letter from Sophia Hunt on Executorship business, accompanying one from Fanny Hunt to MW. — the latter contained a very bad account of the fast-sinking state of Sarah Hunt. — With MW. drove to Stanway to visit our dear children and grandchildren, returning home in the evening by nine o clock. Very affectionately welcomed by all. Inspected the works going on at the Vicarage; the progress made is satisfactory. — Walked to Church Stanway, to Chidley's, Simmons's &c. — Conferred with the former about a payment to be made to him on account of the alterations at the Vicarage. — M[r] and M[rs.] J Scott and M[rs.] Morri-|[39]son called when we were absent from home — The dyspeptic or rheumatic pains under which I have been suffering continue, though somewhat abated.

June 22. Thursday.

Very fine summer weather. — Wrote to Alcocks, Birkbeck & C[o.], desiring them to pay £200 to my account with Mess[rs.] Hoare, from my account with them. — Justice business at home. — Drove to Stow, accompanied by MW, who returned home shortly after we arrived there — Received a letter from M[r] Hare with an inclosure which he proposes that I should forward to Mess[rs.] Cox and Williams, but which needs not to be sent, circumstances being somewhat different than they were when M[r] H. wrote it. — A letter from D[r] Williams, Superintendent of the Gloucester Lunatic Asylum in answer to mine written to him on the 19[th.] Inst. — At the Provident Bank, met M[r] Pole, and M[r] Ford. — At the Workhouse con-|[40]ferred with M[r] Pearce on Union matters — M[r] Ford and myself held a Petty Sessions: M[r] Polhill, with whom I conversed on the affairs of M[r] and M[rs.] Dolphin, was present with us. — Ranke's Reformation in Germany. ——

June 23. Friday.

A colder air, Easterly wind, dull forenoon and afternoon — rainy evening. — Examining M[r] Bloxsome's bill for business done by him during the last half year as Deputy Clerk of the Peace, so preparing for the audit at the approaching Sessions — Justice business at home — Wrote to J. W. Harris desiring him not to sent us any more coal at present, the yard being full.

— Mr Winter called, and partook of luncheon with us: he came to consult me as to a letter he had received from Lord Redesdale, respecting a bill now passing through the house of Lords for the better administration of the duties |41 of Justices of the Peace as to proceedings preliminary to trial in indictable offences; into which it would be desirable to introduce a clause to decide that magistrates residing in an adjoining county should have jurisdiction in contiguous detached parts of counties, not only with regard to indictable offences, but also as to summary punishments and jurisdiction, and ministerial acts. I have endeavoured through C Bathurst to press this on the Committee of the lower house sitting on the same bill. It is important in some neighbourhoods, and especially affects in this the Worcestershire parishes of Daylesford and Evenlode. Ld. R. sends down a draft of a clause, and suggests that it be submitted to me for my approval or correction; I thought it required a slight addition, and Winter will return the clause so amended to Lord R. — He also tendered his services for three of four Sundays, to enable me to |42 make an excursion to the sea, which Mr Hayward has urged, and which probably would be of much service to my health; and we shall, I daresay, avail ourselves of this very friendly offer — Received a letter from Mr Hare on Hunt Trust concerns. — M.W. received from Apphia Witts a tolerably favourable account of our relations at Shrewsbury and Cruck Meole. — Ranke's History of the Reformation in Germany.

June 24. Saturday.

A rainy day — Justice business at home. — Preparing for the public business at the Quarter Sessions at Gloucester next week; going through Mr Bloxsome's bill for business done for the County in his office of Clerk of the Peace. — Wrote on Hunt Trust affairs to Mr Hare, Mr Thornton, and Sophia Hunt. — From the last received a letter on Trust and Executorship business, to which I replied; thus |43 writing to her two letters on the same day. — Received from the Secretary of the fund for extending the religious institutions in the Diocese of Tasmania, increase of missionaries, churches, schools &c. a letter written under the impression that I am County Chairman, with documents to be laid before the Court of Quarter Sessions, recommending the interests of the Church in Van Diemen's land to the good offices of the Magistracy. Answered this letter, that I do not hold the office which the writer supposed me to fill; but that, as a Magistrate going to the Sessions, I will place the papers in the hands of the County Chairman — Wrote to Mr Brookes on Justice and Quarter Sessions business — Ranke's History of the reformation in Germany.

June 25. Sunday.

A very rainy forenoon; the afternoon and evening fine. — Preparing a sermon — Morning service, |44 prayers; afternoon service; prayers and sermon. I preached on the Trinity, the second part of a Sermon on that subject; the former preached on Sunday last. — Received a letter from Mr Price, Coln St. Dennis, as to the proceedings of the County rate committee — Preparing by my papers for the County business to-morrow and the coming Quarter Sessions. — To the family a section from James on the Collects. —

June 26. Monday.

Fine weather; some rain at night. — Left home after an early breakfast in the phaeton for Cheltenham with MW., whom I left there, to pass a few days in lodgings at Mrs. Forget's in

58. Cheltenham Station.

Clarence Street — I proceeded by train from the ~~Great Western~~ ^{Lansdown} Station to Gloucester, where I took up my quarters as usual at the Bell. — I there found a very kind letter from Winter, in answer |[45] to one I had written to him: he most obligingly offers to undertake my clerical duties at Upper Slaughter for three Sundays, so as to allow MW. and myself to make a tour for health and pleasure, and to depart for the sea side on this day fortnight. — To the Shire Hall, where the County business engaged me from 12 to 6 P.M. — Besides the business of the Committee of accounts, two other Committees met — the Prison Comm. and the County rate Committee. The Magistrates present were Purnell, Curtis Hayward, Baker, Parry, Sir M. Crawley Boevy, Raymond Barker, Lysons, and Niblett. — The officials were Bloxsome, Riddiford, Lefroy, Keiley, Fuljames &c. — Mess. rs Purnell, Hayward, Lysons, Baker and myself dined together at the Bell. – Much discussion took place as to various matters of County business to be transacted to morrow. — M.r Riddiford was in attendance |[46] assisting Purnell and myself in auditing accounts &c. M.r Barnett, the Coroner, and M.r Lovegrove, Ass.t Coroner waited on us with reference to their bills — Retired to rest at midnight.

June 27. Tuesday.

The morning and evening fine, rain or damp weather in the course of the day. — Wrote to MW. — Wrote to M.r Whitcomb, requesting him to give me an audience to-morrow morning on Hunt Trust and Executorship affairs. — Attended the Court for transaction of County business from half past ten AM. to half past five PM. — Purnell presided: there was a scanty attendance of magistrates: when fullest the number did not exceed thirty. — As chairman of the Committee of accounts I brought forward, as usual, the financial business of the day, going through and explaining the various items — |[47] Several new magistrates qualified — M.r Hughes, of Downend near Bristol; — M.r Hinton of Daglinworth, near Cirencester; — M.r Peters, Incumbent of Eastington, who married a sister of Curtis Hayward; — Colonel Hicks; — M.r Winterbotham of Stroud, a dissenter, and ci-devant Attorney, a man of talent, and a

59. Cheltenham Station.

liberal, as, I suppose, are most of the rest; and, lastly, a Mᴿ Hume, of Marshfield, formerly in the Army. — Nothing particular occurred as to Prison Management, or other general matters; but the question of the day was the renewal of the licence of Dᴿ Bompas, Superintendent ᵒᶠ a private house for the reception of Lunatics near Bristol. This establishment has been long conducted with credit under the management of Dᴿ Cox, who married a Snooke of Bourton on the Water, and Dᴿ Bompas, his nephew, and father of the present head of the concern. It is on a large scale, |⁴⁸ calculated for the reception of sixty patients of both sexes, of a class above that of paupers, and chiefly persons in good circumstances. Dᴿ B., the father, died about a twelvemonth since, and the Vis. Justices, acting in accordance with law, recognized the younger Dᴿ B. as successor to his Father, and the Court accepted their recommendation in his favour. The present Dᴿ B. is an unprepossessing, heavy-looking, awkward young man of three or four & twenty years of age. — For some time past the entries in the Visiting Journal, both of the Visiting Justices, and of the official Commissioners in Lunacy, have been of an unfavourable tone; the latter chiefly adverted with censure to irregularities in the admission of patients, and in the keeping of the books required by law: the Vis. Justices find fault by insinuation or more openly with the |⁴⁹ treatment of certain patients, whom they consider to have been used harshly, to have been debarred from advantages which would have been beneficial to them, to have been restricted in communications with the Visiting Justices, and two or three instances are particularly dwelt upon, mainly one of a gentleman of education, who, it seems, being subject to violent paroxysms, had been very roughly used by the Keepers, and coerced by a chain attached to his leg at night, unpadded, and fitted with three locks, and this treatment continued for weeks, if not months. — Of the Vis. Justices one only, ~~Mᴿ Moorh~~ Mᴿ Mirehouse was present, his Colleagues, Mᴿ Fripp and Mᴿ Battersby, were absent. It appeared that Mirehouse had been present at all the visits to the Madhouse, so also the Physician appointed as Medical Visitor, and that Mᴿ Battersby or Mᴿ Fripp had been present at other |⁵⁰ visits, and had, with Mirehouse and the Medical Visitor, signed ~~all~~ the entries. Mirehouse felt strongly that the institution ~~was~~ ⁱˢ ill managed, that unnecessary coercion is used, that harshness is the order of the day, that fair privileges and indulgences are denied,

446

that the patients are improperly restricted from intercourse with friends and Vis. Justices; but he shrank from proposing to refuse the licence, being aware that the property would so be grievously depreciated, and much pecuniary loss fall on the Widow and family of the late Dr Bompas, and others who have a share in the concern. This regard for vested interests acted on the minds of Curtis Hayward, myself and others, and caused us to hesitate about refusing the licence altogether, which some magistrates, and among them the County Chairman, in the first instance, contemplated. The un-|51 favourable impression conveyed by the minutes read to the court from the books of the institution was much increased by the appearance and demeanour of Dr Bompas himself: there might be much of embarassment, of awkwardness, of timidity, of slowness of apprehension and speech, but if so, there was an appearance of doggedness, ill-humour, adherence to a harsh system, and not a sufficient appreciation of the great improvements introduced of late years into the ~~system~~ mode of treating lunatics, by the almost entire abandonment of coercion, by soothing, kind, and indulgent management. So deeply sensible were the twenty nine magistrates who voted, that, on D^r B's own shewing, he was not fitted to superintend such an establishment, that, after a long discussion, in which the Chairman, Curtis Hayward, Mirehouse, Capt. Sinclair, and myself, were the leading speakers, it was |52 unanimously voted that the licence should be renewed for six months only, that is till the Epiphany Sessions, and this under a full & clear understanding that Dr Bompas would not be then relicenced, but that the parties interested in the Establishment should then be prepared to submit to the Court the name of some Gentleman with sufficient testimonials of ability, to whom the licence might be renewed. To this arrangement Dr B., probably under the impression that it was hopeless to stem the current running against him, formally assented. — Wrote to Mr Price, Coln St Dennis, on County rate matters, with reference to the parishes of Shipton Oliffe and Shipton Solers, East Leach Martin, and Coln St Dennis, so replying in the name of the County rate Committee to the points raised in the letter which I had received from Price on Saturday, & which |53 I laid before the Committee yesterday. — Receiv'd a note from Mr Whitcombe, who has made an appointment with me for to-morrow morning to discuss Hunt Trust and Exorship matters; also a letter from Sophia Hunt on the same subjects. She proposes to be at Gloucester, coming from Clifton and Bristol by railway on the day after to-morrow, to confer with Mr Whitcombe and me on the business of the Hunt Trust and Executorship. — The dinner party at the Kings Head was very small: Purnell, Mirehouse, Brickdale, Lysons and myself, with a few others, attended –

June 28. Wednesday.

Showers at intervals during the day. — Wrote to MW. — After breakfast went to Mr Whitcombe's office, and conferred with him for an hour on Hunt Trust and Executorship concerns. — Thence to the ~~Court~~ Shire Hall where I remained in Sergeant Ludlow's Court, till a late dinner hour. There were a few |54 appeals, but none of much interest; trials for felony followed. — About ten magistrates dined together at the King's Head, Sergeant Ludlow, Purnell, Mirehouse, Curtis Hayward, myself and others. — A letter from MW.

June 29. Thursday.

Fine weather, but cloudy and chilly. — After breakfast sat in Court till 12 o clock, when I went to the Bell, to meet Sophia Hunt, who had arrived with a day ticket from Bristol by an early train, and had held a conference with Mr Whitcombe: our interview lasted for an hour, being engaged in discussing Hunt Trust and Executorship matters. Her report of the declining state of her sister Sarah leads me to think that her life must soon close — Shopping; and then for an hour in Curtis Hayward's court, before I left Gloucester by train at 3 o clock, |^55 P.M. reaching Cheltenham, and rejoining my wife at M^rs. Forget's lodgings at four. — MW. had received a letter from our dear Sophy with a good account of all at Stanway. — A letter from Messrs. Hoare; Mr Jennings has paid to my account with them £150. 7. 11. — A letter from Mr Chr. Geldard, with the final balance sheet of the Craven Whitsuntide rents; the Directors of the North Western Railway have paid the interest on the principal sum due to us by them. — Cheltenham was in a crowded and tumultuous state to-day. Sir Willoughby Jones, the member elected on the conservative interest at the general election, has been unseated by a Committee on a petition charging treating and bribery, which was considered proved against his supporters. Nothing can be more venal than the borough, as regards the lowest class of voters: no where more party spirit than in Cheltenham; |^56 never was great man more determined than Lord Fitzhardinge to maintain his ascendancy in a borough. Craven Berkeley and Agg Gardner started as rival candidates, Whig and Tory, to fill the vacancy caused by the expulsion of Sir W Jones. — The old arts have been resorted to by the Yellow party, if not by the Blues, and Craven Berkeley is again returned to-day. Every where there is no lack of discordant music, drunken musicians, reeling voters, dingy yellow and green flags — ruffianly fellows ready for a fight, shops closed, and demonstrations of political opinions of the very lowest description. — The recent accounts from Paris are of the most alarming character: the Red Republicans, as they are called, that is, the most violent democrats, socialists, communists and the like, with the ferocious rabble of the Metropolis, have arrayed themselves against the Provisional |^57 Government and the National Assembly, within whose walls the populace found sympathy in many ultra, but influential, and daring politicians. The outbreak must have been preconcerted, as the insurgents were well supplied with arms and ammunition, acting evidently on a well planned system. At one moment it appeared that the government must succumb; but the tide turned in their favour, and after all the desperate fighting which usually marks civil war in a metropolis and crowded streets defended by barricades, the mob party has been put down; the army and the National Guards have obtained a dear bought victory. The fighting lasted four days; cannon were brought up to sweep the streets, and demolish the barricades. Where the money was found, by which the insurgents obtained arms to carry on the war, is a mystery. It was a desperate antagonism of the mob against the bourgeoisie, |^58 a combat of misrule against rule; a renewal of the abortive struggle of May last. Vast numbers, thousands, of the insurgents are taken prisoners, multitudes killed on both sides; much property greatly injured or destroyed. There are, it is said, ten general officers among the killed, and the Archbishop of Paris fell a victim by an assassin's shot, as he was interposing between the insurgents and the military, endeavouring to promote a truce or a cessation of hostilities. Generals Cavaignac and Lamorinére were the officers in command in this frightful struggle, and may now be considered as Dictators; the metropolis is declared to be in a state of siege. The provisional government headed by Lamartine has been dissolved; it consisted of men of discordant principles and opinions; all revolutionists, but some going much further in their opinions towards ultra-democracy than the rest. |[59] Lamartine may be considered as the type of the Conservative section among them, Ledru Rollin, Louis Blanc and others, as the representatives of the Jacobinism of the old Revolution fifty years ago. — The present temporary settlement seems to be that Genl. Cavaignac shall be president of an administration to be nominated by himself, & to hold office, governing the republic, until the National assembly shall have framed the future Constitution. Many representatives, members of the Assembly, are reported among the killed. The outbreak was marked by many acts of savage barbarity on the part of the insurgents. Similar excitement and outrages have burst forth in large towns in the provinces.

June 30. Friday.

A showery day, but fine after 3 PM. — Received a letter from Messrs. Hoare, announcing that they have received £200 on my account from the Craven Bank — A letter from E.F.W. and |[60] dear Sophy with a good account of themselves and children — Wrote to E. Chidley, Stanway; forwarded to him a cheque on Messrs. Hoare for £150 on account of the building going on at the Vicarage, Stanway. — Wrote to Sophy. — Transacted Prov. Bank business with a former servant, Sophia Croome. — Called at the Police Station on Mr Lefroy: looked over the premises with him and Keiley & Hambidge, his deputy and chief Superintendent, with a view to enlargement and improvement of the accommodations for the Constabulary — Shopping. — Our servant brought our open carriage and horses from Upper Slaughter. — We set out on our return home at 3 P.M and reached US. by half past 5 P.M. — Sad weather for haymaking. — Ranke's History of the Reformation in Germany. |[61]

July 1. Saturday.

A cloudy damp day; occasional showers, and a strong blight. — Settling my papers and accounts after my return from the Quarter Sessions. — Mr Pearce called, with whom I conferred on Union business, and signed my name to entries in the minute book, in anticipation of the audit of the accounts of the Union which is fixed for next week. — A letter from the Clerk of the Gloucester Lunatic Asylum announcing a meeting of Visitors for the 11th. Inst. — Visiting sick parishioners — Wrote to Mr C. Geldard, acknowledging the receipt of his letter containing the balance sheet of Craven rents and expenditure — Ranke's History of the Reformation in Germany. —

July 2. Sunday.

Showery weather — Visited the Sunday School. — Visited sick parishioners — Morning service, prayers and Sermon. I preached on the |[62] folly and sinfulness of neglecting the invitation of the gospel. — Rec^d. a circular from the County Gaol, giving notice of a meeting of the Visiting Magistrates — Afternoon Service, prayers. — Preparing a sermon — Ecclesiastical Gazette — To the family a section from Dr James on the Collects. —

July 3. Monday.

A dull forenoon; at noon damp weather; afterwards rain with little intermission. — Preparing a sermon — Justice business at home — Wrote to Mr Thornton on Hunt Trust matters — Visiting sick parishioners — Ranke's History of the Reformation in Germany. —

July 4. Tuesday.

A dull day, but fine — Justice business at home — Preparing a sermon. — Copying the Report for 1847 of our district Committee S.P.G. — We had expected Edward and Sophy to have breakfasted with us on their way |[63] to Stow, this being the day on which the members of the Cricket Club weekly meet, but were disappointed. After luncheon we were on the point of setting out in the phaeton to call on a newly married couple, the Hon. and Rev[d.] — Cholmondeley, and M[rs.] C. — he being a son of Lord Delamere, and she a daughter of Lord Leigh, who have come to reside at Adlestrop house, where he is to be curate to Lord Saye and Sele, when we received the very sad intelligence brought by a servant from Stanway in a note from my Son, that his beloved wife was thrown from her horse yesterday, had fallen violently on her head, and suffered a concussion of the brain. The accident happened in the meadows between Stanway house and the road leading from Winchcomb to Evesham. M[r] Dupre, the curate of Cutsdean, was riding with my son and his wife: the poor sufferer was able to walk home leaning on her husband; but her consciousness was |[64] gone. In a short time M[r] Newman, the Surgeon, from Winchcomb, who had been sent for arrived, and remained with poor Sophy from 6 P.M. yesterday till 11 AM. to-day. GOD be thanked, the remedies used have been so far successful! Consciousness is now restored, and there is no head ache now when the patient is perfectly still. There is reason to hope that there has been only concussion without laceration of the brain. She has enjoyed four hours of sleep. Leeches, mustard plaisters, and calomel appear to have done their proper work. Oh! how this report weighs upon our hearts, and oppresses us! and sends us to our prayers for a favourable issue! — I wrote to my son by the return of his messenger, offering to receive one or all the children; proposing also to postpone our intended journey to Beaumaris, and intimating that we should send to Stanway to-morrow for |[65] further tidings. — Of course we relinquished our intended drive to Adlestrop, and I wrote to Winter to request him to explain to M[r] and M[rs.] C. how we had been prevented from calling on them; also I requested W. to fix the hours at which he proposed taking my clerical duty at Upper Slaughter on the 16[th.] 23[d.] and 30[th.] Inst. if we carried out our scheme of visiting Beaumaris, but intimated that very possibly we might be prevented by the lamentable accident which had occurred at Stanway. — MW. received letters from Sophia Hunt and Rebecca Backhouse: the accounts of Sarah Hunt's state are very bad. — From Edw[d.] Chidley, Stanway, I received an acknowledgment of the draft for £150 which I had sent to him on account of the buildings at the Vicarage, Stanway. — Ranke's Reformation in Germany. —

July 5. Wednesday.

Very fine weather — Wrote to E.F.W. – sent our groom with my |[66] letter, who brought back a very satisfactory report of our dearest Sophy's state; she has rallied wonderfully, and even writes to me herself a very loving note to accompany a longer report from E.F.W. – These tidings, for which GOD be thanked, greatly tend to restore peace to our minds: still we are fully aware that her condition is one which calls for great care & justifies much anxiety — We propose to visit our children on Friday, and setting out on our tour on Monday next: for Edward and Sophy insist on our not postponing it, and, probably, to oppose them in this respect would do harm to the dear object of our solicitude, and induce an apprehension of greater danger than really exists. — Preparing a Sermon. — Copying reports of Stow Distr. Comm. S.P.G. for 1847 — and of the special meeting in February last. — MW. & I set out with the intention of calling on M$^{rs.}$ Dolphin at |^{67} Eyford, but being overtaken on our way thither by Harry Waller, who was also going thither, and judging that it would be better not to interrupt an interview between him and M$^{rs.}$ Dolphin, in which matters would be discussed as to the relative position and circumstances of the lady and her worthless husband, we relinquished our intention of visiting M$^{rs.}$ D. and returned after a long parley with the Farmington Squire ~~and~~ ^{on} the Eyford disagreements and embarrasments. — Visited a sick parishioner — Received a letter from Mr Thornton on Hunt Trust matters; he sent back a letter from Mr Hare which I had forwarded for his perusal. — Justice business at home — Ranke's History of the Reformation in Germany —

July 6. Thursday.

A very fine summer day — Drove with MW. to Stow: she shortly afterwards returned, when she had visited two or three shops. — Transacted business at the Provident Bank, and at the Office of the Gloucestershire Banking Company. |^{68} Called at "the Cottage" on the Vavasours, and partook of luncheon with M^{r} and M$^{rs.}$ Vavasour, and M$^{rs.}$ W.V. — They had been at Stanway yesterday, to visit our dearest Sophy, of whom they brought back a very satisfactory account, and whom they considered to be going on very well. Nevertheless, there is still reason for fear, for a relapse may come on, and the greatest quiet, with the strictest abstinence, is necessary. This was strongly impressed on me to-day by Mr Hayward: if laceration of the brain has happened the consequences may yet be very serious — W. B. Pole also urged upon me the absolute importance of quiet and strict discipline as to food, liquids, and the like in such a case: he has had painful experience on the subject, two near relations having suffered from concussion of the brain. — But still hope in our |^{69} case predominates over fear, for later in the day I received from E.F.W. a very comfortable bulletin, brought by a servant dispatched with these good tidings to comfort us and those at "the Cottage." — Sat at the Justice Room with the Dean of Gloucester and R. Waller — Mess$^{rs.}$ Polhill, W B Pole, and Oakley Hill were also present. — M$^{rs.}$ Pole from Wyck Hill, bringing with her M$^{rs.}$ C R Pole, and M$^{rs.}$ Mundy Pole, had called on MW. in the course of the day, and before my return from Stow, meeting M$^{rs.}$ Dolphin, who was sitting with my wife. — Mr Terry called on us in the Evening. — Received a letter from Mr Jennings with the balance sheet of our London Lady ^{day} rents, both of the houses in Bucklersbury, and of the ground rents in S$^{t.}$ Georges in the East. — A letter from Mr Geldard acknowledging my remittance of £25 as a compensation for his trouble in transacting our Craven concerns, receiving |^{70} our rents &c. for two years – He announces the approaching marriage of his son to a Miss Openshaw, the daughter of a Cotton Manufacturer, at or near Bury in Lancashire. — Received a letter from C Bathurst containing comments on the proceedings at the late quarter Sessions in the matter of Dr Bompas. — A letter from Howell announces that he has had a severe illness, having suffered from inflammation of the bowels and liver; but is now convalescent, and planning to betake himself with part of his family to the sea side. — Received from M$^{rs.}$ Winter a very kind note in answer to my letter to her husband of the 4$^{th.}$ Inst: there are many obliging expressions with reference to dear Sophy's sad accident. W. is gone to attend the commemoration at Oxford, and will reply to my letter as to the hours on which it will be convenient for him to perform the services at Upper Slaughter, on the |^{71} Sundays during which we propose to be absent on the intended tour, when he returns home. Wrote to Sophia Croome, Cheltenham, an old servant, on Provident Bank business.

July 7. Friday.

A dull morning, and a slight shower; the day afterwards fine, till evening, when a shower fell. — Made a rick of hay, part of which is a little damaged, but the larger proportion very good. — Settling my accounts as relates to London Tenants — Visited a sick parishioner. — Drove with MW. to Stanway and back; remaining at the Vicarage for two or three hours, chiefly in the company of my son, and his dear children; but our beloved Sophy was well enough to pass an hour with us. Great comfort it was to be among those most dear to us, and to find the object of our solicitude looking so much herself, pulled down, indeed, but cheerful, and, apparently without much suffering. There was but little of headache or dizziness, and not the slightest |[72] confusion or wandering. We strongly urged on Edward and Sophy the great necessity of quiet, with abstinence, as essential to her recovery. Finding her in so comfortable a state, and fearing to alarm by delaying our contemplated excursion, we consented to set out on Monday next, if there should be no change in Sophy's condition for the worse. The alterations at the Vicarage are going on satisfactorily. — We returned home to dinner. — M[r] and M[rs.] Boudier, M[r] Lefroy, and M[r] Pearce had called during our absence. — A letter from Sophia Hunt brought the intelligence of the death of her sister Sarah, which took place at Clifton; she was quite worn out, and her departure must be considered a happy deliverance for herself and her family. Life had no charms, one would suppose, for her. Of feeble understanding, irritable temperament, and limited acquirements, her health was delicate, |[73] and her personal appearance, from a claret mark, and other deformity of feature, precluded her emerging from the circle of her nearest relations into general society. — Wrote to M[rs.] W. Vavasour a report of dear Sophy's state to-day, a servant having come from Maugersbury to learn such tidings as we had brought. — Ranke's History of the Reformation in Germany. —

July 8. Saturday.

Occasional showers during the day. — Wrote to Mess[rs.] Hoare, desiring them to transfer £35 from my account with them to that of my Son: — to M[r] Jennings, acknowledging the receipt of his balance sheet of rents &c. received from London Tenants, due at Lady-day past, and expenditure on my account: — to Sophia Hunt, in answer to her letter received yesterday. — Justice business at home — Visited a sick parishioner — Preparing for our intended journey on Monday next. — Received a letter |[74] from M[r] Winter, as to the service of my church on the three Sundays of our meditated absence from home, which he kindly undertakes to perform — from Alcocks, Birkbecks & C[o.] Bankers, Settle, with a balance sheet of my banking account with them to June 30: — from the Office of the Clerk of the Peace announcing my reappointment as one of the Board of Vis. Mag. of Gloucester County Gaol. — Ranke's History of the Reformation in Germany. —

July 9. Sunday.

A very rainy morning, forenoon, and afternoon: the evening fine — Morning service — prayers — Afternoon Service, prayers and sermon. I preached on the duty of publishing the gospel to the Heathen and in distant lands; this in obedience to the Queen's letter, and in aid of the funds ~~for~~ of the Society for the Propagation of the gospel in Foreign parts. |[75] The collection made amounted to £1. 12. 8. Received a letter from M[r] Hunt, the District Auditor, addressed to the Chairman and Guardians of our Union, who makes few observations on the management, and no complaint. He completed his audit last week in two days, in an amicable temper, avoiding controversy. This is a satisfactory change; no doubt he has been cautioned by the authorities above, by whom at least on one point his adverse decisions have been pronounced erroneous. Wrote to Mr Pearce; forwarded to him Mr Hunt's letter with suggestions as to the proceedings at the next board meeting — Wrote to the newspaper agent in London, desiring him to forward the St James's Chronicle to me at Beaumaris, and to the Editor of the Gloucestershire Chronicle to the same effect as regards his journal. — Wrote to Mr Winter to settle the appointments for the services at Upper Slaughter on the 16th |^{76} 23^d and 30th Inst., on which days he kindly engages to be my substitute — Wrote to R. Waller, requesting him or his Curate to perform any weekly duty which may occur in my parish during my absence; adverted to magisterial business likely to occur, and to the convenient day to be fixed for the annual meeting of the Stow District Committee S.P.G, on which also the third meeting for the year of the Stow Clerical Society should be held — With the Churchwarden &c. making arrangements as on the eve of leaving home for a month's absence. — British Magazine — To the family a section from James on the Collects. —

July 10. Monday.

Very fine weather. — Justice business at home. — At nine o clock MW. & I left home in our open carriage with our house Servant, Charles Clift, on our excursion to the Sea coast. We had sent our luggage by the carrier |^{77} to meet us at Cheltenham: the carriage & horses to return home with the Groom. — Arrived at the Plough Hotel, Cheltenham at 11 o cl. where we were joined by Elizabeth Simmons, a young person from Stanway, who comes into our service as Lady's maid instead of Amy Hollins, who leaves us. ES. brought a letter from E.F.W. containing a pretty good account of our beloved Sophy, sufficiently favourable to justify us in proceeding on our travels. — Remained nearly two hours at Cheltenham, shopping &c. — I transacted business with Sophia Croome, an old servant, whose money matters I manage in the Stow Prov. Bank. — Proceeded in a fly from the Plough Hotel with servants & luggage to the Birmingham & Gloucester Railway Station at Lansdown, whence we started at 1.5 P.M. for Chester. As far as the Crewe Station the line had been frequently travelled by us before. We reached the Birmingham Station at 3.15 P.M. and |^{78} dined there, leaving that place for Chester at 4.30 PM. By 6.35 PM. we reached Crewe, where we again waited till 7.15 P.M. when our train was again in motion for Chester. The Stations on the line to Chester are near Nantwich, Calveley, Beeston, Tattenhall, and Waverton, of which Beeston is the only first class station: it is at no great distance from the Town of Tarporley. The general character of the country from Crewe to near Beeston is rural, pasture land, flat and uninteresting, but Beeston Rock and ruined castle is a very fine bold feature in a well-wooded country backed by the Peck forton hills, and in the vicinity of Delamere Forest. The insulated rock on which the ruins of the castle stand, frowning over the precipice, is composed of sand stone, very abrupt on one side, but on the other gradually sloping to the general level. Its height is 366 feet, the castle on its crest was formerly considered almost impregnable. |^{79} It was erected in 1220 by an Earl of Chester – and occupied the summit of the cliff, with a large portion of the southern slope of the hill. Little authentic is known of this castle. Leland saw it in ruins in the time of Henry the 8th It was afterwards repaired, and garrisoned for the parliament in the Civil wars. The wooded base of this rock gives a very picturesque tone to the general landscape: the neighbouring hills cluster round and behind it with pleasing outline & foliage; on the side of one of them a very extensive modern, castellated, and yet unfinished mansion contrasts with the old world ruin: this is the property of Mr Tollemache, whose arms give name to a very comfortable looking, modern built, but Tudor ~~looking,~~ style roadside hostelry, which attracted our notice as we paused for a minute or two at the Beeston station — The Railway Station in the outskirts of Chester is a temporary range of buildings, adjoining a very handsome and spacious combination of buildings for the |⁸⁰ same purpose, now nearly completed. These are intended as the united terminus of four distinct railways, that to Birmingham by Crewe, that to Birkenhead, that to Holyhead, that to Shrewsbury. — Taking a fly at the Station we betook ourselves to the Royal hotel, in one of the main streets of the city, having passed thro' the suburb, and beneath an archway substituted for one of the ancient gates of entrance. We reached our quarters at about a quarter past 8 PM. and found them comfortable. The distance travelled this day was to Cheltenham Station

this day was to Cheltenham Station	16 miles
Birmingham d^o	46
Crewe d^o	52
Chester d^o	21
Hotel — nearly	<u>1</u>
	<u>136</u>

July 11. Tuesday.

Beautiful weather — I rose early and walked round the far famed walls of the City of Chester. — The whole circuit is one mile threequarters, and about one hundred |⁸¹ yards. These walls are the only entire specimen of ancient fortification remaining in the Kingdom. There is an excellent walking path of about two yards in width, the outer side being guarded by a stone parapet of about four feet high, and the inner by wooden or iron railing. There are four main entrances into the city, at each of which carriages & horses pass through, and these respectively front one of the cardinal points. These entrances are formed by lofty arches, substituted for the ancient gates, thrown from one side of the street to the other, and over them the walk on the walls is continued. These walls were in most parts, especially on the north and east sides, guarded by towers, so as not to be beyond bowshot of one another. Many of these have been taken down, one or two remain entire, or nearly so. I ascended to the walls by a staircase adjoining the Eastern gate, & bent my course towards the Southern entrance. To the East is a considerable suburb, with an ancient Parish Church, a dark and timeworn |⁸² and spacious structure, of the red crumbling sandstone of which the principal public buildings, walls, cathedral, towers, and the like, are constructed. The River Dee soon met my eye, having traversed, or encircled a large portion of North Wales, it approaches the ancient city, and forms for some considerable distance a kind of horse shoe circuit on its southern and western sides, before it seeks the estuary by which it empties itself into the Irish sea – The line of the walls here sinks to the margin of the river, a broad & rapid stream, flowing beneath an ancient Bridge over ~~which~~ which the road passes to Wrexham. On the other side of the bridge opposite to the city is a suburb, and the city is entered by one of those arches which I have described above. Close to the bridge and arch is a huge ugly range of buildings forming a cornmill, where much business appears to be carried on: this, doubtless, is the site of an ancient mill. Continuing on |83 the river's side, lofty walls rise to the right, the ground here being the base of the hill or promontory on which the old Castle was erected, ~~large~~ some remains of which, but modernized, now ~~remain~~ subsist and still furnish barracks for a small body of military. On the site of the castle are erected the County Gaol and the Court houses, County Hall and other buildings for the transaction of the public ~~business~~ business, – with barracks for officers. Continuing along the base of this hill and gradually ascending, having an extensive meadow to the left bounded by the Dee, making a curve, the new bridge came in view: but I did not approach to inspect it closely: a noble single arch spans the stream, the width of which is 200 feet. It is of the same bold character as that over the branch of the Severn at Over near Gloucester, and was finished in 1832, being formally opened in October in that year. The approach to this bridge from the city is by a road from the Centre |84 of Bridge Street, which passes by the Castle Esplanade, and reaches the bridge by an embankment thrown over the Valley. Crossing this road, I caught a very striking view of the noble public buildings by which it passes, but did not go near enough to notice the details. There is a Shire hall with a spacious portico, also other stately buildings, and a wide area in front enclosed by a semicircular wall, surmounted with iron railings, in the centre of which is the grand entrance of Doric architecture. These buildings appear to great advantage, standing detached from the city, with open fields adjacent to them, and so not crowded, nor the view of them obstructed. The Gaol is on the rear of the Courthouses, and on the slope of the hill, descending towards the old bridge. Still pursued the line of the ancient city wall; to the right a modern, Grecian Church, and the County Infirmary, green fields intervening between |85 them and the wall: on this side also are some detached mansions: below, to the left, a spacious meadow forming the racecourse, bounded by the Dee: the races are of a superior kind, and well frequented: the grand stand, and other accommodations for spectators, are permanent buildings. Beyond the race course, approached by an embankment is the railway bridge over the Dee, on the line leading to Shrewsbury in one direction and ~~the~~ to Holyhead in another. This bridge is constructed of iron and was, not long after it was first opened for traffic, the scene of a sad catastrophe, one of the iron girders having given way, under the pressure of a passing train and so precipitated it into the river and on the rocks beneath, causing serious loss of life with destruction of property: the damage however, was afterwards effectually repaired and the passage is now considered to be perfectly secure. Where the wall forms an angle towards the North West, and adjacent to a |86 Tower, still nearly entire, and connected with other outworks partly in ruins, probably, a sally port, the line of railway from the Station to the bridge is cut thro' the walls, and traverses the interior by a deep cutting through the red sand stone rock. Proceeding onwards, there are two towers in more or less preservation, from one, which may be ascended by a few steps to a small level platform, there is an extensive view, to the Northward — The other, more entire, called the Phoenix Tower, fronts the East, and from its summit the unfortunate Charles I. beheld the defeat of his forces on Rowton heath, when on their way to relieve the garrison of Chester, then in a state of siege. — In making the circuit of the walls the attention is drawn on this side to a canal flowing beneath them, and excavated, as it were out of the soft sand stone rock: — at some parts of the walk the line of wall extends beyond the |87 present town, lawns and fields being interposed between the fortification and the houses: elsewhere the houses, or their roofs, cluster close beside, or beneath, the path which the summit of the walls affords. Shortly before I had concluded my circuit I found myself passing the spacious, but gloomy, grave crowded cemetery of the Cathedral, which rose in crumbling masses of red sand stone, solid, yet in apparent dilapidation, and by no means a pleasing pile. It was the Eastern end, which I here viewed, with the tower and transepts. – After breakfast MW. and I repaired to the morning service at the Cathedral, the approach to which is by mean and narrow lanes; the building being much elbowed by old and gloomy houses appears to less advantage than it would if more detached; but the crumbling stone and frequent repairs give it a heavy, dilapidated and patched appearance. The interior however is far more attractive than |[88] the exterior, exhibiting the usual ~~grave~~ grave, lofty, and graceful lines of an English cathedral. The service was well performed, but the congregation very small; two dignitaries, the officiating minor Canon and the choir, forming at least one half in number of those present. Much enjoyed this opportunity of Cathedral service. — The inner choir is not very spacious, but very cathedral like, and there are many detached portions which might have detained us, and which are on different accounts very interesting, had we been disposed to linger, or sought a guide. But time pressed; we had much to do before the day closed, and other remarkable points in this quaint old town were to be observed. The chief part of the Cathedral was erected during the reigns of the three last Henries: but the original of the church is traced up to the 7[th.] Century. — Strolled in the Rows, and |[89] on the walls, and in the principal streets with MW. – The great peculiarity of Chester is the Rows — in the four main streets, which intersect each other at a central point, in like manner as at Gloucester, indicating an origin from Rome. A ground story based on the level of the street, and used for shops, dwellings, and the like, is the basis of a kind of paved or boarded gallery, passing before the front of the first story of the house, which is mostly occupied as a shop, the gallery being open on the side of the street, and the second story projecting over it, and being supported by timber uprights at intervals, and occasionally by other pillars; the remaining stories of the house, equally with the second story, projecting over the gallery, and ranging with the ground story. This continuous gallery is accessible at intervals from the streets by flights of steps; it is of irregular height and construction, according to the difference there may be in one house or the next, or as it may be of older or more recent date, more or less |[90] altered or repaired. The shops opening on these Rows are generally the best in the Town, and the galleries are the general resort of pedestrians, covered & sheltered from sun or rain. The effect is that a middle story seems to have been cut out of all the houses. Pennant says that "these rows appear to have been the same with the ancient <u>vestibules</u>, and to have been a form of building preserved from the time when the old city was possessed by the Romans. They were built before the doors, midway between the streets and the houses; and were the places were dependants waited for the coming out of their patrons." Possibly the carriage ways may, in course of time, have been greatly sunk below their ancient level, which may at first have been that of the Rows. – As it is, the principal streets are thus provided to a considerable extent with a rude portico, or covered way, scooped, as it were, out of the houses on each side. Many of the houses are of quaint old timber |[91] work, some with pithy moral sentences introduced in the plaister work: there are many public and private edifices worthy of observation and curious, of which we could take only a passing glance. — Left our hotel in a fly, so as to reach the Railway station in time for the train departing for Bangor at 1.45

PM. we took our tickets for the whole distance, with permission to stop at Conway for an hour or two, and so to proceed to Bangor by a later train. We very soon shot through the cutting in the sand stone rock, and the line constructed within the circuit of the city walls, leaving the race course to the left, and crossing the Dee unharmed by the bridge which soon after it was opened was the scene of a grievous calamity. Here we entered on a level plain of great extent parallel with the Æstuary of the Dee, and bounded to the left by the hills and mountains of Denbighshire & Flintshire. Not long after crossing the river the line of railway towards Rhuabon, which is eventually to termi-|[92] nate at Shrewsbury, but now is incomplete from the former to the latter town, diverges from that on which we were travelling. The line of rail till near Conway is conducted as nearly as possible along the coast of the estuary of the Dee, often on the very sand or mud margin of the river, here forming a wide firth, the opposite side being a projecting part of Cheshire separating the mouths of the Dee and Mersey — the hundred of Wirrall. — It is a fertile tract, for the most part, through which we passed — with promising crops of corn — The railway appears well constructed, and well managed. The first station is at Queen's ferry about seven miles from Chester, the next at Flint between twelve and thirteen miles from Chester. Flint is close on the æstuary of the Dee, opposite to Parkgate on the Cheshire side of the River, which we had observed as we travelled from Queen's ferry. This poor town |[93] gives name to the County, and was once considered the county-town, but for many years the assizes have been held at Mold, about six miles distant. Flint itself is a chapelry in the parish of Northop, and is considered to be of Roman origin, as it occupies even now a rectangular, entrenched area, and Roman remains have been discovered in the place and its neighbourhood. From the Station we saw the County hall, and County Gaol, not very imposing structures; the houses generally appear mean, and dingy. This place has a considerable trade in exporting lead ore, there being large smelting houses, and close to the town there are also extensive collieries. Flint is one of several contributory boroughs returning one member to parliament: the others are Caergwle, Caerwys, Overton, Rhuddlan, S[t.] Asaph, Holywell & Mold. The dark remains of Flint Castle stand on a rock in the marsh at the bottom of the town, so near the river that at high |[94] water the walls are washed by the tide — The ruins are still considerable, presenting the relics of four ~~square~~ towers at the angles of a square court containing about an acre of ground. Founded by Henry 2. or Edward 1. the castle was for two or three centuries possessed alternately by the English and Welsh princes. In 1399 it was in possession of Percy, Earl of Northumberland who betrayed into [it] the unfortunate Richard 2 who from hence was led captive to Chester on his route to London, to be deposed, and eventually murdered. The old Chronicler, Stowe, gives an interesting account of what passed prior to his capture, and during his transit through that portion of North Wales which he traversed from Conway to Chester. In the civil wars Flint castle was garrisoned for the King, but eventually surrendered to General Mytton. It was dismantled in 1646. — But the main historical interest |[95] in these tottering walls and towers, and this paltry looking town, is derived from the captured king, whose character Shakespeare so beautifully pourtrays — we are sent to his Richard 2. and we are delighted. — The next Station is not far distant from the flourishing town of Holywell, about 17 miles from Chester. Here the hills descend nearer to the Æstuary of the Dee, and the town, to the left of the Station, lies at their feet, and partly on their slope. The name of the place is derived from a sacred spring dedicated of old

60. Chester.

to a Saint Winifred, of whom a wild, romantic legend was coined, probably not without the privity of the monks of the adjacent abbey of Basingwerk, of which few remains are to be seen. This very copious spring, gushing with great force from a cavity in the rock, and forming a hasty brook, quickly finding its issue in the firth of the Dee, was supposed to be endued with great health restoring virtues; was therefore in by gone ages inclosed in an elegant |[96] reservoir, surmounted by a chapel, and specially visited by Roman catholics having a lively faith in its renovating qualities; and the superstition has descended to our days. The gushing waters, however, have been converted to other than sanatory purposes, several mills being erected along their short course: of these there are extensive cotton and copper works, with an iron foundry &c. — The district immediately round the Holywell is distinguished for the richness of its mineral treasures, particularly for its mines of lead and calamine, which appear to have been worked from a very early period. The town and its environs are very populous; there are several gentlemens seats in the neighbourhood, with numerous villas. It would seem that the surrounding country abounds in picturesque scenery: undulating vallies being well contrasted with the lofty hills by which they are enclosed, and richly wooded eminences, which command extensive and |[97] varied prospects by sea and land. The stations after that near Holywell, are at Mostyn, Prestatyn, and Rhyl: the line of the coast is followed. Mostyn is near the point of Air, which maybe considered as the entrance to the South of the Æstuary of the Dee. Hence the coast has an inclination to the South West, forming a shallow but wide bay the Western limit of which is the mountainous peninsula — stretching into the Irish sea, called Orme's Head. Opposite Air point the projecting portion of Cheshire separating the mouths of the Dee and the Mersey sinks into the Irish Sea; beyond the eye catches no land. To the left, as Rhyl is approached, the interior presents the fine vale of Clwyd, with its river descending from the Welch mountains of the interior, and passing by or near Denbigh, S[t.] Asaph and Rhyddlan with its ruined Castle, which is conspicuous at no great distance: the Clwyd falling into the sea at Rhyl, a chapelry, of Rhuddlan, about two miles below the |[98] latter place. Looking at

Rhuddlan, we are reminded of the politic and able Edward 1., and the so called Statute of Rhuddlan made at a parliament held there, and designed to favour the monarch's schemes for the subjugation of Wales. Crossing the Morva Rhuddlan, or Marsh of that place, between it and the sea, the mind reverts to a great battle fought here between the ~~Danes~~ Saxons and Welsh in the 8th. Cent. — the celebrated Welsh air, Morva Rhyddlan, was composed in commemoration of the disastrous issue of this engagement, which ended in the defeat and slaughter of the Welsh, those who escaped the sword being drowned by the influx of the tides into the Marsh. Rhuddlan Castle presents still considerable remains: its origin may be traced to the beginning of the 11th. Century — and its foundation to Welsh princes, the place being of considerable importance as a stronghold in the frequent contests between the Welsh and Normans. Here Richard 2. |[99] rested for a short halt on his way from Conway to Flint, accompanied by the Earl of Northumberland, before his deposition. In the civil wars it was held for the King, but was surrendered to Genl. Mytton, the parliamentary commander, in 1646, being soon after dismantled. — The Station close to Rhyl is about 30 miles from Chester, and presented a lively, bustling scene: for Rhyl is a thriving sea bathing place, much frequented, and loungers were crowding about, some to meet friends, some to speculate on the travellers; passengers and portmanteaus and carpet bags were on the move — There is a modern stone chapel of no great size — good hotels, it is said, and lodging houses, and a fine sand by the sea shore. The place, as we learnt next day, was crowded: for some fellow travellers of ours, whom we met at Beaumaris, had in vain endeavoured to procure accommodation. — The next Station is near Abergele, about 34 miles from Chester. Here is a small and ancient market Town, about a mile from |[100] the sea shore: the bay opposite to it is sometimes called by its name, being the indentation of the coast from Great Orme's Head to Air point. Abergele and some houses on the sands are more or less frequented by persons seeking sea air, bathing, and healthful walks and drives on fine and extensive sands. Inland there are interesting rides or drives towards and among the picturesque hills and valleys, and mountain streams. Many ancient, as well as modern seats and villas, abound in this vicinity, among which is conspicuous Gwyrch, a modern castellated mansion on an eminence, commanding a superb sea view. The limestone quarries in this neighbourhood furnish vast quantities of rock which being blasted and broken are exported to Liverpool and other places. Llandulas, a village by which the railway passes is supposed to be the place where Richard 2. was surrounded and taken by a band of soldiers |[101] secreted by the Earl of Northumberland for the purpose of forcing him into the hands of Bolingbroke, who was at Flint. — Here is a tram road several miles in length, constructed from the sea to some limestone quarries in the interior, being on an incline of rapid ascent all the way. Advancing towards Conway, the railway is carried further from the margin of the sea, crossing the low land which connects the line of mountain now dipping into the plain, with the bold projecting promontary, which terminates in the mighty cliff called Great Orme's Head. To the left the hills form a kind of foreground to the distant mountains, and enclose on one side the fine vale of the Conway, over which to the West tower lofty and mountainous heights, the Northern extremity of the great Caernarvonshire range: in the valley flows the rapid Conway, expanding into a sort of lake above the romantic town and castle, contracted again under the walls of |[102] the ancient fortress, then widening into a small Æstuary, bounded on one side by the rugged coast, and frowned upon by the lofty Penmaen Mawr, and its lesser rocky subordinates, clustering round its base, — bounded on the other by the high promontory before mentioned gradually rising to its greatest eminence above the cape called Great Ormes Head, which forms the Eastern entrance to the Menai ~~Strait~~ Straits It is hard to fancy a more striking and interesting combination than Conway presents to the traveller. The eye wanders from one object to another; now resting on the mountain-girt valley and river receding inland, now on the picturesque, walled, and turretted town, now on the expanding river and its bay, more pleasing at high tide, now scanning the distant promontary, now bent on the elegant suspension bridge, and again seeking to penetrate the more recent and

61. Phoenix Tower, Chester.

more singular invention for |103 the crossing at the river's mouth, the tubular tunnel, alas! parallel to the suspension bridge, by which, the railway traveller, crossing in profound darkness, is brought up to a halt at the Station within the ancient walls of this mountain stronghold; and there we are, with all the bustle of a station, 45 miles from Chester. But what is a tubular tunnel? I had conceived to myself a huge tubular metallic trunk, somewhat of a circular or oval shape, resting at each end on strong abutments, crossing a wide breadth of water. Nor was I wrong, except as to the presumed circular or oval shape. It is, in fact, a gigantic metallic box or chest, with top, bottom, and sides, and the two ends open, the entrance and exit being by stone gate ways and arches. The darkness is as in an ordinary tunnel: the noise somewhat different; for you are made sensible that you are passing between walls of metal, with a ceiling and floor of metal. As yet there is only one tubular tunnel here, with one line of rails, so that there |104 can be only one train crossing at a time; but a second tunnel, to be erected parallel to the present one, is in progress, the workmen being busily engaged in its construction, and in no long time the double tubular bridge will be finished and at work. Its contiguity to the Suspension bridge is very unfavourable to the latter, ruining the effect of its light and airy elegance. The suspension bridge was both useful and ornamental: the tubular tunnel is a wonderful triumph of art and engineering skill, very useful, but very ugly. One is greately impressed, on looking at these two great works thus side by side, with the gigantic speed with which human ingenuity has been permitted of late to advance: the suspension bridge, a few years ago, was a wonder of the nation, now it becomes almost a toy, a superfluity; steam and iron tracks have superseded what appeared a fine and bold effort to facilitate travelling on an important line |105 heretofore much impeded, and even sometimes render^ed hazardous by an inconvenient ferry. Now the great channel of travelling and traffic is through the tubular tunnel, the Suspension bridge is frequented ^only by the inhabitants ~~only~~ of the town and neighbourhood. A single stage coach, a few light carriages, market carts, horsemen, and pedestrians pass at intervals over the suspension bridge; while ever and anon the thundering, steaming, screaming, prolonged train plunges into the dark jaws of the tunnel, freighted with goods and passengers in profusion, or the pilot engine dashes through it, or the luggage train, or waggon train loaded with materials for construction of the works, rumble along in busy succession. The suspension bridge was begun in the spring of 1822, and completed in the summer of 1826 — It was an undertaking chiefly at the public cost, and very expensive. The chains are fastened on the east side of the river, in a solid rock, which, before the construc-|[106] tion of the bridge was insulated, and on the west side, after passing under the walls of the castle to a distance of 54 feet, are securely bolted into the rock on which the fortress is built. From the eastern extremity an embankment, 671 yards in length, and 30 yards in breadth, has been raised on the sands between the island and the shore, and from the western extremity a road has been cut through the solid rock, under the North East side of the castle, to the distance of 175 yards, thus making the whole extent of the bridge with its approaches more than 900 yards. On this road a handsome lodge of two towers, corresponding in design with the remains of the castle, forms an arched entrance from the town to the bridge. — The length of the bridge between the centres of the supporting towers is 327 feet: its height above high water mark is 18 feet, and the height of the pillars over which the chains pass 42 feet from the platform – |[107] Connected with the suspension bridge, a new line of road in the direction of Bangor passes through the Town, leaving it by a gate way through the North West wall, thence proceeding round the huge mountain Penmaen ~~Mawr~~ Bach, along the northern precipitous declivity of which it is carried by an excavation in the solid rock, in some places 80 feet high and extending more than a mile in length. This new line of road of more than 4 miles extent joine̶d̶s the old road at a point beyond a precipitous and dangerous descent which had made the intercourse between Bangor and Conway proverbially alarming and insecure. I am told by those who have travelled by the new line that it is a stupendous work, most well-worthy of observation. The traveller works his way round the mountain as if on a cornice cut out and projecting from it, precipice above, precipice below, the rocky pass on the one side the wide expanse of sea on the other, dividing |[108] the astonished wayfarer's attention. This, of course, is lost to the traveller by the railway; but if time should permit, it would be well to engage a carriage, & pass over this striking mountain terrace — I return to the Conway Station — Emerging from the tunnel, the ancient walls are penetrated by a wide modern arch; above, to the right, is the castle, close by a mouldering overhanging tower of which the line is constructed; to the left the wall is traced bounding some yards forming part of the railway premises, and the train halts beneath a bridge forming a communication over the railway from one part of the town to another, or, perhaps, to the gateway leading on to the new line of road connected with the suspension bridge — At the Station we left the carriages, reserving our tickets to proceed by a later train, deposited our luggage in the office, and sought the Castle Hotel. Our guide |[109] was a porter from the Inn, the first native we had conversed with, whose short, staccato accent in speaking the to him foreign tongue of English fell oddly on the ear. The interior of the town is generally speaking, homely and mean; after crossing an open space, where we had a view of ~~a hom~~ an ordinary looking, ancient parish church, we descended a street terminated below by a tower and narrow gateway with a pointed arch opening on the quay. In this street, to the left, is a quaint old mansion house with two courts, and grotesque carvings, called Plas Mawr, (the great place.) with all the pretensions of a first rate dwelling on a

62. Conway Quay.

confined scale, but now tenanted, as it would seem, by pauper families. — We reached the Conway station at about half past three P.M. and purposed proceeding to Bangor by the next train a few minutes after 6 PM. Having taken refreshments at the hotel, we sallied forth to explore the curious old place, under the |[110] guidance of an old inhabitant, who, however, remained but for a short time with us, as his services were not permitted within the Castle walls. Proceeding towards the gate way leading to the quay, we turned by a street to the left, which soon brought us to the foot of the walls, and to the wicket leading into our guide's rude garden, from whence he assured us, and with truth, we should command a good view of the Town and Castle. Clambering up to a seat which topped the old dilapidated wall, we rested for a time surveying the very curious prospect before us. The Town lay before us foreshortened, as it were, the Castle in front of us, crowning the rocky eminence which overhangs the mouth of the River; beyond are beheld the line of Country through which we had travelled, to our left was the peninsula stretching towards Great Orme's head; this is separated from the town by the bay into which the Conway falls: we rested, as |[111] were, against the bold outlier of the gigantic Carnarvonshire range of mountains, which here parts the vale of Conway from the line of coast opposite to Anglesey, and bordering the Menai Straits. Conway is the most perfect specimen now remaining in Great Britain of a Saracen town — a triangular area, occupied by houses, streets, Church &c. – girt with walls, there being no suburb, no buildings without the mural enclosure. Looking at the majestic towers of the old castle, one is reminded of the station the poet Gray selected for his bard —

> "On a rock whose haughty brow
>   Frowned oer old Conway's foaming flood,
>   Robed in a sable garb of woe,
>   With haggard eyes the poet stood" ——

The Conway, however, is not here, at least, a foaming flood, but a gently flowing, rapid stream, pursuing its course through a smiling mountain-bound valley; at high water the river at high water is more than half a |[112] mile broad. The lofty walls surrounding the town are nearly a mile in circumference, were defended by 24 towers, and there were four gates. It has been conjectured that the present Conway was the Conovium of the Romans; but probably Caer Rhun, five miles higher up the river, on the same side, was the site of Conovium. The Castle and its walls were erected by Edward 1. about 1283, when he repaired several other castles in Wales, in order to guard against the insurrections of Llywellyn. From this period it was held by the English. Having taken this bird's eye view of the place, we pursued our route to the castle, diverging a little to the quay thro' the gateway in the walls previously mentioned. Desolation and dilapidation are the characteristics of some of the houses in this quarter: few, indeed, in the town are much above the condition of cottages. And the quay exhibits no appearance of |[113] trade or activity; neither commerce nor manufactures have settled at Conway. — Approaching the castle and the gateway at its foot, leading to the Suspension bridge, we found access to the ruin by a wicket carefully locked till the janitress from a neighbouring house admitted, but did not accompany us. To the Castle gate we ascended by a narrow path, passing the former fosse by a little wooden bridge, and encountering no other person than a tourist like ourselves, who had been exploring the interior. It is, indeed, a very picturesque ruin. From each end of the town walls at an angle of the river, on a slate rock, rose a curtain, terminated by a round tower, running to some distance into the water, to impede the approach of an enemy. The castle was defended by eight large round towers, flanking the sides and ends, from each of which rose a slender turret, commanding an extensive prospect over the surrounding country. Of these turrets four |[114] only remain. The walls are embattled, and from 12 to 15 feet in thickness, and nearly entire, except one of the middle towers on the south side, adjoining the entrance to the railway station, the lower part of which has fallen down the rock. This was caused by the inhabitants taking away some of the stones from the foundations for their own use. The upper part of the tower is entire, suspended at a vast great height above, and projecting near thirty feet over the walls below, exhibiting in the breach vast strength of walling. The principal entrance to the castle is to the North West. The hall is now the most remarkable apartment. Its dimensions are 130 feet long, 30 broad, and about 20 high. It was lighted by nine windows, six of which were towards the river, and three towards the court. The roof was supported by eight arches. — Pacing the green turf which spreads itself within, where stones or rubbish do not |[115] encumber the ground, or ivy and brambles do not usurp a supremacy, and looking forth on the country to the East, down on the suspension bridge, and tubular tunnel, and listening to the noise of the workmen hammering the metal, and rivetting the joints of the additional tube now in preparation, or watching the masons busy in erecting portals to the tubes, or catching the hissing noise of steam engines, or obtaining a glimpse of railway signal posts, the contrast between the beginning of the fourteenth and the middle of the nineteenth century is strongly forced on the mind. Then monarchs, recently returned from wars in the Holy land, were engaged in building Saracenic strongholds to restrain and coerce the rude and uncivilized borderers and mountaineers, whose fertile valleys, and rugged Alpine fortresses the English Sovereign felt it a necessary policy to seize: — and when the struggle was over well it was for the Welch that they were subdued. — for on the track of conquest, civiliz-|[116] ation, comparative security, better laws, and diminished

63. Conway
Castle.

strife, internal as well as external, ensued. Now wars and rumours of wars have little to frighten the inhabitants of Conway; their walls and their castle are mouldering away; for the clank of arms and the din of strife they listen to the scream of the engine, the hissing of the steam, the heavy rumbling of the train, the hammering of artizans; are roused into periodical bustle as each train arrives at the station, and try to make a profit as they may from the passers by. — In the civil wars, Conway Castle was garrisoned for the King, but it was ultimately surrendered to General Mytton for the parliament, though it escaped that general dismantlement to which most other fortresses were subjected. After the restoration Charles 2. granted the castle to the Earl of Conway, from whom it has descended to the Marquis of Hertford. In 1665, notwithstanding the remonstrances of the gentlemen |[117] of the county, all the iron, timber, and lead was taken from the Castle, and transported to Ireland, under pretence of being used in the King's service. Thus it was reduced to its present state — a noble and picturesque ruin. — We lingered in its courts till it was time to retrace our steps to the inn, and railway station, where we sat in readiness for a train from Chester which arrived a few minutes after six P.M. and conveyed us to Bangor station, a distance of fourteen miles, about a quarter before seven o clock. There is one intervening station, at Aber, about five miles from Bangor, but the train did not stop there. Between Conway and Aber the pass is very mountainous and difficult, but the arduous task of the Engineer has been ably performed, though, of course, at a great expence; the lofty eminences terminating to the North the Carnarvonshire range of mountains, here dip precipitously into the sea — Penmaen Bach, and Penmaen Mawr, the principal giants, though the former |[118] is designated Bach, or small, in contradistinction to the latter, surnamed Mawr, or great, are magnificent masses of limestone, with a cap of scanty herbage surmounting rocky precipices, and steep beds of crumbling stone. Penmaen Mawr, and, perhaps, its lesser brother, is the scene of active enterprize, several companies having opened quarries, laid tram-roads on inclined planes, and erected quays on the beach for the getting & shipping of the stone, now in much request at Liverpool, Manchester, and elsewhere — I have no clear notion how the railway is conducted above and underground through the iron bound promontory which we penetrated before coming out clear from the roots of Penmaen Mawr: but the view as we approach Aber Station, on the alluvial flat stretching at the base of the Carnarvonshire range of mountains, bordering on the Bay of Beaumaris, the mouth of the Menai Straits, as far as the outlier which separates |*119* this level from the separate valley in which Bangor is situate, is exceedingly striking. To the left lofty mountains, overlooking a fertile tract, to the right, distant five or six miles, the wooded shores of Anglesey, and the low hills bordering on the straits, with the white town of Beaumaris reposing on the beach beneath the groves surrounding Sir Richard Bulkeley's seat at Baron Hill — more seaward the expanding bay opening into the Irish Sea — Penmon, the North Eastern promontory of Anglesey, with the contiguous low, but still elevated, Puffin's Island, or Priestholm, forming the western entrance of the bay, while Great Orme's head on the Eastern entrance projects with a bold and lofty mountain cliff to breast the surge — looking like an Island — for the low marshy isthmus uniting it to the high ground forming one side of the Conway bay, and opposite to that Town, is hardly discernible by the naked eye. Rapidly advancing towards our goal, Penrhyn Castle |*120* is seen in a park, well encircled by wood, on a projecting part of the shore of the Menai Strait, a bold and conspicuous object, the seat of Dawkins Pennant Esqʳ, a modern castellated mansion, in the Norman style of architecture – Before us rises a bold hill of moderate height ~~proje~~ detached, as it were, at right angles from the line of the Caernarvon-Shire or Snowdonian range, and abruptly terminating in a wooded knoll over looking Penrhyn Castle, and Harbour. Through this the line of rails penetrates — patet jauna atra — and we enter a long tunnel — appearing longer still than it is by the slow rate and caution with which we were conducted through it. The railway having been first opened so lately as on the 1ˢᵗ· of June, the works at this tunnel are still unfinished, and many men are yet employed in its interior. Therefore we proceeded slowly with the perpetual scream of the steam whistle, lights flashing, |*121* as we advanced, from the torches and lanthorns used by the workmen. But with much noise there was no danger, and we emerged at the threshold of a handsome station, the present terminus of the Chester and Holyhead railway — Then followed the usual bustle — omnibus, car and coach tendering their services — and, in a few minutes, having taken our places in an Omnibus, servants and luggage being duly provided for, we were on the move for Bangor city and the Penrhyn Arms hotel — Here I foregathered with Mʳ Price, of Tibberton Court near Gloucester, a merchant of that port, a very clever and intelligent young man, for some time very favourably known to me as a brother magistrate, and who, having married a lady, whose fortune was mainly derived from the coffers of the wellknown Gloucester Banker and Miser Jemmy Wood, has not been afraid to accept an invitation to offer himself as representative of the city with which he is connected |*122* by birth, and by business — and though he has not succeeded now, yeilding to the preponderance of the Whig candidate, Captain Berkeley, and the popularity of the Conservative candidate, Mʳ Hope, who has the support of a strong party, it is very likely that he may hereafter attain the object of his ambition. He was on his way to Caernarvon and Tremadoc, and at the door of the Penrhyn Arms Hotel we parted in the hurry of securing apartments and looking after our packages. The hotel is a mile and a half distant from the

64. Beaumaris.

Station; in reaching it we traversed the whole length of Bangor, which appears to be a poor town, with one main and narrow street, expanding about the middle, where in a low situation stands the ancient long and low Cathedral, more likely a respectable parish Church than the mother church of a See; but in good repair, neat and well kept. Emerging from the town, as the houses on |123 each side became more detached, we ascended a gentle acclivity which brought us to the door of the huge hostelry, where civility seems to reign, and we were soon accommodated with a comfortable sitting and bed room. The first impulse was to seek the beautiful garden attached to this Inn, and it excelled the report we had heard of it. Lawns, gravel walks, beds of flowers, in profuse bloom, a dense foliage of shrubbery, and underwood, with commodious seats at choice points of view, and tourists of all ages & both sexes, promenading, were exceedingly attractive. This little paradise crowns the summit of a gently rising cliff slightly projecting into the bay which the Menai straits here form — beneath lies Penrhyn harbour, the property of Col. Dawkins Pennant, with its quay and pier, pushing out into the deep, lined with numerous sloops or other vessels of no great tonnage, employed in the carriage of slates, quarried at the vast slate quarries of that wealthy gentleman, a |124 few miles distant among the mountains, and brought hither by a tram road, on a gently inclined plane — A little beyond the buildings forming the harbour, a dark ivy covered gateway and tower rise, forming an entrance into the park and grounds of Penrhyn Castle — Onward and seaward the eye rests on the beautiful bay of Beaumaris, that town full in view, with the low, but not flat, coast of Anglesey, terminating with Puffin Island, fronting Orme's Head, and thence the eye returning to the point from which this almost matchless prospect is taken, ranges along the giant chain of mountains to which I have so often alluded, commencing with Penmaen Mawr — We viewed this lovely scene at high tide, and not even the low water can divest it of its beauty — for the land outlines vary not — but at low tide the Menai Straits are contracted to a narrow channel, & the fine bay becomes for some hours a |125 wide expanse of treacherous sands, called the Lavan sands, across which there are

466

tracks communicating with ferries, and sad are the tales recorded of mournful accidents in years gone by. But I have only partially described the view from the garden in the direction to the mouth of Beaumaris Bay. Opposite are the richly wooded banks of the Menai strait on the Anglesey side, about two miles distant — where the Strait narrows to one mile is Garth point, on the Caernarvonshire side. This bold headland ^{affords} at ~~the~~ ^{its} extremity ~~of which is~~ a ferry station, by which a constant communication is kept up with the opposite island; ~~and~~ on the base of this foreland, as it curves in towards Bangor, the spot on which we stand forming the opposite entrance of the little bay, are many houses, a kind of suburb to the Cathedral city, while the bay itself forms a harbour for the coasters, trading with Bangor. – Having partaken of the refreshment of tea, we sallied forth for an evening walk; |[126] being recommended to climb an ascent directly opposite to the doors of the hotel, and which soon brought us to a natural terrace of green fields, affording a superb prospect. The eye ranged over the objects above described as seen from the garden, looking Northward — the Islands, the bay, the promontory, the Mountain range, the level at their feet, with Penrhyn Castle and Park; but it reached also into the recesses of the mountain towards the Alpine valley of Nant Francon, flanked by the gigantic twin Mountains, Carnedd David, and Carnedd Llewellyn, that splendid pass through which the great Irish road from the Metropolis by Shrewsbury and Holyhead has been constructed. Descending from this height, and daylight still serving us, we prolonged our walk towards the beach bordering the little bay, and in the direction towards Garth Point, but found ourselves entangled in some mean streets leading to the strand, not very savoury, |[127] nor frequented by the better sort of people. Extricating ourselves from these, we found our way by a circuitous course, taking the high road leading from Bangor to Garth Ferry, and after many a weary step, reached the city and its main street by a by-street, so retracing our way, by the same road as we had passed over in the Omnibus to our spacious and crowded, but comfortable hotel.

65. Flint Castle.

July 12. Wednesday.

Very fine summer weather. — Before and after breakfast enjoying the delicious garden of the hotel, and its splendid views. — Left for Beaumaris at 11 AM. in a hired Barouche — the distance charged eight miles. — Passed through Bangor to the Railway Station. — The city lies between two high ridges of slate rock; the precipitous side of one of these, richly planted with flourishing trees, where there is sufficient soil, overhangs the narrow valley up which the town extends, the opposite ridge, terminating in Garth point, as the first named just above the |[128] Penrhyn Arms Hotel, is less abrupt, and studded with residences, and buildings scattered here and there on its sides, besides those erected more continuously at its foot. The mouth of this little valley is the small bay of Bangor, and the wooded bank across the Strait beyond is the coast of Anglesey — From the site of the Station, which we passed, ascended a steep hill, with a small County Infirmary, splendidly situate, not far from its summit. That we are in the land of blue slate the mounds separating the enclosures evince, which in many instances are constructed of long narrow strips of slate let into the soil, and being placed at a little distance, each is bound at the top to its neighbour by a band of hoop iron — That we are out of England is testified by the Welsh language generally spoken by the middle and lower classes, and by the costume of the peasant women, whom we met walking or in the light carts which we passed — a black |[129] mens beaver hat surmounting a snow white cap, a cotton print bedgown, woollen petticoat, blue check apron, and usually a basket on the left arm, the notable good woman industriously knitting woollen stockings as she walks or drives along. — Having reached the top of the hill terminating in Garth Point, the road is carried along a high terrace commanding splendid views — that Northward I have already described — to our right is the winding line of the Menai Strait, resembling a broad river, fringed on the Anglesey side by a beautiful belt of wood — To the left is the Caernarvonshire range of mountains, stretching Southward, at a considerable distance from the shore of the Menai Strait, towards Llanberris, Snowdon, Beth Gellert &c. Before us, at the further extremity of the Menai Strait, is the coast line extending Southward from Caernarvon, on the direct road

66. *Menai Bridge.*

to which place we were now travelling. Perhaps, at about a mile beyond the railway station, the first view of the |¹³⁰ Menai Bridge is caught, spanning the strait at its narrowest part. It usually happens that reality falls short of expectation, but it was not so in this instance: the elegance, the height, the delicacy of the construction, the beauty of the strait and its shores, the boldness of the conception, the impression forced on the mind that this is really a wonder of science and of art, combine to captivate, and even awe the beholder — Gently descending towards it, on the left, adjacent to the road are seen the works of the Holyhead railway, now fast advancing to completion; much of the space between the ~~Sta~~ Bangor station and the Menai Bridge must be traversed by a tunnel. On the right, and on a wooded lawn sloping to the water, is the Menai Bridge Hotel, said to be a most comfortable resort for the traveller, and most delightfully situate. But we are arrived at the lodge or entrance to the Bridge where toll is paid, and leaving |¹³¹ the carriage, we walked across, that we might more fully and leisurely examine its construction, and enjoy the prospect. There are three lines of road — ~~a~~ ᵗʷᵒ carriage ways outside by which horsemen, cattle and carriages pass to or from the Caernarvon Shire or the Anglesey side: the arrangement being such that the one line is kept by those going Westward, the other by those travelling Eastward; between these two lines, separated by an iron fence, in fact, by some of the chain work of which the whole fabric is constructed, is the line for footpassengers. The site of the bridge is closely contiguous to that of the so called Bangor ferry, which it has wholly superseded, which was occasionally in stormy weather impracticable, so delaying the transit of the mails & travellers on the main road between London and Dublin by Holyhead. The ferry itself was very ancient, probably substituted for fords by which, in ages long past, the island of Anglesey was approached; for we read of Roman and English armies so |¹³² forcing an entrance into the Island. And, indeed, little doubt can be entertained that Anglesey was at one time a peninsula joined to the mainland by a narrow isthmus at this point; the character of the rocky sides of the strait, the insular masses of rock still encumbering the channel, and making the navigation at this reach dangerous, lead to this conclusion. The whole Strait is of dangerous navigation, strong and adverse currents and tides, shifting sands, and sunken rocks, combine with the narrowness of the strait to render the passage difficult: It was originally in contemplation to span the strait by an enormous iron-bridge on the old construction, and Telford, the late eminent engineer, furnished plans and estimates with that design; but the expence would have been enormous, and the enterprize was doubtful, as to its success: this project being abandoned, the same skilful person suggested a bridge on the |¹³³ suspension plan, and carried out the design with admirable science at a far less price than the projected iron bridge would have cost. In developing his plan Mr Telford proposed that the iron hanging bridge should consist of one opening of 560 feet between the points of suspension; in addition to which there should be seven arches, four on the coast of Anglesey, and three on that of Caernarvonshire, each 60 feet in the span, making the total length of the bridge 910 feet: the height above the level of high water line to be 100 feet. The road way to embrace two carriage ways each 12 feet in breadth, with a footpath of 4 feet between them. The whole to be suspended from four lines of strong iron cables, by perpendicular iron rods placed five feet apart; these rods to support the roadway framing. — The suspending power was calculated at 2016 tons, and the weight to be suspended, exclusive of the cables, 343 tons, leaving a disposable power of 1674 tons. The four sides |¹³⁴ of the roadways to be made of

67. Menai Bridge.

framed iron work, firmly bound together for seven feet in height, with a similar work for five feet in depth below the cables. The weight of the whole bridge between the points of suspension to be 489 tons. The abutments to consist of the masonry, comprising the extreme stone work, the two piers, and the seven arches before mentioned, each of the two piers to be 60 feet by 40½ feet wide at high water mark, having a foundation of rock. Upon the summit of the two main piers a frame to be erected of castiron work, of a pyramidal form for the purpose of raising the cables from which the bridge was to be suspended. Such was, if one may so speak, the specification. The first stone was laid in 1820, and in 1825, the first chain was thrown over the strait. The general opening of the bridge took place on Jan. 30. 1826. And its construction when completed may be thus sum-|[135] med up: the extreme length of the chain from the fastening in the rocks is about 1715 feet: the height of the road way from high water line is 100 feet; each of the seven small piers from highwater line to the spring of the arch is 65 feet; the span of each arch is 52½ feet; each of the suspending piers is 53 feet above the road; there are two carriage ways of 12 feet each, with a footpath between them of 4 feet; the length of the suspended part of the road from pier to pier is 553 feet; the carriage roads pass through two arches in the suspending piers, 9 feet wide by 15 feet high to the spring of the arches. To counteract the contraction and expansion of the iron from the effects of change in the atmosphere, a set of rollers are placed under cast-iron saddles on the tops of the suspending piers where the chains rest; the vertical rods, an inch square, suspended from the chains, support the sleepers for the flooring of the road way, the rods being placed 5 feet from each other. — |[136] The chains, 16 in number, consist of 5 bars each: length of the bar 10 feet, width 3 inches by one inch, with six connecting ~~links~~ lengths at each joint, 1 foot 4 inches by 8 inches, and 1 inch thick, secured by two bolts at each joint, each bolt weighing about 50 pounds; and the total number of the bars in the cross-section of the chain is 80 — Such is the scientific combination of strength with due regard to

470

lightness in the whole of this matchless erection, that though placed in a perpetual current of air, suspended over a narrow strait often much agitated, and the force of the wind at certain times exceedingly impetuous, it maintains its ascendancy ~~of~~ over the warring elements with perfect solidity and security: some eleven years ago some damage, indeed, was experienced in a violent storm, but engineering skill soon devised additional braces and appliances which have resisted all subse-|[137] quent buffetings of raging gusts. — In walking over the bridge there is something to be admired at every step: — the effect of a passing carriage; the vibration caused even by a hand applied to the suspending rods; the depth to the level of the water; the fine view of the straits in both directions; on the Anglesey side, some two or three miles off, the lofty pillar erected in honour of the Marquis of Anglesey; — the diminutive appearance of persons on the shore; the excellence and strength of the workmanship; the beauty of the arches over the road at the suspension piers; the echo in them; all conspired to delight and to detain us. From the further side of the bridge, leaving MW. in the carriage, I descended to the foot of the rock forming the Western foundation, and sought the entrance to an excavation which leads by a narrow & low, winding, and rather ascending passage tunneled out of the rock for about 100 yards to the chamber in which all the 16 chains |[138] suspending the bridge are brought down through a shaft, and firmly bound together into the solid rock. The guide precedes with a torch, the way is somewhat damp with trickling moisture, and, to a chest and lungs like mine somewhat the worse for wear, and very susceptible of underground exploration, producing panting, heaving, and oppression, rather difficult: yet very interesting is the dark vaulted cavity within, where the immense cables descending through the shaft are brought into one massive combination, and bound, as it were to their good behaviour, fast anchored fathoms deep, in the native rock, whence apparently no violence can dislodge them, and even the mighty elements in their wrath would seem powerless — On the opposite shore is a similar provision for security — Passed on the edge of the water, whence viewed the noble structure to very great |[139] advantage. From this point, certainly, the best view is obtained, inasmuch as by being in contact with its proportions on <u>terra firma</u>, a better idea can be formed of its real, and, indeed, wonderful dimensions. — My attention was drawn to a very ancient and small church, in a most picturesque situation on a little islet immediately on the South of the Bridge — Dedicated to S[t.] Tysilio, a Welch Saint of course, called after him Llantysilio, scarcely 40 feet long, and just twenty broad, with a humble bell ~~turret~~ [gate] at the Western end, and at the Eastern, an elegant window of the 14[th.] Century, the nave being probably 700 or 800 years old, there stands this diminutive house of GOD, sufficient, probably, at the date of its first construction for the rude and scanty worshippers of the district, in striking contrast with the huge span, the massive abutments and piers, the ~~scientific~~ [bold] combinations of science and |[140] art, which the cultivated powers of the 19[th.] Century, and the demands of a vastly increased population, and gigantic traffic, and needful intercourse for travellers bound on complicated national or private affairs to traverse even the remote parts of the Kingdom, require. — But there remains another contrast to be noticed: from the Menai Bridge, looking Southward, we saw the huge railway tunnel, to be called the Britannia Bridge, in progress of erection, and already far advanced towards completion. It is parallel to the Menai Bridge, more than a mile distant, and, no doubt, disfigures the prospect from its somewhat elder sister. It is, or will be, a triumph of engineering skill, a vast and gigantic work, but must also be far more useful

68. Entrance to
Menai Bridge.

than ornamental. A huge pier rises in the centre of the channel, on which the extremities of two tubes meet, ~~the~~ opposite ends |[141] resting on abutments on the opposite shores of the strait. When completed on the same principle as the tubular tunnel at Conway, this dark bridge will bear the vast traffic by railway across the strait, and so in great measure supersede the Menai Bridge —— Twenty three years have passed since this latter was finished, deemed a stupendous effort of skill, and of vast benefit to the public — now, in this brief interval — a revolution has taken place, old modes of conveyance yeild to new, unheard of projects are carried out with a success only rivalling their boldness, and hundreds of tons, and of passengers, are to be steamed across the beautiful strait in an iron box, and in profound darkness. Whether man will here too subdue or control the elements remains to be proved; but it is noticed that the tubular tunnel will be 11 feet higher than the Suspension Bridge, and present an unbroken surface to be buffetted by the boisterous |[142] winds sweeping through the strait, and so those are not wanting who predict calamity, but they are, probably, snarling critics, prophets of ill, boding evil without a full understanding of the construction of the tunnel, and the provision made for security. — On the Anglesey side of the Menai Bridge rises a pretty large scattered village, which owed its origin to the old Ferry, and its increase to the new bridge — there are little villas, & neat residences, shops, and public houses, and a pleasant and dry site, with a fine prospect; but I saw no Church near, save the little Llantysilio, secluded, oddly built on a miniature islet, and accessible only when the tide is down. The road to Holyhead is carried inland in the same direction as the Bridge, that to Beaumaris, turns to the right at the end of the bridge. It is exquisitely beautiful; it follows the line of the winding and indented shore of the Menai; |[143] on emerging from the village the eye rests on little islets, inlets, and creeks, evidencing the disruption of Anglesey at some remote age from the Caernarvonshire shore: proceeding, the road at one time commands an extensive view of the noble bay, and its lofty encircling mountains; at another time it enters

*69. South Stack
lighthouse,
Anglesey.*

shady oak woods, amid which rocks are frequently jutting out, while a wall, and the foliage of the trees growing out of the precipitous bank, are the protection of the traveller as he passes on the edge of a steep descent, the foot of which is washed by the waves, which may be heard chafing against the rocks below. Wherever there is sufficient space between the road and the margin of the Strait, tasteful villas and dressed ground succeed each other. At length, emerging from the woods, the wanderer beholds the whole bright panorama: Beaumaris, backed by groves, is at his feet, on the margin of the strait, while Orme's Head, Penmaen Mawr, the Nant Francon Mountains, and the more dis-|[144] tant range of Snowdonia, with Penrhyn Castle and Bangor, form an almost matchless prospect. Passing at the foot of the last declivity a little common, projecting into the Strait, and noticing to the left the lodge and entrance to Baron Hill, the seat of Sir Rich[d.] Bulkeley, we drove by some pretty cottage residences fronting the sea, and what may be called the port of Beaumaris, where a few small colliers and other vessels were lying. It must be owned that Beaumaris looks best at a distance; for the town is small, the houses very ordinary, and without appearance of trade or commerce. The principal street, the Castle Street, contains the chief hotel, the Bulkeley Arms, where we were set down, and this establishment is on a large scale, and apparently well conducted. The rooms from the street, to the back of the house, command a fine view of the strait, and the garden opens on the strand. But our object was to secure lodgings, in search of |[145] which we sallied forth, and soon found that there was very little choice. Our wish, of course, was to select a house with a sea view: but there are but few of these, all of them on "the green", a spacious level common intervening, between the town and the ruined Castle, and the sea, being surrounded with a gravel drive or walk, protected from the shingly beach by a low wall, furnished with stone seats, and <u>the lungs</u> of the place. Contiguous to this are two modern rows of houses, a few of them very large and spacious, the rest of less magnitude;

all, or almost all of these, being lodging houses, but not one vacant. So after hunting from one extremity of the place to the other, and disappointed in several instances, we at last ~~took~~ anchored in Castle Street, very near the old Castle, and the green, engaging for three weeks the residence of two ladies, who had retired to lodgings in the Country, to ruralize and economize by letting their house at £4. 4. a week. True it is we looked out into the dull, quiet street, but we had a very well |[146] furnished and roomy drawing room, an excellent, clean, and comfortable bedroom; another to spare, if needed; and good accommodation for our servants, with a clean, tidy servant of the ladies, left behind as cook and housemaid for the lodgers. Add to this a dull, but commodious parlour for breakfast, luncheon, and dinner, and we had no reason to complain: for though the view was not always before our eyes – in five minutes — yes, in two — we were on the public walks. — Dined at the hotel, and drank tea in our new house: settled ourselves comfortably in our apartments, and spent an hour on the Green, lingering till the bright moonlight, admiring the magnificent strait, bay, and mountains. Many were the promenaders on the public walk.

July 13. Thursday.

Very hot summer weather: — but hazy, so that the mountains on the Caernarvonshire side of the strait were only indistinctly seen — Received a letter |[147] from my son with an improved account of our dear Sophy's health; and this was confirmed by a letter from M[rs.] W. Vavasour, who, though she had not been at Stanway, had learnt at "the Cottage," that our dear daughter is going on well. The elder Vavasours called at Stanway on Monday last, on their road to Cheltenham, where they are gone to visit Lady Arbuthnot — A letter from Mess[rs.] Hoare announced that they had transferred £35 from my account to that of my Son. — Wrote to E.F.W. — Walked to Llanfaes, a little hamlet about a mile distant from Beaumaris: from the Green the road leads over some rising ground which forms a projection into the Strait, and descends to a little bay which indents the shore. Here a little snug harbour invites some of the craft navigating the strait, it being a sheltered anchorage for vessels waiting the turn of the tide. Contiguous is a gentleman's seat — the Friary — a beautiful sea side retreat: embowered in foliage, close |[148] on the beach, and commanding magnificent views of the Caernarvonshire mountain range across the Strait. Near the entrance to this place the road turns inland, and the spire of Llanvaes Church, already before seen, invites the pedestrian. It is a sweet, retired spot; two or three cottages are near — the Church modern, except as to the old low tower, and this surmounted by an elegant and recent spire — the style very simple, and rural, ~~one~~ [a] nave and a chancel, with lancet windows — trees and meadows encircle the church and village. Between it and Beaumaris are the parkish grounds & fine woods of Baron Hill, the seat of Sir R. Bulkeley, and very near to Llanfaes, overlooking it, the well placed mansion of M[r] Hampton Lewis, which, however, he does not himself occupy, residing at or near York. This gentleman is a first cousin of M[rs.] Aston, being the son of a sister of her father, M[r] Chambers. — At Llanvaes was formerly a house of Fran-|[149]ciscan friars, founded in the 13[th.] century; of this there are only very obscure remains. – Sat and sauntered in the evening on the Green. —

July 14. Friday.

Very fine weather, ~~but rather hazy on the Caernarvonshire side of the Straits, and at the mouth of the bay.~~ Less hot than yesterday. — Wrote to Howell — Read Report S.P.G. for

1847. — Walked by the strand to the foot of the first hill on the road to the Menai Bridge. Sauntered on the common, and by the Beach, opposite to Penrhyn Castle, harbour, and the Bangor bay. Greatly enjoyed the fine view of the mountains and strait – watching the vessels passing to and fro: the deep channel runs on the Anglesey side, and even at low tide there is a constant succession of sloops and trading vessels, chiefly those engaged in the slate trade, passing to or from Penrhyn harbour, Bangor, and other places of deposit for slate on the Caernarvonshire side of the strait. Add to these fishing and pleasure boats, with daily |¹⁵⁰ steamers plying to and from between Liverpool Beaumaris and the Menai Bridge. These perform their voyage in five or six hours. The passengers and goods for Beaumaris are landed at a substantial and commodious pier of recent erection, projecting from the strand to the channel, so as to be always accessible. About 9 AM. is the hour of departure for Liverpool from the Pierhead, about 3 P.M. the packets come from Liverpool. — In the evening sat or sauntered on the green: whither we had also resorted in the afternoon. — Ranke's Reformation in Germany.

July 15. Saturday.

Very fine weather, but rather hazy on the Caernarvonshire side of the Strait, and at the mouth of the bay — Received short letters from E.F.W. and from Mrs. W. Vavasour, who had been at Stanway: both gave a very comfortable report of our dearest Sophy's progress towards recovery. — Wrote to C Bathurst. — Read⁸ |¹⁵¹ · Report S.P.G. for 1847. — Walked with MW. on the green, and to the common opposite Bangor & Penrhyn Castle and harbour, which I had visited ʸᵉˢᵗᵉʳᵈᵃʸ — More steamers on the qui vive to day: an extra boat made the voyage to and from Liverpool — An excursion steamer called for passengers on a trip to Dublin and back. Next week an excursion is planned to the Isle of ~~Wight~~ ᴹᵃⁿ and back — Irish Oysters brought from the coast of County Wicklow for sale at Liverpool, when the market is overstocked there, are brought by the undertakers hither in bags, and deposited in shallow pools on the beach of the Straits at this projecting point; there they improve, and are ready to be brought into the market at a favourable time. This I learnt from an Irishman busy in so distributing the contents of his sacks of Oysters. — On the green in the evening — Our man servant much indisposed — Ranke's Reformation in Germany. |¹⁵²

July 17. Sunday.

Very fine summer weather. — A letter from Sophia Hunt, dated from Stoke Doyle, with particulars as to the funeral of her sister Sarah — of her will — and other matters, relating to the Hunt family, especially as to her brother Edward — Wrote to Mrs. W. Vavasour — To divine service in the parish Church at 11 AM: there are three services on the Lord's day; an early service in Welch, and an evening service in the same language. The service in the forenoon is in English. — The Church is a spacious edifice, situate with its church yard in the middle of the town, approached by a street at rightangles with the street in which our house stands, Castle Street. It has a low and ordinary looking tower, a nave, and side aisles and spacious chancel, all covered with lead & embrasured. The church is a chapel dedicated to St. Mary, in the parish of Llandegnan, which place is distant between two |¹⁵³ and three miles in the direction towards, but not on the road to, the Menai Bridge. From the importance of the town in which it is situate, Beaumaris Church has become the most considerable in the commot, or hundred. The nave and side aisles are of the end of the fourteenth century, the chancel of the fifteenth. The richly carved oaken roof of the church is well worthy of note: in the chancel the carved stall work, probably brought from the monastery at Llanfaes, has been judicious^ly arranged. Galleries have been erected in the aisles, another serves at the West end, below the tower, for an organ loft, and affords accommodations to a choir of singers and school children – The church is pewed in the good old fashion of narrow and high boxes without lids. One or two square pews of large dimensions are probably appropriated to the owners of large estates, or official dignitaries. We sat in a very quiet, comfortable, but too closed pew, |[154] attached to the house which we occupy. The chancel contains, besides some ancient monumental tablets and inscriptions, a white marble monument by Westmacott, in memory of the late Lord Bulkeley, who died in 1822: this beautiful piece of sculpture represents Faith directing the view of the dejected widow towards the bust of her husband, and to heaven. Besides this, in the centre of the chancel, facing the Communion table is a beautiful marble statue of a female kneeling in an attitude of devotion on a pedestal, bearing monumental inscriptions in English and Welch. This was erected, by Ternouth, to the memory of Charlotte Mary, first wife of Sir R. B. W. Bulkeley Bar^t, and daughter of Lord Dinorben. The service was well performed by two Clergymen, ~~the~~ parts of the service being tolerably chanted; — the preacher treated of faith and good works. — After service I had an interview |[155] with Mr Wynne Jones, a medical gentleman of the place, whom I had called in to prescribe for our man servant, whose head and stomach appear to be much out of order. — An early dinner: after which I walked to Llanvaes Church, to attend divine service in English, commencing at 5 P.M. — The interior of this simple village Church is well arranged with stalls in the nave and very low square pews, holding many worshippers, in the Chancel. The woodwork, roof &c. coloured as old oak, the Chancel windows of painted glass, some monuments, recent and of older date, in the Chancel; one especially to the memory of M^r & M^rs. Hampton Lewis. — There was a large congregation, every place being fully occupied, chiefly by persons of the better sort, of whom a large proportion from Beaumaris. The service was well performed, with great simplicity, and in a devotional tone, both as regarded the Minister and the people. Plain village psalmody was led by |[156] three or four villagers at the communion rails, assisted by a villager of the female sex, neatly attired in the Welsh garb, with snow white cap surmounted by a high crowned, broad-brimmed beaver mens hat. The Sermon treated of the great mercy of GOD in the redemption of fallen man, and in the conversion of the world from ignorance, vice and idolatry to the pure religion of Christ. — After the service was concluded, I followed the main stream of the congregation to Beaumaris by a different road from that which I had come. The new line led, below Mr Hampton Lewis's house, and near to Baron Hill, through well wooded pastures, and hayfields, commanding magnificent views of the Caernarvonshire mountain range, of the Bay, and Strait, with a striking prospect of the old Castle and Church, and town of Beaumaris, which is approached by a road leading to lodges and gates opening into the domains of Baron Hill, and Mr Hampton Lewis, the |[157] former being remarkable for fine single trees, or groupes of timber, and for large herds of grazing cattle, and the high ground above the mansion richly clothed with wide spreading plantations extending in the direction parallel to the Strait, and towards Menai bridge — After tea with MW. sat or strolled on the green. — Report of S.P.G. 1847. —

<u>*July 17. Monday.*</u>
Less sunshine, but a fine summer day. — Our man servant seems nearly recovered. — Wrote letters to Mess.rs Coutts, desiring them to remit to M.r Edw.d Hunt at Dapoolee near Bombay the dividends of Stock under his sister's will and that of M.rs Mary Hunt, to which he is entitled, and as to which M.r Hare, Miss Sophia Hunt and I are Trustees. — To M.r Edward Hunt, informing him of the directions given to Mess.rs Coutts, together with information and advice as to his money matters — To M.r Boye, Paymaster of Pensioners at Dapoolee; sent |¹⁵⁸ him a copy of my letter to Edward Hunt, explaining to him his position, and begging him to advise him for the best. This gentleman, with whom I have before corresponded, appears a judicious & kind hearted person, and to exercise a very salutary influence over the mind of the weak and feeble minded E.H. — Received a letter from M.r Pearce with particulars as to the late visit of M.r Hunt, the Auditor of our Union, who had found no fault, nor indulged in any ill humour. — Walked with MW. on the road to Llanfaes, going by the Baron Hill grounds, as far as to one of the fields near the seat of M.r Hampton Lewis, which, being on high ground, commands a splendid view of the bay, mountains, and strait, with Llanfaes Church and hamlet, as a foreground on the one side, Beaumaris, its Church, and Castle, Baron Hill, and the woods encircling or backing it, and the town, being very attractive objects in |¹⁵⁹ another direction. — Walked also on the Green — This walking would be very enjoyable, were I not suffering ever since I left home, more or less, from tender feet, chiefly owing to corns bruised by new shoes. — Ranke's Reformation in Germany. —

<u>*June 18. Tuesday.*</u>
A cloudy day, yet not with out gleams of sun, the wind cold, and boisterous towards night. — Received a letter from E.F.W. – with a pretty good account of our dear Sophy. — Wrote to Sophia Hunt on Executorship affairs &c. Our walk to day was into the grounds adjoining the old castle, which are open to the public, and exceedingly enjoyable, leading on the outskirts of the Town towards Baron Hill, and the road leading towards Llanfaes which he we had followed yesterday. These grounds are either meadow or pasture, the latter presenting fine herds of cattle — the size of the fields is large, and all are well timbered. The entrance to the Castle is by a gateway, at |¹⁶⁰ the bottom of Castle Street, very near our house. There is a porter's lodge, where the Key may be procured which opens the Castle gate. The site of the Castle adjoins the Green, so often mentioned. It was the last of the three great fortresses, Conway and Caernarvon being the other two, erected by Edward 1. to hold in awe his new and unwilling subjects on both sides of the Menai. For this purpose he fixed on a flat near the water side, with a view of surrounding it with a fosse, for the double purpose of defence, and bringing small craft to unload their cargoes under the walls – This fosse and canal have long since been filled up; but a large iron ring to which the craft were fastened, is still in its place at the great east gate. Within the castle is an area or square of 190 feet, with obtuse corners; on the right is the chapel, the only entire room in all Edward the 1.st buildings, its stone arched roof having saved |¹⁶¹ it at the general dilapidation. The entrance gate ways continue tolerably entire, though unroofed, also the towers are generally standing, and venturous visitors may with little risk make the circuit of the walls, on the summit. — Opposite to the south east entrance is the great hall, 70 feet long, and 23 broad, with a

range of five elegant windows. Though, on the whole, this was a fortress of great size, yet its low situation, and the unusual width of its nearly circular towers, takes off considerably from its height and appearance. In the Castle Court a space has been set apart for a fives court, and the inhabitants or visitors avail themselves of the opportunity to practise the active game, so conducive to health and agility. — This castle is reported to be the scene of the massacre of the bards by Edward 1., who does not appear to have thought himself secure in his newly acquired dominions so long as this influ-|[162] ential order remained to raise the song, and string the harp to deeds of patriotic resistance. — A more recent assembly of bards within these old walls deserves to be mentioned. Within the area of the Castle in August 1832, was held a congress of bards, or Eisteddfod, under the patronage of Sir R B W Bulkeley. What gave peculiar éclat to the meeting was the presence of her present Majesty, then Princess Victoria of Kent, accompanied by her Mother, the Duchess of Kent. During several months of this summer the Royal party had resided at Plas Newydd, the seat of the Marquis of Anglesey. This mansion is situate, perhaps two or three miles beyond the Menai Bridge, on a curve of the Menai Strait, on a lawn sloping to the edge of the water. On the side of the London and Holyhead road, about midway between the Menai Bridge and Plas Newydd, stands the Anglesey column, |[163] erected to commemorate the military exploits of the distinguished Marquis. It was completed in 1817: the height from the base is 100 feet; the summit of the hill on which it is built 260 feet above the level of the sea. — Having explored the castle, we betook ourselves to the Pier, at the hour, when the Liverpool steam packet arrives. Admission to this pier is obtained by the payment of a light toll — the accommodation afforded by it is very great, especially to those who visit Beaumaris by the steamers. We lingered, watching the disembarkation of passengers, luggage and goods — all of which were in abundance — there was the usual bustle, the kind greeting of friends, and the natural anxiety as to the security of packages: but all passed away in a brief space of time, and on the vessel steamed for Garth Ferry, where, in the midchannel, it would discharge its Bangor freight & |[164] passengers into boats, and seek its final destination for the evening & night at the Menai Bridge — perhaps, at Caernarvon — Planning with a Livery Stable man, to whom we were recommended as a civil person, with good carriages for hire, an excursion into the mountain scenes of Capel Curig, Llanberris, & the roots of Snowdon: but the weather was threatening, and of course our setting out uncertain. — Sauntered on the Green in the evening. — An excursion steamer from the Isle of Man arrived. — Ranke's History of the Reformation in Germany.

July 19. Wednesday.

A very wet and squally day — hardly any intermission of rain. The waters of the Strait much agitated. — Of course our proposed excursion into Caernarvonshire was postponed — Received a letter from C. Bathurst — Wrote letters to Mr Geldard, to E.F.W. and to Mr Pearce — Reading the |[165] report for 1847 of the S.P.G — and the Bishop of Colombo's Journal of his Visitation Tour (Bp. Chapman) — Scarcely able to catch an interval, however short, of clear weather for a walk — made one essay in the afternoon, & was driven home again on making another effort in the Evening. — Following one of the main streets, that in which the Church is passed, pursued the road leading to the summit of the hill, and by one of the entrances to Baron Hill; after piercing through the plantations this appears to be a main road into the interior of the island — From the Green noticed vessels, said to be Guernsey or Jersey craft, dredging for oysters on the coast between Beaumaris and Penmon Point. — Beauties of England & Wales. — Ranke's Reformation in Germany. —

July 20. Thursday.

A very showery and squally day: yet in the afternoon it was sufficiently fair to permit of a walk, and the |[166] evening was fine, though windy and cold — Wrote to Messrs. Hoare desiring them to send me £35 in Bank post bills. — to Mr Wellford, after a very long silence. — Bp. of Colombo's Journal of his Visitation Tours in Ceylon. — Beauties of England and Wales. — Mr T. Turner's (Gloucester) Tour in Wales. — In exploring, near the entrance of Beaumaris from the Menai Bridge road, met with a secluded and beautiful walk by the side of a little brook which hurries down a wooded dell to empty itself into the Straits. A public footpath leading by flour mills ascends the hill, and overlooks the narrow dell with its tangled wood: deviated from this public path into the walks and drives passing through the demesne, and woods of Baron Hill, which the considerate possessors place so far at the disposal of their neighbours, the inhabitants and visitors of Beaumaris, that they are allowed to walk through them in all directions. The |[167] timber is very fine, the pastures rich, browsed by fine horned cattle, and at every vista is enjoyed the splendid view of the Menai Straits, and the Caernarvonshire range of mountains. Such liberality in the great man of the country is at once well judged and kind; nor does it seem to be at all abused. — In the forenoon the sea was much agitated; I heard that a small vessel laden was driven ashore between Beaumaris and Penmon — Ranke's history of the Reformation in Germany.

July 21. Friday.

A rainy forenoon, the afternoon fine; the evening sour, and damp — Received a very comfortable letter from E.F.W. with a favourable account of his dear wife, and a few dear little affectionate lines in her own hand. — Also a letter from Howell, who with his daughters, Laura & Constance, Macleod &c. proposes to visit Weymouth very shortly. — A letter from Messrs. Coutts in answer to mine of the 17th. Inst. — Walked towards Llanfaes |[168] as far as the Friars, the seat of a Mr Thompson, a merchant of Liverpool, which I have before noticed, and thence followed a footpath through fields, close on the edge of the shore, in the direction for Penmon: the whole walk commands a superb view of the bay of Beaumaris, the Menai Straits, and the Caernarvonshire Mountains. — Strolled on the Green in the evening. — Bp. of Colombo's Visitation Tour. — Beauties of England and Wales. — Colonial Church Chronicle — Ranke's Reformation in Germany. — |

Diary
1848

July 22. Saturday. — A sour, windy, cloudy day, with more or less rain; squally, especially in the evening, and at night. — Wrote to my son. — Colonial Church Chronicle — Beauties of England and Wales. — Ranke's Reformation in Germany. —— In my morning walk I ascended a steep hill by a road leading into the interior from the entrance to the town in the direction to the Menai Bridge; the summit commands fine views of the Straits, Bay of Beaumaris, and the Caernarvonshire range of mountains. Beyond is an undulating upland country, with rocky pastures, and grass fields, some not mown, others in swarth, or the hay making more advanced in progress. The wood extends no further than to the brow of the hill overhanging the Menai straits: beyond it is comparatively a treeless track,

Diary
1848

<u>*July 22. Saturday.*</u>

A sour, windy, cloudy day, with more or less rain; squally, especially in the evening, and at night. — Wrote to my son. — Colonial Church Chronicle — Beauties of England and Wales. — Ranke's Reformation in Germany. — In my morning walk I ascended a steep hill by a road leading into the interior from the entrance to the town in the direction to the Menai Bridge; the summit commands fine views of the Straits, Bay of Beaumaris, and the Caernarvonshire range of mountains. Beyond is an undulating upland country, with rocky pastures, and grass fields, some not mown, others in swarth, or the haymaking more advanced in progress. The wood extends no further than to the brow of the hill overhanging the Menai straits: beyond it is comparatively a treeless track, |[2] reminding me of the country near Settle or above Giggleswick; though there are many arable fields with crops of oats, barley and vetches: passed also a field of turnips, drilled, and horse hoed: returned into Beaumaris by another road, descending the hill into the town by one of the lodges leading to Baron hill, and so through Church Street. — Our evening walk led us, after pursuing for some distance the road to the Friars, through fine pastures on the left, till we joined the road leading by the Baron Hill demesne from Llanfaes into the upper end of Church Street This, like all our other walks, commands splendid views of the Bay, mountain range, &c. — From what appears in the newspaper as a report of proceedings in the Tracy Peerage case before the Committee of Privileges in the House of Lords, it would seem that the claimant, and those who assist him and support him with means to carry |[3] out his pretensions, have resorted to fraud and conspiracy in concocting evidence; the Attorney General, for the crown, has produced witnesses to shew that the alleged tomb-stone, which may be called the corner-stone of the claimant's case, purporting to have been placed over the grave of William Tracy, a son of Mʳ Justice Tracy, in Castle Brack Churchyard in Ireland — this W.T. being the person from whom the claimant professes to be lineally descended — which tombstone also in a broken state, having been used as flooring in a cottage, but of which witnesses for the claimant averred that they recollected it in the Churchyard, was produced at the bar of the House of Lords — this tomb stone is now alleged to have been a fraud and a fabrication, witnesses for the Crown coming forward to swear, — the one that he selected the stone from a quarry for the purpose of being engraved, the other that he helped to engrave the inscription, broke it, smoked |[4] so as to give it the appearance of antiquity, and all this recently, and with a view to its production in evidence to support the claim. The case is deferred till next Sessions to give the claimant time to rebut these allegations — The news from Ireland is very alarming; the revolutionists seem bent on an outbreak. In the absence of the Lord Lieutenant, now in

England, the Lords Justices, acting in his name, have proclaimed Dublin, Cork, Waterford, and Drogheda, under a recent Act of Parliament passed for the preservation of order and security, by which, after a proclamation of certain places or districts, government is armed with great and extraordinary powers to seize arms, or insurgents, and take other prompt measures to repress rebellion. — The Clubs generally organized by the republican party, in which the most inflammatory language is used, and the most inciting resolutions are passed, the |[5] members being generally drilled in preparation for an active campaign, arms being widely and secretly distributed, rescue prisoners who have been apprehended by the civil authorities, set the laws at defiance, and seem resolved to proceed to open insurrection. Government is sending to the disturbed districts large reinforcements of police and military, being also diligent in arresting the spouters and publishers of sedition. In short, a crisis seems to be come, and a collision is unavoidable. — We are told that there are many Irish visitors at Beaumaris: the alarms so prevalent in the spring, and anticipated civil war, influenced many families to leave Ireland and betake themselves to an adjoining quiet retirement in England.

July 23. Sunday.

Fine weather, with the exception of one shower in the afternoon: cloudy at times, with a cold breeze, particularly in the evening. — Attended the morning service at the parish Church: D[r] Jones, the In-|[6]cumbent, preached an excellent sermon on the Gospel for the day. — After an early dinner, I walked to the evening service at Llanfaes: the church was very crowded — A sermon was preached in aid of the funds of the Society for the Propagation of the gospel; and a collection made — Strolled in the evening on the green. — Colonial Church Chronicle — Beauties of England & Wales.

July 24. Monday.

A showery day. — The morning and forenoon fine, and sufficiently tempting to encourage us to set out on an excursion into Snowdonia. — A letter from Mess[rs.] Hoare, who forward me £35 in Bank Post bills. — The carriage we had engaged was a neat small phaeton with a head, and driving seat; drawn by one active and safe horse, driven by a civil, unobtrusive, well trained youth, the son of the proprietor of the horse and carriage, and used to act as guide on |[7] the line of road which we meant to take. — Our drive as far as the Penrhyn Arms at Bangor offered no new features, but our admiration of the scenery of the Straits, and of the Menai Bridge increases with our acquaintance with these objects. In the channel opposite to Bangor is lying a large three master, an American, arrived for a cargo of slate. — Descending the hill beyond the Penrhyn Arms Hotel, we followed the line of the celebrated Holyhead road as far as the village of Llandegai. On our left were Penrhyn Castle, its park, and home grounds, our daily object from the Green at Beaumaris, an imposing grey pile, of modern erection, but in the Norman style. The principal entrance to the Park, near the village of Llandegai, is a very ~~imposing pile~~ noble combination of tower, turret, and gateway. The village of Llandegai, with its neat church, farm houses and cottages, all in the very best order, modern-built, |[8] and erected in a style to correspond with, and not to discredit, the splendid castellated mansion close at hand, betokens the taste and the wealth of the owners and founders. Though, in fact, this is a very ancient village, the parish extending very far into the interior; — more than fifteen miles from the shore of the Menai straits, far into the

70. Snowdon.

mountainous regions of Snowdon, including a widely extended district, abounding with almost every species of mineral treasure. The scenery is beautifully picturesque and impressively grand, comprehending on one side a vast amphitheatre of mountains, and on the other a fine view of the Menai Straits — This magnificent panorama may be enjoyed in perfection from the towers or other apartments of the stately castle, raised with princely ~~magnificance~~ cost in the adjacent park — built of Mona marble — that material and the slate of the country |[9] being made available in every possible way; but we did not seek admission, preferring the grand creations of nature to the grandest efforts of man's skill in architecture, design and decoration. — At Llandegai the road to Conway and Chester turns off to the left: we pursued up the valley the great Holyhead road, constructed with so much skill through the mountainous district of North Wales, from Shrewsbury, by the eminent engineer, Telford, a great and costly national work, but now very much superseded by the modern railways leading from the Metropolis, and, indeed, from all other great and populous places and districts, to Liverpool, and now by Chester to Holyhead, so opening up a more rapid communication with Dublin. Shortly after leaving Llandegai we crossed the Chester and Holyhead railway by a bridge, not far from the mouth of the Tunnel by which it pierces the lofty hill forming one |[10] side of the narrow valley in which the city of Bangor stands. To the right of us, and generally parallel with, and close to the road, is the tramway by which the slates are transported from the Dolawen Slate quarries to the port of Penrhyn. The mouth of the beautiful valley is rich in meadow, pasture, corn and wood. To the left of us flowed the mountain river Ogwen, which we accompanied even to its source; here it is a clear, dark, foamy, rocky torrent, its banks fringed with wood, now brawling over rapids, now reposing in placid reaches. As we advanced the mountains closed in, as it were, to the right and to the left; on the right Marchlyn Mawr, I believe, to the left the giant masses of Carnedd David and Carnedd Llewellyn. Here and there we noticed the rude, white washed, and slate roofed cottages of the peasantry and quarrymen, all of one story in height. As we approached the great |[11] slate works, the houses were more numerous, the population evidently denser, and the cottages formed into groupes, till at last we entered what may be called a town, with its inns, and shops, and two enormous meeting houses, one, Bethesda, a congregational chapel, staring at a huge Calvinist Methodist chapel on the opposite side of the road. Near at hand is a church built and endowed by the Penrhyn, that is, now, the Dawkins Pennant family: thus they, the great lords of the land, the great improvers of the district, are not unmindful of the spiritual interests of the humble workmen, peasantry, and tenantry on their fine estate, of those whose labours, otherwise liberally paid, contribute to the developement of those natural treasures of the soil, from which so great a revenue is derived. Near the point also, embosomed in trees, on the margin of the Ogwen, is a villa, occasionally |[12] resorted to by the family, Ogwen Bank. Near it we deviated from the main road, crossing the Ogwen, and approaching the slate quarries through a dense plantation, which somewhat sheltered us from a sharp and short pelting shower. But the sun broke out again as we reached the works, and the moisture so quickly evaporated or drained off the slaty pathways, that we found no inconvenience in walking over the quarries. Having procured the services of an intelligent guide we ascended by an inclined plane used for letting down on rails the loaded slate carts by means of chains worked by windlasses; we obtained as we advanced a distinct notion of the vast range of works. The dark towering mountain is gradually in the course of being removed piece-meal — Its height is divided into stories, accessible by inclined planes, communicating from one range to another: |[13] These ranges or stories resemble, on a gigantic scale, the rows of steps on an ancient Grecian or Roman theatre; they are sufficiently wide to afford ample space for the passage of workmen, visitors, waggons and horses, with deposits of slate, working sheds, and machinery; sufficiently lofty to afford a large surface of rock above the spacious ledge to be quarried by the workmen, who throng the precipitous sides, looking like busy bees or birds, digging, boring and hammering, as they cling to the face of the cliff, suspended by ropes on which they hang, if their uncertain footing should give way. Four men form a gang; two are engaged in getting the slate; the other two split and dress them. The average wages of a good man are 23/- or 24/- weekly: if the rock be good, and works well, without much refuse, the above would be the net earnings after paying for tools, blasting powder, and |[14] other requisites. There are generally 1500 men of all sorts employed on the works; the clearing away of the unproductive portions of the rock is done by the yard; many men are employed with horses in driving the loaded tram carts; the labourers, on warning of the approaching explosion of a blast, retire to the sheds; numerous workmen are employed in excavating tunnels, in managing water wheels and machinery required for draining the works; others ply the carpenter's or wheelwright's, or blacksmith's, trades. Some portion of the slate rock is of a red colour, this, though equally good, is less esteemed than the blue slate; large portions of the mountain are beds of another rock not convertible into slate; these are got rid of as refuse, or left in insulated masses; one lofty pyramidal rock of this kind occupies a central position in the space which has been long |[15] since exhausted of slate. In splitting the slates, which process is performed in sheds on the ledges, the thick fragment is more readily divided into laminæ when it has been recently gotten than when it has been long exposed to the variations of the atmosphere, — to heat or cold. One workman is engaged in splitting; the thinner laminæ are, when just parted, more or less elastic, after the manner of whale bone; another workman sits and squares the

71. Snowdon.

slates, cutting off, by a rapid process, by a mallet and fixed knife, the irregular edges; thus forming a slate into different sizes denominated Queens, Duchesses, Countesses &c. according as the dimensions are larger or smaller — The blasting is so arranged as to be between 12 o clock and 1 PM; in the hour allotted for dinner. We were present at this hour. The signal is given from the top of the mountain by a loud blast of a discordant horn; this warns the workmen and others to |[16] retire, and seek a place of shelter. Placed at one end of the ledge on which we had been surveying the works we watched the process. Frequent and loud explosions resounded on all sides; it was not one volley, but a kind of running fire, each explosion being indicated by a volume of ascending smoke, and here and there the crash of falling fragments of rock: but, generally speaking, no great quantity of the material is shivered or dislodged; the purpose is best answered by the loosening of the masses. Accidents to the workmen are, of course, common; and the proprietors maintain a hospital in the vicinity, whither the many who are injured and wounded in the works are conveyed for medical or surgical attendance. — I was told that, of the workmen, hardly three in a hundred can speak English. The attendants at Church are said to be more numerous than for-|[17] merly: in the dissenters' chapels Welsh is the language in which the services are performed: there are Sunday Schools in which English is taught, but very few profit by the instruction; for the learners forget at home and in the works the slender knowledge of the foreign tongue acquired on the Sundays. The men are always paid in money; and there is nothing approaching to the truck system. Descending from the ledge which we had traversed from one end to the other, greatly interested by all we had seen, we bought two or three little specimens of slate, inkstands formed like a miniature shoe, hardly larger than a man's thumb, with other diminutive knick knacks were offered to us, contrasting with the huge masses which lie about formed for cisterns, troughs, baths, tombstones, chimney pieces & the like. It is calculated that two hundred tons of slates are daily conveyed from the quarries by the tram-|[18] road to Port Penrhyn. These quarries were discovered as far back as the reign of Elizabeth. A late Lord Penrhyn greatly improved the method of working them, more than sixty years ago: it is said that the tram road which he constructed, six miles in length, cost him £170,000. — Having resumed our seats in our carriage we proceeded by a private road from the works to regain the turnpike road from which we had deviated. In so doing we crossed the Ogwen, by an ornamental bridge thrown over a bustling, brawling, rocky reach of the mountain torrent, overarched by spreading trees, just above where a picturesque fall tumbles over huge obstructing masses of rock. Onwards we went, to the mouth of the Nantfrancon Vale, the Beavers Hollow — the glen in past ages having been, it is said, the resort of those animals. At first we caught beautiful glimpses of the river and its rapids hurrying on under |[19] bowery foliage: but the trees soon became rare, the mountains closing in on both sides. — Slight showers of rain came on, but did not much incommode us: in one respect we were benefited by them, and their predecessors of the past week, for they elicited the watery treasures of the mountain sides in diminutive cataracts, silvery streamlets, bounding, leaping, flashing, dashing, splashing, between the rocks and by the shale beds on every side. One, of greater pretension than its neighbours, probably never failing, to the left of the road, rushes down the green mountain face from the summit to the base in a serpentine channel. The construction of the road calls for admiration, as it follows the sinuosities of the base or side of the mountain, well protected by a strong parapet wall, sometimes on a level with the valley, sometimes much above it. Now comes a slow, almost imperceptible, gradual ascent: the thin strip of narrow meadow in the valley manifestly |[20] is becoming less worth cultivation, more boggy, more encumbered with masses of dislodged rock, hurled by the winter storms, in bygone years or ages, from the mountains summits or sides: the stream is contracted to a mere thread: and its margin is little better than turbary.[1] The mountains at the upper end of the valley form a Scene singularly grand; on each side the hollow seems guarded by a huge conical rock, Trivaen on the right, Braich du on the left. These, with the Glyder Vach, and Glyder vawr, and some other mountains, fill up the distance, and apparently close the vale. In front of us, just to the right of the road, by which we had been gradually ascending to the higher level of lake Ogwen, through a dark, rifted chasm in the rocky pass, tumbled a noble cataract in three successive falls, down a height of 100 feet. These are called the falls of Benglog, and are the outlet of Lake Ogwen: the scene is exceedingly striking. |[20] Having gained the higher level, and turned our back on the Alpine valley of Nant-francon, we reached the margin of Lake Ogwen, reposing in a bason of rocks, or mountain hollow, beside which the road passes for half a mile, a cold-looking, clear tarn, ruffled in the sharp breeze, curling with foam-crested wavelets. Not a tree, or a bush is to be seen. The lake is said to abound in trout. — The road proceeds for some miles through a wide moor-like valley, much such a district as one meets on the summits of Craven Hills; the hills on high ground on each side low, little cultivation, and poor vegetation; the few cottages rude, the buildings and fences homely and neglected; mountain sheep and black cattle graze the hill-sides; such meagre hungry meadows as there are were under the scythe, and the thin population busy with a thinner crop: the implement reminded us of Craven fashions, a long unwieldy scythe blade, in a longer and |[21] more unwieldy straight handle. Found that we had reached the watershed of this moorland tract, when the rivulets took a[n] west-wa east-ward

---

1.   Turbary – from the same root as turf. A tract of land where peat may be dug for fuel – a peat bog.

72. Beddgelert.

course; before they had flowed Westward to form the Ogwen, now they took a contrary direction, and eventually empty themselves into the Conway river; the hill sides seem alive, during this showery season, with springing waters; tumbling streamlets rush down every hollow and crevice, to form a brook, which soon swells into a respectable mountain torrent — Again reminded of Craven by the smell of peat smoke, turf-stacks, and detached masses of rock frequent in the pastures: not less so by the rude walls separating the fields, and the gaps in them without gates, or only the ghost of gates of by gone years. – The descent becomes more rapid into the valley through which the Holyhead road is carried Eastward towards Shrewsbury; leaving that road we turned to the ~~left~~ right to Capel Curig. |[22] At this point, looking up the Capel Curig valley, the view is closed by the peaks of Snowdon and kindred mountains; the prospect is extremely grand. Pass a square mass of building, stabling on a large scale for the adjacent inn — cross the mountain torrent by a bridle; — to the left the neat little chapel dedicated to a Welsh saint, with its quiet cemetery, and two or three cottages nestling close to the grave yard, under the shelter of some trees — beyond, overhung by a shrubby cliff of no great height, and topped by trees, blocking up, as it were, the narrow entrance of the vale, the long straggling mass of buildings forming the hotel, with appendant stabling, coach houses, and other offices – Here we were ushered into an odd looking combination of parlours and passages, with one upper story of bedrooms, our apartment looking into a quaint garden, meet accompaniment to a quaint house; for the whole building on this side is constructed with a coating of blue slate pinned to the wall, even to the |[23] chimneys, such being probably in this Alpine valley the best preservative against rain & wind, and snow and frost. Here we baited for above two hours of fair weather, and enjoyed a good dinner on Welsh salmon and Welsh mutton, both excellent in their kind — Passing through the garden of our hostelry, we crossed a rude mountain bridge passable only on foot, thrown over the outlet of ~~one or~~ two mountain pools, which form a bason for the rivulets by which the Capel Curig valley and its mountain barriers are drained. From the bridge the view of Snowdon and its compeers is exceedingly striking, and at its foot, two slouched hatted and cloaked tourist artists were attentively transferring to their sketch books the mountain scene. A boat kept here invites travellers to explore the upper portion of these lakelets which extends ~~for~~ some distance up the valley, under the huge mountain Moel Siabod, whose height is 2878 feet, rising from the margin of these pools. |[24] Up the copse clad root of this mountain we strolled for a short walk, enjoying the fine mountain view up the valley towards Snowdon. As the glen is bounded on the one side by Moel Siabod, so on the other by the lofty barriers of Marchwyl Mawr, and Glydir Vawr and Bach. It is a splendid wild mountain dell; at our feet the pools curled by the stirring breeze into more than a ripple — Proceeding in the direction by which we had approached the hotel, and over the bridge and by the Chapel, the eye rested on the fine not unwooded valley through which the mainroad is carried towards Cernioge, Llangollen & Shrewsbury; we were fortunate in the alternations of light and shade so noticeable on a showery day, and particularly ~~noticed~~ observed a very striking outline of projecting pinnacled cliffs in fine sunlight backed by a loftier and gloomy precipice — We had hitherto travelled about 22 miles; the distance from Beaumaris to Bangor |[25] being seven miles, from thence to Capel Curig fifteen. — The latter place is situate in a district abounding with mineral wealth; much calamine has been obtained here — From the hotel, as a point for starting, many interesting objects are within reach, as Dolwyddelau Castle, beneath Moel Siabod, Eastward — Rhaiadr y Wennol, or the Waterfall of the Swallow – and others. — At half past four P.M. we set out for Llanberris, distant ten miles: our route lay up a long desolate valley, not unlike that between Ingleborough and Whernside mountains, on the road from Ingleton to Hawes. The mountain tops were capped with clouds: gusty rain came scudding along; the showers and the wind were cold; but every where there was interest in the rocks and rivulets, and rude bridges, and scattered cottages or crumbling walls. At the head of what I term the Capel Curig valley, the road to Bedd Gellert down Nant Gwynnant, |[26] or the Vale of Gwynnant, deviates from that which we were to pursue. This pass between towering mountains, in the very heart's core of Snowdonia, is said to be one of the most beautiful glens in Wales, wood, lake, torrent, rock, meadow, and mountain contributing to its perfections. We viewed it from its origin, as we toiled up a long steep ascent, the road being formed along the bare side of Glydir Vawr, precipice below, precipice above, a recent work of engineering, opening a more ready communication through these wild passes than heretofore was attainable. As our good horse slowly but steadily toiled up the hill, we enjoyed amid scudding mists, or gusty rain, at brief intervals, striking views down the rifted sides of the mountains, and along the wider valley below. At length, in a heavy shower and strong blast, we surmounted the acclivity, by winding round the shoulder of the mountain to the summit overlooking the valley of Llanberris. Here we entered on the |[27] farfamed Llanberris pass: all is rock and defile, and barrenness; hardly a vestige of vegetation; peaked summits towering above rugged dark cliffs. The traveller believes each to be the veritable Snowdon; but the monarch lies still further and higher up, on the left hand as our road led us; he reveals not the terrors of his brow. At Gorphwysfa, a dreary abode, the place of rest on the top of the pass, a track to the left leads to the peak of Snowdon; this is one of the roads by which the giant is sought by younger and more adventurous tourists than ourselves. Some ascend from Beddgellert, and descend by Gorphwysfa: some reverse the order; others, and this, I believe, is the more easy track, ascend from Llanberris and Dolbadarn tower, returning to the point from which they

73. Penrhyn Castle.

started, or descending to Beddgellert, or Gorphwysfa — From this resting place the distance to Llanberris is four miles; the descent into the valley is rapid, |[28] full of horrors to the horror loving or seeking, a narrow defile, precipices on either side, stony, slaty, shaly, rocky desolation. Towards the foot of the declivity is a slender slip of peaty greensward, intersected by a silvery, thread-like rivulet, incessantly acquiring breadth & force from contributory rills and miniature cascades leaping down the mountain sides – Vast masses of rock hurled from the summit, or loosened and dashed to the bottom in times long past, arrest the attention on each side of the road: one more especially of enormous size, far exceeding in its dimensions the famous Bowderstone in Borrowdale, is said, or fabled, to have afforded a home to a goodwife tending her cows in the glen, and making a house of an angle which two of its sides formed with the ground. The village of Llanberris is truly Alpine, a congregation of low roofed cottages, clustering in a nook of green meadows, under the towering eminences encircling it, near its |[29] humble low church, now unroofed, as it is undergoing repair. As in Switzerland, the slated roofs of the cottages are secured from being stripped by the fury of winter storms, by fragments of stone of ponderous bulk, binding down the slates (as it were, to their good behaviour. The village is said to have derived its name from S[t.] Peris, a British saint, who is traditionally reported to have resided on this spot with Padarn, an anchorite of the sixth century, who reared a cell or small chapel in a meadow, below Dolbadarn Castle, to which he gave a name, not far from the junction of the two Llanberris lakes. Adjacent to the church is a holy well, dedicated to the patron saint, once in high repute, but now neglected, the spread of knowledge penetrating even into the defiles of the Welch mountains dissipating even the popular superstition in respect of the supposed wonder-working, vatidical,[2] or healing fountains. The parish of Llanberis is very |[30] extensive comprising several of the loftiest mountains in the principality. "Nature has here," says Camden, speaking of

---

2.   Vatidical – this should be fatidical – gifted with prophetic powers.

these parts of Caernarvonshire, "reared huge groupes of mountains, as if she intended to bind the island fast to the bowels of the earth, and made a safe retreat for the Britons in time of war. For here are so many crags and rocks, so many wooded vallies, rendered impassable by so many lakes, that the lightest troops, much less an army, could never find their way among them. These mountains may be truly called the British Alps: for besides that they are the highest in the whole Island, they are, like the Alps, bespread with broken crags on every side, all surrounding one, which, towering in the centre, far above the rest, lifts its head so loftily as if it meant not only to threaten, but to thrust it into the sky." Tho' now almost entirely denuded of wood, ancient tradition, and records, and the code of Welch laws attest that this district was truly |³¹ a forest: The upper vale of Llanberris thro' which we had been travelling is in the language of the country called Cwm-glas, or the green hollow. — The upper lake of Llanberis³

74. *Penrhyn Slate Quarries, Snowdonia.*

adjoins the village and the road along which we travelled passes by its margin till an ascent conducts over a spur of the mountain, beneath overhanging rock and crags, among which the miner toils by a steep and rugged path to copper shafts, or conveys to the water edge the extracted ore. This lake, called also Llyn Peris, is about a mile in length, and nearly half a mile in breadth; it is a very deep pool reposing in the bosom of gigantic mountains. Arrived at the top of the ascent, Dolbadarn tower, which we had seen before us for some time past, crowned a rocky knoll, over hanging a meadow, washed by the foot of the upper lake; to the left was a recent plantation of flourishing larch and ~~fur~~ ᶠⁱʳ creeping up the root and foot of the |³² mountain, cottages nestled at the base of another eminence, several houses betokened our approach to a place of much resort, and a few minutes brought us to the door of a huge hotel, the Royal Victoria, where we were hospitably received, the Welch harper, the bustling landlord, his smart and somewhat giddy daughters, being all on the alert on a new arrival. Installed in an apartment commanding a superb view of the now widely expanded valley, and the lower lake, with a comfortable adjacent bedroom. Walked out to explore the locality, and soon reached the Knoll on which Dolbadarn tower stands, a ~~lonle~~ lonely beacon in ruin. Dolbadarn properly signifies Padarn's meadow which the castle overlooks. It is the only fortress remaining in all the narrow passes of North Wales. Of the five narrow passes by which the mountain district might be penetrated from the coast of Caernarvonshire or Anglesey, this was the central, and it alone retains |³³ any remains of the stronghold by which

---

3.   As with previous examples, Francis Witts is not precise with his spelling of proper names, and slips from 'Llanberris' to 'Llanberis' and back again.

each was fortified. What here survives is a round tower only, its inner diameter ten yards, and its height twenty five yards. The British Kings acted on a small scale, compared with the Norman: this fort could only have accommodated a small garrison. It this castle Owen Goch was confined for upwards of twenty years, for having joined in a rebellion against his brother Llewellyn ap Gryffyd, the last prince of Wales. It seems to have been long in ruins, for in Leland's time there was only a piece of a tower left. The view from hence is exceedingly splendid, embracing the two lakes, extending nearly three miles, with the various interesting objects by which they are surrounded, especially the enormous chain of mountains bounding the vale. The horror of the higher lake and glen melting into the beauty of the lower lake and valley is peculiarly striking; the two sheets of water are |³⁴ united by a natural canal or river, which passes through the meadow below the tower; this meadow parts the upper from the lower lake. Opposite, on the other side of this stream, the frowning mountains rise precipitously from the water's edge: the base is clothed with brush wood, the sides, of sheer slate rock, are quarried for slates; this range of quarries, very extensive, but far less so than those we had visited in the morning, are the property of Mᴿ Asheton Smith, who has great estates here — The slate procured is conveyed by a tramway carried on the opposite side, from the quarry, along the margin of the lower lake, proceeding thence to a port or wharf on the ~~margin~~ ᵇᵃⁿᵏ of the Menai strait; there it is shipped for exportation. Our hotel is the property of Mᴿ Smith, occupying with its large range of stabling and offices, the slope of the projecting hill or knoll on the edge of whose rocky cliff the remains of the castle stand: the base of this |³⁵ hill on one side is clothed with a young larch plantation, through which walks are formed, leading from the garden attached to the hotel to the tower — Through this I returned, listening to the sound of a distant waterfall, which feeds a torrent rushing from its basin, and hurrying across the main roads beneath the Hotel and the Tower to the foot of the Upper Lake. The immediate vicinity of the hotel was crowded by boys tendering their services as

75. Llanberis.

guides to Snowdon, to the waterfall, to the slate quarries, or to the castle. Lower down in the Valley, a quarter of a mile distant, is another and smaller hotel, Dolbadarn Inn. The windows of this much smaller hostelry must command a noble view of the lower lake, of Dolbadarn tower, and of the gigantic mountains enclosing the upper lake and glen, as also of the recess to the right, with its plantations, cottages, torrent, and waterfall; but it is a little too remote from |[36] the ruin, and from the mouth of the gorge, forming the entrance of the defile leading to Llanberis village and pass. — From the public journals of the day it appears that Ministers have applied to Parliament for an act to be instantly passed to suspend the Habeas Corpus act in Ireland till Mar. 1. 1849 — in both houses the proposition received almost unanimous acquiescence, the impression being almost universal that the Irish insurrection, which may be now considered as not only organized, but in active operation, must be put down at all hazards with the strongest energies which the government can exert; the humane provisions of the law need to be suspended, the hands of the executive need to be strengthened, and the military and police must be brought to bear on the rebels, high or low. —

July 25. Tuesday.

Very wet and showery weather till nearly 2 P.M: afterwards fine |[37] till 8 P.M. when a shower came on — After breakfast I stole out in a transient gleam of fair weather to the point where the stream connecting the two lakes falls into the lower from the upper. A rude bridge spans the little river, leading to the tram road by which the slate is conveyed from the quarries to its port of embarkation. A few pleasure boats were moored at the head of the lower lake. Nothing can exceed the beauty of the scene which meets the eye at this point — the ruined tower, crowning its promontory; the fine sheets of water filling the hollow; especially the upper lake stretching to the village and church of Llanberris, with its circle of rugged and towering mountains. For those who embark on the lower lake the peak of Snowdon forms a splendid back ground. Char used to abound in these lakes, but have disappeared since the copper mines have been worked — |[38] Taking advantage of another brief interval of fair weather, MW. and myself set out to visit Ceunant Mawr cataract – nearly half a mile distant from our hotel, at the termination of a deep glen. We selected two boys as our guides, one of whom, thirteen years of age, was exceedingly intelligent: his father had been for an equal number of years a Snowdon guide, and among the travellers whom he had escorted he named the King of Saxony: the boy was already arrived at the dignity of a guide on his own account, exhibiting a written testimonial which a party of pedestrians bore to his activity, carefulness, and intelligence. From the boy I collected that his English had been partly taught him by his father, but that his study of the foreign tongue had been greatly helped by a winter passed on the Menai strait, where he had worked at the Britannia tunnel bridge. Very few of the Llanberris peasantry learn or can speak |[39] English. — Passed by some rude low whitewashed cottages; crossed by a humble foot bridge the brawling torrent fed by the water fall as it hurries to empty itself in the lake; leaving on the left hand the bason which the cataract forms, and which is encircled by copse wood, we ascended a steep hill by a path, which brought us on a turfy eminence, opposite to, and looking down upon the mountain stream, as it hurried down the rocky cleft: the fall is oblique, a broad smooth ledge of rock intercepting the downward leap of the stream, and giving it for some distance a rapid and sideward direction, while some of the body of water leaps in the opposite direction over the edge of the interposing bed of rock, from which the torrent falls precipitously in a mass of foam, fringed by brushwood foliage into a deep rocky bason. Ceunant Mawr signifies the Waterfall of the Great chasm. It is upwards of |[40] sixty feet in height, and is formed by the torrent from Cwm Brwynog. From the elevation which we had attained we watched for a little while a pedestrian party setting out for the top of Snowdon, breasting the ascent above the valley, destined soon to be overtaken by heavy rain, but, if they persevered, likely to be rewarded by a fine afternoon, and bright weather, when they attained the summit. — Having again returned to the hotel, I ventured with umbrella and cloak, and accompanied by one of our boy-guides, to explore the locality of the Slate quarries opposite to Dolbadarn tower, but the heavy rain drove me back, not till I was well soaked, and needed to dry my gripping garments. — About 1000 men are usually employed at the Dinorwic Slate quarry, and about 100 tons daily, throughout the year, are said to be conveyed by the tramway, a distance of nine miles, to the shipping port, at Velin Heli, on the Menai straits. — About one o clock so |[41] impetuous was the downfall of rain, that it seemed as if we should be weather bound; but a sudden change ensued, the sky cleared up, all was bright sunshine, and we prepared for departure after a luncheon, or early dinner. We left the Victoria Hotel for Caernarvon at half past two o clock: the distance is eight miles. The early part of the drive is beautiful, the road skirts the lower lake amid and along outliers of the mighty mountains now rapidly sinking into a comparative level. Looking backward, the view of the pass of Llanberis, and the magnificent Snowdon group, is surpassingly grand. — Shall we ever see them more? it is very improbable — "time has thinned my flowing hair, and all but bent me with his iron rod:" to my mind recurred the old lines reported to have been uttered by Queen Mary of Scots in a mountain valley in Derbyshire — "Buxtona, quæ calidæ |[42] ulebrabere nomine lymphæ, / Post hac mihi non adeunda, vale. At the foot of the lake a bridge leads, I believe, to a very

76.
Caernarvon Castle.

perfect Roman station called Dinas Dinorwic, partly natural and partly artificial. The bridge crosses the Seiont river, the drain of the Llanberris lakes and valley, which discharges itself into the Menai at Caernarvon. About a mile beyond the bridge on the left of the road we were travelling stands Bryn Bras Castle, a modern mansion, the residence of a Mr Williams. The country, as we advanced, became uninteresting; the land is indifferent; yet the crops of barley and oats were promising; on our left were round topped hills, outliers of the Snowdon chain, but unpicturesque in outline: Still further, southward, rising out of the plain, and remote, giving one to recollect the Malvern range, as being detached, and overlooking a level country, yet much bolder and more mountainous in their outline than the Malvern Hills, — the Rivals, the English |[43] version of the Welch Yr Eifl, leading one to suppose that a visit into that peninsular part of Caernarvonshire, in which are the towns of Pwlheli, Nevin &c., would reward the traveller. Further on the scenery improves, as the traveller again approaches the Seiont river winding between high wooded banks, on its way to Caernarvon, where, passing near the site and remains of the ancient Roman Station Segontium, to which it seems to have given a name, it falls into the sea at the mouth of the Menai Straits, forming the harbour of Caernarvon. Having crossed the river, the Castle of Caernarvon with its many towers rose before us in the level; beyond it the bay forming the entrance of the Menai Strait; still more remote the flat level of Anglesey; on the horizon the high lands about Holyhead. Nearer Caernarvon we passed some handsome villas on rising ground, and noticed to the right of the Town a rocky knoll which must com-|[44] mand a very fine and extensive view. — Entered Caernarvon, as I believe, through the suburb of Llanbeblig, the church of which village is the mother church to the Chapel of St. Mary's in Caernarvon, which seems originally to have been the Chapel of the Garrison. Caernarvon is much lauded as the metropolis of North Wales, and a commodious town, beautifully situate, in a fine country, and in the vicinity of many interesting objects, but appeared as we drove towards the Market place, and castle precincts, in a street leading out of which was our Inn, the Sportsman, a mean place. Here we remained for an hour and half, while our horse was baited, and strolled out to explore; the Castle, of course was our principal object, and it is very well worth visiting. The entrance is through a lofty gateway, over which is yet left a mutilated figure, supposed to be that of Edward 1. In this gateway there are the grooves of no less |[45] than four portcullises, evidences of the former strength of the fortress. The building is large, but irregular, and much more shattered within than, from viewing it on the outside, no one would be led to imagine – The towers are chiefly octagonal, but three or four of them have each ten sides; among the latter is the Eagle Tower, the largest and by far the most elegant in the whole building. This tower, which received its name from the figure of an eagle still left at its summit, though much mutilated, stands at one end of the oblong court of the castle, and three handsome turrets issue from it. It was in the Eagle tower that Edward, the first Prince of Wales, afterwards Edward 2 was born in 1284. At the other end of this court and opposite to this tower is a gate called the Queen's Gate. It is said to be that through which the faithful Eleanor, Queen of Edward 1, first entered the Castle. The state apartments are large and |[46] commodious, but all is in a state of utter dilapidation. The floors and staircases, throughout the castle, are, with one or two exceptions, beaten in and demolished. A narrow gallery or covered way formerly extended round this fortress, by which, during a siege, a communication could be had with the other parts without danger. One side presents this gallery, along which

*77. Eagle Tower,
Caernarvon Castle.*

we passed, still entire. It was next to the outer wall, and was lighted by narrow slips which served as stations from whence arrows and other missile weapons could be discharged upon the enemy. The castle occupies the whole west end of the town; and was a place of such strength as, before the introduction of artillery, to withstand the most furious attacks of an enemy. The exterior walls are in general about nine feet thick. It is bounded on two sides by water; the mouth of the river Seiont washes the quay which extends below the castle, and, doubtless, in ancient times |[47] reached the foot of the castle walls: the Eagle tower and adjacent portion of the castle fronts the bay, and the space between it and the water is also a part of the Quay. A ditch probably was carried round the castle on the land side. From whatever point or from whatever distance it is viewed, Caernarvon castle has a romantic singularity and air of dignity, being both a picturesque and a striking object. Its ivy-clad walls appear in parts to be fast going to decay, while in others they even yet retain their ancient exterior. Caernarvon probably had its origin in an ancient Roman city Segontium, about half a mile distant – The name is properly Caer yn Arvon — the walled town in the district opposite to Anglesey. Arvôn or Armôn signifies opposite to Mona. Segontium is mentioned in the itinerary of Antoninus. It appears to have been the principal station of the Romans in North Wales, all the rest being |[48] subordinate. The walls round Caernarvon are even yet nearly entire, bearing much the same external appearance which they did in the time of their founder, Edward 1. They have in them a number of round towers, and two principal gates, entrances to the town. Over one of these is the town hall. Of late the town has been greatly enlarged outside the walls. Along the side of the Menai is a broad terrace walk, extending from the quay to the north end of the town walls. The county hall, a building devoid of architectural merit, stands nearly opposite the castle gates: near it is the county prison, to which purpose one of the ancient towers has been converted. Our ramble led us along the quay: there were many traders alongside the pier, and the appearance of much business: but the principal article in demand is slate, many thousands of which are stacked on the quay ready for exportation. These are brought from the inland quarries, chiefly by tramways: Cil gwyn, the white |[49] recess, in the parish of Llanlyffni: Cefndu, the black ridge, in the parish of Llanrug; and Alltdu, the Black cliff, in the mountains on the North East side of the lakes of Llanberis, furnish the largest quantities — Caernarvon would seem to offer much amusement in excursions to the lovers of sailing, and there are many objects of interest both on the Caernarvonshire coast and in Anglesey, which may be visited in boats — In the open square or Market place contiguous to the Castle we visited a small bookseller's shop, and purchased several views of the scenery which we had visited. — At six in the evening we again were on the way to Beaumaris, and passed out of the town by the Uxbridge Arms, a very handsome hotel in the outskirts, fronting the Menai Straits, and adjoining Forthill, the rocky knoll which I mentioned as seen on approaching Caernarvon. The distance to Beaumaris is twelve miles — |[50] The strait was seen by us to advantage, for the tide was high, but the road, which is excellent, does not pass through a tract of much interest; it is level on both sides, affording good sites for comfortable villas. On the opposite shore of the strait we had a view of Plas Newydd, the seat of the Marquis of Anglesey. As we proceeded, the road retires in-land, being no longer continued along the coast line: but we again touched on the Strait at a little port for shipping slate, with a sheltered creek, in which several vessels were lying, and where there is an inclined plane for tramwaggons conveying slate, as I suppose, from the Llanberis quarries. Again proceeding inland, and losing the sea, we passed Vaenol, a seat of M[r] Asheton Smith, and through a well timbered tract, in which is Bryntirion, the seat of a M[r] Griffiths. Somewhat beyond, on the right hand, a road leads into the hill country, being a line by which Llan-|[51] beris may be reached without going round by Caernarvon. Soon afterwards we returned to the edge of the Straits at the Menai Bridge, which we crossed, and by half past seven arrived at our lodgings at Beaumaris, having greatly

78. *Caernarvon Castle.*

79. *Caernarvon Castle, Queen's Gate.*

enjoyed our short excursion — We found that visitors had sought us out yesterday: Mrs. Hunt had been so obliging as to drive over with her family from her residence at Glangwnna, between Caernarvon and Llanberis; she had been informed of the circumstance that we were staying at Beaumaris by Miss S. Hunt. This was an unexpected civility and compliment, as we had no personal acquaintance with this very distant relative, who is the widow of the late Rowland Hunt of Boreatton: she resides in North Wales at a place near which we had passed this morning, not knowing that we were in its vicinity, with her two sons and daughter. The elder son will |52 soon attain his majority, and come into possession of his Shropshire estates. Whether Glangwnna belongs to the Hunt family, or to the Lloyds, a Shrewsbury family, Bankers, Mrs. Hunt having been a Miss Lloyd, I am not sure. – My son, as a schoolboy at Shrewsbury, had experienced much kind civility, from the Hunts, being a frequent guest at Boreatton, at West Felton, the residence of Mr. Thos. Hunt, who is incumbent of that parish, and brother of Rowland Hunt the elder, and George Hunt, and at Ruyton, where the widow Mrs. Hunt, grandmother of the present possessor of Boreatton, resided with her daughter, Miss Hunt. — Ranke's History of the Reformation in Germany. —

July 26. Wednesday.

A rainy forenoon: the afternoon fine, but close and cloudy; the evening cold with a fresh breeze. — Received a letter from E.F.W. with a very comfortable account of our dearest Sophy, who has been to church, and has taken a |53 drive, and called on Lady Wemyss, who with her Lord, the ladies Charteris, and Mr. Wildman, are now staying at the mansion house at Stanway, for the usual fortnight's annual visit. — MW. received a letter from Eliza Daniell, announcing the death of Mr. George Barr, at Henwick; where he resided with his sister, Mrs. Walker, and Miss Barr. Mr. G.B. had long been in a precarious state of health.

His decease is a great trouble to M$^{rs.}$ Cha$^{s.}$ Barr, who was much attached to him, looking up to him as a guide and adviser. He was a useful man of business, Executor to the late Charles Barr, one of the Trustees of the marriage Settlement on the marriage of M^r and M$^{rs.}$ C.B., my son, and a cousin of M$^{rs.}$ C.B., Mr Daniel, one of the Comm$^{rs.}$ in Bankruptcy for the Birmingham district, being the others. — Eliza Daniell proposes to visit us at Upper Slaughter in September. — Walked before dinner in the |^{54} direction of the Menai Bridge; in the evening on the green. — Ranke's History of the Reformation in Germany. —

July 27. Thursday.

A fine day: cold & rough in the forenoon; in the afternoon & evening less boisterous. — Received a letter from Winter: all well at Upper Slaughter — A letter from the Clerk of the Gloucester Lunatic Asylum, announcing a meeting of Visitors for Aug. 1. — A letter from Mess$^{rs.}$ Hoare, announcing that Lady Wilmot Horton has paid to my account with them £194. 3. 4 — being half a year's Interest on a mortgage loan of £10000 — less Income Tax. — Wrote a long letter to E.F.W. — Walked in the beautiful grounds and plantations adjoining Baron Hill: — in the evening on the green — Colonial Church Chronicle — Ranke's History of the Reformation in Germany — The people at Liverpool are in great uneasiness in consequence of |^{55} of[4] the crowds of dissaffected Irish congregated there. It appears that clubs consisting of persons holding the most revolutionary opinions are organized there, and that among the populace there is great sympathy with the rebel Irish. It is represented that the disaffected at Liverpool have secretly provided arms, and fear is entertained, now that the crisis is come in Ireland, that disturbances will break out at Liverpool. Government has, therefore, detached a considerable military force to be encamped near Liverpool; the Police force is largely recruited, the constables being drilled for active service: and a petition has been presented in the House of Commons, praying that the Act for the suspension of the Habeas Corpus Act may be extended so as to operate not only in Ireland, but also to comprehend Liverpool.

July 28. Friday.

Fine weather: in the Evening overclouded and damp. — Wrote to |^{56} M$^{rs.}$ C. Barr, condoling with her on the death of Mr George Barr: — to M$^{rs.}$ Hunt of Glangwnna, apologizing for not returning her visit, and acknowledging her politeness in calling upon us. — I took a very pleasant walk to, and beyond Llanfaes, returning by the shore, enjoying beautiful views of the bay and the Caernarvonshire mountains. — Beauties of England and Wales — Colonial Church Chronicle — Ranke's History of the Reformation in Germany.

July 29. Saturday.

Heavy rain had fallen in the night; but the weather was fine, though dull — & not much sunshine — Wrote to Mr Winter that we purpose returning home on the 5$^{th.}$ Aug: — to Mr Thomas, Newspaper Agent, London, desiring him not to forward our S$^t.$ James's Chronicle elsewhere than to Upper Slaughter, after the receipt of my letter. — Engaged the comfortable open carriage in which we had visited the Caernarvonshire mountain scenery for a |^{57} little

---

4.　Inadvertently duplicated on the change of folio.

excursion to Penmon and back: the distance is four miles and a half, and we were about three hours. The road leads by "the Friars;" — diverging from the main road, we passed through devious lanes, the roads being but indifferent, and kept along, or at a little distance from the shore of the bay, which is every where indented with little recesses or bay-lets, and more or less rocky. We passed some fine fields of wheat, barley, and oats – inland, low hills rose to our left. In a grove on a knoll was Trér Castell, now occupied as a farm house, an old castellated mansion. Here, in a style of rude hospitality, in the 13th. Cent. lived Sir Tudor ap Gronwy, who did homage to Prince Edward, as the first prince of Wales, at Chester, in the 29th. Edw. 1. He had three sons, Ednyfed of Trér Castell, Gronwy of Penmynnyd, and Rhys of Arddreinniog, who were styled the three temporal lords of Anglesey: the three spiritual lords being the |58 archdeacon of Anglesey, the president of Holyhead, and the prior of Penmon. — Further on we came to the lofty wall surrounding Penmon Park, a rude looking tract of land rising to a considerable eminence, and well stocked with deer and rabbits. This park, anciently the property of the monks of Penmon, now belongs to the great land owner of the district, Sir Richard Bulkeley: on a high point in the park, there is a very curious and ancient Stone Cross, or crossed stone — Nearer to Penmon church and ruins is a wharf, tram road, and stage, constructed for the purpose of conveying from a very large adjacent quarry limestone for exportation, which by this means is put on board small vessels lying close to the stage. — Passing the lonely church, ruins, and offices of Penmon priory, we pursued a road which led to the summit of a hill forming the North Eastern promontory of Anglesey, facing Great Orme's head. Here we left our Carriage & |59 enjoyed the magnificent prospect, walking on a delicious short turf with occasional wide patches of fern. A few cottages are on the skirts of this common, some corn fields border it; to the North lies Priestholm, or Puffin Island, called also Inys Seiriol, separate from Anglesey by a narrow channel, on the margin of which are two bright-whitened lighthouses, with adjoining cottages for those who are in charge of them. These are on the Anglesey shore: Puffin Island rises opposite steeply sloping to its centre, while the other sides of the Island sink much more precipitously to the seashore. We noticed no habitation on the Island, though, I believe, there is a dwelling inhabited by a family having in charge a signal post. The herbage of the Island supports a few sheep, and a multitude of rabbits, with myriads of sea birds, especially of that species, which has given the common appellation to the Island. |60 Glannauch is another name of this island. It is about three quarters of a mile distant from the shore of Anglesey, of an oval shape, about a mile in length and half a mile in breadth. Seiriol, a Saint, of the 6th. century, erected here his cell. Near the centre of the island are the remains of an old square tower, adjacent to which are the ~~remai~~ ruins of other buildings, shewing the site of a religious house, subordinate to the priory of Penmon. The tower may have been in part erected as a land mark to navigators, for the coast here is dangerous, the channel difficult, the sands treacherous, and shipwrecks abound. Religious edifices on sea coasts were often so elevated as to be guides to mariners: The priests or monks might in emergency do the duty of lighthouse, or coast guard men; would be at hand to rescue the drowning, or to bury the dead: to save life and property, or take under their charge stranded goods. Prince Owen Gwynnedd, was the |61 foundeᵈ of this house and of Penmon; also of Holyhead and Bangor, being a contemporary of King Arthur. The island would appear to be an interesting spot to naturalists; the vast concourse of sea birds, the peculiarity and rarity of many fishes found in its waters, and even its scanty botany, would afford much for research. The name Glannauch is equivalent to Ynys Lenach, "the Priest's Island" — Standing here on the <u>Head of Mona</u> — <u>Pen Mon</u> — surveying on a calm day the magnificent prospect, looking out on the scarcely ruffled sea, yet is it impossible not to recur to the terrors which have often invested the promontory with the deepest gloom, more especially in the lamentable wreck of the Rothsay Castle Steamer, on the night of Aug. 17. 1831. On the morning of that day the ill fated vessel left the pier head, Liverpool, for Beaumaris, the number of passengers and seamen |62 being between 120 and 140 souls. The weather became rough and the wind adverse: for three hours the vessel was beating about the Great and Little Ormeshead, and night came on, the sea running high, and the tide ebbing. It was near midnight when opposite the tower on Puffin Island the steam became so low that the engine could not keep the vessel on her proper course. The worst fears of the passengers were realized; the crisis was come; the vessel struck on what is called the spit of the Dutchman's bank, where she remained immovable till she went to pieces. At least one hundred persons are known to have perished, and twenty one were ascertained to be saved. Subsequent investigation proved that the vessel was not sea-worthy; that there were no guns on board to make signals of distress; that during the time of peril the captain and the mate were in a state of intoxication; and that on the part of the former there had been great mismanagement and obstinacy. |63 Our friend Winter was staying at Beaumaris at the time of this sad catastrophe. The light house has been since erected; but calamities still occur; last winter a fine bark was wrecked near this point, and its dismantled hull lies aground near the entrance to Beaumaris from the Menai Bridge. One more glance to fix the spot on our memory before we bend our steps to the ruins of Penmon Priory — to the left is the portion of the Island of Anglesey extending North Westward towards Amlwch, and the Paris mountain Copper Mines — The exposed bay formed by the sweep of the coast affords a fine sea view, contrasting with the less open bay of Beaumaris bounded by the Orme's-head promontory on the right. — Descending to the sequestered hollow, where the monks of Penmon took up their abode, our driver directed us first to a holy well in a corner of a neglected garden, where we |64 found a beautiful fountain under a rock, gushing out beneath an ancient roof; the stream now available for domestic purposes, which in days of superstition had been thought powerful to cure. The Church forms one side of a little court yard, the other being the ivied ruins of the refectory: a third side is partly dwelling house, and partly the southern transept of the cruciform church against the gable of which the dwelling has been erected. It is tenanted by a Keeper employed by Sir R. Bulkeley, whose wife conducted us over the Church. The southern door way of entrance is modern: the interior in part very ancient and very interesting. I shall describe it in the words of a skilful antiquary, who has contributed to the Archaeological Journal some very valuable remarks on some of the Churches in Anglesey. He speaks of the beautifully secluded retreat of Penmon Priory — and of the Commot or Hundred of Tyndaethway, as washed by the blue strait of Menai |65 on the one side, and the stormy inlet of Traeth Cosp (Redwharf bay) on the other. Of the churches of this district generally he observes that the existing transepts and chancels were mostly added in the thirteenth and fourteenth centuries, but that in the conventual establishment of Penmon the original form of the building was, no doubt, that which it still retains, cruciform. But even in this church, which can be hardly classed with the ordinary parochial edifices of the island, the only fenestral openings in the nave are small circular-headed loop holes contemporary with the building, twenty four inches by nine externally, but expanding within to a considerable size. The early portions of the churches seem never to have been paved or floored, and such is the case with the nave and transepts of Penmon Church: the earth, like the soil in the peasants cottages, is beaten hard, more or less even, and is generally |⁶⁶ dry. The universal covering of the roofs of these Anglesey churches is the schistose stone which composes the largest geological formation in the island. The only approaches to stone-vaulting are to be found at Penmon and Ynys Seiriol. Here the towers of the two churches are covered with low conical quadrilateral spires, or rather pointed roofs, in the formation of which no wood is employed, but the stones keep lapping over each other from the lowest course laid on the side walls until at length they meet in the apex. A much later example of this rude vaulting, if it may be so called, is in the monastic pigeon house at Penmon, a curious square building of the fifteenth century, almost unique in its kind: the towers above mentioned are about sixteen feet square at Penmon, and eighteen feet by twelve feet at Ynys Seiriol, but in the pigeon house the area is twenty one feet square, and the quadrilateral vaulting approaches to the domical form, |⁶⁷ (like the roofs used by Delorme in the Tuileries, and other French châteaux) and it is entirely covered by stones laid in this manner, without any wood in the whole building, and with a light louvre or lanthorn in the midst. Penmôn church is remarkable for an early font: a quadrangular carved stone stands on a square pedestal: the interior is excavated into a circular bason for immersion; the basis is wider than the upper part: the shaft, if it may so be called, tapers, and is carved in its upper portion, in panneling, after a cross fashion; but the compartments vary, as to the carving. It is not easy to describe this antique relic in words, a drawing can alone represent it faithfully. There is also a water stoup of the same date as the font — near the door of the church: a like remains of antiquity, unless it be a copy, I had noticed at Llanfaes church; and here again a drawing is needed to delineate this ancient article of |⁶⁸ church furniture with accuracy. Penmon was an Augustine priory. With the house on Ynys Seiriol it owes its foundation to Maelgwyn Gwynedd, king of Wales, in the sixth century, and was re-founded by Llewellyn ap Jorwerth, prince of Wales, at the beginning of the thirteenth Century. The nave & south transept are of early date; the chancel of the fifteenth century; the northern transept has been destroyed. The south transept was used as a chapel, and a curious series of small circular-headed arches, with zigzagged mouldings, and filletted shafts, formed seats round its sides for the monks and their attendants. The South door by which you enter the disused nave is a good specimen of round headed early English the agnus dei is rudely sculptured in the pediment; zigzag and filletted mouldings with low side pillars, are all in tolerable preservation. Two ancient belfry windows with double lights will not fail to attract the notice of the curious in such |⁶⁹ details. The churchyard is a sequestered, green, and lonely spot — a few monuments and inscriptions met the eye: in some cases the memorials of the departed were engraved in Welsh: one head stone was a good copy of the South door way to the Nave. — The only portion of the fabric used for divine worship is the Chancel. Our guide, the Keeper's wife, told us that a Dᴿ Owen, resident at Beaumaris, is the Incumbent, this being a perpetual curacy, annexed to Llanvaes, and both in the patronage of Sir R B W Bulkeley: the officiating curate comes from Bangor, as we heard, or, in the homely language of the good woman, — "Dᴿ O. gets a man to do it." — We entered her house, and glanced at her roomy Kitchen and parlour, both well furnished: I understand the

*80. Penmon
Priory, Anglesey.*

Welsh peasantry, on settling in life, make a point of providing one or more chests of drawers of a bureau shape, which they highly value both on account |[70] of their convenience, and of the credit and respectability, which the possession of such articles of furniture confers. The house is built up against the gable of the South transept of the Church, perhaps on the site of the prior's lodgings, and at right angles with the ruined and ivy-clad remains of the refectory, and other conventual buildings — Altogether the place and its remains, with the adjoining park, promontory, and contiguous island, are very interesting, and would well repay a second visit. — We returned to Beaumaris by 4 P.M. — Walked on the Green in the evening — Archaeological Journal — Ranke's Reformation in Germany.

July 30. Sunday.

A shower in the forenoon, very heavy rain in the evening. — Received a letter from M[r] Thornton on Hunt Trust affairs — Wrote to the Innkeeper at Beeston in Cheshire that we propose sleeping at his Inn on Friday night, on our return into Gloucestershire, if we can be accommoda-|[71] ted. We had noticed on our way to Chester this neat road side inn, near a station on the railway, and as it would divide the homeward journey from Bangor conveniently, obviating the necessity of sleeping at Chester, which would require two removals of ourselves, servants and luggage from the Chester Station to the Hotel in the Town by fly, and back to the Station, we preferred the country hostelry to the city hotel. — Attended the morning service at the Church at Beaumaris: the same Clergyman who preached last Sunday week delivered a very good discourse on the rejection of Christ by the Gergesenes, who bade him depart from their coasts. — I walked to Llanvaes to the afternoon service; rain came on before I arrived there, and fell very heavily as I returned. The service was performed by the Clergyman who officiated on last Sunday week. His sermon was on the text that all things work for good to |[72] them that love the Lord. — Preparing a sermon. — Beauties of England and Wales — Colonial Church Chronicle. —

July 31. Monday.

A fine day, but cloudy at times, and the air cool and fresh: rain at night. — Wrote to M[r] Hare and M[r] Thornton on Hunt Trust matters; forwarding to the former the letter I had received yesterday from the latter. Wrote to the Innkeeper at the Penrhyn Arms, Bangor, desiring him to reserve apartments for us on next Wednesday afternoon. — Walked to the Point, — on the Green &c. — Beauties of England and Wales — Ranke's Reformation in Germany. —

Aug. 1. Tuesday.

A rainy forenoon; the afternoon and evening fine. — Received a letter from my son, with a very satisfactory report of dear Sophy and of all at Stanway Vicarage. It is suggested that we should stop at Ashchurch Station on our return homewards on Saturday next, and thence pro-|[73] ceed by Stanway to Upper Slaughter. E.F.W. and Sophy accept our invitation to visit us for a week after our return home, coming to us on the 14[th.] Inst. — Replied to this letter, declining to call on our children on Saturday, as such an arrangement would delay our arrival at home till an inconveniently late hour, and would be attended with trouble as regards luggage. — Walked in the Baron Hill grounds; — on the Green &c. — In exploring a part of the town not before visited, behind the church, passed the small, but ponderous looking and gloomy gaol: near it also is an endowed grammar school. — The Assizes begin to-morrow — the Commission to be then opened. — In conversation with an intelligent old sailor on the Green, I learnt that the average rate of agricultural labourers wages is nine shillings weekly: the peasantry live much on oaten bread and butter milk. My communicative sailor was very conservative in his opinions; highly |[74] indignant with the Chartists, Repealers, Irish insurgents and hoc genus omne. — Beauties of England and Wales — Colonial Church Chronicle, — Ranke's Reformation in Germany. —

Aug. 2. Wednesday.

Weather very fine till the evening, when a very heavy shower fell — Received a letter from the landlady at Beeston who will be glad to accommodate us at her Inn on Friday night: — from M[r] Lovegrove, of Gloucester, deputy coroner, a circular: he solicits my vote and interest for the office of coroner, when it shall be vacant by the death of his principal, M[r] Cooke, who, however, is not in worse health than for a long time past: but competitors have commenced an active canvass: — M[r] Pruen, a Solicitor, of Cheltenham, a M[r] Russel, of the same place, and a M[r] Smith of Winchcombe. — Packing up, paying bills, and preparing to leave Beaumaris — Wrote to Charles Bathurst. — Walked on the Green, Castle fields &c. — Looked |[75] into the Court house, adjacent to the Castle, and in the open space at the bottom of Castle Street. This homely building had been opened in anticipation of the Assizes, this being the Commission to day: the interior arrangements are better than the exterior would lead one to expect. The approaching business caused a little bustle in the quiet town: the Sheriffs carriage was moving about, and country gentlemen seemed to be congregating, in preparation for the usual Assize business. — After an early dinner we set out for Bangor in a comfortable carriage with a pair of horses, hired of the civil person who had supplied us with vehicles for our excursion into the mountain district and to Penmon. As we bade, probably, a last farewell to unpretending, tranquil Beaumaris, we met at "the Point" — the High Sheriff & his Chaplain, other attendants and Javelin men, with his carriage, and a few spectators |[76] awaiting the arrival of the Judge, whom shortly afterwards, and before we reached the Menai Bridge, we passed travelling in his carriage & with a lady. — Before six o clock we reached the Penrhyn Arms, where we found prepared for us a comfortable sitting room opening out into the delightful garden, and a bedroom rather too [more] elevated than might have been wished, but with which it would have been unfair to find fault, as the hotel was crowded with guests. — The public journals published in London this morning, one of which I procured a sight of, announce a most serious outbreak in Ireland. Apparently, a decisive blow has been struck at an obscure place in Tipperary, where Smith O'Brien, with other leaders, at the head of a large body of insurgents, collected among the collieries, came into a contact with a small force of police, not exceeding sixty: these being judiciously posted in a house on a common which was strongly built, detached from others, and |[77] containing several apartments, sustained a sort of siege, firing from the windows, killing a few, and wounding more of the mob. A panic seems to have seized on the rebels, who fled in every direction: other police came up, and assisted in dispersing the main body, making many prisoners. It was not long before a considerable body of military, amounting to 1500, under the command of General Macdonald, came up, surrounding the district, and scouring it in every direction. Smith O'Brien appears to have acted feebly, without discretion or decision, and even to have exhibited a lack of courage. It is not known whither he and other leaders acting with him have fled; one is said to have been grievously wounded in the skirmish: it is expected that the apprehension of the misguided chief and his associates is unavoidable. In the meantime government displays great activity and vigour; overwhelming preparations are made to quell the insurrec-|[78] tion, and suppress the revolutionary movement.

Aug. 3. Thursday.

Beautiful weather — After breakfast we went in an open carriage, drawn by one horse on an excursion to Aber; the distance being six miles. Passed by the Holyhead road along the Penrhyn Park wall, to the principal gateway, and the village of Llandegai; so far by the same road as we had travelled on our excursion to the interior of Caernarvonshire. — At Llandegai we left the Holyhead for the Chester road; which runs nearly parallel to the railway, both passing through a flat alluvial plain bordering on the Menai Straits as far as Penmaen Mawr; to the right we had the chain of mountains, or outliers from them projecting into the plain. As we proceeded we commanded fine views of Beaumaris & its bay: also of the mountain range. The culture was various; crops of wheat, barley, and turnips, all fine; some of the hay crop was still out; there was much turfy and indifferent land, |[79] and much that would be greatly improved by draining: we passed some fields of potatoes, and of these a part was sadly damaged by the blight, the ravages of which appear to be gaining strength. — At Aber there is a pretty rural church, and school house, with a neat small road side inn: not far off is a comfortable looking mansion on a small scale. The village is at the mouth of a valley, into which a lane leads from the high road, and at some little distance from the church. We soon found ourselves in an unadulterated Welch hamlet; the cottages were rude and low, their rough slated roofs overgrown with stone-crop, no order observed in the position of the houses, which were dotted about promiscuously; the walls both of the cottages, and of the gardens, or orchards, built of rude round stones picked up from the fields; pigs were wandering about the narrow lanes; the road way narrow and bad. To our left |[80] was a conical mound towering over the village and its brawling brook, the scene of an old world legend. On this mount was a castle belonging to Llywellyn the great. Here he detected an intrigue between his frail wife, and William de Breos, a stout baron, who had been taken prisoner by Llywellyn, at the siege of Montgomery, in the reign of Henry 3. During that captivity he gained the affections of his captor's lady. The intrigue did not come to the knowledge of the prince till after the Baron had obtained his ransom. The indignant and injured husband, craftily solicited a visit from his manumitted prisoner. De Breos fell into the snare, and the revengeful prince hung him on a hill opposite his castle, from whence he shewed him to his wife, having before sarcastically asked her what she would give for ~~her~~ a sight of her lover. Tradition has handed down a Welch distich, which has been thus translated

>Lovely princess, said Llywellyn |[81]
>>What will you give to see your Gwylim?
>To which the princess replied,
>>Wales and England, and Llywellyn,
>I'd give them all to see my Gwylim —

The mountain stream which flows down the valley of Aber rejoices in the truly Welch sounding name of Gwyn-gregyn — the stream of the white shells; and it is fitly so called from the loads of cockle-shells continually emptied into the stream by the villagers, picked by them on the Lavan sands, which are celebrated for these shell-fish — Coccos-Lavan. Across these sands, when the tide is out, one may walk for four miles, to meet a ferry boat, conveying the passenger to Beaumaris, six miles distant from Aber. But this route is seldom taken since the Menai Bridge has been erected; and it was always an unsafe route: for in foggy weather many have been lost in undertaking the hazardous enterprize. The bell of Aber church, presented for the purpose by Lord |[83] Bulkeley in 1817, is rung in hazy weather, nor is it prudent to attempt to cross without a guide, for the sands frequently shift. The glen down which the torrent flows runs in a straight line a mile and a half between the mountains, and is bounded on one side by a magnificent rock, called Maes y Gaer. Passing the mill at Aber, which, having been lately repaired, is not now so picturesque an object as it has appeared to former travellers, we followed the margin of the brawling, foamy, rocky, dark brown, clear stream. Mountains towered over the defile on either side; the road was apparently as unsafe as one could well travel in a remote and rocky dell; but one hardly heeded the insecurity, so entirely ~~was~~ were the eye and mind occupied with the beautiful combinations of verdure, foliage, mountain, rock and water: every turn seemed to furnish a fresh picture. – At a single arched bridge leading to a divergent valley, which one |[83] longed to explore, down which another tempting brook hurried under the shelter of alders and other shrubby plants, we left our carriage, which could proceed no further, and walked towards the upper end of the defile, crossing by a half ruinous wooden footbridge. — MW. persevered for more than half the distance to the head of the valley, and then sat down on a rock to await my return from the waterfall. Nothing can be more beautiful than the secluded glen, visited, as it was, on a lovely day. If we looked to its mountain-bound extremity, a copious waterfall leaping down a cliff greeted us; on each side were rocky steeps; verdure and brushwood clothed the bed of the valley, down which the stream hurried; fern and fragments of rock diversified the turfy path which we pursued; a solitary cottage as rude as its accompaniments, sent forth two or |*84* three healthy children to offer us a cup of fresh and cool milk; the mountain sheep and dark cattle grazed about us; and when we paused for a moment to rest, and looked backward down the valley, beyond the village of Aber, and between the mountains forming its mouth, the eye roamed across a portion of Beaumaris Bay, and rested on the promontory of Pen Môn, and Puffin Island. A short scramble among shaly rocks and banks brought me to the upper end of the glen closed in by a precipitous cliff, and encumbered by fallen fragments of rock which centuries had accumulated in many a pitiless, pelting storm. Down a cleft worn by the torrent leaped the waterfall, poured from the summit in a narrow gush of foam The quantity of water projected is very considerable, dashing, perhaps, for sixty feet, down the precipitous face of rock — a kind of miniature pisse-vache or Staubbach — exceedingly beautiful, not forming any deep |*85* pool or basin at the foot of the mountain, but losing itself in a mass of rocky fragments, from which it extricates itself, beneath a shaly slope to form the torrent of the glen, aided by two or three contributory spouts, bounding in slender courses down contiguous channels in the mountain side. Returning to rejoin my wife, exchanged a few words with a party ascending to the head of the dell; other sight seekers, and among them portly seniors of both sexes, apparently not much used to a Welch scramble, were toiling along; while we closed a very enjoyable excursion, returning to the Penrhyn Arms, which we reached by half past two o clock — Having rested myself, I strolled to Bangor, and explored the purlieux of the Cathedral, situated in a low hollow, contiguous, to the narrow, mean, but main Street of the Town: there is not much in the exterior to attract attention; it has the appearance |*86* of a spacious, well kept parish church in a good country town; and, I believe, has been much and judiciously restored — by the members of the present chapter, especially by the Dean, Mᴿ Cotton, a Clergyman highly and justly esteemed. — The Bishop's Palace is behind and adjacent to the Cathedral, in a lower situation than it; embowered in trees, old and comfortable looking, ~~but~~ confined, but very neat, with a quaint flower garden in front, which bespeaks, no doubt, the care bestowed upon it by Bishop Bethell's worthy sister, who has for many years resided with him. Had our stay in their immediate vicinity been less transient, and even had I not ascertained that the Bishop was engaged to-day at a distance in the consecration of a chapel, I should have had pleasure, with MW., in renewing our old acquaintance with him and his sister; for when he presided over the See of Gloucester, we had enjoyed their |*87* hospitality and been in frequent intercourse with them. The Cathedral is said to have been founded in the sixth century by Daniel, son of Dinoth, Abbot of Bangor Iscoed, in Flintshire, the great monastery of British monks, under the auspices of Maelgwyn Gwynnedd, King of Wales, founder of Penmôn, and patron of Taliesin, the Bard. It was destroyed in the 11ᵗʰ· century, was ravaged in the 13ᵗʰ· again devastated in the 15ᵗʰ· and restored in the 16ᵗʰ· The building so reedified remains to the present time, and was greatly improved in 1837, at a considerable expence, chiefly by the praiseworthy and unwearied exertions of the present Dean, who was then Precentor and senior Vicar — In the evening I took a lovely walk, pursuing the path we had followed on the evening of our first arrival at the Penrhyn Arms Hotel. Now I ~~pursued~~ traced the road further than on that occasion, enjoying the magnificent |[88] prospect of the sea and the mountains; having nearly reached a point above the mouth of the railway tunnel, I followed a steep footway which led to the summit of the high range of hill which forms one side of the Bangor Valley, descending into the town by a precipitous path; on both sides enjoying very commanding prospects — Ranke's Reformation in Germany. —

Aug. 4. Friday.

Beautiful weather till the evening, which was showery. — After breakfast strolling with MW. in the enjoyable gardens of the Hotel. — I then took a walk along the shore beneath the hotel, in a mean part of the suburbs of Bangor, by what may be called its port, to Garth point, which forms one extremity of the little bay in which vessels resorting to Bangor lie — There is a sort of suburb stretching towards Garth point, which is the extremity of the hilly range which closes in the Bangor valley on the Menai Bridge side: this projecting |[89] eminence terminating abruptly at the Menai Strait, presents fine situations with splendid and commanding views for villas. Several are built overhanging the strait, and sites for many more are unoccupied. An excellent road leading from Bangor to the point is carried round the ~~point of the~~ promontory on a kind of cornice or ledge above the Strait, commanding glorious prospects, and extending to the main road which conducts from Bangor to Menai Bridge — Garth point and Ferry is a lively and interesting, bustling spot — the transit into Anglesey is exactly one mile broad, and the little ferry boat is constantly plying to and fro, its white sail trimmed, as the case may be, for the Anglesey or Caernarvonshire side of the strait. The view from Garth Point across to the wooded shore of Anglesey, and over the bay of Beaumaris, bounded by Great Orme's Head, and Puffin Island, with |[90] the gentle slope of Anglesea, and Beaumaris on the one hand, and the bold mountain range opposite to it on the other, is exquisitely fine. The Anglesey ferry house is overhung by the dense foliage which clothes the bank of the Straits on that side, and may be distant between two or three miles from Beaumaris. At Garth point a little fleet of pleasure boats invited to a sail on the gently rippled surface of the lovely and land locked inlet; of one of these I availed myself, and crossed to Port Penrhyn, at the foot of the Penrhyn Arms pleasure ground, there to embark with MW. on a little sail towards the Menai Bridge. We enjoyed this little excursion extremely, tacking backwards and forwards in a light breeze, and making ourselves acquainted from the strait which we were navigating with the several beautiful villas and pleasure grounds, nestling amid the oak woods which close the Anglesey shore. The most |[91] interesting are those of Mr Beevor, Mr Roberts, and Mr Williams. We proceeded so far in the direction of the Menai Bridge as to command a fine view of that structure, and from the centre of the Strait we took a last view of towering Snowdon — Returning to our hotel, we partook of an early and cold dinner, and prepared to close our agreeable sojourn in North Wales — Soon after three o clock we trusted ourselves to the Omnibus plying to the Railway station, where we arrived in safety, though not without alarm. The day was hot, the horses overdriven, the streets of Bangor narrow, and very ill adapted for the rapid transit of huge lumbering carriages crowded with passengers and luggage. Much is said of the perils of the Railroad; but I greatly prefer that mode of conveyance to travelling in ill constructed coaches, driven by rash and awkward coachmen, drawn by |[92] worn out, ill tempered, ~~or worn out~~ animals. Once in a collision with a returning Omnibus our wheels were locked, and a horse thrown down; hardly was the beast on his legs again, and urged forward, (for the rail system brooks no delay,) than we clashed with a driver of a car — a pause — a scold — and on again — the way into the station yard is up a slight ascent, this and the yard within had been lately coated with fresh limestone, loose and unbound; over this the wretched horses were lashed to the entrance of the Station Booking Office — the express train was come in — was waiting — steam up — porters hurrying — passengers bustling and bewildered; — out we got, to notice one of the miserable animals, which had dragged us, down and apparently strangled in his collar, the end of over exertion — cads and drivers and porters loosening the harness — whether the poor beast lived or died then & there, I know not; for time |[93] hardly sufficed to purchase the tickets, settle ourselves in a coach, and load the luggage, ere we plunged into the long tunnel which commences at the Station, and penetrates the mountain barrier which on the Chester side closes in the narrow valley of Bangor. When we travelled to Bangor from Chester, the railway was only open to the former place — now it is in one sense open to Holyhead: since the 1st. of August the trains have traversed the whole line except in passing the Menai Strait, which will not be accomplished for many months – perhaps more than a twelvemonth may elapse before the vast Britannia tunnel is completed: so now the trains reach on the Caernarvonshire side only to the vicinity of the Menai Bridge — across this, by a contract made with the toll-owners, passengers and luggage are conveyed in Omnibusses, and thence |[94] on the Anglesey shore to a point where the line of railway commences after the Straits are crossed, or will be crossed, by the tunnel, when the rail system is resumed, and the traveller is conveyed by steam power to Holyhead, the haven where he would be. This, however, must be a hurrying process; and the travelling world will be glad, no doubt, to trust themselves, after due assurance of its safety, to the wondrous tunnel, when it is completed. We performed our transit to Chester rapidly and agreeably, recognizing, and, as far as the speed would permit, improving our acquaintance with, the interesting country we had passed thro', on our way to Beaumaris. We were particularly struck with the mountain & rock scenery bordering on the railway between the giant Penmaen Mawr, at the root of Penmaen Bach & Conway — At Chester station, where we arrived by about 20 min. past 5 in the afternoon, we left the express |[95] train, which does not stop at the Beeston station; and waited till half past five, when another train started for Crewe. — Since we were here the old temporary station at which we halted on our arrival from Birmingham, and from whence we set out for Bangor, has been abandoned; the contiguous, and splendid new station having been completed, being a very commodious range of buildings, platforms & skylighted rail terminus, constructed on the most approved plan. Half an hour's travelling brought us to the Beeston Station and Inn; the latter proved as comfortable and clean, as quiet and orderly as we had anticipated: very commodious apartments had been prepared for us. — Both before and after tea, I strolled about the vicinity on a turnpike road in two directions; there is neither town nor village near; but the railroad and a canal, and a few scattered cottages with a farm house. Enjoyed pre-|[96] views of the ~~fine~~ noble rock and ruined castle at a mile distant, which would, doubtless, well reward the visitor; on an adjoining well wooded height, the proprietor, Mr. Tollemache, is erecting a spacious castellated mansion. The distant hills are commanding, the country, immediately about our Inn, is undulating, and fertile, chiefly meadow and pasture, with hedges and hedgerow trees — On our route, after we had passed Conway, we found the harvest begun, much wheat being reaped. — The crops were apparently fine.

Aug. 5. Saturday.

After a rainy night a showery day. — Breakfasted; and at fifty minutes past nine o clock, set out by rail for Birmingham, where we arrived at one in the Afternoon. — Partook of luncheon at the Railway Refreshment room, and started at 2 P.M. by train for Cheltenham, arriving at the Lansdown Station by 4 P.M, and reaching the Plough Hotel by half past four. At Cheltenham we re-|[97] mained an hour, shopping, and quitting the Plough in one of the comfortable carriages which that establishment supplies, at half past five, we reached home by half past seven o'clock. Found all well at Upper Slaughter. — Letters awaited me — from Mr Braickenridge on Hunt Trust business — and from Mr Hare on the same, who enclosed for my perusal a letter from Mr Tilleard to Mr Thornton; — also a letter from C Bathurst on Magistrates' business: he encloses a letter on which he seeks my opinion. — It appears that Mr Vavasour performed divine service in my church on Sunday last, in consequence of Winter being indisposed.

Aug. 6. Sunday.

Fine weather, but cold and cloudy. — Visited the Sunday School. — Preparing a sermon. — Morning service, prayers. Afternoon service, prayers and a sermon. I preached on David and Araunah — A letter from Mr Hare in answer to one |[98] written by me to him before I left Beaumaris. — A circular from Gloucester Gaol, announcing a meeting of Visiting Justices there on the 10$^{th.}$ Inst. — A packet of Quarterly papers, S.P.G. — Remitted to the Treasurer S.P.G. £1. 16. 2. the amount received by me as a collection in aid of that society after a sermon preached by me in obedience to the Queen's letter on the day before we left home for Beaumaris. —

Aug. 7. Monday.

Fine weather. — Visiting sick parishioners. — Justice business at home. — Mary Ryan called on us; full of uneasiness as to proceedings at Eyford. She represents M$^{rs.}$ Dolphin as bent on making extensive repairs, additions and alterations to the mansion house at Eyford; as resolved to dismantle, and even pull down, the farm house at the Parks, erected only a few years ago for the residence of Mr Polhill, and since occupied by W. Smith, Moore &c; — on these expences |[99] she seems determined to enter, in despite of encumbrances or embarrassments, wilfully and irritably refusing to listen to contrary advice. — Drove with MW. to Adlestrop to call on M^r and M$^{rs.}$ Cholmondeley, which we had proposed to do on the very day on which we heard of dear Sophy's sad accident, and then deferred. — We did not find them at home; they were at Stoneleigh Abbey. — Called on the Winters at Daylesford, who were out. — Called at the Vavasours, at "the Cottage:" M$^{rs.}$ V. was not at home, but we were received by Mr Vavasour. — Met and chatted with Mr Wiggin, Mr Pole, Mr W. B. Pole &c. — Transacted business at the office of the Gloucestershire Banking Company at Stow. — Received a letter from E.F.W. with a very good account of our dear daughter, who has ridden out on horseback, and proposes to accompany her husband to the Archery meeting at Stow to-morrow. |[100] We hope this is not venturing too much. Lord Wemyss and family have left Stanway. — E.F.W. wishes his mother and me to drive to see him and Sophy on Friday next; when we may inspect the works now in progress at the Vicarage. — Our dear grand children are quite well. — My son has engaged to go on Wednesday next to Tysoe in Warwickshire, returning home on Thursday, to be present at the christening of the first born child of William Howell, who is now residing there as Curate. His marriage to Miss Willan has been the result of a long attachment, but the lady brought him little fortune, and his father, very blameably, as I think, makes no pecuniary provision for him. It is true that William has displeased his father by his violence and eagerness of temper, particularly at the time of his sister Emmeline's strange misconduct, or derangement, whichever it might be; but the |[101] young man's general deportment is free from reproach, and it may be that mental infirmity would account both in him and in his eldest sister, for much that gives the parent just uneasiness & displeasure. Yet he never made a proper allowance to his son, and has, I grieve to say, failed generally in the paternal duties; turning his back, as it were, and leaving his eldest son and daughter without due countenance and provision; and not making himself beloved by his younger daughters. E.F.W. is invited to be Godfather to W. Howell's infant. — Ranke's History of the reformation in Germany. —

Aug. 8. Tuesday.

Fine weather on the whole; but not without a tendency to rain. — Wrote to E.F.W, that it will not be in our power to visit him and Sophy at Stanway on Friday next, as we have accepted an invitation to dine at Mᵣ W. B. Pole's on that day. — Sent my letter to Stow to be delivered to him |[102] there, when he arrives to attend at the Archery Meeting. — Wrote to Mᵣ Thornton on Hunt Trust business. — Also to Sewell and Newmarch, reminding them that Mᵣ Lockhart's half year's interest was is still unpaid — But I this day received a letter from them, announcing that they had paid £102. 18. 2. on that account to my credit with the Gloucestershire Banking Cᵒ· at Stow. — Received a letter from Sophia Hunt on Hunt Executorship business. — Walked with MW. to Eyford: called on Mʳˢ· Dolphin, who is bent on her new plans of pulling down one house, and repairing another — The new farm house at the Parks to be demolished, the old mansion house, miserably out of repair, to be renovated and enlarged. Alas! for this folly! Her late favourite scheme of procuring a divorce from her husband is now abandoned: her friends, Waller, Bowen, & myself, had warned her against it: now her London Solicitors, Vizard and Lemon, inform her that it is a hopeless project. Met with poor |[103] old Bowen on a visit at Eyford; he is but feeble, and in a very suffering state. — Justice business at home. — Ranke's Reformation in Germany. —

Aug. 9. Wednesday.

Fine weather, with the exception of one sharp shower, the skirts of a thunderstorm more severe elsewhere, about mid-day several loud claps of thunder. — Wrote to Sewell and Newmarch, acknowledging the receipt of the half-year's interest from Mᵣ Lockhart, on Mortgage of his property. — To C Bathurst as to points of Sessions practice and magistrates' duty, on which he had sought from me information and an opinion. — A letter from Mʳˢ· C Barr, in answer to my letter of condolence to her on the death of Mᵣ George Barr. She represents Mʳˢ· Walker's state of health as very precarious. — Visiting poor and sick parishioners. — Preparing for the annual meeting of the Stow Distr. Comm. S.P.G. which is fixed for the 23^d. Inst. — Ranke's |^104 History of the Reformation in Germany. — Smith O'Brien has been arrested by a Railway guard at the Thurles Railway Station; he was taking a ticket for Limerick, when apprehended; worn in appearance, exhausted, looking miserably, as one hunted down; perhaps he was reckless, and may have thrown himself purposely in the way of capture. It appears that since the affair at Ballingarry he has been secreted in the houses of peasantry; after his apprehension he was forthwith conveyed to Dublin, and to Kilmainham Prison. — Other leaders in the insurrection have hitherto escaped arrest, but very many parties implicated in the rebellion have been seized at Dublin, and in the provinces, chiefly notorious and violent Clubbists; arms and ammunition, secreted in many quarters, have been found and captured. A large military force is poured into the disturbed districts, and Lord Hardinge has been appointed to the chief command |^105 in the insurgent ~~district.~~ country The mountain of Shivenamon, the strong hold of the rebels, is surrounded; the soldiery and constabulary force are scouring the country, and patrolling in every direction. Frequent rumours of contemplated outbreaks in different parts are in circulation; but no rising has yet taken place since that at Ballingarry; nor anything further occurred than attempts to rescue prisoners. Thus the insurrection is put down, but the bad spirit still subsists. —

Aug 10. Thursday.

The weather fine, except that a heavy, but partial, thunderstorm fell early in the afternoon. — Drove to Stow, accompanied by M^rs. W. who, after setting me down there, returned home. — A letter from Mr Thornton on Hunt Trust affairs, accompanying a letter from Mr Tilleard for my perusal. — A note of invitation from M^rs. Pole, to a dinner party at |^106 Wick Hill on Thursday next: therefore I wrote a few lines to dear Sophy, naming that we should accept the invitation for her and Edward as well as for ourselves, and praying her to bring with her to Upper Slaughter, a dress suited for company — To the Provident Bank, where I met Mr Pole. — Transacted business at Mr Brookes's office, and at the office of the Gloucestershire Banking company. — Attended at the Workhouse, where I presided at the fortnightly meeting of the Guardians of our Union. — Ranke's History of the reformation in Germany.

Aug 11. Friday.

A dull close forenoon; damp weather in the afternoon and evening, ending in decided rain. — Justice business at home — Wrote to Mr Beman on magisterial business, respecting which he had consulted me yesterday — Preparing notices of the annual district meeting of the S.P.G. at Stow on the 23^d. Inst. |^107 — Visited sick parishioners. — We dined at M^r W B Pole's at Upper Swell, meeting M^r and M^rs. Pole, M^r and M^rs. C. R. Pole, M^r and M^rs. W. Vavasour, Miss Penyston, and Mr Clarke — A pleasant party — After dinner four from Wick Hill joined the circle — two sons and two daughters of C. R. Pole.

Aug. 12. Saturday.

Moist weather in the morning, but afterwards fine — Wrote to Sophia Hunt on Hunt Executorship affairs. — Dispatched a messenger with notes and handbills, announcing the annual meeting of the Stow District Comm. S.P.G. as fixed for the 23^d. Inst. — Canon Ford called, and partook of luncheon with us. He came to inform us that the consecration of the new Church erected at Cerney Wick, in his parish of South Cerney, is fixed for the 24th. Inst.

and to invite us to be present on the occasion. It seems also that he has com-|[108] municated on the matter with Edward and Sophy, who have agreed to be present. Much planning how all the journeying to & fro is to be effected on that day. — Mrs. R. Waller walked from Bourton, attended by her second son, and joined our party at luncheon, — with whom we walked back as far as to Lower Slaughter. — Mrs. Dolphin also called upon us. — Received letters from Mr Hare and Mr Thornton with inclosures on Hunt Trust matters forwarded for my perusal — Officiated at the funeral of an infant of T. S. Collett. — Visited Mrs. Jos. Collett – Rec^{d.} a note from R. Ellis, Stow, as to the purchase of a lot of sheep. — Justice business at home — A letter from C Bathurst on Magisterial and Quarter Sessions law and practice — Ranke's History of the Reformation in Germany. —

Aug. 13. Sunday.

A dull, close, overclouded day, with a moist atmosphere, but hardly to |[109] be called rain till the evening. Visited the Sunday School — Preparing a Sermon — Morning service, prayers, sermon and the administration of the Lord's supper. — I preached on the disobedient prophet — 16 Communicants. —— Evening service, prayers. — Received a letter from S. B. Hunt on Hunt Executorship business and trust matters. — Also from the Treasurers of the S.P.G. in acknowledgment of the receipt of a cheque for £1. 16. 2 which had been collected at my church under the authority of a Queen's letter. —— MW. had written a note to our dear Sophy by one of our village choir, who had gone to Stanway for the day; I received an answer late in the evening written by E.F.W. giving a good account of all at the Vicarage. We had wished them to pass the next week ~~after next~~ here as well as this week, and to accompany us to the consecration of the church at Cerney Wick; but this, it appears, cannot be, because |[110] my son and daughter have engagements in the beginning and end of the week near Stanway, and have planned with M^{r} and Mrs. Bowly to visit them at Siddington, and under Mr Bowly's guidance to inspect Cirencester Agricultural College. Their plan is to go to Cirencester and Siddington on next Wednesday week, to attend at the consecration at Cerney Wick on Thursday, and to return home on that evening. We hope to see them here to-morrow. — Preparing a report for the Ann. meeting of the Stow district Committee S.P.G. — To the family a section from Dr James's work on the Collects. —

Aug. 14. Monday.

A very rainy day — Wrote to Mr Thornton and Mr Hare on Hunt Trust matters. — Preparing a report to be read at the annual meeting of the Stow district Committee S.P.G on the 23^{d.} Inst. — Our dear children and grandchildren came from Stanway to pass a few days with us. We greatly enjoyed their society. Sophy looks |[111] thin, but says she is quite well, and is in good spirits.

Aug. 15. Tuesday.

A dull, damp morning, after rain during the night: in the afternoon the weather was fine. — My son went to Stow to join the Cricketers, and returned to us between our dinner & tea time. — My wife and daughter with my two elder grandchildren drove to call on Mrs. J. T. Rice at Great Risington. — I was engaged in preparing the report to be presented next week at the annual meeting of the Stow Distr. Comm. of the S.P.G. — Received a letter from Mr Thornton enclosing one from Mr Hare to him on Hunt Trust affairs. — In the evening E.F.W. read ~~out~~ to us a very eloquent sermon by Dr Cumming of the Scotch Church, London, on Liberty, being the first of a series of three on Liberty, Equality and fraternity: very suitable to the times, very sound in principles, both religious and political. — |^112

Aug. 16. Wednesday.

Damp, or rainy in the forenoon, and early part of the afternoon; afterwards fine — Wrote to F. Aston, requesting him to order posthorses at the Kings Head, Northleach, to be ready to take us to the consecration of the church at Cerney Wick on the 24th. Inst: and to bring our carriage back. We mean to go to N Leach with Stow posthorses, which will await our return from S. Cerney; we proposed also to take M^rs. Aston or Mary Aston with us to Cerney Wick — Wrote to C Bathurst on public matters and judicial business. — M^rs. Vavasour, Mr W. Vavasour & M^rs. W.V. drove hither, and passed an hour or two with us, not coming, as we expected, in time for luncheon, having been prevented by the damp weather — E.F.W. rode to Bourton to call on Mr W. Stenson. — I walked with dear Sophy and Broome. — Received a letter from Major Graham, the Registrar General, addressed to me as Chairman of our Union: |^113 he is dissatisfied with the conduct of Mr Pearce as Superintendant Registrar of this district, and thinks of dismissing him: he wishes to ascertain from me whether it is likely that there will be difficulty in procuring an efficient successor. — Received a letter from Mr Raymond Cripps, the Treasurer of our Union, who intimates that, as it is necessary, in consequence of the decease of his brother William, who was one of his sureties for the due discharge of his office as Treasurer, that another be substituted in his name, he would propose either his brother Frederick, or his brother in law W. Pye, Rector of Sapperton. — Rec^d. a letter from Mr Sadler, Rector of Sutton under Brailes, as to the parochial subscriptions from thence to the Stow Distr. Comm S.P.G. — MW. received a letter from Eliza Daniell, who proposes to visit us early in September — In the evening E.F.W. read to us |^114 D^r ~~Chalmers~~ Cumming's able discourse on equality. —

Aug. 17. Thursday.

Fine weather on the whole, though at times damp and dull. — Preparing for business at Stow. — To Stow in my carriage, accompanied by dear Sophy, who went to visit her parents at "the Cottage," and returned to Upper Slaughter with E.F.W. who had followed us to Stow in his own carriage, conveying my youngest grandson and his nurse to "the Cottage", to be seen by Grandpapa and Grandmamma Vavasour. — E.F.W. with W. Vavasour and others engaged in practising on the Cricket field — I transacted business at the ~~Cricket~~ Savings Bank, meeting Mr Pole and Mr R. Waller: — also at the office of the Gloucestershire Banking Company; and at the Workhouse, where I conferred with Mr Pearce on many points of Union business, and on the letter I had received from the Registrar General as to his dismissal. — |^115 Met and conferred there with Mr Wilkins. — To the Justice-room where the Dean of Gloucester and R Waller were my colleagues, and Mr Winter was our Assessor. — Returned home to dress for dinner at Wyck Hill, whither we went, accompanied by our children — M^r and M^rs. C Pole entertain very handsomely; much good cheer, and a well appointed table – the guests, besides ourselves, were M^r & M^rs. C. R. Pole, their two sons and two daughters, M^r and M^rs. J. T. Rice, M^r and M^rs. Winter, Captain Leigh, and Mr Lewes. ——

Aug. 18. Friday.

A fine forenoon, the afternoon and evening damp and rainy — Wrote to the Registrar General in reply to his letter received on Wednesday. — E.F.W, Sophy, and Broome went to call on the Wallers and M^r W Stenson at Bourton on the Water — I accompanied them in their carriage as far as to the |^{116} Lower Slaughter Turnpike house, and walked back. — Received a letter from Mr Hare on Hunt Trust business, accompanied by letters from Mess$^{rs.}$ Cox and Williams to Mr Hare, and from Mr Braikenridge to Cox & Williams. — Received a letter from Mr Wiggin accompanying a list of the Oddington parochial contributions to the Soc. for propagation of the Gospel. — M^r and M$^{rs.}$ Cholmondeley called upon us, and appear very pleasing young people. — Notes passed between R Waller and myself on Justice business — Preparing for the annual district meeting S.P.G. to be holden at Stow on Wednesday next. — Enjoyed a domestic evening with my beloved children and grandchildren — E.F.W. read to us Dr Cumming's sermon on Fraternity. — The weather very unpropitious for the operations of the harvest — it is reported that wheat and other grain is sprouting: and there are bad accounts everywhere as to the potatoe blight. — |^{117}

Aug. 19. Saturday.

After a rainy night a wet morning; a showery forenoon; a fine afternoon and evening. — Our dear children and grandchildren left us for Stanway — Tax business and Justice business at home — Called at Lower Swell, on John Perkins, whom I found much in the same state as when I saw him last, weak, and unequal to much exertion. Settled accounts with him as to parochial contributions to S.P.G. — Received a letter from C Bathurst in answer to my last on Justice business. — MW. received a letter from Mr Woodroffe announcing that his wife had given birth to a son, and is doing well — Ranke's history of the reformation in Germany. —

Aug. 20. Sunday.

Showery weather — distant thunder. — Visited the Sunday school. — Preparing sermons. — Morning Service, prayers. — Afternoon service, prayers and Sermon. I preached on the duty of |^{118} parents. — Received a letter from F. Aston, making arrangements as to our journey on Thursday next to attend the consecration of the church at Cerney Wick. — A letter from Mr Winter with a list of books to be ordered for the Stow Book Society. — A letter from Ch. Bathurst in reply to my last, giving his opinion that the Small tenements act is virtually repealed by the County Courts Act. — A letter from Chr. Geldard respecting the money due to us for the purchase of land at Ravenflatt by the directors of the North Western Railway Company: the arrangement made is that £1000 shall remain for three years on mortgage, or, at least, with deposit of deeds, at five per cent interest, the directors paying in cash the balance, between five & six hundred pounds. — A letter from R W Hippisley with a cheque for the amount of subscriptions to S.P.G. from the parochial association at Stow. — Preparing the Report for the annual meeting Stow |^{119} District committee S.P.G. to be held on Wednesday next. — To the family a Section from Dr James's work on the Collects. — An uneasy feeling prevails as to the temper and movements of the Chartist faction, who have been making demonstrations of strength and insurrection in London, at Manchester, Birmingham, Ashton under Lyne, & other places: their movements have been successfully opposed, and many arrests have been made: but it is plain that a bad feeling is prevalent. — In Ireland other leaders of the Insurgents besides Smith O Brien have been apprehended, rebellion being kept under by military & constabulary force. The great anxiety caused by the evil spirit prevalent in Ireland is ~~great~~ much increased by the alarming state of the weather, and its anticipated ill effects on the harvest, and by the extensive damage and unsoundness of the potatoe crop. Trials of prisoners for treason, and ~~pl~~ political |*120* felonies are in progress in Dublin. ——

Aug 21. Monday.

After a rainy night a wet morning, and frequent showers in the forenoon and afternoon. — Tax business at home — Wrote to F. Aston that MW. & I would call on Thursday next at the Vicarage, Northleach, to convey one of his family in our carriage to the consecration of the Church at Cerney Wick. — Wrote to Rodwell, with an order for books for the Stow Book Society. — Wrote to Chr. Geldard, assenting to the proposition made by the Directors of the North Western Railway as to the payment of a portion of the money payable by them to us for land purchased for their works at Ravenflatt, and that the balance remain on loan for three years, as explained in the letter I rec^d. from C.G. yesterday. — Having received a note from Canon Ford, addressed to E F. W. or myself, requesting the use of the tent belonging to the Stow Cricket Club, for the purposes of the consecration at Cerney Wick |*121* on Thursday, replied to him that E.F.W. being returned to Stanway he had better apply to W. Vavasour, or other member of the cricket club, for the use of the tent, and I named the arrangements we had made for being present at the Consecration — Rec^d. from the Misses Ford a note with the amount of the collection made at Little Risington in aid of the S.P.G. an annual contribution, the receipt of which I acknowledged. — Visited parishioners — J Davis, M^rs. Collett, W. Gregory. — Preparing report of the Stow distr. Comm. S.P.G. to be presented at the annual meeting on Wednesday. — Rec^d. a letter from Mr Hare on Hunt Trust business, he returns to me a letter from Mr Thornton to me which I had sent for his perusal. — Ranke's History of the Reformation in Germany. —

Aug. 21. Tuesday.⁵

A rainy morning; frequent showers during the forenoon and afternoon, one accompanied with thunder and lightning; |*122* a damp evening; weather very unpropitious for the harvest. — Tax business with W. Gregory — Justice business at home. — Preparing annual report and other documents for the annual meeting of the Stow Distr. Comm. S.P.G. to be held to-morrow — Rec^d. a note from Mr Hurd, covering his subscription to the S.P.G. — which I acknowledged. — Rec^d. a letter from the Registrar General, who, out of deference to my favourable report to him of Mr Pearce, consents to retain him in his office — A letter from C Bathurst with further thoughts on the subject of his last to me — Ranke's History of the Reformation in Germany. —

Aug. 23. Wednesday.

Fine weather with the exception of a slight shower about midday. — Justice business at home — Wrote to Mr Pearce, forwarding to him the letter I had received yesterday from the

---

5.   An uncorrected dating error.

Registrar General, together with Poor Law documents, and directions as to the business |*123*
to be transacted at the meeting of the Guardians to-morrow, at which it will not be in my
power to preside. I forwarded a copy of a proposed minute and resolution as to the relief
of casual poor, wayfarers, mendicants &c. — Drove to Stow, accompanied by my wife to
attend the annual meeting of the Stow district Comm. S.P.G. — Transacted business at the
office of the Gloucestershire Banking Company — To the library — At the Unicorn, sat to
receive subscriptions and contributions from the members of the district committee S.P.G.
The annual meeting commenced at ~~the~~ 2 P.M. — Owing to the absence of the Dean of
Gloucester, who shrinks from attending on such occasions, from weariness, and dislike of
being confined long together in one place or posture, and to the absence of the Rural Dean
who was gone with his family to South Cerney to make preparations for the Consecration
of the Church |*124* at Cerney Wick to-morrow, M^r. Hippisley, as Rector of Stow, was called
on to preside; other Clergymen present were Messrs. Waller, Sadler, Morrison, Lewes, Terry,
Potter, Wiggin, and Boggis: several ladies were present, my wife, M^rs. Wiggin, M^rs. Hippisley,
accompanied by Miss Taunton & Miss Digby, M^rs. Scott Junr. Miss Morrison, the Misses
Hall — there was rather a more numerous attendance than usual of small subscribers and
favourers, particularly females and children, and some tradesmen of the place. The annual
report was read by me as Secretary and Treasurer — That it should be adopted was moved by
M^r. Wiggin, and seconded by M^r. Potter in an appropriate speech. — M^r. Sadler moved and I
seconded a resolution of confidence in the S.P.G. both of us addressing the company at some
length — M^r. Waller moved and M^r. Morrison seconded a resolution |*125* of thanks to me as
Secretary and Treasurer which gave me an opportunity of again addressing the meeting at
some length — Thanks were voted to the Chairman, & the meeting was dissolved. It is, as I
have experienced for many years, very difficult to gather in this neighbourhood a really good
meeting – there is so much of apathy, so little zeal, so fastidious a feeling, so much, (shall it
be said?) love of pleasure — an archery meeting, a cricket party, or a ball are very popular,
but the anniversary of a Church Society is shunned as tiresome. However the purse is opener
than the heart – for nearly £100 have passed through my hands since the last annual meeting
in the shape of contributions from this district to the parent Society — M^rs. Witts returned
home after the meeting: I remained to be present at the third dinner for the year of the Stow
Clerical Society. M^r. Morrison was in |*126* the Chair, Messrs. Sadler, Lewes, Boggis, R Waller,
Potter, Wiggin and myself attended. M^r. Potter was elected Chairman for the next year: R
Waller re-elected to be Secretary – Returned home, fatigued, to tea.

Aug. 24. Thursday. S^t. *Bartholomew's day.*

MW's birthday: entering on her 63^d. year. May GOD protect and preserve her to be a comfort
to her husband and children, and all connected with her! She has been my faithful and true
partner for forty years and more, an affectionate wife and mother, a good daughter, bearing
with the infirmities and faults of her nearest connections patiently, and doing her utmost to
promote their peace and prosperity. Her health, though very indifferent, is not worse than it
has long been; her removal hence would be a great blow to me, which GOD avert! — The
morning fine; heavy showers in the forenoon and afternoon, yet with in-|*127* tervals of fine
weather, and the evening fine. — Rose and breakfasted early; left home in our chariot with
post horses, to attend the consecration of the Church at Cerney Wick. A little after we had

passed over Bourton Bridge we overtook R. Waller, who had walked forward, and whom we had arranged to take with us in the rumble of the carriage. At Northleach we alighted at the King's Arms, and sent the chariot to the Vicarage, to take up Mary Aston, who was fixed to be our inside passenger. — Mr A. and Sophy had gone to Cirencester yesterday to be the guests of Mr Powell, and M$^{rs.}$ Aston remained at home, M$^{rs.}$ Keysall being on a visit at the Vicarage — When we arrived within a mile of Cirencester, we crossed the turnpike road leading from that town to Barnsley and Bibury; having followed a connecting highway, and with Preston Church and |^{128} Parsonage on our left hand, we fell into the turnpike road leading from Cirencester to Cricklade, near the village of Siddington, and passed along it in the direction for Cricklade, having on our right the residence of Mr Bowly, a gentleman who married, to his second wife, my cousin Maria Whalley, and who, as a farmer, brewer, and man of business, taking a lead in the management of the Cirencester Union, and in all questions relating to agriculture and the general prosperity of the country, takes very right and moderate views, and, being able to express himself in public with much facility and clearness, and sound reasoning, has acquired deservedly considerable reputation as a leading man in the district in which he resides. — When we reached the Thames and Severn canal, which passes near South Cerney, we deviated from the turnpike road to the right, and soon arrived at the little hamlet of Cerney Wick. |^{129} It was a few minutes after eleven, when we arrived at the wicket leading through the Church yard to the spruce little Chapel like sacred edifice, which was already crowded, the service having but just commenced on the punctual Bishop presenting himself with his suite, even before he was expected — R Waller and I put on our Surplices, hoods & scarves, in a cottage by the road side, and, after some little difficulty, obtained seats for ourselves and the ladies near the pulpit and reading desk in the aisle, the stoled Clergy being mostly congregated in the Chancel. — The Bishop was accompanied by his Chancellor, Dr Phillimore, and his two chaplains, Murray Browne, and Barrow, the former being his usual attendant in that part of the diocese which forms the Archdeaconry of Gloucester, and the latter in the Archdeaconry of Bristol — The services of the day were read by M^r |^{130} Mangin, the Curate of South Cerney, a very estimable and useful Clergyman; the first lesson was read by Mr Howman, the Rector of Barnsley, and Rural dean of Fairford Deanery, who is also Honorary Canon of Bristol. — the second lesson was read by Mr Powell, the Incumbent of Cirencester; and the Sermon, appropriate to the occasion, was preached by the Vicar, Mr Ford. It was the same discourse, altered for the occasion, which he had preached when Stow Church was reopened for divine service after its recent restoration. — Parts of the service were chanted by a village choir and Sunday school boys, but, of course, ~~this part of the service~~ the musical performance would not bear criticism — The holy communion was administered to between 50 & 70 of the congregation, and the collection made at the offertory amounted to above £67. which will be appropriated towards payment of what is still lacking in the funds for the erection of the Church, |^{131} and the endowment of a minister. — The ground enclosed for a church yard was consecrated in the usual solemn and impressive manner, the Cricket Tent from Stow being set up to shelter the Bishop and Clergy from the passing showers. — Nothing can be more suitable, unpretending & simple than this little Church. The Architect, M^r S$^t.$ Aubyn, of a good Devonshire, or Cornish family, and nephew of M$^{rs.}$ Marmaduke Vavasour, was present, and well deserved the compliments he received. His works in Ecclesiastical architecture are chiefly to be found in the more Western Counties, but he was selected to erect this church, because, many years since, when he was a pupil of our County Surveyor, Mr T. Fulljames, of Gloucester, he was engaged for a long time, as Clerk of the Works, in superintending the building of Edward's College, South Cerney, the |^{132} charitable institution erected as a refuge for the Wives and daughters of poor Gloucestershire Clergymen deceased. Cerney Wick Church is calculated to hold a congregation not much exceeding one hundred; is of the Early English style of architecture; perfectly simple and plain, and devoid of sculpture or architectural enrichment — yet the effect of the simple lines and angles, every part harmonizing with the other, is graceful and attractive. The entrance is by a porch on the North, the village road passing on that side of the Church; the nave, without aisles, is divided by a pointed arch from the Chancel; there are two West windows, of equal dimensions, an East window, with stained glass: a small stone pulpit, and a rail and desk for the minister — one on the Northern, the other on the Southern side of the arch separating the nave from the chancel. — Encaustic tiles are used in the elevated part of the Chan-|^{133} cel, within the railing, and a sedile on the South side of the Communion table; like that in the Chancel at Stow, will accommodate two officiating Clergymen. On the communion table, a handsome wrought cloth is the work and gift of the ladies of Mr Mangin's family. — Nothing appears to be deficient in the interior fitting up of the Church; the congregation are accommodated in plain open stalls; near the porch is a capacious immersion font; not far from it, an alms-box, of antique form, with inscription, and mediæval hinges & iron work — in the iron work of the entrance door attention has been paid to the old patterns handed down from former centuries – the roof of the church and chancel, of stone slating, is of a lofty pitch, without tower or spire, or bell turret, yet not without a small bell to be tolled for |^{134} prayer within the humble chapel. — The funds for the erection of this ~~hum~~ interesting little edifice arise principally from the benevolence of three individuals possessed of landed property within the hamlet, and chiefly resident within its bounds, so feeling the inconvenience of distance from their parish Church, perhaps two miles off. These parties, named Sutton, Biddle, and another, are of one family by intermarriage, and Mr Sutton is a yeoman cultivating his own estate: Contributions from other sources were obtained; from the Church Building Society, from the Diocesan Church Building Society, from M$^{rs.}$ Sheppard, a benevolent lady now deceased, who was ever forward in promoting by her liberal gifts the erection of new temples to the Lord; from a Church Building Association at Manchester; from Dr Warneford, from Mr Ford &c. — |^{135} The number of Clergymen present on the occasion amounted to thirty — among those not yet enumerated was my Son, who with his dear wife slept at Cirencester last night, having arrived there yesterday, and, after visiting the Agricultural college, had dined with the Bowlys at Siddington: they propose returning to Stanway in the evening. Their report as to the dear children was very comfortable. — Then there were Mr Hippisley and Mr Wiggin — Mr Aston with his younger daughter — Canon Prower, from Purton, my ancient college acquaintance and contemporary, now a Wiltshire Rural Dean and as such raised by Bp Monk to the profitless dignity of honorary canon of Bristol Cathedral: — F. Biscoe, of Turkdean, accompanied by his wife and her sister, Miss Middleton — Matthew Hale Estcourt, now curate to his |^{136} father near Tetbury, where a second and newly erected church was consecrated by the Bishop yesterday; — Mr Bolland, the incumbent of Siddington, accompanied by his sister; — Mr Boudier, a clerical son of the Rector of Farmington, was present, escorting his mother; Mr Price from Coln S$^t.$ Dennis came with a son and daughter;

Mr Foster, the Incumbent of Colne Rogers; Mr Pye, Rector of Sapperton, who brought with him his lady and daughter; Mr H. Cripps, the Rector of Preston; Mr Barker, Rector of Daglinworth; Mr Beadon, Rector of Latton; Mr Tuson, Rector of Minety — with others, whose names and persons were unknown to me. — Divine Service being concluded, the greater part of the Clergy, with the ladies, followed the Bishop, his Chancellor, and his chaplains, conducted by Mr Ford and the ladies of his family, to the residence of Mr Sutton, the principal |^137 resident proprietor and occupier of the hamlet, in whose comfortable, low browed house, and shady pleasure ground, many kind greetings of old acquaintance, and recognitions took place. Thence all adjourned to an orchard near the Church, where, in a spacious tent, borrowed from the Cirencester Archery club, were congregated a large and goodly party, seated at two long tables and a cross, or high table, the Clergy, ladies, and others who had been present at the ceremonial of the day, to meet the Bishop, and partake of a bountiful & handsome collation prepared by the hospitable Vicar. More than a hundred guests were assembled, and the attendants occupied the seats when the more privileged classes had retired. Due honour and compliment were paid to the Bishop by the Vicar, who very justly eulogized the liberality and piety of the worthy persons with whom originated the design of building |^138 the church; Mr Ford also passed just commendation upon his excellent Curate, Mr Mangin, who seems very deservedly popular with the parishioners, and has, perhaps, even more than his vicar, contributed to the successfully carrying out the good design, acting with singular judgment, and with zeal well tempered with discretion. He modestly and unaffectedly, yet warmly acknowledged the compliment received by him, and the Bishop bore his part with dignity and propriety in the reciprocation of kind expressions towards the Vicar and his Curate, and those liberal inhabitants with whom the good design now accomplished originated. These replied by Mr Sutton, as their organ, in plain and suitable terms, thanking the company for their good will & the kind expression of it — The Bishop retired with his staff to prosecute his official duties in the consecration of a church-yard, or addition to one, at the not distant village of Marston-Maisey — |^139 About 4 P.M. the party broke up; those whose residences were remote, and among them ourselves, with R Waller and Mary Aston, to our respective homes; some who lived within less distance repaired to the Schoolroom at South Cerney, where tea and coffee were provided by Mr Ford and his family or Mr Mangin for the lingering guests. — We deposited M. Aston at the Vicarage, Northleach, and set down R Waller at Bourton Bridge, reaching home by 8 P.M. —

Aug 25. Friday.

A dull, cloudy, close day; no rain, except a few drops in the evening. — Settled accounts and arranged my papers relating to the Stow district meeting S.P.G. held on Wednesday. — Visited a sick parishioner — Wrote to Chr. Geldard to thank him for a present of grouse. — The Misses Hall called when we were taking a walk. |^140 Ranke's History of the Reformation in Germany. —

Aug. 26. Saturday.

After a rainy night and morning, a close, cloudy day, with a damp atmosphere; some showers in the afternoon — Justice business at home — Wrote to Ch. Bathurst in reply to his last letter as to the County rate and Small tenements acts. — Wrote to Turner, fishmonger, London, ordering a dish of fish for a dinner party on Wednesday next. — Transacted tax business with E. Lea. — Received a letter from Ch. Geldard as to leaving £1000 – part of the purchase money of land at Ravenflatt bought by the North Western Railway Company on a mortgage loan with the directors of that undertaking. — After luncheon I left home in my open carriage to visit my children at Stanway Vicarage, purposing to remain there till Monday, exchanging duties with my Son to-morrow. |[141] Very affectionately received by my Son and daughter, and their children — The alterations and improvements at the Vicarage are proceeding satisfactorily — M[r] Stott called, making a long visit. — An enjoyable evening — More electioneering strife and bustle at Cheltenham. A committee of the House of Commons has unseated M[r] Agg Gardener, the Conservative Member, on a plea of treating by his partizans: but this does not reinstate Craven Berkeley in the representation; for he was unseated for bribery in 1847, and so is disqualified for representing this borough during the present parliament. —

Aug. 27. Sunday.

A rainy morning: the day damp, close and hot; some rain fell. — E.F.W. went to Upper Slaughter to officiate there, and returned to Stanway to dinner. He found all well at US. and brought me a few lines from MW: — also a letter from |[142] C. Bathurst on public matters. — At Stanway morning service and Sermon. I preached in aid of the funds of the Soc. for the Propagation of the Gospel under the authority of the Queen's letter; the collection amounted to £1. 13. 8 — At the afternoon service I preached on the love of GOD to man in the incarnation of our Blessed Saviour — The newspapers announce the death of M[rs.] Walker at Henwick Hall: a fresh, but not unlooked for distress to M[rs.] C. Barr. — I had much enjoyment in the Society of my dear children and grandchildren. —

Aug 28. Monday.

A rainy morning: the day close and damp, but the forenoon, afternoon, and evening fine. — Engaged with E.F.W. in hearing a case of sheepstealing. — Left Stanway about one P.M: as I returned home called at Temple Guiting on poor old Bowen, whom I found in a very suffering and feeble state. — On my way fell in with M[r] Lovegrove, deputy coroner, who had been calling at Upper Slaughter to solicit my vote and |[143] interest in his favour in the event of the decease of M[r] Cook, the Coroner, which however does not seem likely soon to take place, he being, though infirm through palsy, a hearty old man. Yet it behoves M[r] L. to press his claims, seeing that others are canvassing for the office — M[r] Pruen, Sol[r] Cheltenham, and a M[r] Smith of Winchcombe. I promised to support M[r] Lovegrove — Arrived at home by 4 P.M — Rec[d.] a letter from M[r] Wilton, the County Treasurer, with a mass of County accounts, being the abstract of the Treasurer's annual statement of Receipts and Expenditure from Easter ~~184~~ Sess[ns.] 1847 to Easter Sess[ns.] 1848 – to be examined by me — A letter from M[r] Hare on Hunt Trust business, with enclosures from Mess[rs.] Cox and Williams to M[r] Hare, and from M[r] Braikenridge to Mess[rs.] Cox and Williams. — Found all well at home — Ranke's History of the Reformation in Germany. —

Aug. 29. Tuesday.

At last a fine day, though |[144] for the most part close and cloudy. — Justice and tax business at home. — Visiting sick and poor parishioners — Wrote to M[r] Tilleard and M[r] Hare on

Hunt Trust business, forwarding to the former the letter I received yesterday from Mr Hare with its enclosures — Remitted to the Treasurers of the Society for the Propagation of the Gospel a cheque on Mess$^{rs.}$ Hoare for the amount of the collection made at Stanway on Sunday last. — Preparing a Sermon — Examining the Treasurer's abstract of the County accounts. — Ranke's History of the Reformation in Germany.

Aug. 30. Wednesday.

A fine day with the exception of a slight shower in the Evening. — Examining the Abstract of the Receipts and Expenditure of the County of Gloucester as prepared by the Treasurer, pointed out two or three trifling errors in a letter to the Treasurer, and sent the papers back for publication in the County Newspapers, and for distribution among the Magistrates. — Received a letter |^{145} from C. Bathurst on Magisterial questions. — MW. heard from Miss Daniell who proposes to visit us, and to arrive here on Saturday next. – Entertained several of our neighbours at dinner: the party consisted of M^r and M$^{rs.}$ C. R. Pole, with their eldest son and a daughter, — M^r and M$^{rs.}$ Vavasour, — M^r and M$^{rs.}$ Winter — M^r and M$^{rs.}$ Boudier — and M^r and M$^{rs.}$ Scott. — All passed off pleasantly. ——

Aug. 31. Thursday.

With the exception of a few drops of rain in the afternoon, the weather fine: distant thunder. — Justice business at home. — Drove to Stow — Received a letter from Mr Tilleard on Hunt Trust business: he returns to me the documents which I had forwarded to him with his advice. — A letter from Sophia Hunt on Hunt affairs, which do not move pleasantly in any quarter. — A letter from C. Bathurst on questions relating to the office of magistrate. — Transacted |^{146} business at the Provident Bank; at the office of the Gloucestershire Banking Company; at Mr Morgan's office on tax business. — Visited the Workhouse, and conferred with Mr Pearce on Union and Workhouse matters. — Met R. W. Ford and R. Waller at the Provident Bank, and accompanied them to the Justice room, where we held a long sitting, being engaged with Justice business and Assessed taxes matters. – Winter and W. Vavasour were present. — Ranke's history of the Reformation in Germany.

Sept. 1. Thursday.

A very fine day. — Wrote to Rodwell, to order a book for the Stow library — To Mess$^{rs.}$ Cox and Williams on Hunt Trust business in the terms suggested by Mr Tilleard; — replied to the letter which I received yesterday from Mr Tilleard, sending him a copy of my letter to Mess$^{rs.}$ Cox and Williams. — The Misses Hall and Mr Ford called upon us; the latter consulted me as to publishing |^{147} the consecration sermon which he preached at Cerney Wick: I encour^{a}ged his so doing. — With MW. called on M$^{rs.}$ Dolphin, who is in great trouble, owing to disappointments in law affairs and other annoyances. — Ranke's History of the Reformation in Germany.

Sept. 2. Saturday.

Very fine weather — Wrote to Mr Hare on Hunt Trust business, forwarding for his perusal Mr Tilleard's late letter to me, with copies of my answer to him, and of my late letter to Mess$^{rs.}$ Cox and Williams. — Justice business at home: in reference to one of the cases brought before me, I wrote letters to Mᵣ Winter, Mᵣ Makepeace, and Mᵣ Hayward. — Drove with MW. to call on the Poles at Wyck Hill; but found none of the party at home — As we returned met and conversed with Mᵣ Terry. — We expected the arrival of Eliza Daniell to-day, |[148] but she never came. She has been visiting, at Gloucester, a Major and Mʳˢ· Wornum, whose acquaintance she had formed at Leamington. — MW. wrote a note to her, to be conveyed by the carrier on Monday, to ascertain the reason why she has not come to us agreeably to promise. — Visiting sick parishioners — Ranke's Reformation in Germany.

Sept. 3. Sunday.

Fine weather — Visited the Sunday School. — Preparing a sermon. — Morning service, prayers. — Afternoon service, prayers and Sermon — I preached on duty to Pastors and Teachers. — Received a letter from Mᵣ H. H. Wilton, County Treasurer, in acknowledgment of my note written to him when I returned to him the Abstract of the County accounts. — Also a letter from Mᵣ Tilleard on Hunt Trust affairs — By a letter received by MW. from Eliza Daniell to-day, it seems that her not arri-|[149] ving here yesterday proceeded from her having been persuaded to stay with her friends at Gloucester till to-morrow when she proposes to come to us. — Ecclesiastical Gazette — To the family a section from Dᵣ James on the Collects — It appears, as to the Cheltenham election, that Craven Berkeley, being disqualified by the decision of the Committee of the House of Commons from sitting for that borough, his supporters and himself, under the directions, no doubt, of the real patron, Lord Fitzhardinge, put forward Mᵣ Grenville Berkeley, as candidate, to supply the place of his cousin, Craven, until the latter, in a new parliament, is qualified to resume his seat. Grenville Berkeley is son of the late Admiral B. and married a sister of Lord Leigh; low in politics, as of a Whig family, not unwilling to be a nominee of his powerful |[150] relation, but a gentlemanly and well conditioned person. — Grantley Berkeley, as sworn antagonist of his brother, the Peer, tries to make mischief, and suggests to the voters to elect Sir E. Lytton Bulwer, but that scheme fails: threatening from Grantley that his cousin Grenville shall be petitioned against, if elected, on the ground that he ~~was~~ is disqualified to sit, by reason of bribery and corruption perpetrated by him at the Election for West Gloucestershire in 1847, when Lord Fitzhardinge brought Grenville forward in opposition to Grantley, but was foiled — Truly, these Berkeleys are a united set — a set of discreditables — Lastly, the anti-Berkeley party at Cheltenham, unable to prevail on any respectable Conservative to enter into the Arena, there being so much of dirt and corruption on all hands, invite the Turn-coat Bickham Escott, once Conservative, now Radical, but |[151] retaining in either phase his impudence, volubility, and ambition, to contest, with Grenville, the prize which the latter is almost sure to win. The Election takes place to-morrow — the nomination took place yesterday. —

Sept. 4. Monday.

Very fine weather — Wrote very fully to Sophia Hunt on the questions at issue with Mᵣ Geo. Hunt, on the danger of being involved in a Chancery suit, and the advisableness of referring matters to arbitration. — Tax business with W. Gregory. — Justice business at home. — Our dear children and grandchildren arrived from Stanway on a visit to us. — Miss Daniell, whom we expected to-day did not make her appearance. — Received a letter from Winter as to the insane woman, Willoughby, of Adlestrop, respecting whom I had written to him. —

Sept. 5. Tuesday.

Fine and warm weather |[152] the general character of the day; but heavy rain fell between 2 & 3 P.M. — Wrote to M[r] Hare, forwarding to him the letter I received on Sunday from M[r] Tilleard — Very busy in cleaning the brook in the pleasure ground, with fishing, to the great delight of my grandchildren. — A letter came from Miss Daniell, explaining her non arrival yesterday was owing to inconveniences anticipated from travelling through Cheltenham on the day of the election — The lady did join our circle late in the evening. — Grenville Berkeley was elected yesterday representative for Cheltenham by a majority of 160 over Bickham Escott. – Received from M[r] Bloxsome's office a copy of the new County rate. — From Busby and Jennings, Moreton, a bill for goods supplied.

Sept. 6. Wednesday.

Fine weather. — Wrote to Rev[d.] E. Hawkins with an account of subscriptions &c. received from members of the Stow Distr. Comm. S.P.G. accompanying a |[153] remittance to the Treasurers of the Society — Justice business at home. — E.F.W. rode before breakfast to Maugersbury to the W. Vavasours, to meet M[r] Franks, now on a visit there: — my son returned to us before dinner. — MW. and Sophy drove to call on M[rs.] Ford and the Misses Hall at Little Risington and Bourton on the Water. — I walked with Miss Daniell — Received a note from M[r] Moore, Med. Off. of the Union, urging the importance of precautions being taken by the Guardians in anticipation of a possible outbreak of cholera: the ravages of this frightful epidemic with reason dreaded. — A letter from M[r] Pearce on Union matters. —

Sept 7. Thursday.

Very fine weather — Sophy accompanied me to Stow after breakfast. We took Frederick with us, that he and his Mamma might pass some hours at "the Cottage", and at Maugersbury, |[154] with the two families of the Vavasours, and return with me to Upper Slaughter after I had concluded the business of the day. – E.F.W. rode to Stow, to join the luncheon party at M[r] Vavasour's — After his dinner here, Broome, attended by his squire, Tom Whitford, rode on his poney to join the party at "the Cottage", returning home to us before 6 P.M. – I called twice at "the Cottage", when I conveyed Sophy and Freddy, and when I called to take them home with me. — Transacted business at the Provident Bank, tax business with M[r] Morgan's clerk; conferred with the Superintendent of the Constabulary, and with the Churchwarden of Stow. — At the Union Workhouse presided for three hours at the fortnightly meeting of the Guardians: few attended, the farmers being much occupied with their harvest. — Passed a very enjoyable evening surrounded by my children and precious grandsons. —

Sept. 8. Friday.

A dull, autumnal day, |[155] with a shower about 5 P.M. — Wrote to Mess[rs.] Coutts on the money matters of the Hunt family; as to the division of the sum left by M[rs.] Mary Hunt to Sarah Hunt, which now upon her decease becomes divisible between her surviving brothers and sisters. — Accompanied MW. and Miss Daniell in our open carriage to Stow, intending to proceed with them to call on M[r] and M[rs.] Scott, at Banksfee; but learning at Stow that certain parties had been apprehended for a felony, and been taken to Upper Slaughter, for examination before me, I left the ladies to make the visit, and walked home attended by dear

Broome, whom I encountered at Stow, having gone with E.F.W. and Sophy in their carriage to call on M^r and Mrs. Pole at Wyck Hill; not having found them at home, they were on their way to call at "the Cottage", whence they proceeded to Upper Swell, and visited Mrs. W. B. Pole; Mr. W.B.P. was from |*156* home. I greatly enjoyed my walk from Stow by Hyde Mill with my dear grandson, attended to the business, and at last all our circle were reunited at dinner. — Received from Sophia Hunt a very strange, ill-judged, and fretful letter, founded on false views and prepossessions respecting the Hunt Trust affairs: — from Mr Hare a very proper letter on the same business; — from the office of the Soc. for the Prop. of the Gospel an acknowledgment for the remittance made by me two or three days since.

Sept. 9. Saturday.

Fine weather — Our dear children and grandchildren left us for Stanway to our great regret. E.F.W. and Sophy with the younger children went before our luncheon. Broome with his attendant, Tom, and on his poney, remained till after luncheon. — Justice business at home. — Received a letter from Mr Hare on Hunt trust business. — Wrote to him on the same, forwarding to him for his |*157* perusal and approval the letter I wrote yesterday to Messrs. Coutts, which he will forward if he is satisfied with it — Walked with E. Daniell. — "Dr Francis, sketches of Indian Scenery and Customs;" a collection of lithographs, with illustrative letterpress, by a Physician in the East India Company's Service, a nephew of Mr Francis, some time since curate of Great Risington. —

Sept. 10. Sunday.

A rainy day. — Visited the Sunday School. — Morning service, prayers and sermon. I preached on the character of John the Baptist. — Afternoon service – prayers. — Received a letter from the Clerk of the Worcester Union, who requests my opinion as to the qualifications and characters of two candidates for the office of Governor of the Workhouse of that Union, both of whom are known to me: one is Moore, late Clerk of the County Gaol, Gloucester: the other |*158* Harwood, at one time Porter at our Union Workhouse. — A letter from Mr Hare, who forwards for my perusal a letter received by him from Messrs. Cox and Williams, and returns to me a letter from Mr Tilleard which I had sent to him. — Preparing a Sermon. — To the family a section from Dr James's work on the Collects.

Sept 11. Monday.

Fine weather — Justice business at home. — Wrote to Mr Knott, Clerk to the Worcester Union, with testimonials as to the characters and qualifications of Moore and Harwood, candidates for the office of governor of the Worcester Workhouse — Wrote to Mr Tilleard, forwarding for his opinion the letter from Cox and Williams which Mr Hare had sent to me for my perusal, and which reached me yesterday. — MW. and Eliza Daniell drove to Bourton &c. — In their absence Mrs. Scott, Mrs. R. Scott, and Mrs. Morrison called on us, but were not |*159* admitted; also Mrs. Dolphin —— I called on E. Lea's family as to the funeral of his niece, who died yesterday at Rendcomb, and is to be buried here on Friday. — Dr Francis's sketches of Indian scenery and customs.

Sept. 12. Tuesday.

Very fine weather — Wrote to Mr Fletcher, Stow Brewery, to order a cask of beer. — To Sophia Hunt on Hunt Trust business, and as to the distribution of £2179. 16. 8. 3 P^r C^t. Cons. divisible between herself and surviving brothers and sisters on the decease of her sister Sarah, agreeably to the will of M$^{rs.}$ Mary Hunt — To my son, explaining to him that in consequence of the funeral of the late Miss S. Lea, we shall be unable to visit him and his at Stanway on Friday next, but that we hope to fulfil that engagement on Saturday or Monday. — Mr Wilkins called on me on different matters of Justice business — |^{160} I walked with E. Daniell — Dr Francis's sketches of Indian Scenery and Customs. —

Sept. 13. Wednesday.

Fine weather — Wrote to C Bathurst on points of Justice business, acts of Parliament lately passed &c. — Wrote to Howell. — Walked with Eliza Daniell — Attended a vestry meeting, at which it was agreed to rest satisfied with the assessment of the parish to the County rate, as made by the County Rate Committee — Mr Terry called on us. — Sir W. Scott's Fair maid of Perth. —

Sept. 14. Thursday.

Fine weather — Drove to Stow — MW. and Eliza Daniell accompanied me, returning home after calling at one or two shops. — To the Provident Bank and Library — To the Police Station where I unexpectedly meet the Chief Constable, whom I engaged to return with me to Upper Slaughter to dine and sleep. — To the Workhouse, where transacted business, and conferred on Union matters with M^r |^{161} M^r [6] Pearce; visited the Wards &c. — Went again to the Provident Bank, where met Mr Pole, M^r R Waller, and Morrison — To the Justice room, where much, and some serious, business awaited the Dean of Gloucester, Mr Ford, M^r R Waller and myself — Mr Lefroy was in attendance. – Of gentlemen present there were W Vavasour, Mr Mangin, W B Pole, Mr Chamberlayne &c. — The last named is passing a few days with W. Vavasour at Maugersbury, having left his family at Tunbridge Wells. He came into the neighbourhood to be present, two or three days ago, at the annual meeting of the Stow and Chipping Norton Agricultural Society, which was held at Chipping Norton, under the presidency of Mr Evans of Dean. Mr Chamberlayne is named as the President for the ensuing year, and of the anniversary meeting, which will be held at Stow. — Lefroy returned home with me in my open |^{162} carriage, sending his horse to my stable by a policeman. — Received a letter from Mess$^{rs.}$ Cox and Williams on Hunt Trust business: they send the copy of a letter from Mr Braikenridge, threatening a suit in Chancery, if the proposal of an arbitration of matters in dispute be not accepted in ten days — A letter from Mr Tilleard in answer to my last to him.

Sept. 15. Friday.

Beautiful weather — Mr Lefroy left us after breakfast, for Moreton to visit his station there, meaning to ride across the country, visiting other police stations, to Cheltenham. — Wrote to Mess$^{rs.}$ Busby and Jennings, Moreton, with a cheque for goods supplied. — Wrote to Mr Tilleard, with a copy of the letter sent by Mr Braikenridge to Mess$^{rs.}$ Cox and Williams,

---

6.   Inadvertantly duplicated on the change of folio.

threatening a suit in Chancery. — Wrote to Miss S. Hunt, apprizing her that such a letter had been received. — Wrote to Mr Thornton a letter to meet him on his return |^163 to Llanwarne from a foreign tour, with a resumé of all that has ~~passed~~ passed in respect of the Hunt Trust affairs during his absence: forwarded to him for his perusal and consideration all the correspondence which has been carried on during his absence from England. — Mr C. R. Pole called upon us. — Officiated at the funeral of Miss Sarah Gregory Lea. — Received a letter from Mr Hare on Hunt Trust business — a letter from Messrs. Coutts as to the transfer of Stock from the names of Mr Hare and myself to those of the brothers and sisters of Miss Sarah Hunt deceased, together with a power of Attorney to be executed — a letter from the Accountant of the Bank of England enquiring as to the power of Attorney for the above transfer for which application had been made — a letter from Miss S. Hunt as to Hunt Executorship and Trust matters, in |^164 which she details proceedings and communications with Mr G. Hunt and his family who are now resident temporarily at Wadenhoe; Miss S.H. still disinclined to refer the matters in dispute as to the Hunt Trust to arbitration. — Received a pamphlet addressed to the Magistrates of the County of Gloucester, stated to be written by Dr Charles Bompas, in which he complains of the injustice done to him and his family by the decision of the Magistrates at Trinity Quarter Sessions as to the renewal of the licence of the Fishponds asylum for the insane, now limited to six months, with the understanding that he is to retire from the management at the expiration of that period, and that a competent superintendent be nominated for the approval of the Court, whose qualifications for the office shall be well attested. — Sir W. Scott's Fair maid of Perth. —

Sept. 16. Saturday.

Beautiful weather — Wrote to Sophia Hunt that, having |^165 forwarded the correspondence with Mr Tilleard and others as to the Hunt Trust disputes to Mr Thornton and Mr Hare, it would not be in my power to comply at present with her wish that I should communicate it to Mr Whitcombe. — Justice business at home — Drove with MW. and Eliza Daniell to Stanway. Very kindly received by our dear children and grandchildren, and passed four hours with them very agreeably: partook of luncheon with them. All were well: and the improvements and alterations at the Vicarage are going on apparently as one would wish. — Returned home to a late dinner — M^r and M^rs. R W Hippisley had called on us during our absence: so also M^rs. R. Waller, likewise Mr Moore, Medical officer of our Union, with the new sanitary act, as to which he is desirous of conferring with me. — Rec^d. a letter, announcing a meeting of the Shareholders |^166 of the Gloucester and Berkeley canal — From C Bathurst a letter respecting the pamphlet, lately published by Dr Charles Bompas. — From Mr Knott, Clerk to the Worcester Union, a letter to acquaint me that Mr Moore, late Clerk to the County Gaol, Gloucester, has been elected Governor of the Workhouse of the Worcester Union. — Reading D^r C Bompas's pamphlet. —

Sept. 17. Sunday.

Fine weather. — Visited the Sunday School. — Preparing a sermon. — Morning service; prayers. Afternoon service; prayers and sermon. I preached on the great danger of little sins. — Received a letter from Howell. — Also heard from Mr Hare on Hunt Trust matters. — To the family a section from James on the Collects.

Sept. 18. Monday.

Fine weather — Wrote to Mr Hare on Hunt Trust concerns; sent to him for his execution the |^{167} power of Attorney which I had signed for the transferring of the amount of 3 per C^t· Cons. standing in our names, to the different members of the Stoke Doyle Hunt family in equal proportions, being under the will of M^{rs}· M Hunt divisible among them on the decease of their sister Sarah. Mr Hare will forward the power of Attorney to Messrs· Coutts. — Mr Moore called; with whom I conferred on the sanitary state of the district, and on the provisions of the new Sanitary act — Frederick Aston, the younger, accompanied his sister Sophy on horseback to call upon us, and staid to luncheon with us. — Walked with MW. and Eliza Daniell to Lower Slaughter and the Turnpike gate: as we returned we were overtaken by M^r and M^{rs}· Vavasour in their open carriage, coming to call on us: the ladies got into the carriage with M^{rs}· V. while Mr V. and I walked |^{168} across the fields and joined them at our house. — A letter from Messrs· Busby and Jennings, Moreton in Marsh, acknowledging my cheque for £3. 1. 0. — Sir W. Scott's Fair Maid of Perth. —

Sept 19. Tuesday.

Beautiful weather — Justice business at home. — Wrote to the County Chairman as to the pamphlet published by D^r C Bompas. — To the Editor of the Law Times, desiring to be furnished with a new periodical — the Magistrate. — Preparing for the annual meeting of the Stow Book Society on Tuesday next. — Drove with MW. and Eliza Daniell to Bourton on the Water; called on the Wallers, but they were not at home. — I walked home from Bourton — Received a letter from Mr Tilleard on Hunt Trust affairs: Mr Thornton is not to arrive at home from abroad so soon as was expected — A letter from Sophia Hunt, who reports Mr Capron's opinion on the Hunt Trust controversy: she |^{169} also sends me a copy of the opinion given by Mr Parker, a Chancery barrister, on a case submitted to him by Mr Braikenridge for Mr George Hunt — A note from R W Hippisley announces a Ruri-decanal meeting as fixed for Sept. 29. — Fair Maid of Perth.

Sept. 20. Wednesday.

Fine weather — Preparing for the annual meeting of the Stow Book Society on Tuesday next. — Walked to Eyford, to visit the aged wife of Thomas Pinchin, who is dangerously ill; administered the communion to the old couple, and their neighbours. — Copied Mr Parker's opinion as to the Hunt Trust dispute, a copy of which I received yesterday from Sophia Hunt — Drove to Stow with MW. and Eliza Daniell; at the Library met Mr Ford by appointment, whom I accompanied to the Unicorn Inn, where we sat for the transaction of magisterial business in |^{170} Petty Sessions; the principal case being an order of removal from Bourton on the Water to Long Compton of the wife and child of Moses Roff. A former order regarding the same parties had been quashed by consent in consequence of some technical errors, or informalities in its wording. An order of maintenance in the Lunatic Asylum at Gloucester, saddling the parish of Long Compton with the charges, was made yesterday, as to Moses Roff himself, now detained in that establishment, by Curtis Hayward and Lysons — Messrs· Wilkins, and Brookes, and Taplin assisted to-day as Clerks. — With Mr Ford looked at recent alterations in the Church at Stow, which are carried, we thought, rather too far. The Rector, with the advice and assistance of his friend

Mr Wiggin, whose taste leads him much in the line of mediæval architecture and church decoration, has been enriching the chancel by painting the sedile of a rich |[171] blue colour, on which in gold are painted the sacred monagram, perpetually repeated, with stars &c. — Above the communion table, on the wall, on each side of the East window, are inscribed in ancient gothic characters the ten commandments. All this is Wiggins's own handiwork. The picture of the Crucifixion, presented some years ago by M[r] Chamberlayne, has been removed from above the communion table, where it blocked up the East Window, into the body of the Church, where it is fixed over the stalls assigned to the donor, as Lord of the Manor of Stow and Maugersbury. M[r] Chamberlayne has been wrought upon to consent to this, and also to contribute to the placing of a painted window over the communion table, at some future time, when also a new window is to be inserted into the South Wall of the Chancel, which is to contain in painted glass the Chamberlayne Arms; these formerly, painted |[172] in distemper, disfigured by a huge daub the wall of the aisle, above the Manor pew. Both pew and coat of arms have been done away with in the late improvements — While Ford and I were engaged at Stow, the ladies made fruitless calls on the elder and younger Vavasours, drove to Oddington, visited the Church at Stow &c. — When our business was concluded we returned home.

Sept 21. Thursday.

Very fine weather — Received a letter from C Bathurst — D[r] C. Bompas forwards a copy of his pamphlet to each magistrate in the county. — I drove to Stow. — Attended at the Provident Bank. — Thence to the Workhouse, where I presided at the fortnightly meeting of the Guardians, from 12 to 4 PM. — Returned to dinner — While I was at Stow M[r] Clarke had called to take leave of us: he has resigned the curacy of Icomb, and goes |[173] to Town: he is to be succeeded by M[r] Ogle, a son of an Oxford Physician, who is already known in the neighbourhood as a cricketer.

Sept 22. Friday.

Showery weather — Eliza Daniell left us to visit M[rs.] Barr at Henwick: we conveyed her in our phaeton after an early breakfast to Cheltenham, where we arrived between 11 & 12 AM. and left it soon after 3 PM. when E.D. set out for Worcester by the railway. — We drove to the Plough; — shopping — with E.D. walked to Pittville &c. — Had luncheon at Hooper's, the Pastry cook, where excellent mutton chops may be had: there we fell in with M[r] Close, who resorted thither for a basin of soup. Entered into a lively conversation with him on Church Architecture, Tractarianism &c. — when he surprized E.D. by his hilarity and conversational talent, |[174] who had expected to find in the evangelical M[r] Close, a sour and starched Puritan. — We reached home by quarter past five — A letter from M[r] Hare on Hunt Trust business: he sends me copies of letters received by him from Cox and Williams, and written by him to M[r] Braikenridge — Ranke's Reformation in Germany. |

Diary
1848

1

Sept. 23. Saturday — Showery weather —
Wrote to Sophia Hunt on Hunt Trust affairs.
—— To Miss Moorhouse, with a cheque for
£5. in anticipation of the usual payment
made by us at Martinmas, she having soli-
cited this accommodation in a letter received
by M.W. yesterday —— To Davison, Newman
and C.º with a cheque in payment for groce-
ries supplied, and with an order for more
—— Justice business at home. —— Preparing for the discussion to be held at the
Ruridecanal meeting at Stow on the 29.ᵗʰ
—— Visiting poor parishioners —— Received
a letter from M.ʳ Thornton on Hunt Trust
affairs, written from London on his return
from Germany —— From P. B. Purnell on
the recent publication of D.ʳ C. Bompas, and
other county business. —— Ranke's History
of the reformation in Germany. ——

Witts Family Papers F365

Diary
1848

Sept. 23. Saturday.

Showery weather — Wrote to Sophia Hunt on Hunt Trust affairs — To Miss Moorhouse, with a cheque for £5. in anticipation of the usual payment made by us at Martinmas, she having solicited this accommodation in a letter received by MW. yesterday — To Davison, Newman and C[o.] with a cheque in payment for groceries supplied, and with an order for more — Justice business at home — Preparing for the discussion to be held at the Ruridecanal meeting at Stow on the 29[th.] — Visiting poor parishioners — Received a letter from M[r] Thornton on Hunt Trust affairs, written from London on his return from Germany — From P. B. Purnell on the recent publication of D[r] C. Bompas, and other county business. — Ranke's History of the reformation in Germany. — |[2]

Sept. 24. Sunday.

A fine day. — Visited the Sunday school — Preparing a sermon —— Morning service – prayers and sermon. I preached on the eternity of hell torments. — Afternoon service, prayers — M[rs.] Dolphin and Miss Walmesley called after the second service — Officiated at the funeral of the aged Anne Pinchin. — Preparing for the question to be brought forward at the Ruri-decanal meeting on Friday next. — Received a letter from M[r] Hare on Hunt Trust concerns: he returns to me a letter from Mess[rs.] Coutts which I had sent for his perusal. — To day is the birthday of my youngest grandson; he is a noble and promising boy, now entered on his third year. GOD preserve and protect him and his two lovely brothers! — Ecclesiastical Gazette — To the family a section from D[r] James on the Collects. —

Sept. 25. Monday.

A dull morning fol-|[3] lowed by a fine day — Wrote to C Bathurst, sending for his perusal the letter I had rec[d.] from Purnell on the late pamphlet of D[r] Bompas. — To M[r] Thornton on Hunt Trust affairs, forwarding for his perusal M[r] Parker's opinion, as taken on the part of M[r] Hunt, with letters from M[r] Hare which M[r] T. had not seen; gave him particulars of my late letters to Miss S. Hunt. — Preparing for the discussion expected at the Ruri-decanal meeting on Friday next. — Ranke's Reformation in Germany.

Sept. 26. Tuesday.

A damp and rainy day — Wrote to M[r] Moore, Med. Off. of our Union, on sanitary measures, especially the recent act passed for the removal of nuisances, and in anticipation of this country being again visited by Asiatic cholera. — Preparing for the discussion to be raised at Stow at the ruri-decanal meeting on Friday next — I drove to Stow to attend the |⁴ annual meetings of the Stow District Committee of the Society for the Promotion of Christian Knowledge, and of the Stow Book Society. — Transacted business at the office of the Gloucestershire Banking Company, and with R G K Brookes, as Magistrates' Clerk. — Preparing for the two annual meetings, by examining the accounts with Mᵣ Ford, as the Treasurer and Secretary of Promotion of Christian Knowledge Distr. Comm. and Treasurer of the Book Society — The meeting of the religious Society, at the Unicorn Inn, was a miserable, lukewarm affair. Ford does not strive to infuse into it life or spirit, but contents himself with an uninteresting and meagre report: the proceedings are with closed doors, after the old sleepy fashion — The subscribers pay their quotas, the depository of books is kept up, the neighbourhood is supplied with Bibles, Common Prayer books, Testaments and tracts, |⁵ but there is little or no energy, life, or spirit. To day the Dean of Gloucester presided: Messʳˢ Ford, Morrison, Hutchinson and myself composed the attendance; and of these one, Hutchinson, was not a district subscriber. — These things ought not to be so; but I cannot interfere, or stimulate the Secretary, Ford: it is, with a local distaste for such assemblages, and with a prevalent indifference to the interests of religion and the church, as much as I can do, to keep alive a better feeling as regards the religious Society of which I am the district Secretary — the Soc. for the Propagation of the Gospel — Such indifference does not prevail as to more secular gatherings, as was proved by the assembling of the members of the Stow Book Society at their annual dinner. In the absence of Lord Say and Sele, the appointed chairman, Mᵣ Pole presided: he had brought with him his son, C R. Pole, and his grandson, a younger Charles, an officer in the Guards; Capt. Leigh, Messʳˢ W. Vavasour, Winter, Ford, Hutchinson, Hippisley, |⁶ Morrison, Wiggin and myself made up the party, which passed off pleasantly. Mᵣ Ford and myself were re-elected to the respective posts of Treasurer and Secretary. — Received letters from Davison, Newman & Cᵒ who acknowledge the receipt of a cheque which I lately sent time in payment for groceries — from E.F.W., who was prevented attending at the book society dinner to-day, as he was engaged at a Justice meeting at Winchcomb, and the elder Vavasours are staying at the Vicarage at Stanway — all are well there. — Eliza Daniell has written to MW. from Henwick, and gives a good report of Mʳˢ Barr and her children —

Sept. 27. Wednesday.

A rainy day — Wrote to E.F.W. in answer to his letter received yesterday, that I should desire Messʳˢ Hoare to transfer from my account with them to his account with them the sum of £50: — this is a present, not on the current income account. —— Wrote to |⁷ Messʳˢ Hoare to the same effect. — Wrote to Rodwell, Bookseller, for a supply of books for the Stow Book Society. — Wrote to R. Waller as to the Petty Sessions at Stow to-morrow, and a special Sessions fixed for Monday next. — Arranged the minutes and resolutions of the Book Society meeting held yesterday. — Preparing for the subject to be discussed at the Ruri-decanal meeting on Friday. — Received a letter from Mᵣ Thornton on Hunt Trust business: he forwards a copy of a letter of his to Mʳˢ Hunt. — From Sophia Hunt received a formal letter addressed to the three Hunt trustees, in which she declines personal communication on the matters in dispute with them individually, and desires that any proposition they may have to make be forwarded to M[r] Whitcombe as the Solicitor employed by her family: this accompanies a private letter to me, in which she details transactions with M[r] George Hunt as to the furniture |[8] at Wadenhoe, its sale by auction &c. — I cannot but lament and feel annoyed at the temper in which the family at Stoke Doyle conduct the controversy as far as they are concerned, respecting the Hunt succession & their claims as conflicting with those of M[r] Hunt. It is ungrateful, unjust, and irritating to treat the Trustees with suspicion and distrust: but S.H. has conceived a prejudice, which is wholly unfounded, and persists in upholding her own false impressions, as if they were infallibly just, and her own angry views as if they were undeniably well grounded. — A letter from a Major Kennedy of Cheltenham, enquiring the character of our late servant Amy Hollis — Ranke's History of the Reformation in Germany. —

Sept. 28. Thursday.
A rainy day. — Wrote to Major Kennedy with a character of Amy Hollis: — to M[r] Thornton |[9] to whom I forwarded Sophia Hunt's formal letter addressed to the Hunt Trustees, which reached my yesterday: I commented on the present state of our trust concerns, and replied to the contents of M[r] T's letter rec[d.] yesterday. — Received a letter from M[r] Thornton on Hunt Trust matters: he returns to me letters which I had forwarded for his perusal. — From M[r] Hunt a strange letter, in which he calls upon me to give up the £1000. 3 P[r] C[t.] Cons. which the Hunt Trustees have retained to await the final settlement of the matters in debate, expressing himself as if the above mentioned reserve were wholly and solely my act: he wants the money, he says, to invest it in the purchase of land, and pledges himself to make it good when called upon so to do. It is impossible to avoid the conclusion that M[r] H., with ungovernable ill-temper, and rooted false prejudice on the whole points in dispute, and a most grasping disposition |[10] pursues the end he aims at in a spirit calculated to lead one to suspect his sanity — A letter from Bathurst: he returns me Purnell's letter respecting the pamphlet recently published by D[r] Bompas, which I had forwarded for his perusal. — Justice business at home. — Drove to Stow. — To the Provident Bank, — to the office of the Gloucestershire Banking Company, and to the Workhouse, at all which I transacted business of a public or private nature. — Wrote to Rodwell, Bookseller, London, for a book to be supplied to the Stow Library. — With R W Ford held a petty Sessions at the Unicorn Inn — W. Vavasour attended — Home to dinner — Ranke's History of the Reformation in Germany. ——

Sept. 29. Friday. Michaelmas day.
Very rainy weather — M[r] Arkell of Butler's Court, Boddington, near Gloucester, who married one of the daughters of the |[11] late T. Smith of Eyford, and is now staying with E. Lea, called to consult me on the best course to be adopted in his parish as to a dispute concerning assessment to the Poor rates, an adjudication having been made by the Magistrates of the Cheltenham bench, which appears to have been decided in error. I recommended the line to be taken by the parties considering themselves aggrieved with a view to a rehearing of the case. — After breakfast I drove to Stow, to attend morning service there preliminary to the meeting of the Clergy of the deanery at a ruridecanal synod, as the Rural dean calls our periodical meetings. Once in the year, it is agreed, the Clergy assemble on these occasions to partake together of the Holy Sacrament of the Lord's supper. — The unfavourable

weather may have been the cause why so few of my reverend brethren attended — The Rural Dean, Hippisley, who read the prayers, Hellier, Wiggin, Potter, |*12* Terry and myself were all who communicated. — At the national Schoolroom M.ʳ Hellier read a long paper, carefully prepared, in a philosophical tone, shewing much research, to the purport that the almost universal belief of mankind in a future state ought to be considered as a proof of the immortality of the soul. — Much of this essay was derived from Cudworth's intellectual system. — I followed, confirming the view of the reader: observing that the general belief of the soul's immortality was probably the result of some primæval revelation. I advocated to the opinions of Socrates as developed in Plato's Phædon, comparing passages from that dialogue with texts from the New Testament. I pointed out ᵗʰᵃᵗ the ancient Egyptians held the doctrine of the soul's immortality, and even recognized that of the resurrection of the body. But I further shewed that however |*12* general such a belief was, it was only entertained as a speculative opinion, not held by the many, held doubtful by the wisest, inoperative as a principle of holy living and dying, not practical, and, therefore, worthless. I concluded by urging our great obligations to GOD who sent his son to abolish death, and illustrate, clear up, make sure, the doctrine of life and immortality (2 Tim. 1.10) Some remarks were made by Potter and Terry — It was arranged that the former should at the next meeting read a paper as to the legality of a man marrying his deceased wife's sister, so far as that disputed point, now about to be agitated in the houses of Parliament, is settled in holy writ. — I returned home by 4 P.M. — Received a letter from M.ʳ Thornton, who returns to me the Hunt Trust documents which I had forwarded to him with ~~any~~ ʰⁱˢ comments thereon. —— A letter from C. Bathurst on the case of |*13* the refusal of the Court of Quarter Sessions to grant a licence to D.ʳ Bompas to superintend the private madhouse at the Fishponds near Bristol longer than to the Epiphany Sess.ⁿˢ — A letter from Mess.ʳˢ Hoare announces that they have transferred £50 from my account with them to that of my Son. — Ranke's History of the reformation in Germany. —

Sept. 30. Saturday.

A third rainy day in succession. — Wrote to M.ʳ G. Hunt in reply to his letter received on Thursday; stating that I should communicate its contents to my co-trustees — Wrote to M.ʳ Thornton, sending him the letter I had received from M.ʳ Hunt with a copy of my answer to him; also replied to M.ʳ T's letters of the 25.ᵗʰ 26.ᵗʰ and 27.ᵗʰ Inst. on Hunt Trust affairs. — Justice business at home — Received a letter from Mess.ʳˢ Hoare, announcing that |*14* M.ʳ Jennings has placed to my account with them, £148. 3. 0. — Visited the daughter of one of my parishioners, who has returned home from service in a very declining state of health. — Suffering much from pains in my right arm and shoulder, rheumatic or dyspeptic. — Visited John Davis and William Gregory. — Ranke's History of the Reformation in Germany. —

Oct. 1. Sunday.

Fine weather, but damp in the morning. — Attended the Sunday School — Preparing a sermon. — Morning service. — Prayers, and the ministration of the Holy Communion: 25 Communicants. — Afternoon service: prayers and sermon; I preached on seriousness in religion, an indispensable disposition of mind. — Rec.ᵈ a letter from a Cheltenham tradesman with a bill — Ecclesiastical Gazette — To the family one of the "Family Sermons". —

Oct. 2. Monday

The forenoon fine; a rainy afternoon. — Wrote to Sophia Hunt on |[15] Trust and Executorship business — Also to Lord Sherborne, requesting him to contribute towards the payment of the bill due to Mess[rs.] Wilkins and Kendall for proceedings taken to stop the practice and abate the nuisance of turning out animals in the street of our village — Drove to Stow with MW., who went to call on M[rs.] W. Vavasour at Maugersbury, while I was engaged with M[r] Ford at a special petty Sessions for making an order of filiation in a case in which the defendant had procured the services of an attorney from Shipston — The business being over, I walked to Maugersbury, where I rejoined my wife, and returned home thence with her. — Ranke's History of the Reformation in Germany.

Oct 3. Tuesday

Fine weather. — Wrote to Purnell on the matter of D[r] Bompas, communicating to him my own views, & those entertained by Bathurst as to the |[16] course which may be taken by D[r] B. and his friends and supporters, and which ought to be pursued by the Court at the Michaelmas Sessions. — M[r] J. Blandford having come to Upper Slaughter to visit his little property, and his tenants, called upon us. — Walked to Eyford with MW: called on M[rs.] Dolphin and Miss Walmesley — Visited a sick parishioner. — Received a letter from Sophia Hunt [to MW] on Hunt Trust business: though she has formally declined holding any correspondence with the Trustees, and desired that all communications may be made through her Solicitor, she thus breaks through [or evades] that prudent resolution, and dilates into an ebullition of angry feeling against M[r] Hunt with suspicion of M[r] Thornton's impartiality and integrity; repeating excited and angry conversations which have passed at Stoke and Wadenhoe between M[r] Hunt on the one hand, and herself and sisters on the other. — |[17] Received letters from M[r] Hare and M[r] Thornton on the same worrying business: the former returns to me several letters on the trust affairs which I had forwarded to M[r] Thornton, and he to M[r] Hare. — Ranke's History of the Reformation in Germany. —

Oct 4. Wednesday.

A rainy day. —— Wrote to Sophia Hunt in reply to the letter which MW. had received from her yesterday: reminded her that such letter is inconsistent with the formal notice given by her to the Trustees that she would decline further correspondence with them unless it passed through the medium of her Solicitor: repeated that the Trustees cannot move unless the differences between the Representatives of the late Life-tenant and the Remainder man be settled, or unless all parties agree to an arbitration; begged her to spare me the fruitless harrassing of reiterated explanations to |[18] no purpose; pointed out to her that the contents of her last letter, as reporting an angry conversation with M[r] G. Hunt were such as I could not communicate to my co-trustees; entreated her to spare my wife the annoyance of being made the medium of communications on matters of business. — Preparing a sermon. — Received a letter from E.F.W: all well at Stanway Vicarage; my son details the particulars of past engagements in which he has been in the society of Lord Ellenborough the Mess[rs.] Dent &c. — Lord E. has procured for him admission to a dinner at which his Lordship is shortly to preside at Cheltenham, and which is to be given by the East Indian Officers now resident there, to the gallant hero of Scinde,[1] Sir Charles Napier, whom my son has lately met with a large party of East Indians at Southam; Sir C.N. being a visitor at Cheltenham to recruit his health. — Received a notice of a |[19] meeting of Visiting justices at Gloucester Gaol, fixed for the 11[th.] Inst. —— Visited a sick parishioner; — also the Lea family. — Ranke's History of the Reformation in Germany. —

Oct. 5. Thursday

Fine weather — Wrote to E.F.W. in answer to a question respecting the County rate assessment, which he had asked me in his letter received yesterday — Drove to Stow with MW. who returned home after calling at two or three shops. — To the Provident Bank, where I met M[r] Pole, C R Pole, Winter, and Perkins. — Transacted business with M[r] Taplin, assistant clerk to the Magistrates. — To the Workhouse, where I presided at the fortnightly meeting of the Guardians of our Union: there was much business. A discussion arose on a motion made that a Collector of rates should be appointed for the parishes of the Union, to supersede, to a certain extent, |[20] the Overseers in that department of the duties: it being considered by some that such an officer would collect and pay over the rates with more regularity and expedition, than under the present system, and that at a moderate expence. But the dread of increased expenditure in the way of remuneration, and the dislike of increasing the staff of paid officers, operated, principally with the representatives of the smaller parishes, to the rejection of the project, which was proposed by the Vice Chairman, who was prevented by indisposition from supporting his plan — The town was very full to-day, this being a statute fair for the hiring of agricultural and other servants, — a custom more honoured in the breach than in the observance: the congregating so many young, thoughtless, and ignorant persons is a fruitful source of immorality, intoxication and licentiousness. — Returned home to a late dinner. — A letter from M[r] Thorn-|[21] ton: he rather leans to assenting to the request of M[r] Hunt that the £1000 — 3 P[r] C[t.] Cons. which the Trustees retain till the settlement of the matters in dispute; but to this I am very adverse, and expect that M[r] Hare will concur with me — Our position, as Trustees, badgered on all sides, is exceedingly unpleasant. — MW. received a letter from M[rs.] Backhouse: she proposes coming on a visit to us with two of her daughters about the 17[th.] Inst. — Ranke's History of the Reformation in Germany —

Oct. 6. Friday

On the whole, a fine day, but cloudy and close; slight showers in the afternoon. — Justice business at home — Made an excursion in our open carriage to Hook-norton, and back; MW accompanied me. The object was to inspect a private madhouse there, in which a number of Gloucestershire pauper lunatics are maintained, for whom the County |[22] Asylum at Gloucester does not furnish accommodation. So greatly has mental malady increased with the increase of population, that the provision made for the reception of the insane paupers is insufficient, and hopeless chronic cases are removed to two private establishments — this at

---

1. The campaign in Sind lasted from January to April 1843. Sir Charles remained in Cheltenham for several months, and whilst there wrote a pamphlet advocating the organisation of a baggage corps for the Indian Army. He was called to serve once more in India in the spring of 1849, and remained there almost two years. For detail see *Biographical Index.*

Hook Norton, and another at Fairford. — At the turnpike gate our letter bag brought a letter from Mr Hare as to the £1000 3 P^r C^t. Cons. retained by the Trustees of the Hunt property, which Mr Hunt asks to have paid over to him on certain conditions. Mr Hare agrees with me that, under the sanction of the opinion given to us by Mr Turner & Mr Bates, we ought not to consent to Mr Hunt's demand. — From Purnell I received a letter on the subject of Dr Bompas's pamphlet, and on the proceedings consequent thereon, which must engage at the coming Quarter Sessions the grave attention of the Court. — Passing through Stow, I was |²³ detained for a short time by Justice business. — Near Oddington we met and held a parley with Mr Wiggin. He highly praised a speech which he believed to have been spoken by me at the late meeting of the Winchcomb Agricultural Association, and the report of which he had read in the Morning Herald. I explained to him that my Son had delivered himself of that speech, a report of which E.F.W. had sent to me by the post to-day, as given in a Cheltenham newspaper, in which the proceedings of the day were fully detailed, and which paper my Son requested me, when I had read it, to forward to the Vavasours at the Cottage. — It is, indeed, a very excellent and appropriate address, alluding to the revolutionary outbreaks on the continent, contrasting them with the tranquillity at home, and dilating on the false and true senses in which the words liberty, equality, & fraternity are & |²⁴ ought to be understood. — Lord Ellenborough and Mr Holland justly complimented my Son for the ability & talent and sound principles which he had developed — other speeches by them and ^my Son are the leading features of the report. — Pursued the nearest road to Hooknorton, turning from the turnpike road at the top of Salford hill; found the cross road very indifferent; but still a wellbeaten track, running on the summit of the ridge which separates Oxfordshire from Warwickshire, and commanding extensive views on each side, over Chipping Norton, Salford, Churchill &c. – to the right: Long-Compton, Whichford, Brailes &c. on the left. When my son held the curacy of Whichford we had travelled this way as far as Long Compton Hill, but the road beyond I had not passed over for many years. It leads by Little and Great Rollright, and close by the ancient Druidical circle of Rollright Stones. Between Rollright and Hooknorton the road |²⁵ is very hilly. Hooknorton is fifteen miles from Upper Slaughter – a long rambling village, with several good houses, where persons of comfortable independence may be presumed to reside, built on undulating ground, the parish containing 6000 acres, and the village 1500 inhabitants. There are several shops superior to those usually met with in a country village, and two or three decent public houses, at one of which we found admission into a comfortable parlour, and procured an acceptable luncheon of bread and cheese and porter — This little inn was not far distant from the establishment which I came to visit, having promised to inspect it, as the one of the Visiting Magistrates of the Gloucestershire County Asylum, whose residence was the nearest to it. Leaving MW. at "the Bell", I called and introduced myself to Mr Mallam, the Superintendent and proprietor, a gentleman of the Medical |²⁶ profession, his whole pauper establishment I inspected, which appeared to me liberally and humanely conducted. His first class patients, with whom I had no concern, are accommodated in his own house — the paupers in another & separate range of buildings, with gardens, and land in which spade husbandry is followed, and the patients are employed, whose state justifies their being set to work. There are 15 Glostershire paupers, male and female, in nearly equal numbers, under his charge; most of these are very bad, chronic, fatuous, or epileptic cases. — A county asylum being opened at ^for Oxfordshire, and a charitable establishment existing at Headington, the Warneford Asylum, Mr Mallam has lost the Oxfordshire County Pauper inmates, ~~which~~ ^{who} used to throng this house, which has for many years been open under different proprietors, as a private mad house; but as many neighbouring Counties are as yet without County Asylums, the number |^{27} of pauper patients maintained here is still very considerable. Those whom I came to visit were chiefly persons of impaired strength and decayed bodily constitution, yet they seemed clean and comfortable, well clothed, fed and lodged, and the manner of Mr M. in his intercourse with the poor creatures was gentle, kind and judicious. I could detect no offensive smells, and very few were under coercion: there were one or two coercion-chairs, and one in use by a restless, noisy, patient, merely strapped in it round his waist — chains there were none to be seen — the attendants brought me one or two straps which appeared to have lain by for a considerable time without being used: the dormitories were clean & well-ventilated for the most part; and there was a sufficient padded room. — Before returning home we visited the fine old church, which was partially restored some years ago, but needs a more |^{28} thorough and judicious reparation: the Chancel is much dilapidated, and the pews should be replaced by open seats. There is a very curious Norman or early English immersion font, of a circular shape, with rude sculpture: there is a very well preserved wooden screen and rood loft, the access to the latter being by a staircase constructed in the pier of the arch separating the nave from the chancel: the nave is flanked by North and South Aisles: the tower at the West end should be thrown open to the nave, and so would be procured a fine architectural vista with good East and West windows: in this case the singers gallery would be removed. The Church is of a late date, — say of the Reign of Hen. 7. — with clerestory and a low pitched roof — after the fashion of the neighbouring, but more elaborate church of Chipping Norton. The church at Great Rollright also is in the same style, but without aisles: they have both |^{29} handsome towers with numerous pinnacles. – We reached home before 6 P.M. — Ranke's History of the reformation in Germany. —

Oct. 7. Saturday

A fine day, very close & warm, and somewhat damp; a second midsummer. — Wrote to M$^{rs.}$ W. Vavasour as to a book which she had been desirous of ordering into the book society, that it is out of print; — to Mr Thornton a long letter on Hunt Trust affairs, — that I consider it right not to relinquish our hold on the £1000 — 3 P^r C$^t.$ Cons, which Mr Hunt demands: — to C Bathurst on Dr Bompas's affair, forwarding the rough copy of my letter to Purnell on that subject, and his answer. — Received a letter from Mr Hare, on Hunt trust matters: he returns to me three or four letters from Miss Sophia Hunt, one from Mr G. Hunt, and a copy of my reply to the latter, which had been sent for his consideration — |^{30} Ranke's History of the Reformation in Germany. ——

Oct. 8. Sunday

Close, warm, fine weather. — Visited the Sunday School. — Preparing a sermon. — Morning service – prayers and sermon. I preached on the widow's son raised. – Afternoon service — prayers. — Received a letter from Lord Sherborne in answer to mine respecting the proceedings taken with a view to stop the nuisance of turning cattle loose to graze in the village of U Slaughter: his Lordship, who rarely exhibits a liberal or confiding temper, hesitates as to paying his share of the expence. — Received a report of the proceedings of the half yearly meeting of the proprietors of the Gloucester & Berkeley canal — Ecclesiastical Gazette — To the family a sermon from the "Family sermons." — Somewhat indisposed with a slight attack of diarrhoea: much caution is necessary as to the state of the |[31] bowels at this time: for the Malignant Cholera, which has long been raging in Russia, Poland and Germany, has invaded this country, apparently in the direction from Hamburg, where it has been very active: serious cases are reported at Hull, Sunderland and Edinburgh. —

Oct. 9. Monday

Rainy weather in the forenoon and afternoon; high wind at night. — Wrote to Curtis Hayward, as Chairman of the Visitors of the Lunatic Asylum in Gloucester, a report of the state of Hooknorton madhouse, and of the Gloucestershire pauper patients in confinement there; I also communicated with him on the question respecting the Fishponds private lunatic asylum which is likely to be agitated at the approaching Quarter Sessions. — Wrote to E.F.W. inviting him, Sophy, and Broome to visit us for a night or two, when the Backhouses are our guests. — |[32] MW. received a letter from M[rs.] Backhouse: she and her daughters propose coming to us on Saturday the 14[th.] Inst. — A letter from M[r] Hare who sends a copy of a letter received by him from Mess[rs.] Cox and Williams on Hunt Trust business. — Justice business at home — Visiting sick parishioners — Indisposed with diarrhoea, but the medicine I took seems likely to correct the tendency; — Ranke's History of the reformation in Germany. —

Oct 10. Tuesday

A showery forenoon: the afternoon fine. — Wrote to Howell; — to M[r] Thornton on Hunt Trust affairs, forwarding to him the note &c. which I received yesterday from M[r] Hare; — to M[r] Ford, asking him to attend the Quarter Sessions, there to uphold the Chairman and his friends who are likely to be opposed on the question of the measure adopted at the Trinity Sessions as to the granting a conditional licence to D[r] |[33] Bompas, for holding the private madhouse at the Fishponds till the Epiphany Sessions. — As M[r] F. called upon us, I delivered to him this letter — he brought and presented to us a printed copy of his Sermon preached at the consecration of the church at Cerney Wick. — Ranke's History of the Reformation in Germany — Justice business at home.

Oct. 11. Wednesday.

A fine day. — Suffering from an attack of lumbago, coupled in the evening with diarrhoea, which left me very languid. — Justice business at home — With MW. drove to call on the Aston family at Northleach. On the road we met M[rs.] A. and Mary, going in their carriage to pay a visit to M[rs.] Ford; but they insisted on returning with us to Northleach. There we found M[rs.] Watkins on a visit at the Vicarage, with the Vicar, Frederick Jun[r] and Sophy Aston. Partook of luncheon with them, and passed an hour or two |[34] pleasantly. Leaving MW. at the Vicarage I walked with F. Aston and his son to the Bridewell, meeting by the way M[r] Price & M[r] Fulwar Craven, who had been holding a Petty Session at the Committee Room in the Bridewell. — Inspected the Bridewell, where I met M[r] Thorpe, the Chaplain, and advised as to the enlargement of the Chapel. A workman was fixing a Clock to strike the quarters; — an ingenious piece of mechanism, but to cost £60 – and one of a like construction to be supplied to each of the four houses of correction in the County — MW. with the ladies from the Vicarage called for me at the Bridewell, and we reached home by 5 P.M. — M^rs. Aston has been much of an invalid, suffering from a complaint in the throat, which is greatly abated: she consulted Mr Charles Fowler, of Cheltenham, an eminent surgeon. — Received a letter from C. Bathurst on the affair of Dr Charles Bompas — M^rs. W. Vavasour had called |^35 at Upper Slaughter during our absence. — Ranke's History of the Reformation in Germany. —

Oct. 12. Thursday.

A fine day. — Justice business at home. — Wrote to C Bathurst on the Fishponds controversy. — Drove to Stow, accompanied by M.W. who did not remain there long. — Received letters — from Mr Thornton on Hunt Trust affairs; he forwards to me a letter which he had received from M^rs. Hunt; — from C Bathurst on the proceedings relative to Dr Bompas. — To the Provident Bank, where Mr Lefevre acted as sole Clerk, Mr Pain being confined to his bed by a fit of the gout: there I met Sadler, Winter, and Morrison. — To the Workhouse, where I conferred with Mr Pearce on Union matters. — At the Unicorn held a petty Sessions, assisted by the Dean of Gloucester; the other magistrates of the division being absent from home — |^36 J. T. Rice and Winter attended in the Justice room. — Consulted Mr Hayward about the tendency to diarrhoea, the lumbago, and dyspeptic ailments from which I have been lately suffering. — Returned earlier than usual to dinner — The Asiatic cholera has broken out in London — Smith O'Brien, after a long trial at Clonmel, has been found guilty of high Treason. — Ranke's History of the Reformation in Germany.

Oct. 13. Friday

Fine weather: the air cool — Wrote to Rodwell for a supply of books for the Stow book society. — to Mr Thornton, returning to him the letter from M^rs. Hunt which he had sent for my perusal yesterday — to the Governor of the House of Correction at Northleach, with a warrant of commitment for reexamination of a prisoner brought before me to-day on a charge of felony. — The recent acts passed, by Mr Attorney Genl. Jervis's suggestion, as to magisterial business, |^37 and which in many respects introduce great improvements into the administration of that department of the law, require much attention and caution as to proceedings, the practice being greatly altered. — Received from the Gloucester Lunatic Asylum a notice of a meeting of Visitors fixed for the 24th. Inst. — Ranke's History of the Reformation in Germany. —

Oct. 14. Saturday

Showery weather — Much engaged with Poor Law and Justice business — Many persons called upon me between 10 AM. and 2 P.M. and others between 4 and 5 P.M. —— Among them were the district Inspector of Weights and Measures — the Relieving Officer of our Union — the Keeper of the House of Correction at Northleach — and Mr Brookes, as Magistrates Clerk — Received a letter from Curtis Hayward in reply to mine on the state of the Gloucestershire Pauper Lunatics, confined in the private madhouse at Hook- |^38 Norton, and expressing his thoughts as to the proceedings which will be fit to be taken at the coming Quarter Sessions in regard to Dr Bompas's asylum at the Fishponds. — A letter from Sophia Hunt from Hastings, whither she and her sisters have betaken themselves on a short excursion:

my advice is sought as to the erection of a monument in Wadenhoe Church in memory of Caroline Hunt, the wording of the inscription &c. — From E.F.W. a letter giving an account of his late engagements: being engaged to pass the week after the Quarter Sessions with the Vavasour's at "the Cottage", Sophy and he cannot accept an invitation from us during that week: E.F.W. purposes meeting me next week at the Quarter Sessions — from Tuesday till Thursday: all at Stanway Vicarage are well. — Dear Sophy wrote also to MW. — Received a letter from Mr Bailey, Lord Sherborne's agent, containing a refusal to |^{39} contribute on his Lordship's part towards the law expences incurred in abating the nuisance of cattle, pigs & donkeys, turned to graze in the village green of Upper Slaughter — This ungracious act was not unexpected by me: though the expence incurred was materially advantageous to the peer's interests as Lord of the Manor, establishing his rights, and the result — the abatement of the nuisance, a great advantage to his tenant. — From Geo. Wellford I received a long letter, in his usual strain — conveying the intelligence of the death of his sister. M$^{rs.}$ Hayley, some weeks ago — At a late hour of the evening M$^{rs.}$ Backhouse, with her daughters Mary and Fanny, arrived from Cheltenham. After visiting Miss Backhouse at Wavertree, and the family of Mr Nicholson, near Warrington, they had been staying a few days with some friends near Cheadle, and from thence travelled by railway to |^{40} Cheltenham. —

Oct. 15. Sunday

Rainy weather — Wrote to Mess$^{rs.}$ Hoare, desiring them to transfer £47. 15. 0 from my account with them to that of my Son. — Preparing a Sermon — Getting ready my papers and documents for the Quarter Sessions. — Wrote to Mr Pearce on Union business. ——— Morning service, prayers: afternoon service, prayers and Sermon. I preached on the love of GOD. — Received a letter from Mr Thornton on Hunt Trust matters. —

Oct 16. Monday

A rainy morning: the weather wet for the greater part of the day. — After an early breakfast, I left home at 8 AM. for Gloucester to attend the Quarter Sessions. — To Cheltenham in my phaeton, and thence by the Great Western line to Gloucester in the same carriage with Lord Ellenborough, who was travelling to London. — Took up my quarters, as usual, at the Bell Hotel, where I found a letter |^{41} awaiting me from C. Bathurst with further hints as to the case of the Fishponds private madhouse. Conferred on that and other difficult county matters with the County Chairman. — Thence to the Shirehall, where the Magistrates present during the day were, P. B. Purnell, Curtis Hayward, Lysons, Brook Hunt, Gambier Parry, Goodrich, Sayers, Col. Browne, Barwick Baker, and myself — The officials in attendance were Bloxsome, Riddiford, Lefroy, Keiley, Fulljames, Wilton, Whitehead — A meeting of the Prisons Committee was held, at which reports were received from the County surveyor on alterations, and the progress made in public works, and many points of improvement and management were considered. — The County rate committee held a meeting, — the members present being Purnell, Curtis Hayward and myself, at which the repre-|^{42}sentatives of many parishes attended, complaining that the assessment on them was too high. In all cases we explained to the parties the principle on which the assessments were made, attended to the arguments and the facts which they adduced, raised a few, relieved more, and satisfied the larger proportion that the assessments were fair and honestly made — Besides these committee meetings, the ordinary business of the committee of accounts was transacted. — The magistrates who dined together at the Bell were Purnell, Curtis Hayward, Gambier Parry, Barwick Baker, Brooke Hunt, and myself — Much conversation with anxious deliberation as to the case of the Fishponds Lunatic Asylum, and the measures most proper to be taken in respect thereof, under the full persuasion that a large and influential party will attend the Court to-morrow, calling for a reversal or, at least, a reconsideration of the decision |[43] as to that establishment which was unanimously come to at the Trin. Quarter Sessions. — Mr Hale joined us in the evening. — From 9 P.M. till midnight I was engaged with Riddiford in auditing the County accounts. —

Oct. 17. Tuesday

Weather fine, but cold — Breakfasted at the Bell with Purnell and Hale. — At 10 AM. to the Court, where the usual routing business was transacted till 2 PM. — accounts passed — prison books examined and read — in all which I took the customary part as Chairman of the committee of accounts. — A very large concourse of magistrates, the number amounting in all to 70, and more, had assembled, to take part in the discussion to be raised as to the course to be taken at the last Quarter Sessions in respect of the private madhouse at the Fishponds. — The pamphlet |[44] published in the name of Dr C. Bompas, but probably the production of his Uncle, Mr Grace Smith, a Barrister, and recently appointed Judge of a county court district in Wilts and Somerset, had been generally circulated, and is artfully written both as to what it urges, and what it suppresses. The Proprietors of this asylum, being dissenters, and of liberal opinions in politics, and having a strong local interest in and near Bristol, were likely to be supported by dissenters and liberals, and to be favourably regarded by the Lord Lieutenant, who has long been very diligent in maintaining a parliamentary ascendancy at Bristol, one of the Representatives being a younger brother of his holding extreme liberal opinions. The bias on the mind of the Lord Lieutenant was brought to operate on the magistrates who follow in his wake, and are customarily found to vote at his suggestion. |[45] Nor were those wanting who felt a tenderness for the Bompas family, and a respect for the rights of property: it being understood that the establishment formed for many years past the provision for the maintenance & bringing up of a large family, — that a large capital was embarked in the concern, and that the denial of a licence would be a grievous injury to the family — the widow and the children of the late Dr Bompas. — The allegation on the part of the complainants, the Trustees and members of the family, was that a decision had been hastily and harshly come to by a comparatively small body of magistrates; that the decision should be revised, and opportunity given to disprove the imputations on which it rested: the demand was made that the resolution of the last court should be rescinded, and |[46] that the parties interested might be allowed to prove that the course adopted was uncalled for, as would appear by a strict and searching investigation to which the managers of the establishment were most ready to accede. — They claimed to be heard by counsel, who appeared at the bar, — Mr Keating and Mr Cother, of whom the former had been retained ~~by~~ with a fee of Forty Guineas; but the County Chairman strenuously and successfully objected to hearing counsel: inasmuch as it was ~~unusually~~, and contrary to precedent, that professional advocates should plead before the Magistrates on the day set apart for the transaction of the ordinary county business, there being no cause and no prosecution, no litigant parties, but simply a motion to be made by some number of the Court that a resolution come to at a former sessions, should be revised or rescinded. The hearing of Counsel being refused, M[r] Grace Smith, as a party |[47] deeply concerned, being acting Trustee for the Bompas family, set forth the claim made on their behalf for a reversal of the decision of the last Quarter Sessions, and that a evidence be granted in the usual manner for a twelvemonth; at the same time most confidently offering to submit to a thorough investigation of all the matters charged against the Establishment and the management. The County Chairman replied, stating the law of the case, and recapitulating the facts; vindicated the proceedings taken at the Trinity Sessions; but proposed that, to avoid all appearance of unfairness or haste, the investigation called for by the parties interested should be entered upon. The question then arose by whom should that enquiry be conducted. It was obvious that it would be very difficult for the upholders of the resolution passed at the Trinity Sessions, and the supporters |[48] of the Fishponds family to agree as to the nomination of a committee; Purnell, therefore, proposed that the matter should be referred to a body composed of all the magistrates already serving as Visitors of the County Lunatic Asylum, and of the private madhouses near Bristol, near Cheltenham, and near Fairford: these would number twenty eight Justices, presumed to be men of experience and conversant with the law as regarded the detention of the insane, whether in public or in private institutions. It would be optional with magistrates so named to attend or not — the investigation might be conducted on the spot, or in its neighbourhood. The Lord Lieutenant professed that his object was full enquiry of the most stringent kind, urged that counsel might be employed on both sides, and that the evidence when taken should be published from the shorthand writers notes, and all this was agreed to, parties ~~not~~ not probably ~~not~~ weighing very accurately the heavy cost likely to be incurred. By this |[49] arrangement, which was carried by a very large majority against a small section, who proposed that a committee of nine Magistrates should be appointed to watch over the future conduct of D[r] C Bompas, to whom a licence should be granted for seven months, over and above the six months licence under which he now acts, and which will expire at the Epiphany Sessions, all the 28 Magistrates now acting as Visitors of lunatic asylums within the County are appointed Visitors for those private Madhouses which are in the Bristol neighbourhood — not the establishment only at the Fishponds, — but the others kept by M[r] Ogilvie, ~~M[r]~~, D[r] Fox, M[r] Eyre &c. — The plan suggested by the County Chairman, besides being perfectly fair as relates to the parties impeached, is in strict accordance with the Act of Parliament under which private madhouses are regulated; whereas the scheme proposed by the favourers of D[r] Bompas was |[50] at once illegal and impracticable. — The arrangement now made will comprize me as one of the Visitors of the County Lunatic asylum; and I ~~had~~ have promised Purnell to stand by him and assist in the enquiry if the scheme were carried out: but it is likely to be a laborious and very anxious duty, with considerable personal responsibility & cost; — involving journeys to Bristol and detention there for some days at a cold and bad season of the year. — The Lord Lieutenant, the County Chairman, Curtis Hayward, M[r] Fripp, (a Bristol magistrate) M[r] Winterbotham (a Stroud Magistrate) and myself were the principal speakers — Fripp and Winterbotham supporting the Bompas party with much talent and judgment. — Several gentlemen qualified as magistrates to-day; among them was Lord Campden, eldest son of the Earl of

Gainsborough, and now residing on the paternal property near Campden, in a new house lately erected there: his Lordship seems desirous of taking an active |⁵¹ part in public business, but labours under great disadvantages; being deaf, and having a painful impediment in his speech. — Mᴿ Dorrington, Clerk to the H. of Commons, and purchaser of the Lyppiatt Park estate, and Captain Pearson, residing at Upton Sᵗ· Leonards, whom I had met at Prinknash before Howell left the county, were among those who qualified. — When the discussion respecting the Bristol private madhouses was brought to a close the court was speedily thinned, and the remaining business being ~~brought to a close,~~ terminated there was time for a stroll before dinner, in which I was joined by my Son, Mᴿ Holland Corbet, and Lysons. We directed our course to the fine and large newly constructed dock which is almost finished, and which greatly extends the accommodation to be had in the port of Gloucester: curiously situated in the heart of the busy mart of commerce, |⁵² overtopped by towering warehouses, and on the margin of a wharf, with adjacent railway tracks, is a small mariners church, with a strictly ecclesiastical exterior, almost completed, and likely to be a great benefit to those for whose use it is designed. All these additions and improvements of the port are made very accessible by the construction of a wide and new street, leading from Southgate Street to the docks, by the formation of which an obscure, unwholesome mass of mean dwellings has been annihilated. In the same direction also is a new and handsome custom-house, of late erection. — Twenty magistrates dined together at the Bell, Purnell presiding. Lord Campden, Gambier Parry, &c. were of the party, and the evening passed pleasantly. —

Oct. 18. Wednesday

A very cold day, with a North Easterly wind. In the early part of the morning snow fell. — Wrote to Charles Bathurst, giving him an account of what had passed yesterday as to the private madhou-|⁵³ses in Gloucestershire near Bristol, and the proposed investigation into the condition and management of that at the Fishponds, under the superintendence of Dᴿ C. Bompas. — Received a letter from my wife, who forwards one from a medical gentleman, a candidate for the office of surgeon to the House of Correction at Little Dean. — Breakfasted with the Magistrates at the Bell. — To the ~~Court,~~ Shire Hall where I remained till 5 P.M. attending to the business in Serjeants Ludlow's Court: there was one appeal; afterwards we proceeded with the trial of prisoners. — After a walk to the dock &c. with E.F.W., he and I dressed for dinner, having accepted an invitation to the Lysons's at Hempstead Court — whither we proceeded in a fly. — We met Mᴿ Phelps of Chevenage and his sister. — Mᴿ Peters, of Eastington, a Clergyman & Magistrate, but not in the habit of attending Quarter Sessions, with his lady, a sister of |⁵⁴ Mʳˢ· Lysons; Purnell was also of the party, to which, after dinner, having just arrived by the Railway train, was added Capt. Lysons, brother of our host, recently returned from Canada, where his regiment is stationed, and on leave of absence — He turned out to be an old schoolfellow of my son's, and pupil of Dᴿ Butler at Shrewsbury. We had a handsome entertainment and very pleasant party: Lysons's house abounds in works of art, painting, antiquities, and vertu, chiefly collected by his antiquarian & tasteful Uncle and Father. Mʳˢ· Lysons & Mʳˢ· Peters also delighted us by singing beautifully together. — Purnell, E.F.W. and myself returned to Gloucester in the same fly. ——

Oct. 19. Thursday.

Very cold weather, but not so severe as yesterday. — Breakfasted at the Bell, with my brother magistrates. — Afterwards till midday attended in Sergeant Ludlow's Court at the trial of Prisoners — Arranged various matters of account connected with the County |⁵⁵ finance, and gave directions as to the business within the province of the County rate committee. — Took leave of my son, who proposes to return to Stanway to-day. — Left Gloucester by a train before one o clock. Found my Servant with carriage and horses waiting for me at Cheltenham; he brought a letter from MW. — Called on public business at the Police Station, and conferred with the deputy Chief Constable, having met Mr Lefroy at Gloucester in the forenoon. — Reached home between 4 & 5 PM — All well, and the Backhouse ladies had walked along the road to meet me. — Received a letter from Mrs. Matthews, late Emily Reade, residing with her husband near Shepton Mallet, who forwards a letter addressed to me by her sister, Mrs. Irvine, long resident at Brussels, written in a strange rambling, romantic, and complaining strain; she accuses her husband, from whom she is separated, and her son, who seems to up-|⁵⁶ hold his Father in his alienation from his wife, of treating her with harshness, in curtailing her pecuniary supplies, and insisting on her returning to England, to which she has the greatest repugnance. She entreats my influence in her favour, addressing me as a Trustee of her marriage settlement: but I have no intercourse with Capt. Irvine or his son, and, if I had, should be very unwise to interfere in family quarrels, where blame, no doubt, attaches to both parties, and on one side at least there is a strangeness bordering on insanity. — A letter from Messrs. Hoare, announcing that they have transferred £47. 15. from my account with them to that of my Son. —

Oct 20. Friday

A dull day: an Easterly wind, with some rain — Transacted business with my tenant, J W Harris. — Wrote to invite M^r and Mrs. Vavasour, and Mr Boggis to dinner on Wednesday next. — Justice business at home — Settling bills |⁵⁷ with tradesmen, Stow Fair being at hand. — Preparing a Sermon. — Wrote to Mrs. Matthews, Alham House, near Shepton Mallet, as to the letter which she had forwarded to me from her sister Irvine, intimating that I shall decline any interference between her and her husband or son, having no intercourse with them, nor being at all acquainted with the relation the parties have borne to each other for many years past, or with the circumstances on the one part or the other which have led to alienation. Requested Mrs. Matthews to communicate this to her sister. — Walked with Mrs. Backhouse and her daughters. — Received a letter from C Bathurst in reply to mine written from Gloucester giving an account of what passed on Tuesday there relative to the Fishponds private madhouse — A letter from Hobbs, a Wine merchant in London, who has forwarded to me some Madeira |⁵⁸ which I had ordered through the agency of Mr E. Slatter of Cirencester. —

Oct. 21. Saturday

Damp and rainy weather in the morning and forenoon; finer in the afternoon. — We had intended to have gone with the Backhouses to Stanway to call on my Son and daughter, but the unfavourable state of the weather prevented us. — Much engaged with the Justice business at home. — Wrote a note to Mr Wilkins, Bourton on the Water, as to a case which I propose hearing with other magistrates at his office on Monday next. — Took a walk with M^{rs.} and the Misses Backhouse. — Received a letter from C. Bathurst, who consults me about the employment of lay Scripture readers in populous districts. Col. Kingscote and other well meaning men of the Low Church party are anxious to introduce them into the Forest of Dean. — A letter from Mr Thornton on Hunt Trust affairs: he returns me letters from Mr Hare |^{59} which I had sent for his perusal. —

Oct. 22. Sunday

Very rainy weather till 4 P.M. when the rain ceased. — Preparing a Sermon. — Wrote to Turner, fishmonger, London, to send fish for a dinner party on Wednesday next: — To Mr Terry, inviting him to dine with us on that day. — Morning Service, prayers and sermon: — I preached on diligence in our duties. — Afternoon service, prayers. — Received a letter from Mr Jennings with the balance sheet of our London Midsummer rents and outgoings; — from Howell as to placing his son John at Carshalton, a preparatory school from which the pupils, if found sufficiently prepared, proceed to Woolwich academy, there to receive a military education preparatory to their being appointed to commissions in the Artillery or in the Corps of Engineers — H. has received this appointment for his son from the Marquis of Anglesey, Master General of the Ordnance. |^{60} A note from Vavasour, who accepts for himself our invitation to dinner on Wednesday next, and will come accompanied by E.F.W. and Sophy, who will then be staying at "the Cottage". —

Oct. 23. Monday

Very rainy; in the evening, and at night very stormy. — Wrote to Tagart, Cheltenham, Chemist, for a box of squill pills:^{2} — to Sophia Hunt, to whom I sent what I considered an improved and corrected copy of an inscription for the monument about to be erected at Wadenhoe in memory of her sister, Caroline: Retaining, as far as possible, the words of the inscription sent for my judgment, I had rearranged it, and altered what appeared ambiguous or equivocal. — To C. Bathurst on the employment of Scripture readers. — To Mr Jennings acknowledging the receipt from him of the balance sheet of our London rents, & outgoings — M$^{rs.}$ Backhouse and her daughters drove in our carriage to Oddington and back to call on M^r and M$^{rs.-}$ |^{61} Wiggin, a most unpropitious day for a drive, but they were bent on paying this visit to their connections — I walked to Bourton to meet Robt Waller, at Mess$^{rs.}$ Wilkins & Kendall's office to deal with the case of a lunatic, R. Fox, who had been brought before me on Saturday last charged with annoying and insulting Mr R. Ashwin of Bourton, and his family. Mr Wells, the Apothecary, having pronounced the man to be of unsound mind, made an order for his removal to Gloucester Lunatic Asylum, of which establishment he had previously been an inmate, but removed to his parish at Milton in Oxfordshire, and not properly restrained there from wandering abroad to his old haunts with old delusions — I walked home in heavy rain, sadly inconvenienced by shortness of breathing, and pain in the chest; till I approached Lower Slaughter Turnpike Gate, when I was overtaken by my Car-|^{62}riage, which the ladies, after its return from Oddington, had sent to bring me home — Business at home preparatory to Stow fair — Paid E. Chidley, Builder, Stanway, £200 on account of the improvements and additions at Stanway Vicarage —

2.   Squill pills – Squill is a Mediterranean plant of the lily family *Drimia maritima*, with a long spike of white flowers and a large bulb – also called the sea onion. Extracts from the white variety were used in cough mixtures.

Oct. 24. Tuesday

A fine day overhead — very dirty under foot. — Settling bills with different tradesmen — Justice business at home. — Drove to Stow, this being Stow Fair day. — To the Provident Bank, where I met Winter, W B. Pole, and E.F.W. — Received a letter from Mr Heaton, assistant chaplain at the County Gaol, Gloucester, who suggests to me that convicts might, with economy & saving to the County purse, be dispatched from Gloucester to their destination at Milbank or Pentonville prisons by third class, instead of second class trains. — A letter from the Hon. James Dutton, Bibury about a case of felony to be tried at the Sessions in which a servant of his is [63] witness and prosecutor — Replied to this letter from Stow. — Called on the Vavasours at the Cottage, where I partook of luncheon, meeting and enjoying the society of my dear Son and daughter and ^{their} children — Also saw M^r and M$^{rs.}$ Vavasour. — With E.F.W. to Mr Brookes's office, where Magistrates' business, felonies and misdemeanours incident to the fair, was adjudicated upon by us. — Visited the Workhouse, and conferred with Mr Pearce and Dunford on Union business. — After accompanying Sophy and dear Broome to the booths & sights of the Fair, returned home by 5 PM. — A pleasant Evening with our guests, the Backhouses. —

Oct. 25. Wednesday

A showery day — Justice business at home — Settling Stow fair bills. — Replied to the letter which I received yesterday from Mr Heaton. — Wrote to Mr Aitkens at Castle Church near Stafford, to obtain information sought for by the Backhouses, as to the tunes played [64] by the chimes in the tower of the newly restored church at Stafford, which being, as it is said, secular tunes, had excited the censure of a connection of theirs who has become a convert to Popery. My impression is that all chimes, at home and abroad, are generally set to popular secular Airs. — Walked with the Backhouse ladies. — A circular from the County Gaol, announcing a meeting of visiting Magistrates — A note from Mr Pantin, informing me that he has paid to Mr Ford, to be handed to me, his annual subscription to the Society for the Propagation of the Gospel. — Transacted parish business with the Overseer. — A dinner party — M^r and two Misses Ford, Dulcibella and Sophia, — E.F.W. and Sophy coming from "the Cottage", with Mr Vavasour, and Mr Terry, were our guests. —

Oct. 26. Thursday

Fine weather. — I drove to Stow — Received a circular from the Clerk of the Peace's office, notifying my appointment as one of the Visiting Magistrates of the County Gaol. — To the Provident [65] Bank, where I met Mr Pole, R. Waller, Ford, the Curate of Cutsdean, (M^r Du Pré) and others. — To "the Cottage", where were dearest Sophy and her precious children; the latter, with their attendant, were sent to Upper Slaughter in my carriage to visit their grandmother and cousins, returning to Stow in the carriage, when it is brought to ~~bring~~ ^{convey} me home to dinner. M$^{rs.}$ Vavasour I also saw at "the Cottage"; and E.F.W. was gone to call on the W. Vavasours at Maugersbury, whence he would ride to take luncheon with his Mother and her guests, returning to Sophy at "the Cottage", which all of the name of Witts will leave to-morrow for Stanway — To the Workhouse, where I conferred with Mr Pearce on Union matters. — To the Justice room, where Ford and R Waller sat with me on the Magisterial bench: there was much business to be done, partly remanets[3] from Stow Fair — E.F.W. on his return from Upper Slaughter, joined us at the Unicorn — Reached home to a |[66] late dinner; tired and sleepy in the evening. —

Oct. 27. Friday.

A very rainy forenoon; the afternoon fine, but showery towards evening — M^rs. Backhouse and her daughters left us at half past eleven for Town, travelling to Oxford by Burford in a fly, and thence by railway: they had been very pleasant and friendly visitors. — Wrote to Mr Pantin, with a receipt for his subscription to the S.P.G. which I had received from Mr Ford yesterday: — to Mr Pain about books ordered into the Stow library. — Preparing a sermon. — Justice business at home — Received a letter from M^rs. Matthews, who forwards to me the address of her sister, M^rs. Irvine, at Brussels. I suppose I must write to the latter, thought I have no inclination so to do. — Called on parish business at Edwd. Lea's and William Gregory's; illness in both families. — Ranke's History of the Reformation in Germany. —

Oct. 28. Saturday

A showery day: in the |[67] evening a thunderstorm. — Justice business at home; Mr Brookes called, and assisted me as Clerk — Wrote to M^rs. Irvine, at Brussels; declined to interfere in her disputes with her husband and son — Wrote to Alder, Upholsterer, Cheltenham; with a remittance for an article of furniture lately supplied by him. — Suffering greatly from an attack of lumbago, with flying rheumatic pains in other parts. — Ranke's History of the Reformation in Germany. —

Oct. 29. Sunday.

A fine day. — Being much indisposed, rheumatic, and dyspeptic, I wrote a note to Mr Hayward, requesting him to visit and prescribe for me — He came in the evening and ordered aperient medicine, Calomel, Colocynth, James's powders &c., with a strong embrocation; suffered much from lumbago and rheumatic pains in my left arm. — Nevertheless I |[68] performed all my clerical duties, morning prayers, and evening prayers, preaching a sermon on religious meditation. — Preparing a Sermon — Ecclesiastical gazette — MW. received a letter announcing the safe arrival of the Backhouse ladies at Hans Place on Friday evening. —

Oct. 30. Monday.

A rainy morning early, but fine afterwards. — Suffering very much all day from lumbago and other rheumatic pains, with flatulence and drowsiness. — Justice business at home. — Wrote to Lord Redesdale on the County rate assessment with reference to a correspondence his Lordship has had with Mr Bloxsome, and which was laid before the County rate Committee at the last Quarter Sessions. — M^rs. W. Vavasour called on us. — Received a letter from Mr Thornton on Hunt Trust business: he forwards the copy of a letter from Mr Tilleard, and a letter from M^rs. Hunt. |[69]

---

3.   Remanets – a case or suit of which the hearing has been postponed.

Oct. 31. Tuesday

A wet morning; but the weather fine afterwards. — Mr Hayward visited me; my suffering from lumbago and dyspepsia less than for two or three days past, but I am still much out of order: I had slept well last night, but a continuance of applications internally & externally are necessary to correct the flatulence, and other derangement of the stomach, and the lumbago. — — Justice business at home. — Wrote to Mr Thornton and Mr Hare on Hunt Trust business. — Rec^d a letter from Fanny Backhouse, who fancies she has heard of a curate in Lancashire who may suit Mr Wiggin, who is looking out for assistance at Oddington. — Ranke's History of the Reformation in Germany. —

Nov 1. Wednesday.

A dull and somewhat foggy day without rain. — Justice business at home — Wrote to E.F.W. — |70 Wrote to Mr Wiggin, to whom I sent the parts of the letter I received yesterday from Fanny Backhouse which concerned him. — To Mr Bailey, Lord Sherborne's man of business, in answer to his letter of the 12th Ult. with further explanations as to the nuisance in this village, which is now checked, and the expence attendant on the law proceedings necessary to abate it, which Lord S. declines to assist in paying. — Received a letter from Mrs Irvine, from Brussels, forwarded by her sister, Mrs Matthews, being a duplicate of the one already received by me, and which I have lately answered. — A letter from Mr E. Hunt from India in reply to one written by me to him from Beaumaris, and as to remittances to be made to him, his position under the Company's service &c. — A letter from Alder, Cheltenham, Upholsterer, in acknowledgement of the remittance which I lately made to him — A letter from Mr Aitkens in |71 answer to mine to him with inquiries as to the tunes played on the chimes in Stafford Church tower: — they are secular, it is true; but the machinery of the old tunes is repaired; the selection of tunes is not new, but old. — Ranke's History of the Reformation in Germany — Eccl. Gazette — My health is improved; there is less of rheumatism, less of flatulence. —

Nov. 2. Thursday.

A fine day — Mr Hayward called early, and, finding me so much better, allowed me to attend to my usual public business at Stow. — Engaged with W. Gregory and the traveller from the Durdham Downs Nurserymen, who called for payment of a bill — MW. accompanied me to Stow in the open carriage, returning home, after having set me down at the Provident Bank — Received a letter from Mr Thornton, who forwards to me a letter he had received from Mr Hare on Hunt Trust business — |72 A letter from the Clerk of the Peace notifying my appointment as one of the Visitors of the Private Madhouses in Gloucestershire in the neighbourhood of Bristol, together with a copy of the resolution passed at the late Quarter Sessions in respect of the Fishponds lunatic establishment. — Transacted business at the Provident Bank, where I met W B Pole — To the Workhouse, where I presided at the fortnightly meeting of the Board of Guardians from 12 to 4 PM. — The Dean of Gloucester attended to make a representation of certain nuisances in the parish of Oddington, tending to disease, and more or less accounting for a low fever which has been prevalent there — ill drained tenements, want of privies, accumulations of filth &c., fit matters for enquiry and to be brought under the jurisdiction of the magistrates, agreeably to the recent Act for the correction and removal of Nuisances by which the Boards of Guardians are constituted a medium for bringing such evils |73 under the cognizance of the local magistrates. — Capt. Leigh called upon me, as a magistrate, to bring under my notice what he believed to be misconduct on the part of the Parish Officers of Broadwell, and rate payers there, especially Beman, against whom he entertains a strong prejudice. I explained to him that though the matter of which he complained appeared ill-judged, no offence had been committed which could be dealt with by law — Returned home by 5 P.M. not the worse for my day's work: the unpleasant symptoms, flatulence, and rheumatic or dyspeptic pains, abated. — Ranke's History of the Reformation in Germany: an interesting and instructive work concluded. —

Nov. 3. Friday

A fine morning and forenoon; the afternoon showery, the evening stormy and windy. — Justice business at home — Wrote to Mᵣ Brookes on Magisterial matters. — To Miss S. B. Hunt, forwarding to her the letter I had received from her |74 brother Edward, with copies of my letters to him, to Mᵣ Boye, and to Messʳˢ Coutts in July last. — To Fanny Backhouse in answer to her letter, sending her Aitkens's letter to me about the Stafford chimes — To Rodwell, to order a book for the Stow Book Society. — Received a letter from Mᵣ Bailey in answer to mine of the 1ˢᵗ Inst; he writes less adversely as to the claim made by me on Lord Sherborne, but cannot at present trouble him on the subject, as he is in the Isle of Wight in a bad state of health. — Dᵣ Arnold's lectures on modern history — Not wholly free from rheumatic or dyspeptic pains, but greatly relieved. —

Nov. 4. Saturday.

A frosty morning; a very cold day, some flickering snow — Mᵣ Hayward called, and considered my health to be improved: he wishes me to continue the medicines he has prescribed. I am not free from rheumatic pains, but they are less acute — Wrote to Merrett, tailor, Cheltenham, to order |75 some clothes. — Wrote to Mʳˢ C. Barr — To Mᵣ Bloxsome; as to desiring the Clerks of Petty Sessions to make returns of penalties under Jervis's Act; suggested that it might be necessary, under the act for the regulation of private madhouses, that the Shorthand writer to be employed at the coming investigation as to the management of the Fishponds private lunatic Asylum should be sworn in as an Assistant Clerk to the Visitors. — Justice business at home. — Wrote to Mᵣ Makepeace recommending a more frequent visiting of the parish of Great Barrington by the Rural police — A letter from Mᵣ Whitcombe, private to myself, accompanying a letter addressed to me in common with my Co-trustees, Hare and Thornton: these letters are to the effect that Miss S. Hunt is ready to take a forward movement towards the settling of the questions in debate between the representatives of Miss M C Hunt, and |76 Mᵣ Geo. Hunt: nothing can be more desirable than that these parties should meet each other halfway, and adjust their differences; but the principals are impracticable, the controversy is complicated; the professionals employed are not fully confided in by those whom they represent; are also not disposed to view each others line of action in a favourable light; each fears that the other will take undue advantage of the other and his client; and thus this turn in the affair, though promising, may end in nothing — In the meantime the three Trustees act harmoniously together — I this day received a letter on Hunt Trust affairs from Mᵣ Hare, who returns to me a letter of Mᵣ Thornton's to me, which I had sent for his perusal. — Recᵈ a letter from F. Aston, written from Froyle in Hants, the residence of his sister, M^rs. Watkins; he forwards to me a prescription for an embrocation for Rheumatism which M^rs. W. had promised to send. F.A. has taken his daughter Sophy on a visit to her Aunt, with |^77 whom he proposes to pass a fortnight, and will there meet his midshipman son from Portsmouth. — A letter from E.F.W. brought by the attendant boy, with a good account of all at Stanway Vicarage: the boy to sleep here to night, and to return to-morrow morn^g. with a packet of books which my Son requests ^me to send him, being publications of the Committee of Privy Council on Education, and pamphlets on the same subject by Dr Hook, Dr Kay Shuttleworth, and Mr Burgess, all bearing upon the education of the humbler classes of society. My son wishes to prepare himself for a meeting of the Mechanics institute at Winchcomb on Wednesday next, when Mr Holland is to make an address ~~to~~ ^on the advantages of education to the labouring classes, and E.F.W. is to preside ~~at~~ ^on the occasion. — Our children wish us to visit them on Nov. 20 and the following days. — Called on W. Gregory and his wife; both failing in health – Forty called on me to state that he can no longer afford to rent |^78 the house and premises, which he now occupies of me. He is reduced to a very low condition, and must remove into less highly rented tenement – I consented to release him, and to allow him to remain where he is till Christmas at a reduced rent: it is very doubtful whether I shall easily find a tenant for these premises; my business will be to put them in good repair, and to finish work which has never been completed, laying floors in a part of the house, and otherwise putting it into thorough order, to receive a tenant should anyone offer himself, or to be ~~rent~~ ready as a farm house for a new tenant, if the Davis's should retire from business, or their occupation of my rectory farm expire with themselves; both being aged and infirm, but not needing the house, as occupying one belonging to Mr John Cook, which they rent together with a small estate attached to it. — Called on W. Gregory: both he and his wife are failing. — Dr Arnold's lectures on modern history. —

Nov. 5. Sunday

A frosty morning; a cold |^79 day, — a tendency to rain. — Visited the Sunday school. — Morning service; prayers for the 5th. Nov. and I preached a sermon suited to the commemoration. — Evening prayers — A letter from Sophia Hunt, as to the inscription proposed for the monument in memory of Caroline Hunt: the surviving sisters contemplate a removal from Northamptonshire, and the purchase of a house at Bath — Preparing a sermon — Ecclesiastical gazette – To the family one of the Family Sermons. —

Nov. 6. Monday

A fine day for the season. — Justice business at home — Wrote to Mr Whitcombe in answer to his letters received on the 4th. and to Mr Thornton on that communication from Mr Whitcomb, forwarding to Mr T. the private letter I had received from Mr W. — Received a letter from Lord Redesdale in answer to |^80 that which I wrote to him some days ago, on county rate matters. — Visited the daily School. — Dr Arnold's Lectures on Modern history. —

Nov. 7. Tuesday

A cold day; weather fine, except a slight shower in the afternoon — Wrote to Mr Hare, sending him a copy of the letter I wrote yesterday on Hunt Trust affairs to M^r ~~Thornton~~ Whitcombe

81. Upper Swell church and parsonage.

— Wrote to Sophia Hunt in answer to her letter as to the language of the inscription proposed for the monument to be erected to the memory of M C Hunt. — Justice business at home — Drove with MW. to Stow: transacted business at the library and at Mᵣ Brookes's office. — Shopping — Conversations with Mᵣ Hayward and Mᵣ Boggis — Drove to Upper Swell: called on Mᵣ and Mʳˢ· W. B. Pole: both of whom we saw. Visited the old village church, with Mᵣ W.B.P. – admired the ancient Norman doorway, and arch separating the nave from the Chancel. Mᵣ |⁸¹ Pole, of Wick Hill, has presented to the parishioners a very substantial plain oak communion table, with chairs of the same material, which he had intended for his church at Wick Risington, as a peace offering in consequence of the objection made by him to the placing of a stone communion table by the Rector, which created some time ago much uneasiness – but Mᵣ Cooke or his family held the proffered table & chairs very cheap, and spoke disparagingly of the taste and style displayed in them – whereupon the Squire took umbrage and transferred them to Upper Swell – There is really nothing to find fault with, and the Rector of Wick erred sadly in not accepting what was proffered in a conciliatory spirit. But my good old acquaintance is sorely led in trammels by his wife and children; and they are full of ultra-fancies, as to Church services, furniture, architecture and the like, closely bordering on Tractarianism. |⁸² The stone communion table has been removed to a parish church in Oxfordshire with which Mᵣ Cooke is connected. — Heard a bad account of the state of Bowen's health. — Recᵈ· a letter from Mᵣ Moore as to the sanitary state of our Union. — Ecclesiastical gazette — Arnold's Lectures on Modern History. —

Nov. 8. Wednesday

Frosty weather — a fine day. — Justice business at home. — Wrote to Mᵣ Ford, Mᵣ Waller, Mᵣ Wells, Mᵣ Hayward, Mᵣ Pearce, and Mᵣ Morrison, preparatory to the Petty Sessions to be held at Stow to-morrow, when I purpose to direct the attention of the magistrates, medical officers of the Union, Clerks to the Magistrates and Union, and others, to the sanitary state of the district, and to the measures necessary to be followed in conformity with the notifications of the central board of health recently issued, as a Government proceeding, under the existing |*183* alarm as to the Asiatic Cholera, and with reference to the Nuisance prevention Act — Walked to Eyford: called on M^rs. Dolphin, who with Miss Walmsley was gone to Upper Guiting to visit poor Bowen, who is said to be dangerously ill — Received letters from Mr Thornton and Mr Whitcombe on Hunt trust business: the former sends for my perusal a letters from M^r and M^rs. Hunt, and a copy of a letter to Mr Tilleard: — a letter from the clerk to the Lunatic Asylum at Gloucester, in which it is announced that my letter to Curtis Hayward reporting on the condition of the private madhouse at Hook-norton has been entered on the minutes of the meetings of the Visitors of the Glouc. Lunatic Asylum, as furnishing a statement respecting a number of chronic cases of pauper patients, belonging to the county of Gloucester placed under the charge of the head |*184* of the manager of the Hook-norton establishment. — Received a letter from Mr Bloxsome in reply to one written by me as to the returns of penalties to be made to each Quarter Sessions by Petty Sessions Clerks, and as to the approaching investigation into the management of the Fishponds private madhouse near Bristol. — A letter from Mr Latcham, Clerk to the magistrates appointed Visitors of the private madhouses in Gloucestershire, near Bristol, apprizing me, as one of the Visitors appointed at the last Sessions, that a meeting of Visitors is appointed for the 13th. Inst. to meet at the Fishponds private madhouse, when the books of the establishment will be examined, and the patients visited: that then an adjournment for a few days will take place; and that it is proposed that the enquiry be resumed on a day to be fixed at the Committee room at the Lawford's gate Bridewell: from this |*185* letter I collect that my attendance on the 13th. may be dispensed with, and that I need not travel to Bristol till the "enquiry", properly so called, begins at Lawford's Gate. — A few lines from E.F.W. to his mother brought by a team which had conveyed a load of corn to Stanway, give a good report of our children and grandchildren. — Dr Arnold's lectures on modern history.

Nov. 9. Thursday

Snow had fallen in the night; a frosty morning, soon followed by sunshine melting the snow where it had influence, but elsewhere the roads very slippery. — Preparing for public business at Stow. — MW. accompanied me thither in the open carriage, returning home after having set me down. — Received a letter from Sophia Hunt, who returns the copies of letters to her brother Edward, Mr Boye, and Messrs. Coutts, together with Mr E. Hunt's letter to me |*186* which I had sent for her perusal. She writes wholly on her brother Edward's circumstances and affairs. — To the Provident Bank, where I wrote a letter to my Son, requesting him to obtain the signature of a parishioner to an authority empowering a certain person to receive the money due to a depositor in our Savings Bank. — At the Prov. Bank I met Mr Ford, Mr Pole, Mr Morrison, Mr Perkins &c. — Mr Pearce had previously called on me at Mr Pain's with documents from the Poor Law Board &c. He reported to me that the half yearly audit of accounts for our Union had passed off satisfactorily. — Mr Ford gave a very unfavourable report of poor Bowen's state; it is believed that he is very near his end; effusion of water on the chest, and injury to the spine, are spoken of. — To the Justice room, where the magistrates assembled were the Dean of Gloucester, Mess.rs. Ford, Pole and myself. — Others present |⁸⁷ were Mess.rs. Morrison, Winter, W B Pole, Henry Ford, F. Aston Jun.r, Wiggin, Beman &c. — Proceedings were taken under the Nuisances Prevention Act as to cottages in Oddington in a filthy state from defect of drainage, insufficient privies &c. and so likely to generate cholera or other epidemic or endemic disease. A bad, low fever has been prevalent at Oddington for some time past. Orders were made on several owners of cottages at Oddington to remedy the evils complained of. — Having secured the attendance of the medical officers of the Union, with the exception of M.r Hayward, who was called away on professional business, I took the opportunity of explaining to the magistrates, clergymen, officials connected with the Union, & others present, the actual state of the law as to nuisance, epidemic disease, especially cholera, & the like. Our Union, in common with most others in the Kingdom, in anticipation of |⁸⁸ the impending scourge of cholera, is placed in a long list of those to which the precautionary measures prescribed by the Privy Council, and Central Board of health, apply. These measures are to be promulgated and put in force through and by the Boards of Guardians. The regulations issued give great responsibility and discretionary power to Guardians, Medical officers, and other officers of Unions, enjoining a very close and stringent superintendance as to every thing which affects public health, the removal of nuisances injurious to health, the prevention of cholera and other epidemic or endemic diseases, and the treatment of the sick in infected places. — Other magisterial business followed — Home to a late dinner — Arnold's lectures on Modern history. —

Nov. 10. Friday.

A sharp frost and very fine day. — Wrote to M.r Thornton and M.r Hare on Hunt Trust business, forwarding to the former the last letter I had received from |⁸⁹ M.r Whitcombe, together with letters from M.rs. Hunt which he had sent for my perusal; and to M.r Hare the letter which I received on Wednesday from M.r Thornton, with copies of M.r Whitcombe's last letter to me, and M.r Thornton's late letters to M.r Hunt and M.r Tilleard — Wrote to Cotterel and Rich, Kensington, with an order for candles. — Wrote to M.r Pain, as to M.rs. R. Scott becoming a member of the Stow Book Society. — Wrote to the Clerk of the Gloucester Infirmary, desiring that a boy from Longborough, sent thither with an order from the Union board, now nearly expired, may be retained there on the recommendation of MW. or myself. — Received a letter from M.r Thornton, who returns some letters and copies of letters which I had sent for his perusal: also a letter form M.r Hare for my perusal, and a copy of a letter written by M.r Thornton to |⁹⁰ M.r Whitcombe. — Received from Eyford very unfavourable reports of M.r Bowen's declining stage. — Walked to Bourton on the Water, and conferred with H. Hartwell as to the repairs and reletting of one of E.F.W's cottages there now vacant. — D.r Arnold's Lectures on Modern History. —

Nov. 11. Saturday

A moist, damp day, but no decided rain. — Wrote to M.r Braickenridge on Hunt Trust matters; but, as I received a letter from him, I did not send my letter. M.r B. informs me that he has forwarded the Hunt Trust accounts to Mess.rs. Whitcombe and C.o., with a statement of the claims made by M.r Hunt on the Trustees: as he offers not to urge the heaviest of those claims, it is to be hoped that an arrangement may now be made within a reasonable time — Wrote to Lord Redesdale in answer to the letter lately received by me respecting County rate assessments, and the erection of chapels to Union |[91] Workhouses. — Wrote to E.F.W. —— Rec[d.] a letter from M[r] Hare on Hunt Trust affairs. — Justice business at home as to extending the furlough of a soldier in declining health, which occasioned me to write to L[t.] Col. Warren, C.B. commanding the 18[th.] Inf. Reg. quartered at Dublin — D[r] Arnold's Lectures on Modern History. —

Nov. 12. Sunday.

A fine winter's day. — Visited the Sunday School. — Morning Service, prayers. — Afternoon Service, prayers and Sermon. — I preached on Enticement to sin. — Wrote to Mess[rs.] Whitcombe, Helps, and Wemyss, forwarding to them the letter I had received yesterday from M[r] Braikenridge. — Received a letter from E.F.W. in which he gives an account of a meeting of the Winchcombe Mechanics Institute at which he presided on Wednesday last, and at which M[r] Holland read a lecture on the Educa-|[92] tion of the humbler classes of society. My Son and others dilated on the same subject in their speeches. — E.F.W. has been very kind in his attentions to poor Bowen, now lying on his death bed, and experiencing the tenderest nursing from M[rs.] Dolphin & Miss Walmesley, who have taken up their abode at the parsonage to watch by his bedside. M[r] Hurd and M[r] Billingsley, as well as M[r] Ford, have been unvaried in acts of kindness towards the dying man. B. having expressed a wish to see M[r] Dolphin, the latter hastened to his old friend and had a short and trying interview with him a few evenings since. Coming from his residence in Hants, and taking a conveyance at Stow, he introduced himself to the sick chamber so as to avoid encountering his wife, who was aware of his arrival, but secluded herself with her friend, Miss Walmesley; ~~so that~~ but, of course the being in the same house together caused M[rs.] |[93] Dolphin much agitation and excitement. Poor B. lingers still on the verge of the grave. The ladies are said to be greatly exhausted. All are well at Stanway Vicarage — Received a letter from M[r] Hare with several inclosures on Hunt Trust matters — letters from M[r] Thornton, M[r] Tilleard &c. — Preparing a sermon — Ecclesiastical Gazette. — Read to the family one of the Family sermons. —

Nov. 13. Monday.

A very fine winter's day. — Williams, my son's tenant at Bourton on the Water, against whom he has been obliged to take proceedings in the County Court, as being in arrear of rent, called to endeavour to make an arrangement with me — Received a letter from M[r] Vavasour, informing [me] of the decease of a brother of M[rs.] V., a half pay officer, at Jersey: he has long been in a deplorable state of health. Marmaduke Vavasour, when resident at Broadwell, |[94] ~~whence~~ [once] brought this gentleman to dinner at Upper Slaughter. — Wrote to my Son, explaining the position in which he is placed in respect of his Bourton tenant, Tho[s.] Williams: — answered the letter received yesterday from Stanway, but not promising certainly to visit him and his next week, agreeably to their invitation, because it is not unlikely that I may be then summoned to Bristol on the Fishponds enquiry. — Replied to M[r] Vavasour's note. — Wrote to Mess[rs.] Hoare, desiring them to transfer £35 from my account with them to that of my Son. — Visited W. Gregory and John Davis, both invalids — Preparing a Sermon. — A letter from Lord Redesdale on County rate assessment, and on my position as Chairman of the Stow on the Wold Union, in answer to my letter to his Lordship of Saturday last. — Dᵣ Arnold's Lectures on Modern History. — |⁹⁵

Nov. 14. Tuesday

Fine weather. — Preparing a sermon — Wrote to Mᵣ Hare and Mᵣ Thornton on Hunt Trust business, sending to each inclosures, being letters or copies of letters which had been sent for my perusal. — Wrote to Mᵣ Bloxsome for information, whether a land Surveyor of Worcester, by name Webb, had ever been employed so as to be recognised by the County rate Committee. Lord Redesdale is desirous of employing this person to value the parish of Batsford with a view to the more correct assessment of that parish to the County rate, and has asked me to sanction his being so employed. — Wrote to a young female parishioner, now absent from the village, to inform her that a place of service is now open for her, if she pleases to accept of it. — Recᵈ a letter from Messʳˢ Whitcombe & Cᵒ who return me the letter addressed to me lately by Mᵣ |⁹⁶ Braikenridge, having taken a copy of it, as a document concerning the Hunt Trustees and the Executors of Miss M C Hunt. — The reports from Eyford of Mᵣ Bowen are rather more favourable. — Dᵣ Arnold's Lectures on Modern History.

Nov. 15. Wednesday

Fine, cold weather — Preparing a Sermon. — A letter from Miss F. Backhouse, who returns me the letter from Mᵣ Aitkins which I had sent for her perusal. — A letter from Mᵣ Hare on Hunt Trust matters, with enclosures of letters which I had sent for his perusal. — A letter from Messʳˢ Cotterel and Rich, Kensington, with an invoice of candles &c. sent agreeably to order — A letter from Messʳˢ Hoare, announcing that they have transferred £35 from my account to that of my Son. — I drove to Temple Guiting to visit poor old Bowen: he is considered somewhat better in health, but cannot be regarded as out of danger. He is confined to |⁹⁷ his bed in a state of great weakness, but is in possession of his mental faculties; expresses himself to be resigned and ready to quit this life; seems very much pleased with the kind attention of neighbours and friends; very grateful for their watching over him, and especially for the assiduous and unwearied nursing of Mʳˢ Dolphin and of her friend Miss Walmesley, whose devotedness is very remarkable. It is an euthanasia⁴ for an old man, without wife or children, or relations near at hand, or to whom he has attached himself, to be so tended in his last hours; it tells well for the amiable character of him who receives, as also for the tenderness and charity of those who confer the benefit. — When I returned home from U. Guiting I found Dulcy Ford, and her brother Henry, now settled on a Curacy in the County of Durham, but on a visit to his friends at L Risington, with F. Aston Junᵣ visiting MW. — |⁹⁸ On my road to and from Guiting, engaged in reading documents issued by the Board of Health &c. as to epidemic diseases, cholera &c. — Finished Dᵣ Arnold's Lectures on modern history. —

Nov. 16. Thursday.

Fine weather. — Wrote a note to Mᵣ Vavasour with a message from Miss Walmesley to Mʳˢ V. which the former had requested me to deliver. — Preparing for the public business of

4.   Euthanasia – in this sense a gentle and easy death.

the day at Stow — whither I drove, accompanied by MW. who returned home shortly after setting me down at the Provident Bank, where at a later hour I met Mr Pole. — Transacted business at the office of the Gloucestershire Banking Company, where I met Raymond Cripps. — To the Workhouse, where I presided at the fortnightly meeting of the Guardians: there was much business — especially as related to the sanitary state of the country, the regulations of the Central Board of Health, with prevention of cholera and other epidemic disease — Engaged |^{99} in Union business till 4 P.M. — At Mr Brookes's office transacted county court business relating to my Son's tenant at Bourton on the Water, much in arrear of rent. — A letter from Mr Latcham, Clerk to the Visiting Justices of the Gloucestershire Private Madhouses in the vicinity of Bristol, announcing that the Visitors will meet at Lawford's Gate Bridewell on the morning of the 22^d Inst. to begin the enquiry as to the alleged mismanagement and misconduct of the Superintendent of the Fishponds private asylum. — A circular letter from Mr Heaton, the Assistant Chaplain of the County Gaol at Gloucester, intimating that he intends to offer himself as a candidate for the office of Assistant Chaplain to the House of Correction at Westminster, soliciting my interest with any of the Magistrates who are Electors, of whom he sends a printed list. — A letter from Mr Thornton, who returns to me a letter addressed to me by Messrs Whitcombe |^{100} and C^o, which I had sent for his perusal, with comments on the negociations now in progress as to the Hunt Trust affairs — Mrs Richardson's Life of Louisa, Queen of Prussia — that beautiful, admirable creature, whom I saw, as a boy, at Weimar, who shone so brightly as Queen, wife, and mother; whose misfortunes were as remarkable as her graces.[5] —

Nov. 17. Friday

A showery day: a stormy and windy evening. — Received a letter from E.F.W. brought by a coal waggon from Stanway, with a parcel of books which he returns, and a Cheltenham newspaper recording the proceedings and speeches at a late meeting of the Winchcombe Mechanics Institute, at which my Son presided, and Mr Holland lectured on the education of the Working Classes. — E.F.W. invites us so earnestly to go to Stanway next week, that his mother may remain there during my absence at Bristol, that I replied by letter |^{101} that we will accept his invitation, going on Monday. I propose to proceed thence to Bristol on Tuesday Evening, returning at the end of the week to rejoin my wife, and accompany her home. — Wrote to Mr Heaton that I have no acquaintance with any of the magistrates with whom the appointment of Assistant Chaplain of the Westminster bridewell rests, and cannot therefore help him in his canvass. — Wrote to Mr Brookes respecting the action entered in the County Court by my Son against T. Williams, the tenant of one of his cottages for arrear of rent. — Justice business at home. — Preparing a sermon. — Received from Mr Bloxsome a letter in reply to that which I had written to him, with enquiries respecting a land Surveyor at Worcester whom Lord Redesdale wishes to employ in the valuation of the parish of Batsford for the County rate — A letter from Mr Thornton on |^{102} Hunt Trust business — The like from Mr Hare, who forwards to me a letter he had received from Mr Thornton, as Mr Thornton forwarded one received by him from Mr Tilleard. — Visited W. Gregory, Churchwarden, on parish business — Mrs Richardson's Life of Louisa, Queen of Prussia. —

---

5.   Mrs. Charles Richardson, *Memoirs of the Private Life and Opinions of Louisa, Queen of Prussia*. London: 1847.

Nov. 18. Saturday

Showery, and cold weather: heavy rain and wind in the evening. — Wrote to Mr Thornton on Hunt Trust business, enclosing to him the letter rec^d. by me yesterday from Mr Hare — Wrote to Mr Hare, forwarding to him the letter from Mr Tilleard which Mr Thornton had sent for my perusal, together with the letter which I received from Mr Thornton yesterday. — Wrote to Lord Redesdale as to Surveyors and valuations for assessment of Gloucestershire parishes to the County Rate — Preparing a Sermon — Walked to Lower Slaughter Turnpike |^103 gate — met Henry Ford and his sister Dulcy, with whom chatted — M^rs. Richardson's Life of Louisa Queen of Prussia.

Nov. 19. Sunday

Rain had fallen during the night; the day fine; the evening stormy — Visited the Sunday School. — Morning service, prayers and sermon: I preached on the unforgiving servant: — Evening service, prayers. — Preparing a sermon. — Ecclesiastical Gazette — To the family a sermon from the "family sermons". —

Nov. 20. Monday.

After a stormy and rainy night, a tolerably fine day, till the evening, when heavy rain and wind came on; the night stormy. — Wrote to Mr Hare on Hunt Trust business. — Justice business at home. I was assisted by Mr Brookes, acting as Clerk. — At half past twelve MW. and I set out for Stanway in our open carriage. By the way I called for a few minutes at |^104 the parsonage, Temple Guiting, leaving MW. in the carriage. Was admitted to the chamber of the poor dying man, who laid in a comatose state, apparently very near his end: but while I stood by his bed side he opened his eyes, recognized me, and extended his hand with a friendly pressure. M^rs. Dolphin was seated by him, watching over him — Arrived at the Vicarage, where found all well, except that our dear Sophy was suffering from a cold. — Passed a very pleasant evening with our dear children and grand-children — Well satisfied with all the alterations and improvements.

Nov. 21. Tuesday

A showery day. — Engaged with my son in justice business — Sophy's ~~col~~ cold less oppressive. — Young Frederick Aston, having ridden over from Northleach to see the two Messrs. Cooke, Father & Son, whom he occasionally visits, partook of luncheon at the Vicarage — At four PM. I left my dear circle ~~at~~ at |^105 Stanway in my open carriage for Ashchurch, where I met a train, at three quarters past five o clock, proceeding from Birmingham to Bristol. My servant drove back to Stanway with the phaeton and horses. I reached the Station at Bristol at about 8 P.M. and took a fly to the White Lion, where I expected to have met some at least of the Magistrates appointed to conduct the enquiry as to the alledged misconduct and bad management of Dr Bompas. I had omitted to ascertain by letter to Purnell where he intended to take up his temporary abode, and through misapprehension supposed the White Lion would be the head quarters. But I was mistaken, and neither saw nor heard anything of my colleagues. Passed the rest of the evening in the somewhat comfortless ~~hotel;~~ coffee room and retired to bed in a large old fashioned double bedded room, which I made as comfortable as I |^106 could with a good fire.

Nov. 22. Wednesday.

A very rainy day — After breakfast in the coffee room at the White Lion, went in a fly to Lawford's Gate House of Correction, where, in the Committee room of the prison, a spacious apartment, and detached from the portions of the building in which the prisoners are lodged, the enquiry as to the alleged improper management of the Fishponds private madhouse is to be carried on. The Magistrates present were Purnell, Curtis Hayward, Gambier Parry, W P. Price, Gyde, Milward, Fripp, Battersby, and Mirehouse. The last three are from the neighbourhood of Bristol, and stated visitors, more or less, for several years past, of the Establishment. M[r] Milward, a barrister and magistrate, residing near Lechlade, and M[r] Gyde, of Cheltenham, might be regarded as partizans of D[r] Bompas: M[r] Fripp and M[r] W P. Price as leaning in that direction, the rest of us as |[107] under a persuasion that the establishment had been misconducted, but open to conviction if the evidence should prove us to be in error. The Medical Visitor, D[r] Lyon, a Scotch Physician, resident at Bristol, was also in attendance. — The Professional men engaged on the part of the County to conduct the enquiry were M[r] Stone, of Bristol, a provincial Counsel, of considerable standing, and talent — Mess[rs.] Stanley and Warbrough, Sol[rs.] of Bristol, M[r] Latcham, Bristol, Sol[r] the stated Clerk to the Visitors of the private madhouses near Bristol in Gloucestershire, with his son, and M[r] Riddiford — On behalf of D[r] Jos. Bompas, the party whose management was impeached, appeared that rising and eminent counsel, Keatinge, well known to most of the Magistrates, as leader of the Sessions bar at Gloucester, a man of much legal knowledge, strictly honourable, gentlemanlike and judicious, instructed by Mess[rs.] Livett, Sol[rs.] Bristol, advisers of |[108] the Bompas family, the members of which mustered in strength, headed by M[r] Grace Smith, formerly a provincial barrister of Bristol, a man of great experience, knowledge in his profession and acuteness, and now Judge of a County Court, his district being in Somersetshire and Wilts. There appeared also M[r] N. Smith, an eminent surgeon of Bristol, uncle to D[r] Bompas, and brother of M[r] Grace Smith, M[r] Charles Bompas, brother of D[r] Joseph Bompas, and D[r] Beddome from London, D[r] Jos, Bompas's father in law. Of these M[r] Grace Smith was the most forward in the matter before us; as acting Trustee for the Bompas family, his management in the concern, though not direct, was most influential: it would seem that he has some private and personal motives for keeping things at the Fishponds in statu quo; for retaining the present superintendence, for combating the allegations against the management, and |[109] fighting the battle to the last. To him may be ascribed the pamphlet published and circulated by D[r] Jos. Bompas, and his efforts by every channel have been directed towards impressing on the minds of magistrates that the imputations on the management of the asylum are unfounded, or at least exaggerations, and that the Superintendent is the victim of ill will entertained against him by individual magistrates, particularly, by Purnell and Mirehouse. — There were present also two medical men conversant with lunacy, D[r] Conolly, and D[r] Wood: the former, subpoenaed on the part of the Magistrates to whom the enquiry is entrusted, to watch the case, hear the witnesses examined, and himself testify his judgment on the matter. D[r] C. is the very highest authority in the Kingdom on lunacy: his mind has been for many years bent to the subject. As a superintendent of private madhouses, and as the head of the great Middlesex Lunatic |[110] Asylum at Hanwell, he has enjoyed great experience, and obtained a high reputation.

He is also the head of a system, which is now very generally adopted and acted upon; the system of non-coercion, gentleness, generous diet, amusing, and engaging the minds of the patients, as far as mind is left, and so healing the disease, where possible, or mitigating it, in all which he has been eminently successful, and extensively followed by others having charge of lunatics. Still there are those who do not go the same length of excluding all coercion, maintaining that there are cases in which it must be resorted to — thus there is a school of total non coercionists, and ~~of~~ another of partial coercionists; one of the adherents of the latter school is Dr Wood, a personal friend of Dr Joseph Bompas, and the resident medical man of Bethlehem Hospital. It follows, therefore, that our present enquiry is likely to assume the character, to a certain extent of a battle-|*111* field between Coercionists and Noncoercionists: and it is to be noted that the County Lunatic Asylum at Gloucester, with which ~~most~~ some of the magistrates present, (Purnell, Curtis Hayward, Gambier Parry, W. P. Price & myself) are connected as Visitors is, and has long been conducted on a non coercion principle — Preliminaries having been settled, and books and documents put in, Dr Joseph Bompas was subjected to examination by Counsel, and by the Magistrates who conduct the enquiry. His replies were confused and evasive, and very unsatisfactory; much may be ascribed to his peculiar habit and character of mind; — there is no doubt that he is a young man well trained in the medical profession, studious, and competent to discharge the general duties of a physician; but there is a lack of energy, a vis inertiæ,[6] an inability to express himself intelligibly, an apparent tendency to throw a mist round all his replies, as if |*112* he were incapable of speaking truth truthfully. His temper may be somewhat ruffled, he probably speaks with timidity in presence of his Uncle, Grace Smith, who apparently has much controul over his mind; he is placed in a novel and trying position, questioned and cross questioned by acute and adverse lawyers and magistrates; an object of suspicion, believing himself to be pre-condemned, as he supposes the leading judges before whom he stands to be strongly prejudiced against him. And, then, he must be aware that the system on which his establishment has been conducted, will not bear close enquiry — that it is based on old principles, now, in a great measure, exploded; that new light has not burst fully on the Fishponds, that there are many vulnerable points, much of the management that cannot be defended. Some facts elicited in his examination to-day told strongly against the establishment, shewing negligence, irregularity as to entries, and other deviations of a serious kind |*113* whereby the Act governing such institutions was undeniably and habitually infringed. |

---

6. Vis inertiæ – a tendency to remain inactive or unprogressive.

1

Diary
1849

Dec. 10. . Monday — Foggy weather, but dry — Lefroy left us after breakfast for Cheltenham — Mr Thorp, Chaplain of the Bridewell at North leach, called, partly to ascertain from me what deductions were likely to be made from his stipend in consequence of the deliberations of the County Finance Committee; partly to obtain from me a testimonial of his good conduct as the Chaplain of one of the Gloucestershire Houses of Correction, which he might transmit, with the testimonials of other magistrates, to the authorities in the County of Norfolk, he proposing to offer himself as Candidate for the vacant Chaplaincy of the Bridewell at Swaffham, the income of which is double of that now received by him. Wrote such a testimonial in his favour. ——— Mr Brookes called, with a document for my signature relating to the proposed amalgamation of the 2 Evesham district of turnpike roads with the Tofs and

Witts Family Papers F366

There is a gap in the diaries from 22 November 1848 to 10 December 1849.

Diary
1849

Dec. 10. Monday

Foggy weather, but dry — Lefroy left us after breakfast for Cheltenham — Mr Thorp, Chaplain of the Bridewell at Northleach, called, partly to ascertain from me what deductions were likely to be made from his stipend in consequence of the deliberations of the County Finance Committee; partly, to obtain from me a testimonial of his good conduct as the Chaplain of one of the Gloucestershire Houses of Correction, which he might transmit, with the testimonials of other magistrates, to the authorities in the County of Norfolk, he proposing to offer himself as Candidate for the vacant Chaplaincy of the Bridewell at Swaffham, the income of which is double of that now received by him. Wrote such a testimonial in his favour. — Mr Brookes called, with a document for my signature relating to the proposed amalgamation of the 2^d Evesham district of turnpike roads with the Foss and |^2 Cross district, and the district extending from Chapel House to Bourton on the hill — Justice business at home. — Visiting sick parishioners — Mrs Collett and her son, Samuel, — Matthew Davis, — Widow Townsend, — W. Gregory and wife — Looked in at the day school. — A letter from Purnell: he was taken ill soon after I left the Committee at Gloucester on Wednesday last, and has been an invalid since. He informs me that the Lord Lieutenant has apprized him that Mr Francillon, the Judge of the County Court, has consented to officiate as Chairman for the trial of prisoners in the second court at Quarter Sessions: thus I shall be released from that onerous duty. The County will obtain the services of an experienced barrister; but neither in point of talent, family connection, landed property, or agreeable manners, is Mr F. likely to win the regard of the Magistrates, or respect of the bar — Preparing a Sermon. — Quarterly Review. |^3 Article on the signs of death. —

Dec. 11. Tuesday.

A cold, raw day; one sleet shower, otherwise fair. — Replied to the letter which I received from Purnell yesterday. — Received a letter from Mr Thornton, who forwards to me a note he had received from Mr Williams as to the case prepared to be submitted to Counsel in respect to the controversy in relation to the Hunt Trust concerns, which Mr W. wishes to lay before Mr Thornton, who has engaged to go over it with him on Thursday next. — Wrote to Mr Hare and Miss S. Hunt on the Hunt Trust affairs, apprizing them that a case will shortly be laid before ^{an} eminent chancery Queen's Counsel, for an opinion, as to the course to be pursued, with especial reference to my position as one of the Trustees, and also one of the Executors of the late Miss M. C. Hunt. My letters to both parties were accompanied by enclosures, of former correspondence on the same subject. — Received a circular from the |⁴ Secretary of the Society for the Propagation of the Gospel as to the remittance of balances of subscriptions for the current year before its close — A person called seeking a recommendation to the infirmary at Gloucester, which I could not furnish. — Preparing a sermon. — Quarterly Review — Article on the Construction of the Britannia and Conway tubular bridges, by Sir F. B. Head. —

Dec. 12. Wednesday

A cold, raw day, frost in the afternoon. — Wrote to Lieut. Col. Browne, Stouts-hill, requesting him to furnish me with the address of the place where may be procured an application for sores occasioned by friction in bed-ridden persons, which he had mentioned when I met him at Hardwick court, and which may be useful in the case of a parishioner now confined to her bed — Wrote to F. Aston, in answer to his letter lately received — Drove to Stow: attended the annual meeting of the Trustees and Managers of the Stow Provident Bank, at which the Dean of Gloucester |⁵ presided. Mʳ Pole, Mʳ Ford, Mʳ Morrison, Mʳ Wiggin, Mʳ Winter, Mʳ W. B. Pole, Mʳ Ogle, Capt. Leigh, Mʳ Du Pré, and myself were present. The balance sheet and the report of the proceedings were very satisfactory. The institution maintains its steady course of usefulness, and the officers conduct the business with fidelity and regularity. — Mʳ Wiggin called the Rural Dean and myself to private counsel respecting a correspondence which has given uneasiness to him. It seems that W. with the general approval of his parishioners has planned to build a new church at Oddington on a new site, the old church being much dilapidated, and very inconveniently placed. He proposes to erect a new structure at an expence of £1500 of which sum £500 to be supplied from his own resources, £500 by contributions from friends, and from the Church building Societies, and £300 from the parishioners by a charge on the Church rates to be spread over ten years: the remaining |⁶ £200 to be collected as he may be able, for which, however, W. will make himself responsible. But Sir J. C. Reade, to whom he has applied for his sanction, yet not claiming his support in a pecuniary way, because his property in the parish is on sale, opposes the project, probably because he considers it may injure the sale of his mansion house and estate. We encouraged Mʳ W. to persevere in his scheme, trying, however, by all means to conciliate the baronet. To the parish the project is beneficial on the ground of economy, as the repairs of the old Church would far exceed the sum required of the rate payers for a new one; the new site would be far more convenient also than the old, and would be given by Mʳ Langstone. I fear, W. will find Sir John a very impractible person. — Mʳˢ· Ford, and Sir C. Imhoff both seriously indisposed. — Quarterly review — Sir F. B. Head's article on the Britannia and Conway tubular bridges.

Dec. 13. Thursday.

A dark day, fog and im-|⁷palpable sleet falling, and freezing on the surface rendered the roads very slippery. — Wrote to Mʳ Pantin, with a receipt for his subscription to the Society for the propagation of the Gospel for 1849 which Mʳ Ford handed to me yesterday. — Drove to

Stow, where attended the Provident Bank, and later in the day met there Mr Wiggin, Mr J. T. Rice and Mr W B Pole. — – To the Union Workhouse, where I presided at the fortnightly meeting of the Guardians till 3 PM. — The Relieving Officer being ill and unable to attend was a great inconvenience. The applicants for relief numerous; fever lingering at Broadwell; contracts entered into for provisions at low prices. — A letter from my son with a pleasant account of all at Stanway Vicarage — M^rs. Dolphin sent to request me to visit her to-day; but I had set out for Stow; a second message fixes me for to-morrow. — Quarterly Review — Sir F. B. Head's article on the Britannia and Conway tubular |^8 bridges.

Dec. 14. Friday.

A most, foggy, mild day: wind in the evening. — Wrote to C Bathurst with particulars of what had passed in the finance Committee at Gloucester in the last two weeks. — Rec^d. a letter from him, enquiring as to my health — A letter from Mr Thornton accompanying a copy of the questions to be submitted to counsel (Mr Wood Q.C.) on my part as Executor of the will of the late M. C. Hunt, and one of the Trustees of T. W. Hunt's estate with reference to the matters complained of by Mr George Hunt. — A letter from L^t. Col. Browne in reply to mine written to him on Wednesday last. — M.W. received a letter from Miss Knight, who wishes to hear my opinion as to the real state of M^rs. Dolphin's health — Went to Eyford by appointment, where I found M^rs. and Miss Kirby (Miss Knight's sister and niece) from Cheltenham, who had been passing a day or two with M^rs. Dolphin: conferred with M^rs. K. as to the melancholy state of M^rs. D. and the probabi-|^9 lity that her bodily powers may sink at no distant period under the pressure of disease engendered or aggravated by mental agony caused by apparently irremediable embarrasments and strife in which she is involved by the misconduct of her husband, and her own imprudent entanglement with his property, coupled with habits of expence indulged in by herself, her income having too often been wasted on foolish projects and fancies, while important demands were put aside. Joined with M^rs. D. by her bedside in prayer, M^rs. K. being present, using the Visitation service. M^rs. D. less exhausted, and seemingly suffering less than when I visited her last week, but under the influence of a strong sedative to which she habitually resorts. — A very painful interview — Visited other sick parishioners — M^rs. Rogers, the Widow Townsend, Saml. Collett, the Gregorys. — Quarterly Review — Sir F. B. Head's article on the Britannia and Conway Tubular |^10 bridges.

Dec. 15. Saturday.

A moist, foggy day, approaching to rain in the forenoon, less thick in the afternoon — Wrote to my Son in reply to his letter received on Thursday, a long letter. — Also to Miss Knight, giving her an account of what had passed at Eyford on my two late visits to M^rs. Dolphin, and expressed my opinion as to the distressing state of her health, and the piteous condition of her affairs — Justice business at home: J B Collett's hill barn broken open and robbed: the perpetrators not detected — Letter from Sophia Hunt on Hunt Trust and Executorship concerns in the wonted flighty and unsatisfactory style — Quarterly Review. Article on Peace agitators, those dangerous politicians, who counsel a large reduction of the army, navy, and ordnance on a dreamy assumption that nations may be brought to accommodate their differences by arbitration. —

Dec. 16. Sunday

Fine, open weather, and mild — Owing to the indisposition of the mistress |[11] the Sunday School children had a holiday. — Visited a sick parishioner, Louisa Humphris, who appears in a very suffering state, from chronic internal disease: her step-daughter too in a bad state from unhallowed pregnancy.[1] — Morning service — prayers; — evening service, prayers and sermon. I preached on the wisdom of GOD in man's redemption. — Received a letter from L[t.] Col. Browne, who kindly sends me further particulars as to the plaister respecting which I lately wrote to him. — A circular announces the result of the meeting at Bristol of the Council appointed for carrying into effect the project of a Training School near Bristol for Mistresses. The situation selected, as most eligible, is at the Fishponds; resolutions were passed with a view to an increase of funds &c. — Preparing a sermon. — Eccl. Gazette —

Dec. 17. Monday

After heavy rain during the night, a mild, open day. — Wrote to M[r] Hare, on Hunt Trust business, sending him a copy |[12] of the queries submitted to Counsel, and of M[r] Thornton's letter which accompanied them — Two circulars, one from the office of the Clerk of the Peace, the other from Gloucester Gaol, announcing for the 20[th.] Inst. meetings of magistrates, — the Gloucestershire finance committee, — and the Board of Visiting Justices, — which I shall not be able to attend. — Justice business at home — committed a man charged with turnip stealing. — The barn breakers, who stole fowls & barley from J B. Collett's barn, have not yet been detected. — Preparing a sermon. — Visited E Lea on parish business, which also brought W. Gregory and W. Bateman to me in the Evening — Visited sick parishioners — Louisa Humphris, her step-daughter and Mary Forty. — Quarterly review. Article on the Ornithology of Sussex.

Dec. 18. Tuesday.

A moist, rainy day, the weather in the afternoon less wet [than] in the forenoon, but the evening stormy with wind and rain — |[13] Wrote to Mess[rs.] Cox and Williams, expressing my concurrence in the proceeding recommended as to a case being laid before counsel in the Hunt trust and executorship concerns with reference to the course to be taken by me in my joint capacity of Trustee of T. W. Hunt's estate, and Exor. to the will of M C Hunt — To M[rs.] C. Barr in answer to a letter I had received from her some time since — To Mess[rs.] Hoare, requesting them to send the continuation of my account — To W. Humphris, Cheltenham, in answer to a letter received by me from him to-day respecting his being a candidate for the place of Underwarder in the Separate prison at Gloucester County gaol — To Mess[rs.] Sewell and Newmarch, in reply to a letter received from them by me to-day, in which they ask for information as to the place of interment of a late M[r] Howell of Prinknash Park. I referred them to T. J. Howell — Received a letter from a female in distress, writing from Bristol, by name Villiers, and asking for pecu-|[14]niary aid to help her to establish herself in a school. The writer is unknown to me, but refers to M[r] Gambier Parry, and M[r] Brooke Hunt as parties who have befriended her. — A letter from C. Bathurst in reply to mine giving an account of the proceedings of the finance Committee at Gloucester, the nomination of M[r]

---

1.   Unhallowed – not of a hallowed or sacred character. Presumably the step-daughter was unmarried.

Francillon to be second Court Chairman, my visits to Hardwick Court & Stancombe Park &c. — Preparing a Sermon. — Visited sick parishioners — M^rs. Rogers and M^rs. Ryan at Eyford: called to enquire after M^rs. Dolphin, who did not admit me, having had a bad night — Justice business at home — Quarterly Review. Article on the state of Ireland. —

Dec. 19. Wednesday.

A fine, clear winter's day — Wrote to Miss S. B. Hunt, with the information that a case on the present posture of the Hunt Trust matters had been submitted to Mr Wood, Q.C., and, in answer to her letter received by me a few days ago, consented to pay |^15 to herself and sisters, residuary legatees under M^rs. M. Hunt's will, £130, part of the balance of that Executorship account, standing to my credit in the bank of Messrs. Yorke, Oundle — A circular from Gloucester gaol as to a meeting of Visiting Justices on the 24th. Inst. — Business with R. Prosser as to Income Tax assessed on him in regard of his profits in trade. — Visited sick parishioners, Eliz. Gardner, and Mary Forty. — M^rs. Boudier with her nieces, Jemima and Dulcy Ford, called — My dear Grandson, Frederick, this day six years old; a lovely boy; happy, we suppose, in going to Dumbleton to bring his elder brother home for the Christmas holidays. — Quarterly Review — Article on the state of Ireland. —

Dec. 20. Thursday

A slight snow shower had fallen early, on which a sharp frost followed, making the roads slippery: the weather cold — Justice business at home with Samuel Collett, making a complaint of an attempt to |^16 defraud him by two ~~young~~ young labourers of this parish. The case after wards heard at Stow, and the misdoers, who had not succeeded in their endeavour, mulcted in costs. — Drove to Stow — Received a note from Messrs. Cox and Williams shewing that the case in our Hunt dispute is gone before Mr Wood Q.C. — A kind and long letter, chiefly on his family concerns, from my old friend John Round, dated from Torquay, where he has been residing for sometime past with his daughter, M^rs. Story, and her husband, the former having been recommended by her medical adviser to resort to a mild climate for the correction of a disposition to pulmonary complaint; she has derived much benefit from so doing — A letter from Messrs. Hoare, Bankers, accompanying a continuation of my banking account with them since the balance sheet last rendered, a twelvemonth ago — To the Unicorn Inn by 11 AM. to a meeting of Income Tax Commissioners, where I was |^17 joined by Mr Ford, and Mr Waller, who sat with me hearing appeals under Sched D. of the Income Tax act as to trade, professions &c. — with a few cases under Schedules A & B. as owners and occupiers. Mr Credland attended as Surveyor of the District in the room of Mr Longhurst, dismissed. Mr C. a well educated, and well-mannered man, conducting himself in his office in a very becoming and satisfactory manner. — At half past 2 P.M. with Waller and Ford began to sit as Magistrates till 4. P.M. — Mr Wiggin, Mr Watson Pole, Mr Hippisley, Mr Ogle, and a gentleman with him, as also Mr Vavasour, earlier in the day, were present. — The press of business prevented me from attending at the Provident Bank, where, I understand, a communication was received from the Commissioners for the reduction of the National debt, requiring certain returns to be made intended to test the propriety of the management of the institution. This course adopted |^18 in consequence of a late discovery that the Actuary of the Rochdale Savings Bank, not being duly watched and checked by the Trustees and Managers of the establishment, has embezzled upwards of £70000 of the deposits, this being only detected upon his sudden death. The man, a Quaker, by name Haworth, had borne a very high character, was considered equally valuable for his integrity & business habits, and was employed as an agent in coal-mines by the Smith family, who are related to the Vavasours, and, indeed, M[rs.] Vavasour and my Son, as two of the Executors of Lady Burdett, one of that opulent family, have been in correspondence with this Howorth on her mining property: they, however, are not acting Executors. — M[rs.] W. Vavasour had gone in my carriage to Upper Slaughter to pass some ~~other~~ hours with MW. and returned to the Cottage, when the carriage came for me at 4. P.M. — Heard from her and M[r] V. a pleasant account of |[19] [our] dear children, who were at Stow on Monday last. — Quarterly Review. Article on the state of Ireland. — M[r] Ford, M[r] R. Waller, M[r] Hippisley, M[r] Ogle &c. dined together at the Unicorn, this being the annual audit of the Trustees of the Cope Charity: I have for several years ceased to attend, being afraid of the fatigue, good cheer, and cold air, after a day of business. M.W's indifferent health, coupled with the severity of the season, and my tendency to derangement of the biliary system, if I live otherwise than abstemiously, lead us very much to decline engagements; thus we excused ourselves from joining a dinner party at the Dean of Gloucester's at Oddington yesterday.

Dec. 21. Friday.

A cold day, with an Easterly wind; a slight tendency to sleet and snow; a snow shower in the Evening. — Examining my banking account with Mess[rs.] Hoare: wrote to them as to a presumed error which I discovered in the balance sheet received yesterday — |[20] M[r] Kimber, of Bourton on the Water, called respecting a fine imposed on him for not attending according to his summons as a Grand Juror at the last Sessions at Gloucester; much conversation with him as to M[rs.] Dolphin. — Received a letter from Mess[rs.] Cox and Williams, accompanying a copy of the opinion given by M[r] Wood Q.C. on the case submitted to him as to the present posture of affairs relating to the Hunt Trust and Executorship. M[r] W. makes no comment on the opinion, which I consider, on the whole, satisfactory, as exonerating the Trustees from any breach of trust, confirming the opinion of Mess[rs.] Turner and Bates that we are to wait for an attack from, & not commence proceedings against M[r] Geo. Hunt; — that Miss M. C. Hunt's Estate is liable for dilapidations on the Wharf, while she was Life Tenant; and that the mode of proceeding to a winding up of the Exorship is by my filing a bill against my |[21] Co-Executrix to administer, which would bring M[r] Hunt, if so advised, into Court to make his claim, or, if he should not so proceed, would provide for a sum to be set apart to meet his claim when made and substantiated. But M[r] Wood recommends an arrangement by all parties out of Court. — A note containing a bill from a Cheltenham Tradesman — Grimes, the Bookbinder. — A letter from M[r] Hare on Hunt Trust business, who returns letters &c. which I had sent for his perusal. — Preparing a sermon — Quarterly Review — Article on the state of Ireland.

Dec. 22. Saturday.

Some little snow had fallen last evening, or during the night — the day cold and frosty. — Wrote to M[r] Thornton on our Hunt Trust business. — With Churchw[dn.] Gregory, settling the list of poor parishioners to receive the bread charity on Christmas Eve

— Received a letter from the County Chairman, who sends me a printed copy of his report |[22] made at the Michaelmas Quarter Sessions on the Lunatic asylums near Bristol, chiefly as to those under the management of M[r] Ogilvie, and the Bompas family: — not printed at the expence of the County, but by the alleged Lunatics friends Society. Purnell expects a crowded meeting of Magistrates at the Epiphany Sessions; the Lord Lieutenant to appear with his party in full force, probably to oppose the reduction in numbers of the Constabulary; other propositions in the way of reform likely to be brought forward. — M[r] Ford and M[r] Greene, the Curate of Lower Guiting, met by appointment at my house; the latter to be licensed to his cure, and to take the oaths, the Rural Dean being Commissary. M[r] G. partook of luncheon with us. — M[rs.] Dolphin sent a messenger, desiring me to call on her to-day; but the appointment with M[r] Ford and M[r] Greene, who remained till past four o clock, prevented my obeying M[rs.] D's summons. — Quarterly Review — |[23] Article on the late Roman revolution. —

Dec. 23. Sunday

A sharp frost, and fine winter's day. — The continued indisposition of the Schoolmistress prevented the holding of the Sunday School. — Preparing a sermon. — Wrote to M[rs.] Dolphin, apologizing for not having called on her yesterday, and proposing to wait on her to-morrow. — Morning service, prayers & sermon. I preached on false consciences, consciences biassed by the desires & interests of the unrenewed heart, and worldly minded man — Afternoon service, prayers. — Received a letter from T. J. Howell, family intelligence and political gossip. By a new arrangement of the Factory office, he is to superintend the factories in Ireland with a small, and, as H. thinks, inadequate increase of salary. — A notice from Gloucester Gaol of a meeting of Visiting Justices to enquire into and report upon the duties of the Chaplains, and the time consumed by them in the fulfilment of those duties |[24] — Eccl. Gazette. — To the family a sermon from the "family sermons". —

Dec. 24. Monday

A thick fog, moist atmosphere, and some rain: a thaw set in before mid-day. — Wrote a few lines to M[r] Hare, forwarding to him copies of the opinion given on our Hunt Trust affairs by M[r] Wood, and of the letters I wrote on the 22[d.] to M[r] Thornton — Received a letter from M[r] Bloxsome, desiring to know whether he should forward to me his bills on the county, as Clerk of the Peace, as usual in the week before the Sessions, for my inspection. I replied in the affirmative, that I might make myself acquainted with the items; but said I should not exercise any judgment as to the charges, as it had been settled in Committee that two Magistrates who had been Solicitors should be added to the committee of accounts with a view to the audit of this class of bills. — M[r] Kimber called for my advice as to the fine imposed on him for non attendance at the Mich[as.] |[25] Quarter Sessions, when summoned thither as a grand juror; it seems that he can only recover the amount of the fine by memorializing the Commissioners of the Treasurer for its remission. — Justice business at home — M.W. has been of late so much indisposed, and appeared to suffer particularly to-day from the cold, and has such shortness of breath, with debility, and restless nights, that I wrote to desire M[r] Hayward to visit her; however, from some cause, he did not come — Visited and prayed with M[rs.] Dolphin, and

M[rs.] Rogers: the former very ill, confined chiefly to her bed, and much agitated by painful correspondence on business — the latter a patient sufferer under an incurable internal malady. — Quarterly Review. Article on the late Roman Revolution.

Dec. 25. Tuesday.

Christmas day. — A sharp frost, and fine forenoon: after mid-day a fog came on with thaw. — M[r] Hayward visited |[26] MW. at breakfast time, and found her much out of order; much nervous excitability, a tongue very much furred, a bad pulse &c. but trusts there is no essential mischief at work, and that a course of alterative medicine with care may restore her to a comfortable state.[2] There is no need of confinement to her room or bed. GOD grant that he may be of service, and that his favourable view of her case may prove correct! She was well enough without inconvenience to attend the morning service, and to partake of the Holy Communion. — Morning service — prayers, — sermon — (on the day) — and the sacrament administered to 21 communicants. — Letter from E.F.W. containing very pleasant accounts of all at Stanway Vicarage; dear Broome has returned from school for the holidays, very happy and blooming; with a prize and a good character; fond of reading and improved. — Bad reports of the health of Lady Wemyss, who has had a succession of paralytic attacks, and is not |[27] likely to survive long: her declining state operates unfavourably on the shattered constitution of her Lord. — M[r] Billingsley seriously indisposed. — A letter from M[r] Thornton, who desires to know my views as to the recent opinion on the Hunt affair given by M[r] P. Wood; his reading of it concurs with mine, which he as by this time ascertained from my letter of the 22[d.] Inst. — A letter from Mess[rs.] Hoare, explaining satisfactorily the error made by their clerks, which had led to an entry in the balance sheet of my banking account, as to which I required to be informed. — Preparing a sermon. —

Dec. 26. Wednesday

A moist, foggy day: milder air. — Wrote to E.F.W. informing him of his mother's indisposition and that M[r] Hayward is in attendance; that the symptoms are not such as to alarm, or lead me to relinquish my attendance at the Quarter Sessions next week: invited him and dear |[28] Sophy with their precious Broome to visit us for two nights in the week after next. Broome has been promised to us. — To Mess[rs.] Hoare, in reply to their letter received yesterday, and desired them to transfer £35 from my account with them to that of my son. — To M[r] James Walker, Northleach, with a cheque for oats supplied, and with an order for more — To Lady Jane Charteris, a letter of condolence and enquiry, on hearing of the precarious state of Lady Wemyss's health. — Visited sick parishioners — Mary Forty, Matthew Davis, the Townsends. — Business with an applicant for parochial relief. — Quarterly Review — Article on the late Roman revolution — MW. languid under the influence of medicine, but not worse than for some days past, and had enjoyed a pretty good night's rest. —

Dec. 27. Thursday

A fine forenoon, except as to an occasional threatening of rain or snow: in the afternoon frost came on, and towards |[29] night snow fell. — M[r] Hayward called at breakfast time,

---

2. Alterative – improving bodily function, digestion etc. A medicine for such purpose.

and visited MW. whose pulse he found too quick, and the tongue still foul; she is languid from the effect of aperient medicine administered with a view to correct the disordered action of the liver. He proposes to continue the same medicines somewhat modified. She is certainly not worse, and the symptoms indicate a deranged condition of the biliary organs. — Wrote a few lines to E.F.W. to be conveyed by the person who came from Stanway with a load of coal. — Drove to Stow: — to the Savings Bank, where transacted business; the Comm[rs.] for the Reduction of the National debt require that the Trustees and Managers shall advertise for, and require the production of the pass-books of depositors, that, as far as is practicable, all may be brought in, and certified to correspond with the entries in the ledger by the signature of two managers; this is in accordance with the Savings Bank |[30] Act, but has hitherto not been insisted on in our establishment, owing to the scattered character of our depositors, who are not concentrated in one principal town or district, but live far and wide. Consulted with M[r] Pole, M[r] Morrison, M[r] Wiggin and M[r] W. B. Pole, how this requisition of the Comm[rs.] could be best acted upon, and arranged a plan. It is certain that we shall not be able to call in a considerable portion of our pass-books, as many or our depositors reside far beyond our immediate reach. The plan is good, with reference to the gross defalcations in the Rochdale Savings Bank, as a means of testing the sound management, careful supervision, and integrity of managers and their clerks. — Transacted business with M[r] Brookes, signing certificates, recognizances, &c. — Business at the office of the Gloucestershire Banking Company. — To the Workhouse; presided for three hours at the fortnightly meeting of the Guardians of our Union — Returned home by 5 P.M. — Fairfax |[31] Correspondence:[3] civil wars tem. Ch.1. —

Dec. 28. Friday

A good deal of snow had fallen during the night, or early this morning; a sharp frost, and drifting wind. — Wrote to Mess[rs.] Brown, wine merchants, Cirencester, with a remittance for wine supplied by them — To M[r] Hawkins, Secretary to the Society for the propagation of the Gospel, with a small remittance for Subscriptions received by me from members of our District Committee to the close of the year, and since the date of my last remittance in October — Received a letter from M[r] Bloxsome, who is seriously indisposed, containing a portion of his bill for business done for the county during the last half year — from the Clerk of the Peace's office a circular, notifying a meeting of the Prisons Committee to be held at Gloucester on the 31[st.] Inst. — A packet from Stanway, containing a letter to MW. from Sophy; the boy was sent on purpose, in consequence of a note having been received |[32] this morning addressed M[rs.] Witts, Stanway, Stow on the Wold, being an invitation to dinner to-morrow at Adlestrop House from M[r] and Lady Caroline Leigh, inviting also E.F.W. and Sophy, if they are at home, evidently written in a strange ignorance and misapprehension of our localities, which, indeed, they have shewn before. I dispatched a servant immediately with a note to M[r] Leigh, calculated to undeceive him and his lady as to the places of residence of ourselves, and our children, explaining why Lady C.L's note had not been sooner answered, and declining the invitation in consequence of M.W's health being now so indifferent that it precluded our going out — The Stanway

---

3.   *The Fairfax Correspondence: Memorials of the Civil War.* Edited by Robert Bell, 1849.

Packet also contained a very delightful letter to E.F.W. from Mr Garratt, speaking in very affectionate and gratifying terms of our dear Broome, his excellent conduct in school, and his attention to his lessons. — Another letter was sent in the packet, received from Gosford |^{33} House, written by Col. Wildman, giving a melancholy report of Lord and Lady Wemyss, both of whom are confined to their beds, he very feeble and declining, and she speechless after a series of paralytic attacks, yet may linger some time in her hopeless condition. Lord Elcho, and all the daughters of the Earl and Countess are at Gosford. These letters from Col. Wildman and Mr Garratt I sent back by the messenger to Stanway, with a note I had written to our dear Sophy. — A letter from C Bathurst, containing his considerations, formerly and now, as to the payments to be made to the Clerk of the Peace, in remuneration of his services to the county, which he wishes me to lay before the Committee of accounts, when that subject comes under discussion next week. — A letter from Mr Thornton expressing his first thoughts as to the course to be taken in respect to the opinion lately given by Mr Wood on our Hunt Trust affairs, on |^{34} the same subject he proposes to write again shortly. — A letter from Mr Hare, who gives his impressions as arising out of a perusal of the opinion lately given by Mr Wood. — A letter from Messrs Hoare, announcing that they have transferred £35. from my account with them to that of my Son — Visited parishioners — the Leas — the Davises — and Mrs Rogers; read prayers with the last — M.W. appears languid, probably, from the aperients administered to her; but in no way worse than when Mr Hayward was called in; if any thing, better. — Fairfax Correspondence —

Dec. 29. Saturday

A cold day, and a hard frost. — Perusing Mr Bloxsome's bill on the County, of which he sent me a continuation, but not a conclusion, in a letter received by the post. — A letter from Miss S. B. Hunt, and an indemnity from her and her sisters, the co-residuary legatees of Mrs M. Hunt, to hold me harmless in respect of any claim which |^{35} may still be made on the estate of the late Mrs M. Hunt, over and above what I shall have retained in my hands, when I have paid to their account £130, part of the balance standing to my account, as her Executor, with Messrs Yorke, Bankers, Oundle. S.B.H. writes in a flighty manner on general subjects, and with the usual perversity on other Hunt Trust and Executorship difficulties. — A letter from Messrs Hoare announces that Mr Jennings has paid to my account with them £173. 2. 2. — A friendly letter from F. Aston, as a companion to his usual annual present of an Oxford Almanac — E.F.W. rode over from Stanway to see his Mother, and remained with us for two hours, bringing a good account of all the dear ones at the Vicarage. — Before he left us, Mr Hayward called to visit MW., whom he found rather improved since he last saw her; but the pulse, though reduced, is still too high; |^{36} and the tongue foul: she has experienced languor to day and yesterday from the use of purgatives; has something of a cough; but the breathing is more free. H. proposes to discontinue for the present the aperient, to administer a sedative, and to continue the Alkali and Taraxacum mixture — On the whole there seems an improvement. — John Cox called to consult me as to a Coroner's inquest on the body of his mother who died suddenly to-day — Fairfax Correspondence. —

<u>*Dec. 30. Sunday*</u>

A frosty and fine winter's day — Still no Sunday School, owing to the continued serious illness of the Schoolmistress — Morning Service, prayers; afternoon service, prayers & sermon — preached on the close of the year — An acknowledgment from the Treasurers S.P.G. of the remittance made by me on Friday last. — Preparing papers for the Quarter Sessions business and meeting of the Committee of accounts to-morrow. — MW. seems still to improve in health; more freedom in breathing; sleeps |[37] better; but did not venture to Church — To the family a sermon from "Family Sermons" — Wrote a note to G. Pain as to form of advertisement from Trustees and Managers of Savings Banks, giving notice to depositors to send in their deposit books for comparison with the ledger.

<u>*Dec. 31. Monday.*</u>

A sharp frost; and cold day: the roads very slippery. — Rose early to breakfast, so as to set out for Gloucester at a quarter before eight. — Left MW. after a tolerably comfortable night with good hope that she is gradually recovering a better state of health. — Met M[r] Lefroy at the Great Western station, and travelled with him by the railway to Gloucester; where arrived before 11 o clock. — To the Bell Hotel, where breakfasted, and conferred for more than an hour on County business with M[r] Purnell and M[r] Gambier Parry, Riddiford &c. — To the Shire Hall, where entered on the business of the Committee of accounts, auditing bills &c. — The |[38] members attending were Mess[rs.] Curtis Hayward, Lysons, Brooke Hunt, G. Parry, Baker &c. Mess[rs.] ~~Bloxb~~ Bloxsome, Wilton, Lefroy, Riddiford, Keiley, Whitehead &c. were officials in attendance. — A meeting of the Prisons Committee had been called, at which M[r] Ricardo, and one or two other Magistrates, who do not usually attend on the Monday in the Sessions week, were present, but nothing was transacted out of the ordinary routine of business. Much discussion as to the proceedings of the morrow, report of the proceedings of the County expenditure committee &c. — At

82. Colesbourne.

the Bell the Magistrates who dined together were the County Chairman, Curtis Hayward, Gambier Parry and myself — From 9 P.M. to midnight busily engaged in the audit of accounts, and discussion of business for to-morrow. — Received a letter from C Bathurst who announces that he does not mean to be present to-morrow. |[39]

1850

Tuesday Jan. 1.

Hard frost, severely cold weather. — At the opening of the Court in the Shire hall there were but few magistrates present: but in the course of the day many more flocked in, till the gathering was larger than I ever recollect to have witnessed. About 105 were recorded on M[r] Bloxsome's list, and the business was protracted to an unusually late hour so that the dinner hour was delayed till seven. Among the leading Magistrates were the Lord Lieutenant, the Duke of Beaufort and Lord Ellenborough, the Hon. Grantley and Craven Berkeley, & James Dutton, Sir M H. Beach and Sir W. Codrington, Barts, the Hon. G. G. C. Talbot &c. — Three new Magistrates qualified, Sir John Key, (ci-devant Lord Mayor of London) the Rev[d.] Bourne, Rector of Weston Subedge, and M[r] Elwes Jun[r] of Colesborne. My son came with T. Wynniatt about midday, and returned with him after the principal business was over; he had |[40] been brought to Cheltenham in W's coach, and went back by the same conveyance. — He gave a very pleasant report of his wife and children — I went through the customary routine of presenting and commenting upon the bills brought in, in my capacity of Chairman of the Committee of accounts. — The Lord Lieutenant, adverting to the retirement of Sergeant Ludlow, and the elevation of Curtis Hayward to the senior chair as Judicial Chairman, whereby the second Judicial chair was vacated, it having been fully understood that I only held it at the last Sessions temporarily, proposed that M[r] Francillon should fill that post, to which he acceded, nemine contradicente, but many in their secret souls not being quite satisfied. F. is an amiable, quiet, industrious man, well versed in Sessions practice, as a barrister, who had long practised there, but deficient in family, connection, talent, or superior education, slow but painstaking. — The thanks of the Court voted to |[41] Sergeant Ludlow at the Mich. Sess[ns.] had been beautifully transcribed on vellum and were transmitted to him, signed by the County Chairman. — A very well deserved vote of thanks was moved by Lord Fitzhardinge, and seconded by the Duke of Beaufort, recognizing the great services rendered by Purnell to the County, and to the community at large, in his unwearied and persevering labours, in respect of the conditions of the Private Lunatic Asylums in this County; he being justly congratulated on the valuable results of the investigations made by him and other Magistrates associated with him, in the development and exposure, together with the correction of serious abuses, as also in the liberation of some patients improperly detained, and the improved treatment of others, who had been subjected to management which, if it had not aggravated their maladies, which is very probable, had reduced them below the condition of |[42] comfort to which from their station they were entitled. — As to the Fishponds Asylum the Bompas family has retired with M[r] Nath[l.] Smith from the management, by an arrangement of their own making, and a licence for seven months was this day granted to D[r] Cox. a member of the same family, but who had been alienated from them, in consequence of his joining the Church of England on seceding from the Baptist denomination, to which the rest of his connections belonged. Dr Cox is a physician, conversant with insanity, having practised at London and Naples, and at the latter had peculiar opportunity for acquiring information as to the treatment of the insane in a large national establishment. He professed himself to-day to be entirely dissociated from those who had hitherto conducted the house, and to be resolved on following the improved system, such as is introduced into the first rate public hospitals for the insane in this kingdom. — Mr Ogilvie has |[43] made no movement towards a renewal of the licence heretofore granted to the Ridgway House private asylum, and, so doing, has tacitly admitted the justice of the censures passed on his establishment in the County Chairman's reports. — Purnell in his report presented to the Court this day, entered into further details, with recapitulations as to the proceedings in relation to the Fishponds and other private asylums near Bristol, as also to Dr Connolly's at Charlton, and Dr Hitch's at Sandywell Park, the latter of which he commended, while he spoke with something of censure of the former. — Next followed a long report prepared by the County Chairman as to the history ~~and~~ of the prison management ~~of the~~ and Gaol system in the county, commencing with the shameful condition of the gaol & bridewells in the days of Howard, the philanthropist, tracing the alterations, improvements, and new buildings suggested by, and carried on under |[44] the superintendence of Sir George Onesiphorus Paul, the disciple of Howard, and the great reformer of prison discipline in this County, into which he introduced a very valuable code of rules, with the Penitentiary and Houses of Correction, now existing, and affording a pattern, which other counties emulously followed. The Chairman then detailed the theory of modern Prison-directors, seeking to modify and, perhaps, to improve Sir G. O. Paul's system; the introduction of principles and plans from the United States of America; the Solitary and the Separate Systems; the projects for religious, moral, and instructional improvement, all involving material changes in the structure of the buildings, all adopted and enforced by successive governments, and so urged by the Home Secretaries, as to render extensive alterations at a great expence every where unavoidable. He shewed how the Magistracy of the County, during the period in which he had held the chair, had |[45] met the pressure from the Home office; had resisted demands made so far as to save the existing Gaol and Houses of Correction, which the government had doomed, and the sacrifice of which, together with the erection of one huge central prison would have entailed an enormous expence, which had been spared by a careful alteration and remodelling of the existing structures together with the erection within the walls of the County Gaol of a spacious new prison on the Separate system. It was shewn that everything required had been accomplished by an outlay of ~~from £30000 to~~ rather more than £40000 gradually expended, which would have required £180000 on the plan suggested by the government; and that the contemplated alterations being now completed, no outlay for new works on the prisons would be required, as far as could be foreseen, for a long series of years, which circumstance would relieve the ratepayers of the County |[46] from the payment of, say, £6000 per ann. equal to one penny in the pound on the assessment, so reducing the taxation on the rate payers from about sixpence in the pound to five pence on the estimated value of the real property of the county, which reduction might be carried still further, say, by another halfpenny in the pound, if a contemplated diminution of the Rural Constabulary were acceded to. The report having been read, and a suggestion having been made by me that it should be circulated in the form of a pamphlet, so as to reach the ratepayers generally as well as the Magistrates of the County, in which all concurred, M[r] Hopkinson proposed a resolution of thanks to the Chairman and Members of the Prisons Committee, by whom all the alterations had been successfully and judiciously and economically carried out. This resolution was seconded by the Duke of Beaufort, and emanated with much propriety from M[r] H. as a leader in the |[47] demand for reduction of expenditure, and with others as uninformed as himself, and as rarely applying ~~himself~~ themselves to the administration of county affairs, or watching the proceedings by habitual attendance at the Sessions, wont to entertain and express an opinion that the Magistrates by whom the financial concerns of the county were conducted, had been recklessly extravagant, a charge which had been more than insinuated. The prisons committee is, indeed, a numerous body, but the main business had been done by a few, and to those few, of whom I was one, this resolution of the Court could not be otherwise than satisfactory. — The report of the County Expenditure committee was next read, and in part adopted. As relates to reduction of salaries the recommendation of the Committee was approved, viz. that salaries exceeding £50 and not exceeding £100 should be reduced 5 P[r] C[t.] — that those excee[4] |[48] £100 and not exceeding £200 should be reduced 10 P[r] C[t.] – and that all exceeding £200 sh[d.] be reduced 15 P[r] C[t.]; but it was agreed that this rule as to the Chief Constable's salary should be so applied that the reduction in his case should be made on £300 per ann. only, as his original salary, and not upon £550 his present salary, inasmuch as the £250 added was meant to cover forage and travelling expences, which on his first appointment he was allowed on production of bills — The dismissal of the Assistant Chaplain was a recommendation also affirmed, it being understood that he should be retained for six months, to allow time for him to procure some other situation. — The reduction of the salary of the County Treasurer from £155 to £60 per ann. was also assented to. — The appointment of M[r] Mullings and M[r] Winterbotham on the Committee of accounts, with a view to the regulation of the charges of the Clerk |[49] of the Peace, whether professional as a Solicitor, or as the officer of the Court in matters not strictly professional, was confirmed: it being considered very desirable that these gentlemen, who had been in great practice, as Attorneys, should bring their experience in taxation to bear on this class of bills. — It was agreed that the printing of the County should be thrown open to competition by contract. — The reconsideration of the system of charges, as relates to the County Surveyor was assented to. — The discharge of the Inspectors of Weights and Measures at the Trinity Sessions was agreed to, the duties of that department to devolve upon the Superintendents of Police — Other minor recommendations of the Committee of expenditure were adopted. But the reduction of the numbers of the Constabulary, as proposed by the Committee, was strenuously and successfully resisted. Many causes |[50] concurred in this issue. The Constabulary is firstly a very popular force with the gentry at large, and the Chief Constable has made many friends. The leading men in point of rank, the Lord Lieutenant, the Duke of Beaufort, and Lord Ellenborough, had pledged themselves in its favour, by a junction of interests and influence at its first establishment, and were bound, in consistency, to uphold the system in its integrity. The Lord Lieutenant, when bent

---

4.   The word not completed on the change of folio.

on a measure is wont to rally his forces, and can do so by the good organization of his party, and does so act without scruple, and almost always succeeds. The Cheltenham magistrates, as representing a very large population with interests of their own dissociated from those of the County at large, were biassed in favour of non reduction of the Police force, because such reduction would necessarily withdraw many officers from the town, and lessen the amount of protection there. — On the other hand the Committee of Expenditure included |[51] many leading persons (Curtis Hayward, Col. Browne, Col. Kingscote, G R Barker, myself, and others) entertaining the highest opinion of the excellence of the Constabulary System, as now carried out in Gloucestershire, and unwilling to see the force crippled or diminished: yet we felt the force of the pressure from without, as regards the depreciation in the value of real property, and the products of the land, urged by the agricultural interest, not without an impeachment of those who had managed the financial matters of the County, as having conducted affairs on a reckless, extravagant plan. — True, the enquiries, instituted at the committee meetings, wholly disproved this popular impeachment, but it behoved the members of the Committee to shew a disposition to meet the complaints of the impoverished rate payer, not to irritate the already irritated by rash refusal to listen to complaint, and to offer to try an |[52] experiment of reduction, even though at the risk of lessening the efficiency of the force, and even though making even this concession with reluctance. Something to this effect I said in explanation of the vote for reduction of one fifth in number of the Constabulary which I was about to give, such diminution being calculated to relieve the rate payers to the extent of about £3000 per ann; and what I said was subsequently presented to the attention of the meeting in other words by Curtis Hayward. But neither of us, nor the County Chairman, who really approved of the reduction on principle, could avail against a combined and vigorous maintenance of the fitness & propriety of ~~main~~ preserving the force undiminished, on the other side. – The Lord Lieutenant, the Duke of Beaufort, and the Earl of Ellenboro' were unanimous and decided in their disapproval of any curtailment of the corps. The speech of Lord Ellenborough was a very brilliant, eloquent, impressive appeal; but |[53] with great excellence in many ways it combined much of fallacy and sophistry. The result was a division, in which the Ayes, the supporters of the recommendation of the Committee of expenditure numbered only 31, while the Noes, or party for the retaining the Police in full force amounted to 51. Besides these at least 23 Magistrates did not vote, having left the court before the division, being under obligation to save their trains, since time, tide, & steam wait for no man. For myself I confess I was in no way vexed with the result: I prefer the maintenance of the force on the full scale; though, out of deference to a strong public feeling, I was prepared to endeavour to work the machine with less power, and, therefore, no doubt, less efficiency. Those who have taken a leading part in the management of county financial affairs have shewn their readiness to try to reduce the expenditure so much complained of, |[54] if the county be not relieved to the extent hoped for, let those bear the blame who insisted on maintaining the Police force undiminished, and could not find any other way of economizing the public outlay. But, after all, nearly £6000 per ann. will be saved by the completion of the building expences as to Gaols and bridewells – this saving, however, would have taken place without any clamour on the part of the rate payers, and without any Committee of expenditure — When the exciting subject of the Constabulary was thus disposed of nearly four fifths of the assembled magistracy disappeared, hastening to their respective homes; the little business which remained to be done was quietly & hurriedly dispatched; and by half past seven a party of twenty Justices sat down to table at the King's Head. The Duke of Beaufort, and Sir C W. Codrington (between whom I sat) were of the party; also the heir of the Sherborne peerage. — In the course of the day |[55] I wrote a few lines to my dear wife.

Jan. 2. ~~Tuesday~~ Wednesday.

A continuance of the same severe frost. — Received a letter from MW. who believes herself to be rather better than when I left her, and writes that M[r] Hayward reports more favourably. To the same effect I had an assurance in the course of the day from M[r] Brookes of Stow, who had been desired by Hayward to mention that he found my wife better when he visited her on Monday. — Attended for the whole day from 10 AM. to past 5 P.M. in the Crown Court, where the time was fully occupied after the old fashioned way in the hearing of appeals, some of which were interesting, nice points of law being mooted. Of late years appeals have grown much into disuse; but to day we had them of all classes — settlement, appeal against poor rates, against a conviction in a game case, and against a conviction in bastardy. — M[r] Francillon after mid-day took his seat |[56] as Chairman in the second court, — trying prisoners. — After dinner at the Kings Head, where only ten Magistrates assembled, I went, with M[r] Purnell, and his two sons, Curtis Hayward, R. Waller, and M[r] Hartley to attend the performance of the Oratorio of Elijah at the Shire Hall, where a very full company was assembled. This really enjoyable treat was afforded by the Gloucester Choral Society aided by four professional singers — Machin, a Bass, and Lockey, a tenor: with two Misses Williams, the one having a contralto, the other a soprano voice. This oratorio, which is likely to rank in public estimation next to the glorious Messiah, is by the late celebrated German composer, Felix Mendelsohn Bartholdy, and is a splendid composition. We arrived about the middle of the first part, and so lost some fine portions, especially a grand chorus, of which I had often heard great commendation; but the treat was great though thus curtailed. Perhaps, |[57] Elijah bears rather too large a proportion of the whole work, and the part must be very fatiguing to the performer: the music allotted to him was correctly, but rather tamely, executed by Machin. Lockey, a delightful tenor, and good musician, sang very well in the music appropriated to Obadiah; I liked him still better when I heard him on a like occasion, at the Mich[s.] Sessions, in the Creation: I was also greatly pleased with the Misses Williams who performed ~~there~~ their parts with great skill and taste, and have a fine quality of voice — Considering the boldness of the attempt, the little training, and the miscellaneous character of those who constitute the chorus, shopmen & shopwomen, clerks to mercantile houses, or in Attorneys offices, milliners, and servants &c., it is wonderful to hear so much harmony, such good time, such correctness. M[r] Amott, the Organist of the Cathedral, an accomplished Musician, was |[58] leader, M[r] Morgan played the organ, doing all that could be accomplished by an excellent instrument, but such a noble work as the Elijah is but very inadequately rendered in the absence of a full accompaniment of wind & stringed instruments. — Returned from the Oratorio, where I had met many friends and acquaintances, to tea at a late hour at the Bell, where sat in conversation with the Purnells, R Waller, M[r] Hartley &c. till 1 AM. —

<u>Jan 3. Thursday.</u>

A change in the weather; a gentle thaw. — After breakfast, attended for two hours in Hayward's court at the trial of prisoners: busy also in auditing the accounts of fines and penalties paid to the County Treasurer by the different Clerks of Petty Sessional divisions. — Settling bills, and left the Railway Station at half past twelve by the Broad gage, travelling with a brother magistrate, Mr Machin, from the Forest of Dean. — Found my servant, with my carriage and horses waiting for me at the Plough; he brought a few |⁵⁹ lines from MW. who represents herself as somewhat better in health than when I left her. — Remained above an hour in the town, shopping and paying bills — Reached home as it was getting dark. — I cannot say that I find much improvement in my dear wife's health, but the breath is relieved, & other symptoms do not seem aggravated — A number of letters awaited my return — The Revd. A. Marsden, Vicar of Gargrave, writes to solicit a subscription towards the rebuilding of his church, which is in a very decayed condition. He claims our aid on the ground of our possessing more than 100 acres in the parish, besides that portion of our Ravenflatt farm which lies in the township of Coniston. I was not aware that so large a proportion of the Scale House farm ~~was~~ ^{is} in the parish of Gargrave — Lady Jane Charteris, in reply to my letter of enquiry as to the health of Lord and Lady Wemyss, writes a melancholy account |⁶⁰ of ~~her~~ both her parents: Lady W. paralytic and almost speechless, confined to her bed, but without immediate apprehension of her decease; and my Lord, confined to his bed with effusion of water on the chest, yet that somewhat relieved. — Mr Greaves, the Poor Law Inspector, sends me two copies of queries to be answered as to the condition of the labourers in the Stow on the Wold Union at this season, and in the corresponding season last year; — what is the rate of wages as compared with those last year, — what fall there is in the price of the necessaries of life, and the like. An answer is requested by Jan. 20. and I may advise with experienced parties on the subject. — Messrs. Brown, Wine merchants, Cirencester, send an acknowledgment of my cheque remitted to them for a supply of sherry. — Mr Sadler writes to know whether I should like to possess a lithograph portrait of my old friend Mr Malcolm, the Rector of Toddenham, & late Rural dean of Campden deanery. It seems |⁶¹ that his nephew has prevailed upon him to sit for his portrait, and that it is proposed to engrave a lithographic print to ~~such~~ be a memorial of so good a man, which his friends and acquaintance may obtain at a charge of ten shillings for each lithograph — Good Mr Lumbert sends me a cheque for three pounds as his liberal gift to the poor of the parish of Upper Slaughter, as usual at this time of year. — From Dr Warneford I also found a letter giving me authority to quote him as one who highly values the Rural police establishment in this county, and would very unwillingly be deprived of their services. This was written with a view to my mentioning his name and sentiments at the Quarter Sessions, if needful, but his letter should have arrived a week sooner. — A note from Mr Brookes, Stow, announces a turnpike meeting at Stow for the 10.th. Inst. — A printed circular from Bristol announces a meeting |⁶² of the members of the Council for the management of the Training school for Schoolmistresses near Bristol for a day in the next week. —

<u>Friday Jan. 4.</u>

A fine mild forenoon, a little rain in the afternoon. — Mr Hayward called, and visited MW. but did not find any marked improvement in her state: the breathing is relieved, and the pulse somewhat lower, but the debility and restless nights continue. — Wrote to EFW. inviting him and Sophy with Broome to visit us early in next week. — A letter from Mr Thornton on Hunt Trust affairs; he suggests the style of letter to be written by Cox and Williams to Mr Braikenridge, and the furnishing Mr Whitcombe with a copy of Mr Wood's opinion for his consideration, and to report thereon to Miss S. B. Hunt. — Walked to Eyford: had an interview with Mrs. Dolphin, whom I found very ill, and very full of a visit she had received during this week from her brother, Mr Stavely, and his lady: prayed by her bed-side, |63 and conversed with her on business matters. — Fairfax Correspondence.

<u>Jan 5. Saturday</u>

Frost had succeeded the mild open weather of yesterday, with a considerable fall of snow. — Wrote to Messrs. Yorke, Bankers, Oundle, directing them to pay to the credit of Miss S. B. Hunt with Messrs. Coutts, London, £130 being part of the balance standing to my credit on their books, as Executor of Mrs. M. Hunt deceased — Wrote to Sophia Hunt to the effect that I had so instructed the Messrs. Yorke; informed her that Mr Wood had given his opinion on the case submitted to him as to the position of the several parties concerned in the Hunt Trust controversy, and that I should desire Messrs. Cox & Williams to send to Mr Whitcombe a copy of the case and opinion that he may advise Miss S.H. thereon. — Visiting sick parishioners — M. Forty, M. Townsend, M. Davis &c. — Fairfax Correspondence. — MW. continues in much the |64 same state as for some time past.

<u>Jan. 6. Sunday.</u>

Frosty weather: the ground covered with snow. — Owing to the continued illness of M. Forty, the Sunday School closed — Mr Hayward called to visit MW. and made some change in her medicine: the pulse lower, but the debility great. — Morning service – prayers and a Sermon: I preached a discourse appropriate to the Epiphany, on the obstacles and dangers attending the profession of Christianity: — evening service, prayers. — Preparing a sermon. — Eccl. Gazette.

<u>Jan 7. Monday</u>

Same weather as yesterday — Wrote to Messrs. Cox and Williams on the course to be pursued now that the opinion of Mr Wood has been given us as to the Trust questions at issue between the Trustees of the late T. W. Hunt, Mr Geo. Hunt, and the Representatives of Miss M. C. Hunt; directed that a copy of the case and opinion should be transmitted to Mr Whitcombe; sent to Messrs. C. & W. the letters on the subject I had |65 received from Mr Thornton to assist Mr Williams in coming to a conclusion as to the steps to be further taken particularly as to opening a correspondence on the basis of the letter sketched by Mr Thornton with Mr Braikenridge, with a view to an accommodation — Wrote to W. Ayrton, our tenant at Scale House, desiring information from him as to the quantity of land occupied by him in the parish of Gargrave, and how much he holds in the Chapelry of Rilston; also as to the monies raised or to be raised for the restoration of the Church at Rilston, whether by donation, or rate, or both, and explained that I had not received an answer to a letter I had written on this matter to the Rector of Burnsal, asking for such information as a guide to us to what amount it behoved us to subscribe to the funds for the rebuilding of

Rilston Chapel, a question which now assumes a different shape, as we are called on for a subscription towards the restoration of Gargrave Church, |[66] on the ground of our being landed proprietors in that parish in respect of our Scale House farm to a much larger extent than I was aware — Wrote to M[r] Marsden in reply to his letter, requesting a contribution towards the rebuilding of Gargrave Church, expressing our intention to contribute, but declining to state the amount until the enquiries I had made as to the extent of our acreage in his parish & in the Chapelry of Rilston were answered. — Received a letter from my son, who excuses himself, Sophy and Broome from accepting our invitation to visit us this week, as the return of the frost affords them at Stanway the enjoyment of skating, which they might otherwise entirely lose. — Administered the Sacrament of our Lord's Supper privately to Mary Townsend and two of her widow neighbours — M[r] Hayward again called on us; did not find M[rs.] Witts worse; indeed the pulse improved; but privately intimated a wish that if it could be conveniently arranged, we should |[67] before long call in a Physician, he being desirous to have his view of her case confirmed or corrected, as the state of ill health may be of long continuance, and as possibly there may be latent mischief which has escaped his detection. — Visited M. Forty's Father & Sister, and the Gregory's — M[rs.] G. confined to her bed, and seriously ill since yesterday. — Fairfax Correspondence. —

Jan. 8. Tuesday

Snow lies, frost continues — While I was writing to my son in answer to his letter received yesterday, I had a note from M[rs.] Dolphin informing me that she yeilded yesterday to M[r] Haywards's importunities, and had consented to be visited by D[r] Baron in consultation with him to-day; that she expected him and M[r] H. to meet at Eyford at 2 P.M. and supposed I would embrace the opportunity of consulting him on my dear wife's case. Having without much difficulty prevailed on her to admit of a visit from D[r] Baron, I finished my letter to E.F.W. |[68] with the intelligence that he was likely to be here to-day, and wrote to M[rs.] Dolphin and M[r] Hayward, to express how well satisfied we should be to avail ourselves so easily of D[r] Baron's skill — Wrote to M[r] Jackson Clark, to obtain some sovereigns, that I might be prepared with the necessary fee, not having any gold by me in the house, and received a note from him with ten sovereigns by the return of our Servant. — Wrote to M[r] Beman, to whom I sent one of the papers of queries transmitted to me by M[r] Greaves, that he might reply to them, wither directly to the Poor Law Inspector, or by communicating his answers to me that I might embody them with mine — Wrote to M[r] ~~Sader,~~ Sadler expressing the satisfaction it would give me to be allowed to possess myself of a copy of the lithograph portrait of the excellent M[r] Malcolm — Wrote to D[r] Warneford, explaining to him that his letter to me as to the valuable services of the Rural Constabulary had reached |[69] me so ~~that the~~ late that I had not been able to avail myself of its contents at the discussion on the County day in last week; but that the decision then come to had placed the force on such a secure footing that there was no reason to apprehend that it would be crippled or curtailed. — Frederick Aston Jun[r] walked from Little Risington to pay us a morning visit. He is staying there for a day or two with his sisters, and gave a good report of all his family circle. — D[r] Baron came about 4 P.M. from Eyford with M[r] Hayward, and remained for an hour during which he closely investigated my dear wife's case, examined her person &c. — In 1841 and 1842, when she had been suffering much in the same manner as now from derangement of the biliary system, with chronic affection of the kidneys, Dr B. had frequently prescribed, during our visits to Cheltenham; and after mature consideration he now pronounced that he saw no cause for |^{70} serious alarm, no reason to believe there was any organic mischief, nor a worse state of things than when he had before visited his patient He considered her constitution to be delicate, excitable, & liable to nervous irritation, that she was likely to be in indifferent health for some time, that care and watchfulness were very needful, and that the treatment followed by Mr Hayward was so judicious that he should only slightly modify the medicines. – This, of course, was a very comfortable view of the case. GOD grant the good, old skilful doctor may have judged rightly! a considerable burden is taken from off my mind — I understood Dr Baron to express an opinion that he did not consider M$^{rs.}$ Dolphin's life in present danger, but that the cloud of cares and vexations & harassing business in which she is involved tends to render life and health in her case precarious. — Fairfax correspondence. —

Jan. 9. Wednesday.

No change in the weather — |^{71} Wrote to my son, reporting to him the result of Dr Baron's visit yesterday. — Wrote to Howell in answer to a letter received from him some time ago, and acknowledging for MW. a kind letter written by Laura Howell enquiring after her health. — Received a letter from Mr Ward Hunt, son of Mr Geo. Hunt, a circular addressed to me in common with my co-trustees, Thornton and Hare, in which, seeing that an accommodation of matters in dispute appears impracticable on the present footing, he proposes, on his own part, an arbitration on certain conditions with a view to the settlement of the points at issue: but in his scheme he does not include Miss S.B.H. as Executrix of her deceased sister Caroline, which, as we are advised, both by Mess$^{rs.}$ Turner and Bates, and Mr Wood, is an indispensable condition to be insisted on by us. — From Mr Williams I also received a letter with inclosures containing copies of three letters which had |^{72} passed between him and Mr Braikenridge in which the latter had peremptorily refused to recede from any of the statements contained in a case drawn up by him on behalf of his client, which we and our professional advisers considered to be false colouring, and irrelevant. Mr W. argues from this correspondence that to attempt to bring matters to a conclusion by any amicable proceeding is hopeless, and that it only remains for me to file a bill as recommended in the opinion given by Mr Wood. — Mr W. also sends a copy of the letter addressed by him to Mr Whitcombe, accompanying the copy of the case and opinion ~~sent~~ given by Mr Wood, that Mr Whitcombe may consider and report on the same to Miss S. B. Hunt. — I wrote by return of post in reply to Mr Williams, to whom I forwarded the letter received from Mr Ward Hunt, suggesting the propriety of his communicating it to Mr Whitcomb. — To Mr Thornton I also wrote, forwarding to him Mr Williams's |^{73} letters received by me to-day with the enclosures, and also a copy of the letter I had written to Mr Williams in reply. — Received a letter from Grimes, Bookbinder, Cheltenham, correcting an error made in Thursday last when I paid him a bill for work done for me, and for the Stow Book society. — MW. remains very much in the same state as yesterday — Fairfax correspondence.

Jan. 10. — Thursday

No change in the weather; snow on the ground; the roads very slippery — A coal waggon brought us a supply of fuel from Stanway, and I availed myself of the opportunity to write a few lines to inform our children of their dear Mother's state. — It remains much the same, great languor, with drowsiness, high pulse, a pretty good appetite, and no acute pain: the nights disturbed by frequent waking, the result of irritation in the bladder. Mr Hayward called on MW. while I was at Stow. — Drove thither and to the Provident Bank, where I transacted busi-|^{74}ness, meeting Mess$^{rs.}$ Winter, W B Pole, & Wiggin — Transacted business at the office of the Gloucestershire Banking Company — Paying bills — Attended a turnpike meeting, at which Lord Redesdale presided, and which was summoned for the purpose of considering a proposition for a union of turnpike trusts in this neighbourhood, under the provisions of an Act passed in the last sessions of Parliament, which was brought in by Lord Redesdale. — The Dean of Gloucester, Mr Winter, Sir Charles Rushout, Mr W. B. Pole, Mr Ford, Mr Jarrett, and myself attended. The plan proposed was the union of the Foss and Cross district with the Evesham second district, and the district of roads between Chapel House and Bourton on the Hill, all interlacing with one another, all on nearly an equal footing as to materials, debts, management &c., and therefore capable of being managed together more economically than if kept separate. The Trustees were unanimous as to the propriety of the measure; |^{75} and the necessary steps as directed by the Act were taken, so as to complete the union in the time prescribed by the Act. — Visited the Workhouse, where the Guardians were assembled under the chairmanship of Mr Comely, whom I begged to retain his post, as my other engagements precluded my taking the customary lead. — Home by 5 PM. — Received a letter from Mess$^{rs.}$ Sewell and Newmarch, announcing that they had paid to my account with the Gloucestershire Banking Company at Stow £102. 18. 2 being the half year's interest due on Dec. 23. by Mr Lockhart on a mortgage of his property. — A letter from Mess$^{rs.}$ Yorke, bankers at Oundle, announcing that, in conformity with my instructions they had desired their London bankers to pay £130 to the account of Miss S. B. Hunt with Mess$^{rs.}$ Coutts, from the balance standing to my credit on their books, as Executor to the Estate of the late M$^{rs.}$ Mary Hunt. — Two |^{76} circulars reached me from Gloucester, the one announcing a meeting of the Visiting Justices at the Gaol, the other a meeting of the Visitors of the County Lunatic Asylum. — In the evening read a short pamphlet which had been presented to me by Lord Redesdale, being his lately published remarks on regeneration in baptism. The subject is suggested by the proceedings now before the High Court of appeal (the Privy Council) instituted by the Rev$^{d.}$ Gorham against the judgment of the ecclesiastical Judge, Sir H. Jenner Fust, in a case brought before him as to the legality of a decision come to by the Bishop of Exeter, who, having declined to institute Mr Gorham to a benefice in his diocese, to which he had been presented by the Lord Chancellor, justified such refusal on the ground of views as to regeneration in the baptism of infants at variance with the doctrine of the Church of England a set forth in the Articles, and in the liturgy, and other recognized documents of the Church of England. Mr Gorham takes the Calvinistic view of |^{77} the Sacrament of baptism, the Bishop maintains the High Church doctrine, and the Judge in the Doctors Commons, after elaborate arguments by Advocates pro & con, pronounced in favour of the Bishop. From this decision the appeal has been going on for sometime past, very learned and laboured agu arguments being adduced by counsel on both sides, and the decision of the Court is expected on an early day, being awaited with much anxiety. In the meantime Lord R. has applied his vigorous mind, as a layman, to the subject, and comes to the conclusion that the high Church doctrine on the point is clearly, literally & ~~very~~ unequivocally deducible from the texts in Holy Scripture, more especially in the New Testament, bearing on the point. He does not look at the matter as a question of Church doctrine, divinity or antiquity; does not enquire into the authorities or arguments of divines, or schools, or churches; but sifts the texts, compares, and concludes. There may be some-|[78] what fanciful and fine drawn in some of his reasonings, but he makes out his case that the doctrine set forth in the Church formularies is the obvious and fair conclusion to be drawn from the words of Scripture touching the mystery of the new birth; and it is most refreshing & gratifying to see a lay-peer, a busy participator in political debates, a man of business habits, and withal a keen sportsman, grappling with such a subject, admitting its high importance, professing a profound reverence for revelation, acting on a deep faith, and unquestioning reliance on the world of GOD. — M[r] Ford had also given me a short printed address, which he delivered some time ago at South Cerney, on occasion of presenting the Rev[d.] E. N. Mangin, his late curate there, with a service of plate, (tea and coffee &c.) subscribed for by the parishioners. M[r] Mangin has been lately presented by the Bishop of Gloucester ~~with~~ [to] the very populous and important, but inadequately endowed benefice of Horsley in this diocese, under a due |[79] sense of M[r] Mangin's excellent character, and peculiar discretion mingled with zeal in the discharge of ~~his~~ parochial ministrations. Indeed, he well merits a more remunerative position in the church: having conducted the spiritual charge intrusted to him at South Cerney with singular judgment & success. M[r] F. dilates on his many good deeds with a becoming appreciation of his worth, and of the obligation he has conferred on himself as Vicar, and on the parishioners of South Cerney.

Jan 11. Friday.

A continuation of the same cold and wintry weather. — Wrote to Mess[rs.] Sewell and Newmarch acknowledging their letter received yesterday, and the sum remitted by them to my account with the Gloucestershire Banking Company at Stow — Wrote to Mess[rs.] Hitchman, wine & spirit merchants, Chipping Norton with a remittance for brandy supplied by them last summer – Received a letter from Cox & Williams, who returns me M[r] Ward Hunt's circular proposing an arbitration as regards the |[80] Hunt disputes. M[r] Williams thinks it may lead to a settlement, provided the Representatives of Miss M C Hunt are admitted ~~into the~~ [as] parties to the proposed arbitration, and he has sent a copy of M[r] Ward Hunt's letter with remarks to that effect to M[r] Whitcombe — I wrote a line or two to M[r] Thornton, to whom I forwarded the letter just received from Cox & Williams. — A letter arrived from the Office of the Clerk of the Peace, announcing my appointment as one of the Visiting Magistrates of the County Gaol. — From M[r] Pearce I received a letter with particulars of the prices of articles contracted for in our Union for the use of the Workhouse in Dec. 1848 & Dec. 1849; also the number of Persons, inmates of the Stow on the Wold Workhouse, in the first quarter of 1848 & 1849 respectively: these returns I had called for yesterday as data to be used in replying to the queries proposed by M[r] Greaves the Poor Law inspector. — M[r] Winter called with prisoners caught last evening in lawless |[81] plunder of post and railing on Sir Ch. Imhoff's property at Daylesford. Convicted the two depredators, and sentenced them for non payment of penalties to different periods of imprisonment at Northleach House of Correction, with hard labour. — M[r] Winter partook of our luncheon. — M[rs.] R Waller called to enquire after MW. accompanied by one of her boys, and sat sometime with us. — My wife did not seem the worse for receiving these visitors, but remains much the same as for some days past. — Fairfax Correspondence. — Visited the Gregory family.

Jan. 12. Saturday.

A snowy day, with little intermission till the evening; but not a heavy fall — J Lardner, Inspector of Weights and measures, called to solicit a testimonial from me as a candidate for the vacant place of Relieving Officer in the Chipping Norton Union. Wrote a qualified commendation addressed to the Chairman & Guardians; confining myself to his qualifications as conversant with accounts, |[82] and writing a good hand; stating also that his accounts as Inspector of Weights and Measures had passed through my hands for several years, during which he had given satisfaction in that employment. — Received a letter by coal waggon from Stanway from E.F.W. who, with dear Sophy and Broome, proposes to visit us for two nights, coming on Thursday next: replied to this letter. — A letter from Mr Thornton on Hunt Trust matters, with a copy of the reply he has written to Mr Ward Hunt's letter — A letter from Mr Marsden, Vicar of Gargrave, in which he states the amount of acreage of which we are owners in his parish, partly in the Scale House, and partly in the Ravenflatt farms, as a guide to me in respect of the subscription to the rebuilding of the Church at Gargrave, which he seeks to obtain — Wrote to the Messrs. Yorke, Oundle, in answer to their letter received on Thursday; & forwarded to them the Banking Book, containing my account as Executor of the late |[83] M^rs. Mary Hunt, that they may enter up the account and the remittance made to Messrs. Coutts on account of Miss S. B. Hunt — Mr Hayward called on my poor wife: he found her languid, and the pulse intermittent: proposed some change in the medicines, and seemed anxious as to the disturbance of her rest by frequent necessity of leaving her bed to in consequence of irritation of the bladder. — Fairfax correspondence.

Jan. 13. Sunday.

A severe frost, with an East wind: very cold, slippery, and pinching; the snow on the ground will protect vegetation — The illness of the Schoolmistress prevents the children assembling in the Sunday School. — Morning service, prayers: afternoon, prayers and sermon. I preached on "GOD the giver of all good things." — Received a letter from W. Ayrton, our tenant at Scale House, with particulars of Gargrave and Rilston, the amount of tithe payable in each, the amount |[84] of poor rates to which the farm is assessed in each &c. He presses for a reduction of rent. — Miss C Knight writes from Tanfield, Mr Hutchinson's, in answer to a letter from me respecting the state of M^rs. Dolphin written some weeks since: it seems that M^rs. D. in correspondence, or by her amanuensis, Mary Anne Ryan, has exaggerated expressions which have fallen from me in my interviews with M^rs. D., making it appear that I greatly blame Capt. Frobisher and Miss Knight as to certain transactions of the one, and assumed neglect on the part of the other. Miss K. writes to explain. It is a peculiarly delicate position to be placed in, as Clergyman to administer the consolations of religion to one in great distress both of mind, body and estate, and to be obliged to hear half confidences, ex parte[5] statements and complaints, and yet not at liberty to argue, to remonstrate, or

---

5.   Ex parte – on behalf of or with reference to only one of the parties concerned.

undeceive, since any attempt so to do would agitate, and irritate one so seriously ill, as regards bodily health, and so decidedly |[85] unpersuadable. — A letter from M[r] Hare on Hunt Trust business, with reference to the documents lately forwarded to him by M[r] Thornton, and which I had sent to the letter, and also to the "circular" lately written to the Trustees by M[r] Ward Hunt, and the answer he [(Hare)] has made to the same — A letter from C Bathurst as to the late proceedings at the Quarter Sessions with reference to the Constabulary. — Preparing a Sermon — Eccl. Gazette. ——

Jan. 14. Monday.

Very severe frost, and boisterous East wind; exceedingly cold weather. — M[r] Comely called by appointment, with whom I conferred on the condition of the labouring class within this union, with reference to the replies which are sought to the queries sent to me by M[r] Greaves, the Poor Law Inspector. — Justice business at home. — Wrote to Miss Knight in answer to her letter rec[d.] yesterday. — Wrote to M[r] Marsden |[86] with a cheque on the Craven Bank for £5. as my contribution to the restoration of the Church at Gargrave. — Examining the banking account forwarded to me by the Bankers at Settle, which I found correct. — Expected a visit from M[r] Hayward, but he failed us. I fancied I observed some improvement in M.W's health. — M[r] Boggis called on us. — Visited and prayed with M[rs.] Rogers, who seems to continue in the same state. — Fairfax Correspondence.

Jan. 15. Tuesday.

Frost continues, but less cold than yesterday. — Wrote to M[r.] W. Ayrton in answer to his letter received from him on Sunday last. — Received a letter from M[r.] Mullings, informing me that the 31[st.] Inst. will suit him and M[r] Winterbotham for a meeting of the Committee of accounts, to deliberate on the bills of the Clerk of the Peace, the scale of allowance of such bills, and other county charges to be revised by the Committee. He had communicated to the |[87] same effect with the County Chairman, Curtis Hayward, and M[r] Bloxsome. I replied, expressing a readiness to keep the appointment made, and that I would write to M[r] Riddiford suggesting that M[r] B. Hunt, M[r] G. Parry, M[r] Baker, and M[r] Lysons should also have notice of the meeting. — Wrote to Riddiford with comments on the business to be done at the proposed meeting on the 31[st.] desiring that the other members of the Comm. of acc[ts.] should have notice to attend &c. — I have omitted to mention a letter received from M[r.] Murray Browne, the Bishop of Gloucester's Chaplain on Monday —; he writes to me in consequence of a letter addressed to him by M[r] Ford on Thursday last, in answer to one received from M.B. that day, announcing that a deputation from the Society for the Propagation of the gospel is about to make a circuit through the diocese, with the approval of the Bishop, and to |[88] be attended by M.B. as on a former occasion two years ago. The deputation will probably consist of the under Secretary of the Institution, M[r] Vernon, accompanied by M[r] Pope, the Missionary of the Society in the province of Tinivelly, in Southern India, of whose successful labours in forming a church of Oriental converts we have heard so much, and who is so justly esteemed for zeal combined with discretion. Being now in England, the Society are making him available for enlarging its sphere of action, engaging him as a powerful advocate. Ford, being about to leave home, desired MB. to correspond with me, as Secretary of the District Comm.

S.P.G., that the necessary arrangements may be made. Friday Feb. 1. is the day fixed by MB. for a mid-day meeting at Stow; and it will devolve on me to arrange that details. The illness of my poor wife precludes my offering the hospitality of my house; but Ford would receive the party, if they could avail themselves |[89] of his invitation; but it is likely that they will come from a distant point to Stow, & proceed thence the same day to an evening meeting at Moreton, holding a meeting on the following day at Campden. — I omitted also to ~~ment~~ mention another letter received on Monday from Mess[rs.] Hitchman & C[o.] Chipping Norton, acknowledging the receipt of a cheque which I had forwarded to them — M[r] Hayward called, and cheered me by noticing some improvement in MW's health; symptoms rather more favourable — Walked to Eyford, to call on M[rs.] Dolphin; but, finding that M[rs.] Kirby and her daughter were there, and also the steward, M[r] Paxton, with a gentleman on business, and judging that M[rs.] Dolphin had been much occupied, and that my visit had better be deferred, I returned without seeing any of the parties — Visited M[r] & M[rs.] Davis; settled my half-yearly account with them as to rent &c. — Visited M[rs.] Gregory, very ill, and |[90] confined to her bed with an attack of influenza — read prayers in her sick chamber. — Fairfax Correspondence. —

Jan. 16. Wednesday.

The weather rather less severe: frost with a N.W. wind; a thick atmosphere; in the evening sleet or very fine snow fell. — Wrote to M[r] Graves,[6] Poor Law Inspector, forwarding to him the answers I had prepared to his circular of queries as to the present condition of the labouring classes, so far as regards those in the Stow on the Wold Union — Wrote to C Bathurst in answer to his letter received on Sunday — Also to M[r] Turner, Treasurer to the Gloucester Infirmary, with a cheque for £16. 16. 0, being the amount of annual subscriptions for 1850, from myself and my wife, the Upper Slaughter and Stanway Charities, and the Stow on the Wold Union. — Received a letter from M[r] Hare, who returns to me letters from Cox and Williams, which I had forwarded to M[r] Thornton for his perusal, and which he had sent on to M[r] Hare. — Visited sick |[91] and aged parishioners — Mary Forty, M[rs.] Jos. Collett, Widow Townsend, Matt. Davis — MW. does not appear so well to day as yesterday: she suffers from greater difficulty of breathing — Fairfax Correspondence.

Jan. 17. Thursday.

Frost, snow on the ground: very wintry weather — After breakfast wrote a note to M[r] Hayward, begging his early attendance on MW. whose difficulty of breathing was much increased. But his engagements prevented his arrival till between 2 and 3 P.M. when he pronounced her to be suffering from an attack of influenza, supervening on the complaints which have been disordering her, the Bronchial tubes being much impeded and respiration painfully obstructed. This new disease, originating in the severe winterly weather, the air being bitterly cold with East wind and fog or rime, penetrating every chamber, is calculated to cause much alarm, her constitution being greatly enfeebled by previous disease. Resort was immediately had to the application |[92] of a mustard plaister to the chest, which did not seem to give much relief; other medicines were prescribed and procured from

---

6.   *Sic.* Previously used spelling is Greaves.

Stow, and administered in the course of the evening. But the poor sufferer was greatly oppressed, and exceedingly lethargic; & though sitting up till the usual hour of rest, and enjoying the society of our Son and daughter, and our Grandson Broome, who arrived to dinner, she was very distressingly harassed in her breathing, with a high pulse and much appearance of distress in the countenance. — I determined on not going to Stow, as usual, on Thursday, making public business give way to private duty and anxiety. — I occupied myself in preparing a letter in reply to the circular addressed to me and my Co-Trustees by M<u>ʳ Ward Hunt</u>; and having received a "private" letter from M<u>ʳ Thornton</u> on the subject of our Trust business, with intimations from him as to the bad state of Mʳ Geo. Hunt both in bodily & |⁹³ mental health, as also in respect of the course taken by ~~Geor~~ Ward Hunt, the correspondence between Messʳˢ· Cox and Williams & Mʳ Braikenridge &c., I determined on sending the sketch of my proposed answer to Ward Hunt for his (Thornton's) perusal and comments thereon, which I despatched by the post. — Wrote also to M<u>ʳ Bury</u>, the Incumbent of Burnsal, that we proposed to subscribe £15 towards the restoration of Rilstone Chapel, desiring to know to whom and when I should remit a cheque to that amount — Wrote to <u>W. Ayrton</u>, acknowledging his letter as to the acreage of his farm in Gargrave & Rilstone, and referring him to Mʳ Geldard on the next rent day, for any deduction on his rent which might then appear just — Wrote a note to M<u>ʳ Clark</u> at the Bank, Stow, to whom I forwarded, to be placed to my credit in that establishment, the cheque I had received from J. Davis. — Great enjoyment in seeing my darling school-|⁹⁴ boy, who is everything that can be desired at his age – His younger brothers are left at Stanway quite well. Their parents very affectionate to me and my poor wife, whose state appears very precarious.

Jan. 18. Friday

Snow fell during the forenoon and afternoon; rain followed towards evening with a thaw. — No improvement in my dear wife's health: the remedies applied yesterday do not seem to have succeeded in reducing the irregularity of the pulse, or relieving the impeded respiration — She continued in a very suffering, exhausted state; chiefly confined to her bed till towards dinner time, receiving her dear children, her grandchild and myself more or less in the sick chamber. Mʳ Hayward also paid his visit, prescribed a blister, and changed the medicine. In the evening we all passed some time in the sick chamber. — A very anxious and trying day. — Several parties called on Justice business — |⁹⁵ William Vavasour rode from Stow with enquiries on the part of the other members of his family, written and verbal. — Mʳ and Mʳˢ· C Pole and others sent enquiries after our dear invalid. — <u>Miss Sophia Hunt</u> wrote a letter of kind enquiry, not mixed up with business. — From M<u>ʳ Thornton</u> ᵍⁱᵛᵉˢ a further expression of his opinion as to our present position in respect of the Hunt Trust, in sending for my perusal a letter received by him from Mʳ Hare. — M<u>ʳ Riddiford</u> replied to my letter as to a meeting of the Committee of accounts on the 31ˢᵗ· Inst. saying that the County Chairman has instructed him to call such meeting on the 28ᵗʰ· Inst, which he hopes will suit me as well. I expect to receive a further communication from Mʳ R. on county business to be transacted at the meeting of such committee — A letter from M<u>ʳ Pearce</u>, who sends me a copy of the answers sent by Mʳ Beman to the Queries proposed by Mʳ Graves, Poor |⁹⁶ law Inspector — From M<u>ʳ Graves</u> I received a few lines acknowledging the receipt of my answers to those queries.

— From the <u>Lunatic Asylum Gloucester</u> I received a notice of a meeting of Visitors fixed for Jan 28th. which leads me to think there must be some mistake as to that day being appointed for a meeting of the committee of accounts. — Transacting Provident Bank business with W. Gregory. — My children are a great comfort to me and their mother by their tender and affectionate solicitude about us in this time of serious illness and apprehension.

Jan 19. Saturday

The thaw continues — When Mr Hayward visited our patient he observed some improvement in the pulse and respiration, but the blister had not risen well, and was again applied, but with hardly more result. Still the breath was somewhat relieved, and the drowsiness less. MW. did not leave her bed till 3 P.M. or her chamber at all during the day. The same medicine as |⁹⁷ yesterday repeated, and the weakness not so extreme. My dear children and Broome remained with us till near 3 P.M. then returning to Stanway, and promising to revisit us next week, as circumstances may suggest. — Sophy replied to a kind note of enquiry which I received from <u>Mrs. Winter</u>, and E.F.W. to the letter I had received yesterday from <u>Sophia Hunt</u>. — A letter from the <u>Gaol, Gloucester</u>, with the announcement of a meeting of Visiting Justices on the 24th. Inst. — Spent the Evening for the most part in the sick chamber: my poor wife sitting up, and liking to hear me read aloud, and taking interest in the Fairfax correspondence.

Jan. 20. Sunday

A very hard frost, with a keen N.E. wind, and very cold air. — Mr Hayward called as I was going to the evening service, so that I missed seeing him; but he considered that my poor wife was better, the respiration being improved. |⁹⁸ There appeared, indeed, greater strength, and she sat up in tolerable comfort, though at times very drowsy, from 3 P.M. till bed-time. It had been judged better that I should sleep in another room, and that MW's maid sh^{d.} occupy a bed in the dressing room, an arrangement which saved me, as my rest had been more or less disturbed by my wife's restless nights. — Morning service — prayers and sermon; I preached on "GOD the giver of ^{all} good things," 2^{d.} part. Afternoon service, prayers — Letters received were from <u>C Bathurst</u> on the proposed taxation of the bills of the Clerk of the Peace, and other economical reforms to be undertaken by the Committee of accounts: – he sends for my perusal and consideration a letter he has received from Mr Clifford MP. chairman of the Herefordshire Quarter Sessions, on the proceedings of our county magistrates in the way of reduction &c. at the last Quarter Sessions, with his view of the questions raised as to |⁹⁹ the payment of the bills of the Clerk of the Peace, salary to that officer &c. — <u>Somebody</u> has sent me, without any indication of the name of the author, or other means of conjecturing as to the donor, a newly published book, a 12mo., entitled "Letters to a Niece" — about half of which I read, and found it to be a very shrewd, judicious, right-minded view of the line to be taken in society, at home, in respect of education, accomplishments, employment and conversation ~~of~~ ^{by} young ladies in the better classes of life. — From <u>Purnell</u> I received a basket of wild fowl, a kind remembrance at this season. — From <u>Riddiford</u> a letter on business to be brought before the Committee of accounts on the 28th. Inst. chiefly as to advertizing for tenders for printing, and clothing of the Rural Police —— From the <u>Lunatic Asylum</u>, Gloucester, a circular notifying that the meeting of Visitors which had been fixed for the |[100] 28th. Inst. is postponed till the 30th. — From Mr. Marsden an acknowledgment of my cheque for £5. as our contribution towards the rebuilding of the Church at Gargrave; he seems well satisfied with what we have done, and approves of our subscribing in a larger proportion towards the restoration of Rilstone Chapel. —

Jan. 21. Monday

Hard frost, and Easterly wind. Snow fell in the afternoon, but not heavily — MW. continues in much the same state as yesterday: there may be a slight improvement in respiration, but great languor and drowsiness. Hayward visited her at midday, and partook of luncheon with me: he considered his patient to be slowly mending. A removal from the sick chamber at present not to be expected — A servant from Stanway brought a note of enquiry from E.F.W. who reached home well on Saturday with his dear wife and child, but found Freddy somewhat ailing. It is to be hoped that a little |[101] medicine will set all right. — Replied to this note with a hope expressed that the loved trio will visit us again on Thursday next; if there be no occasion to summon them sooner, which GOD grant there may not be! — Wrote to Purnell, to thank him for his present of wild fowl, and to explain how I am now circumstanced, but that if I should be unable to attend on the Committee of Accounts on the 28th. I will take care to forward such documents as may assist the members in their deliberations. — Answered Riddiford's letter received yesterday, to the same effect as regards the doubt about my attendance on the Committee of accounts; gave some hints as to advertizing for tenders for printing, and clothing for the constabulary — Wrote to Lane, printer, Stow, to prepare him to be ready to execute some printing to-morrow, as soon as I shall be able to furnish him with copies of notes and handbills announcing a special meeting at Stow of |[101] the District Committee S.P.G. — Received a letter from Bathurst on Ricardo's proposition for an auditor of the County accounts — It now appears that the "unknown" author of "Letters to a niece" is Bathurst: I suspected this yesterday, detecting his views and turn of mind in the book. — Fairfax Correspondence — Justice business at home. Two of my parishioners, Benfield and H. Gardner, charged on suspicion of stealing peas, while thrashing that grain for their employer. I fear it is true; but the case is not clear: I referred the business to R. Waller.

Jan. 22. Tuesday

A frost in the morning: in the afternoon it thawed gently. — Wrote to E.F.W. with a report of his mother's state, in wh. we detected improvement, and Hayward, when he called, considered she was better. Still there is oppression in breathing, feebleness, drowsiness, and intermittent pulse with a foul tongue — Received a letter from Mrs. Dolphin of Hallow, Worcestershire, the mother of the |[102] unworthy Vicar of Lower Guiting, whose wife has opened a preparatory school for boys at Clifton, and in which her husband is to teach Latin & Writing, the eldest child being sent to a commercial school near Bristol; Mrs. Dolphin Senr wishes me to intercede with the Bishop that part of the proceeds of the sequestered benefice may be applied towards the education of the son. — I forwarded this letter to Ford, desiring him, if he thought right, to state the case to the Bishop, as Rural Dean, saying that I consider the expediency of the proceeding of opening a school in the diocese as very doubtful, and have no intention of going out of my way to advocate the cause of the family, my connection with the affair having ceased, when the Commissioners had concluded the Enquiry. I shall await M͏ͬ Ford's answer before I reply to M͏ʳˢ· Dolphin's letter. I also communicated to Ford the contents of the letter I had received from Murray Browne as to the |¹⁰³ proposed special meeting of the district committee S.P.G. at which he is to attend at Stow with a deputation. — Not having received another letter from M. Browne, with further information as to this intended meeting, and the time being short, I wrote to the printer, <u>Lane</u>, with copies of notes and handbills announcing such meeting for Feb. 1. to be printed by him and put in circulation by me in the usual manner. — Wrote also to <u>R W Hippisley</u>, who, when Murray Browne first communicated on the subject with Ford, was absent from home, to inform him of the design of holding a meeting at Stow, and of the arrangements in progress. — Rec͏ᵈ· a letter from a <u>M͏ͬ Charles Wordsworth</u>, Paper Buildings, Temple, saying it had been reported that I meant to sell the Scale House property, and wishing, if it were so, to know the price. — Replied to this <u>M͏ͬ Wordsworth</u> that no such intention had ever been entertained by us. — Set out for Eyford, |¹⁰⁴ with the intention of calling on M͏ʳˢ· Dolphin, but met her servant by the way, bringing a bottle of Sirop de Guimauve (Mallows) as a present from her to my wife, — a mucilaginous compound healing to one suffering from hoarseness, I presume — and bearing also a message that she was more indisposed, and could not see me if I thought of visiting her to-day. <u>I wrote a few lines</u>, thanking her for her kind remembrance of MW. — Wrote to <u>Turner</u>, Fishmonger, London, for a barrel of Oysters. — Justice business at home. — Visited sick parishioners — M͏ʳˢ· Gregory, and M͏ʳˢ· Rogers, with both of whom I prayed, & M͏ʳˢ· Collett — Fairfax Correspondence. —

Jan. 23. Wednesday

Mild weather, and very fine winter day. — M͏ͬ Hayward visited MW. and considered that her state is slowly improving. Same medicine continued, and no removal from the chamber. The languor and drowsiness still subsist. |¹⁰⁵ Transacting business with the tax collector — Received a letter from <u>Bathurst</u>, — merely a line or two, desiring me to forward to M͏ͬ Clifford MP., in town, the letter he had written to me before the Epiphany Sessions on the remuneration of the Clerk of the Peace. — <u>This I did</u>, requesting Col. Clifford to return the letters to me by Saturday's Post, that I many receive them in time to take with me to Gloucester, should I be able to attend a meeting of the Committee of accounts there on the 28ᵗʰ· — Received a letter from <u>R W Hippisley</u>, in answer to mine addressed to him yesterday. — A letter from <u>M͏ͬ Thornton</u> with further, but not final thoughts as to the answer to be sent by me to Ward Hunt. — A note from <u>M͏ʳˢ· Dolphin</u>, who wished to see me to-day: and accordingly I walked to Eyford, and had a long interview with her, in her bed; prayed with her; entered at length on many subjects serious and of a business nature. She is in a very suffering |¹⁰⁶ excitable state: professes great anxiety for my poor wife, to whom she sends a religious work, one of ~~which~~ D͏ͬ Baron's recommendation — "Winslow on Grace and Truth" — a modern publication — Repairs in the house at Eyford are in progress — While I was absent M͏ͬ Vavasour called, but could not wait my return: he walked to enquire after MW. — Fairfax Correspondence.

Jan 27. Thursday[7]

Weather very ~~wet~~, ^moist^ as far as relates to thaw, without rain, roads very heavy. — MW. continues much as yesterday: there may be a slight improvement, but languor and drowsiness continue; the respiration more free. — I went to Stow. — To the Provident Bank, where at a later hour I met Winter and W. B. Pole, with Lewes. — Presided till 3 P.M. at the fortnightly meeting of the Guardians of the Union, with the usual amount of business. — Received letters from Miss Knight with very kind enquiries after |[107] my dear wife — From Messrs. Hoare, who announce that Lady Wilmot Horton has paid to my account with them £194. 3. 4, as half yearly interest on mortgage, less income tax. — From Lefroy with an enquiry after MW., and mentioning the need there is that measures be taken by the County for the supply of clothing for the constabulary — From Ford, with kind enquiries as to my poor wife's health: he returns the letter received by me from M^rs. Dolphin, of Hallow, and concurs with me in opinion as to its contents. — From T. Turner, Treasurer to the Gloucester Infirmary, who sends me receipts for the different Infirmary subscriptions, the amount of which I had remitted to him. — Capt. Irvine R.N. called upon me at the Workhouse, and expressed his intention of paying me a visit on Saturday, to confer with me respecting the terms on which he is with his wife, and the trust in which I am concerned as to the settlement |[108] made twenty seven years ago on his marriage with Miss Reade: — he is feeble & deaf, as may be expected at nearly fourscore, but energetic, and now staying for a short time at his relation's, Mr Chamberlayne's house at Maugersbury, for change of air — My dear son and daughter with my eldest grandson arrived from Stanway to dinner, and their presence was a great comfort to me. Part of the evening was spent in the sick room, and the invalid was much pleased to receive them.

Jan. 25. Friday

For the most part a fine open winter's day, towards the evening a little rain fell. — Mr Hayward's visit was satisfactory: he reported favourably of the progress of his patient, and considered that the bronchial mischief was nearly removed, while other symptoms were relieved. MW. took great pleasure in visits from her children and grandson frequently thro'out the day. — Dispatched a messenger with |[109] notes and handbills announcing to the members of the Stow district committee S.P.G. and to others the intended special meeting at Stow on Feb. 1. when a deputation from the Parent Society is expected to attend. — Wrote to Murray Browne, sending him one of the handbills, and so acquainting him with the arrangements made — Wrote to Lefroy, in answer to his letter received yesterday — Received Letters from Mr Thornton and Mr Hare, with enclosures as to the pending proceedings and correspondence arising out of the circular of Mr Ward Hunt, and other ~~the~~ matters connected with the T. W. Hunt Trust. — E.F.W. and Sophy drove to Stow after luncheon to pass an hour at "the Cottage"; going in our carriage, and returning to dinner — I walked out with my lovely grandson, and called on sick parishioners, M^rs. Rogers and M^rs. Gregory — Mr Boggis called to enquire after my wife, and sat |[110] some time with me. — While I was out M^r and M^rs. Pole called to make enquiries. — E.F.W. was kind enough to reply for me to a letter I had received some time since from F. Aston, and to report as to the

---

7.   A dating error; it was 24 January 1850.

health of his mother; while dear <u>Sophy</u> undertook to answer the letter I received yesterday from <u>Miss Knight</u>. — Greatly enjoyed the society of my dear children, and grandson, in the dining room, and in the invalid's apartment. —

Jan. 26. Saturday

Some rain fell once or twice during the day, much having fallen during the night: the evening was frosty. — A decided improvement in the state of my dear wife: she being much less feeble and faint, and the breath less oppressed, yet still weak and restless at night. — Wrote to Messrs. Hoare, desiring them to transfer £50 from my account with them to that of my Son. — Received a letter from Mr. Thornton on Hunt Trust |[111] business; he encloses for my perusal a letter he has received from Mr Tilleard — — A letter from <u>Col. Clifford</u> MP. who returns me the letters from C. Bathurst which I had forwarded for his perusal — Mr Ford called, and partook of our luncheon, conferring with me on the meeting of the District Comm. S.P.G. at Stow fixed for Friday next, and on Justice business — Captain Irvine also called upon me, and joined our party at luncheon, after an interview with me on the subject of his marriage Settlement, his dissentions with his wife, his grievances, his Son's past life and future prospects, and relations subsisting between him and his wife &c. — The conclusion forced upon me, and corresponding with the impression conveyed by a former conference several years ago, is that the poor man labours under a strange delusion as to his intercourse with his wife, amounting to a monomania — that the match was most unhappy, — |[112] that on both sides there have been bad temper, and unsoundness of mind, and on the lady's part want of principle and extravagant notions as to the rights of women, with a rooted dislike of & contempt for her husband: she has used him and her son ill; and deserves the annoyances which her own strange course have in great measure brought upon her. Feeble, & deaf, and strange in manner, barring the delusions under which he labours, the old man has a sort of talent, information, and observation, rendering him not an unpleasant companion when abstracted from the matters which irritate his mind. — E.F.W., Sophy, and Broome left us for Stanway between 3 & 4 P.M. having been for two days a great comfort to us. — M^r and Mrs. Hurd very kindly sent their son to call on me with friendly enquiries as to Mrs. W.'s health. — Fairfax Correspondence. |

1

Diary
1850

Jan. 27. Sunday — A very hard frost. ——
Morning service, prayers; afternoon service,
prayers and sermon. I preached on "God, the
giver of all good things" — third part ——
Mr. Hayward called in the forenoon, and
visited MW. who, though weak, seemed
freer from obstruction in breathing, stronger
than of late, still drowsy, and the legs being
somewhat swollen indicate debility. ——
Received a letter from Mr. Whitcombe with
a paper of proposals for an arbitration of the
matters in dispute arising out of the Estate
of T. W. Kent. He has forwarded these proposals to Cox & Williams, and to Brauken-
ridge; and thus a hope is renewed that we
may see an end of this controversy. ——
Wrote to Mr. Thornton, to whom I forwarded
Mr. Whitcombe's letter with the proposals,
as also a copy of a letter which I wrote to
Ward Hunt, in which I assumed that an

Witts Family Papers F367

Diary
1850

Jan. 27. Sunday

A very hard frost. — Morning service; prayers; afternoon service, prayers and sermon. I preached on "GOD, the giver of all good things" — third part — Mr Hayward called in the forenoon, and visited MW. who, though weak, seemed freer from obstruction in breathing, stronger than of late, still drowsy, and the legs being somewhat swollen indicate debility. — Received a letter from Mr Whitcombe with a paper of proposals for an arbitration of the matters in dispute arising out of the Estate of T. W. Hunt. He has forwarded these proposals to Cox & Williams, and to Braikenridge, and thus a hope is renewed that we may see an end of this controversy. — Wrote to Mr Thornton, to whom I forwarded Mr Whitcombe's letter with the proposals, as also a copy of a letter which I wrote to Ward Hunt, in which I assumed that an l[2] arbitration being now assented to by the Representatives of the late life-tenant, as well as by himself and the trustees, there would be a readiness to agree upon the terms of the reference, and to proceed in it without delay. — Winslow's "Grace and Truth." —

Jan. 28. Monday.

Very boisterous and stormy, and wet weather, especially in the morning: but not much rain in the forenoon & afternoon — MW. appearing pretty well, I left home after an early breakfast for Cheltenham, where I arrived in my open carriage by ten o clock, and went thence by train to Gloucester, where I had an appointment to meet other Magistrates on the Committee of accounts — Reached the Shire Hall by 11 AM. where I found Messrs. Purnell, C. Hayward, Gambier Parry, Lysons, Brooke Hunt, Mullings and Winterbotham. Presided at this meeting till half past three P.M. the subjects under deliberation being the rate of remuneration to the Clerk of the Peace for his numerous & various services l[3] generally, as also for other services performed as Attorney — the machinery of the Registration of voters for the two divisions of the County, and the cost thereof as payable out of the County Rates, and charged to the County by the Clerk of the Peace: into ~~those~~ this matter we went minutely, and the probable result of our enquiries will be a saving of considerable amount on this department of business particularly, if not on the other general bills of the Clerk of the Peace. We further decided on advertising for tenders for the printing required for the County transactions, and on advertising for tenders for the Clothing of the Rural Constabulary. — Left Gloucester by the train for Cheltenham at 4 P.M., not having been brought into contact with the Bishop or his Chaplain, Murray Browne, or others who had been assembled at a meeting on behalf of the Society for the Propagation of the Gospel holden to-day at the Tolsey, at which the |⁴ Revᵈ· G. M. Pope & Mᵣ Vernon, one of the Secretaries of the Parent Society, attended as a deputation, and who are to visit us at Stow on the 1ˢᵗ· of February. — I travelled to Cheltenham, as I had from thence in the morning to Gloucester, with W. P. Price, our High Sheriff. — Called at the Police Station, where I conferred with Lefroy and Keiley on the advertising for tenders for clothing &c. for the Constabulary — I afterwards partook of some refreshment at Lefroy's lodgings, whence I set out soon after 5 P.M. for Upper Slaughter, arriving at home by half past seven o clock — Found my dear wife rather more languid to-day than yesterday, but in main points probably in a satisfactory state of progress.

Jan. 29. Tuesday.

A fine open day. — Mᵣ Hayward called, and was satisfied with the condition of his patient, who seems slowly gaining ground; but is still very languid, with restless nights, and exceedingly drowsy in the evening. The pulse fuller, and less inter-|⁵ mittent. — Wrote to E.F.W, with a report of his mother's health. — Received a formal announcement of the death of poor Lady Wemyss at Gosford on the 26ᵗʰ· Inst. officially forwarded, as it would appear, by the Undertaker. A good, kindhearted woman, an excellent wife and mother, and one who has gone through many trials, and placed her trust in GOD through Jesus Christ, is thus removed from the world. — A letter from Miss S. B. Hunt, partly with enquiries as to my dear wife's state, and partly on Hunt Trust business &c. — A circular from the Gaol at Gloucester, announcing a meeting of Visiting Justices for Feb. 4. — MW. received a letter from Mʳˢ· Geldard enquiring after her health: the intelligence of her illness seems to have reached Craven. — A letter from Messʳˢ· Hoare announces that they have transferred £50 from my acctᵗ· with them to that of my son. — Mᵣ Ford came by appointment to transact some justice |⁶ business here — the commitment of a wretched man charged with an offence against nature — The Rural Dean brought his wife and daughter Dulcy with him, but MW. felt unequal to receive them in the sick room — Mᵣ and Mʳˢ· W. B. Pole, with Mʳˢ· W. Vavasour rode to make personal enquiries as to my wife's health, but did not dismount. — Fredᵏ· Aston Junᵣ came for the same purpose from Northleach with kind remembrances from his parents, and partook of luncheon with me. — I should have mentioned on Sunday a kind visit received by me from W. Perkins and his niece, calling with like friendly enquiries. I am happy to say they were able to give a comfortable report of the state of the worthy Vicar of Lower Swell, who has been for the past week in a very precarious state from an attack of Typhus fever; he is now pronounced out of danger. He has been very skilfully treated by Hayward — Visited my parishioner, Mʳˢ· Gregory, |⁷ still very much indisposed, and prayed with her. — Fairfax Correspondence. —

Jan. 30. Wednesday.

Fine, open weather. — MW. much in the same state as for two or three days past, with somewhat more power, and less drowsiness, but still languid, and the voice weak. — Wrote to Lady Jane Charteris a letter of condolence on the death of Lady Wemyss. — To Rodwell, Bookseller, London, to order books for the Stow Book Society. — To Mᵣ Hutchinson, Batsford, in answer to a letter received from him to-day, in which he asks for information from me, as far as I can give it, as to the movements of the deputation of the S.P.G. now on their circuit through the diocese, particularly as to their appointments after the proposed meeting at Stow on Friday. H. appears not to have been fully instructed on these points by <u>Murray Browne</u>, — from whom I received a letter, announcing that the deputation |⁸ purpose to be at Stow by mid day, and to hold an evening meeting at Campden on Friday. — Justice business at home. — To Eyford, where called on Mrs. Dolphin, still confined to her room, but, perhaps, not so ill as she imagines, or would appear; very much engaged in perplexing business, but her energy carrying her into various matters; expressing great anxiety about my poor wife and sending her ~~variou~~ nice comforts suited to an invalid. Our conversation a melange of serious and sacred topics, with communications on business matters, advice as to everyday occurrences &c. — Wrote to the Coachmaker, <u>Garratt</u>, at Cheltenham, whether he can, and if he can, on what terms he would supply Mrs. D. with a Brougham on hire. — Fairfax Correspondence —

Jan. 31. Thursday

A sharp frost, soon yeilding to thaw, with thick fog, and in the afternoon and evening heavy rain. — My wife much as yesterday, but restless and |⁹ sleepy in the evening. I had left home before Hayward visited her; but I understood him to be satisfied with her progress, and that the pulse was improved. — Wrote to <u>Mrs. Dolphin</u>, Hollow, in answer to a letter received from her several days since, respecting her miserable son's family, declining to intrude on the Bishop with any proposition on their part — To Stow — Received a letter from <u>Mr Hutchinson</u>, whose arrangements are now made plain, as to the visit of the deputation of S.P.G. to Campden, by a letter he had received from Murray Browne. — A letter from <u>Mr Thornton</u> on Hunt Trust affairs, arbitration &c. he returns letters which I had sent for his perusal. — A letter from <u>Mr Wiggin</u>, from the Deanery at Gloucester, with inquiries after MW's health. Sir John Reade has relinquished his opposition to W's scheme of building a new church at Oddington, so that the project is likely to |¹⁰ be executed without uneasy strife — Called at the Rectory on the Hippisleys, and made arrangements with the Rector of Stow to receive the deputation at luncheon to-morrow. — Attended at the Provident Bank, where met Mr Pole, W B Pole, Morrison, Ford &c. — With Ford as my colleague sat from 2 to 4 P.M. as Magistrate at the Justice room — engaged also in hearing appeals to the Assessed Taxes charges — Fairfax Correspondence. —

Feb. 1. Friday.

A finer day than yesterday, damp, but not rainy: high wind. — Preparing for the special meeting S.P.G. at Stow to-day. — Drove thither; called at the Rectory, where met Ford, who had come to preside at the meeting, as Rural Dean; we were joined by Messrs. Vernon, one of the Secretaries of the Parent Society, and Mr Pope, Missionary in the district of Tinivelly in the Diocese of Madras. — With them partook of luncheon at M^r |¹¹ Hippisley's. Had expected to meet Murray Browne, but he has not latterly accompanied the deputation. The meeting was called for half past one, but the chair was not taken by Mr Ford till 2 P.M. – Twelve or fourteen clergymen of the district attended, no layman of the higher class, very few of the inferior sort, half a dozen ladies, wives & daughters of clergymen, a few females, from Stow and its vicinity, of the better sort, and a score of children, chiefly the upper class of the school at Risington, brought by the Ford family. This small attendance augers very ill for the missionary zeal of the neighbourhood: in good truth, the apathy and indifference on such subjects are great and discreditable. It must also be allowed, that the weather & season are very unpropitious for such meetings and that illness is very prevalent. Mr Vernon, being much indisposed, was not able to address the company at much length, but what he said was to the purpose and |^{12} well delivered. Mr Pope's address was long and exceedingly interesting, detailing his experience for ten years as a Missionary in Southern India; he is by descent of Wesleyan origin; calm, composed, measured in tone, rather too low in voice, but very fluent, very impressive, very clear in his explanations. He first drew a picture of the horrible superstitions of Hindooism, their wretched immorality and gross abominations, their doctrine of fatalism, metempsychosis, and absorption into the Deity: the grossness of the idolatry practised, and the crimes to which it leads as Suttee, Thuggism, and Infanticide. On the other hand he laid before us the churches of Southern India, how, one by one, individuals, families, villages come over to the true faith; how carefully, methodically, laboriously, they are educated, trained, and instructed: and how, by degrees, a net work of Christian parishes may be spread over Southern India if only the efforts be continued, more and more |^{13} Missionaries, Catechists and Schoolmasters be sent. Mr Pope is evidently a talented, and earnest, and practical man; he is come home for two years to recruit his health. — I proposed a vote of thanks to the deputation, which was followed by one acknowledging the services of the Chairman, our Rural Dean, and the meeting separated, £6. 13. 10½ having been collected at the door in aid of the general purposes of the Society. Soon afterwards Mr Vernon and Mr Pope proceeded to Campden, where they are to be present at an evening meeting, over which Hutchinson is to preside. — I returned home by 5 P.M. — A letter from Lefroy as to the Uniform and clothing of the Rural Constabulary, and advertising for tenders for the different articles used. — MW. seems to gain but little ground towards recovery: certainly there is more of power, and the respiration is much relieved: but there remains great debility, with drowsiness. — |^{14} Fairfax correspondence. — I omitted yesterday to mention the birth-day of our dear grandson, Broome, now ten years old: a very promising boy; may GOD preserve and protect him, and give him grace to be a blessing and a praise to his parents & near connections!

Feb. 2. Saturday

Damp weather and mild, some rain, and much stormy wind in the even^g· and towards night. — Mr Hayward visited MW. and thought her going on comfortably. The bowels are still constipated, but the pulse is fuller, less fast, and less intermittent; he does not appear to be uneasy about the continued drowsiness. — Hayward partook of my luncheon. — Letters from Mallory, Cheltenham, Ironmonger, as to a Joyces's Stove, which he has sent me, but is not yet delivered by the carrier: — from E.F.W. with a pleasant account of him & his, but containing reports of ill health in several of his neighbours; — to this letter I replied, with |^{15} tidings of his Mother's state. — MW. received a letter from Apphia Witts, giving a poor account of the health of herself and her Brother John; both have been great invalids, but are better, and M$^{rs.}$ J. Witts ill, but not seriously so. — I wrote letters also to Mr Riddiford, and to Lefroy, on the advertising for tenders for the clothing of the Rural Constabulary. — Walked to Eyford, and administered the sacrament privately to M$^{rs.}$ Dolphin, who continues in the same state, and has always some new vexation or distress to communicate. — Finished the Fairfax Correspondence — Began the first volume of Lord Campbell's Lives of the Chancellors.

Feb. 3. Sunday

A fine day, no frost, but cold, late in the afternoon. — Morn^{g.} service, prayers, and a sermon. I preached on "Life a Journey." Evening service, prayers. — Received a letter from Mr Chamberlayne, from Ventnor, a kind enquiry after MW's health. — No marked |[16] change in her state: if the progress to recovery be slow, it is not interrupted by a relapse. — Preparing a Sermon — C Bathurst's letter to a Niece — Winslow's grace and truth. —

Feb. 4. Monday

A fine, mild day — Recording the proceedings of the Special general meeting of our district Comm. S.P.G. on Friday: wrote an account of it to Mr Hawkins, Secretary to the parent society, with a remittance of the amount collected. — Received a letter from Chr. Geldard, with notice that he had paid to my account with the Craven Bank the interest due on Jan. 1. for one year on the £1000 lent to the North Western Railway Company, after paying the half year's tithe rent — charge due to the Vicar of Gigleswick, with one or two minor matters: — replied to his letter, with an account of my wife's state of health as to which especial & kind enquiry had been made. — Visited sick |[17] parishioners, Mrs. Gregory, with whom I prayed — Widow Townsend &c. — While so engaged, and superintending workmen at the Church land cottages, Hayward called on MW. and pronounced, as I was told, that there is an improvement in MW's pulse; he ordered a slight change of medicine, she was less overpowered with sleep in the evening than usual of late. — Lord Campbell's Lives of the Chancellors.

Feb. 5. Tuesday

A fine forenoon and afternoon, followed by rain in the evening with a heavy storm of wind. — MW. remains in much the same state, with a good appetite, less debility, and somewhat less drowsiness. The symptom which makes me most anxious is the swelling of the legs. — Wrote to Mr Thornton on Hunt Trust matters, sending him the copy of the opinion given by Mr Barber, which I had received from S. B. Hunt, also returning to him the letter he had forwarded to me for my perusal, which he had received |[18] from Mr Tilleard; and a letter received by me to-day from Mr Hare, from Town, acquainting me with particulars of an interview he had with Mr Williams. — Wrote also to Mr Williams on the same interminable topics, as to the proposed arbitration, and sent him back the bill of the Surveyors for valuing the Wharf on the behalf of the Trustees, which he had forwarded to Mr Hare, and he had sent for the opinion of myself and Mr Thornton, who agreed that it should be paid. — Conferred with my Co-trustees, E Lea and J B Collett, as to the propriety of beginning to build cottages on the Church land property near the Church in substitution for the four ruinous tenements now standing, and which are hardly fit for the decent or wholesome dwelling of the labourers, by whom they are occupied — Visited sick and aged parishioners: prayed with the widow Rogers; visited Mrs. Collett, Widows Gardner, E. Wilcox's wife, |[19] and Mrs. Dix for Mary James; — dispensing parochial charities. — Lord Campbell's Lives of the Chancellors.

Feb. 6. Wednesday.

After a tempestuous night a fine, but windy day: some damage done to our buildings, a large tree blown down on the Rectory farm; also damage in the pleasure ground at Stanway Vicarage. — Mr Hayward called; he considers his patient in many respects to be going on favourably; the pulse, though too rapid; has almost ceased to be intermittent; there is more strength; but he admits the oedema in the lower extremities to be an unpleasant symptom, and is thinking what remedy he may with safety apply. — Wrote to Miss S. B. Hunt, in answer to her last letter, with particulars as to MW's state of health; on Hunt Trust matters also; and forwarded to her a copy of my reply to M[r] Ward Hunt's circular — Having received a line or two from C Bathurst who is anxious about my plans |[20] from which he apprehends my anxieties may continue or be increased, replied to him in a short letter, in which I adverted to a letter received by me to-day, from a M[r] Bolden, whom I believe to be secretary to the Alleged Lunatics Friends Society, in which it is intimated that many members of that society entertain a desire to present Purnell with some valuable testimonial of gratitude in acknowledgment of the great public services rendered to the nation at large by his energetic, devoted, and persevering investigations into the state & abuses of the Private Lunatic Asylums in Gloucestershire: my opinion is sought as to the proper way of moving in this direction, as regards the Magistracy of this county. The Society have printed the address of thanks moved on this subject to the County Chairman at the last Quarter Sessions, with the speeches on that occasion of the Lord Lieutenant, Duke of Beaufort, and County Chairman, a few copies of which are sent to me, as also a |[21] copy of the Gloucester Journal of last week on account of a paragraph extracted from the Sun, lauding the exertions of the County Chairman and Gloucestershire Magistrates, and recommending a public testimonial. — M[r] Potter called, with whom I conversed on his proposed application to the Magistrates of the Warwickshire, for the vacant Chaplaincy of their County Gaol; and promised him a testimonial of character and fitness for the office. He partook of luncheon here; as did also our dear children from Stanway, who rode over to visit their Mother, and stayed between two and three hours, bringing a very good report of their dear trio of boys. — Lord Campbell's Lives of the Chancellors. —

Feb. 7. Thursday.
A fine day. — Wrote to Tagart, Chemist, Cheltenham, to send some pills, which are wanted — MW. remains nearly in the same unfavourable |[22] state, still confined to her room — — Drove to Stow. — Received a letter from Lefroy on Constabulary clothing &c. — From Riddiford on the same subject, and on other County business — From Mess[rs.] Cox and Williams on Hunt Trust business, advising us to concur with M[r] Ward Hunt and Miss Hunt in an arbitration, if they will agree to one, otherwise to remain passive. — M[rs.] Guydickens wrote very kindly to MW. with enquiries as to her health; gives a comfortable report as to her own state and that of her sister; at their very great age they retain the powers of activity (particularly E.G. in works of charity) and of corresponding, conversing with friends, and reading; though Miss G. suffers from deafness and general feebleness. — Attended at the Provident Bank, where met M[r] Pole, W B Pole, Morrison, Winter, and Charles Lindow with W. Vavasour — Presided at the fortnightly meeting of the guardians |[23] of the Union from half past twelve till 3 P.M: much typhus fever prevails in the district: — at Broadwell, Donnington, Salford, Oddington, Churchill &c. — Home by 5 P.M. — Lord Campbell's Lives of the Chancellor (Thomas a Becket.)

Feb. 8. Friday.

A fine day, milder weather — M^r. Hayward visited MW. and recommended her to go downstairs in the evening, where she sat in the dining room from half past six till ten: very lethargic in the evening; the breath rather failed in the effort to return to her chamber: other symptoms and appearances much the same. — Wrote to M^r. Bolden, from whom I received a letter on Wednesday as to a contemplated testimonial to the County Chairman, approving the proposition, & making suggestions in conformity with a letter I had rec^d. in Dec. last from Purnell, which explained what he would prefer, in the event of such a |^24 project being set on foot. — Wrote to the County Chairman, with the letter I had rec^d. from M^r. Bolden for his perusal, and the rough draft of my reply. — Wrote to Riddiford, in answer to his letter received yesterday, directing him to advertize in the County papers for tenders for printing &c. — Having rec^d. a note from Jackson Clark, accompanying a letter addressed to John Pegler by Serg^t. Banning, of the Constabulary, by which it appeared that he had not as yet benefited in any way by the subscription raised for him, as a testimony of approval of his courage and good conduct in apprehending the burglar, David Johns, at a great personal risk, wrote to my Son, forwarding him the letter so written, and desiring him to look into the business, and report as to the true state of the case — Wrote to M^r. Thornton, to whom I sent for his perusal the letter received by me yesterday from Messrs. Cox & Williams. |^25 Received an acknowledgment from the Soc. Prop. Gosp. of the remittance I had made of the collection at the meeting at Stow this day week, together with a kind note from the Rev^d. E. Hawkins, Sec. S.P.G. thanking me for my long and steady support of the Society. — Walked to Eyford, where had a long interview with M^rs. Dolphin: prayed with her. I thought her in better health; but she believes herself to be in a declining state. — Lord Campbell's lives of the Chancellors — (Th^s. a Becket).

Feb. 9. Saturday

A stormy and showery day. — Justice business at home with M^r. Kimber, and afterwards with M^r. Makepeace. — MW. continues in the same, to me not very satisfactory state; not worse but hardly perceptibly better. — Wrote to M^r. Chamberlayne in reply to his kind letter of enquiry after my wife: also to M^r. Wiggin, answer^g. a letter from him with like obliging enqui- |^26 ries, and congratulated him on the prospects of accomplishing without opposition from Sir John Reade or others his favourite plan of rebuilding the church at Oddington — Wrote to M^r. Potter, a short note to accompany a letter to the Chairman and Justices of the County of Warwick, as a testimonial in favour of M^r. P. who offers himself as a Candidate for the office of Chaplain of the County Gaol at Warwick. — Received a letter from C Bathurst in answer to mine written to him on Wednesday last, and on the proposed testimonial to the County Chairman — Also a letter from M^r. Thornton, who sends me the copy of a letter he had written to M^r. Ward Hunt — Lord Campbell's Lives of the Chancellors. ——

Feb. 10. Sunday

A fine day. — Morn^g. service – prayers: administered the Holy Communion to 14 Communicants. Afternoon Service, prayers and sermon. I preached on Christian Charity. — M^r. Hayward called |^27 on MW. He admitted her case to be complicated, that she was better in one respect, and worse in another — the worse being the effusion in the lower extremities — The nights continue to be disturbed, the debility great, and the drowsiness very oppressive in the evening. She left her bed room by 11 AM. and occupied the little sitting room upstairs, till the evening, when she came in to the dining room, and remained with me there from half past six till past ten — A circular from <u>Gloucester Gaol</u>, announcing a meeting of Visiting Justices for the 18[th.] Inst. — Preparing a Sermon — C Bathurst's letters to a Niece — Winslow's grace and truth.[1] —

Feb. 11. Monday

A stormy and rainy day — Justice business at home — Wrote letters to <u>Apphia Witts</u> and M[rs.] <u>Guydickens</u> in reply to those MW. had lately rec[d.] from these connections, giving a report of her health &c. — Wrote to Mess[rs.] |[28] <u>Davison Newman & C[o.]</u> Fenchurch Street, with a remittance for groceries supplied, and an order for more. — Preparing a Sermon — Making transcript of last year's entries in my parish registers. — MW. remains in nearly the same state, not leaving her small sitting room: perhaps there was a slight improvement. — Lord Campbell's Lives of the Chancellors. ——

Feb. 12. Tuesday

A snowy morning, but, there being no frost, the snow was soon melted: the weather afterwards fine; frosty at night — Wrote a long letter on County business &c. to <u>C Bathurst</u> — Also a short note to M[r.] <u>Riddiford</u> in answer to a letter received from him on matters relating to County Management, accompanying a circular addressed to members of the Committee of accounts, convening them to Gloucester on the 18[th.] Inst. The business is to receive tenders for constabulary clothing, for printing, and for an auditor or accountant to audit County |[29] bills under the direction of the Committee of accounts prior to each Quarter Sess[ns.] I do not mean to be present at this meeting; the business may well be left to my colleagues: there is no principle to be argued, or new proposition to be discussed; and in my poor wife's failing state of health I am desirous of not leaving her for a longer time than I can avoid. — Received a letter from <u>Purnell</u> on County business: he returns to me the letter I received from M[r] Bolden; and approves of my reply. — A letter from M[rs.] <u>Dolphin</u>, Mother of the Vicar of Lower Guiting; she writes to acknowledge in proper terms the letter I addressed to her lately. — M[r] Hayward called; and found MW. very languid, but did not think her worse than on his last visit: indeed the pulse was better. She joined me before tea in the dining room, having passed the earlier part of the day in her little sitting room upstairs — Visited and prayed |[30] with my parishioner, M[rs.] Gregory. — Lord Campbell's Lives of the Chancellors.

Feb. 13. Wednesday – Ashwednesday.

A sharp frost, and very fine, but cold day — Morning service – prayers – with the Commination service. — Received a friendly letter from <u>George Wellford</u> — A letter from M[r] <u>Hooper Wilton</u>, who is very sore about the late curtailment of his salary as County Treasurer; and wishes the question to be revived at the Easter Quarter Sessions, with a view to which he has addressed a letter to the County Chairman, a copy of which he forwards to me, but does not mean to correspond with other Magistrates on the subject. — A letter

---

1. Octavius Winslow (1808-1878), *Grace and Truth*, 1849.

from M̲ʳ̲ ̲P̲o̲t̲t̲e̲r̲, gratefully acknowledging the favourable terms in which I had couched the testimonial on his behalf as Candidate for the vacant chaplaincy of G̶ the County Gaol at Warwick, which I forwarded to him a few days since. — A letter from |³¹ M̲e̲s̲s̲ʳ̲ˢ̲·̲ ̲D̲a̲v̲i̲s̲o̲n̲,̲ N̲e̲w̲m̲a̲n̲ ̲&̲ ̲C̲º̲· with an acknowledgment of the cheque I had forwarded to them. — Visited and prayed with Mʳˢ· Rogers. — To Eyford, but Mʳˢ· Dolphin, alleging indisposition, declined seeing me; visited t̶o̶ ᵗʷᵒ aged and infirm cottagers there. — On my return found Mʳˢ· W. Vavasour, who had walked from "the Cottage," to visit MW. and had been sitting with her for a quarter of an hour. She remained some time with me before she set out on her return, accompanied by her maid. — MW. seems much the same as for some days past; passing the evening with me in the dining room, and the rest of the day in her little sitting room — Lord Campbell's Lives of the Chancellors. —

Feb. 14. Thursday

A very foggy day. — Wrote to M̲ʳ̲ ̲H̲.̲ ̲W̲i̲l̲t̲o̲n̲ in reply to his letter received by me yesterday. — Drove to Stow. — Received a letter from F̲r̲e̲d̲e̲r̲i̲c̲k̲-̲|³² N̲e̲w̲m̲a̲r̲c̲h̲, informing me that the annual meeting of the Northleach Turnpike Trust is fixed for Mar. 13. — M̲ʳ̲ ̲M̲u̲l̲l̲i̲n̲g̲s̲ has sent me a copy of the Bill brought into the House of Commons for the appointment of County Financial Boards, to consist of Magistrates, one for each Union elected by the Ex officio Guardians of that Union, and elected Guardians, one from each Union to be chosen by the elected members, — a very doubtful and hazardous project. — Attended at the Provident Bank, where I met Mʳ Pole and Mʳ Morrison. — With R. Waller sat as magistrate at the Justice room for two hours, transacting the public business of the district. Mʳ Ford was absent in London. — Mʳ W. B. Pole, and J. T. Rice attended the Justice meeting. — Home by 5 PM. — Mʳ Hayward did not call to-day as expected: MW. remains much in the same state as for some days past leavᵍ· her bed room by 11 AM. and occupying her |³³ small sitting room till nearly teatime, and then joining me in the dining-room — Quarterly Review — Art. on the natural history of man. —

Feb. 15. Friday.

A very fine forenoon, and in the afternoon dull weather, windy in the evening. — Mʳ Hayward made an early visit, having been prevented attending yesterday. All seems much the same with our patient as of late; drowsiness, quick pulse, dry mouth, restless nights; the digestive organs, and the kidneys, appear in a better order, but the dropsical symptoms are not materially abated; and H. evidently considers them as serious, not denying, in answer to my questions, that there is anasarca,² with a short cough common in that disease, and that MW's state may be feared to be a breaking up of the constitution — So great is the sleepiness, that it once came on in the evening, while MW. was standing, and, relaxing all the muscular power, she |³⁴ fell prostrate; but without hurting herself. I fear recovery is not to be expected: all must be done to support, and mitigate suffering, and avert pain. — I drove to Northleach, taking up R. Waller at Bourton Bridge by appointment, to conclude an examination as to settlement, and an order of removal, left incomplete yesterday, the party to be removed being

---

2. Anasarca – A generalized oedema of subcutaneous tissue, usually with accumulation of fluid. Dropsy was the general name given to a condition marked by an excess of fluid in the tissues or cavities of the body.

a prisoner. After doing this business, and going over the House of Correction, accompanied by the Chaplain, Mr Thorpe, we called at the Vicarage, and paid a short visit to the Astons, all of whom, with the exception of the younger Frederick, who was gone to Cheltenham, we saw: — thence to get into my carriage at the King's Head, where we met Mr Francillon, the Judge of the County Court, who had just been holding a Sitting. — Home soon after one o'clock, and found a letter from E.F.W. We had rather hoped to have seen him and, perhaps, Sophy, but they are prevented |³⁵ coming for a few days by one of their horses having cast a shoe, and broken its hoof. — A good report of the health of all. My son sends back the letter written by Pol. Serg^{t.} Banning to Mr Pegler, with explanations as to the proposed annuity to be bought for him with the monies subscribed for him. — A letter from C Bathurst in answer to my last. — Quarterly Review; On the Natural History of man.

Feb. 16. Saturday

A fine day, but windy and cold in exposed places — MW. much in the same state, but suffering from pain in the lower extremities, torpor, and shortness of breath late in the evening rather more than usual. — Wrote to E.F.W. in answer to his letter received yesterday, with a report as to his poor mother's declining state — To Messrs. Hoare, directing them to place £30 from my account with them to that of my Son. — To Baily & Jones, Booksellers, Cirencester, in answer to |³⁶ a circular received from them some days ago, that I should prefer a quarto copy of the forthcoming Remains of Roman art at Cirencester, by Chas. Newmarch and Buckman. — To C Bathurst a short note in answer to his received yesterday — To Mr Mullings, to thank him for sending me a copy of the Bill now before the H. of Commons for the establishment of elective County financial Boards, with some comments on the subject. — From Mr Thornton I received a letter on Hunt Trust business: he returns me a letter from Messrs. Cox and Williams, which I had sent for his perusal. — Mr J. T. Rice having written me a note, complaining of his having been appointed Overseer of Great Risington, nearly a twelvemonth ago, and enquiring whether he can divest himself of the office, into which he thinks he was improperly thrust, replied to him by stating the law as to the appointment of |³⁷ overseers, adding that I do not see how he can get rid of the office. —— Visiting aged parishioners, and dispensing to them Mr Lumbert's charity. — Justice business at home. — Quarterly Review — Art. on Clergy relief bill – strangely so called for it was a bill for the relief of persons in holy orders of the Church of England, declaring their dissent from the doctrines of the Church.

Feb. 17. Sunday

A fine day — Mr Hayward called, and did not see any change for the worse in MW's case: he purposes trying digitalis with a view to the absorption of the water accumulated in the lower extremities, and to reduce the rapid pulse. I thought she passed the day rather more comfortably than usual. — Morning Service – prayers and sermon. I preached on Fasting and the duties connected with it. — Afternoon service – prayers — Preparing a Sermon. — Winslow's Grace and Truth. — |³⁸

Feb. 18. Monday

A very fine day. — MW. much in the same state; had the comfort of a visit from our dear children, who rode over to see us, and remained with us from half past one to half past four o clock; they gave good accounts of their three dear boys. — Busy with Churchwarden Gregory in giving directions for the repair of buildings on the Church land cottage property. — Preparing a Sermon. — Wrote to <u>Round</u> — Quarterly Review — Art. on Clergy Relief Bill – Copying report Stow Distr. Comm. S.P.G. 1849.

Feb. 19. Tuesday

Fine weather — Mr Hayward visited MW. in whom their appeared no material change: he now alters the medicine, administering digitalis, hoping to reduce the quick pulse, and to disperse the water in the lower extremities by absorption. There is a fear least this medicine may be too lowering, but no tendency that way was discoverable during the day: great drowsiness in the evening, and shortness of breath in going |^39 upstairs to bed. — Copying report Stow Distr. Comm. S.P.G. for 1849. — Walked to Eyford: M^rs. Dolphin alleged indisposition, and declined seeing me. – Called on the Ryans. — A letter from <u>M^rs. Guydickens</u> in answer to mine announcing the serious illness of MW., very kindly expressed. — A letter from <u>Hoare</u>, intimating that they have transferred £30 from my account with them to that of E.F.W. — A letter from <u>C Bathurst</u> in answer to my last. — Quarterly review. Art. on Clergy Relief Bill. —

Feb. 20. Wednesday

A fine forenoon; rain or moist atmosphere in the afternoon — MW. much in the same state as yesterday — Copying Report District Comm. S.P.G. for 1849. — Rec^d. a letter from <u>Riddiford</u> with particulars as to the meeting of the Comm. of accounts at Gloucester on Monday as to receiving and determining ^on tenders for Printing, Constabulary Clothing &c. – satisfactory; but, some of the arrangements not being |^40 concluded, there was an adjournment till the 25th. Inst. of which I also received notice by a <u>circular</u> from the County Gaol. — Visited my co-trustee & churchwarden, Lea, to advise with him and his wife on distribution of clothing from the parochial charity to the poor &c. — Visited a sick parishioner, M^rs. Gregory. — Mr Wilkins called to consult me as to a dispute with W. Vavasour, as to the amount of rent to be paid by him for land which he held to Mich^s. last under Mr Chamberlayne — also to give me his opinion as to the proper interpretation of the decree under which our Church and Charity Estate trust is regulated. He considers that we have only power to repair tenements, not to take them down and rebuild. — Read the account of the trial and execution of Lord Russell in the end of Charles the 2^d's reign from "the Town — its memorable characters and events, by Leigh Hunt."^3 —

Feb. 21. Thursday

A fine, but cold day — |^41 Mr Hayward visited MW. and was of opinion that the digitalis was operating on the system favourably, the pulse being lower, and the general system not reduced by it: other symptoms remain as before; languor, swelling of the lower extremities, and drowsiness, but the latter less intense — Drove to Stow. — Received a letter from <u>Mr Mullings</u> on the County rates Finance Board Bill, thanking me for hints given on that subject,

---

3.   James Henry Leigh Hunt (1784–1859), *The Town: Its Memorable Characters and Events. St Paul's to St James's*; London: 1848.

which, with others suggested by Curtis Hayward, he will embody with his own remarks in speaking on the bill. — A circular from a Society at Bath, organized with a View to check the desecration of the Lords day, and particularly, to petition the Legislature that all work in the post office department throughout the empire may be discontinued. — Attended at the Savings Bank, where met Mr Pole, Mr Winter, W. B. Pole, and Morrison; transacted |42 business there; called at the office of the Gloucestershire Banking Company; shopping. — Presided for three hours or more at the fortnightly meeting of the Guardians of our Union. — Conference with Vavasour and Mr Wilkins as to the matter in dispute as to rent between Mr Chamberlayne & W. Vavasour. — Home to a late dinner — Concluded the account of the trial and execution of William, Lord Russell, from "The Town &c. by Leigh Hunt."

Feb. 22. Friday

A fine day. — MW. remains nearly in the same state; the breath was very painfully obstructed in going upstairs to bed. — W. Vavasour called on me after breakfast, to give his view & version of the matter disputed between him and Mr Wilkins as to the allowance claimed by him on account of extra manure laid on the land he rented from Mr Chamberlayne: W.V. very sore on the subject, very confident he is right; but not otherwise |43 than friendly in his bearing towards me — Wrote to E.F.W. with a report of his poor Mother's state, on the matter of Banning's annuity, on the question as to W. Vavasour's right to repay himself for extra manure laid on Mr Chamberlayne's land &c. — Wrote to Riddiford on County matters, and business appertaining to the Committee of accounts — Visited Mr Davis, who is unwell. — Quarterly Rev. Art. on Agriculture — Draining. —

Feb. 23. Saturday

Fine weather. — MW. visited by Mr Hayward: the complaints seem very little if at all varied; but slight, if any improvement — — Examining the Bill for the establishment of County Financial Boards, which appears to me very objectionable. — Walked to Eyford: admitted to Mrs. Dolphin's bedside; prayed with her; the usual amount of complaint, revelations as to the past and present evils, with the usual volubility — |44 The Misses Hall called when I was absent — Justice business at home. — Quarterly review. Art. on Agriculture — Draining.

Feb. 24. Sunday

Very fine weather — Morning service – prayers: Afternoon service, prayers and sermon. Preached on Christ's temptation. — A letter from Apphia Witts in answer to mine to her; Kind enquiries as to MW. — better report of the writer's health, as also of that of her Brother and sister-in law — Letter from H. H. Wilton; influenced, perhaps, by my late letter to him, he withdraws the letter he had written to the County Chairman complaining of the reduction of his salary as County Treasurer; so that question will not be mooted at the next Quarter Sessions. — David Ricardo has drawn up, and caused to be printed, and circulated among the Magistrates of Gloucestershire, certain tables illustrating the Receipt and Expenditure of the County at decennial periods from |45 1800 to 1840, and for each year since 1840: he addresses these in a quiet letter to the County Chairman, whose speech or report at the last Q.S. on the expenditure as to the County Gaol and Bridewells he prefixes to his tables; as a postscript he appends some remarks from the Commissioners' report on rates in favour of his scheme for the appointment of an Auditor of county expenditure. — My poor wife hardly seemed so well to day, as she has been; but there was no material change in her condition — Eccl. Gazette — Preparing a sermon — Winslow's Grace and Truth. —

Feb. 25. Monday

Very fine weather — Much justice and other business at home. Mr Comely called to consult me as to the Assessment of his parish for Poor Rates, and the late, and, as alleged, incorrect valuation made by Mr W. Croome — The Relieving officer called for my opinion |^46 on certain Union matters — Mr Makepeace came with a case of felony committed at Burford, and the stolen property partly found at Stow — remanded two prisoners for further examination. — Mr Hayward paid his visit to his patient; water was detected in the arm and under the eyes, showing the extension of anasarca; great debility, shortness of breath, and drowsiness; the appetite less good. The appearances very discouraging. — Mr Ogle called to enquire after MW., being on his way to Stanway. — M^rs· R. W. Scott and Miss Morrison very kindly drove from Longborough to make enquiries after my wife — A circular from Bristol, from Mr Barrow, announcing a meeting of the Committee for managing the Female Training School mistresses institution — Visited E. Lea and W. Gregory, Churchwardens, to engage the attendance of M^rs· Lea and W.G. to-morrow to assist me in |^47 distributing clothing to the poor of the parish. — Quarterly Review – Art. on Agriculture — Draining. —

Feb. 26. Tuesday

Very fine weather — My 67th· birthday; GOD be thanked for his loving kindness in granting me time to make ^my peace with him before I go hence & be no more seen! May he send his Holy Spirit to influence me more and more to penitence, to contrition, to amendment of life! May I be daily advancing in holiness, weaned from the love of this world and its false maxims, fixing my affections more and more on heaven, and heavenly things! May my faith in the Redeemer be ever on the increase, may I fully & exclusively rely on the atonement he has wrought for sin, may I walk more carefully in the ways of his laws and in the paths of his commandments! GOD grant me grace to live in peace and charity with all men, striving to do all the good I can, as regards |^48 the temporal, spiritual and eternal welfare of others! Soften to me, O Lord, the heavy trial I now endure in the grievous sickness of my dear wife, and strengthen me and her to bear up patiently, and to meet the fatal issue to be expected at no distant day! May I in all things set a good example to others, may I overcome the sins that most beset me! let my conversation be edifying, and my preaching faithful, sound, and earnest! — Engaged in the forenoon with M^rs· Lea and W. Gregory in distributing to my poor parishioners calico and flannel, partly from the charity fund of the parish trustees, partly from the Sacrament Alms fund. — M^rs· Lea visited my wife in her sitting room for a short time, and was shocked to find her so feeble and suffering — Justice business at home. — John Illes met with a bad hurt in falling from the top of a waggon load of wood at Eyford, working for me in bringing home faggots & |^49 poles I had bought there at the Wood Sale. I dispatched the groom to bring Mr Hayward to see him, who found that the poor old man had fractured his right blade-bone. H. came to visit us, when he had attended to this case, and found MW. very much exhausted, and sadly feeble; the weakness seems to increase, the water spreads, the lower extremities being much swollen, the breath greatly impeded; still there is a full, though a rapid pulse. The present course of medicine is to be continued — M^r and M$^{rs.}$ C Pole called to enquire after MW. when I was walking out. — Quarterly Rev. Art. on the Memoirs of Lord Cloncurry & John O'Connell.

Feb. 27. Wednesday

A foggy morning: the air colder, but the day fine, yet not so fine as of late. — Visited John Illes, whom I found as well as could be expected. — Making extracts from the Register as to the baptisms of the two sons of E. Lea who are |^{50} about to emigrate to Australia, and preparing commendatory letters addressed to Colonial Bishops and others, which they may produce at the place of their destination in proof that they are members of the Church of England, bearing good characters. — Justice business at home. — MW. received a kind letter from <u>Fanny Backhouse</u>, written in ignorance of my poor wife's sad state of health. — A circular from <u>R G K Brookes</u>, announcing a Turnpike meeting of the United Stow and Moreton Trusts. — Great comfort in a visit from our dear children, and two younger grandchildren. E.F.W. rode, and met dear Sophy who drove hither with the boys, their nurse and the Lad (page). All were well, and gave a comfortable report of dear Broome. It was thoughtful and judicious to afford the poor suffering grandmother this opportunity of embracing and blessing these dear children, whom we dare not invite to stay with us, as they would |^{51} unavoidably cause hurry and noise to the invalid. The beloved party staid with us for three hours or more, and had a comfortable meal with me. Edward and Sophy promised to come again to dine and sleep on Friday, to return on Saturday to Stanway. They observed a change for the worse in their poor Mother, all whose discouraging symptoms continue unabated. — I had written a few lines by post to <u>E.F.W.</u> begging him to come hither on Friday, if he should not visit us to-day. — Lord Campbell's Lives of the Chancellors.

Feb. 28. Thursday

A fine day, but foggy. — Mr Hayward called after breakfast, and found no improvement in his patient. The diuretic medicines administered do not appear to act properly: and the water accumulates, in the upper extremities as well as in the lower. Fear is entertained that there may be effusion in the abdomen. The depression, torpor, and debility great, and the appetite |^{52} less good. In the afternoon I again saw H. at Stow, who had received from Dr Baron an answer to a letter he had addressed to him with a full description of MW's state and his treatment. Dr B. replies by expressing his sorrow, and his fear that there is effusion in the chest: he prescribes, making a slight modification in the medicines now administered by Hayward. The hope of recovery seems cut under our feet: to me, for some days past, it has only appeared a question of time. May GOD support her in the last struggle, and may the close be without grievous pain or distress! May he guide & bear up me and mine! — Drove to Stow. — The only <u>letter</u> a circular announcing a meeting of Visiting Justices at Gloucester Gaol. — Attended at the Provident Bank, where I met Mr Pole, W. B. Pole, and M^r DuPré: the last consulted me as to the course he ought to take to obtain a payment of £20 per ann |^{53} to which, as instructed by the acting member of the Chapter of Christ Church, Oxford, (the patronage of the Perpetual Curacy of Temple Guiting belonging to them,) he is entitled from the Misses Talbot, as of the great tithes under the College, which, however, they do not recognise as an obligation. It seems Bowen received that amount from Mr Talbot up to his death, but as a gratuity, not as a due: and that it has never been paid since. The Chapter assert that it is a condition under which the property is held by Mr Talbot's representatives. — Transacted business at the office of the Gloucestershire Banking Company — Conferred with Mr Vavasour and Mr Wilkins as to the claim made by W. Vavasour for payment from Mr Chamberlayne for extra manure laid on the lands late in W.V's occupation — It seems that Captain Leigh, one of the parties to whom Mr Chamberlayne had |⁵⁴ proposed that the question might be referred, has decided it in favour of W.V. I think he has erred in that decision — Presided at a meeting of the Trustees of the Stow and Burford division of the Chipping Norton, Banbury & Burford trust. – Present Mr Pole, W. B. Pole, Winter, Ford, R Waller. As magistrates, Ford, R. Waller, and myself held afterwards a long sitting; much and varied business. Of gentlemen bystanders or assessors, there were Vavasour Senr, Ogle, Boggis, Potter, besides those mentioned above —— Detained till 5 P.M. R. Waller and Boggis came homewards as far to Lower Slaughter Turnpike in my carriage with me, being pedestrians — Lord Campbell's Lives of the Chancellors. —

Mar. 1. Friday.

Very fine weather — No improvement in MW's state: she seems weaker, and had a restless night. — Wrote to <u>Fanny Backhouse</u>, to acknowledge |⁵⁵ her late letter to my poor wife; informed her of the precarious state in which she lies, which I requested her to communicate to the rest of her family, as also to Miss Backhouse at Wavertree, and thro' her to Miss Gardner. — MW. received a very nice letter from her dear Grandson <u>Broome</u>, from Dumbleton. — Visited John Illes, who is going on as well as can be expected after his late accident. — M^r and Mrs. W. B. Pole rode to enquire after my dear wife, and called upon me. — I walked to the Vicarage at Lower Swell, to enquire after the health of John Perkins: saw Mrs. Perkins, and sat with her for a short time. P. is yet very weak; though convalescent, not able to do the duties of his church; he was gone to lie down. — Our dear E.F.W. and Sophy arrived soon after five P.M. on horseback from Stanway to dine and sleep here; they had been at |⁵⁶ Stow, and visited the Vavasours for a couple of hours. It was a great comfort and indulgence thus to enjoy their society, and to confer together on the trial which awaits us, and on that with which it has pleased GOD in his justice, wisdom, and mercy to visit us. — Wrote to M^r <u>Bryan</u>, Stow, Mercer &c., with a cheque for flannel supplied for distribution to the poor. —

Mar. 2. Saturday

A less fine day; a cold, and rather damp air in the afternoon — Mr Hayward paid his usual visit, and found his patient not worse, if any thing, rather better, with less effusion about her; and she had passed a better night. The medicines, as modified by Dr Baron, seem to suit the case; and H. appears not to anticipate immediate danger, or sudden change. – We sat with the poor invalid during the forenoon, who was feeble, restless, and drowsy; and this was the case in the evening. — E.F.W. and Sophy left us between 3 & 4 P M. promising a visit |⁵⁷ next week, and prepared for a sudden summons. — Received a letter from <u>Riddiford</u>, with satisfactory statements as to county matters, tenders for constabulary clothing, appointment of Mr S. Mayer as Auditor of accounts &c. — A note from <u>Mrs. Winter</u>, kindly expressed with a quantity of the tops of the Broom (Spartium Scoparia) of which my poor wife takes an infusion. — Visited infirm & sick parishioners — John Illes, and Mrs. Rogers; — prayed with the latter. — Quarterly Review – Art. on Free Trade. — This was ~~Mar. 3 Su~~ my dear Son's 37th. birthday: GOD bless him and his! he is in many and essential respects a truly well intentioned, very estimable, and very useful character; a good husband, son, and father; endowed with considerable talents, and of extensive knowledge in many directions; his faults are for the most part constitutional; great energy begets eagerness, and impe-|[58] tuosity in the pursuit of favourite objects, with some lack of self-denial and self control.

Mar. 3. Sunday.

A cold day, but fine weather, till evening, when, after a slight shower before dark, there came on window and hail with some rain. — MW. much the same as for some time past; no abatement, I fear, of the general effusion; much torpor, and feebleness. — Morning service, prayers and a Sermon. I preached on the joy which is in heaven on the repentance of a Sinner. — Afternoon service – prayers: — then the funeral of Mary, late wife of Matthew Davis, a poor weak, creature, released after many years of slow wasting and decay. — A kind & proper letter from Fanny Backhouse in answer to mine written on Friday — A circular from the Gloucester lunatic Asylum, announcing a meeting of Visitors — Preparing a sermon. — Ecclesiastical gazette — Winslow's Grace & truth.

Mar. 4. Monday

Fine weather, but cold — |[59] Visited John Illes, who was considered by his attendants to be worse. Sent my groom to hasten Mr Hayward to attend him; who, when he arrived, found the poor man suffering under an attack of pleurisy. H. visited MW. who continues in a very precarious state; every evil symptom rather on the increase than abated; suffering from shortness of breath, effusion ~~of~~ in the whole system, restlessness, weariness, torpor — a melancholy condition; but GOD gives me strength to bear up. — Justice business at home — Wrote a note to Mr Price, the Attorney and Petty Sessions Clerk at Burford, on a case which I sent for adjudication to the Oxfordshire Magistrates — I had written a note to Mr Hayward to summon him hither. — Received a letter from Mr Joyner Ellis on the subject of a testimonial to Mr Purnell, in acknowledgment of his great services in the late enquiries into the state |[60] of the private mad-houses near Bristol. J.E. writes to me, no doubt, with the privity of the Lord Lieutenant: deprecates the origination of the testimonial in any other quarter than in Gloucestershire — this with reference to the movement made by the alleged lunatics friends Society; — proposes a meeting of parties favourable to the measure at the coming Sessions; consults me as to the proper persons to whom preliminary notices should be sent &c. — Mr Vavasour wrote a note of enquiry as to MW's health to which I replied — Visited a poor sick parishioner, the widow Townsend. — Quarterly Review — Art. on Free Trade. —

Mar. 5. Tuesday

Early hoar frost; a very fine day. — Hayward visited MW. and found little alteration in her condition: all the symptoms much the same as of late. — Wrote to E.F.W. with a report of his poor Mother's state — To Mr Joyner Ellis, in answer to his |[61] letter received yesterday. I forwarded to him the letter I had received from Mr Bolden, Secr. to the Alleged Lunatics friends Society, on the subject of a permanent testimonial to Mr Purnell in acknowledgment of the great services rendered by him to the cause of humanity, in persevering in the enquiries into abuses in Lunatic private Asylums in the County of Gloucester, together with my answer to the same, as shewing the inclination of P's mind on the subject: – intimated that the precarious state of MW's health rendered it very doubtful whether I could attend the approaching Sessions or Assizes. — To <u>Purnell</u> I wrote shortly, sending him the letter written to me by Joyner Ellis, with a copy of my reply to the same. — Visited John Illes who is in a dangerous state from pleurisy. — Mrs. R. Waller called to enquire after MW. and went into her dressing-room to sit for a quarter of an hour with her — she was much |⁶² shocked at seeing her so greatly altered — Received a circular letter from the <u>Gloucester and Berkeley Canal</u> office as to the affairs of that company. — Quarterly review. Art. on Free Trade. — Justice business at home.

Mar. 6. Wednesday

A hoar frost early: a fine day. — MW. continues in the same state; she admitted to her dressing room to day Anne Yearps, a respectable old servant of ours, married to a tradesman of Lower Slaughter, who was anxious to see her. Much conversation, and very satisfactory, with my dear wife, as to arrangements which she wishes me to make in the event of her death; remembrances to her son and grandchildren, to her daughter in law, friends and servants &c. — Mr Hayward called, and continues the present course of medicine. If I may judge by his conversation, he does not anticipate a fatal termination at an early period; thinks it possible the disease may be checked, but not eradi-|⁶³ cated. — I attended by the dying bed of John Illes, whose life cannot, it would seem, be long protracted, and administered the Holy Communion to him, two brothers Collett, and his sister Restall from Naunton. — Justice business at home — "Leaves from the Diary of a Subaltern," — a young officer, who has made the late campaigns in the Punjaub.⁴ — Quarterly Review — Art. on Free Trade.

Mar. 7. Thursday

A fine day. — Poor John Illes breathed his last about midnight. — W. Gregory called on me on parish business at breakfast time — Justice and other business at home — Drove to Stow. — Received a letter from <u>S. B. Hunt</u>, not much to the purpose, on Hunt Trust matters: she forwards, for my perusal, letters she has received from Mr Whitcombe, there is wrong headedness in the management of this worrying affair, both on the part of |⁶⁴ Mr G. Hunt, and on that of Miss S. Hunt. — MW. received kind letters from her cousins, <u>R. Backhouse</u>, and <u>M. Gardner</u>, both now informed of her alarming illness — At Stow — attended a meeting of Trustees of the Stumps Cross turnpike trust, and of the United Stow and Moreton Turnpike Trust — into the business of which we entered, after auditing the accounts of the three trusts hitherto distinct, of which the Union is composed. Lord Redesdale presided — Other Trustees present were, Mr Pole, Mr W. B. Pole, Mr Winter, Mr Colvile, Mr Jarratt, Mr Malcolm, M^r R Waller, and myself – Officials present, Messrs. Brookes, Clerk, Stokes,

---

4. Ensign Daniel Augustus Sandford (1829-1849). Sandford was of the 2nd European Regiment. He was son of John Sandford, Archdeacon of Coventry. Sandford served in the Punjab in 1848 (medal and 2 bars, wounded). *Leaves from the journal of a Subaltern during the campaign in the Punjab.*

Surveyor, and Clark, Treasurer — These were all re-appointed officers of the United Trust: Mr Stokes exhibiting some ill-humour. — After the meeting transacted Justice business with R. Waller as my colleague — We were joined by Mr Vavasour, who accompanied us to |65 the Provident Bank office, where met the two Poles, Winter, Lewes, and Morrison — R Waller accompanied me as far as to Lower Slaughter Gate in my carriage on my return home. — MW. continues very much in the same feeble, torpid state; breath short, and the whole frame dropsical — Leaves from the diary of a subaltern — The business of the turnpike trusts prevented my attending at the meeting of the Board of Guardians to-day. I wrote to Mr Pearce to explain that I should be unable to preside.

Mar. 8. Friday.

A foggy morning, and dull forenoon; a fine afternoon & evening — Mr Hayward visited his patient: little, if any change in her condition, and the same treatment followed. — Engaged in preparing for MW's ~~document~~ signature a document expressive of her wishes in the event of her decease. — E.F.W. rode over from Stanway, and passed three hours with us. He brought |66 a good report of his dear wife and children. — Mr Lefroy called here on a circuit to visit his police Stations, and partook of luncheon with E.F.W. and myself. It was arranged that, after visiting the men at Bourton, Stow, and Moreton, he should return to a late dinner at Stanway Vicarage. Conference on Constabulary and other county business. — Leaves from the diary of a Subaltern.

Mar. 9. Saturday.

Foggy morning, and forenoon; fine afternoon and evening — M.W. in much the same state; if anything weaker. She admitted to her morning sitting room for a few minutes Mrs. Winter, who, with Mr W., kindly drove from Daylesford to enquire after her. — The Misses Hall from Bourton on the Water called with like enquiries; both parties sat a little time with me. — Wrote letters to Miss S. B. Hunt, and Mr Thornton, on Hunt Trust business — replied to the letter of the former received by me on Thursday; forwar-|67 ded to the latter for his perusal the letter then received from S.B.H. the answer I had made to it, (a copy) and the two letters from Mr Whitcombe to S.B.H. which she had sent for my perusal. — Wrote to dear Broome, to acknowledge the letter lately received from him by his poor Grandmother. — Wrote a note to Mr Hayward respecting medicine wanted, and reported on MW's state. — Recd. a few lines from Mr Thornton, mentioning that he is going from home, and furnishing me with an address which will find him on Wednesday next. — A kind & feeling letter from Purnell with reference to my present great anxiety, expressing regret that I had been troubled with correspondence about a matter personal to himself, the contemplated testimonial on which Mr Joyner Ellis wrote to me. — A letter from the office of the Clerk of the Peace as to meetings to be held at Gloucester |68 on the 18th. Inst. — the day before the Quarter Sessions. — My attendance then or at the Q.S. is out of the question, and I have intimated this to Purnell, J. Ellis, & Riddiford — A note from Mr Morrison with the names of books which Mrs. R Scott wishes me to order into the Book Society — Officiated at the funeral of John Illes — Leaves from the Journal of a Subaltern.

Mar. 10. Sunday

A hoar frost in the morning; a fine day. — Mr Hayward called, and thought MW. weaker and more sinking; the last two or three nights have been more disturbed; the pulse is feebler; the feebleness very distressing: in the afternoon there seemed rather a revival of power; but great weakness and drowsiness, and the appetite somewhat fails — Morning service: prayers: — afternoon service prayers and sermon. I preached on the fruits of the Spirit exemplified in the character of Joseph. — A short interview with two Misses Kirby, connections of M$^{rs.}$ |[69] Dolphin, now staying at Eyford. — Read the judgement of the committee of Privy Council in Gorham v. Bp. of Exeter, a very important document as regards the Church. The decision is so far in favour of Gorham that it is held that the Bishop was not justified in refusing him institution to the Benefice to which he had been presented. Institution must therefore be granted; it being thus laid down that low church opinions on baptismal regeneration do not amount to false doctrine. The committee do not profess to assert the true doctrine as either on the one side or the other; but on a close review and criticism of the articles and formularies of the Church, certain first principles of judging being first laid down, they hold that the Church has left the question of baptismal regeneration open, having no where formally and dogmatically or authoritatively limited and defined the sense she |[70] entertains on this much controverted doctrine; insomuch that notwithstanding strong expressions in devotional portions, and in rubrics, it must be held that the point is yet left undecided, and that each member and minister of the Church is at liberty on this article to form his own conclusions according to his understanding & conscience — The Archbishops of York & Canterbury take this view, from which the Bishop of London dissents, these three being the Clerical members of the Board – the legal authorities who have sat in Committee are unanimous with one dissentient. — Preparing a Sermon — Ecclesiastical Gazette. —

Mar. 11. Monday

Beautiful weather, after a frosty morning — Wrote to E.F.W. reporting on his poor Mother's declining state, and advising that he should not attend at the Quarter Sessions next week, least he should be absent at the hour of need. Concluded my note after Mr Hayward had visited |[71] us. — H. thought MW. somewhat revived since he had seen her yesterday: but the water accumulated bespeaks increased dropsy; the appetite fails; the powers both of mind and body grow more languid; the torpor is undiminished. — Wrote to Mr Riddiford, to whom I forwarded minutes of the meeting of the Committee of accounts on Jan. 28. to be presented at the coming Quarter Sessions — Justice business at home — Miss Herbert, daughter of an Eyford tenant, was married to-day to G. A. Lees; formerly farming bailiff to M$^{rs.}$ Dolphin, and, since, holding the like situation at Cirencester Agricultural College — a Scotchman, and clever, enterprizing person, as the destination of the couple shews; for they will shortly embark for Hamburgh, whence they will proceed to Warsaw, Lees being engaged to superintend the farming concerns of a Polish |[72] nobleman and great landed proprietor, whose son has been for some time studying agriculture at the Cirencester College, and who has already, I believe, sent English labourers and live stock &c. with a view to introduce English systems into his country — Quarterly Review – Art. on Free Trade.

Mar. 12. Tuesday.

A hoar frost and fine day — Hayward visited MW. who was peculiarly languid and exhausted after a bad night, before she rose from bed: the appetite continues to fail. In the afternoon and evening there was a revival of power, but great drowsiness, and inability to move. The medicines changed; the digitalis which, probably increased the languor, being discontinued — Wrote to E.F.W. a report of his poor Mother's condition. — To Rodwell for a supply of books for the Stow library — To Mr Joyner Ellis in answer to a note received from him to-day, by which it appears that preliminary notices have |[73] been circulated by him, with the approval of Lord Fitzhardinge, to convene a meeting of magistrates friendly to the presentation of a testimonial to the County Chairman to record his valuable services to humanity in the investigation of abuses in private madhouses; such meeting to be held in the Clerk of the Peace's office at the Shire Hall on the 29th. Mar. being the first day of the Sessions. I expressed my regret that I was unable at present to take part in the good work. — Visited Mrs. Dolphin, in her bed; still very complaining as to health; full of painful details as to her embarrassed affairs and lawsuits; but also very fluent on parish gossip and the concerns of the Village — Quarterly Rev. — Art. on Venice and the revolutionary proceedings in Italy in 1848 – 49. — Preparing a sermon.

Mar. 13. Wednesday

A hoar frost in the |[74] morning, a fine bright day. — Preparing a sermon. — My dear Son and daughter rode from Stanway to visit us, remained with us from 2 till 5 P.M. and then rode back. They brought a good account of our two dear grandchildren at Stanway, but were fraught with tidings of ill health and fatal accident as regarded others of their neighbourhood and acquaintance. Mr Hayward called while they were here, and made his report of my poor wife's state: though she had passed a nearly sleepless night, and the dropsical symptoms are unabated, there was more power, and a fuller pulse; yet nothing on which to build hope — H. named to us the recent decease in town of our old friend John Browne of Salperton, far advanced in years, of an inflammatory disease of the larynx which has long threatened to bring him to the grave. — Received a few lines from C Bathurst, anxious to have how matters are proceeding here as regards MW's state. He forwards for my considera-|[75]tion a letter addressed to him by a Medical man at St. Briavels, who complains of not being called upon to perform a post mortem examination by Barnett, the Coroner: B. suggests that it may be proper to enquire into the case at the Quarter Sessions. I answered, returning the letter, & saying that the alarming illness of my wife would prevent me from attending the Q.S. and that if he thought the matter worthy of enquiry, he had better send the letter he had received to Curtis Hayward — Quarterly Rev. — Art. on Venice.

Mar. 14. Thursday

Fine weather — Preparing a sermon — MW received a kind letter of enquiry from Laura Howell — From Mr. Wilkins notice of a Turnpike meeting at Chipping Norton — Hayward visited MW: found her languid and the dropsical symptoms unabated. Later in the day there was a feebleness amounting almost to fainting |[76] and for a time severe pain in the lower extremities: great drowsiness in the Evening. — E.F.W. sent his servant with a note to his Mother, and a footstool so formed of tin as to be capable of being filled with hot water, and to keep the feet warm — He wrote also to me, acknowledging my last two notes to him, which did not reach him till this morning: he has made up his mind, in consequence of his mother's state, not to attend at the Quarter Sessions next week. — Rec^d. a note from M^r. Vavasour, announcing the decease of M^rs. Walter Vavasour, second wife & widow of a deceased Brother of M^rs. Vavasour of the Cottage. — Drove to Stow. Attended at the Provident Bank, where I met Mr Pole, Winter, W B. Pole, Morrison, Ford and R. Waller. — Afterwards with Ford and R Waller to the Justice room, where we transacted magisterial business from 2 to 4 P.M. – |^77 Mr Bourne, the Rector of Weston sub Edge had come to meet me, to consult me as to the Assessment of his parish to the County rate: he had been in correspondence with Purnell, but to little purpose. I recommended him to meet the County Rate Committee at Gloucester on Monday next, and explained to him the principle of the Assessment, adding that if there were no error in the calculation, he would hardly succeed in getting the Assessment materially reduced — Mr B. is a young Magistrate, promising to be useful; and qualified at the last Sessions — Mr Winter and W B Pole attended our Petty Sessions. — Wrote to Messrs. Hoare, desiring them to transfer £50 from my account with them to that of my son. — Quarterly Rev. — Art. on Venice & its revolution in 1848. —

Mar. 15. Friday

A frosty morning, fine but cold day, and Easterly wind. — |^78 MW. very weak, and at times during the day suffering greatly from languor and pain — Justice business at home, with Mr Brookes, Makepeace, and others. — Wrote to E. F. W in reply to his note received yesterday and with a report as to his poor mother's state — To M^r. Vavasour, acknowledging his note received yesterday, with the news of M^rs. W. Vavasour's decease, reporting on MW's state — To R. Waller, to whom I sent C Bathurst's letters to a niece, that he might convey them to Purnell at the Q.S. next week. — Called on E. Lea, and John Davis, and others on parish business &c. J D. very much indisposed, and his wife not much better then himself — Handed to E. Lea copies of the Register of baptism of his two sons about to emigrate to Australia, with letters commendatory in their favour. — Quarterly Review. Art. on Venice.

Mar. 16. Saturday

An easterly wind, and cold day; for the most part hazy, with a slight |^79 inclination at times to rain. — Much engaged with persons on Justice business in the forenoon. — Mr Hayward called — visited MW. – little if any change in her condition; perhaps, on the whole, less distress and discomfort during the day. — Letters from S. B. Hunt, who writes very kindly as to MW's painful state, very enigmatically and vaguely, and un^intelligibly, as to Hunt Trust concerns. — From C Bathurst a line or two of kind sympathy with me under my present affliction — From Messrs. Hoare, announcing that they have transfered £50 from my account with them to that of my Son — From Canon Ford, explaining that he did nor call here yesterday, as M^rs. Dolphin had postponed receiving him till Monday, when he purposes visiting me on his way to Eyford, and speaks of justice business which he wishes to be transacted here on that day. I replied to his note, intimating that I should be glad to see him, but that I |^80 believed he could not do what he wished; the changes in the law would prevent him; and of these changes my worthy friend takes little or no note — From <u>Lord Saye & Sele</u> with a cheque for Adlestrop subscriptions for 1850 to the Stow District Comm. S.P.G. — To this letter <u>I replied</u>, acknowledging the receipt of the cheque, and sending receipts. — Lord Campbell's Lives of the Chancellors — Quarterly Review. Art. on Lord Clarendon and the Orange men in Ireland (the Dolly's Brae affair)[5]

Mar. 17. Sunday.

A frosty morning, cold air, and Easterly wind. — M[r] Hayward visited MW. who continues in nearly the same state — her nights very restless — her mind in the intervals of sleep more or less wandering — appetite improved — dropsical appearances not diminished — much dosing by day, especially in the evening. H. finding diuretic medicine unavailing, began a course of purgatives as hydragogues to-day; using gamboge[6] &c. — Morning service; prayers |[81] and sermon. I preached on the Spirit of GOD manifested in his fruits, with reference to the character of Joseph – Afternoon service – prayers. — Preparing a sermon. — Eccl. Gazette. —

Mar. 18. Monday.

A sharp frost, followed by a fine day, but the wind Easterly. — M[r] Hayward called: little, if any perceptible difference in my poor wife's state. — Justice business at home. — I had expected Canon Ford to call on his way to Eyford, but he came not, and I heard M[rs] Dolphin had sent to countermand his visit, on the plea of increased illness. — M[r] and M[rs] W B Pole very kindly called to enquire for MW. and sat with me for some time — Wrote to <u>M[r] Thornton</u>, sending him a copy of the portion of S. B. Hunt's last letter to me which related to business — Wrote a note to <u>E.F.W.</u> with a report of his Mother's state. — Lord Campbell's Lives of the Chancellors. — |[82]

Mar. 19. Tuesday.

A dry day, cold, and, for the most part, sour and hazy. — MW. suffered much to day from languor, & faintness, increased distension and shortness of breath: yet moved from her bed room to her little sitting room, & thence in the evening to the dining room, as had been accustomed: very feeble and lethargic in the evening. Yet she enjoyed seeing her children; dear Edward and Sophy riding from Stanway, and passing three hours with us. M[r] Walsh also, from Winchcombe, very kindly drove to call here, and make personal enquiries as to my poor wife's health and state. — A good report of our dear Grandchildren. — Union business at home. — Wrote letters conveying a report of MW's health to <u>Miss Lonsdale</u>, <u>Miss Witts</u>, <u>M[rs] Guydickens</u>, and <u>Miss E. F. Backhouse</u>. — Received letters from <u>M[r] Thornton</u> on Hunt Trust business; he returns two letters from M[r] Whitcombe to Miss S. B. Hunt, which I had sent for his perusal: — from <u>G. F. Newmarch</u> |[83] the annual statement of the Northleach district of turnpike roads: — and another circular. — Visited a poor parishioner — Ja[s] Townsend. — Lord Campbell's Lives of the Chancellors.

5. Dolly's Brae was a Catholic village through which an Orange Order march took place in 1849. On the return Catholic Ribbon Men attacked the marchers and there were fatalities on both sides.
6. Gamboge – A gum resin used as a purgative (and also for dyeing purposes as a yellow pigment) from various Asian trees of the genus *Garcinia*.

Mar. 20. Wednesday.

A dry, but cold, and dull day. — Hayward visited MW. whom he found exceedingly languid and exhausted, in part because she had taken a very active aperient, Elaterium,[7] which he had administered with a view to drawing off water from the System by the alvine excretions. In this he succeeded, and the system rallied, so that the great exhaustion went off, and in the evening the drowsiness was not so overpowering as usual. H. considers that there is latterly much increase of effusion generally, and the recumbent position is become very inconvenient; so that the poor patient cannot lay long in bed — and sits up in an arm chair near the fire |[84] during the greater part of the night, in which posture she can sleep more than when lying down. — In the afternoon she was well enough to see M^rs. Vavasour for a few minutes, who had driven from Stow, accompanied by Mr V. — Attended a Vestry, to audit the accounts of the Overseers of the Poor, and Surveyors of the Highways of the parish. — Read prayers with James Townsend — Copying report district Comm. S.P.G. for 1849 — Lord Campbell's Lives of the Chancellors.

Mar. 21. Thursday.

A very cold air, and dull day. — A visit from Mr Hayward who found his patient suffering from a restless and uneasy night; he purposes to renew the treatment with Elaterium; the day passed off tolerably in the usual change of rooms &c. — Justice business at home — Drove to Stow — Received a letter from Mr Mackersy the Incumbent of Kirkby Malhamdale, soliciting a subscription to a Sunday School |[85] room which it is in contemplation to build at Airton, a township in his parish; his claim on us being that part of the Ravenflatt property is in that Township — To the Provident Bank, where I met Morrison, W B Pole, and Winter — Wrote there a letter to Rodwell, the London Bookseller, as to a book to be supplied to our Library, a mistake having been made by him as to my last order. — To the Workhouse, where I arrived about one o clock, the business having begun much earlier, Messrs. Comely and Godwin, presiding over the relief in the separate districts — I undertook to carry on the remaining business, minutes, audit of bills and correspondence till 3 P.M., when I transacted some Justice business at the Police Office — and proceeded thence to "the Cottage," where I found our dear Sophy, who had ridden from Stanway with E F W. to visit her parents; her husband was engaged at |[86] the Unicorn Inn with other gentlemen on the affairs of the Cricket Club — I saw him there for a minute or two, as I drove out of the town, and reported to him on his poor mother's state — At "the Cottage" I also saw M^r and M^rs. Vavasour, Capt. Leigh, Mr Hutchinson and Mr Winter. —— Mr Vavasour drove with me homeward as far as Lower Slaughter Turnpike Gate, whence he walked back — Lord Campbell's Lives of the Chancellors. —

Mar. 22. Friday.

A cold, sour day; some rain in the afternoon, wind, and the mercury falling in the evening. — An early visit from Mr Hayward, who found his poor patient in a state of great exhaustion, owing to the violence of a medicine, Elaterium, taken on going to bed last night. It had, however, answered the purpose in draining the cavities of the body of a large accumulation of

---

7. Elaterium – A precipitate from the juice of the squirting cucumber *Ecballium elaterium*, used at this period as a drastic purgative and emetic.

water: the sufferer revived in the afternoon, but the appetite was bad, and the tense condi-|[87] tion of the frame from effusion under the skin unabated. Sleep in a recumbent posture for a continuance is impossible to be had without a sense of suffocation, so that the night as well as the day is mostly passed in an arm chair: — Received a letter from our dear <u>Broome</u>, with kind enquiry as to his poor Grandmother, and joyful anticipations of the Easter holidays near at hand — A printed circular craving aid, and shewing forth the spiritual destitution of the parish of <u>Skipton.</u> — A letter from M[r] <u>Joyner Ellis</u> informs me that a good beginning was made at the Sessions on Tuesday last as to a testimonial to the County Chairman, recognizing his great services to the cause of humanity in his difficult and harassing, and judicious investigations into the state of the private madhouses in this County. <u>I replied</u> in a few lines expressive of satisfaction that the project was well launched, and of regret that I had |[88] been prevented joining in the good work by my personal attendance. —— A kind letter from Fanny Backhouse, written on the receipt of my last to her, and expressive of much anxiety as to my dear wife's illness. — Wrote to <u>M[r] Mackesy,</u>[8] Incumbent of Kirkby Malhamdale, promising a contribution of Five Pounds towards the erection of a Schoolhouse at Airton when the building shall have been commenced. — Wrote to <u>M[r] Tagart</u>, Chemist, Cheltenham, for a supply of pills. —— Wrote to <u>E.F.W.</u> with a report of his dear Mother's state and Hayward's treatment. — Walked to Eyford to call on M[rs] Dolphin, who was not prepared to see me to-day. — Visited M[rs] Rogers, who still lingers, and is bed-ridden; prayed by her. — Lord Campbell's Lives of the Chancellors. — Quarterly Review – Art. on Lord Clarendon and the Orangemen of the North of Ireland — Rev[d] W. J. E. Bennett's (Perp. Curate |[89] of S[t] Paul's Knightsbridge) two Sermons — The Church, the Crown, and the State — their Junction or their separation — Bearing reference to the Judicial Comm. of the Privy Council — and the case of Gorham V. Bp. of Exeter — an exposition of Ultra High Church views, which has attracted much notice — M[r] B. being a popular and leading preacher of his class.

Mar 23. Saturday.

A very cold day; heavy clouds at times, alternating with sunshine; snow showers passing away quickly, and occasionally flickering snow. — Hayward found MW. very languid and low, after a bad night; continued the cordial medicine of myrrh and salicene, probably to be succeeded by another dose of elaterium — In the evening our patient revived, and was comparatively alive & alert; but the appetite bad, the extremities very much swollen, & very tense. — Wrote to <u>S. B. Hunt</u>, with |[90] an account of my poor wife's state, and some comment of the business part of her last letter — MW. received a very kind and proper letter from <u>Jane Lonsdale</u>, in reply to the letter I had written to her, announcing my poor wife's serious illness. — A circular from <u>R W Hippisley</u> giving notice of a decanal meeting to be held on April 3. — Visited and prayed by James Townsend — Lord Campbell's Lives of the Chancellors — Copying Report Stow Distr. Comm. S.P.G. for 1849.

Mar 24. Sunday.

Weather very cold; frost very hard. — M[r] Hayward came, as usual, before morning service, and found MW. better than yesterday; less distress, less nervous irritability, after a better

8.   Mackesy; spelt as Mackersy on 21 March.

night. She continued pretty well during the day, but the appetite for solid food failing, and the dropsical affection very overpowering. — Morning service — Prayers — Palm Sunday. — Afternoon service — Prayers and sermon. — I |[91] preached on the Tree of Life, with reference to the Sacrament to be administered next Sunday. — Received a letter from Sophia Hunt, announcing that she and Mr Geo. H. have agreed on an arbitration &c. – A circular announcing a meeting of the diocesan board of education at Gloucester on the 27th. Inst. — Eccl. Gazette — Bennett's sermons on the Church, the Crown, and the State. —

Mar 25. Monday.

A hard frost, and very cold weather. A snow shower in the Evening. — MW. did not suffer so much by the dose of Elaterium which she had taken, as before: the evacuation very copious, but the exhaustion less. Hayward visited her, and was satisfied with the operation of the medicine. Less torpor, but the appetite bad; and the helplessness from swollen limbs and body unabated. — Wrote to Mr Thornton, and Sophia Hunt on Hunt Trust concerns: forwarding to the former the |[92] letter I had received from the latter yesterday; and to the latter I returned two letters from Mr Whitcombe which she had sent for my perusal. — Wrote to E.F.W with an account of his poor mother's state. — – To Mr Vavasour a report of MW's condition — To M^rs. Dolphin the like in answer to a kind letter received from her with a hot water pillow, which she hopes may be used with advantage: she dilates very fully on her own ailments and troubles. — Preparing a Sermon — Lord Campbell's Lives of the Chancellors.

Mar. 26. Tuesday.

A hard frost, and bright morning followed about noon by a very heavy snow storm, lasting for some hours with little interruption, and lying very thick on the ground. — MW. passed a bad night, and was very much exhausted in the forenoon, but rallied in the afternoon and evening. — Received a letter from dear Sophy, writing for her husband, who was engaged, entertaining |[93] F. Aston Junr as a guest. The note brought by a coal waggon. Good tidings of all at the Vicarage; but the melancholy news announced of the death of M^rs. Whalley, at Toddington, on Saturday last after a premature confinement, the Infant having also died. W. Whalley better in health and spirits than he has lately been, but much overpowered: the case very pitiable; a marriage of a very few years standing; one little girl survives; the husband nervous and of uncertain health; death coming hastily, soon after the husband and wife had removed into a handsome new house provided for the Vicar by his patron, Lord Sudeley, which at their time of life they might reasonably hope to enjoy together for several years. But I had noticed the altered & aged appearance of M^rs. Whalley, when I saw her last autumn; and he is a nervous, debilitated man of his years. — Replied to dear Sophy's letter with a report of my poor wife's state. — A letter from Messrs. Hoare announces |[94] that Mr Jennings has paid to my account with them £144. — Preparing a Sermon. Lord Campbell's lives of the Chancellors — A packet of pills from Tagart, Cheltenham.

Mar. 287. Wednesday.

A deep snow lying on the ground, a hard frost, and bright sun melting the snow, but not where it was sheltered from its rays. — Travelling very bad; which, no doubt, prevented us the comfort of a visit from our dear children, which had been promised. — Hayward called, and found his patient improved in some respects; the Elaterium treatment seems to have drawn off much water from the cavities & upper part of the body, but the dropsy in the lower extremities appears unabated; there is much less drowsiness, but hardly less debility, and no greater ability of moving: the appetite is indifferent, but the mind appears less clouded. The treatment is to be continued; myrrh and salicene are administered between the doses of Elaterium to recruit and invigorate the |[95] system. — Preparing a Sermon. — Rec[d.] a letter from <u>Miss S. B. Hunt</u>, and another from M[r] <u>Thornton</u> — both referring to Hunt Trust concerns, and with kind notice of MW's illness: — a note from M[r] <u>Morgan</u>, Stow, desiring me to call on him to receive the £2. awarded to me as Prizes for cattle exhibited by me at the annual meeting of the Stow and Chipping Norton Agricultural Society. — <u>A circular</u>, announcing the meeting of the Stow Clerical Society, for Wednesday next. — Lord Campbell's Lives of the Chancellors. —

Mar. 28. Thursday.

A sharp frost, cold air, and bright sun, melting the snow where it had influence. — M[r] Hayward visited MW.: the Elaterium continues to operate satisfactorily, but leaves considerable languor, and the power of moving the lower extremities seems rather less; yet there is a reduction of puffiness in some parts of the body. MW. did not leave her |[96] chamber during the day. — A circular from the <u>Clerk of the Peace's office</u>, announcing my appointment as one of the Visiting Justices of Gloucester Gaol. — Wrote to M[r] <u>Thornton</u>, to whom I forwarded for his perusal the business part of the letter which I received from S. B. Hunt yesterday – i.e. a copy. — Drove to Stow. — Attended at the Prov. Bank where I met M[r] Pole, M[r] Morrison &c. — To the Justice room, where a long sitting, M[r] Ford and R. Waller being my colleagues — much business — Mess[rs.] Whitmore Jones, Vavasours, Sen[r] and Jun[r], Ogle, Winter, Lewes, W B Pole were assessors. — Wrote from Stow to Rodwell respecting a new book to be supplied to the Library — Lord Campbell's Lives of the Chancellors. —

Mar. 29. Friday.

Good Friday — A hard frost, less cold air, and bright weather. — MW. continues in a weak state; the debility in the earlier part of the day being greater than afterwards. Much pain & exhaustion, but the |[97] effusion diminished: the appetite indifferent, the drowsiness less, the inability of moving unabated. — Wrote to <u>E.F.W</u> with a report of his poor mother's state — Divine Service with a Sermon at 11 AM. I preached on the Faith of Abraham as shewn in the sacrifice of Isaac, & that as prefiguring the sacrifice and voluntary death of Christ. — Letters from <u>Howell</u>, with kind enquiry as to my poor wife, and particulars of his own family — From M[r] <u>Bury</u>, the incumbent of Burnsall, apologizing for long silence, acknowledging my two letters to him concerning the restoration of Rilston Church, which is now likely to be well done, as the late M[r] Waddilove of Rilston, who died a short time since, has left by will £1000 to meet other subscriptions, and £200 towards the building of a schoolhouse there. M[r] Bury sends me also a lithograph of his chapel at Conistone recently |[98] restored under his superintendence: his letter shews him to be a good, zealous, painstaking Clergyman. — A circular <u>from the Gaol, Gloucester,</u> addressed to me as visiting Magistrate, announcing a meeting of Visitors — A kind letter from M[rs.] <u>Guydickens</u>, requesting to hear from me as to the state of MW. — A letter from <u>E.F.W.</u> explaining how the deep snow prevented him and Sophy from visiting us on Wednesday last or on the following day; he proposes, with his dear wife & Broome, to come next week to sleep here for a night, in which case I should send to fetch them, and to convey them back. — A circular with reference to the religious wants of the <u>Diocese of Tasmania</u>, with a view to contributions in aid of the cause of the Church there — A circular addressed to proprietors of the <u>Gloucester and Berkeley canal</u>, with suggestions as to the management of the concern. — Winslow's "grace & truth" |⁹⁹

Mar. 30. Saturday.

A cold day; Easterly wind. — Mʳ Hayward called; little change in his patient's condition; great exhaustion after a bad night, but not such as to induce a doubt as to the further administration of the Elaterium — Justice business at home, which led to my writing a letter to <u>Mʳ Biscoe</u> as to a settled parishioner of Turkdean — Wrote to <u>E.F.W.</u> with an account of his poor mother's state, and to fix him and his wife & eldest boy to visit us next week. After this letter had been dispatched, my son rode to see us, coming from Winchcomb, where he had been attending at a Petty Sessions, after divine service at Stanway. I was at Eyford, visiting Mʳˢ· Dolphin, when he came, but returned on being sent for. E.F.W. remained with us till half past five P.M. — Wrote to <u>Messʳˢ· Hoare</u>, desiring them to transfer from my account with them to |¹⁰⁰ that of my son £47. 10. 0 — Received a letter on Hunt Trust affairs from <u>Mʳ Thornton</u>. — Lord Campbell's Lives of the Chancellors. ——

Mar. 31. Sunday. Easter-day.

A mild, damp atmosphere; two or three showers of rain — Morning service; prayers, sermon, and communion: 17 of the congregation partook of the holy rite; I preached a Sermon suited to the day, on the resurrection of the body. — Afternoon service, prayers. — Between the services Mʳ Hayward visited MW. who was much, but not too much exhausted by the dose of Elaterium she had taken, and which operated satisfactorily. There is great debility, but a diminution of effusion; less ~~top~~ torpor, but much nervousness and excitability; — the mind is less clouded, but still feeble; at times great palpitation of the heart; the appetite bad, & the power of moving not improved. — Preparing a Sermon. — Eccl. Gazette. — Winslow's "Grace & truth". |¹⁰¹

Apr. 1. Monday.

Fine and mild weather till the evening, when rain and wind came on. — MW. continued nearly in the same state as before. She now does not leave her dressing room for the dining room in the evening, nor her bed chamber till afternoon. Great debility, and pain in the body and lower extremities with palpitation of the heart: is more alert in the evening than in the former part of the day. — Wrote to <u>Mʳ Thornton</u> and <u>Miss S. B. Hunt</u>, on Hunt Trust matters — To <u>Mʳ Whitmore Jones</u> with information as to the removal of Superintendent Edwards, late stationed at Campden, from the Gloucestershire Constabulary. W.J. wished for information on the subject, when I saw him on Thursday last, E. having been appointed a Constable at Charlbury. I obtained more correct knowledge on the subject than I possessed before from E.F.W on Saturday last. — Wrote to the |¹⁰² <u>Revᵈ· W. Bury</u>, Rector of Burnsall, with a cheque for £15, as our contribution towards the restoration of Rylstone Church — Justice business at home — Preparing a sermon. — Lord Campbell's Lives of the Chancellors. —

Apr. 2. Tuesday.

A spring like soft air, and, with the exception of two or three showers, a fine day. — Wrote to Messrs. Gorman and C.^o. — with an order for an Octave of Manzanilla Wine[9] — also to Messrs. Butt, with an order for six dozen of Marsala Wine.[10] — Wrot Preparing a sermon — Justice business at home — Received a letter from Messrs. Hoare, announcing that they had transferred £47. 10. 0 from my account with them to that of my Son. — Our dear children with our eldest Grandson arrived from Stanway to pass two nights here. Poor Sophy had been suffering from one of her periodical headaches, but in the Evening had thrown it off. Broome looks very well, and the other children are well too. — Mr Hay-|[103] ward called late to visit MW. whom he found in a state of great languor; having suffered much from palpitation. She continues very feeble, but was carried into the dining-room to enjoy the society of her children in the Evening. It seems that on Sunday Mr H. considered his patient to be less well than on some previous visits: to-day he thought her better than when he saw her last: certainly she is in a very precarious state. —

April 3. Wednesday.

A mild pleasant forenoon, with a slight shower or two. In the afternoon and evening frequent & almost continuous showers of rain with wind. — Mr Hayward called and visited his patient, staying here till after luncheon. She was exceedingly prostrate and exhausted in the morning and forenoon; but more alert and revived in the afternoon and evening, when she could enjoy more or less the society of her children and grandson. — Awaiting Hayward's coming, it was impossible for me to go to Stow to be present |[104] at the first ruri-decanal meeting for the season. — Received a letter from Mr Biscoe in reply to that which I addressed to him on a matter of justice business. — M.^r and M.^rs. Vavasour called and made a long visit. — Justice business at home. — Enjoying the society of my dear children and grandson. —

April 4. Thursday.

A stormy and rainy day with little interruption. — Our dear children and grandson, returned to Stanway to-day in our carriage by Stow, calling at "the cottage", where they found Willm. Vavasour ill, and confined to his bed with a feverish cold. E.F.W. and Sophy had proposed not to set out till afternoo Mr Hayward had visited his patient; but he was detained elsewhere so late that he did not arrive here till 2 P.M. and they had set out between 12 & 1 P.M. which was necessary, as my horse & carriage were to come back in the evening. I had meant to have accompanied my children to Stow, to attend the Board of Guardians, in which case the |[105] carriage would have taken me up on its way back, when the business was over, but, as Hayward did not come early, this arrangement was

---

9. An octave is a small wine cask containing an eighth of a pipe, 13½ gallons (approximately 61.4 litres). The *Oxford English Dictionary* states the first recorded use of it to be 1880, so this usage antedates the dictionary by thirty years. Manzanilla is a specially refreshing style of sherry that is made quite naturally in the seaside sherry town of Sanlúcar de Barrameda.

10. This is the first reference in the diaries to Marsala. The wine comes from Trapani province in Sicily, and was developed by John Woodhouse, an English merchant. Woodhouse 'invented' Marsala in 1773 by adding two gallons of grape spirit to each of the 105 gallon barrels which he shipped to England. The victualling of Nelson's ships in 1798 spread the popularity of the drink.

impracticable. E.F.W was met at Stow by his servant and horse, & rode to Moreton to give orders as to the Cricket ground, proceeding thence to join his wife at home — Hayward found MW. in a very low and pitiable state, but less prostrate than yesterday: she had received her children &c. in her bed room, and did not remove into her sitting room till near dinner time. In the morning the exhaustion is usually greater than later in the day, when the strength seems to rally: but the pain, oppression, languor, and total helplessness are very distressing. H. thinks it justifiable to continue the treatment by Elaterium as long as the system will bear it; because it will drain the effusion, abate the torpor, and check the advance of water to the vitals; but he does not disguise from me |[106] that he has no hope of permanent benefit from the use of this or any other remedy, tho' it may be expedient to resort to scarifying. MW. is fully sensible of her own danger, and a patient sufferer. — Preparing a Sermon. — I received a few lines from dear <u>Sophy</u> on her return home, with a good report of dearest Freddy and Georgy. — A circular from a <u>Cheltenham tradesman.</u> Lord Campbell's Lives of the Chancellors —

April 5. Friday.

Fine weather. — Preparing a sermon. — Wrote to <u>Howell</u> in answer to his letter of enquiry as to MW's state received at the end of last week: to M^r <u>J. Walker</u>, Northleach, with an order for Oats, and a cheque in payment of a quantity of oats supplied some time ago. — Rec^{d.} a letter from Messrs. <u>Gorman & Co.</u> in answer to mine addressed to them, announcing that they have sent to me an Octave of Manzanilla wine by Ward's Waggon — A letter from the <u>Gaol</u> at Gloucester announcing a meeting of Visiting Justices — |[107] An envelope containing a bill from M^r <u>Mallory</u>, the Cheltenham Ironmonger. — MW. was in a very feeble, low and helpless state, worse in the early than in the latter part of the day, but no material change in her condition. — Lord Campbell's Lives of the Chancellors.

Apr. 6. Saturday.

Fine weather, except as to a shower in the afternoon. — Wrote to <u>E.F.W.</u> with a report of his poor Mother's health. — Mr Hayward called; he found the operation of the Elaterium to have been as satisfactory as could be expected, but the exhaustion was considerable; yet there was a rallying after midday, and a tolerably comfortable evening. The fatigue and palpitation consequent on the least movement indicate too surely the accumulation of fluid, probably, in the pericardium. — A letter from M^r <u>Bury</u>, acknowledging my cheque for £15. in aid of the restoration of Rilstone |[108] Church. — Canon Ford called, and gave me particulars of what had passed at the Ruridecanal meeting on Wednesday last, as to the discussion raised on Mr Boggis's paper and a resolution passed in respect of the Gorham controversy – The Rural dean left a paper to be filled up with Statistics as to this parish to be prepared for the Bishop in anticipation of his Triennial Visitation this year. — Preparing a Sermon — Copying the Stow Distr. Comm. annual report S.P.G. for 1849. — Lord Campbell's Lives of the Chancellors.

Apr. 7. Sunday.

Weather fine — Little change in MW's state; in the morning very low and exhausted, rallying after midday, but more drowsy, and no improvement in any of the unfavourable symptoms

— Morning service prayers — Afternoon Service, prayers and sermon. I preached on the duty of trusting in GOD — Attended at the Sunday School in the afternoon — |[109] Preparing a sermon. — Eccl. Gazette — Winslow's "grace and truth." —

Apr. 8. Monday.

A spring day, mild with soft showers. — Wrote to Howell a few lines on a point which I had omitted to notice in my late letter to him: — To E.F.W with particulars of his Mother's state; this letter I did not close till after Hayward had visited his patient. — His report of her state was not more favourable: a bad symptom had shewn itself — defective secretion of urine, so much as to amount to a stoppage for several hours; yet this does not appear to be retention in the bladder, but a failure in the kidneys to secrete; and, no doubt, the organic malady is in the Kidneys. Much feebleness, but, as usual, a rally in the afternoon and evening. We thought, however, there was more effusion, and the pulse did not forbid the administration of the Elaterium at bed time — Justice business at home, which led me to |[110] write a note to Mᴿ Jos. Clifford, Littlebarton. — Preparing a sermon. — Visiting and praying with a sick parishioner — Widow Townsend. — Lord Campbell's Lives of the Chancellors.

April 9. Tuesday.

A mild, spring like day, with frequent genial showers. — Mᴿ Hayward visited us. MW. was in the forenoon and early afternoon in a state of great prostration, owing in part to copious evacuation the result of the Elaterium, but she rallied later in the day; the secretion of urine exceedingly defective, distressing pain from that cause, and from the effusion, principally in the lower extremities. — Preparing a sermon. — A letter from Mᴿ Thornton covering the copy of one to him from Mᴿ W. Hunt, by which it appears that the belligerents have at last agreed to settle their differences on the Representatives of M C Hunt paying £200 to Mᴿ G. Hunt, as money paid to the former by the Trustees in excess and in error on the Wharf account: — a settlement this |[111] which, if it had been made long ago, would have saved much expence, much anger, much bootless correspondence.[11] The arrangement is, I apprehend, equitable; it leaves still some questions as to costs to be settled, which I presume must be referred to a competent umpire. — A letter from Mᴿ Jennings, accompanying my half year's balance sheet of rents received by him from London tenants to Christmas 1849. — Justice business at home. — Lord Campbell's Lives of the Chancellors.

April 10. Wednesday.

Very fine weather — MW. very feeble and languid in the early part of the day, and suffering from various causes; among them a new distress, the involuntary discharge of urine, ~~causin~~ creating much discomfort: there was a revival in the afternoon and evening, but total helplessness, and disinclination to solid food. — She was able to receive and in a degree to enjoy a visit from our dear children, who |[112] came on horseback from Stanway, and remained with us for three hours, bringing a good account of their dear little boys — Wrote to Mᴿ Thornton in reply to his letter received yesterday, that I was prepared to go along with him in the measures he should approve as to the winding up of the Hunt

---

11. Bootless – unavailing, to no purpose.

controversy. — Wrote to M<u>r</u> Jennings in answer to his letter received yesterday; admitting the correctness of the balance sheet &c. — Wrote to M<u>r</u> Pearce for information where a material could be procured at Stow, which under existing circumstances is required in the sick room — He <u>replied</u> to my note and sent the article wanted by the groom, whom I sent with the message — Preparing a document as to the Statistics of this parish for the Rural Dean — Lord Campbell's lives of the Chancellors — Received a letter from M<u>r</u> Thornton, who forwards to me a copy of his answer to the last letter he has received from Mr Ward |*113* Hunt, announcing the arrangement for a compromise come to between Mr G. Hunt and Miss S. B. Hunt. |